OPERAS
IN GERMAN

OPERAS IN GERMAN

A Dictionary

Margaret Ross Griffel

Adrienne Fried Block, Advisory Editor

GREENWOOD PRESS
New York • Westport, Connecticut • London

Library of Congress Cataloging-in-Publication Data

Griffel, Margaret Ross.
    Operas in German : a dictionary / Margaret Ross Griffel.
        p. cm.
    Includes bibliographical references.
    ISBN 0-313-25244-0 (lib. bdg. : alk. paper)
    1. Opera—Dictionaries.   I. Title.
ML102.06G75 1990
782.1'03—dc20   89-17025

British Library Cataloguing in Publication Data is available.

Library of Congress Catalog Card Number: 89-17025
ISBN: 0-313-25244-0

First published in 1990

Greenwood Press, 88 Post Road West, Westport, CT 06881
An imprint of Greenwood Publishing Group, Inc.

Printed in the United States of America

∞

The paper used in this book complies with the
Permanent Paper Standard issued by the National
Information Standards Organization (Z39.48-1984).

10 9 8 7 6 5 4 3 2 1

CONTENTS

In memory of my father
Karl F. Ross (1915–1984)

PREFACE AND ACKNOWLEDGMENTS

Although a sizable number of opera dictionaries and encyclopedias are available, those devoted exclusively to operas in a single language are extremely rare. The present dictionary addresses itself wholly to operas written to a German text, whether from a source originally in German or from a German translation. The main body of this dictionary provides entries on the operas themselves, rather than musical terms, characters, composers, performers, and other personages: in this way each of the roughly 380 operas can be given a thorough treatment. This principal section is augmented by an appendix of some 1250 additional opera titles, and appendices on composers, librettists, authors, sources, and a chronology, and indexes of characters and performers.

Almost all of the composers represented here were born in German-speaking countries or areas controlled by Germany or the Austro-Hungarian Empire before 1919. Among the few notable exceptions is the Italian-born Ferruccio Busoni, all of whose operas were written to German texts and received premieres in German-speaking cities. Composers who wrote operas in more than one language are represented by their German works only. One example is Kurt Weill, who was born in Dessau but died in New York. He wrote his first operas to German librettos but his later ones to English texts; this dictionary covers just his German works. Mozart, Haydn, Handel, and Henze are other composers who wrote operas in more than one language. This volume excludes works that received their premieres in German but were meant to be performed in another language (e.g., Milhaud's opéras-minutes, first given at Baden-Baden in German, and the first part of Berlioz's *Les Troyens*, which had its premiere in Karlsruhe as *Die Eroberung Trojas*). The earliest opera in the dictionary is Heinrich Schütz's *Dafne*, considered the first German opera (1627, Torgau). The latest entry, Willy Decker's *Ein Mitternachtstraum*, dates from May 1989.

The operas are listed alphabetically (excluding the article, which is placed at the end of the title; the exceptions are those works beginning with the genitive "des," in which case the entry is under "d"), and where there is more than one opera per title, the versions are listed chronologically. Each entry includes the title, with the English translation and alternate titles in parentheses; a descriptive term as needed, e.g., "Singspiel"; the number of acts; the composer's name; the librettist's name, the original language, and the original source of the text; the date, place, and cast of the first performance; similar information for the first U.S. and British performances, if applicable; a brief plot summary; the main characters (names and vocal ranges); some of the especially important or noteworthy numbers cited by name; additional information, where appropriate, including comments on special musical problems, techniques, or other significant aspects; and other settings of the text, including non-German ones, and/or other operas involving the same story or characters. Each entry also contains information on the first and critical editions of the scores and librettos, and a bibliography, ranging from scholarly studies to journal articles and reviews, a discography, and, in the few instances where they are available, information on video recordings. Frequently cited bibliographical sources are given in abbreviated form, as are certain journal titles and publishers (see List of Abbreviations following).

As mentioned above, there are also six appendices. The first contains operas in German not covered in the main section because of limitations of space, or dearth of information. This appendix includes the title, composer, number of acts, librettist, date and city of premiere, and information on published scores and librettos. The second is an alphabetical listing of composers, with their places and years of birth and death, followed by a list of their operas included in this volume. The third appendix lists the names of librettists and provides information similar to that in the composer appendix. The fourth is an appendix of authors whose works inspired or were adapted for the librettos of the operas mentioned in the dictionary; similarly the fifth appendix contains the sources used by the librettists. The first index mentions the main characters listed in each opera entry, and the second the performers who sang in the operas' premieres. The chronology lists the date of composition or first performance, the city of the premiere, the short title of the opera, and the composer.

Completing the volume is a bibliography which is intended to help the reader obtain more detailed information on subjects touched on in this work. Classified sections include other dictionaries and encyclopedias on operas, works on performance information, collections of plot summaries, general bibliographies on operas, sources on cities where opera premieres took place, works on the history of operas in German, and selective bibliographies on individual German opera composers.

I am happy to thank a number of people whose assistance in preparing this book was invaluable. Firstly, thanks go to the librarians of various New York institutions, including Jane Gottlieb, at the Juilliard School Library; David Lane and Elliott Kaback, at the Hunter College Library; William Schank, at the Library of the Graduate School, City University of New York; Susan Sommer and the late Marie Bergbüchler, at the Library of the Performing Arts, Lincoln Center; and Thomas Watkins, at the Music Library, Columbia University.

Secondly, my appreciation goes to the editors at Greenwood Press: Adrienne Fried Block, for her initial interest in this project and her valuable suggestions concerning the scope of the book; Marilyn Brownstein, for accepting the manuscript; and William Neenan and Susan Baker, for seeing it through production. My thanks are also due my colleague Chuck Bartelt, for her help and computer acumen, which saved my manuscript more than once.

And finally, untold thanks to my infinitely patient and helpful family: my mother, Anny Ross, for her loving encouragement and assistance; my son David for his expert aid and advice in using the computer; and finally, to my husband, Michael, for his immeasurable editorial help, musicological suggestions and expertise, and careful reading and correction of the text.

LIST OF ABBREVIATIONS

GENERAL ABBREVIATIONS

AGA	Alte Gesamtausgabe
alto	contralto
ARD	Arbeitsgemeinschaft der öffentlich-rechtlichen Rundfunkanstalten der Bundesrepublik Deutschland
AW	Ausgewählte Werke
bar	baritone
BBC	British Broadcasting Corporation
col	coloratura
comp.	composer, composed, compiled
diss.	dissertation
Dlle.	demoiselle
ed.	editor, edited, edition
Fr	French
Frl.	Fräulein
fs	full score
GA	Gesamtausgabe
Ger	German
It	Italian
Mad.	Madame
Mlle.	Mademoiselle
mezzo	mezzo-soprano
Mme.	Madame
Mr.	Mister, Monsieur
mss	manuscript score
MW	Musikalische Werke
ORF	Österreichischer Rundfunk, Vienna, Salzburg
orig.	original
perf.	performed

repr.	reprinted, reprint
rev.	revised
RIAS	Rundfunk im amerikanischen Sektor von Berlin
sop	soprano
SW	Sämtliche Werke
ten	tenor
transl.	translated
vs	vocal score
ZDF	Zweites Deutsches Fernsehen, Mainz

BIBLIOGRAPHIC ABBREVIATIONS

AcM	*Acta musicologica*
AMP	Associated Music Publishers
AMw	*Archiv für Musikwissenschaft*
AmZ	*Allgemeine musikalische Zeitung*
AnMus	*Analecta musicologica*
Bär	Bärenreiter
B&B	Bote & Bock, originally E. Bote & G. Bock
B/*GA*	*Ludwig van Beethovens Werke: Vollständige kritisch durchgesehene überall berechtigte Ausgabe.* Leipzig: B&H, 1862–1865. Supplement, 1888.
B/*SW*	*Ludwig van Beethoven: Werke: Supplemente zur Gesamtausgabe.* Edited by Willi Hess. Wiesbaden: B&H, 1959–71.
B&H	Breitkopf & Härtel
B/*LS*	Clive Brown. *Louis Spohr. A Critical Biography.* Cambridge: Cambridge University Press, 1984.
BO	Boosey & Hawkes
B/*OOR*	Alan Blyth, ed. *Opera on Record.* Discographies compiled by Malcolm Walker. London: Hutchinson & Co., 1979.
BSS	B. Schott's Söhne
C/*DDO*	Félix Clément and Pierre Larousse. *Dictionnaire des opéras.* 2 volumes. Revised by Arthur Pougin. Paris: Larousse, 1905. Reprinted New York: Da Capo Press, 1969.
CM	*Current Musicology*
C/*MS*	Milton Cross and Karl Kohrs. *More Stories of the Great Operas.* Garden City, N.Y.: Doubleday & Co., 1971.
C/*MW*	Peter Cornelius. *Musikalische Werke.* 3 volumes. Edited by Max Hasse. Leipzig: B&H, 1903. Reprint Farnborough, Hants: Gregg, 1971.
C/*NMC*	Milton Cross. *The New Milton Cross Complete Stories of the Great Operas.* Revised and enlarged version. Edited by Karl Kohrs. Garden City, N.Y.: Doubleday & Co., 1955.
COH	*Cambridge Opera Handbooks.* Cambridge, London, and New York: Cambridge University Press.
C/*PCK*	*Peter Cornelius als Komponist, Dichter, Kritiker und Essayist.* Edited by Hans Federhofer and Kurt Oehl. Regensburg: Gustav Bosse Verlag, 1977.

D/*CDD*	Karl Höll. *Carl Ditters von Dittersdorfs Opern für das wiedergestellte Johannisberger Theater*. Heidelberg: Carl Winters Universitätsbuchhandlung, 1913.
DDT	Denkmäler Deutscher Tonkunst
D/*FB*	Edward Dent. *Ferruccio Busoni. A Biography*. London: Oxford University Press, 1933.
DG	Deutsche Grammophon
DJbMw	*Deutsches Jahrbuch der Musikwissenschaft*
D/*MO*	Edward Dent. *Mozart's Operas*. 2nd edition. London: Oxford University Press, 1947.
D/*RS*	Norman Del Mar. *Richard Strauss*. 3 volumes. New York, London, Philadelphia: Chilton Books, 1962, 1969, 1972. Reprint Ithaca: Cornell University Press, 1986.
D/*RWD*	Carl Dahlhaus. *Die Musikdramen Richard Wagners*. Velber: Friedrich, 1971. Translated by Mary Whittall as *Richard Wagner's Music Dramas*. New York: Cambridge University Press, 1979.
DTÖ	Denkmäler der Tonkunst in Österreich
EDM	*Das Erbe deutscher Musik*
E/*ELO*	David Ewen. *The Book of European Light Opera*. New York: Holt, Rinehart and Winston, 1962.
ENO	*English National Opera Guides*. Edited by Nicholas John. London: Calder; New York: Riverrun.
G/" 'T'O"	Margaret Ross Griffel. " 'Turkish' Opera from Mozart to Cornelius," Ph.D. dissertation, Columbia University, 1975. Ann Arbor, Michigan: Xerox University Microfilms, Order No. UM 75–27, 421.
G/*RO*	Arthur Groos and Roger Parker, eds. *Reading Opera*. Princeton: Princeton University Press, 1988.
H/*FMO*	Spike (Patrick) Hughes. *Famous Mozart Operas*. Second revised edition. New York: Dover, 1972.
H/*SW*	*Paul Hindemith: Sämtliche Werke*. Edited by Kurt von Fischer and Ludwig Finscher. Mainz: BSS, 1975.
HiFi	*Hi Fidelity*
HiFi/MA	*Hi Fidelity/Musical America*
HJb	*Hindemith Jahrbuch*
JAMS	*Journal of the American Musicological Society*
J/*WB*	Ute Jung. *Walter Braunfels (1882–1954)*. Regensburg: Bosse, 1980.
K/*KOB*	*The Definitive Kobbé's Opera Book*. Edited, revised and updated by the Earl of Harewood. New York: G. Putnam's Sons, 1987.
K/*NO*	Kim H. Kowalke, ed. *A New Orpheus. Essays on Kurt Weill*. New Haven: Yale University Press, 1986.
L/*CO*	Andreas Liess. *Carl Orff*. Second edition, Zurich: Atlantis, 1977.
MA	*Musical America*
M/*AGA*	*Felix Mendelssohn-Bartholdy. Werke: kritisch durchgesehene Ausgabe*. Edited by Julius Rietz. Leipzig: B&H, 1874–77.
MB/*LA*	*Leipziger Ausgabe der Werke Felix Mendelssohn-Bartholdys*, series V. Edited by Karl-Heinz Köhler. Leipzig: Deutscher Verlag für Musik. 1966–.
ML	*Music and Letters*

Mf	*Die Musikforschung*
MGes	*Musik und Gesellschaft*
M/*IRR*	Kurtz Myers, comp. *Index to Record Reviews.*
MJb	*Mozart-Jahrbuch des Zentralinstituts für Mozartforschung*
MMR	*Monthly Musical Record*
M/*MW*	*W. A. Mozarts Werke.* Edited by L. von Köchel et al. Leipzig: B&H, 1877–83; supplements 1877–1910.
M/*NMA*	*W. A. Mozart. Neue Ausgabe sämtliche Werke.* Edited by E. F. Schmid, W. Plath, W. Rehm. Kassel: Bärenreiter, 1955–.
M/*OM*	William Mann. *The Operas of Mozart.* London: Cassell; New York: Oxford University Press, 1977.
MQ	*The Musical Quarterly*
MR	*The Music Review*
M/*RSC*	William Mann. *Richard Strauss. A Critical Study of the Operas.* London: Cassell, 1964.
MT	*The Musical Times*
NRMI	*Nuova rivista musicale italiana*
N/*SGO*	Ernest Newman. *Stories of the Great Operas and their Composers.* New York: Alfred A. Knopf, 1930.
NY	*The New Yorker*
NYT	*The New York Times*
NZM	*Neue Zeitschrift für Musik*
OAA	*Opernstudien: Anna Amalie Abert zum 65. Geburtstag.* Edited by Kurt Hortschansky. Tutzing: Hans Schneider, 1975.
OJ	*Opera Journal*
ÖMz	*Österreichische Musikzeitschrift*
ON	*Opera News*
OQ	*Opera Quarterly*
P/*HM*	A. Dean Palmer. *Heinrich Marschner, 1795–1861. His Life and Stage Works.* Ann Arbor, Mich.: UMI Research Press, 1980.
PRMA	*Proceedings of the Royal Musical Association*
R/*EKO*	Wolfgang Rogge. *Ernst Kreneks Opern.* Wolfenbüttel and Zurich: Mosler Verlag, 1970.
RIM	*Rivista italiana di musicologica*
RMI	*Rivista musicale italiana*
Scho/*SW*	Arnold Schoenberg. *Sämtliche Werke.* Mainz and Vienna: BSS, UE, 1970–.
Schu/*AGA*	*Franz Schubert's Werke. Kritisch durchgeseh'ne Gesammtausgabe: Dramatische Werke,* series XV. Edited by J. N. Fuchs. Leipzig: B&H, 1884–1897. Reprinted New York: Dover, 1965.
Schu/*NGA*	*Franz Schubert. Neue Ausgabe sämtliche Werke.* Kassel: Bärenreiter, 1964–.
S/*DSG*	Ronald Sanders. *The Days Grow Short.* New York: Holt, Rinehart, and Winston, 1980.
S/*FS*	*Franz Schreker.* Edited by H. Schreker-Bures, H. H. Stuckenschmidt, W. Oehlmann. Vienna: Elisabeth Lafite, 1970.
S/*FSS*	*Franz-Schreker Symposium.* Edited by Elmar Budde and Rudolf Stephan. Berlin: Colloquium, 1980.

S/"MJ"	Georg Schünemann. "Mendelssohns Jugendopern," *ZMW* V (1922–23), 505–45.
SIMG	*Sammelbände der Internationalen Musik-Gesellschaft*
Sm	*Studia musicologica*
SMZ	*Schweizerische Musikzeitung*
SzMW	*Studien zur Musikwissenschaft*
UE	Universal Edition
W/*CMW*	John Warrack. *Carl Maria von Weber*. 2nd edition. Cambridge, England: Cambridge University Press, 1976.
W/*FL*	Anton Würz. *Franz Lachner als dramatischer Komponist*. Dissertation, Max Ludwig University, Munich, 1927.
W/*MW*	*C. M. von Weber. Musikalische Werke*. Augsburg: Dr. Benno Filser Verlag, 1926–1928.
W/*RWW*	*Richard Wagners Werke*. Edited by Michael Balling. Leipzig: B&H, 1912–29.
W/*SW*	*Richard Wagner: Sämtliche Werke*. Edited by Carl Dahlhaus. Mainz: Schott, 1970–.
Wo/*SW*	Hugo Wolf. *Sämtliche Werke*. Edited by H. Jancik et al. Vienna: Doblinger, 1960–.
ZIMG	*Zeitschrift der Internationalen Musik-Gesellschaft*
ZMw	*Zeitschrift für Musikwissenschaft*

A BRIEF HISTORY OF GERMAN OPERA

Thoroughly "German" opera, that is, opera composed by a native of a German-speaking country to a libretto written in German, and in a basically German musical style, did not come into being until the 1670s. The repertoire in the seventeenth century consisted mainly of Italian works written by Italians who held appointments at the major courts. Vienna was a prime example. Its court composer was Antonio Draghi (1635–1700), and his librettist was Nicolò Minato (ca. 1630–1698). When the Austrian Johann Josef Fux (1660–1741) became court composer in Vienna in 1713, he wrote works in a basically old-fashioned style and in Italian, as evidenced by his *feste teatrali*. The court poet was Pietro Metastasio (1698–1782), who took up residence in 1730. Carlo Pallavicino (1630–1688) led the first permanent opera house in Dresden, for which he wrote *Gerusalemme liberata* in 1687; he began his tenure there in 1672. Agostino Steffani (1654–1728) was active in Munich and Hanover. Unlike other Italian composers of the period, who concentrated on spectacles and mythological stories, he used librettos concerned with subjects from German history.

Heinrich Schütz's (1585–1682) *Dafne* (1627, Torgau), considered the first German opera, was an adaptation and translation of Ottavio Rinuccini's (1552–1621) text, which had been set by Jacopo Peri (1561–1633) in 1597 in Florence and by Marco da Gagliano (1582–1643) in 1608 in Mantua. Schütz's music is lost. The earliest German opera for which the music has been preserved is the "spiritual pastorale" *Seelewig*, set by Sigmund Theophil Staden (1607–1655) and performed in Nuremberg in 1644. The text is by Georg Philipp Harsdörffer (1607–1658).

The first extensive native German school of opera arose in Hamburg; its development was spurred by the opening of the Theater am Gänsemarkt in 1678. The house was inaugurated with a work by a pupil of Schütz, Johann Theile (1646–1724), whose *Der erschaffene, gefallene und wieder aufgerichtete Mensch* appeared on January 12. In the next sixty years the house played host to a mainly German repertoire. After the last German work was presented at the theater in 1738, an Italian troupe took over. In addition to religiously-inspired works such as Theile's, secular ones were also popular, including many of Steffani's pieces, given in translation, and Italianate works of German composers also active in other northern cities, such as Johann Philipp Krieger (1649–1725) in Weissenfels and Georg Caspar Schürmann (1672–1751) in Brunswick.

The main librettists in Hamburg were Christian Heinrich Postel (1658–1705), Lucas von Bostel (1649–1716), and Barthold Feind (1678–1721). The leading composers were Nikolaus Adam Strungk (1640–1700), whose *Alceste* inaugurated the opera house in Leipzig in 1693, Johann Wolfgang Franck (1644–1710), whose operas included *Aeneas* and *Alceste* (both 1680, Hamburg), Johann Philipp Förtsch (1652–1732), whose works have not survived, and Johann Sigismund Kusser (1660–1727), who studied under the French master Jean-Baptiste Lully (1632–1687) and brought a more international style to the Hamburg opera house; his operas were also drawn from classical sources and included *Ariadne* and *Jason* (both 1692, Brunswick) and *Erindo* (1694, Hamburg).

Hamburg was still the center of German operatic writing in the early eighteenth century, and its foremost and most prolific composer was Reinhard Keiser (1674–1739). He was a student of Kusser and produced some 70 works, among them *Almira*, which provided a model for Handel's own setting. In musical style, his operas ran the gamut from the Baroque to the *stil galant* of the eighteenth century and were often filled with virtuoso passages, heard especially in those with Italian texts interspersed with the German, such as *Claudius* (1703). His most famous work is *Croesus*, set to a text by Minato in 1710 and revised for a revival in 1730. Among Keiser's successors in Hamburg were Johann Mattheson (1681–1764) and Christoph Graupner (1683–1760). Georg Philipp Telemann (1681–1767), building on Keiser's comic *Der lächerliche Printz Jodelet* (1726, Hamburg), produced comic works in the Italian opera buffa style, including *Der gedultige Sokrates* (1721, Hamburg) and the intermezzo *Pimpinone* (1725, Hamburg). George Frideric Handel (1685–1759) began his operatic career in Hamburg; his German works include *Almira* (1705, Hamburg), itself modeled on Keiser and a mixture of Italian and German styles and texts, with ballets and comic scenes; *Nero* (1705, Hamburg); and *Die verwandelte Daphne* and its sequel, *Der beglückte Florindo* (both 1708, Hamburg).

The demise of the Hamburg opera house in 1738 effectively brought an end to north German opera for the next thirty years, until the emergence of the Singspiel. The north German Singspiel was influenced by the English ballad opera and the French *comédie mêlée d'ariettes*. Charles Coffey's (late 17th century–1745) *The Devil to Pay* (1728) and *The Merry Cobbler* (1735) became the basis for Christian Felix Weisse's (1726–1804) *Der Teufel ist los* (1752, Leipzig) and its sequel, *Der lustige Schuster* (1759, Lübeck), set by J.C. Standfuss (d. after 1759). The version of Johann Adam Hiller (1728–1804) appeared in 1766 in Leipzig as *Der Teufel ist los, oder Die verwandelten Weiber*. Hiller is considered the founder of the north German Singspiel, which was typified by stories about the lower middle class, with a pastoral setting; the plots are usually comical in nature, and the action is developed through spoken dialogue. The majority of musical numbers are simple in structure, with strophic songs common and choruses and extended finales, rare in the earlier Singspiel.

Hiller's large output of Singspiels includes his most popular work, *Die Jagd* (1770, Weimar), also to a text by Weisse, itself based on Jean-Michel Sedaine's (1719–1797) *Le Roi et le fermier*, set by Pierre Monsigny (1729–1817) in Paris in 1762. One of Hiller's students, Christian Gottlob Neefe (1748–1798) (who, in turn, was a teacher of Beethoven) wrote several Singspiels, among them the exotic *Adelheit von Veltheim* (1780, Frankfurt), considered a forerunner of Mozart's *Die Entführung aus dem Serail*. Another composer interested in the Singspiel was Georg Benda (1722–1795), whose output includes *Der Jahrmarkt* (1775, Gotha) and *Das tartarische Gesetz* (1787, Leipzig).

Benda also developed the melodrama, a work in which one or more actors recite their lines to music (a monodrama having one spoken part, a duodrama two). Examples include his *Ariadne auf Naxos* (1775, Gotha), a duodrama. The techniques of melodrama were used in scenes of later German works, such as the grave-digging scene in Beethoven's *Fidelio* and in several of Franz Schubert's works (*Des Teufels Lustschloss* and *Fierrabras*, for example).

Other important Singspiel composers were Anton Schweitzer (1735–1787), with his *Alceste* (1773, Weimar), and Johann André (1741–1799). André's *Belmont und Constanze* (1781, Berlin) appeared a little over a year before Mozart's work on the same subject, *Die Entführung* (1782, Vienna); the similarities in text prompted Christoph Friedrich Bretzner (1748–1807), André's librettist, to charge Mozart with plagiarism. Many Singspiels of the time used exotic subject matter and even Oriental-sounding music (the works were sometimes called "Turkish" operas because of their location and/or characters); the fascination with the exotic continued unabated well into the nineteenth century, as evidenced by Ludwig Spohr's *Zemire und Azor* (1819, Frankfurt), Giacomo Meyerbeer's *Wirth und Gast* (1813, Vienna), Carl Maria von Weber's *Abu Hassan* (1811, Munich) and, on a much grander scale, *Oberon* (1826, London), and Peter Cornelius's *Der Barbier von Bagdad* (1858, Weimar).

Another north German, Johann Friedrich Reichardt (1752–1814), developed the *Liederspiel*, a comedy that consisted of popular songs connected by dialogue. Other writers of *Liederspiel* included Friedrich Heinrich Himmel (1765–1814), Karl Eberwein (1786–1868), and Bernhard Anselm Weber (1764–1821); the designation was also used by Felix Mendelssohn for *Die Heimkehr aus der Fremde* (1829). The initial public performance (August 3, 1789) of Reichardt's *Claudine von Villa Bella*, one of several operas set to Goethe's text, marked the first time an opera was sung in Berlin to a German text.

The Singspiel in south Germany and Austria developed differently because of the influence of the Italian opera buffa, and it tended to have a lighter and more farcical nature. Its growth received added impetus with the formation of a national opera theater, supported by Emperor Joseph II. The famed Burgtheater of Vienna opened on February 18, 1778, with Ignaz Umlauf's (1746–1806) *Die Bergknappen*.

The classic Viennese Singspiel was represented by Karl Ditters von Dittersdorf (1739–1799), whose lively and popular works include *Doctor und Apotheker* (1786, Vienna), *Hieronymus Knicker* (1789, Vienna), and *Die Liebe im Narrenhause* (1787, Vienna). Peter Winter (1754–1825) was another successful Singspiel composer. His *Das unterbrochene Opferfest* (1796, Vienna) was wildly successful. The works of Johann Schenk (1753–1836) included his one-act *Der Dorfbarbier* (1796, Vienna). Rounding out this group was the prolific Wenzel Müller (1767–1835), with *Das Sonnenfest der Braminen* (1790, Vienna) and *Die Schwestern von Prag* (1794, Vienna).

Wolfgang Amadeus Mozart (1756–1791) wrote five German operas. His earliest effort was the one-act Singspiel *Bastien und Bastienne* (1768, Vienna). *Zaïde* (1779), a melodrama, was set to a plot similar to his later *Die Entführung aus dem Serail*; it lay unfinished at his death and was completed in 1838 by Johann Anton André, who also gave the work its title (the premiere was delayed until 1866, in Frankfurt). *Die Entführung* (1782, Vienna) was Mozart's first major success. Set in an exotic locale, it represents the pinnacle of the so-called "Turkish" operas. Musically, alongside its exotic touches, it features elements from comic and serious opera, the main characters having large, virtuoso, Italianate numbers, while the secondary roles are given less complex, Lied-like pieces. Also important are the ensembles and choruses, and its finale is an extended vaudeville (a finale during which each character sings a verse), the model for those of many future operas, German and otherwise. It was followed by the one-act *Schauspieldirektor* (1786, Vienna).

Mozart's last German opera, a combination of Singspiel and serious opera elements, was *Die Zauberflöte* (1791, Vienna). Again, the simpler music accompanies the comic characters, while the more ornate writing is given to the serious characters, as evidenced by the coloratura arias for the Queen of the Night. The complex libretto, by Emanuel Schikaneder (1751–1812), has been taken by some to be a political critique and contains unmistakable Masonic symbolism. Various composers tried to imitate the work's style and success, the most obvious being Peter Winter, with *Das Labarint* (1798, Vienna); the text to the Winter piece, again by Schikaneder, is actually the sequel to *Zauberflöte*.

An important line of development in early nineteenth-century opera was the so-called rescue opera, a genre whose text featured the saving of a main character in distress by the heroic efforts of others, such as a spouse or child. It was similar to the eighteenth-century abduction plots and was given an impetus by the French Revolution; it was particularly popular in France. Luigi Cherubini's *Les Deux Journées* (1800) was set to a libretto by Jean-Nicolas Bouilly (1763–1842), who also wrote the text for Pierre Gaveaux's (1761–1825) *Léonore* (1798). The same text was adapted for a German version by Ludwig van Beethoven

(1770–1827). The result was *Leonore* (1805, Vienna), Beethoven's only completed opera, which he revised twice, in 1806 and 1814, the third version going under the title *Fidelio, oder Die eheliche Liebe*. The work combined elements of the French opéra-comique with those of the German Singspiel and was an important model for future German operas.

There were two main trends in late eighteenth- and early nineteenth-century Singspiel. The first, represented by Joseph Weigl (1766–1846), concentrated on sentimental tales, as in his *Schweizerfamilie* (1809, Vienna). The second featured legendary or romantic themes. Into this group can be fitted the *Oberon* (1789, Vienna) of Paul Wranitzky (1756–1808); *Das Donauweibchen* (1798, Vienna) of Ferdinand Kauer (1751–1831); and *Fanchon, das Leiermädchen* (1801, Berlin), *Die Sylphen* (1806, Berlin), and *Der Kobold* (1813, Vienna) of Friedrich Heinrich Himmel. Others writing in this vein were Johann Zumsteeg (1760–1802), with *Die Geisterinsel* (1798, Stuttgart), and E.T.A. Hoffmann (1776–1822), whose literary texts inspired or were used by several other composers, including Gasparo Spontini. Hoffman's major operatic work was *Undine* (1816, Berlin), its story being a later version of *Das Donauweibchen*. Hoffmann's work was particularly effective in its portrayal of supernatural elements.

Ludwig Spohr (1784–1859) completed nine operas, among them *Faust* (1816, Prague), considered a leading example of German romantic opera. Spohr originally wrote it as a Singspiel but revised it as a grand opera (1852), with added numbers and recitative. Its overture features important themes from the opera, and it contains a high degree of musical and dramatic cohesiveness. Carl Maria von Weber conducted the 1816 premiere. Spohr's *Jessonda* (1823, Kassel), with its continuous music, was also an important German romantic opera.

Of Franz Schubert's (1797–1828) sixteen operatic works, only six were performed during his lifetime, and he was often criticized for a lack of drama in his operas. Of his output, most are Singspiels, and one is a melodrama. He was most successful with *Alfonso und Estrella* (1822, first performed at Weimar in 1854), *Die Verschworenen* (1823, performed at Frankfurt in 1861), and *Fierrabras* (1823, produced at Karlsruhe in 1897). As in the case of Schubert, Felix Mendelssohn's (1809–1847) operatic output, long considered inconsequential, has been reevaluated and revived in recent years. It includes *Die beiden Pädagogen* (1821, first performance 1962, Berlin), *Die Heimkehr aus der Fremde* (1829, Berlin), which had some success on English-speaking stages as *Son and Stranger*, and *Die Soldatenliebschaft* (1820, first performed at Wittenberg, 1962). Robert Schumann's (1810–1856) one completed opera, *Genoveva* (1850, Leipzig), has been taken to task for its dearth of drama, despite much beautiful music.

Carl Maria von Weber (1766–1826) was interested in Romantic subjects from the very beginning of his operatic output, as evidenced by the incomplete *Das Waldmädchen* (1800, Freiburg), to become the later *Silvana* (1810, Frankfurt), and *Rübezahl* (1805, not performed). His first success, written in the tradition of the exotic "Turkish" operas, was the delightful one-act Singspiel *Abu Hassan* (1811, Munich). Impressed by works such as E.T.A. Hoffmann's *Undine* and

Spohr's *Faust*, Weber resolved to develop a truly German opera, unified in all its aspects, the end-line of which was to be the operas of Richard Wagner. In this vein, Weber composed *Der Freischütz* (1821, Berlin) and *Euryanthe* (1823, Vienna). *Der Freischütz*, with its colorful depictions of Nature, rousing choruses, and spectacular use of supernatural elements, remains the most popular opera in the repertoire between *Fidelio* and Wagner's early works. *Euryanthe* is musically impressive despite its complex libretto. His last work, *Oberon* (1826, London), although it contains beautiful numbers, is hindered by an impractical libretto which mixes fairy-tale and medieval elements and lengthy dialogue. His plans to revise the work were halted by his early death.

Heinrich Marschner (1795–1861) also stood firmly in the camp of German Romantic opera with his fourteen works. They include his first success, *Der Vampyr* (1828, Leipzig), set to a typical Romantic text, this one concerning a Dracula-like figure. His next impressive opera, *Der Templer und die Jüdin* (1829, Leipzig), was a setting of Sir Walter Scott's (1771–1832) *Ivanhoe* (1820). *Hans Heiling* (1833, Berlin) is considered Marchner's finest work, and its title character has certain similarities to the Dutchman of Wagner's *Der fliegende Holländer*.

Not all German composers of the first decades of the nineteenth century turned their efforts to Romantic opera. The Singspiel was still of interest, as evidenced by the works of Conradin Kreutzer (1780–1849), with his famed *Das Nachtlager in Granada* (1834, Vienna). Comic opera was the provenance of Albert Lortzing (1801–1851), whose works still enjoy success today in German-speaking countries. They include his early *Ali Pascha von Janina* (1816, Münster), a serious "Turkish" opera, and the comedies *Die beiden Schützen* (1837, Leipzig), *Zar und Zimmermann* (1837, Leipzig), and *Hans Sachs* (1840, Leipzig), which uses the same major character as Wagner's *Die Meistersinger*. The major contribution of Friedrich von Flotow (1812–1883) to the comic repertoire is the charming *Martha* (1847, Vienna). Otto Nicolai (1810–1849), after writing several Italian operas, created one masterpiece, the ebullient *Die lustigen Weiber von Windsor* (1847, Berlin), but his life was cut short by a stroke soon after the premiere.

The last major contributor to the field of German comic opera at mid-century was Peter Cornelius (1824–1874), whose delightful *Der Barbier von Bagdad* (1858, Weimar) was set to a story from *The Thousand and One Nights*. With a witty text by Cornelius himself, some delicate melodies, and exotic musical passages, the modest work was doomed by the disastrous reception at its premiere, the result of an anti-Liszt cabal at Weimar. Its failure caused Cornelius to turn to a much heavier compositional style along the lines of Wagner, as evidenced by *Der Cid* (1865, Weimar) and the unfinished *Gunlöd* (1874, Weimar).

The major figure in German opera in the nineteenth century and beyond was Richard Wagner (1813–1883); his fourteen operas, all to his own texts, fall into several styles. His two earliest efforts were *Die Feen* (1833, first performance 1888, Munich) and *Das Liebesverbot* (1836, Magdeburg). The first was in the

German Romantic tradition, while the second incorporated elements of the Italian style of Bellini, Donizetti, and Meyerbeer. Wagner's next operas were more in the tradition of grand opera, *Rienzi* (1842, Dresden), *Der fliegende Holländer* (1843, Dresden), *Tannhäuser* (1845, Dresden), and *Lohengrin* (1850, Weimar). All focused on heroic figures and advanced the technique of the Leitmotiv, a musical motive that identifies a person, place, thing, idea, or occurrence. In *Tristan und Isolde* (1865, Munich), he entered a new stage, as he set out to compose music dramas. In *Tristan* Wagner stretches the limits of tonality, develops the technique of Leitmotiv even further, and blurs the lines between the various musical units to obtain a continuous musical flow. *Tristan*'s extreme avoidance of cadences, abundance of chromaticism, and several scenes of rapturous love music helped to establish it as the seminal German music drama of the late Romantic era.

Die Meistersinger von Nürnberg (1868, Munich), Wagner's only comic work, represented a partial "retreat" from *Tristan*, with its more identifiable numbers, strict contrapuntal passages, and diatonic harmonies. He then concentrated on the finalization of his concept of *Gesamtkunstwerk*, a combination of all the arts, music, drama, visual arts, poetry, and song (as described in his treatise *Das Kunstwerk der Zukunft*, 1849). The result was the cycle *Der Ring des Nibelungen*, consisting of: *Das Rheingold* (1869, Munich), *Die Walküre* (1870, Munich), *Siegfried* (1876, Bayreuth), and *Götterdämmerung* (1876, Bayreuth). The *Ring* abounds in orchestral depictions of Nature, intricate scenes exploring the depths of human behavior, and extremely difficult and lengthy vocal passages demanding heroic stamina. This tetralogy has long been considered the *ne plus ultra* of the German operatic repertoire. *Parsifal* (1882, Bayreuth), his final work, is steeped in the religious symbolism of the Holy Grail.

The writing of Romantic operas continued after Wagner's three masterpieces. Composers interested in this style included those of Max Bruch (1838–1920), with his *Die Loreley* (1863, Mannheim), and Karl Goldmark (1830–1915), with his *Die Königin von Saba* (1875, Vienna).

Wagner's influence on contemporaneous and subsequent composers was enormous; they either tried to follow in his footsteps or took immense pains to write in a totally different style. Among those in the Wagner camp one may include Franz von Holstein (1826–1878), e.g., with *Die Hochländer* (1876, Munich); August Klughardt (1847–1902), e.g, *Iwein* (1879, Neustrelitz); Felix Draeseke (1835–1913), e.g., *Herrat* (1892, Dresden); Max Zenger (1837–1911), e.g., *Wieland der Schmied* (1880, Zurich); Hans Huber (1852–1921), e.g., *Kudrun* (1896, Basel); and Cyrill Kistler (1848–1907), e.g., *Baldurs Tod* (1905, Düsseldorf). Others were Felix Weingartner (1863–1942), especially his *Sakuntala* (1884) and *Orestes* (1902), Heinrich Zöllner (1854–1941), e.g., *Faust* (1887, Munich), and August Bungert, who completed one cycle, the four-part *Die Odyssee* (1898–1903, Dresden), and started a second, *Die Ilias*. The early works of several composers also showed distinct Wagnerian influence. Among them are Wilhelm Kienzl (1857–1941), especially his *Der Evangelimann* (1895, Berlin); Max von Schillings (1868–1933), with *Pfeifertag* (1899, Schwerin); Richard Strauss with *Guntram* (1894, Weimar) and *Feuersnot* (1901, Dresden); and Eugen d'Albert (1864–1932), in *Kain* (1900, Berlin).

One reaction against Wagner's style was to concentrate on comic opera in a lighter vein, following the models provided by Albert Lortzing, Otto Nicolai, and Peter Cornelius. Among these comic writers were Hermann Goetz (1840–1876), with *Der widerspenstigen Zähmung* (1874, Mannheim), and Hugo Wolf, with *Der Corregidor* (1896, Mannheim); neither work was very successful. The works of E. N. von Reznicek (1860–1945) were more popular, especially his *Donna Diana* (1894, Prague). D'Albert's *Die Abreise* (1898, Frankfurt) was also well received, and several works of Richard Strauss brought the genre to perfection.

A compromise between pro- and anti-Wagner sentiment could be found in the genre of the Volksoper, which often used Wagnerian techniques but set popular tales. In this group may be included the works of Ignaz Brüll, with *Das goldene Kreuz* (1875, Berlin); Viktor Nessler (1841–1890), with *Der Trompeter von Säckingen* (1884, Leipzig) and *Der Rattenfänger von Hamelin* (1879, Leipzig); Kienzl's *Der Evangelimann* and *Don Quixote* (1898, Berlin); Julius Bittner (1874–1939), with *Das höllisch Gold* (1916, Darmstadt) and *Der liebe Augustin* (1916, Vienna); and Richard Heuberger (1850–1914), with *Barfüssele* (1905, Dresden).

Similarly, the Märchenoper, while Wagnerian musically, turned to the realm of the fairytale for its subject matter. Alexander Ritter (1833–1896) contributed *Der faule Hans* (1885, Munich) to this genre; also active in this type of writing were Zöllner, with his *Die versunkene Glocke* (1899, Berlin), and Ludwig Thuille (1861–1907), with *Gugeline* (1901, Bremen) and *Lobentanz* (1898, Karlsruhe). The high point was reached with Engelbert Humperdinck (1854–1921); an early example was the tremendously popular *Hänsel und Gretel* (1893, Weimar), followed by the less successful *Dornröschen* (1902, Frankfurt) and *Königskinder* (1910, New York). His student, Leo Blech (1871–1958), contributed *Alpenkönig und Menschenfeind* (1903, Dresden) and *Aschenbrödel* (1905, Prague). Siegfried Wagner (1869–1930), forever in the shadow of his famous father, achieved some success with *Der Bärenhäuter* (1898, Munich) and *Der Kobold* (1904, Hamburg).

The genre which was furthest afield from the realm of Wagnerian opera was that of the light-hearted Viennese operetta, influenced by the works of Jacques Offenbach and extremely popular in the German-speaking world. Among its early proponents were Franz von Suppé, whose *Martl* (1848, Vienna) and *Der Tannenhäuser* (1852, Vienna) parodied *Martha* and *Tannhäuser*, respectively—his *Boccaccio* (1879, Vienna) was quite successful; Johann Strauss, Jr. (1825–1899), whose many triumphs included the very popular *Die Fledermaus* (1874, Vienna), *Eine Nacht in Venedig* (1883, Berlin), and *Wiener Blut* (1898, Vienna); Carl Millöcker (1842–1899), especially *Der Bettelstudent* (1882, Vienna); Carl Zeller (1842–1898), with *Der Vogelhändler* (1891, Vienna); C. M. Ziehrer

(1843–1922), with *Die Landstreicher* (1899, Vienna); and Heuberger, with *Der Opernball* (1898, Vienna). In the early twentieth century its adherents included Franz Lehár (1870–1948); his works dominated the genre, especially *Die lustige Witwe* (1905, Vienna), *Der Graf von Luxemburg* (1909, Vienna), and *Zigeunerliebe* (1910, Vienna). Also active were Oscar Straus (1870–1954), with *Der tapfere Soldat* (1908, Vienna); Leo Fall (1873–1925), with *Die Dollarprinzessin* (1907, Vienna); and Emmerich Kálmán (1882–1953), who drew on his Hungarian background to create *Die Csárdásfürstin* (1915, Vienna) and *Gräfin Maritza* (1924, Vienna). The operetta lost its vitality by the 1930s, and it was effectively killed off by the rise of the Nazis.

In the field of opera in the early twentieth century, there were several movements which interested German-speaking composers. Among them was Impressionism, as heard in Franz Schreker's (1878–1934) most famous opera, *Der ferne Klang* (1912, Frankfurt). Verismo was another attraction. Its adherents included d'Albert, with *Tiefland* (1903, Prague), and Schillings, with *Mona Lisa* (1915, Stuttgart). The influence of Wagner was still being felt in the works of Hans Pfitzner (1869–1949), as in *Der arme Heinrich* (1895, Mainz), *Palestrina* (1917, Munich), and *Das Herz* (1931, Berlin). Conservatism was evident in the works of Alexander von Zemlinsky (1871–1942), as in *Eine florentinische Tragödie* (1917, Stuttgart), and in the output of his student Erich Korngold (1897–1957), with *Violanta* (1916, Munich) and *Die tote Stadt* (1920, Hamburg). Other conservative composers included Franz Schmidt (1874–1939) (e.g., *Notre Dame*, 1914, Vienna); Paul Graener (1872–1944) (e.g., *Friedemann Bach*, 1931, Schwerin); Julius Weismann (1879–1950) (e.g., *Leonce und Lena*, 1925, Freiburg); and Walter Braunfels (e.g., *Die Vögel*, 1920, Munich).

Ferruccio Busoni (1866–1924), born to an Italian father and German mother, wrote in an eclectic style which took as its ideal the operas of Mozart and rejected those of Wagner. He used set numbers in his works, ranging from the early *Die Brautwahl* (1912, Zurich), to his final opera, *Doktor Faust* (1922, Dresden), left unfinished at his death and completed by Philipp Jarnach (1892–).

Richard Strauss (1864–1949) was another composer eventually attracted to the neoclassic idiom. His first success was the musically continuous *Salome* (1905, Dresden), which shocked the music world with its lurid plot and obvious sexuality. His next work, *Elektra* (1909, Dresden), his first collaboration with the librettist Hugo von Hofmannsthal (1874–1929), pushed tonality to the extreme with its harsh dissonances, and it again featured continuous music and overwhelming orchestral passages. But he soon turned away from the radically adventuresome path with the subsequent *Der Rosenkavalier* (1911, Dresden); its plot was a far cry from the decadence of *Salome* and the vengeance of *Elektra*. The work was much more diatonic than its predecessors and featured as its main character a direct descendant of Mozart's Cherubino. It also contained numerous sections of almost chamber-music passages, in an effort to allow the singer's words to be heard clearly. His desire to achieve an even balance between words and music culminated in *Ariadne* (1912, Vienna), and after such large-scale digressions as the massive *Die Frau ohne Schatten* (1919, Vienna) and the *Rosenkavalier*-like *Arabella* (1933, Vienna), Strauss ended his operatic production with the delicate *Capriccio* (1942, Munich); its very plot concerned the debate between words and music.

Strauss, in his long life, stood apart from the musical trends of the time. A genre that gained importance in the 1920s and 1930s was the political opera. Among its representatives was Kurt Weill (1900–1950), influenced by the flourishing cabaret in his native Berlin. He teamed up with the iconoclastic Bertolt Brecht (1898–1956) and produced such politically provocative works as *Die Bürgschaft* (1932, Berlin) and *Der Silbersee* (1933, Leipzig). Max Brand's (1896–1980) *Maschinist Hopkins* (1929, Duisburg) concerned the struggle of the workers against their oppressive employers. Also interested in politically meaningful plots were Hanns Eisler (1898–1962), with *Dantons Tod* (1929, Berlin); and Ernst Krenek (1900–), with *Der Diktator* and *Schwergewicht* (both 1928, Wiesbaden) and *Karl der Fünfte* (1938, Prague). The works of Paul Hindemith (1895–1963) included strong political viewpoints, as in *Mathis der Maler* (1938, Zurich), which concerned an uprising of the peasants against the governing authority. Non-classical influences such as jazz influenced such works as Weill's famed *Die Dreigroschenoper* (1928, Berlin) and *Aufsteig und Fall der Stadt Mahagonny* (1930, Berlin) and Krenek's *Jonny spielt auf* (1927, Leipzig).

Another development in German opera before World War II was Expressionism. The stage had been set by the harmonic daring of Strauss's *Elektra*, and it was carried to its ultimate by Arnold Schoenberg (1874–1951), with the introduction of twelve-tone writing and Sprechstimme in *Erwartung* (1909, first performed 1924, Prague) and *Die glückliche Hand* (1924, Vienna). It was continued by Schoenberg's disciple, Alban Berg (1885–1935), with *Wozzeck* (1925, Berlin) and *Lulu* (1937, Zurich), two works with profoundly gripping characterizations, tightly organized musical structures, and colorful orchestration. *Alkestis* (1924) by Egon Wellesz (1885–1974) was also a twelve-tone opera.

Carl Orff (1895–1982) favored a return to a simpler style and elements from popular folk songs. The results included the "scenic cantata" *Carmina burana* (1937, Munich), *Der Mond* (1939, Munich), *Die Kluge* (1943, Frankfurt), and the later *Die Bernauerin* (1947, Stuttgart).

After 1933 in Germany and 1938 in Austria many prominent composers were forced to flee because of their Jewish ancestry, as in the case of Weill, Schoenberg, and Korngold, or their political "unacceptability," as with Hindemith and Krenek.[1] Weill turned his efforts to musical theater in the United States, while Korngold wrote the scores for numerous Hollywood movies. Hindemith and Krenek also came to the United States. The apolitical Richard Strauss, long berated for not leaving Germany, was at first honored by the Nazis but eventually became a persona non grata, after he insisted adamantly that the name of his Jewish librettist, Stefan Zweig (1881–1942), be left on the playbill of the premiere of *Friedenstag* (1938, Munich). Other prominent composers to remain in Germany were Carl Orff and Werner Egk (1901–1983), whose radio opera *Columbus* (1933, Bavarian radio) and imposing *Peer Gynt* (1938, Berlin) were followed by the post-war *Der Revisor* (1957, Schwetzingen), *Irische Legende* (1955, Salzburg), and *Die Verlobung in San Domingo* (1963, Munich). The Swiss composer Othmar Schoeck (1886–1957), whose earlier successes included *Erwin und Elmire* (1915, Zurich) and *Penthesilea* (1927, Dresden), was criticized for allowing his final opera, *Das Schloss Dürande*, to receive its first performance in Berlin in 1943.[2]

Leaders after the Second World War included Rudolf Wagner-Régeny (1903–1969), whose early success, *Der Günstling* (1935, Dresden), was equalled by the late *Das Bergwerk zu Falun* (1961, Salzburg). The music of Gottfried von Einem (1918–), although often dissonant, keeps to the sphere of tonality; his first work, *Dantons Tod* (1947, Salzburg), has been joined by the notable *Der Prozess* (1953, Salzburg), *Der Zerrissene* (1964, Hamburg), the scaled-down *Besuch der alten Dame* (1971, Vienna), and the religiously controversial *Jesu Hochzeit* (1980, Vienna). Many of his librettos were written by the prolific Boris Blacher (1903–1975), whose many successes include *Die Flut* (1946, Dresden), the radio play *Abstrakte Oper Nr. 1* (1953, Hessian radio) and *Preussisches Märchen* (1952, Berlin). Paul Dessau (1894–1979), who settled in New York in 1939, returned to Germany in 1948 and lived in the eastern zone. His postwar output, often concerned with politically meaningful plots, included *Das Verhör des Lukullus* (1951, East Berlin), *Puntila* (1966, East Berlin), *Einstein* (1974, East Berlin), and *Leonce und Lena* (1979, East Berlin). Another pre-war composer whose works received premieres in Germany after the war is Ernst Krenek; among them is *Pallas Athene weint* (1955, Hamburg) and *Der goldene Bock* (1964, Hamburg). The eclectic Swiss composer Rolf Liebermann (1910–) updated the *Fidelio* story in his *Leonore 40/45* (1952) and turned to Greek literature for *Penelope* (1954, Salzburg) and to Molière for *Die Schule der Frauen* (1957, Salzburg), while Wolfgang Fortner (1907–1987) looked to García Lorca for the plots of *Die Bluthochzeit* (1957, Cologne) and *In seinem Garten* (1962, Schwetzingen)

Similarly, Giselher Klebe (1925–) has often turned to classics of literature for his texts; examples include *Die Räuber* (1957, Düsseldorf) and *Das Mädchen aus Domrémy* (1976, Stuttgart), both adaptations of Schiller plays. The large output of Hans Werner Henze (1926–) encompasses a variety of styles and choices of librettos. It includes *Das Floss der Medusa*, dedicated to Che Guevera (its scheduled premiere in 1968 was postponed until 1977, London, because of the controversy it generated), the idyllic *Elegie für junge Liebende* (1961, Schwetzingen), and the satirical *Junge Lord* (1965, Berlin) and *Die englische Katze* (1984, Schwetzingen). Non-Germans active in recent years include the Czech composer Bohuslav Martinů (1890–1959), whose *Griechische Passion* received a posthumous premiere in 1961, in Zurich. Korean-born Isang Yun (1917–) has written several operas, based on ancient Oriental stories, to German librettos

(*Geisterliebe*, 1971, Kiel; and *Sim Tjong*, 1972, Munich). Polish-born Krzystof Penderecki (1933–) has written *Der Teufel von Loudun* (1969, Hamburg) and *Die schwarze Maske* (1987, Salzburg). Bernd Alois Zimmermann (1918–1970) used a multimedia approach in his one operatic work, *Die Soldaten* (1965, Cologne). This trend has been continued by Karlheinz Stockhausen (1928–), with the cycle *Licht*; to date it includes *Donnerstag* (1981, Milan), *Samstag* (1984, Milan), and *Montag* (1988, Milan).

NOTES

1. For a detailed study of the Austrian-born composers, critics, musicians, and scholars whom the Nazis forced into exile or killed, see *ÖMz* XLIII/4 (April 1988) and XLIII/12 (December 1988). Hans Gál, Erich Korngold, Ernst Krenek, Marcel Rubin, Arnold Schoenberg, and Egon Wellesz receive individual discussions. The extensive list at the back of each volume includes Ralph Benatzky, Max Brand, Emmerich Kálmán, Bernhard Paumgartner, Robert Stolz, Oscar Straus, Ernst Toch, Viktor Ullmann, Jaromir Weinberger, and Alexander von Zemlinsky.

2. See Hanns-Werner Heister and Hans-Günther Klein, eds., *Musik und Musikpolitik im faschistischen Deutschland* (Frankfurt: Fischer, 1984), especially Klein's "Viel Konformität und wenig Verweigerung," 145-62, which examines the operas of Werner Egk, Ottmar Gerster, Hermann Reutter, Richard Strauss, and Rudolf Wagner-Régeny; and Hubert Kolland's "Wagner und der deutsche Faschismus," 126–35. But see also the caution in Stephen Hinton's review, in *ML* LXVII [1986], 188–90.

OPERAS
IN GERMAN

=A

Abgebrannte Haus, Das. See *Die Feuersbrunst.*

Abreise, Die (The Departure), comic opera in one act by Eugen d'Albert; libretto (Ger) by Ferdinand von Sporck after August von Steigentesch's play (1813). First performance October 20, 1898, Frankfurt. First U.S. performance October 30, 1973, Provo, Utah, Brigham Young University, with Donna Dalton (Gilfen's wife), Ray Arbizu (Trott), and Gene Larson (Gilfen); conducted by Ralph Laycock. First British performance September 3, 1925, London, King's Theatre (Hammersmith) (in English), with M. Bond and A. Skalski.

In this tale Trott attempts to get Gilfen to take a trip, so that Trott can pursue Gilfen's neglected wife. The plan backfires, however, when the wife realizes that she really loves only her husband, and in the end Trott is sent off.

Major roles: Trott (ten), Gilfen (bar), and Luise, Gilfen's wife (sop).

SCORES: fs (Leipzig: M. Brockhaus, c. 1898); vs ed. Ferdinand von Sporck (Leipzig: M. Brockhaus, c. 1898).

LIBRETTO: German (Leipzig: M. Brockhaus, c. 1898).

BIBLIOGRAPHY: Joseph Rosenstock, "Reports: U.S.," *ON* XXXVIII (December 22, 1973), 30 [on U.S. premiere].

Abstrakte Oper Nr. 1 (Abstract Opera No. 1), opera in seven scenes by Boris Blacher; idea and libretto (Ger) by Werner Egk. First performance June 28, 1953, Hessian radio; conducted by the composer. First stage performance October 17, 1953, Mannheim, Nationaltheater; conducted by Herbert Albert. First U.S. performance April 19, 1956, Boston, Boston University. Revised in 1957.

Each scene of this work focuses on one human emotion; for example, fear, love, pain. The text is a series of meaningless syllables.

Major roles: soprano, tenor, and baritone.

SCORE: vs ed. composer (Leipzig, c. 1898; Berlin-Wiesbaden: B&B, c. 1953).

BIBLIOGRAPHY: David Drew, "The Berlin Festival," *Opera* IX (1958), 21–23; Walther Harth, "Turbulente Premiere in Mannheim: Blachers 'Abstrakte Oper Nr. 1,'" *Melos* XX (1953), 326–27 [on premiere].

DISCOGRAPHY: University of Illinois Group, conducted by Zimer, Wergo 600017.

Abu Hassan, comic opera in one act by Carl Maria von Weber; libretto (Ger) by Franz Karl Hiemer after the tale of "The Sleeper Awakened, or The Dead Alive," second part, from the *Thousand and One Nights*. First performance June 4, 1811, Munich, Residenztheater, with Josepha Flerx-Lang (Fatime), Georg Mittermaier (Abu Hassan), and Joseph Muck (Omar); conducted by the composer. First U.S. performance (in the London version) November 5, 1827, New York, Park Theatre; first U.S. performance (Ger) September 8, 1877, New York. First British performance April 4, 1825, Drury Lane Theatre, in an English translation by William Dimond and with the music adapted by Thomas Simpson Cooke. The work was quite successful in the nineteenth century and is occasionally revived today, especially by smaller opera groups.

The story is set in Bagdad and concerns the poor Abu Hassan and his wife, Fatime, who are trying to fend off their many creditors, especially the lecherous Omar, who is also after Fatime. The pair devise a scheme to collect money by going separately to the Caliph and his consort and telling them that Hassan and Fatime have died, thereby making the rulers give the "widower" and "widow" funeral presents. The deception is of course uncovered, but the generous Caliph forgives the indigent pair.

Major roles: Abu Hassan, favorite of the Caliph (ten); Fatime, Hassan's wife (sop); Omar, a money changer (bass); Harun al Raschid, Caliph of Bagdad (speaking role); and Zobëide, his wife (speaking role).

The opera contained eight numbers at the premiere; Weber added two more (Nos. 4 and 8) for an 1812 performance in Gotha. The music, set in a "Turkish" style (with exotic rhythms, melodies, and instruments), evokes memories of Mozart's *Die Entführung aus dem Serail*,* particularly in Fatime's mock-tragic aria (No. 8), "Hier liegt, welch' martervolles Los," which recalls Constanze's "Martern aller Arten." The characters of Omar and Mozart's Osmin bear certain similarities, too. Other musical highlights of *Abu Hassan* include the opening duet of Fatime and Hassan, "Liebes Weibchen, reiche Wein," the exuberant chorus of the creditors (No. 3), "Geld! Geld! Geld!," and the spirited overture in A minor, with themes from the ensuing work. A plot similar to the Weber opera may be found in Antonio Veretti's *Il Favorito del re*, with a libretto by Arturo Rossato, first performed in Milan on March 17, 1932.

SCORES: fs ed. Willy-Werner Göttig (Offenbach am Main: Verlag der Seiboldschen Buchdruckerei Werner Dohany, 1925; reprinted Farnborough, Hants: Gregg International Publishers, 1968); vs (Bonn and Cologne: N. Simrock, ca. 1819).

BIBLIOGRAPHY: Percival R. Kirby, "Weber's Operas in London," *MQ* XXXII (1946), 343–46; W/*CMW*, 112–22.

DISCOGRAPHY: Hallstein, Schreier, Adam, Dresden State Opera Chorus, conducted by Rögner, Eurodisc 80 608 MR (1); Moser, Gedda, and Moll, Bavarian State Opera, conducted by Sawallisch, EMI/Electrola 1C065–30148—both reviewed by John W. Freeman, "Records," *ON* XLVII (July 1982), 37—and Schwarzkopf, Witte, Bohnen; conducted by Ludwig, Berlin Radio Symphony and Chorus, Varèse/Sarabande 81093 (1).

Adelheit von Veltheim (Adelheit of Veltheim), play with music in four acts by Christian Gottlob Neefe; libretto (Ger) by Gustav Friedrich Wilhelm Grossmann. First performance September 23, 1780, Frankfurt. The work was fairly popular and appeared on German stages until about 1800.

In its story and music this opera has strong resemblances to the later *Die Entführung aus dem Serail** of Mozart. Adelheit, like Constanze, has been captured by pirates and is in the Pasha's harem, which is guarded by the Osmin-like Mehmet (except that Mehmet is cultured and not particularly cruel). Karl plans to free his beloved by using a ladder to scale the seraglio wall and getting Mehmet drunk. The plans are thwarted, but the generous Pasha, like his Mozartean counterpart, frees the European lovers.

Major roles: Achmet, Pasha (Bassa) of Tunis (castrato or tenor); Adelheit, a young German woman (sop); Karl von Bingen, beloved of Adelheit and a German passing himself off as Osman, a gardener (ten); Mehmet, overseer of the seraglio (bass).

Among the musical parallels to Mozart's work are Mehmet's drinking songs "Da trink ich" (Act I) and "Kurz ist unser Leben" (Act II); Karl's sorrowful monodrama in the second act, "Vertraute meines Kummer," in which he accompanies himself with a lute (as in Belmonte's Romance "Im Mohrenland"); and the two choral finales which end Acts III and IV, "Dank dem Bassa" and "Opfert im jauchzende Gesänge" (see Mozart's Janissary choruses "Singt dem grossen Bassa" and "Bassa Selim lebe lange"). Musical exoticism can be found in these two choral numbers and in the overture and the "Sinfonia di guerra" which separates the last two acts of *Adelheit*.

LIBRETTO: German (Leipzig: Dykische Buchhandlung, 1781).

BIBLIOGRAPHY: Irmgard Leux, *Christian Gottlob Neefe* (Leipzig: Kistner & Siegel, 1925), 75.

Adonis (Der geliebte Adonis) (Adonis) (The Beloved Adonis), opera in three acts by Reinhard Keiser; libretto (Ger) by Christian Heinrich Postel. First performance spring (?) 1697, Hamburg.

Venus is in love with the mortal Adonis but both are pursued, in turn, by Mars, and by Eumene and Dryante. Mars, urged on by the jealous Dryante, changes himself into a boar and kills Adonis while he is hunting. Venus punishes Dryante by changing her into an oak tree and brings Eumene and Philistus together.

Major roles: Adonis (alto); Venus (sop); Mars (bass); Philistus, a shepherd and friend of Adonis (ten); Dryante and Eumene, shepherdesses in love with Adonis (2 sop); Gelon, a comic shepherd (ten); and Proteus (bass).

SCORE: fs, 1697 libr. repr. in *Handel Sources*, III, ed. John H. Roberts (New York: Garland Publishing, 1986).

Agnes von Hohenstaufen (Agnes of Hohenstaufen), opera in three acts by Gasparo Spontini; libretto (Ger) by Ernst Raupach. First performance ("lyrisches Drama") (first act only) May 28, 1827, Berlin. First complete performance, revised as a "grosse historisch-romantische Oper," June 12, 1829, Berlin, Königliches Opernhaus; third version, as a "grosse historisch-romantische Oper," 1837, Berlin. Revived May 6, 1954 (in Italian), Florence, Maggio Musicale, with Lucille Udovick (Agnes), Dorothy Dow (Irmengard), Franco Corelli (Henry of Brunswick), and G. G. Guelft (the Emperor); conducted by Vittorio Gui; revived again later that month in Florence, with Renata Tebaldi in the title role, conducted by Tulio Serafin.

The story, set at the Hohenstaufen court in Mainz, 1194, concerns Agnes, who is in love with Henry, the Count Palatine and son of the rebel Henry, Duke of Saxony. Plotting against their marriage is Emperor Henry VI, who forbids Agnes to marry any family member of his political enemies and demands that she marry his ally, the French King Philip, who disguises himself as the Duke of Burgundy and pursues Agnes himself. Despite the warnings, Agnes secretly marries her beloved. A catastrophic ending is avoided when her new father-in-law surrenders to the emperor. The ruler is touched by this gesture and gives his blessing to Agnes' wedding.

Major roles: Agnes, daughter of the Countess Irmengard (sop); Irmengard (sop); Count Henry (Heinrich) of Brunswick (ten), son of the rebel Duke of Saxony; Emperor Henry (Heinrich) VI of Hohenstaufen (bass); and King Philip of France/Duke of Burgundy (bar).

Spontini's last opera, *Agnes*, contains among its musical numbers Enrico's beautiful lament in Act II and Agnes' prayer.

BIBLIOGRAPHY: Elizabeth Forbes, "On Radio and TV," *Opera* XXV (1974), 746; Luigi Ronga, " 'L'Agnes di Hohenstaufen' . . . ," *RMI* LVI (1954), 247–57; Claudio Sartori, "Florence" [review of first Italian performance, 1954], *Opera* V (1954), 470–74.

DISCOGRAPHY: Udovick, Dow, Corelli, F. Albanese, Mascherini, Colzani, Guelfi, Florence May Festival, conducted by Gui, Melodram Mel–27055 (2 compact discs) (Italian); this 1954 performance is reviewed by John W. Freeman, *ON* LIV, no. 5 (November 1989), 55.

Ägyptische Helena, Die (The Egyptian Helen), opera in two acts by Richard Strauss; libretto (Ger) by Hugo von Hofmannsthal after a fragment by Euripides. First performance June 6, 1928, Dresden, Opera House, with Elisabeth Rethberg

(Helena), Curt Taucher (Menelaus), Maria Rajdl (Aithra), Helene Jung (the Seashell), Friedrich Plaschke (Altair), and Guglielmo Fazzini (Da-Ud); conducted by Fritz Busch. First U.S. performance November 6, 1928, New York, Metropolitan Opera, with Maria Jeritza (Helena), Rudolf Laubenthal (Menelaus), Editha Fleischer (Aithra), Clarence Whitehill (Altair), and Marion Telva (the Seashell); conducted by Artur Bodanzky. The opera was shortened for a 1933 performance in Salzburg and revised again in 1940. Modern revivals include a concert performance (the original version) on April 27, 1979, in New York's Carnegie Hall, with Gwyneth Jones (Helena), Matti Kastu (Menelaus), Barbara Hendricks (Aithra), Willard White (Altair), Curtis Rayam (Da-Ud), and Birgit Finnilä (the Seashell).

In this variation on the Helen of Troy story, the sorceress Aithra, who is also the beloved of Poseidon, learns from the Omniscient Seashell that Menelaus is planning to kill his wife, Helena, whom he has just brought back from Troy. Menelaus' ship is wrecked in a storm, and he and Helena alight on an island, where they are met by Aithra. She gives Menelaus a magic potion which makes him think that Helena spent ten years in Egypt, rather than with Paris.

Major roles: Helena (sop); Menelaus (ten); Hermione, their child (sop); Aithra, an Egyptian, daughter of the king (sop); Altair (bar); Da-Ud, his son (ten); and the all-knowing Seashell (alto).

For detailed synopses and musical analyses, see D/RS, II, 310–51; K/KOB, 835–37; and M/RSC, 215–41.

The opera includes Helena's beautiful aria "Zweite Brautnacht! Zaubernacht, überlange" (Act II). It is one of the few operas that have an inanimate object (the Seashell) as a major character.

SCORES: vs ed. Otto Singer (Berlin: A. Fürstner, 1928, and London: Fürstner, 1928).

BIBLIOGRAPHY: "Die ägyptische Helena," *Richard Strauss Blätter*, IV (Vienna: Internationale Richard Strauss-Gesellschaft, 1972); Andrew Porter, "Musical Events," *NY* LV (June 4, 1979), 146, 149 [on 1979 Carnegie Hall performance]; Patrick Smith, "Our Critics Abroad . . . " [New York performance], *Opera* XXX (1979), 785–86.

DISCOGRAPHY: Jones, Hendricks, Finnilä, Kastu, Rayam, and White, Jewel Chorale, Detroit Symphony, conducted by A. Dorati, London OSA–13135 (3); reviewed by John W. Freeman, "Records," *ON* XLIV (May 1980), 44.

Alceste, opera in five acts by Anton Schweitzer; libretto (Ger) by Christoph Martin Wieland. First performance May 28, 1773, Weimar, with Josepha Hellmuth (Parthenia), Friedrich Hellmuth (Admet), Franziska Koch (Alceste), and Friedrich Günther (Herkules).

Alceste, wife of Admet, King of Thessaly, volunteers to die in place of her husband. She is rescued from Hades by Herkules.

Major roles: Admet, King of Thessaly (ten); Alceste, his wife (sop); Parthenia, her sister (sop); and Herkules (bass).

The Schweitzer work was composed with the aim of creating a German national opera. It consists mostly of solo numbers and has one chorus piece. Among its numbers is Admet's Act IV "O Jugendzeit"/"O flieh, geliebter Schatten."

Other German treatments of the Alceste story include Nikolaus Adam Strungk (1693, Leipzig); Georg Caspar Schürmann's *Getreue Alceste* (1719, Brunswick); Ernst Wilhelm Wolf (1780, Weimar); Friedrich Benda (1786, Berlin); and Egon Wellesz's *Alkestis* (1924, Mannheim).

SCORES: fs (Leipzig: Schwickert, 1774); repr. in *German Opera 1770–1800*, III, ed. Thomas Bauman (New York and London: Garland Publishing, 1986); vs (Leipzig: Schwickert, 1774).

LIBRETTO: German, repr. in *German Opera 1770–1800*, XVIII, *Librettos I*, ed. Thomas Bauman (New York: Garland Publishing, 1986).

BIBLIOGRAPHY: Anna Amalie Abert, "Der Geschmackswandel auf der Opernbühne, am Alkestis-Stoff dargestellt," *Mf* VI (1953), 214–35.

Alchymist, Der oder **Der Liebesteufel,** opera in one act by Johann Schuster; libretto (Ger) by August Gottlieb Meissner. First performance March 1778, Dresden. Johann André's version April 11, 1778, Berlin.

Louise is in love with Bellnitz, but she is thwarted by her father, Tarnow, an alchemist who will not let her wed until he has discovered the philosopher's stone. The lovers are aided by Christine, Louise's maid, and Heinrich, Bellnitz's servant, who bribes Louise's brother Gustel to switch the silver in his father's apparatus for gold. Magister Kybbutz, Louise's stuffy tutor, enters and threatens to betray the lovers, but Tarnow's sudden appearance forces him to take refuge in a trapdoor with Gustel. Heinrich, hiding in the fireplace, pretends to be a demon and warns the superstitious Tarnow that he will be coming to get him unless he substitutes a young woman in his place. Bellnitz, taking the part of the demon, enters and forces Tarnow to agree to let him marry Louise. The young couple go through the trapdoor. When Frau Tarnow appears and Heinrich tells what has really happened, Tarnow tries to go back on his promise, but, on threat of being revealed as having dealt with the devil, he is convinced to let his daughter wed and, in the bargain, to give up his experiments.

Major roles: Tarnow, an alchemist (bar); Frau Tarnow (sop); Louise, their daughter (sop); Gustel, her ten-year-old brother (sop); Christine, Louise's chambermaid (sop); Bellnitz, Louise's lover (ten); Heinrich, his servant (bass); Magister Kybbutz, Gustel's pedantic tutor (bass).

SCORE: fs ms repr. in *German Opera 1770–1800*, V, ed. Thomas Bauman (New York and London: Garland Publishing, 1985).

LIBRETTO: German (Leipzig, 1778); repr. in *German Opera 1770–1800, Librettos I*, ed. Thomas Bauman (New York and London: Garland Publishing, 1985).

Alchymist, Der (The Alchemist), Romantic opera in three acts by Ludwig Spohr; libretto (Ger) by Fr. Georg Schmidt [Karl Pfeiffer, who wrote under a pseudonym because his employer, the Elector of Kassel, disapproved of his employees' public connection with literary ventures], after Washington Irving's "The Student of Salamanca," published in the collection *Braceridge Hall* (1822). First performance July 28, 1830, Kassel, Kurfürstliches Hoftheater, with Herr Weber (Vasquez), Dlle. Bamberger (Inez), Herr Wild (Alonzo), Herr Föppel (Ramiro), and Dlle. Trant (Paola). It was revived in 1925 in Essen.

The action revolves around a Moorish castle in Spain. It concerns the alchemist Felix de Vasquez and his daughter Inez, who is being courted by Alonzo and Don Ramiro, who is also the lover of the gypsy Paola, a dispossessed Moorish princess. When Vasquez is arrested by the Inquisition and sentenced to death because of the machinations of Ramiro, Alonzo secures a pardon from the judges, defeats Ramiro in a duel, and brings on general rejoicing by the people.

Major roles: Don Felix de Vasquez (bass), Inez (sop), Don Alonzo (ten), Don Ramiro (bass), and Paola (sop).

The music is infused with exoticism, heightened by Spohr's use of the harp, triangle, tambourine, and castanets. This local color is particularly evident in the C-minor overture. The opera contains spoken dialogue as well as recitative.

SCORE: vs (Berlin: Schlesinger, 1831).

BIBLIOGRAPHY: B/*LS*, 202–8.

Alessandro Stradella, Romantic opera in three acts by Friedrich von Flotow; libretto (Ger) by W. Friedrich [Friedrich Riese] after the "comédie mêlée de chant" of P. A. A. Pittaud de Forges and Paul Duport of 1837, which included several airs by Flotow. First performance December 30, 1844, Hamburg, Stadttheater. First U.S. performance November 29, 1853, New York. First British performance June 6, 1846, London, Drury Lane Theatre, with music arranged by Julius Benedict.

The famous Italian composer Stradella is, in this opera, in love with Leonora. But their marriage plans are interrupted by assassins, who have been hired by the jealous and wealthy Bassi, who wants Leonora for himself. When the cutthroats hear the composer sing, however, they repent and ask his forgiveness.

Major roles: Alessandro Stradella, a composer (ten); Leonora (sop); the pupil of the wealthy Bassi (bass).

Together with *Martha*,* this was Flotow's most successful work. The opera's musical highlights include a trio, "Ruhig, leise, stille, sacht" (No. 11a), an a cappella trio in the third act, and Stradella's hymn "Jungfrau Maria" (No. 12), which ends the work.

Other operas on this subject are by César Franck (1844, not performed); Doppler (1845, Vienna, according to C/*DDO*, I); and Sirico (1863).

SCORE: vs ed. composer (Hamburg: J. A. Böhme, ca.1844).

LIBRETTO: German, ed. Georg Richard Kruse (Leipzig: P. Reclam jun. [1910]).

8

Alexandre bis. See *Zweimal Alexander*.

Alfonso und Estrella (Alfonso and Estrella), opera in three acts by Franz Schubert; libretto (Ger) by Franz von Schober. Composed September 1821–February 1822. First performance June 24, 1854, Weimar, under the direction of Franz Liszt. First U.S. performance (concert) November 11, 1978, Detroit, Ford Auditorium, with Elisabeth Söderström (Estrella), Curtis Rayam (Alfonso), Peter Lagger (Adolfo), William Parker (Troila), and Steven Kimbrough (Mauregato); conducted by Antal Dorati. First British performance September 7, 1968, Edinburgh Festival, with Richard Lewis (Alfonso), Phyllis Curtin (Estrella), Josef Greindl (Adolfo), and John Shaw and Thomas Hemsley (the rival kings); conducted by Alexander Gibson.

The Romeo-and-Juliet type of story (albeit with a happy ending) is set in Moorish Spain. It concerns the lovely Estrella, whose father, Mauregato, has illegally seized the throne from Troila, whose son Alfonso falls in love with Estrella. Their marriage plans are blocked by Adolfo, who wants to wed Estrella himself, but Alfonso defeats him and thereby secures happiness for himself and his beloved.

Major roles: Estrella (sop); Alfonso (ten), son of the deposed Troila (bass); Mauregato, Estrella's father (bass); and Adolfo, Mauregato's evil general (bass).

Despite a weak libretto, the opera contains a number of beautiful pieces, including the finale to the first act (No. 10), "Glänzende Waffe den Krieger erfreut."

SCORE: fs (without the overture), Schu/*AGA*, XV/5 (1892).

BIBLIOGRAPHY: Maurice Brown, "Schubert's Two Major Operas. A Consideration of the Actual Possibility of Stage Production," *MR* XX (1959), 104–18; ———, "Schubert: Discoveries of the Last Decade," *MQ* LVII (1971), 351–78; Jay Carr, "Reports: U.S.," *ON* XLIII (January 27, 1979), 58–59 [on U.S. concert premiere]; Jack Hiemenz, "Opera Everywhere. Detroit" [on U.S. premiere], *HiFi/MA* XXIX (March 1979), 23–24; Andrew Porter, "Musical Events," *NY* LIV (December 1, 1978), 65–68, 70, 72 [on U.S. premiere]; Conrad Wilson, ". . . *Alfonso and Estrella*," *Opera* XIX (Festival issue 1968), 50–51 [on British premiere].

DISCOGRAPHY: Prey, Mathis, Adam, Fischer-Dieskau, and Schreier, conducted by Suitner, Berlin Radio Chorus, Staatskapelle Berlin, EMI IC 157–30816/18 (3); reviewed by Andrew Porter, "Classical Records. Schubert: Alfonso und Estrella," *HiFi* XXIX (May 1979), 90–92; John W. Freeman, "Records," *ON* LXIII (March 3, 1979), 41.

Alkmene, opera in three acts by Giselher Klebe; libretto (Ger) by the composer after Heinrich Kleist. First performance September 25, 1961, Berlin, Deutsche Oper, with Thomas Stewart (Jupiter), Evelyn Lear (Alkmene), Richard Lewis (Amphitryon), Lisa Otto, Tom Krause, and Walter Dicks; conducted by Heinrich Hollreiser.

The story is a treatment of the Amphitryon legend, with a prologue on Mount Olympus, during which Jupiter appears to Alkmene. Jupiter then assumes the form of Alkmene's husband, the Theban general Amphitryon, who is in fact away at war.

Major roles: Jupiter (bass); Alkmene (sop); Amphitryon (ten); Merkur (bass); Sosias, servant of Amphitryon (bass); and Cleanthis, Sosias' wife (sop).

Among the musical highlights are Alkmene's Act II arioso, "Wie soll ich Worte finden," and the subsequent duet with Jupiter.

SCORE: vs ed. composer (Berlin: B&B, 1961).

LIBRETTO: German (Berlin: B&B, 1961).

BIBLIOGRAPHY: H. H. Stuckenschmidt, "West Berlin House Opens," *Opera* XII (1961), 780–81 [on premiere].

Almira, opera in three acts by George Frideric Handel; libretto (Ger-It) by Friedrich C. Feustking after the Italian libretto by Giulio Pancieri, set by Boniventi (1691). The complete title is *Der in Krohnen erlangte Glücks-Wechsel* oder *Almira, Königen von Castilien.* First performance January 8, 1705, Hamburg, Theater am Gänsemarkt.

Almira has ascended to the throne of Castile on the death of her father. Although he wished her to wed Consalvo, she is pursued by Osman, who is betrothed to Edilia. The queen herself is in love with Fernando, whom she mistakenly believes to be in love with Edilia. Edilia, meanwhile, is enamored of Raymondo, the King of Mauritania, while the unscrupulous Osman becomes interested in Bellante. Almira imprisons Fernando, but she has him released when she realizes he is innocent of betraying her love. He turns out to be the long-lost son of Consalvo and therefore is suitable for the queen to wed. Osman gets the hand of Bellante, and Raymondo that of Edilia.

Major roles: Almira, Queen of Castile (sop); Edilia, princess (sop); Bellante, Princess of Aranda (sop); Raymondo, King of Mauritania (bass); Consalvo, Prince of Segovia (bass); Osman, his son (ten); Fernando, secretary to the queen (ten); and Tabarco, page to Fernando (ten).

Handel's first opera, *Almira* contains forty-one arias in German and fifteen in Italian. Reinhard Keiser produced his own version in 1706, in Hamburg.

SCORES: fs, *Georg Friedrich Händel's Werke*, LV, ed. Friedrich Chrysander (Leipzig: Ausgabe der Deutschen Handelgesellschaft, 1873).

LIBRETTO: (Hamburg: 1704), repr. in *The Librettos of Handel's Operas*, I, ed. Ellen T. Harris (New York and London: Garland Publishing, 1989).

BIBLIOGRAPHY: Percy Robinson, "Bach's Indebtedness to Handel's *Almira*," *MT* XLVIII (1907), 309–12.

DISCOGRAPHY: excerpts in *Early German Opera from the Goose Market*: Otto, Siemeling, Yano, Schmidt, Prey, Brauer, and Adam, Günther Arndt Chorus, Berlin Philharmonic, conducted by Brückner-Rüggerberg, Angel 36273; reviewed by C. J. Luten, *ON* XXX (May 7, 1966), 30.

Alpenkönig und Menschenfeind (King of the Alps and Misanthrope), opera in three acts by Leo Blech; libretto (Ger) by Richard Batka after Ferdinand Raimund's play of the same name. First performance January 10, 1903, Dresden. Revised as *Rappelkopf* and performed 1917, Berlin.

The opera is set in the Alps, in 1830. The ever-suspicious and misanthropic Rappelkopf makes life miserable for his womenfolk and servants. Astragalus, King of the Elves, appears and changes Rappelkopf into his brother-in-law while assuming Rappelkopf's form himself. Astragalus' subsequent horrid behavior cures the real Rappelkopf of his nastiness.

Major roles: Astragalus, Alpenkönig (bar); Rappelkopf (bar); Sabine, his wife (alto); and Marthe, his daughter (sop).

Other operas on the subject include Wenzel Müller's *Der Alpenkönig* (1828, Vienna); and Mark Lothar's *Rappelkopf* (1958, Munich).

SCORE: vs ed. Egon Pollak (Berlin: B&B, c. 1903).

Alruna, die Eulenkönigin (Alruna, Queen of the Owls), "grand Romantic opera in three acts" by Ludwig Spohr; anonymous libretto (Ger). Composed in 1808 in Gotha. Excerpts performed in winter 1809, Weimar court, but withdrawn by the composer.

In this mixture of human and magical characters, the knight Herrmann loves Bertha, daughter of Count Bruno, who will not permit them to marry unless his stolen property is recovered. A second pair of lovers consists of Franz, Herrmann's squire, and Clara, Bertha's maid. In the second act Herrmann and Franz are caught in a storm in a forest, which is the realm of the sorceress Alruna, who tries to seduce and bewitch Herrmann. When her efforts fail, she conjures up a magical play which portrays Bertha as unfaithful, but Herrmann leaves and returns home to discover whether his beloved has in fact betrayed him.

In Act III Alruna and her helpers search for Herrmann, who has found Franz at the gravestone of the knight's ancestor Udo, one of Alruna's erstwhile victims. The ghost of Udo, not unlike the Commendatore in *Don Giovanni*, speaks from the grave; he offers his descendant a magical shield to break Alruna's power. In the final scene Herrmann uses the shield to foil Alruna's plan to abduct Bertha and her father, and the ghost of Udo joins in at the end.

Major roles: Alruna (sop), Bertha (sop), Herrmann (ten), Bruno (bass), Franz (bass), and Udo's ghost (bass).

The plot has as its antecedents several German Romantic operas, especially Carl Friedrich Hensler's libretto for *Das Donauweibchen*,* which has as its main character a supernatural being. Musically, its overture recalls that of *Die Zauberflöte*,* and Spohr himself admitted that he deliberately imitated the Mozart work. Spohr uses the technique of musical reminiscences, for instance in the Act I Finale, which quotes the music of the lovers' first duet (No. 1). Alruna's third-act scena is another such example. Although Spohr abandoned the opera after a rehearsal in Weimar, he had the overture published and used Bertha's aria (No. 13) in the Adagio of his Notturno, Op. 34 (1815) and parts of Nos. 8 and 9 in his 1811 opera *Der Zweikampf mit der Geliebten.**

SCORES: The overture was published as Op. 21 (Offenbach: André, 1812).

BIBLIOGRAPHY: B/*LS*, 53–56; Eugen Schmitz, "Louis Spohrs Jugendoper 'Alruna,' " *ZIMG* XIII (1911–1912), 293–99.

Antigonae, opera in three parts by Carl Orff; libretto (Ger), a setting of Friedrich Hölderlin's translation (1803) of the Sophocles play. First performance August 9, 1949, Salzburg, with Res Fischer (Antigonae), Maria Ilosvay (Ismene), Benno Kusche (the leader of the chorus), Hermann Uhde (Kreon), Helmut Krebs (the watchman), Lorenz Fehenberger (Haemon), Hilde Zadek (Eurydike), Ernst Häfliger (Tiresias), and Josef Greindl (the messenger); conducted by Ferenc Fricsay. First U.S. performance (concert) April 21, 1968, New York, Brooklyn Academy of Music, with Inge Borkh (Antigonae), Elizabeth Mannion (Ismene and Eurydike), John Ostendorf (the leader of the chorus), Carlos Alexander (Kreon), Leo Goeke (the watchman), William Lewis (Haemon), Norman Page (Tiresias), and J. B. Davis (the messenger); conducted by Thomas Scherman.

Antigonae, daughter of Oedipus and Jocasta, defies Kreon's orders not to bury Polyneices, her brother. Kreon ignores the warnings of the seer Tiresias and condemns Antigonae to be buried alive. Her fiancé, Haemon, son of Kreon, joins her in death, and his mother, Eurydike, kills herself on hearing of the tragedy.

Major roles: Antigonae (sop); Ismene (alto); Eurydike (sop); Kreon (bar); Haemon (ten); Tiresias (ten); the messenger (bass); a watchman (ten); and the leader of the chorus (bar).

In writing the work Orff stressed that he intended to have the emphasis on the words of the play. Therefore there is no traditional singing but rather declamation, with and without accompaniment, depending on the situation.

There are some thirty operas on this story, including those by Giuseppe Maria Orlandini (1718, Venice); Nicola Antonio Zingarelli (1790, Paris); and Arthur Honegger (1927, Brussels).

SCORES: fs (Mainz: BSS and New York: Schott Music, 1959); vs (Mainz: BSS, 1949).

LIBRETTO: German (Mainz: BSS, 1949).

BIBLIOGRAPHY: Virginia Pleasants, "Salzburg Festival Regains Flavor of Cosmopolitanism," *MA* LXIX (October, 1949), 6 [on premiere]; Milos O. Pták, "Current Chronicle. Austria. Salzburg," *MQ* XXXVI (1950), 105–[on premiere]; Herbert Weinstock, "Our Critics Abroad . . . New York" [on U.S. premiere], *Opera* XIX (1968), 552–53.

DISCOGRAPHY: See M/*IRR*, 281–82.

Arabella, lyrical comedy in three acts by Richard Strauss; libretto (Ger) by Hugo von Hofmannsthal after his novella *Lucidor—Characters for an Unwritten Comedy* (1910). First performance July 1, 1933, Dresden, with Viorica Ursuleac

(Arabella), Alfred Jerger (Mandryka), Margit Bokor (Zdenka), Camilla Kallab (Adelaide), Elice Illiard (Fiakermilli), Friedrich Plaschke (Waldner), and Martin Kremer (Matteo); conducted by Clemens Krauss. First U.S. performance February 10, 1955, New York, Metropolitan Opera (in English), with Eleanor Steber (Arabella), George London (Mandryka), Hilde Gueden (Zdenka), Ralph Herbert (Waldner), and Blanche Thebom (Adelaide); conducted by Rudolf Kempe. First British performance May 17, 1934, London, Covent Garden, with Viorica Ursuleac (Arabella), Margit Bokor (Zdenka), Ruth Berglund (Adelaide), Elice Illiard (Fiakermilli), Alfred Jerger (Mandryka), Berthold Sterneck (Waldner), and Martin Kremer (Matteo); conducted by Clemens Krauss.

In an attempt to recapture the success of Der Rosenkavalier,* Strauss again set the opera in Vienna, albeit in modern times, with the focus on the pretty Arabella, daughter of the indigent Count Waldner. Her family lives in a seedy hotel, and she is pursued by many admirers, while her sister, Zdenka, is forced to parade as a young man to save the family the expense of another daughter (and giving Strauss the excuse for having a "trouser" role like Octavian). Mandryka, a wealthy country landowner, comes to court Arabella but is hurt by her seeming indiscretions with Matteo, who is seducing Zdenka, thinking she (he) is Arabella. Identities are straightened out at the end, Arabella accepts the hand of Mandryka in marriage, and Zdenka is allowed to wed her beloved Matteo.

Major roles: Arabella (sop); Zdenka, her sister (sop); Mandryka (bar); Count Waldner, retired cavalry officer and father of Arabella and Zdenka (bass); Adelaide, his wife (mezzo); Matteo, an officer (ten), and Count Elemer (ten), suitors of Arabella; and Fiakermilli (sop).

For detailed synopses and musical analyses, see C/NMC, 56; D/RS, III, 386–439; K/KOB 837–41; and M/RSC, 243–69.

Hofmannsthal died before the opera was completed, which may explain why it is less polished than Der Rosenkavalier. Nonetheless, it contains many exquisite moments, including, in the first act, the duet of Arabella and Zdenka, "Er ist der Richtige," Arabella's closing "Mein Elemer," and the duet of the heroine and Mandryka, "Ich habe eine Frau gehabt"; in the second, Fiakermilli's coloratura passages; and, in the third, Arabella's aria that closes the work, "Das war sehr gut, Mandryka."

The story of Vincenz Franz Tuczek's Arabella oder Die Schreckensfolgen der Eifersucht, 1818, Pest, bears no relation to the Strauss work.

SCORE: vs ed. Felix Wolfes (Berlin-Grunewald: J. Oertel and London: Fürstner Ltd., 1933).

LIBRETTO: German (Berlin: A. Fürstner, 1933).

BIBLIOGRAPHY: Peter G. Davis, "At the Top of the Steps," ON XLVII (February 26, 1983), 28–30; Alan Jefferson, "An Introduction to 'Arabella,' " Opera XVI (1965), 9–12; Joachim H. Meyer, "Arabella's Dresden Premiere," ON XIX (February 21, 1955), 14–15; Harold Rosenthal, "London Opera Diary," Opera XVI (1965), 221–26; John Simon, "The Right One," ON XLVII (February 26, 1983), 16–19, 30.

DISCOGRAPHY: See Alan Jefferson, "Opera on the Gramophone," *Opera* XVIII (1967), 25–31.

VIDEO: Putnam, Rolandi, Sarfaty, Bröcheler, Korn, Lewis, and Bradley, London Philharmonic Orchestra, Glyndebourne Chorus, conducted by Haitink, Thorn EMI HBO Video.

Arden muss sterben (Arden Must Die), opera in two acts by Alexander Goehr; libretto (Ger) by Erich Fried after an anonymous sixteenth-century play, *Arden of Faversham*. First performance March 5, 1967, Hamburg, Staatsoper, with Toni Blankenheim (Arden), Kerstin Meyer (Alice Faversham), and Manfred Schenk (Black Will); conducted by Charles Mackerras. First British performance April 17, 1974, London, Sadler's Wells, conducted by Meredith Davies.

The opera is set around Faversham and London in the sixteenth century and concerns Arden, a rich entrepreneur, whose dealings have filled many people with the desire to kill him. The third attempt on his life is made by Shakebag and Black Will, employed by Arden's wife, and the two landowners Greene and Reede, whose fortunes were ruined by Arden. The plotters kill their prey but are caught by the police.

Major roles: Arden, a rich businessman (bass); Alice Faversham, Arden's wife (mezzo); Shakebag (ten) and Black Will (bass), both employees of Alice; Greene, a landowner (bar); and Reede, a landowner (bass).

Other treatments of the Arden story include Rudolf Raimann's *Arden Enok* (1894, Budapest); Max Wedert's *Enoch Arden* (1909, Essen); and Ottmar Gerster's *Enoch Arden* (1936, Düsseldorf).

SCORE: vs German-English, transl. Geoffrey Skelton (London: Schott and New York: AMP, 1967).

BIBLIOGRAPHY: Erich Fried, "Mein Libretto für Goehr," *Melos* XXXII (1967), 110–14 [on premiere]; Christopher Shaw, " 'Arden Must Die,' " *Tempo* CX (September 1974), 42–43 [on British premiere]; John Warrack, "Goehr's New Opera," *Opera* XVIII (1967), 369–71.

Ariadne (Die schöne und getreue Ariadne) (Ariadne [The Beautiful and Faithful Ariadne]), opera in three acts by Johann Georg Conradi; libretto (Ger) by Christian Heinrich Postel. First performance 1691, Hamburg. The opera was arranged and revised by Reinhold Keiser as *Die betrogene und nachmals vergötterte Ariadne* and was performed on November 26, 1722, in Hamburg.

This is the earliest known German setting of the Ariadne legend. The manuscript was lost and rediscovered only in 1972 (see the article by George Buelow below). Kusser's version followed in 1692 in Brunswick.

Major roles: Ariadne; Phaedra; and Theseus.

Most of the arias are in da capo form, and the orchestra is very active. The composer uses the solo motto technique extensively to begin arias, as in Phaedra's "Liebe muss verständig seyn" (Act I, scene 2).

BIBLIOGRAPHY: George J. Buelow, *"Die schöne und getreue Ariadne* (Hamburg: 1691): A Lost Opera by J. G. Conradi Rediscovered," *Acm* XLIV/1 (1972), 108–21; Paul Nicolai, *Der Ariadne-Stoff in der Entwicklungsgeschichte der deutschen Oper* (Viersen: J. H. Meyer, 1919).

Ariadne auf Naxos (Ariadne on Naxos), "ein Duodrama mit musikalischen Zwischensätzen" in one act by Georg Benda; libretto (Ger) by Johann Christian Brandes after a cantata by Heinrich Wilhelm von Gerstenberg, originally written for Anton Schweitzer. First performance January 27, 1775, Gotha, with Charlotte Brandes (Ariadne).

Ariadne, in helping Theseus escape from the lair of the Minotaur on Crete, has fallen deeply in love with him. They take refuge on Naxos, but Theseus feels he must return to his native Greece and he leaves the sleeping Ariadne. When she awakes and awaits in vain for his return, Ariadne learns from an Oread, a mountain nymph, that Theseus has deserted her, and that her rescue will come in a thunderstorm, after she has offered herself to Neptune. Understanding that death is the only solution, Ariadne climbs the cliff, where she is struck by lightning and falls into the sea.

Major roles: Ariadne, daughter of King Minos of Crete (spoken); Theseus, son of King Aegeus of Athens (spoken); and the voice of an Oread.

The opera represents the first and most successful of the German melodramas. Among its admirers was Mozart. *Ariadne und Bacchus* was set by Maria Teresa Paradis in 1791, in Laxenburg; the music is lost.

SCORES: fs composer (Leipzig: Im Schwichertschen Verlage [1781]); repr. in *German Opera 1770–1800*, IV, ed. Thomas Bauman (New York and London: Garland Publishing, 1985); vs (Leipzig: Im Schwichertschen Verlage, 1778); vs ed. Alfred Einstein (Leipzig: C. F. Siegel, 1920).

LIBRETTO: German (Vienna: J. B. Wallishausser, 1810); repr. in *German Opera 1770–1800*, XVIII, *Librettos I*, ed. Thomas Bauman (New York and London: Garland Publishing, 1985).

BIBLIOGRAPHY: Fritz Brückner, *Georg Benda und das deutsche Singspiel* (Leipzig: B&H, 1904), 19–23.

Ariadne auf Naxos (Ariadne on Naxos). FIRST VERSION: opera in one act by Richard Strauss; libretto (Ger) by Hugo von Hofmannsthal, to be given after Molière's "comédie-ballet" *Le Bourgeois Gentilhomme* (1670), for which Strauss had written incidental music. First performance of first version October 25, 1912, Stuttgart, with Maria Jeritza (Ariadne), Margarethe Siems (Zerbinetta), and Hermann Jadlowker (Bacchus); conducted by the composer. First U.S. performance January 18, 1969, New York, Carnegie Hall (concert), with Claire Watson (Ariadne), Beverly Sills (Zerbinetta), Robert Nagy (Bacchus), John Reardon (Harlequin), Malcolm Smith (Truffaldino), John Ferrante (Brighella), James Billings (Scaramuccio), Benita Valente (Najade), Eunice Alberts (Dryade), and Carole Bogard (Echo); conducted by Erich Leinsdorf. First British performance May 27, 1913, London, His Majesty's, with Eva Plaschke von der Osten (Ariadne), Hermine Bosetti (Zerbinetta), Otto Marak (Bacchus), and Carl Armster (Harlequin); conducted by (Sir) Thomas Beecham. SECOND VERSION: opera in a prologue and one act by Richard Strauss; libretto (Ger) by Hugo von Hofmannsthal. First performance October 4, 1916, Vienna, with Maria Jeritza (Ariadne), Selma Kurz (Zerbinetta), Lotte Lehmann (the Composer), Béla Koernyei (Bacchus), and Hans Duhan (Music Teacher and Harlequin); conducted by Franz Schalk. First U.S. performance November 1, 1928, Philadelphia, Civic Opera, with Peterson, Boykin, Williams, House; conducted by Alexander Smallens. First British performance May 27, 1924, London, Covent Garden, with Elisabeth Schumann (the Composer), Lotte Lehmann (Ariadne), Maria Ivogün (Zerbinetta), Karl Fischer-Niemann (Bacchus), and Karl Renner (the Music Teacher and Harlequin); conducted by Karl Alwin.

The 1912 premiere was considered unsuccessful: the opera lovers were bored by the play, and the theater lovers, by the following musical portion. Strauss rewrote the work as a comic prologue, which is set in the luxurious palace of a "bourgeois gentilhomme," who has engaged the services of a young composer, cast as a "trouser" role (perhaps to remind the audience of the hero of *Der Rosenkavalier**), as well as those of a commedia del l'arte troupe. As the prologue unfolds, the composer learns, to his horror, that since time is at a premium, his serious opera about the desertion of Ariadne by Theseus must be performed and end at the same time as the comedy, so as to ensure that the invited company may enjoy the subsequent fireworks display. This news is broken to the composer by the stuffy Major-domo, cast as a speaking part (a holdover from the original version). The composer sinks into despair, which is somewhat tempered by his appreciation of the attributes of Zerbinetta, the attractive female member of the comedic troupe. The guests take their seats for the evening's entertainment, and the prologue ends.

The opera itself opens with three Rhine Maiden–like nymphs offering encouragement to Ariadne, who sings of her longing for death in "Es gibt ein Reich." The opera also includes two brilliant coloratura arias by Zerbinetta, "Grossmächtige Prinzessin" and "Noch glaub' ich dem einen ganz mich hörend," and ends with a glorious extended duet by Bacchus and Ariadne, "Du schönes Wesen?"

For detailed synopses and musical analyses, see C/*NMC*, 57–67; K/*KOB*, 823–28, and M/*RSC*, 145–67.

Major roles in the Prologue: the Major-domo (speaking part), the Music Master (bar), the Composer (sop), the Tenor (later Bacchus) (ten), the Dancing Master (ten), Zerbinetta (sop), the Prima Donna (later Ariadne) (sop), Harlequin (bar), Scaramuccio (ten), Truffaldino (bass), and Brighella (ten). In the opera: Ariadne (sop); Bacchus (ten); three Nymphs, Naiad, Dryad, Echo (sop, alto, sop); Zerbinetta (sop); Harlequin (bar); Scaramuccio (ten); Truffaldino (bass); and Brighella (ten).

Other Ariadne operas include Bohuslav Martinů's *Ariadne*, which was performed in 1961 at Gelsenkirchen, to a French text. See also *Ariadne** and *Ariadne auf Naxos.**

SCORES: first version: vs ed. Otto Singer (Berlin: A. Fürstner, 1912); second version: fs (London and New York: BO, 1943).

LIBRETTO: first version: German (Berlin: A. Fürstner, 1912); second version: German (Berlin: A. Fürstner, 1916).

BIBLIOGRAPHY: Anthony Besch, "Ariadne auf Naxos," *MT* CII (1962), 18–19; Richard Brett and John Potter, "Threads and Mazes," *ON* XL (March 20, 1976), 16–18; Donald Daviau and George Buelow, *The 'Ariadne auf Naxos' of Hugo von Hofmannsthal and Richard Strauss*, Studies in German Languages and Literature, LXXX (Chapel Hill: University of North Carolina Press, 1975); Charlotte Erwin, "Richard Strauss's *Ariadne auf Naxos*: An Analysis of Music Style Based on a Study of Revision" (diss., Yale University, 1976);————, "Richard Strauss's Presketch Planning for *Ariadne auf Naxos*," *MQ* LXVII (1981), 348–65; Karen Forsyth, *Ariadne auf Naxos by Hugo von Hofmannsthal and Richard Strauss: Its Genesis and Meaning* (Oxford: Oxford University Press, 1982); Speight Jenkins, "Reports: U.S.," *ON* XXXIII (February 22, 1969), 32 [on U.S. premiere of first version]; Willi Schuh, "Metamorphosen einer Ariette von Richard Strauss," in *OAA*.

DISCOGRAPHY: 1911 version: Normann, Varady, Gruberova, Frey, Bär, Fischer-Dieskau, Leipzig Gewandhaus Orchestra, conducted by Masur, Philips 422–84–2 PH2 (2 compact discs); Price, Gruberova, Troyanos, Kollo, Berry, Kunz, London Philharmonic, conducted by Solti, London 13131 (3 tapes). 1916 version: Schwarzkopf, Seefried, Streich, Otto, Hoffman, Schock, Unger, Cuénod, Prey, Ollendorf, Philharmonia Orchestra, conducted by Karajan, Angel CDMB–69396 (2 compact discs) (mono); Tomowa-Sintow, Battle, Baltsa, Lakes, Prey, Vienna Philharmonic, conducted by Levine, DG 419225–2 GH2 (2 compact discs).

Arlecchino oder **Die Fenster** (Harlequin or The Window), theatrical caprice in one act by Ferruccio Busoni; libretto (Ger) by the composer after a play by Carlo Gozzi. First performance (together with the composer's *Turandot**) May 11, 1917, Zurich, Stadttheater, with Käthe Wenck (Colombina), Eduard Grunert (Leandro), Alexander Moissi (Arlecchino), Wilhelm Bocholt (Sèr Matteò), Augustus Milner (Abbate Cospicuo), Heinrich Kuhn (Dottore Bombasto), and Ilse Ewaldt (Annunziata); conducted by the composer. First U.S. performance (semi-staged) October 11, 1951, New York, Carnegie Hall, with William Wilderman (Sèr Matteò), James Pease (Abbate Cospicuo), J. Alden Edkins (Dottore Bombasto), David Lloyd (Leandro), Martha Lipton (Colombina), Pauline Polisi (Annunziata), and John Brownlee (Arlecchino); conducted by Dimitri Mitropoulos. First fully staged U.S performance December 10, 1982, Houston, Grand Opera (in an English translation by Edward Dent), with Timothy Noble (Abbate Cospicuo), Carroll Freeman (Leandro), Wendy White (Colombina), Raymond Hickman (Sèr Matteò), William Dansby (Dottore Bombasto), Grethe Holby (Annunziata), and Robert Langdon Lloyd (Arlecchino); conducted by John De Main. First British performance (concert) January 27, 1939, BBC, with William

Parsons (Sèr Matteò), Dennis Noble (Abbate Cospicuo), Norman Allin (Dottore Bombasto), Steuart Wilson (Arlecchino), Jan van der Gucht (Leandro), and Olive Groves (Colombina); conducted by Clarence Raybould. First stage performance June 25, 1954, Glyndebourne, with Ian Wallace (Sèr Matteò), Fritz Ollendorf (Dottore Bombasto), Geraint Evans (Abbate Cospicuo), Elaine Malbin (Colombina), Kurt Gester (Arlecchino), and Murray Dickie (Leandro); conducted by John Pritchard.

Arlecchino (Harlequin) plays four roles: rogue, soldier, husband, and conqueror. The story opens with Sèr Matteò, a tailor, reading Dante while Harlequin makes love to the tailor's wife. Harlequin escapes through a bedroom window and dons the guise of a soldier. When Harlequin ignores the accusations of his wife, Colombina, that he has been cheating on her, she turns her attention to Leandro.

Major roles: Arlecchino (speaking role); Sèr Matteò, tailor (bar); Abbate Cospicuo (bar); Colombina, Arlecchino's wife (sop); Leandro, a fop (ten); Dottore Bombasto (bass); Annunziata, Matteò's wife (silent role).

The opera is a stylistic mixture of atonality, polytonality, and *Sprechstimme*.

Another opera on the same character was *L'Arlequin*, in five acts, by Max d'Ollone, with a French libretto by Jean Sarment, first performed at the Opéra in Paris on December 24, 1924.

SCORES: fs (Leipzig: B&H, c. 1918); vs ed. Philipp Jarnach (Leipzig: B&H and New York: AMP, 1917, 1954); rev. vs ed. E. J. Dent (Wiesbaden: B&H, 1968).

LIBRETTO: German (Leipzig: B&H, n.d.); new version (Wiesbaden: B&H [1956]).

BIBLIOGRAPHY: Ferruccio Busoni, "The Meaning of *Arlecchino*," "Apropos of *Arlecchino*," in *The Essence of Music and Other Papers*, transl. Rosamond Ley (London: Rockliff Publishing Corp., 1957; repr. New York: Dover, 1965), 66, 67–70; Henry Cowell, "Current Chronicle," *MQ* XXXVIII (1952), 134 [on U.S. premiere]; Scott F. Heumann, "Houston," *Opera* XXXIV (1983), 390–92; ———, "U.S.: Reports," *ON* XLVII (February 26, 1983), 40; Raoul Meloncelli, "Arlecchino ovvero Le Finestre," *Chigiana* XXXI/11 (1976), 369–72; Robert Sabin, "Philharmonic Opens Season with Busoni's Arlecchino," *MA* LXXI (1951), 9 [on U.S. premiere]; Ronald Stevenson, "Ferruccio Busoni's 'Arlecchino,' " *MT* XCV (1954), 307–8.

Arme Heinrich, Der (Poor Henry), opera in three acts by Hans Pfitzner; libretto (Ger) by James Grun after a medieval legend. First performance April 2, 1895, Mainz, with Cruvelli, Neumann, Heydrich; conducted by the composer.

Set in about 1100 in Swabia and in a cloister in Salerno, the story concerns the knight Heinrich; he is awaiting the return of his trusted Dietrich, who is supposed to bring him a miraculous cure from Italy. Dietrich returns empty-handed and says that Heinrich can find peace only if a maiden is willing to give up her life for him. This news is overheard by the young Agnes, who decides to sacrifice herself. She meets Heinrich at a cloister in Salerno and offers to give up her life. At the last moment, Heinrich is unable to permit her to do so, and he forces open the door behind which Agnes is about to die. His act of saving Agnes cures him.

Major roles: Heinrich, a German knight (ten); Dietrich, one of Heinrich's men (bar); Hilde, Dietrich's wife (dramatic sop); Agnes, their daughter, about fourteen (sop); the doctor, a monk in the Salerno cloister (bass).

SCORE: vs ed. composer (Leipzig: Max Brockhaus, ca. 1904).

LIBRETTO: German (Leipzig: Max Brockhaus, n.d.).

BIBLIOGRAPHY: Franz Hirtler, *Hans Pfitzners 'Arme Heinrich'* (diss., Freiburg, Albert-Ludwig University, 1939).

Aufsteig und Fall der Stadt Mahagonny (The Rise and Fall of the City of Mahagonny), opera in three acts by Kurt Weill; libretto (Ger) by Bertolt Brecht. First performance March 9, 1930, Leipzig, with Mali Trummer, Walter Zimmer, Magda Dannenberg, Paul Beinert, Theodor Horand; conducted by Gustav Brecher. First U.S. performance (six excerpts sung) February 23, 1952, New York, Town Hall, with Beatrice Lind, Gabor Carelli, Maria Zorella; conducted by Maurice Levine. First complete U.S. performance (in English) April 28, 1970, New York, Anderson Theater, with Val Pringle (Trinity Moses), Frank Porretta (Jimmy), Estelle Parsons (Begbick), and Barbara Harris (Jenny); directed by Carmen Capalbo. First British performance (in English) January 16, 1963, London, Sadler's Wells, with April Cantelo (Jenny), Patricia Bartlett (Begbick), Ronald Dowd (Jimmy), and Inia Te Wiata (Trinity Moses); conducted by Sir Colin Davis.

The satirical work is set in the imaginary, materialistic, and pleasure-seeking city of Mahagonny. Among its denizens are Jenny and her sister prostitutes and Jimmy and his lumberjack friends: Jenny and Jimmy become lovers. When Jimmy cannot pay for his drinks, he is tried, convicted, and given a sentence deemed appropriate by the inhabitants, death.

Major roles: Leocadia Begbick (alto); Fatty, the bookkeeper (ten); Trinity Moses (bar); Jenny Hill (sop); Jimmy Mahoney (ten).

This work represented the composer's first collaboration with Brecht. It appeared initially as a *Songspiel*, under the title *Mahagonny*,* in 1927. Among its famous numbers is the "Alabama Song," sung by Jenny.

For a detailed plot and musical analysis, see K/*NKC*, 1100–1108.

SCORE: vs ed. Norbert Gingold (Vienna: UE, 1929); David Drew (Vienna: UE, 1969).

LIBRETTO: German (Vienna: UE, 1929).

BIBLIOGRAPHY: Peter Branscombe, "Brecht, Weill and Mahagonny," *MT* CII (1961), 483–86; Geraldine De Courcy, "Opera Satire on Modern Life Creates Uproar" [on premiere], *MA* L (April 10, 1930), 6; David Drew, "Background to Mahagonny," *Opera* XIV (1963), 84–89; Andrew Porter, "Musical Events," *NY* LV (December 3, 1979), 141–42, 144, 146, 148; John Simon, "Exquisitely at Odds," *ON* XLIV (December 1, 1979), 9–12; Patrick J. Smith, "Protest or Classic," *ON* XLV (April 4, 1981), 911; Ralph Zachary, "Sin City Comes to Fun City," *ON* XXXIV (March 14, 1970), 9–12.

DISCOGRAPHY: Lenya, conducted by Brückner-Rüggeberg, North German Radio Orchestra and Chorus, CBS M3X–37874 (3), MXT–37874 (tape).

Aurora, "grosse heroische Oper" in three acts by E. .T. A. Hoffmann; libretto (Ger) by Franz von Holbein. Composed 1811–1812. The premiere, planned for the summer of 1813 in Vienna, did not take place. The opera was first performed, in a version by Lukas Böttcher, on November 5, 1933, in Bamberg.

Major roles: Aurora (sop); Cephalus (sop); Erechtheus, king of the Athenians (bar); Procris, his daughter (sop); Dejoneus, king of the Phliotis (bass); Polybius, Athenian general (bass); Philacrus, chief of the guards of Dejoneus (ten).

A setting by Anton Schweitzer was performed in 1772 at Weimar; Franz Gläser's version in 1836, Berlin; August Bungert also composed a version in the 1880s.

SCORES: The Introduction to the second act was published by P. Greef in "E. T. A. Hoffmann als Musiker und Musikschrifsteller" (Cologne and Krefeld, 1948), 233–39; and No, 11 by E. Kroll in "Über den Musiker E. T. A. Hoffmann," *ZMw* IV (1922), 550ff.

BIBLIOGRAPHY: Gerhard Allrogen, *E. T. A. Hoffmanns Kompositionen: Ein chronologisch-thematisches Verzeichnis* (Regensburg: G. Bosse, 1917), 84–91; Lukas Böttcher, "E. T. A. Hoffmanns 'Aurora.' Eine noch unbekannte Oper. Zu ihrer Uraufführung am 5. Nov. 1933 in Stadttheater zu Bamberg," *ZMw* C, Heft 12 (December 1933), 1241–43; Erwin Kroll, "E. T. A. Hoffmann als Bühnenkomponist," *Musik* XV, no. 1 (1922), 99–115.

B

Baal (Babel), opera in twenty-five scenes by Friedrich Cerha; libretto (Ger) by the composer after Bertolt Brecht. First performance August 7, 1981, Salzburg, Kleines Festspielhaus, with Theo Adam (Baal), Helmut Berger-Tuna (Ekart), Heiner Hopfer (Johannes), Marjana Lipovsek (Emilie), Gabriele Sima (Johanna), Emily Rawlins (Sophie), and Martha Mödl (Baal's mother); conducted by Christoph von Dohnányi.

The story, set in the early part of this century, concerns the drunken poet Baal, who rejects the praises of the bourgeois society around him and goes on a search for happiness and fulfillment among the lower elements of society. Included is a Faust-like episode in which Baal abandons Sophie, the most important of his female victims, when she becomes pregnant.

Major roles: Baal (bar); Ekart, his friend (bass); and Sophie, his victim (sop).

The score is written mostly in twelve-tone language; it includes jazz elements and such compositional procedures as passacaglia.

Other operas on Babel include *Baals Sturz* of Joseph Weigl (1820, Vienna) and Erich Sehlbach's *Baal* (1960), which was not performed.

BIBLIOGRAPHY: Corey Field, "Music Reviews," *MLA Notes* XXIX (September 1982–June 1983), 960–61; Horst Koegler, "Reports: Foreign," *ON* XLVI (November 1981), 53–54 [on premiere]; Kenneth Loveland, "Salzburg" [on premiere], *MT* CXXII (1981), 693; David Patrick Stearns, "Cerha's 'Baal' Premiered," *HiFi/MA* XXXII (April 1982), 38–39.

Bakchantinnen, Die (The Bacchantes), opera in two acts by Egon Wellesz; libretto (Ger) by the composer after *The Bacchae* of Euripides. First performance June 20, 1931, Vienna, Staatsoper, with Herr Jerger (Dionysos), Herr Manowarda (Teiresias), Herr Markhoff (Kadmos), Frau Pauly (Queen Agave), Herr Kalenberg (Pentheus), and Herr Radin (servant of Pentheus); conducted by Clemens Krauss.

The Euripides play tells of the saga of Agave, daughter of the King of Thebes, Kadmos. Zeus appears to her sister, Semele, as a mortal. Fearing that her own son, Pentheus, will be threatened, Agave urges her sister to demand that Zeus show himself in his godly form. When he does, Semele dies, but Zeus saves their child, Dionysos. The opera opens with the return of Dionysos to Thebes; he is seeking revenge for the death of his mortal mother. He causes the women of Thebes to leave their homes and get caught up in the debaucheries of his festivals. Pentheus comes back to Thebes after victorious battles, to find that his own mother has joined the revelers. He is determined to attend one of the festivals in disguise, but he is undone when Dionysos makes him appear to the participants as a wild animal to be sacrificed. Agave and the Bacchantes kill him, whereupon she awakes from her trance and realizes what has happened.

Following the tradition of Greek tragedies, Wellesz emphasizes the chorus to a great extent in this work.

A later setting of the story is Giorgio Federico Ghedini's *Le Baccanti* (1948, Milan); see also *Die Bassariden** by Hans Werner Henze.

SCORE: vs (Berlin: B&B, 1930).

BIBLIOGRAPHY: Robert Schollum, *Egon Wellesz* (Vienna: Österreichische Musikzeit-schrift und Bundesverlag, 1963), 37–43.

Barbier von Bagdad, Der (The Barber of Bagdad), opera in one act by Johann André; libretto (Ger) by the composer after Charles Montenoy de Palissot's play *Le Barbier de Bagdad* (1777). First performance February 19, 1783, Berlin, Döbbelins Theater.

The story is quite similar to Peter Cornelius' version of 1858 (see next entry). In the André setting, Almanzor and Zulima are in love. Zulima's slave and confidante, Fatme, arranges a rendezvous, but her plans are interrupted by the bothersome Barber, who has been brought to shave Almanzar by Osmin, Almanzor's servant. Almanzar flees to the house of Zulima's father, the Cadi, in order to escape the Barber's clutches, and Osmin is beaten in the confusion that follows. Almanzor hides in his beloved's room during the commotion but is discovered. The furious Cadi relents at Fatme's urging, however, and the young lovers are reunited.

Major roles: Almanzor (ten), Zulima (sop), Osmin (bass), Fatme (sop), the Barber (ten), and the Cadi (bass).

The thirteen numbers of the opera do not contain any apparent exoticisms. The loquaciousness of the Barber is portrayed in his duet with Almanzor (no. 7). The concluding ensemble, which praises love, ''Singet laut, die Liebe lebe,'' is among the more interesting pieces of the work.

Another setting of the story was made by H. C. Hattasch, with a first performance around 1793 in Hamburg.

LIBRETTO: German (Leipzig: Esslingersche Buchhandlung, 1772).

Barbier von Bagdad, Der (The Barber of Bagdad), opera in two acts by Peter Cornelius; libretto (Ger) by the composer after ''The Tailor's Story'' from the *Thousand and One Nights*. First performance December 15, 1858, Weimar, with Herr Caspary (Nureddin), Herr Roth (the Barber), Herr Knapp (the Cadi), Rosa von Milde (Margiana), Fräulein Wolf (Bostana), and Herr Milde (the Caliph); conducted by Franz Liszt. The premiere was a disaster, due in large part to the anti-Liszt factions, led by Franz von Dingelstedt. First U.S. performance January 3, 1890, New York, Metropolitan Opera, with Emil Fischer (the Barber), Paul Kalisch (Nureddin), and Sophie Traubmann (Margiana); conducted by Walter Damrosch. First British performance December 9, 1891, London, Savoy, with students of the Royal College of Music. The work was never performed again during Cornelius' lifetime. In an effort to make it more successful, Felix Mottl revised and reorchestrated it; the new version was first performed on February 1, 1884, in Karlsruhe. The opera was revived in its original version by Max Hasse on June 6, 1904, at Weimar, and it is occasionally performed today as Cornelius intended it. Modern U.S. revivals include one on March 6, 1967, New York, Fashion Institute of Technology (by Mannes College and the State University of New York at Stony Brook), with David Ronson (the Barber), William Woodruff (Nureddin), and Karen Roewade (Margiana); conducted by Carl Bamberger.

The wealthy young Nureddin falls hopelessly in love with the lovely Margiana, whom he has seen but not met. The girl's companion, Bostana, arranges for the two young people to meet, but matters are complicated by the Barber, to whom Nureddin has gone for a shave. Nureddin enters Margiana's house but must hide in her fiancé's treasure chest when her father returns. When the chest is opened Nureddin seems dead, but he is revived, and the generous Caliph allows the two to be wed.

Major roles: Nureddin, in love with Margiana (ten); Abul Hassan, the Barber (bass); Baba Mustapha, the Cadi (ten); Margiana, his daughter (sop); Bostana, confidante of Margiana (alto); and the Caliph (bar).

For a detailed plot synopsis, see K/*KOB*, 281–85.

The delicate score contains many delightful moments, such as the Barber's boastful and wordy patter song of the first act, ''Bin Akademiker,'' and the second-act love duet of Nureddin and Margiana, ''So mag kein andres Wort.'' Cornelius employs a more subtle kind of exoticism than earlier ''Turkish'' operas; one such example is the ''Thema des Muezzinrufs'' of the orchestral interlude. His text, which he wrote himself, is quite witty and full of plays on words, and his inclusion of the rose to represent love anticipates *Der Rosenkavalier* by nearly fifty years. This is the only one of Cornelius' three operas which deliberately avoids the influence of Wagner.

SCORE: fs, C/*MW*, III (Leipzig: B&H, 1904).

LIBRETTO: ed. Georg Richard Kruse (Leipzig: P. Reclam Junior [1858]).

BIBLIOGRAPHY: K. W. Bartlett, "Peter Cornelius and 'The Barber of Bagdad,' " *Opera* VII (1956), 469–72; G/" 'T'O," 398–429; Max Hasse, *Peter Cornelius und sein 'Barbier von Bagdad.' Die Kritik zweier Partituren* [on Mottl's revisions] (Leipzig: B&H, 1904); Herbert Horst, "Zur Textgeschichte des *Barbier von Bagdad*," in C/*PCK*, 121–28; Edgar Istel, "Peter Cornelius," *MQ* XX (1934), 260–90; Egon Voss, *"Der Barbier von Bagdad* als komische Oper," in C/*PCK*, 129–38; Leo Wurmser, "Cornelius and His 'Barber,' " *Opera* XVI (1965), 868–73.

DISCOGRAPHY: Schwarzkopf, Gedda, and Czerwenka, conducted by Leinsdorf, EMI 2047/8 (2).

Bärenhäuter, Der (The Idler), opera in three acts by Siegfried Wagner; libretto (Ger) by the composer. First performance January 22, 1899, Munich, Nationaltheater, with Andreas Moers (Hans), Georg Sieglitz (the Devil), Frl. Hoffmann (Luise), and Heinrich Knote (the mayor); conducted by Ernst von Possart.

The plot of the composer's first opera concerns the young Hans Kraft, who is lured by the Devil to the reaches of Hell and its sinful pleasures. As punishment Hans must return to earth as a dirty idler and be released from this life only if a maiden is true to him for three years. Although spurned by most of the women, he is welcomed by Luise. Hans is thereby redeemed.

Major roles: Hans Kraft, a young soldier (ten); the Devil (buffo bass); and Luise, youngest daughter of the mayor (sop).

Along with its fairy-tale elements, this work has musical elements similar to those of Richard Wagner and also Engelbert Humperdinck.

SCORE: vs ed. Eduard Reuss and Julius Kniese (Leipzig: M. Brockhaus, 1898).

BIBLIOGRAPHY: Zdenko von Kraft, *Der Sohn* (Graz: Leopold Stocker, 1969), 85–90; Peter Pachl, *Siegfried Wagners Musik-Dramatische Schaffen* (Tutzing: Hans Schneider, 1979), 90–93.

Bassariden, Die, (The Bassarids), opera seria with an intermezzo in one act by Hans Werner Henze; libretto (English) by W. H. Auden and Chester Kallman after *The Bacchae* of Euripides. First performance (in a German translation by Maria Basse-Sporleder) on August 6, 1966, Salzburg, with Ingeborg Hallstein, Kerstin Meyer, Vera Little, Loren Driscoll, Helmut Melchert, Kostas Paskalis, William Dooley, and Peter Lagger; conducted by Christoph von Dohnányi. First U.S. performance (in the original English) August 7, 1968, Santa Fe, with Joan Caplan (Semele's nurse), Regina Sarfaty (Agave), Evelyn Mandac (Autonoe), Loren Driscoll (Dionysus), Charles Bressler (Teiresias), John Reardon (Pentheus), Thomas Jamerson (the captain), and Peter Harrower (Cadmus); conducted by the composer. First British performance September 22, 1968, London, BBC, with Carlyle, Sarfaty, Watts, Young, Egerton, Bryn-Jones, and Griffiths; conducted by Downes. First British stage performance October 10, 1974 (in English), London, Coliseum, with Josephine Barstow (Autonoe), Katherine Pring (Agave), Dennis Wicks (Cadmus), Gregory Dempsey (Dionysus), Norman Welsby (Pentheus), and Tom McDonnell (the captain); conducted by the composer.

The new King of Thebes is Pentheus. He decrees that Semele, whose tomb is revered by the devotees of Dionysus, the Bassarids, was really loved by a mortal, not by Zeus, so that her son, Dionysus, is not a god. When Pentheus' grandfather, Cadmus, tries to advise him to reverse the decree, Pentheus ignores his warnings and orders members of the Bassarid cult to be arrested by his guards. He goes to Mount Cythaeron, where the Bassarids have gathered. When he is discovered, he pleads in vain with his mother, Agave, one of the group, to save him. She returns to Thebes with the severed head of her son, whereupon she is made to realize what has happened. Dionysus appears and orders the city to be burned to the ground, in revenge for the disgrace done to his own mother.

For a detailed plot synopsis, see K/*KOB*, 926–31.

Major roles: Dionysus (ten); Pentheus, King of Thebes (bar); Kadmos (Cadmus), his grandfather (bass); Teiresias, a blind seer (ten); captain of the guards (bar); Agave, daughter of Kadmos and mother of Pentheus (mezzo); Autonoe, her sister (high soprano); and Beroe, an old slave (mezzo).

The opera is set in the form of a symphony, in four movements, each of which represents a change of mood. The first movement concerns the ascent of Pentheus; the second, the dismay of Cadmus; the third, the hunting down of the Bassarids by Pentheus' guards; an intermezzo, in which Agave and Autonoe, her sister, laugh at Pentheus' behavior; and the fourth, the death of the king and the burning of Thebes.

See also *Die Bakchantinnen** by Egon Wellesz.

SCORE: vs (Ger-Eng) (Mainz: BSS and New York: AMP, 1966).

BIBLIOGRAPHY: Terry Apter, " 'Tristan' and 'The Bassarids,' " *Tempo* CXII (March 1975), 27–30 [on British stage premiere]; Alan Blyth, "Henze's New Opera," *Opera* XVII (1966), 608–10; Paul Griffiths, "The Bassarids: Hans Werner Henze Talks to Paul Griffiths," *MT* CXV (1974), 831–32; Everett Helm, "Current Chronicle. Austria," *MQ* LIII (1967), 408–15 [on premiere]; Frank Merkling, "Reports: U.S.," *ON* XXXIII (September 21, 1968), 20–21 [on U.S. premiere]; Andrew Porter, "Salzburg. Henze's 'Bassarids,' " *MT* CXII (1966), 886–87; Harold Rosenthal, "Salzburg. The Bassarids. Aug. 26," *Opera* XVII (Autumn 1966), 50–54; James Helme Sutcliffe, "Reports: Foreign," *ON* XXXVIII (December 7, 1974), 36 [on British stage premiere].

Bastien und Bastienne, (Bastien and Bastienne), Singspiel in one act by Wolfgang Amadeus Mozart; libretto (Ger) by Friedrich Wilhelm Weiskern, after Charles S. Favart's *Les Amours de Bastien et Bastienne*, itself a parody of Jean-Jacques Rousseau's *Le Devin du village*. First performance September 1768, Vienna, at the home of the hypnotist Anton Mesmer. First U.S. performance October 26, 1916, New York (in English). First British performance December 26, 1894, London, Daly's.

In this pastoral setting the shepherdess Bastienne is in love with Bastien, who in turn loves a wealthy girl. The shepherdess complains to the magician Colas, who tells her to make Bastien jealous. After a lover's quarrel Bastienne and Bastien are reconciled.

Major roles: Bastienne (sop), Bastien (ten), and Colas (bass).

Although composed mainly of simple arias and duets in Lied form, this early Mozart piece contains elements of his more mature operatic style. One example is the beautiful melody of Bastien's love song, "Meiner Liebsten schöne Wangen."

SCORE: fs ed. Rudolph Angermüller, M/*NMA* II/5, 3 (1974).

BIBLIOGRAPHY: Rudolph Angermüller, "Johann Andreas Schachters 'Bastienne'-Libretto," *Mitteilungen der Internationalen Stiftung Mozarteum* XXII (1974), 4–28; ———, "Mozart und Rousseau. Zur Textgrundlage von *Bastien und Bastienne*," *Mitteilungen der Internationalen Stiftung Mozarteum* XXIII (1975), 22–37; Alfred Loewenberg, "*Bastien and Bastienne* Once More," *ML* XXV (1944), 176–81; M/*OM*, 55–67; Alfred Orel, "Die Legende um Mozarts Bastien und Bastienne," *SMz* XCI (1951), 137–43.

DISCOGRAPHY: See M/*IRR*, 179.

Beiden Pädagogen, Die (The Two Pedagogues), Singspiel in one act by Felix Mendelssohn; libretto (Ger) by Johann Ludwig Caspar after the comedy *Les deux Précepteurs* of Eugène Scribe. Composed in 1821. First performance May 27, 1962, Berlin, Opernstudio der Deutschen Hochschule für Musik, at the Komische Oper.

The story concerns Robert, who wants to make his son Carl a well-educated person. Kinderschreck, the schoolmaster (whose comical name translates as "terror of children") advises Robert on how to accomplish this, but to the schoolmaster's chagrin, a Viennese "professor" is engaged for the task, one Luftig, who turns out to be a former lover of Hannchen. Identities are sorted out in the end, and Robert is allowed to wed his beloved, Elise, while the unmasked Luftig is reunited with Hannchen.

Major roles: Herr von Robert, squire (bass); Carl, his son (ten); Elise, Robert's niece (sop); Kinderschreck, the town schoolmaster (bar); Hannchen, his niece, a gardener on Robert's estate (sop); and Luftig, a servant (bar).

Among the musical highlights is Kinderschreck's "Probatum est, dies ruf ich mir" (No. 4), which reveals his unbearable stuffiness.

SCORE: No score or libretto was published during Mendelssohn's lifetime; modern fs in MB/*LA*, V/1 (1966).

BIBLIOGRAPHY: Karl-Heinz Köhler, "Das Jugendwerk Felix Mendelssohns," *DJdMw* VII (1962), 18–35; S/"MJ," 515–24.

DISCOGRAPHY: Fuchs, Laki, Dallapozza, Fischer-Dieskau, Hirte, and Wewel, Munich Radio Orchestra, conducted by Wallberg, EMI 1C065–45416; reviewed by John W. Freeman, "Records," *ON* XLVII (July 1982), 37.

Beiden Schützen, Die (The Two Sharpshooters), comic opera in two acts by Albert Lortzing; libretto (Ger) by the composer after Joseph Patrat's *Méprises par resemblance*, set by A. E. M. Grétry in 1786. First performance February

20, 1837, Leipzig. First U.S. performance (in German) December 13, 1859, New York. First British performance (in English, as *The Random Shot*), March 31, 1898, London, St. George's Hall.

The innkeeper Busch is awaiting the return of his soldier son Gustav, who has been away for ten years. Instead, Wilhelm, the illegitimate son of Magistrate Wall, appears with Schwarzbart, who has swapped identities with Gustav. Wilhelm goes along with the scheme since he is in love with the innkeeper's daughter, Suschen. When the real Gustav returns, his father does not recognize him, and he is thrown into jail. Karoline, daughter of the magistrate and fiancée of the real Gustav, has in the meantime fallen in love with the jailed soldier, a situation which upsets Suschen. Eventually, however, identities are straightened out, to everybody's satisfaction.

Major roles: Magistrate Wall (bass); Karoline, his daughter (sop); Wilhelm, his son, soldier in the First Sharpshooter Battalion (bar); Peter, his cousin (ten); Busch, an innkeeper (bass); Suschen, his daughter (sop); and Gustav, his son, a soldier in the Third Sharpshooter Battalion (ten).

SCORES: vs composer (Leipzig: J. Wunder, 1838; Leipzig: C. F. Peters, 1882).

Belmont und Constanze oder **Die Entführung aus dem Serail** (Belmont and Constanze or The Abduction from the Seraglio), "Operette" in three acts by Johann André; libretto (Ger) by Christian Friedrich Bretzner. First performance May 25, 1781, Berlin, with Marie Niklas (Constanze).

The story is virtually the same as that of Mozart's *Die Entführung aus dem Serail*,* a fact that Bretzner publicized in his angry article "Ein gewisser Mensch namens Mozart," in the *Berliner Litteratur- und Theater-Zeitung* (1782). Belmont has come to the abode of the Pasha to free his beloved, Constanze, who was captured, along with Blonde and Pedrillo, by pirates; she is now in the Pasha's seraglio. As in Mozart's version, Blonde is pursued by the comic-evil Osmin, and Belmont passes himself off as an architect to gain entrance to the Pasha's estate. Similarly, Pedrillo gets Osmin drunk, and the Europeans try to escape using a ladder. The major change is the ending, in which the Pasha is about to condemn Belmont to death when he discovers that the young man is in reality his long-lost son.

Major roles: Pasha (Bassa); Selim (speaking part); Constanze, beloved of Belmont (sop); Blonde, servant to Constanze (sop); Belmont, a Spaniard (ten); Pedrillo, servant of Belmont and overseer of the Pasha's garden (ten); and Osmin, overseer of the country house of the Pasha (bass).

"Turkish" color is provided by "Janissary" music at the entrance of the Pasha, "Singt dem grossen Bassa Lieder" and "exotic" passages in, for example, the overture, e.g., unisons and uncommon tonal relationships. Pedrillo sings a mock martial aria, "Frisch zum Kampfe," before his drinking duet with Osmin, "Vivat Bachus! Bachus lebe." Again, as in *Die Entführung*, Pedrillo sings the romance "Im Mohrenland gefangen war."

Also set by Christian Ludwig Dieter and given its first performance on August 27, 1784, in Stuttgart.

SCORE: fs ms repr. in *German Opera 1770–1800*, VI, ed. Thomas Bauman (New York and London: Garland Publishing, 1985).

LIBRETTO: German (Leipzig: Carl Friedrich Schneider, 1781); repr. in *German Opera 1770–1880*, XVIII, *Librettos I*, ed. Thomas Bauman (New York and London: Garland Publishing, 1985).

Benvenuto Cellini, opera in four acts by Franz Lachner; libretto (Ger) freely translated from the text of H. A. Barbier and A. F. L. de Wailly, which Hector Berlioz set in 1838. First performance October 7, 1849, Munich, Court Opera, with Herr Härtinger (Cellini), Herr Pellegrini (Cardinal Salviati), Fräulein Rettich (Bianca), Herr Sigl (Balducci), Fräulein Diez (Aseanio), and Herr Kindermann (Fieramosca). There were only two more performances that year, and it then disappeared from the repertoire.

In this opera the goldsmith Cellini is in love with Bianca, daughter of the papal treasurer Balducci, much to the latter's displeasure. The father wishes her to marry the sculptor Fieramosca. Cardinal Salviati promises to help Cellini if he completes a gold statue of Perseus for the cleric. Cellini triumphs in the end.

BIBLIOGRAPHY: W/*FL*, 86–101.

Berggeist, Der (The Mountain Gnome), opera in three acts by Ludwig Spohr; libretto (Ger) by Georg Döring. First performance March 24, 1825, Kassel, for the marriage of Princess Marie of Hesse-Kassel to Duke Bernhard Erich of Saxe-Meiningen.

In this story the king of the gnomes, the Berggeist, hears about the joys of human love and decides to kidnap a mortal woman, Alma, who is preparing to wed Oskar. Troll, another gnome, kidnaps Alma's maid, Ludmilla. Convinced by the ladies to help them flee, Troll tricks the Berggeist, and the three escape. In the end, both gnomes decide that human love is not for them anyway.

Major roles: Alma (sop), Ludmilla (sop), Oskar (ten), the Berggeist (bass), and Troll (ten).

Spohr's librettist used as the basis of his story Carl August Musäus' "Wie Rübezahl zu seinem Namen kam," part of his *Volksmärchen der Deutschen* (1782–1787), although Döring changed the comic Rübezahl into the more serious Berggeist.

The opera itself is through-composed and has very little secco recitative. The music is quite effective, but it could not overcome the defects of the weak libretto, and the opera disappeared from the repertoire within a dozen years. Other settings of the plot include the various versions of *Rübezahl,** Peter Lindpaintner's *Der Bergkönig* (1825, Stuttgart), and Kuno Stierlin's *Der Berggeist* (1921, Münster); none of these was successful.

SCORE: vs (Leipzig: C. F. Peters, 1825).

BIBLIOGRAPHY: B/*LS*, 167–71.

Bergknappen, Die (The Miners), Singspiel in one act by Ignaz Umlauf; libretto (Ger) by Paul Weidmann. The first performance February 18, 1778, the first opera of the newly created German *Nationalsingspiel* at the Burgtheater in Vienna, with Katharina Cavalieri (Sophie), Wilhelmine Stierle (Delda), Josef Ruprecht (Fritz), and Herr Fuchs (Walcher). It was preceded by a private performance for Emperor Joseph II on January 16 of the same year.

Sophie and Fritz are in love, but their happiness is threatened by Walcher, Sophie's guardian, who wants her for himself. Delda, a gypsy, promises to help Fritz because of a secret she knows, that Sophie is, in fact, Walcher's daughter and was stolen from him by another gypsy. After a number of difficulties, Walcher allows the pair to wed.

Major roles: Sophie (sop), Fritz (ten), Walcher (bass), and Delda (sop).

Other operas on the subject are by Karl Hellwig (1820, Dresden, after Theodor Körner); C. Oestreich (1839, Weimar); and Michael Hertz, as *Gwarkowie* (1880, Warsaw).

SCORE: fs ed. Robert Haas, DTÖ, XXXVI, Jg. I/36 (1911).

BIBLIOGRAPHY: Alfred Heuss, "Zu Umlauf's Singspiel: *Die Bergknappen*," *ZIMG* XIII (1911–1912), 164–71.

Bergwerk zu Falun, Das. (The Mine at Falun), opera in eight scenes by Rudolf Wagner-Régeny; libretto (Ger) by the composer after Hugo von Hofmannsthal. First performance August 16, 1961, Salzburg, with Elisabeth Schwarzenberg (Anna), Hermann Uhde (sailor), Sona Cervena (Mine Queen), and Max Lorenz (the ghost); conducted by Heinz Wallberg.

The story concerns a young sailor, Elis Fröbom, who is lured by the Mine Queen to leave the sea and work in a mine. On the day of his wedding to the daughter of the mine's owner, he deserts her. Wagner considered setting E. T. A. Hoffmann's tale *Die Bergwerke zu Falun* but only reached the stage of writing a prose sketch. There are certain similarities between the Hoffmann work and Richard Wagner's *Tannhäuser** (see Marc A. Weiner's article, listed below).

Major roles: Anna (sop), a sailor (bar), the Mine Queen (alto), and a ghost (ten).

SCORE: vs ed. composer (Berlin: B&B, 1961).

BIBLIOGRAPHY: Martin Bernheimer, "Current Chronicle. Salzburg," *MQ* XLVIII (1962), 120–21; Lionel Dunlop, "Reports from Abroad," *MT* CII (1961), 640 [on premiere]; Günter Hausswald, "Bericht,"*Musica* XV (1961), 543–44 [on premiere]; Rudolf Wagner-Régeny, "Die Musik zum 'Bergwerk zu Falun,'" *ÖMZ* XVI (1961), 357–58; Marc A. Weiner, "Richard Wagner's Use of E. T. A. Hoffmann's 'The Mines of Falun,'" *19th Century Music* V (1982), 201–14.

Bernauerin, Die (The Bernauer Woman), "ein bairisches Stück" in a prologue and two acts by Carl Orff; libretto (Bavarian dialect) by the composer after a fifteenth-century story based on the historical figure of Agnes Bernauer. First performance June 15, 1947, Stuttgart, with Godela Orff (Agnes); conducted by B. Wetzelsberger. First U.S. performance March 21, 1968, Kansas City, University of Missouri (in an English translation by Fritz Andre Kracht), with Cheryl Reineke (Agnes), Everett McGill (Albrecht), John Bruce (a monk), and Lynn Penticuff (announcer); conducted by William Fischer.

Young Duke Albrecht marries the commoner Agnes, despite the strenuous objections of the old duke. The enraged ruler has Agnes kidnapped, accused of witchcraft, and drowned in the Danube. As Albrecht is set to march against his father, he receives the news that his father has died, making him the ruler of Bavaria.

Major roles: announcer; Albrecht, Duke of Bavaria and Prince of Voheburg; Kaspar Bernauer, barber-surgeon; Agnes Bernauer, his daughter; and Duke Ernst, father of Albrecht.

The work is basically a spoken drama with music, with operatic writing in the love scene and finale. The chorus plays an important part, and *Sprechstimme* is also employed.

The story was also set by L. Kaufmann and Josef Messner, under the title *Agnes Bernauer* (neither work was performed). Karl Krebs' *Herzog Albrecht* received its premiere in Hamburg in 1833, and in a revised version, as *Agnes Bernauer*, in Dresden in 1858.

SCORE: vs (Mainz: BSS, 1946).

BIBLIOGRAPHY: John Haskins, "Reports: U.S.," *ON* XXXII (May 18, 1968), 26 [on U.S. premiere].

Besuch der alten Dame, Der (The Visit of the Old Lady), opera in three acts by Gottfried von Einem; libretto (Ger) by Friedrich Dürrenmatt after his tragicomedy of the same name (1956). First performance May 23, 1971, Vienna, State Opera, with Christa Ludwig (Claire Zachanassian), Eberhard Wächter (Alfred III), Hans Beirer (the mayor), and Hans Hotter (the teacher); conducted by Horst Stein. First U.S. performance October 25, 1972, San Francisco, with Regina Resnik and Richard Cassilly; conducted by Maurice Peress. First British performance May 31, 1973, Glyndebourne (in an English translation by Norman Tucker), with Kerstin Meyer (Claire), Alan Crofoot (the mayor), Bell, and Garrard; conducted by John Pritchard.

Set in a small Central European town, the story concerns Claire, originally from the town, who has returned as the richest woman in the world. She meets Alfred III, who got her pregnant and ran her out of town in disgrace. Claire has been forced to become a prostitute but then marries many times, the last time to an extremely wealthy man. She has returned to her birthplace to offer a fortune to the townspeople on the condition that they kill her one-time lover Alfred. At first expressing horror at her suggestion, the people gradually reveal their greed. Then Alfred dies, ostensibly from heart failure. The town gets the money and Claire her revenge.

Major roles: Claire Zachanassian, washerwoman, now a multimillionairess (mezzo); Alfred III (bar); his wife (sop); his daughter (sop); his son (ten); the mayor (ten); the priest (bass-bar); and the schoolmaster (bar).

SCORES: vs (London: BO, 1970); English-German vs transl. Norman Tucker (London: BO, 1972).

LIBRETTO: German (London: BO, 1970); English-German, transl. Norman Tucker (London: BO, 1972).

BIBLIOGRAPHY: Rudolf Klein, "Von Einems Dürrenmatt-oper *Der Besuch der alten Dame*," *ÖMz* XXVI (1971), 302–6; Friedrich Saathen, "Committed Opera: Gottfried von Einem's 'The Visit of the Old Lady,' " *Tempo* CIV (1973), 23–29; Hans Heinz Stuckenschmidt, "Von Einems *Der Besuch der alten Dame*," *Tempo* XCVIII (1972), 28–30.

Bettelstudent, Der (The Beggar Student), operetta in three acts by Carl Millöcker; libretto (Ger) by F. Zell [Camillo Walzell] and Richard Genée. First performance December 6, 1882, Vienna, Theater an der Wien, with Felix Schweighofer (Count Ollendorf) and Alexander Girardi (Jan Janitzky). First U.S. performance October 19, 1883, New York, Thalia Theater (in German), with Marie Geistinger, Seebold, Schmitz, Friest, and Schulze; October 29, 1883, New York, Casino Theater (in English), with Rose Leighton (Countess Nowalska), Bertha Ricci (Countess Laura), William T. Carlton (Symon), and Fred Leslie (Colonel Ollendorf). First British performance April 12, 1884, London, Alhambra Theatre (in English), with Fanny Leslie and Marion Hood (Symon).

The Polish General Ollendorf is rejected by Laura, daughter of a countess, and in order to get revenge he arranges for the humble beggar student Symon to pretend to be a wealthy gentleman. Laura falls in love with Symon, who tries to explain to her who he really is, only to have his letter intercepted by Ollendorf. Humiliated, Symon thinks of killing himself, but his friend, Janitsky, helps the Polish king regain his throne and thereby wins a high station for himself and Symon. The newly ennobled Symon is therefore able to propose to Laura.

Major roles: Palmatica, Countess Nowalska (mezzo); Countess Laura, her daughter (sop); Countess Bronislawa, Laura's sister (sop); Symon, the Beggar Student (ten); Jan Janitzky, Symon's friend (ten); and Colonel Ollendorf (bass).

For a detailed synopsis, see K/*KOB*, 300–303.

The composer's most famous work. Also set by Peter Winter (1785, Munich) and Johann Schenk (1796, Vienna).

SCORE: English vs (New York: White-Smith Music, ca. 1883).

BIBLIOGRAPHY: Walter Ducloux, "The Beggar Student. Carl Milloecker," *OJ* IV/2 (1971), 21–23.

DISCOGRAPHY: See M/*IRR*, 162–64.

Bluthochzeit, Die (Blood Wedding), opera in two acts by Wolfgang Fortner; libretto (Ger) by Enrique Beck after Federico García-Lorca's tragedy *Bodas de sangre* (1933). First performance June 8, 1957, Cologne, with Natalie Hinsch-Gröndahl (mother), Anny Schlemm (bride), Irmgard Gerz (mother-in-law), Emmy Lisken (Leonardo's wife), Ernest Gratwohl (Leonardo), Otto Wilhelm (the bridegroom), Alexander Schödler (bride's father), Helga Jenckel (Death), and Gerhard Nathge (the Moon); conducted by Günter Wand. First British performance June 30, 1958, BBC, with Natalie Hinsch-Gröndahl (mother); conducted by Günter Wand.

In this work a young girl runs away with her former fiancé on her wedding day. He and the groom are then killed in a fight.

Major roles: the mother (sop), the bride (sop), the maid (mezzo), Leonardo's wife (alto), Leonardo's mother-in-law (alto), the child (young sop), the Moon (ten), Leonardo (bar), the bridegroom (speaking role), and the bridegroom's father (speaking role).

The opera includes much dialogue. It is written mostly in serial style, with diatonic sections interspersed.

Other settings of the García-Lorca text include Juan José's *Bodas de sangre* (1979, Buenos Aires), and Sandor Szokoloy (1966, Wuppertal).

BIBLIOGRAPHY: anonymous, "Klebes 'Räuber' und Fortners 'Bluthochzeit,' " *Melos* XXIV (1957), 22–24; Iain Hamilton, "Radio Opera," *Opera* IX (1958), 541–42 [on rebroadcast of premiere]; Heinrich Lindlar, ed., *Wolfgang Fortner* (Rodenkirchen/Rhein: P. J. Tonger, 1960), 76–86 [press reviews of the premiere]; William Marshall, "News. Germany," *Opera* VIII (1957), 505–6 [on premiere].

Boccaccio, opera in three acts by Franz von Suppé; libretto (Ger) by F. Zell [Camillo Walzell] and Richard Genée. First performance February 1, 1879, Vienna, Carl-Theater, with Antonie Link (Boccaccio) and Rosa Streitmann (Fiametta). First U.S. performance April 15, 1880, Philadelphia, Chestnut Street Theater (in English); April 23, 1880, New York, Thalia Theater (in German). First British performance 1882, London, Royal Comedy Theatre, with Violet Cameron (Boccaccio).

Pietro, the Prince of Palermo, is sent to Florence to marry Fiametta, the illegitimate daughter of the Duke of Tuscany. She in turn is in love with Boccaccio. On the eve of his engagement, Pietro watches a play by Boccaccio which ridicules the marriage of two people who do not love each other. Taking his cue, Pietro gives up his claim to Fiametta and leaves the way free for Boccaccio.

Major roles: Fiametta, foster daughter of Almbertuccio (sop); Boccaccio, a writer (ten/sop); Lambertuccio, a Florentine (ten); Scalza, a merchant (bar); Beatrice, his wife (sop); Peronella, Lambertuccio's wife (alto); and Pietro, Prince of Palermo (ten).

For a detailed plot synopsis, see K/*KOB*, 278–81.

Among the highlights is Fiametta's song of love to Boccaccio, "Hab ich nur deine Liebe."

SCORES: vs. ed. C. F. Konradin (Hamburg: Aug. Cranz, 187–); vs transl. D. Smith (English-German) (Boston: O. Ditson & Co., 1880).

LIBRETTO: German (Hamburg: A . Cranz, 187–).

DISCOGRAPHY: excerpts: Rothenberber, Görner, Hoppe, Prey, Böhme, and Grimm, Gärtnerplatz Theater, conducted by Michalski, Odeon SME083940; reviewed by C. J. Luten, "Records," *ON* XXXI (January 7, 1967), 34; complete: Rothenberger, Moser, Dallapozza, Prey, Böhme, Bavarian Symphony, conducted by Boskovsky, Arabesque 8096L (2), 9096L (tape).

Boulevard Solitude, lyric drama in seven scenes by Hans Werner Henze; libretto (Ger) by Grete Weil after a scenario by Walter Jockisch, based on Abbé Prévost's tale *Manon Lescaut*. First performance February 17, 1952, Hanover, Landestheater, with Sigurd Claus (Manon), Walter Buckow (Des Grieux), and Theo Zilliken (Lescaut); conducted by Johannes Schüler. First U.S. performance August 2, 1967, Santa Fe, with Patricia Brooks (Manon), Lorin Driscoll (Des Grieux), and George Fortune (Lescaut); conducted by Robert Baustian. First British performance (in English) June 25, 1962, London, Sadler's Wells Theatre, with April Cantelo (Manon), John Carolan (Des Grieux), and Peter Glossop (Lescaut); conducted by Leon Lovett.

In this modernization of the *Manon Lescaut* story, the settings include a railway station, Armand's attic apartment, the university library, a dope den, and a square in front of a prison. And in this version Manon is arrested not because she is unable to take action to save herself (as in the Puccini version), but because Des Grieux takes time to steal a painting in order to sell it and get money.

Major roles: Manon Lescaut (sop); Armand Des Grieux, a student (ten); Lescaut, Manon's brother (bar).

Musically, the opera combines lyrical melody with twelve-tone technique. It includes a number of beautiful instrumental interludes.

SCORE: vs (Mainz: BSS and New York: Schott Music Corporation, 1951).

BIBLIOGRAPHY: Horst Koegler, "Summer Festivals. Hanover" [on premiere], *Opera* III (1952), 364–66; William S. Mann, "London Opera Diary"?, *Opera* XIII (1962), 556–58 [on British premiere]; George Martin, "Reports. U.S." [on U.S. premiere], *ON* XXXII (September 9, 1967), 20–21.

Brautwahl, Die (The Marital Selection), musical fantasy-comedy in three acts and an epilogue by Ferruccio Busoni; libretto (Ger) by the composer after a story by E. T. A. Hoffmann. First performance April 13, 1912, Hamburg, with Von Scheidt (Leonhard), Lohfing (Manasse), Wiedemann (Voswinkel), Marak (Edmund Lehsen), Birrenkoven (Thusman), and Fräulein Puritz-Schumann (Albertine); conducted by Brecher. This was the first of the composer's operas to be performed.

The story concerns the parvenu Voswinkel, who is confronted with the difficult choice of a husband for his daughter. Her suitors include the middle-aged Thusman, Baron Bensch, and the fiery young Edmund Lehsen, with whom Albertine has already fallen in love. Leonhard, who has magical powers and paternal feelings toward Edmund, arranges a lottery in which his protegé wins the hand of Albertine; the other two aspirants still emerge satisfied.

Major roles: Voswinkel, a councillor (bar); Albertine, his daughter (sop); Thusman, a minor government official (ten); Edmund Lehsen, a young artist (ten); Baron Bensch (ten); Leonhard, a goldsmith (bar); and Manasse, an old man (bass).

SCORES: fs (Berlin: Harmonie-Verlag, c. 1914); vs ed. Egon Petri (Berlin: Harmonie-Verlag, 1912).

BIBLIOGRAPHY: H. H. Stuckenschmidt, "Brautwahl," *SMz* CII (1962), 344–51; Leonhard Thurneiser, "Die Brautwahl, eine Berlinische Oper Busonis,"*Melos* V (1925), 22–28.

Bürgschaft, Die (The Pledge), opera in three acts by Franz Schubert; anonymous libretto (Ger) after Friedrich von Schiller's ballade, which Schubert set as a Lied (1815). Composed 1816, first act, second act, entr'acte and No. 16 of Act III completed. First performance March 7, 1908, Vienna, Wiener Schubertbund (concert).

Schubert used part of the ballade music as an orchestral prelude in No. 14 of the opera, Möros' scene and aria "O göttliche Ruhe!" The original libretto and dialogue of the opera are lost. In the Schiller ballade, Möros is arrested after trying to kill the tyrant and is sentenced to be crucified. He receives a stay of execution to save his sister's husband, on the condition that he leave his friend as a hostage. His friend will be killed in his place if he does not return in three days. Möros reunites his sister and her husband, but on the way back he is slowed down by thieves and a raging brook. When he enters the city he is warned by Philostratus that it is too late to save his friend, and that Möros should flee. Möros declares that he, too, is willing to die, and, moved by this display of true loyalty, the king frees both.

Major roles: Möros (bass), Dionys (bass), Anna (sop), Ismene (sop), Julus (sop), Theages (bass), and Philostratus (ten).

SCORE: fs Schu/*AGA*, XV/7, no. 13 (1893).

Bürgschaft, Die (The Pledge), opera in the three acts by Franz Lachner; libretto (Ger) by K. von Biedenfeld after Friedrich Schiller. First performance October 30, 1838, Pest, with Dlle. Schindler, Herr Fischer, Herr Watzinger, and Herr Mink; conducted by the composer.

The story is set in ancient Greece. After the cessation of fighting, brought on by Dionysus, the populace is celebrating the peace, all except Moeros, who seeks revenge for his father. He is prevented from killing the tyrant by Aeakos and is reminded by his friend Prokles of his duty to free Polyxena, who is desired by Dionysus. Prokles, who also loves Polyxena, agrees to take Moeros' place in prison. After the wedding of Helene, Moeros' sister, to Philomen, Aeakos and his men come and seize Helene and her attendants. In the subsequent fighting, Moeros kills Aeakos in a torrential stream. Prokles anxiously awaits the return of his friend and refuses Dionysus' offer of freedom if he will renounce his belief in Moeros' loyalty. Just as Prokles is about to be hanged, Moeros appears. Moved by this show of true devotion, Dionysus pardons Moeros and asks for the friendship of the noble companions.

BIBLIOGRAPHY: W/*FL*, 29–49.

Bürgschaft, Die (The Pledge), opera in a prologue and three acts by Kurt Weill; libretto (Ger) by Caspar Neher on a parable by Johann Gottfried von Herder, "Der afrikanische Rechtspruch." First performance March 10, 1932, Berlin, Deutsche Oper, with Wilhelm Rode, Hans Reinmar, Josef Burgwinkel, Charlotte Müller, Irene Eisinger, and Ruth Berglund; conducted by Fritz Stiedry. Revived October 1957, Berlin, Städtische Oper, with Josef Greindl (David Orth), Tomislav Neralic (Mattes), and Irene Dalis (Anna); conducted by Artur Rother.

Set in the make-believe land of Urb, the opera concerns two friends, Johann Mattes, a cattle farmer, and David Orth, a grain dealer. Orth sells his friend two sacks of grain, knowing full well that one of the sacks contains a lot of money but believing that Mattes needs the money and will pay him back when he can. Mattes discovers the money and, believing Orth knows nothing of it, decides to keep his discovery to himself. Somehow three extortionists learn of the treasure, and when Mattes refuses to pay them, they ran off to tell Orth the truth. Mattes reaches the house before them, but when he offers to return the money, Orth will have nothing to do with it. A judge decides that the son of Mattes should marry the daughter of Orth, and the money serve as a dowry. Before the action can be taken, however, the two men are arrested through the intervention of a neighboring "Great Power," and they are sent to jail. They both return as wealthy men, but when things deteriorate around them, the people seek revenge by going after Mattes, who has cheated them. This time Orth refuses to shelter him, and he turns him over to the vengeful mob, who wound him mortally. Orth tells his dying erstwhile friend that he did not betray him, but that everything had occurred according to the law of money and power.

Major roles: Johann Mattes (bar); Anna, his wife (mezzo); Luise his daughter (sop); David Orth (bass); Jakob, his son (ten); the Judge of Urb (ten); and Ellis, the Commisar (ten).

The chorus plays an important role in this work, offering commentary on the events as they unfold. Especially noteworthy is its "Four Gates" cantata in the last act.

SCORE: vs ed. Erwin Stein (Vienna: UE, 1931).

BIBLIOGRAPHY: David Drew, "Topicality and the Universal: The Strange Case of Weill's *Die Bürgschaft*," *ML* XXIX (1958), 242–55; ———, "The Berlin Festival," *Opera* IX (1958), 24–25 [on Berlin revival]; Fritz Stege, "Berliner Musik," *ZfM* XCIX (1932), 309–10 [on premiere].

C

Capriccio, conversation piece in music in one act by Richard Strauss; libretto (Ger) by Clemens Krauss. First performance October 28, 1942, Munich, with Viorica Ursuleac (the Countess), Hildegarde Ranczak (Clairon), Horst Taubmann (Flamand), Hans Hotter (Olivier), Walter Höfermayer (the Count), and Georg Hann (La Roche); conducted by Clemens Krauss. First U.S. performance (in English) April 4, 1954, New York, Juilliard, with Gloria Davy (the Countess), Mary Mackenzie (Clairon) William Blankenship (Flamand), Frederick Gersten (Olivier), Robert Rue (the Count), and Thomas Stewart (La Roche); conducted by Frederic Waldman. First British performance September 22, 1953, London, Covent Garden, with Maud Cunitz (the Countess), Hertha Töpper (Clairon), Benno Kusche (La Roche), and Karl Schmitt-Walter (the Count); conducted by Robert Heger.

Set in the Paris of Gluck's time, the opera debates whether words or music is more important, as personified by the poet Olivier and the composer Flamand. Both love Countess Madeleine, who at the end renegs on her promise to select one or the other.

For a detailed synopsis, see K/*KOB*, 851–55.

Major roles: the Countess (sop); Clairon, an actress (alto); Flamand, a musician (ten); Olivier, a poet (bar); the Count, the Countess' brother (bar); and La Roche, director of a theather (bass).

In keeping with his wish not to overwhelm the singers with the orchestra, Strauss provided reduced instrumentation for his last stage work.

For detailed synopses and musical analyses, see C/*MS*, 51–64; D/*RS*, III, 180–245; and M/*RSC*, 359–86.

SCORES: fs (Berlin: Grunewald–J. Oertel, 1942); vs ed. Ernst Gernot Klussmann (Berlin: Grunewald, 1942).

LIBRETTO: German (Berlin: Grunewald, 1942).

BIBLIOGRAPHY: Richard F. Goldman, "Current Chronicle . . . ," *MQ* XL (1954), 391–94 [on premiere]; Richard Strauss, preface to the score, transl. Maria Massey, *Juilliard Review* I/2 (Spring 1954), 4–6, 9; Roland Tenschert, "The Sonnet in Richard Strauss's Opera 'Capriccio,' " *Tempo* XLVII (Spring 1958), 7–11.

DISCOGRAPHY: Schwarzkopf, Fischer-Dieskau, Wächter, Gedda, Hotter, Ludwig, Christ, Moffo, Troy, and Schmitt-Walter, conducted by Sawallisch, Philharmonia Orchestra, Angel CL–3580–3 (3).

Cardillac, opera in three acts by Paul Hindemith; libretto (Ger) by Ferdinand Lion after E. T. A. Hoffmann's *Das Fräulein von Scuderi*. First performance November 9, 1926, Dresden, Sächsische Staatstheater, with Claire Born (the daughter), Grete Nikisch (the lady), Max Hirzel (the officer), Robert Burg (Cardillac), and Ludwig Eybisch (the cavalier); conducted by Fritz Busch. First U.S. performance July 26, 1967, Santa Fe, with Doris Yarick (the daughter), Saramae Endich (the lady), Ragnar Ulfung (the officer), John Reardon (Cardillac), and John Stewart (the cavalier); conducted by Robert Craft. First British performance (concert) December 18, 1936, London, B.B.C., with Noel Eadie, Miriam Licette, John McKenna, Arthur Fear, Norman Walker, and Dennis Noble; conducted by Clarence Raybould. First British stage performance March 11, 1970, London, Sadler's Wells, with Ann Pashley, Elizabeth Robson, John Wakefield, Frank Olegani (the gold merchant), and John Cameron (Cardillac); conducted by Leon Lovett. Hindemith revised the work in 1952, when he wrote it in four acts and provided a new text. First performance of this version June 20, 1952, Zurich, with Hillebrecht, Müller-Bütow, Herbert Brauer (Cardillac), and Lichtegg; conducted by Victor Reinshagen.

The story is set in seventeenth-century Paris and concerns the master goldsmith Cardillac, who is so enamored of his works that he kills anyone who buys them. He is discovered through the love of a soldier for his daughter and is killed by an angry mob at the end.

Major roles: Cardillac, a goldsmith (bar); his daughter (sop); the lady (sop); the officer (ten); the cavalier (ten); and the gold merchant (bass).

For a detailed synopsis, see K/*KOB*, 881–84.

Although the principals have several set numbers, most of the lyricism is left for the orchestra.

SCORES: fs H/*SW* 1/4 (1979); vs ed. Otto Singer (Mainz: BSS, c. 1926); rev. ed. of vs ed. composer (Mainz: BSS and New York: AMP, 1952).

LIBRETTO: German (Mainz: BSS, 1926); new version (Mainz: BSS, 1954).

BIBLIOGRAPHY: Martin Bernheimer, "Current Chronicle . . . ," *MQ* XLVIII (1962), 115–17; Kurt Honolka, "Cardillacs Wiederkehr," *Musica* VI (1952), 301–2; Ian Kemp, "Hindemith's *Cardillac*," *MT* CXI (1970), 268–71; George Martin, "Santa Fe," *ON* XXXII (September 9, 1967), 20 [on U.S. premiere]; Patrick Smith, "And Yet More Festivals. Santa Fe," *Opera* XIII (1967), 81–82 [on U.S. premiere]; Ralf Steyer, "Munich Cardillac," *Opera* XVII (1966), 70–73; Joseph Wechsberg, "World Reports. 'Cardillac' in Vienna," *Opera* XV (1964), 240–41.

DISCOGRAPHY: Kirschstein, Söderström, Grobe, Katz, Fischer-Dieskau, and Kohn, conducted by Keilberth, Cologne Radio Orchestra, DG 139435–36 (2); reviewed by M. H. Herbert, "Recordings. Cardillac," *OJ* I/1 (Spring 1983), 133–34.

Carmina burana (Songs from Benediktbeuren), scenic cantata in a prologue, three parts, and an epilogue by Carl Orff; texts (Latin, middle high German, old French) by the composer, Michel Hofmann, and Wolfgang Schadewaldt after thirteenth-century songs from a Latin codex of the monastery of Benediktbeuren. First performance June 8, 1937, Frankfurt, Staatsoper, with Clara Ebers and Jean Stern; conducted by B. Wetzelsberger. First U.S. performance (concert) January 19, 1954, San Francisco; (stage) October 3, 1958, San Francisco, with Elaine Malbin and Manton; conducted by Leopold Ludwig. First British performance January 26, 1960, London, Royal Festival Hall.

Major roles: soprano, tenor, baritone.

The work is divided into three parts: "In Springtime," "In the Tavern," and "The Court of Love."

SCORES: fs Latin (Mainz: BSS and New York: AMP, 1937); vs (Latin) (Mainz: BSS, 1937).

DISCOGRAPHY: See M/*IRR*, 282–83.

Catharina Cornaro, Königin von Cypern (Catharina Cornaro, Queen of Cyprus), opera in four acts by Franz Lachner; libretto (Ger) by Alois Büssel, a translation of J. H. Vernoy de Saint-George's French libretto (set by Jacques Halévy as *La Reine de Chypre* and first presented three weeks after the Lachner work). First performance December 3, 1841, Munich, with Karoline Hetznecker (Catharina), Ernst Friedrich Dietz (Marco), Aloys Bayer (Jakob), and Giulio Pellegrini (Onofrio). Revised version October 15, 1845, Berlin, Königliches Opernhaus.

In the story, set in fifteenth-century Venice, Catharina is engaged to Marco Vernero, but she has been promised by the Venetian council to the King of Cyprus. After Catharina is wed, Marco discovers that the Venetians are planning to kill the Cypriot king, the same man who had once saved Marco's life. Marco goes to Cyprus and leads the Cypriots to victory over the attacking Venetians. The dying king, poisoned by his enemies, led by Onofrio, leaves his wife and young child in the care of Marco.

Major roles: Marco Vernero, Venetian nobleman (ten); Catharina (Caterina) Cornaro (sop); and Jakob von Lusignan, King of Cyprus (ten); and Onofrio, member of the Venetian council (bass).

This was Lachner's most successful work.

The story was also set by Gaetano Donizetti as *Caterina Cornaro* (1844, Naples); Michael Balfe as *The Daughter of St. Mark* (1844, London); and Giovanni Pacini, as *La Regina di Cipro* (1846, Turin).

SCORES: vs (1841 version: Mainz: Schott, 1842); vs (1845 version: Mainz: Schott, ca. 1846); piano potpourri in *Opern-Bibliothek für das Pianoforte*, II, no. 29 (Wolfenbüttel: n.p., 18—).

LIBRETTO: German (1841 version: Mainz: Schott, 1842); (1845 version: Mainz: Schott, ca. 1846).

BIBLIOGRAPHY: Alex Duncker, ed., *Costüme und Decorationen der Oper Catharina Cornaro von Franz Lachner* (Berlin: n.p., 1846); W/*FL*, 66–85.

Christophorus, oder Die Vision einer Oper (Christophorus, or The Vision of an Opera), opera in a prologue, two acts, and epilogue by Franz Schreker; libretto (Ger) by the composer. Composed 1924–1927. The originally scheduled premiere was blocked by the Nazis, since the composer was half Jewish. First performance October 1, 1978, Freiburg, with Luis Glockner (Anselm), Steven Kimbrough (Christophorus), Jan Alofs (professor), and Patricia Stasis (Lisa); conducted by Klaus Weise.

The story concerns Anselm, a young composer, who is unable to write an opera. Both he and his alter ego, Christophorus, are drawn to Lisa, the daughter of Anselm's professor, Maestro Johann.

BIBLIOGRAPHY: Christopher Hailey, "Freiburg. Schreker's 'Christophorus' Premiered," *HiFi/MA* XXIX (February 1979), 34–35; ———, "Zur Entstehungsgeschichte der Oper *Christophorus*," in S/*FSS*, 115–40; Edward A. Reed, "Reports: Foreign," *ON* XLIII (December 16, 1978), 40 [on premiere].

Cid, Der (Master Warrior), lyric drama in three acts by Peter Cornelius; libretto (Ger) by the composer after Corneille's tragedy *El Cid* (1637). First performance May 21, 1865, Weimar, with Rosa von Milde (Chimene) and Feodor von Milde (the Cid). Performed in a revised version by Hermann Levi, April 21, 1891, Munich. Revived in its original form, reconstructed by Max Hasse, June 9, 1904, Weimar.

The opera, which takes place in Burgos around 1064, concerns Ruy Diaz, who has killed the father of his betrothed, Chimene. She asks the king to revenge her father's death, but this cannot be done until Diaz returns from fighting the Moors. When he comes back, victorious, as the "Cid," the king orders that Chimene carry out the sentence.

Major roles: Chimene, Princess of Lozan (sop); Ruy Diaz, Prince of Vibar, called Campeador (bar); Fernando, King of Castile (ten); and Luyn Calvo, Bishop (low bass).

Other settings of the story include Handel's *Rodrigo* (1707) and *Flavio* (1723, London); Antonio Sacchini's *Il Cidde* (1769, Rome, revived as *Chimène, ou Le Cid*, 1783, Fontainebleau); Giuseppe Farinelli (1797); Johann Kaspar Aiblinger, as *Rodrigo und Zimene* (1821, Munich); Giovanni Pacini (1853); Ludwig Schindelmeisser, as *Der Rächer* (1846, Budapest); Jules Massenet (1855, Paris); and Johann Wagenaar, as *De Cid* (1916, Utrecht).

SCORES: fs ed. Max Hasse C/*MW* IV (1904, repr. 1971); vs ed. Waldemar von Baussern (Leipzig: B&H, c. 1905).

BIBLIOGRAPHY: Erwin Koppen, "Cornelius' *Cid* in thematologischer Sicht," in C/ *PCK*, 139–44.

Cimarrón, El (The Fugitive Slave), "recital for four musicians" in two parts by Hans Werner Henze; libretto (Ger) by Hans Magnus Enzensberger on Miguel Barnet's narrative of Esteban Montejo, *The Autobiography of a Runaway Slave*. First performance (in an English translation by Christopher Keene) June 22, 1970, Aldeburgh Festival, with William Pearson, Karlheinz Zöller, Leo Brouwer, and Stomu Yamash'ta. First U.S. performance March 27, 1971, University of Pittsburgh.

The work consists of fifteen episodes involving four musicians: the singer, flute, guitar, and percussion. It presents the recollections of a 104–year-old runaway slave. The music contains passages that are half spoken and half sung, with some quarter-tone writing.

Major role: Esteban (bar).

BIBLIOGRAPHY: Carsten Wolfgang Becker, "Current Chronicle. Berlin," *MQ* LVII (1971), 314–15; David Matthews, "Henze's *El Cimarrón*," *Tempo* XCIV (Autumn 1970) [on premiere].

DISCOGRAPHY: Pearson, DG 2707.050.

Circe, oder **Des Ulysses Erster Theil** (Circe or Ulysses, First Part), "Singe-spiel" in three acts by Reinhard Keiser; libretto (Ger) by Christian Friedrich Bressand. First performance February 1696, Brunswick. The second part is *Penelope*. Keiser's *Circe* (1734, Hamburg) and *Ulysses* (1722, Copenhagen) are different works altogether. Also Performed 1702, Hambutg.

Circe is the sorceress of Greek mythology who lives on the island of Aeaea. She turns men who meet her into swine, including those of Odysseus, but he escapes her spell and makes her restore his crew to their human forms.

Other settings of the Circe legend include those by Marc-Antoine Charpentier (1675, Paris); Ruperto Chapí y Lorente (1902, Madrid); Herbert Trantow, as *Odysseus bei Circe* (1938); and Werner Egk (1948, Berlin).

SCORE: copy of the fs ms at the Königliche Bibliothek in Berlin (1911, Library of Congress).

Claudine von Villa Bella (Claudine of Villa Bella), opera in three acts by Johann Friedrich Reichardt; libretto (Ger) by Goethe (first set by Ignaz von Beecke in 1780, Vienna). First performance (private) July 29, 1789, Charlottenburg, Schlosstheater. First performance (public) August 3, 1789, Berlin, Opernhaus. Modern revival May 1932, Königsberg (in a version by Joseph Müller-Blattau).

In the Goethe comedy, Claudine, the fiancée of Pedro, becomes interested in the vagabond Crugantino. When Crugantino turns out to be Pedro's brother, Claudine returns to her first love.

Other settings of the Goethe text include those by Johann André (1778); Claus Schall, as *Claudine af Villa Bella* (1787, Copenhagen); Johann Christoph Kienlen (1810, Munich); and Franz Schubert (see following entry).

Claudine von Villa Bella (Claudine of Villa Bella), Singspiel in three acts by Franz Schubert; libretto (Ger) by Goethe. Composed 1815. First performance April 26, 1916, Vienna, Gemindenhaus, Wieden, by the Wiener Schubertbund (with piano accompaniment, arranged by Adolf Kirchl). Revived May 26, 1978, Vienna, Kammeroper.

Major roles: Lucinde (sop), Pedro (ten), Alonzo (bass), Claudine (sop), Rugantino (ten), and Basco (bass).

Extant are only the overture and the first act, and the vocal lines for nos. 9 and 10, an ariette by Pedro, and a duet by Claudine and Pedro.

SCORES: fs (overture, first act) Schu/*AGA*, XV/11 (1893); Schu/*NGA* II/12.

Claudius (Die verdammte Staat-Sucht, oder **Der verfuehrte Claudius)** (Claudius [The Damned State Mania, or the Misled Claudius]), ''Sing-Spiel'' in three acts by Reinhard Keiser; libretto (Ger) by Heinrich Hinsch. First performance possibly spring 1703, Hamburg. Revived on November 21, 1718, and July 17, 1726, Hamburg, as *Claudius, Roemischer Kayser* (with changes).

Calpurnia, although engaged to Callistus, is in love with Silius, who in turn loves Messalina, wife of the emperor, who encourages him and urges Claudius' removal. Rejected by Silius, Calpurnia regains her affection for her betrothed. Eventually the conspiracy to overthrow Claudius is defeated, Messalina and Silius are imprisoned, and Claudius gives his blessing to Calpurnia and Callistus.

Major roles: Claudius, Emperor of Rome (bass); Messalina, his wife (sop); Narcissus, Callistus, and Pallas, favorites of Claudius (sop, 2 altos); Calpurnia, betrothed of Callistus (sop); Silius, a Roman prince (ten); and Curtius Rufus, a Roman general (ten).

Handel borrowed some twenty numbers from Keiser for his own operas, including *Trionfo*, *Agrippina*, *Radamisto*, *Sosarme*, and *Athalia* (see the Roberts edition below).

The opera contains fifty-six airs in German and eleven in Italian.

SCORE: ms ed. John H. Roberts, in *Handel Sources. An Anthology of Handel's Borrowings*, III (New York: Garland Publishing, 1986; also 1703 libretto).

Cleopatra (Die betrogene Staats-Liebe, oder **Die erretete Unschuld** oder **Germanicus, Römischer General)** (Cleopatra [Betrayed Love of State, or Innocence Saved, or Germanicus, Roman General]), opera in three acts by Johann Mattheson; libretto (Ger) by Friedrich Christian Feustking. First performance October 20, 1704, Hamburg, with the composer singing and conducting.

Other settings of the Cleopatra story include Kusser's (1691, Brunswick); Graun's *Cleopatra e Cesare* (1742, Berlin); Domenico Cimarosa's *Cleopatra* (1789, St. Petersburg); Sebastiano Nasolini's *La Morte di Cleopatra* (1791, Vicenza); Victor Massé's *La Nuit de Cléopâtre* (1885, Paris); Melisio Morales' *Cleopatra* (1891, Mexico); August Enna's *Cleopatra* (1894, Copenhagen); Jules Massenet's *Cléopâtra* (1914, Monte Carlo); and Theo Goldberg's *Kleopatra* (1952, Karlsruhe).

SCORE: fs ed. George J. Buelow, *EDM*, LXIX (1975).

BIBLIOGRAPHY: George Buelow, "An Evaluation of Johann Mattheson's Opera *Cleopatra* (Hamburg, 1704)," in *Studies in 18th Century Music*, ed. H. C. Robbins Landon and Roger Cluysman (London: Allen & Unwin, 1970), 92–107.

Cola Rienzi. See **Rienzi**.

Columbus, radio opera in three parts by Werner Egk; libretto (Ger) by the composer. First performance July 13, 1933, Munich radio; conducted by the composer. First performance (concert) April 4, 1934, Munich, Tonhalle; conducted by the composer. Revised for the stage in 1941. First performance January 13, 1942, Frankfurt, Städtische Bühnen Opernhaus, with Clara Ebers, Hellmut Schweebs, and Jakob Sabel; conducted by Franz Konwitschny. Revised May 17, 1951, Berlin, Städtische Oper.

This treatment of Christopher Columbus examines his discoveries, conflicts, and death.

Major roles (1941 version): Columbus (bar), Ferdinand (ten), and Isabella (sop).

Other operas on the explorer include those by Pietro Ottoboni (1690, Rome); Francesco Morlacchi (1828, Genoa); Ramón Carnicier (1831, Madrid); Alberto Franchetti's *Cristoforo Colombo* (1892, Genoa); Erwin Dressel's *Armer Kolumbus* (1928, Kassel); Darius Milhaud's *Christophe Colomb* (1930, Berlin, original French text); Vassilenko (1938); and Walter Böhme's *Kolumbus* (1950, Reichenbach).

SCORE: vs ed. composer (Mainz: BSS, c. 1942).

LIBRETTO: first version: German, (Munich: Franz, 1933); 1941 version: German (Mainz: BSS and New York: Schott Music, c. 1942).

BIBLIOGRAPHY: Otto Oster, "Werner Egks 'Columbus,' " *ZMw* C (1933), 1233–35 [on radio premiere].

Corregidor, Der (The Magistrate), opera in four acts by Hugo Wolf; libretto (Ger) by Rosa Mayreder-Obermeyer after Pedro de Alarcón's story *El Sombrero de tres picos* (1874). First performance June 7, 1896, Mannheim, with Frl. Hohenleitner (Frasquita); Rüdiger (the Magistrate), and Joachim Krömer (Tio Lukas); conducted by Röhr. First U.S. performance (concert) January 5, 1959, New York, Carnegie Hall (in an English translation by Phyllis and George Mead) with Nadine Conner, Martha Lipton, Norman Kelley, Hugh Thompson, and

Donald Gramm; conducted by Thomas Scherman. First British performance (in an English translation by Geoffrey Thomas Dunn) July 13, 1934, London, Royal Academy of Music, with Janet Hamilton-Smith (Frasquita), Clifford Deri (Tio Lukas), and Bernard Lewis (the Corregidor); conducted by (Sir) John Barbirolli.

Frasquita, the wife of the jealous miller Tio Lukas, takes advantage of the amorous overtures of the elderly magistrate (Corregidor) to teach her husband a lesson and to obtain a post for her nephew. Overcome by her attentions, the Corregidor falls in the dust and vows revenge on the miller. He sends his officer with a warrant for the miller's arrest. When he is taken away, Frasquita hears a call for help. When she opens her door, she finds a drenched Corregidor, wet from having fallen into the brook. Frasquita leaves to search for her husband, and the Corregidor takes off his clothes and makes himself comfortable in the miller's bed.

The miller returns and, seeing the sleeping magistrate, jumps to the wrong conclusion. He then puts on the dry clothes and goes to the Corregidor's house to confront Doña Mercedes, wife of the Corregidor. The Corregidor meanwhile awakens and has to don the miller's attire. He too returns to his home, where he is humiliated and, along with the once jealous miller, chastened.

Major roles: Frasquita, wife of Tio Lukas (mezzo); Tio Lukas, the miller (bar); Don Eugenio de Zuniga, the magistrate (buffo tenor); and Doña Mercedes, his wife (sop).

This is Wolf's one completed attempt in the genre. In it he tried to create "a comic opera, and, in fact, a completely ordinary comic opera, without having the gloomy, world-saving ghost of Schopenhauer philosophy in the background" (Edgar Istel, *Die moderne Oper* [Leipzig: B. G. Teubner, 1915], p. 21).

The story was also set by Riccardo Zandonai as *La farsa amorosa* (1933, Rome) and by Manuel de Falla as the ballet *El sombrero de tres picos* (1919, London).

SCORES: vs (Mannheim: K. Ferdinand Heckel, 1896); vs (Leipzig: C. F. Peters, 1919).

BIBLIOGRAPHY: "F. B.," "Wolf's 'Corregidor' at the R.A.M.," *MT* LXXV (1934), 746 [on British premiere]; Werner Bollert, "Hugo Wolf's *Corregidor*," *Musica* XIV (1960), 143–47; Peter Cook, *Hugo Wolf's 'Corregidor': A Study of the Opera and Its Origins* (London: Author, 1976); Imogen Fellinger, "Die Oper im kompositorischen Schafen von Hugo Wolf," *Jahrbuch des Staatlichen Instituts für Musikforschung 1971* (1972), 87–99; Robert Hernried, "Hugo Wolf's *Corregidor* at Mannheim," *MQ* XXVI (1940), 19–30; Hans-Josef Irmen, "Hugo Wolf und seine rheinischen Freunde Engelbert Humperdinck, Hermann Wette und Arnold Mendelssohn," *Beiträge zur rheinischen Musikgesellschaft* CV (1974), 37–73; Mary Ellis Pelz, "Reports," *ON* XXIII (February 2, 1959), 26–27 [on U.S. premiere]; Fritz Schachermeyr, "Der 'private' und 'offentliche' Hugo Wolf," *ÖMz* XXVIII (1973), 438–43.

DISCOGRAPHY: Erb, Fuchs, Bohme, Wessely, Frick, Hermann, Teschemacher, Hann, and Rott, conducted by K. Elmendorff, Saxon State Orchestra, Urania US 5208/3 (3).

Croesus (Der hochmütige, gestürtzte und wieder erhabene Croesus) (Croesus [The Haughty, Overthrown, and Again Elevated Croesus]). "Sing-Spiel" in three acts by Reinhard Keiser; libretto (Ger) by Lucas von Bostel after Nicolò Minato's text (first set by Johann Philipp Förtsch in 1684, Hamburg). First performance 1711, Hamburg, Operntheater. Revised version December 6, 1730, Hamburg. First U.S. performance of the 1730 version (concert, abridged) December 5, 1967, with Rita Shane (Elmira); Bernard Krysen (Croesus); Hughes Cuénod (Atis); Gene Boucher (Cyrus); and Dorothy Coulter (Clerida); conducted by Newell Jenkins.

Croesus, King of Lydia, goes off to fight Cyrus the Great and leaves Prince Eliates in charge, a move which upsets Oriantes. Oriantes is in love with Elmira, who in turn loves Atis, the mute son of the king. Although Croesus is defeated, he is saved from death by Atis, who regains his voice and foils a plot by Oriantes. Croesus is then imprisoned for his rebellion and condemned to death by Cyrus, who refuses to accept a ransom for him or let Atis, Elmira, or Clerida take his place. Cyrus finally yields on the advice of Solon. Atis weds Elmira, and Eliates Clerida, while Oriantes is pardoned.

Major roles: Croesus, the Lydian king (1711, ten; 1730, bass); Atis, his son (1711, bass; 1730, sop); Clerida, a Lydian princess (sop); Elmira, a Medean princess (sop); Oriantes (bass) and Eliates (ten), Lydian princes; Cyrus (bar); and Solon (ten).

Among the musical numbers are several that are through-composed, such as "Hoffe noch" and "Ihr stummen Fische" of Elmira and "Elmira, wo bleibest du?" There are also buffo elements, including the quartet "Clerida, du hältst gefangen" and several ballets. The 1730 version has thirty-seven new arias.

SCORES: fs, *DDT*, I/37–38 (1912); rev. Hans Joachim Moser (Wiesbaden: B&H, 1958); vs (Wiesbaden: B&H, 1967).

LIBRETTO: German (1711 version: Hamburg: Friedrich Conrad Greflinger, 1711; 1730 version: 1730, Hamburg).

BIBLIOGRAPHY: Frank Merkling, "Reports: U.S.," *ON* XXXII (December 30, 1967), 31 [on the U.S. premiere]; Mary Peckham, "Report from New York: First American Performance of Keiser's *Croesus*" [on the U.S. premiere], *CM* VI (1968), 81–83.

DISCOGRAPHY: in *Early German Opera from the Goose Market*: Otto, Siemling, Yano, Schmidt, Prey, Brauer, and Adam, Günther Arndt Chorus, Berlin Philharmonic, conducted by Brückner-Rüggeberg, Angel 362773, reviewed by C. J. Luten, "On Records," *ON* XXX (May 7, 1966), 30.

Csárdásfürstin, Die (The Gypsy Princess), operetta in three acts by Emmerich [Imre] Kálmán; libretto (Ger) by Leo Stein and Béla Jenbach. First performance November 13, 1915, Vienna, Johann Strauss Theater, with Mizzi Günther (Sylva Varescu). First U.S. performance September 24, 1917 (*The Riviera Girl*, with several numbers by Jerome Kern) New York, New Amsterdam Theater, with Wilda Bennett, Carl Gantwoort, and Gene Lockwood. Its New York run was a failure. First British performance May 20, 1921, London, Prince of Wales Theatre, also in English, with Sári Petráss (Sylva), Billy Leonard, Mark Lester, and Phyllis Titmuss. The London engagement faired no better than its New York counterpart.

The cabaret singer Sylva Varescu is pursued by Prince Edwin, who wishes to marry her, despite his obligation to marry Countess Stasi and the opposition of his father. The singer realizes that such a match would be impossible. She attends the engagement party of the Prince and the Countess, during which she reminds the Prince of his worthless promises to wed her. When she flees, the Prince follows her and again tells her of his wishes to marry her. His father, originally opposed to the marriage, relents when he is reminded of his own earlier love for a singer.

Major roles: Sylva Varescu (sop); Prince Edwin (ten); and Countess Stasi (sop).

One of Kálmán's most successful operettas in the German-speaking world, it contains such favorites as the Viennese "Machen wir's den Schwalben nach" and the Hungarian czardas, which appears first in the overture.

SCORE: vs (Leipzig: J. Weinberger, 1916).

LIBRETTO: German (Vienna: J. Weinberger, 1944).

For information on discography, see M/*IRR*, 85–86.

Cubana, La (The Cuban Woman), "a cruel and obscene vaudeville" in five scenes by Hans Werner Henze; libretto (Ger) by Hans Magnus Enzensberger after Miguel Barnet's novel *La Canción de Rachel*. First performance March 4, 1974, New York, WNET (in English), with Lee Venora (young Rachel), Lili Darvas (old Rachel), and Alan Titus (the trio of men in Rachel's life). First stage performance May 28, 1975, Munich. First British performance October 19, 1978.

The action centers around the aged Rachel, once a famous music hall singer and actress, as she relives her past through a series of flashbacks.

Major roles: Young Rachel, a beauty in the cabaret (sop); Rachel's lovers—Eusebio, a rich young man (bar), Paco, an artist (bar), and Federico, a student (bar)—old Rachel (speaking role); Lucile, a young whore (mezzo); Alberto/Yarini (ten); Don Alfonso, a circus director (bass bar); El Cimarrón, a former slave (bass bar); a critic/theater director (ten); and Ofelio, Rachel's maid (sop).

The music mixes melodic writing with dissonance; the score includes dialogue and *Sprechstimme*.

SCORE: vs ed. Wilfried Steinbrenner (Mainz: BSS and New York: Schott, 1974).

BIBLIOGRAPHY: Bernard Jacobson, "Henze's 'La Cubana,' "*Opera* XXIX (1978), 953–56; ———, "TV," *ON* XXXVIII (March 16, 1974), 25 [on premiere].

= D =

Dafne, the "first German opera" by Heinrich Schütz; libretto (Ger) by Martin Opitz after Ottavio Rinuccini's text, set by Jacopo Peri (1597, Florence). First performance April 13, 1627, Torgau, for the wedding of George II of Hesse-Darmstadt and Sophie Eleonora of Saxony.

The music is lost.

In this first known German setting of the Daphne legend, the daughter of a river god is loved by Apollo and escapes from him by being turned into a laurel tree. Subsequent German versions include Richard Strauss' work *Daphne*.*

BIBLIOGRAPHY: Martin Gregor-Dellin, "Der erste deutsche Oper," in *Heinrich Schütz* (Munich: Piper, 1984), 146–53; Siegfried Köhler, "*Dafne* und die Folgen: Anmerkungen zum Opernschaffen des Heinrich Schütz," in *Der Komponist und sein Adressat*, ed. Siegfried Bimberg (Halle: Martin Luther University, 1977), 40–45.

Dame Kobold (Lady Sprite), "musikalische Komödie" in three acts by Gerhard Wimberger; libretto (Ger) by the composer and Wolfgang Rennert after Hugo von Hofmannsthal's free translation of Calderón's play *La Dama Duende*. First performance September 24, 1964, Frankfurt, Opernhaus, with Sylvia Stahlman (Donna Angela), Kurt Wehofschitz (Cosme), Anny Schlemm (Isabel), Heinz Hoppe (Don Manuel), Georg Stern (Don Luis), Sona Cervana (Donna Beatriz), and Hans Wilbrink (Don Juan); conducted by Wolfgang Rennert.

The newly widowed Donna Angela is forced to live in seclusion at the home of her brother Don Luis. In an effort to escape her dreary existence, she leaves the house to see the entertainment on the palace grounds. She is pursued by her rakish brother, who does not recognize her because of her veil. Seeking to avoid being discovered, she stops two strangers, Don Manuel and his servant, Cosme, who have just come to town to stay with, of all people, Don Juan, brother of Don Luis. At her request, the pair detain Don Luis, who wounds Don Manuel in a duel. Eventually Don Juan joins the group, and by the time identities are straightened out, Donna Angela has made her way safely back home.

After she tells her maid, Isabel, of her adventure, Isabel informs her mistress of a secret panel that leads to the guest room of Don Manuel. After the two ladies gain access to the room, Donna Angela leaves Don Manuel an unsigned love note, and Isabel creates havoc among his effects, so that when he and Cosme return, the latter is convinced there is a phantom prowling around. Don Manuel suspects that the phantom is Don Luis' mistress, and he begins an ardent correspondence with his "phantom" visitor. The deception continues with the help of Donna Beatriz, Angela's cousin and the love interest of Don Juan and the object of Don Luis' unwanted attentions. Donna Angela becomes trapped in Don Manuel's room and tells him her true identity as well as of her love for him. Don Luis comes upon the pair and claims that the family honor can be saved only if Don Manuel marries his sister. Don Manuel happily complies.

Major roles: Donna Angela, a young widow (sop); her brothers Don Luis (high bass) and Don Juan (bar); Donna Beatriz, Donna Angela's cousin (mezzo); Don Manuel (ten); Cosme, his servant (buffo tenor); Isabel, maid of Donna Angela (sop); and Rodrigo, Don Luis' servant (bass).

A modernized "number" opera with extensive dialogue, the score contains sections of "cool jazz," with saxophone and guitar featured in the orchestra.

Also set by Felix Weingartner (1916, Darmstadt); and Kurt von Wolfurt (1940, Kassel).

BIBLIOGRAPHY: Hans Georg Bonte, "Uraufführung von Wimbergers 'Dame Kobold,' " *ÖMz* XIX (1964), 544; G. A. Trumpff, "Calderon mit cool jazz," *NZM* CXXVII (1964), 483–84 [on premiere]; Ruth Uebel, "Reports," *ON* XXIX (December 12, 1964), 31 [on premiere].

Dantons Tod (Danton's Death), opera in two parts by Gottfried von Einem; libretto (Ger) by the composer and Boris Blacher, freely adapted from Georg Büchner's drama (1835). First performance August 6, 1947, Salzburg Festival, with Paul Schöffler (Danton), Josef Witt (Robespierre), Julius Patzak (Camille Desmoulins), Maria Cebotari (Lucile), and Herbert Alsen (Herrmann); conducted by Ferenc Fricsay. First U.S. performance March 9, 1966 (in an English translation by Ruth and Thomas Martin), New York, City Opera, with John Reardon (Danton), Mauro Lampi (Robespierre), William Dupree (Camille Desmoulins), and Sylvia Grant (Lucile); conducted by Ernst Märzendorfer.

The story is set in revolutionary Paris, in 1794. Camille Desmoulins warns his friends Danton and Hérault that two more innocent victims are needed for the guillotine. Robespierre promises the bloodthirsty crowd more victims, an action which Danton criticizes. When Danton leaves, St. Just advises Robespierre to have Danton and his friend Hérault arrested and convicted, although it might cost Robespierre the friendship of Camille. Lucile, Camille's wife, fears it will cost Camille his life, also. The second part opens in front of the prison, which holds the bewildered Danton and Camille. Although Danton initially sways some of the crowd in his favor, he, along with Camille and Hérault, are condemned. Lucile, now crazed, lies down on the ground and sings "Es ist ein Schnitter, der heisst Tod," as the opera closes.

For a detailed plot analysis, see K/*KOB*, 898–900.

Major roles: Georg Danton (bar); Camille Desmoulins, deputy (ten); Robespierre (ten); Herrmann, president of the revolutionary tribunal (bar); Lucile, wife of Desmoulins (sop).

The music is in a neoclassical style. It incorporates a French march in the introduction to the second part and includes several powerful choral scenes.

Hanns Eisler set the Büchner text in 1929 (Berlin); other treatments of Danton include John Eaton's *Danton and Robespierre* (1978, Bloomington, Indiana).

SCORES: fs (Vienna: UE, 1961); vs (Vienna: UE, 1947).

LIBRETTO: German (Vienna: UE, 1947).

BIBLIOGRAPHY: John Ardoin, "America," *Opera* XVII (1966), 360–61 [on U.S. premiere]; Dominik Hartmann, "Bekenntnisoper unserer Zeit. Zu Gottfried von Einems Dantons Tod," *ÖMz* XXII (1967), 594–97; Hans Rutz, "Gottfried Einem und seine Oper 'Dantons Tod,' " *ÖMz* II (1947), 175–78.

DISCOGRAPHY: Laki, Mayr, Hollweg, and Hiestermann, conducted by Wallberg, Munich Radio Orchestra, Bavarian Radio Chorus, Orfeo S–102842H (2) (recorded live at Salzburg, August 13, 1983).

Daphne, bucolic tragedy in one act by Richard Strauss; libretto (Ger) by Joseph Gregor. First performance October 15, 1938, Dresden, with Margarethe Teschemacher (Daphne), and Torsten Ralf (Apollo); conducted by Karl Böhm. First U.S. performance (concert) October 7, 1960, Brooklyn, Little Orchestra, conducted by Thomas Scherman; first staged U.S. performance July 29, 1964, Santa Fe, with Sylvia Stahlman (Daphne), George Shirley (Apollo), Donald Gramm (Peneios), and Glade Peterson (Leukippos); conducted by John Crosby.

Daphne, the daughter of the fisherman Peneios and Gaia, is loved by the shepherd Leukippos, who invites her to attend a Dionysian festival with him. When she refuses, he comes dressed as a girl. Also present at the festival is Apollo, who wants Daphne for himself. When Leukippos reveals his true identity and challenges Apollo, the god strikes him dead. Daphne is inconsolable, and Apollo asks Zeus to change her into a laurel tree.

For a detailed synopsis, see K/*KOB*, 846–48.

Major roles: Peneios, a fisherman (bass); Gaia, his wife (alto); Daphne, their daughter (sop); Leukippos, a shepherd (ten); and Apollo (ten).

Other operas on the Daphne legend include those by Jacopo Peri (1597, Florence); Giulio Caccini (1600, lost); Marco da Gagliano (1608, Mantua); Heinrich Schütz's *Dafne*;* Attilio Ariosti (1696); Giuseppe Aldrovandini (1696); Alessandro Scarlatti (1700); George Frideric Handel's lost *Der beglückte Florindo, oder Die verwandelte Daphne* (1708, Hamburg); Emanuele d'Astorga (1709, Genoa); Giuseppe Mulé (1928, Rome).

SCORES: fs (Berlin-Grunewald: J. Oertel, 1938); vs ed. Ernst Gernot Klussmann (Berlin: A. Fürstner, 1938, 1940).

BIBLIOGRAPHY: Kenneth Birken, *Friedenstag and Daphne: An Interpretive Study of the Literary and Dramatic Sources of Two Operas by Richard Strauss* (New York & London: Garland Publishing, 1989); Bryan Randolph Gilliam, "Richard Strauss's *Daphne*: Opera and Symphonic Continuity" (diss., Harvard University, 1984); Richard Franko Goldman, "Current Chronicle, U.S.,"*MQ* XLVII (1961), 98–100 [on U.S. premiere]; M/*RSC*, 313–29; *Richard Strauss Blätter*, III, *Daphne* (Vienna, 1972); Allen Young, "Reports," *ON* XXIX (October 17, 1964), 24 [on U.S. stage premiere].

DISCOGRAPHY: Popp, Wenkel, Goldberg, Schreier, Moll, Bavarian Radio Symphony and Chorus, conducted by Haitink, Angel-EMI DSK–3941 (2), reviewed by John W. Freeman, "Records," *ON* XLVIII (March 17, 1984), 45, released later in compact-disc format, EMI Angel CDS 7–493–9 (2); Gueden, Little, Wunderlich, King, Schöffler, Vienna State Opera Chorus, Vienna Symphony, conducted by Böhm, DG 2721–190 (2), reviewed by John W. Freeman, *ON* XLIV (October 1979), 67.

Des Teufels Lustschloss (The Devil's Pleasure Palace), Singspiel in three acts by Franz Schubert; libretto (Ger) by August von Kotzebue. First version 1813–1814; second version 1814, revised by Antonio Salieri. First performance December 12, 1879, Vienna, Musikvereinssaal. First U.S. performance July 15, 1988, Boston, Kresge Auditorium. Performed (concert) January 14, 1990, New York, Hunter College, with Rodney Nolan, Hermann Prey, Carolyn James, Lisa Saffer, Werner Klemperer, and Mimi Lerner; conducted by Bruno Weil.

Luitgarde has been taken from her uncle by Oswald, and the two young people come upon a haunted castle, where the knight and his squire, Robert, attempt to break the spell. The action continues, as Oswald and Luitgarde are faced with several life-threatening situations. In the end the castle disappears and the two find themselves together with Luitgarde's uncle, who explains that the entire adventure was devised by him to test Oswald's faithfulness and courage.

Major roles: Luitgarde (sop), Oswald (ten), Robert (bass), an innkeeper (sop), and an Amazon (sop).

The score contains an impressive melodrama in the second act for Oswald (no. 14), and a two-part canon (no. 21), "Hab ich dich wieder," followed by a notable three-part canon; the first number is clearly inspired, according to A. Hyatt King, by "O namenlose Freude" of Beethoven's *Fidelio*.*

Also set by Johann Friedrich Reichardt (1802, Berlin); Christian Ludwig Dieter (1804, Stuttgart); and Franz Weiss (1820, Pest).

SCORE: fs Schu/*AGA*, XV/1 (acts I and III from second version, II from first) (1888); Schu/*NGA*, II/1 (nyp).

LIBRETTO: German (Leipzig: Paul Gotthelf Kummer, 1801).

BIBLIOGRAPHY: A. Hyatt King, "Music for the Stage," in *The Music of Schubert*, ed. Gerald Abraham (Port Washington, N.Y.: Kennikat Press, 1969), 210.

Dido, Königin von Carthago (Dido, Queen of Carthage), opera in three acts by Christoph Graupner; libretto (Ger) by Heinrich Hinsch. First performance spring 1707, Hamburg. The music is lost.

There are dozens of settings of the Dido story, which concerns the Queen of Carthage and her love affair with and abandonment by Aeneas of Troy. These include Francesco Cavalli's *La Didone* (1641, Venice); Henry Purcell's *Dido and Aeneas* (1700, London); Domenico Sarro's *Didone abbandonata* (1724, Naples, the first of many settings of the Metastasio text); Bernhard Klein's *Dido* (1823, Berlin); and Hector Berlioz's *Les Troyens à Carthage* (1863, Paris). The *Dido* of Ferdinand Andergassen (1892–1964) was not performed.

LIBRETTO: German (Hamburg, 1707).

Diktator, Der (The Dictator), tragic opera in one act by Ernst Krenek; libretto (Ger) by the composer. First performance May 6, 1928, Wiesbaden. First U.S. performance December 5 (in English), December 6 (in German), 1980, Minneapolis, Scott Hall; conducted by Jacqueline Jones.

The story, set in Switzerland, concerns two couples, the dictator and his possessive wife, and a blind army officer and his gentle, weak wife, Maria. Seeking revenge against the dictator for having caused her husband's blindness, Maria is shot by the gun with which she had intended to kill him.

Major roles: the dictator (bar); Charlotte, his wife (sop); the officer (ten); and Maria, his wife (sop).

SCORES: fs (Vienna: UE, 1928); vs composer (Vienna: UE, c. 1928).

LIBRETTO: German (Vienna, UE, 1927).

BIBLIOGRAPHY: Kathleen Grandchamp, "Reports: U.S.," *ON* XLV (March 7, 1981), 27 [on U.S. premiere]; R/*EKO*, 73–82.

Doctor (Doktor) und Apotheker (Doctor and Apothecary), comic opera in two acts by Karl Ditters von Dittersdorf; libretto after Gottlob Stephanie, Jr. First performance July 11, 1786, Vienna, Kärntnertortheater. First British performance (in English, by J. Cobb, with additional music by Stephen Storace), October 25, 1788, London, Drury Lane Theatre. First U.S. performance 1795, Boston.

The story is set in a small city in southern Germany around 1780. Gotthold, the son of Dr. Krautmann, is in love with Leonore, the daughter of the apothecary Stössel. Unfortunately, the fathers are bitter enemies, and Leonore's parents want her to marry Captain Stürmwald. The young lovers are saved by the intervention of Leonore's mother, who has been won over by Gotthold. In a subsidiary plot, Stössel's niece, Rosalie, also gets her man, Sichel, a surgeon.

Major roles: Stössel, the apothecary (bass); Claudia, his wife (mezzo); Leonore, their daughter (sop); Rosalie, Stössel's niece (sop); Krautmann, the doctor (bass); Gotthold, his son (ten); and Stürmwald, a captain (ten).

The music includes the comical exchange between the two fathers, "Sind sie ein Charlatan" (Act II).

SCORES: vs (Mainz: B. Schott [1786]); vs ed. Heinrich Burkhard (Vienna: UE, 1935).

LIBRETTO: German (Stuttgart: Reclam, 1961).

DISCOGRAPHY: Uhrmacher, Woodward, Meier, Schöne, Stamm, Lang, and Unger, Rhenish State Philharmonic, conducted by Lockhart, RBM 3101/3 (3); reviewed by John W. Freeman, "Records," *ON* XLVI (April 3, 1982), 36.

Doktor Faust (Doctor Faust), poem for music in two prologues, an entr'acte, and three main scenes by Ferruccio Busoni. Composed 1922, completed by Philipp Jarnach; libretto (Ger) by the composer after Christopher Marlowe's *Doctor Faustus* (1589). First performance May 21, 1925, Dresden, with Meta Seinemeyer (Duchess), Theo Strack (Mephistopheles), and Robert Burg (Doktor Faust); conducted by Fritz Busch. First U.S. performance (concert) December 1, 1964, New York, Carnegie Hall, with Ingrid Bjoner (Duchess of Parma), George Shirley (Mephistopheles), and Dietrich Fischer-Dieskau (Doktor Faust), American Opera Society; conducted by Jascha Hornstein. First U.S. stage performance January 25, 1974, Reno, Nevada. Revived August 5, 1977, Vienna, Virginia, Wolf Trap (in an English translation by Edward Dent), with Richard Stilwell (Faust), Kenneth Riegel (Mephistopheles), Noelle Rogers (Duchess of Parma), John Lankston (Duke), and Donnie Ray Albert (Wagner); conducted by Cal Stewart Kellogg. First British performance (concert broadcast, in an English translation by Edward J. Dent), March 17, 1937, London, Queen's Hall, with May Blyth (Duchess of Parma), Parry Jones (Mephistopheles), Dennis Noble (Doktor Faust), Foster Richardson (Wagner), and Henry Wendon (Duke); conducted by (Sir) Adrien Boult. First British stage performance (with closing scene reconstructed by Anthony Beaumont) April 25, 1986, London, Coliseum, with Thomas Allen (Doktor Faust), Graham Clark (Mephistopheles), and Eilene Hannan (Duchess of Parma); conducted by Mark Elder.

In this treatment of the Faust legend, set in medieval Wittenberg, Münster, and Parma, Faust makes his agreement with the Devil, seduces Margaret (who does not appear in the opera), and tells of his one true love, a duchess, who, according to Mephistopheles, has died. Unlike the Charles Gounod setting, which is based on Goethe, this opera ends with Faust's redeeming himself (the end was set by Jarnach). In another significant change from the Gounod version, Faust is cast as a baritone and Mephistopheles as a tenor.

Major roles: Doktor Faust (bar), Mephistopheles (ten), Wagner (bar), the Duchess of Parma (sop), and the Duke of Parma (ten).

For a detailed plot synopsis, see K/*KOB*, 988–93.

Another setting is Hermann Reutter's *Doktor Johannes Faust* (1936, Frankfurt). Ignaz Walter's *Doktor Faust* (1797, Bremen) uses the Goethe version. See also *Faust*.*

SCORES: vs ed. Egon Petri and Michael von Zadora (Leipzig: B&H, c. 1926, new ed. Wiesbaden: B&H [1965]).

LIBRETTO: German (Potsdam: G. Kiepenheuer, 1920); (Leipzig: B&H, c. 1925, rev. ed. Wiesbaden: B&H [1965]).

BIBLIOGRAPHY: Luciano Alberti, "Italy . . . Florence," *Opera* XV (1964), 80–81; Anthony Beaumont, "Busoni's 'Doctor Faust': a Reconstruction and Its Problems," *MT* CXXVII (1986), 196–99; Martin Bernheimer, "Current Chronicle. Holland," *MQ* XLVIII (1962), 518–20; Ferruccio Busoni, "The Score of *Doktor Faust*," in *The Essence of Music and Other Papers*, transl. Rosamond Ley (London: Rockliff Publishing Corp., 1957; repr. New York: Dover, 1965), 70–76; Winton Dean, "Opera. Doctor Faust," *MT* CXXVII (1986), 344 [on British stage premiere]; D/*FB*, 290–313; P. Walter Jacob, "Faust in der Oper," *Das Musikleben* VI (1953), 256–60; Robert Jacobson, "Reports: U.S. Festivals," *ON* XLII (October 1977), 62 [on revival]; "McN," "London Concerts," *MT* LXXVIII (April 1937), 361–62 [on British premiere]; Frank Merkling, "Reports," *ON* XXIX (January 2, 1965), 31; Roy Pascal, "Four Fausts: From W. S. Gilbert to Ferruccio Busoni," *German Life and Letters* X (1956–1957), 263–74.

DISCOGRAPHY: Hillebrecht, Cochran, de Ridder, Schmidt, Fischer-Dieskau, Kohn, Sotin, and Rintzler, Chorus and Orchestra of Bavarian Radio, conducted by Leitner, DG 2709.032 and SLPM–139291–93 (3); DG 427–413 (compact discs/tapes).

Dollarprinzessin, Die (The Dollar Princess), operetta in three acts by Leo Fall; libretto (Ger) by Alfred Maria Willner and Fritz Grünbaum after a comedy by Emmerich Gatti and Thilo Friedrich Wilhelm von Trotha. First performance November 2, 1907, Vienna, with Mizzi Günther, Louis Treumann, and Louise Kartousch. First U.S. performance September 6, 1909, New York, Knickerbocker Theater (in an English translation by George Grossmith, Jr., with additional music by Jerome Kern), with Valli Valli (Alice) and Donald Brian (Freddy). First British performance September 25, 1909, London, Daly's, with Lily Elsie (Alice), Joseph Coyne (Couder), W. H. Berry, Robert Michaelis, Gabrielle Ray, and Gladys Cooper.

The operetta, set in New York and Canada, involves the wealthy widower John Couder, who is looking for a wife. He sends his brother Tom to Europe to find a woman who is of high birth, and the brother returns with Olga, a cabaret singer masquerading as a Russian countess. Although she is recognized by Baron von Schlick, the stable master, and by the struggling Fred[d]y Wehrburg, enamored of Alice, Couder's daughter, the "Dollar Princess," they keep Olga's secret to themselves. Freddy, put off by Alice's bold announcement of their engagement and her haughtiness brought on by her father's money, flees to Canada, where he becomes wealthy in his own right. When he invites Couder to Canada, along with his Couder's new wife and Alice, Freddy is reconciled with his former love, but Couder realizes that Olga has married him because of his riches alone; he divorces her.

Major roles: John Couder (comedian); Alice, his daughter (sop); Dick, his nephew; Fred[d]y Wahrburg (ten); Baron Hans, Freiherr von Schlick (buffo bass); Olga Lambinski (comedienne); and Tom Couder.

SCORE: vs (Berlin: Harmonie, 1907).

Don Ranudo, comic opera in four acts by Othmar Schoeck; libretto (Ger), by Armin Rüeger after Ludvig Holberg's comedy. First performance April 16, 1919, Zurich, Stadttheater; conducted by Robert F. Denzler.

The story takes place in a small Spanish town around 1750. Don Ranudo de Colibrados, a Spanish grandee from an ancient family, and his wife, Olympia, are poverty stricken, a situation that can be changed only if their daughter Maria marries the rich Don Gonzalo di las Minas. The parents find this a horrible prospect, since they want their child to marry a nobleman. Their scheming servant Pedro devises a plan to dress Don Gonzalo as a Moorish prince, a ruse which fools the noble pair. They are furious when they discover the truth.

Major roles: Don Ranudo di Colibrados, an old nobleman (bass); Dona Olympia, his wife (alto); Maria, their daughter (sop); Gonzalo de las Minas, a young would-be prince (ten); Pedro, a servant of Don Ranudo (bar).

SCORES: fs (Leipzig: B&H, 1919); vs ed. Otto Singer (Leipzig: B&H, 1919).

LIBRETTO: German (Leipzig: B&H, 1919).

BIBLIOGRAPHY: Hans Bärlocher, "Don Ranudo im Marionettentheater zu Bischofszell, eine Reminiszenz," *SMz* LXXXV/5 (1945), 92–93; Hans Corrodi, *Othmar Schoeck*, 2d ed. (Frauenfeld: Hans Huber, 1936), 109–28; Werner Vogel, *Thematisches Verzeichnis der Werke von Othmar Schoeck* (Zurich: Atlantis Verlag, 1956), 79–83.

Donauweibchen, Das (The Danube Maid), "ein romantisches komisches Volksmärchen mit Gesang nach einer Sage der Vorzeit" in two parts (three acts each) by Ferdinand Kauer; libretto (Ger) by Karl Friedrich Hensler. First performance of part I January 11, 1798, Vienna, Theater in der Leopoldstadt. First performance of part II February 13, 1798, Vienna, Theater in der Leopoldstadt. First U.S. performance December 17, 1859, New York.

In this early version of the *Undine** story (which has parallels to the plot of *Lohengrin,** e.g., the themes of jealousy and secret identities), the knight Albrecht von Waldsee is engaged to Bertha von Burgau. Before his marriage he finds himself in the same Danube neighborhood where he was involved four years earlier with a young maiden, who is in reality a transformed Danube water sprite, Hulda; she bore him an illegitimate daughter, Lilli, of whom he knows nothing. He learns that when he was injured, he was saved only by the intervention of Hulda, who asked in return that he visit her one month of the year. Hulda appears in disguise to Bertha and requests that she raise Lilli as a foundling. Albrecht returns to Hulda briefly, who shows him their daughter, and demands of him three days of love every May.

In Burgau the jealous Hedwig and the knight Bodo attempt to prevent the wedding of Bertha and Albrecht. Bodo fights Albrecht, who is victorious but spares Bodo when the spirit of his grandfather intervenes. Albrecht returns to Burgau, and the plans for the wedding proceed. During the festivities Hulda appears in disguise and puts a spell on the wedding guests; she takes Albrecht with her. The first part of the opera ends here.

In the second part, Hulda's spell is over and the wedding festivities continue. Hulda, now dressed as a beggar, gives the bridal pair a gift of two doves, with the advice that as long as the doves thrive, so will Bertha and Albrecht be happy. The malicious Hedwig and Bodo, failing in their attempt to have the doves killed, force Kaspar, a confidant of Albrecht, to reveal Lilli's identity. Kaspar and the singer Minnewart then free the birds. Albrecht, desperate to rid himself of Hulda's control, reveals that he is Lilli's father. Hulda takes her revenge by striking Bertha with a lightning bolt and reclaims Lilli. As Bertha is laid out in her coffin, Hulda relents when she see Albrecht's grief, and restores Bertha to life; she brings the couple back to her enchanted world.

Major roles: Hulda (sop); Lilli, her daughter (sop); Kasper (bar); Minnewart, a singer (bar); speaking roles: Albrecht von Waldsee; Bertha, his wife; Bodo von Triesnitz; and Hedwig von Lindenhorst.

Julius Hopp's operetta appeared in Vienna in 1866.

SCORE: vs (Leipzig: P. Reclam, n. d.).

BIBLIOGRAPHY: Jürgen Schläder, " 'Das Donauweibchen' von Ferdinand Kauer," in *Undine auf dem Musiktheater* (Bonn-Bad Godesberg, 1979), 99–227.

Donna Diana, comic opera in three acts by Emil Nikolaus von Reznicek; libretto by the composer after C. A. West's translation of Moreto's comedy. First performance December 16, 1894, Prague, Deutsches Theater. Revised by Julius Kapp, November 15, 1933, Berlin.

The story is set in Barcelona, in 1890. The toreador Don Cesar is in love with the beautiful Donna Diana, daughter of the mayor, but she does not seem to share his feelings. His manager, Perin, advises him that the only way he can get her interested is by ignoring her. This he does several times, although he almost falls into a trap when she asks him to accompany her to a dance. At a ball in the house of the mayor, Don Diego, Donna Diana is being pursued by many admirers. She wants to upset Don Cesar by telling him that she has saved the last dance for Don Luis. The two finally discard their pride, declare their true love for each other, and ask her father for permission to marry.

Major roles: Don Diego, mayor of Barcelona (bass); Donna Diana, his daughter (sop); Donna Laura and Donna Fenisa, his nieces (sop, alto); Don Cesar, toreador (ten); Perin, his manager (bar); and Don Luis, sugar refiner (ten).

Also set by Heinrich Hofmann (1886, Berlin).

SCORES: vs (Leipzig: J. Schuberth, 1895); vs ed. Julius Kapp (Vienna: UE, 1933).

Donnerstag (Thursday), "opera" in three acts by Karlheinz Stockhausen; libretto (Ger) by the composer. First performance of entire work April 3, 1981, Milan, La Scala, with Markus Stockhausen, trumpet; Robert Gambill and Paul Sperry, tenors; Michele Noiret, dancer (Michael); Annette Meriweather, soprano; Suzanne Stephen, basset horn; Elisabeth Clarke, dancer (Eve); Matthias Hölle, bass; Mark Tezak, trombone; Alain Louafi, dancer/mime (Lucifer); and Majella Stockhausen, piano solo; conducted by Peter Eötvös. Part of the composer's projected cycle *Licht*,* with an "opera" for every day of the week. First British performance September 16, 1985, London, Covent Garden.

The story revolves around three main spirits presented as a singer, an instrument, and a dancer: Michael, the archangel (trumpet, tenor, dancer); Eve, the mother (soprano, basset horn, dancer); and Lucifer, the father (bass, trombone, dancer/mime). The work consists of three "acts":

1. Michaels Jugend (Michael's Youth) 1980.
2. Michaels Reise um die Erde (Michael's Journey around the Earth). First performance 1978, Paris. A "concerto" for trumpet and chamber orchestra; no vocal parts.
3. Michaels Heimkehr (Michael's Homecoming) in three scenes. First performance June 14, 1980, Amsterdam, Concertgebouw. Includes the three soloists, chorus, and orchestra. In it, Saint Michael comes back to the heavenly palace.

BIBLIOGRAPHY: Aliki Andris-Michalaros, "Reports: Foreign," *ON* XLVI (September 1981), 44–45 [on premiere]; Peter Britton, "Stockhausen's Path to Opera," *MT* CXXVI (1985), 515–21; Menno Feenstra, "Reports: Foreign," *ON* XLV (September 1980), 63 [on premiere of third "act"]; Dominic Gill, "Stockhausen's 'Thursday,' " *Opera* XXXII (1981), 585–88 [on premiere]; Roger Smalley, "Music in London," *MT* CXXVI (1985), 679.

DISCOGRAPHY: Meriweather, Gambill, Sperry, and Hölle, West German Radio Chorus (Cologne), Hilversum Radio Chorus and Orchestra/Ensemble Intercontemporain (Paris), conducted by Stockhausen, DG 2740–272 (4); reviewed by John W. Freeman, "Records," *ON* XLVIII (March 3, 1984), 45.

Dorfbarbier, Der (The Village Barber), comic opera in one act by Johann Schenk; libretto by Joseph and Paul Weidmann. First performance October 30, 1796, Vienna, Burgtheater. First U.S. performance December 15, 1847, New York.

Lux, the barber, has his eye on his ward, Suschen, who is secretly in love with Joseph. The schoolmaster Rund is determined to help the young pair and he forms a plan. Joseph is to tell Lux that he has been poisoned and has willed his entire fortune to Suschen. Rund then convinces Lux to allow Suschen to marry Joseph quickly, so that no other relatives may claim his money. Lux falls for the scheme and is of course the loser in the end.

Major roles: Lux, barber (bass); Suschen, his ward (sop); Rund, a schoolmaster (bass); Joseph, son of a tenant farmer (ten); Adam, Lux's partner (ten); Margarethe, widow of a smith (sop); and Peter, a tailor (bass).

A version by Johann Adam Hiller appeared in 1771, in Leipzig.

SCORES: fs ed. Robert Haas, DTÖ, LXVI (Vienna: UE, 1927); vs ed. Richard Kleinmichel (Vienna: UE, ca. 1914).

Dorfjahrmarkt, Der. See *Der Jahrmarkt.*

Drei Pintos, Die (The Three Pintos), comic opera in three acts by Carl Maria von Weber; libretto (Ger) by Theodor Hell after the story *Der Brautkampf* by Carl Seidel. Unfinished, 1821, completed by Gustav Mahler, 1888, with a new text by Weber's grandson, Carl von Weber. First performance January 20, 1888, Leipzig, Neues Stadt-Theater, with Baumann (Clarissa), Artner (Laura), Rothhauser (Inez), Emanuel Hedmont (Gaston), Hübner (Gomez), Grengg (Pinto), Schelper (Ambrosio), Köhler (Pantaleone), and Proft (landlord); conducted by Gustav Mahler. Revived May 22, 1978, Vienna, Volksoper, with Carl von Weber's libretto, with Adolf Dallapozza and Christian Boesch; conducted by Friedemann Layer. First U.S. performance June 6, 1979, St. Louis, with Joseph McKee (Pinto), Alan Kays (Gaston), Neil Rosenshein (Gomez), Sheryl Woods (Clarissa), Faith Esham (Laura), and Jane Kamp (Inez); conducted by Bruce Ferden. First British performance April 10, 1962, London, John Lewis Theatre, with Denis Brandt (Gaston), Michael Maurel (Ambrosio), and Pauline Tinsley (Clarissa); conducted by David Lloyd-Jones.

In the story, Don Pinto, who is on his way to Seville to wed Clarissa, is interrupted by his rivals Don Gaston and Ambrosio, who attempt to teach him how to court his intended. When this fails, Gaston passes himself off as Pinto, only to find that Clarissa really loves Gomez; he therefore gives Gomez the Pinto papers. When the real Don Pinto arrives and reveals what has happened, Don Pantaleone, father of the bride-to-be, is furious, but all turns out well in the end.

The plot is given in detail by John Warrack, ''School and Amateur Performances,'' *Opera* XIII (1962), 423–25; see also W/*CMW*, 256–72 for an analysis.

Major roles: Don Pinto (bass); Clarissa (sop); Don Gaston (ten); Ambrosio (bar); Gomez (ten); and Don Pantaleone, Clarissa's father (bar).

After Weber's death, his heirs asked Giacomo Meyerbeer to complete Weber's work, consisting of seven pieces, but he was unable to do so and returned the materials in 1852 Mahler took on the task. He completed the scoring and composed an interlude of themes from the opera. He also added other music by Weber, with the resulting amalgam of early German Romanticism and Mahleresque touches; see, for example, the interlude of Act II.

LIBRETTO: German-Italian, ed. Luigi Rognoni (Turin: Unione Tipografico-Editrice Torinese, 1975).

BIBLIOGRAPHY: Heinz Becker, "Meyerbeers Ergänzungsarbeit an Webers nachgelassener Oper *Die drei Pintos*," *Mf* VII (1954), 300–12; Herta Blaukopf, "Eine Oper 'Aus Weber,' " *ÖMz* XXXIII (1978), 204–8; Kurt Blaukopf, "Der Symphoniker in der Oper. Zu neuen Ergebnissen in der Mahler-Forschung," *HiFi-Stereophonie* XV (1976), 1076–78; Birgit Heusgen, *Studien zu Gustav Mahlers Bearbeitung und Ergänzung von Carl Maria von Webers Opernfragment "Die drei Pintos"* (Regensburg: Gustav Bosse, 1983); Robert Jacobson, "Reports: U.S.," *ON* XLIV (September 1979), 51–52; Andrew Porter, "Musical Events," *NY* LV (July 2, 1979), 70–72 [on U.S. premiere]; John Warrack, "Mahler and Weber," *MT* CVII (1967), 120–23; Karl Laux, "In Erinnerung gebracht. 'Die drei Pintos,' " *Musikbühne 76: Probleme und Informationen* (1976), 89–111.

DISCOGRAPHY: Popp, Hollweg, Orey, Moll, Kruse, and Lövas, Netherlands Vocal Ensemble, RCA PRL 3-9-63 (6).

Dreigroschenoper, Die (The Threepenny Opera), opera in a prologue and three acts by Kurt Weill; libretto by Bertholt Brecht after Elisabeth Hauptmann's translation of John Gay's *The Beggar's Opera* of 1728, with additional lyrics from Kipling and Villon. First performance August 31, 1928, Berlin, Theater am Schiffbauerdamm, with Lotte Lenya (Jenny), Harald Paulsen (Macheath), Roma Bahn (Polly), Kurt Gerron (the Streetsinger), Rosa Valetti, Erich Ponto, and Kate Kühl; conducted by Theo Mackeben. First U.S. performance April 13, 1933, New York, Empire Theatre (in an English translation by Gifford Cochran and Jerrold Krimsky), with Steffi Duna (Polly), Rex Evans (Sheriff Brown), Evelyn Beresford (Mrs. Peachum), Marjorie Dille (Jenny), and Josephine Huston (Lucy); conducted by Macklin Marrow. First British performance (in English, in the Marc Blitzstein version) February 9, 1956, London, Royal Court Theatre, with Daphne Anderson (Polly), Bill Owen (Mackie), Georgia Brown (Lucy), Eric Pohlmann (Peachum), and Maria Remusat (Jenny); conducted by Berthold Goldschmidt.

In the updating of the plot, Brecht attempted to highlight the political and social corruption of the Germany of the 1920s. Polly, daughter of Peachum, head of the Beggar's Guild, weds her robber lover Macheath, here called Mackie Messer (Mack the Knife). Polly's parents are furious that she has married a thief and they threaten to inform on him. When Polly tells Macheath of the danger, he hides in a brothel, where his past and present unfold in the "Zuhälter" ballad. Macheath is arrested, betrayed by his old friend Jenny, head of the brothel, who has been bribed by Mrs. Peachum. Polly visits Macheath in jail and meets a former lover Lucy, daughter of Brown, the police chief who has assisted the thief. After the ladies quarrel, Mrs. Peachum removes Polly, and Lucy helps Macheath escape. But, betrayed again by Jenny, Macheath's freedom is short-lived; he is recaptured and sentenced to be hanged. Just before he is to be executed, he is saved by a pardon from the Queen herself, who grants him a castle and pension. The crowd offers thanks in the closing chorale, "Verfolgt das Unrecht nicht zu sehr."

For a detailed synopsis and musical analysis, see *S/DGS*, 112–28.

Major roles: Jenny (chanteuse), Polly (sop), Macheath (ten), Mr. Peachum (bass), Mrs. Peachum (mezzo), Lucy (sop), streetsinger (ten), and Brown (bass).

The work was a phenomenal success in Germany until it was banned by the Nazis because Weill was Jewish and the opera itself was considered degenerate. Initially a failure at its 1933 U.S. premiere, it enjoyed a rebirth in a modernized version (text only) by Marc Blitzstein, which opened off Broadway on March 10, 1954. After a short break it reopened on September 20, 1955, and ran for 2,500 performances. The work includes the famous "Moritat," which gained fame through the United States as "Mack the Knife" and launched the career of the pop singer Bobby Darin, who revived it in 1959. The song was also a favorite vehicle for Louis Armstrong. The score of the Weill work mixes classical writing together with blues and Tin Pan Alley styles.

SCORES: vs ed. Norbert Gingold (Vienna: UE, 1928); miniature score (Vienna: UE, 1972).

LIBRETTO: German (Vienna: UE, 1928).

BIBLIOGRAPHY: John Fuegi, "Most Unpleasant Things with the Threepenny Opera: Weill, Brecht, and Money," in K/NO, 157–82; Donald Mitchell, "Kurt Weill's 'Dreigroschenoper' and German Cabaret Opera in the 1920's," The Chesterian (July 1950), 1–6; Félice Pastorello, L'Opéra de quat' sous de Bertolt Brecht, mises en scène d'Erich Engel et Gaston Baty. Les voces de la création théatrales VII (Paris, 1979).

DISCOGRAPHY: Lenya and Arthur, conducted by Rae, Polydor 820260–1E, 820260–2 (compact disc), 820260–4E (tape) (Eng). Lenya, Neuss, Trenk-Trebitsch, Hesterberg, and Schellow, conducted by Brückner-Ruggeberg, CBS 78279 (2); reviewed by William W. Kearns, in OQ I/2 (Summer 1983), 175–76, a reissue of the 1950s recording, also available on tape: M2T–37864. Liane, Felbermayer, Roswaenge, and Jerger, Vienna State Opera Orchestra and Chorus, conducted by Adler, Vanguard CSRV–273E. Excerpts: Lenya, Gerron, and Mackeben (Ger), Teldec 641991 AJ (m).

E

Einstein, opera in a prologue, three acts, an epilogue, and two intermezzos by Paul Dessau; libretto (Ger) by Karl Mickel. First performance February 16, 1974, East Berlin, Staatsoper, with Theo Adam (Einstein), Peter Schreier and Rainer Süss (two physicists), and Horst Hiestermann (Hanswurst); conducted by Otmar Suitner.

The story traces the scientist's life from the rise of the Nazis to power in the 1930s in Germany to the first antiwar demonstrations in the United States in the 1960s. The action is explained by Hanswurst in the prologue.

Major roles: Einstein (bar), two physicists (ten, bass), and Hanswurst (ten).

SCORES: fs (Berlin: B&B, 1973); vs ed. Horst Karl Hessel (Berlin: B&B, 1973).

BIBLIOGRAPHY: *Opernschaffen der DDR in Gespräch. Entwicklungstendenzen 1949–1974 im Überblick. Aus Kolloquien zu 'Levins Mühle' und 'Einstein'* (Berlin, 1974); Gerd Rienäcker, "*Einstein*—analytische Bemerkungen zur Oper von Paul Dessau," *MGes* XXIV/12 (December 1974), 711–16; James Helme Sutcliffe, "Reports, Foreign. East Berlin," *ON* XXXVIII (May 1974), 35–36 [on premiere].

Electra. See *Elektra*.

Elegie für junge Liebende (Elegy for Young Lovers), opera in three acts by Hans Werner Henze; libretto (Ger) by Ludwig Landgraf, Werner Schachtel, and the composer after the English text by W. H. Auden and Chester Kallman. First performance (in German) May 20, 1961, Schwetzingen Festival, with Eva-Maria Rogner (Hilda), Dietrich Fischer-Dieskau (Mittenhofer), Karl Christian Kohn (doctor), Friedrich Lenz (Toni), Lillian Bennigsen (Carolina), and Ingeborg Bremert (Elisabeth). First performance with English text July 13, 1961, Glyndebourne, with Elisabeth Söderström, Dorothy Dorrow, Kerstin Meyer, André Turp, Carlos Alexander, and Thomas Helmsley; conducted by John Pritchard. First U.S. performance April 29, 1965, Juilliard, with Lorna Haywood and Janet

Wagner (Mittenhofer's mistress and secretary), Rita Shane (Hilda), Jack Davison (Mittenhofer), and Robert Jones (Toni); conducted by Christopher West.

The story concerns the great poet Gregor Mittenhofer, who looks for inspiration in the tragedies of others. He goes to the Schwarzer Adler Inn in the Alps every year to be moved by the despair of Hilda Mack, still waiting for the return of her husband, who vanished on their honeymoon forty years ago. When the husband is found frozen in a glacier, the poet turns to the young lovers Toni, his stepson, and Elisabeth. They meet their deaths at the Hammerhorn mountain, having been sent there by the poet. He then writes his "Elegy for Young Lovers," which he reads to the audience as the opera ends.

For a detailed synopsis, see K/*KOB*, 921–26.

Major roles: Gregor Mittenhofer, poet (bar); Hilda Mack (sop); Toni, Mittenhofer's stepson (ten); and Elisabeth (sop).

SCORES: English-German vs (Mainz: BSS, c. 1961).

BIBLIOGRAPHY: Martin Bernheimer, "Current Chronicle. Munich," *MQ* XLVIII (1962), 118–20; ———, "World Reports. America . . . Opera Workshop . . . New York," *Opera* XVI (1965), 572–73; Hans Werner Henze, "On Writing 'Elegy for Young Lovers,' " *Opera* XII (1961), 433–434; Frank Martin, "New York Novelties," *ON* XXX (September 25, 1965), 22 [on U.S. premiere]; Andrew Porter, "Elegy for Young Lovers," *MT* CII (1961), 418–19 [on Glyndebourne premiere].

Elektra, opera in one act by Richard Strauss; libretto (Ger) by Hugo von Hofmannsthal after Sophocles' drama. First performance January 25, 1909, Dresden, Königliches Opernhaus, with Ernestine Schumann-Heink (Klytämnestra), Annie Krull (Elektra), Margarethe Siems (Chrysothemis), Johannes Sembach (Aegisthus), and Carl Perron (Orestes); conducted by Ernst von Schuch. First U.S. performance (in French) February 1, 1910, New York, Manhattan Opera, with Jeanne Gerville-Réaches (Klytämnestra), Mariette Magarin (Elektra), and Gustave Huberdeau (Orestes). First British performance February 19, 1910, London, Covent Garden, with Edyth Walker (Elektra), Anna Mildenburg (Klytämnestra), Frances Rose (Chrysothemis), and Friedrich Weidemann (Orestes); conducted by (Sir) Thomas Beecham.

The scene opens on Elektra, who, unkempt and wild-eyed, is mourning the death of her father, Agamemnon, at the hands of her mother, Klytämnestra, and the mother's lover, Aegisthus. Her one thought is to avenge her sire, and she taunts and berates her mother, who cannot understand her hatred. Elektra's only ally is her gentle younger sister, Chrysothemis, who does not wish to be part of any revenge. The Queen, terrified by Elektra's threats, is overjoyed at the news that Orestes, her son, is dead. Hearing this, Elektra is determined to become her father's avenger. When a hooded messenger appears, she does not recognize him at first but then realizes that he is her long-absent brother. He goes into the palace, slays his mother, and, when Aegisthus arrives, kills him also. These events lead Elektra to a frenzied joy and maniacal dancing, and she collapses, dead. Chrysothemis falls in despair on her sister's lifeless body.

For detailed synopses and musical analyses, see C/*NMC*, 195–202; *COH*, ed. Derrick Puffett (1989); D/*RS*, I, 287–333; K/*KOB*, 810–15; and M/*RSC*, 63–95.

Major roles: Klytämnestra, widow of Agamemnon (mezzo); Elektra and Chrysothemis, her daughters (sop, sop); Aegisthus, Klytämnestra's lover (ten); and Orestes, son of Klytämnestra and Agamemnon (bar).

This opera was the first in a series written by Strauss with Hugo von Hofmannsthal. The terrors of the libretto are echoed in the strident harmonies and extended polytonality, and the contrasts between harsh dissonance and lush late-Romantic writing. The harshness of the music led one of the singers, Schumann-Heink, to call the opera "ein furchtbares Gebrüll" (a fearful screeching) and the local press to have a field day, one cartoonist penning what he called the "Elektra" chair. The premiere was just short of a disaster, but the opera was much more enthusiastically received at subsequent performances, and it is a standard at most major opera houses today. Strauss himself was not satisfied with the direction toward modernity that he took, first with *Salome** and then with *Elektra*; and his next work, *Der Rosenkavalier*,* represented a striking break and a return to a more conservative, lush style of writing, one which Strauss kept to for the rest of his creative life.

Other settings of the Electra story include Christian Cannabich's monodrama (1781, Mannheim); J. C. F. Häffner's *Electra* (1787, Stockholm); and Vittorio Gnecchi's *Cassandra* (1905, Bologna). The similarities of Gnecchi's work to the later Strauss opera were pointed out by the Italian critic Tebaldini (see below), who accused Strauss of plagiarism (Gnecchi did send Strauss a copy of the score of *Cassandra*), but Gnecchi never joined in the dispute.

SCORES: fs (London, New York: BO, 1943); vs ed. Otto Singser (Berlin: A. Fürstenau, 1908).

LIBRETTO: German (Berlin: A. Fürstenau, 1908).

BIBLIOGRAPHY: Mosco Carner, "Witches' Cauldron," *ON* XXXV (February 27, 1971), 24–26; Michael Horwath, "Tebaldini, Gnecchi, and Strauss," *CM X* (1970), 74–91; George Marek, "Cry of Anguish," *ON* XLIX (December 8, 1984), 16–18; Günther von Noé, "Das Leitmotiv bei Richard Strauss, dargestellt am Beispiel der *Elektra*," *NZM* CXXXII (August 1971), 418–22; John Potter and Suzanne Potter, "Prophetic Avenger," *ON* XLIV (February 9, 1980), 17–18, 36; Regina Resnik, "On Singing Clytemnestra," *Opera* XVI (1965), 161–63; Giovanni Tebaldini, "Telepatia Musicale," *RMI* XVI (March 1909), 400–412.

DISCOGRAPHY: See Alan Jefferson, B/*OOR*, 562–65, 566.

Elisabeth Tudor, opera in three acts by Wolfgang Fortner; libretto (Ger) by Matthias Braun, revised by the composer. First performance October 23, 1972, Berlin.

A treatment of the struggle of Elizabeth I and Mary, Queen of Scots, for the throne of England.

Major roles: Maria Stuart (sop); Elisabeth Tudor, Queen of England (mezzo); Duke of Norfolk (bar); Duke of Leicester (bar); Nicolas Bacon (counter-ten); Cecil (bass); Arundel (ten); Walsingham (bass); and Gresham (ten).

Other operas on this subject include Gaetano Donizetti's *Maria Stuarda* (1834, Naples) and Thea Musgrave's *Mary, Queen of Scots* (1977, Edinburgh).

Emma und Eginhard. See *Die Last-tragende Liebe*.

Ende einer Welt, Das (The End of a World), opera in one act by Hans Werner Henze; libretto (Ger) by Wolfgang Hildesheimer. First performance December 4, 1953, NWOR, Hamburg; November 30, 1965, Frankfurt (staged). First British performance (staged) March 8, 1966, London, St. Pancras Town Hall, with Monica Sinclair, John Kentish, Angela Moran; conducted by Frederick Marshall.

A group of snobbish culture seekers are gathered at the house of the Marchesa Montetristo, on the island of San Amerigo, near Venice. The guests continue their bizarre activities, despite the fact that their island is sinking.

Originally written as a radio opera, the work was converted into a piece for the stage, a transition which critics felt was unsuccessful (see below).

Major roles: Herr Fallersleben (ten); Marchesa Montetristo (alto); Dombrowska (ten); Signora Sgambati, astrologer (col sop); Gloch, cultural dignitary (bass); Professor Kuntz-Sartori, politician (bar).

SCORE: German-English fs ed. Heinz Moehn (Mainz: BSS, 1965).

LIBRETTO: German (Frankfurt, 1953).

BIBLIOGRAPHY: Harold Rosenthal, "London Opera Diary," *Opera* XVII (1966), 404–5 [on British stage premiere]; Hildegard Weber, "World Reports," *Opera* XVII (1966), 370–71 [on stage premiere].

Engel von Prag, Der (The Angel from Prague), opera in three acts by Cesar Bresgen; libretto (Ger) by the composer after themes from Leo Perutz's novel *Nachts unter der steinernen Brücke*. First performance 1979, Salzburg, Landestheater, with Klaus Wallprecht (Rudolf II), Hans Günther Nöcker (Arcimboldo), Kathleen Kaun (Esther), and Eberhard Storz (Rabbi Löw); conducted by Josef Wallnig. Revised 1985.

The story takes place in Prague in 1587. Emperor Rudolf II falls in love with the angelic Esther, a married Jewish woman. When she returns his love, the plague breaks out in the city. The plague stops only when Esther admits her adultery and dies. The town is thus saved.

Major roles: Emperor Rudolf II (bar); Esther, wife of Mordechai Meisl (sop); Arcimboldo, the Emperor's painter (bass); Count Nostiz (ten); Count Palffy (ten); Zdenko von Lobkowitz, councillor (bass); Count Malaspina (bass); Rabbi Löw (bass); Mordechai Meisl (ten); and Angel Maggid (mezzo).

BIBLIOGRAPHY: Pierre Cossé, "Bresgen-Oper in Salzburg uraufgeführt," *ÖMz* XXXIV (1979), 100–102.

Englische Katze, Die (The English Cat), "a story for singers and instrumentalists" by Hans Werner Henze; libretto (Eng) by Edward Bond after Honoré de Balzac's *Peines de coeur d'une chatte anglaise* (1840). First performance June 2, 1983, Schwetzingen, Schlosstheater, in a German translation by Ken Bartlett, with Roland Bracht (Arnold), Elisabeth Glauser (Babette), Inga Nielsen (Minette), Regina Marheinek (Louise), Martin Finke (Lord Puff), and Wolfgang Schöne (Tom); conducted by Dennis Russell Davies. First U.S. performance (in English) July 28, 1983, Santa Fe, with Inga Nielsen (Minette), Scott Reeve (Tom), Michael Myers (Lord Puff), Kurt Link (Arnold), Kathryn Gamberoni (Louise).

The satirical story centers around a community of cats and other animals who dress and act like human beings. It opens on the impending marriage of the aged Lord Puff, president of the Royal Society for the Preservation of Rats, to Minette. This union is opposed by the devious Arnold, Puff's nephew, and Tom, who is in love with Minette himself. The marriage finally takes place.

Tom returns after a stint in the marines and tries to get Minette to run off with him, but they are apprehended by the Royal Society, and Tom is put on trial. He is freed after the disclosure that he is the long-lost son of Lord Fairport and is therefore the richest cat in England. He then turns his attentions to Babette, Minette's sister, and is about to sign a will giving Babette his entire fortune, when he is stabbed by Lucian, who then tells the Royal Society that Tom killed himself. Tom's money thereby reverts to the Society, and the opera ends with Louise, a mouse who had become an honorary cat, declaring that she has lost her trust in the cat species.

Major roles: Lord Puff (ten); Arnold, his nephew (bass); Tom (bar); Minette (sop); Babette, her sister (mezzo); Louise, a mouse (sop); and Lucian, a fox (ten).

The score, despite its occasional dissonance, is written in a neoclassical style and is very melodious.

BIBLIOGRAPHY: Horst Koegler, "Reports: Foreign," *ON* XLVIII, No. 2 (August 1983), 42 [on premiere]; John Rockwell, "Opera: In Santa Fe, Henze's 'English Cat,'" *NYT*, July 29, 1985.

Entführung aus dem Serail, Die (The Abduction from the Seraglio), comic Singspiel in three acts by Wolfgang Amadeus Mozart; libretto (Ger) by Gottlob Stephanie the Younger, an alteration of C. F. Bretzner's text for Johann André's *Belmont und Constanze.** The Bretzner and Stephanie texts were so similar, in fact, that Bretzner attacked Mozart in print for "stealing" his libretto. First performance of the Mozart version July 16, 1782, Vienna, Burgtheater, with Katharina Cavalieri (Constanze), Therese Teyber (Blonde), Valentin Adamberger (Belmonte), J. E. Dauer (Pedrillo), Ludwig Fischer (Osmin), and D. Jautz (Pasha Selim); conducted by the composer. First U.S. performance February 16, 1860, New York, Brooklyn Operatic Circle (in Italian, as *Belmonte e Con-*

stanze); October 10, 1862 (in German), New York, German Opera House. First British performance November 24, 1827, London, Covent Garden, in a version by Christoph Kramer (with extra characters), with Mme. Vestris, Miss Hughes, Mr. Sapio, Mr. Benson, and Mr. Wrenn.

This work represents the apex of the so-called "Turkish" opera, a genre in great vogue from the seventeenth to the middle of the nineteenth century. It is a variation of a theme popular in eighteenth- and nineteenth-century European literature, that of young European men freeing their sweethearts from the clutches of pirates, Turkish sultans and pashas, and so forth. In the Mozart setting, the story unfolds at the country house of a Turkish pasha in North Africa in the sixteenth century. Constanze, a European, has been kidnapped and put into the harem of Pasha Selim, who has not yet claimed his rights to her. Also taken captive are her maid, Blonde, who has caught the eye of the villainous and lecherous Osmin, and Pedrillo, servant of Constanze's fiancé, Belmonte. Belmonte comes to the Pasha's villa and passes himself off as an architect. He plans to free Constanze, Pedrillo, and Blonde by getting Osmin hopelessly drunk. The plan misfires when Osmin comes to his senses before the Europeans can make their escape. Despite the fact that Belmonte had tried to take away Constanze and is the son of the Pasha's mortal enemy, the Turk generously frees the Europeans, and the opera ends happily for all except the mean-spirited Osmin.

For detailed synopses and musical analyses, see C/*NMC*, 212–18; D/*MO*, 67–87; H/*FMO*, 19–45; K/*KOB*, 79–83; and M/*OM*, 289–320.

Major roles: Constanze, a noblewoman (sop); Blonde, her maid (sop); Belmonte, a young Spanish nobleman (ten); Pedrillo, his servant (ten); Osmin, overseer of the Pasha's harem (bass); Pasha Selim (speaking role).

Mozart introduces exoticism into the opera by using the "Turkish" battery of the bass drum, cymbals, and triangle in various numbers such as the overture and the Janissary chorus "Singt dem grossen Bassa Lieder" (Act I, No. 5). He also achieves an "Oriental" effect by employing unusual intervals and modulations, as in Pedrillo's romance "Im Mohrenland gefangen war" (Act III, No. 18) and "Singt dem grossen Bassa," cited above. Among the florid Italianate numbers of the opera is Constanze's concerto-like aria "Martern aller Arten" (Act II, No. 11). This is in sharp contrast to the comic numbers such as the raucous drinking duet of Osmin and Pedrillo, "Vivat Bacchus, Bacchus lebe" (Act II, No. 14), in which the European tries to get the seraglio keeper drunk.

Die Entführung, Mozart's second large-scale stage work, represents an important point in the history of the Viennese Singspiel because of its high level of excellence. It skillfully blends elements from comic and serious opera, with the main characters singing large virtuoso arias in the Italian style, while the secondary parts have simpler, Lied-like numbers. Choruses and ensembles are also significant, and the work ends with an extended vaudeville, involving all the characters, and with the mood changing typically from sadness to joy. Earlier "Turkish" models for Mozart's work include Gluck's *La Rencontre imprévue* (1764, Vienna); Franz Joseph Haydn's setting of the same story, *L'incontro improvviso* (1775, Esterháza); Christian Gottlob Neefe's *Adelheit von Veltheim** (1780, Frankfurt); Mozart's own unfinished *Zaïde** (1780); and André's *Belmont und Constanze**. Later "Turkish" operas include Carl Maria von Weber's *Abu Hassan** (1811, Munich) and Peter Cornelius' *Der Barbier von Bagdad** (1858, Weimar). Justin Knecht also composed a setting of the Stephanie text (see following entry).

SCORES: fs (Bonn: Simrock, 1821); ed. Gerhard Croll, M/*NMA*, series II/12 (1982); vs (Vienna, 1785).

LIBRETTO: German (Vienna: Logenmeister, 1782).

BIBLIOGRAPHY: Rudolph Angermüller, " 'Les époux ésclaves ou Bastien und Bastienne à Alger.' Zur Stoffgeschichte der 'Entführung aus dem Serail,' " *MJb 1978* (1979), 70–88; Thomas Bauman, *Die Entführung aus dem Serail*, COH (1988); G/" 'T'O," 272–94; Hans Keller, "The *Entführung's* Vaudeville," *MR* XVII (1956), 304–13; Walter Preibisch, "Quellenstudien zu Mozart's *Entführung aus dem Serail*. Ein Beitrag zu der Geschichte der Türkenoper," *SIMG* X (1908–1909), 430–76; Bence Szabolcsi, "Exoticisms in Music," *ML* XXXVII (1956), 323–32; Helmut Wirth, "Gluck, Haydn und Mozart—drei Entführungs-Opern," in *OAA*, 25–35.

DISCOGRAPHY: See M/*IRR*, II, 182–83.

Entführung aus dem Serail, Die (The Abduction from the Seraglio), Singspiel in three acts by Justin Knecht; libretto (Ger) after Gottlob Stephanie the Younger. First performance February 2, 1787, Biberach.

The story and characters are the same as the earlier Mozart setting (see previous entry).

Knecht makes some attempts at exoticism, especially in the Janissary chorus and Osmin numbers. His setting of the Osmin-Pedrillo duet is in a folksong-like style, as is Pedrillo's Romance, and his "Martern aller Arten" receives a spirited treatment; he provides it with a "martial" theme reminiscent of the Mozart version. Knecht's vaudeville finale recalls earlier themes of the opera.

BIBLIOGRAPHY: Walther Preibisch, *Quellenstudien zu Mozarts "Entführung aus dem Serail." Ein Betrag zur Geschichte der Türkenoper* (Halle: Erhardt Karras, 1908) [some musical examples].

Ersten Menschen, Die (The First Humans), opera in two acts by Rudi Stephan; libretto (Ger) by Otto Borngräber. First performance (posthumous) July 1, 1920, Frankfurt. The opera was revived on January 31, 1988, in Bielefeld, with Ingeborg Schneider (Chawa), John Pickering (Chabel), Herbert Adami (Kajin), and Monte Jaffe (Adahm); conducted by David de Villiers.

The story revolves around the first human beings, Chawa, Adahm, Chabel, and Kajin, who search for a meaning to their existence. The naive Chawa (Eve) looks for love and the happiness of giving birth, while her spouse, Adahm (Adam) turns to work. Chabel (Abel) is concerned with God, while his brother, Kajin

(Kain), pursues earthly pleasures. Both boys desire their mother, and Kajin kills his sibling out of jealousy.

Stephan completed his only opera in 1914. He was killed during World War I, when he was twenty-eight years old.

BIBLIOGRAPHY: Matthias Henneberger and Rein A. Zondergeld, "Reports," *Opera* XXXIX (1988), 476, 478 [on revival].

Erwartung (Expectation), monodrama in one act by Arnold Schoenberg; libretto (Ger) by Marie Pappenheim. Composed 1909. First performance June 6, 1924, Prague, with Marie Gutheil-Schoder; conducted by Alexander von Zemlinsky. First U.S. performance November 15, 1951, New York. First British performance (concert) January 9, 1931, BBC broadcast, with Margot Hinnenberg-Lefebre; conducted by the composer. First British performance (staged) April 4, 1960, London, Sadler's Wells, with Heather Harper; conducted by Leon Lovett.

Set in a forest, the Expressionist work, which uses *Sprechstimme*, concerns a woman who is searching for her lost lover. When she emerges from the forest, she stumbles over the dead body of her paramour. Schoenberg himself described the piece as "a nightmare" and insisted that a real forest, not an abstract one, be used as a setting to enhance the nightmarish effect.

For a detailed synopsis, see K/*KOB*, 860–61.

Major role: a woman (sop).

SCORES: fs (Vienna: UE, 1916); vs ed. Edward Steuermann (Vienna: UE, 1922).

LIBRETTO: German (Vienna: UE, 1911).

BIBLIOGRAPHY: Sieghart Döhring, "Schönbergs *Erwartung*," in *Arnold Schönberg* (Berlin: Akademie der Künste, 1974); Martin Just, "Schönbergs *Erwartung*, Op. 2, No. 1," in *Kongress-Bericht Berlin. 1974*, 425–27; Seigfried Mauser, "Forschungsbericht zu Schönbergs *Erwartung*," *ÖMz* XXXV (1980), 215–19; Josef Rufer, *The Works of Arnold Schoenberg* (New York: Free Press of Glencove, 1963), 35–36.

DISCOGRAPHY: Martin, BBC Symphony, conducted by Boulez, CBS 13M–37863 (3). Pilarczyk, NW German Philharmonic, conducted by Scherchen, Wergo 50001. Pilarczyk, Washington Opera, conducted by Craft, Columbia M2S–679 (2); reviewed by C. J. Luten, "Records," *ON* XXXIII (April 12, 1969), 34. Wyner, Orchestra of the 20th Century, conducted by Weisberg, CRI SD–503.

Erwin und Elmire (Erwin and Elmire), Singspiel in two acts by Johann Friedrich Reichardt; libretto (Ger) by Goethe (1775) after Oliver Goldsmith's *Edwin and Angelina*. First performance ca. March 1793, Berlin. Revived summer 1987, East Berlin, Staatsoper, with Lis Nilsson (Elmire), Ralph Eschrig (Erwin), Roman Trekel (Valerio), and Yvonne Füssel (Rosa); conducted by Ernst Stoy.

Erwin, dissatisfied by Elmire's flightiness, disappears. In despair Elmire, heeding Valerio, seeks the advice of a hermit who lives in the hills. Valerio's attentions to Elmire in turn arouse the jealousy of his own beloved, Rosa. Valerio gets to the hermit's hut first and, finding Erwin there, tells him to dress as the recluse. Erwin hears Elmire confess to her lack of commitment and her real love for Erwin, and both pairs of lovers are reunited.

Major roles: Elmire (sop), Erwin (ten), Valerio (bass), and Rosa (sop).

SCORE: vs (Berlin: Im Verlage der Neuen Berlinischen Musikhandlung, 1793).

BIBLIOGRAPHY: James Helme Sutcliffe, "In Review," *ON* LII (December 19, 1987), 39–40 [on revival].

Erwin und Elmire (Erwin and Elmire), songs to the *Schauspiel* of Johann Wolfgang von Goethe with prelude and intermezzo by Othmar Schoeck. First performance November 11, 1916, Zurich, Stadttheater; conducted by Max Kaempfert.

In this version of the Goethe story (see the Reichardt setting in the previous entry), Elmire seeks the advice of a friend, called Bernardo, who directs her to a hermit. The hermit turns out to be Erwin.

Schoeck set eighteen numbers to the Goethe text.

Major roles: Erwin (ten), Elmire (sop), Olympia (alto), and Bernardo (bass).

Other treatments of the text include those by Johann André (1775, Frankfurt); and Georg Joseph Vogler (1781, Darmstadt).

SCORE: vs ed. F. H. Schneider (Leipzig: B&H, 1919).

BIBLIOGRAPHY: Hans Corrodi, "Erwin und Elmire," in *Othmar Schoeck, eine Monographie*, 2d ed., 95–109 (Zurich, 1936); Werner Vogel, *Thematisches Verzeichnis der Werke von Othmar Schoeck* (Zurich: Atlantis Verlag, 1956), 71–78.

Euryanthe, grand heroic-Romantic opera in three acts by Carl Maria von Weber; libretto (Ger) by Helmina von Chézy after a French Romance. First performance October 25, 1823, Vienna, Kärntnertortheater, with Henriette Sontag (Euryanthe), Anton Haitzinger (Adolar), Therese Grünbaum (Eglantine), Anton Forti (Lysiart); conducted by the composer. First U.S. performance December 23, 1887, New York, Metropolitan, with Lilli Lehmann. First British performance (in German) June 29, 1833, London, Covent Garden.

The French knight Lysiart bets Count Adolar that Lysiart can seduce any woman, including Euryanthe, Adolar's fiancée. Each wagers his entire fortune. Euryanthe is tricked by the evil Eglantine, who loves Adolar, into revealing Adolar's family secret. His sister, Emma, killed herself after her beloved was killed in battle. Using this secret, Lysiart denounces Euryanthe for unfaithfulness before the court; Adolar is forced to give up his estates. He attempts to kill the disgraced Euryanthe in the desert but is prevented by a serpent's attack, which Euryanthe foils. Left alone to die, Euryanthe is found by a hunting party of the king. Just as Eglantine is to wed Lysiart, Adolar arrives. Eglantine reveals her part in the plot and is stabbed by Lysiart. Adolar and Euryanthe are reunited, and the opera ends.

Major roles: Euryanthe of Savoy (sop), Eglantine of Puiset (mezzo), Count Adolar of Nevers (ten), and Count Lysiart of Forêt (bar).

For a detailed plot synopsis, see K/*KOB*, 136–40.

The plot has similarities to Wagner's later *Lohengrin*.* The characters of Eglantine and Lysiart have their counterparts in Ortrud and Telramund, and Adolar's secret in Lohengrin's hidden origins; both secrets being uncovered by the heroine of the respective operas. Musical highlights of the Weber include the stirring overture, the ensemble "Ich bau auf Gott und meine Euryanthe," the love duet "Hin nimm die Seele mein," and the revenge duet of Lysiart and Eglantine in the second act, "Dunkle Nacht, du hörst den Schwur!"

SCORES: fs ed. E. Rudorff (Berlin: Schlesinger, 1866, repr. Farnborough, Hants: Gregg, 1969); vs ed. composer (Vienna: S. A. Steiner & Co., 1824).

BIBLIOGRAPHY: Anna Amalie Abert, "Webers 'Euryanthe' und Spohrs 'Jessonda' als grosse Opern," in *Festschrift für Walter Wiora*, ed. Ludwig Finscher, et al. (Kassel: Bär, 1967), 435–40; Charles Groves, " 'Euryanthe'—Too Little Known and Recognized,' " *Opera* XXVIII (1977), 1026–29; Michael C. Tusa, "Richard Wagner and Weber's *Euryanthe*," *19th Century Music* IX (1986), 206–21; John Warrack, "A Note on Helmina von Chézy," *Opera* XXVI (1975), 349–53; ———, "Weber and 'Euryanthe,' " *Opera* IX (1958), 481–86; ———, W/*CMW*, 280–301.

DISCOGRAPHY: Hunter, Norman, Gedda, Krause, and Vogel, conducted by Janowski, Dresden State Orchestra, Leipzig Radio Chorus, Angel 4AVC–34067 (3 tapes).

Evangelimann, Der (The Evangelist), "musikalisches Schauspiel" in two acts by Wilhelm Kienzl; libretto (Ger) by the composer after a story by Leopold Florian Meissner (1894). First performance May 4, 1895, Berlin, Staatsoper, with Bertha Pierson (Martha), Marie Goetze (Evangelica), Eloi Sylva (Mathias), Paul Bulss (Johannes), and Josef Mödlinger (Engel); conducted by Karl Muck. First U.S. performance November 3, 1923, Chicago, Great Northern Theater, with Mörike, Metzger, Ritter, and Zador. First British performance July 2, 1897, London, Covent Garden, with Marie Engle (Martha), Louise Meisslinger (Magdalena), Ernest Van Dyck (Mathias), David Bispham (Johannes), Lempriére Pringle (Friedrich), conducted by Philippe Flon.

The story takes place in the first part of the nineteenth century at the Benedictine cloister of St. Othmar in lower Austria and in Vienna. It concerns Johannes Freudhofer, who sets fire to the monastery in which he teaches and has his brother Mathias imprisoned for the crime. When the woman both brothers love, Martha, kills herself, Johannes becomes an evangelist. He confesses his misdeeds on his deathbed, and the brothers are reconciled.

Major roles: Friedrich Enel, justice administrator at the cloister of St. Othmar (bass); Martha, his niece and ward (sop); Magdalena, her friend (alto); Johannes Freudhofer, schoolteacher (bar); and Mathias Freudhofer, his younger brother (ten).

The musical highlights include "O schöne Jugendtage mit eurem stillen Glück" and "Selig sind, die Verfolgung leiden" from the second act.

SCORE: vs ed. composer (Berlin: B&B, 1894).

DISCOGRAPHY: Donath, Wenkel, Jerusalem, Hermann, and Moll, Bavarian Radio, conducted by Zagrosek, EMI 1C–165–46–191/3; reviewed by John W. Freeman, "Records," *ON* XLVI (April 3, 1982), 36. Excerpts: Rothenberger, Höffgen, Gedda, Lenz, Crass, and Kusche, conducted by Heger, Odeon SMC–80965; reviewed by C. J. Luten, *ON* XXXI (January 7, 1967), 34. Zeumer, Feldhoff, and Schock, conducted by Gierster, Eurodisc 86865. Excerpts: Konya, Ericsdotter, and Boese, Bavarian Radio Choir and Orchestra, conducted by Stein, DG 3306–036.

F

Faust, Singspiel in two acts by Ludwig Spohr; libretto (Ger) by Joseph Karl Bernard. First performance September 1, 1816, Prague, conducted by Carl Maria von Weber. Revised as a Romantic opera in three acts. First performance of second version July 15, 1852, London, Covent Garden, with Jeanne Castellan (Kunigunde), Anna Zerr (Röschen), Enrico Tamberlik (Count Hugo), Mr. Stigelli (Franz), Mr. Soldi (Wohlhaldt), Luigi Mei (Wagner), Giorgio Ronconi (Faust), and Karl Formes (Mephistofeles); conducted by the composer.

In this version of the legend, the opera opens with Faust, having tired of a life of sensual pleasures, seeking to use his diabolical powers, given to him by Mephistofeles, for the good of humankind. To this end he plans to wed Röschen, but he is thwarted by Röschen's former suitor, Franz, and the citizenry, who suspect Faust of murder. Faust is forced to flee.

In his second attempt, Faust tries to help Count Hugo rescue Kunigunde, Hugo's fiancée, who is being held by Sir Gulf. Unfortunately, in the course of assisting Hugo, Faust falls in love with Kunigunde himself and, at her wedding to Hugo, seduces her with the help of a potion provided by Mephistofeles. Realizing what has happened, Hugo challenges Faust to a duel and is killed. Röschen, who has attended the wedding in disguise, is driven to suicide by Faust's unfaithfulness; Mephistofeles gloats with a band of witches on the Blocksberg. Kunigunde, no longer under the spell of the potion, realizes that Faust has killed Hugo; she tries to stab Faust but is prevented from doing so by Mephistofeles, who discloses that he is the reason for Faust's power. The opera ends as Mephistofeles and his cohorts drag Faust down to hell.

Major roles: Faust (bass); Mephistofeles (bass); Count Hugo (ten); Kunigunde, his fiancée (sop); Gulf, a knight (bass); Röschen (sop); Franz (ten); Wohlhaldt (ten); Wagner (ten); and Sycorax, a witch (sop).

Among the musical highlights is Mephistofeles' calling of the witch Sycorax, "Sycorax hebe Dich aus Deiner Kluft!" (in No. 15 of first version, No. 18 of second). The score also features Spohr's first extensive use of leitmotives; the most prominent of these are the ones for hell and love. In the 1852 version, recitatives replaced the spoken dialogue, and the work was expanded from two acts to three, with entr'actes included.

Other settings of the Faust legend not based on Goethe include Ferruccio Busoni's *Doktor Faust** (1925, Dresden); Hermann Reutter's *Doktor Johannes Faust* (1936, Frankfurt); Hans Ulrich Engelmann's *Doktor Fausts Höllenfahrt* (1951, Hamburg); and Reutter's *Don Juan und Faust* (1950, Stuttgart).

SCORES: a combination of both versions, with ms score ed. Jonathan Stracey and introduction by Clive Brown, *Selected Works of Louis Spohr*, I (New York: Garland Publishing, 1990); vs (Leipzig: Peters, 1822); English vs ed. W. S. Rockstro (London: Boosey, 1852); rev. version vs ed. Karl Gotthelf Böhme (Leipzig: Peters, 1854).

LIBRETTOS: German (Vienna, 1814, first version, and Kassel, 1854, second version; both are reproduced in the Stracey-Brown edition).

BIBLIOGRAPHY: Clive Brown, "Spohr, Faust and Leitmotif," *MT* CXXV (1984), 25–27; B/*LS*, 76–79; E. M. Butler, *The Fortunes of Faust* (Cambridge: Cambridge University Press, 1952); Siegfried Goslich, *Beiträge zur Geschichte der deutschen romantischen Oper zwischen Spohrs 'Faust' und Wagners 'Lohengrin,'* (Berlin: Victor Otto Stamps, 1937).

Feen, Die (The Fairies), opera in three acts by Richard Wagner; libretto (Ger) by the composer after Carlo Gozzi's *La donna serpente* (1762). Composed in 1833. First performance June 29, 1888, Munich, Königliches Hof- und National-Theater, with Lilli Dressler (Ada), Anton Fuchs (Morald), Max Mikorey (Arindal), Adrienne Weitz (Lora), Gustav Siehr (Gernot), Victoria Blank (the fairy king, set here as an alto role), and Emilie Herzog (Drolla); conducted by Franz Fischer. First U.S. performance February 24, 1982 (concert, cut), New York, New York City Opera, with Penelope Daner (Ada), June Anderson (Lora), John Alexander (Arindal), and Frederick Burchinal (Morald); conducted by Antonio de Almeida. First British performance (in English), May 17, 1969, Midland Music Makers, University of Aston, with Robert Kirk (Gernot), and conducted by Lee; May 2, 1976, BBC Radio 3, with John Mitchinson (Arindal), April Cantelo (Ada), Paul Hudson (Gernot), Teresa Cahill (Drolla), Lorna Heywood (Lora), and Tom McDonnell (Morald), and conducted by Edward Downes.

The story concerns Prince Arindal of Tramond, who is in love with the fairy Ada, although he does not know who she is. When he asks her her identity, she disappears, since she is not human. In despair, the prince follows Ada to the underworld kingdom to be with her and gives up his humanity.

Major roles: Ada (sop); Lora, sister of Prince Arindal (sop); Arindal (ten); Morald, Lora's lover (bar); Gernot, servant of Arindal (bass); the fairy king (bass, set for alto at first performance); and Drolla, Laura's companion (sop).

Other settings of the Gozzi tale include Friedrich Himmel's *Die Sylphen* and Alfredo Casella's *La donna serpente* (1932, Rome).

SCORES: fs ed. Michael Balling, W/*RWW*, V (1912; repr. New York: Da Capo Press, 1971); vs ed. K. Ferd. Heckel (Mannheim: K. F. Heckel, ca. 1888).

BIBLIOGRAPHY: David Hamilton, "At the Start," *ON* XLVI (February 27, 1982), 14, 16 [on U.S. concert premiere]; Bryan Magee, "Early Wagner in the Highlands," *Opera* XX (1969), 649–50 [on British premiere]; George Movshon, "Early Wagner: A Pair," *HiFi/MA* XXXII (June 1982), 19 [on U.S. premiere]; Andrew Porter, "Musical Events," *NY* LVIII (March 22, 1982), 146, 149 [on U.S. premiere]; Patrick J. Smith, "America. Early Wagner," *Opera* XXXIII (1982), 486 [on U.S. premiere].

DISCOGRAPHY: Moll, Studer, Laki, Hermann, Bavarian Radio Orchestra and Chorus, conducted by Sawallisch, Orfeo CD062 (3 compact discs).

Fernando, Singspiel in one act by Franz Schubert; libretto (Ger) by Albert Stadler. Composed in 1815. First performance April 13, 1907, Vienna, Wiener Schubertbund (concert); August 18, 1918, Magdeburg, arranged by Bernhard Engelke. First British performance May 15, 1960 (concert), London, Public Lane Opera with Hazel Schmid and Kenneth Bowen, accompanied by Patricia Kew. First U.S. performance (concert) October 13, 1975, New York, Alice Tully Hall, with Judith Raskin (Philipp), Berenice Bramson, and Grayson Hirst; conducted by Jens Nygaard.

Major roles: Philipp (sop), Fernando (ten), Eleonore (sop), Köhler (bass), and Jäger (bass).

The seven numbers of the work include a romance by Philipp and a grand finale, "Himmlische Göttin."

SCORES: fs, Schu/*AGA*, XV/2 (1888); Schu/*NGA*, II/2 (nyp).

DISCOGRAPHY: Mathis, Sima, Hopfner, and Holl, conducted by Zagrosek, Austrian Radio Symphony and Chorus, Orfeo S–109841 A.

Fernando und Yariko (Die Wilden und die Gesitteten) (The Savages and the Civilized People), Singspiel in three acts by Benedikt Schack; libretto (Ger) by Karl von Eckhartshausen after Nicolas Chamfort's *La Jeune Indienne* (1765), a reworking of Joseph Addison's tale of *Inkle and Yariko* (1711). First performance December 3, 1784, Vienna, Leopoldstadt Theater (as *Die Wilden*).

The story is a treatment of the noble savage theme. The English merchant Inkle and his servant Pedril have been marooned on an island near the American coast, where they are aided by the native girl Yariko, who has fallen in love with Inkle. The Europeans are joined by the Spanish admiral Consalvo and Fernando, his son, who have also been shipwrecked. The intolerant Consalvo feels that all "savages" should be killed, a belief not shared by his son. Yariko's brother, Azor, and another native, Zerim, find the Europeans and condemn them to death before they realize that Fernando had once spared their lives. Azor then agrees to save Fernando and even his cruel father, and Pedril prevents Inkle from betraying Yariko to save his own skin.

Inkle repays Yariko's kindness by trying to betray her once more by selling her to Steley, a slave trader who has landed on the island. Only Pedril and Fernando, among the Europeans, behave decently. In the end, Inkle, Steley, and Consalvo are put out to sea for their treachery, and Pedril and Fernando remain behind, with Fernando hoping to win Yariko's affection.

Major roles: Consalvo, admiral of a Spanish fleet (bass); Fernando, his son (ten); Inkle, a merchant (ten); Pedril, Inkle's servant (bass); Yariko, a savage (sop); and Steley, a slave trader (spoken).

The score includes twenty-eight numbers. Among them is Yariko's aria "O Inkle! Wie ich liebte dich" (No. 19).

The libretto was set as *Fernando und Yariko* by Franz Christoph Neubauer in 1788 in Zurich. Another version is Samuel Arnold's *Inkle and Yariko* (1787, London). *Inkle und Yariko* by Ferdinand Kauer appeared in 1807.

SCORE: fs (Zurich, 1788); repr. in *German Opera 1770–1800*, IX, ed. Thomas Bauman (New York and London: Garland Publishing, 1986).

LIBRETTO: German, the same.

Ferne Klang, Der (The Distant Sound), opera in three acts by Franz Schreker; libretto (Ger) by the composer. First performance August 18, 1912, Frankfurt, Opernhaus, conducted by Krähmer. The opera was revived at Kassel on September 13, 1964; conducted by Christoph von Dóhnanyi.

A young musician, Fritz, gives up his true love, Grete, to search for a "lost chord," and he meets the sinister Doktor Vigelius. In the meantime, Grete's father offers her hand in marriage to the innkeeper, much to her horror. In despair, she flees to "La casa di maschere" in Venice, where she is greeted as the Queen of the Festival and is transformed into the worldly Greta. As the third act opens, Fritz's new opera is to be performed. Greta, meanwhile, has become a prostitute. Although the first two acts are greatly acclaimed, the third is a disaster. The next morning Fritz, ailing, hears the story of Greta from Vigelius. Suddenly she appears, and the former lovers are reunited. Dying, Fritz hears the music that he had been searching for all along.

Major roles: Fritz (ten) and Grete/Greta (sop).

The non-functional harmony of the composer's first opera is quite like that of Debussy, and there is much tonal ambiguity. The orchestration is very full, and Schreker also uses leitmotifs. The work is considered the most experimental of the composer's output.

SCORE: vs ed. Ferdinand Rebay (Vienna: UE, 1911).

LIBRETTO: German, the same.

BIBLIOGRAPHY: Erno Balogh, "A Distant Sound," *ON* XXIX (December 19, 1964), 6–7; Nicholas Chadwick, "Franz Schreker's Orchestral Style and Its Influence on Alban Berg," *MR* XXXV (February-May 1974), 29–46; Andrew D. McCredie, "Overseas Reports. German. Schreker Revival," *Opera* XV (1964), 748–49; Gösta Neuwirth, *Die Harmonik in der Oper 'Der ferne Klang' von Franz Schreker* (Regensberg, 1972); Werner

Oehlmann, "Schreker und seine Oper," in S/*FS*, 63–69; Winfried Zillig, "Schreker's Der ferne Klang," *MT* CV (1964), 652–54.

DISCOGRAPHY: Grigorescu and Harper, Hagen Opera Chorus and Philharmonic Orchestra, conducted by Halasz, Marco Polo (Harmonia Mundi) 8.223270–271 (2 compac discs).

Fest der Winzer, Das, oder **Die Weinlese** (The Feast of the Vintners, or The Vintage), Singspiel in three acts by Friedrich Ludwig Aemilius Kunzen; libretto (Ger) by Johann Jakob Ihlée. First performance May 3, 1793, Frankfurt, with Margarethe Schick.

Although Luise is in love with the young Gürge, a worker in the vineyard, her father, the Mayor, is determined that she wed the unpleasant schoolmaster Barthel, who arranges with the hunter Wolf to frame Gürge for poaching. When Gürge is arrested, Luise turns to the Landowner and his daughter for help. The Landowner helps to free Gürge and also discovers that Barthel is a fraud. In place of jail, Barthel loses his job and half his property, and he must pay for the wedding feast of Luise and Gürge.

Major roles: Luise, daughter of the Mayor (sop); the Mayor (bar); Gürge, a worker (ten); the Landowner (bass); and Barthel, the schoolmaster (bass).

The score includes several rousing choruses and Gürge's "Der Wein, der Wein ist Goldes werth" (No. 2), which was published separately and has appeared in several anthologies.

SCORES: fs ms repr. in *German Opera 1770–1800*, XI, ed. Thomas Bauman (New York and London: Garland Publishing, 1986); vs as *Vinhøsten* (Copenhagen, 1798).

LIBRETTO: German, repr. in *German Opera 1770–1800*, XIX, *Librettos II*, ed. Thomas Bauman (New York and London, 1986).

Feuersbrunst, Die (Das abgrebrannte Haus) (Conflagration [The Burning House]), Singspiel/marionette opera in two acts by Franz Joseph Haydn; anonymous libretto (Ger). Composed ca. 1776, for the marionette theater at Esterháza Castle. The work, considered lost until 1962, was reconstructed by H. C. Robbins Landon from a manuscript score at Yale University. Performed in this version (as *Das brennende Haus*) July 18, 1963, Bregenz, and in May 1982, Vienna, Theater an der Wien, with Paul Wolfrum (Hanswurst), Wolfgang Mayr (Steckel), Christopher Doig (nobleman and ghost), Jaroslav Stajnc (Odoardo); and Elisabeth Kales (Colombina); conducted by Bernard Klebel.

In this "Hanswurst" comedy, the Papageno-like hero, Hanswurst, appears in various disguises in an attempt to win Colombina away from Leander. Colombina is the daughter of the newly rich Odoardo; it is his house that is consumed by fire (at the end of the first act). Hanswurst wins Columbina's hand in the end.

Class distinctions are emphasized by the use of Viennese dialect for characters such as Hanswurst and *hochdeutsch* for those such as Leander. The distinctions carry over to the music: Hanswurst's arias feature folk-like melodies; Colombina's numbers are very delicate.

Major roles: Hanswurst, chimneysweep (bar); Steckel, porter at the inn (ten); Odoardo, a well-to-do peasant in charge of the Count's estate (ten); Colombina, his daughter (sop); Leander, a dandy (ten); a ghost, Steckel's father (ten).

Robbins Landon has dated the score by the composer's use of clarinets, which were employed at Esterháza from 1776 to 1778; the third movement of the overture comes from Haydn's *L'infedeltà delusa* of 1773; the first two movements of the overture were composed by his pupil Ignaz Pleyel. The work itself has twenty-seven numbers, including arias, duets, dances, a ballet, and choruses. The original dialogue is lost.

SCORES: fs ed. H. C. Robbins Landon (London: Schott & Co., 1963); vs ed. Roderick Biss, the same.

BIBLIOGRAPHY: Christopher Norton-Welsh, "Reports: Foreign," *ON* XLVII (August 1982), 32 [on revival]; H. C. Robbins Landon, "Foreword" to fs; ———, "Haydn's Marionette Operas . . . ," *Haydn Yearbook* I (1962), 111–97; Nick Rossi, "Joseph Haydn and Opera," *OQ* I/1 (Winter 1983), 75–77.

Feuersnot (Lack of Fire), *Singgedicht* in one act by Richard Strauss; libretto (Ger) by Ernst von Wolzogen after a tale in Johann Wilhelm Wolf's *Sagas of the Netherlands* (1843). First performance November 21, 1901, Dresden, with Annie Krull (Diemut) and Karl Scheidemantel (Kunrad); conducted by Ernst von Schuch. First U.S. performance December 1, 1927, Philadelphia, with Stanley, Salzinger, Raseley, Albert Mahler, and Nelson Eddy; conducted by Alexander Smallens. First British performance July 9, 1910, London, His Majesty's, with Fay, Oster, and Robert Radford; conducted by (Sir) Thomas Beecham.

The story is set in Seindlingerstrasse in Munich, on Midsummer Day. The hero, Kunrad, kisses the daughter of the mayor, Diemut. Shocked by his action, she lures him to be lifted up to her balcony by way of a basket; halfway up, she leaves him dangling, to become the laughingstock of the townsfolk. In a rage Kunrad asks the Wizard for help, and all fires in the town are extinguished. They are restored only after Diemut reconsiders and accepts Kunrad's love.

Major roles: Ortlof Sentlinger, the mayor (bass); Diemut, his daughter (sop); and Kunrad, an alchemist (bar).

The hero is the personification not only of Strauss, but of his idol, Wagner, and their initial rejection by the people of Munich.

SCORE: vs ed. Otto Singer (Berlin: A. Fürstner, 1901).

LIBRETTO: German (Berlin: A. Fürstner, 1901).

BIBLIOGRAPHY: William Mann, "Feuersnot," M/*RSC*, 21–38; K. Schultz and S. Kohler, *Richard Strauss: Feuersnot* (Munich: Bavarian State Opera, 1980).

DISCOGRAPHY: Cunitz and Cordes, Bavarian State Opera Orchestra and Chorus, conducted by Kempe, Melodram 103 (m). Varady, Weikl, Berger-Tuna, Lenz, Schenk, and Engen, Bavarian Radio, conducted by Fricke, Acanta 40–23530 (2); reviewed by John W. Freeman, "Records," *ON* XLIX (December 8, 1984), 61.

Fidelio oder **Die eheliche Liebe** (Fidelio or Conjugal Love), opera in three acts by Ludwig van Beethoven; libretto (Ger) by Joseph Sonnleithner after Jean Nicolas Bouilly's *Léonore* ou *L'Amour conjugal*, set by Pierre Gaveaux in 1798 (Paris). First performance November 20, 1805, Vienna, Theater an der Wien (see *Leonore**). Stefan von Breuning altered and reduced the opera to two acts in 1806, and in 1814 Georg Friedrich Treitschke gave it the form in which it is usually performed today. First performance of the second version March 29, 1806, Vienna, Theater an der Wien. First performance of the third version May 23, 1814, Vienna, Kärntnertortheater, with Anna Milder (Fidelio), Mlle. Bondra (Marzelline), Herr Radichi (Florestan), Johann Michael Vogel (Don Pizarro), Carl-Friedrich Weinmüller (Rocco), and Herr Frühwald (Jaquino); conducted by Michael Umlauf. First U.S. performance September 9, 1839 (in English), New York, Park Theatre, with Inverarity, Manvers, Giubilei, and Martyn. First British performance May 18, 1832, with Wilhelmine Schröder-Devrient and Anton Haitzinger; conducted by Chelard.

Don Florestan has been imprisoned by his political enemy, the evil Don Pizarro. Leonore, determined to free her husband, gains entry to the prison by dressing as a man and calling herself Fidelio. She offers to assist the jailer Rocco, whereupon his daughter Marzelline spurns the attentions of her sweetheart Jaquino in favor of this new "helper." Fidelio (or Leonore) locates her husband and intercedes when Pizarro comes to kill him after hearing that his superior, Don Fernando, is coming to visit. Rocco tells Don Fernando of Pizarro's evil deeds, Pizarro is arrested, and Florestan is freed, along with the rest of the prisoners; this scene has come to represent a symbol of freedom in the modern era.

For detailed synopses and musical analyses, see C/*CS*, 236–40; *ENO* IV (1980); K/*KOB*, 127–32; and N/*SGO*, II, 168–99.

Major roles: Florestan, a Spanish nobleman (ten); Leonore, his wife (sop); Don Pizarro, overseer of the state prison (bass-bar); Rocco, a jailer (bass); Marzelline, his daughter (sop); Jaquino, a turnkey (ten); and Don Fernando, the prime minister (bass).

Beethoven, who searched long for a suitable story to set, was drawn to this particular libretto because of its emphasis on the idealized love of a woman for her husband, a love for which the composer searched his entire life, and for its theme of the triumph of justice over evil. He worked incessantly to perfect the opera, ergo the several versions and the four overtures: the Leonore Overtures No. 1 (for a Prague performance); No. 2 (for the 1806 version); No. 3 (for the original version); and the *Fidelio Overture*, in E, which serves to open the 1814 version. Among the many musical gems of the score are the first-act quartet "Mir ist so wunderbar," written in canon, and Leonore's anguished recitative and aria "Abscheulicher! Wo eilst du hin/Komm Hoffnung," also in the first act. In the second, are Florestan's despairing recitative and aria "Gott, welch Dunkel hier/In des Lebens Frühlingstagen" and his joyous duet with Leonore, "O namenlose Freude." The opera ends with a chorus of rejoicing, "Heil sei dem Tag, heil sei der Stunde.'' Beethoven's work had a tremendous impact on subsequent German operas, many of which, such as *Die Meistersinger** end with "Heil" choruses.

SCORES: fs first version, B/*SW*, ed. Willi Hess, supplement II, XI-XIII (1967, 1970); second version, B/*SW*, ed. Willi Hess, XI-XIII (1967, 1970); third version, B/*GA*, series XX/206 (1865); vs first version (Leipzig, 1905); second version (Leipzig, 1810); third version (Vienna, 1814).

LIBRETTO: German (Vienna: Anton Pichler, 1805).

BIBLIOGRAPHY: Emily Anderson, "On the Road to Fidelio (1814)," *Opera* XII (1961), 82–88; Kurt Blaukopf, "Die Funktion der Leonoren-Ouvertüren in *Fidelio*," *HiFi-Stereophonie* IX (1970), 290–94; Jens Brincker, "Leonore and Fidelio," in *Festkrift Jens Peter Larsen*, ed. Nils Schiørring et al. (Copenhagen, 1972), 351–68; Mark Brunswick, "Beethoven's Tribute to Mozart in *Fidelio*," *MQ* XXXI (1945), 29–32; "Fidelio," *L'Avant-scène opéra* X (May-June 1977), 1–29; Walter Graf, "Zum klanglichen Ausdruck in Beethovens "Fidelio," in *Beethoven-Studien, Festgabe* (Vienna, 1970), 253–70; Joachim Herz, "Questions about 'Fidelio,' " *Opera* XXXI (1980), 435–39; Willi Hess, *Beethovens Oper Fidelio und ihre drei Fassungen* (Zurich: Atlantis, 1966); ———, "Fünfzig Jahre im Bühne von *Leonore-Fidelio*," *Beethoven Jahrbuch* IX (1973–1977), 167–84; Edgar Istel, "Beethoven's *Leonora* and *Fidelio*," *MQ* VII (1921), 226–51; Ludwig Misch, "*Fidelio* als ethisches Bekenntnis," in *Beethoven-Studien* (Berlin: W. de Gruyte, 1950), 143–49; Johanna Rudolph, "Realismus und Anticipation in Werken Beethovens. Zum Weschselwirkung der Künste am Beispiel der *Egmont*-Musik und des *Fidelio*-Problems in Shakespeares *Cymbeline*," *Beethoven Kongress. Berlin 1970*, 249–68; ———, in *Shakespeare Jahrbuch* CVIII (1972), 64–82; Martin Ruhnke, "Die Librettisten des *Fidelio*," in A/*OAA*, 121–40; Erich Schenk, "Über Tonsymbolik in Beethovens *Fidelio*," *Beethoven-Studien, Festgabe* (Vienna, 1970), 223–52; Rudolf Steglich, "Das melodische Hauptmotiv in Beethovens *Fidelio*," A/*Mw* IX (1952), 51–67; Alan Tyson, "The Problem of Beethoven's 'First' *Leonore* Overture," *JAMS* XXVIII (1975), 292–334; ———, "Yet Another 'Leonore' Overture?" *ML* LVIII/2 (1977), 192–203.

DISCOGRAPHY: See Lord Harewood, B/*OOR*, 119–130 and M/*IRR*, 182–83.

Fierrabras (Fierabras), opera in three acts by Franz Schubert; libretto (Ger) by Josef Kupelwieser after the French romance *Fierabras* and the German saga *Eginhard und Emma*. Composed 1823. First performance (several numbers) May 7, 1835, Vienna, Theater in der Josefstadt; conducted by Conradin Kreutzer. First performance (abridged, staged) February 9, 1897, Karlsruhe; conducted by Felix Mottl. First U.S. performance May 9, 1980, Philadelphia, Walnut Street Theater, with Paul Spencer Adkins (Fierrabras), Gregory Stapp (Karl) Cecilia Dempsey (Emma), Marla McDaniel (Florinda), and Richard Pendergraph (Roland); conducted by Alessandro Siciliani. Produced by the BBC in 1971. First staged British performance February 19, 1986, Oxford, Oxford University Opera Club, with Paul Wilson (Fierrabras), Ann Todd (Emma), Alison Truefit (Florinda), Neil Lunt (Eginhard), and Christopher Parke (Roland); conducted by Clive Brown.

The piece is set against the background of the war between Charles (Karl) V of Spain and the Moors, with a love story between the warring rulers' offspring as the centerpiece. Charles has defeated the Moors and has taken Fierrabras, son of their leader, as prisoner. Fierrabras is in love with Emma, Charles' daughter, as is Eginhard, a Spanish knight; Fierrabras' sister, Florinda, loves Roland, also a Spanish knight. In the end, it is Eginhard who wins the hand of Emma. Fierrabras converts to Christianity and joins Charles' forces.

The opera contains numerous choruses, including the women's chorus "Den Siegen lass uns schmücken" and "O theures Vaterland" for unaccompanied men's voices.

Major roles: Emma (sop), Eginhard (ten), Fierrabras (ten), Roland (bass), and Karl (bass).

The story was also set by Georg Philip Telemann as *Die Last-tragende Liebe, oder Emma und Eginhard.**

SCORES: fs, Schu/*AGA*, XV/6, no. 10 (1886); Schu/*NGA*, II/8 (nyp).

LIBRETTO: German, ed. Christian Pollack (Tutzing: Hans Schneider, 1988).

BIBLIOGRAPHY: Maurice Brown, "Schubert's *Fierrabras*," *MT* CXII (1971), 338–39; ———, "Two Major Operas. A Consideration of the Possibility of Actual Stage Production," *ML* XX (1959), 104–18; Winton Dean, "Oxford," *MT* CXXVII (1986), 224 [on British premiere]; Andrew Porter, "Musical Events," *NY* LVI (May 26, 1980), 113–17 [on U.S. premiere]; Gary Schmidgall, "Reports: North America," *ON* XLV (August 1980), 29–30 [on U.S. premiere]; Daniel Webster, "Philadelphia. AVA Opera Theater: Schubert Premiere," *HiFi/MA* XXX, (1980), 24.

Figaro lässt sich scheiden (Figaro Gets Divorced), opera in two acts by Giselher Klebe; libretto (Ger) by the composer after Ödon von Horvath. First performance June 28, 1963, Hamburg.

Despite the title, Figaro is merely separated from—and then reunited with—Susanna.

Major roles: Figaro (bar) and Susanna (sop).

The score features extensive musical quotes from Mozart's *Le Nozze di Figaro* (1786, Vienna).

Other operas that treat the Figaro story include Karl Ditters von Dittersdorf's *Die Hochzeit des Figaro** (1789); *Rosina* by Hiram Titus (1980, Minneapolis); and the parody *The Abduction of Figaro* by P. D. Q. Bach [Peter Schickele] (1984, Minneapolis).

SCORE: vs (Berlin: B&B, 1963).

LIBRETTO: German, the same.

BIBLIOGRAPHY: Heinz Joachim, *Opera* XIV (1963), 602–3 [on premiere].

Fledermaus, Die (The Bat), operetta in three acts by Johann Strauss, Jr.; libretto (Ger) by Karl Haffner and Richard Genée after Henri Meilhac and Ludovic Halévy's vaudeville *Le Reveillon* (1872), which, in turn, was based on Roderich Benedix's 1859 comedy *Das Gefängnis*. First performance April 5, 1874, Vienna, Theater an der Wien, with Jani Szika (Eisenstein), Marie Geistinger (Rosalinde) Frau Charles-Hirsch (Adele), Herr Rüdinger (Alfred), Frl. Rittinger (Prince Orlovsky), Herr Rott (Dr. Blind); and Herr Lebrecht (Dr. Falke); conducted by the composer. First U.S. performance November 21, 1874, New York, Thalia Theater. First British performance December 18, 1876, London, Alhambra. The New York and London premieres were unsuccessful, and the work achieved popularity in the United States and Britain first in its revivals in 1911 and 1910, respectively.

Dr. Falke, still smarting from a practical joke that left him dressed as a bat on a public bench, plans an elaborate revenge on his friend Gabriel von Eisenstein. It is New Year's Eve, and he convinces Eisenstein to delay going to jail for a minor offense in order to attend a masked ball given by the Russian Count Orlovsky. When the friends leave, Rosalinde, Eisenstein's wife, has to contend with the arrival of a former lover of hers, Alfred, who pretends to be Eisenstein when Frank, the jail warden, comes to take Eisenstein to jail. The warden therefore takes Alfred instead and afterwards goes to the ball disguised as a Frenchman. Others in attendance include the Eisenstein maid, Adele, disguised as an actress, and Rosalinde, whose disguise as a Hungarian countess fools her husband to the point of his attempting to seduce her. The main characters wind up at the jail, trying to sort out the various identities; in the end all are unmasked and order is restored.

For a detailed synopsis see C/*NMC*, 248–58 and K/*KOB*, 285–90.

Major roles: Eisenstein, a wealthy socialite (ten); Rosalinde (sop); Adele (col sop); Alfred (ten); Dr. Falke (bar); Prince Orlovsky (mezzo or male voice); Dr. Blind, Eisenstein's lawyer (ten); Frank, the jail warden (bar); Frosch, the jailer (speaking comedian); and Ida, Adele's sister (sop).

The operetta, often performed on New Year's Eve, contains a gala section in the second act, during which guest artists perform their favorite arias. Among the work's fixed outstanding numbers are the sparkling overture, Rosalinde's lovely "Täubchen, das entflattert ist," and the drinking song finale "Trinke, Liebchen, trinke schnell." In the second act are the comical duet of the pretend Frenchmen, "Mein Herr Marquis"; Rosalinde's mock exotic csárdás, "Klänge, der Heimath"; and the luscious finale, sung by the entire company, "Brüderlein and Schwesterlein." The third act, which has an extended comical dialogue by the jailer, Frosch, a part often taken by an outstanding comic actor, also features the closing finale, "O Fledermaus!"

SCORES: fs *Johann Strauss. Sämtliche Werke*, series II/3, ed. Fritz Racek (Vienna: Doblinger, 19—); vs (Vienna: Friedrich Schneider, 1974).

LIBRETTO: German (Vienna: Gustav Lewy, ca. 1874).

BIBLIOGRAPHY: Franz Mailer, " 'Glücklich ist wer vergisst.' Aus der Geschichte der *Fledermaus* in Wein," *ÖMz* XXIX (1974), 217–25; Leonard Stocker, "Notes on Die Fledermaus," *OJ* VIII/1 (1975), 19–22.

DISCOGRAPHY: See Alan Blyth, B/*OOR*, 532–41.

VIDEO: Te Kanawa, Prey, Hechele, and Luxon, Royal Opera, Covent Garden, conducted by P. Domingo, Thorn/EMI TVD 2791 or NVC/BBC FLEO1 (2).

Fliegende Holländer, Der (The Flying Dutchman), opera in three acts by Richard Wagner; libretto (Ger) by the composer after an episode in Heinrich Heine's *Memoiren des Herrn von Schabelewopski* and inspired by Wagner's experience in a storm when crossing the North Sea in 1839. P. L. P. Dietsch set the opera *Le Vaisseau-fantôme*, with a text by P. H. Foucher and B. H. Révoil, based on Wagner's scenario, which Wagner had sold; the Dietsch version was first performed on November 9, 1842, in Paris, at the Opéra; it was a failure. The Wagner premiere took place on January 2, 1843, in Dresden, at the Hofoper, with Wilhelmine Schröder-Devrient (Senta), Michael Wächter (the Dutchman), Karl Risse (Daland), Therese Wächter (Mary), S. Reinhold (Erik), and Wenzel Bielczizky (steersman); conducted by the composer. First U.S. performance November 8, 1876, New York (in Italian, as *Il Vascello Fantasma*), with Pappenheim, Baccei, Preusser, and Sullivan; conducted by Carlberg. First British performance July 23, 1870, Drury Lane Theatre (in Italian, as *L'Olandese damnato*), with Charles Santley (the Dutchman), Ilma Di Murska (Senta), Julius Perotti (Erik), Allan James Foli (Daland), and Iginio Corsi (the steersman); conducted by Luigi Arditi.

In the story, the Dutchman has been condemned to sail the seas for all eternity because of his blaspheming; he can be redeemed only by finding a woman who will love him faithfully until she dies. A storm brings his ship to land near the vessel of Daland, who is tempted by the stranger's wealth to encourage him to marry Daland's daughter, Senta, although she is already pledged to the young Erik. Senta, obsessed with the Dutchman's picture, welcomes the stranger and promises him her love, despite the pleas of her fiancé. Overhearing Erik's entreaties, however, the Dutchman resolves to leave and sails off. But Senta gives him the ultimate proof of her loyalty by throwing herself into the sea. The damned ship sinks, and the Dutchman and Senta, now saved, ascend to Heaven.

For detailed synopses and musical analyses, see C/*NMC*, 259–63; K/*KOB*, 162–67; and N/*SGO*, I, 286–318.

Major roles: the Dutchman (bar); Daland (bass); his daughter, Senta (sop); Mary, Senta's nurse (alto); Erik, a huntsman (ten); and the helmsman (ten).

Although written as a German Romantic opera, with set pieces such as duets, arias, and ballads, Wagner's work represents his first important use of the leitmotif, in this case to represent the storm and salvation, among others. The story itself contains a theme which appears in many of the composer's later works, that of the main character's search for the love of a pure woman (as in *Lohengrin** and *Tannhäuser*,* for example, where the heroine also dies). Wagner also stresses here and elsewhere the idea of salvation through love, for example, in the famed "Senta's Ballad" of Act II. Other striking numbers include the Dutchman's recitative and aria of the opening act, "Die Frist ist um," and the powerful overture, with its open fifths and chromatics to signify the storm and the following section, which is major and diatonic, to represent the calm.

The similarities to and differences from the Dietsch version are traced by Barry Millington (see below), who points out the parallel characters of the cursed seafarer, a daughter given in marriage to a stranger by a greedy father, and her leaping to her death.

The opera was only fairly successful at Dresden, but it was given in other cities and shortly thereafter became very popular, as it remains to this day. In addition to the Dietsch version, G. Rodwell composed *The Flying Dutchman* or *The Phantom Ship* (1827, New York).

SCORES: fs ed. Carl Dahlhaus, W/*SW*, IV/1–5 (1970); vs ed. C. F. Meser (Dresden, 1844).

LIBRETTO: German (Dresden, n.p., 1843).

BIBLIOGRAPHY: Carolyn Abbate, "Erik's Dream and Tannhäuser's Journey," in G/ *RO*, 129–47; Gerald Abraham, " 'The Flying Dutchman': Original Version," *ML* XX (1939), 412–19; John Deathridge, "An Introduction to 'The Flying Dutchman,' " ENO Opera Guide, XII, ed. Nicholas John (London, 1982); Peter Gülke, "Motivarbeit unterhalb der Leitmotive: Beobachtungen und Überlegungen bei Wagners Fliegendem Holländer," *Musikbühne 75*, ed. Horst Seeger (Berlin, 1975), 51–65; Edgar Istel, "Autographie Regiebemerkungen Wagners zum 'Fliegenden Holländer,' " *Die Musik* XII (1912–1913), 214–19; Hellmut Kühn, "Wagners Senta und der nordische Exotismus," *NZM* CXXI/2 (1974), 85–90; Gustave Leprince, "*The Flying Dutchman* in the Setting by Philippe Dietsch," *MQ* L (1964), 307–20; Paul Machlin, "Wagner, Durand and 'The Flying Dutchman': The 1852 Revisions of the Overture," *ML* LX (1974), 410–28; ———"A Sketch for the 'Dutchman,' " *MT* CXVII (1976), 727–29; Barry Millington, " 'The Flying Dutchman,' 'Le Vaisseau fantôme' and Other Nautical Yarns," *MT* CXXVII (1986), 131–35.

DISCOGRAPHY: See William Mann, B/*OOR*, 338–45.

VIDEO: Balslev, Estes, Salminen, Bayreuth Festival Orchestra, conducted by Nelsson, Philips.

Florentinische Tragödie, Eine (A Florentine Tragedy), opera in one act by Alexander von Zemlinsky; libretto (Ger) by Max Meyerfeld, an abridged version in German of Oscar Wilde's play. First performance January 30, 1917, Stuttgart, Hoftheater, with Felix Fleischer (Simone), Helene Wildbrunn (Bianca), and Rudolf Ritter (Guido Bardi); conducted by Max von Schillings. First U.S. performance April 22, 1982, New York, Manhattan School of Music; conducted by John Crosby. First professional U.S. performance August 9, 1984, Santa Fe, Sante Fe Opera, with Edward Craft (Simone), John Stewart (Guido), and Lisa Turetsky (Bianca); conducted by Dennis Russell Davies.

The story is set in Renaissance Florence, where a hardworking merchant, Simone, discovers his young wife, Bianca, with her noble lover, Prince Guido; when her husband kills her lover, Bianca is again attracted to her husband.

Another setting is by Richard Flury (1929, Solothurn).

SCORE: vs ed. composer (Vienna: UE, 1916).

BIBLIOGRAPHY: Robert Jacobson, "U.S.: Reports," *ON* XLIX (November 1984), 46 [on professional U.S. premiere]; Andrew Porter, "Musical Events," *NY* LVIII (June 14, 1982), 108–109, 110 [on U.S. premiere]; Stanley Sadie, "Music in London," *MT* CXXVI (1985), 739; Horst Weber, "In the Maze of Emotions," *Opera* XXXIV (1983), 841–46.

Floss der Medusa, Das (The Raft of Medusa), "oratorio volgare e militare" in two parts by Hans Werner Henze; libretto (Ger) by Ernst Schnabel. The premiere set for December 9, 1968, did not take place. The West Berlin choir refused to sing under a red flag and a banner to Che Guevara, to whom the piece was dedicated. First performance (concert) December 17, 1977, London, Albert Hall, with Phyllis Bryn-Julson (Death); conducted by David Atherton.

The tale, based on a historical incident and immortalized in Géricault's famous painting, involves the sinking of a French frigate, the *Medusa*, after which the officers took the lifeboat and left the rest of the men to die on a makeshift raft. Only a mulatto sailor survived, and the Henze work encompasses his chilling tale.

Major roles: Death (sop), Jean-Charles (bar), and Charon (speaker).

The story was also set by Friedrich von Flotow as *Die Matrosen* (1845, Hamburg), an enlargement of *Le Naufrage de la Méduse* (1839, Paris), which he wrote with Pilati.

SCORE: vs ed. Henning Brauel (Mainz: BSS, 1968).

BIBLIOGRAPHY: Wolfgang Becker, "La Zattera di Henze," *NRMI* IV/3 (1970), 488–92; Andrew Porter, "Musical Events" *NY* (December 17, 1977), 170 [on the London premiere]; Wolfram Schwinger, "Der Fall Medusa. Henzes neues Oratorium wurde nicht uraufgeführt," *Musica* XXIII (1969), 41–42.

DISCOGRAPHY: Moser, Fischer-Dieskau, and Regnier, Choir and Orchestra of North German Radio, conducted by Henze, DGG 139–382; reviewed by Robert Henderson, "Henze," *MT* CXII (1971), 145.

Flut, Die (The Flood), opera in one act by Boris Blacher; libretto (Ger) by Heinz von Cramer. First performance December 20, 1946, Radio Berlin. First staged performance March 4, 1947, Dresden. First U.S. performance April 19, 1956, Boston, Boston University School of Fine Arts. First British performance March 8, 1960, London, St. Pancras Town Hall, with Mary Illing (the girl), Edward Byles (young man), and Donald Campbell (banker); conducted by Meyer Fredman.

The opera, set on a desert island, concerns a girl, a young fisherman, an irresponsible young man, and a rich old banker, who are shipwrecked. When the banker offers gold to anyone who will save them, he is killed by the young man. When the tide recedes unexpectedly, the girl and young man go off together, leaving the fisherman to dream.

Major roles: the girl (sop), the young man (ten), the banker (bass), and the fisherman (bar).

The vocal lines are patterned after speech, and there are a few set arias. Igor Stravinsky's television opera *The Flood* (1962, CBS) concerns Noah and his wife during the building of the ark.

SCORE: fs (Berlin: B&B, 1962); vs ed. Johannes O. Hasse, English text by Dorothy de Reeder and Kurt Heinrich Hansen (Berlin: B&B, c. 1947).

LIBRETTO: German (Berlin: B&B, 1946).

BIBLIOGRAPHY: Arthur Jacobs, "Two Operas New to London," *Opera* XI (1960), 182–83 [on British premiere].

Forza della virtù, La oder **Die Macht der Tugend** (The Force of Virtue), opera in three acts by Reinhard Keiser; libretto (Ger) by Friedrich Christian Bressand after the Italian libretto of Domenico David, set by Carlo Francesco Pollarolo (1693). First performance Carnival, 1700, Hamburg.

After a marriage has been arranged between the king of Castile, Fernando, and a French princess Clotilde, Clotilde is distressed to discover the coldness of her husband-to-be. Fernando admits to the captain of his guards, Alfonso, that he desires Anagilda, not knowing that his captain is also in love with her. Hoping to gain the throne, Anagilda tells Fernando that she cannot accept his love unless he gives up Clotilde, which he promises to do, and she ignores her father Sancio's pleas not to sully their family's name. Anagilda conspires to have Clotilde arrested for adultery, and Alfonso takes her away to prison.

When Clotilde's trial ends in a quick guilty verdict, Rodrigo, Fernando's courtier, in love with Clotilde, is determined to rescue her. Meanwhile, Anagilda exults in her upcoming coronation and Clotilde's death. Just as Clotilde prepares to stab herself with Fernando's sword, Rodrigo enters and tries to strike the king. But Coltilde places herself between the men, and Fernando, moved by her devotion, frees her. Anagilda tries to stab Clotilde, but she is foiled by Alfonso, who succeeds in having the would-be assassin spared. Rodrigo is also spared, and Clotilde is finally crowned queen.

Major roles: Fernando, king of Castile (ten); Coltilde, his wife, a French princess (sop); Anagilda, his mistress (sop); Rodrigo, a nobleman in love with Clotilde (bass); Alfonso, captain of the royal bodyguard, in love with Anagilda (alto); Sancio, Anagilda's father (bass); and Padiglio, Fernando's servant (ten).

According to John Roberts (see below), this opera was the source of many Handel borrowings, for example, sections in his *La Resurrezione*, *Acis*, *Rodelinda*, and *Water Music*.

SCORE: ms repr., ed. John H. Roberts, *Handel Sources. An Anthology of the Sources of Handel's Borrowings*, II (New York: Garland Publishing, 1986).

Francesca da Rimini, opera in three acts by Hermann Goetz, completed by Ernst Frank; libretto (Ger) by the composer after Dante's *L'Inferno*, V, 116–42. First performance (posthumous) September 30, 1877, Mannheim. First British performance (in an English translation by M. E. Browne) December 3, 1908, London, His Majesty's Theatre.

The story concerns two lovers, whose lives end in tragedy when they are betrayed by a jealous rival.

Also set by Riccardo Zandonai (1914, Turin), among others.

SCORE: vs ed. Ernst Frank (Leipzig: F. Kistner [1878]).

LIBRETTO: German ed. Georg Richard Kruse (Leipzig: P. Reclam Junior [1910]).

BIBLIOGRAPHY: Edgar Istel, "Hermann Goetz," *ZIMG* III, no. 5 (February 1902), 177–88.

Frau ohne Schatten, Die (The Woman without a Shadow), opera in three acts by Richard Strauss; libretto (Ger) by Hugo von Hofmannsthal. First performance October 10, 1919, Vienna, with Maria Jeritza (the Empress), Lotte Lehmann (the Dyer's Wife), Aagard Oestvig (the Emperor), Richard Mayr (Barak), and Lucie Weidt (the Nurse); conducted by Franz Schalk. First U.S. performance September 18, 1959, San Francisco, with Edith Lang (the Empress), Marianne Schech (the Dyer's Wife), Sebastian Feiersinger (the Emperor), Mino Yahia (Barak), and Irene Dalis (the Nurse); conducted by Leopold Ludwig. First British performance May 2, 1966, London, Sadler's Wells, Hamburg Opera, with Enriqueta Tarrés (the Empress), Gladys Kuchta (the Dyer's Wife), Ernst Kozub (the Emperor), and Franz Crass (Barak); conducted by Leopold Ludwig.

The story revolves around two couples, the Emperor and his half-supernatural Empress, and the dyer Barak and his wife. The Empress is unable to bear a child because she cannot cast a shadow; unless she has a child, however, her husband will be turned to stone. The nurse leads her to the selfish dyer's wife, who is willing to part with her shadow for payment. When Barak convinces the Empress not to accept the shadow, her nobility restores her husband to life, and she receives a shadow. Barak is reconciled with his spouse.

Major roles: the Empress (sop); the Emperor (ten); the dyer's wife (sop); Barak, the dyer (bass-bar); and the nurse (mezzo).

For detailed synopses and analyses, see C/*MS*, 119–37; D/*RS*, II, 151–218; K/*KOB*, 828–31; and M/*RSC*, 169–91.

This massive work, with its symbol-laden text, contains some of Strauss' finest orchestral writing.

SCORE: fs (London: Fürstner and B&H, 1946); vs ed. Otto Singer (Berlin: A. Fürstner, 1919).

LIBRETTO: German, the same.

BIBLIOGRAPHY: Walther Gurewitsch, "In the Mazes of Light and Shadow. A Thematic Comparison of *The Magic Flute* and *Die Frau ohne Schatten*," *OQ* I/2 (Summer 1983), 11–18; Kurt Oppens, "*Die Frau ohne Schatten* blickt in den Spiegel. Strauss Opern und ihre Quellen in der Literatur,'' *Oper* (1967), 37–43; *Richard Strauss Blätter* II (1971), VII (1976) [entire issues]; Walter Ritzer, *"Die Frau ohne Schatten.* Gedanken zum Libretto,'' *ÖMz* XXIX (1974), 328–40; Harold Rosenthal, "London Diary,'' *Opera* XVII (1966), 499–501 [on British premiere]; Lynn Shook, "The Myth and the 'Shadow,' '' *Opera* XVIII (1967), 454–59; Frank J. Warnke, "Theater of the Supernatural: Roots of Hofmannsthal's Libretto,'' *ON* XLII/19 (April 1, 1978), 10–14.

DISCOGRAPHY: Nilsson, Rysanek, Hesse, King, and Berry, conducted by Böhm, Vienna State Opera, DG 415472–1 GJ3 (3), 415472–2 GH3 (3 compact discs), 415472–4 GH3 (3 tapes).

Freischütz, Der (The Free-Shooter), Romantic opera in three acts by Carl Maria von Weber; libretto (Ger) by Friedrich Kind after Apel and Laun's *Gespensterbuch.* First performance June 18, 1821, Berlin, Schauspielhaus, with Caroline Seidler (Agathe), Carl Stümer (Max), Johanna Eunicke (Aennchen), Heinrich Blume (Caspar), Herr Wauer (Cuno), Herr Rebenstein (Ottokar), Herr Wiedemann (Kilian), and Herr Hillebrand (Samiel); conducted by the composer. First U.S. performance March 2, 1825, New York (in English), with Kelly, De Luce, Keene, Clarke, and Richings. First British performance July 22, 1824, London, Lyceum (in English with music adapted by William Hawes) with Miss Noel, Miss Povey, John Braham (Max), Mr. Baker, Mr. Bartley, and Mr. Bennett.

The story takes place shortly after the Thirty Years' War. The hunter Max, who is in love with the forester's daughter, Agathe, must win a shooting contest in order to become the head ranger. In his desperation to win he seeks the assistance of the hunter Caspar, who has sold his soul to the evil Samiel and is obligated to bring him another soul. Samiel agrees to give the magic bullets to Max, who ignores Agathe's pleas not to go to the Wolf's Glen to get them. The bullets help Max win the contest, and he fires his last shot at a white dove. The shot kills Caspar, who had planned to have Agathe killed instead. When Samiel comes to claim Max, an old hermit appears and says that Max will be spared in answer to Agathe's prayers.

For detailed synopses and musical analyses, see C/*NMC*, 275–84; K/*KOB*, 132–40; N/*SGO* II, 260–305; and W/*CMW*, 210–39.

Major roles: Ottokar, ruling prince (bar); Cuno, princely forester (bass); Agathe, his daughter (sop); Aennchen, her friend (sop); Caspar and Max, young hunters (bass, ten); Samiel, the wild hunter (speaker); Kilian, a rich peasant (bar); and a hermit (bass).

The overture, in symphonic first-movement form, consists almost completely of melodies from the opera and sets the stage for the first truly Romantic German opera. The famous Wolf's Glen ("Wolfsschlucht") scene, at the end of the second act, is the epitome of Romanticism; it depicts the supernatural by various musical means such as string tremolo and choruses singing in unison. Other striking sections include Max's soliloquy in the first act, "Durch die Wälder,'' Agathe's beautiful prayer of the second act, "Leise, leise, fromme Weise'' and her cavatina of Act III, "Und ob die Wolke.'' Also noteworthy are the third-act bridesmaids' chorus "Wir winden dir den Jungfernkranz" and the hunters' chorus that opens the final scene, "Was gleicht wohl auf Erden," and the hermit's cautionary aria that ends the work, "Leicht kann des Frommen Herz auch wanken."

Julius Hopp's parody appeared in Vienna in 1867.

SCORES: fs (Berlin: Schlesinger'sche Buch u. Musikhandlung, 1843; repr. Farnborough, Hants: Gregg International, 1969); fs autograph facsimile ed. Georg Knepler (Leipzig: Peters, 1978); fs ed. Joachim Freyer (Leipzig: Peters, 1977); vs ed. Carl Zulehner (Mainz: BSS, 1822).

LIBRETTO: German (Berlin, n.p., ca. 1821).

BIBLIOGRAPHY: *L'Avant-scène opéra* CV (1988), entire issue; Attila Csampai and Dietmar Holland, eds., *Carl Maria von Weber. Der Freischütz: Texte, Materialien, Kommentare* (Reinbeck bei Hamburg: Ricordi-Claussen and Bosse, Leck, 1981); Carl Dahlhaus, "Weber's *Freischütz* und die Idee der deutschen Oper," *ÖMz* XXXVIII/7–8 (1983), 380–83; Edward J. Dent, "Der Freischütz," *Opera* V (1954), 137–44; Harry Goldschmidt, "Die Wolfsschlucht—eine schwarze Messe?," *Beiträge zur Musikwissenschaft* XXX (1988), 8–27; same issue, Joachim Herz, "Aspekte der Freischütz-Interpretationen," 37–41; Kurt Pahlen, *Carl Maria von Weber. Der Freischütz* (Munich: Wilhelm Goldmann Verlag, 1982); George R. Price, "Washington Irving's Librettos," *ML* XXIX/ 4 (1948), 348–55; William Upton, "Max and Agathe vs. Rudolph and Agnes, et al.," *Notes* IV/2 (1946–1947), 217–24; Hermann von Waltershausen, *Der Freischütz: Ein Versuch über die musikalische Romantik* (Munich: H. Bruckmann, 1920).

DISCOGRAPHY: See B/*OOR*, 131–41.

VIDEO: Ligendza and Kramer, Würtemburgische Staatsoper, Stuttgart, NVC DEFF01.

Freunde von Salamanca, Die (The Friends from Salamanca), Singspiel in two acts by Franz Schubert; libretto (Ger) by Johann Mayrhofer. Composed in 1815. First performance (Nos. 4, 8, 9, 12) December 19, 1875, Vienna, Musikverein; conducted by Johann Herbeck. First performance (staged) May 6, 1928, Halle, with dialogue by Günther Ziegler. The libretto and consequently the spoken dialogue have been lost.

Major roles: Olivia (sop), Eusebia (sop), Laura (sop), Alonso (ten), Diego (ten), Tormes (ten), and Fidelio (bass).

SCORES: fs, Schu/*AGA* XV/2, no. 4 (1888); Schu/*NGA* II/3 (nyp).

DISCOGRAPHY: Mathis, Moser, Prey, and Holl, Austrian Radio, conducted by Guschlbauer, DG 2702–126 (2); reviewed by John W. Freeman, "Records," *ON* XLVI (February 27, 1982), 37.

Friedenstag (Day of Peace), opera in one act by Richard Strauss; libretto (Ger) by Joseph Gregor (see below) after Calderón's *La Rendención de Breda* (1625). First performance July 24, 1938, Munich, with Viorica Ursuleac (Maria), Hans Hotter (Commandant), Ludwig Weber (Holsteiner), Georg Hann (Sergeant-Major), Julius Patzak (the Private), and Peter Anders (the Piedmontese); conducted by Clemens Krauss. First U.S. performance April 2, 1957, Los Angeles, University of Southern California; conducted by Walter Ducloux. First British performance March 28, 1985, London (concert), with Florian Cerny (Commandant), Roger Bryson (Holsteiner), John Treleaven (Sergeant-Major), and Marie Hayward Segal (Maria); conducted by Nicholas Cleobury.

The story is set during the Thirty Years' War, in 1648, just before the Peace of Westphalia ends the fighting. Facing impending starvation and dwindling ammunition, the Commandant of the town of Breda refuses to surrender to the attacking Holstein forces. He devises a plan to blow himself up along with the garrison and his young wife, Maria, just as the enemy thinks the town is giving up. Moments before the fuse is to be lit, the Commandant is informed that the enemy desires peace. Urged by his wife, he accepts the offer of peace, and the former foes embrace each other.

For a detailed synopsis, see K/*KOB*, 844–46.

Stefan Zweig was the original librettist for the work, but the Nazis opposed a second collaboration between Strauss and the Jewish writer (*Die schweigsame Frau** was the first). Rather than work in secret, as the composer had suggested, Zweig convinced the reluctant Strauss to accept Gregor. Gregor is the ostensible librettist of the opera, therefore, but Zweig worked closely with him to hammer out the details. The fact that the Nazis permitted an opera that praises peace and brotherhood to be performed in 1938 is remarkable in itself.

Major roles: Commandant of the besieged town (bar); Maria, his wife (sop); a Sergeant-Major (bass); a Piedmontese (ten); and the Holsteiner, commanding the besieging army (bass).

"Ein feste Burg" is quoted several times in the opera, including in the final scene, as peace is at hand. The work closes with a joyful choral hymn in C major, "Wagt es zu denken, wagt zu vertrauen."

SCORES: fs (Berlin-Grunewald: J. Oertel, 1938); vs ed. Ernst Gernot Klussmann (Berlin: A. Fürstner, 1938, 1940).

BIBLIOGRAPHY: Martin Bernheimer, "Current Chronicle. Munich," *MQ* XLVIII (1962), 117–18; Kenneth Birken, *Friedenstag and Daphne: An Interpretive Study of the Literary and Dramatic Sources of the Two Operas by Richard Strauss* (New York and London: Garland Publishing, 1989); Julian Budden, "Music in London. Revivals," *MT* CXXVI (1985), 357; Harald Kaufmann, *Ästhetische Manipulationen bei Richard Strauss. 'Friedenstag' und 'Schweigsame Frau'* (Vienna, 1969); M/*RSC*, 299–312; Pamela H. Potter, "Strauss's *Friedenstag*: A Pacifist Attempt at Political Resistance," *MQ* LXIX (1983), 408–24.

Fürstin Tarakanowa, opera in three acts by Boris Blacher; libretto (Ger) by the composer and Karl Koch. First performance February 5, 1941, Wuppertal.

On the basis of a false document, Princess Tarakanowa, who lives in the house of Duchess Tschernomski in Livorno, believes that she is a daughter of the dead Tsarina Elisabeth, giving her a claim to the Russian throne, now held by Catherine the Great. The Russian admiral Orloff, whose fleet has stopped in

Livorno, has been given the job of apprehending Tarakanowa, and he invites her to a party, which she attends, despite the warnings of the Duchess. Orloff, overcome by Tarakanowa's beauty, is temporarily confused but then resolves to carry out his mission. The Polish lieutenant Krasinski attempts to open Tarakanowa's eyes to Orloff's deception, but in vain. She accompanies Orloff to his ship and is arrested.

Major roles: Princess Tarkanowa (sop), Admiral Orloff (bar), Lieutenant Krasinski (ten), and Duchess Tschernomski (mezzo).

=G

Gedultige Sokrates, Der (The Patient Socrates), comic opera in three acts by Georg Philipp Telemann; libretto (Ger) by Johann Ulrich von König after Nicolo Minato's *La Patienza di Socrate con due moglie*, set by Antonio Draghi in 1680 and by Antonio Caldara in 1731. First performance January 28, 1721, Hamburg. The opera was revived in 1934, in Krefeld.

The story, set in Athens during the war with Sparta, involves a fictional law by which each man must be married to two ladies at the same time. Socrates is not spared; in addition to the nagging Xantippe, he is saddled with the uncouth but patient Amitta. A side story involves a one-time pupil of Socrates, Melito, who is forced to choose two wives from the three women selected by his father. When Melito is unable to decide, Socrates is called in to make the decision.

Major roles: Socrates, a philosopher (bar); Xantippe and Amitta, his wives (sops); Rodisette and Edronica, Athenian princesses (sops); Melito and Antippo, Athenian princes (tens); Nicia, the Prince, Melito's father (bass); Aristophanes, a satiric poet and enemy of Socrates (ten); Alcibiades and Xenophon, students of Socrates (tens); and Plato (bass).

The music ranges from da capo arias to folklike pieces. It also includes pastoral scenes.

SCORES: fs ed. Bernd Baselt, *Werke*, XX (Kassel: Bär, 1967); vs ed. Bernd Baselt (Leipzig: Deutscher Verlag für Musik, 1966).

Geisterinsel, Die (The Island of Ghosts), Singspiel in three acts by Johann Friedrich Reichardt; libretto (Ger) by Friedrich Wilhelm Gotter and Friedrich Hildebrand von Einseidel after Shakespeare's *The Tempest*. First performance July 6, 1798, Berlin, Nationaltheater, with Margarethe Schick (Miranda). The libretto was originally written for Mozart, who died just at its completion.

In this version of the Shakespeare play, Miranda, banished to an island with her father, Prospero, is decorating the grave of the kind spirit Maja, when she learns that the evil Sycorax and her son, Caliban, are coming to threaten her and her father this very evening. Ariel, a spirit and Prospero's servant, comes with the news that he has sighted a ship. The wicked Caliban, thwarted in his attempts to seduce Miranda, promises to gain his revenge when Prospero is helpless to stop him. The act ends as a storm is gathering and the island's inhabitants see a ship in distress.

Prospero discovers Fernando, son of the king of Naples, near the shore. When Miranda falls in love with the young man almost immediately, Prospero intervenes and tells him he must be tested before he can have her love. Meanwhile, as Fabio, one of Fernando's companions, goes off to find his friend, Caliban tricks two other companions, Stefano and Oronzio, to help him dispose of Prospero.

Fernando and Miranda are counting corals at Maja's grave, but he is unable to control himself and prostrates himself before Miranda. The lovers are dispersed by thunder and lightning, and when the ground opens up to release Sycorax, Maja also appears in earthly form and blocks the path of the witch. Caliban, Oronzio, and Stefano fail in their attempt to kill the sleeping Prospero; their target is really a vision conjured up by Ariel. Caliban then throws himself into the sea. A ship lands and from it disembarks Ruperto, who had originally banished Miranda and Prospero. He informs them that the tyrant of Milan has been killed and the populace is demanding Prospero's return. Prospero thanks the faithful spirits who had served him for nine years and destroys his magic staff.

Major roles: sung: Prospero, former duke of Milan and a magician (bass); Miranda, his daughter (sop); Fernando, prince of Naples (ten); Fabio, a noble youth (sop); Ariel, a sylph (sop); Caliban, a gnome, son of Sycorax (bass); spoken: Ruperto, a sailor; pantomime: Maja, a shade (to be played by the leading tragic actress); Sycorax, a shade (to be played by the leading tragic actor).

The score is noteworthy for its emphasis on male voices, for example "Hurtig!" (no. 30), a quartet for basses. The opera also includes among its highlights Miranda's aria "Trockne, trockne deine Thränen" (Act II, no. 22), set in rondeau form and written specifically for Margarethe Schick.

Johann Rudolf Zumsteeg's setting of the text was first performed on November 7, 1798, in Stuttgart. Another setting was made by Friedrich Fleischmann for a performance on May 19, 1798, in Weimar. See also *Der Sturm.**

SCORES: fs ms repr. in *German Opera 1770–1800*, VII, ed. Thomas Bauman (New York and London: Garland, 1985); vs (Berlin: Neue berlinische Musikhandlung, 1799).

LIBRETTO: German, repr. in *German Opera 1770–1800*, XX, *Librettos III*, ed. Thomas Bauman (New York and London: Garland Publishing, 1986).

Geisterliebe (Love of Spirits), opera in two acts by Isang Yun; libretto (Ger) by Harald Kunz. First performance June 20, 1971, Kiel, with Martha Mödl (Priestess), Takao Okamura (Son-Long), Martin Häusler (Pan Hon-San), Ingeborg Helmreich (Ah-Hsiu), and Pamela MacFarland (Liang-Kung); conducted by Hans Zenda.

Two ghosts in the form of vixens want to be united in love with a human being. The object of their love is a young teacher. They have a demon take the form of a mandarin and a mendicant monk to express their love and convince the teacher to sacrifice himself for them. He dies, and they obtain human existence.

Major roles: narrator (alto); Pan Hon-San, a young teacher (ten); Son-Long, a demon (bass); Ah-Hsiu, a fox (sop); and Liang-Kung, a fox (mezzo).

SCORE: vs ed. Wolfgang Gayler (Berlin: B&B, 1971).

BIBLIOGRAPHY: James Helme Sutcliffe, "Reports: Foreign," *ON* XXXVI (September 1971), 27 [on premiere].

Genoveva, opera in four acts by Robert Schumann; libretto (Ger) by Robert Reinick after Ludwig Tieck's *Das Leben und Tod der heiligen Genoveva* (1799) and Friedrich Hebbel's *Genoveva* (1843). First performance June 25, 1850, Leipzig, with Mayer, Günther-Bachumann, Wiedemann, and Brussin; conducted by Reitz. First British performance December 6, 1893, London, Drury Lane Theatre. Revived October 26, 1975, Zwickau; conducted by Hans Storck.

The story is set in medieval times. It concerns the noble Genoveva of Brabant, whose husband, Siegfried, has left to join a crusade. She is framed by the villainous Golo, whose overtures she has rejected, and by the sorceress Margaretha, who convinces Siegfried of his wife's infidelity by means of a magic mirror. Genoveva is almost killed before her husband overcomes these machinations and returns to her.

Major roles: Genoveva (sop); Golo (ten); Margaretha, a sorceress (alto); and Siegfried (bar).

Other settings include L. Huth's *Golo und Genoveva* (1838, Neustrelitz); José Rogel's zarzuela *Genoveva de Brabante* (1868, Madrid); Jacques Offenbach's comic *Geneviève de Brabant* (1859, Paris); Alexander Ecklebe (1937, Hagen); Natanaël Berg (1947, Stockholm); and Detlev Müller-Siemens' *Genoveva* oder *Die weisse Hirschkuh* (1977).

SCORES: fs, Robert Schumann, AGA, series IX, no. 3, 1–309 (Leipzig: B&H, 1886; repr. Farnborough, Hants: Gregg International, 1967); vs (Leipzig: B&H, ca. 1886).

BIBLIOGRAPHY: Walter Ducloux, "Schumann's Theatre Revisited," *ON* XXI (November 19, 1956), 12–14; Linda Siegel, "A Second Look at Schumann's *Genoveva*," *MR* XXXVI (1975), 17–41; Reinhold Sietz, "Zur Textgestaltung von Robert Schumanns 'Genoveva,' " *Mf* XXXIII (1970), 395–410; James Helme Sutcliffe, "Genoveva Revived," *Opera* XXVII (1976), 273–75; Hellmuth Christian Wolff, "Schumanns 'Genoveva' und der Manierismus des 19. Jahrhunderts," in *Beiträge zur Geschichte der Oper* (Regensburg: Bosse, 1969), 89–94.

DISCOGRAPHY: Fischer-Dieskau, Moser, and Schreier, Gewandhaus Orchestra of Leipzig, conducted by K. Masur, EMI C157–02.914/16 (3).

Geschichte von Aucassin und Nicolette, Die (The Story of Aucassin and Nicolette), opera in two acts by Günter Bialas; libretto (Ger) by Tankred Dorst
after a thirteenth-century fable. First performance December 12, 1969, Munich,
with Friedrich Lenz, Raimund Grumbach, and Keith Engen (the three Antons);
Hans Wilbrink (Aucassin); Ingeborg Hallstein (Nicolette); Karl Christian Kohn
(the king); Hans Günter Nöcker (Vizgraf); and Lilian Benningsen (the wet nurse);
conducted by Matthias Kuntzsch.

The tale is narrated by the three Antons. Aucassin, the son of a count, is in
love with Nicolette, a Moorish girl, and so the count sends his son into battle.
When his father dies, Aucassin becomes the count and is reunited with his
beloved.

Major roles: Aucassin (bar); Nicolette (sop); Garin von Beaucaire (bass);
Cirage, a black nurse (alto); Vizgraf/teacher (bass-bar); and King Karthago (ten).

BIBLIOGRAPHY: Desmond Graham, "Reports: Foreign," *ON* XXXIV (February 7,
1970), 29–30 [on premiere]; Wolfram Schwinger, "Die zweite Oper von Bialas," *Musica*
XXIV (1970), 31–33 [on premiere].

Gespenst von Canterville, Das (The Ghost of Canterville), television opera in
one act by Heinrich Sutermeister; libretto (Ger) by the composer, freely adapted
from Oscar Wilde's tale. First performance September 6, 1964, Mainz, ZDF,
with Barry McDaniel (the ghost); Maria von Ilosvay (Miss Umney); Lisa Otto
(Mrs. Otis); Doris Herbert (Virginia); and Benno Hoffmann, Charles Brauer,
and Franz Schaftheitlin (speaking roles); conducted by Kurt Graunke.

The opera opens in the lobby of a London hotel, with all the characters present.
It moves to the old English castle called Canterville, which is haunted by a
ghost. This does not intimidate the new owners of the castle, the Otis family,
who in fact must be "saved" by their pretty daughter, Virginia.

Major roles: the ghost (bar); Lord Canterville (speaking part); Miss Umney
(mezzo); Washington Otis (ten); Virginia Otis (sop); Hiram B. Otis, American
minister (speaking role); Mrs. Barbara Otis (sop); and Simon Canterville, student
(speaking part).

BIBLIOGRAPHY: Erich Limmert, "Oper für Nachtschwärmer," *NZM* XXV (1964),
504.

Gespenstersonate (Ghost Sonata), chamber opera by Aribert Reimann; libretto
by the composer and Uwe Schendel after August Strindberg. First performance
September 25, 1984, Berlin, Hebbel Theater, with David Knutson (Arkenholz),
Hans Günter Nöcker (Director Hummel), Horst Hiestermann (the "Colonel"),
Martha Mödl (the Mummy); and Gudrum Sieber (the "Colonel's" daughter);
conducted by Friedemann Layer.

The nightmarish plot is set in the seemingly solid home of the "Colonel."
The characters are tied to each other by guilt, secrets, and crimes, and in the
course of the work the players are unmasked, as they wait for death. The cripple

reveals that the "Colonel," a former servant, had once stolen his fortune, and that the cripple is the real father of the "Colonel's" daughter. The "Colonel," further, is a murderer, and he hangs himself on his wife's orders. The happiness of a young couple, a student, and the daughter is destroyed, and when the student begs Christ for help, the young girl falls dead.

Major roles: the student, Arkenholz (ten); the old man, Director Hummel (bar); the Mummy, the "Colonel's" wife (mezzo); the "Colonel" (ten); and the young lady, supposedly the "Colonel's" daughter (sop).

The chamber opera is accompanied by twelve instrumentalists. The modern score includes quarter-tone writing and a prepared piano.

Also set by Julius Weismann (1930, Munich).

BIBLIOGRAPHY: James Helme Sutcliffe, "Reports: Foreign," *ON* XLIX (March 2, 1985), 32 [on premiere].

Gezeichneten, Die (The Stigmatized Ones), opera in three acts by Franz Schreker; libretto (Ger) by the composer. First performance April 25, 1918, Frankfurt, conducted by Ludwig Rottenberg. Revived January 20, 1979, Frankfurt, Opera, with June Card (Carlotta), Barry Mora (Count Tamare), Günter Reich (Duke Adorno), and Werner Götz (Alviano); conducted by Michael Gielen.

After writing the libretto for Alexander von Zemlinsky, Schreker decided to compose the music himself. The story, set in Renaissance Italy, concerns the hunchbacked nobleman Alviano Salvago, who shuns the object of his love, Carlotta, because of his ugliness. His handsome and unprincipled rival, Count Vitelozzo Tamare, goes after Carlotta. When the hunchback finds the two together, he kills the Count, but he becomes insane when Carlotta rejects him.

Major roles: Alviano Salvago (ten), Carlotta (sop), and Count Vitelozzo Tamare (bar).

SCORE: vs ed. Walter Gmeindl (Vienna: UE, 1916).

LIBRETTO: German (Vienna: UE, 1918).

BIBLIOGRAPHY: Nicholas Chadwick, "Franz Schreker's Orchestrational Style and Its Influence on Alban Berg," *MR* XXXV/1 (February–May 1974), 29–46; Christopher Hailey, "Reports: Foreign," *ON* XLIII (March 24, 1979) [on 1979 revival]; Wolfgang Molkow, "Die Rolle der Kunst in den frühen Opern Franz Schrekers," *S/FSS*, 83–94; Paul Moor, "Frankfurt Opera Gains Fresh Momentum . . . Die Gezeichneten," *HiFi/MA* XXIX (June 1979), 39; Werner Oehlmann, "Schreker und seine Oper," in *S/FS*, 71–75.

Giuditta, opera in three acts by Franz Lehár; libretto (Ger) by Paul Knepler and Fritz Löhner. First performance January 20, 1934, Vienna, Staatsoper, with Richard Tauber and Jarmila Novotna; conducted by the composer. Although the forty-two performances were sold out, the opera was skewered by the Viennese press and has not enjoyed much success since. It was Lehár's last full-scale work.

The story concerns Giuditta, a passionate woman who deserts her husband for an Italian soldier. The soldier becomes a nightclub pianist, and she ends up alone as a bitter nightclub singer.

Major roles: Manuel Biffi (bar); Giuditta, his wife (sop); and Octavio, a captain (ten).

The title character's sensuous fourth-scene waltz, "Meine Lippen, sie küssen so heiss," is still a favorite in the concert repertoire of sopranos.

BIBLIOGRAPHY: Bernard Grun, *Gold and Silver* (London: W. H. Allen, 1970), 246–53; Victor Junk, "Wiener Musik," *ZMW* CI (1934), 310–12 [on premiere].

DISCOGRAPHY: Moser, Linder, Gedda, and Finke, Munich Radio Orchestra and Chorus, conducted by Boskovsky, Angel DS–3947 (2); Gueden, Loose, Kmentt, Dickie, Majkut, Berry, Czerwenka, and Pröghöf, Vienna State Opera and Chorus, conducted by Moralt, London A4333 (3).

Glückliche Hand, Die (The Lucky Hand), "Drama mit Musik" in one act by Arnold Schoenberg; libretto (Ger) by the composer. First performance October 14, 1924, Vienna, Volksoper, with Alfred Jerger (the Man), Hedy Pfundtmayr (the Woman), and Josef Hustinger (the Gentleman); conducted by Fritz Stiedry. First U.S. performance April 11, 1930, Philadelphia, Academy of Music, with Ivan Ivantzoff (the Man); conducted by Leopold Stokowski. First British performance (public) October 17, 1962, London, Royal Festival Hall, with Derrick Olsen (the Man); conducted by Michael Gielen.

The allegorical story opens with a man in the clutches of a mythological monster. He is urged by a chorus of six men and six women to believe in reality and reject what is unobtainable. In subsequent scenes the protagonists do not notice those around them, and the work closes with the man again in the grasp of the monster, with the chorus commenting on his difficult and hopeless search.

Major role: the Man (bar).

The music is, like that of *Erwartung*,* a mixture of singing and *Sprechstimme*. The work attempts to relate all the stage elements to each other, e.g., speech, color, and movement. Schoenberg was particularly concerned with emphasizing the symbolism of colors, which vary according to the action and music.

SCORES: fs (Vienna: UE, 1916); vs ed. Eduard Steuermann (Vienna: UE, 1923).

LIBRETTO: German (Vienna: UE, 1911).

BIBLIOGRAPHY: Richard Beck, "The Sources and Significance of *Die glückliche Hand*," *Kongress-Bericht Berlin* (1974), 427–29; John Crawford, "*Die glückliche Hand*: Further Notes," *Journal of the Arnold Schoenberg Institute* IV/1 (June 1980), 68–76; ———, "*Die glückliche Hand*: Schoenberg's *Gesamtkunstwerk*," *MQ* LX (1974), 583–601; Erwin Stein, "Schönberg's Fantastic 'Glückliche Hand,' " *MA* (February 25, 1930), 7, 31, 50; Ena Steiner, "*The Happy Hand*: Genesis and Interpretation of Schoenberg's *Monumentalkunstwerk*," *MR* XLI (1980), 207–22; Oscar Thompson, "Philadelphia. Orchestra and League of Composers Sponsor American Premiere of 'Die glückliche Hand,' " *MA* L (April 25, 1930), 5, 14.

DISCOGRAPHY: Oliver, Columbia Chorus and Orchestra, conducted by Craft, Columbia M2S–679 (2), reviewed by C. J. Luten, "Records," *ON* XXXIII (April 12, 1969), 34. Nimsgen, conducted by Boulez, BBC Symphony and Chorus, CBS 13M–37883.

Goldene Bock, Der (The Golden Ram), opera in four acts by Ernst Krenek; libretto (Ger) by the composer. First performance June 16, 1964, Hamburg, with Helga Pilarczyk (Medea), Tom Krause (Jason), Helmut Melchert (Pelias), Elisabeth Steiner (Glaukis), Ilse Hollweg (Nephele), Toni Blankenheim (Chattahoochie), and Vladimir Ruzdak (Athamas); conducted by the composer.

In this modernized and sometimes graphically brutal version of the Greek legend, Athamas sends his nephew, Jason, to America, to recover the golden fleece. Jason finds it, with Medea's help, on an Indian reservation. He needs a way to get money for his family, so he and Medea, now his wife, get jobs as a servant couple to Pelias, the brother-in-law of Athamas. Pelias has become a rich American shipping magnate (a parody of Aristotle Onassis). Jason, who has tired of Medea, turns his attentions to Glaukis, and when Medea discovers this, she tricks Jason into killing Glaukis; Medea then kills her children, whom Jason had fathered. Jason, hounded by the police because of the many unexplained deaths, returns to Greece. But he is prevented from entering his homeland by a customs official, who seizes the fleece. Jason, realizing his efforts were in vain, dies.

Major roles: Medea (sop); Athamas, king of Joklos (bar); Pelias, his brother-in-law (ten); Jason, his nephew (bar); Espali, an exiled prince (bar); Glaukis, his daughter (sop), and Chattahoochie, an Indian (bar).

The music features twelve-tone writing.

SCORES: fs (Kassel: Bär, 1964); vs (Kassel: Bär, 1964).

LIBRETTO: German (Kassel: Bär, 1964).

BIBLIOGRAPHY: Ruth Berges, "Reports," *ON* XXIX (December 12, 1964), 31 [on premiere]; Hans Joachim, "Antike ohne Illusionen," *NZM* CXXV (1964), 310–11 [on premiere].

Götterdämmerung. *See* **Der Ring des Nibelungen**.

Grab des Mufti, Das oder **Die zwey Geizigen** (The Mufti's Grave or The Two Misers), Singspiel in two acts by Johann Hiller; libretto by August Gottlieb Meissner after C. G. Fenouillot de Falbaire's setting for A. E. M. Grétry's *Les Deux Avares* (1770, Fontainebleau). First performance 1779, Leipzig?

Although this is not an abduction story, it is set in a "Turkish" locale (Smyrna) and it has certain similarities to Mozart's *Die Entführung*.* The lovers Karl and Wilhelmine are being mistreated by their miserly relatives, Gripon and Martin, who have fled France because of their shady dealings. The two misers have not only cheated their young wards but also plan to rob the grave of the Mufti in search of treasure. The faithful Madelon overhears the plan and warns the lovers, who triumph in the end and receive their rightful inheritance. Exoticism is featured in the second act, which includes several Janissary numbers, e.g., "Es lebe der Wein," which is similar to Mozart's "Vivat Bacchus."

Major roles: Karl (ten); Wilhelmine (sop); Madelon, Wilhelmine's confidante (sop); Martin (ten); and Gripon (bass).

Also set by Gotthilf von Baumgarten (1778, Breslau).

LIBRETTO: German (Leipzig: Dykische Buchhandlung, 1776).

Graf von Gleichen, Der (The Count of Gleichen), opera in two acts by Franz Schubert; libretto (Ger) by Eduard von Bauernfeld. Composed 1827 (unfinished). First performance December 15, 1865, Vienna, Redoutensaal, edited and conducted by Johann Herbeck (Introduction); October 10, 1868, Vienna, Redoutensaal, edited and conducted by Herbeck (Nos. 5a, 7).

Seeking a "Turkish-Christian" mixture, the librettist wrote a story which combines characters from both worlds. Returning from the East, the Graf von Gleichen has brought home a second wife. He is able to reconcile her with his first wife, a European.

Major roles: Graf von Gleichen (bass), Fatime (sop), Kurt (ten), Hassan (bass), and Suleika (sop).

Schubert left the opera in a fragmentary state.

The story was also set by Franz Volkert (1815, Vienna); Karl Eberwein (ca. 1822, Weimar); and A. Wandersleb (1847, Gotha).

SCORES: fs, Schu/NGA, II/14 (nyp); facs. ed. Ernst Hilmar (Tutzing: Schneider, 1988); vs ed. Johann Herbeck (Vienna: C. A. Spina's Nachfolger, ca. 1868).

LIBRETTO: German (Vienna: Karl Fromme, 1907).

BIBLIOGRAPHY: Alexander Ringer, "On the Question of 'Exoticism' in 19th Century Music," *Sm* VII (1965), 122.

Graf von Luxemburg, Der (The Count of Luxemburg), operetta in three acts by Franz Lehár; libretto (Ger) by Alfred Maria Willner and Robert Bodanzky. First performance November 12, 1909, Vienna, with Otto Storm (René), Annie von Ligety (Angèle), Louise Kartousch (Juliette), and Max Pallenberg (Prince Basil). First U.S. performance September 16, 1912, New York, Amsterdam Theater (in English, with a text by Glen MacDonough), with George Leon Moore (René), Anne Swinburne (Angèle), Frank Moulan, and Fred Walton. First British performance (in English, with a text by Basil Hood), with Bertram Wallis (René), Lily Elsie (Angèle), Huntley Wright, and W. H. Berry.

Set in Paris at the turn of the century, the story concerns Prince Basil, who is in love with the singer Angèle. Since he does not wish to marry a commoner, he arranges for the poor Count René to go through with a marriage in name only and then divorce, leaving the ennobled Angèle free for the Prince. René and Angèle have come disguised to the wedding; when René sees his "bride" at the theater and falls in love with her, he does not realize who she is. After they discover their true identities, Angèle is angered that René would have agreed to such an arrangement, but her own feelings get the better of her. The Prince is unable to wed her, since the Czar is forcing him to wed a real Countess, leaving René and Angèle free to enter into a real marriage. All ends happily.

Major roles: René, Count of Luxemburg (ten), Angèle (sop), and Prince Basil (bar).

Striking numbers include Angèle's entrance in the first act, as she considers the "marriage" she is about to undertake, "Heut noch werd' ich Ehefrau," and her farewell to a singing career, "Soll ich? Soll ich nicht?"

SCORE: vs (Vienna: Glocken-Verlag, c. 1909).

LIBERTTO: German (Vienna: W. Karczag & K. Wallner, c. 1909).

DISCOGRAPHY: Popp and Gedda, conducted by Mattes, Vienna Operetta Records VOR 500 (2). Schramm and Schock, conducted by Stolz, Vienna Operetta Records VOR 560 (1). Excerpts: Jenkins and Tierney, Sadler's Wells Opera Orchestra, conducted by Wordsworth (Eng). That's Entertainment 1050.

Gräfin Maritza (Countess Maritza), operetta in two acts by Emmerich Kálmán; libretto (Ger) by Julius Brammer and Alfred Grünwald. First performance February 28, 1924, Vienna, with Betty Fischer (Countess Maritza), Hubert Marischka (Tassilo), Max Hansen (Baron Zsupán), Richard Waldemar, and Hans Moser. First U.S. performance September 18, 1926, New York, Schubert Theater (in an English adaptation by Harry B. Smith), with Yvonne d'Arle (Countess Maritza), Walter Woolf (Tassilo), Odette Myrtil (the gypsy Manja), Vivian Hart, Harry K. Morton, George Hassell (Prince Populescu, originally Baron Zsupán in the original version) First British performance 1938, London, with Maria Losseff (Countess Maritza), John Garrick (Tassilo), and Douglas Byng (Count Zsupán).

In an effort to raise money for his sister Lisa's dowry, the former army officer Count Tassilo, using the pseudonym Torok, gets a job with the wealthy Countess Maritza. The Countess, anxious to rid herself of unwanted suitors, says that she has become engaged and stages an elaborate party. To her dismay, one of her guests, Baron Kolomon Zsupán claims to be her intended, and she cannot deny it without creating a scene. The Countess starts to flirt with Torok but discovers his true identity and, feeling that he has come to work for her in order to obtain her fortune, demands that he depart. Suddenly, Princess Bozena Guddenstein, Torok's aunt, appears and reveals that she has assumed all Torok's debts and has given him a substantial sum to live on. Realizing her suspicions were unfounded, the Countess reveals that she is in love with Torok.

Major roles: Countess Maritza (sop); Tassilo (ten); and Baron Zsupán (bar).

This popular operetta includes the famous aria of Tassilo/Torok, "Komm, Zigan, komm, Zigan, spiel mir was vor," containing typical "gypsy" melodies. It enjoyed a run of 318 performances when it opened in 1926.

SCORE: English vs ed. Arthur Stanley, Eddie Garr (London: B. Feldman & Co., 1938).

LIBRETTO: German (Leipzig and Vienna: W. Karczag, 1924).

DISCOGRAPHY: See M/*IRR*, 85–86.

Griechische Passion, Die (The Greek Passion), opera in two acts by Bohuslav Martinů; libretto (English) by the composer after Jonathan Griffin's English translation of Nikos Kazentzakis' novel *Christ Recrucified*. First performance (English) June 9, 1961, Zurich, Stadttheater, with Sandra Warfield (Katerina), Heinz Borst (Fotis), James Pease (Grigoris), and Glade Peterson (Manolios); conducted by Paul Sacher. First performance (Ger) June 1971, Zurich. First U.S. performance April 26, 1981 (Brian Large's English version), New York, Metropolitan Opera, the Indiana University School of Music, with Tim Noble (Grigoris), David Rampy (Panait), Rebecca Field (Katerina), and Daniel Brewer (Manolios); conducted by Bryan Balkwill. First British performance April 29, 1981, Cardiff, Welsh National Opera, with John Mitchinson (Manolios), Richard Van Allan (Grigoris), Helen Field (Katerina), and Arthur Davies (Yannakos); conducted by Sir Charles Mackerras.

Martinů's last opera was written with a performance at Covent Garden in mind (where it was performed in 1985). The libretto exists in English and German versions. The story is set on a stony, barren mountain in Greece. The plot intertwines the themes of villagers chosen for the annual Passion play and the plight of refugees uprooted by the Turks. The shepherd Manolios is selected to play Christ, and the young widow Katerina is cast as Mary Magdalen, and both urge the villagers to accept the refugees, against the opposition of the priest. As the story unfolds, Manolios is killed by Panait, who is to play Judas.

For a plot synopsis, see K/*KOB*, 1303-7.

Major roles: Katerina (sop); Grigoris (b-bar); Manolios (ten); Fotis (b-bar); Panait (ten); and Yannakos, a peddler (ten).

BIBLIOGRAPHY: Winton Dean, "Reports," *Opera* XXXII (1981), 744–46 [on British premiere]; Elisabeth Forbes, "Music in London," *MT* CXXVI (1985), 107; Nicolas Kenyon, "Musical Events" [on the U.S. premiere], *NY* (May 18, 1981), 166; Brian Large, "Martinů's 'Greek Passion,' " *Opera* XXXII (1981), 344–49 [on British premiere]; John Warrack, "Martinů's New Opera at Zurich," *Opera* XII (1961), 510–12.

DISCOGRAPHY: Cullis, Field, Savory, Mitchinson, Lawton, and Tomlinson, Czech Philharmonic Chorus, Brno State Phil, conducted by Mackerras, Supraphon 1116–3611/ 2 (2, in English), reviewed by John W. Freeman, *ON* XLVI (March 6, 1982), 37.

Grossmüthige Tomyris, Die (The Generous Tomyris), Singspiel in three acts by Reinhard Keiser; libretto (Ger) by Johann Joachim Hoë, a translation of Domenico Lalli's *L'Amor di figlio non conosciuto*, set by Tommaso Albinoni and Alessandro Scarlatti in 1715 as *Tigrane* (Venice, Naples). First performance July 1717, Hamburg, Theater an der Gänsemarkt. Revived winter 1978, Hamburg (concert), with Faye Robinson (Tomyris), Gabriele Fuchs (Meroë), and Anthony Rolfe Johnson (Tigranes); conducted by Jürgen Jürgens.

Tomyris is in love with Tigranes, one of her young officers. He in turn loves Meroë, whose father, Cyrus, was killed by Tomyris. When an attempt is made on Tomyris' life, Tigranes, fearing that Meroë will be implicated, takes the blame for the act. The infuriated queen condemns Tigranes to death, but Meroë confesses her guilt. Tomyris becomes magnanimous and forgives the wrongdoing.

For a detailed plot summary, see the *Kritischer Bericht* of the full score, edited by Klaus Helm.

Major roles: Tomyris, Queen of Messagets (sop); Meroë, Princess of Persia and Cyrus' daughter (sop); Policares, King of Lydia (ten); Doraspe, King of Damascus (bass); Tigranes, army commander (ten); Orontes, a general (bass); and Laytyrus, confidant of Meroë (ten).

The work includes Tomyris' beautiful aria "Strahlt, ihr Sterne, meine Liebe."

SCORE: fs ed. Klaus Zelm (Munich: G. Henle, 1975).

LIBRETTO: German (Hamburg: Greflinger, 1717).

BIBLIOGRAPHY: Hans Christoph Worbs, " 'Die grosssmüthige Tomyris' in Hamburg," *Musica* XXXII (1978), 265–66 [on revival].

Gülnare, oder **Die persische Sklavin** (Gulnare, or the Persian Slave Girl), Singspiel in one act by Franz Xaver Süssmayr; libretto (Ger) by Friedrich Karl Lippert after J. B. Marsollier's *Gulnare, ou l'Esclave persanne* [sic], set by Nicolas Dalayrac in 1798, in Paris. First performance July 5, 1800, Vienna, Kärntnertortheater.

This exotic work is set in a seraglio near Ispahan, capital of Persia. It involves the beautiful and clever Gülnare, who is in love with her master, Osmin, a kindly man, unlike his Mozartean namesake in another, earlier exotic opera, *Die Entführung aus dem Serail*.* Osmin is forced to put Gülnare up for sale because he needs money to ransom his father. He and the girl arrive at the court of the Persian prince Dely to seek a buyer. A likely customer is the old and miserly Ibrahim, a high official, but Gülnare begs Dely to spare her such a fate. The kindly ruler pays the ransom and reunites Gülnare with her beloved Osmin.

Major roles:. Gülnare (sop); Osmin (ten); Ibrahim (bass); Seid, servant of Dely (ten); and Dely, a Persian prince (ten).

Echoes of "Es lebe Sarastro" in *Die Zauberflöte** may be found in the chorus of tenor slaves in "Der Fürst von seltnen Gaben." Other noteworthy numbers include Gülnare's Romance, "Liebe, wer kann deiner Macht widerstehen," in which she is accompanied by a mandoline and harp, and Ibrahim's comic "Ich liebe wohl ein schönes Weib." The opera closes with the joyful finale praising love, "Liebe, du Göttin der Herzen."

SCORE: no printed score; copyist's score in Vienna, Nationalbibliothek, Musiksammlung (K. T. 198).
LIBRETTO: German (Vienna: J. Wallishausser, 1800).

Gunlöd, opera in three acts by Peter Cornelius; libretto (Ger) by the composer. Composed 1864–1874, unfinished. Completed by Carl Hoffbauer. First performance with alterations by Ernst Lassen on May 6, 1891, Weimar.

Disillusioned by the failure of *Der Barbier von Bagdad,* * Cornelius decided to follow a strictly Wagnerian path in his third (and last) opera. He chose his subject matter from the early Scandinavian mythology of the *Edda.* Taken from the *Hâmavâl* 12, 13, the story concerns Odin (Wodan), the God of Light, who has gained access to the giant Suttung's castle by turning himself into a worm. Warned by Gunlöd (Gunlada), Suttung hides the golden goblet that is filled with the precious mead. Gunlöd, overcome by love, gives Odin the mead, and he flees with it. The text ends with the death of Suttung and Gunlöd. Cornelius sketched but did not complete a fourth act. He dedicated the text to Wagner.

Major roles: Odin (ten), Suttung (bass) Gunlöd (mezzo), and Hela (alto).

SCORES: fs ed. Max Hasse, *Peter Cornelius, Werke,* V (Leipzig: B&H, 1905); vs, the same (c. 1894).

BIBLIOGRAPHY: Anna Amalie Abert, "Zu Cornelius' Oper *Gunlöd,*" in C/*PCK*, 145–54.

Günstling, Der (The Favorite), opera in three acts by Rudolf Wagner-Régeny; libretto (Ger) by Caspar Neher. First performance February 20, 1935, Dresden.

The opera is set in London about 1550. Renard wants to prove to Queen Mary that Fabiani is unfaithful and thereby ruin him. Fabiani tells Gil that he has seduced the latter's wife, Jane, and Gil swears revenge. Fabiani's treachery is unveiled to the Queen, who, despite her love for him, lets him be punished, and Gil and his wife are reunited.

Major roles: Queen Mary (Maria) Tudor of England (sop); Fabiano Fabiani, an adventurer and favorite of the Queen (ten); Gil, a man of the people (bar); Jane, an orphan and Gil's wife (sop); Simon Renard, a minister (bass); and Erasmus, an old man from Naples (speaking part).

SCORE: vs (Vienna: UE, 1934).

Günther von Schwarzburg, Singspiel in three acts by Ignaz Holzbauer; libretto (Ger) by Anton Klein. First performance January 5, 1777, Mannheim, with Herr Raaf (Günther), Herr Fischer (Rudolf), Mlle. Danzy (Anna), Mlle. Strasser (Asberta), and Herr Hartig (Karl).

The story is set in and around Frankfurt. Anna is in love with Karl and wishes to wed him; she is encouraged by his mother, Asberta, who believes that such a union would help Karl become the new emperor. Rudolf, Anna's father, also supports the union, but Asberta plots against him, since he supports Günther for the position. Günther is elected but, through Asberta's machinations, is poisoned. Anna disappears and is presumed dead. Karl, who has laid seige to the city, is warned by a disguised Anna that it was his mother who caused all the trouble. Anna and Karl enter the court, where Karl asks Rudolf for Anna's hand in marriage and tells the dying Günther that he is his friend. Günther names Karl as his successor and, as he expires, calls for unity and peace.

Although the work is called a Singspiel, it contains recitatives and was designed as the first step in the creation of a grand national opera in German.

Major roles: Günther, Count of Schwarzburg (ten); Rudolf, Count Palatine and Elector (bass); Anna, his daughter (sop); Asberta, widowed Queen of Bohemia (sop); and Karl, King of Bohemia and son of Asberta (ten).

SCORE: fs ed. Hermann Kretzschmar, *DDT*, VIII–IX (1902), rev. Hans Joachim Moser (Wiesbaden: B&H, 1957).

Guntram, opera in three acts by Richard Strauss; libretto (Ger) by the composer. First performance May 10, 1894, Weimar, with Heinrich Zeller (Guntram) and Pauline de Ahna (Freihild). Strauss shortened the opera and thinned out the orchestration in 1940. First U.S. performance January 19, 1983, New York, Carnegie Hall (concert), with Ilona Tokody (Freihild) and Reiner Goldberg (Guntram); conducted by Eve Queler.

Using the works of Richard Wagner as a cue, Strauss set his first opera in a medieval German town, complete with knights and Minnesingers. The hero, Guntram, belongs to a secret society, the Streiter der Liebe, which has vowed to end the suffering caused by Duke Robert's harsh rule. Another member is his teacher, Friedhold. Guntram falls in love with the Duke's wife, Freihild, after he prevents her from killing herself. He kills the ruler in a fight, but he is filled with guilt and he renounces his beloved and his secret society. He leaves in an effort to find salvation.

For a detailed plot summary and musical analysis, see M/*RSC*, 1–20.

Major roles: Freihild, daughter of the old Duke (sop); Duke Robert, her husband (bar); Guntram, a singer (ten); and Friedhold, a singer (bass).

The opera includes a long monologue by Guntram, "Ein glückliches Los," in the first act and his "Ich schaue ein glänzend prunkendes Fest" in the second, which recalls Lohengrin's narrative.

SCORES: fs (Munich: J. Aibl, 1894); vs ed. Otto Singer (Munich: J. Aibl, 1894).

BIBLIOGRAPHY: George Movshon, "Guntram," *HiFi/MA* XXXIII (June 1983), 18 [on U.S. premiere]; Andrew Porter, "Musical Events," *NY* (February 28, 1983), 100, 102, 103 [on U.S. premiere].

DISCOGRAPHY: Windgassen, South German Radio Orchestra, conducted by Rischner (Ital), Melodram 103 (m); Tokody, Goldberg, Sólyom-Nágy, and Gáti, Hungarian State Orchestra, Hungarian Army Chorus, conducted by Queler (Ger), CBS 12M–39737 (2).

=H

Hamlet, opera in three acts by Humphrey Searle; libretto (Ger) by the composer, a shortened version of the Shakespeare text. First performance March 5, 1968, Hamburg, Staatsoper, with Sylvia Anderson (Ophelia), Kerstin Meyer (the Queen), Ronald Dowd (Claudius), Tom Krause (Hamlet), Toni Blankenheim (Polonius), Willi Hartmann (Laertes), and Heinz Blankenburg (Horatio); conducted by Matthias Kuntzsch. First British performance April 18, 1969, London, Covent Garden, with Anne Howells (Ophelia), Patricia Johnson (Gertrude), Ronald Dowd (Claudius), Victor Braun (Hamlet), and David Hughes (Laertes); conducted by Edward Downes.

The setting sticks very closely to the Shakespeare version, with six minor characters deleted. The music is written in a twelve-tone idiom, and the characters have themes that are derived from the basic series. The work opens with an orchestral section to evoke the ghost. Among the highlights is Ophelia's mad scene, written in a modernistic folksong style.

Major roles: Ophelia (sop); the Queen (mezzo); Claudius (ten); Hamlet (bar); and Polonius (bar).

Other settings of the Shakespeare play include Francesco Gasparini (1705, Venice); Domenico Scarlatti (1715, Rome); Luigi Caruso (1789); Gaetano Andreozzi (1792, Padua); Josef Schuster's "Karrikatur" (1809, Vienna); Saverio Mercadante (1822, Milan); Max Maretzek (1843, Brünn); Antonio Buzzolla (1848, Venice); Alexander Stadtfeld (1853, perf. 1857, Darmstadt); Franco Faccio (1865, Genoa); Ambroise Thomas (1868, Paris); Julius Hopp, in the parody *Hammlet* [sic] (1874, Vienna); Aristide Hignard (1888, Nantes); Edward Keurvels (1891, incidental music); Leslie Heward (1916, unfin.); Janis Kalnins' *Hamlets*, in Estonian (1936, Riga); Sándor Szokolay's *Hamlet*, in Hungarian (1968, Budapest); Hans Ulrich Engelmann's *Ophelia* (1969, Hanover); Pascal Bentoiu's *Hamlet*, in Rumanian (1971, Bucharest); Kelterborn's *Ophelia* (1984, Schwetzingen); and Wolfgang Rihm's *Hamletmaschine* (1987, West Berlin).

BIBLIOGRAPHY: Frank Granville Barker, "Reports," *ON* XXXIII (June 14, 1969), 31 [on British premiere]; Andrew Porter, "Reports," *MT* CIX (1968), 457–58 [on premiere]; James Helme Sutcliffe, "Reports: Foreign," *ON* XXXII (April 20, 1968), 29 [on premiere].

Hans Heiling, Romantic opera in a prologue and three acts by Heinrich Marschner; libretto (Ger) by Eduard Devrient after Theodor Körner. First performance May 24, 1833, Berlin, with Caroline Grünbaum (Anna) and Eduard Devrient (Hans Heiling); conducted by the composer. First British performance December 2, 1953 (in an English translation by Peter Branscombe), Oxford, with Jack Townend (Hans Heiling), Thetis Balcker (Queen of the Earth Spirits), Barbara Rawson (Anna), and Inez Holmes (Gertrud); conducted by Jack Westrup.

Like Wagner's Flying Dutchman, Heiling is a half-human, half-spirit character in love with a mortal woman, in this case the peasant girl Anna. When she finds out who he is, she flees to her former lover, the hunter Konrad. Hans swears revenge on the two, but his mother, the Queen of the Earth Spirits, convinces him to return to the underworld.

Major roles: Hans Heiling (bar); Anna, his beloved (sop); his mother, Queen of the Earth Spirits (sop); Gertrud, Anna's mother (alto); and Konrad, a huntsman (ten).

Much of the music is written in a Singspiel-like style, while forward-looking elements can be found in the choral writing and the extended use of chromatic passing tones. Among the vocal highlights are the melodrama and Lied at the opening of the second act.

SCORES: fs ed. Gustav F. Kogel (Leipzig: C. F. Peters, 190–); vs ed. Gustaf F. Kogel (Leipzig: F. Hofmeister, ca. 1893).

BIBLIOGRAPHY: Peter Heyworth, "Opera in London," *Opera* V (1954), 54–55 [on British premiere].

Hans Sachs, opera in three acts by Albert Lortzing; libretto (Ger) by the composer, Philipp Reger, and Philipp Jakob Düringer after a play by the same name by Johann Ludwig Franz Deinhardstein. First performance June 23, 1840, Leipzig.

The story has a number of resemblances to Wagner's later *Die Meistersinger von Nürnberg** (see the Laue book below). The older shoemaker, Hans Sachs, is in love with Kunigunde, daughter of the goldsmith Steffen. He tricks his opposition, the alderman Eoban Hesse, at a song competition judged by Emperor Maximilian I, and he wins the hand of his beloved. The other two lovers are Kordula, the niece of Sachs, and the young apprentice shoemaker, Börg.

Major roles: Emperor Maximilian I (bass-bar); Master Steffen (bass); Kunigunde, his daughter (sop); Kordula, his niece (sop); Hans Sachs, master shoemaker (bar); Börg, his apprentice (buffo ten); and Eoban Hesse, councillor in Augsburg (ten).

Adalbert Gyrowetz composed *Hans Sachs im vorgerückter Alter* in Dresden in 1834, and excerpts of the Singspiel were performed on December 26, 1836, and December 26, 1837, in Vienna.

SCORE: vs ed. Richard Kleinmichel (Vienna: UE, 1912).

BIBLIOGRAPHY: Hellmuth Laue, *Die Operndichtung Lortzings* (Würzburg, 1932), 102ff; Hans Christoph Worbs, *Albert Lortzing* (Reinbeck bei Hamburg: Rowohlt Taschenbuch, c. 1979), 54–57.

Hänsel und Gretel (Hansel and Gretel), opera in three acts by Engelbert Humperdinck; libretto (Ger) by Adelheid Wette, sister of the composer, after a tale by the brothers Grimm. First performance December 23, 1893, Weimar, with Kayser, Schubert, Tibelti, Finck, and Wiedley; conducted by Richard Strauss. First U.S. performance October 8, 1895 (in English), New York, with Jacques Bars (Peter), Jeanne Douste (Gretel), Marie Elba (Hänsel), Meisslinger, Gordon, Brani, and Johnston, and conducted by Anton Seidl; November 25, 1905 (in German). First British performance December 26, 1894, London, Daly's Theatre (in an English translation by Constance Bache), with Elba, Douste, Edith Miller (the witch), Lennox, and Copland, and conducted by Louis Arditi; June 24, 1895, London, Drury Lane Theatre (in German).

Hänsel and Gretel, children of a poor couple, are sent into the woods to gather strawberries after their mother finds them playing instead of working. They lose their way in the forest, and, after singing the beautiful prayer, "Abends will ich schlafen gehen, vierzehn Engel um mich stehn," they fall asleep. When they awaken, their search for food leads them to a gingerbread house, inhabited by a witch. She locks up Hänsel to fatten him up and forces Gretel to work for her, but the clever girl pushes her into the oven, freeing all the children who had been turned into gingerbread cookies. The parents of Hänsel and Gretel, who have been searching for their offspring, are joyously reunited with them.

For detailed synopses and musical analyses, see C/*NMC*, 296–301; K/*KOB*, 303–304; and N/*SGO*, III, 258–90.

Major roles: Gretel (sop); Hänsel (mezzo); Gertrude, the mother (mezzo); Peter, the father (bar); and the witch (mezzo, sometimes sung by a man).

In addition to the prayer cited above, the score has among its beautiful moments Gretel's touching folk song of the first act, "Ein Männlein steht im Walde" and the orchestral prelude before the second act, which is subtitled "The Witches' Ride." The opera has been immensely successful from its start, and today it is a favorite among younger audiences and is often performed during the Christmas season.

Johann Friedrich Reichardt's Singspiel *Hänschen und Gretschen* was performed in 1772 in Leipzig. Peter Schickele, writing under the pseudonym P. D. Q. Bach, has composed the parody *Hansel and Gretel and Ted and Alice*.

SCORES: fs ed. composer (Mainz: BSS, 1895); vs, the same (1894).

LIBRETTO: German (Elberfeld: Sam. Lucas, ca. 1893).

BIBLIOGRAPHY: Bruno Bettelheim, "Lessons for Life," *ON* XLIII (December 23, 1978), 11–14, 39; Hans Josef Irmen, "Auf dem Wege zu 'Hänsel und Gretel,' " in *Die Odysee des Engelbert Humperdinck* (Siegburg: Druck Schmitt 1975), 53–75.

DISCOGRAPHY: See M/*IRR*, 72.

Happy End, comedy with music in three acts by Kurt Weill; text (Ger) adapted by Elisabeth Hauptmann from a story by Dorothy Lane, song texts by Bertolt Brecht. First performance September 2, 1929, Berlin, Theater am Schiffbauer-damm, with Carola Neher (the lieutenant), Oscar Homolka (Bill), Peter Lorre (Dr. Nakamura), Kurt Gerron (Sam), and Helene Weigel ("the Fly"); conducted by Theo Mackeben.

The sparse plot revolves around a young Salvation Army worker who is trying to protect the souls of a group of gangsters and falls in love with one of them, Bill. It is not unlike the story of the 1950 *Guys and Dolls*, based on Damon Runyon's 1932 short story, "The Idyll of Sarah Brown."

Major roles: Salvation Army lieutenant (female); Bill, a gangster (male); Dr. Nakamura (male); and "the Fly" (female).

The creators of the piece intended to capture the spirit and success of *Die Dreigroschenoper*,* but the discord accompanying its creation and its tumultuous first production led to its early exit from the repertoire. Brecht himself remained dissatisfied with the work and removed it from his collected opus. The musical highlights include "Surabaya Johnny," the "Bilbao Song," and the "Sailor's Song."

SCORE: vs (Vienna: UE, 1929).

BIBLIOGRAPHY: S/*DS*, 137–40.

DISCOGRAPHY: Lenya, conducted by Brückner-Ruggeberg, CBS Special Products COS–2032.

Harmonie der Welt, Die (The Harmony of the World), opera in five scenes by Paul Hindemith; libretto (Ger) by the composer. First performance August 11, 1957, Munich, Prinzregenttheater, with Liselotte Fölser (Susanna), Hertha Töpper (Katharina), Richard Holm (Wallenstein), Josef Metternich (Kepler), Luise Camer (his daughter), and Marcel Cordes (Tansur); conducted by the composer.

The action, which takes place between 1608 and 1630, concerns the life of the astronomer Kepler, especially his musical theories of planetary motion. It includes several substories, such as the rise and fall of Wallenstein; Kepler's love affair with Susanna, who becomes his wife; his mother, who is almost hanged for being a witch; his assistant Ulrich, who ultimately turns against him; and Tansur, a street vendor, who becomes the major domo of Wallenstein.

Major roles: Emperor Rudolf II/Ferdinand II/Sol (bass); Johannes Kepler, a mathematician (bar); Susanna, Kepler's eventual wife/Venus (sop); Katharina,

Kepler's mother/Luna (alto); Tansur, a street vendor and major domo of Wallenstein (bass).

The work is symphonically conceived, and the orchestra plays a major role.

SCORE: vs composer (Mainz: BSS, 1957).

LIBRETTO: the same.

BIBLIOGRAPHY: Andres Brimer, "Die erste Textfassung von Paul Hindemiths Oper 'Die Harmonie der Welt,' " in *Festschrift für einen Verleger* (Mainz: Ludwig Strecker, 1973), 203–41; Everett Helm, "Harmony of the World," *MR* XVIII (1957), 320–21; Alfred Rubeli, "Johannes Keplers Harmonik in Paul Hindemiths Oper *Die Harmonie der Welt*," in *Kepler Symposium*, ed. Rudolf Haase (Linz: Linzer Veranstaltungsgesellschaft, 1982), 107–16; Frank J. Warnke, "Germany. Celestial Harmonies," *ON* XXII (October 14, 1957), 6–7 [on premiere].

Häusliche Krieg, Der. See *Die Verschworenen.*

Heimkehr aus der Fremde, Die (The Return from Abroad), *Liederspiel* in one act by Felix Mendelssohn; libretto (German) by Karl Klingemann. First performance December 26, 1829, Berlin (private); April 10, 1851, Leipzig (public). First British performance (as *Son and Stranger*, in an English translation by H. F. Chorley) July 7, 1851, London, Little Haymarket.

The village magistrate, who is celebrating his fifty years in office, is saddened because of the absence of his son, Hermann. His ward, Lisbeth, who is the fiancée of Hermann, has been true to him all this time. A stranger, the boorish Kauz, appears in the village, and tries to make Lisbeth forget about Hermann. Hermann himself returns secretly and takes Lisbeth into his confidence. She dismisses Kauz's clumsy advances, put forth in his patter song "Ich bin ein vielgereister Mann," somewhat like Beckmesser, in *Die Meistersinger*,* during a serenade under her window at night. Hermann then locks up Kauz. The next morning, when Kauz is released and he tries to pass himself off as the long-lost son, Hermann steps forth and unmasks his competitor.

Major roles: the magistrate (bass), the mother (alto), the ward Lisbeth (sop), Kauz (bass), and Hermann (ten).

The work, which consists of fourteen numbers, is written in a very simple style. It was penned for the silver anniversary of the composer's parents, at whose house it was first performed.

SCORES: fs ed. Julius Rietz M/*AGA*, Series XV/8, no. 122 (Leipzig: B&H, 1848); vs (Leipzig: B&H, 1850).

BIBLIOGRAPHY: Eric Werner, *Mendelssohn. Leben und Werk in neuer Sicht* (Zurich: Atlantis, 1980), 187–91.

DISCOGRAPHY: Donath, Schwarz, Schreier, Fischer-Dieskau, and Kusche, conducted by Wallberg, Munich Radio Orchestra and Chorus, Arabesque 1838, A–9138 (tape).

Hero und Leander, opera in seven scenes by Günter Bialas; libretto (Ger) by Eric Spiess after Franz Grillparzer's lyric tragedy *Des Meeres und der Liebe Wellen* (1831). First performance September 8, 1966, Mannheim, with Ursula Rheins (Hero), Georg Volker (Leander), and Franz Mazura (priest); conducted by Horst Stein.

Following the Greek legend, Leander of Abydos and Hero are deeply in love. Leander swims across the Hellespont every night to see his beloved, who lives in Sestos. When Leander drowns, Hero throws herself into the sea.

Major roles: Hero (sop), Leander (bass), priest (bass), Naukleros (ten), and Janthe (alto).

The work has a choral hymn as its prologue.

Other settings of the legend include Paul Caró's version (1912, Breslau).

SCORE: vs ed. Heinz Moehn (Kassel, New York: Bär, 1966).

BIBLIOGRAPHY: G. A. Trumpff, "Das Musikleben. Mannheim," *NZM* CXXVII (1966), 397–98 [on premiere].

Hieronymus Knicker, comic opera in two acts by Karl Ditters von Dittersdorf; libretto (Ger) by Christian August Vulpius. First known performance July 7, 1789, Vienna, Leopoldstadttheater.

The aging Hieronymus Knicker wishes to marry, and he opposes the match between his niece, Luise, and Karl Feldberg. He is tricked into consenting to their marriage, and in the end he is stuck with Henriette, to whom he had once proposed in a moment of weakness.

Major roles: Hieronymus Knicker (bass); Luise, his niece (sop), and Ferdinand, his nephew (ten) (both are his wards); Karl Feldberg, Luise's lover (ten); Henriette, Luise's maid (sop); Röschen, daughter of a farmer (sop); and Tobias Filz, a rich merchant (silent role).

The work contains an overture and twenty-two numbers.

SCORE: vs (Leipzig: Seigfried Schmiedt, 1792).

BIBLIOGRAPHY: D/ *CDD*, 5–17.

Hin und zurück (There and Back), "Sketch mit Musik" by Paul Hindemith; libretto (Ger) by Marcellus Schiffer. First performance July 17, 1927, Baden-Baden with J. Klemperer, Mergler, Lothar, Giebel, and Pechner; conducted by Ernst Mehlich. First U.S. performance April 22, 1928, Philadelphia. First British performance July 14, 1958, London, Sadler's Wells, the Opera de Camera of Buenos Aires, with Chevaline, Valori, and Feller; conducted by Sivieri.

In this satirical story the husband murders his unfaithful wife, but the plot is then reversed; the wife comes back to life, the lover leaves, and the husband puts back his revolver.

The whole work takes about twelve minutes.

Major roles: Robert (ten); Helene, his wife (sop); the professor (bar); and the male nurse (bass).

SCORE: vs composer (Mainz: BSS, 1927).

Hochzeit, Die (The Wedding), unfinished opera in three acts by Richard Wagner; libretto (Ger) by the composer after Johann Gottlieb Büsching's book *Ritterzeit und Ritterwesen* (1823). Composed 1832. The completed portions were first performed on February 13, 1938, in Leipzig, at the Neues Theater. A possible first performance took place in 1833 in Würzburg, at the Musikverein.

Major roles: Kadolt (bass), Admund (ten), Ada (sop), Arindal (ten), Hadmar (bass), Lora (sop), and Harald (ten).

Wagner abandoned the work, his first opera. Only the introduction, chorus, and septet remain.

SCORE: fs ed. Michael Balling, W/ *RWW*, XII (1912; repr. 1971).

BIBLIOGRAPHY: F. Muncker, "Richard Wagners Operntext 'Die Hochzeit,' " *Die Musik* I (1901–1902), 1824; Edgar Istel, "Wagners erste Oper 'Die Hochzeit' auf Grund der autographen Partitur dargestellt," *Die Musik* IX (1909–1910), 331–51; Max Koch, "Die Quellen der 'Hochzeit,' " *Richard Wagner Jahrbuch* IV (1912), 105.

Hochzeit des Camacho, Die (The Wedding of Camacho), opera in two acts by Felix Mendelssohn; libretto (German) by Karl Klingemann after an episode in Miguel de Cervantes' *Don Quixote*. First performance April 29, 1827, Berlin, Schauspielhaus. First U.S. performance (concert) May 1, 1875, Chicago. The dialogue is lost.

The plot opens with the farmer Carrasco, who has arranged to have his daughter, Quiteria, marry Camacho, a rich landholder. Quiteria, however, is in love with Basilio, a poor student. In order to prevent the planned marriage, Basilio stages a mock suicide, in which he supposedly stabs himself. A priest is summoned for the final rites, but Basilio refuses to give his final confession unless he is betrothed to Quiteria. Don Quixote, one of Camacho's wedding guests, takes Basilio's side and convinces Camacho to allow the wedding of Basilio and Quiteria, since Quiteria will be a widow by the next day anyway. The priest unites the pair, whereupon Basilio springs up and shows himself to be uninjured—and a happy bridegroom to boot!

This is Mendelssohn's only completed opera. It includes various set pieces, such as Basilio's first-act monologue (no. 3) "Noch tröstet mich das Vorgefühl" and the ballet entr'acte for the wedding ceremony in the second act (no. 14) in which Cupid's warriors are victorious over the champions of wealth (seemingly a bit of social criticism on the part of the librettist). Mendelssohn adds local color here by including a bolero and fandango.

Major roles: Quiteria (sop); Basilio (ten); Camacho (bass); Carrasco (bass); Don Quixote (bass); and Sancho (bass).

SCORE: fs in M/*AGA* XV, no. 121; vs (Leipzig, 1829).

BIBLIOGRAPHY: Heinrich Eduard Jacob, *Felix Mendelssohn und seine Zeit* (Frankfurt: S. Fischer Verlag, 1959), 70–81; S/"MJ," 506–507.

Hochzeit des Figaro, Die (The Marriage of Figaro), Singspiel in two acts by Karl Ditters von Dittersdorf; libretto (Ger) probably by the composer after Beaumarchais' *La folle Journée, ou Le Mariage de Figaro* (1785). First performance possibly 1789, Brünn. It was repeated on June 15, 1801, in Graz. The music is lost.

The characters are the same as in Mozart's *Le Nozze di Figaro* of 1786, but, although Dittersdorf probably hoped to capitalize on the success of the earlier work, his own version soon sank into obscurity.

For another treatment of the Figaro story, see *Figaro lässt sich scheiden.**

LIBRETTO: German (Brünn: Johann Sylvester Siedler, 1789).

BIBLIOGRAPHY: D/*CDD*, 38–40.

Im Weissen Rössl, (The White Horse Inn), operetta in three acts by Ralph Benatzky; libretto (Ger) by Erik Charell and Hans Müller after a farce by Oscar Blumenthal and Kadelburg, *Zum weissen Rössl* (1897). The work includes music by Robert Stolz, Bruno Granichstädten, Eduard Künneke, and Robert Gilbert. First performance November 8, 1930, Berlin, with Trude Lieske (Frau Josepha), Paul Hörbiger (the Emperor), Max Hansen (Leopold), Camilla Spira, and Sig Arno. First U.S. performance October 1, 1936, New York, Center Theater, as *The White Horse Inn*, with a book by David Freedman and lyrics by Irving Caesar, with William Gaxton and Kitty Carlisle. First British performance April 8, 1931, London, Coliseum, in an English translation by Harry Graham, with Amy Augarde, Friedrich Leisteg, Clifford Mollison, Bruce Carfax, Lea Seidl, and George Gee.

Frau Josepha, the proprietess of an inn on the Wolfgangsee in Austria, is loved by two men, Leopold, her headwaiter, and Erich Siedler, a lawyer who is a frequent guest at the hotel. Leopold's jealousy leads to a fierce quarrel with Josepha, and she fires him, only to change her mind when she learns that Emperor Franz Josef is to be a guest at the inn. Leopold again loses his temper when he sees Josepha with Siedler. In despair, the innkeeper confides to the Emperor that she loves Siedler, but the monarch advises her that she would be better off with Leopold. When Leopold comes to say farewell, Josepha tells him that he is no longer her headwaiter but, rather, he has a new post—as her husband. Siedler consoles himself with a new love, the young Ottilie.

Major roles: Frau Josepha, an innkeeper (sop); Leopold, the headwaiter (ten); Erich Siedler, a lawyer (bar), and Emperor Franz Joseph (bar).

The work was immensely popular. Among its many highlights are the love song "Es muss ein wunderbares sein" and the waltz "Im weissen Rössl am Wolfgangsee." Robert Stolz's "Die ganze Welt ist himmelblau" and "Mein Liebeslied muss ein Walzer sein" are additional highpoints.

DISCOGRAPHY: Hallstein, Körner, Köth, Schock, and Philipp, conducted by Fehring. Eurodisc 80838XE (2).

In seinem Garten liebt Don Perlimplín Belisa (In His Garden Don Perlimplín Loves Belisa), opera in four scenes by Wolfgang Fortner; libretto (Ger) by Enrique Beck after Federico García Lorca's erotic play *Amor de Don Perlimplín con Belisa en su jardin* (1931). First performance May 10, 1962, Schwetzingen, Rokokotheater, with Lisa Montoya (Belisa), Helen Raab (Marcolfa), Maria Kallisti (Belisa's mother), and Ernst Gutstein (Don Perlimplín); conducted by Wolfgang Sawallisch.

Don Perlimplín, a rich, older man, has married the young Belisa. In order to keep her happy, he invents a young lover who writes her poetry. Unable to live up to the ideal he has created and to reveal that he is the author of the poems, Perlimplín kills himself.

Major roles: Belisa (sop), mother (col sop), and Perlimplín (bar).

Also set by Vittorio Rieti (1952, Urbana, Illinois); and Balduin Sulzer (1984, Linz).

SCORE: vs ed. Markus Lehmann (Mainz: BSS, 1962).

BIBLIOGRAPHY: Ernst Thomas, "Das Musikleben," *NZM* CXXIII (1962), 276–78 [on premiere].

Inganno fedele, L', oder **Der getreue Betrug** (The Faithful Deception), opera in three acts by Reinhard Keiser; libretto (Ger-It) by Johann Ulrich König. First performance October 1714, Hamburg, Schau-Platz.

This complex story takes place along the Elbe. In the first act, Asterie, dressed as the gypsy Cloris, bemoans the faithlessness of her beloved Sireno, in the aria "Um einen schönen Ungetreuen." She meets the lovers Ismene and Celindo and she learns, to her horror, that Sireno is in love not with her but with Silvamire. When Asterie warns Sireno, he replies with the Italian aria "Per compiacerti, o cara" (a mixture of German and Italian was not uncommon in Keiser's later works; it is present also in Handel's 1705 opera *Almira**). Grulla appears with her wounded foster son Polidor, whom Silvamire nurses, whereupon he declares his love for her. At the opening of the second act, Sireno takes back his ring from Asterie, and she gets another admirer, Celindo, who sings "Locken, die auch Löwen zähmen." The meeting of Ismene and Polidor is interrupted by the appearance of Silvamire, and then by the incensed Sireno, who sings "Vor meiner Rache Strahl."

The third act begins in a large concert room. The various lovers discuss their problems as a cantata is performed. The scene changes to a pastoral setting. Asterie is abducted by a group of four masked shepherds, and her cries draw the attention of Silvamire, Ismene, and Polidor. The masked men, led by Celindo, discover that their prey is not the intended Ismene. The errant Sireno thinks that

Asterie is the spirit of his beloved Cloris. Grulla explains that Polidor and Ismene are really twins. The various lovers are reconciled, including Sireno and Asterie.

Major roles: Silvamire, a noble and rich shepherdess; Asterie, a noble shepherdess, dressed as a gypsy and called Cloris; Ismene, a noble shepherdess, called Melissa, confidante of Silvamire; Sireno, a noble shepherd and lover of music; Polidor, called Melisso, a noble shepherd and lover of art; Celindo, a noble shepherd and lover of the hunt; Elpin, a cow and animal herder; Grulla, an old fisherman's widow and foster mother of Polidor.

SCORES: selections (Hamburg: Friederich Conrad Greflingern, 1714); ed. Max Schneider, new version Hans Joachim Moser (Wiesbaden: B&H, 1958).

Ino, melodrama in one act by Johann Friedrich Reichardt; libretto (Ger) by Johann Christian Brandes. First performance September 4, 1779, Leipzig.

Ino, the daughter of Cadmus, has raised the child of Semele and Jupiter after Semele's death. The goddess Juno, who had brought about Semele's demise, now plots to undo Ino, and she begins by getting Ino's husband, Athamas, to have an affair with Nephele, his first wife. The contrite Athamas returns to Ino, but Juno tells him that he and his sons will be spared only if he kills Ino. He is driven mad by the Furies and kills one son, Learch, after which Ino and the second son, Melizert, jump into the sea, and Athamas runs off. Saved by Jupiter, Ino and Melizert emerge from the sea in a chariot drawn by a Triton.

Major roles: Ino (spoken); Athamas, her husband (spoken); Juno (spoken); a voice (spoken); and two singing choruses.

SCORES: fs ms (Leipzig, 1779); repr. in *German Opera 1770–1800*, IV, ed. Thomas Bauman (New York and London: Garland Publishing, 1985); vs (Leipzig, 1779).

LIBRETTO: German (Berlin, 1781), repr. in *German Opera 1770–1800*, XX, *Librettos III*, ed. Thomas Bauman (New York and London: Garland Publishing, 1985).

Intermezzo, "bürgerliche Komödie" in two acts by Richard Strauss; libretto (Ger) by the composer. First performance November 4, 1924, Dresden, with Lotte Lehmann (Christine) and Joseph Correck (Storch); conducted by Fritz Busch. First U.S. performance (concert) February 11, 1963, New York, New York State Theater (in English), with Phyllis Curtin (Christine), Donald Bell (Storch), Robert Lewis (Baron Lummer), and Mary Davenport (Anna); conducted by Thomas Scherman. First performance (staged, in an English translation by Andrew Porter) February 25, 1977, Philadelphia, Curtis Institute, Walnut Street Theater, with Julia Conwell (Christine) and Carlos Serrano (Storch); conducted by Dino Yannopoulos. First British performance September 2, 1965, Edinburgh, King's Theatre, with Hanny Steffek (Christine), Hermann Prey (Storch), Ferry Gruber (Baron Lummer), and Gertrud Freedman (Anna); conducted by Meinhard von Zallinger.

Strauss wanted to write an opera on a realistic theme. Failing to interest Hofmannsthal in this idea and rejecting Hermann Bahr's sketches for it, Strauss decided to write his own libretto. The result was unabashedly autobiographical. The conductor Robert Storch is married to a talkative and nagging wife, Christine (i.e., Richard and Pauline Strauss). After one of their many arguments, he sets off on a trip to Vienna, leaving the bored Christine to fend for herself. Taking the advice of her maid, Anna, she goes tobogganing, where she meets the young and handsome (but indigent) Baron Lummer. Christine decides to make him her protegé and says that her husband will provide financial support for him.

Christine intercepts a love note she believes was intended for Robert. Enraged, she sends her husband a telegram informing him that she wants a divorce. The telegram interrupts his game of skat (a favorite pastime of Strauss) with some friends, including the conductor Stroh, for whom the love letter was really intended. Stroh finally convinces Christine of her husband's innocence, Baron Lummer gets to meet Robert, and the Storches decide to stay married.

For detailed synopses and musical analyses, see K/*KOB*, 832–35, and M/ *RSC*, 193–214.

Major roles: Christine Storch (sop); Hofkapellmeister Robert Storch, her husband (bar); Anna, the maid (sop); and Baron Lummer (ten).

The opera has never enjoyed great popularity, perhaps because of its rather tasteless story and the lack of extended musical numbers. It does contain beautiful symphonic interludes that connect the fourteen scenes (the interludes are sometimes performed in concert) and an appealing monologue by Christine in the first act, "Ein hübscher Mensch."

BIBLIOGRAPHY: Felix Aprahamian, "Reports," *ON* XXX (November 6, 1965), 30 [on British premiere]; Paul Hamburger, "Strauss's 'Intermezzo,' " *Tempo* CX (September 1974), 2–5; Everette Helm, "Concert Opera," *MA* LXXXIII (April 1963), 28–29 [on U.S. concert premiere]; Frank Merkling, "Reports," *ON* XXVII (March 23, 1963), 32 [on U.S. concert premiere].

DISCOGRAPHY: Popp, Fuchs, Dallapozza, Finke, Fischer-Dieskau, Hirte, Grumbach, Wilsing, and Moll, Bavarian Radio Symphony, conducted by Sawallisch, Electrola IC165–30983/5 (3); reviewed by John W. Freeman, "Records," *ON* XLV (March 7, 1961), 28; released in compact disc format, EMI Angel CDS 7–49337 (2).

VIDEO: Lott and Pringle, Glyndebourne Festival, RM ARTS/BBC INTO1V.

Irische Legende (Irish Legend), opera in five scenes by Werner Egk; libretto (Ger) by the composer after W. B. Yeats' drama *The Countess Cathleen* (1892). First performance August 17, 1955, Salzburg, Festspielhaus, with Inge Borkh (Cathleen), Margarete Klose (Oona), and Kurt Böhme (Aleel); conducted by George Szell. Revised version February 26, 1975, Augsburg, Stadttheater.

Seven animals conspire to seize the souls of humankind by means of starvation and other catastrophes. Wandering the land with her old nurse, Oona, and her lover, the poet Aleel, the Countess Cathleen eventually saves Aleel and the rest of humankind.

Major roles: Cathleen (sop), Aleel (bar), the tiger (bar), the vulture (ten), Oona the nurse (alto), and the apparition of Faust (bass).

The music is written in a twelve-tone style, with four chords as its basis. It also incorporates rhythms from jazz, Indian, and Arab music.

SCORE: vs (Mainz: BSS, 1957).

LIBRETTO: German (the same).

BIBLIOGRAPHY: Ernest de Weerth, "Salzburg: Legends," *ON* XIX (October 17, 1955), 22 [on premiere]; Hans Keller, "Dodecaphoneys," *MR* XVI (1955), 323–29; Hans Werba, "Musik der freien Entscheidung: Werner Egks *Irische Legende*," *ÖMz* X (1955), 231–36.

Irrelohe (Flames of Madness), opera in three acts by Franz Schreker; libretto (Ger) by the composer. First performance March 27, 1924, Cologne, conducted by Otto Klemperer.

The work opens with a song by the aging barmaid Lola, "Einst war ich schön, einst war ich jung," in which she tells her son Peter of Castle Irrelohe's terrible curse: all the men of the noble family are wild and bloodthirsty, and even the scholastic Count Heinrich will one day succumb to his heritage. She refuses to tell Peter who his father is, but her secret is revealed by Christobald, an old man, who recalls that, at a wedding feast thirty years ago at which he was performing, the count raped Lola. Peter, finding out who his father is, is left alone to his thoughts, and he is joined by Eva, daughter of the forester, who tells him that she has met the young Count Heinrich. Peter fears that he will lose Eva to the royal scion.

In the second act, Eva comes to the castle to meet Heinrich and tells him that she is drawn to him. He asks her to marry him, and a beautiful love scene ensues, "Ich kenne kein Auge auf dieser Erden." The act closes with a joyful chorus that is dampened by demonic spirits, "Ein einziges Feuer sei Irreloh'!"

As the third act opens, Eva bids farewell to Peter, who asks that she promise not to dance the bridal dance with Heinrich. When she leaves, Peter, feeling he has been possessed by demons, asks his mother to restrain him. The bridal procession begins, and Lola reprises her opening song, "Einst war ich schön." When the bride and groom appear, Peter grabs Heinrich, who kills the crazed boy; Lola's warning that they are brothers comes too late. Christobald reports that Irrelohe is in flames, and Heinrich collapses, filled with remorse for having killed his brother. Eva lifts him up, telling him that love has overcome wild passion. The work closes with a stirring duet, "In uns ist Sonne, in uns ward es Tag!"

Major roles: Lola (alto), Peter (bar), Heinrich (ten), and Eva (sop).

In addition to the vocal numbers cited above, the opera contains striking orchestral preludes to the first and third acts. It is Schreker's only opera that ends optimistically, with light conquering darkness. The experimental score includes harsh harmonies, bitonality, and polytonality.

SCORE: vs (Vienna: UE, 1923).

BIBLIOGRAPHY: Werner Oehlmann, "Schreker und seine Oper," in S/*FS*, 79–82.

J

Jacobowsky und der Oberst (Jacobowsky and the Colonel), opera in four acts by Giselher Klebe; libretto (Ger) by the composer after Franz Werfel. First performance November 2, 1965, Hamburg, with Oskar Czerwenka (Jacobowsky), Gerhard Stolze (the Colonel), Arlene Saunders (Marianne), and Erwin Wohlfahrt (Szabunievitz); conducted by Leopold Ludwig. First U.S. performance June 27, 1967, New York, Metropolitan (Hamburg State Opera), with the same cast; conducted by Matthias Kuntzsch.

The plot is based on a true story. It concerns Jacobowsky, a Polish Jewish refugee, who meets the Polish Colonel Stjerbinsky on the coast. The latter is waiting to be rescued by an English submarine. Marianne, who is at first attracted to the Colonel, eventually is drawn to Jacobowsky.

Major roles: Jacobowsky (bass), Colonel Stjerbinsky (ten), Szabunievitz (bar), and Marianne (sop).

SCORE: vs (Berlin: B&B, 1965)

LIBRETTO: German (Berlin: B&B, 1965).

BIBLIOGRAPHY: Frank Merkling, "Reports: U.S.," *ON* XXXII (September 9, 1967), 19 [on U.S. premiere]; James H. Sutcliffe, "Reports: Foreign," *ON* XXX (December 18, 1965), 31–32 [on premiere].

Jagd, Die (The Hunt), Singspiel in three acts by Johann Adam Hiller; libretto (Ger) by Christian Felix Weisse after Charles Collé's *La Partie de chasse de Henri IV*, this based on Jean Michel Sedaine's *Le Roi et le fermier*, set by Pierre Monsigny (1762, Paris). First performance January 29, 1770, Weimar, by the Koch troupe.

Christel, son of the village judge Michel, is in love with Hannchen, who has disappeared with the evil Count von Schmetterling. Röse, who loves Töffel, may not wed until her brother Christel does. In the midst of preparing for the impending arrival of the hunting party of the king, Töffel is approached by Hannchen, who tells him how the Count kidnapped her and how she miraculously escaped. She gives Töffel a letter for Christel, in which she explains these happenings. Christel, who has been unable to find his beloved, receives her letter. The lovers are about to meet when they are sent fleeing by an approaching storm, which also separates the king from his party. He is able to scare off two poachers and meets Michel, to whom he describes himself as a member of the king's party. Michel offers the king the comforts of his modest home.

The disguised king witnesses the reunion of Michel and Christel and hears how popular he is in the town. He also hears from Hannchen of the evil deeds of Count von Schmetterling. When Töffel brings in the two poachers, they try to pass themselves off as members of the king's party; the ruler recognizes one of them as the wicked Schmetterling, whom he promptly banishes. The king then bestows a dowry of 2,000 Thaler on each of the two young couples.

Major roles: the king (bass); Michel, a village judge (ten); Marthe, his wife (sop); Christel, their son (ten); Röse, their daughter (sop); Töffel, Röse's lover (bass); and Hannchen, a farmer's daughter (sop).

The work was very popular throughout Germany in the late eighteenth and nineteenth centuries; it reappeared in Leipzig in 1905. It includes the Romance "Als ich auf meiner Bleiche," sung by Hannchen in Act II (No. 17), and the serious aria "Welche königliche Lust!" of Act III (No. 37).

Also set by F. A. Holly (1772, Prague); Johann Schenk (1799, Vienna).

SCORES: fs ms repr. in *German Opera 1770–1800*, I, ed. Thomas Bauman (New York and London: Garland Publishing, 1985); vs (Leipzig: B. C. Breitkopf & Sohn, 1771).

LIBRETTO: German (Berlin: C. U. Ringmacher, 1776); repr. in *German Opera 1770–1800*, XX; *Librettos III*, ed. Thomas Bauman (New York and London: Garland Publishing, 1985).

Jahrmarkt, Der (Der Dorfjahrmarkt) (The Annual Fair/The Annual Village Fair), Singspiel in one act by Georg Benda; libretto (Ger) by Friedrich Wilhelm Gotter. First performance February 10, 1775, Gotha, Schlosstheater, by the Seyler troupe. Johann Adam Hiller divided the piece into two acts and added some music; first performance of this version October 26, 1775, Dresden. The work was also known as *Lucas und Bärbchen*.

The simple story concerns a young peasant couple, Lukas and Bärbchen. Their love is tested by the attentions to Bärbchen by a lieutenant, who tries to get the sergeant Fickfack to induct Lukas. When Lukas flees, he is arrested. He is saved by the actions of the colonel, who demotes the lieutenant.

Major roles: Lukas, a young peasant (ten); Bärbchen, his bride (sop); Eva, his mother (sop); Lenchen, a Tyrolean (sop); the colonel (ten); Fickfack, a sergeant (bass); and the lieutenant (speaking role).

The seventeen numbers include an opening drinking song "Trinkt, trinkt" and Lukas' mournful "Ach, ich liebte sie so zärtlich."

SCORES: fs ed. Th. W. Werner, DDT LXIV (1930); rev. Hans Joachim Moser (Wiesbaden: B&H; Graz: Akademische Druck- u. Verlagsanstalt, 1959); vs as *Der Dorffahrmarkt* (Leipzig, 1776).

LIBRETTO: German, as *Der Jahrmarkt* (Leipzig, 1778).

Jakob Lenz, chamber opera by Wolfgang Rihm; libretto (Ger) by Michael Fröhlich after Georg Büchner's novella *Lenz.* First performance March 6, 1980, Karlsruhe, Badisches Staatstheater, with Paul Yoder (Lenz), Mark Munittrick (Pastor Oberlin), Julius Best (Kaufmann), and Michael Lesch (narrator); conducted by Frithjof Haas. First U.S. performance summer 1981, Bloomington, Indiana University, with Michael Smartt (Lenz), Robert Borg (Pastor Oberlin), and Joseph Levitt (Kaufmann); conducted by Thomas Baldner.

Jakob Lenz (1751–1792), a German poet and protégé of Goethe, went mad and died penniless on the streets of Moscow. This opera covers the period in which a Pastor Oberlin near Strasbourg took care of the writer.

The atonal music is played by an orchestra of eleven instrumentalists. The score, reminiscent of Berg, includes old chorale tunes mixed with modern dissonances.

BIBLIOGRAPHY: Robert Croan, "Reports: North America," *ON* XLVI (December 5, 1981), 51 [on U.S. premiere]; Andrew Porter, "Musical Events," *NY* (January 11, 1988), 80, 82; Edward A. Reed, "Reports: Foreign," *ON* XLIV (June 1980), 41–42 [on premiere].

Janus, opera in three acts by Reinhard Keiser; libretto (Ger) by Christian Heinrich Postel. First performance 1698, Hamburg.

Livia, the wife of the Roman Emperor Augustus, schemes to have her son by an earlier marriage, Tiberius, become the next emperor by having him marry Julia, Augustus' daughter by his first wife, even though Tiberius is betrothed to Agrippina. The victorious general Valerius, whose forces have subdued Parthia, returns to find that his beloved Agrippina is no longer interested in him. Since peace has returned, Augustus says that he will close the temple of Janus, and he offers Valerius any reward he chooses. When Valerius asks for Agrippina, Livia has her abducted.

Philanax comes to tell Valerius that Agrippina has drowned herself in the Tiber, and Tiberius is also told of this turn of events. Agrippina, meanwhile, is told that Tiberius has imprisoned her so that he can wed Julia. Philanax summons the major characters to the temple of Janus, where Livia informs them that Agrippina, who is still alive, is in reality the twin of Tiberius. Since Tiberius cannot marry his sister, he agrees to wed Julia, and Agrippina decides to wed Valerius. In a bow to a contemporary German ruler, Leopold of Austria (1640–1705), the librettist concludes the opera by having a priestess prophesy that in the future Leopold, like Augustus before him, will restore peace after more than a thousand years of fighting.

Major roles: Augustus, Emperor of Rome (bass); Livia, his wife (sop); Tiberius, son of Livia by her first husband (alto); Julia, daughter of Augustus by his first wife (sop); Agrippina, betrothed of Tiberius (sop); Valerius, in love with Agrippina (alto); and Philanax, confidant of Augustus (ten).

The opening of this early Keiser work bears a certain resemblance to "O ruddier than the cherry" of George Frideric Handel's *Acis and Galatea*. The opera is one of the several sources of Handel works (see the Roberts edition below).

SCORE: mss, 1698 libr. repr. in *Handel Sources. An Anthology of the Sources of Handel's Borrowings*, ed. John H. Roberts, I (New York: Garland Publishing, 1986).

Jasager, Der (The Yea-Sayer), school opera in two acts by Kurt Weill; libretto (Ger) by Bertolt Brecht after Elisabeth Hauptmann's translation of Arthur Waley's English adaptation of the Japanese Noh play *Taniko*. First performance June 23, 1930, Berlin; conducted by Kurt Drabek. First U.S. performance April 25, 1933, New York, Henry Street Settlement Music School (in an English translation by Alice Mattulath); conducted by Lehman Engel. First British performance December 1965, BBC; first stage performance March 24, 1966, London, Central Foundation Boys' School; conducted by Patrick Connelly.

The story, a type of morality play, revolves around a teacher and a group of students traveling on a mountain. One of the group needs to bring medicine to his sick mother. When he himself becomes ill, the teacher is informed that the group will be able to continue only by gripping the rocks hand over hand, which the ailing boy obviously cannot do. According to custom he is to be thrown off the mountain to his death in order to avoid a slow and lonely death, but, also following custom, he must be asked for his consent. After the group agrees to bring his mother the needed medicine, he agrees, becoming therefore a "Jasager." The chorus comments after he dies, "Wichtig zu lernen vor allem ist Einverständnis" (Above all one must learn mutual understanding).

The work, meant to be performed by amateurs, is written in a simple style.

For a detailed plot and musical analysis, see *S/DGS*, 159–68.

SCORE: vs (Vienna: UE, 1930, 1957).

BIBLIOGRAPHY: Arthur Jacobs, "Music in London," *Opera* XVI (1966), 418 [on English stage premiere].

Jery und Bätely, Singspiel in one act by Johann Friedrich Reichardt; libretto (Ger) by Johann Wolfgang von Goethe. First performance March 30, 1801, Berlin. Revived June 16, 1916, Weimar.

Bätely is a young, independent Swiss girl. Her brother, Thomas, whom she has not seen since childhood, comes and pretends to be a roughneck. Taking his threats seriously, Jery, who is in love with Bätely, valiantly defends her. Jery's brave efforts win Bätely's love.

First set by Karl Siegmund von Seckendorff (1780, Weimar). The many other

settings include Peter Winter (1790, munich); Schaum (1795, Oels); Gottlob
Benedikt Bierey (ca. 1803, Dresden); Conradin Kreutzer (1810, Vienna); Frey
(ca. 1810, Mannheim); Rietz (1825, Germany); Adolphe Adam's *Le Chalet*
(1834, Paris); Gaetano Donizetti's *Betly, ossia La Capanna Svizzera* (1836,
Naples); and Ingeborg von Bronsart (neé Starck) (1873, Weimar).

Jessonda, opera in three acts by Ludwig Spohr; libretto (Ger) by Eduard Heinrich
Gehe after Antoine Marie Lemierre's tragedy *La Veuve de Malabar*. First per-
formance July 28, 1823, Kassel. First U.S. performance February 15, 1864,
Philadelphia. First British performance June 18, 1840, London, Prince's.

Set in India, the story concerns the young widow Jessonda, who is to be
burned on the funeral pyre of her deceased husband, the Rajah of Goa. This
course of action is being urged by the High Priest, Dandau, and opposed by the
young priest, Nadori. Awaiting her doom, Jessonda reveals to her sister, Amazili,
that she was forced to marry the old rajah, although she was really in love with
a Portuguese general. Nadori appears, with the ritual message of death, and
instantly he falls in love with Amazili. He is determined to save Jessonda from
her gruesome fate.

The Portuguese army has landed and is approaching the city. At the Portuguese
camp, the general, Tristan d'Achuna, has returned to avenge the death of murdered Portuguese traders. He still mourns for his lost love, an Indian girl who
mysteriously vanished with her family. Not knowing the true nature of the
impending religious rite, he allows it to go on. When he recognizes Jessonda
as his true love and when he is informed by Nadori of the real purpose of the
ceremonies, he is reminded that he has promised not to interfere. The frustrated
general withdraws. As the third act opens, the despairing Tristan learns that the
truce is no longer valid. Dandau has attacked the Portuguese ships. Nadori leads
the Portuguese army through a secret passage into the city, and the forces arrive
just as Jessonda is to be sacrificed. Tristan is reunited with his beloved Jessonda,
and Nadori with her sister Amazili.

Major roles: Jessonda (sop), Amazili (sop), Dandau (bass), Nadori (ten), and
Tristan d'Achuna (bar).

The most successful and highly regarded of Spohr's operas, the work has
continuous music. Unlike his earlier works, it uses the chorus and ballet to a
great extent and replaces spoken dialogue with recitative. It also includes a
leitmotif to represent Tristan's oath and the beautiful duet in the second act,
"Schönes Mädchen."

Other settings include, as *Lanassa*, incidental music by Johann André (1781);
Johann Nepomuk Komareck's sequel (1792), adapted by Karl Reger as *Marie
von Montalban* oder *Lanassas zweiter Teil* for Peter von Winter (1800, Munich);
Vincenz Franz Tuczek's *Lanassa* oder *Die Eroberung von Malaba* (1805, Pest);
and Simone Mayr's *Lanassa* (1818, Venice).

SCORES: fs ed. G. Kogel (Leipzig: Peters, 1881); repr. in *Selected Works of Louis Spohr*, II, ed. Clive Brown (New York: Garland Publishing, 1989); vs (Leipzig: Peters, 1824).

LIBRETTO: German (Berlin: G. Mode's Verlag, 187–).

BIBLIOGRAPHY: B/*LS*, 157–63; Clive Brown, "Spohr's *Jessonda*," *MT* CXXI (1980), 94–97; Louis Spohr, "Aufruf an deutsche Komponisten," *AmZ* XXIX (July 16, 1823), 457–64 [discusses the principles he used in composing *Jessonda*].

Jesu Hochzeit (The Wedding of Jesus), "mystery opera" in two acts by Gottfried von Einem; libretto (Ger) by Lotte Ingrisch, with extensive quotes from the Bible. First performance May 18, 1980, Vienna, Theater an der Wien (televised), with Karan Armstrong (Death/Judas Iscariot), Per-Arne Wahlgren (Jesus), Eberhard Waechter (Joseph), Elisabeth Steiner (Mary), Anna Gjevang (Mary Magdalene), Lucy Peacock (Lazarus), and Thomas Moser (the Angel); conducted by David Shallon.

The story describes the life and death of Jesus. The "marriage" refers to his confrontation and spiritual union with the female Death. The subject matter of the text, which offended many religious Catholics, led to charges of sacrilege and a request for a court order barring its performance on charges of blasphemy.

It is a "number" opera which uses specific tonalities for the main characters.

Major roles: Death (sop); Jesus (ten); Joseph (bar); and Mary (mezzo).

SCORE: fs (Berlin: B&B, ca. 1981).

LIBRETTO: German, the same.

BIBLIOGRAPHY: Rudolf Klein, "Gottfried von Einems Oper *Jesu Hochzeit*. Zur Uraufführung der Wiener Festwochen," *ÖMz* XXXV (1980), 189–99; Christopher Norton-Welsh, "Reports: Foreign," *ON* XLV (September 1980), 59 [on premiere]; ———, "Vienna. Von Einem furore," *Opera* XXXI (1980), 57–58 [on premiere].

Jonny spielt auf (Johnny Strikes Up), opera in two acts by Ernst Krenek; libretto (Ger) by the composer. First performance February 10, 1927, Leipzig, with Cleve, Schulthess, Beinert, Horand, and Spilcker; conducted by Gustav Brecher. First U.S. performance January 19, 1929, New York, Metropolitan Opera, with Michael Bohnen (Daniello) and Friedrich Schorr (Jonny); conducted by Artur Bodanzky. First British performance (in English) October 6, 1984, Leeds, Leeds Grand Theatre, with Gillian Sullivan (chambermaid), Penelope Mackay (Anita), Kenneth Wollam (Max), Lyndon Terracini (violinist), and Jonathan Sprague (Jonny); conducted by David Lloyd-Jones.

The work takes place in a middle European city. Anita, a singer, is in love with Max, a composer. On a trip to Paris she meets Daniello, with whom she also falls in love. Jonny, a Black jazz musician, is determined to get Daniello's priceless violin. He frames first Anita, then Max for the theft, and Max is arrested. Jonny frees Max, as the troupe is about to leave the train station for Amsterdam. Waving the violin triumphantly, Jonny climbs atop a signal post and then to the station clock, which is transformed into a globe and causes people all over the world to dance the Charleston.

Major roles: the composer Max (ten); the singer Anita (sop); Jonny, a Black jazz violinist (bar); Daniello, a violin virtuoso (bar); and Yvonne, the chambermaid (sop).

Krenek incorporates jazz elements into the score.

SCORE: vs composer (Vienna: UE, 1926).

BIBLIOGRAPHY: R. S. Ginell, "Review," *HiFi/Ma* XXXVI (September 1986), 19–20; Noel Goodwin, "Reports: Foreign," *ON* XLIX (January 19, 1985), 42–43 [on British premiere]; R/*EKO*, 55–72.

DISCOGRAPHY: excerpts: Lear, Popp, Blankenship, Feldhoff, and Stewart, Vienna Academy Chamber Chorus and Orchestra of the Volksoper, conducted by Hollreiser, Mace MXX–9094.

Judith, opera in two acts by Siegfried Matthus; libretto (Ger) by the composer after Friedrich Hebbel's drama (1840). First performance September 28, 1985, East Berlin, Komische Oper, with Werner Haseleu (Holofernes), Eva-Maria Bundschuh (Judith), Horst-Dieter Kaschel (the captain), Wolfgang Hellmich (the orderly), Hans-Otto Rogge (Ephraim), Hans-Martin Nau (Osias), Manfred Hopp (Daniel), and Vladimir Bauer (Ammon); conducted by Rolf Reuter.

Major roles: Judith (sop) and Holofernes (bar).

The story is a mixture of the Biblical tale, from Book IV of the Apocrypha, and Hebbel's play. It concerns the Biblical heroine, Judith, who saves Bethulia from being destroyed by Holofernes, general of Nebuchadnezzar, by getting Holofernes drunk and decapitating him. When Judith realizes that her actions have not changed her countrymen for the better, she hangs herself.

The work includes striking music for the two principals and moving choral passages.

BIBLIOGRAPHY: James Helme Sutcliffe, "Reports: Foreign," *ON* L, No. 8 (January 4, 1986), 40–41 [on premiere].

Junge Lord, Der (The Young Lord), opera in two acts by Hans Werner Henze; libretto (Ger) by Ingeborg Bachmann after Wilhelm Hauff's fable *Der Scheik von Alexandria und seine Sklaven* (1827). First performance April 7, 1965, Berlin, Deutsche Oper, with Loren Driscoll (Lord Barrat), Barry McDaniel (secretary), Vera Little (Begonia), Edith Mathis and Donald Grobe (the young lovers), and Patricia Johnson (Baroness von Grünwiesel); conducted by Christoph von Dohnányi. First U.S. performance February 17, 1967, San Diego (in an English translation by Eugene Walter), with Glenn Cole (Lord Barrat), Richard Fredricks (the secretary), Norma Lynn and Kenneth Riegel (the young lovers), Claramae Turner (Baroness von Grünwiesel); conducted by Walter Herbert. First British performance October 14, 1969, London.

The story concerns an older, snobbish English aristocrat, Sir Edgar, who moves to a German town and brings his "nephew," the young Lord Barrat of the title, who is feted and lionized by the residents. During his engagement party celebrating his betrothal to Luise, the niece of a baroness, the nephew is revealed to be a circus ape. Luise returns to Wilhelm, her first love.

Major roles: Sir Edgar (mime); his secretary (ten); Lord Barrat (high ten); Baroness von Grünwiesel (mezzo); Luise, her ward (sop); and Wilhelm (ten).

For a detailed synopsis, see K/*KOB*, 932–35.

In the score Henze uses less polytonality and atonality than in his previous works, and he includes, among the ensembles and choruses, a full-fledged aria.

SCORE: vs ed. Peter Hartman (Mainz: BSS, 1965).

BIBLIOGRAPHY: James H. Sutcliffe, "Reports: Foreign," *ON* XXX (September 25, 1965), 26–27 [on premiere].

DISCOGRAPHY: Mathis, Jasper, Otto, Hohnson, Hesse, Little, McDaniel, Grobe, Driscoll, Krebs, Treptow, Röhrl, Sardi, and Krukowski, Deutsche Oper Berlin, conducted by Dohnányi, DG 139257/9 (3), reviewed by C. J. Luten, "Records," *ON* XXXII (March 16, 1968), 34.

K

Kabale und Liebe (Intrigue and Love), opera in two acts by Gottfried von Einem; libretto (Ger) by the composer and Lotte Ingrisch after Friedrich Schiller's tragedy (1784). First performance December 17, 1976, Vienna, with Bernd Weikl (Ferdinand), Hans Beirer (the President), Anja Silja (Luise), Brigitte Fassbaender (Lady Milford), Walter Berry (the miller), and Martha Mödl (the miller's wife); conducted by Christoph von Dohnányi.

The aristocratic Ferdinand is in love with Luise, the miller's daughter, but their match is opposed by Ferdinand's father. When he listens to a jealous troublemaker, he unknowingly causes the young lovers' demise.

Major roles: Ferdinand (bar); Luise (sop); her father, the miller (bass); his wife (mezzo); the President (bar); and Lady Milford (mezzo).

Also set by Giuseppe Verdi as *Luisa Miller* (1849, Naples).

BIBLIOGRAPHY: Robert Breuer, "Catching up with Einem," *ON* XLI (December 4, 1976), 46, 48–49; Rainer Wagner, "Klassiker Opernverschnitt," *Musica* XXXI (1977), 141–42 [on premiere].

Kaiser von Atlantis, Der oder **Der Tod dankt ab** (The Emperor of Atlantis or Death Abdicates), opera in four scenes by Viktor Ullmann; libretto (Ger) by Peter Kien. Composed in 1944 while the composer and librettist were prisoners at the Terezín concentration camp. Stage rehearsal October 1944, with Marion Podolier, Hilde Aronson-Lindt, David Grünfeld, Walter Windholz, and Karel Berman. When the authorities learned the nature of the work, they refused to let it be performed. Both Ullmann and Kien died at Auschwitz, but the score somehow survived and was rediscovered in London by Kerry Woodward. First performance December 16, 1975, Amsterdam, Netherlands Opera Foundation, Centrum Bellevue, with Adriaan van Limpt (Pierrot), Tom Haenen (Death), Meinhard Krack (the Emperor), and Lodewijk Meeuwsen (Loudspeaker); conducted by Kerry Woodward. First U.S. performance May 10, 1975, Philadelphia; first U.S. stage performance spring 1977, San Francisco, Spring Opera Theater, with William Dansby (Death) and Ralph Griffin (the Emperor); conducted by Kerry Woodward.

Emperor Überall is so busy killing humankind that Death rebels and forces people, including the despairing Pierrot, to endure life's endless suffering. The ruler is therefore forced to sacrifice himself to Death, so that the natural cycle can resume.

Major roles: Emperor Überall (bar), Loudspeaker (bass), a soldier (ten), Pierrot (ten), Death (bass), the Drummer (mezzo), and a girl (sop).

For a detailed synopsis of the work, see K/*KOB*, 889–91.

The light nature of the music, played by a small orchestra, holds forth until the stirring final hymn, "Ein feste Burg," set to modern harmonies. Although the composer studied with Schoenberg, the score, which has echoes of Wagner and Mahler, contains no atonality.

BIBLIOGRAPHY: Alfred Frankenstein, "Review," *HiFi/MA* XXVII (October 1977), 30–31 [on U.S. stage premiere]; Joel Kasow, "Holland," *Opera* XXVII (1976), 276–77 [on premiere]; Hugh R. N. Macdonald, " 'Der Kaiser von Atlantis,' " *Tempo* CXVI (March 1976), 42–44 [on premiere].

Kalte Herz, Das (The Cold Heart), opera in three acts by Norbert Schultze; libretto (Ger) by Kurt E. Walter after Wilhelm Hauff's fairy tale. First performance November 7, 1943, Leipzig. The opera was revised in 1983.

Peter, a poor charcoal gatherer, gives his mother the last of his money so that she can pay her rent. But this means that he cannot take his beloved, Lisbeth, to the dance. He begins to dream, and in his dreams he discovers that his desire to dance as well as the king of the ball and to have as much money as the rich Ezechiel will come true if he trades in his heart for one of stone. Peter awakens, and Lisbeth gives him a stone in the shape of a heart. He is able to sell the stone for 19 ducats, which is enough money to buy back his mother's house from Ezechiel.

Major roles: Peter Munk, a poor coal miner (ten); Lisbeth (sop); the mother (alto); and Ezechiel, a woodcutter (bar).

This children's opera, written by the composer of the famous song "Lili Marleen," is one of several by the composer for young audiences.

Karl der Fünfte (Charles the Fifth), opera in two acts by Ernst Krenek; libretto (Ger) by the composer. First performance June 15, 1938, Prague, Deutsches Theater. New version, first performance May 11, 1958, Düsseldorf, Deutsche Oper am Rhein, Opernhaus, with Valerie Bak, Ingeborg Lasser, Elisabeth Schwarzenberg, Karl Wolfram, and Walter Raninger; conducted by Reinhard Peters.

The work examines the failure of the ruler's idea for an international empire that is Christian and controlled by the Habsburgs. The Holy Roman Emperor reflects on the main events of his life as he speaks to his young confessor: his troubles with Martin Luther, his disputes with the Pope, and his denunciation as a heretic.

Major roles: Karl V (bar), Eleanore (sop), Isabella (sop), Francisco (ten), and Franz (ten).

The opera is completely twelve-tone. Its anti-Nazi slant caused its 1934 premiere in Vienna to be cancelled, and it was first heard in Prague four years later.

SCORES: fs, vs (Vienna: UE, 1933).

LIBRETTO: German (Vienna: UE, 1933).

BIBLIOGRAPHY: Heinz-Klaus Metzger and Rainer Riehn, eds., *Musik-Konzepte* XXXIX/XL (October 1984): Ernst Krenek, "Studien zu meinem Bühnenwerk 'Karl V,' " 20–34; Claudia Maurer, "Schöne und 'scheene' Musik," 38–52; and Heinz-Klaus Metzger, "Plus ultra. Notizen zu Kreneks Karl V," 53–66; R/*EKO*, 111–20; Claudia Maurer Zenck, "Musikalisches Welttheater: Kreneks *Karl V*. Zur konzertanten Wiedergabe der Oper bei den Salzburger Festspielen", *ÖMZ* XXXV (1980), 370–72.

Kaufmann von Smyrna, Der (The Merchant of Smyrna), "Operette" in one act by Georg Joseph Vogler; libretto (Ger) by Christian Friedrich Schwan after Nicolas Chamfort. First performance 1771, Mannheim.

The plot, like the later *Die Entführung aus dem Serail*,* focuses on the "generous Turk" theme. It concerns the plight of Dornal and Amalie, two Christians who have been captured by pirates and put on sale as slaves in Smyrna. Dornal is bought by Hassan, a rich Turk who himself was freed by a Christian, and Amalie is bought by Zayde, Hassan's wife. Both Europeans are released by Hassan, after he learns that it was Dornal who freed him from slavery.

Major roles: Hassan, a Turk and resident of Smyrna (bass); Zayde, his wife (sop); Dornal, a Frenchman from Marseilles (ten); Amalie, his fiancée (sop); Kaled, a slave dealer (bass); Fatmé, a slave of Zayde (sop); and André, Dornal's servant (ten).

This "Turkish" opera, which predates Mozart's opera by some eleven years, features Kaled, a comic-evil character along the lines of Osmin, as well as the Pedrillo-like André. Among the musical numbers is Dornal's aria about his beloved, "Schöner ist die Rose nicht." Vogler continued to be fascinated by exotic themes, and he composed *Samori*, which was performed in Vienna in 1804. Among Vogler's pupils was Carl Maria von Weber, whose exotic works include *Abu Hassan** and *Oberon*.*

The Schwan text was also set by Karl David Stegmann (1773, Königsberg)— his work opens with a three-part sinfonia designated "alla turca"; Andreas Franz Holly (1775, Berlin)—Holly's version, which was his most successful opera, concludes with a plea for brotherhood, "Seyd ihr nicht alle Kinder eines Blutes"; Johann Nikolaus Franz Seydelmann (1778, Dresden); Ignaz Walter (1783, Prague); and Peter Ritter, revised into two acts (1790, Mannheim).

SCORE: fs ms repr. in *German Opera 1770–1800*, VIII, ed. Thomas Bauman (New York, London: Garland Publishing, 1986).

LIBRETTO: German (Mannheim: C. F. Schwan, 1771; repr. in *German Opera 1770–1800*, XXI, *Librettos III*, ed. Thomas Bauman (New York and London: Garland Publishing, 1986).

Kluge, Die (The Wise Woman), opera in one act by Carl Orff; libretto (Ger) by the composer after the Grimm fairy tale "Die Geschichte von dem König und der klugen Frau." First performance February 20, 1943, Frankfurt, Staatsoper, with Wackers, Gonszar, and Staudenmeyer; conducted by O. Winkler. First U.S. performance December 7, 1949, Cleveland, Karamu House. First British performance July 27, 1959, London, Sadler's Wells (in an English translation by Caryl Brahms and Ned Sherrin), with April Cantelo (the daughter) and Joseph Ward (the king); conducted by Brian Priestman.

When a peasant finds a golden mortar on the king's land, he disregards his daughter's advice to either throw the gold away or bury it, and the goes to the monarch for an expected reward. Instead, the peasant is thrown into jail, since the king was awaiting the return of the missing pestle as well. Hearing the peasant's cries, the king listens to the prisoner's story and demands that the wise daughter be brought to him. He poses three questions which, if she answers them correctly, will win her freedom. Her correct answers so impress the king that he makes her his queen and frees all his prisoners, including her father. When she intercedes on behalf of a donkey driver, the king, tired of her cleverness, demands that she leave but he lets her take whatever she holds dearest with her in a trunk. The girl drugs the king and puts him in the trunk. When he awakes, she tells him that one cannot love and be clever at the same time. The two are reconciled.

Major roles: the king (bar); the peasant (bass); the wise woman, daughter of the peasant (sop); the prison warden (bass); the man with the donkey (ten); and the man with the mule (bar).

For a detailed synopsis, see K/*KOB*, 879–80.

The score includes a vivacious drinking scene, "Fides ist geschlagen tot" in the seventh scene. The orchestra is cast in an accompanying role to the vocal lines in the work.

SCORE: vs (Mainz: BSS, 1942).

BIBLIOGRAPHY: L/*CO*, 92–98; William Mann, "Sadler's Wells," *Opera* 10 (1959), 620–21 [on British premiere].

DISCOGRAPHY: Schwarzkopf, Christ, Kuen, Cordes, Perry, Frick, Kusche, Neidlinger, and Wieter, Philharmonia Orchestra, conducted by Sawallisch, Angel 3551B/L or Arabesque 8021 (2).

Kobold, Der (The Goblin), opera in three acts by Siegfried Wagner; libretto (Ger) by the composer. First performance January 29, 1904, Hamburg, Stadttheater, with Johanna Neumeyer (Getrud), Katharina Fleischer-Edel (Verena), Max Dawison (the Count), Charlotte Schloss (the Countess), Josefine von Artner (Jeanette), Alois Pennarini (Friedrich), Max Lohfing (old Eckhart), and Hans Mohwinkel (Trutz); conducted by Carl Gille. The opera was among the composer's greatest successes.First British performance (concert) October 12, 1980, London, Queen Elizabeth Hall, Pro Opera, with Carmen Reppel (Verena), Heikki Torvanen (Eckhart), and Stephen Williams (Trutz).

Verena, whose brother was murdered, possibly by their mother, fends off an attack by the Count and sacrifices herself for her lover, thereby releasing the Kobold, the soul of her dead sibling.

Major roles: Getrud, innkeeper; Verena, her daughter; the Count; the Countess; and the maid, Jeannette.

The story was also set by Friedrich Heinrich Himmel (1813, Vienna).

LIBRETTO: German (Leipzig: M. Brockhaus, ca. 1904).

BIBLIOGRAPHY: William Mann, "In Concert," *Opera* XXXII (1981), 90–91.

König Hirsch oder **Die Irrfahrten der Wahrheit** (The Stag King or Truth Going Astray), opera in three acts by Hans Werner Henze; libretto (Ger) by Heinz von Cramer after Carlo Gozzi's *Il Re Cervo*. First performance September 23, 1956, Berlin, Städtische Oper, with Sandor Konya (the King), Tomislav Neralic (the Governor), Helmut Krebs (Checco), Martin Vantin (Coltellino), and Helga Pilarczyk (the girl); conducted by Hermann Scherchen. Revised and shortened as *Il Re Cervo*, 1964, Kassel, with Ticho Parly in the title role; conducted by the composer. First U.S. performance, as *Il Re Cervo*, August 4, 1965, Santa Fe, with George Shirley (the King) and Donald Gramm (the state elder); conducted by Robert Baustian.

The rightful King, left in the forest as a young child by the evil Governor, has been raised by wild animals. A grown man, he returns to his kingdom, but his attempts to claim his title and select a wife are thwarted by the Governor, and he is forced once again to return to the forest, where he enters the body of a stag. Meanwhile, the Governor takes over the body of the monarch and terrorizes the kingdom. Longing for the world of humans, the Stag King comes back to the city. When the Governor is killed by his own henchmen, the King assumes his human form once more.

Major roles of *König Hirsch*: the Stag King (ten); the Governor (bass-bar); Costanza, the girl (sop); Checco, a melancholy musician (buffo ten); and Coltellino, a murderer (buffo ten). Major roles of *Il Re Cervo*: Leandro, the king (ten); Costanza, a maid (sop); and Tartaglia, state elder (bar).

For a detailed synopsis, see K/*KOB*, 914–18.

SCORE: vs ed. Heinz Moehn (Mainz: BSS and New York: AMP, 1964).

134

BIBLIOGRAPHY: From *Chigiana* XXXI/11 (1977): Heinz von Cramer, "Il mio libretto per *Re cervo*," 295; Hans Werner Henze, "La genesi di *Re cervo*," 297–302 [reprinted from *Essays* (Mainz, 1964)]; and Mila Massimo, "Troppe canzoni per *Re cervo*," 303–5; Horst Koegler, "King Stag at Bay," *ON* XXI (November 5, 1956), 22–23 [on premiere]; Robert C. Marsh, "Reports," *ON* XXX (September 25, 1965), 23 [on U.S. premiere]; H. H. Stuckenschmidt, "Hans Werner Henze's 'König Hirsch,' " *Opera* VII (1956), 728–32 [on premiere].

Königin von Saba, Die (The Queen of Sheba), opera in four acts by Karl Goldmark; libretto (Ger) by S. H. Mosenthal. First performance March 10, 1875, Vienna, Staatsoper, with Johannes Nepomuk Beck (King Solomon), Viktor Freiherr von Rokitansky (High Priest), Marie Wilt (Sulamith), Gustav Walter (Assad), Theodor Lay (Baal-Hanan), Amalie Materna (the Queen of Sheba), and Frl. Siegstädt (Astaroth). First U.S. performance December 2, 1885, New York, Metropolitan Opera, with Lilli Lehmann, Marie Krämer-Widl, Albert Stritt, and Adolf Robinson; conducted by Anton Seidl. First British performance August 29, 1910, London, Kennington Theatre, with Woodall, Wheatly, and Winckworth; conducted by Eugène Goossens.

Sulamith is awaiting the return of her fiancé, Assad, who has been sent by King Solomon to meet the Queen of Sheba. Assad, meanwhile, has secretly fallen in love with the Queen, who returns his feelings, but, in the presence of the court, she denies ever having met him before. With the help of Astaroth, Assad secretly meets the Queen. When his marriage to Sulamith is about to take place, Assad flings away the ring and pledges his love to the Queen. Assad is condemned to death for his deed, but the Queen asks for mercy, and Solomon, after a plea from the innocent Sulamith, banishes Assad to the desert. The Queen follows him there, but he casts her away and dies in the arms of his faithful Sulamith.

Major roles: King Solomon (bar); High Priest (bass); Sulamith, his daughter (sop); Assad, favorite of Solomon (ten); Baal-Hanan, captain of the guards (bar); the Queen of Sheba (mezzo); Astaroth, her slave (sop); and temple watchman (bass).

The Queen of Sheba was also the subject of operas by Charles Gounod (*La Reine de Saba*, 1862, Paris); Xavier Leroux (*Astarté*, 1901, Paris); and Rui Coelho (*Belkis*, 1938, Lisbon).

SCORE: vs (Bremen: Schweers & Haake, ca. 1878).

LIBRETTO: German (Vienna: Wallishausser, 1875).

DISCOGRAPHY: Sólyom, Gregor, Kincses, Jerusalem, Miller, Takács, Kalmár, and Polgár, Chorus and Orchestra of the Hungarian State Opera, conducted by Fischer, Hungaroton SLPX 1279–82 (3, in Hungarian); reviewed by John W. Freeman, "Records," *ON* XLV (January 31, 1981), 36; Paul Henry Lang, "Goldmark's Exotic *Queen of Sheba* in a Splendid Revival," *HiFi* XXXI (April 1981), 70–72; and Christopher J. Thomas, "Recordings," *OQ* II/2 (Summer 1984), 138–39.

Königskinder (The King's Children), opera in three acts by Engelbert Humperdinck; libretto (Ger) by Ernst Rosmer [Elsa Bernheim]. First performance December 28, 1910, New York, Metropolitan Opera, with Geraldine Farrar (the goose girl), Louise Homer, Otto Goritz, Albert Reiss, Adamo Didur, and Hermann Jadlowker (the prince); conducted by Alfred Herz. First performace in a German-speaking city January 14, 1911, Berlin. First British performance November 27, 1911, London, Covent Garden, with Annie Gura-Hummel (the goose girl), Otto Wolff, Langendorff, and Hofbauer; conducted by Franz Schalk. Originally produced as a play with music January 23, 1897, Munich; October 13, 1897 (in English), London, Court Theatre; April 29, 1898, New York (in German).

A goose girl lives in the forest with a witch, who forces her to bake a magical bread; whoever eats half of it will die. The girl, who has never seen a human being, meets the disguised prince in the town, and they fall immediately in love. The fiddler asks the witch who will be the next king. She says that it will be the one who enters the city when the clock chimes midday. When this turns out to be the unknown prince, accompanied by the goose girl, the townspeople, feeling they have been deceived, turn on them and drive them out. Unable to find their way back to the prince's royal parents, and suffering from hunger and cold, the young couple trade his crown for some old bread from the woodsman. Unknown to any of them, it is the witch's fatal dough. The prince and the goose girl, eat it and fall into a permanent sleep. They are found by the fiddler and some children, who build them a funeral bier.

For a detailed synopsis, see K/*KOB*, 304–306.

Major roles: the prince (ten), the goose girl (sop), the fiddler (bar), the witch (alto), and the woodsman (bass).

SCORE: vs ed. Rudolf Siegel (Leipzig: Max Brockhaus, 1910).

DISCOGRAPHY: Donath, Schwarz, Ankersen, Wenkel, Dallapozza, Prey, Ridderbusch, and Unger, Bavarian Radio Chorus, Munich Radio Orchestra, conducted by Wallberg, EMI 1D–157–30–698/700Q (3); reviewed by John W. Freeman, "Records," *ON* XLII (April 1, 1978), 41.

Kreuzfahrer, Die (The Crusaders), grand opera in three acts by Ludwig Spohr; libretto (Ger) by the composer and his wife, Marianne, after August von Kotzebue's play (1803). First performance January 1, 1845, Kassel, Hoftheater.

The work takes place in 1097, in the camp near Nicea and the cloister. The knight Balduin, given up for dead, returns to his camp after escaping from his Saracen captivity, with the help of Adhemar, the papal legate. Balduin can find no news, however, about his betrothed, Emma, who was still in Germany when he was captured. Another crusader, Bohemund, returns with a valuable prisoner, the daughter of an Emir. Emma, meanwhile, has come to the Holy Land. Failing to find her beloved, she resolves to enter a convent, which is run by the harsh Abbess Cölestine, who hates Emma; the nun had entered the convent herself after being rejected by Emma's father, and she warns Emma that the punishment for breaking the rules of the convent is entombment.

In the crusader's camp Fatime, the Emir's daughter, is being harassed by her captors. Feeling an injustice is being done, Balduin offers to be her champion in a duel with Bohemund. Although he is wounded, Balduin is the victor and he earns the eternal gratitude of the Emir, who promises to aid him if he is ever in need. Balduin is brought to the convent to be healed; it is the very convent where Emma has been admitted as a nun. She faints when she realizes whom she is attending to, and the Abbess, finding Emma in Balduin's arms, condemns her to be entombed. After an attempt to free Emma has failed, despite the help of the gatekeeper, Balduin is in despair, until the Emir arrives with his troops. Just as Emma is to be entombed, the Saracens' attack is announced. The legate Adhemar also arrives and decides that, because Emma was engaged, she was not really a nun anyway and can return to Balduin. The opera ends happily.

For a detailed plot and musical analysis, see B/*LS*, 286–91.

Major roles: Balduin von Eichenhorst (ten); Bohemund von Schwarzeneck (bass); Adhemar, Bishop of Puy, papal legate (bar); the Emir of the Seljuk Turks (bass); Fatime, his daughter (sop); Cölestine, Abbess of the cloister (sop); Bertha, the gatekeeper (mezzo); and Emma of Falkenstein, a pilgrim (sop).

The story has several parallels to Sir Walter Scott's *Ivanhoe* (1819), set by Heinrich Marschner as *Der Templer und die Jüdin*.* Spohr's opera is through-composed. It opens with a brief orchestral prelude, which leads into a soldiers' chorus. The solos and ensembles themselves are fairly brief, and the action is carried on in the arioso sections, which are extensive.

SCORE: vs (Hamburg and Leipzig: Schuberth, 1845).

L

Labarint, Das oder **Der Kampf mit den Elementen** (The Labyrinth or The Battle with the Elements), opera in two acts by Peter Winter; libretto (Ger) by Emanuel Schikaneder. First performance June 12, 1798, Vienna, Theater auf der Wieden. Revived October 23, 1930, Kiel, as *Papagenos Hochzeit*, in an arrangement by Georg Hartmann.

Schikaneder wrote the libretto as a sequel to Mozart's *Die Zauberflöte*.* It contains the main characters of the Mozart work plus new ones, among them Tipheus and Sistos, new allies of the Queen of the Night; and Monostatos. The story opens after Pamina and Tamino's wedding, when the Queen of the Night and her forces attack Sarastro's kingdom and force the newlyweds to seek shelter in the labyrinth. Pamina is captured and promised to Tipheus by the Queen of the Night. Monostatos disguises himself as Papageno to seduce Papagena, but he is captured by his intended prey and her beloved. Tamino is finally able to get back Pamina by using the magic flute, and he fights Tipheus in a duel to decide which side will be victorious. Tamino triumphs and throws Tipheus into a flaming abyss, and the Queen of the Night falls to her death. Harmony is once more restored.

Winter's work borrows heavily from *Die Zauberflöte*,* but it never achieved the success of the earlier Mozart opera, nor did it measure up to it artistically.

BIBLIOGRAPHY: Donald G. Henderson, "The Magic Flute of Peter Winter," *ML* LXIV (1983), 193–205.

Lächerliche Printz Jodelet, Der (The Ridiculous Prince Jodelet), comic opera in five acts by Reinhard Keiser; libretto (Ger-It) by Johann Praetorius after Calderón's *El alcaide de si mismo* and Paul Scarron's comedy *Jodelet ou Le Maître Valet* (1645). First performance 1726, Hamburg, with Mr. Westenholtz (Fernando); Mlle. Monjo, the Elder (Laura); Mr. Riemschneider (Federich); Mr.

Bahn (Eduard); Mlle. Monjo, the Younger (Isabella); Madame Kayserin (Erminde); Mlle. Kayserin (Julia); Mr. Petersen (Octavius); Mr. Riemschneider (Jodelet); Mr. Buchhöffer (Nicolo); Mr. Möhring (Henriquez); and Mr. Scheffel (Sanchez). Revived 1930, Hamburg.

Major roles: Fernando, King of Naples; Laura, his princess; Federich [sic], Crown Prince of Sicily, going by the name of Leonhard; Eduard, his brother, Isabella, Princess of Salerno; Erminde, a lady at court; Julia, confidante of Laura; Octavius, Federich's confidant; Jodelet, a foolish person, thought to be Prince Federich; Nicolo, his neighbor; Henriquez, captain of the footmen; and Sanchez, a cavalier.

The opera has arias in German and Italian; one example of the latter is Erminde's "Belle donne, voi che sapete" of the fifth act.

SCORE: fs ed. Friedrich Zeller, *Publikationen älterer Musikwerke*, XVIII (1892).

BIBLIOGRAPHY: Klaus Zelm, "Stilkritische Untersuchungen an einem Opernpasticcio. Reinhard Keisers *Jodelet*," in *Festschrift Heinz Becker*, ed. Jürgen Schläder and Reinhold Quandt (Laaber: Laaber-Verlag, 1982), 10–25.

Lampedo, melodrama in one act by Georg Joseph Vogler; libretto (Ger) by Christian Friedrich Lichtenberg after Marcus Junianus Justinus' *Historiae Philippicae*. First performance July 11, 1779, Darmstadt, Hoftheater, with Crown Princess Louise Karoline Henriette (Lampedo); conducted by Crown Prince Ludewig.

Queen Lampedo has led the Amazons to a great and bloody victory over the Scythians, and she is determined to get revenge by killing the king, Argabyses, and other prisoners. Tomiris, the high priestess, brings in the king, but as Lampedo is about to kill him with her dagger, she finds that she cannot. Finally, renouncing the Amazon practice of killing their captives, Lampedo frees the prisoners. Argabyses then vows to protect her crown, and the former enemies celebrate the peace.

Major roles: Lampedo, Queen of the Amazons (spoken); Argabyses, Scythian king and the queen's prisoner (spoken); Tomiris, Amazon high priestess (spoken).

The score includes a storm scene and a chaconne, which ends the work.

SCORE: fs ms repr. in *German Opera 1770–1800*, IX, ed. Thomas Bauman (New York and London: Garland Publishing, 1986).

LIBRETTO: German (Darmstadt: J. J. Will, 1779); repr. in *German Opera 1770–1800*, XXI, *Librettos III*, ed. Thomas Bauman (New York and London: Garland Publishing, 1986).

Land des Lächelns, Das (The Land of Smiles), operetta in three acts by Franz Lehár; libretto (Ger) by Ludwig Herzer and Fritz Löhner. First performance October 10, 1929, Berlin, Metropole Theater, with Richard Tauber (Prince Sou-Chong). First U.S. performance September 5, 1946, New York, Schubert Theater (in English, as *Yours Is My Heart*), with Richard Tauber. First British performance May 8, 1931, London, Drury Lane, with Richard Tauber (Sou-Chong). *Das Land des Lächelns* was a reworking of the composer's unsuccessful operetta *Die gelbe Jacke*, first performed in Vienna on February 9, 1923, to a text by Viktor Léon (Viktor Hirschfeld).

Lisa, daughter of the Viennese Count Lichtenfels, falls in love with Prince Sou-Chong, a Chinese diplomat. She marries him and returns to Peking. But her happiness is shattered when, according to family custom, he takes four more wives, which reduces her to the role of lowly fifth wife. Meanwhile, Gustav von Pottenstein, himself in love with Lisa, has come to Peking as a military attaché and turns his attentions to Mi, Sou-Chong's sister. The two agree to help Lisa extricate herself from her miserable life, but her escape is thwarted. The Prince, who could condemn Lisa to death, instead allows her to return to Vienna with Gustav. Sou-Chong and Mi remain behind to mend their broken hearts.

Major roles: Count Ferdinand Lichtenfels; Lisa, his daughter (sop); Count Gustav von Pottenstein (ten); Prince Sou-Chong (ten); and Mi, his sister (soubrette).

The musical high point, itself lifted from *Die gelbe Jacke*, is "Dein ist mein ganzes Herz," an aria with which Tauber was closely identified.

DISCOGRAPHY: See M/*IRR*, 100–01.

Landarzt, Ein (A Country Doctor), radio opera in one act by Hans Werner Henze; libretto (Ger) by the composer after Franz Kafka's short story of the same name. First performance May 27, 1953, NWDR, Hamburg, with Hans Werner Fiedler (the doctor). Stage version 1964. First performance in this version November 30, 1965, Frankfurt, Stadttheater, with Ernst Gutstein (the doctor), Kurt Wehofschitz (the stable boy), and Marlise Wendels (Rosa); conducted by Wolfgang Rennert. First U.S. performance August 15, 1968, Aspen, Colorado, Opera Workshop (in an English translation by Wesley Balk), with Robert Shiesley (narrator); conducted by John Nelson. First British performance March 8, 1966, London, St. Pancras Festival, with John Cameron (the doctor); conducted by Frederick Marshall.

This dramatization of the Kafka story is presented as a monologue for baritone, with backcloth projections to illustrate the narration. The country doctor, in need of a horse, sends the maid Rosa to search for one. When she is unsuccessful, he goes himself and comes upon a strange figure with two powerful steeds, who seizes Rosa. The doctor finds himself at the bedside of a young patient and is forced into the boy's bed by the family. The doctor escapes on one of the horses, but he realizes that he will never see his home again.

Major roles: the country doctor (bar), the stable boy (ten), the patient (deep boy's voice), the father (bass), Rosa (sop), the daughter (sop), and the mother (alto).

SCORE: vs ed. Heinz Moehn, English text by Wesley Balk (Mainz: BSS, 1965).

BIBLIOGRAPHY: Ronald Crichton, "Henze Triple Bill," *MT*, CVII (1966), 420 [on British premiere]; Barbara Haddad, "Reports," *ON* XXXIII (October 12, 1968), 35 [on U.S. premiere]; Friedrich Hommel, "Das Musikleben," *NZM* CXXXVII (1966), 14–15 [on stage premiere]; Heinz Joachim, "Henze komponiert Kafkas 'Landarzt,' " *Melos* XIX (1952) 22–23 [on premiere].

DISCOGRAPHY: soloists, conducted by S. Ehrling, Swedish Radio Symphony. In *Swedish Radio Symphony Orchestra: 1928–1979*, Bis LP 331/333 (5) (Swedish).

Landstreicher, Die (The Tramps), operetta in a prologue and two acts by C. M. Ziehrer; libretto (Ger) by L. Krenn and C. Lindau. First performance June 29, 1899, Vienna, Sommertheater, with Herr Tuschl (Prince Adolar Gilka), Frl. Dorn (Mimi), Herr Matscheg (August Fliederbusch), and Frl. Augustin (Bertha); conducted by the composer. First U.S. performance (as *The Strollers*, with new music by Ludwig Englander) June 24, 1901, New York, Knickerbocker Theater, with Francis Wilson, Irene Bentley, Harry Garfoil, and Eddie Foy.

The plot concerns August Fliederbusch and his wife, Bertha. Having had no luck in any business, they have become tramps. They find a pearl necklace and a thousand mark bill and proceed to order a sumptuous meal. The suspicious innkeeper has them arrested. The pair is held in the magistrate's office, where they meet Prince Adolar Gilka and his beloved, the dancer Mimi, for whom he had bought the pearl necklace. The tramps manage to lure the couple into their own cell and then steal their fancy clothes. Properly attired, the tramps pretend to be the royal couple at a fancy resort. They are found there by the prince, who now needs help to recover the necklace, which has been stolen by Mimi. When Bertha is able to trick Mimi into handing over the necklace, the grateful Gilka agrees to hire the couple. It then turns out that the necklace is fake.

Major roles: Prince Adolar Gilka; Mimi, a dancer; August Fliederbusch; and Bertha, his wife.

The work was very favorably received, and its waltz number, "Sei gepriesen, du lauschige Nacht," was repeated at the premiere by popular request. It reached its 100th performance on June 20, 1900.

Lange Weihnachtsmahl, Das (The Long Christmas Dinner), opera in one act by Paul Hindemith; libretto (German and English version) by the composer after Thornton Wilder's tale. First performance December 17, 1961, Mannheim, Nationaltheater, with Elisabeth Thoma, Eva-Maria Molner, Gertrud Schretter-Petersik, Petrina Kruss, Erika Ahsbahs, Thomas Tipton, Jean Cox, Frederick Dalberg, and Georg Völker; conducted by the composer. First U.S. performance (in English) March 1963, New York, Juilliard School.

The story, beginning in the dining room of the Bayard home at Christmas, covers ninety dinners in the Bayard household.

Major roles: Lucia (sop), Mother Bayard (alto), Roderick (bar), Brandon (bass), Charles (ten), Geneviève (mezzo), and Leonora (high sop).

SCORE: vs ed. composer (Ger-Eng) (Mainz: BSS, 1961).

LIBRETTO: the same.

BIBLIOGRAPHY: Everett Helm, "Reviews," *MA* LXXXIII (May 1963), 20 [on U.S. premiere]; Horst Koegler, "Reports," *Opera* XIII (1962), 178 [on premiere]; Norbert J. Schneider, "Thorton Wilder und Paul Hindemith. Zu ihrem Briefwechsel anlässlich der Entstehung von The Long Christmas Dinner," *HJb* XI (1982), 137–88; Willi Schuh, "Paul Hindemith—Thorton Wilder: 'Das lange Weihnachtsmahl,' " *SMz* CII (1962), 36–40.

Langwienzige Weg in die Wohnung der Natascha Ungeheuer, Der (The Tedious Way to the Place of Natasha Monster), "spiritual odyssey in Marxist terms" in seventeen scenes by Hans Werner Henze; libretto (Ger) by the composer after Gàstón Salvatore. First performance May 17, 1971, Rome (in Italian).

The episodes show the political awakening of Gastón Salvatore, son of a Chilean diplomat. Natascha is the symbol of the fashionable new left; her name means, in fact, monstrous, colossal, or frightful.

Major role: one vocalist.

BIBLIOGRAPHY: Werner Oehlschlägel, "Hans Werner Henzes 'Natascha Ungeheuer,' " *Musica* XXV (1971), 370–71 [on premiere].

Lanzelot, opera in fifteen scenes by Paul Dessau; libretto by Heiner Müller and Ginka Tscholakowa after themes by Hans Christian Andersen and the fairy-tale comedy *The Dragon* (1943) of Yevgeni Schwarz. First performance December 19, 1969, East Berlin, with Siegfried Vogel (Lanzelot), Rainer Süss (the dragon), Renata Krahmer (Elsa), Horst Hiestermann (the mayor), and Eberhard Büchner (Heinrich); conducted by Herbert Kegel.

In the story Lanzelot saves the heroine Elsa from the dragon and the dragon-like mayor and his son Heinrich. The tale contains parallels between the characters and their situations to actual political figures considered heroes and villains.

Major roles: Lanzelot (bar), the dragon (bass), Elsa (sop), the mayor (ten), and Heinrich, his son (ten).

SCORES: fs (Berlin: Henschel-Verlag, 1970); vs (the same).

LIBRETTO: German (Berlin: B&B, 1970).

BIBLIOGRAPHY: Wolfgang Seiffert, "Berlin—Ost," *NZM* XXXI (1970), 57–60 [on premiere]; James Helme Sutcliffe, "Reports: Foreign," *ON* XXXIV (February 14, 1970), 30–31.

Last-tragende Liebe, Die oder **Emma und Eginhard** (Burdensome Love, or Emma and Eginhard), opera by Georg Philipp Telemann. First performance 1728, Hamburg. Revived May 23, 1973, Magdeburg, Maxim Gorky Theater; conducted by Roland Wambeck.

142   LEAR

The story is set in Charlemagne's palace in Aachen. The emperor's daughter has an affair, but, just as she is to be beheaded, she is saved by a celestial voice. The characters also appear in Schubert's *Fierrabras*.*

SCORE: fs ed. Hellmuth Christian Wolff (Kassel: Bär, 1957).

BIBLIOGRAPHY: James Helme Sutcliffe, "Reports. Foreign...Magdeburg," *ON* XXXVIII (September 1973), 60 [on modern revival].

Lear, opera in two parts by Aribert Reimann; libretto (Ger) by Claus H. Henneberg after Shakespeare's play *King Lear*. First performance July 9, 1978, Munich, with Dietrich Fischer-Dieskau (Lear), Julia Varady (Cordelia), Colette Lorand (Regan), Helga Dernesch (Goneril), David Knutson (Edgar), Werner Götz (Edmund), and Rolf Boysen (the Fool); conducted by Gerd Albrecht. First U.S. performance June 12, 1981, San Francisco, San Francisco Opera (in English), with Helga Dernesch (Goneril), David Knutson (Edgar), Thomas Stewart (Lear), Emily Rawlins (Cordelia), Rita Shane (Regan), Jacques Trussel (Edmund), William Lewis (Kent), Robert Lloyd (the Fool), and Chester Ludgin (Gloucester); conducted by Gerd Albrecht.

A faithful treatment of the Shakespeare play, in which the monarch divides his kingdom among his three daughters, Goneril, Regan, and Cordelia. Only Cordelia is true to her father.

For a complete synopsis, see K/*KOB*, 936–38.

Major roles: Cordelia (lyric sop), Goneril (dramatic sop), Regan (dramatic-lyric sop), Lear (bar), Edmund (ten), Edgar (ten), Kent (ten), Gloster/Gloucester (bass-bar), and the Fool (speaking role).

The work has several orchestral interludes, including the portrayal of the storm in the first act. It ends with Lear's singing a dirge for his murdered daughter and then expiring.

The play was also set by Ghislanzoni (*Ré Lear*, 1937, Rome).

BIBLIOGRAPHY: Stephanie von Buchau, "Reports: U.S.," *ON* XLVI (October 1981), 30 [on U.S. premiere]; Andrew Porter, "Musical Events," *NY* (July 27, 1981), 71–73 [on U.S. premiere]; Klaus Schulz, ed., *Aribert Reimanns 'Lear'* (Munich: Deutsher Taschenbuch Verlag, 1984).

DISCOGRAPHY: Varady, Dernesch, Lorand, Fischer-Dieskau, Holm, Nöcker, Knutson, Götz, and Boysen, Bavarian State Opera, conducted by Albrecht, DG 2709–089 (3); reviewed by John W. Freeman, "Records," *ON* XLIV (December 1, 1979), 44.

Leben des Orest, Das (The Life of Orestes), opera in five acts by Ernst Krenek; libretto (Ger) by the composer. First performance January 19, 1930, Leipzig; conducted by Gustav Brecher. First U.S. performance November 20, 1976, Portland, Oregon, Civic Auditorium, with Victor Braun (Orest), Sylvia Anderson (Klytämnestra), William Wilderman (Thoas), Glade Peterson (Agamemnon), Kenneth Riegel (Aegist), Barrie Smith (Iphigenie), Linda Cook (Thamar), Anita Salta (Elektra), and Alyce Rogers (Anastasia); conducted by Stefan Minde.

When war breaks out against Troy, Agamemnon is convinced by Aegist to sacrifice his son, Orest, to rally the people. Orest's mother, Klytämnestra, sends her son to safety with his nurse, Anastasia. Agamemnon then decides to sacrifice his daughter Iphigenie, but she is rescued by the gods. After ten years, during which time Klytämnestra has taken Aegist as a lover, Agamemnon returns from Troy. Aegist has Agamemnon poisoned from a cup brought by another daughter, Elektra. Orest also returns home and, roused by Elektra, kills his mother and Aegist. He himself is forced to flee by the enraged mob, which kills Elektra.

Iphigenie has come to the land of King Thoas, who falls in love with her. Orest appears, pursued by the Furies for his deed. He is led to his sister by Thamar, Thoas' daughter, and tells Iphigenie of the terrible happenings at home. The siblings resolve to leave, and Thamar and Thoas accompany them. Orest goes before the court in an attempt to be rid of his curse. His fate is to be decided by rolling three black and three white dice. At the roll, an additional white die appears; one that Anastasia had left as an offering in Athens. Orest is freed, the people rejoice, and he is united with Thamar.

Major roles: Agamemnon, King of Greece (ten); Klytämnestra, his wife (mezzo); Elektra (sop); Iphigenie (mezzo); Orest (bar); Aegist (ten); Anastasia, nurse to the royal children (alto); Thoas, King in the North (bass); and Thamar, his daughter (sop).

The eclectic score mixes several styles, including jazzlike elements and foxtrot rhythms.

SCORES: fs (Vienna: UE, 1930); vs (Vienna: UE, 1929).

LIBRETTO: German (Vienna: UE, 1929).

BIBLIOGRAPHY: Martin Bernheimer, "Our Critics Abroad," *Opera* XXVII (1966), 126–28; "M.C.," "Portland," *MA* XXVI (March 1976), 28 [on U.S. premiere]; R/ *EKO*, 82–96.

Lenardo und Blandine, melodrama in two acts by Peter Winter; libretto (Ger) by Josef Franz von Göz after Gottfried August Bürger's ballade of the same name. First performance June 25, 1779, Munich, National-Schaubühne, with Karoline Heigl (Blandine).

In this story, similar to *Lucia di Lammermoor*, the noble Lenardo falls in love with Blandine, who is the daughter of his father's enemy, the king. Therefore, the young man disguises himself as a gardener in order to woo her. The king, however, has chosen a prince to marry his daughter. In despair, Lenardo and Blandine wed secretly, and, when they meet to plan their escape, they are overheard by the prince, who summons Blandine's father. The opera opens on this secret meeting, and when Blandine leaves, the king and the prince kill Lenardo. Not knowing of this, Blandine waits with increasing desperation for her beloved's return. When she discovers the truth, she goes mad and dies. Her father, realizing his mistake only now, stabs the prince, who had urged him to take Lenardo's life in the first place.

Major roles (all spoken): the king; Blandine, his daughter; Lenardo, a noble disguised as a gardener; and a prince.

The text was also set by Johann Georg Staudinger (1780, Weissenburg am Nordgau); and Anton Zimmermann (1782, Vienna).

SCORE: facsimile of fs ed. Thomas Bauman (New York and London: Garland Publishing, 1986).

LIBRETTO: German, in *Versuch einer zahlreichen Folge leidenschaftlicher Entwürf*, I (Augsburg, 1783; repr. New York and London: Garland Publishing, 1986), 92–103.

Leonce und Lena, opera in two acts by Paul Dessau; libretto (Ger) by Thomas Körner after Georg Büchner. First performance November 27, 1979, East Berlin, Staatsoper, with Eberhard Büchner (Leonce), Carola Nosseck (Lena), and Rainer Süss (King Peter); conducted by Otmar Suitner.

Prince Leonce of Popo and Princess Lena of Pipi are both fleeing from a prearranged marriage. They meet, fall in love, and return to court as a happy couple. Overjoyed, the prince's father, King Peter, abdicates his throne in favor of his son.

Major roles: King Peter of Popo (bass); Prince Leonce, his son (ten); Princess Lena of Pipi (sop); and Valerio (ten).

Also set by Julius Weismann (1925, Freiburg); Eric Zeisl (1952, Los Angeles); and Kurt Schwaen (1961, East Berlin).

SCORES: fs and vs (Berlin: Henschel-Verlag, 1978).

BIBLIOGRAPHY: Georg-Friedrich Kühn, "Signale aus dem Lande Noch-Nicht. Paul Dessaus letzte Oper *Leonce und Lena*," *HiFi-Stereophonie* XXIX (1980), 176 [on premiere].

Leonore, opera in three acts by Ludwig van Beethoven (first version of *Fidelio**); libretto (Ger) by Joseph Sonnleithner after Jean Nicolas Bouilly's French libretto *Léonore ou L'Amour conjugal* for Ferdinand Paër. First performance November 20, 1805, Vienna, Theater an der Wien, with Anna Milder (Leonore), Louise Müller (Marzelline), Joseph Demmer (Florestan), Sebastian Mayer (Pizarro), Herr Rothe (Rocco), Herr Weinkopf (Don Fernando), and Herr Caché (Jaquino); conducted by Ignaz von Seyfried. First U.S. performance August 4, 1967, Lenox, Massachusetts, Tanglewood Festival, with Hanne-Lore Kuhse (Leonore), George Shirley (Florestan), Tom Krause (Pizarro), Ara Berberian (Rocco), and Mary Ellen Pracht (Marzelline); conducted by Erich Leinsdorf. Stefan von Breuning altered and reduced the opera to two acts in 1806, and in 1814 Georg Friedrich Treitschke gave it the form in which it is usually performed today, also in two acts, as *Fidelio*. First performance of the second version March 29, 1806, Vienna, Theater an der Wien, with the same cast except with Joseph August Röckel as Florestan.

See *Fidelio* for a synopsis of the plot and the voices. The 1805 version begins with the so-called Leonore Overture No. 2. The Leonore Overture No. 3, a revision of No. 2, written for the second version, is often played in the break between the first and second scenes of Act II of *Fidelio* and includes the famous trumpet call signaling freedom. The Leonore Overture No. 1 was composed for a performance planned for Prague.

Other settings include Pierre Gaveaux's *Léonore, ou L'Amour conjugale* (1798, Paris); Paer's *Leonora, ossia L'Amour coniugale* (1804, Dresden); Hüttenbrenner's *Leonore* (1835, Graz); Mercadante's *Leonora* (1844, Naples); and Rolf Liebermann's *Leonore 40/45** (1952, Basel).

BIBLIOGRAPHY: Willy Hess, *Beethovens Oper Fidelio und ihre drei Fassungen* (Zurich Atlantis Verlag, 1966); ———, "Fünfzig Jahre im Bühne von *Leonore-Fidelio*," *Beethoven Jahrbuch* IX (1973–1977), 167–84; Edgar Istel, "Beethoven's *Leonora* and *Fidelio*," *MQ* VII (1921), 226–51; Speight Jenkins, "Reports: U.S.," *ON* XXXII (September 23, 1967), 20–21 [on U.S. premiere]. See the *Fidelio* bibliography for further entries.

DISCOGRAPHY: Moser, Cassilly, Adam, Riddersbusch, and Donath, Leipzig Radio Chorus and Staatskapelle Dresden, conducted by Blomstedt, EMI 157–02 (3).

Leonore 40/45, "opera semiseria" in two acts by Rolf Liebermann; libretto (Ger and French) by Heinrich Strobel. First performance March 26, 1952, Basel.

Monsieur Emile, described as a guardian angel for the characters of the opera, describes the happenings. The work opens in a German apartment in 1939. Hermann is listening to a performance of *Fidelio,** which is interrupted by the announcement that the country is mobilizing for war. His son, Alfred, an oboist, is called up. The scene switches to the Parisian apartment of Germaine, who fears that war will come. In the Paris of 1941–1942, Huguette, Germaine's musician daughter, meets Alfred, now a soldier, at a concert. Eventually, the two become lovers, but they are separated when Alfred is taken prisoner. With the help of Monsieur Emile, the Leonore-like Huguette finds Alfred, who as a prisoner of war has been assigned to work for the instrument maker Lejeune; she eventually wins freedom for Alfred. The guardian angel again intercedes when the various bureaucrats forbid the couple to marry. The work ends with the chorus "Alles wendet sich zum Guten in der besten aller Welten," a fugal sextet for the principals.

Major roles: Huguette (sop), Germaine (alto), Alfred (ten), Hermann (bass), Lejeune (buffo bass), and Monsieur Emile (bar).

Along with musical quotes at appropriate moments from works such as *Fidelio, Pagliacci,* and Franz Liszt's *Liebestraum,* the score employs bitonality and twelve-tone technique.

BIBLIOGRAPHY: Hans Curjel, "Current Chronicle," *MQ* XXXIX (1953), 267–75 [on premiere]; K. H. Ruppel, " 'Leonore 40/45,' " *Melos* XIX (1952), 148–51 [on premiere].

Libussa, opera in three acts by Conradin Kreutzer; libretto (Ger) by Josef Karl Bernard. First performance December 4, 1822, Vienna, Kärntnertortheater, with Caroline Ungher-Sabatier, Anton Hartzinger, Franz Anton Forti, and Karl Friedrich Weinmüller.

The story is set in Bohemia in the early Middle Ages. When Wladislaw saves Princess Libussa from a bear, she falls in love with him but does not reveal her true identity, telling him to come to the castle in order to see her again. In the meantime, the nobles Domoslaw and Tursko are vying for Libussa's hand; she has announced that she will choose one of them as her husband. Wladislaw comes to court, but Libussa, wishing to test his love for her, switches identities with Dobra, who immediately is drawn to the young man herself. Wladislaw is banished, and he seeks solace from Botak, his foster father. Domoslaw hatches a plot against Libussa in order to assure the matrimonial throne for himself, but Libussa decides to choose Wladislaw. This moves Dobra, who is still in love with him herself, to reveal that she is not the princess. Libussa then discloses that Wladislaw is actually Przemsyl, the son of the noble Schima and brother of Dobra. Wladislaw is declared the new prince.

Major roles: Libussa, Princess of Bohemia (sop); Dobra, a young woman at her court (sop); Wladislaw (ten); Domoslaw (bass); Tursko (ten); and Botak (bass).

Other settings include one by Frantisek Škroup (*Libušin Sňatek*, 1850, Prague); and Bedřich Smetana (*Libuše*, comp. 1869–1872, perf. 1881, Prague).

SCORE: vs (Vienna: Pennauer, 1822).

LIBRETTO: German (Vienna: Wallishausser, 1823).

Licht, an epic by Karlheinz Stockhausen, comprising an opera for each day of the week. *Montag,** *Donnerstag,** and *Samstag** have been performed.

BIBLIOGRAPHY: Robert Frisius, "Auf der Suche nach verlorenen Polyphonie. Tendenzen in Stockhausens 'Licht'-Zyklus," *NZM* 145 (July-August 1984), 24–27.

Liebe der Danae, Die (The Love of Danae), opera in three acts by Richard Strauss; libretto (Ger) by Joseph Gregor on a sketch by Hugo von Hofmannsthal. Composed 1938–1940, dress rehearsal August 14, 1944, Salzburg, with Viorica Ursuleac (Danae), and Hans Hotter (Jupiter), conducted by Clemens Krauss; but the theaters were then closed. First performance August 14, 1952, Salzburg, with Annelies Kupper (Danae), Paul Schöffler (Jupiter), Josef Gostic (Midas), and Esther Rethy (Europa); conducted by Clemens Kraus. First U.S. performance (professional) August 18, 1982, Santa Fe, Santa Fe Opera, with Ashley Putnam (Danae), Victor Braun (Jupiter), Dennis Bailey (Midas), Ragnar Ulfung (Pollux), Mary Jane Johnson (Xanthe), and James Hoback (Mercury); conducted by John Crosby.

The work opens at the court of King Pollux, who is in debt because of his luxurious life-style. The king's four nephews try to remedy this situation by carrying a portrait of Pollux's beautiful daughter, Danae, to various prospective husbands. They succeed in arousing the interest of the very wealthy Midas, whose touch turns everything to gold. Attempting to win over Danae for himself, Jupiter appears to the lovely Danae in the guise of Midas. On the wedding night Danae is changed into a golden statue by Midas' touch, but Midas still refuses to give way to the god, and he lets Danae decide with whom to stay. When she chooses Midas, he is stripped of his wealth and is forced to live with Danae in poverty. Jupiter again attempts to win Danae, but once again she rejects him. Moved by her genuine devotion to her earthly husband, Jupiter blesses the pair.

For a detailed synopsis, see K/*KOB*, 848–51.

Major roles: Jupiter (bar); Pollux, King of Eos (ten); Danae, his daughter (sop); Xanthe, her servant (sop); Midas, King of Lydia (ten); the four kings, nephews of Pollux (2 ten, 2 bass); and their wives, Semele, Europa, Alkmene, Leda (2 sop, mezzo, alto).

The musical highlights include the orchestral interlude of the first act, the Golden Rain, in which Jupiter appears to Danae, and the a cappella octet of the four nephews and their wives, after the nephews have seen Midas. Also impressive are the two closing scenes of the opera. The work met with mixed reviews at its premiere (see below), and it is rarely revived today.

SCORE: vs ed Ernst Gernot Klussmann (Berlin-Grunewald: J. Oertel, 1944).

LIBRETTO: German (the same).

BIBLIOGRAPHY: Robert Jacobson, "Reports: U.S.," *ON* XLVII (November 1982), 38, 40 [on U.S. professional premiere]; Hans Keller, "Salzburg: A Sick Orphan," *MR* XIII (1952), 300–02 [on premiere]; Dolf Lindner, *Richard Strauss/Joseph Gregor: Die Liebe der Danae: Herkunft, Inhalt und Gestaltung eines Opernwerkes* (Vienna: Oesterreichischer Diana Verlag, 1952); Richard RePass, " 'Die Liebe der Danae' at Salzburg," *MT* XCIII (1952), 462–63 [on premiere]; Signe Scanzoni, "Danae in Salzburg," *ON* XVII (October 13, 1952), 26–27 [on premiere]; Willi Schuh, ed., *Hugo von Hofmannsthal: Danae oder Die Vernunftheirat* (Frankfurt, 1952); Roland Tenschert, "A 'Gay Myth.' The Story of 'Die Liebe der Danae,' " *Tempo* XXIV (Summer 1952), 5–11.

Liebe im Narrenhaus, Die (Love in the Insane Asylum), Singspiel in two acts by Karl Ditters von Dittersdorf; libretto (Ger) by Gottlieb Stephanie the Younger. First performance April 12, 1787, Vienna, Kärntnertortheater.

Trübe wants his daughter Constanze to wed Bast, the head of an insane asylum, because Bast is his friend and he stands to inherit a fortune from a dying brother. Bast invites the father and daughter to visit him at his place of work, to be amused by the inmates, a thought which horrifies Constanze, who is in love with Albert. In order to thwart Trübe's plans, the faithful Clärchen contrives to have Albert become an inmate of the asylum, and Bast, expecting his brother to die momentarily, rushes to his sibling's side in order to ensure his inheritance. Clärchen is able to release Albert and Orpheus, a patient who has regained his senses and to whom she is attracted. But before the lovers can make their escape,

Bast returns in a foul mood. His brother has died but has left his estate to somebody else. When Bast tries to contest the will, he discovers that the beneficiary is, of all people, Albert, the brother's son. Trübe quickly agrees to let Constanze marry Albert, and Clärchen decides to wed the cured Orpheus.

Major characters: Bast, supervisor of the asylum (bass); Trübe, his friend (bass); Constanze, Trübe's daughter (sop); Clärchen, her lady in waiting (sop); and Albert, Constanze's lover (ten).

Offended by the tasteless treatment of the opera's unfortunate characters, later producers of the work sometimes discarded the libretto and put the music to a new setting; in one such case, it was recast as *Orpheus der Zweyte*, with alterations of the text by F. L. Schröder; this version was performed on December 8, 1788 in Hamburg.

SCORES: fs ed. Thomas Bauman (New York and London: Garland Publishing, 1986); vs (Mainz: Schott, ca. 1790).

LIBRETTO: German (Vienna: Logenmeister, 1787; repr. New York and London: Garland Publishing, 1986).

Liebesverbot, Das oder **Die Novize von Palermo** (Forbidden Love or The Novice of Palermo), "grosse komische Oper" in two acts by Richard Wagner; libretto (Ger) by the composer after William Shakespeare's play *Measure for Measure*. First performance March 29, 1836, Magdeburg, with Karoline Pollert (Isabella), Friedrich Krug (Friedrich), Herr Freimüller (Luzio), and Herr Schreiber (Claudio); conducted by the composer. Revived February 13, 1983, Munich, National Theater, with Hermann Prey (Friedrich) and Sabine Hass (Pamela); conducted by Wolfgang Sawallisch. First U.S. performance July 9, 1983, Waterloo Music Festival, Stanhope, New Jersey, with Jeanne Distell (Isabella), Alessandra Marc (Mariana), Margaret Chalker (Dorella), Roger Roloff (Friedrich), Donald Grobe (Luzio), Howard Hensel (Claudio), Edward Craft (Brighella), and Howard Bender (Pontio Pilato); conducted by Gerard Schwarz. First British performance February 15, 1965, London, University College, with Davies, Jenkins, Bentley, and Kallipetis; conducted by Badacsonyi.

The plot of the opera is inspired by the Shakespeare play, with the action shifted to Sicily. The governor of Sicily, Friedrich, has decreed that having sex is punishable by death. In order to save her brother, Claudio, who has been condemned by this law, Isabella, a novice, agrees to accept the advances of the governor. But Isabella escapes her fate by having Mariana, Friedrich's estranged wife, take her place. Friedrich is therefore forced to withdraw the unpopular law.

Major roles: Friedrich, the German governor of Sicily (bass); Luzio and Claudio, two young nobles (ten); Isabella, Claudio's sister and a novice (sop); Mariana, a novice (sop); Brighella (bass); and Dorella, former maid to Isabella (sop).

BIBLIOGRAPHY: Hans Engel, "Über Richard Wagners Oper 'Das Liebesverbot,' " in *Festschrift für Friedrich Blume* (Kassel: Bär, 1963), 80–91; Bernard Holland, "Opera:

Early Wagner Effort Has U.S. Premiere in Jersey,'' *NYT* (July 11, 1983) [on U.S. premiere]; Edgar Istel, "Richard Wagners Oper 'Das Liebesverbot' auf Grund der handschriftlichen Originalpartitur dargestellt," *Die Musik* VIII, no. 9 (1908–1909), 3–47; Thomas P. Lanier, "Reports: U.S.," *ON* XLVIII (October 1983), 96 [on U.S. premiere]; Rodney Milnes, "On Radio," *Opera* XXVII (1976), 970–72 [on British premiere]; Andrew Porter, "Musical Events," *NY* (July 25, 1983), 62–65 [on U.S. premiere].

SCORES: fs in W/*RWW*, XIV (1923, repr. 1971); vs ed. Otto Singer (Leipzig: B&H, 1923); English-German text ed. Edward Dent (Wiesbaden: B&H, 1982).

DISCOGRAPHY: Soffel, Linser, Whitmarsh, Kräussel, Lorig, and Gelling, Bayreuth Youth Festival 1972, conducted by Bell, Mixture MXT 3001/3 (3). Gale, Cantelo, Young, Caley, Jenkins, Herincx, and Elvon, conducted by Downes, BBC Northern Symphony and Singers, Pantheon C–87689 (3) (tape).

Lohengrin, opera in three acts by Richard Wagner; libretto (Ger) by the composer after an anonymous German epic. First performance August 28, 1850, Weimar, Court Theater, with Rosa Agathé-Milde (Elsa), Hans Feodor Milde (Telramund), and Josephine Fastlinger (Ortrud); conducted by Franz Liszt. First U.S. performance April 3, 1871, New York, Stadt Theater, with Lichtmay, Friderici, Habelmann, Vierling, Franosch, and Theodor Formes (Lohengrin); conducted by Adolf Neuendorff. First British performance May 8, 1875, London, Covent Garden, with Emma Albani (Elsa), Anna D'Angeri (Ortrud), Ernest Nicolini (Lohengrin), and Victor Maurel (Telramund); conducted by Auguste-Charles-Leonard-François Vianesi.

After the shimmering orchestral prelude in A, which, according to Wagner himself, represents the Holy Grail, the opera opens upon the virtuous Elsa of Brabant, who has been accused of killing her brother Gottfried by the evil Count Friedrich of Telramund, assisted by his heathen wife Ortrud. King Heinrich orders that Elsa be brought before him and answer the charges. Elsa then delivers her beautiful "Einsam in trüben Tagen," known as "Elsa's Dream," in which she tells of seeing a knight who will act as her defender. But when the call goes out for just such a champion, there is no response. Just as Elsa loses all hope of being saved, an unknown knight appears in a boat, drawn by a swan. He offers to defend Elsa and wed her on the condition that she not ask him his real identity, warning, "Nie sollst du mich befragen," set to an ominous A-minor motive. She agrees, and Lohengrin defeats Friedrich in the ensuing battle but spares his life. The act ends with the joyful praises of the crowd, "Heil! Heil dir, Held!''

In striking contrast, the second act opens with a gloomy prelude in F-sharp minor, presaging the trouble to come. It is night, and Friedrich, following his humiliating defeat, is ready to flee, but he is encouraged by his wife, who says she will trick Elsa into unmasking the unknown knight. Elsa, preparing for her nuptials, sings the simple but effective thanks to her champion, "Euch Lüften, die mein Klagen." She is joined by the sly Ortrud, who offers to help her prepare for her wedding. Dawn breaks, and a flourish of trumpets in C announces the approach of the bridal party. Elsa, accompanied by her bridesmaids, enters to the strains of the beautiful E-flat chorus "Gesegnet soll sie schreiten," but she is challenged by Ortrud and Friedrich, who accuse Lohengrin of sorcery and shake Elsa's confidence in her intended, at the same time raising doubts among the crowd. Lohengrin rejects the charges, and the king orders the ceremony to continue.

The third act begins with a robust prelude in G, which gives way to the famous Bridal Chorus, in B-flat, "Treulich geführt." Lohengrin and Elsa are finally alone in the bridal chamber, where they sing their magnificent duet, "Das süsse Lied verhallt." Torn by the poisonous insinuations of Ortrud, Elsa finally asks the fatal question. Just then Friedrich breaks in with four accomplices who try to kill Lohengrin. The knight slays Friedrich instead and, with great sadness, tells Elsa he will reveal his identity to the assembled community in the morning. The final scene opens after another brilliant prelude, this one in E-flat. The knight reveals, in the famous Narration, "In fernem Land," that he is Lohengrin, the son of Parsifal and a knight of the Holy Grail, whose mission is to defend virtue as long as his identity is secret. Since he has been forced to tell who he is, he must leave, and so he bids farewell, in "Mein lieber Schwan." Just as Lohengrin is to depart, his faithful swan is transformed into Gottfried. Lohengrin leaves, and Elsa dies in Gottfried's arms.

The famous 1859 parody by Nestroy, *Lohengrün*, with music by Carl Binder, was revised in 1870 by Franz von Suppé, as *Lohengelb*. This version was revived by the Vienna Chamber Opera in an adaptation by Kurt Huemer and Ernst R. Barthel on March 14, 1984. Among the comic characters are Hinundherrufer, the knight Uffo, and the drunken Gaugraf/Landgrave.

For detailed synopses and musical analyses, see C/*NMC*, 309–17; K/*KOB*, 174–84; and N/*SGO*, I, 63–95.

Major roles: King Heinrich, the Falconer (bass); Lohengrin (ten): Elsa von Brabant (sop); Friedrich von Telramund, Brabantine Count (bar); and Ortrud, his wife (sop).

LIBRETTO: German (Weimar, n.p., 1850).

SCORES: fs (Leipzig: B&H, 1852); vs (Leipzig: B&H, 1851).

BIBLIOGRAPHY: Thomas Cramer, *Lohengrin. Edition und Untersuchung* (Munich: Fink, 1971) [critical edition and commentary]; E. Kloss, "Richard Wagner über 'Lohengrin': Aussprüche des Meisters über sein Werk," *Richard Wagner-Jahrbuch* III (1908), 132–88; Heinrich Porges, "Über Richard Wagners 'Lohengrin,' " *Bayreuther Blätter* XXXII (1909), 173ff; John and Suzanne Potter, "Figure of Romance," *ON* XLIX (February 16, 1985), 30–31, 46; Ulrich Siegele, "Das Dramen der Themen am Beispiel des *Lohengrin*," in D/*RWD*, 41–51.

DISCOGRAPHY: See Charles Osborne, B/*OOR*, 354–62.

Loreley, Die, opera in four acts by Max Bruch; libretto (Ger) by Emanuel Geibel (originally written for Felix Mendelssohn) after an old legend. First performance

June 14, 1863, Mannheim. First British performance February 18, 1986, London, Bloomsbury Theatre, University College Opera, with Penelope Chambers (Lenore); Mark Hamilton (Otto); Elizabeth Brice (Bertha); Brindley Sherratt (Hubert); and Howard Charles (Reinald); conducted by Christopher Fifield.

The slighted heroine, Lenore, gets revenge on her former lover, Otto, at his wedding feast to Bertha. The story has such Romantic elements as knights, the supernatural, and religious trappings.

Major roles: Archbishop of Mainz (bass); Bertha, his niece, Countess von Stahleck (sop); Count Palatine Otto (ten); Hubert, the innkeeper (bass); Lenore, his daughter (sop); and Reinald, a Minnesinger (bar).

Other settings are by Ignaz Lachner (1846); Felix Mendelssohn (fragments performed 1851, Leipzig); Wallace (as *Lurline*, 1860); Alfredo Catalani (as *Elda*, 1880, Turin; revived as *Loreley*, 1890, Turin); Mohr (1884); Pacius (1887); Hans Sommer (1891, Brunswick); Albert Becker; and Emil Naumann.

SCORES: fs, vs composer (Breslau: F. E. C. Leuckart, 1862).

BIBLIOGRAPHY: Winton Dean, " 'Die Loreley," *MT* CXXVII (1986), 220–21 [on British premiere]; Reinhold Sietz, "Die musikalische Gestaltung der Loreleysage bei Max Bruch, Felix Mendelssohn und Ferdinand Hiller," in *Max Bruch-Studien*, ed. Dietrich Mämpner (Cologne: Arno Volk Verlag, 1970), 14–45.

Ludovicus Pius, oder **Ludewig der Fromme** (Louis the Pious), opera in three acts by Georg Caspar Schürmann, with numbers by André Campra, André Destouches, and Karl Heinrich Graun; libretto (Ger) by Christian Ernst Simonetti. First performance February 1726, Brunswick.

The story concerns Ludwig I (778–840), the successor of Charlemagne, whose older sons resent his trying to create a kingdom for Charles, his son by his second wife.

Major roles: Ludwig the Pious, Roman Emperor (ten); his sons Lotharius, Pipinus, and Claudius (bass, sop, sop); Adelheid, royal princess (sop); Judith, sister of Welfus, intended bride of the emperor (sop); Robertus, Count of Burgundy, in love with Adelheid (ten); and Welfus, Count of Altorff in Swabia (ten).

SCORES: fs ed. Robert Eitner, *Publikationen älterer Musikwerke*, XVII (1890).

Lulu, unfinished opera in three acts by Alban Berg; libretto (Ger) by the composer after Frank Wedekind's *Erdgeist* (1895) and *Die Büchse der Pandora* (1901). First performance June 2, 1937, Zurich, with Hadzic, Bernhard, Baxevanos, Feher, and Stig; conducted by Robert Denzler. First U.S. performance August 7, 1963, Santa Fe, with Joan Carroll, Elaine Bonazzi, George Shirley, and Donald Gramm: conducted by Robert Craft. First British performance October 1, 1962, London, Sadler's Wells, with Evelyn Lear; conducted by Leopold Ludwig. First performance of the complete opera February 24, 1979, Paris, Paris Opéra (completed by Friedrich Cerha), with Teresa Stratas (Lulu); Franz Mazura

(Dr. Schön); Kenneth Riegel (Alwa), Yvonne Minton (Countess Geschwitz), Robert Tear (the Painter), Gerd Nienstedt (the Animal Trainer), and Toni Blankenheim (Schigolch); conducted by Pierre Boulez. First complete U.S. performance July 29, 1979, Santa Fe, (in an English translation by Arthur Jacobs), with Nancy Shade (Lulu); William Dooley (Dr. Schön); Barry Busse (Alwa), Andrew Foldi (Schigolch), Lenus Carlson (the Acrobat), Leo Goeke (the Painter), Katherine Ciesinski (Countess Geschwitz), Joseph Frank, and Claudia Catania (the Student); conducted by Michael Tilson Thomas.

The work opens with a prologue, in which an Animal Trainer presents his circus troupe, a menagerie that includes the femme fatale Lulu. Lulu is the mistress of her mentor, Dr. Schön, who prompts her to marry the aged Dr. Goll; Goll dies of a heart attack when he sees her making love to the Painter. She then weds the Painter, who cuts his throat when Dr. Schön tells him of Lulu's infamous past. Alwa, Dr. Schön's son, breaks his own engagement because of her, but she weds the father instead, while continuing to flirt with others, including the lesbian Countess Geschwitz, an Athlete, a Student, and Schigolch, a scoundrel whom she believes to be her father. The despairing Dr. Schön hands Lulu a gun to shoot herself, but instead, she shoots him and is imprisoned for the deed. After Lulu is hospitalized with cholera, Countess Geschwitz, who has fallen in love with Lulu, lets herself become infected and switches places with Lulu. After escaping to Paris with Alwa, Lulu ends up as a prostitute in London, supporting Alwa and Schigolch. When Geschwitz finds Lulu, they both become the victims of Lulu's final "client," Jack the Ripper.

For a detailed plot synopsis, see C/*MS*, 237–59 and K/*KOB*, 873–78; for a detailed study of the opera, see George Perle, *The Operas of Alban Berg*, II: *Lulu* (Berkeley: University of California Press, 1980).

Major roles: Lulu (sop); Dr. Schön (bar); Countess Geschwitz (mezzo); Alwa (bar); the Painter (ten); Schigolch (bass); Rodrigo, Athlete/Animal Trainer (bass); and the Student (alto).

Although Berg left a short score for the third act and set in full score everything up to second ensemble of Act III, his wife, Helene, blocked its reconstruction, and the third act of Leo Stein's vocal score, made by Berg's pupil Erwin Stein was suppressed; Universal published the vocal score in 1936, with only the first two acts. *Lulu* was therefore performed in its first forty years of existence as an incomplete work, with the two acts Berg had completed, and the third consisting of a pantomime to the *Lulu Symphony* (comprising the Rondo, Ostinato, and Song of Lulu from the second act; the Variations from the third; and the Adagio from Acts I and III). Mrs. Berg died in 1976, and, at the request of Universal, the Austrian composer Friedrich Cerha completed the reconstruction (see George Perle's review below). The opera was given in its finished version in 1979 (see above).

Friedrich Kuhlau's *Lulu*, after a tale from Christoph Martin Wieland's *Dschinnistan*, was performed in Copenhagen in 1824.

SCORE: vs Edwin Stein (two acts) (Vienna: UE, 1936).

LIBRETTO: German (first two acts) (Vienna: UE, c. 1937); German-English (three acts) (Vienna: UE, 1978).

BIBLIOGRAPHY: Claus-Hennig Bachmann, *"Lulu* bisher: . . . ein Anschlag auf den Dramatiker Berg. Herstellung des dritten Aktes—Grespräch mit Friedrich Cerha," *NZM* CXL (1979), 264–66; Mosco Carner, "Berg and the Reconsideration of 'Lulu,' " *ML* CXXIV (1982), 477–79; Friedrich Cerha, *Arbeitsbericht zur Herstellung des 3. Acts der Oper Lulu von Alban Berg* (Vienna: UE, 1979); Gerold Fierz, " 'Lulu' Returns to Her Birthplace," *Opera* XXXI (1980), 659–64; Dale Harris, "Paris. 'Lulu'—Complete at Last," *HiFi/MA* XXIX(August 1979), 38–39; Arthur Holmberg, "Opening Pandora's Box," *ON* XLV (December 20, 1980), 15–16, 18, 20, 22; Douglas Jarman, "The Completed Lulu," *MT* CXXII (1981), 106–7; ———, "Rhythmic and Metric Techniques in Alban Berg's *Lulu,*" *MQ* LVI (1970), 349–66; Rudolf Klein, "Friedrich Cerhas Arbeitsbericht zur Herstellung des III. Aktes der Oper *Lulu* von Alban Berg," *ÖMz* XXXIV (1979), 130–41; ———, "Pariser Premiere löst nicht alle Probleme. Alban Bergs *Lulu* in der von Friedrich Cerha hergestellten dreiaktigen Fassung," *ÖMz* XXXIV (1979), 144–48; Ernst Krenek, "Zur Vollendung von Alban Bergs *Lulu*-Fragment," *Musica* XXXI (1977), 401–3; Thomas P. Lanier, "Reports: U.S.," *ON* XLIV (October 1979), 44 [on complete U.S. premiere]; George R. Marek, "Earth Spirit: Playwright Frank Wedekind and Lulu," *ON* XLI/21 (1977), 16–19; Karl Neumann, "Wedekind's and Berg's *Lulu,*" *MR* XXXV (1974), 47–57; Dika Newlin, "Out of Pandora's Box. How a Ziegfield Girl [Louise Brooks] Filmed Lulu," *ON* XLI/21 (1977), 20–22; George Perle, "Auf der Sache nach *Lulu,*" *Der Monat* XIX/222 (1967), 63–65; ———, "The Cerha Edition," *Perspectives of New Music* (1979), 251–59; ———, "The Character of Lulu: A Sequel" [to Donald Mitchell's "The Character of Lulu: Wedekind and Berg's Conceptions Compared," *MR* XV (1954)], *MR* XXV (1964), 311–19; ———, "The Complete 'Lulu,' " *MT* CXX (1979), 115–20; ———, "Current Chronicle, Edinburgh," *MQ* LIII (1967), 101–8; ———, "Inhaltliche und formale Strukturen in Alban Bergs Opera *Lulu,*" *ÖMz* XXXII (1977), 427–41; ———, "Die Personen in Bergs *Lulu,*" *AMw* XXIV (1967), 283–90; Andrew Porter, "Musical Events," *NY* LIII (April 4, 1977), 125–31 [fragments of Act III]; ———, "Musical Events," *NY* LVI (January 5, 1981), 64–66 [Metropolitan Opera, with Act III complete]; ———, "Musical Events," *NY* LV (March 12, 1979), 123–25 [premiere of complete opera, Paris]; Manfred Reiter, *Die Zwölftontechnik in Alban Bergs Oper 'Lulu'* (Regensburg: G. Bosse 1973); Volker Scherliess, "Alban Bergs analytische Tafeln zur *Lulu*-Reihe," *Mf* XXX (1977), 452–64; Arthur Schoep, "Lulu by Alban Berg," *OJ* VIII/2 (1975), 15–18; Harold C. Schonberg, "Opera: Sante Fe Troupe Offers Complete Lulu," *NYT* (July 30, 1979) [complete U.S. premiere]; ———, "Paris Will See All of Lulu," *NYT* (February 18, 1979), 17; Michael Steinberg, "An Essay in Virtuosity. Explaining Berg's Score," *ON* XLI/21 (1977), 32–35; David Stevens, "Reports: Foreign," *ON* XLIII (June 1979), 28, 29 [on 1979 premiere]; Florence Stevenson, "Lulu's Last Stand: Jack the Ripper," *ON* XLI/21 (1977), 36.

DISCOGRAPHY: Lear, Johnson, Fischer-Dieskau, and Grobe, Orchester der Deutschen Oper Berlin, conducted by Böhm, with unfinished third act, DG 139 273/75 (3). Stratas, Minton, Schwarz, Riegel, and Mazura, Paris Opera, conducted by Boulez, with third act completed by Cerha, DG 415489–1 GH4 (4), 415489–2 GH3 [ADD] (3 compact discs).

Lustige Witwe, Die (The Merry Widow), operetta in three acts by Franz Lehár; libretto (Ger) by Victor Léon and Leo Stein (originally for Richard Heuberger) after Meilhac's *L'Attaché*. First performance December 28, 1905, Vienna, Theater an der Wien, with Mizzi Günther (Hanna, the Merry Widow) and Louis Treumann. First U.S. performance October 21, 1907, New York, New Amsterdam Theater, with E. Jackson and D. Brian. First British performance June 8, 1907, London, Daly's Theatre, with J. Coyne.

The Merry Widow, Hanna Glawari, meets an old friend, Count Danilo, at a reception for the ambassador from Pontevedro, Baron Mirko Zeta. Danilo, who was in love with Hanna, has not seen her since she married the rich Glawari, and her husband's death has left her quite wealthy. The Baron suggests to Danilo that he marry Hanna in order to secure her fortune for Pontevedro; Danilo rejects the idea because he does not want Hanna to think he is after her money. Zeta's wife, Valencienne, meanwhile, would like Hanna to marry Camille, an admirer of Valencienne. Hanna tries to find out whether Danilo really loves her, and when he becomes enraged after seeing her with Camille, she knows he has passed the test. She tells everyone that she will retain her fortune only if she does not remarry. When Danilo tells her of his love, she explains that her story was a ruse, and that her marrying would not jeopardize her wealth.

Major roles: Baron Mirko Zeta (bass); Valencienne, his wife (sop); Count Danilo Danilowitsch, secretary to the Baron (ten); Hanna Glawari (sop); and Camille de Rosillon (ten).

The tuneful score includes such favorites as Hanna's aria at a garden party in the second act to entertain her guests, entitled the "Viljalied," and the waltz that is the opera's signature.

LIBRETTO: German (Vienna: Ludwig Doblinger, ca. 1905).

BIBLIOGRAPHY: Bernard Grun, *Gold and Silver* (London: W.H. Allen, 1970), 111–30.

DISCOGRAPHY: See M/*IRR*, 101–2.

Lustigen Musikanten, Die (The Merry Musicians), opera in two acts by E. T. A. Hoffmann; libretto (Ger) by Clemens Brentano. First performance April 6, 1805, Warsaw, with Herr Wurm (Ramiro), Mme. Beyer (Azelie), Herr Franz (Piast), Mme. Wöhner (Fabiola), Mlle. Busch (lame boy), Herr Schönau (Rinaldo), Herr Knaust (Pantalon), and Herr Beyer (Tartaglia); conducted by Wojciech Boguslawski. (Hoffmann's name was not included on the theater program.)

Major roles: Ramiro, Prince of Samarkand (ten); Azelie, Princess of Famagusta, his sister (sop); Piast, an old blind man (bass); Fabiola, his daughter (sop); a lame boy, cared for by Piast (sop); Rinaldo, melancholy hero of Samarkand (ten); Pantalon, mayor of Famagusta (low bass); and Tartaglia, minister of Samarkand (bass).

Also set by Peter Ritter (1804, Mannheim).

SCORE: vs in *Werke*, IV/5, ed. Gerhard Allroggen (Mainz: BSS, 1975).

BIBLIOGRAPHY. Gerhard Allroggen, *E. T. A. Hoffmanns Kompositionen* (Regensburg: G. Bosse, 1970), 43–61; Günter Wöllner, "Romantische Züge in der Partitur der 'Lustigen Musikanten,' " *Mitteilungen der E. T. A. Hoffmann-Gesellschaft* XII (1966), 20–30.

DISCOGRAPHY: excerpts: Schweizer, Schmidt, Schulze, and Lang, Berlin Radio, conducted by Zagrosek, Musica Mundi VMS–1616: reviewed by John W. Freeman, "Records," *ON* XLIX (January 19, 1985), 44.

Lustigen Weiber von Windsor, Die (The Merry Wives of Windsor), opera in three acts by Otto Nicolai; libretto (Ger) by S. M. Mosenthal after Shakespeare's play (1601). First performance March 9, 1849, Berlin, Court Theater, with August Zschiesche (Falstaff): conducted by the composer. First U.S. performance March 16, 1863, Philadelphia. First British performance May 3, 1864, London, Her Majesty's Theatre (in Italian), with Therese Tietjens (Frau Fluth), Vitali, Jura, and Charles Santley (Falstaff).

Sir John Falstaff, a rotund, middle-aged knight, is forever pursuing the ladies. He is taught a lesson when his targets are two married ladies, Frau Fluth and Frau Reich. They discover his duplicity and agree to meet him in Windsor Forest, but they arrange for him to meet a group of elves instead. A secondary story concerns Anna Reich, who is in love with the poor Fenton but is pursued by Dr. Cajus and Junker Spärlich. In the end, Anna gets her way.

Major roles: Sir John Falstaff (bass), Herr Fluth (bar), Herr Reich (bass), Fenton (ten), Junker Spärlich (ten), Dr. Cajus (bass), Frau Fluth (sop), Frau Reich (mezzo), and Anna Reich (sop).

For a detailed plot synopsis, see K/*KOB*, 150–52.

The comic elements of the plot are emphasized by the overweight title character, a bass; his operatic "descendants" many be said to include the title role in Cornelius' *Der Barbier von Bagdad** and Baron Ochs in *Der Rosenkavalier.** Falstaff's first entrance, in the Act I finale, is preceded by a royal fanfare. Any knightly pretensions are quickly dispelled by the mocking strings that accompany his vocal line. Comedy in *Die Weiber* is also provided by the two clumsy suitors of Anna, the bumbling Junker Spärlich, and Dr. Cajus, whose German is no better than that of Valzacchi in *Der Rosenkavalier*. Among the many musical highlights of Nicolai's work are the atmospheric overture, which portrays the moonlit Windsor Forest and cites themes from the opera, and Falstaff's drinking song (accompanied by a chorus) of Act II (No. 11), "Als Büblein an der Mutter Brust." Also noteworthy are Fenton's Romance (No. 7b) of the same act, "Horch, die Lerche singt;" his duet with Anna (No. 7c), "Fenton! Mein Mädchen!;" and the choral paen to the moon in Act III, "O süsser Mond!" This was Nicolai's first (and only) German opera. He died two months after its premiere.

Karl Ditters von Dittersdorf's *Die lustigen Weiber und der dicke Hanns* (1796, Oels) is an earlier German setting of the Shakespeare play. Other settings include

Giuseppe Verdi's *Falstaff* (1893, Milan) and Ralph Vaughan Williams' *Sir John in Love* (1929, London).

SCORES: fs (1849, repr. Berlin: E. Bole & G. Bock 187—); vs (Berlin: B&B, ca. 1852).

LIBRETTO: German (Berlin: Deckerschen Geb. Ob. Hofbuchdruckerei, 1849).

BIBLIOGRAPHY: Julia Liebscher, "Biedermeier-Elemente in der deutschen Spieloper— Zu Otto Nicolais 'Die lustigen Weiber von Windsor,' " *MF* XL (1987), 229–37; Helmut Wirth, "Natur und Märchen in Webers *Oberon* . . . und Nicolais *Die lustigen Weiber von Windsor,*" in *Festschrift Friedrich Blume*, ed. A. A. Abert et al. (Kassel: Bär, 1963), 389–97).

DISCOGRAPHY: See M/*IRR*, 273–74.

Lysistrate, opera in three acts by Paul Kont; libretto (Ger) by the composer after Ludwig Seeger's translation of Aristophanes. First performance March 19, 1961, Dresden, with Ingeborg Kollmana (Lysistrate); conducted by Klaus Tennstedt.

The plot concerns a group of Greek women who, in the twenty-first year of the Peloponnesian War, convince the wives of Sparta and Athens to refuse their husbands until the fighting stops.

Major roles: Lysistrate and Kalonike (mezzos), Lampito (alto), and Kinesias (ten).

The score, written in a modern vein, uses Dorian and Lydian modes. The choral sections employ declaimed *Sprechgesang*.

SCORE: vs ed. Gerhard Kiel (Berlin: VEB Lied der Zeit musikverlag, n. d.).

BIBLIOGRAPHY: Joseph Wechsberg, "Germany," *Opera* XII (1961), 454–55 [on premiere]; Franz Willnauer, "Dresden," *NZM* CXXII (1961), 200–201 [on premiere].

═M═

Madame Pompadour, operetta in three acts by Leo Fall; libretto (Ger) by Rudolph Schanzer and Ernst Welisch. First performance September 9, 1923, Berlin, Berliner Theater, with Fritzi Massary (Madame Pompadour) and Ralph Arthur Roberts (René). First U.S. performance, with a libretto by Clare Kummer, November 11, 1924, New York, Martin Beck Theatre, with Wilda Bennett (Madame Pompadour). First British performance, as *Pompadour*, with the text adapted by Frederick Lonsdale and Harry Terraine, December 20, 1923, London, Daly's, with Evelyn Laye (Madame Pompadour), Derek Oldham (René), Huntley Wright (Calicot), Bertram Wallis (King Louis XV), and Elsie Randolph. The New York opening was a flop, while the English production ran for 469 performances.

The story is set around the historical characters of Madame Pompadour, who is the mistress of the French King Louis XV and, at the same time, the lover of René.

Major roles: Madame Pompadour (sop); René (ten); Calicot, a poet (ten); and Louis XV (bar).

The operetta's many highlights include Madame Pompadour's waltz of the first act, "Heut' könnt' einer sein Glück bei mir machen" and her duet with René that follows, "Ich bin dein Untertan."

SCORE: vs (Berlin: Drei Masken Verlag, c. 1922).

Mädchen aus Domrémy, Das (The Girl from Domremy), opera in two acts by Giselher Klebe; libretto (Ger) by the composer after Friedrich Schiller's *Die Jungfrau von Orleans* (1801). First performance June 19, 1976, Stuttgart, with Irmgard Stadler (Johanna), Enriqueta Attres, Günter Reich, Raymond Wolansky (Dunois), and Toni Krämer (Karl VII); conducted by Janos Kulka.

A treatment of the Joan of Arc story, in which Joan is in love with Lionel, her enemy. The opera ends with her death.

Major roles: Johanna (sop); King Karl (Charles) VII of France/Pierre Couchon/ Bishop of Beauvais (ten); Prince Dunois, bastard of Orléans/Brother Martin Ladvenu (bar); and Agnes Sorel, Karl's mistress (sop).

The score mixes twelve-tone writing and tonality, *Sprechgesang*, and a leit-motif for Joan.

BIBLIOGRAPHY: Peter Elvins, "Reports: Foreign," *ON* XLI, No. 3 (September 1976), 60–61 [on premiere]; Kurt Honolka, "Germany," *Opera* XXVII (1976), 862–63 [on premiere]; Wolf-Eberhard von Lewinski, "Konzentration auf einen ewigen Konflikt. Anmerkungen zu Giselher Klebes Oper *Das Mädchen aus Domrémy*," *Musica* XXX (1975), 305–8.

Mahagonny (Das kleine Mahagonny), *Songspiel* by Kurt Weill; libretto (Ger) by Bertolt Brecht. First performance July 18, 1927, Baden-Baden, with Lotte Lenya (Jessie), Irene Eden (Bessie), Erik Wirl (Charlie), Georg Ripperger (Billy), Karl Giebel (Bobby), and Gerhard Pechner (Jimmy); conducted by Ernst Mehlich. First U.S. performance May 23, 1971, New Haven, Yale Repertory Theater (in an English translation by Michael Feingold); conducted by Gustav Meier.

This is the first version of what was to become *Der Aufsteig und Fall der Stadt Mahagonny*.*

Major roles: Jessie (soubrette), Bessie (soubrette), Charlie (ten), Billy (ten), Bobby (bass), and Jimmy (bass).

For a detailed plot summary and musical analysis, see *S/DS*, 86–93.

SCORES: vs (Vienna: UE, 1927); vs ed. David Drew (Vienna: UE, 1963).

BIBLIOGRAPHY: David Drew, "The History of Mahagonny," *MT* CIV (1963), 18; Hans Heinsheimer, "Rise and Fall and Resurrection," *ON* XLIV (December 1, 1979), 28, 30–34.

DISCOGRAPHY: Dickinson, Liddell, Thomas, Langridge, Luxon, Partridge, and Rippon, London Sinfonietta, conducted by Atherton, DG 2709–064 (3); reviewed by John W. Freeman, "Records," *ON* XLI (April 2, 1977), 48.

Manuel Venegas, unfinished opera in three acts by Hugo Wolf; libretto (Ger) by Moritz Hoernes after Pedro Alacrón's "El niño de la bola." First performance March 1, 1903, Mannheim.

The story takes place in a small town in southern Spain. Manuel Venegas is the son of a military hero who not only spent his entire fortune but died in debt to the usurious Elias Perez. Manuel, a wastrel raised by the priest Don Trinidad, has met Soledad, Elias' daughter, and has fallen in love with her. Her father has forbidden the union, but Manuel is determined to have her and he amasses a fortune. Still repulsed by the father, he swears to kill anyone who takes Soledad from him. Although she loves Manuel, her father forces her on his deathbed to accept Antonio, whom she marries and with whom she has a son.

The operatic action begins when Manuel returns once again to the town, this time with priceless jewels and a dagger. It is the day of a special religious festival, during which any man can win a dance with a girl of his choice. Despite the lies and warnings of the jealous apothecary, Vitriolo, Manuel refuses to flee and begins to dance with Soledad. In the middle of the dancing, Antonio grabs the dagger and stabs him.

Major roles: Manuel Venegas (ten); Antonio Arregui (bar); Don Trinidad, priest (bass); Vitriolo, apothecary (ten); Soledad, Antonio's wife (sop); and Donna Maria, mother of Soledad (alto).

Also set by Richard Heuberger (1889).

SCORES: fs ed. Hans Jancik, Wo/*SW* XIII (1960); v.s. (Vienna, 1902).

Martha, oder Der Markt von Richmond (Martha, or The Fair of Richmond), opera in four acts by Friedrich von Flotow; libretto (Ger) by W. Friedrich, an operatic version of the ballet pantomime "Lady Henriette ou La Servante de Greenwich," a scenario by Vernoy de Saint-Georges and music by Flotow, Burgmüller, and Deldevez (1844, Paris). First performance November 25, 1847, Vienna, Kärntnertortheater, with Anna Zerr (Lady Harriet), Josef Erl, Alois Ander, and Karl Formes. First U.S. performance November 1, 1852, New York, Niblo's Garden, with Anna Bishop, Jacques, Guidi, Leach, Strini, and Rudolph; conducted by Bochsa. First British performance June 4, 1849, London, Drury Lane Theatre.

The story is set in Richmond, England, in 1710. Lady Harriet Durham and her maid, Nancy, attend a fair dressed as two country girls, Martha and Julia. They are hired as servants by two young farmers, Lionel and his foster brother Plunkett. Lionel falls in love with Martha, and Plunkett with Julia. After upsetting the household, the ladies flee. Nancy is reunited with Plunkett, and Harriet with Lionel, when it is revealed that he is really the Earl of Derby.

Major roles: Lady Harriet, maid of honor to Queen Anne (sop); Nancy, her maid (alto); Sir Tristram Mickelford, Lady Harriet's cousin (bass); Plunkett, a young farmer (bar); Lionel, his foster brother (ten); and the Sheriff of Richmond (bass).

For detailed synopses, see C/*NMC*, 367–74 and K/*KOB*, 152–57.

The opera, once immensely popular in its Italian version, has not maintained its place in the repertoire. Among its once-famous numbers are Martha's "Die letzte Rose" ("The Last Rose of Summer"), which she sings in the second act at the urging of Lionel, and his expression of love for her in the third, "Ach, so fromm."

SCORES: vs (Leipzig: A. Cranz, 1840); (Vienna: H. F. Müller, ca. 1848).

LIBRETTO: German (Vienna: Anton Pichler's sel. Witwe, 1847).

BIBLIOGRAPHY: Edward Dent, "A Best-Seller in Opera," *ML* XXII (1941), 139–54.

DISCOGRAPHY: See M/*IRR*, 373.

Masagniello Furioso oder **Die Neapolitanische Fischer-Empoerung** (Mad Masagniello, or The Neapolitan Fishermen's Uprising), opera in three acts by Reinhard Keiser; libretto (Ger) by Barthold Feind. First performance June 1706, Hamburg. Revived October 11, 1967, East Berlin, Staatsoper.

The plot concerns the 1647 uprising of Neapolitan fishermen, headed by Thomas Aniello, against their Spanish masters. It also forms the basis of Auber's *La Muette de Portici* (1828, Paris), which appeared in New York in 1829 as *Masaniello*.

Maschinist Hopkins, opera in three acts by Max Brand; libretto (Ger) by the composer. First performance April 13, 1929, Duisburg. First British performance (radio) September 17, 1986, Radio 3.

The work is set in the United States, around 1920. It opens with Bill and his beloved, Nell, trying to deceive her foreman husband Jim by falsifying the work records. Jim catches them in the act but is killed in the following struggle when he falls against the machinery. In the next five years Bill becomes a rich industrialist and plans to close up the factory to cover up his crime. Hopkins discovers Bill's plans, forces Nell to betray his secret, and tells Bill of Nell's betrayal. Nell becomes a prostitute and Bill, losing his mind, tries to destroy the machinery. He is stopped by Hopkins, and the opera ends with Hopkins announcing the start of another workday.

Major roles: Jim, the foreman (bass); Nell, his wife (sop); Bill, a machinist (ten); Hopkins, another machinist (bar).

Although the opera did well initially, it disappeared from the repertoire within a few years. The musical style is eclectic, with one number in a thoroughly jazz style. Clive Bennett (see below) claims that the work predates *Lulu** in its use of the structural device of recapitulation for psychological-dramatic inversion, especially in the last twenty minutes, and that Berg knew the Brand work well.

BIBLIOGRAPHY: Clive Bennett, "Maschinist Hopkins: A Father for Lulu?," *MT* CXXVII (1986), 481–84.

SCORE: vs ed. Erwin Stein (Vienna: UE, c. 1928).

LIBRETTO: German (Vienna: UE, c. 1928).

Massimilla Doni, opera in four acts by Othmar Schoeck; libretto (Ger) by Armin Rüeger after Honoré de Balzac's story of the same name. First performance March 2, 1937, Dresden, with Heinrich Tessmer (Duke Cattaneo), Kurt Böhme (Capraja), Rudolf Dittrich (Emilio Memmi), Arno Schellenberg (Prince Vendramin), Torsten Ralf (Genovese), Felice Hüni-Mibacsek (the Duchess); and Erna Sack (Tinti); conducted by Karl Böhm.

The story takes place in Venice, in 1830. The young Emilio, who comes from an aristocratic Venetian house whose fortunes have faded, is in love with Massimilla, the fiancée of Duke Cattaneo, for whom she has little feeling. Emilio's attentions are diverted by the seductive Tinti, a singer. Driven to attempt suicide by her betrayal, Emilio is rescued by the caring Massimilla, who has been summoned by Vendramin, his friend. The work closes with her touching cradle song. Interwoven in the plot is the quarrel of Duke Cattaneo and his friend, Capraja, over music.

Major roles: Duke Cattaneo, an old crank (ten); Capraja, his friend, patron of Genovese (bar); Emilio Memmi, a young nobleman (ten); Prince Vendramin, his older friend (bar); Genovese (ten); Duchess Massimilla Doni, fiancée of the duke (sop); and Tinti, a singer patronized by Cattaneo (sop).

SCORE: vs (Vienna: UE, 1936).

LIBRETTO: German, the same.

BIBLIOGRAPHY: Hans Corrodi, "Othmar Schoeck's 'Massimilla Doni,' " *ML* XVIII (1937), 391–97; Karl Heinrich David, "Über Othmar Schoecks 'Massimilla Doni,' " *SMz* LXXVII/1 (1937); Gerhard Pietzsch, " 'Massimilla Doni,' Othmar Schoecks neue Oper," *Die Musik* XXX (March 1, 1937).

Mathis der Maler (Mathis the Painter), opera-oratorio in seven scenes by Paul Hindemith; libretto (Ger) by the composer on the subject of the sixteenth-century German painter Matthias Grünewald. First performance May 28, 1938, Zurich, with Asger Stig (Mathis), Peter Baxevanos (Cardinal Albrecht), Hans Schwalb (Ernst Mosbacher), Albert Emmerich (Riedlinger), Simon Bermani (Rat Capito), Judith Hellwig (Ursula), Leni Funk, and Georgine von Milinkovic; conducted by Robert F. Denzler. First U.S. performance February 17, 1956, Boston. First complete U.S. performance (in an English translation by Walter Ducloux) April 17, 1966, Los Angeles, University of Southern California, with George Gibson (Mathis), Rafael Enriquez (Cardinal Albrecht), Joan Robb (Ursula), and Joan Barber (Regina); conducted by Walter Ducloux. First British performance (concert) March 15, 1939, London, Queen's Hall, with Dennis Noble (Mathis), Parry Jones (Cardinal Albrecht), Stiles Allen (Ursula), Muriel Brunskill (Countess Helfenstein), John McKenna (Rat Capito), Noel Eadie (Regina), and Norman Walker (Lorenz von Pommersfelden); conducted by Clarence Raybould. First performance (stage) August 29, 1952, Edinburgh, with Helmut Melchert (Cardinal Albrecht), Anneliese Rothenberger (Regina), and Mathieu Ahlersmeyer (Mathis); conducted by Leopold Ludwig. The premiere was set for Berlin in 1934, but the Nazis, fearing the consequences of showing a revolt against authority, banned the work. Hindemith was forced to leave Germany.

The story details the efforts of Mathis Grünewald to help the peasants in the Peasants' War of 1542. When his efforts fail, he escapes with Regina and gives up politics in favor of art.

For a detailed plot synopsis, see K/*KOB*, 885–89.

Major roles: Albrecht von Brandenburg, Cardinal, Archbishop of Mainz (ten); Mathis, a painter in his service (bar); Riedlinger, a rich Mainz citizen (bass); Hans Schwalb, leader of the protesting peasants (ten); Ursula, Riedlinger's daughter (sop); and Regina, Schwalb's daughter (sop).

SCORES: fs (Mainz: BSS, 1939); vs ed. composer (Mainz: BSS, 1935).

LIBRETTO: (Mainz: BSS, 1935).

BIBLIOGRAPHY: Andres Briner, "Entstehung und Aussage der Oper *Mathis der Maler*," *Melos* XXXVII (1970), 437–46; James E. Paulding, "Mathis der Maler—The Politics of Music," *HJb* V (1976), 102–22; Edward Sackville-West, "Mathis der Maler. Analysis of the Opera," *Opera* III (1952), 536–41, 546; Norbert J. Schneider, "Prinzipien der rhythmischen Gestaltung in Hindemiths Oper *Mathis der Maler*," *HJb* VIII (1979), 7–48.

DISCOGRAPHY: See M/*IRR*, 65.

Medea, "ein mit Musik vermischtes Drama" in one act by Georg Benda; libretto (Ger) by Friedrich Wilhelm Gotter. First performance May 1, 1775, Leipzig, Koch's Theater.

A treatment of the Medea story, in which, after she has helped Jason obtain the Golden Fleece, Medea kills her sons by Jason when he deserts her for Kreusa. In utter despair, Jason stabs himself.

Major roles (all spoken): Medea, Jason, their sons, and Kreusa, the daughter of the King of Corinth and Jason's betrothed.

Among the other settings are Francesco Cavalli's *Giasone* (1649, Venice); Antonio Gianettini's *Medea in Atene* (1675, Venice); Johann Siegmund Kusser's *Jason* (1692, Brunswick); Marc-Antoine Charpentier's *Médée* (1693, Paris); Joseph-François Salomon's *Médée et Jason* (1713, Paris); Luigi Cherubini's *Médée* (1797, Paris); Johann Simone Mayr's *Medea in Corinto* (1813, Naples); Giovanni Pacini's *Medea* (1843, Palermo); Darius Milhaud's *Médée* (1939, Antwerp); and B. A. Zimmermann's *Medea* (not performed).

SCORES: fs ed. J. Trojan, *Musica Antiqua Bohemica*, II/8 (Prague: Supraphon, 1976); vs (Leipzig: Im Schwickertschen Verlage, 1778).

LIBRETTO: German (Gotha: Ehinger, 1775).

Meistersinger von Nürnberg, Die (The Mastersingers of Nuremberg), opera in three acts by Richard Wagner; libretto (Ger) by the composer. First performance June 21, 1868, Munich, with Franz Betz (Hans Sachs), Kaspar Bausewein (Pogner), Gustav Hölzel (Beckmesser), Franz Nachbaur (Walther von Stolzing), Max Schlosser (David), Mathilde Mallinger (Eva), and Sophie Diez (Magdalene); conducted by Hans von Bülow. First U.S. performance January 4, 1886, New York, Metropolitan Opera, with Auguste Seidl-Krauss (Eva), Marianne Brandt (Magdalene), Albert Stritt, Herr Krämer, Emil Fischer (Hans Sachs), Otto Kemlitz, Herr Lehmler, and Josef Staudigl (Pogner); conducted by Anton Seidl. First British performance May 30, 1882, London, Drury Lane Theatre, with Rosa Sucher (Eva), Josephine Schefsky, Hermann Winkelmann (Walther von Stolzing), Landau, Eugen Gura (Hans Sachs), Ehrke, Kraus, and Koegel; conducted by Hans Richter.

An imposing C-major overture, with its contrapuntal elements, sets the scene, which opens in the church of St. Katherine. The congregation includes Eva, the daughter of Veit Pogner, the goldsmith, and Magdalene, her nurse. They are joined by young Walther von Stolzing, a visiting knight, who is in love with Eva. She explains that he may wed her only if he wins the song contest of the Guild of Mastersingers. The apprentice David explains the rules to Walther, and the Mastersingers enter for the preliminary trial. Walther is introduced, and explains, in the aria "Am stillen Herd," how he learned the art of singing. He then presents his song entry, "Fanget an! So rief der Lenz in den Wald." Although the venerable cobbler Hans Sachs and Pogner approve, the rest of the Guild members, especially the jealous town clerk, Beckmesser, do not, since the song breaks most of the traditional rules. In despair and anger Walther stalks off. Sachs is left to ponder the state of affairs.

In the second act Sachs muses over Walther's song and his own love for Eva; but he realizes he is too old for her and, sensing that she loves Walther, he decides to help the younger man. When Beckmesser comes to court Eva, Sachs interrupts his serenade with blows from his hammer. An uproar ensues, during which the entire neighborhood joins in, and Beckmesser is soundly thrashed. The appearance of the watchman disperses the crowd.

The third act opens in Hans Sachs' shop, after a magnificent orchestral prelude. Sachs muses about the state of the world in his aria "Wahn! Wahn! Überall Wahn!," after which he is joined by Walther, who tells him of his dream, in which the "Preislied" came to him. The two men discuss Walther's song, and the shoemaker makes suggestions to improve Walther's chances at winning the competition. Overhearing this, Beckmesser waits until the two have left and then he steals what he thinks is Walther's new creation. He waves the paper in Sach's face and accuses him of trying to make him lose the competition, whereupon Sachs gives Beckmesser the song as a present. Beckmesser leaves, and Eva enters, pretending that one of her shoes is too tight. Walther then comes in dressed in his knight's costume, and then Magdalene and David come in, and all join in in the sparkling quintet "Selig wie die Sonne meines Glückes lacht." An extended instrumental interlude, which reprises part of the overture, leads to the finale, scene 5. The various guilds enter, singing and waving their banners. When Hans Sachs appears, he is saluted by the hymn "Wach'auf, es nahet gen den Tag," which he acknowledges with "Euch wird es leicht." The song competition then begins. The first contestant is Beckmesser, who, not understanding the piece he tried to steal from Walther, makes a fool out of himself as he tries to fit the words to his own tune. Walther steps forward and sings the verses in the proper manner; this is the famous "Preislied" ("Morgenlich leuchtend im rosigen Schein"), set in a perfect Bar form. All are moved by his beautiful piece, and he wins the contest unanimously. At first he rejects the gold chain of the Masters' Guild, but Sachs urges him to take it ("Verachtet mir die Meister nicht"). Walther accepts the praise of the crowd and the hand of his beloved Eva, and Hans Sachs receives the final salute from the throng, "Heil Sachs! Hans Sachs!"

For detailed synopses and musical analyses, see C/*NMC*, 391–99; K/*KOB*, 197–214; and N/*SGO*, I, 41–62.

Major roles: Eva (sop), Walther (ten), Hans Sachs (bass or bass-bar), Magdalene (sop or mezzo), David (ten), Beckmesser (bass), Pogner (bass), and Kothner (bass).

Sachs is also the hero of operas by Adalbert Gyrowetz (1834) and Albert Lortzing (1840, see *Hans Sachs**).

SCORES: fs (London, Mainz: BSS, 1868); W/*SW*, IX/1, IX/2, ed. Carl Dahlhaus (Mainz: BSS, 1970); vs (Mainz: BSS, 1868).

LIBRETTO: German (Mainz: B. Schott's Söhne, 1862).

BIBLIOGRAPHY: Kurt Atterberg, "Midsummer Madness," *ON* XXXVI (January 15, 1972), 21–23; Robert Donington, "Wagner and *Die Meistersinger*," *ON* XL (April 17, 1976), 18–19; Ludwig Finscher, "Über den Kontrapunkt der *Meistersinger*," in D/*RWD*, 303–12; Anthony Lewis, "A 'Pretty' Theme and the Prize Song," *MT* CXVII (1976), 732–33; William E. McDonald, "Words, Music and Dramatic Development in *Die Meistersinger*," *19th Century Music* I (1978), 246–60; George R. Marek, "Nuremberg's Cobbler Poet," *ON* XLI/8 (1976), 19–20; Curt Mey, *Die Meistersinger in Geschichte und Kunst* . . . (Walluf bei Wiesbaden: Sändig, 1903; facsimile of 1901 edition); H. H. Stuckenschmidt, "The Real Beckmesser?" *ON* XL (April 17, 1976), 30–33; Jens Wildgruber, "Das Geheimnis der 'Barform' in Richard Wagners Die Meistersinger von Nürnberg," in *Festschrift für Heinz Becker*, 205–13.

DISCOGRAPHY: See Richard Law, B/*OOR*, 376–92.

Miriways, Singspiel in three acts by Georg Philipp Telemann; libretto (Ger) by J. S. Müller. First performance May 26, 1728, Hamburg.

The generous Persian ruler Miriways is secretly married to Samischa. Their daughter, Bemira, who is not aware of her true parentage, has been raised by the widow Nisibisis. Bemira falls in love with Sophi, favorite general of Miriways, and Sophi has been promised the throne if he marries the daughter of Miriways. Since Sophi is unaware that the ruler's daughter and his beloved are one and the same, he refuses his sovereign's request. Further complications arise from two suitors for Nisibisis' hand, Murgah and the evil Zemir. After many difficulties all ends well, with Zemir falling into disgrace and Sophi marrying Bemira.

This work stands midway between Telemann's comic and heroic works. Among its numbers is a March of the Persians (Act 2, scene 12) and Zemir's comic "Ja, ja, es muss mir glücken" (Act 1, scene 7), in which he expresses his intention to win the widow's hand through cunning. "So lustig," sung by the character Sandor (Act 3, scene 4), is a drinking song written in a rapid patter style.

BIBLIOGRAPHY: Mary Peckham, "The Operas of Georg Philipp Telemann," Ph.d. diss., Columbia University, 1972.

Mona Lisa, opera in two acts by Max von Schillings; libretto (Ger) by Beatrice Dovsky. First performance September 26, 1915, Stuttgart, with Hedy Iracema-Brügelmann and Carl Johan Forsell. First U.S. performance March 1, 1923, New York, Metropolitan Opera, with Barbara Kemp (Mona Lisa) and Michael Bohnen (Francesco); conducted by Artur Bodanzky.

A lay brother at a Carthusian monastery tells a couple honeymooning in Florence the tale of Mona Lisa. The young wife of Francesco del Giocondo is in love with Giovanni de Salviati. When Francesco locks the lover in a cupboard, which leads to his suffocation, Mona Lisa pushes her husband in and kills him. At the end the visiting couple turns out to be a modern version of Mona Lisa and Francesco, and the brother that of Giovanni.

Major roles: Francesco del Giocondo/a traveler (bar); Mona Lisa, his wife/a woman (sop); and Giovanni de Salviati/lay brother (ten).

SCORE: vs (Vienna: UE, 1914).

LIBRETTO: German-English (New York: F. Rullman, 1922).

BIBLIOGRAPHY: Clemens N. Gruber, "Max von Schillings—An Almost Forgotten Composer," *Opera* XXXIII (1983), 963–68.

Mond, Der (The Moon), opera in three acts by Carl Orff; libretto (Ger) by the composer after the Grimm tale *Der Mond*. First performance February 5, 1939, Munich, Staatsoper, with Julius Patzak; conducted by Clemens Krauss. First U.S. performance October 16, 1956, New York, City Center, with Kelly and Norman Treigle; conducted by Joseph Rosenstock.

The narrator tells the story of a country on which the moon has never shone. When four boys from this country visit another country and see the moon, they decide to steal it. They become heroes in their homeland, and when they grow old they each request that a quarter of the moon be buried with them when they die. Their request is granted, and after the last expires, the country is plunged into darkness once more. When the four put the moon back together again and hang it up, the underworld is bathed in light, awakening the dead. The chaos this brings on reaches to the heavens, and Peter finally decides that this must stop in order to preserve the world. He takes the moon and hangs it from a star. The moon subsequently shines on the earth.

Major roles: the narrator (ten); four boys who steal the moon (ten, two bar, bass); a peasant (bar); an old man, Peter, who preserves order in the heavens (bass); a small child, who discovers the moon in the heavens (speaking part).

SCORE: vs (Mainz: BSS, 1939).

BIBLIOGRAPHY: L/*CO*, 88–92.

DISCOGRAPHY: Christ, Philharmonia Chorus and Orchestra, conducted by Sawallisch, Angel 3567B/L (2). Büchner, Klotz, Lunow, Teschler, Terzibaschian, and Süss, Radio Symphony Orchestra and Chorus Leipzig, conducted by H. Kegel, Phillips 6700 0 83 (2); reviewed by Rodney Miles, "New Records," *Opera* XXVII (1976), 358.

Montag (Monday), opera in three acts by Karlheinz Stockhausen; libretto (Ger) by the composer. First performance May 7, 1988, Milan, La Scala. Part of the *Licht** cycle.

The plot celebrates woman and the cycle of birth and focuses on the character of Eve. It consists of "Eve's First Birth" (Act I); "Eve's Second Birth" (Act II), which covers the birth of the first human children; and "Eve's Magic" (Act III), in which men appear.

The score is performed by twenty-one musicians, which includes fourteen solo voices, six instrumentalists, a mime/actor, choruses, and six synthesizers. The main soloists are not singers but two solo instrumentalists, a basset hornist and a flutist.

BIBLIOGRAPHY: Henning Lohner, "Light Work," *ON* LII (May 1988), 15–16.

Mörder, Hoffnung der Frauen (Murder, the Hope of Wives), opera in one act by Paul Hindemith; libretto (Ger) by Oskar Kokoschka. First performance June 4, 1921, Stuttgart, Landestheater; conducted by Fritz Busch.

The story takes place in olden times. The expressionist drama focuses on sexual conflict.

Major roles: the husband (bar), the wife (sop), first warrior (ten), second warrior (bass), third warrior (ten), first maiden (sop), second maiden (alto), and third maiden (sop).

SCORES: fs (Mainz: BSS, 1921); vs ed. Hermann Uhticke, the same.

BIBLIOGRAPHY: W. Nagel, "Mörder, Hoffnung der Frauen. Uraufführung," *NMZ* XLII (1921), 300.

DISCOGRAPHY: Schnaut, Grundheber, et al., conducted by Albrecht, Berlin Radio Symphony, Wergo WER–6–132, WER–60132–50 (compact disc).

Moses und Aron (Moses and Aaron), unfinished opera in two acts (several sketches for third act) by Arnold Schoenberg; libretto (Ger) by the composer after the Old Testament, Exodus 3–4, 20–31, 32. Composed 1932. First performance March 12, 1954, Hamburg, NWDR, with Hans Herbert Fiedler (Moses) and Helmut Krebs (Aron). First stage performance June 6, 1957, Zurich, with Hans Herbert Fiedler (Moses) and Helmut Melchert (Aron); conducted by Hans Rosbaud. First U.S. performance November 30, 1966, Boston, Back Bay Theatre (in an English translation by Allen Forte), with Donald Gramm (Moses) and Richard Lewis (Aron); conducted by Osborne McConathy. First British performance June 28, 1965, London, Covent Garden, with Forbes Robinson (Moses) and Richard Lewis (Aron); conducted by Sir Georg Solti.

The opera covers the period when Moses received the Ten Commandments while Aron urged the Hebrews to build a Golden Calf and Moses reappeared and shattered the holy tablets. The opera ends with Moses sinking to the ground in despair. The last act would have dealt with Moses' triumph in the desert.

For a detailed synopsis, see K/*KOB*, 862–66.

Major roles: Moses (bass speaking role) and Aron (ten).

Schoenberg completed the music and text for the first two acts. He wrote the text for the first scene of the third and sketched a few measures of the music.

SCORES: fs, English-German (Mainz: BSS, 1958); fs ed. Christian Martin Schmidt, Scho/SW, III/8/1–2 (1977, 1978); vs, English-German, ed. Winfried Zillig and Allen Forte (Mainz: BSS, 1957).

LIBRETTO: German (Mainz: BSS, ca. 1957).

BIBLIOGRAPHY: John D. Drummond, "The Background, Shape and Meaning of Twelve-Tone Music: An Examination via *Moses und Aron*," *Soundings* III (1973), 18–25; John W. Freeman, "Voice in the Wilderness," *ON* XXX (May 7, 1966), 14–15 [on first U.S. performance]; Eberhardt Klemm, "Schönbergs Oper *Moses und Aron*," in *Arnold Schönberg—1874 bis 1951 . . .*, ed. Mathias Hansen and Christa Müller (Berlin: Akademie der Künste der DDR, 1976), 75–79; René Leibowitz, "Das unmögliche Meisterwerk," *ÖMz* XXVIII (1973), 215–19; Oliver Neighbour, "Moses and Aaron," *MT* CVI (1965), 422–25; Hans F. Redlich, "Schoenberg's Religious Testament," *Opera* XVI (1965), 401–7; Harold Rosenthal, "London. Opera Diary," *Opera* XVI (1965), 601–5 [on British premiere]; Erwin Stein, "Moses und Aron," *Opera* VIII (1957), 485–89 [on premiere]; Egon Wellesz, "Schönbergs Magnum opus," *ÖMz* (1973), 209–14; Pamela C. White, *Schoenberg and the God-Idea: The Opera 'Moses und Aron'* (Ann Arbor, Mich.: UMI Research Press, 1985); Gilliam Widdicombe, "London Opera Diary," *Opera* XVII (1966), 752–53; Karl H. Wörner, "Current Chronicle. Germany," *MQ* XL (1954), 403–12 [on premiere]; ———, *Schoenberg's 'Moses and Aaron'* transl. Paul Hamberger (London: Faber, 1963).

DISCOGRAPHY: See M/*IRR*, 394.

Murieta, musical theater in three acts by Jens-Peter Ostendorf; libretto (Ger) by the composer after Pablo Neruda's play *The Glory and Death of Joaquin Murieta*; translated into German by Klaus Möckel. First performance October 25, 1984, Cologne, with Allan Evans (Murieta), Delores Ziegler (Theresa), Peter Haage (Reyes), Matthias Hölle (Dreifinger), and Marga Schiml (the Tempter); conducted by Steuart Bedford.

The story concerns a Chilean peasant, Murieta, who comes to California during the Gold Rush and becomes a bandit who robs from the rich to give to the poor. The Ku Klux Klan kills his wife, Theresa, and he is beheaded by the Klan when he visits her grave. The Chileans get his head back, and it becomes a symbol of freedom and independence.

Major roles: Murieta (bar), Theresa (lyric sop), Reyes (buffo ten), Dreifinger (bass), and the Tempter (dramatic alto).

Alexei Rybnikov's *The Star and Death of Joaquin Murieta* (1975) is another treatment of the subject.

BIBLIOGRAPHY: Elizabeth Forbes, "Reports: Foreign," *ON* XLIX (February 2, 1985), 36 [on premiere].

=N

Nacht in Venedig, Eine (A Night in Venice), operetta in three acts by Johann Strauss, Jr.; libretto (Ger) by F. Zell [Camillo Walzell] and Richard Genée. First performance October 3, 1883, Berlin, for the opening of the Friedrich-Wilhelm-Städtisches-Theater, with Ottilie Collin (Annina) and Jani Szika (Caramello). First U.S. performance (in English) April 24, 1884, New York, Daly's; January 8, 1890 (in German, as *Venetianische Nächte*). First British performance May 25, 1944, London, Cambridge Theatre. New version by Erich Korngold and Ernst Marischka 1931, Berlin.

The Duke of Urbino is attracted to Barbara, the wife of Delacqua, an elderly senator of Venice. He arranges for his barber, Carmello, to go to Venice and bring Barbara back for a ball he is giving. The barber returns, but with his girlfriend Annina, disguised as Barbara, and Barbara as Annina. The duke eventually finds out he has been tricked, but he accepts his fate good-naturedly.

For a detailed synopsis and musical analysis, see K/*KOB*, 290–94.

Major roles: the Duke of Urbino (ten); Delacqua, a senator (bar); Barbara, his wife (mezzo); Annina, a young fish seller (sop); and Caramello, a barber (ten or bar).

The text was written at about the same time as *Der Bettelstudent*,* and Strauss wanted to set the latter. He was eventually convinced to let the fledgling composer Millöcker have the second text, which he regretted when *Eine Nacht* was a miserable failure at its premiere. The score nonetheless has beautiful music, including the "Lagunenwalzer," "Ach wie so herrlich zu schau'n," and Caramello's paen to Venice, "Sei mir gegrüsst du mein holdes Venetia." The operetta has fared better since its opening night, beginning with its Vienna premiere on October 9, 1883, and it is occasionally revived.

SCORE: vs ed. Erich Korngold and Ernst Marischka (Brussels: A. Cranz, 1924).

BIBLIOGRAPHY: Andrew Lamb, "Nights in Venice," *MT* CXVII (1976), 989–92.

DISCOGRAPHY: excerpts: Köth, Schirmacher, Schock, and Curzi, Berlin Symphony, conducted by Schmidt-Boeicke, Eurodisc 258–375 (compact disc).

Nachtlager in Granada, Das (The Night Camp in Granada), opera in two acts by Conradin Kreutzer; libretto (Ger) by Karl Johann von Braun after the drama by Friedrich Kind. First performance January 13, 1834, Vienna, Theater in der Josefstadt, with Anna Segatta (Gabriele), Josef Pöck (Gomez), Josef Emminger (Gomez), Franz Borschizki (Ambrosio), and Karl Rott (Vasco). Revised version March 9, 1837, Vienna, Kärntnertortheater. First U.S. performance December 15, 1862, New York. First British performance May 13, 1840, London, Prince's Theatre. Revivals include one in 1947, Hamburg, and one in 1980, Messkirch, Upper Swabia, conducted by Heinz Bucher.

The opera takes place in Spain in 1550. The shepherdess Gabriele loses a little dove and is comforted by Gomez. Her uncle Ambrosio wants Gabriele to marry Vasco. The dove is returned by an unknown hunter, the Spanish Crown Prince, who unmasks Vasco and his accomplices as robbers. Gabriele and Gomez are reunited.

Major roles: Gabriele (sop); Gomez, a young hunter (ten); Vasco, a shepherd (bass); Ambrosio, a shepherd and Gabriele's uncle (bass).

Among the interesting musical numbers are the hunter's Romance of the first act, "Ein Schütz bin ich," and the closing choral prayer "Schon die Abendglocken klangen." Act II includes Gabriele's "Moorish" Romance, "Leise wehet, leise wallet," and the terzet of the hunter and the two lovers, "Trenne nicht das Band der Liebe." This was Kreutzer's most successful work.

SCORES: fs, revised version (Leipzig: A. Cranz, 1925); vs (Bremen: Cranz n. d.), ed. Gustav F. Kogel, revised version (Leipzig: C. F. Peters, 187–; Leipzig: A. Cranz, 1925).

LIBRETTO: German, first version (Vienna: Trentsensky & Vieweg, n.d.); revised version (Leipzig: B&H, n.d.)

DISCOGRAPHY: Arnold Schoenberg Chorus, Akademischer Orchesterverein, conducted by Etti, Preiser SPR 3271/72 (2).

Nebucadnezar (Der gestürtzte und wieder erhöhte Nebucadnezar, König zu Babylon unter dem grossen Propheten Daniel) (The Downfallen and Again Risen Nebucadnezar, King of Babylonia under the Great Prophet Daniel), Singspiel in three acts by Reinhard Keiser; libretto (Ger) by Menantes [Christian Friedrich Hunold]. First performance Carnival, 1704, Hamburg.

The Babylonian king Nebucadnezar has captured Jerusalem and taken Daniel, Sadrach, Mesach, and Abednego among his prisoners. When the king has a dream, Daniel is able to interpret it and is rewarded by being made a prince. Sadrach, Mesach, and Abednego refuse to bow before a golden image of Nebucadnezar, and they are thrown into a fiery furnace, but they are saved by an angel. Hearing this, the king declares that their religion must be respected.

Darius, a Median prince, is in love with Barsine, the king's daughter, but his way is blocked by the jealous Adina, the king's wife, who drives away the king when he becomes half-mad and tries to poison Barsine. She fails in her attempt, and the lovers flee. Through the intercession of Daniel, Nebucadnezar regains his sanity, and Adina, realizing her mistake, consents to let Barsine and Darius wed. Beltazer, son of the king, wins the hand of the princess Cyrene, whom he has been pursuing. The opera ends in general rejoicing at the court of Nebucadnezar.

Major roles: Nebucadnezar, king of Babylon (bass); Adina, his wife (sop); Barsine, his daughter (sop); Cyrene, a mediam princess (sop); Beltsazer, son of Nebucadnezar (ten); Darius, a Mede prince (sop); Daniel, the prophet and later prince of Babel (ten); Cores, a high-ranking nobleman (ten); Sadrach, Mesach, and Abednego, Jewish princes (altos).

Other settings of the Nebucadnezar story include Giuseppe Verdi's *Nabucco (Nabucodnosor)* (1842, Milan) and Benjamin Britten's *The Burning Fiery Furnace* (1966, Suffolk).

SCORE: ms repr. in *Handel Sources. An Anthology of the Sources of Handel's Borrowings*, III, ed. John H. Roberts (New York: Garland Publishing, 1986).

LIBRETTO: German (Hamburg: Greflinger, 1704, repr. with score).

Nero (Die durch Blut und Mord erlangete Liebe, oder Nero) (Love Won through Blood and Murder), Singspiel in two acts by George Frideric Handel; libretto (German) by Friedrich Christian Feustking. First performance 1705, Hamburg.

The story begins with the funeral of the emperor Claudius, father of Octavia, Nero's wife. Nero's attentions soon turn to Poppea, who is also admired by Tiridates, although he is engaged to Princess Cassandra. Nero ultimately banishes Octavia, despite the pleas of Seneca and his mother, Agrippina, who is also exiled. Included in the action is Nero's setting fire to Rome. The work concludes with the double marriage of Poppea and Nero and Cassandra and Tiridates, and Poppea's coronation.

Major roles: Nero, Roman emperor; Agrippina, his mother; Octavia, his empress and wife; Sabina Poppea, a noble Roman; Tiridates, the Armenian crown prince; Cassandra, crown princess of Media, in love with Tiridates; and Seneca, counselor to the emperor.

Monteverdi treated the same events in *L'incoronazione di Poppea* (1642, Venice).

Most of the music is lost.

LIBRETTO: German (Hamburg, 1705); repr. in *The Librettos of Handel's Operas*, I, ed. Ellen T. Harris (New York and London: Garland Publishing, 1989).

Neu-modische Liebhaber Damon, Der (The Fashionable Lover Damon), "ein scherzhaftes Singspiel" in three acts by Georg Philipp Telemann; libretto (Ger) by the composer. First performance June 1724, Hamburg.

The satyr Damon of Thessaly, after being driven away, has conquered Arcadia with the help of a group of satyrs. In payment for his victory he tries to seduce all the nymphs. Tyrsis, a shepherd who helped to bring about Damon's original expulsion, arranges for all to think he is dead, and he reappears dressed as the nymph Caliste. With the help of Mirtilla, Tyrsis' sister, Arcadia is freed from the ill-bred lover Damon.

Major roles: Tyrsis, an Arcadian shepherd, disguised as the nymph Caliste (mezzo); Mirtilla, a nymph in love with Laurindo (sop); Elpina, a nymph in love with Laurindo (sop); Laurindo, a shepherd (bar); Ergasto, a shepherd (bass); Damon, a satyr (bass); Nigella, an Egyptian gypsy, Damon's wife (sop); Hippo, a jolly satyr (ten); and Pales, Damon's young son (silent role).

SCORE: fs ed. Bernd Baselt, in *Werke*, XXII (Kassel: Bär, 1969).

LIBRETTO: German (Hamburg: Caspar Jakhel, 1724).

Neues vom Tage (News of the Day), comic opera in three parts (two acts) by Paul Hindemith; libretto (Ger) by Marcellus Schiffer. First performance June 8, 1929, Berlin, Kroll's; conducted by Otto Klemperer. Revised 1953. First U.S. performance August 12, 1961, Santa Fe, with Loren Driscoll, Marguerite Willauer, and Elaine Bonazzi; conducted by the composer.

The story pokes fun at the lengths to which sensational newspapers go to obtain their stories. It concerns the couple Eduard and Laura, who have decided to get a divorce. Their decision is seconded by the reporter Mrs. Pick, who makes the situation worse by photographing Laura in her hotel bath with the dashing Hermann, who is from the "Universum" Agency.

Major roles: Laura (sop); Eduard (bar); Baron D'Houdoux, president of "Universum" (bass); Mrs. Pick, a reporter (alto); and the handsome Mr. Hermann (ten).

SCORES: fs (Mainz: BSS, c. 1929); vs ed. Franz Willims, the same (repr. 1954).

LIBRETTO: the same.

BIBLIOGRAPHY: Robert Bright, "Success at Santa Fe," *Opera* LXI (1961), 703–5 [on U.S. premiere]; Hans Mersmann, "Paul Hindemith: Neues vom Tage; Oper in 3 Teilen," *Melos* VIII (1929–1930), 369–71; Andrew Porter, "Musical Events," *NY* LV (March 19, 1979), 132–33 [on N.Y. premiere].

Nurmahal, oder Das Rosenfest von Caschmir (Nurmahal, or The Rose Festival of Kashmir), opera in two parts by Gasparo Spontini; libretto (Ger) by Carl Alexander Herklots after Spicker's German translation of Moore's *Lalla Rookh* (1817). First performance May 27, 1822, Berlin, Opernhaus, with Karl Adam Bader (Dscheangir); Caroline Seidler (Nurmahal); Eduard Devrient (Bahar); Josefine Schulze (Zelia); and Anna Milder-Hauptmann (Nanuma).

The work is based on the fourth story of Thomas Moore's poem, "The Light of the Harem," in which Nurmahal, wife of the Mongolian emperor, wins back her husband's love through a magic spell.

Major roles: Dscheangir, a Mongolian emperor (ten); Nurmahal, his wife (sop); Bahar, his confidant (bar); Zelia, Bahar's sister; and Nanuma (sop).

This was the composer's first German opera. The musical highlights include, in the first act, Zelia's "Welch Gefühl durchströmt mein Wesen" and her duet with Dscheangir "Hat der Lenz," and in the second act "Ich fühl im liebende Herzen" and the duet of Nanuma and Nurmahal, "Pflücke die Blumen." The bachanale was originally written for a revival of Antonio Salieri's *Les Danaïdes* in 1817 in Paris.

Moore's work also provided the basis of Félicien David's *Lalla-Roukh* (1862, Paris) and Anton Rubinstein's *Feramors* (1863, Dresden).

SCORE: vs (Berlin: A. M. Schlesinger, c. 1826).

BIBLIOGRAPHY: Alberto Ghislanzoni, *Gasparo Spontini* (Rome: Author, 1951), 148–51.

Nusch-Nuschi, Das, "ein Spiel für burmanische Marionetten" in one act by Paul Hindemith; libretto (Ger) by Franz Blei. First performance June 4, 1921, Stuttgart; conducted by Fritz Busch.

The story concerns a philanderer in an Eastern country who is castrated as punishment for his lack of virtue. The subject matter caused a scandal at the premiere.

Major roles: Mung Tha Bya, King of Burma (bass); Ragwent, the crown prince (speaking part); Field Marshall Kyce Waing (bass); the master of ceremonies (bass); and the hangman (bass).

The work includes a quotation from King Marke's music in *Tristan**.

SCORES: conducting score (Mainz: BSS, 1921); vs ed. Reinhold Merten (Mainz: BSS, 1921).

BIBLIOGRAPHY: J. Hermann, "Gegenwartsmusik," *Musica* XII (1958), 212.

O

Oberon, opera in three acts by Carl Maria von Weber; libretto by James Robinson Planché after William Sotheby's translation of Christoph Martin Wieland's *Oberon* (1780) and the French Romance *Huon de Bordeaux*. First performance April 12, 1826, London, Covent Garden, in English, with Mary Anne Paton (Rezia), John Braham (Huon), Lucia Elizabeth Vestris (Fatima), John Fawcett (Sherasmin), Charles Bland (Oberon), Harriet Cawse (Puck), and Mary Anne Goward (mermaid). First German performance, translated by Theodor Hell, December 23, 1826, Leipzig. First U.S. performance October 9, 1828, New York.

The story opens in the fairy kingdom of Oberon and Titania, who have quarreled. Oberon will not be reconciled with his wife until he can be shown an example of a truly loving couple. Puck tells him of the French knight Huon de Bordeaux, who has insulted the Emperor Charlemagne and has been banished until he makes Rezia, the daughter of the Caliph of Bagdad, his bride. Oberon causes Huon to dream of the lovely Rezia, and he immediately falls in love with her. In order to spirit her away, he is given a magic horn. Huon and Sherasmin, his squire, escape from Bagdad with Rezia and Fatima, her confidante, but they lose the horn and are shipwrecked. The four are seized by pirates and sold as slaves to the Emir of Tunis, Almansor. The Emir attempts to seduce Rezia, and his wife attempts to seduce Huon, but their overtures are refused, and the young lovers are condemned to death. Fortunately, Sherasmin finds the magic horn, and the four are saved. The lovers return to France, and Huon receives a pardon from Charlemagne. Oberon is convinced that he has found a faithful couple.

For a detailed synopsis and musical analysis see K/*KOB*, 140–46.

Major roles: Oberon, King of the Elves (ten); Titania, his wife (silent role); Puck (mezzo); Harun al Rashid, Caliph of Bagdad (speaking role); Rezia, his daughter (sop); Fatima, her confidante (sop); Almansor, Emir of Tunis (speaking role); Roschana, his wife (speaking role); Huon (Hüon) of Bordeaux (ten); and Sherasmin (Scherasmin), his squire (bar).

Weber's last opera includes among its highlights Huon's aria in the first act "Von Jugend auf in dem Kampfgefild." Two of Rezia's arias are especially noteworthy, "Ozean, du Ungeheuer," after the lovers are shipwrecked (Act II), and "Arabien, mein Heimatland," when she is a prisoner of the Emir of Tunis. Another striking piece is the quartet of the lovers after they escape death, "Über die blauen Wogen, über die Fluten hier" (Act II). Although occasionally performed, the opera has had limited success because of its plodding text and complicated plot. The composer died less than two months after its premiere. Its magnificent overture, still played as a concert piece today, contains the magic horn call and features various themes of the opera's numbers.

Among other settings of the story are those by Paul Wranitzky, *Oberon** (see below); Friedrich Kunzen, *Holger Danske* (1789, Copenhagen); and Georg Christoph Grosheim, *Titania, oder Liebe durch Zauberei* (1972, Kassel).

SCORES: fs (Berlin: Schlesinger'sche Buch-und Musikhandlung, ca. 1881; repr. Farnborough, Hants: Gregg International, 1969).

LIBRETTO: English (London: Hunt and Clarke, 1826).

BIBLIOGRAPHY: *L'Avant scène opéra* LXXIV (1985) (entire issue); Anthony Burgess, *Oberon Old and New* (London: Hutchinson, 1985); Egon Komorzynski, " 'Zauberflöte' und 'Oberon,' " *MJb 1953* (1954), 150–61; Andrew Porter, "Musical Events," *NY* LIV (March 13, 1978), 118–22 [on New York revival]; Ernest Sanders, "Oberon and Zar und Zimmermann," *MQ* XL (1954), 521–32; Horst Seeger, "Das 'Original-Libretto' zum 'Oberon,' " *Musikbühne 76* (1976), 33–87; John Warrack, "Weber and 'Oberon,' " *Opera Annals* IV (1957), 65–72; ———, " 'Oberon' und der englische Gechmack . . . ," *Musikbühne 76* (1976), 15–31; ———, W/*CMW*, 321–44; Helmut Wirth, "Natur und Märchen in Webers *Oberon* . . . ," in *Festschrift Friedrich Blume*, ed. A. A. Abert et al. (Kassel: Bär, 1963), 389–97.

Oberon, König der Elfen (Oberon, King of the Elves), "romantische komische Oper" in three acts by Paul Wranitzky [Pavel Vranicky]; libretto (Ger) by Karl Ludwig Gieseke after Christoph Martin Wieland's poem and Frederike Sophie Seyler's 1789 libretto *Hüon und Amande*. First performance November 7, 1789, Vienna, Theater auf der Wieden. Revived May 2, 1980, Schwetzingen Festival; conducted by Alicia Mounk.

The opera begins with the quarrel between Oberon and Titania and continues with the love problems of Ritter Hüon and Rezia, the daughter of the Sultan of Bagdad.

The story was also set, in a Danish version, under the title *Holger Danske*, by Friedrich Kunzen, receiving its premiere on March 31, 1789, in Copenhagen, and by Carl Maria von Weber in 1826 (see above entry).

SCORE: vs (1791, Berlin?).

BIBLIOGRAPHY: G. Bobrik, *Wielands . . . Oberon auf der deutschen Singspielbühne* (1909); Horst Koegler, "Reports: Foreign," *ON* XLV (August 1980), 35 [on 1980 revival]; Egon Komorzynski, " 'Zauberflöte' und 'Oberon,' " *MJb 1953* (1954), 153–54.

Octavia (Die römische Unruhe oder Die edelemüthige Octavia) (The Roman Unrest or the Noble Octavia), opera in three acts by Reinhard Keiser; libretto (Ger) by Barthold Feind. First performance August 5, 1705, Hamburg.

Octavia is the noble wife of Nero, whom he has killed in order to marry his mistress, the notorious Poppea. Other settings of the Octavia-Nero story include Monteverdi's *L'Incoronazione di Poppea* (1642, Venice) and Handel's *Nero** (1705, Hamburg), with which the later Keiser opera was competing for the attentions of audiences in Hamburg.

SCORE: fs in the supplement to Handel's GA, ed. Max Seiffert, VI (Leipzig, 1902; repr. Farnborough, Hants: Gregg, 1968).

Oedipus der Tyrann (Oedipus the King), opera in one act by Carl Orff; libretto (Ger) by Friedrich Hölderlin after Sophocles. First performance December 11, 1959, Stuttgart; conducted by Ferdinand Leitner.

This is a setting of the Oedipus story, in which Oedipus unknowingly kills his father and marries his mother, Jocasta, sister of the regent Kreon of Thebes. When the seer Tiresias discloses Oedipus' identity, Jocasta hangs herself and Oedipus scratches out his eyes.

Major roles: Oedipus, a priest, Kreon, Tiresias, and Jocasta.

The work includes seventy-two percussion instruments (six pianos), and the text is spoken, sung, chanted, and declaimed by unspecified voices.

Also set by Igor Stravinsky, as *Oedipus Rex* (1927, Paris).

SCORE: vs (Mainz: BSS, 1959).

BIBLIOGRAPHY: L/*CO*, 145–56.

DISCOGRAPHY: Varnay, Stolze, Harper, Buchta, Cramer, Nöcker, Kohn, and Engen, Bavarian Radio Symphony and Chorus, conducted by Kubelik, DG 139251/3 (3); reviewed by C. J. Luten, "Records," *ON* XXXII (February 10 1968), 34.

Omphale, opera in three acts by Siegfried Matthus; libretto (Ger) by Peter Hacks. First performance September 7, 1976, Weimar, Nationaltheater, with Uta Priew, Volker Schunker, Helmut Bante, Peter Slakow, and Lothar Heublein; conducted by Lothar Seyfarth.

The Queen of Lydia, Omphale, exchanges clothes with Heracles, her slave and lover. Omphale wears the lion's skin, and Hercules is attired in women's clothing. The status quo returns when Heracles slays the monster Lityerses, who has held captive the shepherd Daphnis and Pimplea, his beloved; and Omphale gives birth to three sons.

Major roles: Omphale (sop); Heracles (bar); Daphnis (ten); and Pimplea (sop).

Also set by André Destouches (1700, Paris).

BIBLIOGRAPHY: Paul Moor, "Siegfried Matthus' 'Omphale,' " *HiFi*/*MA* XXVII (January 1977), 34–35 [on premiere].

Opernball, Der (The Opera Ball), operetta in three acts by Richard Heuberger; libretto (Ger) by Viktor Léon [Viktor Hirschfeld] and Heinrich von Waldeberg after Delacour [Alfred-Charlemagne Lartigue] and Alfred Néoclès Hennequin's farce *Les Dominos roses* (1876). First performance January 5, 1898, Vienna, Theater auf der Wieden. First U.S. performance May 24, 1909, New York.

The story is set, as is part of *Die Fledermaus*,* at a masked ball, in this case one taking place at the Opéra in Paris. Two cheating husbands and old school friends, Beaubisson and Duménil, dance with two attractive ladies, who happen to be the wives of each of the men. Also involved are Hortense, the maid, and the young navel cadet, Henri, her partner at the dance.

Major roles: Beaubisson (bass), Madame Beaubisson, his wife (alto), Henri, Beaubisson's nephew (ten), Angèle, his wife (sop), Georges Duménil (ten), Marguérite, his wife (sop), and Hortense, Duménil's chamber maid (sop).

The famous "Im chambre séparé," originally sung as a duet, is often performed in concert as a soprano solo.

SCORE: vs (Vienna: V. Kratochwill & Co., c. 1898).

Opernprobe, Die, oder **Die vornehmen Dilettanten** (The Opera Rehearsal or The Noble Dilettantes), comic opera in one act by Albert Lortzing; libretto (Ger) by the composer after Johann Friedrich Jünger's *Die Komödie aus dem Stegreif* (1794). First performance January 20, 1851, Frankfurt, with Karoline Denemy-Ney, Samuel Friedrich Hassel, Robert Leser, Carl Anton Meinhold, and Therese Tietjens.

The servants of the music-loving count are holding an orchestra rehearsal, directed by Hannchen, the chamber maid. Before the scheduled opera performance the tenor takes sick. In steps the disguised Adolf von Rheinthal, who is trying to avoid a marriage arrangement made by his uncle; the young baron is accompanied by his servant, Johann, and both volunteer to sing at the performance. Hannchen has guessed their real identities and tells the baron's fiancée of her discovery. The old baron appears unexpectedly at the rehearsal, where Adolf and Johann improvise a scene about an uncle meeting his missing nephew accidentally. Fantasy turns to reality, as the work ends with engagement festivities.

Major roles: the count (bass); the countess (mezzo); Luise, their daughter (sop); Hannchen, the chamber maid (sop); Baron Rheinthal (bass); Adolf von Rheinthal, his nephew (ten); and Johann, the nephew's servant (bar).

SCORE: vs ed. Richard Kleinmichel (Vienna: UE, ca. 1910).

LIBRETTO: German (Berlin: Litfass, 1851).

BIBLIOGRAPHY: Hans Hoffmann, *Albert Lortzing* (Düsseldorf, Droste Verlag, 1987), 353–58; Elmar Wulf, " 'Die Opernprobe' von G. A. Lortzing," in *Untersuchungen zum Operneinakter in der Mitte des 19. Jahrhunderts* (diss., University of Cologne, 1963).

Orpheus und Eurydike (Orpheus and Euridice), opera in three acts by Ernst Krenek; libretto (Ger) by Oskar Kokoschka. First performance November 27, 1926, Kassel.

Major roles: Orpheus (ten), Eurydike (sop), Amor (silent role), and Psyche (sop).

Among the many operas concerning the Orpheus legend is Carl Orff's *Orpheus* (1925, Karlsruhe), which is based on the Monteverdi setting. A later German setting is by Hans Haug (1954, Lausanne).

SCORE: vs (Vienna: UE, 1925).

BIBLIOGRAPHY: R/*EKO*, 40–54.

P

Paganini, operetta in three acts by Franz Lehár; libretto (Ger) by Paul Knepler and Béla Jenbach. First performance October 30, 1925, Vienna, Johann-Strauss Theater. First British performance 1938, London, with Richard Tauber (Paganini).

The famous violinist Paganini is admired by the villagers of a town near Lucca, Italy, and among his admirers is a mysterious lady, to whom Paganini is also attracted. He discovers that she is the Princess Maria Anna Elisa, the sister of Napoleon and wife of Prince Felix of Lucca. He accepts her invitation to come to her palace, and her husband is tolerant until Paganini shows a sudden interest in the prima donna Bella Giretti, who happens to be the Prince's mistress. Elisa's love suddenly turns to hatred, and she tries to have Paganini arrested, but when she hears him playing, her love is rekindled. Faced by both Elisa and Bella, Paganini decides to give up women and turn his attentions to his art.

Major roles: Maria Anna Elisa, Princess of Lucca and Piombino (sop); Prince Felix Bacchiocchi, her husband (ten); Niccolo Paganini (ten); and Bella Giretti, prima donna at the Royal Opera in Lucca (sop).

Among the many popular numbers of the operetta are the hero's "Gern hab' ich die Frau'n geküsst" and "Niemand liebt dich so wie ich," and the duet "Hab' nur dich allein."

SCORE: vs ed. Gustav Volk (Berlin: Crescendo Theater-Verlag, 1925).

LIBRETTO: German (Viena: Glocken Verlag, 1936).

BIBLIOGRAPHY: George Jellinek, "Franz Lehár and the 'Tauber Operetta,'" *HiFi/Stereo Review* XVIII/1 (1967), 68–72.

DISCOGRAPHY: Gedda and Rothenberger, Chorus and Symphony Orchestra of the Bavarian Staatsoper, conducted by Boskovsky, EMI C 157–30.751/53 (2).

Palestrina, opera in three acts by Hans Pfitzner; libretto (Ger) by the composer. First performance June 12, 1917, Munich, Prinzregententheater, with Karl Erb

(Palestrina) and Maria Ivogün (Ighino); conducted by Bruno Walter. First U.S. performance May 14, 1982, San Francisco, with Quade Winter (Palestrina), Kenneth Criste (Cardinal Borromeo), Sara Ganz (Ighino), and Vicki Van Dewark (Silla); conducted by Kent Nagano. Performed June 13, 1981, Dublin, Abbey Opera, Collegiate Theatre, with Stuart Kale (Palestrina), Kathleen Murphy (Silla), Donald Stephenson (Bishop), and Barnaby Mason (Cardinal); conducted by Anthony Shelley.

The opera opens in Palestrina's house, where his young student, Silla, is attempting to write a piece in the new monodic style. Ighino, the composer's son, is concerned about his father, who has not been able to work since the death of his wife. Cardinal Borromeo appears in order to ask Palestrina to compose a mass to save the older contrapuntal style, which is threatened by the new way of writing.

Undecided, Palestrina sees a vision of nine great composers of the past, who urge him to undertake the Cardinal's request. The result is the *Missa Papae Marcelli*. It is performed at the Sistine Chapel, with the Pope in attendance, and it is enthusiastically received. The composer is blessed by the Pope and named to head the chapel. Left alone, Palestrina is unaffected by his great success. He sits down at the organ and begins to play.

For a detailed synopsis, see K/*KOB*, 856–60.

Major roles: Pope Pius IV (bass); Carlo Borromeo, Roman Cardinal (bar); Palestrina (ten); Ighino, his son (sop); Silla, Palestrina's pupil (mezzo); and Masdruscht, Bishop of Trent (bass).

SCORE: vs ed. Felix Wolfes (Berlin and Paris: Adolph Fürstner, 1916).

LIBRETTO: the same.

BIBLIOGRAPHY: Stephanie von Buchau, "Reports: U.S.," *ON* XLVII (August 1982), 36 [on U.S. premiere]; Karl Friess, "Palestrina," *NZM* LXXXIV (1917), 206–7 [on premiere]; Franz Grassberger, "Dokumente zur Wiener Erstaufführung des *Palestrina*," *ÖMz* XXIV/4 (April 1969), 234–45; *MT* (1981), 547 [on Dublin premiere]; Jon Newsom, "Hans Pfitzner, Thomas Mann and The Magic Mountain," *ML* LV (1974), 136–50; Herbert von Stein, "Äusserungen Hans Pfitzners über eine thematische Analyse zu *Palestrina*," *Mitteilungen Hans Pfitzner Gesellschaft* XXVIII (1972), 2–11; Christopher Norton Welsh, "Overseas Report. Austria. Pfitzner's 'Non-Opera,' " *Opera* XVI (1965), 120–22.

DISCOGRAPHY: Fischer-Dieskau, Prey, Ridderbusch, Mazura, Fassbänder, DG 427–417 (compact discs and tape).

Pallas Athene weint (Pallas Athena Weeps), opera in a prologue and three acts by Ernst Krenek; libretto (Ger) by the composer. First performance October 17, 1955, Hamburg, with James Pease, Heinz Sauerbaum, Helmut Melchert, Hermann Prey, Arnold van Mill, Helga Pilarczyk, and Militta Muszely; conducted by Leopold Ludwig.

The action takes place in Athens and Sparta during the last phase of the Peloponnesian War. The plot concerns the fall of Athens to Sparta. It opens with

Pallas Athene crying for her beleaguered citizens, who did not value their freedom. The main action involves Sokrates and three of his students: the general Alkibiades, who eventually betrays the navy to Sparta and flees with the wife of the King of Sparta, only to be killed by Spartan lances; Meletos, who conspires against Alkibiades and leads Athens under Spartan rule; and the pacifist Meton, who becomes a victim of Meletos.

Major roles: Pallas Athene (mezzo); Sokrates (bass-bar); Alkibiades, Meletos, and Meton, his friends and pupils (2 ten, bar); Althaea, priestess of Eleusis (sop); Nauarchos (bar); Agis, king of Sparta (bass); Queen Timaea (sop); Lysander, general (ten); Brasidas, captain (bar); and Ktesippos, his son (ten).

The twelve-tone music contains no set pieces. Among its most noteworthy sections are the orchestral intermezzi.

SCORE: vs (Mainz: BSS, c. 1955).

BIBLIOGRAPHY: Horst Koegler, "Modern Hamburg," *ON* XX (December 12, 1955), 13 [on premiere].

Parsifal, "Bühnenweihfestspiel" in three acts by Richard Wagner; libretto (Ger) by the composer after Wolfram von Eschenbach's poem *Parzival* (ca. 1210). First performance July 26, 1882, Bayreuth, with Amalie Materna (Kundry), Hermann Winkelmann (Parsifal), Theodor Reichmann (Amfortas), August Kindermann (Titurel), Karl Hill (Klingsor), and Emil Scaria (Gurnemanz); conducted by Hermann Levi. First U.S. performance (stage) [which violated the German copyright] December 24, 1903, New York, Metropolitan Opera House, with Milka Ternina (Kundry), Alois Burgstaller (Parsifal), Anton Van Rooy (Amfortas), Robert Blass (Gurnemanz), Otto Goritz (Klingsor), and Marcel Journet (Titurel); conducted by Heinrich Conried. First British performance February 2, 1914, London, Covent Garden, with Eva von der Osten (Kundry), Heinrich Hensel (Parsifal), Paul Bender (Amfortas), and Paul Knüpfer (Gurnemanz); conducted by Arthur Bodanzky.

In order to get revenge for having been barred from the brotherhood of the Knights of the Holy Grail, the evil sorcerer Klingsor has his slave Kundry lure Amfortas, king of the Knights, into a magic garden. Amfortas is carrying the Holy Spear, the one that pierced the side of Christ on the Cross; Klingsor seizes it and wounds Amfortas. Henceforth he can be cured only if he is touched by the Spear held by a Guileless Fool, one who can resist all temptations. These events are recounted in Gurnemanz's monologue of the first act, "O wunden-wundenvoller heiliger Speer!" Parsifal enters the scene, amid preparations for the gathering of the Knights of the Holy Grail in Montsalvat for the Communion Feast. Included in this act is the beautiful orchestral interlude known as the Transformation Scene.

The second act opens in Klingsor's castle, which Parsifal enters. At first attracted by the beauty of the transformed Kundry and the Flower Maidens, Parsifal suddenly understands Amfortas' agony in "Amfortas! Die Wunde!."

Kundry replies with "Seit Ewigkeiten harre ich deiner," in which she explains how she has been cursed since she laughed at Christ on the Cross. Klingsor attacks Parsifal with the Holy Spear but misses him; Parsifal grasps it, makes the sign of the cross with it, and thereby destroys Klingsor and his castle.

As Act III begins, many years have passed, during which Parsifal has wandered over the earth. He comes back to Montsalvat on a Good Friday and recounts his travels to Gurnemanz in his "Der Irrnis und der Leiden Pfade." Gurnemanz then baptizes Parsifal and Kundry. They join the knights in the castle, during which Amfortas begs the knights to slay him so that the Grail can be redeemed. Parsifal steps forward, the Holy Spear in his hand. Saying that the wound can be cured only by the weapon that inflicted it, in "Nur eine Waffe taugt," he touches the king, thereby relieving his suffering. Kundry, also redeemed, dies.

For detailed synopses and musical analyses, see C/*NMC* 439–47; *COH*, ed. Lucy Beckett (1981); K/*KOB*, 263–77; and N/*SGO*, I, 124–57.

Major roles: Kundry (sop), Parsifal (ten), Amfortas (bar), Gurnemanz (bass), Klingsor (bass), and Titurel (bass).

Also set by Adolf von Doss as *Percifal* (1883, Liège).

SCORES: fs (London and Mainz: BSS, 1883); SW, XIV (1970); vs ed. Joseph Rubinstein (Mainz: BSS, 1882); vs ed. Richard Kleinmichel, H. and F. Corder, German-English (Mainz: BSS, ca. 1885).

LIBRETTO: German (Mainz: BSS, 1877).

BIBLIOGRAPHY: Hans-Joachim Bauer, *Wagners 'Parsifal.' Kriterien der Kompositionstechnik* (Munich, 1977); Lucy Beckett, "*Parsifal* as Drama," *ML* LII (1971), 259–71; Jacques Chailley, *'Parsifal' de Richard Wagner* (Paris, 1979); M. Owen Lee, "Grand Illusion," *ON* XXXVIII (April 20, 1974), 14–15; Dietrich Mack, "Von der Christianisierung des *Parsifal* in Bayreuth. Ein Brief Felix Weingartners an Hermann Levi," *NZM* CXXX (1969), 467–68; Barry Millington, "Parsifal: Facing the Contradictions," *MT* CXXIV (1983), 97–98; Adolf Nowak, "Wagners *Parsifal* und die Idee der Kunstreligion," in D/*RWW* 161–74; Andrew Porter, "Musical Events," *NY* (February 21, 1983), 112, 114–16, 119 [on Hans Jürgen Syberberg's film]; John Potter and Suzanne Potter, "Compassion Beyond Passion," *ON* XLIII (April 7, 1979), 31; Heinrich Reinhardt, *Parsifal. Studien zur Erfassung des Problemhorizonts von Richard Wagners letztem Drama* (Straubing: Donau, 1979); Michael Steinberg, "Portrait of the Artist," *ON* XLVII (April 9, 1983), 22–24, 40; James Helme Sutcliffe, " 'Parsifal.' Summation of a Musical Lifetime," Part 1, *Opera* XXXIII (1982), 685–92, Part 2, 805–12; Richard Wagner, *Dokumente zur Entstehung und ersten Aufführung des Bühnenweihfestspiels 'Parsifal,'* eds. Martin Geck and Egon Voss, in W/*SW*, XXX (1970); ———, *'Parsifal.' Dichtung, Entwurf, Schriften* (Leipzig: B&H, 1914; repr. Walluf bei Wiesbaden: Sändig, 1973); Peter Wapnewski, "Parzival und Parsifal oder Wolframs Held und Wagners Erlöser," in *Wagner: Von der Oper zum Musikdrama*, ed. Stefan Kunze (Bern and Munich: Francke, 1978), 47–60.

DISCOGRAPHY: See Robin Holloway, B/*OOR*, 440–51.

VIDEO: actors: Jordan, Sperr, Lloyd, Kutter/Krick, Haugland, and Clever; singers: Schoene, Tschammer, Lloyd, Goldberg, Haugland, and Minton; conducted by Jordan, Kultur VHS 1195 (2).

Peer Gynt, opera in three acts by Werner Egk; libretto (Ger) by the composer freely adapted from Henrik Ibsen's play (1867). First performance November 24, 1938, Berlin, Staatsoper, with Mathieu Ahlersmeyer (Peer Gynt), Käte Heidersbach (Solveig), Margarete Arndt-Ober (Aase), Hilde Scheppan (Ingrid), Benno Arnold (Mads), Gustav Rödin (the old man), and Else Tegenhoff (the Redhead); conducted by the composer. First U.S. performance February 23, 1966, Hartford, Hartt College of Music (in an English version by Walter Ducloux); conducted by Moshe Paranov.

The composer has reduced the five acts to a prologue and three acts. Although uninvited, Peer Gynt attends the wedding of his onetime fiancée, Ingrid, who is marrying the dumb Mads. When another girl, the pure Solveig, refuses to dance with him, Peer kidnaps Ingrid and runs off with her. They meet the old man, who is the king of the trolls, and the Redhead, who is his daughter; Peer abandons Ingrid for her. When Peer gets tired of the trolls, he escapes to the mountains, where he is joined by the faithful Solveig. Their happiness is ruined by the appearance of the Redhead, whereupon Peer flees. He is finally brought to trial because of his misdeeds on earth, but his mother's wish that he receive one more chance is granted, and he returns to his house in the mountains, where Solveig is waiting. Her fidelity and love set him free.

Major roles: Peer Gynt (bar), Solveig (sop), Aase (alto), the old man (ten), the Redhead (sop), Ingrid (sop), and Mads (ten).

The work contains syncopation and jazz; despite these "foreign" elements, the Nazis allowed it to be performed.

Also set by Viktor Ullmann (not performed).

SCORE: vs ed. Hans Bergese (Mainz: BSS, c. 1938).

LIBRETTO: (Mainz: BSS, 1938).

BIBLIOGRAPHY: William Miranda, "Hartford," *ON* XXX (April 9, 1966) [on U.S. premiere]; Moshe Paranov, "In the Hall of the Mountain King," *ON* XXX (February 26, 1966).

DISCOGRAPHY: Sharp, Perry, Wulkopf, Hopf, and Hermann, Munich Radio Orchestra, Bavarian Radio Chorus, conducted by Walberg, Orfeo S005823R (3).

Penelope, "opera semi-seria" by Rolf Liebermann; libretto (Ger) by Heinrich Strobel. First performance August 17, 1954, Salzburg, Festspielhaus, with Christel Goltz (Penelope), Anneliese Rothenberger (Telemachos), Carl Dönch (Leiokritos), Walter Berry (Eurymachos), Peter Klein (Demoptolemos), Rudolf Schock (Ercole), Theo Baylé (Achille), and Kurt Böhme (Odysseus); conducted by George Szell.

In this version of the story, based on a real incident from World War II, Penelope's husband is missing and believed dead. After she marries Ercole, she receives a letter telling her that her husband is alive. Achille tells Penelope that Odysseus has died on the way home, but when she returns to her villa she finds Ercole hanged.

Major roles: Penelope (sop); Telemachos (sop); Leiokritos, Eurymachos, and Demoptolemos, freemen (bar, buffo bass, ten); Ercole (ten); Achille (bar); and Odysseus (bar).

The work contains twelve-note writing and significant choral sections.

Among the many settings of the story is one by Gabriel Fauré (1913, Monte Carlo).

SCORE: fs (Vienna: UE, 1954); vs ed. H. E. Apostel (Vienna: UE, 1954).

LIBRETTO: German (Vienna: UE, 1954).

BIBLIOGRAPHY: *Opera* V (1954), 607–8 [on premiere].

Penthesilea, opera in one act by Othmar Schoeck; libretto (Ger) by the composer after Heinrich von Kleist's play, based on an episode in *The Iliad*. First performance January 8, 1927, Dresden, Sächsische Staatsoper, with Irma Tervani (Penthesilea) and Friedrich Plaschke (Achilles); conducted by Hermann Kutzschbach. First British performance 1957, with Derrik Olsen (Achilles) and Ingrid Steger (Penthesilea).

The story takes place on the Trojan battlefield. Achilles kills Penthesilea, Queen of the Amazons, after she has aided the Trojans, but her beauty and valor make him lament his deed.

Major roles: Penthesilea, Queen of the Amazons (mezzo); Prothoe and Meroe, Amazon princesses (sops); a high priestess of Diana (alto); and Achilles and Diomedes, Greek kings (bar, ten).

Also set by Rudo Ritter (1927, Würzburg).

SCORE: vs ed. Karl Krebs (Zurich: Hüni, 1927).

LIBRETTO: German (Kassel: Bär, 1927).

BIBLIOGRAPHY: Richard Eidenbenz, "Über Harmonik und tonale Einheit in Othmar Schoecks 'Penthesilea,' " *Schweizerisches Jahrbuch für Musikwissenschaft* IV (1929), 94–130.

DISCOGRAPHY: Smith, Janku, Scherler, Kostia, Hermann, Blankenship, and Widmer, Cologne Radio Symphony Orchestra, Choruses of the NDR of Hamburg and the WDR of Cologne, conducted by Macal, BASF H9 22485–6.

Peter Schmoll und seine Nachbarn, (Peter Schmoll and His Neighbors), opera in two acts by Carl Maria von Weber; libretto by J. Türk[e] after C. G. Cramer. Composed 1801–1802. First performance probably March 1803, Augsburg.

The rich Dutch merchant Peter Schmoll lives in France with his daughter, Minette, and two friends, Helmers and Abbé Saurin. When the French Revolution breaks out, Helmers flees with his young son, Carl, and the Abbé goes to search for them. Schmoll and his daughter, along with Hans Bast, his assistant, also emigrate and take up residence in an old castle on the German border. The opera begins at this point, with the trio "Das sind die schöne Früchte," sung by Schmoll, Minette, and Bast. Minette, now sixteen years old, falls in love with

Carl, an overseer of the horse dealer Michelsen. The two sing of their love in No. 10, "Der edle, schöne, junge Mann," and the act comes to a close with a trio of the lovers and Bast, who is suspicious of the young man.

Carl finds an old, confused man by the wayside, who sings of his lost son, "Wie der bange Pilge zittert." Schmoll, having been confined to the castle all this time, decides to venture out, with Carl's help. When Schmoll becomes ill during the journey, he is restored to health by a hermit, who turns out to be the Abbé Saurin. The old man's memory is jogged by the mention of Peter Schmoll's name, and the former recognizes that Carl is his lost son. The opera ends happily, with the finale (No. 20), "So hab' ich."

Major roles: Peter Schmoll (bar), Minette (sop), Carl (ten), and Bast (bass buffo).

For a detailed plot synopsis and musical analysis, see W/*CMW*, 38–39.

The dialogue is lost from this early Weber work, written when the composer was just fifteen. Various editors have tried to reconstruct the work for subsequent performances, including Hans Hasse's version for a production on May 18, 1943, at Freiburg.

SCORES: fs ed. A. Lorenz, We/*MW*, II/1 (1926); vs ed. Meinhard von Zallinger, text Willy Werner Göttig (Frankfurt and New York: Henry Litolff's Verlag/C. F. Peters, 1963).

Philemon und Baucis oder **Jupiters Reise auf der Erde** (Philemon and Baucis, or Jupiter's Trip to the Earth), puppet opera in one act by Franz Joseph Haydn; libretto (Ger) possibly by Phillip Georg Bader after Gottieb Konrad Pfeffel's play (1763), based in turn on Ovid's *Metamorphoses*, Book 8. Written for the visit of Maria Theresa to Esterháza on September 2, 1773, with Elisabeth Griessler (Baucis), Johann Haydn, Michael Ernst, and Eleonora Jäger; conducted by the composer. Performed as a Singspiel in 1776. *Der Götterrat*, in one act, with a libretto by P. G. Bader, is the *Vorspiel* for the work.

The poor Philemon and Baucis are so hospitable to Jupiter, that he offers to grant them any wish they desire.

Major roles: Baucis (alto); Philemon, her husband (bass); Aret, her son (ten); Narcissa, his wife (sop); Jupiter and Merkur (speaking roles).

This was Haydn's first marionette opera. It includes Philemon's aria (No. 4) "Ein Tag, der allen Frieden bringt."

Set by Gounod as *Philémon et Baucis* (1860, Paris).

SCORES: fs in *Werke*, XXIV/1 (1971), ed. Jürgen Braun; vs ed. Karl-Heinz Füssl.

BIBLIOGRAPHY: H. C. Robbins Landon, "Haydn's Marionette Operas," *Haydn Year-book* I (1962), 111–99; Joseph Müller-Blattau, "Zu Haydns Philemon und Baucis," *Haydn-Studien* II (1969), 66.

DISCOGRAPHY: See M/*IRR*, 32.

Pietro von Abano, Romantic opera in two acts by Ludwig Spohr; libretto (Ger) by Karl Pfeiffer after Ludwig Tieck's novel (1825). First performance October 13, 1827, Kassel.

Set in medieval Padua, the story concerns the noble Antonio of Florence, who has just returned to wed Cäcilia but finds that the funeral procession he meets is bearing the corpse of his beloved. Pietro joins the mourners, who are unaware that he had desired her himself and that he intends to bring her back to life through sorcery. Cäcilia's parents, the Podesta and Eudoxia, cannot believe the bishop's warnings that Pietro is evil. The scene changes to a forest, where Rosa, Cäcilia's twin, who had been kidnapped as an infant by her nurse, Pancrazia, and given to bandits, is lamenting her separation from her family. Antonio wanders into the forest and meets Rosa. Although he at first takes her to be Cäcilia, she explains the real situation, and the two plan to escape. Just as they are about to depart, Idefonso and his bandits return, and Antonio is wounded and forced to run away. Pietro appears and, with the help of Beresynth, Pietro succeeds in reviving the dead girl, who is horrified by his powers. Antonio finds her in Pietro's house and reluctantly agrees to assist her in restoring her soul by permitting her to be blessed and die. Rosa returns and accompanies Antonio to the cathedral, where they interrupt the consecration of Pietro as rector. Cäcilia dies in peace, Pietro is condemned, and Antonio and Rosa are betrothed.

Major roles: Pietro von Abano (bar); his servant, Beresynth (ten); Bishop of Padua (speaking role); Ambrosio, the Podesta (bass); Eudoxia, his wife (sop); Cäcilia/Rosa, their daughters (sop); Pancrazia (spoken); and Antonio Cavalcanti, her fiancé (ten).

The opera was not well received, perhaps because of its morbid plot, and its inclusion of a bishop in the cathedral scene displeased the Church, despite the fact that his part was spoken. Spohr was forced to alter the work for a subsequent performance.

Musically, the opera is a combination of older elements, such as formal arias and ensembles, and newer ones, such as extended scenes. The work includes parallels to Weber's *Der Freischütz,** specifically the chorus of spirits in the Act I finale and the Wolf Glen scene, as noted by Clive Brown (see below).

SCORE: vs (Berlin: Schlesinger, 1828); facsimile of autograph, with a modern transcription of the libretto, in *Selected Works of Louis Spohr,* III, ed. Clive Brown (New York and London: Garland Publishing, 1989).

BIBLIOGRAPHY: B/*LS,* 183–89.

Pimpinone (Der ungleiche Heirat oder **Das herrsch-süchtige Camer-Mädgen Pimpinone)** (The Unequal Marriage, or The Tyrannical Chamber Maid Pimpinone), intermezzo in one act by Georg Philipp Telemann; libretto (Ger) by Johann Philipp Praetorius after Pietro Pariati's Italian libretto *Pimpone,* written for Tomaso Albinoni (1708). First performance September 27, 1725, Hamburg.

The plot is similar to *La serva padrona*, in that the chamber maid Pimpinone gets to marry her master.

SCORES: fs ed. T. W. Werner, *EDM*, VI (1936); vs (Mainz: BSS and New York: AMP, 1955).

Preciosa, "Romantische Schauspiel mit Musik" in four acts by Carl Maria von Weber for P. A. Wolff's play, after Miguel de Cervantes' novel *La Gitanella* (1613). First performance March 14, 1821, Berlin, Hoftheater.

A beautiful young gypsy catches the eye of a young aristocrat, who leaves his home to be with her. In the end she turns out to be the daughter of a noble family, who had been kidnapped by gypsies when she was a child. She is therefore able to wed her aristocratic admirer.

In an attempt to add authenticity to the exotic nature of the work, Weber includes numbers based loosely on Spanish tunes, such as No. 5 (Act I), "Im Wald," with its bolero rhythms, and the dances in No. 9 (Act III). The three melodramas, Nos. 3, 4a, and 11, are quite effective.

Other settings of the text include those by J. P. C. Schulz (1812, Leipzig) and Ignaz von Seyfried (1812, Vienna).

SCORES: fs (Berlin: Schlesinger'sche Buch u. Musikhandlung, ca. 1842); We/*MW*, II/3, ed. L. K. Mayer (Augsburg, ca. 1932; repr. New York, 1977); vs (Berlin: Schlesinger, 1821).

BIBLIOGRAPHY: Dolores Menstell Hsu, "Carl Maria von Weber's *Preciosa*: Incidental Music on a Spanish Theme," *MR* XXVI (1965), 97–103.

Preussisches Märchen (Prussian Fairy Tale), opera-ballet in five scenes by Boris Blacher; libretto (Ger) by Heinz von Cramer after Carl Zuckmayr's *Der Hauptmann von Köpenick* (1931). First performance September 23, 1952, Berlin, Städtische Oper.

Set in Berlin at the turn of the century, the satirical story concerns the writer Wilhelm Fadenkreutz, a discharged municipal scribe, and his sister, who is desperate to get married. He slips into a captain's uniform, seizes a troupe of soldiers, and occupies the town hall. Confiscating the treasury, he arrests the mayor. When he surrenders at the end, the authorities are unwilling to believe that such an unimposing figure could have fooled the entire town.

Major roles: Wilhelm Fadenkreutz (bar); Auguste, his sister (sop); the mayor (bass); and Adelaide, his daughter (sop).

SCORE: fs (Berlin: B&B, 1950); vs composer (Berlin: B&B, c. 1950).

LIBRETTO: German (the same).

BIBLIOGRAPHY: Kurt Heinz, "In Mannheim," *Melos* XX (1953), 226–27.

Prinz von Homburg, Der (The Prince of Homburg), opera in three acts by Hans Werner Henze; libretto (Ger) by Ingeborg Bachmann after Heinrich von Kleist's drama (1810). First performance May 22, 1960, Hamburg, with Vladimir

Rudzak (the Prince), Lisabette Fölser (Natalie), Helmut Melchert (the Elector), Mimi Aarden (the Electoress), and Heinz Hoppe (Hohenzollen); conducted by Leopold Ludwig. First British performance September 26, 1962, London, Sadler's Wells, with Rudzak, Melchert, and Colette Lorand (Natalie).

The plot concerns Prince Friedrich of Homburg, whose disregard of orders during a battle threatened the Elector's victory. Because of this, the Prince is court-martialed and sentenced to death. The Elector pardons him after the Prince concedes that the death sentence was justified. He is then praised for his military deeds and is allowed to wed his beloved Natalie, niece of the Electress.

For a detailed synopsis, see K/*KOB*, 918–21.

Major roles: Prince Friedrich Artur von Homburg (bar); Prince Friedrich Wilhelm, the Elector of Brandenburg (ten); the Electress (alto); the Electress' niece, Princess Natalie (sop); and Count Hohenzollen (ten).

An earlier setting is by Paul Graener (1935, Berlin).

BIBLIOGRAPHY: Andrew McCredie, "Reports from Abroad," *MT* (1960), 506 [on premiere].

Prinzessin Brambilla (Princess Brambilla), comic opera in two acts by Walter Braunfels; libretto (Ger) by the composer after a story by E. T. A. Hoffmann (1820). First performance March 25, 1909, Stuttgart; conducted by Max von Schillings. Revised 1931, Hanover.

The story takes place at Carnival time in Rome. It has two pairs of characters who mirror each other, the fairy-tale Princess Brambilla and Prince Cornelio, and the human Giacinta, a seamstress, and Giglio, an actor.

SCORES: vs ed. Rudolf Louis (Munich: H. Levy, c. 1908); (Vienna: UE, c. 1930).

LIBRETTO: (Munich: H. Levy, c. 1908).

BIBLIOGRAPHY: Ute Jung, *Walter Braunfels (1882–1954)* (Regensburg: Gustav Bosse, 1980), 59–84.

Protagonist, Der (The Protagonist), opera in one act by Kurt Weill; libretto (Ger) by Georg Kaiser on his play of the same name. First performance March 27, 1926, Dresden, with Curt Taucher (the Protagonist) and Elisa Stünzer (the sister); conducted by Fritz Busch.

The story concerns a traveling theater troupe in England during Elizabethan times. The troupe has been employed by a duke to entertain his guests. Since the guests do not understand English, the players are required to present their entertainment in pantomime. The troupe is headed by the Protagonist, whose sister is in love with a young gentleman. The sister is waiting for the right moment to tell her overly possessive brother of her plans to marry her suitor.

The pantomime chosen for the evening's entertainment concerns a husband and wife, his mistress, and a ribald monk. The rehearsal goes well, and the sister tells her brother of her plans. But the troupe is informed that a bishop will be among the guests, so that a serious story is now in order. The troupe therefore reworks the comedy into a drama in which the husband interrupts his wife with her lover. Unable to distinguish reality from fantasy in his mind, the Protagonist stabs his sister, who is playing the part of the unfaithful wife.

Major roles: the Protagonist (ten), the sister (sop), and the young gentleman (bar).

SCORES: fs (Vienna: UE, 1926); vs (Vienna: UE, 1926).

LIBRETTO: German (the same).

BIBLIOGRAPHY: S/*DGS*, 68–71.

Prozess, Der (The Trial), opera in nine scenes (two parts) by Gottfried von Einem; libretto (Ger) by the composer and Heinz von Cramer after Franz Kafka's novel (1915). First performance August 17, 1953, Salzburg, with Max Lorenz (Joseph K.), Lisa Della Casa (three women: Frl. Buerstner, Frau Gerichtsdiener, and Nurse Leni), Ludwig Hofmann (a manufacturer, passenger, overseer, and priest), Paul Klein (the Student), Alfred Poell (the Lawyer), and Oskar Czerwenka (the Trial Judge); conducted by Karl Böhm. First U.S. performance October 22, 1953, New York, City Center. First British performance May 24, 1973, London, Collegiate Theatre.

The opera presents a treatment of Kafka's surrealistic novel, in which the hero, Joseph K., a bank official, is accused of a crime of which he knows nothing. The opera describes his vain effort to clear himself and his miserable death.

Major roles: Joseph K. (ten), the Student (ten), the Lawyer (bar), Titorelli (ten), the Trial Judge (bar), and three women (sops).

Also set by Gunther Schuller as *The Visitation* (1966).

SCORE: vs ed. composer (Mainz: BSS, 1953).

LIBRETTO: German, the same.

BIBLIOGRAPHY: Trude Goth, "Repercussions on the Trial," *ON* XVIII (February 8, 1954), 32; Max Graf, "*Der Prozess* von Gottfried von Einem," *ÖMz* VIII (1953), 259–64; Willi Reich, "Current Chronicle. Austria," *MQ* XL (1954), 40 [on premiere] ; Signe Scanzoni, "Trial and Tribulation in Salzburg," *ON* XVIII (October 19, 1953), 12 [on premiere].

Prüfung, Die (The Test), opera in one act by Ludwig Spohr; libretto (Ger) by Eduard Henke, Spohr's uncle. Despite promising rehearsals, Spohr cancelled the concert performance of the work at the Gotha court, which was scheduled for 1806.

The "test" refers to Natalie's disguising herself as Ida to see if her lover, Edmund, is faithful.

Only the tenor aria (No. 4) and the overture were later performed.

Major roles: Natalie (sop), Chaus (sop), Edmund (ten), and Count W. (bass).

BIBLIOGRAPHY: B/*LS*, 41–43; Eugen Schmitz, "Louis Spohrs erster Opernversuch," *AMw* VII (1942), 84–89.

Puntila, opera in three acts by Paul Dessau; libretto (Ger) by Peter Palitzsch and Manfred Werkwerth after Bertolt Brecht's *Herr Puntila und sein Knecht Matti* (1940). First performance November 15, 1966, Deutsche Staatsoper, East Berlin, with Rainer Süss (Puntila), Kurt Rehm (the Chauffeur), Irmgard Arnold (Eva), Gertrude Stilo (Smuggler Emma), Edda Schaller (the Apothecary), Sylvia Pavlik (Lisa, the Milkmaid), Erna Roscher (the Telephone Operator), Annelies Burmeister (the Cook), and Henno Garduhn (Elino); conducted by Otmar Suitner.

The setting is Finland in the first half of the twentieth century. Puntila, a farmer, behaves like an unpleasant landowner when he is sober, and like a caring human being when he is drunk. His chauffeur, Matti, deserts his employer because of the former's instability.

The opera contains many sections that are spoken or half sung, and its music uses polytonality.

Major roles: Johannes Puntila, landowner (bass); Matti Altonen, his chauffeur (bar); Fredrick, a lawyer (ten); the Smuggler Emma (alto); the Apothecary (mezzo); Lisa, the Milkmaid (sop); and the Telephone Operator Sandra (sop).

SCORES: fs (Berlin: Henschel-Verlag, 1959); vs (the same); vs ed. Fritz Geissler (Berlin: B&B, 1967).

BIBLIOGRAPHY: James H. Sutcliffe, "Reports: Foreign," *ON* XXXI (December 31, 1966), 31 [on premiere].

R

Räuber, Die (The Robbers), opera in four acts by Giselher Klebe; libretto (Ger) by the composer after Friedrich Schiller's play (1782). First performance June 3, 1957, Düsseldorf, with Elisabeth Schwarzenberg (Amalie), Wilhelm Walter Dicks (Franz), Walter Beissner (Karl), Harold Kraus (Hermann), and Helmut Fehn (the old Count von Moor); conducted by Reinhard Peters.

The text is a condensation of the Schiller work; some of the secondary characters and action have been removed. When Karl Moor, a student, is cheated of his inheritance by his brother Franz, he forms a band of robbers. After he returns to his former home, he finds his father has been locked up by Franz and that it was Franz who deceived him. The insane Franz hangs himself, but Karl, unable to shake off his misdeeds and start a new life, kills Amalie, his beloved, and surrenders.

Major roles: Karl Moor (bass); Franz (ten); the Count, their father (bar); and Amalie (sop).

The atonal score contains, among its complex pieces, the vocally difficult quartet of Act III.

SCORES: vs ed. composer (Wiesbaden: B&B, c. 1956); new ed. (Berlin: B&B, 1962).

LIBRETTO: (Berlin: B&B, 1957).

BIBLIOGRAPHY: Everett Helm, "New Opera by Klebe," *MT* XCVIII (1957), 446–47 [on premiere]; ———, "Operas by Egk, Klebe and Fortner," *MR* XVIII (1957), 226–28 [on premiere].

Rauchfangkehrer, Der (The Chimney Sweep), opera in three acts by Antonio Salieri; libretto (Ger) by Leopold von Auenbrugger. First performance April 30, 1781, Vienna, National-Singspiel.

The story takes place at the home of a wealthy young widow, Frau von Habicht. She and her stepdaughter Nannette are courted by admirers seeking to enrich their own fortunes. Lisel, the cook, is secretly betrothed to Volpino, an Italian chimney sweep, who devises a plan to deceive Frau von Habicht and Nannette, and thereby win some money for himself and his new bride. He convinces the wealthy ladies that he is in fact a marchese, who is about to recover his lost fortune and lands, and he makes each lady fall in love with him by singing Italian arias to her and teaching her the language. His deception is eventually uncovered by Herr von Bär and Herr von Wölf, the erstwhile lovers of Frau von Habicht and Nannette. The ladies now see that they have been foolish, and they welcome the return of their gentlemen and even agree to add to Lisel's dowry.

Major roles: Frau von Habicht, a young widow (sop); Fräulein Nannette, her stepdaughter (sop); Johann, a servant (bass); Franzl, a chambermaid (sop); Lisel, a cook (sop); Herr von Bär, a lover of Frau von Habicht (bass); Herr von Wölf, a lover of Nannette (ten); Volpino, a journeyman chimney sweep (bar); and Herr Tomaso, a master chimney sweep (bass).

Salieri was instructed by the Austrian Emperor, Joseph II, to write an opera in German, and this was the result. Nonetheless, using the plot as an excuse, the composer was able to incorporate several lovely Italian arias among the thirty-three numbers of the score.

SCORE: facs. of fs ms ed. Thomas Bauman (New York and London: Garland Publishing, 1986).

LIBRETTO: German (Vienna: Logenmeister, 1781; repr. New York and London: Garland Publishing, 1986).

Re Cervo, Il. See *König Hirsch.**

Regina, oder **Die Marodeure** (Regina, or The Marauders), opera by Albert Lortzing; libretto (Ger) by the composer, revised by Adolf L'Arronge. Composed 1848. First performance March 21, 1899, Berlin, Opernhaus, in a version by Richard Kleinmichel. Revived December 22, 1983, Linz, Landestheater, in the original version, with Linda Roark-Strummer (Regina), Christopher Doig (Richard), Rudolf Kostas (Stephan), Zdenek Kroupa, Franz Donner, Hans-Günther Müller; conducted by Ernst Dunshirn.

Striking workers are pacified by Richard, the factory manager, who is rewarded by winning the hand of Regina, daughter of the factory owner, Simon. This disappoints the evil foreman Stephan, who joins the strikers. They break up the engagement party, destroy the factory, and abduct Regina, but she shoots Stephan just before he is to blow up the armory and the people who have sought refuge in it.

Major roles: Simon, a factory owner (bass); Regina, his daughter (sop); Richard, the factory manager (ten); and Stephan, foreman of the factory (bar).

SCORE: vs ed. Richard Kleinmichel (Berlin: B&B, 1899).

BIBLIOGRAPHY: Christopher Norton-Welsh, "Reports: Foreign," *ON* XLVIII (March 17, 1984), 41 [on revival].

Reisende Ceres, Die (The Traveling Ceres), Singspiel in three acts by Franz Joseph Haydn; libretto (Ger) by Maurus Lindemayr. Date of composition unknown. First known performance August 6, 1977, Salzburg [Hellbrunn]. The work was considered spurious until recently.

The goddess Ceres, in her travels on earth, meets a rash youth, whom she turns into a lizard when he makes fun of her.

BIBLIOGRAPHY: Eva Badura-Skoda, "An Unknown *Singspiel* by Joseph Haydn?" in *Report of the Eleventh Congress of the International Musicological Society*, ed. H. Glahn (Copenhagen, 1974), 236–39; ———, "Zur Erstaufführung von Joseph Haydns Singspiel *Die reisende Ceres*," *ÖMz* XXXII (1977), 317–24.

Revisor, Der (The Inspector General), comic opera in five acts by Werner Egk; libretto (Ger) by the composer after Nikolai Gogol's *The Inspector General* (1836). First performance May 9, 1957, Schwetzingen, Schlosstheater, with Fritz Ollendorf (the town commander), Friederike Sailer (his daughter), Hetty Plümacher (his wife), Gerhard Stolze (the young man from St. Petersburg), Heinz Cramer, Alfred Pfeifle, Frithjof Sentpaul, Fritz Linke, Fritz Wunderlich, and Gustaf Grefe; conducted by the composer. First U.S. performance October 19, 1960 (in English), New York, City Center; conducted by the composer. First British performance July 25, 1958, London, Sadler's Wells, with Alexander Young in the title role; conducted by Leon Lovett.

The story concerns a corrupt mayor and his advisors, who expect an inspector to visit their town in disguise. Chlestakov, a minor civil servant from St. Petersburg, is stranded there and, mistaken for the official, takes advantage of the situation. Although his real identity is discovered by the nosey postmaster, he escapes before he is unmasked; just as the town officials are in a rage about being deceived, the genuine inspector shows up.

Major roles: Chlestakov (ten), Ossip (bass), the town commander (bass-bar), Anna (alto), Marja (sop), Mischka (ten), the postmaster (ten), the curator (bass), the judge (bass), Bobtschinski (ten), Dobtschinski (bar), a young widow (sop), and the wife of the jailor (mezzo).

The score includes two scenes with Russian folksongs and a French chanson.

SCORE: vs (Mainz: BSS, 1957).

LIBRETTO: German (the same).

BIBLIOGRAPHY: Richard Franko Goldman, "Current Chronicle. New York," *MQ* XLVII (1961), 98–100 [on U.S. premiere]; Everett Helm, "Operas by Egk, Klebe and Fortner," *MR* XVIII (1957), 224–26.

Rheingold, Das. See *Der Ring des Nibelungen.*

Rienzi (Cola Rienzi, der letzte der Tribunen) (Cola Rienzi, the Last of the Tribunes), opera in five acts by Richard Wagner; libretto (Ger) by the composer after Mary Russell Mitford's drama (1828) and the novel by Edward Bulwer Lytton (1835). First performance October 20, 1842, Dresden, Hofoper, with Joseph Tichatschek (Rienzi), Wilhelmine Schröder-Devrient (Adriano), Henriette Wüst (Irene), Wilhelm Dettmer (Stefano Colonna), Johann Michael Wächter (Paolo Orsini), and Giovanni Vestri (Cardinal Raimondo); conducted by Carl Gottlieb Reissiger. First U.S. performance March 4, 1878, New York, Academy of Music, with Pappenheim, Hüman, Adams, Heinrich Wiegand, and Emil Fischer (Stefano); conducted by Menetzek. First British performance January 27, 1879, with Helene Crosmond and Joseph Maas (Rienzi); conducted by Carl Rosa. First U.S. revival January 1977, San Antonio, with Janet Price (Irene), James McCray (Rienzi), Rose Marie Freni (Adriano), and Ara Berberian (Cardinal Raimondo); conducted by John Mauceri.

The story, which takes place in the Roman republic of the fourteenth century, concerns a struggle between the nobles and the common people. Paolo Orsini, a noble, is prevented from abducting Irene, sister of Cola Rienzi, by Stefano Colonna and his son, Adriano. On the urging of Cardinal Raimondo, the papal legate Rienzi, who is a commonor, vows to defend the people and he becomes the tribune. While swearing allegiance to him, the nobles plot to murder Rienzi, and, when they are discovered, they are spared only by the intercession of Adriano. After turning on the nobles, the populace also abandons Rienzi. Adriano warns Irene that her brother is in danger, but when she discovers him praying in the capitol, she refuses Adriano's offer of safety. Adriano joins the siblings in the capitol, and the three die in the blaze set by the mob.

For a detailed plot synopsis and musical analysis, see K/*KOB*, 159–62.

Major roles: Cola Rienzi, papal tribune (ten); Irene, his sister (sop); Paolo Orsini (bass); Stefano Colonna (bass); Adriano, his son (mezzo); and Cardinal Raimondo (bass).

Wagner's first success, the opera follows the lines of grand opera. Along with stirring choruses, it contains the beautiful prayer of Rienzi in Act V, "Allmächt'ger Vater, blick herab!" The famous overture uses the theme of the prayer aria.

SCORES: fs (Dresden and Leipzig: Fürstenau, 1846); fs ed. Reinhard Strom and Egon Voss, *Werke*, III/1 (Mainz: B. Schott, 1974); vs ed. C. F. Meser (Dresden: Fürstner, 1844).

LIBRETTO: German (Dresden, 1842).

BIBLIOGRAPHY: Alan Blyth, "British Opera Diary," *Opera* XXXIV (1983), 1349–52; John Deathridge, "Rienzi . . . a Few of the Facts," *MT* CXXIV (1983), 546–49; ———, *Wagner's 'Rienzi' . . . a Reappraisal Based on a Study of the Sketches and Drafts* (Oxford, 1977); Quaintance Eaton, "Wagner's 'Rienzi,' " *MA* XXVII (August 1977),

30, 38; Martin Geck, *"Rienzi* in Bayreuth," *NZM* CXXIX (1968), 331–33; ———, *"Rienzi-*Philologie," in D/*DRW*, 183–96; William Mann, " 'Rienzi': an Introduction," *Opera* XXXIV (1983), 1066–71; Andrew Porter, "Musical Events," *NY* LII (February 14, 1977), 106–11; Reinhard Strohm, *"Rienzi* and Authenticity," *MT* CXVII (1976), 725–27.

DISCOGRAPHY: Wennberg, Martin, Springer, Kollo, Schreier, Leib, Adam, Hillebrand, conducted by Hollreiser, Angel SELX–3818 (3).

Ring des Nibelungen, Der (The Ring of the Nibelung), cycle of four works by Richard Wagner; libretto (Ger) by the composer after the Nibelung saga. First complete performance August 13, 14, 16, 17, 1876, Bayreuth, Festspielhaus, with Heinrich Vogl (Loge), Eilers (Fasolt), Franz Betz (Wotan, the Wanderer), Grün (Fricka), Elmblad (Donner), Engelhardt (Froh), Haupt (Freia), Reichenberg (Fafner), Karl Hill (Alberich), Max Schlosser (Mime), Luise Jaide (Erda), Albert Niemann (Siegmund), Josephine Schefsky (Sieglinde), Josef Nierung (Hunding), Amalie Materna (Brünnhilde), Lilli Lehmann (Rhinemaiden, Woodbird), Gustav Siehr (Hagen), Eugen Gura (Gunther), Weckerlin (Gutrune), and Marianne Brandt (Waltraute); conducted by Hans Richter. First complete U.S. performance March 4, 5, 6, 11, 1889, New York, Metropolitan Opera, with Lilli Lehmann (Brünnhilde), Katti [Senger-]Bettaque, Julius Perotti, Max Alvary (Loge), Wilhelm Sedlmayer, Emil Fischer (Wotan), and Joseph Beck; conducted by Anton Seidl.

Consists of *Das Rheingold, Die Walküre, Siegfried,* and *Götterdämmerung,* which follow the bibliography of this section.

LIBRETTOS: German (private printing by composer, 1853); English, transl. Andrew Porter as *The Ring of the Nibelung* (London: Dawson and New York: Norton, 1976); reviewed by D. Kern Holoman, "Wagner's *Ring* in Andrew Porter's English," *19th Century Music* I (1977), 62–70.

BIBLIOGRAPHY: Oskar Andree, *Richard Wagners 'Ring des Nibelungen'* (Stuttgart, 1976); Herbert Barth, ed., *Bayreuther Dramaturgie. Der Ring des Nibelungen* (Stuttgart and Zurich: Besler, 1980); Nancy Benvenga, *Kingdom on the Rhine: History, Myth and Legend in Wagner's 'Ring'* (Harwich: Essex, 1983); Pierre Boulez et al., *Historie d'un 'Ring.' Der Ring des Nibelungen (L'Anneau du Nibelung) de Richard Wagner. Bayreuth 1976–1980,* eds. Sylvie de Nussac and François Regnault (Paris: Diapason, Laffont, 1980); Werner Brieg, "Das Schiksalskunde-Motiv im *Ring des Nibelungen,*" in D/*DRW*, 223–33; Reinhold Brinckmann, "Mythos-Geschichte-Natur Zeitkonstellationen im 'Ring,' " in *Richard Wagner—von der Oper zum Musikdrama,* ed. Stefan Kunze (Bern and Munich, 1978), 61–77; Peter Burbridge and Richard Sutton, eds., *Wagner Companion* (New York: Cambridge, 1979); Deryck Cooke, *I Saw the World Ending* (New York: Oxford, 1979) [does not include *Siegfried* or *Götterdämmerung,* since Cooke died before the work was completed]; William O. Cord, *An Introduction to Richard Wagner's Der Ring des Nibelungen. A Handbook* (Athens: Ohio University Press, 1983); John Culshaw, *Reflections on Wagner's 'Ring'* (London and New York, 1976); ———, *The Ring Resounding* (New York: Viking Press, 1967); Robert C. Cumbow, "The Ring Is a Fraud. Self, Totem, and Myth in *Der Ring des Nibelungen,*" *OQ* I/1 (Spring 1983), 107–25;

Carl Dahlhaus, "Formprinzipien in Wagners 'Ring des Nibelungen' " in Carl Becker, ed., *Beiträge zur Geschichte der Oper* (Regensburg, 1969), 95–129; John Deathridge, "Wagner's Sketches for the 'Ring.' Some Recent Studies," *MT* CXVIII (1977), 383–89; Alan Dickinson, "The Structural Methods of *The Ring*," *MMR* LXXXIV (1954), 87–92; J. L. Di Gaetani, ed., *Penetrating Wagner's 'Ring.' An Anthology* (Rutherford, N.J.: Fairleigh Dickinson University, 1978); Robert Donington, *Wagner's Ring and Its Symbols* (New York: St. Martin's Press, 1974); Hans Engel, "Versuche einer Sinndeutung von Richard Wagners *Ring des Nibelungen*," *Mf* X (1957), 225–41; Michael Ewans, *Wagner and Aeschylus. The Ring and the Oresteia* (New York: Cambridge University Press, 1983); Victor Gollancz, "Doubts about 'The Ring,' " *Opera* XV (1964), 583–89; David Hamilton, "How Wagner Forged His Ring," *ON* XXXIX (special "Ring" issue, 1975), 21–26; Robert L. Jacobs, "A Freudian View of *The Ring*," *MR* XXVI (1965), 201–19; Tibor Kneif, "Wagner: eine Rekapitulation—Mythos und Geschichte im *Ring des Nibelungen*," in D/*DRW*, 213–21; M. Owen Lee, "Wagner's *Ring*. Turning the Sky Around," *OQ* 1/2 (Summer 1983), 28–47; Dietrich Mack, "Zur Dramaturgie des *Ring*," in D/*DRW*, 53–63; Francesco Orlando, "Proposte per una semantica del leitmotiv nell' *Anello del Nibelungo*," *NRMI* IX (1975), 230–47; Kurt Overhoff, *Wagners Nibelungen-Tetralogie. Eine zeitgemässige Betrachtung* (Salzburg-Munich: Pustet, 1971); Heinrich Porges, *Wagner Rehearsing the 'Ring*,' trans. Robert L. Jacobs (New York: Cambridge University Press, 1983); George Bernard Shaw, *The Perfect Wagnerite* (1898; 4th ed. repr. New York: Dover, 1967); Patrick J. Smith, "Wotan's Tragic Stature," *ON* XXXIX (special "Ring" issue, 1975), 54–56; Robert van der Lek, "Zum Begriff Übergang und zu seiner Anwendung durch Alfred Lorenz auf die Musik von Wagners 'Ring,' " *Mf* XXXV (1982), 129–47; Richard Wagner, *Der Ring des Nibelungen. Vollständiger Text mit Notentafel der Leitmotive*, ed. Julius Burghold (Munich: Goldmann, Mainz and Schott, 1980); Wieland Wagner, "Thoughts on 'The Ring,' " *Opera* XV (1964), 8–13; Curt von Westernhagen, *The Forging of the 'Ring*,' trans. Arnold Whittall and Mary Whittell (New York: Cambridge University Press, 1976).

DISCOGRAPHY: See Alan Blyth, B/*OOR*, 393–403. Boulez recording reviewed by Rodney Milnes, "The Boulez 'Ring.' Sight and Sound," *Opera* XXXIV (1983), 139–43; Hall recording reviewed by George Movshon, "The 'English Ring' of Sir Peter Hall," *HiFi/MA* XXXIII (December 1983), 28–31.

Rheingold, Das (The Rhine Gold), prologue in one act. First performed separately September 22, 1869, Munich, with Sophie Stehle (Fricka), Henriette Müller (Freia), Emma Seehofer (Erda), Heinrich Vogl (Loge), Max Schlosser (Mime), Franz Nachbaur (Froh), August Kindermann (Wotan), Wilhelm Fischer (Alberich), Kaspar Bausewein (Fafner), Karl Samuel Heinrich (Donner), Anna Kaufmann (Woglinde), Therese Vogl (Wellgunde), and Wilhelmine Ritter (Flosshilde); conducted by Franz Wüllner. First U.S. performance January 4, 1889, New York, Metropolitan Opera, with Fanny Moran-Olden, Max Alvary, Wilhelm Sedlmayer, Albert Mittelhauser, Emil Fischer, Joseph Beck, Alois Grienauer, Ludwig Mödlinger, and Eugene Weiss; conducted by Anton Seidl. First British performance May 5, 1882, London, Her Majesty's Theatre, with Hedwig Reicher-Kindermann (Fricka), Heinrich Vogl (Loge), Max Schlosser (Mime), and Emil Scaria (Wotan); conducted by Anton Seidl.

Alberich, the Nibelung dwarf, gives up love in order to steal the gold from the Rhine Maidens and forge a Ring therefrom, enabling him to rule the world. Wotan, ruler of the gods, has promised to give the giants Fasolt and Fafner the goddess of youth, Freia, for building Valhalla, the dwelling place of the deities, but when he is unable to pay them, they start to drag Freia away. Wotan, with the help of Loge, god of fire, tricks Alberich to get the gold and the Ring, which Alberich curses. Wotan is forced to give the giants the booty, along with the magic helmet, the Tarnhelm, which makes its wearer invisible. The giants quarrel over the treasure, and Fafner kills Fasolt. Wotan has fathered with Erda nine warrior daughters, the Valkyries, but he must father human children in order to regain the Ring and remove the curse. He sires Sieglinde and Siegmund, who are separated at birth and grow up independently, a story which is developed in *Die Walküre*.

For detailed synopses and musical analyses, see *ENO* XXXV (1985); C/*NMC*, 480–85; K/*KOB*, 219–29; and N/*SGO*, I, 158–86.

Major roles: Alberich (bar or bass-bar); Wotan (bar); Loge (ten); Fricka (mezzo); Freia (sop); Erda (mezzo); the Rhine Maidens Woglinde, Wellgunde, and Flosshilde (2 high sops, low sop); Donner (bar); Mime, Alberich's brother (ten); Fasolt (bar); and Fafner (bass).

Among the glorious musical moments are the 136 measures of the opening prelude, a representation of the Rhine River set around an E-flat chord; the orchestral interlude that accompanies the journey of Wotan and Loge to Nibelheim, Alberich's dwelling; and the interlude depicting the working of the dwarfs at the forge. Others include the rainbow music, "Zur Burg führt die Brücke," sung by Froh, and Wotan's paen to Valhalla, "Abendlich strahlt die Sonne Auge."

William Vincent Wallace's *Lurline* (1860, London) has a scene at the bottom of the Rhine.

SCORES: fs (Mainz: BSS, 1873); vs ed. Karl Klingworth (Mainz: BSS, 1861), ed. Richard Kleinmichel, German-English text ed. H. and F. Corder (Mainz: BSS, 1882).

LIBRETTO: German (Zurich, 1853).

BIBLIOGRAPHY: J. Merrill Knapp, "The Instrumental Draft of Wagner's *Das Rheingold*," *JAMS* XXX (1977), 272–95; Peter Nitsche, "Klangfarben und Form. Das Walhallthema in *Rheingold* und *Walküre*," *Melos/NZM* I/2 (1975), 83–88; Otto Schneider, "Vor 100 Jahren: Zur Uraufführung von Wagners 'Rheingold,' " *ÖMZ* XXIV (1969), 589–91.

DISCOGRAPHY: See Alan Blyth, B/*OOR*, 403–7, 436; in English: EMI SLS 5032 (4).

Walküre, Die (The Valkyrie), music drama in three acts. First separate performance June 26, 1870, Munich, Hofoper, with Sophie Stehle (Brünnhilde), Therese Vogl (Sieglinde), Anna Kaufmann (Fricka), Heinrich Vogl (Siegmund), August Kindermann (Wotan), and Kaspar Bausewein (Hunding); conducted by Franz Wüllner. First U.S. performance April 2, 1877, New York, Academy of Music, with Auguste Seidl-Kraus (Sieglinde), Pappenheim, Canissa, Listner,

Bischoff, Preusser, and Blum; conducted by Neuendorff. First British performance May 6, 1882, London, Her Majesty's Theatre; with Hedwig Reicher-Kindermann (Fricka), Therese Vogl (Brünnhilde), Riegler, Albert Niemann (Siegmund), Emil Scaria (Wotan), and Heinrich Wiegand (Hunding); conducted by Anton Seidl.

Siegmund, in flight from his enemies, seeks refuge in a hut inhabited by Hunding and his wife, Sieglinde. She tells Siegmund of the magic sword Nothung, which a stranger, Wotan, had thrust into a tree, and which could not be removed by anyone but a hero. The brother and sister fall in love; he sings the rapturous "Winterstürme," and Sieglinde replies with the beautiful "Du bist der Lenz." Siegmund realizes that it was his father Wotan who thrust in the spear, and he is able to extract it from the tree. With it he fights the enraged Hunding, who has awakened from his drugged sleep.

Brünnhilde, Wotan's favorite Valkyrie daughter, attempts, against her father's orders, to assist Siegmund in his battle, but Wotan intercedes, at the urging of his wife, Fricka, guardian of marriage vows. Wotan shatters Nothung and lets Hunding kill Siegmund. Hunding also dies by Wotan's hand. During the fight Brünnhilde carries off Sieglinde, who is to bear Siegmund's child, Siegfried. The third act opens with the famous "Ride of the Valkyries." They are joined by Brünnhilde, who is trying to escape her father's wrath. As punishment for her disobedience, Wotan puts Brünnhilde to sleep on a rock surrounded by a ring of fire, one that can be penetrated only by a hero. He sings the moving "Leb' wohl, du kühnes, herrliches Kind!" and the opera closes with the glorious and evocative Magic Fire Music.

For detailed synopses and musical analyses, see C/*NMC*, 486–91; *ENO*, XXI (1983); K/*KOB*, 229–42; and N/*SGO*, I, 187–221.

Major roles: Sieglinde (sop), Brünnhilde (sop), Siegmund (ten), Wotan (bar or bass-bar), Fricka (sop or mezzo-sop), Hunding (bass).

Johan Ernst Hartmann's *Balders Død* includes ensembles of Valkyries (1778, Copenhagen).

SCORES: fs (Mainz: BSS, 1874); vs (Mainz: BSS, 1865); vs ed. Richard Kleinmichel, English H. and F. Corder (New York: G. Schirmer, 18—); ed. Karl Klindworth (Mainz: BSS, ca. 1865).

LIBRETTO: German (Zurich, 1853).

BIBLIOGRAPHY: *L'Avant-scène opéra* VIII (January-February 1977) [entire issue]; David Hamilton, "Crux of the Ring: *Die Walküre's* Second Act Unraveled," *ON* XLI/15 (1977), 8–12; Harald Kaufmann, "Orchesterfarben als Dimension des Komponierens. Zur 'Walküre,' " in *Spurlinien. Analytische Aufsätze über Sprache und Musik* (Vienna: Lafite, 1969), 102–6; Peter Nitsche, "Klangfarbe und Form. Das Walhallthema in *Rheingold* und *Walküre*," *Melos/NZM* I/2 (1975), 83–88; John Potter, "Brünnhilde's Choice," *ON* XLVII (March 26, 1983), 9–11.

DISCOGRAPHY: See Alan Blyth, B/*OOR*, 393–403, 407–21, 437–38; in English: EMI SLS 5063 (5).

Siegfried, music drama in three acts. First separate performance August 16, 1876, Bayreuth, Festspielhaus, with Amalie Materna (Brünnhilde), Luise Jaide (Erda), Georg Unger (Siegfried), Max Schlosser (Mime), Franz Betz (the Wanderer), Karl Hill (Alberich), Franz von Reichenberg (Fafner), and Lilli Lehmann (forest bird); conducted by Hans Richter. First U.S. performance November 9, 1887, New York, Metropolitan Opera, with Max Alvary (Siegfried), Lilli Lehmann (Brünnhilde), Ferenczy, and Emil Fischer (the Wanderer); conducted by Anton Seidl. First British performance May 8, 1882, London, Her Majesty's Theatre, with Therese Vogl (Brünnhilde), Heinrich Vogl (Siegfried), Max Schlosser (Mime), Emil Scaria (the Wanderer), and Auguste Seidl-Kraus (forest bird); conducted by Anton Seidl.

Sieglinde has died bearing Siegfried, and he has been raised by the dwarf Mime, brother of Alberich. Mime hopes to mend the shattered sword and reclaim the Rheingold. He is visited by Wotan, disguised as the Wanderer, who tells him that the sword can be forged only by a hero. Realizing that this hero is Siegfried, Mime convinces Siegfried to restore the weapon. The boy does this, in his famous "Schmiede, mein Hammer, ein hartes Schwert" of the first act. In the second act, again at the urging of Mime, Siegfried seeks out Fafner, who has changed himself into a dragon and is guarding the gold. The boy is fearless, and he kills the dragon with his sword. When Siegfried touches the blood of the dead dragon, he acquires the gift of understanding the forest bird's song, "Hei! Siegfried gehört nun der Nibelungen Hort." The bird warns Siegfried, in "O traute Mime dem Treulosen nicht," that Mime is planning to kill him. Siegfried slays Mime instead and, at the bird's urging, takes the Ring and the Tarnhelm and goes off to rescue Brünnhilde from the rock. The final act opens with an extended scene between the Wanderer and Erda, whom he has roused from sleep and who predicts that the gods are doomed. He seeks to block Siegfried's path, but the latter shatters his spear with Nothung. The two part, and Siegfried ascends to the rock, accompanied by a beautiful orchestral interlude, which includes Siegfried's two main themes and the fire music. The final scene is a duplicate of the scene that closes *Die Walküre.* Here Siegfried discovers the sleeping Brünnhilde, who, despite her armor and to his delight, "ist kein Mann" (a line which invariably prompts laughter from the audience). She responds with the glorious "Heil dir, Sonne!" He replies with "Dich lieb' ich," and the scene and opera close with her "Fahr' hin, Walhalls," as she throws herself into Siegfried's waiting arms.

For detailed synopses and musical analyses, see C/*NMC*, 492–98; *ENO*, XXVIII (1984); K/*KOB*, 242–52; and N/*SGO*, I, 222–52.

Major roles: Brünnhilde (sop), Siegfried (ten), Mime (ten), the Wanderer [Wotan] (bass or bass-bar), Alberich (bass), Fafner (bass), voice of the forest bird (sop) and Erda (alto).

The score features only male voices until the third-act meeting of the Wanderer and Erda (with the exception of the forest bird's solos in Act II).

SCORES: fs (Mainz: BSS, 1876; repr. New York: Dover, 1983); vs ed. Karl Klindworth (Mainz: BSS, 1871).

BIBLIOGRAPHY: *L'Avant-scène opéra* XII (November-December 1977) [entire issue] Daniel Coren, "Inspiration and Calculation in the Genesis of Wagner's *Siegfried*," in *Studies in Musicology in Honor of Otto E. Albrecht*, ed. John Walter Hill (Kassel: Bär, 1980), 266–87; ———, "The Texts of Wagner's *Der junge Siegfried* and *Siegfried*," *19th Century Music* VI (1982), 17–30; Carl Dahlhaus, "Das unterbrochene Hauptwerk. Zu Wagners *Siegfried*," D/*DRW*, 235–38.

DISCOGRAPHY: Flagstad, Svanholm, and Herrmann, Everest 475/3; reviewed by William Brown, *OQ* I (1983), 278; T. V. Murray, "Recordings: Lauritz Melchior chante Siegfried," *OQ* I/4 (1983), 136–38 [review of EMI recording SLS 875 (5)]. See also Alan Blyth, B/*OOR*, 393–403, 421–27, 438.

Götterdämmerung (Twilight of the Gods), music drama in three acts. First separate performance August 17, 1876, Bayreuth, Festspielhaus, with Amalie Materna (Brünnhilde), Mathilde Weckerlin (Gutrune), Luise Jaide (Erda), Georg Unger (Siegfried), Eugen Gura (Gunther), Karl Hill (Alberich), and Gustav Siehr (Hagen); conducted by Hans Richter. First U.S. performance (in an abbreviated version) January 25, 1888, New York, Metropolitan Opera, with Lilli Lehmann (Brünnhilde), Auguste Seidl-Krauss (Gutrune), Albert Niemann (Siegfried), Adolf Robinson, and Emil Fischer (Hagen); conducted by Anton Seidl. First British performance May 9, 1882, London, Her Majesty's Theatre, with Therese Vogl (Brünnhilde), Schreiber, Hedwig Reicher-Kindermann, Heinrich Vogl (Siegfried), Heinrich Wiegand (Hagen), Bibert, and Schleper; conducted by Anton Seidl.

The work opens with a prologue, in which the Norns foresee the end of the gods, and Siegfried, seeking adventure, leaves his bride, Brünnhilde, after giving her his ring. His travels are portrayed orchestrally in the famed "Siegfried's Rhine Journey." The scene changes to the hall of the Gibichungs, whose residents include Gunther, his sister, Gutrune, and their half-brother, Hagen, whose father is Alberich. When Siegfried arrives, he is given a drink prepared by Alberich, one which makes him fall in love and marry Gutrune, leaving Brünnhilde for Gunther. Hurt by Siegfried's betrayal, Brünnhilde tells Hagen of Siegfried's one weakness, a blow to his back. Hagen kills Siegfried with a spear thrust. His body is borne off to the magnificent Funeral March. Brünnhilde builds a funeral pyre for her slain husband and sings a heartbreaking farewell, "Wie Sonne lauter strahlt mir sein Licht." The great Immolation Scene follows, in which she rides into the flames, which destroy Valhalla. The Rhine Maidens reclaim their treasure and kill Hagen, and the opera and cycle end.

Götterdämmerung takes about five hours (not counting the intermissions), which makes it the longest German opera in the standard repertoire. It includes the only chorus (Vassals, Act II) in the entire *Ring*, marking a violation of Wagner's own theories against choruses in the music drama.

For detailed synopses and musical analyses, see C/*NMC*, 499–505; *ENO* XXXI (1985); K/*KOB*, 252–63; and N/*SGO*, I, 253–85.

Major roles: Brünnhilde (sop), Siegfried (ten), Hagen (bass), Gutrune (sop), Alberich (bass), and Gunther (bass or bass-bar).

Heinrich Dorn's *Die Nibelungen* of 1844 (Berlin) contains the characters Siegfried, Günther, Brunhild, and Hagen; they all die in the opera, and Chriemhild is the ultimate victor. The libretto was published in 1853.

SCORES: fs (Mainz: BSS, 1876, repr. New York: Dover, 1982); fs in SW, XIII/1–3; vs ed. Karl Klindworth (Mainz: BSS, 1875).

LIBRETTO: German (Zurich, 1853).

BIBLIOGRAPHY: Robert Bailey, "Wagner's Musical Sketches for *Siegfrieds Tod*," in *Studies in Musicology*, ed. Harold Powers (Princeton, N.J.: Princeton University Press, 1968), 459–94; Carl Dahlhaus, "Über den Schluss der Götterdämmerung," D/*RWW*, 97–115; Speight Jenkins, "Wagner's Grand Opera," *ON* XXXVIII (March 23, 1974), 24–25; William Kindermann, "Dramatic Recapitulation in Wagner's *Götterdämmerung*," *19th Century Music* IV (1980), 101–12; Peter John Ryder, "Götterdämmerung—Possible Solutions to Some Wagner Problems," *Opera* XXII (1971), 26–31.

DISCOGRAPHY: Hunter, Curphey, Pring, Masterson, Squires, Attfield, Remedios, Welsby, Haugland, and Hammond-Stroud, English National Opera Chorus and Orchestra, conducted by Goodall, in English, EMI (UK) SLS–5118 (6); reviewed by John W. Freeman, "Records," *ON* XLIII (April 7, 1979), 67. See also Alan Blyth, B/*OOR*, 427–36, 439.

Ring des Polykrates, Der (The Ring of Polycrates), opera in one act by Erich Korngold; libretto (Ger) by Heinrich Teweles. First performance March 28, 1916, Munich, with Maria Ivögun (Laura), and Karl Erb (Wilhelm); conducted by Bruno Walter. First U.S. performance March 17, 1983, New York, Manhattan School of Music, with Richard Decker, Lauren Flanigan, Brian Bruce, Li-Chan Chen, and Joseph Philippe; conducted by C. William Harwood.

The story is a modernization of the Greek legend of King Polycrates, who sacrificed his favorite ring to the gods and was rewarded by its return. The Korngold version concerns a court conductor and his wife, Wilhelm and Laura Arndt. The wife is bothered by an old beau, Peter Vogel, the conductor's best friend. In the end the beau is thrown out.

Major roles: Wilhelm (ten); Laura (sop); Florian Döblinger, a timpanist (ten); Lieschen, Laura's maid (sop); and Peter Vogel (bar).

SCORE: ed. Ferdinand Rebay (Mainz: BSS, c. 1916).

LIBRETTO: German (Mainz: BSS, 1915).

BIBLIOGRAPHY: Robert Jacobson, "U.S.: Reports," *ON* XLVII (June 1983), 48 [on U.S. premiere].

Romeo und Julia (Romeo and Juliet), opera in two acts by Heinrich Sutermeister; libretto (Ger) by the composer after August Wilhelm von Schlegel's translation of the Shakespeare play. First performance April 13, 1940, Dresden. First British performance March 12, 1953, London, Sadler's Wells, with Victoria Elliott (Julia), Rowland Jones (Romeo), and Stanley Lawrence (Friar Laurence); conducted by James Robertson.

Among the many other operatic treatments of the Shakespeare play are Georg Benda's *Romeo und Julie**; Vincenzo Bellini's *I Capuleti e i Montecchi* (1830, Venice); Charles Gounod's *Romeo et Juliette* (1867, Paris); Frederick Delius' *A Village Romeo and Juliet* (1907, Berlin, in German); Riccardo Zandonai's *Giuletta e Romeo* (1922, Rome); and Boris Blacher's *Romeo und Julia.**

SCORE: vs ed. composer (Mainz: BSS, 1940).

BIBLIOGRAPHY: Earl of Harewood, "Opera Diary," *Opera* IV (1953), 305–10.

Romeo und Julia (Romeo and Juliet), opera in three acts by Boris Blacher; libretto (Ger) by the composer after Shakespeare, in a greatly shortened version. Composed 1943–1944. First performance (concert) 1947, Berlin-Zehlendorf; conducted by the composer. First performance (staged) August 8, 1950, Salzburg Festival; conducted by Joseph Krips. First U.S. performance 1953, University of Illinois, Opera Workshop.

Major roles: Romeo (ten), Julia (sop), Lady Capulet (alto), the nurse (alto), Capulet (bass), Tybald (ten), Benvolo (bass), and Peter (ten).

The chorus comments on and even takes part in the action, to the point of handing Julia the poison. The work is scored for chamber orchestra.

SCORE: German-English (Vienna: UE, c. 1950).

LIBRETTO: the same.

Romeo und Julie (Romeo and Juliet), opera in three acts by Georg Benda; libretto (Ger) by Friedrich Wilhelm Gotter after Shakespeare. First performance September 25, 1776, Gotha, Hoftheater, with Franziska Koch (Julie) and Johann Ernst Dauer (Romeo).

Despite the tragic source, this first operatic setting of the Shakespeare play ends happily. The lovers are, in this case, aided by the Kapellet's chaplain, Lorenzo, who tricks Julie's father into saying that he would let her marry the hated Romeo, if it would bring her back to life.

Major roles: Kapellet, a noble of Verona (ten); Julie, his daughter (sop); Romeo Montecchi (ten); Laura, a friend of Julie (sop).

The opera's numbers include the love duet of the second act, "Hat noch ein Paar/Nie hat ein Paar," and the third-act funeral chorus, "Im Grabe winnt Vergessenheit der Sorgen." See also Heinrich Sutermeister's *Romeo und Julia** (1940, Dresden) and Boris Blacher's *Romeo und Julia** (1950, Salzburg).

SCORES: fs facs. of ms, ed. Thomas Bauman (New York and London: Garland Publishing, 1985); vs (Leipzig: Im Verlage der Dykischen Buchhandlung, 1778).

LIBRETTO: German (Leipzig: Im Verlage der Dykischen Buchhandlung, 1779).

BIBLIOGRAPHY: Fritz Brückner, "Georg Benda, und das deutsche Singspiel," *SIMG* V (1903–04), 30–32.

Rosamunde, Fürstin von Cypern (Rosamunde, Princess of Cyprus), Romantic play in four acts (Ger) by Helmina von Chézy, with music by Franz Schubert. First performance December 20, 1823, Vienna, Theater an der Wien.

Rosamunde, the orphaned daughter of the King of Cyprus, has been raised as a shepherdess. In her infancy she was betrothed to Prince Alfonso of Candia. When she reaches eighteen and is about to assume the crown, the prince, summoned by Albanus, a leader of the citizenry of Cyprus, comes to Cyprus in disguise, to test Rosamunde's faithfulness. Albanus seeks the help of Fulgentius, who tries to kill both Rosamunde and her intended. Alfonso, discovering Fulgentius' intentions, gets him to inhale a letter Fulgentius himself had laced with poison. Rosamunde, with Alfonso at her side, mounts the throne.

Schubert's music consists of an overture and nine numbers, including a beautiful Romance for alto, "Der Vollmond strahlt auf Bergeshöh'n" (No. 3b, Act II), and the hunting chorus of the third act, "Wie lebt sich's so fröhlich im Grünen" (No. 8), supported by horns and bassoons.

SCORE: Schu/*AGA* XV/4, part 2; Schn/*NGA* II/9 (nyp).

BIBLIOGRAPHY: Otto Erich Deutsch, "Schuberts *Rosamunde* im Theater an der Wien," *ÖMz* XXXIII (1978), 179–84; Elizabeth Norman, "Schubert's Incidental Music to Rosamunde," *MR* XXI (1960), 8–15.

Rosamunde Floris, opera in two acts by Boris Blacher; libretto (Ger) by Gerhart von Westermann after Georg Kaiser's play (1940). First performance September 21, 1960, Berlin, Städtische Oper, with Britta Melanda (Rosamunde), Alice Oelke, Kerstin Meyer, Helmut Krebs, Thomas Stewart, Peter Roth-Ehrang, Karl Ernst Mercker, Leopold Clam, and Hanns Pick; conducted by Richard Kraus.

The wealthy young Rosamunde Floris has a brief affair with a stranger. When she becomes pregnant she tries to seduce Erwin, who breaks his neck when trying to escape. She marries his brother Bruno, whom she tries to poison. In the end she is caught, and she confesses to having murdered Bruno's ex-fiancée.

Major roles: Rosamunde Floris (sop); Herr Benler (bass); Frau Benler (sop); Bruno and Erwin, their sons (tens); sister Wanda (sop); and Wilhelm (bar).

SCORE: vs ed. composer (Berlin: B&B [1960]).

LIBRETTO: Berlin: B&B [1960]).

Rose von Stambul, Die (The Rose of Istanbul), operetta in three acts by Leo Fall; libretto (Ger) by Julius Brammer and Alfred Grünwald. First performance December 2, 1916, Vienna, Theater an der Wien, with Hubert Marischka and Betty Fischer. First U.S. performance (with additions by Sigmund Romberg) March 7, 1922, New York, Century Theater, with Tessa Kosta.

The libretto is set in Turkey and in a Swiss spa and involves the doings of Kondja Gül, rebellious daughter of the Turkish Pasha. She is in love with a poet is but forced by her father to marry a stranger. The stranger turns out to be her beloved.

Major roles: Kondja Gül (sop) and a poet/stranger (ten).

Among the musical highlights is the title song, "Das ist das Glück nach der Mode" and the waltz "Ein Walzer muss es sein."

The work was highly successful in Vienna and Berlin but flopped in its New York production. It is still occasionally performed.

SCORE: vs (Vienna and Berlin: Verlag Ullstein & Co., 1916).

Rosenkavalier, Der (The Cavalier of the Rose), opera in three acts by Richard Strauss; libretto (Ger) by Hugo von Hofmannsthal. First performance January 26, 1911, Dresden, with Margarethe Siems (the Marschallin), Eva von der Osten (Octavian), Minnie Nast (Sophie), Carl Perron (Baron Ochs), Karl Scheidemantel (Faninal), and Fritz Soot (Italian tenor/Faninal's major domo); conducted by Ernst von Schuch. First U.S. performance December 9, 1913, New York, Metropolitan Opera, with Frieda Hempel (the Marschallin), Margaret Arndt-Ober (Octavian), Anna Case (Sophie), Otto Goritz (Baron Ochs), and Hermann Weil (Faninal); conducted by Alfred Hertz. First British performance January 29, 1913, London, Covent Garden, with Margarethe Siems (the Marschallin), Claire Dux (Sophie), Eva von der Osten (Octavian), and Paul Knüpfer (Baron Ochs); conducted by (Sir) Thomas Beecham.

Set in Vienna in the time of Empress Maria Theresa, the story opens in the bedroom of the Princess von Werdenberg (called the "Marschallin"), who has spent the night with the seventeen-year-old Count Octavian. Their tryst is interrupted by the appearance of the Marschallin's boorish country cousin, Baron Ochs, who has come to ask her for a favor: to suggest someone to carry a silver rose to the Baron's intended, the young Sophie, only daughter of the nouveau-riche Herr von Faninal. A perennial skirt chaser, the Baron makes a play for Octavian, whom the Marschallin has disguised as the maid Mariandel, to avoid his finding out about her indiscretion with Octavian. The Baron chases the "maid," during which he sings his risqué (and quite beautiful) paean to love, "Wo nicht dem Knaben Cupido," until he is interrupted by the beginning of the Marschallin's levee.

The colorful levee features a motley assortment of characters, including an Italian tenor, who sings the beautiful aria, "Di rigori armato il seno," whose second strophe is brought to an abrupt conclusion by the Baron's loud argument with the notary, who is trying to draw up his nuptial agreement. When the mob has been dispersed, the Marschallin impulsively agrees to let her young cousin Octavian, the supposed brother of "Mariandel," be the "Rosenkavalier," and the Baron is sent off, whereupon the scene takes on a chamber-music setting. The Marschallin is left to bemoan the nerve of her crude cousin, in "Da geht er hin,'' and to ponder her fate of growing old, in ''Die Zeit, die ist ein sonderbar Ding,'' to an uncomprehending Octavian. She prophesies that he will leave her for a younger woman, in the exquisite ''Heut' oder morgen.'' The act ends with a delicate violin solo and the Marschallin gazing sadly into a mirror.

In contrast, the second act opens with a lush scene, one of the most striking visual and musical scenes in opera. Set at the garish town house of Faninal, it centers around the Presentation of the Rose by Octavian to the convent-bred Sophie. As he sings ''Mir ist die Ehre wiederfahren,'' she answers with ''Hat einen starken Geruch,'' accompanied by the shimmering chords of the orchestra. The two join voices and immediately fall in love. Their bliss is rudely interrupted by the appearance of the Baron and his ill-mannered retinue, but the introductions are temporarily halted after the Baron's servants run amuck, and the lovers are left alone. When the Baron returns and makes a clumsy pass at Sophie, Octavian challenges him to a duel and wounds him slightly in the arm. Sophie tells her father that she will not marry the boorish Baron, but Faninal replies that she will, even if he is a corpse. Octavian whispers to Sophie not to worry, that he will set things straight. The Baron is left alone on stage, enjoying a letter from ''Mariandel'' in which she agrees to meet him at a country inn. The act closes as the Baron sways to the music of the famous, albeit anachronistic waltz, the hallmark of the opera.

The third act, set at a seedy country inn, starts as a ribald (considered by some as a rather tasteless) farce, with the Baron trying to seduce Mariandel, all the while attempting to keep down the costs of his tryst. The scene has been arranged by Valzacchi and Annina, his accomplice, who were originally rebuffed by the Baron and are now in the employ of Octavian. They arrange to have the police arrive to arrest the Baron for having abandoned Annina, who claims to be his wife, and their many children, and for his attempted seduction of a minor. Pandemonium ensues, especially when Sophie and her father are summoned, and Faninal becomes ill from the apparent scandal. Mariandel is finally revealed to be Octavian, and Sophie believes that her future is ruined. The scene comes to an abrupt halt with the appearance of the Marschallin, who is brought by the Baron's illegitimate son and body servant, Leopold, and the opera reverts to its original elegant status. The Marschallin forces the Baron to renounce his claims to Sophie, and all the characters leave except for the three women. In their incomparable trio, which begins with the Marschallin's reprise from the first act, ''Heut' oder morgen,'' she surrenders her beloved to her younger rival. Faninal reappears and gives his blessing to the union, and he and the Marschallin leave together. The opera closes with the simple and touching duet of Octavian and Sophie, ''Spür nur dich''/''Ist ein Traum.''

For detailed synopses and musical analyses, see C/*NMC*, 512–27; *COH*, ed. Alan Jefferson (1986); D/*RS*, I, 334–420; *ENO*, VIII (1981); K/KOB, 815–23; and M/*RSC*, 95–143.

Major roles: the Marschallin (Feldmarschallin) (sop); Baron Ochs of Lerchenau (bass); Octavian, a young gentleman of a noble family (mezzo); Herr von Faninal, a rich merchant, newly ennobled (bar); Sophie, his daughter (sop); Marianne, her duenna (sop); Valzacchi, an Italian intriguer (ten); Annina, his accomplice (alto); and an Italian tenor (ten).

Hofmannsthal based his plot on various eighteenth-century works, including two Molière plays, *Les Fourberies de Scapin* (1671) and *Monsieur de Pourceaugnac* (1669). The levee scene was probably inspired by William Hogarth's set of engravings, "Marriage à la mode," and the tenor aria's text comes from *Le Bourgeois Gentilhomme* of Lully. One often has the feeling that the Baron was inspired not only by characters such as Falstaff, but also by Strauss himself, whom Hofmannsthal considered to be something of a boor. The character of Octavian is a "trouser" role cast for a mezzo, which was Strauss' custom for a main male character, since he disliked tenors intensely. The role has, among its antecedents, Cherubino of Mozart's *Le Nozze di Figaro*.

SCORES: fs (London and New York: BO, 1934); vs German: Otto Singer, English: Alfred Kalisch (London: A. Fürstner, 1911).

LIBRETTO: German (Berlin: A. Fürstner, 1911).

BIBLIOGRAPHY: Reinhard Gerlach, "Die ästhetische Sprache als Problem im *Rosenkavalier*. Der Text der ersten Szene . . . ," *Melos/NZM* I (1975), 95–101; ———, "Der lebendige Inhalt und die tote Form. Marginalien zum *Rosenkavalier*," *NZM* CXXXV (1974), 411–19; Gerhard Heldt, " . . . aus der Tradition gestaltet: *Der Rosenkavalier* und seine Quellen," in *Ars musica . . . Festschrift Heinrich Hüschen*, ed. Detlef Altenburg (Cologne: Gitarre und Laute, 1980), 233–39; Walter Legge, "Recollections on *Der Rosenkavalier*," *ON* XL (March 20, 1976), 10–14; *Metropolitan Opera Classics Library, Der Rosenkavalier* (New York, 1982); Lyle F. Perusse, " 'Der Rosenkavalier' and Watteau," *MT* CXIX (1978), 1042–44; Otto Schneider, "*Der Rosenkavalier* in Salzburg," *ÖMz* XXIV (1969), 451–53; Willi Schuh, ed., *Der Rosenkavalier: Fassungen, Filmszenarium, Briefe* (Frankfurt, 1971); ———, *Der Rosenkavalier. Vier Studien* (Olten, 1968); Morris Springer, "The Marschallin. A Study in Isolation," *OQ* II/1 (Spring 1984), 56–59; Hans Swarowsky, "Noch einmal: Zum *Rosenkavalier*-Libretto," *ÖMz* XXIV (1969), 584–86; Adam Wandruszka, "Das 'Rosenkavalier'-Libretto," *ÖMz* XXIV (1969), 440–45.

DISCOGRAPHY: See Alan Jefferson, B/*OOR*, 567–76.

VIDEO: Schwarzkopf, Jurinac, Rothenberger, Edelmann, and Kunz, Vienna Philharmonic, Salzburg Festival, conducted by Karajan, Video Arts International VAI-OP–2 (2); Te Kanawa, Howells, Haugland, and Bonney, Covent Garden, conducted by Solti, NVC/BBC DERO1 (2).

Rothe Käppchen, Das, oder **Hilft's nicht, so schadt's nicht** (The Little Red Cap, or If It Doesn't Help, It Doesn't Hurt Either), opera in three acts by Karl Ditters von Dittersdorf; libretto (Ger) by the composer after Filippo Livigni's *Giannina e Bernadone*, set by Domenico Cimarosa (1791, Venice). First performance May 26, 1790, Breslau.

The magistrate of a town, Hans Christoph Nitsche, is jealous, without cause, of his pretty wife, Hedwig. When he locks her out of the house, she gets revenge by tricking him into coming out, slamming the door, and leaving him outside, to be ridiculed by the neighbors. Hedwig seeks help from Sander, her brother, and his wife, Marianne. They get Felsenberg to disguise himself as a merchant and sell Nitsche a red cap guaranteed to make its wearer have a faithful wife. Nitsche is then admired for his "magic" headdress.

Major roles: Lieutenant von Felsenberg (ten); Sander, steward of the castle (ten); Marianne, his wife (sop); Hans Christoph Nitsche, magistrate of the town (bass); and Hedwig, his wife and Sander's sister (sop).

Very popular in German cities through the nineteenth century.

SCORE: vs ed. Ignaz Walter (Mainz: Schott [1792]).

LIBRETTO: German (Cologne: Langen, 1791).

BIBLIOGRAPHY: H/CD, 18–24.

Royal Palace, opera in one act by Kurt Weill; libretto (Ger) by Iwan Goll. First performance March 2, 1927, Berlin, with Delia Reinhardt, Carl Jöken, Leo Schützendorf, and Leonhard Kern; conducted by Erich Kleiber. The composer's orchestration is lost. First U.S. performance October 5, 1968, San Francisco, San Francisco Opera, in a reconstruction; conducted by Gunther Schuller.

The opera takes its title from the name (in English) of the Italian resort hotel in which the action takes place. The heroine, Dejanira, has three men in her life: her husband, "Yesterday's Lover," and "Tomorrow's Lover." After her three men tell of their passion for her, Dejanira complains of her boring life. The opera ends as she drowns herself in a lake.

Major roles: Dejanira (sop), the husband (bass), "Yesterday's Lover" (bar), and "Tomorrow's Lover" (ten).

This is Brecht's first work to employ authentic-sounding jazz themes. The finale, in which Dejanira kills herself, is sung to the accompaniment of a tango.

For a detailed plot and musical analysis, see S/DGS, 71–75.

SCORE: vs (Vienna: UE, 1927).

LIBRETTO: German (the same).

BIBLIOGRAPHY: John Rockwell, "Reports," ON XXXIII (November 23, 1968), 23 [on U.S. premiere].

Rübezahl, unfinished opera in two acts by Carl Maria von Weber; libretto (Ger) by Johann Gottlieb Rhode after the folk legend. Composed 1804–1805.

Rübezahl is a Robin-Hood-like mountain spirit who helps the poor and down-trodden but is merciless toward the proud and evil. He appears as a handsome young man and falls in love with a princess, who rejects his offer of immortality and jewels. The rest of the tale, not set by Weber, relates how the princess tricks Rübezahl into counting turnips (ergo his name), during which time she escapes.

Major roles: Rübezahl; the Princess; the King, her father; and Prince Ratibor, her beloved.

Weber completed three rather undistinguished numbers, of which No. 3, a chorus of spirits, was performed in Mannheim on March 31, 1810. He reworked the overture into an overture entitled *Der Berherrscher der Geister*, Op. 27 (1811).

The tale was also set by Josef Schuster (1789, Dresden); Vincenz Franz Tuczek (1801, Breslau); Franz Danzi (1813, Karlsruhe); Wilhelm Würfel (1824, Prague); Friedrich von Flotow (1853, Frankfurt); Alfred Stelzner (1902, Dresden); Hans Sommer, as *Rübezahl und der Sackpfeifer von Neisse* (1904, Brunswick); and Carl Vogler (1917, Zurich). Gustav Mahler completed the text but not the music for a five-act version (ca. 1879–1883); only the libretto has survived. Hugo Wolf also attempted to set the tale but abandoned his efforts.

SCORES: fs ed. Willibald Kaehler, W/*MW*, II/2, 3 nos. (1928); vs (Leipzig: C. F. Peters, 186–).

BIBLIOGRAPHY: Stephen E. Hefling, "The Road Not Taken: Mahler's Rübezahl," *Yale University Library Gazette* LVII (1983); 145–70 [also discusses the versions by Wolf and Weber]; W/*CMW*, 55–56.

S

Salome, opera in one act by Richard Strauss; libretto (Ger) by the composer after Hedwig Lachmann's translation of Oscar Wilde's play (1894). First performance December 9, 1905, Dresden, with Marie Wittich (Salome), Chavanne, Carl Burrian (Herod), and Carl Perron (Jokanaan); conducted by Ernst von Schuch. First U.S. performance January 22, 1907, New York, Metropolitan Opera, with Olive Fremstad (Salome), Marion Weed (Herodias), Carl Burrian (Herod), and Anton Van Rooy (Jokanaan); conducted by Alfred Hertz. First British performance December 8, 1910, London, Covent Garden, with Aïno Ackté (Salome), Ernst Kraus (Herod), and Clarence Whitehill (Jokanaan); conducted by (Sir) Thomas Beecham.

The story is set in Galilee in about 30 A.D. King Herod has imprisoned John the Baptist, here called Jokanaan. Herod's stepdaughter, Salome, the daughter of the evil Herodias, is attracted to the prophet and arranges a meeting with him. He rejects her advances, although she offers to free him, and he is returned to his cell. Salome acquiesces to Herod's fevered request to dance for him in return for granting her anything she wishes. After her famous Dance of the Seven Veils (usually danced by a stand-in for the singer), Salome names her reward: Jokanaan's head on a platter. The horrified Herod reluctantly agrees and has the prophet killed. When Salome grabs the head and, in a frenzy, kisses its lifeless lips, Herod orders his soldiers to crush the crazed girl to death.

Major roles: Salome (dramatic sop), Herod (ten), Herodias (mezzo), and Jokanaan (bar).

For detailed synopses and musical analyses, see C/*NMC*, 540–43; *COH*, ed. Derrick Puffett (1989); D/*RS*, I, 238–86; K/*KOB*, 806–10; and M/*RSC*, 39–62.

The brutal and suggestive text scandalized early opera audiences and led to harsh diatribes from critics (such as Edgar Istel, who was generally sympathetic to newer works); the Lord Chamberlain succeeded in delaying the London premiere for three years. But the work is counted among Strauss' greatest by modern commentators, and its content raises hardly an eyebrow today.

SCORES: fs (London and New York: BO, 1943); vs ed. Otto Singer (Berlin: A. Fürstner, 1905).

LIBRETTO: German (Berlin: A. Fürstner, 1905).

BIBLIOGRAPHY: Clemens Höslinger, "*Salome* und ihr österreichisches Schicksaal, 1905–1918," *ÖMZ* XXXII (1977), 300–309; Gary Schmidgal, "Imp of Perversity. Strauss' vs. Wilde's Vision of Salome," *ON* XLI (February 12, 1977), 10–13; Helmut Schmidt-Garre, "Salome—Inbild des fin de siècle," *NZM* CXXVIII (1967), 300–10.

DISCOGRAPHY: See Alan Jefferson, "Salome," B/*OOR*, 557–62, 565–66.

Samstag (Saturday), opera in four scenes by Karlheinz Stockhausen: libretto (Ger) by the composer; second of the seven-opera cycle *Licht*.* First performance May 25, 1984, Milan, Palazzo dello Sport, with Matthias Hölle (Lucifer) and the University of Michigan Symphony Band.

The work has one vocalist, Lucifer, who appears in the first and third scenes. It offers a Gnostic view of death as "natural destiny."

BIBLIOGRAPHY: Robert Frisius, "Auf der Suche nach verlorenen Polyphonie. Tendenzen in Stockhausens 'Licht'-Zyklus," *NZM* 145 (July–August 1984), 24–27; Glenn Watkins, "Reports: Foreign," *ON* XLIX (November 1984), 54–55 [on premiere].

Sancta Susanna (Saint Susan), opera in one act by Paul Hindemith; libretto (Ger) by August Stramm. First performance March 26, 1922, Frankfurt, Opernhaus; conducted by Ludwig Rottenberg. First U.S. performance March 17, 1983, New York, Manhattan School of Music; conducted by C. William Harwood.

The story concerns repression, sexual frustration and demonic possession at a convent.

Major roles: Susanna (sop); Klementa (alto); and an old nun (alto).

The music is written as a theme and variations.

SCORES: fs (Mainz, BSS, 1921); vs ed. Hermann Uhticke (Mainz: BSS, 1921).

BIBLIOGRAPHY: S. Günther, "Paul Hindemith: Sancta Susanna, Op. 21," *Melos* IV (1924–1925), 250–60.

DISCOGRAPHY: Donath, Schnaut, Schreckenbach, Berlin Radio, conducted by Albrecht, Wergo WER–60106–50 (Harmonia Mundi) (compact disc), reviewed by John W. Freeman, "Recordings," *ON* LIV, no. 2 (August 1989), 30.

Saul, opera in one act by Herman Reutter; libretto (Ger) by Alexander Lernet-Holenia. First performance July 26, 1928, Baden-Baden. New version, first performance September 17, 1960, Stuttgart, Württembergische Staatsoper, with Paula Brivkalne (the Witch), Gustav Neidlinger (Saul), Hubert Buchta, Lothar Brüning, Heinz Cramer, and Hans-Günther Nöcker; conducted by Karl Maria Zwissler.

The story concerns the visit of Saul with the Witch of Endor.
Major roles: the Witch (sop) and Saul (bar).

SCORE: vs (Mainz: BSS, 1948).

BIBLIOGRAPHY: Kurt Honolka, "Zwei Reutter-Einakter," *Musica* XIV (1960), 728–29 [on premiere of new version].

Schatzgräber, Der (The Treasure Digger), opera in a prologue, four acts and an epilogue by Franz Schreker; libretto (Ger) by the composer. First performance January 21, 1920, Frankfurt. Revived May 28, 1989, Hamburg.

The story is set in a fairytale kingdom. The king (bass) is seeking the advice of his fool on how to retrieve his queen's jewelry, which has been stolen; the queen has become an invalid through her loss, the treasure being the source of eternal beauty. The fool advises the ruler to seek the services of the singer Elis (ten), whose fantastic lute will uncover the gems, and asks as his own reward a wife of his choosing.

The scene shifts to a forest, where Els (sop) has had the queen's treasure stolen, piece by piece. She has the young squire Albi (ten) kill the thieves after they give her their loot. Elis, guided by his lute, finds Els but is bewitched by her; the two fall in love; he abandons his mission temporarily but then decides to return the jewels to their rightful owner. Els is sentenced to be burned as a witch. The fool, however, demands to receive his reward for helping to get the jewels back. To everyone's dismay he requests as his wife Els, who is forced to go with him.

The opera is less experimental than *Der ferne Klang**. It represents a return to a more Romantic idiom and employs Wagnerian-like harmonies.

SCORE: vs (Vienna: UE, 1919).

LIBRETTO: German (Vienna: UE, 1919).

BIBLIOGRAPHY: Matthias Brzoska, *Franz Schrekers Oper 'Der Schatzgräber'* (Stuttgart: Steiner, 1988); S/*FS*, 75–78.

Schauspieldirektor, Der (The Impresario), "Komödie mit Musik" in one act by Wolfgang Amadeus Mozart; libretto (Ger) by Gottlieb Stephanie, Jr. First performance February 7, 1786, Vienna, Schönbrunn Palace, with Katharina Cavalieri (Mme. Silberklang), Aloysia Lange (Mme. Herz), and Valentin Adamberger (Vogelsang). First U.S. performance November 9, 1870, New York (in the German version by Louis Schneider) and October 26, 1916 (in an English translation by H. E. Krehbiel, as *The Impresario*). First British performance May 30, 1857, London, St. James Theatre (in French) and September 14, 1877, Crystal Palace (in an English translation by William Grist, as *The Manager*).

The opera traces the difficulties encountered by a theater manager who has to deal with two jealous prima donnas, each of whom sings an aria to demonstrate her skill, and then a trio with M. Vogelsang. In the end, the manager is able to satisfy both ladies.

Major roles: Mme. Silberklang (sop), Mme. Herz (sop), M. Vogelsang (ten), and the Impresario (speaking part).

The opera has often been given in a revised version and is commonly presented in a contemporary setting.

SCORES: fs M/*MW*, v/16; M/*NMA*, V/15; facsimile of autograph, introd. J. R. Turner (New York: Pierpont Morgan Library, 1976).

BIBLIOGRAPHY: M/*OM*, 343–55; Christopher Raeburn, "Die textlichen Quellen des *Schauspieldirektors*," ÖMz XIII (1958), 4–10.

DISCOGRAPHY: See M/*IRR*, 186–87; also Grist and Schreier, Dresden State Orchestra, conducted by Böhm, DG 2709051.

Schloss Dürande, Das (The Castle of Durande), opera in four acts by Othmar Schoeck; libretto (Ger) by Hermann Burte after Joseph Eichendorff (1837). First performance April 1, 1943, Berlin; conducted by Robert Heger. The composer attended the premiere, which led to Schoeck's being accused of being a Nazi sympathizer and to the work's unpopularity in Switzerland.

The story takes place in southern France around the time of the beginning of the French Revolution, in 1789. It concerns Count Armand of Dürande, who seduces Gabriele, the sister of his huntsman, Renald. When Renald leads an attack against the Count, Gabriele and the Count are killed. Renald then burns the castle.

Major roles: Armand, the young Count of Dürande (ten); the old Count, his father (ten); the Prioress of Himmelpfort (alto); Countess Morvaille (sop); Renald Vomholz, the Count's huntsman (bar); Gabriele, his sister (sop); Nicole, a servant of the count (bass-bar); and a gamekeeper (bar).

SCORE: (Vienna: UE, 1942).

LIBRETTO (Vienna: UE, 1943).

BIBLIOGRAPHY: Willi Schuh, "Idee und Tongestalt in Schoecks 'Schloss Dürande,' " *SMz* LXXXIII, no. 3 (1943), 74–83; Chris Walton, "Othmar Schoeck: Politics and Reputation," *MT* CXXVII (1986), 485–86.

Schmied von Gent, Der (The Smith of Ghent), "grosse Zauberoper" in three acts by Franz Schreker; libretto (Ger) by the composer after Charles de Coster's *Smetse Smee*. First performance October 29, 1932, Berlin, Deutsches Opernhaus, with Wilhelm Rode (Smee), Charlotte Müller (his wife), Josef Burgwinkel (Flipke), Harry Steier (Slimbrock), Georg Groke (Luzifer), Elisabeth Friedrich (Astarte), Rudolf Gonszar (St. Joseph), Anita Gura (St. Maria), and Anton Baumann (St. Peter); conducted by Paul Breisach. The premiere was marred by violent Nazi demonstrations because Schreker was half Jewish. The opera was revived in 1981 in East Berlin, at the State Opera, with Jürgen Freier (Smee) and Uta Priew (his wife); conducted by Rolf Reuter.

The sixteenth-century smith of Ghent, Smetse Smee (bar), his business in ruins because of the jealous smith Slimbrock (ten), strikes a bargain with the

Devil to have seven good years. He is saved from going to Hell through the help of St. Joseph, and he is allowed to enter Heaven.

BIBLIOGRAPHY: Paul Moor, "Schreker's Last Opera, 'The Smith of Ghent,' " *MA* XXXI (November 1981), 36–37; Werner Oehlmann, "Schreker und seine Oper," in *S/ FS*, 86–91.

Schneider Wibbel (Wibbel the Tailor) comic opera in four acts by Mark Lothar; libretto (Ger) by Hans Müller-Schlösser. First performance May 12, 1938, Berlin, Staatsoper, with Karl August Neumann (Wibbel) and Hilde Scheppan (Fin).

The opera takes place during the occupation of the Rhineland by Napoleon's troops, in 1813. While drunk, the tailor Wibbel is sentenced to jail for speaking against the authorities. His friend Zimpel changes places with him but unfortunately dies in jail. The real Wibbel becomes a local hero when the French are defeated.

Major roles: Anton Wibbel, master tailor (bass-bar); Fin, his wife (sop); and Zimpel, one of Wibbel's apprentices (buffo ten).

The story was also set as a musical, under the title *Wibbel*, by Christian Bruhn (1984, Aachen).

Schöne Galatea (Galathee), Die (The Beautiful Galatea), operetta in one act by Franz von Suppé; libretto (Ger) by Poly Henrion [Leonhard Kohl von Kohlenegg]. First performance June 30, 1865, Berlin, Meysels-Theater. First U.S. performance September 6, 1867, New York (in German). First British performance (in English, as *Ganymede and Galatea)* January 20, 1872, London, Gaiety.

In this comic treatment of the Pygmalion legend, when Galatea becomes human, she also turns into a shrew, spurred on by the art enthusiast Mydas and Ganymed, Pygmalion's servant. Just as Pygmalion is about to reduce Galatea to dust with his hammer, she pleads with the gods for help and becomes a statue once more. The sculptor sells his creation to Mydas.

Major roles: Pygmalion, a young sculptor (ten); Ganymed, his servant (alto); Mydas, a lover of art (ten); and Galatea, a statue (sop).

The musical highlights include the brillant overture and the trio "Seht den Schmuck, den ich für Euch gebracht."

SCORE: vs (Vienna: F. Schieber, ca. 1876).

DISCOGRAPHY: Moffo and Kollo, Bavarian Radio Orchestra Choir, Munich Radio Orchestra, conducted by Kurt Eichhorn, RCA-UK RL 25108.

Schule der Frauen, Die (The School for Wives), opera in one act by Rolf Liebermann; libretto (Eng) by Elizabeth Montague after Molière's *L'École des femmes*. First performance December 3, 1955, Louisville, Louisville Philharmonic Society. Expanded to three acts with a libretto (Ger) by Heinrich Strobel. First performance of this version October 14, 1957, Salzburg, with Walter Berry

(Poquelin), Kurt Böhme (Arnolphe), Anneliese Rothenberger (Agnes), Alois Pernerstorfer (Oronte), Nicolai Gedda (Horace), and Christa Ludwig (Georgette), conducted by George Szell.

The old cynic Arnolphe tries to win the hand of the young Agnes; competing for her affections is the young love-struck Horace, son of Arnolphe's friend Oronte. Arnolphe's plan fails when Heinrich, played by the commentator Poquelin, intercedes.

Major roles: Arnolphe (bar); Agnes (lyric sop); Horace (lyric ten); Heinrich/Poquelin (bar); and Georgette, Arnolphe's servant (alto).

Also set by Virgilio Mortari (1959, Milan).

SCORES: fs, first version (Vienna: UE, 1955); vs, first version, in English (Vienna: UE, 1955); fs, second version (Vienna: UE, 1957).

BIBLIOGRAPHY: German (Vienna: UE, 1957).

Schwarze Spinne, Die (The Black Spider), opera in two acts by Willy Burkhard; libretto (Ger) by Robert Faesi and Georgette Boner after a tale by Jeremias Gotthelf (1842). First performance May 28, 1949, Zurich.

Set in a Swiss village, the tale concerns the plight of a group of peasants, who are forced to build a beech avenue leading up to the overlord's castle in one month. Faced by this impossible task, the villagers despair but hesitate to accept the Devil's offer in exchange for the next child that is born in the village. A young woman, strange to the town, agrees to the pact, but the Devil is denied his reward when the next newborn is christened before he can touch it. The Devil takes his revenge by changing the young woman into a black spider, which brings illness and ruin. Only after the spider is confined is the town safe.

Major roles: narrator/priest (speaking-singing role), young woman (sop), and the Devil (bass-bar).

Also set by Josef Matthias Hauer (composed 1932; first performance 1966, Vienna); and Heinrich Sutermeister (1936, Radio Beromünster; 1949, St. Galen).

Schweigsame Frau, Die (The Silent Woman), opera in three acts by Richard Strauss; libretto (Ger) by Stefan Zweig after Ben Johnson's comedy *Epicoene, or The Silent Woman* (1609). First performance June 24, 1935, Dresden, Staatsoper, with Maria Sebotari (Aminta), Mathieu Ahlersmayer (the barber), and Friedrich Plaschke (Sir John Morosus); conducted by Karl Böhm. First U.S. performance October 7, 1958, New York, City Center, with Joan Carroll (Aminta), John Alexander (Henry Morosus), Paul Ukena (the barber), and Herbert Beattie (Sir John Morosus); conducted by Peter Hermann Adler. First British performance November 20, 1961, London, Convent Garden, with Barbara Holt (Aminta), David Ward (Sir John Morosus), Kenneth Macdonald (Henry Morosus), and Monica Sinclair (housekeeper); conducted by Rudolf Kempe.

The retired English admiral Sir John Morosus cannot stand noise. When Morosus disinherits his nephew, Henry, for marrying Aminta, Henry arranges with Morosus' barber to have Morosus "wed" Timida, the so-called Silent Woman (really Aminta in disguise). As soon as the mock ceremony is concluded, however, Morosus' new "wife" becomes a shrill companion. Discovering that this is all a sham, Morosus happily gives his blessing to his clever nephew.

For detailed plot synopses and musical analyses, see D/*RS*, II, 3–51; K/*KOB*, 841–44 and M/*RSC*, 271–97.

Major roles: Sir John Morosus (bass); Schneidebart, the barber (bar); the Widow Zimmerlein, his housekeeper (alto); Henry Morosus, his nephew (ten); and Aminta, Henry's wife (sop).

Since the premiere was scheduled to take place in 1935, after Hitler had assumed power, the Nazi censors attempted to remove the name of Zweig, who was Jewish, from the handbills of the Dresden premiere. When Strauss learned of this and threatened to boycott the premiere, Zweig's name was restored. The opera received several successful performances and was then officially banned in Germany.

The Jonson tale was also set by Antonio Salieri, as *Angiolina ossia Il Matrimonio per susurro* (1800, Vienna); and Mark Lothar, as *Lord Spleen* (1930, Dresden).

SCORE: vs ed. Felix Wolfes (Berlin: A. Fürstner, 1935).

BIBLIOGRAPHY: Norman Feasey, " 'The Silent Woman'—An Introduction," *Opera* XII (1961), 692–97; Harald Kaufmann, "Ästhetische Manipulationen bei Richard Strauss, 'Friedenstag' und 'Schweigsame Frau,' " in *Spurlinien. Analytische Aufsätze über Sprache und Musik* (Vienna: Lafite, 1969) 81–93; Roland Tenschert, "Richard Strauss und Stefan Zweig," *ÖMz* XXIII (1968), 75–79.

DISCOGRAPHY: Scovotti, Burmeister, Büchner, Schöne, Adam, and Jaseleu, Dresden State Opera, conducted by Janowski, Angel SZCX–3867 (3); reviewed by John W. Freeman, "Records," *ON* XLIV (October 1979), 67; David Hamilton, "The Silent Lass with a Strenuous Air," *HiFi* XXIX (October 1979), 89–90. Released in compact-disc format, EMI Angel CDS 7–49340 (2).

Schweizerfamilie, Die (The Swiss Family), opera in three acts by Joseph Weigl; libretto (Ger) by Ignaz Franz Castelli. First performance March 14, 1809, Vienna, Kärntnertortheather. First British performance (in English, as *The Swiss Family*) June 27, 1828, London, Surrey Theatre; July 25, 1832, London, Haymarket Theatre (in German). The very popular work was presented throughout Germany.

The story has parallels to Johann David Wyss' *The Swiss Family Robinson* (1813), in which a Swiss clergyman and his family are shipwrecked on a desert island. The opera, written in a simple, folklike style, contains twenty numbers, among them arias, ensembles, and a melodrama.

Major roles: Emmeline (sop), Gertrud (sop), Jacob (ten), Paul (ten), Durmann (ten), the count (bass), and Richard (bass).

SCORES: vs (Bonn: N. Simrock, ca. 1810); vs (Leipzig:; Philipp Reclam Junior, ca. 1889).

Schwergewicht, oder **Die Ehre der Nation** (Heavyweight, or The Honor of the Nation), "burleske Oper" in one act by Ernst Krenek; libretto (Ger) by the composer. First performance May 6, 1928, Wiesbaden.

The story, set in modern times, is a satire on the world of a sports hero. It takes place in the training gym of the boxing champion Adam Ochsenschwanz, whose wife, Evelyne, is training with Gaston to set the world record for endurance dancing.

Major roles: Adam Ochsenschwanz, master boxer (buffo bass); Evelyne, his wife (sop); Gaston, a dancing master (ten); Professor Himmelhuber (bar); and Anna Maria Himmelhuber, his daughter (mezzo).

SCORES: fs (Vienna: UE, 1928); vs ed. composer (Vienna: UE, 1928).

LIBRETTO: German (Vienna: UE, 1928).

BIBLIOGRAPHY: R/*EKO*, 73–82.

Schwestern von Prag, Die (The Sisters from Prague), Singspiel in two acts by Wenzel Müller; libretto (Ger) by Joachim Perinet after Philipp Hafner's comedy *Die reisenden Komödianten* (1762). First performance March 11, 1794, Vienna, Leopoldstädter Theater. First U.S. performance November 30, 1859, New York. The work was extremely popular in the late eighteenth century and well into the nineteenth.

Major roles: Herr von Gerstenfeld (ten); Herr von Sperlingshausen (ten); Chevalier Chemise (ten); Herr von Brummer (bass); Kunegunde, his wife (sop); Wilhelmine, his daughter from his first marriage (sop); Lorche, her maid (sop); and Kaspar, a houseboy (bass).

The finale of the first act is quite extensive.

SCORE: vs ed. Richard Kleinmichel (Leipzig: Barthold Senff, 1891).

LIBRETTO: (Vienna: J. B. Wallishausser, 1841).

Seelewig, "spiritual pastorale" in a prologue and three acts by Sigmund Theophil Staden; libretto (Ger) by Georg Philipp Harsdörffer. First performance 1644, Nuremberg. The complete title is *Die geistliche Waldgedicht* oder *Freudenspiel, genant Seelewig, Gesangsweis auf Italienische Art gesetzet* (The Sacred Forest Poem, or Play of Gladness, Called Seelewig, Set Vocally in the Italian Manner).

This is the first extant German opera, since the music to Heinrich Schütz's *Dafne** has been lost.

In this allegorical story, the shepherd Künsteling meets the satyr Trügewalt, who wants to win the heart of the shepherdess Seelewig. Since the satyr feels he is very ugly and would be rebuffed by Seelewig, he convinces Künsteling, helped by Reichimuth and Ehrelob, to "kidnap" Seelewig, so that he, Trügewalt, can "rescue" her. Seelewig and Sinnigunda, her friend, dismiss the warnings of the older Gwissulda of impending danger.

Künsteling meets Seelewig and Sinnigunda, and he manages to distract them with presents. He finally gets Seelewig alone, but his actions are observed by Gwissulda and Hertzigild, and he is forced to retreat. Sinnigunda runs away, and Seelewig remains under a tree, where she is trapped by a thunderstorm. The shepherds return empty-handed to the disappointed Künsteling but they promise to try again. The next day, they attempt another scheme; they involve the ladies in a game of blindman's buff, but their efforts are again thwarted by the watchful Gwissulda and Hertzigild. The opera closes with a commentary by an allegorical figure from the prologue.

Major roles: Seelewig, Sinnigunda, and Hertzigild (high voices); Gwissulda, a matron, and Künsteling (alto or high voices); Ehrelob and Reichimuth (ten or medium voices); and Trügewalt (bass).

The through-composed score consists mostly of strophic songs and follows the style of the earlier school dramas.

SCORES: fs ed. Irmgaard Böttcher (Tübingen, 1968–1969); vs ed. Robert Eitner, *Monatshefte für Musik-Geschichte*, XIII (1881), reprinted from G. P. Harsdörffer's *Frauenzimmer Gesprächspiele*, IV (1644), 489–622.

LIBRETTO: in Harsdörffer's *Frauenzimmer Gesprächspiele*, IV (1644); ed. Erich Trunz (Tübingen, 1968–1969).

BIBLIOGRAPHY: Peter Keller, *Die Oper Seelewig von Sigmund Theophil Staden und Georg Philipp Harsdörffer* (Bern and Stuttgart: Paul Haupt Verlag, 1977); Keller, "Stadens Oper *Seelewig*," in Ellen Harris, *Handel and the Pastoral Tradition* (London: Oxford University Press, 1980), chapter 3; Hellmuth Christian Wolff, "Zum Dokumente Deutscher Oper von 1627 bis 1697," in Heinz Becker et al., *Quellentexte zur Konzeption der europaischen Oper im 17. Jahrhundert* (Kassel: Bär, 1981), 163–90.

Sieben Todsünden der Kleinbürger, Die (The Seven Deadly Sins of the Petit Bourgeois), "Ballet-chanté" in seven sections by Kurt Weill; text (Ger) by Bertolt Brecht. First performance June 7, 1933, Paris, Théâtre des Champs Elysées, choreographed by George Balanchine, with Lotte Lenya (Anna I) and Tilly Losch (Anna II); conducted by Maurice Abravanel. First British performance (in an English translation by Edward James and the composer, as *Anna-Anna*) London, July 1, 1933, in the same production as the premiere. First U.S. performance December 4, 1958, in English, New York, with Lenya and A. Kent.

The story centers on the two Annas, one who sings and narrates the events in the life of the silent Anna, a dancer, who searches for money to build a home for her family, which is in Louisiana. The dancing Anna visits seven American cities in her quest and meets a sin in each one of them.

Major roles: Anna I (sop); Anna II (dancer); the Family (tens I and II, bar, bass [Mother] [sic]).

For detailed analyses and background, see K/*NO*, 203–16 and S/*DGS*, 197–201.

The work, written in Weill's popular style, contains elements of the monodrama and cantata.

SCORE: vs ed. Wilhelm Brückner-Rüggeberg (Mainz: BSS, 1956).

LIBRETTO: German (Zurich: Suhrkamp, 1959).

BIBLIOGRAPHY: Andrew Porter, "Musical Events," *NY* LVI (July 7, 1980), 67–68 [1980 revival in St. Louis].

DISCOGRAPHY: Lenya, conducted by Brückner-Rüggeberg, Male Quartet and Chorus, CBS Special Product CSP AKL–5175 (mono); Migenes, Tear, Kale, Opie, Kennedy, London Symphony Orchestra, conducted by Tilson-Thomas, CBS Masterworks MK 44529 (compact disc).

Siebzehn Tage und vier Minuten (Seventeen Days and Four Minutes), opera semibuffa in three acts by Werner Egk; libretto (Ger) by the composer after Pedro Calderón's *El mayor encanto amor*. New version of *Circe* (1948). First performance June 2, 1966, Stuttgart, Staatsoper, with Ruth-Margret Pütz (Circe), Gerhard Stolze (Ulyss), Alfred Pfeifle (Klarin), and Fritz Linke (Leporell); conducted by Ferdinand Leitner.

In this modern treatment of the Ulysses-Circe story, whoever stays longer than seventeen days and four minutes on Circe's island remains her prisoner eternally. After she has changed the seamen Moro and Leporell into wild animals, she turns her attention to Ulyss. Ulyss destroys her power, and demands that she restore his men to their human forms. She agrees, on the condition that he join her in a feast at her palace. Ulyss quickly falls under her power, to the despair of his men. Klarin, however, who, in his animal state, had discovered the secret of the time limit, finally brings Ulyss to his senses.

The eclectic score includes elements ranging from blues to recitative and aria.

Major roles: Circe (sop), Lybia (sop), Asträä (mezzo), Baba (alto), Ulyss (ten), Arsidas (ten), an old woman (sop), a dwarf (ten), Anistes (bar), Klarin (ten), Leporell (bass), and Moro (bass).

BIBLIOGRAPHY: Kurt Honolka, "Musica-Bericht," *Musica* XX (1966), 160 [on premiere].

Siegfried. See *Der Ring des Nibelungen*.

Silbersee, Der (Silver Lake), "ein Wintermärchen" in three acts by Kurt Weill; libretto (Ger) by Georg Kaiser. First performance February 18, 1933, Leipzig, Altes Theater, with Berndt, Carstens, Siedel, Golling, and Sattler; conducted by Gustav Brecher; simultaneously, in Erfurt and Magdeburg; conducted by Georg Winkler. Revived March 20, 1980 (in an English adaptation by Hugh Wheeler and Lys Symonette), New York, New York City Opera, with William Neill (Severin), Joel Grey (Olim), Elizabeth Hynes (Fennimore), and Elaine Bonazzi (Frau von Luber); conducted by Julius Rudel. First British performance (in English) June 18, 1982, Manchester; conducted by Ian Kemp.

Set in a mythical country meant to be Germany, the work concerns Severin, the leader of a group of out-of-work young men. When he leads his gang in a robbery attempt, he is shot by a policeman named Olim, who later regrets his actions. After Severin recovers, Olim uses the money he has won in a lottery to buy a castle for himself and Severin. Frau von Luber, the embittered and once noble housekeeper, plots with Baron Laur to cheat Olim and Severin. Desperate, the two rush into the Silver Lake to drown themselves but find that the lake is frozen. They are encouraged by the voice of Fennimore, the housekeeper's idealistic niece, to go on living.

Among the musical highlights are the "Lied der Fennimore," which the niece sings at the beginning of the second act, and her "Ballad of Ceasar's Death," which she sings to her employers; it describes the demise of tyrants. In another, "Schlaraffenland," Frau von Luber and Baron Laur tell of the way in which the two are successful. The controversial nature of the material and the increasing successes of the Nazis caused the work to be closed down shortly after it opened.

SCORE: vs (Vienna: UE, 1933).

BIBLIOGRAPHY: Robert Jacobson, "Reports: North America," *ON* XLIV (June 1980), 30 [on New York revival]; Robert Jones, "Opera Everywhere. New York City Opera: 'Silverlake,' " *HiFi/MA* XXX (July 1980), 30; Nicholas Kenyon, "Musical Events," *NY* LVI (April 14, 1980), 115–18; S/*DGS*, 190–93.

DISCOGRAPHY: Hynes, Bonazzi, Grey, Neill, and Harrald, N.Y. City Opera, conducted by Rudel, Nonesuch DB–79003 (2) (Eng); reviewed by John W. Freeman, "Records," *ON* XLV (December 20, 1980), 52; and by David Hamilton, *"Silverlake: Der Silbersee* It's Not!" *HiFi* XXXI (February 1981), 57–58. Now also available on compact disc: 79003–2 and tape: D2–790003.

Silvana, Romantic opera in three acts by Carl Maria von Weber; libretto (Ger) by Franz Carl Hiemer after the text of *Das Waldmädchen**. First performance September 16, 1810, Frankfurt, with Caroline Brandt (Silvana), Margarethe Lang (Mechtilde), Dlle. Isermann (Clara), Herr Mohrhardt (Rudolph), Herr Hill (Albert), Herr Berthold (Adelhart), Herr Lux (Krips), Herr Leissring (Fust), Herr Urspruch (Hugo), Herr Krönner (Kurt), and Herr Haas (Ulrich); conducted by the composer. First British performance (in an English translation by C. A. Somerset) September 2, 1828, Surrey Theatre.

On a hunt Krips, the squire of Count Rudolph, glimpses the mysterious Silvana, who lives in the forest. Rudolph appears; he is distressed because he does not love his fiancée, Mechtilde, daughter of Count Adelhart, and he sings of his woes in "So soll denn dieses Herz" (No. 4a). When he meets Silvana, he is immediately taken with her, and he has her drugged and brought back to Adelhart's castle, where he is to compete in a tournament. Back at the castle Adelhart tells Mechtilde that she must wed Rudolph, even if she does not love him. The father reveals that his other daughter, Ottile, was kidnapped by Hanns von Cleeburg, and that the current marriage would restore the family's fortune. Mechtilde, meanwhile, is in love with Albert von Cleeburg, son of the evil Hanns. The tournament begins, and one of the victors turns out to be Albert. When Adelhart attempts to have him arrested, Rudolf and Mechtilde, for their own reasons, defend him. Albert and his men return to Silvana's cave in the forest, during a raging storm, reflected in Introduction (No. 16) and the chorus "Wie furchtbar." They meet the aged Ulrich, who reveals that he had been forced to take Adelhart's daughter to the woods and kill her. Instead, he raised her as his own daughter. The group is interrupted by Adelhart's servant Hugo, who seizes them and drags them back to the castle. Adelhart vents his fury in the aria "Welch schrecklich Loos" (No. 17) and wants Silvana killed. As he attempts to stab her, he is interrupted by Albert, who tells him that it is Adelhart's daughter he is on the verge of killing. Silvana's identity as Ottile is confirmed, and she is allowed to wed Rudolf, while Mechtilde is free to marry Albert. The opera ends joyfully with the chorus "Mit dem Liebesgott im Bunde."

Major roles: Silvana (mime and speaker); Count Rudolph (ten); Mechtilde, his fiancée (sop); Count Adelhart (bass); Albert von Cleeburg (ten); Clara, Mechtilde's nurse (sop); Kurt, Albert's squire (bass); Krips, Rudolph's squire (bass); Fust von Grimbach, a supporter of Rudolph (bass); Hugo, Adelhart's servant (bass); and Ulrich, Silvana's foster father (bass).

SCORES: fs ed. Willibald Kaehler, W/MW, II/2 (Augsburg: Dr. Benno Filser Verlag, 1928; repr. New York, 1977); vs (without ensembles) (Berlin, 1812); complete vs (Berlin, 1828); vs ed. Ferdinand Langer (Leipzig: C. Rühle, ca. 1890).

BIBLIOGRAPHY: W/CMW, 78–86.

Sim Tjong, legend in prologue, intermezzo, and two acts by Isang Yun; libretto (Ger) by Harald Kunz. First performance August 1, 1972, Munich, with William Murray (Sim), Lilian Sukis (Sim Tjong) and Wolfgang Brendel (the Emperor); conducted by Wolfgang Sawallisch.

The angel Sim Tjong is born as a daughter to Li, who dies in childbirth, and to Sim, a landholder who is going blind and is infatuated with his own erudition. Brought up in self-abnegation, she offers her life in order to make her egocentric father see; she is saved, however, and becomes the bride of the Emperor.

Major roles: Sim Tjong, a born-again angel (sop); Sim, her earthly father (bar); Li, her earthly mother/Ik-tjin, her heavenly mother (sop); Paengdok, a neighbor (alto); beggar monk (bass); the Emperor (bar); and Park, a young lover (ten).

LIBRETTO: (Berlin: B&B, 1972).

BIBLIOGRAPHY: Wolfram Schwinger, "Isang Yuns Oper 'Sim Tjong,' " *Musica* XVI (1972), 458–59 [on premiere].

Soldaten, Die (The Soldiers), opera in four acts by Bernd Alois Zimmermann; libretto (Ger) by Erich Bormann after the play by Jakob Lenz (1775). First performance February 15, 1965, Cologne, with Edith Gabry (Marie); conducted by Michael Gielen. First U.S. performance February 15, 1982, Boston, with Phyllis Hunter (Marie); Beverly Morgan (Charlotte); Joseph Evans (Stolzius), Kerstin Meyer (Stolzius' mother), Richard Crist (father), William Cochran

(Baron Desportes), and Rosemarie Freni (Countess de la Roche); conducted by Sarah Caldwell. First British performance August 21, 1972, Edinburgh.

The story concerns the degradation of a young woman, Marie Wesener. She is seduced by two officers, Pirzel and Baron Desportes, although she is in love with a young merchant, Stolzius. Desportes takes up with her for a while but then deserts her, and Marie becomes a prostitute to the soldiers. After Stolzius becomes Desportes' orderly, Stolzius poisons his superior and then himself.

For a detailed synposis, see K/*KOB*, 901–7.

Major roles: Marie Wesener (col sop); her sister Charlotte (mezzo); their father, Wesener, a mechant of fancy goods (bass); Stolzius (high bar); Stolzius' mother (high alto); Baron Desportes, a French nobleman and officer (high ten); and Pirzel, a captain (high ten).

This multimedia work, written for fifteen soloists, also includes speaking roles and dancers. It uses three film screens and projectors and loudspeakers.

Also set by Manfred Gurlitt (1965, Düsseldorf).

SCORE: fs ed. Markus Lehmann and Georg Kröll (Mainz: BSS and New York: Schott, 1966).

BIBLIOGRAPHY: Robert Baxter, "Boston," *Opera* XXXIII (1982), 628 [on U.S. premiere]; Thor Eckert, Jr., "Reports: U.S.," *ON* XLVI (May 1982), 42 [on U.S. premiere]; Wilfred Gruhr, "Zur Entstehungsgeschichte von Bernd Alois Zimmermanns Oper 'Die Soldaten,' " *Mf* XXXVIII (1985), 8–15; Wolf-Eberhard von Lewinski, "Current Chronicle. Germany," *MQ* LI (1965), 555–58 [on premiere]; Andrew Porter, "Musical Events," *NY* LVIII (March 1, 1982), 114, 116 [on U.S. premiere].

DISCOGRAPHY: Gabry, Jenckel, and Kelemann, Cologne Opera, Gürzenich Orchestra, conducted by Gielen, Wergo WER–60030 (3); reviewed by John W. Freeman, "Records," *ON* XLVI (January 23, 1982), 37.

Soldatenliebschaft, Die (Soldier Sweethearts), comic opera in one act by Felix Mendelssohn; libretto (Ger) by Johann Ludwig Casper. Composed 1820. First performance April 28, 1962, Wittenberg, Elbe-Elster-Theater; conducted by Walter Herbst.

The action takes place in Spain at the beginning of the nineteenth century, in and around Elvire's castle. Each night a secret admirer leaves flowers for Elvire. Tonio, who is in love with Zerbine, is convinced that the flowers are being left by one of the officers quartered nearby. Meanwhile, Zerbine is interested in Victor, but neither of them can obtain consent to marry from their respective superiors. Trapped in a tree when he is trying to reach Zerbine's room, Victor notices that Elvire is with Felix, a French colonel. Their secret discovered, Elvire and Felix agree to let Victor and Zerbine wed.

Major roles: Elvire, widowed Spanish countess (sop); Zerbine, her companion (sop); Felix, a French colonel (ten); Victor, a sergeant major (ten); Tonio, a servant of Elvire (bass-bar); and Ernst, a soldier (bar).

BIBLIOGRAPHY: Karl-Heinz Köhler, "Das Jugendwerk Felix Mendelssohns," *DJdMw* VII (1962), 18–35; S/"MJ," 509–15.

Soliman der Zweyte, oder **Die drey Sultaninnen** (Soliman the Second, or the Three Sultanas), Singspiel in two acts by Franz Süssmayr; libretto (Ger) by F. X. Huber after Charles Favart's drama. First performance October 1, 1799, Vienna, Kärntnertortheater.

One of the many "Turkish" operas of the period coming after Mozart's *Die Entführung aus dem Serail,** the work is similarly set in the harem of Soliman, the sultan in Constantinople. He is searching for a sultana and has lavished his attentions on the haughty Elmire, who wishes to return to her parents in Spain. The kindhearted ruler is ready to grant the girl's wish, when his attention is diverted first by Delia and then by the wild and rude German girl, Marianne. Marianne conspires to escape, with the help of Osmin via a ladder. She is caught, of course, but she gets her wish to be the new sultana, since Soliman has fallen deeply in love with her.

The composer uses exotic elements throughout the music, beginning in the overture, which has "Turkish" instruments and na Oriental theme that includes the augmented fourth. The first appearance of the sultan is to exotic music, and Osmin's "Wie die Feuertrommel schmettert" of the second act is also accompanied by "Turkish" instruments. In a throwback to *Die Entführung*, aside from the plot similarities, the composer emphasizes Marianne's advice to Soliman, "Man gewinnt nicht Mädchen Herzen" of the first act, similar to Blondchen's "Durch Zärtlichkeit und Schmeicheln," which she sings to Osmin. There can be no mistaking the deliberateness of including the next "Hier soll ich Soliman erwarten! Mich foltern Marter aller Arten . . . '' in Elmire's second-act aria (No. 12). Süssmayr's second attempt at "Turkish" opera was *Gülnare, oder Die persische Sklavin** of 1800 (Vienna), which was set to music by Dalayrac in Paris (1798).

Other operas to the same story are by Johann Hasse (*Solimano*, 1753, Dresden); Pérez (1757, Lisbon); Naumann (ca. 1772); and Krauss (*Soliman den II, eller De tre Sultaninnorna*, 1789, Stockholm).

SCORE: vs (Vienna: K. K. Hoftheater Musick Verlag in der Burg [1800]).

LIBRETTO: German (Vienna: Johann Baptist Wallishausser, 1807).

Sonnenfest der Braminen, Das (The Sun Festival of the Brahmins), "heroisch-komishches Original-Singspiel" in two acts by Wenzel Müller; libretto (Ger) by Karl Friedrich Hensler. First performance September 9, 1790, Vienna, Leopoldstadt Theater.

The action takes place on an island off the Indian coast, where the priests are preparing for the festival of Brahma. They are scattered by an approaching storm, leaving the Indian maidens Bella and Lora, against the wishes of their father, Kaleph, to rescue the Europeans, Eduard and Barzalo, from their foundering boat. Kaleph reveals that he lost his own son because of the British.

Bella learns from the High Priest that she has been chosen, as the daughter of the sun, to be sacrificed to Brahma, an honor which she does not desire. Eduard, taken by Bella, thinks of why he has come to the island, to rescue his beautiful Laura, kidnapped by the Hottentots. Laura, meanwhile, is being held at the governor's palace; when a British ship enters the harbor, she convinces the governor to allow the sailors to land. The group turns out to include Captain Jansen, Laura's father.

As the second act opens, the Brahmin priests and priestesses are preparing for the sacrifice. Jansen, who has learned of the impending sacrifice, tells Kaleph that, since he was responsible for Kaleph's losing his son, he feels responsible for saving Kaleph's daughter. Jansen hatches a plan with Eduard, who is able, with the help of Pirokko and Mikka, to replace Bella with Barzalo, disguised in her clothing. As the sacrifice is about to occur, a voice states that the sacrificial victim will be spared since there has been a miracle—the victim has been changed by Brahma into a man. Jansen then reveals to Kaleph that Eduard is the son who had been abducted twenty years before.

Major roles: Medan Solana, governor of the island (bass); High Priest of the Brahmins (ten); Kaleph, an old Indian (bass); Bella and Lora, his daughters (2 sop); Lord Jansen, a sea captain (bass); Eduard, a young Englishman (ten); Laura Windsor (sop); Barzalo, Eduard's servant (bass); Pirokko, a gardener (ten); and Mikka, his wife (sop).

SCORE: facsimile of fs ms ed. Thomas Baumann (New York and London: Garland Publishing, 1986).

Spiegel von Arkadien, Der (The Mirror of Arcadia), "Zauber-Oper" in two acts by Franz Xaver Süssmayr; libretto (Ger) by Emanuel Schikaneder. First performance November 14, 1794, Vienna, Theater an der Wien.

The pleas of the lonely Ballamo, stranded on a beautiful Greek island, are answered by the gods, who give him a wife and companion, Philanie. They are joined by Giganie and her burly husband, Metallio, who vow eternal friendship. Two genies, guided by Jupiter, offer the two couples a choice of two baskets, one filled with gold, the other with plants that will turn into fellow humans. The four choose the second, and Metallio blocks the attempts of his evil master, Tarkeleon, to cause harm to Philanie, whom he recognizes to be his enemy's daughter. Tarkeleon manages, however, to convince the people who have sprouted from the gourds to take his poisoned wine, and they get ready to tear Metallio and Giganie apart when the couple is unable to provide more food and drink. Jupiter intervenes and drives Tarkeleon into the sea.

As the second act opens, the new people have been taught that they cannot get food until they have worked for it. In the next scene there are two doors, one marked "The Way to Good" and the other, "The Way to Evil." Tarkeleon reappears, and he offers Metallio a magic mirror which can attract any woman he desires by making him appear to be the person the woman loves best; the one condition for possessing the mirror is that Metallio must ultimately bring these deceived women to Tarkeleon. Metallio thus deceives Philanie, who believes he is Ballamo. When Ballamo overhears the conversation, he thinks his wife has deceived him and taken The Way to Evil, the end of which is the kingdom of Tarkeleon. In desperation he turns to Jupiter and Juno, who urge him to follow Philanie, taking care not to trust appearances. Ballamo is confronted by the other men, who have been convinced by Tarkeleon to kill Ballamo, but Jupiter and Juno intercede, and Ballamo is reunited with Philanie. Tarkeleon is put in chains.

Major roles: Jupiter (bass); Juno (sop); Tarkeleon, an evil genius (bass); Ballamo (ten); Philanie, his wife (sop); Metallio, a viper catcher (bass); Giganie, his wife (sop); and Agathos and Kalos, two genies (2 sop).

The work, written in a Lied-like style, contains a revenge aria by Tarkeleon in the first act (No. 6), "Der Tag der Rache ist erschienen." The genes are not unlike those of *Die Zauberflöte.**

SCORES: facsimile of fs ms ed. Thomas Bauman (New York and London: Garland Publishing, 1986); vs ed. Johann Henneberg (Heilbronn: Johann Anon, n.d.).

Spiegelritter, Der (The Looking-Glass Knight), Singspiel in three acts by Franz Schubert; libretto (Ger) by August von Kotzebue. Fragment composed ca. 1811. First performance December 11, 1949, Lucerne, Radio Beromünster. First U.S. performance (concert) January 30, 1988, New York, 92nd Street Y, with John Cheek (the King of Dumristan), Lorna Haywood (the Queen), Jon Garrison (Prince Almador), Hermann Prey (Schmurzo), and David Shapero (Burudusussu); conducted by Bruno Weil.

Prince Almador, seeking knowledge and love, travels to faraway lands, accompanied by three squires and the comical Schmurzo. He is also assisted by a wizard and a magic mirror, which tells him of danger. The Prince is shipwrecked on the Black Islands, where he rescues Queen Milni from a curse.

Major roles: the King of Dumristan (bass); the Queen (sop); Prince Almador, their son (ten); Schmurzo, the Prince's shield-bearer (bass); and Burudusussu, a wizard (bass).

The fourteen-year-old Schubert composed seven numbers for this work, which ends with the hero's departure. Among the resemblances to *Die Zauberflöte** is the Papageno-like Schmurzo.

Also set by Vincenz Maschek (Masek) (1784, Prague); and Ignaz Walter (1791, Frankfurt).

SCORE: fs Schu/*AGA* XV 7 (1893).

DISCOGRAPHY: Mathis, Moser, Prey, and Holl, Austrian Radio, conducted by Guschlbauer, DG 2707–126 (2); reviewed by John W. Freeman, "Records," *ON* XLVI (February 27, 1982), 37.

Spielwerk und die Prinzessin, Das (The Chimes and the Princess), opera in a prologue and two acts by Franz Schreker; libretto (Ger) by the composer. First performance March 15, 1913, in Frankfurt am Main and in Vienna, at the Hofoper; conducted by Bruno Walter. Although the opera was not successful, Schreker considered it his best work. It was revived in a one-act version, as *Das Spielwerk*, on October 30, 1920, in Munich; also on October 4, 1987, in Wuppertal.

The story takes place in a medieval town. Liese, the rejected wife of Master Florian, builder of an unusual set of chimes, tells her former husband that their son, once a lover of the Princess, is near death, and that he should take the boy into his home. The chamberlain of the castle meets a young journeyman in front of the house and tells him of the love-crazed Princess. The naïve boy is determined to save her from her sickness. His simple flute playing causes Master Florian's chimes, which had been thought to be ruined, to ring again, a happening that the chamberlain interpretes as a special sign. Florian, however, attempts to dissuade the boy from his plan, but his counsel has the opposite effect. The Princess appears and announces her plan to have a wild celebration, during which the chimes will be destroyed by her slave, Wolf, once Liese's lover. Wolf has in fact spoiled the chimes, so that they have brought ruin instead of joy. The young journeyman finally meets the Princess, but he takes her to be a young peasant girl. Night falls, and four men bring in the lifeless body of the son of Liese. The chimes ring obscenely, and the celebration begins, but the Princess fears for her life, since Liese has roused the crowd against her. The journeyman comes to the Princess' rescue, and both go off into the sunset. Florian appears at the celebration and reports that his dead son has struck up a tune on his fiddle. The evil spell of the chimes has been broken: the Princess is saved, and Liese can send her dead son to his last rest.

For a detailed musical analysis and plot synopsis, see *S/FS*, 69–71.

Major roles: Florian (bar), the Princess (sop), a journeyman (ten), and Wolf (bass-bar).

SCORE: vs ed. composer (Vienna: UE, 1912).

LIBRETTO: (Vienna: UE, 1916).

BIBLIOGRAPHY: Thomas Luys, ''Reports: Foreign,'' *Opera* XXXIX (February 1988), 39 [on 1987 revival]; Rudolf Stephan, ''Anmerkungen zur Oper *Das Spielwerk*,'' *S/FSS*, 110–11.

Stumme Waldmädchen Das. See *Das Waldmädchen*.

Sturm, Der (The Storm), opera by Frank Martin; libretto (Ger) after August Schlegel's translation of Shakespeare's *The Tempest*. First performance June 17, 1956, Vienna, Staatsoper, with Christa Ludwig (Miranda), Eberhard Waechter (Prospero), and Willy Dirtl (Ariel); conducted by Ernest Ansermet. First U.S. performance 1956, New York, City Opera.

The story concerns the magician and philosopher Prospero, who rules an enchanted island together with his daughter Miranda. He creates a storm which causes a boat and its passengers to be washed ashore. Among the boat's occupants are Antonio, Prospero's brother, who was responsible, along with Alonso, the king of Naples, another passenger, for seizing the magician's dukedom of Milan and setting him adrift with his daughter. Alonso's son, Ferdinand, is missing and feared drowned, but he has in fact been washed ashore and has met Miranda, with whom he has fallen in love. Alonso and Antonio, in their search for Ferdinand, follow the music of the invisible sprite Ariel, a servant of Prospero. When the evildoers come upon Prospero, he scolds them for their misdeeds and orders them to make amends. Alonso returns the dukedom to Prospero and, discovering that his son is alive, approves of the young couple's union. Prospero gives up his magical powers and releases Ariel from his servitude.

Major roles: Prospero (bass-bar), Miranda (sop), Antonio (ten), Alonso (ten), Ferdinand (ten), and Ariel (dancer).

The opera includes most of the Shakespeare text, and the music is in dodecaphonic style.

The text was also set by Peter Winter (1798, Munich); Wenzel Müller (1799, Vienna); and Anton Urspruch (1888, Frankfurt).

SCORE: vs (Vienna: UE. 1955).

BIBLIOGRAPHY: Erwin von Mittgang, *ON* XXI (October 22, 1956), 15–16 [on premiere].

T

Tannhäuser und der Sängerkrieg auf Wartburg (Tannhäuser and the Battle of the Singers on the Wartburg), opera in three acts by Richard Wagner; libretto (Ger) by the composer. First performance October 19, 1845, Dresden, with Joseph Tichatschek (Tannhäuser), Wilhelm Dettmer (Herrmann), Johanna Wagner (Elisabeth), Wilhelmine Schröder-Devrient (Venus), Anton Mitterwurzer (Wolfram von Eschenbach), and Max Schloss (Walther von der Vogelweide); conducted by the composer. First U.S. performance April 4, 1859, New York, Stadt Theater, with Sidenburg, Pickaneser, Lehmann, and Graf; conducted by Bergmann. First British performance May 6, 1876, with Emma Albani (Elisabeth), Anna D'Angeri (Venus), Carpi, Victor Maurel (Wolfram von Eschenbach), and Capponi; conducted by Auguste-Charles-Leonard-François Vianesi. Revised in the version known as the Paris version, March 13, 1861, Paris Opéra, with Marie Sax (Elisabeth), Fortuna Tedesco (Venus), Albert Niemann (Tannhäuser), Morelli (Wolfram von Eschenbach); conducted by Louis Dietsch. This version was in a French translation by Charles Truinet and had an added ballet in the second act (the so-called Venusberg music). First U.S. performance January 30, 1889, New York, Metropolitan Opera, with Katti (Senger-)Bettaque (Elisabeth), Lilli Lehmann (Venus), Paul Kalisch (Tannhäuser), Alois Grienauer, and Emil Fischer; conducted by Anton Seidl. First British performance July 15, 1895, London, Convent Garden, with Emma Eames (Elisabeth), Adini, Albert Alvarez, Victor Maurel (Wolfram von Eschenbach), and Pol Plançon; conducted by Luigi Mancinelli.

The troubadour Tannhäuser has sought the pleasures of love with Venus at the Venusberg. After a year of dalliance with her, he decides to return to his home, where his beloved, Elisabeth, is waiting for him. He joins a singing contest at the Wartburg Castle. The theme of the contest is love, and when Tannhäuser's turn comes, he humiliates Elisabeth by singing the praises of Venus. For this outburst, he is ostracized and forced to seek forgiveness from the Pope. But the pontiff decrees that Tannhäuser will be forgiven only if the papal staff sprouts leaves. In despair Tannhäuser returns to Venus, but he comes back when he hears Elisabeth has died. He meets her funeral procession, begs forgiveness from her spirit, and dies also. Pilgrims bearing the Pope's staff pass by; the sceptre has borne leaves.

Major roles: Tannhäuser (ten); Herrmann, Landgraf von Thüringen (bass); Wolfram von Eschenbach (bass); Walther von der Vogelweide (ten); Elisabeth, niece of the Landgraf (sop); and Venus (sop).

The many musical highlights include the bacchanale of the opening scene in Venus' abode, "Naht euch dem Strande," and, in the second act, Elisabeth's "Dich teure Halle" and her duet with Tannhäuser, "Gepriesen sei die Stunde." The act concludes with the stirring Entrance of the Guests, "Freudig begrüssen wir die edle Halle." Noteworthy in the third act are the Pilgrim's Chorus, "Beglückt darf nun dich;" Elisabeth's prayer, "Allmächt'ge Jungfrau;" Wolfram's famous Song to the Evening Star, "Wie Todesahnung Dämm'rung;" and Tannhäuser's Rome narrative, "Inbrunst im Herzen, wie kein Büsser."

For detailed plot synopses and musical analyses, see C/*NMC*, 564–70: K/ *KOB*, 168–74; and N/*SGO*, I, 3–40.

In the *Tan[n]häuser* of Mangold (1846, Darmstadt), the hero marries in the end.

SCORES: fs, SW, V/1 (1845); vs ed. Joseph Rubinstein (Berlin: C. F. Messer [A. Fürstner] [1846]).

LIBRETTO: German (Dresden: C. F. Meser, 1845).

BIBLIOGRAPHY: Carolyn Abbate, "Erik's Dream and Tannhäuser's Journey," in G/ *RO*, 129–67; Reinhold Brinkmann, "Tannhäusers Lied," in D/*DRW*, 199–211; Edward Downes, "The Paris Version of 'Tannhäuser,' " *Opera* VI (1955), 693–97; Robert Lawrence, "Hymn to Venus: Praising the Paris Version of *Tannhäuser*," *ON* XLII (January 21, 1978), 8–13; Karl Musiot, "Über die Herkunft eines *Tannhäuser*-Motivs," *Mf* XXI (1968), 45–47; Conrad L. Osborne, "The Spirit of the Wartburg: Wagner Fuses Fact and Fiction," *ON* XLII (January 21, 1978), 24–28; Dietrich Steinbeck, ed., *Richard Wagners Tannhäuser-Szenarium. Das Vorbild der Erstaufführungen, mit der Kostümbeschreibung und den Dekorationsskizzen* (Berlin, 1968); Dietrich Steinbeck, "Zur Textkritik der Venus-Szenen im 'Tannhäuser,' " *Mf* XIX (1966), 412–21.

DISCOGRAPHY: M. Mueller, S. Pilinsky, H. Hanssen, and I. Andresen, chorus and orchestra of the Bayreuth Festival, conducted by Karl Elmendorff [Siegfried Wagner's last production, 1930] (Ger) EMI IC 137–03.130/32 (3). See also John Steane, B/*OOR*, 346–53.

Tapfere Soldat, Der (The Gallant Soldier), operetta in three acts by Oscar Straus; libretto (Ger) by Leopold Jacobson and Rudolf Bernauer after George Bernard Shaw's *Arms and the Man* (1894). First performance November 14, 1908, Vienna, Theater an der Wien, with Max Pallenberg (Popoff). Despite its lukewarm reception at the premiere, the work enjoyed a fantastic success shortly thereafter in the English-speaking world. First U.S. performance (as *The Choc-*

olate Soldier) September 13, 1909, New York, Lyric Theater, with Ida Brooks Hunt, J. E. Gardner, and William Pruette (Popoff). The work ran for 296 performances. First British performance (in an English translation by Stanislaus Strange) September 10, 1910, London, Lyric Theatre, with Constance Drever (Nadina) and C. H. Workman (Bumerli).

The story is a satire on the noble attitude toward war. It concerns a soldier who would rather eat chocolate than fight.

Major roles: Nadina (sop); Bumerli (ten); and Colonel Popoff (bar).

The musical highlights include Nadina's first-act "Mein Held" (My Hero).

Shaw himself was reluctant to have his play linked to an operetta and only grudgingly allowed the plot but not the dialogue to be used for the Straus work. Shaw's intransigence and demand for large royalties forced Louis B. Mayer to turn to another plot source, Ferenc Molnár's *The Guardian*, for the 1941 film *The Chocolate Soldier*, with Nelson Eddy in the title role and Risë Stevens as his wife.

SCORES: vs (Vienna: Ludwig Doblinger, 1908); vs (New York: M. Witmark & Sons, 1909).

LIBRETTO: German (Vienna: Ludwig Doblinger, ca. 1908).

Tartarin von Tarascon (Tartarin of Tarascon), children's opera in five scenes by Manfred Niehaus; libretto (Ger) by the composer after Alphonse Daudet's story (1885). First performance December 4, 1977, Hamburg, Staatsoper, Opera Stabile Studio, with Toni Blankenheim (Tartarin), Heinz Kruse (Max the clown), and Ude Krekow (Madame Mitaine); conducted by Michael Halász.

The mild-mannered Tartarin, a provincial character, is challenged to shoot a lion, and he goes to Africa, where he shoots a donkey instead. He is imprisoned and is released on bail with money saved by the children of his hometown. He returns a hero.

Major roles: Tartarin (bass); Madame Mitaine, the circus director (bass); Max, the circus clown (ten/sop); Babette, Tartarin's housekeeper (mezzo).

Also set by Friedrich Radermacher (1965, Cologne).

BIBLIOGRAPHY: James Helme Sutcliffe, "Reports: Foreign," *ON* XLII (February 18, 1978), 47 [on premiere].

Templer und die Jüdin, Der (The Crusader and the Jewess), opera in three acts by Heinrich Marschner; libretto (Ger) by Wilhelm August Wohlbrück after Sir Walter Scott's *Ivanhoe* (1820). First performance December 22, 1829, Leipzig. First U.S. performance January 29, 1872, New York, Stadt Theater, with Fabbri-Mulder, Rosetti, Bernard, W. Formes, C. Formes, Zschichte, Weinlich, Müller, Dickhoff, Habelmann, and Weisheit. First British performance June 17, 1840, London, Prince's Theatre.

A treatment of the famous Scott tale of the Saxon knight Ivanhoe, who is in love with Rowena, his father's ward. When the beautiful Rebecca, a Jewess, is falsely accused of witchcraft because of her nursing skills and is sentenced to die unless a champion can be found to battle the head of the Knights Templar, Brian de Bois-Guilbert, Ivanhoe steps in to defend her and triumphs. Although he is drawn to Rebecca, Ivanhoe follows his duty and selects Rowena.

Major roles: Rebecca (sop), Rowena (sop), Ivanhoe (ten), and Brian de Bois-Guilbert (bar).

Other settings of the tale include Rossini's pasticcio (1826); Pacini (1832); Otto Nicolai's Italian opera *Il Templario* (1841, Turin); Pisani, as *Rebecca* (1865); and Arthur Sullivan's grand opera *Ivanhoe* (1891).

SCORES: vs German-Italian (Leipzig: Fr. Hofmeister, 1876); ed. Richard Kleinmichel (Vienna: UE, ca. 1912).

LIBRETTO: German (Hanover: Schlüter, 18—).

BIBLIOGRAPHY: P/*HM*, 100–16.

Teufel ist los, Der oder **Die verwandelten Weiber** (The Devil to Pay, or The Metamorphosed Wives), opera in two acts by Johann C. Standfuss; libretto (Ger) by Christian Felix Weisse after Charles Coffey's *The Devil to Pay*, a ballad opera with sixteen songs (1731, London), which was repeated, in a German translation by C. W. von Borcke, on January 24, 1743, in Berlin. First performance October 6, 1752, Leipzig, by the Koch ensemble. The sequel was *Der lustige Schuster* (1759), based on the English sequel *The Merry Cobbler* (1735, London). The score is lost. The work was adapted by Johann Adam Hiller in 1766 (see following entry).

The drunk Jobsen Zeckel neglects his wife, Lene, while Liebreich's wife terrorizes all who come in contact with her, including Microscop, a magician. When Microscop is befriended by Lene, he promises to reward her by making her rich. Microscop switches the identities of the two ladies, so that Zeckel is now hounded by his wife and Liebreich enjoys a sweet spouse. Microscop then modifies his spell by softening Liebreich's character and curing Zeckel of his drunkenness.

Major roles: Herr von Liebreich, a country squire (ten); Frau von Liebreich, his wife (sop); Jobsen Zeckel, a cobbler (bass); Lene, his wife (sop); and Microscop, a magician (bass).

The opera's performance gave rise to a pamphlet war, because its opponents, led by the dramatist and philosopher Johann Christoph Gottsched, felt that the new comic Singspiel, which Standfuss' work represented, was devoid of good taste.

BIBLIOGRAPHY: Gregory Calmus, *Die ersten deutschen Singspiele von Standfuss und Hiller* (Leipzig: B&H, 1908).

Teufel ist los, Der, opera in three acts by Johann Adam Hiller; libretto (Ger) by C. F. Weisse. First performance May 28, 1766, Leipzig.

The composer used many of Standfuss' numbers for his own version.

SCORE: vs (Leipzig: Johann Friedrich Junious, 1770).

Teufel von Loudun, Die (The Devils of Loudun), opera in the three acts by Krzysztof Penderecki; libretto (Ger) by the composer after John Whiting's dramatization of Aldous Huxley's novel, translated by Erich Fried. First performance June 20, 1969, Hamburg, with Tatyana Troyanos, Andre Hiolski, Helmut Melchert, and Bernard Ladysz; conducted by Henrik Czyz. First U.S. performance August 14, 1969, Santa Fe, with Joy Davidson and John Reardon, conducted by Stanislaw Skrowaczewski. First British performance November 1, 1973, London, Coliseum, with Josephine Barstow (Sister Jeanne), Geoffrey Chard (Grandier), Harold Blackburn (Father Barré), and Gregory Dempsey (Adam); conducted by Nicholas Braithwaite.

The story centers on Urbain Grandier, who has led a life of vanity and lechery. When he is accused of being the devil by the prioress Jeanne and her Ursuline nuns, he is put on trial. Even after being tortured Grandier refuses to confess to Father Barré and is then burned at the stake.

For a detailed plot synopsis, see K/*KOB*, 1311–17.

Major roles: Jeanne, prioress of the Ursuline order (sop); Father Grandier, pastor of St. Peter (bar); Father Barré, vicor of Chinon (bass); and Adam, a chemist (ten).

BIBLIOGRAPHY: Frank Granville Barker, "Reports: Foreign," *ON* XXXVIII (December 22, 1973), 32–33 [on British premiere]; Hans Heinz Stuckenschmidt, "*Die Teufel von Loudon* in Hamburg. Uraufführung von Pendereckis erster Oper," *Melos* XXXVI (1969), 322–25; Carol B. Zytowski, "Review. Devils of Loudon," *OJ* III/I (1970), 24–25 [on U.S. premiere].

Tiefland (The Lowlands), opera in a prologue and three acts by Eugen d'Albert; libretto (Ger) by Rudolf Lothar after the Catalan play *Terra Baixa* by Angel Guimerá. First performance November 15, 1903, Prague, German Theater, with Alföldy, Foerstel, Aranyi, and Hunold; conducted by Leo Blech. Revised into a prologue and two acts; first performance January 6, 1905, Magdeburg. First U.S. performance (revised version) November 23, 1908, New York, Metropolitan Opera, with Emmy Destinn (Marta), Erik Schmedes (Pedro), and Fritz Feinhals (Sebastiano); conducted by Alfred Hertz. First British performance October 5, 1910, London, Covent Garden, with Muriel Terry (Marta), John Coates (Pedro), Maggie Teyte (Nuri), and Robert Radford (Tommaso); conducted by (Sir) Thomas Beecham. Revived October 1978, Wexford, Wexford Festival.

The story is set in the Pyrenees and Catalonian lowlands at the beginning of the twentieth century. The wealthy landowner Sebastiano is trying to marry his mistress Marta off to the shepherd Pedro, while still keeping her for himself. When the duplicity of the landowner is discovered, Pedro kills Sebastiano. Pedro and Marta then take refuge in the mountains.

For a detailed synopsis, see K/*KOB*, 803–6.

Major roles: Sebastiano, a rich landowner (bar); Marta and Pepa, servants of

Sebastiano (2 sops); Pedro (ten); Tommaso, the village elder (bass); and Nuri, a servant of Sebastiano (sop).

SCORES: vs (Berlin: B&B [1903]); ed. Otto Singer (Berlin: B&B, c. 1907).

DISCOGRAPHY: See M/*IRR*, 2.

Tödlichen Wünsche, Die (The Deadly Wishes), opera in three acts by Giselher Klebe; libretto (Ger) by the composer after Honoré de Balzac's *La Peau de chagrin* (1831). First performance June 14, 1959, Düsseldorf, with Walter Beissner (Raphael), Kurt Gester (the old man), and Ingrid Paller (the girl); conducted by Reinhard Peters.

The hero, Raphael, gets a piece of magic skin that fulfills his every wish; it, along with his life, grows smaller with each granting of a wish. He is unable to stretch the skin, and he dies a young man.

Major roles: the old man (bar), the girl (sop), and Raphael (ten).

The music contains twelve-tone writing and has references to nineteenth-century pieces, especially *Rigoletto*.

SCORE: vs ed. composer (Berlin: B&B, 1959).

LIBRETTO: (Berlin: B&B, c. 1959).

BIBLIOGRAPHY: Heinrich von Lüttwitz, "Musiktheater des 20. Jahrhunderts," *Musica* xiii (1959), 568–69 [on premiere]; Karl H. Wörner, "Current Chronicle. Germany," *MQ* XLVI (1960), 80–83 [on premiere].

Tomyris. See *Die grossmüthige Tomyris*.

Töpfer, Der (The Potter), "eine komische Oper" in one act by Johann André; libretto (Ger) by the composer. First performance January 22, 1773, Hanau, private theater of the Landgraf and Crown Prince of Hesse.

The potter Michel is agreeable to his daughter Hannchen's desire to marry the young peasant Gürge, but his wife, Marthe, opposes the match and hopes, by winning the lottery, to elevate the family's social status. When the drawing is narrowed to two people, Marthe and Amschel, a Jew, Michel suggests that the prize be split, no matter who is the final winner, so that each party is certain to get a good amount of money. All but Marthe agree to the plan. Gürge, meanwhile, proposes to give Amschel his property if he loses, or receive a thousand thaler if Amschel wins. Convinced she will win, Marthe prepares for the congratulations from the visitors she expects when she becomes wealthy. Finally, Amschel and Michel return with the news—Amschel has won.

Major roles: Michel, a potter (bass); Marthe, his wife (sop); Hannchen, their daughter (sop); Gürge, a young peasant and Hannchen's suitor (ten); and Amschel, a Jew (bass).

The composer's first opera, it was particularly admired by Goethe and was well received in Frankfurt after its first performance there on October 29, 1773. In its mixture of German and French styles, the latter represented especially by the two-movement overture, the work presents a sympathetic portrait of Jews in the figure of Amschel, who uses Yiddish dialect, and of lower-class people, as exemplified by Michel and Gürge. Gürge, for example, sings the praises of country life in No. 5, "In unsern stillen Hütten."

SCORES: fs (Offenbach: Johann André, 1773); ed. Thomas Bauman (New York and London: Garland Publishing, 1986).

LIBRETTO: German (Frankfurt and Leipzig: J. G. Esslinger, 1773); (Berlin: C. U. Ringmacher, 1775; repr. New York and London: Garland Publishing, 1986).

Tote Stadt, Die (The Dead City), opera in three acts by Erich Korngold; libretto (Ger) by Paul Schott after Georges Rodenbach's play *Bruges-la-Morte* (1892). First performance December 4, 1920, Hamburg, with Anny Munchow (Marietta), Maria Olczewska (Brigitta), Richard Schubert (Paul), and Josef Degler (Frank); conducted by Egon Polak; simultaneously, in Cologne, with Johanna Klemperer (Marietta), Katharine Rohr, Karl Schröder, and Karl Renner; conducted by Otto Klemperer. First U.S. performance November 19, 1921, New York, Metropolitan Opera, with Maria Jeritza (Marietta), Marion Telva, and Orville Harrold; conducted by Artur Bodanzky.

The work is set at the end of the nineteenth century, in Bruges. Paul is mourning the loss of Marie, his young wife, amid the surroundings of this "dead" city, which constantly remind him of his grief. He has made one room of his house a shrine to his departed spouse; included among the treasures there is a braid of her beautiful golden hair. Frank, an old friend of Paul's, arrives in Bruges to find a disturbing scene. Paul has invited a woman who reminds him greatly of Marie to the house. When Marietta, as she is called, sings and dances for Paul, he is torn between faithfulness to his dead wife and his attraction to Marietta. When the dancer finally leaves, Paul has a vision in which Marie steps from her portrait and tells him to seek happiness with her double.

Paul then imagines that Brigitta, his old housekeeper, has left him to become a novice because of his faithlessness. He then sees Marietta with the dancer Gaston taking part in a rehearsal for *Robert le Diable*, in which Marie had a part in real life. Torn between his love for Marie and his desire for Marietta, Paul steps forward and, after everyone else has departed, yields to Marietta's seduction after a tempestuous scene.

The third act opens back at his house, where Paul finds Marietta in Marie's room. He watches a religious procession outside with rapt attention, and when she mocks him for his piety and drapes the strands of Marie's hair around her neck, Paul loses control and strangles her with the tresses. Suddenly the vision ends. Nothing has been touched in Marie's room, and Brigitta tells Paul that the dancer has returned for her umbrella. He declines Marietta's veiled request to stay with him, and, as she departs, he vows to leave this mournful city and its painful memories.

Major roles: Marietta (sop); Marie (sop); Paul (ten); and Brigitta (alto).

The opera, which was extremely popular after its premiere, was the first one to be sung in German at the Metropolitan after World War I. Banned by the Nazis, it was revived by Robert Heger in 1955 in Munich. It was also successfully mounted in New York on April 2, 1975, by the City Opera. The work includes the beautiful and sensuous "Mariettas Lied," sung by Marietta to Paul in the first act.

SCORES: fs (Mainz: BSS, 1920); vs ed. Ferdinand Rebay (Mainz: BSS, c. 1920).

LIBRETTOS: German (Mainz: BSS, 1920); German-English (New York: Ricordi, 1921).

BIBLIOGRAPHY: Ann M. Lingg, "Master of Melody," *ON* XXXIX (April 5, 1975), 9–11; Franz Mailer, " 'Abendglanz im Jugendstil.' Anmerkungen, Gedanken und Erinnerungen zur Biographie Erich Wolfgang Korngolds," *NZM* CXXXIII (1972), 628–33.

DISCOGRAPHY: Neblett, Fuchs, Clark, Wagemann, Kollo, De Ridder, Brokmeier, Prey, and Luxon, Bavarian Radio Chorus and Munich Radio Orchestra, conducted by Leindsdorf, RCA ARL–3–1199 (3), RCA 7767–2–RG (compact discs, tapes).

Toten Augen, Die (The Blind Eyes), opera in a prelude and one act by Eugen d'Albert; libretto (Ger) by Hanns Heinz Ewers and Marc Henry [Achille Georges d'Ailly-Vaucheret] after Henry's drama *Les Yeux morts* (1897). First performance March 5, 1916, Dresden, Hofoper.

The story is set in Jerusalem at the time of Jesus. It opens in the countryside, where a shepherd is awaiting the return of his sheep. A harvester stops by and tells the shepherd of his unfulfilled love, a feeling which is alien to the shepherd, who is used to living alone. He goes off in search of a missing sheep, and the scene turns to a Roman house on the outskirts of Jerusalem. It is the residence of the beautiful but blind Myrtocle, who is desperate to regain her sight in order to see her beloved husband, Arcesius. He fears just this situation, since she would then see that he is really ugly and limps.

The crowd is awaiting the appearance of Jesus, who is on his way to Jerusalem. Myrtocle is brought to the waiting throng by her slave Arsinoë. Maria Magdalene, who has heard the story of the lost sheep, leads Myrtocle to Jesus; he heals the blind woman, prophesying at the same time that she will come to curse him for having helped her. Myrtocle returns home and awaits the return of her husband. He comes back accompanied by his handsome friend Galba, but when he hears what has happened, Arcesius withdraws. Myrtocle, who had imagined her husband to be attractive, sees only Galba and thinks he is her husband. He encourages this, having been in love with her for some time. Arcesius, having seen all of this transpire, strangles Galba. Myrtocle realizes the truth of what has occurred and, following the prophecy, curses Jesus. In order to reclaim her happiness she lets herself be blinded by looking into the glaring sun. Arcesius returns and finds her sitting outside, helpless. He leads her back to the house, and the shepherd passes by, holding the lost sheep.

Major roles: the shepherd (ten); the harvester (bar); Arcesius, representative

of the Roman Senate in Jerusalem (bar); Myrtocle, his wife (sop); Aurelius
Galba, a Roman captain and friend of Arcesius (ten); Arsinoë, Myrtocle's slave;
and Maria Magdalene (alto).

The opera, written in an eclectic style, includes an idyllic prelude.

SCORE: vs (Berlin: B&B, c. 1913).

LIBRETTO: the same.

Traum des Liu-Tung, Der (The Dream of Liu-Tung), opera in a prologue, four
scenes, and epilogue by Isang Yun; libretto (Ger) by Winfried Bauernfeind after
a fourteenth-century Chinese legend by Ma-Chi-Yunn, translated by Rudelsber-
ger. First performance September 25, 1965, West Berlin, Akademie der Künste.
Part of *Träume*.* Revised version December 9, 1967, Bonn.

The frivolous student Liu-Tung has horrifying dreams, after which he is converted to Taoism.

Major roles: Liu-Tung, a young student (bar); Ching-Yaug, a hermit (bar);
Pien-Fu, a merchant (ten); Yü-Chan, his wife (sop); Mrs. Wang, an innkeeper
(mezzo); and Tung-Hua, an immortal (bass).

BIBLIOGRAPHY: Horst Koegler, "Reports. Foreign," *ON* XXXII (January 13, 1968):
31 [on revised version].

Traum ein Leben, Der (A Dream Is Life), "dramatisches Märchen" in a
prologue, three acts, and an epilogue by Walter Braunfels; libretto (Ger) by the
composer after Franz Grillparzer. Composed in 1937. A scheduled performance
under Bruno Walter in Vienna was cancelled. First performance March 22, 1950,
Frankfurt, Hessische Rundfunk.

Set in the Orient, it concerns the restless Rustan, who is unwilling to marry
Mirza, his betrothed. He leaves in a quest for love and adventure and becomes
a favorite of the King of Samarkand, helped by Zanga, a slave. He then marries
the king's daughter, Gülnare, after he brings about the monarch's death through
treachery. Realizing his sins, he jumps into a river to drown himself. This episode
causes him to awaken; all this has been a dream, and it causes Rustan to have
a new-found maturity.

Also set by Paul Kont as *Traumleben* (1963, Salzburg) and Franz Mixa (1963,
Graz).

BIBLIOGRAPHY: J/*WB*, 397–405.

Träume (Dreams), a combination of the two one-act operas *Der Traum des Liu-
Tung** and *Die Witwe des Schmetterlings** by Isang Yun; librettos (Ger) by
Harald Kunz. First performance February 23, 1969, Nuremberg; conducted by
Hans Giester.

LIBRETTO: (Wiesbaden: B&B, 1969).

BIBLIOGRAPHY: Gerhard Koch, "Scheidung auf chinesisch. Anmerkung zur Uraufführung von Isang Yuns Oper *Träume*,'' *Opernwelt* X/4 (1969), 28; Eckhart Schwinger, "Isang Yuns Oper 'Träume,' '' *Musica* XXIII (1969), 254–55 [on premiere].

Traumspiel, Ein (A Phantasmagoria), opera in thirteen scenes by Aribert Reimann; libretto (Ger) by Peter Weiss after August Strindberg's drama *A Dream Play* (1902). First performance June 26, 1965, Kiel; conducted by Joachim Klaiber.

This serial work, based on Strindberg's surrealistic play, includes a stark declaimed vocal quintet. Reimann's first opera, it was received coolly at its premiere.

Also set by Julius Weismann (1925, Duisburg).

BIBLIOGRAPHY: Hellmuth Steger, "Aribert Reimanns erste Oper," *Musica* XIX (1965), 269 [on premiere].

Tristan und Isolde, opera in three acts by Richard Wagner; libretto (Ger) by the composer after Gottfried von Strassburg's *Tristan* (ca. 1210), in turn based on Thomas of Britain's *Tristram* (ca. 1150), itself based on an earlier version of the legend. First performance June 10, 1865, Munich, with Ludwig Schnorr von Carolsfeld (Tristan), Malwina Schnorr von Carolsfeld (Isolde), Ludwig Zottmayr (King Marke), Anton Mitterwurzer (Kurwenal), and Anna Deinet (Brangäne); conducted by Hans von Bülow. First U.S. performance December 1, 1886, New York, Metropolitan Opera, with Lilli Lehmann (Isolde), Marianne Brandt (Brangäne), Albert Niemann (Tristan), and Emil Fischer (King Marke); conducted by Anton Seidl. First British performance June 20, 1882, London, Drury Lane Theatre, with Rosa Sucher (Isolde), Marianne Brandt (Brangäne), Hermann Winkelmann (Tristan), and Eugen Gura (King Marke); conducted by Hans Richter.

Set in legendary Brittany and Cornwall, the story revolves around the themes of love, night, and death; each is important in each of the three acts. The orchestral prelude opens with the so-called Tristan chord, which appears later in the work and is often described as a half-diminished seventh chord. The story itself begins with Tristan assigned to take Isolde to wed his uncle, King Marke. Isolde blames Tristan for the death of the man she was to wed, and she asks her nurse, Brangäne, to give her poison. Instead, Brangäne gives her mistress a love potion, and Isolde and Tristan fall passionately in love. Disregarding the danger, the lovers meet while the king is hunting with Melot. Their passion culminates in the ecstatic duet of Act II, scene 2, "O sinkt' hernieder, Nacht," and they disregard Brangäne's warning, "Habet Acht, schon weicht dem Tag die Nacht," that the king and his party are returning. King Marke is devastated by the scene of the lovers. Melot mortally wounds Tristan with his sword, and Isolde leaves with Marke. The dying man is brought back to Britanny by Kurwenal, his retainer, and he can think only of Isolde. Isolde returns to Tristan and, when he expires, she follows him in death after singing the passionate *Liebestod*, "Mild und leise wie er lächelt," perhaps the most famous "number" in all of Wagner. It includes the chromatic motif which begins the prelude of the opera; the theme also appears when the lovers drink the love potion in Act I and, in the second act, when Marke asks Isolde if she will return with him.

For detailed synopses and musical analyses, see C/*NMC*, 595–600; *ENO*/VI (1981); K/*KOB*, 184–97; and N/*SGO*, I, 96–123.

Major roles: Tristan (ten), King Marke (bass), Isolde (sop), Kurwenal (bar), and Brangäne (sop).

Frank Martin's *Le vin herbé* (1942, Zurich) is also based on the Romance of Tristan [see Martin Bernheimer, "Current Chronicle. Munich," *MQ* XLVIII (1962), 525–28].

SCORES: fs (Leipzig: B&H, 1860; repr. New York: Da Capo, 1971, ed. Michael Balling); vs (Leipzig: B&H, 1860); vs ed. Richard Kleinmichel, English, H. & A. Corder (Leipzig: B&H, 1914).

LIBRETTO: German (Leipzig: B&H, 1859).

BIBLIOGRAPHY: Peter Barford, "The Way of Unity: A Study of *Tristan und Isolde*," *MR* XX (1959), 253–63; Robert Beeson, "The *Tristan* Chord and Others: Harmonic Analysis and Harmonic Explanation," *Soundings* V (1975), 55–72; Jacques Chailley, '*Tristan et Isolde' de Richard Wagner* (Paris, 1972); Irmtraud Fleschig, "Beziehungen zwischen textlicher und muskialischer Struktur in Richard Wagners *Tristan und Isolde*," in D/*DRW*, 239–57; Peter Franklin, "Flight from the Green Hill: *Tristan* and the Destiny of the Artist," *MR* XXXVI (1975), 135–39; Arthur Groos, "Appropriation in Wagner's *Tristan* Libretto," in G/*RO*, 12–33; Roland Jackson, "Leitmotif and Form in the *Tristan* Prelude," *MR* XXXVI (1975), 42–53; Joseph Kerman, "Tristan, Madness and Method," *ON* XIX (March 14, 1955), 4–7; Ernst Kurth, *Romantische Harmonik und ihre Krise in Wagners 'Tristan'* (Berlin, 1923; repr. Hildesheim, 1968); Alfred Lorenz, "Die formale Gestaltung des Vorspiels zur *Tristan und Isolde*," *ZMW* V (1922–1923), 455–74, repr. in *Zur musikalischer Analyse*, ed. Gerhard Schumacher (Darmstadt, 1974), 546–57; William Mitchell, "The Tristan Prelude: Techniques and Structure," *The Music Forum* I (1967), 162–203; Harold Truscott, "Wagner's *Tristan* and the Twentieth Century," *MR* XXIV (1963), 75–85; Egon Voss, "Wagners Striche im *Tristan*," *NZM* CXXXII (1971), 644–47.

DISCOGRAPHY: See Robin Holloway, B/*OOR*, 363–75.

Troilus und Cressida, opera in three acts by Winfried Zillig; libretto (Ger) by the composer after Shakespeare's play. First performance February 3, 1951, Düsseldorf. New version 1958.

Set in the Trojan War, the story takes place during a break in the hostilities. The Trojan prince Troilus falls in love with Cressida, and they consummate their love with the help of Pandarus. Cressida's father, Calchas, has his daughter brought to the Greek camp, where she takes up with Diomedes. Troilus, who has joined in a feast in honor of Achilles, discovers his lover's unfaithfulness and returns in sadness to Troy.

Major roles: Troilus (bar); Achilles (ten); Cressida, a Trojan maiden (sop); Kassandra, a seer (sop); and Helena (sop).

The story was also set by William Walton (1954, London), who based the text on the Chaucer poem.

SCORE: vs (new version) (Wiesbaden: Bärenreiter, 1958).

Turandot, opera in two acts by Ferruccio Busoni; libretto (Ger) by the composer after the German translation by K. Vollmöller of Carlo Gozzi's play, which is based on "L'Histoire du Prince Calaf, & de la Princesse de la Chine" in Pétis de la Croix's *Les Milles et un jour, contes persanes* (1710–1712). First performance (together with Busoni's *Arlecchino**) May 11, 1917, Zurich, with Laurenz Saeger-Pieroth (Altoum), Inez Encke (Turandot), Marie Smeikal (Adelma), August Richter (Kalaf), Tristan Rawson (Barak), and Elisabeth Rabbow (Queen Mother); conducted by the composer. First U.S. performance (concert) October 10, 1967, New York, Little Orchestra Society, with Hannelore Kuhse (Turandot); conducted by Thomas Scherman; November 15, 1986 (stage), Hartford, conducted by Gilgoc. First British performance March 8, 1978, London, Cockpit Theatre.

The story is similar to the more famous version by Giacomo Puccini (1926, Milan), with commedia del l'arte characters and the hero Kalaf faced with having to answer three riddles or be executed. The hero perseveres and wins the hand of the Chinese princess. Characters not found in the Puccini version include Barak, an old servant of Kalaf; the Queen Mother of Samarkand, who sings a major rage aria in the opening scene; and Turandot's slave Adelma, who helps Kalaf solve the riddles. Absent from the Busoni version is the character of Liu.

Major roles: Altoum, the Emperor (bass); Turandot, his daughter (sop); Adelma, her servant (mezzo); Kalaf (ten); Barak, his servant (bar); the Queen Mother of Samarkand (sop); and Pantalone and Tartaglia, ministers (basses).

Other versions include those by Carl Maria von Weber (incidental music, 1809); Blumenroeder (1810, Munich); Reissiger (1835, Dresden); J. Zerboni (1838, Vienna); Vesque von Püttlingen (1838); Lövenskjold (1854, Copenhagen); Jensen (*Die Erben von Montfort*, 1865); Bazzini (*Turanda*, 1867, Milan); Rehbaum (1888); Neumeister (1908); and Gottfried von Einem (ballet, 1954, Monaco).

SCORES: fs (Leipzig: B&H, 1919); vs ed. Philipp Jarnach (Leipzig: B&H, c. 1981); new version (Wiesbaden: B&H, 1965).

LIBRETTO: (Leipzig: B&H, c. 1918).

BIBLIOGRAPHY: Sergio Martinotti, "Gozzi e i musicisti romantici tedeschi—'Turandot' di Weber e 'Le fate' di Wagner," *Chigiana* XXXI, n.s. II (1976), 69–123; Raoul Meloncelli, " 'Turandot' di Busoni, con alcune note sull 'possiblià dell'opera,' " *Chigiana* XXXI, n.s. II (1976), 167–86; Andrew Porter, "Musical Events," *NY* LVII (December 22, 1986), 89–90 [on Stamford, Conn. performance]; Fernando Previtali, "La

Turandot di Busoni,'' *Chigiana* XXXI, n.s. II (1976), 249–58; Michael Walsh, ''Berke-ley, Promenade Orchestra: Busoni's 'Turandot,' '' *HiFi/Ma* XXX (May 1980), 35, 40.

DISCOGRAPHY: Malbin, Dickie, Evans, Wallace, Ollendorff, and Gester, Glynde-bourne Festival Orchestra, conducted by Pritchard, Vic LM 1944.

=U

Undine, opera in three acts by E. T. A. Hoffmann; libretto (Ger) by the composer after de la Motte Fouqué's tale. First performance August 3, 1816, Berlin, Royal Opera House, with Herr Blume (Huldbrand), Herr Gern (fisherman), Madame Eunike (his wife), Mlle. Johanna Eunike (Undine), Herr Wauer (Kühleborn,) Herr Eunike (the duke), Mlle. Emil. Willmann (the duchess), and Mlle. Wilhelmine Leist (Berthalda); conducted by Bernhard Romberg.

An earlier setting of the legend is Ferdinand Kauer's *Das Donauweibchen** (1798, Vienna). In the Hoffmann version, the emphasis is on the relationship of Huldbrand and Undine, and her quest for revenge when she is betrayed. Her main human competition is the daughter of the duke, here called Berthalda.

Major roles: Knight Huldbrand von Ringstetten (bar); an old fisherman (bass); his wife (mezzo); Undine, their foster daughter (sop); Kühleborn, a water sprite (bass); the duke (ten); the duchess (sop); and Berthalda, their foster daughter (sop).

The work, discussed extensively by Jürgen Schläder (see below), represents an important step in the development of Romantic opera in Germany, and it is particularly effective musically in the scenes that portray supernatural beings. It also includes numerous folklike melodies and choruses.

The story was also set by K. F. Girschner (Berlin, 1830); Albert Lortzing (see the following entry); Lvov (1848); Semet (1863); Rogowski (1920); and Wolfgang Fortner (1969, Ober Hambach).

SCORES: ed. J Kindermann, AW, I–III (Mainz, 1971–1972); vs ed. Hans Pfitzner (Leipzig: C. F. Peters, 1906).

BIBLIOGRAPHY: Aubrey S. Garlington, Jr., "Notes on Dramatic Motives in Opera: Hoffmann's *Undine,*" *ML* XXXII (1971), 136–45; Jürgen Schläder, *'Undine' von E. T. A. Hoffmann. Undine auf dem Musiktheater* (Bonn-Bad Godesberg: Verlag für systemische Musikwissenchaft, 1979).

Undine, opera in four acts by Albert Lortzing; libretto (Ger) by the composer after de la Motte Fouqué. First performance April 21, 1845, Magdeburg. First U.S. performance October 9, 1856, New York, Niblo's Garden.

In the Lortzing version, the French knight Hugo falls in love with Undine, who he thinks is a girl from the village, and he brings her back to court. Veit, Hugo's squire, has informed Undine's father, Kühleborn, a great water sprite, that Hugo will desert Undine for Berthalda. Undine tells Hugo who she really is, and that she can regain her soul only by finding a human husband who will not betray her. When Berthalda humiliates Undine, Kühleborn reveals that the haughty Berthalda is really the child of the fisherman Tobias and his wife, Martha, who had raised Undine. The disgraced Berthalda is taken in by Hugo and Undine; nonetheless, she procedes to seduce Hugo. The sorrowful Undine returns to her realm. Unable to forget her, Hugo follows her and, with Veit's help, joins her in her watery kingdom.

Major roles: Berthalda, daughter of Duke Heinrich (sop); Hugo von Ringstetten (ten); Kühleborn, a powerful water prince (bar); Tobias, a fisherman (bass); Martha, his wife (alto); Undine, their foster daughter (sop); and Veit, Hugo's squire (ten).

Notable musical aspects include the employment of recurring themes and descriptive music. An example of the latter is the music of the water sprites in Act II, scene 5. Other important numbers include Undine's aria ''Ich scheide nun'' of the first act and her duet with Hugo in the fourth, ''Ich war in meinen jungen Jahren.''

SCORES: fs ed. Kurt Soldan (Leipzig: C. F. Peters, 1925); vs ed. Gustav F. Kogel (Leipzig: B&H, ca. 1875).

DISCOGRAPHY: excerpts: Otto, Schirmacher, Schock, Gruber, Kusche, and Frick, Chorus of the Deutsche Oper, Berlin, and Berlin Symphony Orchestra, conducted by Schüchter, Eurodisc 70728.

=V

Vampyr, Der (The Vampire), opera in two acts by Heinrich Marschner; libretto (Ger) by W. A. Wohlbrück after John William Polidori's *The Vampire* (1819). First performance March 29, 1828, Leipzig, with Eduard Genast (Ruthven), Dorothea Devrient (Emmy), Wilhelmina Streit (Malwina), and August Höfler (Aubry). First U.S. performance October 1980, New York. First British performance August 25, 1829, London, Lyceum.

The Dracula-like vampire Lord Ruthven is permitted to remain on earth another year if he is able, in the space of twenty-four hours, to convert three young ladies to be his brides and to serve the cause of vampirism. His first target is Janthe, who is an easy conquest, but her father, while trying to defend his daughter, wounds Ruthven gravely. Ruthven is aided by Aubry, a young man whose life he had once saved. Aubry promises to keep his silence for a day. Returning to the manor house, Aubry learns that Malwina, Sir Humphrey's daughter, has been betrothed to one Count Marsden, whom Aubry knows to be the vampire, but whose identity he cannot reveal because of his oath.

Ruthven's next intended victim is Emmy who, when she sees him, sings the Romance "Sieh, Mutter, dort den bleichen Mann," a piece not unlike Senta's ballad in Act II of *Der fliegende Holländer*.* Emmy is conquered during the pre-wedding celebrations, which feature the festive quartet "Im Herbst, da muss man trinken." As the twenty-four hours are nearing their end, Aubry tries to delay Malwina's marriage to Ruthven. The clock finally strikes one, and Aubry, released from his promise, reveals Ruthven's identity as a vampire. Ruthven sinks into the underworld, and the grateful Sir Humphrey gives his daughter's hand in marriage to the faithful Aubry.

Major roles: Sir Humphrey, laird of Davenaut (bass); Malwina, his daughter (sop); Edgar Aubry, a relative (ten); Lord Ruthven (bar); Sir John Berkley (bass); Janthe, his daughter (sop); John Perth (spoken role); Emmy, his daughter and fiancée of Dibdin (sop); and George Dibdin, Davenaut's servant (ten).

Also set by Peter Lindpaintner and appearing six months later (see following entry).

SCORE: vs ed. composer (Leipzig: F. Hofmeister, 1828).

LIBRETTO: German (Leipzig: Hartmann, 1828).

BIBLIOGRAPHY: Jack Hiemenz, "New York. Encompass Theatre: Marschner: 'Der Vampyr,' " *HiFi/MA* XXXI (February 1981), 19–20; Pamela C. White, "Two Vampires of 1828," *OQ* V/1 (Spring 1987), 22–57 [compares the Lindpaintner and Marschner settings].

DISCOGRAPHY: Pisarenko, Farley, Tomaszewska-Schepis, Nimsgern, Protschka, Di Credico, Lenz, and Egel, Italian Radio-Television, conducted by Neuhold, Fonit Cetra LMA–30005 (Ital) (3); reviewed by John W. Freeman, "Records," *ON* XLVIII (March 31, 1984), 44. Augér, Tomowa-Sintow, Grobe, Van Kesteren, and Hermann, Bavarian Radio Orchestra and Chorus, conducted by Rieger, Pantheon C–85074 (3) (tape).

Vampyr, Der (The Vampire), opera in three acts by Peter Lindpaintner; libretto (Ger) by Cäsar Max Heigel after his play *Ein Uhr!* (1822) and John William Polidori's *The Vampire* (1819). First performance September 21, 1828, Stuttgart, Hoftheater, just six months after Heinrich Marschner's *Vampyr*,* with Christian Wilhelm Häser (Ignerand), Carl Hambuch (Hippolyt), Katharina Walbach-Canzi (Isolde), and Gustav Pezold (Aubry).

As Isolde's betrothal to Hippolyt is being celebrated, word comes of Isolde's disappearance during a hunt, and Etienne voices the fear that she may have been kidnapped by the vampire rumored to be in the forest. Isolde eventually appears but seems changed. Hippolyt wishes to get on with the marriage; Ignerand tells him that Isolde was betrothed to the son of Count Aubry as a child, but the young man died in Greece. Their conversation is interrupted by the appearance of a young man, Aubry, in reality the vampire, who almost comes to blows with Hippolyt when he learns of the impending marriage.

The scene shifts to Aubry's estate. Aubry has forced Isolde to agree to marry him. While he is waiting for her, Aubry contemplates how to make Lorette his next victim. Lavigne, Lorette's fiancé, meets the distraut Hippolyt in the nearby woods and tells him that he fears that Lorette has already been seduced by Aubry. Knowing that Aubry must claim Isolde before midnight in order to survive, Hippolyt and her father block his way. When the clock strikes twelve, Aubry is dragged down to hell. Isolde, released from Aubry's spell, sinks into Hippolyt's arms.

Major roles: Ignerand, Count of Port d'Amour (bass); Isolde, his daughter (sop); Count Aubry, the vampire (bar); Hippolyt, Count of Damartin, Isolde's fiancé (ten); Etienne, the gardener of Port d'Amour castle (bass); Balbine, Isolde's maid (mezzo); Morton, one of Aubry's tenants (bass); Lorette, Morton's daughter (sop); and Lavigne, her fiancé (ten).

Originally composed with spoken dialogue, the work was revived as *Isolde, Gräfin von Port d'Amour*, on April 20, 1840, in Linz. Its second version contained recitatives and additional text by Franz Ludwig Feodor von Löwe. The premiere of this version took place on April 26, 1850, Stuttgart, Hoftheater.

SCORE: vs (German-Italian) (Leipzig: Peters, 1840).

LIBRETTO: German (Munich: Hübschmann, 1828).

BIBLIOGRAPHY: Pamela C. White: "Two Vampires of 1828," *OQ* V/1 (Spring 1987), 22–57 [compares the Lindpaintner and Marschner settings]; R. Hänsler, *Peter Lindpaintner als Opernkomponist* (diss., University of Munich, 1928).

Venus, opera in three acts by Othmar Schoeck; libretto (Ger) by Armin Rüeger after a story by Prosper Mérimée. First performance May 10, 1922, Zurich, with Curt Taucher (Horace); conducted by the composer.

On the eve of their wedding, a couple, Simone and Horace, vow eternal love. Baron de Zarandelle, Horace's uncle, discovers a statue of the goddess of love, Venus, in his garden. During a masked ball in honor of the upcoming wedding, Horace is attracted to a masked figure who is, in fact, Venus; she kisses him, to Simone's despair, and suddenly disappears. Horace, who has forgotten his bride-to-be, disregards the warnings of her cousin, Raimond, and says, "Die Erde, die dich hält, ist längst für mich versunken. . . . '' He goes in search of Venus after the ball has ended. When he sees the statue, he is inexorably drawn to it. As it embraces him, he is crushed to death.

Major roles: Baron de Zarandelle (ten); Horace, his nephew (ten); Simone, his bride (sop); Raimond, Simone's cousin (bar); and Venus (silent role).

SCORE: vs ed. K. Krebs (Leipzig: B&H, 1925).

Verhör des Lukullus, Das (The Trial of Lucullus), opera in twelve scenes by Paul Dessau; libretto (Ger) by Bertolt Brecht. First performance March 17, 1951, East Berlin, State Opera, with Alfred Hülgert (Lukullus); conducted by Hermann Scherchen. Revised as *Die Verurteilung des Lukullus*, October 12, 1957, East Berlin.

The work opens at the funeral of the Roman general Lukullus, who is tried by a ghostly tribunal. The only person to say anything good about this supposed great man turns out to be his cook.

Major roles: Lukullus, Roman general (ten); the king (bass); the queen (sop); and Lasus, the cook of Lukullus (ten).

The score includes an impressive march at the opening to honor the deceased general. The remainder consists mainly of narrative passages.

SCORES: fs (Berlin: Henschel-Verlag, 1961); vs (the same).

LIBRETTO: German (Berlin: Aufbau, 1951).

DISCOGRAPHY: See M/*IRR*, 331.

Verlobung in San Domingo, Die (The Betrothal in San Domingo), opera in two acts by Werner Egk; libretto (Ger) by the composer after Heinrich von Kleist's novel of the same name (1810). First performance November 27, 1963,

Munich, Nationaltheater, with Evelyn Lear (Jeanne), Margarethe Bence, Hans Günther Nöcker, Fritz Wunderlich (Christoph von Ried), Mino Yahia, Richard Holm, and Karl Christian Kohn; conducted by the composer. First U.S. performance July 12, 1974, St. Paul.

The story takes place during the slave uprising of 1803 on the island of San Domingo, a French colony. Christoph von Ried, an officer, seeks refuge from the fighting and comes to the house of Hoango, an embittered black who hates whites. While Hoango is away, the officer is seemingly befriended by the young Jeanne and her mother, Babekan, who are really awaiting the return of Hoango. When Jeanne falls in love with Christoph, she vows to help her beloved. Unaware that Jeanne is responsible for his escape, Christoph returns and shoots her, learning too late from his uncle that his release was due only to Jeanne's efforts.

Major roles: Jeanne, a young girl (sop); Babekan, her mother, a mulatto (alto); Hoango, a black (bass); Christoph von Ried, a French officer (ten); Gottfried von Ried, his uncle (bass); Mr. Schwarz (ten); and Mr. Weiss (bass).

Also set by Winfried Zillig (1957, NDR; 1961, Bielefeld).

Verschworenen, Die oder **Der häusliche Krieg** (The Conspirators, or The Domestic War), opera in one act by Franz Schubert; libretto (Ger) by Ignaz Franz Castelli after Aristophanes' *Lysistrata*. Composed 1823. First performance August 29, 1861, Frankfurt. First U.S. performance June 16, 1877, New York. Revived January 17, 1975, New York; conducted by Michael Spierman.

This battle of the sexes is set in a Gothic fortress at the time of the Crusades. Countess Ludmilla and her female companions feel that they have been neglected by their husbands and resolve to have an all-out "household war," employing the weapon of the "denial of love." Udolin, dressed as a woman, relays the ladies' plans to his male companions, all of whom have returned from the war. The youthful lovers Astolf and Helene are the first to break the restrictions, in their duet "Ich muss sie finden," and they are finally followed by the other couples; all vow to stay together in the finale, "Wie? Darf ich meinen Augen traun?."

Major roles: Graf Heribert von Lüdenstein (bass); Countess Ludmilla (sop); Count Astolf von Reisenberg (ten); Helene, Astolf's housekeeper (sop); Isella, Ludmilla's confidante (sop); and Udolin, Heribert's page (ten).

SCORES: fs Schu/*AGA*, XV/3, No. 6 [no overture]; Schu/*NGA* II/7 (nyp).

BIBLIOGRAPHY: John W. Freeman, "Reports: U.S.," *ON* XXXIX (March 8, 1975), 33 [on U.S. performance]; Donald Kerne, "Lysistrata à la Schubert," *OJ* IV/2 (1971), 13–15; Fritz Racek, "Franz Schuberts Singspiel Der hüsliche Krieg und seine jetzt aufgefundene Ouvertüre," *Biblos* XII (1963), 136–43.

DISCOGRAPHY: excerpts: Donath, Fischer-Dieskau, Moll, and Schreier, Chorus of the Bavarian Radio and Munich Radio Orchestra, conducted by Wallberg, EMI C065–30743 (1).

Versiegelt (Pawned), comic opera in one act by Leo Blech; libretto (Ger) by Richard Batka and Alexander Pordes-Milo after Ernst Raupach's *Der versiegelte Bürgermeiser*. First performance November 4, 1908, Hamburg, Stadttheater.

The work is set in a small town in about 1830. The widow Frau Willmers leaves an old trunk that is to be pawned at her neighbor Gertrud's house. Gertrud is a young widow who wishes to marry Braun, the mayor, who is not so inclined. He opposes the marriage of his daughter Else to Bertel, the son of Frau Willmer. When Lampe comes to Gertrud's house to move the trunk, Braun, who has been dallying with Gertrud, hides in it. He is released by Else and Bertel and promptly locks the pair in the trunk. Hearing a commotion, Gertrud has the trunk opened; all are surprised when the young couple, not Braun, emerge from their confinement. Braun is now ready to marry Gertrud and allows Else to wed Bertel.

Major roles: Braun, the mayor (bar); Else, his daughter (sop); Frau Gertrud, a young widow (mezzo); Frau Willmers, her neighbor (alto); Bertel, Frau Willmer's son (ten); and Lampe (bass).

SCORE: vs ed. E. Pollak (Berlin: Verlag "Harmonie," ca. 1908).

LIBRETTO: German (Berlin: Verlag "Harmonie," ca. 1908); English (New York: F. Rullman, ca. 1911).

Verurteilung des Lukullus, Die. See *Das Verhör des Lukullus*.

Vestas Feuer (Vesta's Fire), unfinished opera by Ludwig van Beethoven; libretto (Ger) by Emanuel Schikaneder. Composed 1803. Scene completed by Clayton Westermann. First performance (concert), 1982 Spoleto Festival; conducted by Gian Carlo Menotti.

In the opening scene Malo, a slave, tells his master, Porus, that Porus' daughter Volivia loves Sartagones, the son of Porus' enemy. Porus and Malo, who is himself seeking Volivia's hand, spy on the lovers, who sing a duet of eternal fidelity. Porus bursts in on the scene and refuses to accept Sartagones until Sartagones threatens to kill himself. Porus is moved by his actions, and the fragment ends with the three singing a trio of reconciliation, "Nie war ich so froh wie heute."

Major roles: Porus, a noble Roman (bar); Volivia, his daughter (sop); Sartagones, her beloved (ten); and Malo, a slave of Porus (ten).

The libretto was also used by Joseph Weigl (1805, Vienna).

SCORE: vs ed. C. Westermann (New York: GS, 1983).

Vetter aus Dingsda, Der (The Cousin from Nowhere), operetta in two acts by Eduard Künneke; libretto (Ger) by Herrmann Haller and Rideamus. First performance April 15, 1921, Berlin, Theater am Nollendorfplatz, with Ilse Marvenga. First U.S. performance, as *Caroline*, January 31, 1923, New York, Ambassador Theater. First British performance, as *The Cousin from Nowhere*, February 24, 1923, London, Princes Theatre.

The work is set in Holland and concerns a stranger who thinks that a country house is an inn.

Its highlights include the theme song of the stranger, "Ich bin nur ein armer Wandergesell," which became popular in English as "I'm only a Strolling Vagabond."

This was Künneke's most successful work.

Vierjährige Posten, Der (The Four-Year Post), Singspiel in one act by Franz Schubert; libretto (Ger) by Theodor Körner. Composed 1815. First performance September 23, 1896, Dresden (in a version by Robert Hirschfeld).

The hero, Duval, a soldier, comes to a village with his regiment. On guard duty, he is left behind when the regiment departs. He weds one of the village girls, but when his regiment returns four years later, he fears that he will be treated as a deserter. His captain, recognizing him despite his disguise, orders his arrest. A heated argument breaks out among the men as to the justice of the situation. When the general arrives, he hears the entire story and gives Duval an honorable discharge.

Major roles: Walther, the town judge (bar); Käthe, his daughter (sop); and Duval, a former soldier (ten).

The work includes the four-part canon "Freund, eilet euch zu retten!" (No. 4) and the lively No. 6, a march and soldiers' chorus, "Lustig in den Kampf!"

SCORE: fs Schu/*AGA*, XV/2, No. 2 (1888); Schu/*NGA*, II/2, IV/14 (No. 5) (nyp).

DISCOGRAPHY: Donath, Fischer-Dieskau, Moll, and Schreier, Chorus of the Bavarian Radio and Munich Radio Orchestra, conducted by Heinz Wallberg, EMI CO65–30742 (1).

Violanta, opera in one act by Erich Korngold; libretto (Ger) by Hans Müller. First performance March 28, 1916, Munich, Hoftheater, with Emmy Krüger (Violanta), Franz Gruber (Alfonso), and Friedrich Brodersen (Simone); conducted by Bruno Walter. First U.S. performance November 6, 1926, New York, with Maria Jeritza (Violanta), Walter Kirchoff (Alonso), and Clarence Whitehill (Simone); conducted by Artur Bodanzky.

The action takes place in Venice in the fifteenth century. In order to get revenge on her sister's seducer, Alfonso, Violanta arranges for him to come to her home, where her husband, Simone, will kill him. Instead, Violanta falls in love with Alfonso, and she takes the dagger blow Simone intends for Alfonso.

Major roles: Violanta (sop), Alfonso (ten), and Simone (bar).

The opening orchestral prelude contains themes and motifs which are not heard again until the end of the opera, when Violanta confronts Alfonso. Among the noteworthy musical numbers of the opera is Alfonso's ballad, "Der Sommer will sich neigen," which he sings just before he meets Violanta.

SCORE: fs (Mainz: BSS, 1916); vs ed. Ferdinand Rebay (Mainz: BSS, c. 1916).

LIBRETTO: German (Mainz: BSS, 1916).

BIBLIOGRAPHY: Brendan Carroll, ''Korngold's 'Violanta,' '' *MT* CXXI (1980), 695–98.

DISCOGRAPHY: Marton, Jerusalem, and Berry, Bavarian Radio Chorus and Orchestra, conducted by Janowski, CBS M2–35909 (2); reviewed by John W. Freeman, ''Records,'' *ON* XLVI (August 1981), 36.

Vögel, Die (The Birds), ''ein lyrisch-phantastisches Spiel'' in two acts by Walter Braunfels; libretto (Ger) after Aristophanes' *The Birds*. First performance December 4, 1920, Munich, Nationaltheatre; conducted by Bruno Walter.

Two people, Ratefreund and Hoffegut, are traveling through the realm of the birds, a realm which they do not understand. Ratefreund, in his disappointment, returns to the human world, but Hoffegut accepts the love of the nightingale.

Major roles: Hoffegut (ten), Ratefreund (bass), and the nightingale (sop).

SCORES: fs (Vienna: UE, c. 1921); vs (Vienna: UE, c. 1920).

LIBRETTO: (Vienna: UE, c. 1920).

BIBLIOGRAPHY: J/*WB*, 231–60.

Vogelhändler, Der (The Bird Dealer), operetta in three acts by Carl Zeller; libretto (Ger) by Moriz West and Ludwig Held. First performance January 10, 1891, Vienna. First U.S. performances October 5, 1891, New York, in English, as *The Tyrolean*, and in German, on December 26, 1892. First British performance (in German) June 17, 1895, London, Drury Lane Theatre.

The story, which takes place in Bavaria in the eighteenth century, concerns the Tyrolean birdseller Adam, who is in love with the female postal carrier Christel. Adam is pursued by the disguised Countess, who tells him her name is Marie; she gives him a rose as a symbol of love (as in *Der Rosenkavalier**). Meanwhile, Christel, in order to make Adam jealous, accepts the attentions of Stanislaus, the nephew of the gamekeeper. The problems are sorted out at the end, and Christel accompanies Adam back to his native Tyrol.

Major roles: Countess Marie (sop); Baron Stanislaus (ten); Adam, a birdseller from Tyrol (ten); and Christel (sop).

The operetta was extremely popular after its premiere and was a favorite in Vienna for many years.

The musical highlights include the introduction of Christel, ''Ich bin die Christel von der Post,'' complete with a post horn, and the Countess' ''Schenkt man sich Rosen in Tirol.''

DISCOGRAPHY: excerpts: Hallstein, Alexander, and Talmar, conducted by Marszalek, Polydor S 2430–267.

Vom Fischer un syner Fru (The Fisherman and His Wife), dramatic cantata in seven tableaux by Othmar Schoeck; libretto (low and high German) by Philipp Otto Runge after a Grimm fairy tale. First performance October 3, 1930, Dresden, with Claire Born, Max Hirzel, and Ivar Andresen; conducted by Fritz Busch.

The wife of a simple fisherman cajoles him into asking for more and more favors from a great fish that he has caught and thrown back into the sea. The couple loses everything when the wife demands to play God, but in the end they find happiness anyway.

Major roles: the wife (sop), the fisherman (ten), and the fish (bass).

Also set by Gunther Schuller, as *The Fisherman and His Wife* (1970, Boston).

SCORES: fs (Leipzig: B&H, 1930); vs ed. Willi Schuh (low and high German) (Leipzig: B&H, 1930).

BIBLIOGRAPHY: Geraldine de Courcy, "Dresden Hears Opera Novelties by Swiss Composer," *MA* L (November 10, 1930) [on premiere]; Hans Corrodi, *Othmar Schoeck, Eine Monographie*, 2d ed. (Zurich: Atlantis, 1956), 228–40.

DISCOGRAPHY: Malaniuk, Haefliger, and Lagger, Radio Orchestra Beromünster, conducted by E. Schmid, Rimaphon RJLP 30–030.

Von heute auf morgen (From One Day to the Next), opera in one act by Arnold Schoenberg; libretto (Ger) by Max Blonda [Gertrud Schoenberg, the composer's wife]. First performance February 1, 1930, Frankfurt, with Else Gentner-Fischer (the wife), Elisabeth Friedrich (the girl friend), Benno Ziegler (the husband), and Anton M. Töplitz (the singer); conducted by Wilhelm Steinberg. First U.S. stage performance July 26, 1980, Santa Fe (in an English translation by Bliss Herbert), with William Stone and Mary Shearer; conducted by Manahan. First British performance (concert) November 13, 1963, London, Royal Festival Hall with Heather Harper, Erika Schmidt, Herbert Schachtschneider, and Derrik Olsen; conducted by Antal Dorati.

The story details a wife's efforts to keep her husband, despite his attraction to the female companion of a singer.

For a detailed synopsis, see *K/KOB*, 861–62.

Major roles: the wife (sop); the husband (bass-bar); the girl friend (sop); and the tenor (ten).

An early twelve–tone opera with recitatives and arias, this is Schoenberg's only comic work.

SCORES: fs (Berlin-Charlottenburg: Edition B. Balan, 1930); fs ed. Richard Hoffmann and Werner Bittinger, Scho/*SW*, III/7/1–2 (1970); vs ed. Hermann Scherchen (Vienna: Ars Viva Verlag, 1951).

BIBLIOGRAPHY: Geraldine de Courcy, "Germany Continues to Produce Novel Operas," *MA* L (March 10, 1930), 12, 27 [on premiere]; Hans Keller, "Schoenberg's Comic Opera," *The Score* XXIII (July 1958), 27–36; Stephen Wadsworth, "Reports: U.S.," *ON* XLV (November 1, 1980), 35 [on U.S. stage premiere].

DISCOGRAPHY: Schmidt, Harper, Schachtschneider, and Olsen, Royal Philharmonic, conducted by Craft. Columbia M2S–780 (2); reviewed by C. J. Cluten, "Records," *ON* XXXIII (April 12, 1969), 34.

═ W ═

Waffenschmied, Der (The Armorer), opera in three acts by Albert Lortzing; libretto (Ger) by the composer. First performance May 31, 1846, Vienna, with Josef Staudigl (Stadinger), Dlle. Eder (Marie), Herr Becker (Count von Liebenau), and Herr Gehrer (Georg); conducted by the composer. First U.S. performance December 7, 1853, Milwaukee.

Set in Worms in the sixteenth century, the story concerns Count von Liebenau, who is in love with Marie, the daughter of the armorer Stadinger. Liebenau courts Marie in his own dress as a count and as the apprentice smith Conrad. He is overjoyed when Marie says that she loves Conrad, until Stadinger rejects the match in favor of one with Georg, the Count's servant. Identities are straightened out, and the opera ends happily.

Major roles: Hans Stadinger, the armorer and animal doctor (bass); Marie, his daughter (sop); Count von Liebenau (bar); and Georg, his servant (ten).

The score includes Maria's number at the end of the first act, "Reichtum allein tuts nicht auf Erden," in which she sings of her love for Conrad, and Stadinger's third-act aria "Auch ich war ein Jüngling mit lockigem Haar," perhaps a forerunner to Hans Sachs' musings in *Die Meistersinger.**

SCORES: fs ed. Gustav F. Kogal (Leipzig: C. F. Peters, 1922); vs ed. Gustav F. Kogel (Leipzig: C. F. Peters, 1881).

LIBRETTO: (Halle: Hendel, 1909).

DISCOGRAPHY: excerpts: Gueden, Kmentt, Wächter, and Czerwenka, Vienna State Opera and Chorus and Volksoper Orch., conducted by Roonefeld, London 5768.

Wahrer Held, Ein (A True Hero), opera in three acts by Giselher Klebe; libretto (Ger) by the composer after John Millington Synge's *Playboy of the Western World*, translated by Heinrich Böll. First performance January 18, 1975, Zurich, with Sven Olof Eliasson (Christy), Gerlinde Lorenz (Margaret Flaherty), and Ernst Gutstein (Christy's father); conducted by Ferdinand Leitner.

The timid young peasant Christy Mahon runs away from home after he believes he has slain his father. When people react to his deed by treating it as a heroic achievement, Christy's character changes completely, and he sheds his timidity.

Major roles: Christopher Mahon, known as Christy (ten); old Mahon, his father (bar); Michael James Flaherty (bar); Margot Flaherty, known as Pegeen Mike, the daughter (sop); the widow Quin (sop); and Shawn Koegh, Pegeen's cousin (ten).

BIBLIOGRAPHY: Eugene V. Epstein, "Reports: Foreign," *ON* XXXIX (March 22, 1975), 31–32 [on premiere].

Waldmädchen, Das (The Forest Girl), opera in three acts by Carl Maria von Weber; libretto (Ger) by Carl von Steinsberg. First performance November 24, 1800, Freiburg, Buttermarkt Theater, by the Steinberg company. The work was given in Chemnitz under the title *Das stumme Waldmädchen*, on December 5, 1800, and as *Das Mädchen im Spessarter Wald* on December 4, 1804, in Vienna. The text was subsequently adapted by Franz Carl Hiemer for *Silvana.** Only two fragments survive from Weber's first opera, written when he was just thirteen. They are Mathilde's da capo aria and a terzett with Count Arbander, Krips, and Mathilde.

SCORE: fs ed. A. Lorenz, MW, II/1.

BIBLIOGRAPHY: W/*CMW*, 34–35.

Walküre, Die. See *Der Ring des Nibelungen.*

Weinlese, Die. See *Das Fest der Winzer.*

Weisse Rose, Die (The White Rose), opera in eight scenes by Udo Zimmermann; libretto (Ger) by Inge Zimmermann. First performance October 6, 1968, Schwerin. First U.S. performance September 17, 1988, Omaha, with Lauren Flanigan (Sophie) and Peter Kazaras (Hans); conducted by John DeMain.

The story centers around Sophie and Hans Scholl, a real-life German brother and sister, whose abhorrence of the Nazis' persecutions of the Jews and others led them to form a student group called "Die weisse Rose." The small group distributed anti-Nazi pamphlets, but the siblings were arrested in 1943 and beheaded for their actions. Zimmermann's setting takes place in the prison, where the two sit in separate cells and, awaiting execution, recall their past and ponder their unfulfilled wishes.

Major roles: Sophie (sop) and Hans (ten).

The cantata-like work involves two voices and fifteen players. It mixes the lyricism of the protagonists with the strident brass and percussion sections of their opponents.

BIBLIOGRAPHY: Fritz Hennenberg, "Musikdrama und Dialektik: analytische Versuche," *Sammelbände der Musikgeschichte der DDR*, ed. Heinz Alfred Bockhaus and

Konrad Niemann (Berlin: Neue Musik, 1975), 236–71; Bernard Holland, "An Omaha Premiere for 'The White Rose,' " *NYT*, September 17, 1988, C, 12 [on U.S. premiere]; Mark Swed, "The White Rose Blooms," *ON* LIII (September 1988), 26–27.

DISCOGPAPHY: Fontana, Harder, conducted by Zimmermann, Orfeo S–162871.

Widerspenstigen Zähmung, Der (The Taming of the Shrew), opera in four acts by Hermann Goetz; libretto (Ger) by Joseph Viktor Widmann after Shakespeare's play. First performance October 11, 1874, Mannheim, Hof- und Nationaltheater, with Ida Auer-Herbeck (Bianka), Carl Slovak (Lucentio), Eduard Schlosser (Petrucchio), Ottile Ottiker (Katharina), Nina Zottmayr (the widow), and August Knapp (Hortensio); conducted by August Wolff. First U.S. performances January 4, 1886 (in English); March 15, 1916 (in German). Revived (in English) February 25, 1982, New York, Manhattan School of Music, with Lauren Flanigan (Katharina) and Leslie Tennent (Petrucchio); conducted by Bruce Ferden. First British performance October 12, 1878, London, Drury Lane Theatre.

The story, unchanged from the Shakespeare, concerns the difficult daughter of Baptista, Katharina, who upsets his entire household and whose hostile temperament makes her catching a husband seem impossible. Also affected by this is her sweet younger sister, Bianka, who is not allowed to wed any of her suitors before her sister marries. Petrucchio, a visitor from Verona, appears on the scene, marries Katharina, and, by treating her roughly, manages to "tame" her quite speedily.

Major roles: Baptista, a rich nobleman of Padua (bass); Katharina and Bianka, his daughters (sops); Hortensio and Lucentio, Bianka's suitors (bar and ten); Petrucchio, a noble from Verona (bar); and Grumio, his servant (bass).

This delicate comic work uses a small orchestra. Despite having been written in the shadow of *Die Meistersinger von Nürnberg** (which appeared about six years before), it basically avoids the Wagnerian echoes found in other German works of the period and is, rather, in a direct line from Peter Cornelius' *Der Barbier von Bagdad.** Among its numbers is the lovely duet between Lucentio and Bianka of the first act, "O strahlend' Himmelslicht," and Petrucchio's aria at the end of the act, "Sie ist ein Weib, für solchen Mann geschaffen," in which he outlines his plan to subdue Katharina. Highlights in the second act include Petrucchio's "Jetzt gilt's" and Katharina's "Ich möcht ihn fassen," and, in the fourth, Katharina's aria of surrender, "Die Kraft versagt, des Kampfes bin ich müde."

SCORE: vs (Leipzig: F. Kistner [1875]).

BIBLIOGRAPHY: Edgar Istel, "Hermann Goetz," *ZIMG* III (February 1902), 177–88; Andrew Porter, "Musical Events," *NY* LVIII (March 15, 1982), 132; Patrick J. Smith, "Opera Everywhere," *HiFi/MA* XXXII (June 1982), 21–22 [on U.S. revival].

DISCOGRAPHY: See M/*IRR*, 400.

Wiener Blut (Viennese Life), operetta in three acts by Johann Strauss, Jr., adapted for the stage by Adolf Müller, Jr. from earlier Strauss works; libretto (Ger) by Victor Léon and Leo Stein. First performance October 26, 1899, Vienna, Carltheater. First U.S. performance January 23, 1901, New York, Broadway Theater, as *Vienna Life*.

The work takes place in Vienna at the time of the Congress of Vienna, in 1815. It concerns Count Zedlau, a Thuringian delegate, who is having an affair with Franzi, a Viennese dancer. Prince Ypsheim, the Count's superior, mistakenly believes that Franzi is the Count's wife, and that his real wife, Gabriele, is his mistress. The Count convinces Ypsheim to pretend that Franzi is his wife. Matters are complicated at an embassy ball, at which both ladies are present. During the event the Count is attracted to yet another lady, Pepi, whom he plans to meet in the suburb of Hietzing. When the other two ladies find out about this, they surprise the lovers in their rendezvous. Franzi has nothing more to do with the philandering Count and helps his real wife to win her husband back by making him jealous of Gabriele. Franzi consoles herself with the attentions of Prince Ypsheim.

For a detailed plot summary see K/*KOB*, 297–300.

Major roles: Prince Ypsheim-Gindelbach (bass); Count Zedlau (ten); Gabriele, his wife (sop); and Franziska (Franzi) Cagliari, a dancer (sop).

Wiener Blut was a failure at its premiere, perhaps because of its weak text, but it flourished after its revival in 1905 at the Theater an der Wien. Its few highlights include the theme song, the waltz of the second act, sung by the Count and Countess, "Wiener Blut, eig'ner Saft."

DISCOGRAPHY: complete: Schwarzkopf, Koth, Loose, Gedda, and Kunz, Philharmonia Orchestra and Chorus, conducted by Ackermann, Angel CDH–69529 (mono) (compact disc); soloists, Vienna Volksoper Orchestra and Chorus, conducted by Bibl (live performance), Denon C37–7430/1 (compact disc); excerpts: Rothenberger, Holm, and Gedda, Hungarica Philharmonica, Cologne Opera Chorus, conducted by Boskovsky, Angel COM–69095 (compact disc); Schramm, Gueden, Schock, Kusche, Vienna Symphony, conducted by Stolz, Eurodisc 258–370 (compact disc).

Wildschütz, Der, oder **Die Stimme der Natur** (The Poacher, or The Voice of Nature), opera in three acts by Albert Lortzing; libretto (Ger) by the composer, after August von Kotzebue's *Der Rehbock*. First performance December 31, 1842, Leipzig, with Günther, Lanz, Krüder, Düringer, Kindermann, Schmidt, Berthold, and Wallmann. First U.S. performance March 25, 1859, New York, with Hübner, Heyde, Siedenberg, Lehmann, Graf, Fortner, and Quint. First British performance July 3, 1895, London, Drury Lane.

The schoolmaster Baculus accidentally shoots a buck on the estate of Count Eberbach and loses his job. He is afraid to have his fiancée, Gretchen, intercede for him since he knows that the count is a great admirer of young ladies. Baroness Freimann, sister of the count, disguises herself as Gretchen and attends a party on the count's estate with Baculus. The count offers Baculus a bonus if he will give up his claims on Gretchen. He agrees, but when the real Gretchen shows up, the count cancels the bargain. His sister reveals her true identity, Baculus is reinstated as the schoolmaster, and the forgiving Gretchen takes back her errant Baculus.

For a detailed plot synopsis see K/*KOB*, 148–49.

Major roles: Count Eberbach (bar); Baroness Freimann, the count's sister (sop); Baculus, the schoolmaster (bass); and Gretchen, his intended (sop).

Among the noteworthy musical numbers are the first-act duet of Baculus and Gretchen, "A.B.C.D., der Junggesellenstand tut weh" (No. 2), and the comical aria of Baculus in the second act (No. 12), "Fünftausend Taler," in which he discovers he can sell his wife-to-be for a considerable sum.

SCORES: fs ed. Kurt Soldan (Leipzig: C. F. Peters, ca. 1928); vs (Leipzig: B&H, ca. 1843).

LIBRETTO: ed. Wilhelm Kienzl (Vienna: UE, ca. 1900).

DISCOGRAPHY: excerpts: Köth, Holm, Schock, Cordes, and Frick, RIAS Chorus and Berlin Symphony, conducted by Schüchter, Eurodisc 70214. Excerpts: Pütz, Römisch, Schröter, Schreier, Krause, and Van Mill, Orchestra of the Gewandhaus Leipzig, conducted by Schmitz, London OS–26181. Resick, Mathis, Soffel, Schreier, Sotin, and Hornik, (East) Berlin State Orchestra, conducted by Klee, DG 2740–271 (3); reviewed by John W. Freeman, "Records," *ON* XLVIII (March 31, 1984), 44.

William Ratcliff, "Musiktheater" in a prologue, three acts, and two intermezzos by Jens-Peter Ostendorf; libretto (Ger) after Heinrich Heine's tragedy. First performance September 15, 1982, Hamburg, Opera Stabile, with Peter Haage (Ratcliff) Audrey Michael (Marie) and Olive Fredericks (Margarete); conducted by Manfred Schandert.

The work is set in Scotland long ago. Taking as its point of departure the tragedy of Heinrich Heine, it portrays the inner conflicts of William Ratcliff, who has sworn to kill anyone who marries his beloved Marie, the daughter of a Scottish laird. Marie had rejected Ratcliff when he was a student, and she now wishes to wed Douglas. When Ratcliff fails to kill Douglas, Douglas spares his life when he realizes that Ratcliff had aided him in the woods. The wounded Ratcliff goes to Marie, who takes care of him. In the final scene, he kills her, her father, and then himself.

Major roles: Mac-Gregor, a Scottish laird (speaking role); Marie, his daughter (sop); Baron Douglas, her fiancé (speaking role); William Ratcliff (ten); and Margarete, Marie's nurse (alto).

The work, whose action is interpreted by singers, seen and unseen, a dancer, and speakers, includes aleatory passages, taped sections, and minimalist writing. The first act is spoken, to an orchestral accompaniment.

Also set by Cornelius Dopper (1909, Weimar).

BIBLIOGRAPHY: James Helme Sutcliffe, "Reports: Foreign," *ON* XLVII (January 15, 1983), 39–40 [on premiere].

Wir bauen eine Stadt (Let's Build a Town), children's opera by Paul Hindemith; libretto (Ger) by Robert Seitz. First performance June 21, 1930, Berlin.

In this work, written for and performed by children, the characters decide to build a new town. When a stranger asks what type of people will come to the town, the children tell him that all types will come, in all kinds of vehicles, and from various places. The children are supreme here, and the adults come second.

Hindemith wrote the work after observing children at a school in Berlin, and he incorporated their suggestions.

SCORES: fs (Mainz: BSS, 1930); vs (Mainz: BSS, 1930); vs ed. composer (Mainz: BSS, 1958).

DISCOGRAPHY: DG 2546.013 (1).

Wirth und Gast, oder **Aus Scherz Ernst** (Host and Guest, or From a Joke to Seriousness), *Lustspiel* in two acts by Giacomo Meyerbeer; libretto (Ger) by Johann Gottfried Wohlbrück after "The Sleeper Awakened" (first part) from the *Thousand and One Nights*. First performance January 6 1813, Stuttgart, Hoftheater.

The story, which is continued in Carl Maria von Weber's *Abu Hassan,** concerns the young hero, here called Alimelek. He is visited by a stranger who says he is a merchant. Alimelek invites him to dinner, and during the meal the stranger, in reality Harun al Raschid, the caliph of Bagdad, slips a sleeping potion into his host's wine. When Alimelek awakens, he is in the caliph's chambers; he has been carried there by Mesrour, Harun's servant and the head of the eunuchs. Alimelek finds himself dressed in the clothing of the caliph and is convinced by all around that he indeed is the ruler. When the day ends, however, he is drugged and returned to his own home, and his efforts to prove that he is the caliph land him in the insane asylum, until he changes his story. A month later he meets the stranger once again and is drugged; when he awakes this time in the caliph's chambers, he is rewarded with riches and a wife, Irene.

Major roles: Harun al Raschid, the caliph; Irene, his niece; Giaffer, his servant; Alimelek, a young, rich Moslem; and Ibrahim, his servant.

A "Turkish" opera along the lines of the earlier *Die Entführung* and *Abu Hassan*, its exoticism is reflected in several numbers, including the A-minor overture, Irene's Romance (No. 2), and No. 4, a drinking song, also in A minor, which features chromatic writing. The various instrumental interludes use "Turkish" instruments such as the triangle, drum, and cymbals, and the exoticism is maintained in the "Chor der Imans" (No. 9), again in A minor. The work concludes with an extended finale, which opens with a melodrama and ends with a chorus and ballet. It was only moderately successful after its premiere. It was performed in an abridged version in Vienna in 1815, as *Die beyden Kaliphen*, and later that year in Prague, at the urging of the creator of *Abu Hassan*, Carl Maria von Weber.

SCORE: overture ed. August Schulms (Prague: Marco Benc, 18—).

Witwe des Schmetterlings, Die (The Widow of the Butterfly), opera in one act by Isang Yun; libretto (Ger) by Harald Kunz after a sixteenth-century Chinese story. First performance February 23, 1969, Nuremberg. First U.S. performance February 27, 1970, Chicago-Evanston, Northwestern University.

Set in classical China, the story concerns the unhappily married Tschuang-tse. He imagines himself to be a butterfly. After pretending to be dead, he becomes one.

Major roles: Lao-tse (ten); Tschuang-tse (bar); Mrs. Tiän, his wife (mezzo); a young widow (sop); Prince Fu (high bar); and the prince's servant (bass).

The work is a companion to *Der Traum des Liu-Tung*.* Performed together, the two form *Träume*.*

SCORE: vs (Berlin: B&B, 1969).

LIBRETTO: German, the same.

Wozzeck, opera in three acts by Alban Berg; libretto (Ger) by the composer after the play by Georg Bücher (1836). First performance December 14, 1925, Berlin, with Johannsen, Scheele-Müller, Henke, Soot, Leo Schützendorf, and Abendroth; conducted by Erich Kleiber. First U.S. performance March 19, 1931, Philadelphia, Academy of Music (repeated November 19, Philadelphia, and November 23, New York, Metropolitan Opera), with Anne Roselle (Marie); Ivan Ivantzoff (Wozzeck); Ivan Steschenko (the Doctor); Nelson Eddy (the Drum Major)—despite the program notes which list Gabriel Leonoff, according to the assistant conductor Sylvan Levy—(see the Brisk article below); and Edwina Eustis (Margret); conducted by Leopold Stokowski. First British performance January 22, 1952, London, Convent Garden, with Christel Goltz (Marie); Sinclair, Hannesson, Parry Jones (the Captain), Marko Rothmüller (Wozzeck), and Dalberg; conducted by Erich Kleiber.

The bleak story centers around the simpleminded soldier Wozzeck, who is controlled by his haughty Captain and the crazed doctor, who uses him for experiments. Wozzeck's mistress, Marie, is seduced by the drum major, and when Wozzeck becomes suspicious of her, he is taunted by the captain. Wozzeck finds Marie dancing with the drum major, and when he refuses to drink with the latter, the drum major beats him up. Marie repents after reading the Bible story of Mary Magdalen, and she goes walking with Wozzeck, who has become increasing distraught and unhinged. When they pass by a pond, he stabs her. He seeks solace in a tavern but flees after Margret, with whom he has been dancing, sees blood on his hands. He searches for the knife in the pond and drowns in his attempt to find it. The child of Marie and Wozzeck, left alone on his hobbyhorse, cannot comprehend his playmates' declarations that his mother is dead.

Major roles: Wozzeck (bar); the drum major (ten); the captain (ten); the doctor (bass); Marie (sop); Margret (alto); and Andres (ten).

For detailed plot synopses, see C/*NMC*, 619–30 and K/*KOB*, 866–73; for a detailed study of the work, see George Perle, *The Operas of Alban Berg*, I: *Wozzeck* (Berkeley: University of California Press, 1980).

The work combines traditional and new forms, with twelve-tone musical interludes accompanying the scene changes and preludes connecting the scenes. The first act contains five character studies: the captain (suite), Andres (rhapsody), Marie (military march and lullaby), the doctor (passacaglia), and the drum major (rondo), a twelve-tone theme with twenty-one variations. The second act is a symphony in five movements. The third act contains six "Inventions," i.e., the invention on a theme, to Marie's reading of the Bible; the invention on one tone to accompany Marie's murder; the invention on a rhythm, during which Wozzeck thinks about the knife and leaves the public house to search for it; the invention on a sixth chord for Wozzeck's attempt to retrieve the knife and his drowning; the invention on a key, an orchestral interlude between scenes; and the invention on a quaver rhythm, to accompany the closing scene of the children playing in front of Marie's house.

Also set by Manfred Gurlitt (1926, Bremen); K. Pfister (1950, Regensburg).

SCORES: fs ed. H. E. Apostel (Vienna: UE, c. 1955); vs ed. Fritz Heinrich Klein (Vienna: UE, ca. 1923).

LIBRETTO: German (Vienna: UE, c. 1923).

BIBLIOGRAPHY: Barry Brisk, "Leopold Stokowski and *Wozzeck*. An American Premiere in 1931," *OQ* V/1 (Spring 1987), 71–82; Donald Chittum, "The Triple Fugue in Berg's *Wozzeck*," *MR* XXVIII (1967), 52–62; Ernst Hilmar, '*Wozzeck' von Alban Berg. Enstehung—erste Erfolge—Repressionen (1914–1935)* (Vienna, 1975); Arthur Holmberg, "Core of Loneliness," *ON* XLIV (March 8, 1980), 20–23; John W. Klein, " 'Wozzeck'—A Summing Up," *ML* XLIV (1963), 132–39; Otto Kolleritsch, ed., *50 Jahre Wozzeck von Alban Berg. Vorgeschichte und Auswirkungen in der Opernästhetik* (Graz, 1978); Kurt Oppens, "Alban Bergs *Wozzeck*," *Merkur* XXI (1967), 1154–69; George Perle, "The Musical Language of Wozzeck," *Music Forum* I (1967), 204–59; ———, "Woyzeck and Wozzeck," *MQ* LII (1967), 206–19; Peter Peterson, "Wozzecks persönliche Leitmotive. Ein Beitrag zur Deutung der Musik in Alban Bergs *Wozzeck*," *Hamburgische Jahrbuch für Musikwissenschaft* IV (1980), 33–83; Gerd Ploebsch, *Alban Bergs 'Wozzeck.' Dramaturgie und musikalischer Aufbau* (Baden-Baden, 1968); Mark A. Radice, "The Anatomy of a Libretto: The Music Inherent in Büchner's *Woyzeck*," *MR* XLI (1980), 223–33; John Simon, "Meeting of Minds," *ON* LXIX (January 19, 1985), 14–16, 46; Jack M. Stein, "From *Woyzeck* to *Wozzeck*: Alban Berg's Adaptation of Büchner," *Germanic Review* XLVII (1972), 168–80; Konrad Vogelsang, *Dokumentation zur Oper Wozzeck von Alban Berg. Die Jahre des Durchbruchs 1925–32* (Laaber: Laaber Verlag, 1977).

DISCOGRAPHY: Lear, Fischer-Dieskau, Kohn, Melchert, Stolze, and Wunderlich, Chorus and Orchestra of the Deutsche Oper Berlin, conducted by Böhm, DG 2707023 (2). Waechter, Winkler, Laubenthal, Zednik, Matta, and Silja, Vienna Philharmonic, conducted by C. von Dohnányi (Ger), London LDR 72007 (2); reviewed by Oliver B. Ellsworth, "Recordings. *Wozzeck*," *OQ* I/2 (Summer 1983), 155–56.

Wundertheater, Das. (The Miracle Theater), opera in one act by Hans Werner Henze; libretto (Ger) by Adolf Graf von Schack after Miguel Cervantes' *El retablo de las maravillas* (ca. 1605). First performance May 7, 1949, Heidelberg. Second version November 30, 1965, Städtische Bühnen, Kammerspiel, Frankfurt. First British performance March 8, 1966, London, St. Pancras Festival; conducted by Frederick Marshall.

The story, set in "Spain and everywhere," is a satire on society's conventions and the conformity of a small town. The town's small-mindedness and self-deception are brought to the fore by the magical theater of Chanfalla.

Major roles: Chanfalla, the director of the Miracle Theater (ten); Chirinos, his mistress (sop); the Runt, a musician (ten); the Gobernadór (bar); Benito Repollo (bass); and Theresa, his daughter (sop).

SCORE: vs ed. Hans Göhre (Mainz: BSS and New York: AMP, 1949).

BIBLIOGRAPHY: Ronald Crichton, "Henze Triple Bill," *MT* CVII (1966), 420 [on British premiere].

=Z

Zaïde, unfinished opera by Wolfgang Amadeus Mozart; libretto (Ger) by Johannes Andreas Schachtner, rewritten by Karl Gollmick. Composed 1779. First performance January 27, 1866, Frankfurt. First U.S. performance August 8, 1955, Tanglewood, Lenox, Massachusetts, with Christina Cardillo (Zaïde); conducted by Aviva Einhorn.

Soliman, the all-powerful sultan, is infatuated with Zaïde, who is in his seraglio. She, however, has fallen in love with the Spanish Christian slave Gomas, and the two plan to escape with the aid of Allazim, a Turk whose life Gomas saved. As in the later "Turkish" *Die Entführung aus dem Serail,** the lovers are caught and brought before their wronged captor. Mozart stopped composing at this point in the story, but Gollmick continued it and gave it a "happy" ending. Just as the lovers are to be punished by being set adrift on the angry seas, a bolt of lightning reveals a special mark on Allazim, which proves that he is Gomas' long-lost brother, who had been carried off by the Moors as a child. This event is taken as a divine sign by Soliman, who grants the three their freedom.

Major roles: Zaïde (sop), Soliman (ten), Allazim (bass), Gomas (ten), and Osmin (bass).

This work has musical ties to Mozart's later "Turkish" opera via the orchestral beginning of the quartet in *Zaïde* and the middle section of Constanze's aria "Traurigkeit ward mir zum Loose;" the instrumentation and meter are also the same. A melodic similarity to *Die Entführung*'s overture may also be detected in Soliman's rage aria (No. 10), "Der stolze Leu'." Finally, there is a kinship between Zaïde's defiant aria "Tiger, wetze nur die Klauen" and Constanze's famous "Martern aller Arten." Gollmick, in an attempt to capitalize on the appeal of the comic Osmin of *Die Entführung,* enhanced the comic side of *Zaïde*'s Osmin.

Feeling that the work was "not suitable for Vienna, where people prefer comic pieces," Mozart abandoned it and incorporated several of its elements into another of his "Turkish" works, *Die Entführung.** The unfinished overture and finale were completed by Johann Anton André in 1838, who also gave the untitled work its name.

Also opera by J. N. Poissl (1843, Munich).

SCORES: fs and vs (Offenbach am Main: J. André [1838]); fs ed. Friedrich Heinrich Neumann, M/*NMA*.

BIBLIOGRAPHY: Anna Amalie Abert, *"La Finta Giardiniera* und *Zaïde* als Quellen für spätere Opern Mozarts," in *Musik und Verlag. Karl Vötterle zum 65. Geburtstag*, ed. Richard Baum and Wolfgang Rehm (Kassel, 1968), 113–22; Alfred Einstein, "Die Text-Vorlage zu Mozart's *Zaïde*," *Acta* VIII (1936), 30–37; G/" 'T'O," 260–71; Jean-Victor Hocqead, *L'enlèvement au sérail précédée de Zaide* (Paris: Aubier Montaigne, 1980); William Mann, "Zaïde," M/*OM*, 233–49.

DISCOGRAPHY: J. Blegen, W. Hollweg, W. Schöne, T. Moser, R. Holl, P. Pikel, and W. Bellon, Mozarteum Orchestra, conducted by L. Hager, Orfeo S 055832 H(2); reviewed by Christopher Hunt, "Recordings. *Zaïde*," *OQ* II/2 (Summer 1984), 143–44. See also M/*IRR*, 187 for more information on discography.

Zar lässt sich photographieren, Der (The Tsar Lets Himself be Photographed), "opera buffa" in one act by Kurt Weill; libretto (Ger) by Georg Kaiser. First performance February 18, 1928, Leipzig, Neues Theater, with Ilse Kögel, Maria Janowska, and Theodor Horand; conducted by Gustav Brecher. First U.S. performance, as *The Shah Has His Photograph Taken*, October 27, 1949, New York, the Juilliard School; conducted by Dino Yannopoulos.

The story, which takes place in Paris, involves a famous woman photographer, Angèle. While she is preparing to take a photograph of the Tsar, assisted by two male helpers, assassins enter and forcibly take the threesome's places. When the Tsar arrives, he and the false Angèle begin a flirtation. He insists on taking her picture first; knowing that the camera is rigged to fire a shot, she tries to avoid the camera's focus. During the commotion the bodyguard comes in and says that a conspiracy has been uncovered to kill the ruler. The false Angèle makes her escape, and when the real one comes in, the confused Tsar thinks he has been dreaming. He finally settles down to have his portrait taken.

Major roles: the Tsar (bar); Angèle (sop), the assistant (ten), the boy (alto), the false Angèle (sop), the false assistant (ten), and the false boy (alto).

The score includes a tango, here to accompany the "dancing" of the Tsar and the false Angèle around the camera. A male chorus, seated in the orchestra, comments on the important developments in the plot.

SCORE: ed. Erwin Stein (Vienna: UE, 1927).

LIBRETTO: (Vienna: UE, 1927).

BIBLIOGRAPHY: S/*DGS*, 75–77.

DISCOGRAPHY: McDaniel, Pohl, Napier, conducted by Latham-König, Capriccio 60007–1 (compact disc).

Zar und Zimmermann, oder **Die zwei Peter** (Tsar and Carpenter, or The Two Peters), opera in three acts by Albert Lortzing; libretto (Ger) by the composer after Mélesville, Merle, and de Boirie's *Le Bourgemestre de Saardam.* First performance December 22, 1837, Leipzig, with Günther, Frau Lortzing (Marie), A. Lortzing, Richter, and Berthold. First U.S. performance April 8, 1852, Milwaukee, First British performance April 15, 1871, London, Gaiety, in an English translation by J. M. Maddox, as *Peter the Shipwright,* with Blanche Cole, A. Tremaine, Lyall, Charles Santley, and Cook; conducted by Meyer Lutz.

In the story, Peter I, the Tsar, exchanges identities with a carpenter, Peter, and passes himself off as a shipwright in the shipyard of the widow Brown. There he becomes friends with a young Russian, Peter Ivanov, who loves Marie, the niece of Burgomaster Van Bett. Another contender for her affection is the Marquis de Châteauneuf, the French ambassador. When Admiral Lefort, the Russian ambassador, reports that there is unrest in Russia, the Tsar decides to return home. By now the French ambassador has discovered the Tsar's true identity, but Lefort and Lord Syndham, the British ambassador, still believe that Ivanov is the ruler. The real Tsar makes his escape, but he leaves Ivanov with a promotion and permission to wed Marie.

Major roles: Tsar Peter I (bar); Peter Ivanov (ten); Van Bett (bass); Marie (sop); Admiral Lefort (bass); Lord Syndham, English ambassador (bass); Marquis de Châteauneuf (ten); and Widow Brown (alto).

For a detailed plot synopsis and musical analysis, see K/*KOB*, pp. 147–48.

Considered the highpoint of Lortzing's operatic output, along with *Der Wildschütz,** the work contains many musical gems, including the sparkling overture and Van Bett's comical "O, sancta justitia" of the first act. The second act features Marie's lovely bridal aria and the famed sextet "Zum Werk, das wir beginnen." The last act contains the Tsar's "Einst spielt ich mit Szepter, mit Krone" and the duet of Marie and Ivanov, "Darf eine niedre Magd es wagen." Also noteworthy is the ensemble that opens the act, a cantata of praise to the Tsar, "Heil sei dem Tag, da du bei uns erschienen!"

SCORES: fs ed. Gustav F. Kogel (Leipzig: C. F. Peters, 1900); vs ed. Gustav F. Kogel (Leipzig: C. F. Peters, 188–).

LIBRETTO: German (Leipzig: Sturm and Koppe, ca. 1837).

BIBLIOGRAPHY: Ernest Sanders, "Oberon and Zar und Zimmermann," *MQ* XL (1954), 521–32.

DISCOGRAPHY: See M/*IRR*, 122–23.

Zarewitsch, Der, operetta in three acts by Franz Lehár; libretto (Ger) by Béla Jenbach and Heinrich Reichert. First performance February 21, 1927, Berlin, Deutsches Künstlertheater, with Richard Tauber (the Zarewitsch) and Rita Georg (Sonia).

Based on the life of the son of Peter the Great, the story is moved to the nineteenth century. The young Russian prince, called the Zarewitsch, has strong feelings against women until he meets Sonia, a Russian ballerina disguised as a Circassian soldier. The two fall in love but are forced to part when the Zarewitsch must return to his princely duties.

Major roles: the Zarewitsch (ten) and Sonia (sop).

When Sonia meets the prince for the first time, she sings the haunting "Einer wird kommen." Other highlights include the duet of the lovers, "Hab' nur dich allein."

DISCOGRAPHY: excerpts: Della Casa, Funk, Roswänge, and Hendrik, Orchestra of the Tonhalle Zurich, conducted by Reinshagen, London LLP219. Holm, Wisniewska, Schock, Lang, and Gruber, Berlin Symphony, conducted by Stolz, Eurodisc 258–359 (compact disc). Stratas and Ochman, conducted by Mattes. Viennese Operetta Records VOR 960 (1).

SCORE: vs (Berlin: Drei Masken-Verlag, c. 1927).

Zauberflöte, Die (The Magic Flute), opera in two acts by Wolfgang Amadeus Mozart; libretto (Ger) by Emanuel Schikaneder after "Lulu" in the collection *Dschinnistan* (1786) of Christoph Martin Wieland. First performance September 30, 1791, Vienna, Theater auf der Wien, with Franz Xaver Gerl (Sarastro), Benedikt Schack (Tamino), Josefa Hofer (Queen of the Night), Anna Gottlieb (Pamina), Emanuel Schikaneder (Papageno), Barbara Gerl (Papagena), and Johann Joseph Nouseul (Monostatos); conducted by J. B. Henneberg. First U.S. performance April 17, 1833, New York, Palmo's Opera House, with Mrs. Wallack, Mrs. Austin, Mrs. Sharpe, John Jones, Placide, and Horn. First British performance June 6, 1811 (in English), London, Haymarket Theatre, with Griglietti, Bertinotti-Radicati, Cauvini, Signora Cauvini, Righi, Naldi, and Rovedino; conducted by Weichsell and Pucilta.

Set in ancient Egypt, the story opens with Prince Tamino being pursued by a serpent. He faints during the ordeal and is saved by the Three Ladies, attendants of the Queen of the Night. Papageno, the bird catcher, appears, and he introduces himself with the folklike "Der Vogelfänger bin ich" (No. 2). When Tamino awakes, Papageno claims credit for having saved him. For his lying, Papageno is punished by having a lock put on his mouth. The Ladies show Tamino a picture of Pamina, the daughter of the Queen of the Night, and he immediately falls in love with her. The Queen arrives and, in her brilliant and extremely difficult recitative and coloratura aria (No. 4), "O zittre nicht/Zum Leiden bin ich auserkoren," tells Tamino of her daughter's capture by the supposedly evil Sarastro. Tamino, convinced to rescue Pamina, receives a magic flute from the Three Boys to aid him; the cowardly Papageno gets the glockenspiel, or magic bells. The scene switches to a splendid room in which Pamina is being guarded by the evil Monostatos, a Moor, who desires Pamina for himself. Monostatos is frightened off by Papageno, who, he thinks, is the devil. The extended finale (No. 8) opens with the Three Boys directing Tamino to find Pamina; it progresses to Monastatos' gleeful "Das klinget so herrlich," after he is seduced by Papageno's bells; and it ends with the grand chorus that pays homage to Sarastro, "Es lebe Sarastro, Sarastro soll leben." Pamina and Tamino meet for the first time, but they are separated so that Tamino and Papageno can take the tests for initiation into Sarastro's society.

In the second act, Tamino and Papageno begin the proceedings. They are sworn to silence, a task made difficult by the appearance of the Three Ladies, who tell them of the evilness of Sarastro's kingdom. The next scene takes place in a garden where Monastatos is waiting. His aria "Alles fühlt der Liebe Freuden" (No. 13) bewails his inability to be loved. He withdraws when the Queen of the Night appears and sings her second famous aria, "Der Hölle Rache kocht in meinem Herzen" (No. 14). She gives Pamina a dagger with which to kill Sarastro. When Pamina refuses to carry out the deed, Monostatos tries to stab her, but he is prevented from doing so by the arrival of Sarastro. Monostatos goes off to join the Queen. When Pamina begs Sarastro not to punish her mother, he replies with the aria "In diesen heil'gen Hallen" (No. 15), in which he explains his philosophy. Another scenic change focuses on Papageno, who is desperate for a glass of water. An ugly old woman appears with the drink and informs him that she is really only eighteen years and two minutes old and that she has a lover whose name is—Papageno. She disappears before the stunned bird catcher can find out her name. The Three Boys reappear with the magic flute and the bells, and they sing the lovely trio "Seid uns zum zweiten Mal wilkommen" (No. 16). Pamina, believing herself abandoned by Tamino, sings of her despair in the aria "Ach, ich fühl's, es ist verschwunden" and is prepared to die. Papageno, tiring of the initiation rites, wishes instead for "Ein Mädchen oder Weibchen" (No. 20), and, to his surprise, he is rewarded. The old woman, having convinced Papageno to accept her or die by himself, is transformed into Papagena. She is led away, since Papageno has not yet proved himself worthy of her.

The scene changes once again to begin the extended finale (No. 21). Pamina is about to stab herself. She is stopped by the Three Boys, who promise to aid her. She observes Tamino entering his final trial, and she joins him. They are shielded from harm by their love and the music of the magic flute. Their success is marked by the chorus "Triumph! Triumph! du edles Paar!" The action shifts to Papageno, who is about to hang himself since he has been unable to find Papagena. The Three Boys intercede again and bring in the girl. Papageno and Papagena are joined in the joyful "Welche Freude wird das sein." The final victory of Sarastro is delayed by the appearance of the Queen of the Night, the Three Ladies, and the vengeful Monostatos. They are foiled by the light of Sarastro's sun, and the stage reveals Sarastro standing with Tamino and Pamina, both in priestly garments. Sarastro announces that the sun has triumphed, "Die Strahlen der Sonne," and the chorus intones a hymn of thanks to Osiris and Isis, "Heil sei euch Geweihten!"

Major roles: Sarastro, priest of the sun (bass); Tamino (ten); Queen of the

Night (sop); Pamina, her daughter (sop); Papageno, a bird catcher (bass); Monostatos, a Moor (ten); Papagena (sop); and a priest (bar).

For detailed synopses and musical analyses, see C/*NMC*, 631–40; H/*FMO*, 189–238; *ENO*, III (1980); K/*KOB*, 114–23; N/*SGO*, II, 89–121; and M/*MO*, 591–640.

This was the second to the last opera Mozart wrote (although it was performed two weeks after *La clemenza di Tito*). It has been given many interpretations, from being a paean to the illegal Masonic movement to serving as a political critique, in which the Empress Maria Teresa is symbolized by the Queen of the Night, her son Joseph II by Sarastro, and Austria by Pamina. It is regarded as one of the great operas in the repertoire, and it was a huge success from the very start. It spawned many imitations; its actual sequel is Peter Winter's not very successful *Das Labarint** of 1798, again to a text by Schikaneder.

SCORE: fs M/*MW*, V/20; fs ed. Gernot Gruber and Alfred Orel, M/*NMA*, II, 5/19; vs, excerpts (Vienna, 1791–1792).

LIBRETTO: German (Vienna: Ignaz Alberti, 1791).

BIBLIOGRAPHY: Anna Amalie Abert, "Bedeutungswandel eines Mozartschen Lieblingsmotivs," *MJb 1965/1966* (1967), 7–14; J. N. A. Armitage-Smith, "The Plot of *The Magic Flute*,"*ML* XXXV (1954), 36–39; *L'Avant-scène opéra, La Flûte enchantée* (January-February 1976) [entire issue]; E. M. Batley, "Emanual Schikaneder: The Librettist of 'Die Zauberflöte,' " *ML* XLVI (1965), 231–36; ———, "Textual Unity in *Die Zauberflöte*," *MR* XXVII (1966), 81–92; Jacques Chailley, *The Magic Flute, Masonic Opera*, transl. Herbert Weinstock (New York, 1971; French ed. Paris, 1968); ———, "Die Symbolik in der Zauberflöte," *MJb* XV (1967), 100–110; Gerhard Croll, "Papagenos Glockenspiel," *ÖMz* XXIX (1974), 341–45; Herbert Decker, *Dramaturgie und Szene der Zauberflöte* (Regensburg, 1950); Otto Erich Deutsch, "The Première of 'Die Zauberflöte,' " transl. Anne Ross, *Opera* VII (1956), 404–11; Judith A. Eckelmeyer, "Two Complexes of Recurrent Melodies Related to *Die Zauberflöte*," *MR* XLI (1980), 11–25; Karl Fellerer, "Mozarts *Zauberflöte* als Elfenoper," in *Symbolae historiae musicae. Hellmut Federhofer zum 60. Geburtstag*, ed. F. W. Riedel et al. (Mainz: Schott, 1972), 229–47; Gerold Fierz, "Mozarts Zauberflöte unter neuen Aspekten: Das Libretto Schikaneders im Vergleich mit neuerem Übersetzungen," *Acta mozartiana* XXIV (1977), 14–24; Marius Flothius, "Jupiter oder Sarastro?" *MJb 1965/1966* (1967), 121–32; Joscelyn Godwin, "Layers of Meaning in *The Magic Flute*," *MQ* LXV (1979), 471–92; Franz Grasberger, "Zur Symbolik der *Zauberflöte*," *Bericht—Kongress Wien, Mozartjahre 1956* (Graz, 1958), 249–52; Gernot Gruber, "Das Autograph der 'Zauberflöte.' Eine stilkritische Interpretation des philologischen Befundes," Part I, *MJb* XV (1967), 127–49 and Part II, *MJb* XVI (1968–1970), 99–110; ———, "Bedeutung und Spontanität in Mozarts *Zauberflöte*," in *Festschrift Walter Senn zum 70. Geburtstag*, eds. Erich Egg and Ewald Fassler (Salzburg, 1975), 118–30; L. W. Haldemann, "The Triumph of Papageno," *Opera Journal* I/1 (1968), 11–15; Karl Hammer, "Zur Allegorisierung und Aktualisierung der *Zauberflöte*," *Acta mozartiana* XXI/3-4 (1974), 60–65; Daniel Heartz, "La clemenza di Sarastro. Masonic Benevolence in Mozart's Last Opera," *MT* CXXIV (1983), 152–57; Jean-Victor Hocquard, *La Flûte enchantée* (Paris, 1979); Spike Hughes, "Notes of the Flute," *ON* XLI/11 (1977), 12–14; Edgar Istel, "Mozart's *Magic Flute* and Freemasonry," *MQ* XIII (1927), 510–27; Egon von Komorzynski, *"Die Zauberflöte und Dschinnistan,"* *MJb 1954* (1955), 177–94; ———, "Das Urbild der *Zauberflöte,"* *MJb 1952* (1953), 101–9; ———, " 'Zauberflöte' und 'Oberon,' " *MJb 1953* (1954), 150–61; Ann Livermore, *"The Magic Flute* and Calderón," *ML* XXXVI (1955), 7–16; Siegfried Morenz, "Die Zauberflöte: Eine Studie zum Lebenszusammenhang Aegypten—Antike—Abendland" (Münster and Cologne, 1952); Paul Nettl, *Mozart and Masonry* (New York, 1957); Andrew Porter, "Musical Events," *NY* LVI (August 4, 1980), 62, 64, 66; Dorith Riedl, "Pamina und Papageno—Vergleich der beiden Selbstmord-Szenen in der *Zauberflöte,"* *Acta mozartiana* II (June 1970), 34–39; H. C. Robbins Landon, *Mozart and the Masons* (London, 1983); Alfons Rosenberg, "Alchemie und *Zauberflöte,"* *MJb* (1971–72), 402–14; ———, "The First Pamina," *Opera* XVII (1966), 525–27; Katharine Thomson "Mozart and Freemasonry," *ML* LVII (1976), 25–46; Tomislav Volek, "Die erste Aufführung der 'Zauberflöte' in tschechischer Sprache in Prag 1794," *MJb* XV (1967), 387–91; Erik Werba, "Fünfzig Jahre Salzburger Festspiel-*Zauberflöte.* Chronik und Zeiturteil," *ÖMz* XXXIII (1978), 341–47; Eric Werner, "Leading or Symbolic Formulas in *The Magic Flute,"* *MR* XVIII (1957), 286–93; Wolfgang Witzenmann, "Zu einigen Handschriften des *Flauto magico"* AnMc XVIII (1978), 55–95.

DISCOGRAPHY: See Peter Branscombe, "Die Zauberflöte," B/*OOR*, 106–18; and M/ *IRR*, 187–88.

VIDEO: Gruberová, Araiza, Berndel, and Moll, Bavarian State Opera, conducted by Sawallisch, Polygram Video (Ger); Shane, Wells, Holloway, and Hermiston, Canada National Arts Center, conducted by Bernardi, Canadian Broadcasting Corp MAG02 (Eng).

Zauberharfe, Die (The Magic Harp), "Zauberspiel mit Musik" in three acts by Franz Schubert; libretto (Ger) by Georg Ernst von Hofmann. First performance August 19, 1820, Vienna, Theater an der Wien.

The work consists of thirteen numbers, among them five melodramas and six choruses. Schubert's only complete melodrama, it was unsuccessful. He used the overture to the first act in the later *Rosamunde, Fürstin von Cypern,** set to a four-act play by Hemina von Chézy.

Major roles: Palmiren, a troubador (ten); Melinde, Arnulf, and Ida (speaking parts).

SCORES: fs Schu/*AGA*, XV/4, no. 7 (1891); ed. Rossana Dalmonte, Schu/*NGA*, II/4 (1975).

Zemire und Azor, opera in three acts by Ludwig Spohr; libretto (Ger) by J. J. Ihlee after J. F. Marmontel's libretto for A. E. M. Grétry (1771), itself based on P. C. Nivelle de la Caussée's comedy *Amour par amour* (1742). First performance April 4, 1819, Frankfurt.

Set in an exotic locale, namely Persia, alternating between a fairy palace and a country house on the Gulf of Ormus, the story is basically that of the "Beauty and the Beast." Sander, his daughter Zemire, his favorite Fatme, and Ali wander into the forest and come upon a deserted mansion. They enter the abode and are treated to a sumptuous feast, but no host appears to welcome them. When they leave, Sander picks a rose, which arouses the wrath of his unseen host, Azor, a Persian prince who has been changed into a beast. Azor makes Sander promise that his theft will be repaid, at the cost of Sander's daughter, Zemire. The father, brokenhearted, leaves his beloved child behind. The good Zemire, at first resigned to her fate, falls in love with the hideous Azor but begs him to let her see her family once more. Azor agrees and gives her until sunset to return. Much to his surprise, she returns at the promised time, and her faithfulness transforms the ugly beast into a handsome prince.

Major roles: Zemire (sop); Lisbe (sop); Fatme (sop); Azor, a Persian prince (ten); Sander (bass); Ali, Sander's slave (ten); and the fairy (speaking role).

The highly Romantic opera opens with an atmospheric overture, which portrays thunder and sets the stage for the first number, an invisible chorus of spirits, "Wo schwarz die Wolken ziehen." This eerie atmosphere is continued in the chromatic Zwischenakt No. 10, in the key of F minor. The opera also has three Romances, including No. 8, Zemire's "Rose wie bist du reizend und mild," the same text used by Grétry (see below). Azor's Romance, "Unter Palmen schlief ich ein" (No. 13), is accompanied by a solo guitar and recalls Pedrillo's "Im Mohrenland gefangen war" of *Die Entführung aus dem Serail*.* Spohr himself, in his *Autobiography*, admitted that his work was influenced by Rossini's *Tancredi*.

Also set by A. E. M. Grétry (1771, Fontainebleau); Gotthilf von Baumgarten (1776, Breslau); and Garcia (ca. 1827). A sequel, *Der Ring der Liebe* oder *Zemirens und Azorens Ehestand* was set by Ignaz Umlauf in 1786 (Vienna).

SCORE: vs ed. J. F. Schwencke (Hamburg: A. Cranz, 1821).

BIBLIOGRAPHY: B/*LS*, 121–24.

Zerbrochene Krug, Der (The Broken Jug), comic opera in seven scenes by Fritz Geissler; libretto (Ger) by the composer after the comedy by Heinrich von Kleist (1811). First performance August 28, 1971, Leipzig.

The story concerns a Dutch village judge, Adam. On the day he is to be observed in his work by a government official, he discovers the case he is to hear has, as its guilty party, himself. It seems that a Mrs. Marthe Rull is suing for damages to her broken jug, damaged when the judge was retreating from an unsuccessful amorous tryst. His efforts to hide the truth are eventually undone by the official, the lawyer Walter.

Major roles: Walter, a lawyer (bar); Adam, the town judge (bass); Licht, a writer (ten); Mrs. Marthe Rull (alto); and her daughter, Eve (sop).

BIBLIOGRAPHY: Christoph Fritz Sramek, "Fritz Geissler's Oper *Der zerbrochene Krug*," *Musikbühne* LXXVII (1977), 127–46.

Zerrissene, Der (Split Personality), opera in two acts by Gottfried von Einem; libretto (Ger) by Boris Blacher after the play by Johann Nestroy (1844). First performance September 17, 1964, Hamburg, with Tom Krause (Herr von Lips),

Edith Mathis (Madame Schleyer), and Helmuth Melchert (Gluthammer); conducted by Wolfgang Sawallisch.

The wealthy and bored Herr von Lips proposes to Madame Schleyer, a beautiful lady with a tarnished past. This arouses the ire of the locksmith Gluthammer, a former lover of the lady.

Major roles: Herr von Lips (bar); Madame Schleyer (mezzo); Kathi (sop); and Gluthammer (ten).

The music is diatonic and employs functional harmony. The solo numbers often have obbligato instrumental accompaniments, such as No. 9, Kathi's D-major aria, accompanied by a solo flute.

Also set by Peter Kreuder (1941, Stockholm); A. Jenny (1942, Stans).

BIBLIOGRAPHY: Harold Blumenthal, "Reports," *ON* XXIX (December 12, 1964), 30 [on premiere]; Willi Schuh, "First Performances," *Tempo* LXXI (Winter 1974–1975), 22–24 [on premiere].

Zigeunerbaron, Der (The Gypsy Baron), operetta in three acts by Johann Strauss, Jr.; libretto (Ger) by Ignaz Schnitzer after Maurus Jókai's novel *Saffi*. First performance October 24, 1885, Vienna, Theater an der Wien, with Ottile Collin (Saffi), Karl Streitmann (Sandor), Alexander Giradi (Zsupan), Hartmann, and Reisser; conducted by the composer. First U.S. performance February 15, 1886, New York, Casino Theater (in English), with Hall, Fritch, St. John, Castle, Wilson, and Fitzgerald; conducted by Williams. First British performance (amateur, in English) February 12, 1935, London, Rudolf Steiner Hall.

The story is set in Hungary, at the close of the eighteenth century. Sandor Barinkay has come to claim his ancestral estate, which is lying in ruins after the Turkish invasions. The grounds have been seized by Kalman, a pig farmer, who is searching for the treasure he believes the Turks left behind. Sandor's attempts to win the hand of Kalman's daughter, Arsena, are rebuffed; she is in love with Ottokar, and she tells her would-be suitor that he is no longer an appropriate choice for a husband, since he is no longer a baron. He is welcomed instead by the gypsies, who claim him as their gypsy baron, and he falls in love with Saffi, a gypsy maiden. He then discovers the hidden Turkish treasure, which the police attempt to seize. Before they can, however, Saffi is revealed to be the daughter of the noble Pasha. When a squadron of Hungarian hussars appears on its way to fight the Austrians, Sandor and the other gypsies join the contingent. Sandor's bravery in battle earns him an elevation to the rank of baron, and the Emperor, present at the victory feast, grants him his request. He is allowed to wed Saffi.

For a detailed synopsis, see C/*MS*, 435–47 and K/*KOB*, 294–97.

Major roles: Sandor Barinkay (ten); Saffi (sop); Kalman Zsupan, a pig farmer (bass); Arsena, his daughter (sop); and Ottokar (ten).

The work, with its mixture of Viennese and pseudo-gypsy music, is full of famous numbers, including Sandor's "Als flotter Geist" (No. 2), heralding his return to his native land, and Saffi's air (No. 6) "So elend und so treu," both in the first act. Another highpoint is the waltz of the second act, the so-called Schatz waltz, a trio (No. 9) by Saffi, Sandor, and Kalman, sung to accompany the finding of the treasure, "Ha seht es winkt." Also noteworthy is the rousing march (No. 17) of the third act, "Hurrah! die Schlacht mitgemacht."

SCORE: vs (Leipzig: A. Cranz, 1887).

LIBRETTO: German (New York, ca. 1885).

DISCOGRAPHY: Schröder and Anders, conducted by Marszalek, Viennese Operetta Recordings VOR 1941 (1). Schwarzkopf and Gedda, conducted by Ackermann, Viennese Operetta Recordings VOR 1890 (2).

Zigeunerliebe (Gypsy Love), operetta in three acts by Franz Lehár; libretto (Ger) by A. M. Willner and Robert Bodanzky. First performance January 8, 1910, Vienna, Carltheater. First U.S. performance October 17, 1911, New York, Globe Theater, with Marguerite Sylva (Zorika); the New York production was a failure. First British performance (as *Gipsy Love*) London, Daly's, July 1, 1912, with Sári Petrás (Zorika), Robert Michaelis (Józsi), Gertie Millar (Lady Babby, a new part), and W. H. Berry (Dragotin). The London production ran for 299 performances.

This "gypsy" operetta concerns the landowner Dragotin, who wants his daughter, Zorika, to wed the socially suitable Jonel. She, however, is in love with Józsi, a gypsy violinist. When the two attempt to flee, they are thwarted by her old nurse. Zorika seeks refuge from her engagement party near a river, where she remembers the old legend: whoever drinks the waters will be able to see into the future. When she does this, she falls asleep and dreams that she has run off with Józsi, only to see him as the target of beautiful women, including the well-to-do Lady Ilona. She awakens suddenly, to find Jonel there; he has come to take her back to the party. At the party she sees Jóozsi casting his attentions on a girl whose name is Ilona. Realizing that she has been given a glance into the future, Zorika gladly accepts Jonel as her future mate.

Major roles: Peter Dragotin (bar); Zorika, his daughter (sop); Józsi, a gypsy violinist (ten); Jonel Bolescu (ten); and Ilona (sop).

Among the well-known numbers in the operetta are the first-act gypsy song, "Ich bin ein Zigeunerkind," sung by Józsi, Zorika's "Hör' ich Cymbalklänge," and the duet of the lovers Zorika and Józsi, "Es liegt in blauen Fernen."

DISCOGRAPHY: Seegers, Mentzel, Groh, Karell, Chorus and Orchestra of Radio Berlin, conducted by Dobrindt, Urania 205; excerpts: Schramm, Chryst, Schock, Katona, Berlin Symphony, conducted by Stolz, Eurodisc 258–360 (compact disc).

Zweimal Alexander (Alexandre bis) (Two Times Alexander), opera buffa in one act by Bohuslav Martinů; libretto by Kurt Honolka after André Wurmser. Composed 1937. First performance February 18, 1964, Mannheim; conducted by Georg Calder.

In this domestic comedy, the bearded Alexander shaves his whishers off and seduces his wife, Armande, while pretending to be his cousin from Texas.

Major roles: Armande (sop); Alexander, her husband (bar); Oscar, Alexander's cousin (ten); Portrait (narrator, bass); and Philomene (narrator, sop/mezzo-sop).

BIBLIOGRAPHY: G. A. Trumpff, "Martinus 'Zweimal Alexander' . . . " *NZM* CXXV (1964), 159 [on premiere].

Zwerg, Der (The Dwarf), opera in one act by Alexander von Zemlinsky; libretto (Ger) by Georg C. Claren after Oscar Wilde's *The Birthday of the Infanta*. First performance May 28, 1922, Cologne.

In the story a dwarf, who has been captured in the woods, is presented to the Spanish Infanta on her eighteenth birthday. He falls in love with the beautiful princess, but when he sees his reflection in a mirror and realizes how grotesque he is, he dies of a broken heart.

Major roles: the dwarf (ten); the Infanta (sop); Ghita, the Infanta's maid (sop); and the major-domo (bar).

SCORE: vs (Vienna: UE, 1921).

DISCOGRAPHY: (as *Der Geburtstag der Infantin*) Nielsen, Riegel, and Weller, Berlin Radio, conducted by Albrecht, Schwann/Musica Mundi VMS–1626 (3), reviewed by John W. Freeman, "Records," *ON* XLIX (January 19, 1985), 44.

Zwillingsbrüder, Die (The Twin Brothers), Singspiel in one act by Franz Schubert; libretto (Ger) by Georg von Hofmann after the vaudeville *Les deux Valentins*. First performance June 14, 1820, Vienna, Kärntnertortheater, with Johann Michael Vogl as the twins.

The plot concerns the troubles of a set of separated twins, who find each other at the end.

The work includes ten numbers.

Major roles: Anton (ten); Liescher (sop); Franz (bass); Schulze (bass); and Friedrich (bass).

SCORES: fs, Schu/*AGA*, XV/3, no. 5 (1889); Schu/*NGA* II/5 (nyp).

BIBLIOGRAPHY: Reinhard van Hoorickx, "Two Essays on Schubert," *Revue belge de musicologie* XXIV (1970), 81–95.

Zwillingskomödie (Double Trouble), comedy in one act, with a prologue, epilogue, and two choral interludes by Richard Mohaupt; libretto (Ger) by the composer after Plautus' "Menaechmi"; English version by Roger Maren. First performance December 4, 1954, Louisville, Kentucky (in English).

The story concerns the twins Hocus and Pocus, the sons of Docus and Crocus. They were separated at an early age, and when they are reunited, trouble and confusion ensue.

Major roles: Hocus (bass-bar); Pocus (bass-bar); Naggia, wife of Hocus (mezzo); Erotia, a courtesan (sop); Cynthia, Hocus' daughter (sop); Lucio, Cynthia's lover (ten); and Dr. Antibioticus, Lucio's father (ten).

SCORE: vs ed. composer, English-Ger (New York: AMP, 1954).

Zwischenfälle bei einer Notlandung (Incident at a Forced Landing), opera in "2 phases, 14 situations" by Boris Blacher; libretto (Ger) by Heinz von Cramer. First performance February 4, 1966, Hamburg, Staatsoper, with Helmut Melchert (professor), Colette Lorand, Elisabeth Steiner, Carl Schultz, Erwin Wohlfahrt, Hans Sotin, and Herbert Fliether; conducted by Gustav Rudolf Sellner.

The story concerns the eleven survivors of a plane crash, a representation of modern society, who are in the wilderness. The professor goes back to the wreck to get his work. Although he escapes when the plane explodes, he prevents the other survivors from signalling to rescue planes.

Major roles: the millionaire (bass); the tourist (ten); the engineer (bar); the staff officer (bass); the assistant (mezzo); the professor/host (ten); the journalist (ten); and the prima donna (sop).

The composer uses electronically generated sounds in his score, especially in the opening instrumental prelude.

LIBRETTO: (Berlin: B&B, 1966).

BIBLIOGRAPHY: Wolf-Eberhard von Lewinski, "Current Chronicle. Germany," *MQ* LI (1965), 376–79 [on premiere]; Hans Christian Worbs, "Eine Uraufführung von Boris Blacher," *Musica* XX (1966), 114–15 [on premiere].

APPENDIX 1
ADDITIONAL OPERAS IN GERMAN

Abdul und Erinieh, oder **Die Toten,** comic opera in one act by Karl Friedrich Curschmann; libretto by S. tor Hardt; October 29, 1828, Kassel.

Abels Tod, Singspiel by Michael Haydn; libretto by Friedrich Gottlieb Klopstock after Johann Samuel Patzke; ca. 1778.

Abend im Walde, Der, comic opera in two acts by Ernst Wilhelm Wolf; libretto by Gottlob Ephraim Heermann; 1773, Weimar; vs (Riga: Johann Friedrich Hartnock, 1775); libretto (Berlin: C. U. Ringmacher, 1776).

Abenteuer, Der, opera in four acts by Julius Bittner; libretto by the composer; October 30, 1913, Cologne; vs (Berlin: Jungdeutscher Verlag [1913]).

Abenteuer Carl des Zweiten, Ein, opera in one act by J. Hoven [Johann Vesque von Püttlingen]; libretto by S. H. Mosenthal; January 12, 1850, Vienna.

Abenteuer des Casanova, Ein, four one-act operas by Volkmar Andreae; libretto by Ferdinand Lion; June 17, 1924, Dresden; libretto (Dresden: C. C. Meinhold & Söhne, 1925).

Abenteuer des Don Quichotte, Ein, opera by Heimo Erbse (1924–) (not performed).

Abenteuer des Don Quichotte, Ein, opera by Jean Kurt Forest (1909–1975) (not performed).

Abenteuer des Don Quichotte, Ein, opera in five scenes by Robert Kirchner; libretto by the composer; October 25, 1941, Schwerin.

Abenteuer des Ritter Don Quixote von la Mancha, Ein, Singspiel by Friedrich Ludwig Seidel; anonymous libretto; 1811, Berlin.

Abenteuer einer Neujahrsnacht, Der, comic opera in three acts by Richard Heuberger; libretto by Franz Schaumann; 1886, Leipzig; fs, vs (Mainz: Schott [1886]).

Abu Kara, opera by Heinrich Dorn; libretto by L. Bechstein; 1831, Leipzig; vs (Leipzig: F. Hofmeister, 1832).

Achilleus, opera by August Bungert; part of his *Die Ilias** cycle, sketched but not completed.

Achmed und Almanzine, Singspiel by Johann Schenk; libretto after the Théâtre de la Foire; August 14, 1795, Vienna.

Adam und Eva. See *Der erschaffene, gefallene und wieder aufgerichtete Mensch.*

Admiral, Der (Der gewonnene Prozess), comic opera in one act by Georg Joseph Vogler; ca. January 1811, Darmstadt.

Adrast, Singspiel fragment (eight numbers) by Franz Schubert; libretto by Johann Mayrhofer; composed 1817–1819; Nos. 8 and 9 December 13, 1868, Vienna; No. 6 November 14, 1875, Vienna; fs Schu/*AGA*, XV/7 (1893).

Adrast und Isidore, oder **Die Serenate,** opera in two acts by Otto C. E. von Kospoth; libretto by Christoph Friedrich Bretzner after Molière; October 16, 1779, Berlin.

Adrian von Ostade, Singspiel in one act by Joseph Weigl; libretto by Georg Friedrich Treitschke; October 3, 1807, Vienna; libretto (Königsberg: G. K. Haberland, 1813).

Aeneas (des trojanischen Fürsten Ankunfft in Italien), opera in a prologue and three acts by Johann W. Franck; libretto by J. P. Förtsch; 1680, Hamburg; *Arien* (Hamburg: [Georg Rebenlein], 1680).

Aennchen von Tharau, opera in three acts by Heinrich Hofmann; libretto by Roderich Fels [S. Rosenfeld]; November 6, 1878, Hamburg.

Aerndtekranz, Der, opera in three acts by Johann Adam Hiller; libretto by Christian Felix Weisse; spring 1771, Leipzig; vs ((Leipzig: J. F. Junius, 1772); libretto (Prague: J. Eman, 1785).

Aesopus, opera by Georg Philipp Telemann; 1729.

Agamemnons Tod, opera in one scene by Theo Goldberg; libretto by Johannes Hübner; 1949, Berlin.

Aglaja, opera in one act by Leo Blech; libretto by David Kunhardt; ca. 1893; vs (Aachen: Naus, 1893).

Agnes Bernauer, opera in four acts by Karl August Krebs; libretto by August Lewald; January 17, 1858, Dresden; originally called *Herzog Albrecht**.

Agnes Bernauer, opera by Leo Kauffmann (1901–1944); not performed.

Agnes Bernauer, opera by Josef Messner; libretto after Fredrich Hebbel; ca. 1935.

Agnes Sorel, opera in three acts by Adalbert Gyrowetz; libretto by Josef Sonnleithner; December 4, 1806, Vienna; vs (Vienna: Thadé Weigl [1806]).

Ährenleserin, Die, Singspiel by Michael Haydn; libretto by Christian Felix Weisse; July 2, 1778, Salzburg.

Aladin oder **Die Wunderlampe,** Singspiel in one act by Adalbert Gyrowetz; libretto by Ignatz Franz Castelli; February 7, 1819, Vienna; *Arien und Gesänge* (Berlin: n.p. [1819]).

Aladins Wunderlampe, opera by Kuno Stierlin (1886–1967); not performed.

Alarich und Zaïde. See *Die bezauberte Leyer.*

Albigenser, Die, opera in three acts by Jules Deswert; libretto by Wilhelm Rullmann; October 1, 1878, Wiesbaden.

Alceste, opera by Johann Wolfgang Franck; libretto by the composer after Matsen; 1680, Hamburg.

Alceste, opera in a prologue and three acts by Nikolaus Adam Strungk; libretto by Paul Thiemisch after Aurelio Aureli's *Antigona delusa da Alceste* (1660); May 18, 1693, Leipzig.

Alceste, opera in five acts by Ernst Wilhelm Wolf; libretto by Christoph Martin Wieland; 1780, Weimar.

Alceste, Singspiel in two acts by Friedrich Benda; libretto by Christoph Martin Wieland; January 15, 1786, Berlin (concert).

Alchemist, Der, opera by Max Häfelin (1898–1952) (not performed).

Alchemist, Der, opera in one act by Carl Pistor; libretto by the composer; March 12, 1931, Kiel.

Alchemist, Der, opera by Max Lang (1917–) (not performed).

Alchymist, Der, opera in one act by Johann André; libretto by August Gottlieb Meissner; April 11, 1778, Berlin.

Alcidor, opera in three acts by Gaspare Spontini; libretto by Carl Herklots after M. A. J. Rochon de Chabannes; May 25, 1825, Berlin.

Aleida von Holland, opera in three acts by Willem Frans Thooft; libretto by Ernst Pasqué; March 10, 1866, Amsterdam.

Alexander, "grosse heroische Oper" in two acts by Franz Teyber; libretto by Emanuel Schikaneder; June 13, 1801, Vienna.

Alexander, opera in two acts by Theodor Holterdorf; libretto by Friedrich Forster; September 29, 1960, Bremen.

Ali Baba und die vierzig Räuber, school opera in six scenes by Josef Dienel; libretto by Ulrich Kabitz; June 25, 1952, Fellbach.

Ali Hitsch-Hatsch, comic opera in three acts by Simon Sechter; libretto by Theodor Heiter; April 27, 1844, Vienna.

Ali Pascha, opera by Friedrich Goeldner; 1906, Posen.

Ali Pascha von Janina, oder Die Franzosen in Albanien, opera in one act by Albert Lortzing; libretto by the composer; composed 1816; February 1, 1828, Münster.

Alidia, opera in three acts by Franz Lachner; libretto by Otto Prechtler after Edward Bulwer Litton's *The Last Days of Pompeii* (1834); April 12, 1839, Munich.

Alimon und Zaide, oder Der Prinz von Katanea, opera in three acts by Conradin Kreutzer; anonymous libretto; February 24, 1814, Stuttgart; vs (Mainz: B. Schott, 181–).

Alkestis, opera in one act by Egon Wellesz; libretto by Hugo von Hofmannsthal after Euripides; March 20, 1924, Mannheim; vs (Vienna: UE, 1923).

Alles ist Kismet, opera in two scenes by Wolfgang Hofmann; libretto by Peter Thullen; November 29, 1952, Kaiserslautern.

Almanzine, oder Die Höhle Sesam, opera in three acts by Johann Peter Pixis; libretto by Heinrich Schmidt; April 11, 1820, Vienna.

Almira (Der durchlauchtige Secretarius, oder **Almira),** opera in three acts by Reinhard Keiser; libretto by Barthold Feind after Friedrich Christian Feustking's version for George Frideric Handel; 1706, Hamburg; a reworking of the 1704 version.

Almira, Königen von Castilien, opera in three acts by Reinhard Keiser; libretto by Friedrich Christian Feustking; 1704, Weissenfels; the music is lost.

Aloise, opera in two acts by Ludwig Maurer; libretto by Franz Ignaz von Holbein; January 16, 1828, Hanover.

Alpenhirten, Die, opera in three acts by Frederick Wollank; libretto by H. W. Loess; February 19, 1811, Berlin.

Alpenhütte, Die, opera in one act by Conradin Kreutzer; libretto by August von Kotzebue; March 1, 1815, Stuttgart.

Alpenkönig und der Menschenfeind, Der, *Zauberspiel* in two acts by Wenzel Müller; libretto by Ferdinand Raimund; October 17, 1828, Vienna; vs (Hamburg: J. A. Böhme, n.d.; Vienna: Diabelli & Co., n.d.).

Alte Freyer, Der, Singspiel in one act by Johann André; libretto by the composer; October 2, 1776, Berlin; vs (Frankfurt: Johann Christian Gebhard, 1775).

Ameise, Die, opera in three acts by Peter Ronnefeld; libretto by Richard Bletschachy; October 21, 1961, Düsseldorf.

Amelinde, oder **Dy triumphirende Seele . . . ,** "Sing-Spiel" in a prologue, five acts, and epilogue, probably by Johann Jakob Loewe; libretto by Anton Ulrich; April 20, 1657, Brunswick.

Amerika, opera by Frederick Block (1899–1945) (not performed).

Amors Guckkasten, opera in one act by Christian Gottlob Neefe; libretto by J. B. Michaelis; May 10, 1772, Leipzig; vs ed. G. von Westermann (Munich: Drei-Masken-Verlag, 1922).

Amphytrion, "musical comedy" by Rainer Kunad; libretto by Ingo Zimmermann; May 26, 1984, East Berlin.

Amphitryon, opera in four acts by Heinrich Hermann; libretto by the composer after Heinrich von Kleist; August 28, 1958, Magdeburg.

Amphitryon, opera in a prologue and three acts by Robert Oboussier; libretto by the composer after Molière and Heinrich von Kleist; March 13, 1951, Berlin and Dresden; vs (Kassel: Bärenreiter, 1950).

An allem ist Hütchen schuld, opera in three acts by Siegfried Wagner; libretto by the composer; December 6, 1917, Stuttgart; vs (Bayreuth: C. Giessel, 1916).

Anaximanders Ende, chamber opera in one act by Werner Thärichen; libretto by Wolf-dietrich Schnurre; October 3, 1958, Berlin; vs (Berlin: B&B, 19–).

Andreas Wolius, opera in three acts by Fried Walter; libretto by Christoph Schulz-Gellen; December 19, 1940, Berlin.

Andromache, opera in two acts by Herbert Windt; libretto by the composer; February 16, 1932, Berlin.

Andromeda, opera by Johann Sigismund Kusser; February 20, 1692, Brunswick; the work is lost.

Andromeda, opera by Gotthilf von Baumgarten; 1776, Breslau; vs (Breslau: Korn, 1776).

Andromeda, opera in three acts by Johann Friedrich Reichardt; libretto by A. Filistri; January 11, 1788, Berlin.

Andromeda, opera in three acts by Pierre Maurice; libretto by Madeleine Maurice after Seneca; April 23, 1924, Basel.

Angenehme Betrug, Der, oder **Der Carneval von Venedig,** opera in three acts by Reinhard Keiser and Christoph Graupner; libretto by Meister and Mauritz Cuno; summer 1707, Hamburg; selection in *DDT* XXXVIII, ed. M. Schneider (1912).

Anna Blume, lyric scene by Stefan Wolpe; libretto by Kurt Schwitters; 1929.

Antiochus und Stratonica, opera by Christoph Graupner; 1708.

Anton bei Hofe, oder **Das Namenfest,** Singspiel in two acts, possibly by Benedikt Schack; libretto by Emanuel Schikaneder; June 4, 1791, Vienna; fifth of Schikaneder's seven ''Anton'' Singspiels; the work is lost.

Apajune der Wassermann, opera in three acts by Carl Millöcker; libretto by F. Zell [Camillo Walzel] and Richard Genée; December 18, 1880, Vienna.

Apollo's Wettgesang, opera in three acts by Wilhelm Sutor; libretto by Franz Karl Hiemer after Thomas d'Hèle; March 27, 1808, Stuttgart.

Apotheke, Die, opera in two acts by Christian Gottlob Neefe; libretto by Johann Jacob Engel after Carlo Goldoni's *Lo Speziale*; December 13, 1771, Berlin; vs (Leipzig: J. F. Junius, 1772); libretto (Berlin: C. U. Ringmacher, 1775).

Apotheke, Die, Singspiel in two acts by Ignaz Umlauf; libretto by Johann Jacob Engel; June 20, 1778, Vienna.

Arabella, oder **Die Schreckensfolgen der Eifersucht,** opera by Vincenz Franz Tuczek; 1818, Pest.

Arcifano, comic opera by Karl Ditters von Dittersdorf; libretto after Carlo Goldoni's *Arcifano, Rè dei Mattei*; 1777.

Ariadne, opera in five acts by Johann Sigismund Kusser; libretto by Friedrich Christian Bressand; February 15, 1692, Brunswick; rev. R. Keiser November 22, 1722, Hamburg; selections in *Heliconische Musen-Lust* (1700: Paul Treu, Stuttgart).

Ariadne, opera by Hans Haug (1900–1967) (not performed).

Ariadne und Bacchus, opera by Maria Theresia von Paradis; 1791, Laxenburg; the music is lost.

Arme Gespenst, Das, school opera in three acts by Paul Hermann; libretto by the composer after Oscar Wilde; January 18, 1961, Berlin.

Arme Jonathan, Der, operetta in three acts by Carl Millöcker; libretto by Hugo Wittmann and Julius Bauer; January 4, 1890, Vienna; fs (Hamburg: A. Cranz, ca. 1890); libretto (New York: I. Goldmann, 1891).

Arme Konrad, Der, opera in four acts by Jean Kurt Forest; libretto by the composer after Friedrich Wolf; October 4, 1959, East Berlin.

Armer Kolumbus, opera in eight scenes by Erwin Dressel; libretto by Arthur Zweiniger; February 19, 1928, Kassel.

Armin, heroic opera in five acts by Heinrich Hofmann; libretto by Felix Dahn; 1872, Dresden.

Arsene, opera in four acts by Franz Seydelmann; libretto by August Gottlieb Meissner after Charles S. Favart; March 3, 1779, Dresden.

Arzt der Sobeide, Der, opera in three acts by Hans Gál; libretto by Fritz Zoref; November 2, 1919, Breslau; vs (Vienna: UE, 1919).

Aschenbrödel, opera in three acts by Leo Blech; libretto by Richard Batka; December 26, 1905, Prague; vs (Berlin: B&B, ca. 1905).

Ashmedai, opera in two acts by Josef Tal; libretto by I. Eliraz; November 13, 1971, Hamburg.

Astorga, opera in three acts by Johann Joseph Abert; libretto by Ernst Pasqué; May 27, 1866, Stuttgart.

Astutuli, opera in one act by Carl Orff; libretto by the composer; October 20, 1953, Munich; fs (Mainz: BSS, 1953).

Athalia, music by Johann Abraham Peter Schulz for Jean Racine's tragedy *Athalie*; 1786, Berlin; fs ed. Heinz Gottwaldt, *EDM*, LXXI (1977); vs (Kiel: C. F. Cramer, 1786).

Athalia, opera in three acts by Johann Nepomuk Poissl; libretto by Johann Gottfried Wohlbrück after Jean Racine; June 3, 1814, Munich.

Athener Komödie, comic opera by Hans Vogt; libretto by Christopher Middleton after Menander, translated by the composer and Erich Fried; February 18, 1964, Mannheim.

Atmen gibt das Leben, opera in one act by Karlheinz Stockhausen; libretto by the composer; May 22, 1977, Nice.

Atomtod, opera in two acts by Giacomo Manzoni; libretto by E. Jona; March 17, 1965, Milan.

Attila, opera by Karl Winkler (1899–) (not performed).

Aufsichtsrat, Der, opera in one act by Diether de la Motte; libretto by Rolf Schneider; February 1, 1970, Hanover.

Augenarzt, Der, opera in two acts by Adalbert Gyrowetz; libretto by Johann Emanuel Veith after Armand Croizette and Armand François Chateauvieux; October 1, 1811, Vienna; vs (Vienna: Pietro Mechetti [1811]).

Augustus (Der bey dem allgemeinen Welt-friede von dem grossen Augustus geschlossene Tempel des Janus), opera in three acts by Reinhard Keiser; libretto by Christian Heinrich Postel; June 9, 1698, Hamburg.

Aurora, opera by Anton Schweitzer; 1772, Weimar.

Aurora, opera by Franz Gläser; 1836, Berlin.

Aurora, opera by August Bungert, ca. 1885; vs (Berlin: B&B, 188–).

Aus Deutschland, opera in twenty-seven scenes by Maurizio Kagel; libretto by the composer after Heinrich Heine's poems; May 9, 1981, West Berlin.

Ausgerechnet und verspielt, ''Spiel-Oper'' in one act by Ernst Krenek; libretto by the composer; July 25, 1962, Salzburg, ORF.

Austin, Romantic opera in four acts by Heinrich Marschner; libretto by the composer; January 25, 1852, Hanover.

Auszeichnung, Die, chamber opera in four scenes by Hans Poser; libretto by the composer and Karl Vibach after Guy de Maupassant; August 14, 1959, Hamburg, ARD.

Azakia, Singspiel in three acts by Christian Cannabich; libretto by Christian Friedrich Schwan; November 26, 1778, Mannheim.

Baal, opera by Erich Sehlbach (1898–) (not performed).

Baals Sturz (Daniel in der Löwengrube, oder **Baals Sturz),** opera in three acts by Joseph Weigl; libretto by Georg Ernst von Hofmann; April 13, 1820, Vienna.

Babü, Der, opera in three acts by Heinrich Marschner; libretto by Wilhelm August Wohlbrück; February 19, 1838, Hanover; vs (Leipzig: J. Wunder, ca. 1838).

Babylons Pyramiden, opera in two acts by Peter Winter (Act II) and Gallus (Johann Mederitsch) (Act I); libretto by Emanuel Schikaneder after Goethe; October 25, 1797, Vienna; vs (Leipzig: B&H, ca. 1797).

Bad auf der Tenne, Das, opera in ten scenes by Friedrich Schröder; libretto by Günther Schwenn; March 26, 1955, Nuremberg.

Badewanne, Die, radio comedy by Manfred Niehaus; libretto by the composer and Johann M. Kamps after an idea by Ivan Vyscoczyl; April 16, 1970, WDR, Cologne; February 21, 1973 (staged), Bonn.

Baldurs Tod, opera in three acts by Cyrill Kistler; libretto by Edgar von Sohlern; October 25, 1905, Düsseldorf; vs (Bad Kissinger: Verlag der Tagesfragen, 1891).

Banadietrich, opera in three acts by Siegfried Wagner; libretto by the composer; January 23, 1910, Karlsruhe.

Bankette, Die, opera by Georg Katzer; libretto by Gerhard Müller after Plato; April 30, 1988, East Berlin.

Bär, Der, opera in three acts by Kuno Stierlin; libretto by H. Brenner after Ludwig Uhland and Justinius Kerner; November 27, 1938, Osnabrück.

Bär, Der, opera in one act by Erwin Dressel; libretto by Robert Schnell after Anton Chekhov; June 23, 1963, Radio Bern.

Barbier von Sevilla, Der, Singspiel in four acts by Friedrich Benda; libretto by G. F. W. Grossmann after Beaumarchais; May 7, 1776, Leipzig; vs (Leipzig: Schwickert, 1779).

Bärenhäuter, Der, opera in three acts by Arnold Mendelssohn; libretto by Hermann Wette; February 9, 1900, Berlin.

Barfüssele, opera in a prologue and two scenes by Richard Heuberger; libretto by Victor Léon after B. Auerbach; March 11, 1905, Dresden; vs (Leipzig: M. Brockhaus [1905]).

Bartelby, opera in two acts by Walter Aschaffenburg; libretto by Jay Leyda; November 12, 1964, Oberlin, Ohio.

Bartleby, opera in one act by Manfred Niehaus; libretto by the composer after Herman Melville; May 5, 1967, Cologne and Berlin.

Basilius (Der königliche Schäfer, oder **Basilius in Arcadien),** opera in three acts by Reinhard Keiser; libretto by Friedrich Christian Bressand after Flaminio Parisetti; 1694, Hamburg; the music is lost.

Baskische Venus, Die, opera in two acts by Hermann Hans Wetzler; libretto by Lini Wetzler after Prosper Mérimée; November 18, 1928, Leipzig.

Bassa [Pascha] von Tunis, Der, *Operette* in one act by Franz Holly; libretto by Carl Friedrich Henisch; January 6, 1774, Berlin; vs (Berlin, 1775).

Bassgeige, Die, opera in one act by Hans Poser; libretto by Eric Spiess; April 19, 1964, Mainz.

Bassgeige, Die, opera semiseria in five scenes by Arghyris Kounadis; libretto by Siegfried Schoenbohm, Wolfgang Reuter, and the composer after Anton Chekhov; 1977–1978.

Bastien und Bastienne, opera by Ferdinand Kauer; anonymous libretto; 1790, Vienna.

Bauer im Fegefeuer, Der, opera in one act by Manfred Grafe; libretto by the composer after Hans Sachs; February 6, 1958, Meissen.

Bauernhochzeit, opera in one act by Herrmann Reutter; libretto by H. Roth after Johann Gottfried von Herder; February 15, 1967, Mainz.

Bauernliebe, opera in two acts by Ferdinand Kauer; libretto by Franz Xaver Huber; 1802, Vienna; libretto (Vienna: M. A. Schmidt, 1802).

Beatrice Cenci, opera in three acts by Berthold Goldschmidt; libretto by Martin Esslin after Percy Bysshe Shelley; April 13, 1953, London.

Beglückte Florindo, Der, opera in three acts by George Frideric Handel; libretto by Heinrich Hinsch after Ovid; January 1708, Hamburg; most of the music is lost; libretto (Hamburg, 1708; repr. ed. Ellen T. Harris, in *The Librettos of Handel's Operas*, I [New York and London: Garland Publishing, 1989]).

Beiden Figaro, Die, comic opera in two acts by Conradin Kreutzer; libretto by Georg Friedrich Treitschke after Johann Friedrich Jünger; August 13, 1840, Brunswick.

Beiden Neffen, Die. See *Der Onkel aus Boston.*

Belagerungszustand, Der, opera in a prologue and two acts by Milko Keleman; libretto by the composer and Joachim Hess after Albert Camus; January 13, 1970, Hamburg.

Bellerophon, oder Das in die Preussische Krone verwandelte Wagen-Gestirn auf dem frohen Vermählungs-Feste, opera by Christoph Graupner; libretto by Barthold Feind after Pierre Corneille; November 28, 1708, Hamburg; libretto (Hamburg: n.p., 1708).

Bellerophon, Singspiel in three acts by Peter Winter; libretto by J. F. von Binder; July 29, 1785, Munich.

Belmont[e] und Constanze, oder Die Entführung aus dem Serail, Singspiel in three acts by Christian Ludwig Dieter; libretto by Christoph Friedrich Bretzner; August 27, 1784, Stuttgart.

Belsazar, opera by Georg Philipp Telemann; 1723; three arias extant.

Belsazar, opera in one act by Hans Peró; libretto by Paul Knepler; March 12, 1929, Hamburg.

Belshazar, music drama in three parts by Volker David Kirchner; libretto by Harald Weirich; January 25, 1986, Munich.

Beowulf, opera by John Julia Scheffler (1867–1942) (unfinished).

Berenice und Lucilla, oder Das tugenhafte Lieben, opera by Christoph Graupner; libretto by Osiander after Aurelio Aureli; March 4, 1710, Darmstadt.

Bergfest, Das, Singspiel in two acts by Wenzel Müller; libretto by Karl Friedrich Hensler; 1803, Vienna.

Berggeist, Der, opera in three acts by Kuno Stierlin; libretto by Theodor Bohn; April 28, 1921, Münster.

Bergknappen, Die, opera by Karl Hellwig; April 27, 1820, Dresden.

Bergknappen, Die, opera by Johannes Paleschko (1877–1932) (not performed).

Bergknappen, Die, opera by Johannes Quaritsch (1882–) (not performed).

Bergkönig, Der, opera in three acts by Peter Lindpaintner; libretto by Carl Hanisch; January 30, 1825, Stuttgart.

Bergmönch, Der, opera in three acts by Joseph Maria Wolfram; libretto by Karl Borromäus von Miltitz; March 14, 1830, Dresden.

Bergsee, Der, opera in three acts by Julius Bittner; libretto by the composer; November 9, 1911, Vienna; vs (Berlin: K. Fliegel & Co., ca. 1911); libretto (Berlin: Jungdeutscher Verlag, ca. 1911).

Bergsturz, Der, opera in three acts by Joseph Weigl; libretto by Johann Anton Friedrich Reil; December 19, 1812, Vienna.

Bergwerk von Falun, Das, opera by Alma Mahler-Werfel (1879–1964) (not performed).

Bergwerk von Falun, Das, opera by Armin Schibler; composed 1953.

Beständige Argenia, Die, Singspiel by Johann Valentin Meder; 1680, Reval; fs, *EDM*, LXVIII (Mainz: BBS, 1973).

Bestrafte Rachbegierde, Die, Singspiel–marionette opera by Franz Joseph Haydn; ca. 1779; the music is lost.

Besuch auf dem Lande, Der, comic opera in two acts by Conradin Kreutzer; July 8, 1826, Vienna.

Besuch in Saint-Cyr, Ein, opera in three acts by Josef Dessauer; libretto by Eduard von Bauernfeld; May 6, 1838, Dresden.

Betrug durch Aberglauben, oder **Die Schatzgräber,** Singspiel in two acts by Karl Ditters von Dittersdorf; libretto by Ferdinand Eberl; October 3, 1786, Vienna.

Bettelstudent, Der, oder **Das Donnerwetter,** opera in two acts by Peter Winter; libretto by Paul Weidmann after Miguel de Cervantes' story *La Cueva de Salamanca*; February 2, 1785, Munich; vs (1789).

Bettler Namenlos, Der, opera in three acts by Robert Heger; libretto by the composer; April 8, 1932, Munich.

Bezauberte Leyer, Die, oder **Alerich und Zaïde,** comic magic opera by Vincenz Franz Tuczek; libretto by Joseph Alois Gleich; 1809, Vienna; libretto (Vienna: J. B. Wallishausser, 1809).

Bezauberten, Die, Singspiel in one act by Johann André; libretto by the composer after Marie Favart; October 18, 1777, Berlin; vs (Berlin: Christian Friedrich Himburg, 1777).

Bianca und Giuseppe, oder **Die Franzosen vor Nizza,** opera in four acts by Johann Friedrich Kittl; libretto by Richard Wagner after Heinrich König; February 19, 1848, Prague.

Bibiana, oder **Die Kapelle im Walde,** opera in three acts by Johann Peter Pixis; libretto by Louis Lax after Heinrich Cuno; October 8, 1829, Aachen.

Bildnis des Dorian Gray, Das, opera by Rudolf Bella (1890–1973) (not performed).

Bildnis des Dorian Gray, Das, opera in three acts by Roderich Kleemann; libretto by Ingebord Kleemann; May 21, 1965, Zwickau.

Blanda, oder **Die silberne Birke,** opera by Johann Wenceslaus Kalliwoda; libretto by Friedrich Kind; November 29, 1847, Prague.

Blau Bart, opera by Camillo Togni; libretto after Georg Trakl; December 14, 1977, Venice.

Blaue Berg, Der, opera in two acts by Egon Lustgarten; libretto by Lia Spaun-Matthus; May 4, 1945, New York.

Blindekuh, operetta in three acts by Johann Strauss, Jr.; libretto by Rudolf Kneisel; December 18, 1878, Vienna.

Blonde Liselott, Die, Singspiel in three acts by Eduard Künneke; libretto by Richard Kessler; December 25, 1927, Altenburg; vs (Berlin: B&B, 1928); revised as *Liselott* in six scenes, February 17, 1932, Berlin.

Blumen von Hiroshima, Die, opera in three acts by Jean Kurt Forest; libretto by the composer after Editha Morris; June 21, 1967, Weimar.

Blumenmädchen, Das, Singspiel in one act by Friedrich Benda; libretto by Friedrich Rochlitz; July 16, 1806, Berlin.

Boabdil, der letzte Maurenkönig, opera in three acts by Moritz Moszkowski; libretto by Carl Wittkowsky; April 21, 1892, Berlin.

Bon vivant, Le, oder **Die Leipziger Messe,** opera by Reinhard Keiser; libretto by Barthold Feind; 1710, Hamburg; libretto (Hamburg: J. N. Gennagel, 1710).

Boom-Boom Land, aleatory "opera for children and grownups" by Georg Katzer; libretto after Roald G. Dobrovensky's tale *Behind the Treble Clef*; September 30, 1978, East Berlin.

Borgia, opera by Paul Hoeffler (1895–1949) (not performed).

Boris Goudenow, opera by Johann Mattheson; 1710, Hamburg.

Böse Weib, Das, opera in two acts by Arnold Hufeld; libretto after Hans Sachs; February 5, 1939, Tilsit.

Brandenburger Tor, Das, opera by Giacomo Meyerbeer; 1814 (not performed).

Braut von Messina, Die, opera in four acts by Julius Mai; libretto by the composer after Friedrich Schiller; December 11, 1904, Bern.

Bremer Stadtmusikanten, Die, opera in two acts by Richard Mohaupt; libretto by Theo Phil after the brothers Grimm; July 15, 1949, Bremen; vs (Berlin-Grunewald: J. Oertel, 1949).

Bremer Stadtmusikanten, Die, opera in two scenes by Hans Bergese; libretto by Annelies Schmolke after the brothers Grimm; December 20, 1949, Cologne.

Bremer Stadtmusikanten, Die, opera in three scenes by Hans Auenmüller; libretto by Hans-Hermann Krug after the brothers Grimm; July 22, 1972, Thale.

Brücke von San Luis Rey, Die, opera in one act by Hermann Reutter; libretto by the composer after Thornton Wilder; June 20, 1954, Frankfurt radio; December 18, 1954, Essen (staged).

Bruder Lustig, opera in three acts by Siegfried Wagner; libretto by the composer; October 13, 1905, Hamburg; libretto (Leipzig: M. Brockhaus, 1905).

Brüderlein Hund, school opera in three scenes by Cesar Bresgen; libretto by Ludwig Andersen; November 12, 1953, Nuremberg; vs (Mainz: BBS, c. 1953).

Brüderlein und Schwesterlein, opera in three acts by Karl Friedrich; libretto by the composer after Eduard Mörike; March 26, 1949.

Cadmus, opera by Johann Paul Kunzen; 1720, possibly Brunswick.

Cagliostro, opera in three acts by Albert Lortzing; libretto by the composer after Eugène Scribe and J. H. Vernoy de Saint-Georges; composed 1849–1850.

Cagliostro, opera in a prelude and two acts by Otto Wartisch; libretto by the composer; April 3, 1924, Gotha.

Cagliostro in Wien, operetta in three acts by Johann Strauss, Jr.; libretto by F. Zell [Camillo Walzel] and Richard Genée; February 27, 1875, Vienna.

Cara Mustapha (Der unglückliche Gross-Vezier Cara Mustapha), opera in three acts by Johann Wolfgang Franck; libretto by Lucas von Bostel; January 1686, Hamburg; *Arien* (Hamburg: Samuel Viöngen Buchhändler, 1686).

Caramo, oder **Die Fischerstechen,** comic opera in three acts by Albert Lortzing; libretto by the composer after Amabale Vilain de Saint-Hilaire and Paul Duport's *Cosimo*, set by E. P. Prévost (1835, Paris); September 20, 1839, Leipzig.

Carlos Fioras, oder **Der Stumme in der Sierra Morenaza,** opera in three acts by Ferdinand Fränzl; libretto by Wilhelm Vogel; October 16, 1810, Munich.

Carneval von Venedig, Der. See *Der angenehme Betrug.*

Cartouche, comic opera in one act by Heinrich Hofmann; libretto by W. Fellechner; 1869, Berlin.

Casanova, operetta by Ralph Benatzky using melodies of Johann Strauss, Jr.; September 1, 1928, Berlin.

Casanova in der Schweiz, opera in five scenes by Paul Burkhard; libretto by Richard Schweitzer; February 20, 1943, Zurich.

Casanova in Murano, comic opera in three acts by Albert Lortzing; libretto by the composer after the French vaudeville *Casanova au Fort Saint-André* by Charles Victor Varin, Étienne Arago, and Desvergers [Armand Chapeau]; December 31, 1841, Leipzig; vs ed. F. L. Schubert (Leipzig: B&H, 1842); vs ed. Mark Lothar, text ed. Siegfried Mitlacher (Berlin-Grunewald: Johannes Oertel, 1942); libretto in *Albert Lortzings komische Opern*, I (Leipzig: n.p., 1847).

Casilda, opera in four acts by Ernst II; libretto by N. Tenelli [J. H. Millenet]; March 23, 1851, Gotha.

Cephalus und Prokris, opera in one act by Johann Friedrich Reichardt; libretto by K. W. Ramler; July 7, 1777, Hamburg; vs (Leipzig: Schwickert, 1781).

Cherubina, opera in two acts by Leo Blech; libretto by David Kunhardt; 1894; vs (Aachen: T. Naus, c. 1894).

Christelflein, Das, *Spieloper* in two acts by Hans Pfitzner; libretto by the composer after Ilse von Stach; music developed from Pfitzner's incidental music (1906) to Stach's Christmas play; December 11, 1917, Munich; vs (Berlin: A. Fürstner, 1918); vs (London: Fürstner, c. 1943).

Christliche Judenbraut, Die, opera in two acts by Johann Baptist Paneck; libretto by Franz Xaver Girzik; October 18, 1789, Budapest.

Circe, opera in five acts by Reinhard Keiser; libretto by Johann Philipp Praetorius and J. J. van Mauritius; also arias by Leonardo Vinci, George Frideric Handel, and Johann Adolf Hasse; March 1, 1734, Hamburg.

Circe, opera in three acts by Werner Egk; libretto by the composer after Pedro Calderón's *El major encanto amor*; December 18, 1948, Berlin; vs (Mainz: Schott, 1947); revised as *Siebzehn Tage und vier Minuten,** 1966, Stuttgart (see p. 219).

Clarissa, oder **Das unbekannte Dienstmädchen,** opera by Johann Abraham Peter Schulz; 1775, Berlin.

Claudia amata, opera in three acts by Johannes Driessler; libretto by Bettina Brix after Gottfried Keller's *Eugenia*; November 22, 1952, Münster; vs (Kassel: Bär, 1952?).

Claudine von Villa Bella, opera in three acts by Johann André; libretto after Goethe; 1778, Gotha.

Claudine von Villa Bella, opera in three acts by Ignaz von Beecke; libretto after Goethe; June 13, 1780, Vienna.

Claudine von Villa Bella, opera in three acts by Johann Christoph Kienlen; libretto after Goethe; September 9, 1810, Munich.

Cleopatra, opera by Johann Sigismund Kusser; libretto by Friedrich Christian Bressand; 1691, Brunswick; the music is lost.

Coeur As, intermezzo in three acts by Eduard Künneke; libretto by Emil Tschirsch and Otto Berg after Eugène Scribe, October 31, 1913, Dresden; vs (Berlin: O. Wiede, c. 1940).

Colmal, opera in three acts by Peter Winter; libretto by Matthäus von Collin after Ossian; September 15, 1809, Munich.

Contarini, oder **Die Verschwörung zu Padua,** opera in five acts by Henry Hugh Pierson; libretto by M. E. Lindau; April 16, 1872, Hamburg; revived as *Fenice*, April 24, 1883, Dessau.

Corinna, opera in one act by Wolfgang Fortner; libretto by Heiner Schmidt after Gerard Nerval; October 3, 1958, Berlin.

Corsar, Der, opera by Robert Schumann; libretto by O. Marbach after Lord Byron's poem; begun in 1844 but left unfinished.

Costanza sforzata, La/Die bezwungene Beständigkeit, oder **Die listige Rache des Sueno,** opera by Reinhard Keiser; libretto by Barthold Feind; October 11, 1706, Hamburg; libretto in *Barthold Feindes Italienische-Deutsche Gedichte* (Hamburg: Stade, 1708).

Cress ertrinkt, opera in three acts by Wolfgang Fortner; libretto by Andreas Zeitler; June 4, 1931, Bad Pyrmont.

Cyrus und Astyages, opera in three acts by Ignaz Franz von Mosel; libretto by Matthäus von Collin after Pietro Metastasio's *Ciro riconosciuto*; June 13, 1818, Vienna.

Dagmar, opera in three acts by Kurt Striegler; libretto by Robert Bosshart after T. Storm; March 18, 1932, Dresden.

Dame im Traum, opera in three acts by Franz Salmhofer; libretto by Ernst Decsey and Gustav Holm; December 26, 1935, Vienna.

Dame Kobold, opera in three acts by Felix Weingartner; libretto by the composer after Pedro Calderón; February 23, 1916, Darmstadt; vs (Vienna: UE, 1916); libretto (Vienna: UE, 1916).

Dame Kobold, opera in three acts by Kurt von Wolfurt; libretto by E. Kurt Fischer after Pedro Calderón; March 14, 1940, Kassel.

Dämona, das kleine Höckerweibchen, opera by Vincenz Franz Tuczek; May 29, 1805, Pest.

Daniel in der Löwengrube. See *Baals Sturz.*

Dankgefühl einer Geretteten, monodrama by Johann Nepomuk Hummel; March 21, 1799, Vienna.

Dantons Tod, opera by Hanns Eisler; libretto after Georg Büchner's play; 1929, Berlin.

Daphnis und Chloe, opera in one act by Ewald Nacke; June 1913, Hamburg.

Das kommt davon (Wenn Sardakai auf Reisen geht), opera in two acts by Ernst Krenek; libretto by the composer; June 27, 1970, Hamburg.

Das war ich, "Dorfidylle" in one act by Leo Blech; libretto by Richard Batka after Johann Hutt; October 6, 1902, Dresden; vs (Berlin: B&B, 1902).

Des Adlers Horst, opera in three acts by Franz Gläser; libretto by K. von Holtei after Johanna Schopenhauer; December 29, 1832, Berlin.

Des Esels Schatten, school opera in a prologue and six scenes after Richard Strauss, orchestrated by Karl Haussner; libretto by Hans Adler after Christoph Martin Wieland's novel *Die Abderiten* (1774); June 7, 1964, Ettal, Bavaria (private); October 28, 1964, Naples (public).

Des Falkners Braut, opera in three acts by Heinrich Marschner; libretto by Wilhelm August Wohlbrück after Karl Spindler; March 10, 1832, Leipzig.

Des Kaisers Dichter, opera in three acts by Clemens von Franckenstein; libretto by Rudolf Lothar [Rudolf Spitzer]; November 2, 1920, Hamburg.

Des Kaisers neue Kleider, opera in five scenes by Eberhard Werdin; libretto by the composer after Hans Christian Andersen; June 29, 1948, Leverkusen.

Des Kaisers neue Kleider, school opera in two acts by Fritz Westien; libretto by the composer; April 1, 1957, Weimar.

Des Kaisers neue Kleider, opera in five scenes by Bertold Hummel; libretto by Oscar Gitzinger after Hans Christian Andersen; June 19, 1957, Freiburg/Bresgau.

Des Kaisers neueste Kleider, school opera in one act by Otto Kaufmann; libretto by the composer after Hans Christian Andersen; November 13, 1954, Münster.

Des Simplicius Simplicissimus Jugend, opera in three acts by Karl Amadeus Hartmann; libretto by the composer and Wolfgang Petzer after H. J. C. Grimmelshausen; October 22, 1949, Cologne; vs (Heidelberg: Süddeutscher Musikverlag, c. 1949).

Des Teufels Lustschloss, Singspiel in two acts by Christian Ludwig Dieter; libretto by August von Kotzebue; 1802, Stuttgart; the music is lost.

Desiderius, Koenig der Longobarden, opera in a prologue, three acts, and an epilogue by Reinhard Keiser; libretto by Barthold Feind; July 26, 1709, Hamburg; libretto (Hamburg: n.p., 1709).

Diana, oder **Der sich rächende Cupido,** opera in three acts by Reinhard Keiser; libretto by Johann Ulrich König; April 1712, Hamburg.

Diana von Solange, opera in five acts by Ernst II; libretto by Otto Prechtler; December 5, 1858, Coburg.

Dido, Singspiel–marionette opera by Franz Joseph Haydn; 1778; the music is lost.

Dido, opera in three acts by Bernhard Klein; libretto by Ludwig Rellstab; October 15, 1823, Berlin.

Diener zweier Herren, Der, opera in three acts by Arthur Kusterer; libretto by the composer after Carlo Goldoni; March 3, 1936, Freiburg.

Diener zweier Herren, Der, opera in three acts by Waldemar Bloch; libretto by the composer after Carlo Goldoni; June 17, 1961, Graz; vs ed. composer (Vienna: Doblinger, c. 1960).

Dinorah, oder **Die Turnerfarht nach Hütteldorf,** parody of Giacomo Meyerbeer's *Dinorah (Le Pardon de Ploërmel)* (1859, Paris) by Franz von Suppé; May 4, 1865, Vienna.

Diocletianus, opera in a prologue and three acts by Johann Wolfgang Franck; libretto by Lucas von Bostel; March 6, 1682, Hamburg.

Doktor Eisenbart, opera in three acts by Hermann Zilcher; libretto by Hermann W. von Waltershausen after Otto Falckenberg; May 25, 1922, Leipzig and Mannheim; vs (Leipzig: B&H, 1921).

Doktor Eisenbart, opera in three acts by Alfred Böckhamann; libretto by the composer; September 4, 1954, Weimar.

Doktor Faust, opera by Ignaz Walter; libretto by Heinrich Gottlieb Schmieder after Goethe; December 28, 1797, Bremen.

Doktor Fausts Höllenfahrt, opera in one act by Hans Ulrich Engelmann; libretto after Klabund [Alfred Henschke]; June 11, 1951, Hamburg radio; October 7, 1962, Nuremberg.

Doktor Johannes Faust, opera in three acts by Hermann Reutter; libretto by Ludwig Andersen; May 26, 1936, Frankfurt; revised June 8, 1955, Stuttgart.

Don Cesar, operetta in three acts by Rudolf Dellinger; libretto by Oscar Walther [Oscar Friedrich Kunel] after the French play *Don César de Bazan* of Adolphe Phillipe d'Ennery and Pinel Dumanoir; March 28, 1885, Hamburg.

Don Gil von den grünen Hosen, "musikalische Komödie" in three acts by Walter Braunfels; libretto by the composer after Tirso de Molina; 1924, Munich; fs (Vienna and New York: UE, c. 1923); vs the same.

Don Juan in der Fremde, opera in two acts by Hans Haug; libretto by Dominique Müller; December 5, 1930, Basel.

Don Juan und Faust, opera in three acts by Hermann Reutter; libretto by Ludwig Andersen and the composer after Christian Dietrich Grabbe; June 14, 1950, Stuttgart; vs (Mainz: BSS, 1950).

Don Juans Ende, opera in three acts by Gustav Drechsel; libretto by the composer and J. Larska; May 15, 1930, Ansbach.

Don Juans letztes Abenteuer, opera in three acts by Paul Graener; libretto by Otto Anthes; June 11, 1914, Leipzig.

Don Juans Sohn, opera in one act by Hermann Wunsch; libretto by the composer after Almquist and Hauser; January 31, 1928, Vienna.

Don Pedros Heimkehr, opera in three acts with music by W. A. Mozart and by Hans Erismann; libretto by Oscar Wäterlin and Werner Galusser after Lorenzo da Ponte and Giovanni Battista Varesco; January 19, 1952, Zurich.

Don Quichote, der sinnreicher Junker von der Mancha, opera in three acts by Anton Beer-Walbrunn; libretto by Georg Fuchs; January 1, 1908, Munich.

Don Quichotte, operetta by Richard Heuberger; libretto by Heinz Reichert and Fritz Grünbaum; 1910, Vienna; vs (Vienna: L. & S. Natzler, c. 1910).

Don Quichotte der Löwenritter, opera by Georg Philipp Telemann; 1761.

Don Quijote, opera in four scenes by Gerhard Maasz; libretto by Dirks Paulun; October 24, 1947, Hamburg.

Don Quixote, opera in three acts by Wilhelm Kienzl; libretto by the composer after Miguel de Cervantes; November 18, 1898, Berlin.

Don Quixote der Zweyte (Don Chisciotte), Singspiel in two acts by Karl Ditters von Dittersdorf; libretto by the composer; February 4, 1795, Oels.

Don Quixote in dem Mohrengebirge, Singspiel by A. Müller; anonymous libretto; 1727, Hamburg.

Don Quixotte, opera by Ignaz von Beecke; anonymous libretto; 1788, Berlin.

Donna Diana, opera in three acts by Heinrich Hofmann; libretto by Carl Wittkowsky after Agustin Moreto y Cabeña; 1886, Berlin.

Donna Juanita, operetta in three acts by Franz von Suppé; libretto by F. Zell [Camillo Walzel] and Richard Genée; February 21, 1880, Vienna.

Doppelgängerin, Die, opera in three acts by Jan Meyerowitz; libretto by the composer after Gerhard Hauptmann's *Winterballade* (1917); January 29, 1967, Hanover; performed subsequently under the title *Winterballade*.

Dorf im Gebirge, Das, opera in two acts by Joseph Weigl; libretto by August von Kotzebue; April 17, 1798, Vienna; libretto (Königsberg: G. K. Haberland, 1814).

Dorf ohne Glocke, Das, opera in three acts by Eduard Künneke; libretto by Arpad Pasztor; 1919, Berlin; vs (Berlin: Drei-Masken-Verlag, c. 1919).

Dorfbarbier, Der, Singspiel in two acts by Johann Adam Hiller; libretto by Christian Felix Weisse after J.-M. Sédaine's *Blaise le savetier,* set by F. A. D. Philidor (1759, Paris); 1771, Leipzig; vs (Leipzig: Bernhard Christoph Breitkopf und Sohn, 1771); libretto (Berlin: C. U. Ringmacher, 1776).

Dorfdeputierten, Die, opera in three acts by Ernst Wilhelm Wolf; libretto by Gottlob Ephraim Heermann after Carlo Goldoni's *Il Feudataris;* June 15, 1772, Berlin; vs (Weimar: Karl Ludolf Hoffmann, 1773); libretto (Berlin: C. U. Ringmacher, 1774).

Dorfdeputierten, Die, opera in three acts by Johann Lukas Schubaur; libretto by Gottlob Ephraim Heermann; May 8, 1783, Munich.

Dorfdeputierten, Die, Singspiel in two acts by Christian Ludwig Dieter; libretto probably by Gottlob Ephraim Heermann after Carlo Goldoni; October 1786, Stuttgart.

Dorfgala, Der, opera in two acts by Anton Schweitzer; libretto by Friedrich Wilhelm Gotter; June 30, 1772, Weimar; vs (Leipzig: Schwichert, 1777).

Dorfmusikanten, Die, opera by Karel Weis; libretto after a folk story by Josef Kajetán Tyl; April 29, 1907, Prague.

Dorfschule, Die, opera in one act by Felix Weingartner; libretto by the composer; May 13, 1920, Vienna; vs (Vienna: UE, 1919); libretto, the same.

Dorian, opera in five scenes by Hans Leger; libretto by Caroline Creutzer after Oscar Wilde; March 24, 1939, Karlsruhe.

Dorian Gray, opera in eight scenes by Charles Flick-Steger; libretto by Olaf Pedersen after Oscar Wilde; March 1, 1930, Aussig.

Dorian Gray, opera in nine scenes by Robert Hanell; libretto by the composer after Oscar Wilde; June 9, 1962, Dresden.

Doris, "ein musikalisches Schaeferspiel" in two acts by Johann Georg Schürer; anonymous libretto; February 13, 1747, Dresden.

Dornröschen, opera by Karl Mangold; libretto by Eduard Duller; 1851, Darmstadt.

Dornröschen, fairy tale in a prologue and three acts by Engelbert Humperdinck; libretto by E. B. Ebelings-Filhès after Charles Perrault; November 12, 1902, Frankfurt; vs (Leipzig: M. Brockhaus, 1902).

Dornröschen, opera in three acts by Franz Höfer; libretto by Max Müller; November 24, 1918, Nuremberg.

Dornröschen, opera in a prologue and four scenes by Max Herre; libretto by J. C. Brunnes; March 3, 1929, Augsburg.

Dornröschen, Singspiel in four acts by Cesar Bresgen; libretto by Otto Reuther; April 15, 1942, Strasbourg; vs (Potsdam: L. Voggenreiter, 1941).

Dorval, der vierjährige Posten, opera in one act by Louis Zehntner; libretto by the composer after Theodor Körner; April 4, 1913, Basel; revised as *Amfeld der Söldner.*

Drei Walzer, operetta in three acts by Oscar Straus; libretto by Paul Knepler and Armin Robinson; 1935, Zurich.

Drei Wünsche, Die, Singspiel in three acts by Carl Loewe; libretto by Ernst Raupach; February 18, 1834, Berlin.

Drei Wünsche, Die, operetta in a prelude and three acts by Carl Michael Ziehrer; libretto by L. Krenn and C. Lindau; March 9, 1901, Vienna.

Dreispitz, Der, opera in three acts by Hans Korman; libretto by Carl Willnau after Pedro Antonio de Alarcón; February 18, 1936, Altenberg.

Drey Töchter Cecrops, Die, Singspiel in a prologue and five acts by Johann Wolfgang Franck; libretto by Aurora von Königsmarck; 1679, Ansbach; revived in 1680, Hamburg, with new music by Nicolaus Adam Strungk (which led Johann Mattheson to attribute the score to Strungk).

Dumme Gärtner aus dem Gebirge, Der, oder **Die zween Anton,** Singspiel in two acts by Benedikt Schack and Franz Xaver Gerl; libretto by Emanuel Schikaneder; July 12, 1789, Vienna; vs (Bonn, n.d.); first of Schikaneder's seven "Anton" Singspiels.

Durchmarsch, Der, oder **Der Alte muss bezahlen,** opera by Vincenz Franz Tuczek; libretto by Joachim Perinet; November 30, 1808, Vienna; a sequel to *Die christliche Judenbraut.**

Dybuk, Der, opera in three acts by Karlheinz Füssl; libretto by Helmut Wagner after An-Ski; September 26, 1970, Karlsruhe; libretto (Vienna: UE, 1968).

Echo und Narcissus, opera in three acts by Georg Bronner; libretto by Friedrich Christian Bressand; 1693, Brunswick.

Edle Rache, Die, comic opera in two acts by Franz Süssmayr; libretto by Franz Xaver Huber; August 27, 1795, Vienna.

Egon und Emilie, opera in one act by Ernst Toch; libretto by Christian Morgenstern; October 21, 1928, Mannheim; vs (Mainz: BSS, 1928).

Ehrlichkeit und Liebe, *Schauspiel* with songs in one act by Ernst Wilhelm Wolf; libretto by C. J. Wagenseil; 1776, Weimar; vs (Leipzig: Johann Gottlob Immanuel Breitkopf, 1782).

Eifersüchtige Trinker, Der, opera in one act by Max Ettinger; libretto by Friedrich Freksa [Kurt Friedrich]; February 7, 1925, Nuremberg, together with the composer's *Juana.**

Eiserne Heiland, Der, opera in three acts by Max von Oberleithner; libretto by Bruno Hardt-Warden and Ignaz Michael Welleminsky; Janaury 20, 1917, Vienna.

Eiserne Mann, Der, "österreichisches Volksmärchen" in three acts by Wenzel Müller; libretto by Leopold Huber; 1801; libretto (Vienna: M. A. Schmidt, 1801).

Eiserne Pforte, Die, grand opera in two acts by Joseph Weigl; libretto after E. T.A. Hoffmann; February 27, 1823, Vienna.

Ekkehard, opera in five acts by Johann Joseph Abert; libretto by the composer after Joseph Viktor von Scheffel; October 11, 1878, Berlin.

Elbondokani, Singspiel in one act by Johann Rudolf Zumsteeg; libretto by C. F. Haug; December 8, 1803, Stuttgart; vs (Leipzig: B&H, ca. 1802).

Electra, monodrama by Christian Cannabich; September 1, 1781, Mannheim; facsimile of fs, lib. ed. Thomas Bauman (New York and London: Garland Publishing, 1986).

Elga, opera in seven scenes by Erwin Lendvai; libretto by Martha von Zobeltitz after Gerhard Hauptmann's play (1905); December 6, 1916, Mannheim.

Elga, opera in two acts by Rudolf Weisshappel; libretto by the composer after Gerhard Hauptmann's play (1905); June 13, 1965, Vienna, ORF; January 28, 1967, Linz (staged).

Elisabeth von England (Die Königen), opera in four acts by Paul von Klenau; libretto by the composer; March 29, 1939, Kassel.

Elisene, Prinzessin von Bulgarien, opera in three acts by Joseph Rösler; libretto by Ignaz Franz Castelli after Louis Charles Caigniez's *La Forêt de Hermanstadt* (1805); October 18, 1807, Prague.

Elysium, "ein Vorspiel mit Arien" in one act by Anton Schweitzer; libretto by Johann Gregor Jacobi; January 18, 1770, Hanover.

Emerike, oder Die Zurechtweisung, comic opera in two acts by Adalbert Gyrowetz; December 11, 1807, Vienna; libretto (Vienna: J. B. Wallishausser, 1808).

Endlich allein, operetta in three acts by Franz Lehár; libretto by Alfred Maria Willner and Robert Bodanzky; February 10, 1914, Vienna; revised as *Schön ist die Welt.**

Engel kommt nach Babylon, Ein, opera in three acts by Rudolf Kelterborn; libretto by Friedrich Dürrenmatt after his play of the same name; June 5, 1977, Zurich.

Engelberger Talhochzeit, Eine, "Mundartoper" in three acts by Franz Joseph Meyer von Schauensee; 1781.

Englische Patriot, Der, Singspiel by Michael Haydn; ca. 1779, Vienna.

Enoch Arden, opera in a prologue and two acts by Max Wedert; libretto by Fritz Droop; October 7, 1909, Essen.

Enoch Arden, opera in four scenes by Ottmar Gerster; libretto by Carlo Michele von Levetzow after Alfred, Lord Tennyson; November 15, 1936, Düsseldorf.

Entzückende Frau, Eine, operetta in three acts by Richard Heuberger; libretto by Bruno Hardt-Warden, Rudolf Zindler; revision of *Ihre Excellenz**; 1940; vs and libretto (Berlin: J. Weinberger, 1940).

Erbe von Morley, Der, opera in three acts by Franz von Holstein; libretto by the composer; January 23, 1872, Leipzig.

Erbin von Montfort, Die, opera by Adolf Jensen; 1865; revised by Wilhelm Kienzl as *Turandot*, 1888.

Erbschaft, Die, opera by Dieter Nowka; September 27, 1960, Schwerin.

Eremit auf Formentara, Der, opera in two acts by Peter Ritter; libretto by August von Kotzebue; December 14, 1788, Mannheim.

Eremit auf Formentara, Der, Singspiel in two acts by Christian Ludwig Dieter; libretto by August von Kotzebue; January 10, 1791, Stuttgart.

Erindo, oder Die unsträfliche Liebe, opera in three acts by Johann Sigismund Kusser; libretto by Friedrich Christian Bressand; 1694, Hamburg; in *Arien, Duette und Chöre*, ed. Helmuth Osthoff, in *EDM*, II/3 (1938).

Erlösung, Die, opera in three acts by August Scharrer; libretto by Richard Specht after Guido Menasci's *La Redenzione*; November 21, 1895, Strasbourg.

Ermordung Cäsars, Die, opera in one act by Giselher Klebe; libretto by the composer after Shakespeare; September 30, 1959, Düsseldorf; vs (Berlin: B&B, 1960); libretto (Berlin: B&B, 1959).

Eroberte Jerusalem, Die, oder Arminda und Rinaldo, Singspiel in three acts by Georg Caspar Schürmann; libretto by Johann Samuel Müller after Giulio Cesare Corradi's *Gerusalemme liberata*; February 1722, Brunswick.

Eros und Psyche, opera in three acts by Max Zenger; libretto by Wilhelm Schriefer; January 11, 1901, Munich.

Errettete Unschuld, Die, oder Andromeda und Perseus, opera by Johann Wolfgang Franck; libretto after Pierre Corneille's *Andromède;* 1675, Ansbach.

Errettung Thebens, Die, opera in three acts by Rudolf Kelterborn; libretto by the composer; June 23, 1963, Zurich.

Erschaffene, gefallene und wieder aufgerichtete Mensch, Der (Adam und Eva), opera in a prologue and five acts by Johann Theile; libretto by Christian Richter; January 1678, Hamburg.

Erschöpfung der Welt, Die, opera by Mauricio Kagel; libretto by the composer; February 8, 1980, Stuttgart.

Erste Falte, Die, opera in one act by Theodor Leschetizky; libretto by S. H. Mosenthal; October 9, 1867, Prague.

Erwin und Elmire, "Schauspiel mit Gesang" by Johann André; libretto after Goethe; May 1775, Frankfurt; vs (Frankfurt and Leipzig: n.p., 1775).

Erwin und Elmire, Singspiel in one act by Georg Joseph Vogler; libretto after Goethe; December 12, 1781, Darmstadt.

Es war einmal . . . , opera in a prologue and three acts by Alexander vom Zemlinsky; libretto by Maximilian Singer after Holger Drachmann; January 22, 1900, Vienna.

Eselhaut, Die, oder **Die blaue Insel,** Spingspiel in three acts by Johann Nepomuk Hummel; libretto by Geway, March 10, 1814, Vienna.

Esther (Die liebreiche, durch Tugend und Schönheit erhöhte Esther), Singspiel by Nikolaus Adam Strungk; libretto by Johann Martin Köler; 1680, Hamburg.

Esther, opera in two acts by Robert Hanell; libretto by Günther Deicke; October 10, 1966, East Berlin.

Eulenspiegel, opera in two acts by Cyrill Kistler; libretto after August von Kotzebue; revised into one act by H. Levi and L. Sauer; 1889, Würzburg; vs (Bad Kissingen: Verlag der Musikalischen Tagesfragen, ca. 1890).

Evanthia, opera in one act by Paul Umlauft; libretto by the composer; July 30, 1893, Gotha.

Ewige Arzt, Der, school opera in five scenes by Cesar Bresgen; libretto by Paul Kamer after the brothers Grimm; February 10, 1956, Schwyz, Switzerland.

Ewige Feuer, Das, opera in one act by Richard Wetz; libretto by the composer; March 19, 1907, Düsseldorf.

Fabel in C, opera in one act by Heimo Erbse; libretto by the composer; September 2, 1952, Berlin.

Fabel vom seligen Schlächtermeister, Die, opera in three scenes by Rudolf Wagner; libretto by Hans von Savigny; May 23, 1964, Dresden.

Fächer, Der, opera in two acts by Ernst Kunz; libretto by the composer after Carlo Goldoni; May 5, 1929, Zurich.

Fächer, Der, opera in three acts by Ernst Toch; libretto by Ferdinand Lion; June 8, 1930, Königsberg.

Fall des grossen Richters in Israel, Simpson, Der, oder **Die abgekühlte Liebes-Rache der Debora,** opera by Christoph Graupner; libretto by Barthold Feind; 1709, Hamburg; libretto (Hamburg: Spieringische Schriften, 1709).

Fall ist noch weit seltner, Der, oder **Die geplagten Ehemänner,** Singspiel in two acts by Benedikt Schack, a sequel to Martín y Soler's *Una cosa rara*; libretto by Emanuel Schikaneder; May 10, 1790, Vienna.

Fall van Damm, Der, radio opera in one act by Hans Ulrich Engelmann; libretto by Markus Kutter; June 11, 1968, WDR radio, Cologne; April 9, 1974, Münster (staged).

Familie auf Isle de France, Die, opera in three acts by Conradin Kreutzer; libretto by Ignaz Castelli; 1805, Vienna; libretto (Vienna: J. B. Wallishausser, 1805).

Fanchon, das Leiermädchen, opera in three acts by Friedrich Heinrich Himmel; libretto by August von Kotzebue after Joseph Maria Pain and Jean Nicolas Bouilly; May 16, 1804, Berlin; vs (Leipzig: P. Reclam jun., 18–).

Fanferlieschen Schönefüsschen, opera by Kurt Schwertsik; libretto by Karin and Thomas Körner after a fairy tale by Clemens Brentano; November 24, 1983, Stuttgart.

Fantasio, opera in two acts by Ethyl Smyth; libretto by the composer after Alfred de Musset's play; May 24, 1898, Weimar.

Fassbinder, Der, Singspiel in one act by Johann Schenk; libretto by H. Faber; December 17 or 18, 1802, Vienna; libretto (Vienna: J. B. Wallishausser, 1802).

Fatinitza, operetta in three acts by Franz von Suppé; libretto by F. Zell [Camillo Walzel] and Richard Genée after Eugène Scribe's *Circassienne*, set by D. F. E. Auber (1861, Paris); January 5, 1876, Vienna.

Faule Hans, Der, opera in one act by Alexander Ritter; libretto by the composer after Felix Dahn; October 15, 1885, Munich.

Faust, opera in a prologue and four acts by Heinrich Zöllner; libretto by the composer after Goethe; October 19, 1887, Munich; vs (Leipzig: C. F. W. Siegel, 1887).

Faust I. Teil, music drama in four acts by Cyrill Kistler; libretto after Goethe; composed 1905.

Faust und Yorick, opera in one act by Wolfgang Rihm; libretto by Frithjof Hass after Jean Tardieu's play of the same name; October 7, 1977, Hanover.

Feindlichen Nachbarn, Die, chamber opera in one act by Paul Breuer; libretto by Erich Bormann after a story by Wilhelm Busch; January 21, 1949, Cologne.

Feldlager in Schlesien, Ein, Singspiel in three acts by Giacomo Meyerbeer; libretto by Ludwig Rellstab; December 7, 1844, Berlin; parts used for Meyerbeer's *L'Etoile du Nord* (1854, Paris).

Feldprediger, Der, operetta in three acts by Carl Millöcker; libretto by Hugo Wittmann and Alois Wohlmuth; October 31, 1884, Vienna.

Felsenmühle zu Estalières, Die, opera in two acts by Karl Gottlieb Reissiger; libretto by Karl Borromäus von Miltitz; April 10, 1831, Dresden.

Feodora, opera in one act by Conradin Kreutzer; libretto by August von Kotzebue; 1812, Stuttgart.

Feramors, opera in two acts by Anton Rubinstein; libretto by Julius Rodenberg after Thomas Moore's poem "Lalla Rookh"; February 24, 1863, Dresden; originally called *Lallah Rookh* but changed because of Félicien David's opera of the same name (1862, Paris).

Fest auf Haderslev, Ein, opera in three acts by Robert Heger; libretto by the composer; November 12, 1919, Nuremberg.

Fest auf Solhaug, Das, opera in three acts by Vilhelm Stenhammar; libretto by Marie von Borch after Henrik Ibsen; April 12, 1899, Stuttgart.

Fettlösschen, opera by Karl Heinz Wahren; libretto by the composer and Claus Henneberg after Guy de Maupassant's *Boule de Suif*; April 24, 1976, West Berlin.

Feuerprobe, Die, opera in one act by Walter Dost; libretto by Ernst Günther after August von Kotzebue; April 18, 1920, Plauen.

Fido amico, Il, oder Der getreue Freunde Hercules und Theseus, opera by Christoph Graupner; libretto by Breymann; 1708, Hamburg; libretto (Hamburg: n.p., 1708).

Findelkind, Das, oder **Unverhofft kömmt oft,** "Kinder-operette" in one act by Georg Benda; libretto by Christian Felix Weisse; ca. 1787, not performed; vs (Leipzig: Schwickertsche Verlag, ca. 1777).

Fingerhütchen, opera in one act by Heinrich Sutermeister; libretto by the composer after Conrad Ferdinand Meyer; February 12, 1950, Berlin.

Fischer un syne Fru, De, school opera in three acts by Kurt Brüggemann; libretto by the composer after the brothers Grimm; January 25, 1936, Hamburg.

Flammen, opera in one act by Franz Schreker; libretto by the composer and Dora Leen; April 24, 1902, Vienna (concert).

Flaschenpost vom Paradies, Die, opera in one act by Ernst Krenek; libretto by the composer; March 7, 1974, ORF, Vienna.

Flauto solo, "musikalisches Lustspiel" in one act by Eugen d'Albert; libretto by Hans von Wolzogen; November 12, 1905, Prague; vs ed. Egon Pollak (Berlin: B&B, c. 1905); libretto the same.

Flavius Bertaridus, opera by Georg Philipp Telemann; 1729.

Fleurette, oder **Näherin und Trompeter,** operetta by Jacques Offenbach; March 8, 1872, Vienna.

Florentinische Tragödie, Eine, opera in one act by Richard Flury; libretto by the composer after Oscar Wilde; April 9, 1929, Solothurn, Switzerland.

Flotte Bursche, operetta in one act by Franz von Suppé; libretto by Joseph Braun; April 18, 1863, Vienna.

Flucht nach der Schweiz, Die, Singspiel in two acts by Friedrich Wilhelm Kücken; libretto by Karl Blum; February 26, 1839, Berlin.

Folkunger, Die, opera in five acts by Edmund Kretschmer; libretto by S. H. Mosenthal; March 21, 1874, Dresden.

Fortunat, opera in three acts by Xaver Schnyder von Wartensee; libretto by Georg Döring; October 2, 1831, Frankfurt.

Forza dell'amore, La, oder . . . **Helena,** opera by Reinhard Keiser; libretto possibly by Barthold Feind; 1711, Hamburg.

Foscari, Die, opera by Max Zenger; 1863, Munich.

Frasquita, operetta in three acts by Franz Lehár; libretto by Alfred Maria Willner and Heinrich Reichert; May 12, 1922, Vienna; vs (Leipzig: J. Weinberger, 1922).

Frau, die weiss was sie will, Eine, operetta in three acts by Oscar Straus; libretto by A. Grünwald after L. Verneuil; September 1, 1932, Berlin; libretto (Berlin: Drei Masken Verlag, 1932).

Frauen von Troia, Die, opera in two acts by Heinz Röttger; libretto by Eva John; February 10, 1962, Dessau.

Frauenort, oder **Der Kaiser als Zimmermann,** opera by Karl August von Lichtenstein; Bamberg, 1814.

Fredegunda, opera in five acts by Reinhard Keiser; libretto by Johann Ulrich König after Francesco Silvani's *La Fredegonda*; March 4, 1715, Hamburg.

Freikorporal, Der, opera in three acts by Georg Vollerthun; libretto by Rudolf Lothar [Rudolf Spitzer] after Gustav Freytag; November 10, 1931, Hanover; vs (Berlin: E. Bote & G. Bock, 1931); libretto the same.

Fremde, Der, opera in four scenes by Hugo Kaun; libretto by Franz Rauch after *Gevatter Tod* of the brothers Grimm; February 23, 1920, Dresden.

Fremde Erde, opera in five acts by Karol Rathaus; libretto by Kamilla Palffy-Wanick; December 10, 1930, Berlin.

Fremdenführer, Der, operetta in a prelude and three acts by Carl Michael Ziehrer; libretto by L. Krenn and C. Lindau; October 11, 1902, Vienna.

Fremdling, Der, opera in three acts by Heinrich Vogl; libretto by Felix Dahn; May 7, 1899, Munich.

Freund deutscher Sitten, Der, Singspiel in three acts by Otto Carl Erdmann von Kospoth; libretto by G. W. Burmann; September 25, 1778, Berlin.

Fridolin, oder Der Gang nach dem Eisenhammer, Romantic opera in three acts by Conradin Kreutzer; libretto by Johann Anton Friedrich Reil after Friedrich von Schiller; December 16, 1837, Vienna.

Friedemann Bach, opera in three acts by Paul Graener; libretto by Rudolf Lothar after Albert Emil Brachvogel; November 13, 1931, Schwerin; vs (Berlin: B&B, 1931).

Friedensengel, Der, opera in three acts by Siegfried Wagner; libretto by the composer; March 4, 1926, Karlsruhe; vs (Bayreuth: C. Giessel, 1915).

Friederike, Singspiel in three acts by Franz Lehár; libretto by Ludwig Herzer [Ludwig Herzl] and Fritz Beda-Löhner [Fritz Löhner]; October 4, 1928, Berlin.

Friedliche Dörfchen, Das, allegorical Singspiel in one act by Wenzel Müller; libretto by Karl Friedrich Hensler; September 29, 1803, Vienna; libretto (Vienna: M. A. Schmidt, 1803).

Frohsinn und Schwärmerei, *Liederspiel* in one act by Friedrich Heinrich Himmel; libretto by Carl Alexander Herklots; March 9, 1801, Berlin.

Frühling, Der, oder Der Anton ist noch nicht tot, Singspiel in two acts, possibly by Benedikt Schack; libretto by Emanuel Schikaneder; June 18, 1790, Vienna; fourth of Schikaneder's seven "Anton" Singspiels; the work is lost.

Frühlings Erwachen, opera in three acts by Max Ettinger; libretto after Franz Wedekind's play; April 14, 1928, Leipzig.

Frühlingsnacht, opera in one act by Gerhard Schjelderup; libretto by the composer; May 1, 1908, Dresden; revised as *Liebesnächte*, October 18, 1934, Lübeck.

Fuersten der Longobarden, Die, opera in three acts by Ferdinand Kauer; libretto by J. A. Gleich; Vienna, 1808; libretto (Vienna: J. B. Wallishausser, 1808).

Fünf Minuten des Isaak Babel, Die, "scenic requiem" by Volker David Kirchner; libretto by the composer and Harald Weirich; 1980, Wuppertal.

25,000 Gulden, Die. see *Im Dunkel ist nicht gut munkeln.*

Fürstin Ninetta, operetta in three acts by Johann Strauss, Jr.; libretto by Hugo Wittmann and Julius Bauer; January 10, 1893, Vienna.

Fürstin von Granada, Die, oder **Der Zauberblick,** opera in five acts by Johann Christian Lobe; libretto by the composer and Philipp Carl Christian Sonderhausen; September 28, 1833, Weimar.

Füsse im Feuer, Die, opera in one act by Heinrich Sutermeister; libretto by the composer after Conrad Ferdinand Meyer; February 12, 1950, Berlin.

Füsse im Feuer, Die, opera in one act by Armin Schibler; libretto by the composer after Conrad Ferdinand Meyer; April 25, 1955, Zurich.

Galatea, "ein griechisches Märchen" in one act by Walter Braunfels; libretto by Silvia Baltus; January 26, 1930, Cologne; vs score ed. Hellmut Schnackenburg (Vienna: UE, c. 1929); libretto the same.

Galatea Elettronica, opera in two acts by Theo Goldberg; libretto by the composer; May 14, 1969, Bellingham, Washington.

Gärtnermädchen, Das, comic opera in three acts by Ernst Wilhelm Wolf; libretto by C. A. Musäus; 1769, Weimar; vs (Leipzig: B. C. Breitkopf & Sohn, 1774); libretto (Berlin: C. U. Ringmacher, 1775).

Gasparone, operetta in three acts by Carl Millöcker; libretto by F. Zell [Camillo Walzel] and Richard Genée; January 26, 1884, Vienna; vs (Leipzig: A. Cranz, 1884); libretto (New York: Samisch & Golman, 1885).

Gaudeamus, *Spieloper* in three acts by Engelbert Humperdinck; libretto by Robert Misch; March 18, 1919, Darmstadt; vs (Berlin: A. Fürstner, 1919).

Geburth Christi, Die, opera by Johann Theile; 1681, Hamburg.

Gefängnisse, "sinfonisches Drama" in three parts by Gerhard von Keussler; libretto by the composer; April 22, 1914, Prague.

Gefesselte Phantasie, Die, *Zauberspiel* with songs in two acts by Wenzel Müller; libretto by Ferdinand Raimund; January 8, 1828, Vienna.

Geheime Königreich, Das, opera in one act by Ernst Krenek; libretto by the composer; May 6, 1928, Wiesbaden and Cologne; fs, vs, and libretto (Vienna: UE, c. 1928).

Geheimnis des entwendeten Briefes, Das, chamber opera in seven scenes by Boris Blacher; libretto by Herbert Brauer after Edgar Allan Poe; February 16, 1975, Berlin.

Geisterbraut, Die, opera in three acts by Eugen of Württemberg; libretto by the composer after G. A. Bürger's poem; February 22, 1842, Breslau.

Geisterinsel, Die, Singspiel in three acts by Fridrich Fleischmann; libretto by Friedrich Wilhelm Gotter and Friedrich Hildebrand von Einsiedel after William Shakespeare's *The Tempest*; May 19, 1798, Weimar.

Geisterinsel, Die, opera in three acts by Johann Rudolf Zumsteeg; libretto by Friedrich Wilhelm Gotter and Friedrich Hildebrand von Einsiedel after William Shakespeare's *The Tempest*; November 7, 1798, Stuttgart; vs (Leipzig: B&H, 1799).

Geliebte Adonis, Der. See *Adonis*.

Geliebte Stimme, Die, opera in three acts by Jaromir Weinberger; libretto by R. Michel after the composer's Czech version; February 28, 1931, Munich; vs (Vienna: UE, 1930).

Gelöbnis, Das, opera in two acts by Cornelie van Oosterzee; libretto by Gertrud Klett and Luise Wittich after Richard Voss; May 1, 1910, Weimar.

Genesius, opera in three acts by Felix Weingartner; libretto by Hans Herrig; November 15, 1892, Berlin.

Genoveva, opera in four acts by Alexander Ecklebe; libretto by the composer; February 9, 1936, Berlin radio; April 22, 1937, Hagen, Germany (staged).

Genoveva, oder Die weisse Hirschkuh, Hanoverian drama in four scenes and an entr'acte by Detlev Müller-Siemens; libretto by Julie Schrader; 1977.

Gensericus (Der grosse König der Africanischen Wenden Gensericus als Rom- und Karthagens Überwinder), opera in a prologue and three acts by Johann Georg Conradi [also attributed to Johann Sigismund Kusser]; libretto by Christian Heinrich Postel; 1693, Hamburg; revised as *Sieg der Schönheit.**

Genueserin, Die, "grosse romantische Oper" in three acts by Peter Lindpaintner; libretto by Carl Philipp Berger; February 8, 1839, Vienna; libretto (Breslau: Grass, Barth & Co., ca. 1838).

Germanicus (Die errettete Unschuld, oder Germanicus, Römischer General), opera in three acts by Gottfried Grünewald; anonymous libretto; October 1704, Leipzig.

Gernot, opera by Eugen d'Albert; libretto by G. Kastropp; April 11, 1897, Mannheim; fs and vs (Leipzig: Breitkopf & Härtel, c. 1897).

Gervinus, der Narr von Untersberg, oder Ein patriotischer Wunsch, farce with songs in three acts by Franz von Suppé; libretto by A. Berla; July 1, 1849, Vienna.

Geschichte vom schönen Annerl, Die, opera in nine scenes by Leo Justinius Kauffmann; libretto by Eduard Reinacher and Erich Bormann after Clemens von Brentano; June 20, 1942, Strasbourg.

Geschiedene Frau, Die, operetta in three acts by Leo Fall; libretto by Victor Léon [Victor Hirschfeld]; December 23, 1908, Vienna; vs and libretto (Vienna: L. Doblinger, c. 1908).

Gespenstersonate, Die, opera in two acts by Julius Weismann; libretto by the composer after August Strindberg; December 19, 1930, Munich.

... Gestern an der Oder ... , opera in three acts by Jean Kurt Forest; libretto by the composer and J. A. Weindlich; February 17, 1962, Frankfurt/Oder.

Gestiefelte Kater, Der, oder Wie man das Spiel spielt, comic opera in two acts by Günther Bialas; libretto by Tankred Dorst after Ludwig Tieck; May 15, 1975, Schwetzingen.

Getreue Alceste, Die, opera in three acts by Georg Caspar Schürmann; libretto by Johann Ulrich König after Quinault's *Alceste*, 1674; February 1719, Brunswick.

Gewalt des Liedes, Die, comic opera in three acts by Peter Lindpaintner; libretto by Ignaz Vincenz Franz Castelli; March 13, 1836, Stuttgart.

Gewaltige Hahnrei, Der, opera in two acts by Berthold Goldschmidt; libretto by the composer after F. Crommelynck; February 14, 1932, Mannheim; vs (Vienna: UE, c. 1931).

Ghismonda, opera by Eugen d'Albert; libretto by the composer after Karl Immermann; November 28, 1895, Dresden.

Giuditta, opera by Paul Dessau; libretto by M. May; 1912; not performed.

Gläserne Berg, Der, "ein Weinachtsmärchen" by Walter Braunfels; libretto by Elsner and Örtel; 1928, Krefeld.

Gluckerich, Der, oder **Tugend und Tadel der Nützlichkeit,** musical burlesque in three acts by Erich Urbanner; libretto by Ruth von Magenburg after Guy de Maupassant; April 7, 1965, Radio Innsbruck; May 27, 1965, Vienna (staged).

Glückliche Ende, Das, opera in one act by Winfried Wolf; libretto by the composer; May 23, 1954, Nuremberg.

Glücksfischer, Der, opera in two acts by Mark Lothar; libretto by Walter Brandin; March 16, 1962, Nuremberg; vs (Hamburg: Sikorski, 1962).

Gogolori, Der, "Bavarian tale" by Winfried Hiller; libretto by Michael Ende; February 1985, Munich.

Goldene Kreuz, Das, opera in two acts by Ignaz Brüll; libretto by S. H. Mosenthal after A. H. J. Mélesville and Nicolâs Brazier; December 22, 1875, Berlin; fs, vs, and libretto (Berlin: E. Bote & G. Bock, ca. 1876); libretto (Leipzig: P. Reclam jun. [1910]).

Goldene Vogel, Der, opera in three acts by Leo Fall; libretto by Julius Wilhelm and Paul Frank; May 21, 1920, Dresden; vs and libretto (Leipzig: L. Doblinger, 1920).

Goldschmied von Toledo, Der, pasticcio in three acts of works by Jacques Offenbach (especially of *Der schwarze Korsar**), arranged by Julius Stern and Alfred Zamara; libretto by Karl Georg Zwerenz after E. T. A. Hoffmann's *Das Fräulein von Scuderi*; February 7, 1919, Mannheim; vs (Leipzig: UE, 1919); libretto (Vienna: UE, 1919).

Golem, Der, music drama in three acts by Eugen d'Albert; libretto by Ferdinand Lion; November 14, 1926, Frankfurt; fs, vs, and libretto (Vienna and New York: UE, c. 1926).

Gondoliere des Dogen, Der, opera in one act by Emil Nikolaus von Reznicek; libretto by Paul Knudsen; October 29, 1931, Stuttgart.

Göttin der Vernunft, Die, operetta in three acts by Johann Strauss, Jr.; libretto by Alfred Maria Willner and Bernhard Buchbinder; March 13, 1897, Vienna.

Götz von Berlichingen, opera in five acts by Karl Goldmark; libretto by Alfred Maria Willner after Goethe; December 16, 1902, Budapest; revised 1903, Frankfurt; vs (Leipzig: E. Berté, c. 1902).

Graf Hammerstein, opera by Jules Deswert; 1884, Mainz.

Graf von Gleichen, Der, "historische-komische Oper" by Franz Volkert; libretto by Josef Alois Gleich; 1815, Vienna.

Graf von Gleichen, Der, opera by Karl Eberwein; libretto by Schmidt and Peucer; ca. 1822, Weimar.

Graf von Gleichen, Der, opera by A. Wandersleb; 1847, Gotha.

Graf von Gleichen, Der, opera in one act by Franz Mohaupt; libretto by Peter Riedl; March 14, 1901, Reichenberg.

Gringoire, opera in one act by Ignaz Brüll; libretto by Victor Léon [Victor Hirschfeld] after Théodore Faullain de Banville; March 19, 1892, Munich; vs (Leipzig: J. Weinberger [1892]).

Grosse Loos, Das, comic opera in two acts by Ernst Wilhelm Wolf; libretto by F. J. Bertuch after Charles Favart; 1774, Weimar; libretto (Berlin: C. U. Ringmacher, 1776).

Grossindustrielle, Die, opera in one act by Kurt Driesch; libretto by Erich Bormann; May 27, 1953, Cologne; given on December 12, 1953, Dresden, as *Der Indianer*.

Grossmüthige Scipio, Der, opera in a prologue and three acts by Johann Philipp Krieger; libretto is an anonymous translation of Minato's *Scipione Africano*, 1664; November 2, 1690, Weissenfels.

Grüne Heinrich, Der, opera in two scenes by Georg Ebner; libretto by Ernst Hohenstatter after Gottfried Keller; May 12, 1922, Munich.

Grüne Kakadu, Der, opera in one act by Richard Mohaupt; libretto by the composer after Arthur Schnitzler; September 16, 1958, Hamburg.

Gudrun, opera in four acts by Karl Mangold; 1851, Darmstadt.

Gugeline, opera in five acts by Ludwig Thuille; libretto by Otto Julius Bierbaum; March 4, 1901, Bremen; vs (Mainz: BSS, 1900); libretto (Berlin: Schuster & Loeffler, 1899).

Gutsherr, Der, oder **Hannchen und Gürge (Der Schiffspatron),** Singspiel in two acts by Karl Ditters von Dittersdorf; libretto by Johann Friedrich Jünger; March 2, 1791, Vienna.

Guttenberg, opera in four acts by Ferdinand Füchs; libretto by Otto Prechtler; April 1, 1846, Graz.

Habemeajaja, radio opera by Boris Blacher; libretto by Heggars; composed in 1929 and long thought to be lost; January 30, 1987, West Berlin.

Hagbarth und Signe, opera in three acts by Ödön Mihalovich; libretto by Adolf Stern after Adam Gottlob Oehlenschläger; March 12, 1882, Dresden.

Haideschacht, Der, opera in three acts by Franz von Holstein; libretto by the composer after E. T. A. Hoffmann; October 22, 1868, Dresden; fs (Leipzig: B&H, 1869); vs and libretto (Leipzig: B&H, n.d.).

Hamlet, "eine Karrikatur" in three acts by Ignaz Schuster; libretto by Joachim Perinet; 1807, Vienna; libretto (Vienna: J. B. Wallishausser, 1807).

Hamlet, opera in five scenes by Jean Kurt Forest; libretto by the composer after S. Grammaticus and F. de Belleforest; October 15, 1973, East Berlin (concert).

Hamletmaschine, opera by Wolfgang Rihm; libretto by Heiner Müller; 1987, Mannheim.

Hanneles Himmelfahrt, opera in two acts by Paul Graener; libretto by the composer after Gerhard Hauptmann's play (1893); February 17, 1927, Dresden and Breslau; vs (Berlin: B&B, c. 1927).

Hans Hüttenstock, comic opera in two acts by Franz Joseph Leonti Meyer von Schauensee; libretto by the composer; 1769, Lucerne.

Hans Sachs im vorgerückter Alter, Singspiel in two acts by Adalbert Gyrowetz; 1834, Dresden.

Hänschen und Gretschen, Singspiel in one act by Johann Friedrich Reichardt; libretto by J. G. Bock after Jean Michel Sedaine's *Rose et Colas*, set by Pierre Monsigny (1771, Paris); 1772, Leipzig; vs (Riga, 1773); ed. in *Documenta Musicologica* XCVII (1964).

Hansel und Gretel, opera in two acts by Rudolf Semmler; libretto by the composer after Wilhelm Busch; June 9, 1956, Zurich.

Harald, opera in three acts by Franz Xaver Kleinheinz; libretto by Matthäus Stegmayer; March 22, 1814, Budapest.

Harald der Wiking, opera in three acts by Andreas Hallén; libretto by Hans Herrig; October 16, 1881, Leipzig.

Haus ist zu verkaufen, Dies, Singspiel in one act by Johann Nepomuk Hummel; libretto by A. Klebe after Alexandre Duval's *Maison à vendre*; May 5, 1812; based on music from *Die vereitelten Ränke*, September 1806, Eisenstadt.

Häuschen im Walde, Das, oder **Antons Reise nach seinem Geburtsort,** Singspiel in two acts by Benedikt Schack; libretto by Emanuel Schikaneder; possibly January 6, 1795, Vienna; seventh of Schikaneder's seven "Anton" Singspiels; the work is lost.

Heidenkönig, Der, opera in a prologue and three acts by Siegfried Wagner; libretto by the composer; December 16, 1933, Cologne.

Heilige, Die, opera by Manfred Gurlitt; libretto by the composer after C. Hauptmann; 1920.

Heilige Berg, Der, opera in a prologue and two acts by Christian Sinding; libretto by Dora Duncker; April 19, 1914, Dessau.

Heilige Ente, Die, "ein Spiel mit Göttern und Menschen" in a prologue and three acts by Hans Gál; libretto by Karl Michael von Levetzow and Leo Feld [Leo Hirschfeld]; April 29, 1923, Düsseldorf; fs (Vienna: UE, c. 1923); vs (Vienna: UE, c. 1922).

Heilige Katharina, Die, opera in three acts by Otto Böhme; libretto by the composer after Christoph Martin Wieland; May 16, 1919, Chemnitz.

Heimchen am Herd, Das, opera in three acts by Karl Goldmark; libretto by Alfred Maria Willner after Charles Dickens' *Cricket on the Hearth*; March 21, 1896, Vienna; vs (Leipzig: E. Berté, c. 1896).

Heimkehr, Die, opera by Marcel Mihalovici; libretto by Karl Heinrich Rupel after Guy de Maupassant; June 17, 1954, Frankfurt radio; November 9, 1954, Düsseldorf (staged); revised 1955; vs (Berlin-Wiesbaden: B&B, 1954).

Heimliche Ehe, Die (Der Löwe von Venedig), opera in three acts by Peter Gast [Johann Heinrich Köselitz]; libretto by the composer after Giovanni Bertati's *Matrimonio segreto*; January 23, 1891, Danzig.

Heinrich der Löwe, "ein allegorisches Singspiel" in two acts by Carl David Stegmann; libretto by Heinrich Gottlieb Schmieder; July 15, 1792, Frankfurt.

Heinrich der Löwe, opera in four acts by Edmund Kretschmer; libretto by the composer; 1877, Leipzig; vs (Leipzig: F. Kistner, ca. 1877).

Heinrich der Vogler (Heinrich der Vogler, Herzog zu Braunschweig, nachmahls erwehlter Teutscher Kayser), Singspiel in three acts by Georg Caspar Schürmann; libretto by Johann Ulrich König; August 1, 1718, Brunswick.

Heinrich IV und d'Aubigné, opera in three acts by Heinrich Marschner; libretto by Hornbostel and Alberti; July 19, 1820, Dresden.

Heirat wider Willen, Die, opera in three acts by Engelbert Humperdinck; libretto by Hedwig Humperdinck after Alexandre Dumas the Elder's *Les Demoiselles de Saint-Cyr*, 1843; April 14, 1905, Berlin, revised 1935; vs (Leipzig: M. Brockhaus, 1905).

Heiratsantrag, Der, opera in one act by Heinz Röttger; libretto by the composer after Anton Chekhov; October 31, 1960, Magdeburg.

Heisse Eisen, Das, opera in one act by Wax Wolff; libretto by the composer after Hans Sachs; October 10, 1909, Frankfurt.

Heiss[e] Eisen, Das, opera in one act by Werner Wehrli; libretto after Hans Sachs; December 11, 1918, Bern.

Heisse Eisen, Das, opera in one act by Bernhard Paumgartner; libretto by the composer after Hans Sachs; July 24, 1922, Salzburg.

Heisse Ofen, Der, "comic opera in five acts and three intermezzi" by Hans Werner Henze et al.; libretto by Michel and Rosi; March 18, 1989, Kassel.

Helena und Paris, opera in three acts by Peter Winter; libretto by Carl Josef Förg; February 5, 1782, Munich.

Heliantus, opera in three acts by Adalbert von Goldschmidt; libretto by the composer; March 26, 1884, Leipzig.

Henrico IV (Die geheimen Begebenheiten Henrico IV, König von Castilien und Leon, oder Die getheilte Liebe), opera in five acts by Johann Mattheson; libretto by Johann Joachim Hoe; February 9, 1711, Hamburg; *Arien* (Hamburg: Author, 1711).

Hermannsschlacht, Die, opera in five acts by Hippolyte Chélard; libretto by Karl Weichselbaumer; September 12, 1835, Munich.

Hermione, opera in four acts by Max Bruch; libretto by Emil Hopffer after Shakespeare's *A Winter's Tale*; March 21, 1872, Berlin; fs (Berlin: 1872).

Hero und Leander, opera in three acts by Paul Caró; libretto by the composer after Franz Grillparzer; May 31, 1912, Breslau.

Herr Dandolo, opera in three acts by Rudolf Siegel; libretto by Will Vesper after Giovanni Giraud; May 23, 1914, Essen.

Herr in Grau, Der, opera by Heimo Erbse; 1966.

Herrat, opera in three acts by Felix Draesecke; libretto by the composer; March 10, 1892, Dresden.

Herrn Dürers Bild, opera in three acts by Joseph Gustav Mraczek; libretto by Arthur Ostermann after Franz Karl Ginzkey; January 29, 1927, Hanover.

Herz, Das, opera in three acts by Hans Pfitzner; libretto by Hans Mahner Mons; November 12, 1931, Berlin; vs ed. Felix Wolfes (London: Fürstner, 1931); libretto (Berlin: A. Fürstner, 1931).

Herzog Albrecht, opera in four acts by Karl August Krebs; libretto by August Lewald; October 8, 1833, Hamburg; revised as *Agnes Bernauer**.

Herzog Johann Albrecht von Mecklenberg, oder Andreas Mylias, opera in three acts by Friedrich von Flotow; libretto by E. Hobein; May 27, 1857, Schwerin.

Herzog Philipps Brautfahrt, opera in three acts by August Reuss; libretto by Hanns von Gumppenberg; February 22, 1909, Graz.

Herzog Wildfang, opera in three acts by Siegfried Wagner; libretto by the composer; March 23, 1901, Munich.

Hexe von Passau, Die, opera in four scenes by Ottmar Gerster; libretto by Richard Billinger; October 11, 1941, Düsseldorf.

Hexenlied, opera in two acts by Roderich Kleeman; libretto by Ingeborg Reinhold after Ernst von Wildenbruch; March 20, 1948, Zwickau.

Hexen-schabbas, Singspiel–marionette opera by Franz Joseph Haydn; 1773; the music is lost.

Himmelskleid, Das, opera by Ermanno Wolf-Ferrari; libretto by the composer after Charles Perrault; April 21, 1927, Munich.

Hirtenlegende, opera in five scenes by Eugen Bodart; libretto by the composer after Lope de Vega; November 26, 1936, Weimar.

Hochländer, Die, opera in four acts by Franz von Holstein; libretto by the composer after Sir Walter Scott's *Waverly* (1814); January 16, 1876, Mannheim.

Hochzeit auf dem Lande, Die, oder **Hanns Klachel dritter Theil,** Singspiel by Antonín Volanek; libretto by Karl Franz Guolfinger von Steinsberg; 1798, Prague and Leipzig.

Hochzeit auf der Alm, Die, Singspiel by Michael Haydn; May 6, 1768, Salzburg.

Hochzeit des Jobs, Die, comic opera in four acts by Joseph Haas; libretto by Ludwig Andersen; July 2, 1944, Dresden.

Hochzeit des Mönchs, Die, opera in four acts by August Klughardt; libretto by Ernst Pasqué after Conrad Ferdinand Meyer; November 10, 1886, Dessau; vs (Mainz: BBS [1943]).

Höhle von Salamanca, Die, opera in one act by Bernhard Paumgartner; libretto by the composer after Miguel de Cervantes; November 20, 1923, Dresden; vs (Vienna: Wiener Philharmoniker Verlag, 1923).

Hohle von Waverly, Die, opera in three acts by Conradin Kreutzer; libretto by Georg Ott after Adam Gottlob Oehlenschläger; April 6, 1837, Vienna.

Hokus-Pokus, oder **Der Gaukelspiel,** comic opera in two acts by Karl Ditters von Dittersdorf; libretto by Christian August Vulpius; 1790, Vienna.

Höllenberg, Der, heroic-comic opera in two acts by Joseph Wölfl; libretto by Emanuel Schikaneder; November 21, 1795, Vienna.

Höllisch Gold, Das, opera in one act by Julius Bittner; libretto by the composer after a play by Hans Sachs; October 15, 1916, Darmstadt.

Holofernes, opera in two acts by Emil Nikolaus von Reznicek; libretto by the composer after Friedrich Hebbel's *Judith;* October 27, 1923, Berlin; vs (Vienna: UE, 1923).

Holzdieb, Der, opera in one act by Heinrich Marschner; libretto by Friedrich Kind; February 22, 1825, Dresden; vs (Berlin: E. Bote & G. Bock, 188–).

Holzhauer, Der, oder **Die drei Wünsche,** Singspiel in one act by Georg Benda; libretto by Friedrich Wilhelm Gotter after Jean-François Guichard and Nicolas Castet's *Le Bûcheron,* set by F. A. D. Philidor (1763, Paris); January 2, 1778, Gotha; vs (Leipzig: Im Schwickertschen Verlage, 1778).

Homerische Welt, Die, two operatic cycles by August Bungert: *Die Odyssee** and *Die Ilias.**

Husar, Der, opera by Ignaz Brüll; 1898, Vienna.

Hussiten vor Naumberg, Die, opera by Antonio Salieri; 1803, Vienna.

Ida, die Büssende, opera in four acts by Adalbert Gyrowetz; libretto by Franz Ignaz von Holbein; February 26, 1807, Vienna.

Idris und Zenide, comic opera in two acts by Franz Süssmayr; libretto by Karl Ludwig Giesecke after Christoph Martin Wieland; May 11, 1795, Vienna.

Igel als Bräutigam, Der, opera for big and little people in five scenes by Cesar Bresgen; libretto by the composer and Ludwig Andersen; 1948, Esslingen; revised 1951, Nuremberg; vs (Mainz: BSS, 1951); vs (Mainz: BBS, 1956).

Ihre Excellenz, operetta by Richard Heuberger; January 28, 1899, Vienna; revised as *Eine entzückende Frau**; vs (Berlin: J. Weinberger, ca. 1898).

Ilias, Die, unfinished five-part cycle of operas by August Bungert; *Achilleus** and *Klytemnestra** were sketched.

Ilsebill, opera in five scenes by Friedrich Klose; text by Hugo Hoffmann after the brothers Grimm; June 7, 1903, Karlsruhe.

Im Dunkel ist nicht gut munkeln, oder **Irrung über Irrung (Die 25,000 Gulden),** comic opera in two acts by Karl Ditters von Dittersdorf; libretto by Christian Heinrich Spiess; February 1789, Vienna.

Improvisator, Der, opera in three acts by Eugen d'Albert; libretto by Gustav Kastropp after Hans Christian Andersen; February 26, 1902, Berlin; fs and vs (Berlin: B&B, 1902).

Indianer, Der. See *Die Grossindustrielle.*

Indigo und die vierzig Räuber, operetta in three acts by Johann Strauss, Jr.; libretto by Maximilian Steiner; February 10, 1871, Vienna.

Indische Legende, opera in one act by Paul Kont; libretto by Jörg Mauthe; January 30, 1952, Vienna radio; June 17, 1954, Vienna (staged).

Ingewelde, opera in three acts by Max von Schillings; libretto by Ferdinand von Sporck; November 13, 1894, Karlsruhe.

Inkle und Yariko, Singspiel in three acts by Ferdinand Kauer; libretto by J. A. Gleich; Vienna, 1807; libretto (Vienna: J. B. Wallishausser, 1807).

Insel der Liebe, Die, Singspiel by Ignaz Umlauf; libretto by J. H. F. Müller; ca. 1772, Vienna.

Inzwischen, opera in a prologue, three acts, and a postlude by Paul Kont; libretto by the composer after W. H. Auden; January 5, 1967, Vienna, ORF.

Iphigenia in Aulis, opera by Karl Heinrich Graun; libretto by Christian Heinrich Postel; winter 1731, Brunswick; libretto in *Deutsche Literatur*, Reihe 13: *Barock . . .*, III (Leipzig: 1933).

Irene, opera in three acts by Joseph Huber; libretto by Peter Lohmann; June 3, 1881, Stuttgart.

Irrlicht, opera in three acts by Leo Fall; libretto by Ludwig Fernand; January 8, 1905, Mannheim; vs (Berlin: Harmonie, c. 1904).

Irrlicht, Das, oder **Endlich fand er sie,** opera in three acts by Ignaz Umlauf; libretto by Christian Friedrich Bretzner; January 17, 1782.

Irrwisch, Der, oder **Endlich fand er sie,** Singspiel in three acts by Christian Ludwig Dieter; libretto by Christoph Friedrich Bretzner; November 23, 1779, Stuttgart.

Irrwisch, Der, oder **Endlich fand er sie,** opera in three acts by Otto von Kospoth; libretto by Christoph Friedrich Bretzner; October 2, 1780, Berlin.

Island-Saga, opera in three acts by Georg Vollerthun; libretto by Bertha Thierisch; January 17, 1925, Munich.

Iwein, opera by August Klughardt; 1879.

Izeÿl, music drama in three acts by Eugen d'Albert; libretto by Rudolf Lothar after Paul Armand Silvestre and Eugène Morand; November 6, 1909, Hamburg; fs and vs (Berlin: B&B, 1909).

Jabuka, oder **Das Apfelfest,** opera in three acts by Johann Strauss, Jr.; libretto by Max Kalbeck and Gustav Davis; October 12, 1894, Vienna.

Jagd, Die, Singspiel in three acts by Franz Andreas Holly; libretto by C. F. Weisse; May 10, 1772, Prague.

Jagd, Die, comic opera in two acts by Johann Schenk; libretto by Christian Felix Weisse; 1799, Vienna; libretto (Vienna: C. P. Rehm, 1799).

Jason, oder **Die Eroberung des güldenen Fliesses,** opera in five acts by Johann Kusser; libretto by Friedrich Christian Bressand; September 1, 1692, Brunswick.

Jephtas Gelübde, opera in three acts by Giacomo Meyerbeer; libretto by Alois Schreiber; December 23, 1812, Munich.

Jery und Bäteli, Singspiel in one act by Peter Winter; libretto after Goethe; 1790, Munich.

Jochem Tröbs, oder **Der vergnügte Bauernstadt,** opera by J. C. Standfuss; 1759, Hamburg; the music is lost.

Johann Faustus, opera in a prologue and three acts by Hanns Eisler; libretto by the composer; April 11, 1974, Tübingen; libretto (Berlin: Aufbau, 1952).

Johanna d'Arc, opera in five acts by J. Hoven [Johann Vesque von Püttlingen]; libretto by O. Prechtler after Friedrich Schiller's *Die Jungfrau von Orleans*; December 30, 1840, Vienna.

Jorinda und Jorgile, radio opera in two acts by Heinrich Sutermeister; libretto by the composer after the brothers Grimm; April 13, 1934, Munich radio.

Jot, oder **Wann kommt der Herr zurück,** "dialectic" opera in one act by Klaus Huber; libretto by Philip Oxman, German version by Kurt Marti and Dietrich Rischl; July 27, 1973, Berlin.

Juana, opera in one act by Max Ettinger; libretto by Georg Kaiser; February 7, 1925, Nuremberg, together with the composer's *Der eifersüchtiger Trinker*.*

Jubelhochzeit, Die, Singspiel in three acts by Johann Adam Hiller; libretto by Christian Felix Weisse; April 5, 1773, Leipzig; vs (Leipzig: Johann Friedrich Junius, 1773); libretto (Berlin: C. U. Ringmacher, 1773).

Jubelhochzeit, Die, Singspiel in three acts by Ignaz von Beecke; libretto by Christian Felix Weisse; 1782, Mannheim.

Judith, opera in four acts by Albert Franz Doppler; libretto by S. H. Mosenthal; December 30, 1870, Vienna; vs (Vienna: G. Lewy [1870]; libretto, the same (1871).

Judith, opera in three acts by Max Ettinger; libretto by the composer after Friedrich Hebbel; November 24, 1921, Nuremberg.

Judith, opera in four acts by Franz Adam; libretto by Charles Hellem and Paul d'Estoc; May 8, 1948, Strasbourg.

Judith, opera in one scene by Theo Goldberg; libretto by Johannes Hübner; 1950, Berlin.

Jugend (Jugendjahre) Peter des Grossen, Die, opera in three acts by Joseph Weigl; libretto by Georg Friedrich Treitschke after Jean Nicolas Bouilly; December 10, 1814, Vienna.

Julia, opera in three acts by Johann Kusser; libretto by Friedrich Christian Bressand; August 1690, Brunswick.

Julia, opera in five acts by Reinhard Keiser; libretto by Johann Joachim Hoe after Giacomo Francesco Bussani; February 1717?; fs (Hamburg: F. C. Greflinger, 1717).

Julie, oder Der Blumenkopf, Singspiel in one act by Gasparo Spontini; 1806; libretto (Vienna: J. B. Wallishausser, 1806).

Julietta, opera in four acts by Heimo Erbse; libretto by the composer after Heinrich von Kleist; August 17, 1959, Salzburg.

Julius Caesar (Der durch dem Fall des grossen Pompejus erhöhte Julius Caesar), opera by Reinhard Keiser; libretto by Barthold Feind; 1710, Hamburg; libretto (Hamburg: Spieringische Schriften, 1710).

Jungfrau von Orleans, Die, opera in three acts by Emil Nikolaus von Reznicek; libretto by the composer after Friedrich Schiller; June 19, 1887, Prague.

Junggesellen-Wirtschaft, Die, opera in one act by Adalbert Gyrowetz; libretto by Georg Friedrich Treitschke; June 18, 1807, Vienna.

Jüngste Tag, Der, opera by Giselher Klebe; libretto by Lore Klebe after Odön von Horváth's play of the same name; July 16, 1980, Mannheim.

Junker Heinz, opera in three acts by Karl von Perfall; libretto by Franz Grandaur after Wilhelm Hertz's *Heinrich von Schwaben*; April 9, 1886, Munich.

Junker in der Mühle, Der, Singspiel in one act by Johann Nepomuk Hummel; libretto possibly by Heinrich Schmidt; Vienna, November 1813.

Jürg Jenztsch, opera in six scenes by Heinrich Kaminski; libretto by the composer after Conrad Ferdinand Meyer's novel (1876); April 27, 1929, Dresden.

Käficht, Der, opera in one act by Hans Kormann; libretto by Hans P. Schmiedel after August von Kotzebue; January 16, 1925, Leipzig.

Kain, opera in one act by Eugen d'Albert; libretto by Heinrich Bulthaupt; February 17, 1900, Berlin; fs (Berlin: B&B, c. 1900); vs (Berlin: B&B, c. 1899).

Kain, opera in one act by Friedrich Schmidtmann; libretto by the composer after Lord Byron; March 1952, Cologne.

Kain und Abel, opera in one act by Felix Weingartner; libretto by the composer; May 17, 1914, Darmstadt; vs and libretto (Vienna: UE, 1914).

Kaiser Adolph von Nassau, opera in four acts by Heinrich Marschner; libretto by Heribert Rau; January 5, 1845, Dresden.

Kaiser Hadrian, opera in three acts by Joseph Weigl; libretto by Johann Cölestin Mayer; May 21, 1897, Vienna.

Kaiser Jovian, opera in four acts by Rudolph Kelterborn; libretto by Herbert Meier; March 4, 1967, Karlsruhe; vs (Kassel and New York: Bär, 1966).

Kaiserstochter, Die, opera in three acts by Willem de Haan; libretto by Wilhelm Jacoby; February 1, 1885, Darmstadt.

Kalif Storch, opera in four scenes by Joseph Eidens; libretto by Peter Mennicken after Wilhelm Hauff; December 22, 1946, Aachen.

Kalte Herz, Das (Der Kohlenpeter), opera in three acts by Robert Konta; libretto by the composer after Wilhelm Hauff; October 28, 1908, Düsseldorf and Prague.

Kalte Herz, Das, opera in one act by Mark Lothar; libretto by G. Eich; March 24, 1935, Berlin radio.

Kalte Herz, Das, opera in three acts by Kurt Brüggemann; libretto by the composer after Wilhelm Hauff; January 28, 1938, Hamburg.

Karamasows, Die, opera in a prologue and three acts by Paul Coenen; libretto by the composer after Fyodor Dostoyevski; September 3, 1945, Berlin.

Kardinal, Der, opera in one act by Helmut Eder; libretto by Ernst Brauner; June 15, 1962, Vienna, ORF TV; April 22, 1965, Linz (staged).

Karneval in Rom, Der, operetta in three acts by Johann Strauss, Jr.; libretto by Joseph Braun, F. Zell [Camillo Walzel], and Richard Genée after Victorien Sardou; March 1, 1873, Vienna.

Kaspar, der Fagottist, oder **Die Zauberzither,** Singspiel by Wenzel Müller; libretto by M. A. Schmidt; June 8, 1791, Vienna; libretto in O. Rommel, ed., *Die Maschinenkomödie* (Leipzig: Deutsche Literatur, 1935).

Kassandras Tod, "dramatische Kantate" by Hans Chemin-Petit; libretto by the composer after Aeschylus; October 16, 1977, Berlin (concert).

Katakomben, Die, opera in three acts by Ferdinand Hiller; libretto by Moritz Hartmann; February 15, 1862, Wiesbaden.

Kätchen von Heilbronn, Das, opera in five acts by Friedrich Lux; libretto by Friedrich Meck after Heinrich von Kleist; March 23, 1846, Dessau; revised 1847.

Kätchen von Heilbronn, Das, opera in four acts by Karl Reinthaler; libretto by Heinrich Bulthaupt after Heinrich von Kleist; December 7, 1881, Frankfurt.

Kätchen von Heilbronn, Das, opera in three acts by Waldemar Bloch; libretto by the composer after Heinrich von Kleist; June 21, 1958, Graz.

Kathrin, Die, opera in three acts by Erich Korngold; libretto by Ernst Decsey; October 7, 1938, Stockholm; vs (Vienna: J. Weinberger, c. 1937).

Kaufmann von Smyrna, Der, "Operette" in one act by Georg Joseph Vogler; libretto by Christian Friedrich Schwan after Nicolas Chamfort; 1771, Mannheim; libretto (Mannheim: C. F. Schwan, 1771).

Kaufmann von Smyrna, Der, "Operette" in one act by Karl David Stegmann; libretto by Christian Friedrich Schwan after Nicolas Chamfort; 1773.

Kaufmann von Smyrna, Der, "Operette" in three acts by Andreas Franz Holly; libretto by Christian Friedrich Schwan after Nicolas Chamfort; November 13, 1773, Berlin; vs (Berlin, 1775).

Kenilworth, opera in a prologue and three acts by Bruno Otto Klein; libretto by Wilhelm Müller after Sir Walter Scott; February 13, 1895, Hamburg.

Kinder der Heide, Die, opera in four acts by Anton Rubinstein; libretto by S. H. Mosenthal after Karl Beck; February 23, 1861, Vienna.

Kinder der Natur, Die, opera in two acts by Franz Aspelmayr; libretto by L. A. Hoffmann after Pierre Carlet de Marivaux; July 15, 1778, Vienna.

Kirke, opera in a prologue and three acts by August Bungert; libretto by the composer; January 29, 1898, Dresden; part of the cycle *Die Odyssee**; vs and libretto (Leipzig: C. F. Leede, c. 1897); libretto in *Die Odyssee*, part I (Leipzig: C. G. Röder, 1897).

Kirmies, Die, opera in one act by Wilhelm Taubert; libretto by Eduard Devrient; January 23, 1832, Berlin.

Kirschgarten, Der, opera by Rudolf Kelterborn; libretto after Anton Chekhov; December 6, 1984, Zurich.

Kjarten und Gudrun, opera in three acts by Paul von Klenau; libretto by the composer; April 4, 1918, Mannheim; revised 1924 as *Gudrun auf Island*.

Klage der Ariadne, version of Claudio Monteverdi's *Lamento d'Arianna* by Carl Orff; 1925, Karlsruhe; fs (Mainz: BSS, 1931).

Klage der Ariadne, "dramatische Szene" by Hans Chemin-Petit; libretto by the composer after Freidrich Nietzsche; September 15, 1973, Berlin (concert).

Kleider machen Leute, opera in a prologue and three acts by Alexander von Zemlinsky; libretto by Leo Feld after Gottfried Keller; December 2, 1910, Vienna; vs (Vienna: UE, 1922).

Kleider machen Leute, comic opera in a prelude and four acts by Marcel Rubin; libretto by the composer after Gottfried Keller; December 14, 1973, Vienna.

Kleine Aehrenleserin, Die, children's operetta by Johann Adam Hiller; libretto by Christian Felix Weisse; 1778, Leipzig; vs (Leipzig: Crusius, 1778).

Kleine Stadt, Die, opera in three acts by Franz Xaver Lehner; libretto by Herbert Wiesinger after Heinrich Mann; May 26, 1957, Nuremberg.

Kleopatra, opera by Theo Goldberg; 1952, Karlsruhe.

Kluge Jacob, Der, Singspiel in three acts by Otto Carl Erdmann von Kospoth; libretto by J. Wetzel; February 26, 1788, Berlin.

Kluge Wirtin, Die, opera in three acts by Hajo Hinrichs; libretto by Friedrich Lindemann; May 27, 1943, Oldenburg.

Klytemnestra, part of the unfinished *Die Ilias** cycle of August Bungert; sketched but not completed.

Kobold, Der, opera by Friedrich Heinrich Himmel; libretto after Friedrich Wilhelm Gotter; May 22, 1813, Vienna; vs (Vienna: Pietro Mechetti, 18—).

Kohlhaymerin, Die, opera in three acts by Julius Bittner; libretto by the composer; April 9, 1921, Vienna; vs and libretto (Vienna: UE, 1920).

Kolumbus, opera in four acts by Walter Böhme; libretto by the composer; June 13, 1950, Reichenbach.

Kolumbus, opera in three acts by Karl-Rudi Griesbach; libretto by the composer; December 23, 1958, Erfurt.

Komödiantin, Die, opera in three acts by Hans Chemin-Petit; libretto by the composer after Heinz Coubier; June 17, 1970, Coburg.

Komödie der Irrungen, Die, opera in two acts by Karl Lorenz; libretto by the composer after William Shakespeare's *Comedy of Errors*; March 11, 1939, Stettin.

König Alfred, opera in four acts by Joseph Raff; libretto by Gotthold Logau [Henrik Glogau] and the composer; March 9, 1851, Weimar.

König Drosselbart, opera by Diether Noll; libretto by Alexander Stillmark after the brothers Grimm; January 15, 1958, Erfurt.

König Lustig, opera in three acts by Erich Riede; libretto by Reinhold Scharnke; February 1, 1952, Kassel.

König Magnus, opera in one act by Preben Nodermann; libretto by the composer after Birger Moerner; October 8, 1898, Hamburg.

König Manfred, opera in five acts by Carl Reinecke; libretto by Friedrich Roeber; July 26, 1867, Wiesbaden.

König Nicolo, opera in three acts by Hans Chemin-Petit; libretto by the composer after Frank Wedekind; May 6, 1962, Aachen.

König Nicolo, opera in two acts by Rudolf Weishappel; libretto by Harald Kaufmann after Frank Wedekind; February 22, 1972, Vienna.

König René's Tochter, opera by Fritz Behrend; composed 1927; vs (Magdeburg: Heinrichshofen's Verlag, c. 1927).

König Ubü, opera by Franz Hummel; libretto by Roland Lillie after Alfred Jarry's play (1896); March 11, 1984, Salzburg.

König von Samarkand, Der, opera in two acts by Franz Mikorey; libretto by the composer after Franz Grillparzer; March 27, 1910, Dessau.

Königin der schwarzen Insel, Die, opera in two acts by Anton Eberl; libretto by Johann Schwaldopler after Christoph Martin Wieland; May 23, 1801, Vienna.

Königin Mariette, opera by Ignaz Brüll; libretto by F. Zell [Camillo Walzel] and Richard Genée; 1883, Munich; vs (Berlin: B&B, ca. 1883).

Königssohn aus Ithaka, Der, opera in two acts by Franz Anton Hoffmeister; libretto by Emanuel Schikaneder; June 27, 1795, Vienna; vs (Brunswick: Musikalisches Magazin auf der Höhe, no. 88, n.d.).

Konradin von Schwaben, opera in three acts by Conradin Kreutzer; libretto by B. von Guseck; ca. 1810; new text K. R. Weitzmann, March 30, 1812, Stuttgart.

Krach im Offen, Der, school opera in three acts by Armin Kaufmann; libretto by Alfred Jirasek and Willi Pribil; May 27, 1961, Vienna.

Kreidekreis, Der, opera in three acts by Alexander von Zemlinsky; libretto by Klabund [Alfred Henschke] after an old Chinese play by Hui Lan-ki; October 14, 1933, Zurich.

Krieg, Der, Singspiel in three acts by Johann Adam Hiller; libretto by Christian Friedrich Weisse after Carlo Goldoni's *La guerra*; 1772, Leipzig; vs (Leipzig: Bernhard Christoph Breitkopf und Sohn, 1773); libretto (Berlin: C. U. Ringmacher, 1774).

Kriegsgefangene, Die, opera in two acts by Karl Goldmark; libretto by Emil Schlicht [Alfred Formey]; January 17, 1899, Vienna; vs (Leipzig: Schubert, ca. 1897); libretto (Leipzig: Schubert, 1899).

Krumme Teufel, Der, "Pantomine-Singspiel" by Franz Joseph Haydn; libretto probably by Joseph Kurz; 1751 or 1753; first known performance May 29, 1753, Vienna; the music is lost.

Kudrun, opera by Hans Huber; January 29, 1896, Basel.

Kuhreigen, Der, opera in three acts by Wilhelm Kienzl, libretto by Richard Batka after Rudolf Hans Bartsch; November 23, 1911, Vienna.

Kukuska, operetta in three acts by Franz Lehár; libretto by Felix Falzari [Hans Hoffmann]; November 27, 1896, Leipzig.

Kunihild, opera in three acts by Cyrill Kistler; libretto by Ferdinand von Sporck; March 20, 1884, Sonderhausen, Germany; vs (Leipzig: E. W. Fritzsch, 1884).

Kyberiade, opera in three acts by Krzystof Meyer; libretto by the composer after Stanislav Lem's stories *The Friend of the Automathias* and *The Story of the Three Storytelling Machines,* translated by Jörg Morgener; 1986.

Kyffhäuserberg, Der, Singspiel in one act by Heinrich Marschner; libretto by August von Kotzebue; January 2, 1822, Zittau.

Lächeln am Fusse der Leiter, Das, opera by Antonio Bibalo; libretto after Henry Miller's *The Smile at the Foot of the Ladder*; 1965; Hamburg.

Lächerlichen Preziösen, Die, opera in one act by Fritz Behrend; libretto by the composer after Molière; May 22, 1949, Berlin.

Lady Hamilton, opera in three acts by Robert Heger; libretto by the composer; February 11, 1951, Nuremberg.

Lanassa, oder Die Eroberung von Malaba, opera in three acts by Vincenz Franz Tuczek; libretto by the composer after Karl Martin Plümicke's German translation of Antoine Marin Lemierre's *La veuve de Malabar*; December 13, 1805, Pest.

Lancelot, opera in four acts by Theodor Hentschel; libretto by Franz Bittony; 1879; vs (Bremen: Aug. Fr. Cranz, 1879).

Landfriede, Der, opera in three acts by Ignaz Brüll; libretto by S. H. Mosenthal after Eduard von Bauernfeld's comedy; October 4, 1877, Vienna; vs (Berlin: B&B [1877]).

Landgraf Ludwigs Brautfahrt, opera in five acts by Eduard Lassen; libretto by Ernst Pasqué; May 10, 1857, Weimar.

Lanzelot und Elaine, opera in four acts by Walter Courvoisier; libretto by Walter Bergh [Bertha Thiersch] after Alfred, Lord Tennyson; November 3, 1917, Munich.

Laune des Verliebten, Die, opera in one act by Erwin Dressel; libretto by the composer after Goethe; October 30, 1949, Leipzig.

Laura Rosetti, "Schauspiel mit Gesang" by Johann André; libretto by B. C. D'Arien; May 23, 1778, Berlin; vs score (Leipzig: Im Verlage der dykischen Buchhandlung, 1777).

Laura Rosetti, Singspiel by Christian Ludwig Dieter; libretto by B. C. D'Arien; February 9, 1781, Stuttgart; the music is lost.

Legende von der heiligen Elisabeth, Die, opera-oratorio in a prologue and four scenes by Franz Liszt; libretto by Otto Roquette; October 23, 1881, Weimar.

Leichte Cavallerie, Die, operetta in two acts by Franz von Suppé, libretto by C. Costa; March 24, 1866, Vienna; fs (Leipzig: A. Cranz, 1927); libretto (Vienna: F. Ullrich. 1866).

Leiden des jungen Werthers, Die, opera by Hans-Jürgen von Bose; April 30, 1986, Schwetzingen.

Leila, opera in three acts by Henry Hugh Piersen; libretto by Caroline Leonhardt-Lysen; February 22, 1848, Hamburg.

Leonce und Lena, opera in three acts by Julius Weismann; libretto by the composer after Georg Büchner's comedy of the same title, with additions by W. Calé; June 21, 1925, Freiburg.

Leonce und Lena, opera in three acts by Eric Zeisl; libretto by Hugo von Königsgarten and Hans Kafka; May 16, 1952, Los Angeles.

Leonce und Lena, opera in three acts by Kurt Schwaen; libretto by the composer after Georg Büchner's play; October 15, 1961, Berlin.

Leonilde oder Die siegende Beständigkeit, *Schauspiel* in three acts by Georg Caspar Schürmann; libretto by Gottlieb Fiedler; 1703, Brunswick.

Leonore, opera in two acts by Anselm Hüttenbrenner; libretto by Gottfried von Leitner after Gottfried August Bürger's ballad; April 22, 1835, Graz.

Letzte Schuss, Der, opera in two acts by Siegfried Matthus; libretto by the composer and Götz Friedrich after Boris Lavrenyov; November 5, 1967, East Berlin; vs (Leipzig: VEB Deutsche Verlag für Musik, 1969).

Letzte Tage von Pompeji, Die, opera in five acts by Reinhold Montowt; libretto by the composer; March 29, 1900, Lübeck.

Letzte Walzer, Der, operetta in three acts by Oscar Straus; libretto by Julius Brammer and Alfred Grünwald; February 12, 1920, Berlin.

Letzte Zauberer, Der, opera in two acts by Pauline Viardot; libretto by Richard Pohl after the French version by Ivan Turgenev; April 8, 1869, Weimar.

Levins Mühle, opera in nine scenes by Udo Zimmermann; libretto by Ingo Zimmermann after Johannes Brobowski's novel (1973); March 27, 1973, Dresden and Weimar.

Libussa, opera by Paul Kont; 1969.

Lichtenstein, opera in five acts by Peter Lindpaintner; libretto by F. von Dingelstedt after Wilhelm Hauff's novel; August 26, 1846, Stuttgart; libretto (Stuttgart: Fein, ca. 1846).

Lieb' und Treue, *Liederspiel* in one act by Johann Friedrich Reichardt; libretto on Lieder texts of Goethe, Herder, and Salis; March 31, 1800, Berlin.

Liebe auf dem Lande, Die, Singspiel in three acts by Johann Adam Hiller; libretto by Christian Friedrich Weisse after Charles Favart's *Annette et Lubin* and L. Anseaume's *La Clochette*; May 18, 1768, Leipzig; vs (Leipzig: B. C. Breitkopf und Sohn, 1769).

Liebe auf dem Lande, Die, Singspiel in three acts by Franz Süssmayr; libretto by Christian Friedrich Weisse; ca. 1789, not performed.

Liebe Augustin, Der, operetta in three acts by Leo Fall; libretto by Rudolf Bernauer and Ernst Welisch; February 3, 1912, Berlin; revision of the unsuccessful *Der Rebell*, November 29, 1905, Vienna.

Liebe Augustin, Der, Singspiel in four acts by Julius Bittner; libretto by the composer; June 11, 1916, Vienna.

Liebe ist teuer, opera in three acts by Hans Brehme; libretto by Franz Clemens and K. E. Jaroschek after Ernst Raupach; January 21, 1949, Münster; vs (Mainz: Schott, 1949).

Liebe macht kurzen Prozess, oder **Heirat auf gewisse Art,** pasticcio by Joseph Wölfl with Franz Xaver Süssmayr, Johann Baptist Henneberg, Matthäus Stegmayr, Franz Anton Hoffmeister, Ignaz von Seyfried, Jakob Haibel, and J. Triebensei; libretto by Joachim Perinet after J. Rautenstrauch; March 26, 1798, Vienna.

Liebe und Eifersucht, Singspiel in three acts by E. T. A. Hoffmann; libretto by the composer after August Schlegel's translation *Die Schärpe und die Blume* of a Pedro Calderón comedy. Composed in 1807.

Liebelei, opera in three acts by Franz Neumann; libretto on Arthur Schnitzler's play (no alterations); September 18, 1910, Frankfurt.

Liebeskette, Die, opera buffa in two acts by Franz Xaver Lehner; libretto by the composer after Lope de Vega; June 16, 1961, Wiesbaden.

Liebesketten, opera in three acts by Eugen d'Albert; libretto by Rudolf Lother after Angel Guimerá's play *Filla del Mar*; November 12, 1912, Vienna; vs (Mainz: BSS, c. 1912).

Liebestod, opera in one act by Georges Aperghis; libretto by Marie-Noel Rio; March 16, 1982, Strasbourg.

Liebeswogen, opera in one act by Theodor Gerlach; libretto by the composer after Heinrich Heine; November 7, 1903; Bremen; revised as *Das Seegespenst,* 1914.

Liebhaber als Automat, Der, oder **Die redende Maschine,** opera in one act by Johann André; libretto by the composer after C. Dorbeil; September 11, 1782, Berlin.

Liebhaber nach dem Tode, Der, unfinished opera in three acts by E. T. A. Hoffmann; libretto by C. W. Salice-Contessa after Pedro Calderón's *El Galan Fantasma*; composed 1818–1822.

Lied der Nacht, Das, opera in three acts by Hans Gál; libretto by Karl M. Levetzow; April 24, 1926, Breslau.

Lindor und Ismene, opera in one act by Joseph Aloys Schmittbauer; libretto by J. von Soden; June 4, 1777, Lüneburg.

Liselott. See *Die blonde Liselott.*

Lisuarte und Darlioette, oder **Die Frage und die Antwort,** Singspiel in two acts by Johann Adam Hiller; libretto by Daniel Schiebeler after Charles Favart's *La Fée Urgèle*; November 25, 1766, Leipzig; vs (Leipzig: Bernhard Christoph Breitkopf und Sohn, 1768).

Lobetanz, opera in three acts by Ludwig Thuille; libretto by O. J. Bierbaum; February 6, 1898, Karlsruhe; vs (Mainz: BSS, 1897); libretto (Berlin: Verlag der Gewissenschaft Pan, 1895).

Lord Spleen, opera in two acts by Mark Lothar; libretto by Hugo Fritz Koenigsgarten after Ben Jonson's *Epicoene*; November 11, 1930, Dresden.

Loreley, Die, opera by Ignaz Lachner; 1846, Munich.

Loreley, Die, opera by Hans Sommer; April 11, 1891, Brunswick; vs (Leipzig: C. F. Leede, 1890).

Los Alamos, opera in three acts by Marc Neikrug; October 1, 1988, West Berlin.

Lottchen am Hofe, Singspiel in three acts by Johann Adam Hiller; libretto by Christian Friedrich Weisse after Carlo Goldoni and Charles Favart's *Ninette à la cour*; April 24, 1767, Leipzig (Leipzig: Bernhard Christoph Breitkopf und Sohn, 1769).

Lou Salomé, opera in two acts by Giuseppe Sinopoli; libretto by Karl Dietrich Gräwe; May 10, 1981, Munich.

Louise, Singspiel in three acts by Friedrich Ludwig Benda; libretto by Friedrich Ernst Jester; January 16, 1781, Königsberg; vs (Königsberg: Nicolovius [1791]).

Löwe von Venedig, Der. See *Die heimliche Ehe*.

Lübecker Totentanz, Der, opera in one act by Hermann Reutter; libretto after poems of the Marienkirche; January 25, 1948, Göttingen; vs (Mainz: BSS, 1943).

Lucius Verus, oder Die singende Treue, opera in three acts by Reinhard Keiser; libretto by Heinrich Hinsch; 1728, Hamburg; the music is lost; libretto (Hamburg: Stromersche Schriften, 1728).

Lucretia (Die kleinmüthige Selbstmörderin Lucretia), opera in five acts by Reinhard Keiser; libretto by Barthold Feind; 1705, Hamburg; libretto in *Italienische Deutsche Gedichte* (Hamburg: Stade, 1708).

Ludewig der Fromme, opera in three acts by Georg Caspar Schürmann, with numbers by André Campra, André Destouches, and Karl Heinrich Graun; libretto by Christian Ernst Simonetti; February 1726, Brunswick; score ed. Robert Eitner, *Publikationen älterer Musikwerke*, XVII (1890).

Lukretia, opera in two acts by Heinrich Marschner; libretto by A. Eckschlager; January 17, 1827, Danzig.

Lukrezia Borgia, opera in two acts by Walter Herbst; libretto by the composer; July 4, 1946, Strelsund.

Lustige Hochzeit, Die, opera by Reinhard Keiser and Christoph Graupner; 1708, Hamburg; libretto (Hamburg, 1708).

Lustige Krieg, Der, operetta in three acts by Johann Strauss, Jr.; libretto by F. Zell [Camillo Walzel] and Richard Genée; November 25, 1881, Vienna; vs (Hamburg: A. Cranz, ca. 1881); libretto (New York: H. Bartsch, 187–).

Lustige Schuster, Der, oder Der zweyte Theil vom Teufel ist los, opera in three acts by J. C. Standfuss; libretto by Christian Friedrich Weisse after Charles Coffey's *The Merry Cobbler*; January 18, 1759, Lübeck; vs (Leipzig: J. F. Junius, 1771).

Lustige Schuster, Der, Singspiel in three acts by Franz Andreas Holly; libretto by Carl Friedrich Henisch after Charles Coffey's *The Merry Cobbler*; 1770, Prague.

Lustigen Nibelungen, Die, ''burleske Operette'' in three acts by Oscar Straus; libretto by Rideamus [Fritz Oliven]; Vienna, November 12, 1904; libretto (Berlin: Verlag ''Harmonie,'' 1904).

Lustigen Weiber von Windsor, Die, Singspiel in two acts by Karl Ditters von Dittersdorf; libretto by the composer after Shakespeare's *The Merry Wives of Windsor*; June 25, 1796, Oels.

Macbeth, opera in five acts by Wilhelm Taubert; libretto by Friedrich Eggers after Shakespeare; November 16, 1858, Berlin.

Maccabäer, Die, opera in three acts by Anton Rubinstein; libretto by S. H. Mosenthal; April 17, 1875, Berlin.

Madame Bovary, opera in a prologue and two acts by Heinrich Sutermeister; libretto after Gustav Flaubert and contemporary documents; May 26, 1967, Zurich.

Maja und Alpino, oder Die bezauberte Rose, opera in three acts by Joseph Maria Wolfram; libretto by Eduard Heinrich Gehe after Ernst Konrad Friedrich Schulze's poem ''Die bezauberte Rose'' (1818); May 24, 1826, Prague.

Maldoror (Scenen vom Bösen), opera in twenty scenes by Manfred Niehaus; libretto by the composer and Alfred Feussner after the prose work by the Comte de Lautréamont; June 21, 1970, Kiel.

Mann im Mond, Der, "Wunderliches Spiel für Musik" in three acts by Jan Brandt-Buys; libretto by Bruno Hardt-Warden and Ignaz Michael Welleminsky; 1922.

Mann im Mond, Der, fairy-tale opera in six scenes by Cesar Bresgen; libretto by Ludwig Andersen and the composer; May 22, 1960, Nuremberg.

Manon (Schloss de l'Orme), opera by Richard Kleinmichel; January 1883, Hamburg.

Manru, opera in three acts by Ignacy Jan Paderewski; libretto by Alfred Nossig after a novel by Józef Ignacy Kraszewski; May 29, 1901, Dresden.

Manuel Venegas, opera by Richard Heuberger; March 27, 1889, Leipzig; revised as the grand opera *Mirjam*.*

Mara, opera in three acts by Joseph Netzer; libretto by Otto Prechtler; March 16, 1841, Vienna.

Mara, opera in one act by Ferdinand Hummel; libretto by Axel Delmar; October 11, 1893, Berlin.

Marat, operatic version by Walter Haupt of Peter Weiss' play of the same name (1965); June 23, 1984, Kassel.

Märchen von der schönen Lilie, Das, opera in two acts by Giselher Klebe; libretto by the composer after Goethe; May 15, 1969, Schwetzingen; libretto (Kassel and New York: Bär, 1969).

Mareike von Nymwegen, "Legendenspiel" by Eugen d'Albert; libretto by H. Alberti; October 31, 1923, Hamburg; vs (Hamburg: Anton J. Benjamin, 1923).

Marie von Montalban, opera in four acts by Peter Winter; libretto by Karl Reger after Johann Nepomuk Komareck, a sequel to Karl Martin Plümicke's *Lanassa**, set by Vincenz Franz Tuczek (1805, Pest); January 28, 1800, Munich; vs (Mainz: Carl Zulehner, 181–).

Marike Weiden, opera in three acts by Karl-Rudi Griesbach; libretto by the composer; October 7, 1960, Weimar.

Marketendierin, Die, opera in two acts by Engelbert Humperdinck; libretto by Robert Misch; May 10, 1914, Cologne; vs (Berlin: A. Fürstner, c. 1914).

Martl, oder Der Portiunculatag in Schnabelhausen, farce with music in three acts by Franz von Suppé; libretto by Alois Berla; December 16, 1848, Vienna; a parody of Friedrich von Flotow's *Martha** (see p. 159).

Maske, Die, Singspiel in three acts by E. T. A. Hoffmann; libretto by the composer; composed 1799; vs excerpts ed. Friedrich Schnapp (Berlin, 1923); libretto ed. Friedrich Schnapp (Berlin: Verlag für Kunstwissenschaft, 1923).

Maskerade im Serail, Die, oder Die grosse Löwenjagd, Singspiel by Antonín Volanek; libretto by P. Heimbacher; 1792, Prague; the music is lost.

Mathilde von Guise, opera in three acts by Johann Nepomuk Hummel; libretto after Emanuel Mercier-Dupaty's text, set by Jean Pierre Solié (1808); March 26, 1810, Vienna; vs (Leipzig: C. F. Peters, ca. 1828); libretto (Vienna: J. B. Wallishausser, 1810).

Matrosen, Die, opera in four acts by Friedrich von Flotow; December 23, 1845, Hamburg, libretto by W. Friedrich; an enlargement of *Le Naufrage de la Méduse*; libretto by Hippolyte and Théodore Cogniard; May 31, 1839, Paris.

Mauer, Die, opera in one act by Hans Ulrich Engelmann; libretto by Langston Hughes; October 4, 1955, Hamburg.

Max und Moritz, children's opera in seven episodes by Walter Willig; libretto after Wilhelm Busch; December 1, 1979, Freiburg.

Meergeuse, Der, opera in three acts by František Škroup; libretto by J. Karl Hickel; November 29, 1851, Prague.

Meister Andrea, opera in two acts by Felix Weingartner; libretto by the composer after Emanuel Geibel; May 13, 1920, Vienna; libretto (Vienna: UE, 1919).

Meister Guido, opera in three acts by Hermann Noetzel; libretto by the composer; September 15, 1918, Karlsruhe.

Meister Martin und seine Gesellen, opera in three acts by Wendelin Weissheimer; libretto by August Schricker after E. T.A. Hoffmann; April 14, 1879, Karlsruhe.

Meister Martin und seine Gesellen, opera in two acts by Louis Lacombe; libretto by Hugo Riemann after Charles Nuitter's *Le Tonnelier de Nurenberg*, itself after E. T. A. Hoffmann; March 7, 1897, Koblenz.

Melusina, opera in three acts by Conradin Kreutzer; libretto by Franz Grillparzer; February 27, 1833, Berlin; libretto (Vienna: J. B. Wallishausser, 1833).

Melusine, opera in three acts by Karl Grammann; libretto by the composer; September 25, 1875, Wiesbaden.

Melusine, opera in four acts by Aribert Reimann; libretto by Claus H. Henneberg after the play by Yvan Goll; April 29, 1971, Berlin.

Menandra, opera in three acts by Hugo Kaun; libretto by the composer and Ferdinand Jansen after the latter's *Hypatia*; October 29, 1925, Brunswick, Kiel, Osnabrück, and Rostock.

Merkwürdige Frau des Schusters, Die, opera by Udo Zimmermann; libretto after Federico García-Lorca's *Zapatera prodigiosa* (1931); April 25, 1982, Schwetzingen.

Merlin, opera in three acts by Karl Goldmark; libretto by Siegfried Lipiner; November 19, 1886, Vienna; rev. 1904; fs, vs, and libretto (Leipzig: J. Schuberth, 1886).

Merlin, opera in three acts by Philippe Rüfer; libretto by Ludwig Hoffmann after Karl Immermann; February 28, 1887, Berlin; vs (Leipzig: B&H, 1887).

Merlin, opera in three acts by Felix Draeseke; libretto by the composer after Karl Immermann; April 18, 1913, Gotha.

Mira, opera in two acts by Kurt Overhoff; libretto by Arthur Hospelt; March 18, 1925, Essen.

Mirandolina, opera in three acts by Bernhard Scholz; libretto by Theodor Rehbaum after Carlo Goldoni; March 1, 1907, Darmstadt.

Mirjam, oder **Das Maifest,** grand opera in three acts by Richard Heuberger; January 20, 1894, Vienna; revision of his *Manuel Venegas**.

Mischelli und sein Sohn, opera in three acts by Johann Heinrich Clasing; libretto by Anton Kirchner; May 30, 1806, Hamburg; a sequel to Luigi Cherubini's *Les Deux Journées* (1800, Paris).

Miss Julie, opera by Antonio Bibalo; libretto after August Strindberg; 1975, Aarhus; revised March 18, 1984, West Berlin.

Mister Wu, opera in three acts by Eugen d'Albert; libretto by M. Karlev [K. M. von Levetzow] after the English play by H. M. Vernon and H. Owen; unfinished; completed by Leo Blech; September 29, 1932, Dresden; vs ed. H. F. Redlich (Berlin: Adler, c. 1932).

Mitgefühl, Das, *Liederspiel* in one act by Paul Wranitzky; libretto by Friedrich Treitschke; April 21, 1804, Vienna.

Mitschuldigen, Die, opera in three acts by Helmut Reithmüller; libretto by the composer after Goethe; February 3, 1957, Schwerin.

Mitternachtsstunde, opera in three acts by Franz Danzi; libretto by Matthias Georg Lambrecht after Antoine Jean Dumaniant's *La Guerre ouverte*; April 1788, Munich.

Mitternachtstraum, Ein, opera by Willy Decker; libretto after William Shakespeare's *A Midsummer Night's Dream*; May 29, 1988, Cologne.

Mohr von Semegonda, Der, opera in three acts by Ferdinand Kauer; libretto by Anton Gleich; 1805, Vienna; libretto (Vienna: J. B. Wallishausser, 1805).

Moloch, opera in three acts by Max von Schillings; libretto by Emil Gerhäuser after Friedrich Hebbel; December 8, 1906, Dresden.

Mönch von Sendomir, Der, opera in a prologue, three acts, and epilogue by Alfred Lorentz; libretto by Franz Kaibel after Franz Grillparzer; April 9, 1907, Karlsruhe.

Mondnacht, opera in three acts by Julius Bittner; libretto by the composer; November 13, 1928, Berlin; vs and libretto (Vienna: UE, 1928).

Moschopulos, opera in three acts by Rudolf Wagner-Régeny; libretto by the composer after Franz Pocci; December 1, 1928, Gera.

Mudarra, opera in four acts by Bernhard Anselm Weber; libretto by Carl Alexander Herklots; March 10, 1800, Berlin.

Münchhausen, opera in three acts by Mark Lothar; libretto by Wilhelm M. Treichlinger after Gottfried August Bürger; December 6, 1933, Dresden.

Musen, Die, Singspiel in one act by Johann Adam Hiller; libretto by Daniel Schiebeler; October 3, 1767, Leipzig; vs (Leipzig, 1771).

Musikant, Der, opera in two acts by Julius Bittner; libretto by the composer; April 12, 1910, Vienna; vs (Mainz: BSS, c. 1909).

Mysteriöse Herr X, Der, opera in a prelude and three acts by Alfred Uhl; libretto by Theo Lingen; June 8, 1966, Vienna; vs (Vienna: Doblinger, 1966).

Nacht zu Paluzzi, Die, opera in three acts by Franz Xaver Pentenrieder; libretto by J. von Forst; October 2, 1840, Munich.

Nachtigall, Die, opera in four scenes by Alfred Irmler; libretto by Rudolf Gahlbeck after Hans Christian Andersen; May 17, 1939, Düsseldorf.

Nachtigall, Die, opera in three acts by Hans Schanazara; libretto by Herbert Hennies after Hans Christian Andersen; December 31, 1947, Cologne.

Nachtigall und Rabe, opera in one act by Joseph Weigl; libretto by Georg Friedrich Treitschke after Charles Guillaume Etienne's *Le Rossignol*; April 20, 1818, Vienna.

Nachtschwalbe, Die, dramatic nocturne in one act by Boris Blacher; libretto by Friedrich Wolf; February 22, 1948, Leipzig; vs and libretto (Berlin: B&B, c. 1947).

Nackte König, Der, opera in three acts by Rudolf Wagner-Régeny; libretto by Vera Braun after Hans Christian Andersen's *The Emperor's New Clothes*; December 1, 1928, Gera.

Nana, opera in four acts by Manfred Gurlitt; libretto by Max Brod after Émile Zola's novel (1880); April 26, 1933, Darmstadt; vs (Vienna: UE, 1933).

Nanon, die Wirtin vom Goldenen Lamm, operetta in three acts by Richard Genée; libretto by F. Zell [Camillo Walzel] after a comedy by E. G. M. Théaulon and F. V. A. d'Artois; March 10, 1877, Vienna.

Narcissus, opera in a prologue and three acts by Johann Sigismund Kusser; libretto by Gottlieb Fiedler; October 4, 1692, Brunswick; libretto (Wolfenbüttel: Caspar Johann Bismarck, 1700?).

Narrengericht, Das, "Singkomödie" in two scenes and an interlude by Paul Graener; libretto by Otto Anthes; February 20, 1916, Halle; vs (Vienna: UE, c. 1912).

Nausikaa, opera in a prologue and three acts by August Bungert, part of his cycle *Die Odyssee**; libretto by the composer; March 20, 1901, Dresden.

Nausikaa, opera in two acts by Hermann Reutter; libretto by the composer after Goethe; February 15, 1967, Mainz.

Nero, opera in four acts by Anton Rubinstein; libretto by Richard Pohl after Jules Barbier's French version; November 1, 1879, Hamburg.

Netzwerk, opera by Friedrich Cerha; May 31, 1981, Vienna.

Neue Alceste, Die, caricature opera in three acts by Wenzel Müller; libretto by Joachim Perinet after Pauersbach and Richter; June 12, 1806, Vienna.

Neue krumme Teufel, Der, Singspiel in two acts by Franz Joseph Haydn; libretto by Johann Joseph Kurz after Alain René Lesage's *Le Diable boîteux*; 1759, Vienna; the music is lost.

Neue Paris, opera in one act by Louis Maurer; anonymous libretto; January 27, 1826, Hanover.

Neue Semiramis, Die, opera in three acts by Vincenz Franz Tuczek; libretto by Joachim Perinet; June 25, 1808, Vienna; libretto (Vienna: J. B. Wallishausser, 1808).

Neusonntagskind, Das, opera in two acts by Wenzel Müller; libretto by Joachim Perinet after Philipp Hafner's play *Der Furchtsame* (1763); October 10, 1793, Vienna; libretto (Vienna: M. A. Schmidt, 1794).

Nibelungen, Die, opera in five acts by Heinrich Dorn; libretto by E. Gerber; March 27, 1854, Berlin; vs (Berlin: E. Bote & G. Bock, ca. 1855).

Niobe, monodrama in two acts by Heinrich Sutermeister; libretto by Peter Sutermeister; June 22, 1945, Zurich.

Niobe, opera in one act by Winfried Hiller; libretto by Elisabeth Woska after *Niobe* of Aeschylus; August 16, 1977, Vienna, ORF.

Norwegische Hochzeit, opera in two acts by Gerhard Schjelderup; libretto by the composer; March 17, 1900, Prague.

Notre Dame, opera in two acts by Franz Schmidt; libretto by Leopold Wilk after Victor Hugo's novel (1831); April 1, 1914, Vienna.

Oberst Chabert, opera in three acts by Hermann Wolfgang von Waltershausen; libretto by the composer after Honoré de Balzac's *Le Colonel Chabert*; January 18, 1912, Frankfurt; vs (Munich: Drei-Masken-Verlag, 1911).

Obersteiger, Der, opera in three acts by Carl Zeller; libretto by Moritz West [Moritz Georg Nitzelberger] and Ludwig Held; January 5, 1894, Vienna; vs (Leipzig and London: Bosworth & Co., 1894); libretto (New York: I. Goldmann, ca. 1894).

Ochsensmenuette, Die, Singspiel in one act, based on music of Joseph Haydn, arranged by Ignaz von Seyfried; libretto by Georg Ernst von Hofmann after an incident in Haydn's life; December 13, 1823, Vienna; vs revised George Driescher (Mainz: BSS, 192–).

Ödipus, opera in two acts by Helmut Eder; libretto by Weinstock after Sophocles; September 30, 1960, Linz.

Odyssee, Die, music tragedy in four parts by August Bungert, consisting of *Kirke**, *Nausikaa**, *Odysseus' Heimkehr**, and *Odysseus' Tod**.

Odysseus, opera in three acts by Hermann Reutter; libretto by Rudolf Bach; October 7, 1942, Frankfurt; vs (Mainz: BSS, 1942).

Odysseus bei Circe, opera in three acts by Herbert Trantow; libretto by the composer; May 30, 1938, Brunswick.

Odysseus' Heimkehr, opera in a prologue and three acts by August Bungert; libretto by the composer; December 12, 1896, Dresden; the third part of the composer's cycle *Die Odyssee**.

Odysseus' Tod, opera in a prologue and three acts by August Bungert; libretto by the composer; October 30, 1903, Dresden; the last part of the composer's cycle *Die Odyssee**; vs and libretto (Leipzig: C. F. Leede, 1896).

Odysseus und die Sirenen, opera in one scene by Theo Goldberg; libretto by Johannes Kluenner; February 23, 1950, Berlin.

Oedipus, opera by Wolfgang Rihm; libretto by the composer after Sophocles and texts by Friedrich Nietzsche and Heiner Müller; October 4, 1987, West Berlin.

Olympia, "grosse Oper" in three acts by Gasparo Spontini; libretto by E. T. A. Hoffmann, a translation of the French text by Michel Dieulafoy and Charles Brifaut, after Voltaire, for the Paris premiere (1819, Paris); May 14, 1821, Berlin; vs (Berlin, ca. 1823).

Omar und Leila, "romantische Oper" in three acts by Friedrich Ernst Fesca; libretto by Leopold Robert; February 26, 1824, Karlsruhe.

Onkel aus Boston, Der, oder **Die beiden Neffen,** comic opera in three acts by Felix Mendelssohn; libretto by J. L. Caspar; February 3, 1824, Berlin (private).

Opfer, Das, opera in three acts by Winfried Zillig; libretto by Reinhard Goeting; November 12, 1937, Hamburg; vs (Kassel and New York: Bär, 1960).

Opferung des Gefangenen, Die, opera by Egon Wellesz; libretto by Franz von der Stucken after the Aztec legend; 1926, Cologne; vs (Vienna: UE, 1925).

Ophelia, opera in one act by Hans Ulrich Engelmann; libretto by Miriam Goldschmidt; February 1, 1969, Hanover.

Ophelia, opera by Rudolf Kelterborn; libretto by Herbert Meier after Shakespeare's *Hamlet*; May 2, 1984, Schwetzingen.

Orestes, opera in three parts by Felix Weingartner; libretto by the composer after Aeschylus; February 15, 1902, Leipzig; vs (Leipzig: B&H, 1901).

Originale, opera in one act by Karlheinz Stockhausen; libretto by the composer; October 26, 1961, Cologne.

Orontes, opera by Johann Theile; 1678, Hamburg.

Orpheus, opera in five acts by Reinhard Keiser; libretto by Friedrich Christian Bressand; 1698, Brunswick; given in two parts, as *Die sterbende Eurydice, oder Orpheus erster Theil** and *Die verwandelte Leyer des Orpheus, oder Orpheus ander Theil**; libretto (Brunswick: Gruber, 1698).

Orpheus, Singspiel in three acts by Friedrich Benda; libretto by Lindemann; January 16, 1785, Berlin (concert); vs (Berlin: Im Verlage des Autors, Rellstabschen Musikdruckerey [1787]).

Orpheus, a setting of Claudio Monteverdi's opera by Carl Orff; libretto by Dorothee Günther; October 4, 1925, Dresden.

Orpheus ander Theil, opera in three acts by Reinhard Keiser; libretto by Friedrich Christian Bressand; 1702, Hamburg; a revision of *Die verwandelte Leyer.**

Orpheus aus Thracien, opera in a prologue and three acts by Johann Jakob Loewe; libretto by Anton Ulrich, Duke of Brunswick; August 30, 1659, Brunswick; the music is lost.

Orpheus erster Theil. See *Die sterbende Eurydice*; part of *Orpheus.**

Orpheus und der Bürgermeister, children's opera by Paul Dessau; libretto by Robert Seitz; composed 1931.

Palast Hotel Thanatos, opera in one act by Dieter Einfeldt; libretto by Bernd W. Wessling after André Maurois; April 7, 1972, Hanover.

Palmer und Amalia, opera in three acts by Carl Cannabich; anonymous libretto after C. A. G. Pigault-Lebrun's *Le Major Palmer* (1797); August 1803, Munich.

Paris und Helena, oder **Der glückliche Liebeswechsel,** opera in three acts by Johann David Heinichen; libretto possibly by Barthold Feind after *La forza dell'amore*, first set by Reinhard Keiser in 1711; 1710, Naumberg.

Parolo (Frau Denise), opera in one act by Leo Fall; libretto by L. Fernand; 1902, Hamburg.

Peer Gynt, opera by Viktor Ullmann; libretto after Henrik Ibsen; not performed.

Penelope, oder **Des Ulysses zweiter [anderer] Theil,** opera in three acts by Reinhard Keiser; libretto by Friedrich Christian Bressand; February 1696, Brunswick; a different work from Keiser's *Ulysses**, 1722; first performed with *Circe**; the music is lost.

Penthesilea, opera in three acts by Rudo Ritter; libretto by Karl Ritter after Heinrich von Kleist; June 14, 1927, Würzburg.

Periander, "scenes from the life of a tyrant" by Theodore Antoniou; libretto by George Christodoulakis, German translation by Peter Kertz; February 6, 1983, Munich.

Persische Episode, comic opera in four acts by Rudolf Wagner-Régeny; libretto by Caspar Neher after Bertolt Brecht poems; March 27, 1963, Rostock; vs (Vienna: UE, 1951).

Peter der Dritte, opera in three parts by Norbert Schultze; libretto by Ivo Wanja and Karl Vibach; March 21, 1965, Kiel, ZDF; May 30, 1974, Lübeck (stage).

Peter und Susanne, oder **Die österreichische Schwermut,** opera in five scenes by Paul Kont; libretto by Gerhard Fritsch; June 26, 1959, Vienna, ORF; January 29, 1968, Innsbruck (staged).

Pfauenfest, Das, Singspiel in two acts by Johann Rudolf Zumsteeg; libretto by F. A. Werthes; February 24, 1801, Stuttgart.

Pfeifertag, Der, comic opera in three acts by Max von Schillings; libretto by Ferdinand Graf von Sporck; November 26, 1899, Schwerin; vs and libretto (Berlin: B&B, 1899).

Pfiffige Magd, Die, comic opera in three acts by Julius Weismann; libretto by Ludwig Holberg; February 11, 1939, Leipzig; vs and libretto (Mainz: BSS, 1939).

Phaedra, opera in one scene by Theo Goldberg; libretto by Johannes Hübner; 1950, Berlin.

Phasma, oder **Die Erscheinung im Tempel der Verschweigenheit,** Singspiel in two acts by Franz Süssmayr; July 25, 1801, Vienna; libretto (Vienna: J. B. Wallishausser, 1801).

Pluto, opera in five scenes by Paul Kont; libretto by the composer; February 10, 1977, Klagenfurt.

Polnische Jude, Der, opera in two acts by Karel Weis; libretto by Victor Léon and Richard Batka after Émile Erckmann and Pierre Alexandre Chatrian; March 3, 1901, Prague.

Polterabend, Der, Singspiel in one act by August Eberhard Müller; libretto by A. Wolff; 1813 or 1814, Weimar; vs (Leipzig, c. 1820).

Poltis, oder **Das gerettete Troja,** Singspiel by Johann Adam Hiller; libretto by G. S. Brunner after Steinel; ca. 1777; vs (Leipzig: Schwickert, ca. 1777).

Pompadour, La, opera in two acts by Emanuel Moór; libretto by L. von Ferro and A. L. Moór after Alfred de Musset; February 22, 1902, Cologne.

Porsenna, opera by Georg Caspar Schürmann; 1718, Brunswick.

Porzia, opera in three acts by Otto Taubmann; libretto by Richard Wilde after Shakespeare's *Merchant of Venice*; November 14, 1916, Frankfurt; vs (Berlin: Drei-Masken-Verlag, 1916).

Postmeister Wyrin, opera in three acts by Florizel von Reuter; libretto by the composer after Alexsander Pushkin; November 12, 1946, Berlin.

Preis, Der, opera by Karl Ottomar Treibmann; libretto by Harald Gerlach; 1980, Erfurt.

Prinz Eugen, der edle Ritter, opera in three acts by Gustav Schmidt; libretto by Alexander Rost; July 26, 1847, Frankfurt.

Prinz Methusalem, operetta in three acts by Johann Strauss, Jr.; libretto by Karl Treumann after Victor Wilder and Alfred Delacour [Alfred Charlemagne Latrigue]; January 3, 1877, Vienna.

Prinz von Homburg, Der, opera in nine scenes by Paul Graener; libretto by the composer after Heinrich von Kleist; March 14, 1935, Berlin.

Prinz wider Willen, Der, opera in three acts by Otto Lohse; libretto by Rudolf Seuberlich; February 27, 1890, Riga.

Prinzessin auf der Erbse, Die, opera in one act by Ernst Toch; libretto by Benno Elkon after Hans Christian Andersen; July 17, 1927, Baden-Baden; vs (Mainz: BSS, 1927).

Prinzessin Ginara, "Weltspiel und Legende" by Egon Wellesz; libretto by Jacob Wassermann; May 15, 1921, Hanover; vs (Vienna: UE, 1921).

Prinzessin und der Schweinehirt, Die, opera in ten scenes by Hermann Reutter; libretto by Else Helmund after Hans Christian Andersen; December 18, 1938, Mainz.

Prinzessin von Provence, Die, opera in three acts by Johann Nepomuk Poissl; libretto by the composer after Felice Romani, January 23, 1825, Munich.

Procris und Cephalis, Singspiel in three acts by Reinhard Keiser; libretto by Friedrich Christian Bressand; 1694, Brunswick.

Prometheus, scenic oratorio in five scenes by Rudolf Wagner-Régeny; libretto by the composer after Aeschylus; September 12, 1959, Kassel; libretto (Berlin: B&B, 1958).

Psyche (Die wunderschöne Psyche), opera in three acts by Reinhard Keiser; libretto by Christian H. Postel; 1701, Hamburg.

Psyche, Singspiel in two acts by Peter Winter; libretto by C. Mühler; 1790, Munich.

Pulcinella, opera in two acts by Bernhard Krol; libretto by Curt Hotzel; January 24, 1961, Kaiserlautern.

Pygmalion, opera in one act by Georg Benda; libretto an anonymous translation of Jean-Jacques Rousseau's work; September 20, 1779, Gotha; vs ed. composer (Leipzig: Schwickert, 1780).

Pyramus und Thisbe, melodrama in one act by Anton Eberl; libretto by the composer; December 7, 1794, Vienna.

R. Hot, "opera-fantasy in more than one hundred dramatic, comic and fantastic poses" by Friedrich Goldmann; libretto by Thomas Körner after Jacob Michael Reinhold Lenz's play *Der Engländer* (1776); February 27, 1977, East Berlin.

Rächer, Der, opera in three acts by Ludwig Schindelmeisser; libretto by Otto Prechtler after Pierre Corneille's *Le Cid*; April 4, 1846, Budapest.

Raimondin, opera in five acts by Karl von Perfall; libretto by Hermann Theodor von Schmid; March 27, 1881, Munich; revised as *Melusine*, September 30, 1885, Munich.

Rappelkopf, opera in three acts by Mark Lothar; libretto by Wilhelm M. Treichlinger after Ferdinand Raimund; August 8, 1958, Munich.

Raskolnikoff, opera in two acts by Heinrich Sutermeister; libretto by Peter Sutermeister after Fyodor Dostoyevsky; October 14, 1948, Stockholm; libretto (Mainz: BSS, 1948).

Ratcliff, opera in four scenes by Volkmar Andreae; libretto after Heinrich Heine; May 25, 1914, Duisburg; vs (Berlin: A. Fürstner, c. 1918).

Rattenfänger, Der, opera by Friedrich Cerha; libretto by the composer after Carl Zuckmayer's play (1975); September 26, 1987, Graz.

Rattenfänger von Hamelin, Der, opera in five acts by Viktor Ernst Nessler; libretto by Friedrich Hofmann after Julius Wolff; March 19, 1879, Leipzig; vs (Leipzig: J. Schuberth & Co., 1879).

Räuberbraut, Die, opera in three acts by Ferdinand Ries; libretto by Georg Döring; October 15, 1828, Frankfurt.

Rauchfangkehrer, Die (Die unentbehrlichen Verräther ihrer Herrschaften aus Eigennutz), opera in three acts by Antonio Salieri; libretto by Leopold von Auenbrugger; April 30, 1781, Vienna.

Rebekka als Braut, Singspiel by Michael Haydn; libretto after P. F. Reichssiegel; April 10, 1766, Salzburg.

Regenbrüder, Die, opera in two acts by Ignaz Lachner; libretto by Eduard Mörike and Hermann Kurz; May 20, 1839, Stuttgart.

Regnat, Der, oder **Anton in der Türkei,** Singspiel in two acts possibly by Benedikt Schack; libretto by Emanuel Schikaneder; September 15, 1792, Vienna; sixth of Schikaneder's seven "Anton" Singspiels; the work is lost.

Reise, Die, opera by Lars Johan Werle; libretto by Lars Rusen after P. C. Jersild's novel *To Warmer Lands;* March 2, 1969, Hamburg.

Reiter der Nacht, opera in a prologue and eleven scenes by Ernst Hermann Meyer; libretto by Günther Decker after P. Abrahams; November 17, 1973, East Berlin.

Rembrandt van Rijn, opera in four acts by Paul von Klenau; libretto by the composer; first performance January 23, 1937, Berlin.

Revolutionshochzeit, opera in three acts by Eugen d'Albert; libretto by Ferdinand Lion after Sophus Michaelis; September 26, 1919, Leipzig; vs (Berlin-Munich: Drei-Masken-Verlag, c. 1919).

Rheinnixen, Die, operetta by Jacques Offenbach; 1864, Vienna; libretto (Vienna: J. Löwenthal, 1864).

Rinaldo und Alcina, opera in three acts by Maria Theresia von Paradis; libretto by Ludwig von Baczko after Lodovico Ariosto; summer 1797, Prague.

Ring der Liebe, Der, oder **Zemirens und Azors Ehestand,** Singspiel in three acts by Ignaz Umlauf; libretto by Paul Weidemann or Karl Emil Schubert; December 3, 1786, Vienna; a sequel to A. E. M. Grétry's *Zémire et Azor* (1771, Fontainebleau).

Ring des Glückes, Der, oder **Die Quellenfürstin im Alpentale,** *Zauberspiel* in three acts by Conradin Kreutzer; libretto by F. K. Weidmann; December 19, 1833, Vienna.

Ritter Blaubart, opera in three acts by Emil Nikolaus von Reznicek; libretto by Herbert Eulenberg; January 29, 1920, Darmstadt; vs and libretto (Vienna: UE, 1920).

Ritter Pázmán, comic opera in three acts by Johann Strauss, Jr.; libretto by Lajos Dóczy; January 1, 1892, Vienna; vs (Berlin: N. Simrock, ca. 1892).

Robert, oder **Die Prüfung,** opera in two acts by Adalbert Gyrowetz; libretto by Franz Xaver Huber; July 15, 1815, Vienna.

Robin Hood, opera in three acts by Albert Dietrich; libretto by Reinhard Molen; 1879, Frankfurt; vs (Leipzig: Fr. Kistner, ca. 1879).

Robins Ende, opera in two acts by Eduard Künneke; libretto by Maximilian Morris; May 5, 1909, Mannheim.

Robinson und Freitag, radio opera in one act by Theo Goldberg; libretto by Heinz von Cramer; June 24, 1951, Berlin, RIAS.

Rodrigo und Zimene, opera in two acts by Johann Kaspar Aiblinger; libretto by Jacob Sendtner after Pierre Corneille's *Le Cid* (1637); May 1, 1821, Munich.

Rolands Knappen, oder **Das ersehnte Glück,** opera in three acts by Albert Lortzing; libretto by the composer, Georg Meisinger and Carl Haffner; May 25, 1849, Leipzig.

Romanische Lucretia, Die, opera in a prologue and three acts by Kaspar Kasimir Schweitzelsperger; anonymous libretto; 1714, Durlach; vs (Hamburg: n.p., 1715).

Rosamunde, opera in three acts by Anton Schweitzer; libretto by Christoph Martin Wieland; January 20, 1780, Mannheim.

Rose, oder **Pflicht und Liebe im Streit,** opera by Johann Mederitsch; libretto by Gottlob Stephanie, Jr., February 9, 1783, Vienna; libretto (Vienna: Logenmeister, 1782).

Rose von Liebesgarten, Die, opera in a prologue, two acts, and an epilogue by Hans Pfitzner; libretto by James Grun; November 9, 1901, Elberfeld.

Rose von Pontevedra, Die, opera in one act by Josef Forster; libretto by the composer; July 30, 1893, Gotha.

Rosen der Madonna, Die, operetta in one act by Robert Stolz; libretto by Bruno Hardt-Warden and Otto Tumtinz; October 2, 1964, ORF, Vienna.

Rosenfest, Das, opera in three acts by Ernst Wilhelm Wolf; libretto by Gottlob Ephraim Heermann after Charles Favart, 1769; September 4, 1770, Weimar; vs (Berlin: Georg Ludwig Winter, 1771).

Rosengärtlein, Das, "Legende" in three acts by Julius Bittner; libretto by the composer; March 18, 1923, Mannheim; vs (Vienna: UE, c. 1922).

Rossenknecht, opera in one act by Winfried Zillig; libretto by Richard Billinger; February 11, 1933, Düsseldorf; vs (Kassel and New York: Bär, 1959).

Rossini in Neapel, opera in three acts by Bernhard Paumgartner; libretto by Hans Adler; March 27, 1936, Zurich.

Rote Gred, Die, opera in three acts by Julius Bittner; libretto by the composer; October 26, 1907, Frankfurt; vs (Mainz: BSS, c. 1907).

Rote Stiefel, Der, opera in three acts by Heinrich Sutermeister; libretto after Wilhelm Hauff's *Das kalte Herz*; November 22, 1951, Stockholm.

Rübezahl, opera in three acts by Vincenz Franz Tuczek; libretto by G. Bürde; 1801, Breslau.

Rübezahl, Singspiel in two acts by Franz Danzi; libretto by Caterino Mazzola; April 19, 1813, Karlsruhe.

Rübezahl, opera in three acts by Wilhelm Würfel; libretto by Wilhelm Marsano; October 7, 1824, Prague.

Rübezahl, opera in three acts by Friedrich von Flotow; libretto by Gustav Heinrich Gans zu Putlitz; August 13, 1852, Retzien (private); November 26, 1853, Frankfurt.

Rübezahl, "Märchenspiel" by Carl Vogler; libretto by J. Löwenberg; 1917, Zurich.

Rübezahl und der Sackpfeifer von Neisse, opera in four acts by Hans Sommer; libretto by Eberhard König; May 15, 1904, Brunswick.

Rubin, Der, "musikalisches Märchen" in two acts by Eugen d'Albert; libretto by the composer after Friedrich Hebbel's comedy (1851); October 12, 1893, Karlsruhe; vs (Leipzig: B&H, c. 1893).

Rubin, Der, opera in three acts by Albert Jenny; libretto by the composer after Friedrich Hebbel; February 20, 1938, Stans, Switzerland.

Rückfahrt des Kaisers, Die, opera in one act by Johann Nepomuk Hummel; libretto by Johann Emanuel Veith; June 15, 1814, Vienna.

Rufen Sie Herrn Plim!, musical in one act by Mischa Spoliansky; text by Marcellus Schiffer; ca. 1925.

Ruinen vom Paluzzi, Die, opera in three acts by Andreas Romberg; libretto by Johann Friedrich Schink; December 27, 1811, Hamburg.

Rumpelstilzchen, opera in seven scenes by Paul Büttner; libretto by the composer after the brothers Grimm; November 11, 1911, Bamberg.

Runenzauber, opera in one act by Emil Hartmann; libretto by Emma Klingenfeld after Julius Lehmann's text, founded on the Henrik Hertz play *Svend Dyrings Hus*; October 15, 1896, Hamburg.

Ruy Blas, opera by Max Zenger; 1868, Mannheim.

Saidar und Zulima, opera by Heinrich Marschner; 1818, Bratislava.

Sakuntala, opera in five scenes by Franz Schubert; libretto by Johann P. Neumann; composed 1820; June 12, 1971, Vienna (concert) ; fs Schu/*NGA*, II/13.

Sakuntala, opera in three acts by Felix Weingartner; libretto by the composer after Kalidasa's Indian drama; March 23, 1884, Weimar; fs (Kassel: P. Voigt, 1884).

Sakuntala, opera in three acts by Balduin Zimmermann; libretto by H. Schmilinski; April 2, 1905, Erfurt.

Salambo, opera in three acts by Lukas Böttcher; libretto by Aline Sanden after Gustave Flaubert's novel (1862); May 1, 1926, Altenburg.

Salomon, Singspiel in three acts by Georg Caspar Schürmann; libretto by Duke Anton Ulrich von Brunswick or J. C. Knorr von Rosenroth; August 1701, Brunswick.

Salvator Rosa, oder Zwey Nächte in Rom, opera in two acts by Joseph Rastrelli; libretto by Johann Peter Theodor Lyser after E. T. A. Hoffmann's story *Signor Formica* (1819); July 22, 1832, Dresden.

Samori, opera in three acts by Georg Joseph Vogler; libretto by Franz Xaver Huber; May 17, 1804, Vienna; vs (Vienna: Tranquillo Mollo & Co., ca. 1804).

Samson, Richter in Israel, melodrama in three acts Vincenz Franz Tuczek; libretto by J. A. Schuster; August 13, 1808, Vienna.

Sancio und Sinilde (Die in ihrer Unschuld siegende Sinilde), opera in three acts by Karl Heinrich Graun; libretto by Johann Ulrich König after Francesco Silvani's *Il miglior d'ogni Amore per il peggiore d'ogni Odio*, set by Francesco Gasparini (1703, Venice); February 3, 1727, Brunswick.

Sandmann, Der, opera in ten scenes by Arghyris Kounadis; libretto by Peter Siefert after E. T. A. Hoffmann's *Nachtstücke* (1815); February 7, 1987, Hamburg.

Sandro der Narr, opera in three acts by Heinrich Bienstock; libretto by H. H. Hinzelmann [Karl Michael von Levetzow and Leo Hirschfeld]; September 24, 1916, Stuttgart.

Sänger und der Schneider, Der, opera in one act by Friedrich von Drieberg; libretto probably by the composer after Pierre Villiers' and Armand Gouffé's text for Pierre Gaveaux's *Le Bouffe et le Tailleur* (1804, Paris); November 23, 1814, Berlin.

Sangeskönig Hiarne, oder **Das Tyrfingschwert,** opera in four acts by Heinrich Marschner; libretto by Wilhelm Grothe; composed in 1861; September 13, 1863, Frankfurt.

Santa Chiara, opera in three acts by Ernst II, Duke of Saxe-Coburg-Gotha; libretto by Charlotte Birch-Pfeiffer; April 2, 1854, Gotha.

Sappho, opera in three acts by Hugo Kaun; libretto by the composer after Franz Grillparzer's play (1817); October 27, 1917, Leipzig.

Sarema, opera in three acts by Alexander von Zemlinsky; libretto by Arnold Schoenberg after Rudolf von Gottschall's *Die Rose vom Kaukasus*; October 10, 1897, Munich.

Satuala, opera in three acts by Emil Nikolaus von Reznicek; libretto by Rolf Lauckner; December 4, 1927, Leipzig; vs (Vienna: UE, 1928).

Satyros, opera in a prologue and two acts by Waldemar von Baussnern; libretto by the composer after Goethe's poem; January 31, 1923, Basel.

Sawitri, opera in three acts by Hermann Zumpe, completed by G. Rössler; libretto by Ferdinand Graf von Sporck; November 8, 1907, Schwerin; vs (Leipzig, c. 1908).

Scenen aus Mozarts Leben. See *Szenen aus Mozarts Leben.*

Schach dem König!, comic opera in three acts by Ignaz Brüll; libretto by Victor Léon [Victor Hirschfeld] after Schauffer; 1893, Munich; vs (Leipzig: Zimmermann, 1893).

Scharazade, opera in three acts by Bernhard Sekles; libretto by Gerdt von Bassewitz; November 2, 1917, Mannheim.

Schatzmeister, Der, operetta in three acts by Carl Michael Ziehrer; libretto by Alexander Engel and Julius Horst; December 10, 1904, Vienna.

Scherz, List und Rache, opera by Peter Winter; 1790, Munich.

Scherz, List und Rache, Singspiel in one act by E. T. A. Hoffmann; libretto by the composer after Goethe; ca. 1801, Posen.

Scherz, List und Rache, opera in one act by Max Bruch; libretto by L. Brachoff after Goethe; private performance December 14, 1856, Cologne; first public performance January 14, 1858, Cologne; vs (Leipzig: B. Senff, ca. 1858).

Scherz, List und Rache, opera in one act by Egon Wellesz; libretto by the composer after Goethe; March 1, 1928, Stuttgart; vs (Vienna: UE, 1927).

Scherz, List und Rache, opera in two acts by Friedrich Leinert; libretto by the composer after Goethe; March 6, 1961, Hanover.

Schiffspatron, Der. See *Der Gutsherr.*

Schirin und Getraude, opera in four acts by Paul Graener; libretto by Ernst Hardt after his comedy of the same name; April 28, 1920, Dresden; vs (Berlin: Musikverlag EOS [1920]).

Schlaue Müllerin, Die, *Tanzspiel* in one act by Cesar Bresgen; libretto by the composer; 1943; vs (Mainz: BSS, 1943).

Schlaue Susanna, Die, opera in nine scenes by Franz Xaver Lehner; libretto by the composer after Hans Schlegel's translation of Lope de Vega; January 13, 1952, Nuremberg.

Schloss, Das, opera in three acts by André Laporte; libretto after Franz Kafka's novel (1922); December 1986, Brussels.

Schloss am Ätna, Das, opera in three acts by Heinrich Marschner; libretto by August Klingemann (the text was originally called *Adelgunde*); January 29, 1836, Leipzig; vs (Leipzig: G. Wunder, 18—).

Schloss Candra, "heroische Oper" in three acts by Joseph Maria Wolfram; libretto by Eduard Heinrich Gehe; December 1, 1832, Dresden.

Schmied von Marienburg, Der, opera in three acts by Siegfried Wagner; libretto by the composer; December 16, 1923, Rostock.

Schmied von Ruhla, Der, opera in three acts by Friedrich Lux; libretto by Ludwig Bauer; March 29, 1882, Mainz.

Schneekönigin, Die, opera in three acts by Kurt Thies; libretto by Harald Netzband; January 18, 1957, Trier, West Germany.

Schneider Fips, Der, opera in one act by Alfred Lorentz; libretto by Friedrich Goeldner after August von Kotzebue; March 16, 1928, Coburg.

Schneider von Schönau, Die, comic opera in three acts by Jan Brandts-Buys; libretto by Bruno Hardt-Warden and Ignaz Michael Welleminsky; April 1, 1916, Dresden.

Schöffe von Paris, Der, opera in two acts by Heinrich Dorn; libretto by Wilhelm August Wohlbrück; November 13, 1838, Riga.

Schön ist die Welt, operetta in three acts by Franz Lehár; libretto by Ludwig Herzer [Ludwig Herzl] and Fritz Löhner; December 3, 1930, Berlin; a revision of *Endlich allein*.*

Schöne Bellinda, Die, opera in a prologue and three acts by Hans Huber; libretto by Gian Bundi; April 2, 1916, Bern.

Schöne Geschichten, opera by Stefan Wolpe; composed 1929.

Schöne Melusine, Die, opera by Vincenz Franz Tuczek; May 6, 1809, Vienna.

Schöne Müllerin, Die, opera in one act by Otto Dorn; libretto by the composer; November 6, 1906, Kassel.

Schöne Schusterin, Die, oder **Die pücefarbenen Schuhe,** opera by Ignaz Umlauf; 1779, Vienna; libretto in *German Opera Librettos*, XXII (New York: Garland, 1986).

Schreiner, Der, opera by Paul Wranitzky; 1799, Vienna.

Schuhu und die fliegende Prinzessin, Der, opera by Udo Zimmermann; libretto by the composer and Eberhardt Schmidt after the play of Peter Hacks (1966); December 30, 1976, Dresden.

Schuldigkeit des ersten Gebotes, three-part sacred drama, with part I by Wolfgang Amadeus Mozart, part II by Michael Haydn, and part III by Anton Cajetan Adlgasser; libretto by I. A. Weiser; part I performed March 1, 1767, Salzburg; fs, M/*MW*; parts II and III are lost.

Schulkandidat, Der, opera by Maria Theresia von Paradis; 1792, Vienna.

Schuster-Feierabend, Der, opera by Antonín Volanek; 1793, Prague.

Schwanenweiss, opera in three acts by Julius Weismann; libretto by the composer after August Strindberg; September 23, 1923, Duisburg; vs (Mainz: BSS, 1924).

Schwanhild, opera in three acts by Paul Graener; libretto by Otto Anthes; January 4, 1942, Cologne; vs and libretto (Vienna: UE, c. 1941).

Schwarz auf weiss, radio opera in two acts by Kurt Hüber; libretto by Rainer Martin after Jonathan Swift; November 19, 1968, ORF, Vienna.

Schwarze Frau, Die, Singspiel by Adolf Müller; libretto by Meisl, a parody of *La dame blanche* of François Adrien Boieldieu (1825, Paris); December 1826, Vienna.

Schwarze Kaschka, Die, opera in four acts by Georg Jarno; libretto by Victor Blüthgen; May 12, 1895, Breslau.

Schwarze Korsar, Der, operetta by Jacques Offenbach; September 21, 1872, Vienna; basis of *Der Goldschmied von Toledo.**

Schwarze Maske, Die, opera by Krzystof Penderecki; libretto by Harry Kupfer; August 1987, Salzburg Festival.

Schwarze Orchidee, Die, "Opera grotesca" in three acts by Eugen d'Albert; libretto by Karl M. von Levetzow; December 1, 1928, Leipzig; vs and libretto (Vienna: UE, c. 1928).

Schwarze Spinne, Die, Singspiel by Josef Matthias Hauer; libretto by H. Schlesinger after the story of Jeremias Gotthelf [Albert Bitzius] (1842); composed 1932; first performance May 23, 1966, Vienna.

Schwarze Spinne, Die, opera in one act by Heinrich Sutermeister; libretto by Albert Rösler after Jeremias Gotthelf; October 15, 1936, Bern radio; February 16, 1949, St. Gallen (staged).

Schwarzer Peter, children's opera in five scenes by Norbert Shulze; libretto by Walter Lieck after Heinrich Traulsen's *Erica*; December 6, 1936, Hamburg.

Schwarzschwanreich, opera in three acts by Siegfried Wagner; libretto by the composer; November 5, 1918, Karlsruhe; vs (Leipzig: M. Brockhaus, 1911).

Schweigende Dorf, Das, opera in three acts by Wilhelm Neef; libretto by Willi Bredel; May 6, 1961, Plauen, East Germany.

Scirocco, opera in three acts by Eugen d'Albert; libretto by Leo Feld [Leo Herschfeld] and Karl M. von Levetzow; May 16, 1921, Darmstadt; vs (Berlin: Drei-Masken-Verlag, c. 1919).

Seekadett, Der, operetta in three acts by Richard Genée; libretto by F. Zell [Camillo Walzel]; October 24, 1876, Vienna.

Seemannsbraut, Die, opera in three acts by Sigwardt Aspestrand; libretto by the composer; March 29, 1894, Gotha.

Semiramis, oder Die allerletste regierende Königen, opera by Johann Wolfgang Franck; libretto by Heinrich Hinsch after the opera text set by Pietro Andrea Ziani (1670, Venice); 1683, Hamburg.

Seraphine, opera in one act by Heinrich Sutermeister; libretto by the composer after François Rabelais; June 10, 1959, Bern, SRG television; February 25, 1960, Munich (staged).

Sganarelle, opera in one act by Rudolf Wagner-Régeny; libretto by the composer after Molière's farce (1660); April 12, 1929, Essen.

Sicilianische Vesper, Die, "Grosse heroische Oper" in four parts by Peter Lindpaintner; libretto by Heribert Rau; 1843; libretto (Munich: G. Franz, 184–).

Sieben Geislein, "Märchenoper" by Engelbert Humperdinck; libretto by Adelheid Wette; December 19, 1895, Magdeburg; vs (Magdeburg, 1895).

Sieg der Schönheit, revised version of Johann Georg Conradi's *Gensericus**; altered libretto by Christian Friedrich Weichmann and additional music by Georg Philipp Telemann; June 20, 1722, Hamburg.

Siguna, Nordic legend in three acts by Conradin Kreutzer; libretto by the composer; November 20, 1823, Vienna.

Simplicius, Der, opera in three acts by Hans Huber; libretto by Albrecht Mendelssohn-Bartholdy after H. J. C. Grimmelshausen's satire *Simplicius Simplicissimus* (1669); February 22, 1912, Basel.

Simplizius, Der, operetta in three acts by Johann Strauss, Jr.; libretto by Victor Léon [Victor Hirschfeld] after H. J. C. Grimmels-hausen's satire; December 17, 1887, Vienna.

Singende Teufel, Der, opera in four acts by Franz Schreker; libretto by the composer; December 10, 1928, Berlin; vs (Vienna: UE, 1928).

Sinilde. See *Sancio und Sinilda*.

Sirius, opera in one act by Karl Stockhausen; libretto by the composer; April 8, 1977, Aix-en-Provence.

Sizilianer, Der, opera in two scenes by Karl Heinrich David; libretto by the composer after Molière; October 22, 1924, Zurich.

So oder so, opera in five scenes by Diether de la Motte; libretto by the composer; April 10, 1975, Hamburg.

Soldaten, opera in three acts by Manfred Gurlitt; libretto by the composer after the play by J. M. R. Lenz (1776); November 9, 1930, Düsseldorf; vs (Vienna: UE, c. 1930).

Soldatenleben, opera in three acts by Friedrich Wilhelm Hackländer; libretto by the composer; June 4, 1848, Stuttgart.

Sonnenflammen, opera in three acts by Siegfried Wagner; libretto by the composer; October 30, 1918, Darmstadt.

Sophie Katharina, oder **Die Grossfürstin,** opera in four acts by Friedrich von Flotow; libretto by Charlotte Birch-Pfeiffer; November 19, 1850, Berlin.

Sophonisbe, monodrama in one act by Christian Gottlob Neefe; libretto by August Gottlieb Meissner; November 3, 1778, Mannheim; vs (Leipzig: Schwickert, n.d.).

Spanische Nacht, opera in two acts by Eugen Bodart; libretto by the composer after Heinrich Laube; October 16, 1937, Mannheim.

Spiegel der Agrippina, Der, opera in three acts by Hans Haug; libretto by Fridolin Tschudi after Hans Müller; May 24, 1937, Basel.

Spiegelritter, Der, opera in three acts by Ignaz Walter; libretto by August von Kotzebue; September 1, 1791, Frankfurt.

Spiel oder Ernst?, opera in one act by Emil Nikolaus von Reznicek; libretto by Paul Knudsen; November 11, 1930, Dresden; vs (Vienna: UE, 1930); libretto, the same.

Spiel von der Auferstehung des Herrn, Das, opera by Walter Braunfels; libretto by Hans Reinhart after the Alsfelder Passion play; 1954, Cologne radio.

Spiel von König Aphelius, Das, opera in a prelude, five scenes, and a postlude by Heinrich Kaminski; libretto by the composer; January 29, 1950, Göttingen; libretto (Kassel: Bär, 1947).

Spiel von Liebe und Zufall, Das, opera by Gerhard Rosenfeld; libretto by Gerhard Hartmann after Pierre Carlet de Marivaux's play *Le Jeu de l'Amour et du Hasard* (1730); February 27, 1982, Karlsruhe.

Spieldose, Die, opera in three acts by Robert Hanell; libretto by Georg Kaiser; November 30, 1957, Erfurt.

Spielmann, Der, opera in three acts by Kurt Striegler; libretto by P. Neuhaus; November 23, 1949, Coburg.

Spitzentuch der Königin, Das, operetta in three acts by Johann Strauss, Jr.; libretto by Heinrich Bohrmann-Riegen and Richard Genée; October 1, 1880, Vienna.

Sprung über den Schatten, Der, opera in three acts by Ernst Krenek; libretto by the composer; June 9, 1924, Frankfurt; vs (Vienna: UE, c. 1923).

Stadt hinter dem Strom, Die, opera in three acts by Hans Vogt; libretto by Hermann Kasack; May 3, 1955, Wiesbaden.

Steinerne Herz, Das, Romantic opera in three acts by Ignaz Brüll; libretto by Joseph Victor Widmann; 1888, Vienna; vs (Leipzig: C. F. Kahnt Nachfolger, c. 1888).

Stella, opera in three acts by Waldemar Bloch; libretto by Harald Kaufmann after Goethe; July 5, 1951, Graz.

Stella Maris, opera in three acts by Alfred Kaiser; libretto by the composer after the French original of Henry Revers; November 25, 1910, Düsseldorf.

Stephen Climax, opera by Hans Zender; libretto by the composer after the life of St. Simeon Stylites and episodes from James Joyce's *Ulysses*; June 15, 1986, Frankfurt.

Sterbende Eurydice, Die, oder **Orpheus erster Theil,** Singspiel in three acts by Reinhard Keiser; libretto by Friedrich Christian Bressand; 1702, Hamburg; the music is lost; part of *Orpheus.**

Stern geht auf aus Jaakob, Ein, opera in ten scenes by Paul Burkhard; libretto by the composer; December 6, 1970, Hamburg.

Sternengebot, Das, opera in a prologue and three acts by Siegfried Wagner; libretto by the composer; January 21, 1908, Hamburg.

Stier von Olivera, Der, opera in three acts by Eugen d'Albert; libretto by Richard Batka after Heinrich Lilienfein's drama; March 10, 1918, Leipzig; vs (Berlin: B&B, c. 1917).

Stoertebecker und Joedge Michaels, opera in three acts by Reinhard Keiser; libretto by Hotter; 1701, Hamburg; the music is lost.

Strike der Schmiede, Der, opera in one act by Max Joseph Beer; libretto by Victor Léon after François Coppée's play; February 18, 1897, Augsburg.

Strohwitwe, Die, operetta in three acts by Leo Blech; libretto by August Neidhardt; ca. 1920; vs (Berlin: Drei-Masken-Verlag, c. 1920).

Stumme Serenade, Die, opera in two acts by Erich Korngold; libretto by Viktor Clement; November 10, 1954, Dortmund.

Sturm, Der, opera by Peter Winter; 1798, Munich.

Sturm, Der, oder Die bezauberte Leyer, opera by Wenzel Müller; libretto by Karl Friedrich Hensler after Shakespeare; November 8, 1799, Vienna.

Sturm, Der, opera by Anton Urspruch; 1888, Frankfurt; libretto after Shakespeare; vs (Hamburg: Aug. Cranz, ca. 1888).

Sturm auf der Mühle, Der, opera in three acts by Karel Weiss; libretto by Richard Batka after Emile Zola's *Attaque du moulin*; March 29, 1912, Prague, in a Czech translation; March 13, 1914, Vienna (in German).

Sturmvögel, opera in three acts by Gerhard Schjelderup; libretto by the composer; September 19, 1926, Schwerin.

Sturz des Antichrists, Der, opera by Viktor Ullmann; not performed.

Sulamith, opera in five scenes by Anton Rubinstein; libretto by Julius Rodenberg; November 8, 1883, Hamburg.

Sulamith, opera in one act by Paul von Klenau; libretto after the Bible; 1913, Munich.

Sylphen, Die, opera by Friedrich Heinrich Himmel; 1806, Berlin; vs (Berlin: Rudolph Werckmeister, ca. 1806).

Szenen aus Mozarts Leben, Singspiel in one act by Albert Lortzing; 1832; vs and libretto (Berlin: Afa-Verlag H. Dünnebil, 1932, 1933).

Tai Yang erwacht, opera in seven scenes by Jean Kurt Forest; libretto by Friedrich Wolf; September 4, 1960, Halberstadt.

Tamerlan, opera in four acts by Johann Friedrich Reichardt; libretto by Johann Otto Heinrich Schaum after Étienne Morel de Chédeville; October 16, 1800, Berlin.

Tamira, opera by Johann Rudolf Zumsteeg; 1788, Stuttgart.

Tankredi, parody in two acts by Wenzel Müller; libretto by A. Bäurle; April 25, 1817, Vienna.

Tannenhäuser, Der, dramatic poem with music by Franz von Suppé; libretto by H. von Levitschnigg; February 27, 1852, Vienna.

Tan[n]häuser, opera in three acts by Karl Mangold; libretto by Eduard Duller; May 17, 1846, Darmstadt; revised as *Der getreue Eckart*, 1892, Darmstadt.

Tante Simona, opera in three acts by Ernst von Dohnányi; libretto by Viktor Heindl; January 22, 1913, Dresden.

Taras Bulba, opera in three acts by Ernst Richter; libretto by Johann Kempfe after Nikolai Gogol's story (1835); January 21, 1935, Stettin.

Tarquin, opera in two acts by Ernst Krenek; libretto by E. Lavery; May 13, 1941, Poughkeepsie, New York.

Tartarin von Tarascon, opera in three acts by Friedrich Radermacher; libretto by the composer after Alphonse Daudet; July 6, 1965, Cologne.

Tartarische Gesetz, Das, *Operette* in three acts by Johann André; libretto by Friedrich Wilhelm Gotter after Carlo Gozzi *I pittocchi fortunati*; May 31, 1779, Berlin; libretto (2 acts) (Leipzig: Verlag der Dykischen Buchhandlung, 1779).

Tartarische Gesetz, Das, Singspiel in two acts by Johann Zumsteeg; libretto by Friedrich Wilhelm Gotter after Carlo Goldoni; March 28, 1780, Stuttgart.

Tartuffe, opera in four acts by Joseph Eidens; libretto by Willi Aron after Fulda's translation of Molière's comedy (1664); April 7, 1929, Elberfeld.

Tartuffe, opera in two acts by Hans Haug; libretto by the composer after Molière; May 24, 1937, Basel.

Taucher, Der, opera in two acts by Johann Friedrich Reichardt; libretto by G. Bürde after Friedrich Schiller's ballad (1797); March 18, 1811, Berlin; arias and dances (Berlin: A. M. Schlesinger, 18—).

Telemaque, opera in four acts by Georg Caspar Schürmann; libretto possibly by Johann Christoph Frauendorf; June or July 1706, Naumburg; revived as *Telemachus und Calypso*, August 1717, Brunswick.

Testament, Das, opera in two acts by Wilhelm Kienzl; libretto by the composer after Peter Rosegger; December 6, 1916, Vienna.

Teufelsmühle am Wienerberg, Die, opera by Wenzel Müller; libretto by Karl Friedrich Hensler; September 12, 1799, Vienna.

Theophano, opera in three acts by Paul Graener; libretto by Otto Anthes; June 5, 1918, Munich; vs (Vienna: UE, c. 1913).

Theseus, opera by Nikolaus Adam Strungk; libretto by Lucas von Bostel after Philippe Quinault; 1683, Hamburg.

Theseus, opera in three acts by Johann Löhner; libretto by the composer after the setting for Giovanni Domenico Freschi's *Teseo tra le rivali* (1685), with a text by Aurelio Aureli; November 15, 1688, Nuremberg.

Thusnelde, Singspiel in four acts; libretto by Johann Adolf Scheibe, 1749; not set to music but a prototype of the eighteenth-century German Singspiel.

Till, opera by Gerhard Wohlgemuth; September 22, 1956, Halle.

Till Eulenspiegel, opera in two parts and an epilogue by Emil Nikolaus von Reznicek; libretto by the composer after Johann Fischart's *Till Eulenspiegel Reimenweiss* (1572); January 12, 1902, Karlsruhe; revised 1937, Cologne.

Till Eulenspiegel, school opera in one act by Alfred von Beckerath; libretto by the composer; 1949, Fischbachau.

Tiroler Wastel, Der, Singspiel in three acts by Jakob Haibel; libretto by Emanuel Schikaneder; May 14, 1796, Vienna.

Titania, oder Liebe durch Zauberei, Singspiel in two acts by Georg Christoph Grosheim; 1792, Kassel; vs (Bonn, ca. 1792).

Titus Feuerfuchs, oder Liebe, Tücke und Perücke, burlesque opera in two acts by Heinrich Sutermeister; libretto by the composer after Johann Nestroy's *Der Talismann* (1840); April 14, 1958, Basel; vs and libretto (Mainz: Schott, 1958).

Tobias Wunderlich, opera in three acts by Joseph Haas; libretto by H. H. Ortner and L. Andersen; November 24, 1937, Kassel; fs and vs (Mainz: BSS [1937].

Tod des Empedokles, Der, "scenic concerto" in two acts by Hermann Reutter; libretto after Friedrich Hölderin's tragedy (1626); May 29, 1966, Schwetzingen.

Tönenden Sphären, Die, "Operndichtung" in two acts and an epilogue by Franz Schreker; composed 1915; libretto (Vienna: UE, 1924).

Tor und der Tod, Der, chamber opera by Hans Brehme; libretto after Hugo von Hofmannsthal; composed 1928.

Tote Gast, Der, opera in three acts by José Berr; libretto by Rudolf Lothar [Rudolf Spitzer] after Heinrich Zschokke; March 23, 1923, Basel.

Touristen, Die, oder **Das romantische Abenteuer,** opera in three acts by Theodor Stauffer; libretto by the composer; January 1869, Lucerne.

Tragaldabas, oder **Der geborgte Ehemann,** comic opera in four acts by Eugen d'Albert; libretto by Rudolf Lother [Rudolf Spitzer] after Auguste Vacquerie's play; December 3, 1907, Hamburg; fs and vs (Mainz: BSS, c. 1907).

Tragödie der Menschheit, Die, opera by Peter Michael Hamel; libretto by Kurt Peter Hamel, completed by Claus H. Henneberg, after Imre Madách's *The Tragedy of Mankind*; June 27, 1981, Kassel.

Traum, Der, opera in three acts by Joseph Gustav Mraczek; libretto by the composer after Franz Grillparzer's play *Der Traum ein Leben* (1831); February 26, 1909, Brünn.

Traumgörge, Der, opera by Alexander von Zemlinsky; libretto by Leo Feld; composed 1906; first performance October 11, 1980, Nuremberg.

Traumleben, opera in two acts by Paul Kont; libretto by Jörg Mauthe after Franz Grillparzer; December 25, 1963, Salzburg.

Traumspiel, Ein, opera in a prologue and three acts by Julius Weismann; libretto by the composer after August Strindberg's *Dream Play* (1902); April 23, 1925, Duisburg.

Traumwandel, lyric opera in two acts by Karl Heinrich David; libretto by the composer after Ivan Turgenev; January 29, 1928, Zurich.

Trauung, Die, opera in three acts by Volker David Kirchner; libretto by Walter Tiel after Witold Gombrowicz's play (1946); April 27, 1975, Wiesbaden.

Travistirte Zauberflöte, Die, opera by Wenzel Müller; libretto by Karl Meissl; 1818, Vienna.

Treuen Köhler, Die, opera in two acts by Ernst Wilhelm Wolf; libretto by Gottlob Ephraim Heerman; 1773, Weimar; vs (Leipzig: B C. Breitkopf & Sohn, 1774).

Treuen Köhler, Die, opera in two acts by Johann Lukas Schubaur; libretto by Gottlob Ephraim Heermann; September 29, 1786, Munich.

Trilby, opera in one act by Friedrich Hieronymus Truhn; libretto by L. W. Both [L. Schneider] after a vaudeville by Eugène Scribe and P. E. A. Carmouche (1823); May 22, 1835, Berlin.

Trilby, opera in one act by G. A. Schmitt; libretto by L. W. Both [L. Schneider]; December 21, 1845, Frankfurt.

Triumpf der Liebe, Der, opera in four acts by Carl David Stegmann; libretto by Friedrich Ernst Jester; April 4, 1796, Hamburg.

Trojanische Pferd, Das, comic opera by Joseph Wölfl; libretto by Heinrich Gottlieb Schmieder; composed 1799.

Trompeter von Säckingen, Der, opera in four acts by Viktor Ernst Nessler; libretto by Rudolf Bunge after Joseph Victor von Scheffel; May 4, 1884, Leipzig; vs (Leipzig: J. Schuberth & Co., 1884); libretto (English) (New York: Metropolitan Opera, 1887).

Troubadour, Der, opera in five acts by Alexander Ernst Fesca; libretto by Friedrich Schmezer; July 25, 1847, Brunswick.

Turandot, Singspiel in two acts by Franz Danzi; libretto after Carlo Gozzi; February 9, 1817, Karlsruhe.

Tyll, "eine Ulenspiegel-Oper" in three acts by Mark Lothar; libretto by Hugo Fritz Koenigsgarten; October 4, 1928, Weimar.

Überfall, Der, opera in two acts by Heinrich Zöllner; libretto by the composer after Ernst von Wildenbruch's *Die Danaide*; September 7, 1895, Dresden; vs (Berlin: Schlesinger, 1896).

Uhrmacher von Strassburg, Der, opera in three acts by Hans Brehme; libretto by Paul Ginthum; February 25, 1941, Kassel.

Uilenspiegel, opera in three acts by Walter Braunfels; libretto by the composer after Charles de Coster; November 9, 1913, Stuttgart.

Ulysses. Composed of two operas by Reinhard Keiser, *Circe**, 1696, and *Penelope**, 1702.

Ulysses, opera in a prologue, three acts, and an epilogue by Reinhard Keiser; libretto by Friedrich Maximilian Lersner after Henri Guichard; October 11, 1722, Copenhagen.

Undine, opera in three acts by Karl Friedrich Girschner; libretto by La Motte Fouqué; May 19, 1830, Berlin (concert); April 20, 1837, Danzig.

Undine, school opera in one act by Wolfgang Fortner; libretto by Anneliese Schäfer; May 21, 1969, Ober Hambach.

Ungebetenen Gäste, Die, oder **Der Canonicus von Mailand,** comic Singspiel in one act by E. T. A. Hoffmann; libretto by Rohrmann after Alexandre Duval's *Le souper imprévu*; composed 1805; the music is lost.

Ungeheuer, Das, opera in one act by Anton Beer Walbrunn; libretto after Anton Chekhov; April 25, 1914, Karlsruhe.

Unglückliche Liebe zwischen der egyptischen Königen Cleopatra und dem romischen Trium-Vir Antonio, Die, opera by Casimir Schwetzelsperger; 1716, Durlach; the music is lost.

Uniform, Der, opera in two acts by Joseph Weigl; libretto by Georg Friedrich Treitschke after Giuseppe Carpani; February 15, 1805, Vienna.

Unmöglichste von allem, Das, opera in a prologue and three acts by Anton Urspruch; libretto by the composer after Lope de Vega's *El mejor imposible*; November 5, 1897, Karlsruhe.

Unnützte Vorsicht, Die, oder **Die betrogene Arglist,** marionette opera in one act by Joseph Weigl; libretto by F. L. Schmidel; February 23, 1783.

Unsichtbare, Die, opera in one act by Carl David Eule; libretto by Karl Ludwig Costenoble; July 7, 1809, Hamburg.

Unsterbliche Kranke, Der, opera in three acts by Hans Haug; libretto by Bernhard Diebold after Molière's *Le Médécin malgré lui* (1666); February 8, 1947, Zurich.

Unter dem Milchwald, opera in three acts by Walter Steffens; libretto by Erich Fried after the play *Under Milk Wood* by Dylan Thomas (1954); May 10, 1973, Hamburg.

Unter Räubern, opera in one act by Anton Rubinstein; libretto by Ernst Wichert; November 8, 1883, Hamburg.

Unterbrochene Opferfest, Das, opera by two acts by Peter Winter; libretto by Franz Xaver Huber; June 14, 1796, Vienna; vs (Bonn: N. Simrock, 1796); libretto (Berlin, 1797).

Untergang der Titanic, Der, "Mittspieloper" by Wilhelm Dieter Sieberg; libretto by the composer; September 6, 1979, West Berlin.

Untersberg, Der, opera by Johann Nepomuk Poissl; 1829, Munich.

Urteil des Paris, Das, musical comedy in one act by Cesar Bresgen; libretto by Otto Reuther; February 7, 1943; Göttingen, Stadttheater; vs (Mainz: BSS, c. 1943).

Urvasi, opera by Wilhelm Kienzl; February 20, 1886, Dresden; rewritten 1909.

Veilchen, Das, opera in three acts by Julius Bittner; libretto by the composer; December 8, 1934, Vienna.

Verdeckten Sachen, Die, Singspiel in two acts by Benedikt Schack, with Gerl and Lickl; libretto by Emanuel Schikaneder; September 26, 1789, Vienna; second of the seven "Anton" Singspiels by Schikaneder; the work is lost.

Verirrte Taube, Die, opera in one act by Hans Haug; libretto by Walther Franke-Ruta; January 11, 1953, Basel.

Verkehrte Welt, Die, opera by Georg Philipp Telemann; 1728.

Verkündigung, "ein Mysterium" in a prologue and four acts by Walter Braunfels; libretto after Paul Claudel's *L'Annonce faite à Marie* (1910), translated by Jakob Hegner; April 4, 1948, Cologne.

Verlöbnis, Das, opera in one act by Winfried Zillig; libretto by Richard Billinger; November 23, 1963, Linz.

Verlobung in San Domingo, Die, opera in one act by Winfried Zillig; libretto by the composer after Heinrich Kleist's short story (1811); June 26, 1957, Hamburg, NDR; February 25, 1961, Bielefeld (staged); vs (Kassel and New York: Bär, 1960).

Verlorene Sohn, Der, opera in one act by Hermann Reutter; libretto by André Gide, translated by Rilke; March 20, 1929, Stuttgart.

Vernarrte Prinzess, Die, opera in three acts by Oskar von Chelius; libretto by Otto Julius Bierbaum; January 15, 1905, Schwerin.

Verschenkte Frau, Die, comic opera in three acts by Eugen d'Albert; libretto by Rudolf Lothar after F. Antony; February 3, 1912, Troppau; vs (Leipzig: A. Cranz, c. 1911).

Verschwender, Der, opera by Conradin Kreutzer; libretto by Ferdinand Raimund; February 20, 1834, Vienna; vs (Leipzig: P. Reclam, Jr., 1889); libretto (Stuttgart: Reclam, 1952).

Verstöhrte Troja, Das, Singspiel in five acts by Georg Caspar Schürmann; libretto by Johann Christoph Frauendorf; February 1706.

Versuchung, Die, opera in two acts by Josef Tal [Josef Gruenthal]; libretto by Israel Eliraz; July 26, 1976, Munich.

Versunkene Glocke, Die, opera in five acts by Heinrich Zöllner; libretto by the composer after Gerhart Hauptmann's play (1896); July 8, 1899, Berlin.

Vertrauenssache, opera in one act by Ernst Krenek; libretto by the composer; May 23, 1962, Saarbrücken.

Verwandelte Daphne, Die, opera in three acts by George Frideric Handel; libretto by Heinrich Hinsch, a continuation of *Der beglückte Florindo**; February 1708, Hamburg; most of the music is lost; libretto (Hamburg, 1708; repr. ed. Ellen T. Harris, in *The Librettos of Handel's Operas*, I [New York and London: Garland Publishing, 1989]).

Verwandelte Leyer des Orpheus, Die, Singspiel in three acts by Reinhard Keiser; libretto by Friedrich Christian Bressand; 1699, Brunswick; libretto (Brunswick: Gruber, 1699); revived as *Orpheus ander Theil*, Hamburg, 1702; libretto (Hamburg: Neumann und Rahts [1702]); part of *Orpheus**.

Verzauberte ich, Das, opera in four acts by Ottmar Gerster; libretto by Paul Koch after Ferdinand Raimund's *Alpenkönig und Menschenfeind* (1828); June 25, 1949, Wuppertal.

Vespasianus, opera by Johann Wolfgang Franck; libretto by Lucas von Bostel; 1681, Hamburg; *Arien* (Hamburg: Georg Rebentein, 1681).

Vestalin, Die, opera in three acts by Karl Wilhelm Ferdinand Guhr; libretto by Joseph von Seyfried after Étienne de Jouy's libretto, set by Gasparo Spontini as *La Vestale* (1807, Paris); June 3, 1814, Kassel.

Vestas Feuer, opera in two acts by Joseph Weigl; libretto by Emanuel Schikaneder; August 10, 1805, Vienna.

Vice-Admiral, Der, operetta in a prologue and three acts by Carl Millöcker; libretto by F. Zell [Camillo Walzel] and Richard Genée; October 9, 1886, Vienna.

Viel Lärm um nichts, opera in three acts by Hermann Heinrich; libretto by the composer after Shakespeare's *Much Ado About Nothing*; August 18, 1956, Frankfurt/Oder.

Vincent, opera in ten scenes by Rainer Kunad, libretto by the composer after Alfred Matusche's play *Van Gogh* (1966); February 22, 1979, Dresden; fs and vs (Berlin: Henschel-Verlag, 1978).

Viola, opera in a prologue and three acts by Hanns Holenia; libretto by Oskar Widowitz after Shakespeare's *Twelfth Night*; November 17, 1934, Graz.

Virgilius, der Magier von Rom, magic opera in a prologue, five scenes, and an epilogue by Alfred Koerpen; libretto after Virgilius; June 17, 1951, Frankfurt.

Visiones amantes, opera in six scenes by Cesar Bresgen; libretto by Ernst Gartner after O. von Wollenstein; February 17, 1964, Radio Bremen; December 20, 1971, Innsbruck (staged).

Wahrheit der Natur, Die, Singspiel by Michael Haydn; July 1769, Salzburg.

Waisenhaus, Das, opera in two acts by Joseph Weigl; libretto by Georg Friedrich Treitschke; October 4, 1808, Vienna; libretto (Vienna: J. B. Wallishausser, 1811).

Wald, Der, opera in a prologue, one act, and an epilogue by Ethyl Smyth; libretto by the composer; April 9, 1902, Berlin.

Wald, Der, opera in one act by Wolfgang Fortner; libretto by Enrique Beck after Federico García Lorca; June 25, 1953, Hessischer Rundfunk; December 18, 1954, Essen (staged).

Walder, opera in one act by Georg Benda; libretto by Friedrich Wilhelm Gotter after Jean François Marmontel's *Silvain*, set by A. M. E. Grétry (1770, Paris); February 23, 1776, Gotha.

Waldmeister, operetta in three acts by Johann Strauss, Jr.; libretto by Gustav Davis; December 4, 1895, Vienna.

Wallenstein, musical tragedy in six scenes by Jaromir Weinberger; libretto by Max Brod after Milos Kares' Czech original, based on Friedrich Schiller's play (1799); November 18, 1937, Vienna.

Walzer aus Wien, Singspiel in three acts by Johann Strauss, Jr.; libretto by Alfred Maria Willner, Heinz Reichert and Ernst Marischka; 1931, Vienna.

Walzertraum, Ein, operetta in three acts by Oscar Straus; libretto by Felix Dörmann and Leopold Jacobson; March 2, 1907, Vienna; libretto (Vienna: Ludwig Doblinger, 1907).

Wandbild, Das, "Szene und Pantomime" by Othmar Schoeck; libretto by Ferruccio Busoni; January 29, 1924, Zurich.

Wandernden Komödianten, Die, opera by Felix Mendelssohn; 1822.

Was ihr wollt, opera in five acts by Ludwig Hess; libretto by the composer after Shakespeare; March 30, 1941, Stettin.

Was macht der Anton im Winter?, Singspiel in two acts, possibly by Benedikt Schack; libretto by Emanuel Schikaneder; January 6, 1790, Vienna; third of the seven "Anton" Singspiels of Schikaneder.

Weg der Verheissung, Der, biblical drama in four parts by Kurt Weill; libretto by Franz Werfel; composed 1935, not performed; revised as *The Eternal Road*, English text and lyrics by Ludwig Lewissohn; January 7, 1937, New York.

Weg durchs Fenster, Der, opera in one act by Paul Weissleder; libretto by the composer after Eugène Scribe; May 8, 1917, Mainz.

Weg nach Freudenstadt, Der, opera in five scenes by Hermann Reutter; libretto by Sonia Korty; January 25, 1948, Göttingen.

Weibertreue, oder Kaiser Konrad vor Weinsberg, opera in three acts by Gustav Schmidt; libretto by the composer; February 16, 1858, Weimar.

Weinlese, Die, opera in three acts by Johann Schenk; libretto by Wilhelm Christian Dietrich Meyer after Christian Friedrich Weisse's text, set by Johann Adam Hiller as *Die Aerndtekranz** (Leipzig, 1771); October 12, 1785, Vienna.

Weinlese, Die, Singspiel in three acts by Ignaz von Beecke; libretto by Joachim Perinet; 1782, Mannheim.

Weisse Hut, Der, opera in twenty-seven scenes and an intermezzo by Wilhelm Killmayer; French and German text; 1964; premiere 1967.

Weltfrühling, opera in three acts by Hans Huber; libretto by Rudolf Wackernagel; March 28, 1894, Basel.

Wem die Krone?, opera in one act by Alexander Ritter; libretto by the composer; June 8, 1890, Weimar.

Wette, Die, opera in one act by Bernhard Anselm Weber; libretto after P. Guillet's *Un Quart-d'Heure de Silence*, set by Pierre Gaveaux (1804, Paris); January 21, 1805, Berlin.

Wettkampf zu Olmypia, Der, oder Die Freunde, opera in three acts by Johann Nepomuk von Poissl; libretto by the composer after Metastasio's *Olimpiade*; April 21, 1815, Munich.

Widerspenstige Heilige, Der, opera in three acts by Mark Lothar; libretto by the composer after Paul Vincent Carroll's comedy *The Wayward Saint* (1955); February 8, 1968, Munich.

Wiedertäufer, Der, opera by Alexander Goehr; libretto by John McGrath and the composer; April 19, 1985, Duisburg.

Wieland der Schmied, opera in four acts by Max Zenger; libretto by Philipp Allfeld; January 18, 1880, Munich.

Wilde Jagd, Der, Romantic opera in four acts by Viktor Nessler; libretto by Friedrich Hofmann after Julius Wolff; 1881; vs (Leipzig: J. Schuberth & Co., 1882).

Wildfang, Der, comic opera in two acts by Franz Xaver Süssmayr; libretto by Franz Xaver Huber after August von Kotzebue; October 4, 1797, Vienna.

Wilhelm von Oranien, Romantic opera in three acts by Heinrich Hofmann; libretto by Roderich Fels [S. Rosenfeld]; 1882, Hamburg.

William Ratcliff, opera in two acts by Cornelis Dopper; libretto after Heinrich Heine's poem; October 19, 1909, Weimar.

Windsbraut, Die, opera in three scenes by Wilfried Zillig; libretto by Richard Billinger; May 12, 1941, Leipzig.

Winterballade. See *Die Doppelgängerin*.

Wintermärchen, Das, opera in four acts by Balduin Zimmermann; libretto by the composer after Shakespeare's *A Winter's Tale*; March 11, 1900, Erfurt; vs (Vienna: W. Karczag & C. Wallner, c. 1907).

Wintermärchen, Ein, opera in four acts by Karl Goldmark; libretto by Alfred Maria Willner after Shakespeare's *A Winter's Tale*; January 2, 1908, Vienna.

Wirtin von Pinsk, Die, opera in three acts by Richard Mohaupt; libretto by Kurt Naue after Carlo Goldoni; February 10, 1938, Dresden; vs (Vienna: UE, 1937).

Witwe von Ephesus, Die, opera in one act by Hermann Reutter; libretto by Ludwig Andersen after a tale by Petronius; June 23, 1954, Cologne; vs ed. composer (Mainz: BSS, 1941).

Wladimir, Fürst von Novgorod, opera in three acts by Gottlob Benedikt Bierey; libretto by Matthäus Stegmayer; November 25, 1807, Vienna.

Wo die Lerche singt, operetta in three acts by Franz Lehár; libretto by Alfred Maria Willner and Heinz Reichert [Heinrich Blumenreich]; March 27, 1918, Vienna; revision of *A pacsirta*, February 1, 1918, Budapest.

Wozzeck, opera in eighteen scenes and an epilogue by Manfred Gurlitt; libretto after Georg Büchner's drama; April 22, 1926, Bremen.

Wozzeck, opera in three acts by Kurt Pfister; February 25, 1950, Regensburg.

Wunder der Heliane, Das, opera in three acts by Erich Korngold; libretto by Hans Müller after Hans Kaltneker; August 7, 1927, Hamburg; vs ed. Ferdinand Rebay (Mainz: BSS, 1927).

Wunderlampe, Die, "grosses komische Zauberoper" in four acts by Wenzel Müller; libretto by Josef Alois Gleich; 1811, Vienna.

Wüste Insel, Die, opera by Joseph Schuster; 1779, Leipzig.

Yolimba, oder **Die Grenzen der Magi,** opera in one act and four "hymns of praise" by Tankred Dorst; libretto by the composer; May 9, 1970, Munich.

Yü-Nü, opera by Erich Riede; libretto by Willy Werner Göttig after *Die Edelstein-sklaven*; February 25, 1958, Dortmund.

Yvonne, Prinzessin von Burgund, opera in four acts by Boris Blacher; libretto by the composer after Witold Gombrowicz; September 15, 1973, Wuppertal.

Zaide, opera by Johann Nepomuk Poissl; 1843, Munich.

Zauberer, Der, opera in one act by Roderich Mojsisovics; libretto by the composer after Miguel de Cervantes; April 1, 1926, Gera.

Zaubergeige, Die, comic opera in three acts by Werner Egk; libretto by the composer and Ludwig Andersen after Franz Pocci; May 22, 1935, Frankfurt; revised version 1954.

Zauberinsel, Der, opera in a prologue and two acts by Heinrich Sutermeister; libretto by the composer after Shakespeare's *The Tempest*; October 31, 1942, Dresden; vs (Mainz: BSS, 1942).

Zauberlehrling, Der, opera in one act by Johannes Doebber; libretto by Hermann Eiler after Goethe; July 25, 1907, Brunswick.

Zauberspiegel, Der, opera in three scenes by Hans Gál; libretto by Karl Jaroschek; December 19, 1930, Breslau.

Zauberspiegel, Der, television opera in one act by Ernst Krenek; libretto by the composer; September 6, 1967, Bayerische Rundfunk.

Zehn Mädchen und kein Mann, operetta in one act by Franz von Suppé; libretto by Karl Treumann after Adolphe Jaime's and Adolphe Choler's *Six Demoiselles à marier*, set by Léo Delibes (1856, Paris); October 25, 1862, Vienna.

Zemire und Azor, "romantisch-komische Oper" in four acts by C. Gotthilf von Baumgarten; libretto by Karl Emil Schubert and the composer after Jean François Marmontel's *Zémire et Azor*, set by A. M. E. Grétry (1771, Fontainebleau); May 18, 1776, Breslau; continuo score (Breslau: Johann Friedrich Korn, Sr., 1775).

Zerrissene, Der, opera in two acts by Peter Kreuder; libretto by Hans M. Kremer; September 15, 1941, Stockholm.

Zerrissene, Der, opera in three acts by Albert Jenny; libretto by the composer after Johann Nestroy (1844); February 12, 1942, Stans, Switzerland.

Zeus und Elida, opera by Stefan Wolpe; composed 1928.

Zierpuppen, opera in one act by Anselm Goetzl; libretto by Richard Batka after Molière's *Les Précieuses ridicules*; November 15, 1905, Prague; vs (Leipzig: M. Brockhaus, 1906).

Zinnober, opera in three acts by Siegmund von Hausegger; libretto by the composer after E. T. A. Hoffmann's *Klein Zaches*; June 19, 1898, Munich.

Zirkusprinzessin, Die, operetta by Emmerich Kálmán; 1926, Vienna; vs (Leipzig: W. Karczag, 1926).

Zoraide, oder **Der Friede von Granada,** opera in three acts by Karl Ludwig Blum; libretto after the French original; ca. 1818, Berlin.

Zuleima, an opera in one act by Heinrich Beinstock; libretto by Ferdinand Lion; February 18, 1913, Karlsruhe.

Zum Grossadmiral, opera in three acts by Albert Lortzing; libretto by the composer after Alexandre Duval's comedy *La Jeunesse de Henri V*; December 15, 1847, Leipzig; vs ed. F. L. Schubert (Leipzig: B&H, 1848).

Zwei Herzen im 3/4 Takt, operetta by Robert Stolz; September 30, 1933, Zurich.

Zwei Klacheln von Przelautsch, Die, opera by Vincenz Franz Tuczek; 1797, Prague.

Zwei Prinzen, Die, opera in three acts by Heinrich Esser; libretto by M. G. Friedrich [Friedrich Melchior Gredy] after a play by Eugène Scribe and A. H. J. Mélesville; April 11, 1845, Munich.

Zweihunderttausend Taler, opera in three scenes and an epilogue by Boris Blacher; libretto by the composer after Sholem Aleichem; September 25, 1969, Berlin; vs (London and New York: BO, 1970).

Zweikampf mit der Geliebten, Der, opera in three acts by Ludwig Spohr; libretto by Johann Friedrich Schink; November 15, 1811, Hamburg; vs ed. C. F. G. Schwencke (Hamburg: Johann August Böhme, 1813).

Zweite Entscheidung, Die, opera in seven scenes by Udo Zimmermann; libretto by Inge Zimmermann; May 10, 1970, Magdeburg.

Zwingburg, opera in one act by Ernst Krenek; libretto by Franz Werfel after an anonymous scenario; October 21, 1924, Berlin; vs (Vienna: UE, c. 1923).

APPENDIX 2
COMPOSERS

+See Appendix I. *Year of composition.
Right columns include year and city of premiere, and
year of composition if significantly earlier.

Abert, Johann Joseph
      b. Kochowitz, September 20, 1843; d. Stuttgart,
          April 1, 1915
      Astorga+   1866 Stuttgart
      Ekkehard+   1878 Berlin

Adam, Franz
      b. Munich, December 28, 1885; d. there September
          21, 1954
      Judith+   1848 Strasbourg

Adlgasser, Anton Cajetan
      b. Inzell, Bavaria, October 1, 1729; d. Salzburg,
          December 22, 1777
      Schuldigkeit des ersten   1767* not perf
          Gebotes, Die+, pt. 3

Aiblinger, Johann Kaspar
      b. Wasserburg, Bavaria, February 23, 1779; d.
          Munich, May 6, 1867
      Rodrigo und Zimene+   1821 Munich

Albert, Eugen [Eugène] d'
      b. Glasgow, April 10, 1864; d. Riga, March 3,
          1932
      Abreise, Die   1898 Frankfurt
      Flauto solo+   1905 Prague
      Gernot+   1897 Mannheim
      Ghismonda+   1895 Dresden
      Golem, Der+   1926 Frankfurt
      Improvisator, Der+   1902 Berlin
      Izeyel+   1909 Hamburg
      Kain+   1900 Berlin
      Liebesketten+   1912 Vienna
      Mareike von Numwegen+   1923 Hamburg
      Mister Wü+   1932 Dresden
      Revolutionshochzeit+   1919 Leipzig
      Rubin, Der+   1893 Karslruhe
      Schwarze Orchidee, Die+   1928 Leipzig
      Scirocco+   1921 Darmstadt
      Stier von Olivera, Der+   1918 Leipzig
      Tiefland   1903 Prague
      Toten Augen, Die   1916 Dresden
      Tragaldabas+   1907 Hamburg
      Verschenkte Frau, Die+   1912 Troppau

André, Johann
    b. Offenbach, March 28, 1741; d. there June 18,
        1799

Alchymist, Der+	1778	Berlin
Alte Freyer, Der+	1776	Berlin
Barbier von Bagdad, Der	1783	Berlin
Belmont und Constanze	1781	Berlin
Bezauberten, Die+	1777	Berlin
Claudine von Villa Bella+	1778	Gotha
Erwin und Elmire+	1775	Frankfurt
Laura Rosetti+	1778	Vienna
Liebhaber als Automat, Der+	1782	Berlin
Tartarische Gesetz, Das+	1779	Berlin
Töpfer, Der	1773	Hanau

Andreae, Volkmar
    b. Bern, July 5, 1879; d. Zurich, June 18, 1962

Abenteuer des Casanova, Ein+	1924	Dresden
Ratcliff+	1914	Duisburg

Antoniou, Theodor
    b. Athens, February 10, 1935

Periander+	1983	Munich

Aperghis, Georges
    b. Athens, December 23, 1945

Liebestod+	1982	Strasbourg

Aschaffenburg, Walter
    b. Essen, May 20, 1927

Bartelby+	1964	Oberlin, Ohio

Aspelmayr, Franz
    b. Linz, bapt. April 2, 1728; d. Vienna, July
        29, 1786

Kinder der Natur, Die+	1778	Vienna

Aspestrand, Sigwardt
    1856-1941

Seemannsbraut, Die+	1894	Gotha

Auenmüller, Hans
    b. Dresden, October 31, 1926

Bremer Stadtmusikanten, Die+	1972	Thale

Baumgarten, C. Gothilf von
    b. Berlin, January 12, 1741; d. Gross-Strehlitz,
        Silesia, October 1, 1813

Andromeda+	1776	Breslau
Grab des Mufti, Das	1778	Breslau
Zemire und Azor+	1776	Breslau

Baussnern, Waldemar von
    b. Berlin, November 29, 1866; d. Potsdam, August
        20, 1931
    Satyros+   1923 Basel

Beckerath, Alfred von
    b. Hagenau, near Schwerin, April 10, 1901
    Till Eulenspiegel+   1949 Fischbachau

Beecke, Ignaz von
    b. Wimpfen am Necke, near Heilbronn, October 28,
        1733; d. Wallerstein, January 2, 1802
    Claudine von Villa Bella+   1780 Berlin
    Don Quixotte+   1788 Berlin
    Jubelhochzeit, Die+   1782 Mannheim
    Weinlese, Die+   1782 Mannheim

Beer, Max Joseph
    1851-1908
    Strike der Schmiede, Der+   1897 Augsburg

Beer-Walbrunn, Anton
    b. Kohlberg, near Weiden, June 29, 1864; d.
        Munich, March 22, 1929
    Don Quichote+   1908 Munich

Beethoven, Ludwig van
    b. Bonn, bapt. December 17, 1770; d. Vienna,
        March 26, 1827
    Fidelio   1814 Vienna
    Leonore   1805, 1806 Vienna
    Vestas Feuer   1803* perf. Spoleto
                                               (1982)

Behrend, Fritz
    b. Berlin, March 3, 1889; d. there December 29,
        1972
    König René's Tochter+   1927* ?
    Lächerlichen Preziösen, Die+   1949 Berlin

Bella, Rudolf
    b. Hermannstadt [now Sibiu, Rumania], December 7,
        1890; d. Romanshorn, Switzerland, July 14,
        1973
    Bildnis des Dorian Gray, Das+ ?   not perf

Benatzky, Ralph
    b. Mährisch-Budweis [now Moravské-Budejovice,
        Czechoslovakia], June 5, 1884; d. Zurich,
        October 16, 1957
    Casanova+   1928 Berlin
    Im Weissen Rössl   1930 Berlin

Benda, Friedrich (Wilhelm Heinrich)
    b. Potsdam, July 15, 1745; d. there June 19, 1814
    Alceste+   1786   Berlin
    Blumenmädchen, Das+   1806   Berlin
    Orpheus+   1785   Berlin

Benda, Friedrich Ludwig
    b. Gotha, bapt. September 4, 1752; d. Königsberg
       [now Kaliningrad], March 20 or 27, 1792
    Barbier von Sevilla, Der+   1776   Leipzig
    Louise   1791   Königsberg

Benda, Georg [Jiri]
    b. Alt-Benatek, Bohemia, June 30, 1722; d.
      Köstriz, near Gera, November 6, 1795
    Ariadne auf Naxos   1775   Gotha
    Findelkind, Das+   ca. 1787   not perf
    Holzhauer, Der+   1778   Gotha
    Jahrmarkt, Der   1775   Gotha
    Medea   1775   Leipzig
    Pygmalion+   1779   Gotha
    Romeo und Julie   1776   Gotha
    Tartarische Gesetz, Das+   1787   Leipzig
    Walder+   1776   Gotha

Berg, Alban
    b. Vienna, February 9, 1885; d. there December 24,
      1935
    Lulu   1937   Zurich
    Wozzeck   1925   Berlin

Bergese, Hans
    b. Freiburg, May 24, 1910
    Bremer Stadtmusikanten, Die+   1949   Cologne

Berr, José R.
    b. Regensburg, December 29, 1874; d. Zurich, April
      14, 1947
    Tote Gast, Der+   1923   Basel

Bialas, Günter
    b. Belschowitz, Silesia, July 19, 1907
    Geschichte von Aucassin und   1969   Munich
      Nicolette, Die
    Gestiefelte Kater, Der+   1975   Schwetzingen
    Hero und Leander   1966   Mannheim

Bibalo, Antonio
    b. 1922
    Miss Julie+   1975   Aarhus
    Lächeln am Füsse der Leiter,   1965   Hamburg
      Das+

Bienstock, Heinrich
    b. Mühlhausen, July 13, 1894; d. Tübingen,
        December 17, 1918

| **Sandro der Narr**+ | 1916 | Stuttgart |
| **Zuleima**+ | 1913 | Karlsruhe |

Bierey, Gottlob Benedikt
    b. Dresden, July 25, 1772; d. Breslau, May 5, 1840

| **Wladimir, Fürst von Novgorod**+ | 1807 | Vienna |

Bittner, Julius
    b. Vienna, April 9, 1874; d. there January 10,
        1939

Abenteuer, Der+	1913	Cologne
Bergsee, Der+	1911	Vienna
Höllisch Gold, Das+	1916	Darmstadt
Kohlhaymerin, Die+	1921	Vienna
Liebe Augustin, Der+	1916	Vienna
Mondnacht+	1928	Berlin
Musikant, Der+	1910	Vienna
Rosengärtlein, Das+	1923	Mannheim
Rote Gred, Die+	1907	Frankfurt
Veilchen, Das+	1934	Vienna

Blacher, Boris
    b. Niu-chang, China, January 19, 1903; d.
        Berlin, January 30, 1975

Abstrakte Oper Nr. 1	1953	Hessian radio
Flut, Die	1946	Dresden
Fürstin Tarakanowa	1941	Wuppertal
Geheimnis des entwendeten Briefes, Das+	1975	Berlin
Habemeajaja+	?	perf. Berlin (1987)
Nachtschwalbe, Die+	1948	Leipzig
Preussisches Märchen	1952	Berlin
Romeo und Julia	1947	Berlin-Zehlendorf
Rosamunde Floris	1960	Berlin
Yvonne, Prinzessin von Burgund+	1973	Wuppertal
Zweihunderttausend Taler+	1969	Berlin
Zwischenfälle bei einer Notlandung	1966	Hamburg

Blech, Leo
    b. Aachen, April 21, 1871; d. Berlin, August 24,
        1958

Aglaja+	ca. 1893*	?
Alpenkönig und Menschenfeind	1903	Dresden
Aschenbrödel+	1905	Prague
Cherubina+	1894*	?

Blech, L. (cont.)
Das war ich+   1902   Dresden
Strohwitwe, Die+   ca. 1920* ?
Versiegelt   1908   Hamburg

Bloch, Waldemar
b. Vienna, May 5, 1905
Diener zweier Herren, Der+   1936   Freiburg
Kätchen von Heilbronn, Das+   1958   Graz
Stella+   1951   Graz

Block, Frederick
b. Vienna, August 30, 1899; d. New York, January
1, 1945
Amerika+   ?   not perf

Blum, Karl [Carl] Ludwig
1786-1844
Zoraide+   ca. 1818   Berlin

Böckmann, Alfred
b. Essen, January 10, 1905
Doktor Eisenbart+   1954   Weimar

Bodart, Eugen
b. Kassel, October 8, 1905
Hirtenlegende+   1936   Weimar
Spanische Nacht+   1937   Mannheim

Böhme, Otto
b. Falkenstein, May 20, 1874; d. Chemnitz
[now Karl-Marx-Stadt], March 1944
Heilige Katharina, Die+   1919   Chemnitz

Böhme, Walter
b. Leipzig, September 6, 1884; d. Reichenbach,
July 21, 1952
Kolumbus+   1950   Reichenbach

Bose, Hans Jürgen von
b. Munich, December 24, 1953
Leiden des jungen Werthers,   1986   Schwetzingen
     Das+

Böttcher, Lukas
b. Frankfurt, February 13, 1878; d. Bamberg,
March 24, 1970
Salambo+   1926   Altenburg

Brand, Max
> b. Lemberg [now Lvov], April 26, 1896; d. 1980,
> Langenzersdorf
> **Maschinist Hopkins**   1929 Duisburg

Brandt-Buys, Jan
> b. Zutphen, Holland, September 12, 1868;
> d. Salzburg, December 8, 1933
> **Mann im Mond, Der+**   1922* ?
> **Schneider von Schönau, Die+** 1916 Dresden

Braunfels, Walter
> b. Frankfurt, December 19, 1882; d. Cologne,
> March 19, 1954
> **Don Gil von den grünen Hosen+** 1924 Munich
> **Galatea+**   1930 Cologne
> **Gläserne Berg, Der+**   1928 Krefeld
> **Prinzessin Brambilla**   1909 Stuttgart
> **Spiel von der Auferstehung,** 1954 Cologne radio
> **Das+**
> **Traum ein Leben, Der**   1937* perf. Frank-
>   furt (1950)
> **Uilenspiegel+**   1913 Stuttgart
> **Verkündigung+**   1948 Cologne
> **Vögel, Die**   1920 Munich
> **Zauberlehrling, Der**   1952 Hamburg radio

Brehme, Hans
> b. Potsdam, March 10, 1904; d. Stuttgart,
> November 10, 1957
> **Liebe ist teuer+**   1949 Münster
> **Tor und der Tod, Der+**   1928* ?
> **Uhrmacher von Strassburg,**   1941 Kassel
> **Der+**

Bresgen, Cesar
> b. Florence, October 16, 1913
> **Brüderlein Hund+**   1953 Nuremberg
> **Dornröschen+**   1942 Strasbourg
> **Engel von Prag, Der**   1979 Salzburg
> **Ewige Arzt, Der+**   1956 Schwyz
> **Igel als Bräutigam, Der+**   1948 Esslingen
> **Mann im Mond, Der+**   1960 Nuremberg
> **Schlaue Müllerin, Die+**   1943* ?
> **Urteil des Paris, Das+**   1943 Göttingen
> **Visiones amantes+**   1964 Radio Bremen

Breuer, Paul
> b. Zündorf, near Cologne, April 7, 1918
> **Feindlichen Nachbarn, Die+**   1949 Cologne

Bronner, Georg
    b. Hamburg, bapt. February 17, 1667; d. Hamburg,
        buried March 8, 1720
    Echo und Narcissus+   1693   Brunswick

Bruch, Max
    b. Cologne, January 6, 1838; d. Friedenau, near
        Berlin, October 2, 1920
    Hermione+   1872   Berlin
    Loreley, Die   1863   Mannheim
    Scherz, List und Rache+   1856   Cologne

Brüggemann, Kurt
    b. Berlin, March 30, 1908
    Fischer un syne Fru, De+   1936   Hamburg
    Kalte Herz, Das+   1938   Hamburg

Brüll, Ignaz
    b. Prosnitz, Moravia, November 7, 1846; d. Vienna,
        September 17, 1907
    Goldene Kreuz, Das+   1875   Berlin
    Gringoire   1892   Munich
    Königen Mariette+   1883   Munich
    Landfriede, Der+   1877   Vienna
    Schach dem König+   1893   Munich
    Steinerne Herz, Das+   1888   Vienna

Bungert, August
    b. Mühlheim an der Ruhr, March 14, 1845; d.
        Leutesdorf, October 26, 1915
    Aurora+   ca. 1885* not perf
    Die Ilias:
        Achilleus+   ?   not perf
        Klytemnestra+   ?   not perf
    Die Odyssee (Die homerische Welt):
        Kirke+   1898 Dresden
        Nausikaa+   1901 Dresden
        Odysseus' Heimkehr+   1896 Dresden
        Odysseus' Tod+   1903 Dresden

Burkhard, Paul
    b. Zurich, December 21, 1911; d. Zell, near
        Zurich, September 6, 1955
    Casanova in der Schweiz+   1943   Zurich
    Stern geht auf aus Jaakob,   1970   Hamburg
        Ein+

Burkhard, Willy
    b. Evillard sur Bienne, Switzerland, April 17,
        1900; d. Zurich, June 18, 1955
    Schwarze Spinne, Die   1949   Zurich

Busoni, Ferruccio
   b. Empoli, Italy, April 1, 1866; d. Berlin, July
      27, 1924

Arlecchino	1917	Zurich
Brautwahl, Die	1912	Hamburg
Doktor Faust	1922	Dresden
Turandot	1917	Zurich

Büttner, Paul
   b. Dresden, December 10, 1870; d. there October
      15, 1943

Rumpelstilzchen+	1911	Bamberg

Cannabich, Carl (Konrad)
   b. Mannheim, bapt. October 11, 1771; d. Munich,
      May 1 or 2, 1806

Palmer und Amalia+	1803	Munich

Cannabich, Christian
   b. Mannheim, bapt. December 28, 1731; d.
      Frankfurt, January 20, 1798

Azakia+	1778	Mannheim
Electra+	1781	Mannheim

Caró, Paul
   b. Breslau [now Wroclaw, Poland], October 25,
      1859; d. there June 23, 1914

Hero und Leander+	1912	Breslau

Cerha, Friedrich
   b. Vienna, February 17, 1926

Baal	1981	Salzburg
Netzwerk+	1981	Vienna
Rattenfänger, Der+	1987	Graz

Chélard, Hippolyte-André
   b. Paris, February 1, 1789; d. Weimar, February
      12, 1861

Hermannsschlacht, Die+	1835	Munich

Chelius, Oskar von
   b. Mannheim, July 28, 1859; d. Munich, June 12,
      1923

Vernarrte Prinzess, Die+	1905	Schwerin

Chemin-Petit, Hans
   b. Potsdam, July 24, 1902

Kassandras Tod+	1977	Berlin
Klage der Ariadne+	1973	Berlin
König Nicolo+	1962	Aachen
Komödiantin, Die+	1970	Coburg

Clasing, Johann Heinrich
       1779-1829
       Mischelli und sein Sohn+   1806   Hamburg

Coenen, Paul
       b. Saarlouis [Saarleutern], near Saarbrücken,
          December 8, 1908
       Karamasows, Die+   1945   Berlin

Conradi, Johann Georg
       b. ?; d. Oettingen, May 22, 1699
       Ariadne   1691   Hamburg
       Gensericus+   1693   Hamburg
       Sieg der Schönheit, Der+   1722   Hamburg

Cornelius, Peter
       b. Mainz, December 24, 1824; d. there October 1,
          1874
       Barbier von Bagdad, Der   1858   Weimar
       Cid, Der   1865   Weimar
       Gunlöd (completed by Lassen)   1874   Weimar

Courvoisier, Walter
       b. Riehen, near Basel, February 7, 1875; d.
          Locarno, December 27, 1931
       Lanzelot und Elaine+   1917   Munich

Curschmann, Karl Friedrich
       b. Berlin, June 21, 1804; d. Langfuhr, near
          Danzig, August 24, 1841
       Abdul und Erinieh+   1828   Kassel

Danzi, Franz
       b. Schwetzingen, June 15, 1763; d. Karlsruhe,
          April 13, 1826
       Mitternachtsstunde, Die+   1788   Munich
       Rübezahl+   1813   Karlsruhe
       Turandot+   1817   Karlsruhe

David, Karl Heinrich
       b. St. Gall, December 30, 1884; d. Nervi, Italy,
          May 17, 1951
       Sizilianer, Der+   1924   Zurich
       Traumwandel+   1928   Zurich

Decker, Willy
       ?
       Mitternachtstraum, Ein+   1988   Cologne

Dellinger, Rudolf
    b. Graslitz, Bohemia, July 8, 1857; d. Dresden,
        September 24, 1910
    Don Cesar   1885 Hamburg

Dessau, Paul
    b. Hamburg, December 10, 1894; d. East Berlin,
        June 28, 1979
    Einstein   1974 Berlin (East)
    Giuditta+   1912 not perf
    Lanzelot   1969 Berlin (East)
    Leonce und Lena   1979 Berlin (East)
    Orpheus und der   1931* ?
        Bürgermeister+
    Puntila   1966 Berlin (East)
    Verhör des Lukullus, Das 1951 Berlin (East)

Dessauer, Josef
    b. Prague, May 28, 1798; d. Mödling, July 8, 1876
    Besuch in Saint-Cyr, Ein+   1838 Dresden

Deswert, Jules
    b. Louvain, August 15, 1843; d. Ostend, February
        24, 1891
    Albigenser, Die+   1878 Wiesbaden
    Graf Hammerstein+   1884 Mainz

Dienel, Josef
    b. Sebusein, February 22, 1889
    Ali Baba und die vierzig   1952 Fellbach
        Räuber+

Dieter, Christian Friedrich
    b. Ludwigsburg, June 13, 1757; d. Stuttgart, May
        15, 1822
    Belmont und Constanze+   1784 Stuttgart
    Des Teufels Lustschloss+ 1802 Stuttgart
    Dorfdeputierten, Die   1786 Stuttgart
    Eremit auf Formentera, Der+ 1791 Stuttgart
    Irrwisch, Der+   1779 Stuttgart
    Laura Rosetti+   1781 Stuttgart

Dietrich, Albert
    b. Forsthaus Golk, near Meissen, August 28, 1829;
        d. Berlin, November 20, 1908
    Robin Hood+   1879 Frankfurt

Dittersdorf, Karl Ditters von
    b. Vienna, November 2, 1739; d. Neuhof, Pilgram,
        Bohemia, October 24, 1799
    Arcifano+   1777* ?
    Betrug durch Aberglauben+ 1786 Vienna

Dittersdorf, K. (cont.)

Doctor [Doktor] und Apotheker	1786	Vienna
Don Quixote der Zweyte+	1795	Oels
Gutsherr, Der+	1791	Vienna
Hieronymus Knicker	1789	Vienna
Hochzeit des Figaro, Die	1789	Brünn
Hokus-Pokus+	1790	Vienna
Im Dunkel ist nicht gut munkeln+	1789	Vienna
Liebe im Narrenhaus, Die	1787	Vienna
Lustigen Weiber von Windsor, Die+	1796	Oels
Rothe Käppchen, Das	1790	Breslau

Doebber, Johannes
    b. Berlin, March 28, 1866; d. there January 25, 1921

Zauberlehrling, Der+	1907	Brunswick

Dohnányi, Ernst von
    b. Pressburg [now Bratislava, Czechoslovakia], July 27, 1877; d. New York, February 9, 1960

Tante Simona+	1913	Dresden

Dopper, Cornelis
    b. Stadskanaal, near Groningen, February 7, 1870; d. Amsterdam, September 18, 1939

William Ratcliff+	1909	Weimar

Doppler, Albert Franz
    b. Lemberg [now Lvov, Poland], September 12, 1825; d. Stuttgart, March 10, 1900

Judith+	1870	Vienna

Dorn, Heinrich
    b. Königsberg [now Kaliningrad], November 14, 1804; d. Berlin, January 10, 1892

Abu Kara+	1831	Leipzig
Nibelungen, Die+	1854	Berlin
Schöffe von Paris, Der+	1836	Riga

Dorn, Otto
    b. Cologne, September 7, 1848; d. Wiesbaden, August 11, 1931

Schöne Müllerin, Die+	1906	Kassel

Dorst, Tankred
    b. 1925

Yolimba+	1970	Munich

Dost, Walter
    b. Schneeberg/Erzgebirge, near Zwickau, May 26,
        1874; d. Lenggries, Bavaria, July 15, 1947
    Feuersprobe, Die+   1920 Plauen

Draeseke, Felix
    b. Coburg, October 7, 1835; d. Dresden, February
        26, 1913
    Herrat+   1892 Dresden
    Merlin+   1913 Gotha

Drechsel, Gustav
    b. Issigau, February 16, 1874; d. Munich, May 21,
        1939
    Don Juans Ende+   1930 Ansbach

Dressel, Erwin
    b. Berlin, June 10, 1909; d. there December 17,
        1972
    Armer Kolumbus+   1928 Kassel
    Bär, Der+   1963 Bern radio
    Kuchentanz, Der   1929 Kassel
    Laune des Verliebten, Die+   1949 Leipzig

Drieberg, Friedrich von
    1780-1856
    Sänger und der Schneider,   1814 Berlin
        Der+

Driesch, Kurt
    b. Heidelberg, May 15, 1904
    Grossindustrielle, Die+   1953 Cologne

Driessler, Johannes
    b. Friedrichsthal, near Saarbrücken, January 26,
        1921
    Claudia amata+   1952 Münster

Eberl, Anton
    b. Vienna, June 13, 1765; d. there March 11, 1807
    Königen der schwarzen Insel,   1801 Vienna
        Die+
    Pyramus und Thisbe+   1794 Vienna

Eberwein, Karl
    b. Weimar, November 10, 1786; d. there March 2,
        1868
    Graf von Gleichen, Der+   ca. 1822 Weimar

Ebner, Georg
    b. Munich, September 5, 1896; d. Bernau, near
        Berlin, November 6, 1962
    Grüne Heinrich, Der+   1922 Munich

Ecklebe, Alexander
    b. Cosel, Silesia, December 1, 1904
    Genoveva+   1936 Berlin radio

Eder, Helmut
    b. Linz, December 26, 1916
    Kardinal, Der+   1962 ORF TV
    Ödipus+   1960 Linz

Egk [Mayer], Werner
    b. Auchsesheim, Bavaria, May 17, 1901; d. Inning,
        Bavaria, July 10, 1983
    Circe+   1948 Berlin
    Columbus   1933 Bavarian radio
    Irische Legende   1955 Salzburg
    Peer Gynt   1938 Berlin
    Revisor, Der   1957 Schwetzingen
    Siebzehn Tage und vier   1966 Stuttgart
        Minuten
    Verlobung in San Domingo, Die 1963 Munich
    Zaubergeige, Die+   1935 Frankfurt

Eidens, Joseph
    b. Aachen, June 29, 1896; d. there March 15, 1960
    Kalif Storch+   1885 Darmstadt
    Tartuffe+   1929 Elberfeld

Einem, Gottfried von
    b. Bern, January 24, 1918
    Besuch der alten Dame, Der   1971 Vienna
    Dantons Tod   1947 Salzburg
    Jesu Hochzeit   1980 Vienna
    Kabale und Liebe   1976 Vienna
    Prozess, Der   1953 Salzburg
    Zerrissene, Der   1964 Hamburg

Einfeldt, Dieter
    b. Hamburg, April 11, 1935
    Palast Hotel Thanatos+   1972 Hanover

Eisenmann, Willi
    b. Stuttgart, March 3, 1906
    Leonce und Lena+   ?   not perf

Eisler, Hanns
    b. Leipzig, July 6, 1898; d. East Berlin
        September 6, 1962

Dantons Tod+	1929	Berlin
Johann Faustus+	?	perf. Tübingen (1974)

Engelmann, Hans Ulrich
    b. Darmstadt, September 8, 1921

Doktor Fausts Höllenfahrt+	1965	Hamburg radio
Fall van Damm, Der+	1968	Cologne radio
Mauer, Die+	1955	Hamburg
Ophelia+	1969	Hanover

Erbse, Heimo
    b. Rudolstadt, Thuringia, February 27, 1924

Abenteuer des Don Quichotte, Ein+	?	not perf
Fabel in C+	1952	Berlin
Herr in Grau, Der+	1966	not perf
Julietta+	1959	Salzburg

Erismann, Hans
    b. Aarau, Switzerland, January 21, 1911

Don Pedros Heimkehr+	1952	Zurich

Ernst II, Duke of Saxe-Coburg-Gotha
    1818-1893

Casilda	1851	Gotha
Diana von Solange+	1858	Coburg
Santa Chiara+	1854	Gotha

Esser, Heinrich
    b. Mannheim, July 15, 1818; d. Salzburg, June 3,
        1872

Zwei Prinzen, Die+	1845	Munich

Ettinger, Max
    b. Lemberg [now Lvov, Poland], December 27,
        1874; d. Basel, July 19, 1951

Eifersüchtige Trinker, Der+	1925	Nuremberg
Frühlings Erwachen+	1928	Leipzig
Juana+	1925	Nuremberg
Judith+	1921	Nuremberg

Eugen II, Duke of Württenberg
    1788-1857

Geisterbraut, Die+	1842	Breslau

Eule, Carl Dietrich
    b. 1776; d. Hamburg, August 30, 1827

Unsichtbare, Die+	1809	Hamburg

Fall, Leo
  b. Olmütz [now Olomouc, Czechoslovakia], February
      2, 1873; d. Vienna, September 16, 1925
  Dollarprinzessin, Die   1907 Vienna
  Geschiedene Frau, Die+   1908 Vienna
  Goldene Vogel, Der+   1920 Dresden
  Irrlicht+   1905 Mannheim
  Liebe Augustin, Der+   1912 Berlin
  Madame Pompadour   1923 Berlin
  Parolo (Frau Denise)+   1902 Hamburg
  Rose von Stambul, Die   1916 Vienna

Fesca, Alexander Ernst
  b. Karlsruhe, May 22, 1820; d. Brunswick,
      February 22, 1849
  Troubadour, Der+   1847 Brunswick

Fesca, Friedrich Ernst
  b. Magdeburg, February 15, 1789; d. Karlsruhe,
      May 24, 1826
  Omar und Leila+   1824 Karlsruhe

Fleischmann, Friedrich
  b. Markatheidenfeld, near Würzburg, July 18,
      1766; d. Meiningen, November 30, 1798
  Geisterinsel, Die   1798 Weimar

Flick-Steger, Charles
  b. Vienna, December 13, 1899
  Dorian Gray+   1930 Aussig

Flotow, Friedrich von
  b. Teutendorf, near Schwerin, April 27, 1812;
      d. Darmstadt, January 24, 1883
  Alessandro Stradella   1844 Hamburg
  Herzog Johann Albrecht von 1857 Schwerin
      Mecklenberg+
  Martha   1847 Vienna
  Matrosen, Die+   1839 Paris
  Rübezahl+   1852 Retzien
  Sophie Katharina+   1850 Berlin

Flury, Richard
  b. Biberist (Solothurn), March 26, 1896; d.
      there December 23, 1967
  Florentinische Tragödie,   1929 Solothurn
      Eine+

Forest, Jean Kurt
  b. Darmstadt, April 2, 1909; d. Berlin, March
      2, 1975
  Abenteuer des Don Quichotte+ ?   not perf

Forest, J. K. (cont.)
    Arme Konrad, Der+   1959 Berlin (East)
    Blumen von Hiroshima, Die+ 1967 Weimar
    Hamlet+   1973 Berlin (East)
    Tai Yang erwacht+   1960 Halberstadt

Forster, Josef
    1845-1917
    Rose von Pontevedra, Die+   1893 Gotha

Fortner, Wolfgang
    b. Leipzig, October 12, 1907; d. Heidelberg,
        September 11(?), 1987
    Bluthochzeit, Die   1957 Cologne
    Corinna+   1958 Berlin
    Cress ertrinkt+   1931 Bad Pyrmont
    Elisabeth Tudor   1972 Berlin
    In seinem Garten liebt Don 1962 Schwetzingen
      Perlimlín Belisa
    Undine+   1969 Ober Hambach
    Wald, Der+   1953 Hessian radio

Franck, Johann Wolfgang
    b. Unterschwaningen, Franconia, bapt. June 17,
        1664; d. ca. 1710
    Aeneas+   1680 Hamburg
    Alceste+   1680 Hamburg
    Cara Mustapha+   1686 Vienna
    Diocletianus+   1682 Hamburg
    Drey Töchter Cecrops, Die+ 1679 Ansbach
    Errettete Unschuld, Die+   1675 Ansbach
    Semiramis+   1683 Hamburg
    Vespanius+   1681 Hamburg

Franckenstein, Clemens von
    b. Wiesentheid, July 14, 1875; d. Hechendorf,
        August 19, 1942
    Des Kaisers Dichter+   1920 Hamburg

Fränzl, Ferdinand
    b. Schwetzingen, May 24, 1770; d. Mannheim,
        November 19, 1833
    Carlos Fioras   1810 Munich

Friedrich, Karl
    b. Stockheim, near Oberfranken, January 22, 1920
    Brüderlein und Schwesterlein+ 1949 ?

Füchs, Ferdinand
    1811-1848
    Guttenberg+   1846 Graz

Füssl, Karlheinz
    b. Gablonz [now Jablonec, Czechoslovakia], March
       21, 1924
    Dybuk, Der+   1970   Karlsruhe

Gál, Hans
    b. Brunn [now Brno, Czechoslovakia], August 5,
       1890; d. October 3, 1987
    Arzt der Sobeide, Der+   1919   Breslau
    Heilige Ente, Die+   1923   Düsseldorf
    Lied der Nacht, Das+   1926   Breslau
    Zauberspiegel, Der+   1930   Breslau

Gallus. See Johann Mederitsch.

Gast, Peter [Johann Heinrich Köselitz]
    b. Annaberg, Saxony, January 10, 1854; d. there
       August 15, 1918
    Heimliche Ehe, Die+   1891   Danzig

Geissler, Fritz
    b. Wurzen, near Leipzig, September 16, 1921; d.
       Bad Saarow, January 11, 1984
    Zerbrochene Krug, Der   1971   Leipzig

Genée, Richard
    b. Danzig [now Gdansk, Poland], February 7, 1823;
       d. Baden, June 15, 1895
    Manon   1877   Vienna
    Seekadett, Der+   1876   Vienna

Gerlach, Theodor
    b. Dresden, June 25, 1861; d. Kiel, November
       12, 1940
    Liebeswogen+   1903   Bremen

Gerster, Ottmar
    b. Braunfels, Hesse, June 29, 1897; d. Leipzig,
       August 31, 1969
    Enoch Arden+   1936   Düsseldorf
    Hexe von Passau, Die+   1941   Düsseldorf
    Verzauberte ich, Das+   1949   Wuppertal

Girschner, Karl Friedrich
    1794-1860
    Undine+   1830   Berlin

Gläser, Franz
    b. Obergeorgenthal [now Horní Jiretin, Bohemia],
       April 19, 1798; d. Copenhagen, August 29, 1861
    Aurora+   1836   Berlin
    Des Adlers Horst+   1832   Berlin

Goehr, Alexander
    b. Berlin, August 10, 1932
    Arden muss sterben   1967 Hamburg
    Wiedertäufer, Der+   1985 Duisburg

Goeldner, Friedrich
    b. Rawicz, Poland, October 21, 1885
    Ali Pascha+   1906 Posen

Goetz, Hermann
    b. Königsberg [now Kaliningrad], December 7, 1840;
       d. Hottingen, near Zurich, December 3, 1876
    Francesca da Rimini   1877 Mannheim
    Widerspenstigen Zähmung, Der 1874 Mannheim

Goetzl, Anselm
    b. Karolinenthal, Bohemia, August 20, 1878; d.
       Barcelona, January 9, 1923
    Zierpuppen+   1905 Prague

Goldberg, Theodor
    b. Chemnitz [now Karl-Marx-Stadt], September
       29, 1921
    Agamemnons Tod+   1949 Berlin
    Galatea Elettronica+   1969 Bellingham,
                               Wash.
    Judith+   1950 Berlin
    Kleopatra+   1952 Karslruhe
    Odysseus und die Sirenen+ 1950 Berlin
    Phaedra+   1950 Berlin
    Robinson und Freitag+   1951 Berlin radio

Goldmann, Friedrich
    b. April 27, 1941, Siegmar-Schönau
    R. Hot+   1977 Berlin

Goldmark, Karl
    b. Keszthely, Hungary, May 18, 1830; d. Vienna,
       January 2, 1915
    Götz von Berlichingen+ 1902 Budapest
    Heimchen am Herd, Das+ 1896 Vienna
    Königin von Saba, Die   1875 Vienna
    Kriegsgefangene, Die+   1899 Vienna
    Merlin+   1886 Vienna
    Wintermärchen, Ein+   1908 Vienna

Goldschmidt, Adalbert von
    b. Vienna, May 5, 1848; d. Hacking, near Vienna,
       December 21, 1906
    Heliantus+   1884 Leipzig

Goldschmidt, Berthold
    b. Hamburg, January 18, 1903
    Beatrice Cenci+   1953 London
    Gewaltige Hahnrei, Der+ 1932 Mannheim

Graener, Paul
    b. Berlin, January 11, 1872; d. Salzburg,
        November 13, 1944
    Don Juans letztes Abenteuer+ 1914 Leipzig
    Friedemann Bach+   1931 Schwerin
    Hanneles Himmelfahrt+   1927 Dresden,
                                    Breslau
    Narrengericht, Das+   1916 Halle
    Prinz von Homburg, Der+ 1935 Berlin
    Schirin und Getraude+   1920 Dresden
    Schwanhild+   1942 Cologne
    Theophano+   1918 Munich

Grafe, Manfred
    b. Löbau, Saxony, May 25, 1935
    Bauer im Fegefeuer, Der+ 1958 Meissen

Grammann, Karl
    1842-1897
    Melusina+   1875 Wiesbaden

Graun, Karl Heinrich
    b. Wahrenbrück, near Dresden, May 7, 1704; d.
        Berlin, August 8, 1759
    Iphigenia in Aulis+   1731 Brunswick
    Sancio und Sinilde+   1727 Brunswick

Graupner, Christoph
    b. Kirchberg, Saxony, January 13, 1683; d.
        Darmstadt, May 10, 1760
    Angenehme Betrug, Der+ 1707 Hamburg
    Antiochus und Stratonica+ 1708* ?
    Bellerophon+   1708 Hamburg
    Berenice und Lucilla+   1710 Darmstadt
    Dido, Königin von Carthago+ 1707 Hamburg
    Fall des grossen Richters in 1709 Hamburg
        Israel, Der+
    Fido amico, Il+   1708 Hamburg
    Lustige Hochzeit, Die+   1708 Hamburg
        (with R. Keiser)

Grünewald, Gottfried
    b. Eibau [now Eywau], near Zittau, Upper Austria,
        1675; d. Darmstadt, December 19, 1739
    Germanicus+   1704 Leipzig

Guhr, Karl Wilhelm Ferdinand
    b. Militsch, October 30, 1787; d. Frankfurt, July
       22, 1848
    Vestalin, Die+   1814 Kassel

Gurlitt, Manfred
    b. Berlin, September 6, 1890; d. Tokyo, April 29,
       1972
    Heilige, Die+   1920 Bremen
    Nana+   1933 Darmstadt
    Soldaten+   1930 Düsseldorf
    Wozzeck+   1926 Bremen

Gyrowetz, Adalbert
    b. Budweis [now Ceske Budejovice], Bohemia,
       February 20, 1763; d. Vienna, March 19, 1850
    Agnes Sorel+   1806 Vienna
    Aladin+   1819 Vienna
    Augenarzt, Der+   1811 Vienna
    Emerike+   1807 Vienna
    Hans Sachs im vorgerückter 1834 Dresden
       Alter+
    Ida, die Büssende+   1807 Vienna
    Junggesellen-Wirtschaft, Die+ 1807 Vienna
    Robert+   1813 Vienna

Haas, Josef
    b. Maihingen, Bavaria, March 19, 1879; d. Munich,
       March 30, 1960
    Hochzeit des Jobs, Die+ 1944 Dresden
    Tobias Wunderlich+   1937 Kassel

Hackländer, Friedrich Wilhelm
    1816-1877
    Soldatenleben+   1848 Stuttgart

Häfelin, Max
    b. St. Gallen, August 28, 1898; d. there October
       20, 1952
    Alchemist, Der+   ?   not perf

Haibel, Jakob
    b. Graz, July 20, 1762; d. Djakovar [now Dakovo,
       Yugoslavia], March 27 (?) 1826
    Tiroler Wastel, Der+   1796 Vienna

Hamel, Peter Michael
    ?
    Tragödie der Menschheit, Die+ 1981 Kassel

Handel [Händel], George Frideric
    b. Halle, February 23, 1685; d. London, April 14,
        1759

Almira	1705	Hamburg
Beglückte Florindo, Der+	1708	Hamburg
Nero	1705	Hamburg
Verwandelte Daphne, Die+	1708	Hamburg

Hanell, Robert
    b. Toschosch, Bohemia, March 2, 1925

Dorian Gray+	1962	Dresden
Esther+	1966	Berlin (East)
Spieldose, Die+	1957	Erfurt

Hartmann, Emil
    b. Copenhagen, February 21, 1836; d. there July
        18, 1898

Runenzauber+	1896	Hamburg

Hartmann, Karl Amadeus
    b. Munich, August 8, 1905; d. there January 5,
        1963

Des Simplicius Simplicissimus	1949	Cologne
Jugend+		

Hauer, Josef
    b. Wiener Neustadt, March 19, 1883; d. Vienna,
        September 22, 1959

Schwarze Spinne, Die+	1932*	perf. Vienna (1966)

Haug, Hans
    b. Basel, July 27, 1900; d. Lausanne, September
        15, 1967

Ariadne+	?	not perf
Don Juan in der Fremde+	1930	Basel
Spiegel der Agrippina, Der+	1937	Basel
Tartuffe+	1937	Basel
Unsterbliche Kranke, Der+	1947	Zurich
Verirrte Taube, Die+	1953	Basel

Haupt, Walter
    ?

Marat+	1984	Kassel

Hausegger, Siegmund von
    1872-1948

Zinnober+	1898	Munich

Haydn, Franz Josef
    b. Rohrau, Lower Austria, March 31, 1732; d.
       Vienna, May 31, 1809

Bestrafte Rachbegierde,	ca. 1779	?
Die+		
Dido+	1778*	?
Feuersbrunst, Die	1775*	perf. Vienna
		(1982)
Hexen-schabbas+	1773	?
Krumme Teufel, Der+	1753	Vienna
Neue krumme Teufel, Der+	1759	Vienna
Ochsensmenuette, Die+		perf. Vienna
(Haydn music, arr.		(1823)
Seyfried)		
Philemon und Baucis	1773	Esterháza
Reisende Ceres, Die	1777?	Esterháza?

Haydn, Michael
    b. Rohrau, Lower Austria, bapt. September 14,
      1737; d. Salzburg, August 10, 1806

Abels Tod+	1778	?
Ährenleserin, Die+	1778	Salzburg
Englische Patriot, Der+	ca. 1779	Vienna
Hochzeit auf der Alm, Die+	1768	Salzburg
Rebekka als Braut+	1776	Salzburg
Schuldigkeit des ersten	1767*	not perf
Gebotes, Die+, pt. 2		
Wahrheit der Natur, Die+	1769	Salzburg

Heger, Robert
    b. Strasbourg, August 19, 1886; d. Munich, January
      14, 1978

Bettler Namenlos, Der+	1932	Munich
Fest auf Haderslev, Ein+	1919	Nuremberg
Lady Hamilton+	1951	Nuremberg

Heinichen, Johann David
    b. Krössuin, near Weissenfels, April 17, 1683;
      d. Dresden, July 15, 1729

Angenehme Betrug, Der+	1705	Weissenfels?
Paris und Helena+	1710	Naumberg

Heinrich, Hermann
    ?

Viel Lärm um nichts+	1956	Frankfurt/Oder

Hellwig, Karl
    b. Kunersdorf [now Kunowice, Poland], July 23,
      1773; d. Berlin, November 24, 1838

Bergknappen, Die+	1820	Dresden

Hentschel, Theodor
   ?
   Lancelot+   1879 ?

Henze, Hans Werner
   b. Gütersloh, Westphalia, July 1, 1926

Bassariden, Die	1966	Salzburg
Boulevard Solitude	1952	Hanover
Cimarrón, El	1970	Aldeburgh Festival
Cubana, La	1974	New York, WNET
Elegie für junge Liebende	1961	Schwetzingen
Ende einer Welt, Das	1965	Frankfurt
Englische Katze, Die	1983	Schwetzingen
Floss der Medusa, Das	1968*	perf. London (1977)
Junge Lord, Der	1965	Berlin
König Hirsch (Il Re Cervo)	1956	Berlin
Landarzt, Ein	1953	Hamburg
Langwienzige Weg in die Wohnung Natascha Ungeheuer, Der	1971	Rome
Prinz von Homburg, Der	1960	Hamburg
Wundertheater, Das	1949	Heidelberg

Herbst, Walter
   b. Mannheim, April 14, 1907
   Lukrezia Borgia+   1946   Strelsund

Hermann, Heinrich
   ?
   Amphitryon+   1958   Magdeburg

Hermann, Paul
   b. Berlin, February 1, 1904
   Arme Gespenst, Das+   1961   Berlin

Herre, Max
   b. Leipzig, October 30, 1887; d. Augsburg, September 19, 1956
   Dornröschen+   1929   Augsburg

Hess, Ludwig
   b. Marburg, March 23, 1877; d. Berlin, February 5, 1944
   Was ihr wollt+   1941   Stettin

Heuberger, Richard
   b. Graz, June 18, 1850; d. Vienna, October 20, 1914
   Abenteuer einer Neujahrsnacht, Die+   1886   Leipzig

Heuberger, R. (cont.)
    Barfüssele+   1905   Dresden
    Don Quichote+   1910   Vienna
    Entzückende Frau, Eine+   1940   ?
       (rev. of **Ihre Excellenz**)
    Ihre Excellenz+   1899   Vienna
    Manuel Venegas+   1889   Leipzig
    Mirjam+   1894   Vienna
    Opernball, Der   1898   Vienna

Hiller, Ferdinand
    b. Frankfurt, October 24, 1811; d. Cologne, May
       11, 1885
    Katakomben, Die+   1862   Wiesbaden

Hiller, Johann Adam
    b. Wendisch-Ossig, near Görlitz, December 25,
       1728; d. Leipzig, June 16, 1804
    Aerndtekranz, Der+   1771   Leipzig
    Dorfbarbier, Der+   1771   Leipzig
    Grab des Mufti, Das   1779   Leipzig
    Jagd, Die   1770   Weimar
    Jubelhochzeit, Die+   1773   Leipzig
    Kleine Aehrenleserin, Die+   1778   Leipzig
    Krieg, Der+   1772   Leipzig
    Liebe auf dem Lande, Die+   1768   Leipzig
    Lisuarte und Darlioette+   1766   Leipzig
    Musen, Die+   1767   Leipzig
    Poltis+   ca. 1777* ?
    Teufel ist los, Der   1766   Leipzig

Hiller, Winfried
    b. Weissenhorn, March 15, 1941
    Niobe+   1977   Vienna, ORF

Himmel, Friedrich Heinrich
    b. Treuenbrietzen, near Potsdam, November 20,
       1765; d. Berlin, June 8, 1814
    Fanchon, das Leiermädchen+ 1804   Berlin
    Frohsinn und Schwärmerei+ 1801   Berlin
    Kobold, Der+   1813   Vienna
    Sylphen, Die+   1806   Berlin

Hindemith, Paul
    b. Hanau, November 16, 1895; d. Frankfurt,
       December 28, 1963
    Cardillac   1926   Dresden
    Harmonie der Welt, Die   1957   Munich
    Hin und zurück   1927   Baden-Baden
    Lange Weihnachtsmahl, Das 1961   Mannheim
    Mathis der Maler   1938   Zurich
    Mörder, Hoffnung der Frauen 1921   Stuttgart

Hindemith, P. (cont.)
    Neues vom Tage   1929 Berlin
    Nusch-Nuschi, Das   1921 Stuttgart
    Sancta Susanna   1922 Frankfurt
    Wir bauen eine Stadt   1930 Berlin

Hinrichs, Hajo
    b. Oldenburg, March 20, 1911
    Kluge Wirtin, Die+   1943 Oldenburg

Hoeffler, Paul
    b. Barmen, Wuppertal, December 21, 1895; d.
        Berlin, August 31, 1949
    Borgia+   ?   not perf

Höfer, Franz
    b. Griesbach, August 27, 1880; d. Garmisch-
        Partenkirchen, November 13, 1952
    Dornröschen+   1918 Nuremberg

Hoffmann, E. T. A. (Ernst Theodor Amadeus)
    b. Königsberg [now Kaliningrad], January 24, 1776;
        d. Berlin, June 25, 1822
    Aurora   1812* perf. Bamberg
                             (1933)
    Liebe und Eifersucht+   1807* not perf
    Liebhaber nach dem Tode, Der+ 1822* not perf
    Lustigen Musikanten, Die   1805 Warsaw
    Maske, Die+   1799* not perf
    Scherz, List und Rache+ ca. 1801 Posen
    Ungebetenen Gäste, Die+   1805* not perf
    Undine   1816 Berlin

Hoffmeister, Franz Anton
    b. Rothenburg am Neckar, May 12, 1754; d.
        Vienna, February 9, 1812
    Königssohn aus Ithaka, Der+ 1795 Vienna

Hofmann, Heinrich
    b. Berlin, January 13, 1842; d. Gross-Tabarz,
        Thuringia, July 16, 1902
    Aennchen von Tharau+   1878 Hamburg
    Armin+   1872 Dresden
    Cartouche+   1869 Berlin
    Donna Diana+   1896 Berlin
    Wilhelm von Oranien+   1882 Hamburg

Hofmann, Wolfgang
    b. Karlsruhe, July 6, 1922
    Alles ist Kismet+   1952 Kaiserlautern

Holenia, Hans
    b. Graz, July 5, 1890; d. there November 8, 1972
    Viola   1940 Graz

Holly, Franz Andreas
    b. ca. 1747; d. Breslau, May 4, 1783
    Bassa von Tunis, Der+   1774 Berlin
    Jagd, Die+   1772 Prague
    Kaufmann von Smyrna, Der+   1773 Berlin
    Lustige Schuster, Der+   1770 Prague

Holstein, Franz von
    b. Brunswick, February 16, 1826; d. Leipzig, May
       22, 1878
    Erbe von Morley, Der+   1872 Leipzig
    Haideschacht, Der+   1868 Dresden
    Hochländer, Die+   1876 Mannheim

Holterdorf, Theodor
    b. Castrop-Rauxel, Westphalia, January 26, 1910
    Alexander+   1960 Bremen

Holzbauer, Ignaz
    b. Vienna, September 17, 1711; d. Mannheim, April
       7, 1783
    Günther von Schwarzburg   1777 Mannheim

Hoven, J. [Johann Vesque von Püttlingen]
    b. Oppeln [now Opole, Poland], July 23, 1803; d.
       Vienna, October 29, 1883
    Abenteuer Carl des Zweiten, 1850 Vienna
        Ein+
    Johanna d'Arc+   1840 Vienna

Huber, Hans
    b. Eppenberg, June 28, 1852; d. Locarno,
       December 25, 1921
    Kudrun+   1896 Basel
    Schöne Bellinda, Die+   1916 Bern
    Simplicius, Der+   1912 Basel
    Weltfrühling+   1894 Basel

Huber, Joseph
    1837-1886
    Irene+   1881 Stuttgart

Huber, Klaus
    b. Bern, November 30, 1924
    Jot oder Wann kommt der Herr+ 1973 Berlin

Hüber, Kurt
   b. Salzburg, July 9, 1928
   Schwarz auf weiss+   1968   ORF, Vienna

Hufeld, Arnold
   b. Stettin [now Szczecin, Poland), June 16, 1903;
      d. Walsrode, Saxony, September 24, 1960
   Böse Weib, Das+   1939   Tilsit

Hummel, Bertold
   b. Hüfingen/Donaueschingen, November 27, 1925
   Des Kaisers neue Kleider+   1957   Freiburg
                                          and Bresgau

Hummel, Ferdinand
   b. Berlin, September 6, 1855; d. there April 24,
      1928
   Mara+   1893   Berlin

Hummel, Franz
   ?
   König Ubü+   1984   Salzburg

Hummel, Johann Nepomuk
   b. Pressburg [now Bratislava, Czechoslovakia],
      November 14, 1778; d. Weimar, October 17,
      1837
   Dankgefühl einer Geretteten+   1799   Vienna
   Eselhaut, Die+   1814   Vienna
   Haus ist zu verkaufen, Dies+ 1806   Eisenstadt
   Junker in der Mühle, Der+   1813   Vienna
   Mathilde von Guise+   1810   Vienna
   Rückfahrt des Kaisers, Die+ 1814   Vienna

Humperdinck, Engelbert
   b. Siegburg, near Bonn, September 1, 1854; d.
      Neustrelitz, September 27, 1921
   Dornröschen+   1902   Frankfurt
   Gaudeamus+   1919   Darmstadt
   Hänsel und Gretel   1893   Weimar
   Heirat wider Willen, Die+   1905   Berlin
   Königskinder   1910   New York
   Marketendieren, Die+   1914   Cologne
   Sieben Geislein+   1895   Magdeburg

Hüttenbrenner, Anselm
   b. Graz, October 13, 1794; d. Ober-Andritz, near
      Graz, June 5, 1868
   Leonore+   1835   Graz

Irmler, Alfred
   b. Berlin, February 1, 1891
   Nachtigall, Die+   1939   Düsseldorf

Jarno, Georg
   1868-1920
   Schwarze Kaschka, Die+   1895   Breslau

Jenny, Albert
   b. Solothurn, September 24, 1912
   Rubin, Der+   1938   Stans
   Zerrissene, Der+   1942   Stans

Jensen, Adolf
   b. Königsberg [now Kaliningrad], January 12, 1837;
      d. Baden-Baden, January 23, 1879
   Erbin von Montfort, Die+   1865* not perf

Kagel, Maurizio
   b. Buenos Aires, December 24, 1931
   Aus Deutschland+   1981   Berlin (West)
   Erschöpfung der Welt, Die+ 1980   Stuttgart

Kaiser, Alfred
   b. Brussels, March 1, 1872; d. London, February
      10, 1917
   Stella Maris+   1910   Düsseldorf

Kalliwoda, Johann Wenceslaus
   b. Prague, February 21, 1801; d. Karlsruhe,
      December 3, 1866
   Blanda   1847   Prague

Kálmán, Emmerich [Imre]
   b. Siófek, Hungary, October 24, 1882; d. Paris,
      October 30, 1953
   Csárdásfürstin, Die   1915   Vienna
   Gräfin Maritza   1924   Vienna
   Zirkusprinzessin, Die+   1926   Vienna

Kaminski, Heinrich
   b. Tiengen, Schwarzwald, July 4, 1886; d. Ried,
      Bavaria, June 21, 1946
   Jürg Jentsch   1929   Dresden
   Spiel von König Aphelius, 1946* perf. Gött-
      Das+   ingen (1950)

Katzer, Georg
   b. Habelschwerdt, Schleswig, January 10, 1935
   Boom-Boom Land+   1978   Berlin (East)

Kauer, Ferdinand
    b. Klein-Tajax [now Dyákowice], near Znaim [now
       Znojmo], Moravia, January 18, 1751; d.
       Vienna, April 13, 1831

Bastien und Bastienne+	1790	Vienna
Bauernliebe+	1802	Vienna
Donauweibchen, Das	1798	Vienna
Fuersten der Longobarden, Die+	1808	Vienna
Inkle und Yariko+	1807	Vienna
Mohr von Semegonda, Der+	1805	Vienna

Kauffmann, Leo
    b. Dammerkirch [now Dannemarie, Alsace], September
       20, 1901; d. Strasbourg, September 24, 1944

Agnes Bernauer+	1944	not fin.
Geschichte vom schönen Annerl, Die+	1942	Strasbourg

Kaufmann, Armin
    b. Neu-Itzkany, October 30, 1902

Krach im Offen, Der+	1961	Vienna

Kaufmann, Otto
    b. Celle, November 1, 1927

Des Kaisers neueste Kleider+	1954	Münster

Kaun, Hugo
    b. Berlin, March 21, 1863; d. there April 2, 1932

Fremde, Der+	1920	Dresden
Menandra+	1925	Brunswick, etc.
Sappho+	1917	Leipzig

Keiser, Reinhard
    b. Teuchern, near Weissenfels, bapt. January 12,
       1674; d. Hamburg, September 12, 1739

Adonis	1697	Hamburg
Almira+	1704	Weissenfels
Almira+ (rev. 1704 version)	1706	Hamburg
Angenehme Betrug, Der+	1707	Hamburg
Augustus+	1698	Hamburg
Basilius+	1694	Hamburg
Bon vivant, Le+	1710	Hamburg
Circe+	1734	Hamburg
Circe (Des Ulysses erster Theil)	1696	Brunswick
Claudius	1703	Hamburg
Costanza sforzata, La+	1706	Hamburg
Croesus	1710	Hamburg
Desiderius+	1709	Hamburg
Diana+	1712	Hamburg

Keiser, R. (cont.)
Forza dell'amore, La+	1711	Hamburg
Forza della virtù, La	1700	Hamburg
Fredegunda+	1715	Hamburg
Grossmüthige Tomyris, Die	1717	Hamburg
Inganno fedele, L'	1714	Hamburg
Janus	1698	Hamburg
Julia+	1717	Hamburg
Julius Caesar+	1710	Hamburg
Lächerliche Printz Jodelet, Der+	1726	Hamburg
Lustige Hochzeit, Die+ (with C. Graupner)	1708	Hamburg
Masagniello Furioso	1706	Hamburg
Nebucadnezar	1704	Hamburg
Octavia	1705	Hamburg
Orpheus:	1698	Brunwsick
Die sterbende Eurydice (Orpheus erster Theil)+	1702	Hamburg
Die verwandelte Leyer des Orpheus+	1699	Brunswick
(as **Orpheus ander Theil**)+	1702	Hamburg
Penelope (Des Ulysses zweiter Theil)+	1696	Brunswick
Procris und Cephalis+	1694	Brunswick
Psyche+	1701	Hamburg
Stoertebecker und Joedge Michaels+	1701	Hamburg
Ulysses+	1722	Copenhagen

Keiser, R., and C. Graupner
Lustige Hochzeit, Die+	1708	Hamburg

Keleman, Milko
b. Podravska Slatina, Croatia, March 30, 1924
Belagerungszustand, Der+	1970	Hamburg

Kelterborn, Rudolf
b. Basel, September 3, 1931
Engel kommt nach Babylon, Ein+	1977	Zurich
Errettung Thebens, Die+	1963	Zurich
Kaiser Jovian+	1967	Karslruhe
Kirschgarten, Der+	1984	Zurich
Ophelia+	1984	Schweitzingen

Keussler, Gerhard von
b. Schwanenburg, July 15, 1874; d. Niederwartha, August 21, 1949
Gefängnisse+	1914	Prague

Kienlen, Johann Christoph
    b. Ulm, bapt. December 14, 1783; d. Dessau,
       December 7, 1829
    Claudine von Villa Bella+   1780 Vienna

Kienzl, Wilhelm
    b. Waizenkirchen, January 17, 1857; d. Vienna,
       October 3, 1941
    Don Quixote+   1898 Berlin
    Evangelimann, Der   1895 Berlin
    Kuhreigen, Der+   1911 Vienna
    Testament, Das+   1916 Vienna
    Urvasi+   1886 Dresden

Killmayer, Wilhelm
    b. Munich, August 21, 1927
    Weisse Hut, Der+   1964* perf. 1967

Kirchner, Robert
    b. Hanover, April 2, 1889; d. Schwerin, June 16,
       1946
    Abenteuer des Don Quichotte+ 1941 Schwerin

Kirchner, Volker David
    b. Mainz, June 25, 1942
    Belshazar+   1986 Munich
    Fünf Minuten des Isaak Babel+ 1980 Wuppertal
    Trauung+   1975 Wiesbaden

Kistler, Cyrill
    b. Gross-Aitingen, near Augsburg, March 12,
       1848; d. Kissingen, January 1, 1907
    Baldurs Tod+   1905 Düsseldorf
    Eulenspiegel+   1889 Würzburg
    Faust I. Teil+   1905* ?
    Kunihild+   1884 Sonderhausen

Kittl, Johann Friedrich (Jan Bedrich)
    b. Orlik nad Vltavou, May 8, 1806; d. Lissa,
       Prussia [now Leszno, Poland], July 20, 1868
    Bianca und Giuseppe+   1848 Prague

Klebe, Giselher
    b. Mannheim, June 28, 1925
    Alkmene   1961 Berlin
    Ermordung Cäsars, Die+   1959 Düsseldorf
    Figaro lässt sich scheiden 1963 Hamburg
    Jacobowsky und der Oberst 1965 Hamburg
    Jüngste Tag, Der+   1980 Mannheim
    Mädchen von Domrémy, Das 1976 Stuttgart
    Märchen von der schönen   1969 Schwetzingen
       Lilie, Das+

Klebe, G. (cont.)
    Räuber, Die   1957 Düsseldorf
    Tödlichen Wünsche, Die   1959 Düsseldorf
    Wahrer Held, Ein   1975 Zurich

Kleemann, Roderich
    b. Berlin, August 4, 1914
    Bildnis des Dorian Gray, Das+ 1965 Zwickau
    Hexenlied+   1948 Zwickau

Klein, Bernhard
    b. Cologne, March 6, 1793; d. Berlin, September 9,
        1832
    Dido+   1823 Berlin

Klein, Bruno Oskar
    1858-1911
    Kenilworth+   1895 Hamburg

Kleinheinz, Franz Xaver
    1772-1832
    Harald+   1814 Budapest

Kleinmichel, Richard
    b. Posen [now Poznan, Poland], December 31, 1846;
        d. Charlottenburg, August 18, 1901
    Manon+   1883 Hamburg

Klenau, Paul von
    1883-1946
    Elisabeth von England+   1939 Kassel
    Kjarten und Gudrun+   1918 Mannheim
    Rembrandt von Rijn+   1937 Berlin
    Sulamith+   1913 Munich

Klose, Friedrich
    b. Karlsruhe, November 29, 1862; d. Ruvigliana,
        Lugano, December 24, 1942
    Ilsebill+   1903 Karlsruhe

Klughardt, August
    b. Cöthen, November 30, 1847; d. Rosslau, near
        Dresden, August 3, 1902
    Hochzeit des Mönchs, Die+ 1886 Dessau
    Iwein+   1879 Neustrelitz

Knecht, Justin
    b. Biberach, September 30, 1752; d. there December
        1, 1817
    Entführung aus dem Serail, 1787 Biberach
        Die

Koerpen, Alfred
    b. Wiesbaden, December 16, 1926
    Virgilius+   1951   Frankfurt

Kont, Paul
    b. Vienna, August 18, 1920
    Indische Legende+   1952   Vienna, RWR
    Inzwischen+   1967   Vienna, ORF
    Libussa+   1969* ?
    Lysistrate   1961   Dresden
    Peter und Susanne+   1959   Vienna, ORF
    Pluto+   1977   Klagenfurt
    Traumleben+   1963   Salzburg

Konta, Robert
    b. Vienna, October 12, 1880; d. Zurich, October
        19, 1953
    Kalte Herz, Das+   1908   Düsseldorf and
                                   Prague

Kormann, Hans
    b. Leipzig, April 2, 1889
    Dreispitz, Der+   1936   Altenberg
    Käficht, Der+   1925   Leipzig

Korngold, Erich
    b. Brünn [now Brno, Czechoslovakia], May 29, 1897;
        d. Hollywood, November 29, 1957
    Kathrin, Die+   1938   Stockholm
    Ring des Polykrates, Der 1916   Munich
    Stumme Serenade, Die+   1954   Dortmund
    Tote Stadt, Die   1920   Hamburg
    Violanta   1916   Munich
    Wunder der Heliane, Das+ 1927   Hamburg

Kospoth, Otto Carl Erdmann von
    b. Mühltroff, Vogtland, November 25, 1753; d.
        there June 23, 1817
    Adrast und Isidore+   1779   Berlin
    Freund deutscher Sitten, Der+ 1778   Berlin
    Irrwisch, Der+   1780   Berlin
    Kluge Jacob, Der+   1788   Berlin

Kounadis, Arghyris
    b. Constantinople, February 14, 1924
    Bassgeige, Die+   1978 ?
    Sandmann, Der+   1987   Hamburg

Krebs, Karl August
    b. Nuremberg, January 16, 1804; d. Dresden, May
        16, 1880
    Agnes Bernauer+   1858   Dresden
    Herzog Albrecht+   1833   Hamburg

Krenek [Křenek], Ernst
  b. Vienna, August 23, 1900

Ausgerechnet und verspielt+	1962	Salzburg
Das kommt davon+	1970	Hamburg
Diktator, Der	1928	Wiesbaden
Flaschenpost vom Paradies, Die+	1974	Vienna, ORF
Geheime Königreich, Das+	1928	Wiesbaden
Goldene Bock, Der	1964	Hamburg
Jonny spielt auf	1927	Leipzig
Karl der Fünfte	1938	Prague
Leben des Orest, Das	1930	Leipzig
Orpheus und Eurydike	1926	Kassel
Pallas Athene weint	1955	Hamburg
Schwergericht	1928	Wiesbaden
Sprung über den Schatten, Der+	1924	Frankfurt
Tarquin+	1941	Poughkeepsie, N.Y.
Vertrauenssache+	1962	Saarbrücken
Zauberspiegel, Der+	1967	Bavarian radio
Zwingburg+	1924	Berlin

Kretschmer, Edmund
  1830-1908

Folkunger, Die+	1874	Dresden
Heinrich der Löwe+	1877	Leipzig

Kreuder, Peter
  b. Aachen August 18, 1905

Zerrissene, Der+	1941	Stockholm

Kreutzer, Conradin
  b. Messkirch, Baden, November 22, 1780; d. Riga, December 14, 1849

Alimon und Zaide+	1814	Stuttgart
Alpenhütte, Die+	1815	Stuttgart
Beiden Figaro, Die+	1840	Brunswick
Besuch auf dem Lande, Der+	1826	Vienna
Familie auf Isle de France, Die+	1805	Vienna
Feodora+	1812	Stuttgart
Fridolin+	1837	Vienna
Höhle von Waverly, Die+	1837	Vienna
Konradin von Schwaben+	ca. 1810*	?
Libussa	1822	Vienna
Melusina+	1833	Berlin
Nachtlager in Granada, Das	1834	Vienna
Ring des Glückes, Der+	1833	Vienna
Siguna+	1823	Vienna
Verschwender, Der+	1834	Vienna

Krieger, Johann Philipp
    b. Nuremberg, bapt. February 27, 1649; d.
       Weissenfels, February 6, 1725
    Grossmüthige Scipio, Der+   1690 Weissenfels

Krol, Bernhard
    b. 1920
    Pulcinella+   1961 Kaiserslautern

Kücken, Friedrich Wilhelm
    b. Bleckede, Hanover, November 16, 1810; d.
       Schwerin, April 3, 1882
    Flucht nach der Schweiz, Die+ 1839 Berlin

Kunad, Rainer
    b. Chemnitz [now Karl-Marx-Stadt], October 24,
    1936
    Amphitrion+   1984 Berlin (East)
    Vincent+   1979 Dresden

Künneke, Eduard
    b. Emmerich, January 27, 1885; d. Berlin,
       October 27, 1953
    Blonde Liselott, Die+   1927 Altenburg
    Coeur As+   1913 Dresden
    Dorf ohne Glocke, Das+   1919 Berlin
    Robins Ende   1909 Mannheim
    Vetter aus Dingsda, Der+ 1921 Nollendorf-
                                 platz

Kunz, Ernst
    b. Zimmerwald, near Bern, June 2, 1891
    Fächer, Der+   1929 Zurich

Kunzen, Friedrich Ludwig Aemilius
    b. Lübeck, September 4, 1761; d. Copenhagen,
       January 28, 1817
    Fest der Winzer, Das   1793 Frankfurt

Kunzen, Johann Paul
    b. Leisnig, Saxony, August 31, 1696; d. Lübeck,
       March 20, 1757
    Cadmus+   1720 Brunswick?

Kusser, Johann Sigismund
    b. Pressburg [now Bratislava, Czechoslovakia],
       bapt. February 13, 1660; d. Dublin, November
       1727
    Andromeda+   1692 Brunswick
    Ariadne+   1692 Brunswick
    Cleopatra+   1691 Brunswick
    Erindo+   1694 Hamburg
    Jason+   1692 Brunswick

Kusser, J. S. (cont.)
    Julia+   1690   Brunswick
    Narcissus+   1692   Brunswick

Lachner, Franz
    b. Rain am Lech, April 2, 1803; d. Munich, January
        20, 1890
    Alidia+   1839   Munich
    Benvenuto Cellini   1849   Munich
    Bürgschaft, Die   1838   Pest
    Catharina Cornaro   1841   Munich

Lachner, Ignaz
    b. Rain am Lech, September 11, 1807; d. Hanover,
        February 24, 1895
    Loreley, Die+   1846   Munich
    Regenbrüder, Die+   1839   Stuttgart

Lacombe, Louis
    b. Bourges, November 26, 1818; d. St.
        Vaast-la-Hougue, Manche, September 30, 1884
    Meister Martin und seine   ?   perf. Koblenz
       Gesellen+   (1897)

Lang, Max
    b. Zurich, January 11, 1917
    Alchemist, Der+   ?   not perf

Laporte, André
    b. 1931
    Schloss, Das+   1986   Brussels

Lassen, Eduard
    b. Copenhagen, April 13, 1830; d. Weimar, January
        15, 1904
    Landgraf Ludwigs Brautfahrt   1857   Weimar

Leger, Hans
    b. Mannheim, February 21, 1899
    Dorian+   1939   Karlsruhe

Lehár, Franz
    b. Komáron, Hungary, April 30, 1870; d. Bad Ischl,
        October 24, 1948
    Frasquita+   1922   Vienna
    Giuditta   1934   Vienna
    Graf von Luxemburg, Der   1909   Vienna
    Kukuska+   1896   Leipzig
    Land des Lächelns, Das   1929   Berlin
    Lustige Witwe, Die   1905   Vienna
    Paganini   1925   Vienna

Lehár, Franz (cont.)
    Schön ist die Welt+   1930 Berlin
    Wo die Lerche singt+   1918 Vienna
    Zarewitsch, Der   1927 Berlin
    Zigeunerliebe   1910 Vienna

Lehner, Franz X.
    b. Regensburg, November 29, 1904
    Kleine Stadt, Die+   1957 Nuremberg
    Liebeskette, Die+   1961 Wiesbaden
    Schlaue Susanna, Die+   1952 Nuremberg

Leinert, Friedrich
    b. Oppeln, May 10, 1908; d. Freiburg, May 6, 1975
    Scherz, List und Rache+   1961 Hanover

Lendvai, Ernö
    b. Kaposvár, Hungary, February 6, 1925
    Elga+   1916 Mannheim

Leschetizky, Theodor
    b. Lancut, Galicia, June 22, 1830; d. Dresden,
        November 14, 1915
    Erste Falte, Die+   1867 Prague

Lichtenstein, Karl August
    b. Lahm, Franconia, September 8, 1767; d.
        Berlin, September 10, 1845
    Frauenort+   1814 Bamberg

Liebermann, Rolf
    b. Zurich, September 14, 1910
    Leonore 40/45   1952 Basel
    Penelope   1954 Salzburg
    Schule der Frauen, Die   1957 Salzburg

Lindpaintner, Peter (Josef von)
    b. Koblenz, December 9, 1791; d. Nonnenhorn,
        Lake Constance, August 21, 1856
    Bergkönig, Der+   1825 Stuttgart
    Genüserin, Die+   1839 Vienna
    Lichtenstein+   1846 Stuttgart
    Sicilianische Vesper, Die+ 1843* ?
    Vampyr, Der   1828 Stuttgart

Liszt, Franz [Ferenc]
    b. Raiding, near Ödenburg [now Sopron], Hungary,
        October 22, 1811; d. Bayreuth, July 31, 1886
    Legende von der heiligen 1881 Weimar
        Elisabeth, Die+

Lobe, Johann Christian
    b. Weimar, May 30, 1797; d. Leipzig, July 27, 1881
    Fürstin von Granada, Die+   1833 Weimar

Loewe, Carl
    b. Loebjuen, near Halle, November 30, 1796; d.
       Kiel, April 20, 1869
    Drei Wünsche, Die+   1834 Berlin

Loewe, Johann Jakob
    1628-1703
    Amelinde+   1657 Brunswick
    Orpheus aus Thracien+   1659 Brunswick

Lofer, Hans
    b. Hanau, January 9, 1900
    Des Kaisers neue Kleider+   1953 Gelsenkirchen

Löhner, Johann
    b. Nuremberg, bapt. November 21, 1645; d. there
       April 2, 1705
    Theseus+   1688 Nuremberg

Lohse, Otto
    b. Dresden, September 21, 1858; d. Baden-Baden,
       May 5, 1925
    Prinz wider Willen, Der+   1890 Riga

Lorentz, Alfred
    b. Strasbourg, March 7, 1872; d. Karlsruhe,
       April 23, 1931
    Mönch von Sendomir, Der+   1907 Karlsruhe
    Schneider Fips, Der+   1928 Coburg

Lorenz, Karl Adolf
    b. Köslin, Pommern, August 13, 1837; d. Stettin,
       March 19, 1923,
    Komödie der Irrungen, Die+   ?   Stettin (1939)

Lortzing, Albert
    b. Berlin, October 23, 1801; d. there January 21,
       1851
    Ali Pascha von Janina+   1816 Münster
    Beiden Schützen, Die   1837 Leipzig
    Cagliostro+   1850* ?
    Caramo+   1839 Leipzig
    Casanova in Murano+   1841 Leipzig
    Hans Sachs   1840 Leipzig
    Opernprobe, Die   1851 Frankfurt
    Regina   1848* perf. Berlin
                             1899
    Rolands Knappen+   1849 Leipzig

Lortzing, A. (cont.)
 Szenen aus Mozarts Leben+ 1832* ?
 Undine   1845 Magdeburg
 Waffenschmied, Der   1846 Vienna
 Wildschütz, Der   1842 Leipzig
 Zar und Zimmermann   1837 Leipzig
 Zum Grossadmiral+   1847 Leipzig

Lothar, Mark
 b. Berlin, May 23, 1902; d. 1985
 Glücksfischer, Der+   1962 Nuremberg
 Kalte Herz, Das+   1935 Berlin radio
 Lord Spleen+   1930 Dresden
 Münchhausen+   1933 Dresden
 Rappelkopf+   1958 Munich
 Schneider Wibbel   1938 Berlin
 Tyll+   1928 Weimar
 Widerspenstige Heilige, Der+ 1968 Munich

Lustgarten, Egon
 b. Vienna, August 17, 1887; d. Syosset, New York,
  June 2, 1961
 Blaue Berg, Der+   1945 New York

Lux, Friedrich
 1820-1895
 Kätchen von Heilbronn, Das+ 1846 Dessau
 Schmied von Rohla, Der+ 1882 Mainz

Maasz, Gerhard
 b. Hamburg, September 2, 1906
 Don Quijote+   1947 Hamburg

Mahler-Werfel, Alma
 b. Vienna, August 31, 1879; d. New York, December
  13, 1964
 Bergwerk von Falun, Das+ ? not perf

Mai, Julius
 b. Roth am Sand, October 10, 1862; d. Bern, May 2,
  1938
 Braut von Messina, Die+ 1904 Bern

Mangold, Karl
 b. Darmstadt, October 8, 1813; d. Obertsdorf im
  Allgäu, August 4, 1889
 Dornröschen+   1851 Darmstadt
 Gudrun+   1851 Darmstadt
 Tan[n]häuser+   1846 Darmstadt

Manzoni, Giacomo
    b. Milan, September 26, 1932
    Atomtod+   1965 Milan

Marschner, Heinrich
    b. Zittau, August 16, 1795; d. Hanover, December
        14, 1861
    Austin+   1852 Hanover
    Babü, Der+   1838 Hanover
    Falkners Braut, Des+   1832 Leipzig
    Hans Heiling   1833 Berlin
    Heinrich IV und d'Aubigne+   1820 Dresden
    Holzdieb, Der+   1825 Dresden
    Kaiser Adolph von Nassau+   1845 Dresden
    Kyffhäuserberg, Der+   1822 Zittau
    Lukretia+   1827 Danzig
    Saidar und Zulima+   1818 Bratislava
    Sangeskönig Hiarne+   1863 Frankfurt
    Schloss am Ätna, Das+   1836 Leipzig
    Templer und die Jüdin, Der   1829 Leipzig
    Vampyr, Der   1828 Leipzig

Martin, Frank
    b. Geneva, September 15, 1890; d. Naarden,
        November 21, 1974
    Sturm, Der   1956 Vienna

Martinů, Bohuslav
    b. Policka, Bohemia, December 8, 1890; d. Liestal,
        Switzerland, August 28, 1959
    Griechische Passion, Die   1959* perf. Zurich
                                               (1961)
    Zweimal Alexander   1937* perf. Mannheim
        (Alexander bis)   (1964)

Mattheson, Johann
    b. Hamburg, September 28, 1681; d. there April 17,
        1764
    Boris Goudenow+   1710 Hamburg
    Cleopatra   1704 Hamburg
    Henrico IV+   1711 Hamburg

Matthus, Siegfried
    b. Mallenuppen, East Prussia, April 13, 1934
    Judith+   1985 Berlin (East)
    Letzte Schuss, Der+   1967 Berlin (East)
    Omphale   1976 Weimar

Maurer, Ludwig
    b. Potsdam, February 8, 1789; d. St. Petersburg,
        October 25, 1878
    Aloise+   1828 Hanover

Maurer, L. (cont.)
       Neue Paris, Der+   1826 Hanover

Maurice, Pierre
       b. Allaman, November 13, 1868; d. Geneva, December
          25, 1936
       Andromeda+   1788 Berlin

Meder, Johann Valentin
       b. Erfurt, fl. ca. 1755–1800
       Beständige Argenis, Die+   1680 Reval

Mederitsch, Johann [also known as Gallus]
       b. Vienna, bapt. December 27, 1752; d. Lemberg
          [now Lvov, Poland], December 18, 1835
       Babylons Pyramiden+   1797 Vienna
          (with P. Winter)
       Rose+   1782 Vienna

Mendelssohn, Arnold
       b. Ratibor, December 26, 1855; d. Darmstadt,
          February 19, 1933
       Bärenhäuter, Der+   1900 Berlin

Mendelssohn, Felix
       b. Hamburg, February 3, 1809; d. Leipzig, November
          4, 1847
       Beiden Pädagogen, Die   1821* perf. Berlin
                                              (1962)
       Heimkehr aus der Fremde, Die 1829 Berlin
       Hochzeit des Camacho, Die   1827 Berlin
       Onkel aus Boston, Der/   1824 Berlin
          Die beiden Neffen+
       Soldatenliebschaft, Die   1820* perf. Witt-
                                              enberg (1962)
       Wandernden Komödianten, Die+ 1822* not perf

Messner, Josef
       b. Schwarz/Tirol, February 27, 1893; d. St. Jakob
          am Thurn, February 23, 1969
       Agnes Bernauer+   1935 not perf

Meyer von Schauensee, Franz
       1720–1789
       Engelberger Talhochzeit,   1781* ?
          Eine+
       Hans Hüttenstock+   1769 Lucerne

Meyer, Ernst Hermann
       b. Berlin, December 8, 1905
       Reiter der Nacht+   1973 Berlin (East)

Meyer, Krzystof
    b. Kraków, August 11, 1943
    Kyberiade+   1970* ?

Meyerbeer, Giacomo [Beer, Jakob Liebmann]
    b. Vogelsdorf, near Berlin, September 5, 1791; d.
       Paris, May 2, 1864
    Brandenburger Tor, Das+   1814   not perf
    Feldlager in Schlesien, Ein+ 1844   Berlin
    Jephtas Gelübde+   1812   Munich
    Wirth und Gast   1813   Stuttgart

Meyerowitz, Jan
    b. Breslau [now Wroclaw, Poland], April 23, 1913
    Doppelgängerin, Die+   1967   Hanover

Mihalovich, Ödön Péter József de
    b. Fericance, Slovenia, September 13, 1842; d.
       Budapest, April 22, 1929
    Hagbarth und Signe+   1882   Dresden

Mihalovici, Marcel
    b. Bucharest, October 22, 1898
    Heimkehr, Die+   1954   Frankfurt
                                       radio

Mikorey, Franz
    b. Munich, June 3, 1873; d. Garmisch, May 11, 1947
    König von Samarkand, Der+   1910   Dessau

Millöcker, Carl
    b. Vienna, April 29, 1842; d. Baden, December 31,
       1899
    Apajune der Wassermann+   1880   Vienna
    Arme Jonathan, Der+   1890   Vienna
    Bettelstudent, Der   1882   Vienna
    Feldprediger, Der+   1884   Vienna
    Gasparone+   1884   Vienna
    Vice-Admiral, Der+   1886   Vienna

Mohaupt, Richard
    b. Breslau [now Wroclaw, Poland], September 14,
       1904; d. Reichenau, July 3, 1957
    Bremer Stadtmusikanten, Die+ 1949   Bremen
    Graf von Gleichen, Der+   1901   Reichenberg
    Grüne Kakadu, Der+   1958   Hamburg
    Wirtin von Pinsk, Die+   1938   Dresden
    Zwillingskomödie   1954   Louisville

Mojsisovics, Roderich
    b. Graz, May 10, 1877; d. there March 30, 1953
    Zauberer, Der+   1926   Gera

Montowt, Reinhold
    b. Kirpehnen, January 12, 1842; d. there March 14,
       1925
    Letzte Tage von Pompeji, Die+ 1900   Lübeck

Mosel, Ignaz Franz von
    b. Vienna, April 1, 1772; d. there April 8, 1844
    Cyrus und Astyages+   1818   Vienna

Moszkowski, Moritz
    b. Breslau [now Wroclaw, Poland], August 23, 1854;
       d. Paris, March 4, 1925
    Boabdil+   1892   Berlin

Motte, Diether de la
    b. Bonn, March 3, 1928
    Aufsichtsrat, Der+   1970   Hanover
    So oder so+   1975   Hamburg

Mozart, Wolfgang Amadeus
    b. Salzburg, January 27, 1756; d. Vienna, December
       5, 1791
    Bastien und Bastienne   1768   Vienna
    Entführung aus dem Serail, 1782   Vienna
      Die
    Schauspieldirektor, Der   1786   Vienna
    Schuldigkeit des ersten   1767   Salzburg
      Gebotes, Die+, pt. 1
    Zaïde   1779* perf. Frank-
                           furt (1866)
    Zauberflöte, Die   1791   Vienna

Mozart, W. A., M. Haydn, and A. C. Adlgasser
    Schuldigkeit des ersten   1767   Salzburg
      Gebotes, Die+   (pt. 1 only)

Mraczek, Joseph Gustav
    b. Brünn [now Brno, Czechoslovakia], March 12,
       1878; d. Dresden, December 24, 1944
    Herrn Dürers Bild+   1927   Hanover
    Traum, Der+   1909   Brünn

Müller, A.
    ?
    Don Quixote in dem   1727   Hamburg
      Mohrengebirge+

Müller, Adolf
    b. Toina, Hungary, October 7, 1801; d. Vienna,
        July 29, 1886
    Schwarze Frau, Die+   1826 Vienna

Müller, August Eberhard
    b. Nordheim, December 13, 1767; d. Weimar,
        December 3, 1817
    Polterabend, Der+   ca. 1813 Weimar

Müller, Wenzel
    b. Tyrnau, September 26, 1767; d. Baden, August 3,
        1835

Alpenkönig und Menschenfeind+	1828	Vienna
Bergfest, Das+	1803	Vienna
Eiserne Mann, Der+	1801*	?
Friedliche Dörfchen, Das+	1803	Vienna
Gefesselte Phantasie, Die+	1828	Vienna
Kaspar, der Fagottist+	1791	Vienna
Neue Alceste, Die+	1806	Vienna
Neusonntagskind, Das+	1793	Vienna
Schwestern von Prag, Die	1794	Vienna
Sonnenfest der Braminen, Das	1790	Vienna
Sturm, Der+	1799	Vienna
Tankredi+	1817	Vienna
Teufelsmühle am Wienerberg, Die+	1799	Vienna
Travistirte Zauberflöte, Die+	1818	Vienna
Wunderlampe, Die+	1811	Vienna

Müller-Siemens, Detlev
    b. 1957
    Genoveva oder **Die weisse**   1977* ?
      Hirschkuh+

Nacke, Ewald
    ?
    Daphnis und Chloe+   1913 Hamburg

Neef, Wilhelm
    b. Kolin, Bohemia, January 28, 1916
    Schweigende Dorf, Das+   1961 Plauen

Neefe, Christian Gottlob
    b. Chemnitz [now Karl-Marx-Stadt], February 5,
        1748; d. Dessau, January 26, 1798

Adelheit von Veltheim	1789	Frankfurt
Amors Guckkasten+	1772	Leipzig
Apotheke, Die+	1771	Berlin
Sophonisbe+	1778	Mannheim

Nessler, Viktor
    b. Baldenheim, near Schlettstadt, Alsace, January
        28, 1841; d. Strasbourg, May 28, 1890
    Rattenfänger von Hamelin,   1879 Leipzig
    Der+
    Trompeter von Säckingen, Der+ 1884 Leipzig
    Wilde Jagd, Der+   1881 Leipzig

Netzer, Joseph
    1808-1864
    Mara+   1841 Vienna

Neumann, Franz
    1874-1929
    Liebelei+   1910 Frankfurt

Nicolai, Otto
    b. Königsberg [now Kaliningrad], June 9, 1810;
        d. Berlin, May 11, 1849
    Lustigen Weiber von Windsor, 1849 Berlin
    Die

Niehaus, Manfred
    b. Cologne, September 8, 1933
    Badewanne, Die   1973 Bonn
    Bartelby   1967 Cologne and
                            Berlin
    Maldoror+   1970 Kiel
    Tartarin von Tarascon   1977 Hamburg

Nodermann, Preben
    b. Hjörring, Denmark, January 11, 1867; d. Lund,
        Sweden, November 14, 1930
    König Magnus+   1898 Hamburg

Noll, Diether
    b. Merzig, Saarland, Germany, September 21, 1934
    König Drosselbart+   1958 Erfurt

Nötzel, Hermann
    b. Wiesbaden, April 10, 1880; d. Starnberg, near
        Munich, March 8, 1951
    Meister Guido+   1918 Karlsruhe

Nowka, Dieter
    b. Madlow bei Cottbus, Germany, July 7, 1924
    Erbschaft, Die+   1960 Schwerin

Oberleithner, Max von
    b. Märisch-Schönberg [now Sumpert, Moravia],
        July 11, 1868; d. there December 5, 1935
    Eiserne Heiland, Der+   1917 Vienna

Oboussier, Robert
    b. Antwerp, July 9, 1900; d. Zurich, June 9, 1957
    Amphitryon+   1951 Berlin and
                                    Dresden

Offenbach, Jacques (Jacob)
    b. Cologne, June 20, 1819; d. Paris, October 5,
        1880
    Fleurette+   1872* Vienna
    Goldschmied von Toledo, Der+   ---- perf. Mann-
      (pasticcio arr. by Julius   heim (1919)
      Stern and Alfred Zamara)
    Rheinnixen, Die+   1864 Vienna
    Schwarze Korsar, Der+   1872 Vienna

Oosterzee, Cornelie van
    b. Batavia, Java, August 16, 1863; d. Berlin,
        August 8, 1943
    Gelöbnis, Das+   1910 Weimar

Orff, Carl
    b. Munich, July 10, 1895; d. there March 29, 1982
    Antigonae   1949 Salzburg
    Astutuli+   1953 Munich
    Bernauerin, Die   1947 Stuttgart
    Carmina burana   1937 Frankfurt
    Klage der Ariadne+   1925 Karlsruhe
    Kluge, Die   1943 Frankfurt
    Mond, Der   1939 Munich
    Oedipus der Tyrann   1959 Stuttgart
    Orpheus+   1925 Dresden

Ostendorf, Jens-Peter
    b. Hamburg, July 20, 1944
    Murieta   1984 Cologne
    William Ratcliff   1982 Hamburg

Overhoff, Kurt
    b. Vienna, February 20, 1902
    Mira+   1925 Essen

Paderewski, Ignacy Jan
    b. Kurylówka, Podolia, Poland, November 18, 1860;
        d. New York, June 29, 1941
    Manru+   1901 Dresden

Palaschko, Johannes
    b. Berlin, July 13, 1877; d. there October 21,
       1932
    Bergknappen, Die+   ?   not perf

Paneck, Johann Baptist
    ?
    Christliche Judenbraut, Die+ 1789 Budapest

Paradis, Maria Theresia von
    b. Vienna, May 15, 1759; d. there February 1, 1824
    Ariadne und Bacchus+   1791 Laxenburg
    Rinaldo und Alcina+   1797 Prague
    Schulkandidat, Der+   1792 Vienna

Paumgartner, Bernhard
    b. Vienna, November 14, 1887; d. Salzburg, July
       27, 1971
    Heisse Eisen, Das+   1922 Salzburg
    Höhle von Salamanca, Die+ 1923 Dresden
    Rossini in Neapel+   1936 Zurich

Penderecki, Krzystof
    b. Debica, Poland, November 23, 1933
    Schwarze Maske, Die+   1987 Salzburg
    Teufel von Loudun, Der   1969 Hamburg

Pentenrieder, Franz Xaver
    b. Kaufbeuren, Bavaria, February 6, 1813; d.
      Munich, July 17, 1867
    Nacht zu Paluzzi, Die+   1840 Munich

Perfall, Karl von
    b. Munich, January 29, 1824; d. there January 14,
      1907
    Junker Heinz+   1886 Munich

Peró, Hans
    b. Gmünd, Austria, April 28, 1900
    Belsazar+   1929 Hamburg

Pfister, Kurt
    b. Ludwigshafen, January 16, 1895; d. Munich, May
      25, 1951
    Wozzeck+   1950 Regensburg

Pfitzner, Hans
    b. Moscow, May 5, 1869; d. Salzburg, May 22, 1949
    Arme Heinrich, Der   1895 Mainz
    Christelflein, Das+   1917 Munich
    Herz, Das+   1931 Berlin
    Palestrina   1917 Munich

Pfitzner, H. (cont.)
    Rose von Liebesgarten, Die+   1901 Elberfeld

Piersen, Henry Hugh
    b. Oxford, April 12, 1815; d. Leipzig, January 28,
       1873
    Leila+   1848 Hamburg

Pistor, Carl
    b. Menz, January 9, 1884; d. Rostock, August 26,
       1969
    Alchemist, Der+   1931 Kiel

Pixis, Johann Peter
    b. Mannheim, February 10, 1788; d. Baden-Baden,
       December 22, 1874
    Almanzine+   1820 Vienna
    Bibiena+   1829 Aachen

Poissl, Johann Nepomuk
    b. Haukenzell, Lower Bavaria, February 15, 1783;
       d. Munich, August 17, 1865
    Athalia+   1814 Munich
    Prinzessin von Provence, Die+ 1825 Munich
    Untersberg, Der+   1829 Munich
    Wettkampf zu Olympia, Der+ 1815 Munich
    Zaide+   1843 Munich

Poser, Hans
    b. Tannenbergsthal, East Prussia, October 8, 1917;
       d. Hamburg, January 10, 1970
    Auszeichnung, Die+   1959 Hamburg, ARD
    Bassgeige, Die+   1964 Mainz

Quaritsch, Johannes
    b. Magdeburg, February 18, 1882
    Bergknappen, Die+   ?   not perf

Radermacher, Friedrich
    b. Düren, near Aachen, April 14, 1924
    Tartarin von Tarascon+   1965 Cologne

Raff, Joachim
    b. Lachen, near Zurich, May 27, 1822; d.
       Frankfurt, June 24 or 25, 1882
    König Alfred+   1851 Weimar

Rastrelli, Joseph
    b. Dresden, April 13, 1799; d. there November 15,
       1842
    Salvator Rosa+   1832 Dresden

Rathaus, Karol
    b. Tarnopol, Galicia, September 16, 1895; d. New
       York, November 21, 1954
    Fremde Erde+   1930 Berlin

Reichardt, Johann Friedrich
    b. Königsberg [now Kaliningrad], November 25,
       1752; d. Giebichenstein, near Halle, June 27,
       1814

Andromeda+	1788	Berlin
Cephalus und Prokris+	1777	Hamburg
Claudine von Villa Bella	1789	Charlottenburg
Erwin und Elmire	1793	Berlin
Geisterinsel, Die	1798	Berlin
Hänschen und Gretschen+	1727	Leipzig
Ino	1779	Leipzig
Jery und Bätely	1801	Berlin
Lieb' und Treue+	1800	Berlin
Tamerlan+	1800	Berlin
Taucher, Der+	1811	Berlin

Reimann, Aribert
    b. Berlin, March 4, 1936

Gespenstersonate	1984	Berlin
Lear	1978	Munich
Melusine+	1971	Berlin
Traumspiel, Ein	1965	Kiel

Reinecke, Carl
    b. Altona, June 23, 1824; d. Leipzig, March 10,
       1910
    König Manfred+   1867 Wiesbaden

Reinthaler, Karl
    b. Erfurt, October 13, 1822; d. Bremen, February
       13, 1896
    Kätchen von Heilbronn, Das+ 1881 Frankfurt

Reissiger, Karl Gottlieb
    b. Belzig, January 31, 1798; d. Dresden, November
       7, 1859
    Felsenmühle zu Estalieres, 1831 Dresden
    Die+

Reuss, August
    b. Liliendorf bei Nzaim, Moravia, March 6, 1871;
        d. Munich, June 18, 1935
    Herzog Philipps Brautfahrt+   1909 Graz

Reuter, Florizel von
    b. Davenport, Iowa, January 21, 1890
    Postmeister Wyrin+   1946 Berlin

Reutter, Hermann
    b. Stuttgart, June 17, 1900; d. Zurich, January 1,
        1985

Bauernhochzeit+	1967	Mainz
Brücke von San Luis Rey, Die+	1954	Frankfurt radio
Don Juan und Faust+	1950	Stuttgart
Nausikaa+	1967	Mainz
Odysseus+	1942	Frankfurt
Prinzessin und der Schweinehirt, Die+	1938	Mainz
Saul	1928	Baden-Baden
Tod des Empedokles, Der+	1966	Schwetzingen
Verlorene Sohn, Der+	1929	Stuttgart
Weg nach Freudenstadt, Der+	1948	Göttingen
Witwe von Ephesus, Die+	1954	Cologne

Reznicek [Rezniček], E(mil) N(ikolaus) von
    b. Vienna, May 4, 1860; d. Berlin, August 2, 1945

Donna Diana	1894	Prague
Gondoliere des Dogen, Der+	1931	Stuttgart
Holofernes+	1923	Berlin
Jungfrau von Orleans, Die+	1887	Prague
Ritter Blaubart+	1920	Darmstadt
Satuala+	1927	Leipzig
Spiel oder Ernst?+	1930	Dresden
Till Eulenspiegel+	1902	Karslruhe

Richter, Ernst
    b. Dux [now Duchcov, Czechoslovakia], May 26, 1903
    Taras Bulba+   1935 Stettin

Riede, Erich
    b. London, May 3, 1903
    König Lustig+   1952 Kassel
    Yü-Nü+   1958 Dortmund

Ries, Ferdinand
    b. Bonn, bapt. November 28, 1784; d. Frankfurt,
        January 13, 1838
    Räuberbraut, Die+   1828 Frankfurt

Riethmüller, Helmut
    b. Cologne, May 16, 1912; d. Samedan, Switzerland,
       February 28, 1966
    Mitschuldigen, Die+   1957   Schwerin

Rihm, Wolfgang
    b. Karlsruhe, March 13, 1952
    Faust und Yorick+   1977   Hanover
    Hamletmaschine+   1987   Mannheim
    Jakob Lenz   1980   Karlsruhe
    Oedipus+   1987   Berlin (West)

Ritter, Alexander
    b. Navra, Estonia, June 7, 1833; d. Munich, April
       12, 1896
    Faule Hans, Der+   1885   Munich
    Wem die Krone?+   1890   Weimar

Ritter, Peter
    b. Mannheim, July 2, 1763; d. there August 1, 1846
    Eremit auf Formentara, Der+   1788   Mannheim

Ritter, Rudo
    b. Würzburg, November 27, 1889; d. Gaildorf, June
       3, 1966
    Penthesilea+   1927   Würzburg

Romberg, Andreas
    b. Vechta, near Münster, April 27, 1767; d. Gotha,
       November 10, 1821
    Ruinen vom Paluzzi, Die+   1811   Hamburg

Ronnenfeld, Peter
    b. Dresden, January 26, 1935; d. Kiel, August 6,
       1965
    Ameise, Die+   1961   Düsseldorf

Rosenfeld, Gerhard
    b. Königsberg [now Kaliningrad], February 10, 1931
    Spiel von Liebe und Zufall,   1982   Karslruhe
      Das+

Rösler, Joseph
    b. Banská Stiavnica, August 22, 1771; d. Prague,
       January 28, 1813
    Elisene, Prinzessin von   1807   Prague
      Bulgarien+

Röttger, Heinz
    b. Herford, Westphalia, November 6, 1909; d.
       Dessau, August 26, 1977
    Frauen von Troia, Die+   1962   Dessau

Röttger, H. (cont.)
    Heiratsantrag, Der+   1960   Magdeburg

Rubin, Marcel
    b. Vienna, July 7, 1905
    Kleider machen Leute+   1973   Vienna

Rubinstein, Anton
    b. Vikhvatinets, Podolsk district, November 28,
        1829; d. Peterhof, near St. Petersburg,
        November 20, 1894
    Feramors+   1863   Dresden
    Kinder der Heide, Die+   1861   Vienna
    Maccabäer, Die+   1875   Berlin
    Sulamith+   1883   Hamburg
    Unter Räubern+   1883   Hamburg

Rüfer, Philippe
    b. Liège, June 7, 1844; d. Berlin, September 15,
        1919
    Merlin+   1887   Berlin

Salieri, Antonio
    b. Legnago, August 18, 1750; d. Vienna, May 7,
        1825
    Hussiten von Naumberg, Die+   1803   Vienna
    Rauchfangkehrer, Der   1781   Vienna

Salmhofer, Franz
    b. Vienna, January 22, 1900; d. there September
        22, 1975
    Dame im Traum+   1935   Vienna

Schack [Žak], Benedikt
    b. Mirotice, Moravia, February 7, 1758; d. Munich,
        December 10, 1826
    Dumme Gärtner, Der+   1789   Vienna
    Fall ist noch weit seltner,   1790   Vienna
        Der+
    Fernando und Yariko   1784   Vienna
    Verdeckten Sachen, Die+   1789   Vienna
        (with F. X. Gerl)

Schanazara, Hans
    ?
    Nachtigall, Die+   1947   Cologne

Scharrer, August
    b. Strasbourg, August 18, 1866; d. Weherhof, near
        Fürth, October 24, 1936
    Erlösung, Die+   1895   Strasbourg

Scheffler, John Julia
    b. Hamburg, November 29, 1867; d. there March 20,
      1942
    Beowulf+   ?   unfin.

Schenk, Johann Baptist
    b. Wiener Neustadt, November 30, 1753; d. Vienna,
      December 29, 1836

Achmed und Almanzine+	1795	Vienna
Dorfbarbier, Der	1796	Vienna
Fassbinder, Der+	1802	Vienna
Jagd, Die+	1799	Vienna
Weinlese, Die+	1785	Vienna

Schibler, Armin
    b. Kreuzlingen, November 20, 1920; d. Zurich,
      September 7, 1986

Bergwerk von Falun, Das+	1953*	not perf
Füsse im Feuer, Die+	1955	Zurich

Schillings, Max von
    b. Düren, near Aachen April 19, 1868; d. Berlin,
      July 24, 1933

Moloch+	1906	Dresden
Mona Lisa	1915	Stuttgart
Pfeifertag, Der+	1899	Schwerin

Schindelmeisser, Louis
    b. Königsberg [now Kaliningrad], December 8, 1811;
      d. Darmstadt, March 30, 1864

Rächer, Der+	1846	Budapest

Schjelderup, Gerhard
    b. Kristiansand, Norway, November 17, 1859; d.
      Bendiktenbeuern, July 29, 1933

Frühlingsnacht+	1934	Lübeck
Norwegische Hochzeit+	1900	Prague
Sturmvögel+	1926	Schwerin

Schmidt, Franz
    b. Pressburg [now Bratislava], December 22, 1874;
      d. Perchtoldsdorf, near Vienna, February 11,
      1939

Notre Dame+	1914	Vienna

Schmidt, Gustav
    b. Weimar, September 1, 1816; d. Darmstadt,
      February 11, 1882

Prinz Eugen+	1847	Frankfurt
Weibertreue+	1858	Weimar

Schmidtmann, Friedrich
    b. Mönchengladbach, February 2, 1913
    Kain+   1952   Cologne

Schmitt, Georg Aloys
    b. Hanover, February 2, 1827; d. Dresden, October
        15, 1902
    Trilby+   1845   Frankfurt

Schmittbauer, Joseph Aloys
    b. Bamberg, November 8, 1718; d. Karlsruhe,
        October 24, 1809
    Lindor und Ismene+   1777   Lüneborg

Schneider von Wartensee, Xavier
    1786-1868
    Fortunat+   1831   Frankfurt

Schoeck, Othmar
    b. Brunnen, September 1, 1886; d. Zurich, March 8,
        1957

Don Ranudo	1919	Zurich
Erwin und Elmire	1916	Zurich
Massimilla Doni	1937	Dresden
Penthesilea	1927	Dresden
Schloss Dürande, Das	1943	Berlin
Venus	1922	Zurich
Vom Fischer un syner Fru	1930	Dresden
Wandbild, Das+	1924	Zurich

Schoenberg [Schönberg], Arnold
    b. Vienna, September 13, 1874; d. Los Angeles,
        July 13, 1951

Erwartung	1909*	perf. Prague (1924)
Glückliche Hand, Die	1924	Vienna
Moses und Aron	1932*	perf. Hamburg (1954)
Von heute auf morgen	1930	Frankfurt

Scholz, Bernhard
    b. Mainz, March 30, 1835; d. Munich, November 26,
        1916
    Mirandolina+   1907   Darmstadt

Schreker, Franz
    b. Monaco, March 23, 1878; d. Berlin, March 21,
        1934

Christophorus	1927*	perf. Freiburg (1978)
Ferne Klang, Der	1912	Frankfurt
Flammen+	1902	Vienna

Schreker, F. (cont.)
    Gezeichneten, Die   1918   Frankfurt
    Irrelohe   1924   Cologne
    Schatzgräber, Der   1920   Frankfurt
    Schmied von Gent, Der   1932   Berlin
    Singende Teufel, Der+   1928   Berlin
    Spielwerk und die Prinzessin, 1913   Frankfurt
        Das
    Tönenden Sphären, Die+   1915* not perf.

Schröder, Friedrich
    b. Näfels, August 6, 1910; d. Berlin, September
       25, 1972
    Bad auf der Tenne, Das   1955 Nuremberg

Schubaur, Johann Lukas
    b. Lechfeld, bapt. December 23, 1749; d. Munich,
       November 15, 1815
    Dorfdeputierten, Die+   1783 Munich
    Treuen Köhler, Die+   1786 Munich

Schubert, Franz
    b. Vienna, January 31, 1797; d. there November 19,
       1828
    Adrast+   1819* perf. Vienna
                            (1868)
    Alfonso und Estrella   1822* perf. Weimar
                            (1854)
    Bürgschaft, Die   1816 Vienna
    Claudine von Villa Bella   1815 Vienna
    Des Teufels Lustschloss   1814* perf. Vienna
                            (1879)
    Fernando   1815* perf. Vienna
                            (1907)
    Fierrabras   1823* perf. Vienna
                            (1835)
    Freunde von Salamanca, Die 1815* perf. Vienna
                            (1875)
    Graf von Gleichen, Der   1827* perf. Vienna
                            (1865)
    Rosamunde, Fürstin von Cypern 1823 Vienna
    Sakuntala+   1820* perf. Vienna
                            (1971)
    Spiegelritter, Der   1811* perf. Bero-
                            münster radio
                            (1949)
    Verschworenen, Die   1823* perf. Frank-
                            furt (1861)
    Vierjährige Posten, Der   1815* perf. Vienna
                            (1896)

Schubert, F. (cont.)
    Zauberharfe, Die   1820 Vienna
    Zwillingsbrüder, Die   1820 Vienna

Schultze, Norbert
    b. Brunswick, January 26, 1911
    Kalte Herz, Das   1943 Leipzig
    Peter der Dritte+   1965 ZDF radio
    Schwarzer Peter+   1936 Hamburg

Schulz, Johann Abraham Peter
    b. Lüneburg, March 31, 1747; d. Schwedt an der
        Oder, June 10, 1800
    Athalia+   1786 Berlin
    Clarissa+   1775 Berlin

Schumann, Robert
    b. Zwickau, Saxony, June 8, 1810; d. Endenich,
        near Bonn, July 29, 1856
    Corsair, Der+   not perf
    Genoveva   1850 Leipzig

Schürer, Johann Georg
    b. possibly Raudnitz [now Roudnice], Bohemia, ca.
        1720; d. Dresden, February 16, 1786
    Doris+   1747 Dresden

Schürmann, Georg Caspar
    b. Idensen, near Hanover, 1672 or 1673; d.
        Wolfenbüttel, February 25, 1751
    Eroberte Jerusalem, Die+ 1722 Brunswick
    Getreue Alceste, Die+   1719 Brunswick
    Heinrich der Vogler+   1718 Brunswick
    Leonilde+   1703 Brunswick
    Ludovicus Pius   1726 Brunswick
        (Ludwig der Fromme)
    Porsenna+   1718 Brunswick
    Salomon+   1701 Brunswick
    Telemaque+   1706 Naumburg
    Verstöhrte Troja, Das+   1706 ?

Schuster, Ignaz
    b. Vienna, July 20, 1779; d. there November 6,
        1835
    Hamlet+   1807 Vienna

Schuster, Joseph
    b. Dresden, August 11, 1748; d. there July 24,
        1812
    Alchymist, Der   1778 Dresden
    Wüste Insel, Die+   1779 Leipzig

Schütz, Heinrich
    b. (Bad) Köstritz, near Gera, bapt. October 9,
       1585; d. Dresden, November 6, 1672
    Dafne   1627 Torgau

Schwaen, Kurt
    b. Kattowitz [now Katowice], Silesia, June 21,
       1909
    Leonce und Lena+   1961 Berlin

Schweitzer, Anton
    b. Coburg, bapt. June 6, 1735; d. Gotha, November
       23, 1787
    Alceste   1773 Weimar
    Aurora+   1772 Weimar
    Dorfgala, Der+   1772 Weimar
    Elysium+   1770 Hanover
    Rosamunde+   1780 Mannheim

Schweizelsperger, Caspar
    b. Rosenheim, Upper Bavaria, December 3, 1668; d.
       after 1722
    Romanische Lucretia, Die+ 1714 Durlach
    Unglückliche Liebe+   1716 Durlach

Schwertsik, Kurt
    b. Vienna, June 25, 1935
    Fanferliesschen   1983 Stuttgart
    Schönefüsschen+

Searle, Humphrey
    b. Oxford, August 26, 1915; d. London, May 12,
       1982
    Hamlet   1968 Hamburg

Sechter, Simon
    b. Friedberg, Bohemia, October 11, 1788; d.
       Vienna, September 10, 1867
    Ali Hitsch-Hatsch+   1844 Vienna

Sehlbach, Erich
    b. Barmen, Wuppertal, November 18, 1898
    Baal+   1960* not perf

Seidel, Friedrich Ludwig
    b. Treuenbrietzen, June 1, 1765; d. Berlin, May 5,
       1831
    Abenteuer des Ritters Don 1811 Berlin
      Quixote, Ein+
    Dorfbarbier Zweiter Theil, 1807 Berlin
      Der+

Sekles, Bernhard
    b. Frankfurt, March 20, 1872; d. there December 8, 1934
    Scharazade+   1917 Mannheim

Semmler, Rudolf
    b. Dortmund, October 31, 1904
    Hansel und Gretel+   1956 Zurich

Seydelmann, Franz
    b. Dresden, October 8, 1748; d. there October 23, 1806
    Arsene+   1779 Dresden

Sieberg, Wilhelm Dieter
    ?
    Untergang der Titanic, Der+   1979 Berlin (West)

Siegel, Rudolf
    b. Berlin, April 12, 1878; d. Bayreuth, December 4, 1948
    Herr Dandolo+   1914 Essen

Sinding, Christian
    b. Kongsberg, Norway, January 11, 1856; d. Oslo, December 3, 1941
    Heilige Berg, Der+   1914 Dessau

Smyth, (Dame) Ethel
    b. Marylebone, April 22, 1858; d. Woking, May 9, 1944
    Fantasio+   1898 Weimar
    Wald, Der+   1902 Berlin

Sommer, Hans [Hans F. Zincken]
    b. Brunswick, July 20, 1837; d. there April 26, 1922
    Loreley, Die+   1891 Brunswick

Spohr, Ludwig (Louis)
    b. Brunswick, April 5, 1784; d. Kassel, October 22, 1859
    Alchymist, Der   1830 Kassel
    Alruna   1808* not perf
    Berggeist, Der   1825 Kassel
    Faust   1816 Prague
    Jessonda   1823 Kassel
    Kreuzfahrer, Die   1845 Kassel
    Pietro von Abano   1827 Kassel
    Prüfung, Die   1806* not perf
    Zemire und Azor   1819 Frankfurt

Spohr, L. (cont.)
    Zweikampf mit der Geliebten, 1811 Hamburg
    Der+

Spoliansky, Mischa
    b. December 28, 1898, Bialystok, Poland
    Rufen Sie Herrn Plim!+   ca. 1925

Spontini, Gaspare
    b. Maiolati, near Iesi, November 14, 1774; d.
        there January 24, 1851

Agnes von Hohenstaufen	1827	Berlin
Alcidor+	1825	Berlin
Julie+	1806	Vienna
Nurmahal	1822	Berlin
Olimpia+	1821	Berlin

Staden, Sigmund Theophil
    b. Kulmbach, Bavaria, bapt. November 6, 1607;
        buried Nuremberg, July 30, 1655
    Seelewig   1644 Nuremberg

Standfuss, J[ohann?] C.
    d. after 1759

Jochem Tröbs+	1759	Hamburg
Lustige Schuster, Der+	1759	Lübeck
Teufel ist los, Der	1743	Berlin

Stauffer, Theodor
    1826–1880
    Touristen, Die+   1869 Lucerne

Steffens, Walter
    b. Aachen, October 31, 1934
    Unter dem Milchwald+   1973 Hamburg

Stegmann, Carl David
    b. Staucha, near Meissen, 1751; d. Bonn, May 27,
        1826

Heinrich der Löwe+	1792	Frankfurt
Kaufmann von Smyrna, Der+	1773	Königsberg
Triumph der Liebe, Der+	1796	Hamburg

Stenhammar, Wilhelm
    b. Stockholm, February 7, 1871; d. there November
        20, 1927
    Fest auf Solhaug, Das+   1899 Stuttgart

Stephan, Rudi
    b. Worms, July 29, 1887; d. near Tarnopol,
        Galicia, September 29, 1915
    Ersten Menschen, Die   ?   perf. Frank-
                                        furt (1920)

Stierlin, Kuno
    b. Ulm, August 30, 1886; d. Düsseldorf, August 26,
        1967
    Aladins Wunderlampe+   ?   not perf
    Bär, Der+   1938 Osnabrück
    Berggeist, Der+   1921 Münster

Stockhausen, Karlheinz
    b. Mödrath, near Cologne, August 22, 1928
    Atmen gibt das Leben+ 1977 Nice
    Licht:
            Donnerstag   1981 Milan
            Montag   1988 Milan
            Samstag   1984 Milan
    Originale+   1961 Cologne
    Sirius+   1977 Aix-en
                                  Provence

Stolz, Robert
    b. Graz, August 25, 1880; d. Berlin, June 27, 1975
    Rosen der Madonna, Die+ 1964 Vienna, ORF
    Zwei Herzen im 3/4 Takt+ 1933 Zurich

Straus, Oscar
    b. Vienna, March 6, 1870; d. Bad Ischl, January
        11, 1954
    Drei Walzer+   1935 Zurich
    Frau, die weiss was sie will+ 1932 Berlin
    Letzte Walzer, Der+   1920 Berlin
    Lustigen Nibelungen, Die+ 1904 Vienna
    Tapfere Soldat, Der   1908 Vienna
    Walzertraum, Ein+   1907 Vienna

Strauss, Johann, Jr.
    b. Vienna, October 25, 1825; d. there June 3, 1899
    Blindekuh+   1878 Vienna
    Cagliostro in Wien+   1875 Vienna
    Fledermaus, Die   1874 Vienna
    Fürstin Ninetta+   1893 Vienna
    Göttin der Vernunft, Die+ 1897 Vienna
    Indigo und die vierzig   1871 Vienna
        Räuber+
    Jabuka+   1894 Vienna
    Karneval in Rom, Der+   1873 Vienna
    Lustige Krieg, Der+   1881 Vienna
    Nacht in Venedig, Eine   1883 Berlin

Strauss, J., Jr. (cont.)
    Prinz Methusalem+   1877 Vienna
    Ritter Pázmán+   1892 Vienna
    Simplizius, Der+   1887 Vienna
    Spitzentuch der Königin, Das+ 1880 Vienna
    Waldmeister+   1895 Vienna
    Walzer aus Wien+   1931 Vienna
    Wiener Blut   1899 Vienna
    Zigeunerbaron, Der   1885 Vienna

Strauss, Richard
    b. Munich, June 11, 1864; d. Garmisch-
        Partenkirchen, September 8, 1949
    Ägyptische Helena, Die   1928 Dresden
    Arabella   1933 Vienna
    Ariadne auf Naxos   1912 Vienna
    Capriccio   1942 Munich
    Daphne   1938 Dresden
    Des Esels Schatten+ (music   ---- Ettal
    after Strauss,   (Bavaria)
       arr. Haussner)   (1964)
    Elektra   1909 Dresden
    Feuersnot   1901 Dresden
    Frau ohne Schatten, Die   1919 Vienna
    Friedenstag   1938 Munich
    Guntram   1894 Weimar
    Intermezzo   1924 Dresden
    Liebe der Danae, Die   1940* perf. Salzburg
                               (1952)
    Rosenkavalier, Der   1911 Dresden
    Salome   1905 Dresden
    Schweigsame Frau, Die   1935 Dresden

Striegler, Kurt
    b. Dresden, January 7, 1886; d. Wildthurn, near
        Landau, August 4, 1958
    Dagmar+   1932 Dresden
    Spielmann, Der+   1949 Coburg

Strungk, Nicolaus Adam
    b. 1600 or 1601; d. Brunswick, buried October 12,
        1694
    Alceste+   1693 Leipzig
    Esther+   1680 Hamburg
    Theseus+   1683 Hamburg

Suppé, Franz von
    Spalato, Dalmatia [now Split, Yugoslavia], April
        18, 1819; d. Vienna, May 21, 1895
    Boccaccio   1879 Vienna
    Dinorah+   1865 Vienna
    Fatinitza+   1876 Vienna

Suppé, F. von (cont.)
Flotte Bursche+	1863	Vienna
Gervinus+	1849	Vienna
Leichte Cavallerie, Die+	1866	Vienna
Martl+	1848	Vienna
Schöne Galatea, Die	1865	Berlin
Tannenhäuser, Der+	1852	Vienna
Zehn Mädchen und kein Mann+	1862	Vienna

Süssmayr, Franz Xaver
    b. Schwanenstadt, Upper Austria, 1766; d. Vienna,
        September 17, 1803
Edle Rache, Die+	1795	Vienna
Gülnare+	1800	Vienna
Idris und Zenide+	1795	Vienna
Liebe auf dem Lande, Die+	ca. 1789*	not perf
Phasma+	1801	Vienna
Soliman der Zweyte	1799	Vienna
Spiegel von Arkadien, Der	1794	Vienna
Wildfang, Der+	1797	Vienna

Sutermeister, Heinrich
    b. Feuerthalen, Switzerland, August 12, 1910
Fingerhütschen+	1950	Berlin
Füsse im Feuer, Die+	1950	Berlin
Gespenst von Canterville, Das	1964	ZDF
Jorinda und Jorgile+	1934	Munich radio
Madame Bovary+	1967	Zurich
Niobe+	1945	Zurich
Raskolnikoff+	1948	Stockholm
Romeo und Julia	1940	Dresden
Rote Stiefel, Der+	1951	Stockholm
Schwarze Spinne, Die+	1936	Radio Beromünster
Seraphine+	1959	SRG television
Titus Feuerfuchs+	1958	Basel
Zauberinsel, Der+	1942	Dresden

Sutor, Wilhelm
    1774-1828
Apollos Wettgesang+	1808	Stuttgart

Tal [Grünthal], Josef
    b. Pinne, near Poznan [Poland], September 18, 1910
Aschmedai+	1971	Hamburg
Versuchung, Die+	1976	Munich

Taubert, Wilhelm
    b. Berlin, March 23, 1811; d. there January 7,
        1891
Kirmies, Die+	1832	Berlin

Taubert, W. (cont.)
    Macbeth+   1858   Berlin

Taubmann, Otto
    b. Hamburg, March 8, 1859; d. Berlin, July 4, 1929
    Porzia+   1916   Frankfurt

Telemann, Georg Philipp
    b. Magdeburg, March 14, 1681; d. Hamburg, June 25,
        1767
    Aesopus+   1729* ?
    Belsazar+   1723* ?
    Don Quichotte der   1761* ?
        Löwenritter+
    Flavius Bertaridus+   1729* ?
    Gedultige Sokrates, Der   1721   Hamburg
    Last-tragende Liebe, Die   1728   Hamburg
    Miriways   1728   Hamburg
    Neu-modische Liebhaber Damon   1724   Hamburg
    Pimpinone   1725   Hamburg
    Verkehrte Welt, Die+   1728* ?

Teyber, Franz
    b. Vienna, bapt. August 25, 1758; d. there October
        21 or 22, 1810
    Alexander+   1801   Vienna

Thärichen, Werner
    b. Neuhardenberg, August 18, 1921
    Anaximanders Ende+   1958   Berlin

Theile, Johann
    b. Naumburg, July 29, 1646; d. there, buried June
        24, 1724
    Erschaffene...Mensch, Der+   1678   Hamburg
    Geburth Christi, Die+   1681   Hamburg
    Orontes+   1678   Hamburg

Thies, Kurt
    ?
    Schneekönigin, Die+   1957   Trier

Thooft, Willem Franz
    b. Amsterdam, July 10, 1829; d. Rotterdam, August
        27, 1900
    Aleida von Holland+   1866   Amsterdam

Thuille, Ludwig
    b. Bozen [now Bolzano], Tyrol, November 30, 1861;
        d. Munich, February 5, 1907
    Gugeline+   1901   Bremen
    Lobentanz+   1898   Karlsruhe

Toch, Ernst
    b. Vienna, December 7, 1887; d. Santa Monica,
       California, October 1, 1964

Egon und Emilie+	1928	Mannheim
Fächer, Der+	1930	Königsberg
Prinzessin auf der Erbse, Die+	1927	Baden-Baden

Togni, Camillo
    b. Gussago, Brescia, October 18, 1922

Blau Bart+	1977	Venice

Trantow, Herbert
    ?

Odysseus bei Circe+	1938	Brunswick

Treibmann, Karl Ottomar

Preis, Der+	1980	Erfurt

Truhn, Friedrich Hieronymus
    b. Ebling, November 14, 1811; d. Berlin, April 30,
       1886

Trilby+	1835	Berlin

Tuczek, Vinzenz Franz
    b. Prague, February 2, 1773; d. Pest, ca. 1821

Arabella, oder **Die Schrekens- folgen der Eifersucht**+	1818	Pest
Bezauberte Leyer, Die+	1809	Vienna
Dämona+	1805	Pest
Durchmarsch, Der+	1808	Vienna
Lanassa+	1805	Pest
Neue Semiramis, Die+	1808	Vienna
Rübezahl+	1801	Breslau
Samson, Richter in Israel+	1808	Vienna
Schöne Melusine, Die+	1809	Vienna
Zwei Klacheln von Przelautsch+	1797	Prague

Uhl, Alfred
    b. Vienna, June 5, 1909

Mysteriöse Herr X, Der+	1966	Vienna

Ullmann, Viktor
    b. Prague, January 1, 1898; d. Auschwitz, after
       October 1944

Kaiser von Atlantis, Der	1944*	perf. Amster- dam (1975)
Peer Gynt+	?	not perf
Sturz des Antichrists, Der+	?	not perf

Umlauf[f], Ignaz
    b. Vienna, 1746; d. Meidling, near Vienna, June 8,
      1806
    Apotheke, Die+   1778 Vienna
    Bergknappen, Die   1778 Vienna
    Insel der Liebe, Die+   ca. 1772 Vienna
    Irrlicht, Das+   1782 Vienna
    Ring der Liebe, Die+   1786 Vienna
    Schöne Schusterin, Die+   1779 Vienna

Umlauft, Paul
    1853-1934
    Evanthia+   1893 Gotha

Urbanner, Erich
    b. Innsbruck, March 26, 1936
    Gluckerich, Der+   1965 Radio
                                   Innsbruck

Urspruch, Anton
    b. Frankfurt, February 17, 1850; d. there January
      7, 1907
    Sturm, Der+   1888 Frankfurt
    Unmöglichste von allem, Das+ 1897 Karslruhe

Vesque von Püttlingen, Johann. See J. Hoven.

Viardot, Pauline
    b. Paris, July 18, 1821; d. there May 18, 1910
    Letzte Zauberer, Der+   1869 Weimar

Vogl, Heinrich
    b. Munich, January 15, 1845; d. there April 21,
      1900
    Fremdling, Der+   1899 Munich

Vogler, Carl
    b. Oberrohrdorf, Switzerland, February 26, 1874;
      d. Zurich, June 17, 1951
    Rübezahl+   1917 Zurich

Vogler, Georg Joseph
    b. Pleichach, near Würzburg, June 15, 1749; d.
      Darmstadt, May 6, 1814
    Admiral, Der+   1811 Darmstadt
    Erwin und Elmire+   1781 Darmstadt
    Kaufmann von Smyrna, Der 1771 Mannheim
    Lampedo   1779 Darmstadt
    Samori+   1804 Vienna

Vogt, Hans
    b. Danzig [now Gdansk, Poland], May 14, 1911
    Athener Komödie+   1964   Mannheim
    Stadt hinter dem Strom, Die+   1955   Wiesbaden

Volanek, Anton
    b. Jaromer, November 1, 1761; d. Prague, January
       16, 1817
    Hochzeit auf dem Lande, Die+   1798   Prague and
                                        Leipzig
    Maskarade im Serail, Die+   1792   Prague
    Schuster-Feierabend, Der+   1793   Prague

Volkert, Franz
    b. Vienna, February 12, 1778; d. there March 22,
       1845
    Graf von Gleichen, Der+   1815   Vienna

Vollerthun, Georg
    b. Fürstenau, September 29, 1876; d. Strausberg,
       near Berlin, September 15, 1945
    Freikorporal, Der+   1931   Hanover
    Ireland-Saga+   1925   Munich

Wagner, Richard
    b. Leipzig, May 22, 1813; d. Venice, February 13,
       1883
    Feen, Die   1833* perf. Munich
                                      (1888)
    Fliegende Holländer, Der   1843   Dresden
    Hochzeit, Die   1832* perf. Leipzig
                                      (1938)
    Liebesverbot, Das   1836   Magdeburg
    Lohengrin   1850   Weimar
    Meistersinger von Nürnberg,   1868   Munich
       Die
    Parsifal   1882   Bayreuth
    Rienzi   1842   Dresden
    Ring des Nibelungen, Der   1876   Bayreuth
       (complete)
       Das Reingold   1869   Munich
       Die Walküre   1870   Munich
       Siegfried   1876   Bayreuth
       Götterdämmerung   1876   Bayreuth
    Tannhäuser   1845   Dresden
    Tristan und Isolde   1865   Munich

Wagner, Siegfried
    b. Triebschen, near Lucerne, June 6, 1869; d.
       Bayreuth, August 4, 1930
    An allem ist Hütchen schuld+   1917   Stuttgart

Wagner, S. (cont.)
Banadietrich+	1910	Carlsruhe
Bärenhäuter, Der	1899	Munich
Bruder Lustig+	1905	Hamburg
Friedensengel, Der+	1926	Karlsruhe
Heidenkönig, Der+	1933	Cologne
Herzog Wildfang+	1901	Munich
Kobold, Der	1904	Hamburg
Schmied von Marienburg, Der+	1923	Rostock
Schwarzschwanreich+	1918	Karlsruhe
Sonnenflammen+	1918	Darmstadt
Sterngebot, Das+	1908	Hamburg

Wagner-Régeny, Rudolf
    b. Régen [now Szász-Régen], Transylvania, August
        28, 1903; d. East Berlin, September 18, 1969
Bergwerk zu Falun, Das	1961	Salzburg
Fabel vom seligen	1964	Dresden
Schlächtermeister, Der+		
Günstling, Der	1935	Dresden
Moschopulos+	1928	Gera
Nackte König, Der+	1928	Gera
Persische Episode+	1963	Rostock
Prometheus+	1959	Kassel
Sganarelle+	1929	Essen

Wahren, Karl Heinz
    b. Bonn, April 28, 1933
Fettlöschen+	1976	Berlin (East)

Walbrunn, Anton Beer
    ?
Ungeheuer, Das+	1914	Karlsruhe

Walter, Fried
    b. Ottendorf, near Dresden, December 19, 1907
Andreas Wolius+	1940	Berlin

Walter, Ignaz
    b. Radonitz [now Radonice], Bohemia, August 31,
        1755; d. Regensburg, February 22, 1822
Doktor Faust	1797	Bremen
Spiegelritter, Der+	1791	Frankfurt

Waltershausen, Hermann Wolfgang von
    b. Göttingen, October 12, 1882; d. Munich, August
        12, 1954
Oberst Chabert+	1912	Frankfurt

Wandersleb, A.
    ?
Graf von Gleichen, Der+	1847	Gotha

Wartisch, Otto
    b. Magdeburg, November 18, 1893; d.
       Wolfratshausen, April 29, 1969

Cagliostro+	1924	Gotha

Weber, Bernhard Anselm
    b. Mannheim, April 18, 1764; d. Berlin, March 23,
       1821

Mudarra+	1800	Berlin
Wette+	1805	Berlin

Weber, Carl Maria von
    b. Eutin, Schleswig-Holstein, November 18?, 1786;
       d. London, June 5, 1826

Abu Hassan	1811	Munich
Drei Pintos, Die	1821*	perf. Leipzig (1888)
Euryanthe	1823	Vienna
Freischütz, Der	1821	Berlin
Oberon	1826	London
Peter Schmoll und seine Nachbarn	1802	Augsburg
Preciosa	1821	Berlin
Rübezahl	1805	not perf
Silvana	1810	Frankfurt
Waldmädchen, Das [**stumme**]	1800	Freiburg

Wehrli, Werner
    b. Aarau, January 8, 1892; d. Lucerne, June 27,
       1944

Heiss[e] Eisen, Das+	1918	Bern

Weigl, Joseph
    b. Eisenstadt, March 28, 1766; d. Vienna, February
       3, 1846

Adrian von Ostade+	1807	Vienna
Baals Sturz+	1820	Vienna
Bergsturz, Der+	1812	Vienna
Daniel in der Löwengrube+	1820	Vienna
Dorf im Gebirge, Das+	1798	Vienna
Eiserne Pforte, Die+	1823	Vienna
Jugend Peter des Grossen, Die+	1814	Vienna
Kaiser Hadrian+	1897	Vienna
Nachtigall und Rabe+	1818	Vienna
Schweizerfamilie, Die	1809	Vienna
Uniform, Der+	1805	Vienna
Unnutzte Vorsicht, Die+	1783	Vienna
Vestas Feuer+	1805	Vienna
Waisenhaus, Das+	1808	Vienna

Weill, Kurt
    b. Dessau, March 2, 1900; d. New York, April 2,
      1950

Aufsteig und Fall der Stadt Mahagonny, Der	1930	Leipzig
Bürgschaft, Die	1932	Berlin
Dreigroschenoper, Die	1928	Berlin
Happy End	1929	Berlin
Jasager, Der	1930	Berlin
Mahagonny	1927	Baden-Baden
Protagonist, Der	1926	Dresden
Royal Palace	1927	Berlin
Sieben Todsünden, Die	1933	Paris
Silbersee	1933	Leipzig
Weg der Verheissung, Der+	1935*	not perf
Zar lässt sich photographieren, Der	1928	Leipzig

Weinberger, Jaromir
    b. Prague, January 8, 1896; d. St. Petersburg,
      Fla., August 8, 1967

Geliebte Stimme, Die+	1931	Munich
Wallenstein+	1937	Vienna

Weingartner, Felix
    b. Zara, Dalmatia, June 2, 1863; d. Winterthur,
      May 7, 1942

Dame Kobold+	1916	Darmstadt
Dorfschule, Die+	1920	Vienna
Genesius+	1892	Berlin
Kain und Abel+	1914	Darmstadt
Meister Andrea+	1920	Vienna
Orestes+	1902	Leipzig
Sakuntala+	1884	Weimar

Weis, Karel
    b. Prague, February 13, 1862; d. there April 4,
      1944

Polnische Jude, Der+	1901	Prague
Sturm auf die Mühle, Der+	1912	Prague

Weishappel, Rudolf
    b. Graz, March 25, 1921

Elga+	1939	Kassel
König Nicolo	1972	Vienna

Weismann, Julius
    b. Freiburg, December 26, 1879; d. Singen am
      Hohentweil, Lake Constance, December 22, 1950

Gespenstersonate, Die+	1930	Munich
Leonce und Lena+	1925	Freiburg
Pfiffige Magd, Die+	1939	Leipzig

Weismann, J. (cont.)
    Schwanenweiss+   1923 Duisburg
    Traumspiel, Ein+   1925 Duisburg

Weissheimer, Wendelin
    b. Osthofen, Alsace, February 26, 1838; d.
        Nuremberg, June 16, 1910
    Meister Martin und seine   1879 Karlsruhe
      Gesellen+

Weissleder, Paul
    b. Kolbergermünde, August 14, 1886; d. New York,
        August 25, 1960
    Weg durchs Fenster, Der+   1917 Mainz

Wellesz, Egon
    b. Vienna, October 21, 1885; d. Oxford, November
        9, 1974
    Alkestis+   1924 Mannheim
    Bakchantinnen, Die   1931 Vienna
    Opferung des Gefangenen, Die+ 1926 Cologne
    Prinzessin Ginara+   1921 Hanover
    Scherz, List und Rache+   1928 Stuttgart

Werdin, Eberhard
    b. Spenge, October 19, 1911
    Des Kaisers neue Kleider+   1948 Leverkusen

Werle, Lars Johan
    b. Gävle, Sweden, June 23, 1926
    Reise, Die+   1969 Hamburg

Westien, Fritz
    b. Döbeln, near Leipzig, April 10, 1925
    Kaisers neue Kleider, Des+ 1957 Weimar

Wetz, Richard
    b. Gleiwitz [now Gliwice, Poland], February 26,
        1875; d. Erfurt, January 16, 1935
    Ewige Feuer, Das+   1907 Düsseldorf

Wetzler, Hermann
    b. Frankfurt, September 8, 1870; d. New York, May
        29, 1943
    Baskische Venus, Die+   1928 Leipzig

Weydert, Max
    b. Kosnitz, January 1, 1873; d. Dortmund, May 9,
        1939
    Enoch Arden+   1909 Essen

Willig, Walter
    ?
    Max und Moritz+   1979   Freiburg

Wimberger, Gerhard
    b. Vienna, August 30, 1923
    Dame Kobold   1964   Frankfurt

Windt, Herbert
    b. Senftenberg, Cottbus, Saxony, September 15,
        1894; d. Munich, November 22, 1965
    Andromache+   1932   Berlin

Winkler, Karl
    b. Vienna, September 26, 1899
    Attila+   ?   not perf

Winter, Peter [von]
    b. Mannheim, bapt. August 28, 1754; d. Munich,
        October 17, 1825
    Babylons Pyramiden (with   1797   Vienna
        J. Mederitsch)
    Bettelstudent, Der+   1785   Munich
    Colmal+   1809   Munich
    Helena und Paris+   1782   Munich
    Jery und Bäteli+   1790   Munich
    Labarint, Das   1798   Vienna
    Lenardo und Blandine   1779   Mannheim
    Marie von Montalban+   1800   Munich
    Psyche+   1790   Munich
    Scherz, List und Rache+   1790   Munich
    Sturm, Der+   1798   Munich
    Unterbrochene Opferfest, Das+ 1796   Vienna

Wohlgemuth, Gerhard
    b. Frankfurt, March 16, 1920
    Till+   1956   Halle

Wolf, Ernst Wilhelm
    b. Grossenbehringen, near Gotha, bapt. February
        25, 1735; d. Weimar, November 29 or 30, 1792
    Abend im Walde, Der+   1773   Weimar
    Alceste+   1780   Weimar
    Dorfdeputierten, Die+   1772   Berlin
    Ehrlichkeit und Liebe+   1776   Weimar
    Gärtnermädchen, Das+   1769   Weimar
    Grosse Loos, Das+   1774   Weimar
    Rosenfest, Das+   1770   Weimar
    Treuen Köhler, Die+   1773   Weimar

Wolf, Hugo
    b. Windischgraz, Styria [now Slovenj Gradec,
        Yugoslavia], March 13, 1860; d. Vienna,
        February 22, 1903
    Corregidor, Der   1896   Mannheim
    Manuel Venegas   1903   Mannheim

Wolf, Winfried
    b. Vienna, June 19, 1900
    Glückliche Ende, Das+   1954   Nuremberg

Wolf-Ferrari, Ermanno
    b. Venice, January 12, 1876; d. there January 21,
        1948
    Himmelskleid, Das+   1927 Munich

Wolff, Max
    b. Frankfurt, April 3, 1885; d. London, October
        25, 1954
    Heisse Eisen, Das+   1909 Frankfurt

Wölfl, Joseph
    b. Salzburg, December 24, 1773; d. London, May 21,
        1812
    Höllenberg, Der+   1795 Vienna
    Trojanische Pferd, Das+ 1799* ?

Wölfl, J. et al.
    Liebe macht kurzen Prozess+ 1798 Vienna

Wolfram, Joseph Maria
    b. Dobrzan, Bohemia, July 21, 1789; d. Teplitz
        [now Teplice Lazné], Bohemia, September 30,
        1839
    Bergmönch, Der+   1830 Dresden
    Maja und Alpino+   1826 Prague
    Schloss Candra+   1832 Dresden

Wolfurt, Kurt von
    b. Lettin, September 7, 1880; d. Munich, February
        25, 1957
    Dame Kobold+   1940 Kassel

Wollank, Friedrich
    b. Berlin, November 3, 1781; d. there September 6,
        1831
    Alpenhirten, Die+   1811 Berlin

Wolpe, Stefan
    b. Berlin, August 25, 1902; d. New York, April 4,
        1972
    Anna Blume+   1929* not perf

Wolpe, S. (cont.)
　　Schöne Geschichten+　　　　　　1929* not perf
　　Zeus und Elida+　　　　　　　　1928* not perf

Wranitzky [Vraniky], Paul [Pavel]
　　b. Neureisch [now Nova Rise], Moravia, December
　　　　30, 1756; d. Vienna, September 26, 1808
　　Mitgefühl, Das+　　　　　　　1804　Vienna
　　Oberon, König der Elfen　　1789　Vienna
　　Schreiner, Der+　　　　　　　1799　Vienna

Wunsch, Hermann
　　b. Neuss, near Düsseldorf, August 9, 1884; d.
　　　　Berlin, December 21, 1954
　　Don Juans Sohn+　　　　　　　1928　Vienna

Würfel, Wilhelm [Wenzel]
　　b. Plánany, near Kolin [Kolín], Bohemia, May 6,
　　　　1790; d. Vienna, March 23, 1832
　　Rübezahl+　　　　　　　　　　1824　Prague

Yun, Isang
　　b. Tongyong, Korea, September 17, 1917
　　Geisterliebe　　　　　　　　1971　Kiel
　　Sim Tjong　　　　　　　　　　1972　Munich
　　Träume:
　　　　Der Traum des Liu-Tung　1965　Berlin
　　　　Die Witwe des　　　　　　1969　Nuremberg
　　　　　　Schmetterlings

Zehntner, Louis
　　b. Sissach, January 28, 1868; d. Basel, June 3,
　　　　1949?
　　Dorval+　　　　　　　　　　　1913　Basel

Zeisl, Eric
　　b. Vienna, May 18, 1905; d. Los Angeles, February
　　　　18, 1959
　　Leonce und Lena+　　　　　　1952　Los Angeles

Zeller, Carl
　　b. St. Peter in der Au, June 19, 1842; d. Baden,
　　　　August 17, 1898
　　Obersteiger, Der+　　　　　1894　Vienna
　　Vogelhändler, Der　　　　　1891　Vienna

Zemlinsky, Alexander von
　　b. Vienna, October 14, 1871; d. Larchmont, N.Y.,
　　　　March 15, 1942
　　Es war einmal+　　　　　　　1900　Vienna

Zemlinsky, A. von (cont.)
    Florentinische Tragödie, Eine 1917 Stuttgart
    Kleider machen Leute+ 1910 Vienna
    Kreidekreis, Der+ 1933 Zurich
    Sarema+ 1897 Munich
    Traumgörge, Der+ 1906* perf. Nurem-
        berg (1980)
    Zwerg, Der 1922 Cologne

Zender, Hans
    b. 1936
    Stephan Climax+ 1986 Frankfurt

Zenger, Max
    b. Munich, February 2, 1837; d. there August 16,
      1911
    Eros und Psyche+ 1901 Munich
    Foscari, Die+ 1863 Munich
    Ruy Blas+ 1868 Mannheim
    Wieland der Schmied+ 1880 Munich

Ziehrer, C(arl) M(ichael)
    b. Vienna, May 2, 1843; d. there November 14, 1922
    Drei Wünsche, Die+ 1901 Vienna
    Fremdenführer, Der+ 1902 Vienna
    Landstreicher, Die 1899 Vienna
    Schatzmeister, Der+ 1904 Vienna

Zilcher, Hermann
    b. Frankfurt, August 18, 1881; d. Würzburg,
      January 1, 1948
    Doktor Eisenbart+ 1922 Leipzig and
        Mannheim

Zillig, Winfried
    b. Würzburg, April 1, 1905; d. Hamburg, December
      18, 1963
    Opfer, Das+ 1937 Hamburg
    Rossenknecht, Der+ 1933 Düsseldorf
    Troilus und Cressida 1951 Düsseldorf
    Verlöbnis, Das+ 1963 Linz
    Verlobung in San Domingo, 1957 NDR radio
      Die+
    Windsbraut, Die+ 1941 Leipzig

Zimmermann, Balduin
    b. Styrum, December 20, 1867; d. Luckau,
      Brandendburg, November 21, 1948
    Sakuntala+ 1905 Erfurt
    Wintermärchen, Das+ 1900 Erfurt

Zimmermann, Bernd Alois
    b. Bliesheim, near Cologne, March 20, 1918; d.
       Grosskönigsdorf, near Cologne, August 10,
       1970
    Soldaten, Die   1965 Cologne

Zimmermann, Udo
    b. Dresden, October 6, 1943
    Levins Mühle+   1973 Dresden and
                                     Weimar
    Merkwürdige Frau des   1982 Schwetzingen
      Schusters, Die+
    Schuhu und die fliegende 1976 Dresden
      Prinzessin+
    Weisse Rose, Die   1968 Schwerin
    Zweite Entscheidung, Die+ 1970 Magdeburg

Zöllner, Heinrich
    b. Leipzig, July 4, 1854; d. Freiburg, May 8, 1941
    Faust+   1887 Munich
    Überfall, Der+   1895 Dresden
    Versunkene Glocke, Die+   1899 Berlin

Zumpe, Hermann
    b. Taubenheim, April 9, 1850; d. Munich, September
       4, 1903
    Sawitri+   1907 Schwerin

Zumsteeg, Johann Rudolf
    b. Sachsenflur, near Mergentheim, January 10,
       1760; d. Stuttgart, January 27, 1802
    Elbondokani+   1803 Stuttgart
    Geisterinsel, Die+   1798 Stuttgart
    Pfauenfest, Das+   1801 Stuttgart
    Tamira+   1788 Stuttgart
    Tartarische Gesetz, Das+ 1780 Stuttgart

APPENDIX 3
LIBRETTISTS

+See Appendix I.

Abert, Johann Joseph (1874-1954)
Ekkehard+   1878   Abert, J. J.

Adler, Hans
Des Esels Schatten+   1964   Strauss, R.
                                              (arr. Haussner)
Rossini in Neapel+   1936   Paumgartner, B.

Albert, Eugen d' (1864-1932)
Ghismonda+   1895   Albert, E. d'
Rubin, Der+   1893   Albert, E. d'

Alberti (with Hornbostel)
Heinrich IV und d'Aubigne+   1820   Marschner, H.

Alberti, H.
Mareike von Numwegen+   1923   Albert, E. d'

Allfeld, Philipp
Wieland der Schmied+   1880   Zenger, M.

Andersen, Ludwig
Brüderlein Hund+   1953   Bresgen, C.
Doktor Johannes Faust+   1936   Reutter, H.
Don Juan und Faust+   1950   Reutter, H.
   (with H. Reutter)
Hochzeit des Jobs, Die+   1944   Haas, J.
Igel als Bräutigam, Der+   1948   Bresgen, C.
   (with C. Bresgen)
Mann im Mond, Der+   1960   Bresgen, C.
   (with C. Bresgen)
Tobias Wunderlich+   1937   Haas, J.
   (with H. H. Ortner)
Witwe von Ephesus, Die+   1954   Reutter, H.
Zaubergeige, Die+   1935   Egk, W.
   (with W. Egk)

André, Johann (1741-1799)
Alte Freyer, Der+   1776   André, J.
Barbier von Bagdad, Der   1783   André, J.
Bezauberten, Die+   1777   André, J.
Liebhaber als Automat, Der+   1782   André, J.
Töpfer, Der   1773   André, J.

Anthes, Otto
Don Juans letztes   1914   Graener, P.
   Abenteuer+
Narrengericht, Das+   1916   Graener, P.
Schwanhild+   1942   Graener, P.
Theophano+   1918   Graener, P.

Aron, Willi
  Tartuffe+   1929   Eidens, J.

Aspestrand, Sigwardt
  Seemannsbraut, Die+   1894   Aspestrand, S.

Auden, W[ysten] H[ugh] (1907-1973)
  Bassariden, Die   1966   Henze, H. W.
    (with C. Kallman)

Auenbrugger, Leopold von
  Rauchfangkehrer, Die+   1781   Salieri, A.

Bach, Rudolf
  Odysseus+   1942   Reutter, H.

Bachmann, Ingeborg (1926-1973)
  Junge Lord, Der   1965   Henze, H. W.
  Prinz von Homburg, Der   1960   Henze, H. W.

Baczko, Ludwig Franz Josef von (1756-1823)
  Rinaldo und Alcina+   1797   Paradis, M. T.
                                                  von

Bader, P. G.
  Philemon und Baucis   1773   Haydn, F. J.

Baltus, Silvia
  Galatea+   1930   Braunfels, W.

Bassewitz, Gerdt von
  Scharazade+   1917   Sekles, B.

Batka, Richard (1868-1922)
  Aschenbrödel+   1905   Blech, L.
  Kuhreigen, Der+   1911   Kienzl, W.
  Stier von Olivera, Der+   1918   Albert, E. d'
  Sturm auf der Mühle, Der+   1912   Weis, K.
  Zierpuppen+   1905   Goetzl, A.

Bauer, Julius
  Arme Jonathan, Der+   1890   Millöcker, C.
  Fürstin Ninetta+   1893   Strauss, J., Jr.
    (with H. Wittmann)

Bauer, Ludwig (1803-1846)
  Schmied von Rohla, Der+   1882   Lux, F.

Bäuerle, Adolf (1786-1859)
  Tankredi+   1817   Müller, W.

Bauernfeind, Winfried
   Traum des Liu-Tung, Der   1965 Yun, I.

Bauernfeld, Eduard von (1802-1890)
   Besuch in Saint-Cyr, Ein+   1838 Dessauer, J.
   Graf von Gleichen, Der   1827 Schubert, F.

Baussnern, Waldemar von (1866-1931)
   Satyros+   1923 Baussnern, W. von

Bechstein, Ludwig (1801-1860)
   Abu Kara+   1831 Dorn, H.

Beck, Enrique
   Bluthochzeit, Die   1957 Fortner, W.
   In seinem Garten liebt   1962 Fortner, W.
    Don Perlimplín Belisa
   Wald, Der+   1953 Fortner, W.

Beckerath, Alfred von (1901-)
   Till Eulenspiegel+   1949 Beckerath, A. von

Beda-Löhner, Fritz. See Fritz Löhner.

Behrend, Fritz (1889-1972)
   Lächerlichen Preziösen, 1949 Behrend, F.
    Die+

Berg, Alban (1885-1935)
   Lulu   1937 Berg, A.
   Wozzeck   1925 Berg, A.

Berg, Otto
   Coeur As+   1913 Künneke, E.
   (with E. Tschirsch)

Berger, Carl Philipp
   Genüserin, Die+   1839 Lindpaintner, P.

Bergh, Walter
   Lanzelot und Elaine+ 1917 Courvoisier, W.

Berla, Alois
   Gervinus+   1849 Suppé, F. von
   Martl+   1848 Suppé, F. von

Bernard, Joseph Karl
   Faust   1816 Spohr, L.
   Libussa   1822 Kreutzer, C.

Bernauer, Rudolf
  Liebe Augustin, Der+   1912 Fall, L.
    (with E. Welisch)
  Tapfere Soldat, Der   1930 Straus, O.
    (with L. Jacobsen)

Bertuch, Friedrich Justin (1747-1822)
  Grosse Loos, Das+   1774 Wolf, E. W.

Biedenfeld, K. von
  Bürgschaft, Die   1838 Lachner, F.

Bierbaum, Otto Julius (1865-1910)
  Gugeline+   1901 Thuille, L.
  Lobetanz+   1898 Thuille, L.
  Vernarrte Prinzess, Die+   1905 Chelius, O. von

Billinger, Richard (1893-1965)
  Hexe von Passau, Die+   1941 Gerster, O.
  Rossenknecht+   1933 Zillig, W.
  Verlöbnis, Das+   1963 Zillig, W.
  Windsbraut, Die+   1941 Zillig, W.

Binder, J. F. von
  Bellerophon+   1785 Winter, P.

Birch-Pfeiffer, Charlotte (1800-1868)
  Santa Chiara+   1854 Ernst II
  Sophie Katharina+   1850 Flotow, F. von

Bittner, Julius (1874-1939)
  Abenteuer, Der+   1913 Bittner, J.
  Bergsee, Der+   1911 Bittner, J.
  Höllisch Gold, Das+   1916 Bittner, J.
  Kohlhaymerin, Die+   1921 Bittner, J.
  Liebe Augustin, Der+   1916 Bittner, J.
  Mondnacht+   1928 Bittner, J.
  Musikant, Der+   1910 Bittner, J.
  Rosengärtlein, Das+   1923 Bittner, J.
  Rote Gred, Die+   1907 Bittner, J.
  Veilchen, Das+   1934 Bittner, J.

Bittony, Franz
  Lancelot+   1879 Hentschel, T.

Blacher, Boris (1903-1975)
  Fürstin Tarakanowa   1941 Blacher, B.
    (with K. Koch)
  Romeo und Julia   1947 Blacher, B.
  Yvonne, Prinzessin von 1973 Blacher, B.
    Burgund+
  Zerrissene, Der   1964 Einem, G. von

Blacher, B. (cont.)
  Zweihunderttausend Taler+   1969   Blacher, B.

Blech, Leo (1871-1958)
  Alpenkönig und   1903   Blech, L.
    Menschenfeind
  Das war ich+   1902   Pordes-Milo, A.
  Versiegelt   1908   Blech, L.

Blei, Franz (1871-1942)
  Nusch-Nuschi, Das   1921   Hindemith, P.

Bletschachy, Richard
  Ameise, Die+   1961   Ronnenfeld, P.

Bloch, Waldemar (1906-)
  Diener zweier Herren,   1936   Bloch, W.
    Der+
  Kätchen von Heilbronn,   1958   Bloch, W.
    Das+

Blonda, M. [Gertrud Schoenberg]
  Von heute auf morgen   1930   Schoenberg, A.

Blum, Karl (1786-1844)
  Flucht nach der Schweiz,   1839   Kücken, F. W.
    Die+

Blüthgen, Victor
  Schwarze Kaschka, Die+   1895   Jarno, G.

Bock, J.G.
  Hänschen und Gretschen+   1727   Reichardt, J. F.

Böckmann, Alfred (1905-)
  Doktor Eisenbart+   1954   Böckmann, A.

Bodanzky, Robert
  Endlich allein+   1914   Lehár, F.
    (with A. M. Willner)

Bodart, Eugen (1905-)
  Spanische Nacht+   1937   Bodart, E.
  Hirtenlegende+   1936   Bodart, E.

Böhme, Otto (1874-1944)
  Heilige Katharina, Die+   1919   Böhme, O.

Böhme, Walter
  Kolumbus+   1950   Böhme, W.

Bohn, T.
  Berggeist, Der+   1921 Stierlin, K.

Bohrmann-Riegen, Heinrich
  Spitzentuch der Königin,   1880 Strauss, J., Jr.
    Das+ (with R. Genée)

Borch, Marie von
  Fest auf Solhaug, Das+   1899 Stenhammar, V.

Bormann, Erich
  Feindlichen Nachbarn,   1949 Breuer, P.
    Die+
  Geschichte vom schönen   1942 Kaufmann, L.
    Annerl, Die+ (with E.
    Reinacher)
  Grossindustrielle, Die+   1953 Driesch, K.
  Soldaten, Die   1965 Zimmermann, B. A.

Borngräber, Otto
  Ersten Menschen, Die   1920 Stephan, R.

Borromäus von Miltitz, Karl
  Felsenmühle zu   1831 Reissiger, K. G.
    Estalieres, Die+

Bosshart, Robert
  Dagmar+   1932 Stiegler, K.

Bostel, Ludwig van
  Cara Mustapha+   1686 Franck, J. W.
  Croesus   1710 Keiser, R.
  Diocletianus+   1682 Franck, J. W.
  Theseus+   1683 Strungk, N. A.
  Vespanius+   1681 Franck, J. W.

Both, L. W. [Louis Schneider]
  Trilby+   1835 Truhn, F. H.
  Trilby+   1845 Schmitt, G. A.

Brachoff, L.
  Scherz, List und Rache+   1856 Bruch, M.

Brammer, Julius
  Gräfin Maritza   1924 Kálmán, E.
    (with A. Grünwald)
  Letzte Walzer, Der+   1920 Straus, O.
    (with A. Grünwald)

Brand, Max (1896–1980)
  Maschinist Hopkins   1929 Brand, M.

Brandes, Johann Christian (1735-1799)
   Ariadne auf Naxos   1775 Benda, G.
   Ino   1779 Reichardt, J. F.

Brandin, Walter
   Glücksfischer, Der+   1962 Lothar, M.

Brauer, Herbert
   Geheimnis des   1975 Blacher, B.
      entwendeten Briefes, Das+

Braun, Joseph
   Flotte Bursche+   1863 Suppé, F. von
   Karneval in Rom, Der+   1873 Strauss, J., Jr.
      (with F. Zell and R. Genée)

Braun, Karl Johann von Braunthal
   Nachtlager in Granada, 1834 Kreutzer, C.
      Das

Braun, Matthias
   Elisabeth Tudor   1972 Fortner, W.

Braun, Vera
   Nackte König, Der+   1928 Wagner-Régeny, R.

Brauner, Ernst
   Kardinal, Der+   1962 Eder, H.

Braunfels, Walter (1882-1954)
   Don Gil von den grünen 1924 Braunfels, W.
      Hosen+
   Prinzessin Brambilla   1909 Braunfels, W.
   Traum ein Leben, Der   1937 Braunfels, W.
   Vögel, Die   1920 Braunfels, W.
   Uilenspiegel+   1913 Braunfels, W.

Brecht, Bertolt (1898-1956)
   Aufsteig und Fall der   1930 Weill, K.
      Stadt Mahagonny, Der
   Dreigroschenoper, Die 1928 Weill, K.
   Jasager, Der   1930 Weill, K.
   Mahagonny (Das kleine 1927 Weill, K.
      Mahagonny)
   Sieben Todsünden, Die 1933 Weill, K.
   Verhör des Lukullus, Das 1951 Dessau, P.

Bredel, Willi
   Schweigende Dorf, Das+ 1961 Neef, W.

Brenner, H.
   Bär, Der+   1938 Stierlin, K.

Brentano, Clemens (1778-1842)
  Lustigen Musikanten,   1805   Hoffmann,
  Die   E. T. A.

Bresgen, Cesar (1913-)
  Engel von Prag, Der   1979   Bresgen, C.
  Schlaue Müllerin, Die+   1943   Bresgen, C.

Bressand, Friedrich Christian (ca. 1670-1699)
  Ariadne+   1692   Kusser, J. S.
  Basilius+   1694   Keiser, R.
  Circe (Des Ulysses   1696   Keiser, R.
    erster Theil)
  Cleopatra+   1691   Kusser, J.S.
  Echo und Narcissus+   1693   Bronner, G.
  Erindo+   1694   Kusser, J.S.
  Forza della virtù, La   1700   Keiser, R.
  Jason+   1692   Kusser, J.
  Julia+   1690   Kusser, J.
  Orpheus: 1698   Keiser, R.
    Die sterbende Eurydice 1702   Keiser, R.
    (Orpheus erster Theil)+
    Die verwandelte Leyer 1699   Keiser, R.
      des Orpheus (Orpheus
      ander Theil)+
    Procris und Cephalis+ 1694   Keiser, R.

Bretzner, Christoph Friedrich (1748-1807)
  Adrast und Isidore+   1779   Kospoth, O. C. E.
                                     von
  Belmont und Constanze   1781   André, J.
  Belmont und Constanze+ 1784   Dieter, C. F.
  Irrlicht, Das+   1782   Umlauf, I.
  Irrwisch, Der+   1779   Dieter, C. F.
  Irrwisch, Der+   1780   Kospoth, O. C. E.
                                     von

Breuning, Stefan von
  Fidelio   1806   Beethoven, L. van

Breymann
  Fido amico, Il+   1708   Graupner, C.

Brix, Bettina
  Claudia amata+   1952   Driessler, J.

Brod, Max (1884-1968)
  Nana+   1933   Gurlitt, M.
  Wallenstein+   1937   Weinberger, J.

Brüggemann, Kurt (1908-)
  Fischer un syne Fru, De+ 1936   Brüggemann, K.

Brüggemann, K. (cont.)
    Kalte Herz, Das+   1938 Brüggemann, K.

Brunner, G. S.
    Poltis+   ca. 1777 Hiller, J. A.

Brunnes, J. C.
    Dornröschen+   1929 Herre, M.

Buchbinder, Bernhard
    Göttin der Vernunft, Die+   1897 Strauss, J., Jr.
    (with A. M. Willner)

Bulthaupt, Heinrich (1849-1905)
    Kain+   1900 Albert, E. d'
    Kätchen von Heilbronn,   1881 Reinthaler, K.
    Das+

Bundi, Gian
    Schöne Bellinda, Die+   1916 Huber, H.

Bunge, R.
    Trompeter von Säckingen,   1884 Nessler, V. E.
    Der+

Bungert, August (1845-1915)
    Achilleus+   not perf Bungert, A.
    Kirke+   1898 Bungert, A.
    Nausikaa+   1901 Bungert, A.
    Odysseus' Heimkehr+   1896 Bungert, A.
    Odysseus' Tod+   1903 Bungert, A.

Bürde, G.
    Rübezahl+   1801 Tuczek, V. F.
    Taucher, Der+   1811 Reichardt, J. F.

Burkhard, Paul (1911-1977)
    Stern geht auf aus   1970 Burkhard, P.
    Jaakob, Ein+

Burmann, G. W.
    Freund deutscher Sitten, 1778 Kospoth, O. C. E.
    Der+   von

Burte, Hermann [Hermann Strübe] (1879-1960)
    Schloss Durande, Das   1943 Schoeck, O.

Busoni, Ferruccio (1866-1924)
    Arlecchino   1917 Busoni, F.
    Brautwahl, Die   1912 Busoni, F.
    Doktor Faust   1922 Busoni, F.

Busoni, F. (cont.)
   Turandot   1917   Busoni, F.
     (with K. Vollmöller)
   Wandbild, Das+   1924   Schoeck, O.

Büssel, Alois Josef
   Catharina Cornaro   1841   Lachner, F.

Büttner, Paul (1870-1943)
   Rumpelstilzchen+   1911   Büttner, P.

Caró, Paul (1859-1914)
   Hero und Leander+   1912   Caró, P.

Caspar, J. L.
   Beiden Pädagogen, Die 1821   Mendelssohn, F.
   Onkel aus Boston, Der 1824   Mendelssohn, F.
    (Die beiden Neffen)+
   Soldatenliebschaft, Die 1820   Mendelssohn, F.

Castelli, Ignaz Franz (1781-1862)
   Aladin+   1819   Gyrowetz, A.
   Elisene, Prinzessin von 1807   Rösler, J.
    Bulgarien+
   Familie auf Isle de   1805   Kreutzer, C.
    France, Die+
   Gewalt des Liedes, Die+ 1836   Lindpaintner, P.
   Schweizerfamilie, Die 1809   Weigl, J.
   Verschworenen, Die   1823   Schubert, F.

Cerha, Friedrich (1926-)
   Baal   1981   Cerha, F.
   Rattenfänger, Der+   1987   Cerha, F.

Charell, Erik
   Im Weissen Rössl   1930   Benatzky, R.
    (with H. Müller)

Chemin-Petit, Hans (1902-)
   Kassandras Tod+   1977   Chemin-Petit, H.
   Klage der Ariadne+   1973   Chemin-Petit, H.
   Komödiantin, Die+   1970   Chemin-Petit, H.
   König Nicolo   1962   Chemin-Petit, H.

Chézy, Wilhelmina Christiane von (1783-1856)
   Euryanthe   1823   Weber, C. M. von
   Rosamunde, Fürstin von 1823   Schubert, F.
    Cypern

Christodiykalis, George
   Periander+   1983 Antoniou, T.
   (transl. P. Kertz)

Claren, Georg C.
   Zwerg, Der   1922 Zemlinsky, A. von

Clemens, Franz
   Liebe ist teuer+   1949 Brehme, H.
   (with K. E. Jaroschek)

Clement, Viktor
   Stumme Serenade, Die+ 1954 Korngold, E.

Coenen, Paul (1908-)
   Karamasows, Die+   1945 Coenen, P.

Collin, Matthäus von (1779-1824)
   Colmal+   1809 Winter, P.
   Cyrus und Astyages+   1818 Mosel, J. F. von

Cornelius, Peter (1824-1874)
   Barbier von Bagdad, Der 1858 Cornelius, P.
   Cid, Der   1865 Cornelius, P.
   Gunlöd   1874 Cornelius, P.

Costa, C.
   Leichte Cavallerie, Die+ 1866 Suppé, F. von

Costenoble, Karl Ludwig
   Unsichtbare, Die+   1809 Eule, C. D.

Cramer, Heinz von
   Flut, Die   1946 Blacher, B.
   König Hirsch   1956 Henze, H. W.
   Preussisches Märchen   1952 Blacher, B.
   Prozess, Der   1953 Einem, G. von
   Robinson und Freitag+ 1951 Goldberg, T.
   Zwischenfälle bei einer 1966 Blacher, B.
    Notlandung

Creutzer, Caroline
   Dorian+   1939 Leger, H.

Dahn, Felix (1834-1912)
   Armin+   1872 Hofmann, H.
   Fremdling, Der+   1899 Vogl, H.

D'Arien, B.C.
   Laura Rosetti+   1778 André, J.
   Laura Rosetti+   1781 Dieter, C. F.

David, Karl Heinrich (1884-1951)
  Sizilianer, Der+   1924 David, K. H.
  Traumwandel+   1928 David, K. H.

Davis, Gustav
  Jabuka+ (with M. Kalbeck) 1894 Strauss, J., Jr.
  Waldmeister+   1895 Strauss, J., Jr.

Decker, Günther
  Reiter der Nacht+   1973 Meyer, E. H.

Decsey, Ernst
  Dame im Traum+   1935 Salmhofer, F.
    (with G. Holm)
  Kathrin, Die+   1938 Korngold, E.

Deicke, Günther
  Esther+   1966 Hanell, R.

Delmar, Axel
  Mara+   1893 Hummel, Ferd.

Devrient, Eduard (1784-1832)
  Hans Heiling   1833 Marschner, H.
  Kirmies, Die+   1832 Taubert, W.

Diebold, Bernhard
  Unsterbliche Kranke, Der+ 1947 Haug, H.

Dingelstedt, Franz von (1814-1881)
  Lichtenstein+   1846 Lindpaintner, P.

Dittersdorf, Karl Ditters von (1739-1799)
  Don Quixote der Zweyte+ 1795 Dittersdorf, K.
  Hochzeit des Figaro, Die 1789 Dittersdorf, K.
  Lustigen Weiber, Die+   1796 Dittersdorf, K.
  Rothe Käppchen, Das   1790 Dittersdorf, K.

Doczy, Lajos
  Ritter Pázmán+   1892 Strauss, J., Jr.

Döring, Georg
  Berggeist, Der   1825 Spohr, L.
  Fortunat+   1831 Wartensee, X. S.
  Räuberbraut, Die+   1828 Ries, F.

Dörmann, F.
  Walzertraum, Ein+   1907 Straus, O.
    (with L. Jacobson)

Dorn, Otto (1848-1931)
  Schöne Müllerin, Die+   1906 Dorn, O.

Dorst, Tankred (1925-)
  Geschichte von Aucassin,   1969   Bialas, G.
  Die
  Gestiefelte Kater, Der+   1975   Bialas, G.
  Yolimba+   1970   Dorst, T.

Dovsky, Beatrice
  Mona Lisa   1915   Schillings, M.
         von

Draesecke, Felix (1835-1913)
  Herrat+   1892   Draeseke, F.
  Merlin+   1913   Draeseke, F.

Drechsel, Gustav
  Don Juans Ende+   1930   Drechsel, G.
  (with J. Larska)

Dressel, Erwin (1874-1930)
  Laune des Verliebten,   1949   Dressel, E.
  Die+

Drieberg, Friedrich von (1780-1856)
  Sänger und der Schneider,   1814   Driesberg, F. von
  Der+

Droop, Fritz
  Enoch Arden+   1909   Wedert, M.

Duller, Eduard (1809-1853)
  Dornröschen+   1851   Mangold, K.
  Tan[n]häuser+   1846   Mangold, K.

Duncker, Dora
  Heilige Berg, Der+   1914   Sinding, C.

Düringer, Philipp Jakob
  Hans Sachs   1840   Lortzing, A.
  (with P. Reger and A. Lortzing)

Dürrenmatt, Friedrich (1921-)
  Besuch der alten Dame,   1971   Einem, G. von
  Der
  Engel kommt nach Babylon,   1977   Kelterborn, R.
  Ein+

Ebelings-Filhes, E. B.
  Dornröschen+   1902   Humperdinck, E.

Eberl, Anton (1766-1807)
  Pyramus und Thisbe+   1794   Eberl, A.

Eberl, Ferdinand
   Betrug durch Aberglauben+   1786 Dittersdorf, K.

Eckartshausen, K. von
   Fernando und Yariko   1784 Schack, B.

Ecklebe, Alexander (1904-)
   Genoveva+   1936 Ecklebe, A.

Eckschlager, A.
   Lukretia+   1827 Marschner, H.

Eggers, Friedrich
   Macbeth+   1858 Taubert, W.

Egk, Werner (1901-1983)
   Abstrakte Oper Nr. 1   1953 Blacher, B.
   Circe+   1948 Egk, W.
   Columbus   1933 Egk, W.
   Irische Legende   1955 Egk, W.
   Peer Gynt   1938 Egk, W.
   Revisor, Der   1957 Egk, W.
   Siebzehn Tage und vier 1966 Egk, W.
     Minuten
   Verlobung in San Domingo, 1963 Egk, W.
     Die

Eich, Günther (1907-1972)
   Kalte Herz, Das+   1935 Lothar, M.

Eiler, Hermann
   Zauberlehrling, Der+   1907 Doebber, J.

Einem, Gottfried von (1918-)
   Dantons Tod   1947 Einem, G. von
     (with B. Blacher)
   Kabale und Liebe   1976 Einem, G. von
     (with L. Ingrisch)

Einsiedel, Friedrich Hildebrand von (1750-1828)
   Geisterinsel, Die+   1798 Reichardt, J. F.
     (with F. W. Gotter)

Eisler, Hanns (1898-1962)
   Johann Faustus+   1974 Eisler, H.

Eliraz, I.
   Aschmedai+   1971 Tal, J.

Elkon, Benno
   Prinzessin auf der Erbse, 1927 Toch, E.
     Die+

Elsner (with Ortel)
     Gläserne Berg, Der+   1928   Braunfels, W.

Ende, Michael
     Gogolori, Der+   1985   Hiller, F.

Engel, A.
     Schatzmeister, Der+   1904   Ziehrer, C. M.
        (with J. Horst)

Engel, Johann Jakob (1741-1892)
     Apotheke, Die+   1771   Neefe, C. G.
     Apotheke, Die+   1778   Umlauf, I.

Enzensberger, Hans Magnus (1929-)
     Cimarrón, El   1970   Henze, H. W.
     Cubana, La   1974   Henze, H. W.

Erbse, Heimo (1924-)
     Fabel in C+   1952   Erbse, H.
     Julietta+   1959   Erbse, H.

Esslin, M.
     Beatrice Cenci+   1953   Goldschmidt, B.

Estoc, Paul d'
     Judith+   1848   Adam, F.
        (with C. Hellem)

Ettinger, Max (1874-1951)
     Judith+   1921   Ettinger, M.

Eugen of Württemberg
     Geisterbraut, Die+   1842   Eugen of
                                               Württemberg

Eulenberg, Herbert (1876-1949)
     Ritter Blaubart+   1920   Reznicek, E. N.
                                               von

Ewers, Hans Heinz (1871-1943)
     Toten Augen, Die   1916   Albert, E. d'
        (with M. Henry [Vaucheret])

Faber, H.
     Fassbinder, Der+   1802   Schenk, J.

Faesi, Robert (1883-1972)
     Schwarze Spinne, Die   1949   Burkhard, W.
        (with G. Boner)

Falzari, Felix [Hans Hoffmann]
   Kukuska+   1896   Lehár, F.

Feind, Barthold
   Almira+   1706   Keiser, R.
   Bellerophon+   1708   Graupner, C.
   Bon vivant, Le+   1710   Keiser, R.
   Costanza sforzata, La+   1706   Keiser, R.
   Desiderius+   1709   Keiser, R.
   Fall des grossen Richters   1709   Graupner, C.
     in Israel, Der+
   Julius Cäsar+   1710   Keiser, R.
   Lucretia+   1705   Keiser, R.
   Masagniello Furioso   1706   Keiser, R.
   Octavia   1705   Keiser, R.
   Paris und Helena+   1710   Heinichen, D.

Feind, Barthold?
   Forza dell'amore, La+   1711   Keiser, R.

Feld, Leo [Leo Hirschfeld] (1869-1924)
   Heilige Ente, Die+   1923   Gál, H.
     (with K. M. von Levetzow)
   Kleider machen Leute+   1910   Zemlinsky, A. von
   Scirocco+   1921   Albert, E. d'
     (with K. M. von Levetzow)
   Traumgörge, Der+   1906   Zemlinsky, A. von

Fellechner, W.
   Cartouche+   1869   Hofmann, H.

Fels, Roderich [S. Rosenfeld]
   Aennchen von Tharau+   1878   Hofmann, H.
   Wilhelm von Oranien+   1882   Hofmann, H.

Fernand, Ludwig
   Irrlicht+   1905   Fall, L.
   Parolo (Frau Denise)+   1902   Fall, L.

Feussner, Alfred
   Maldoror+   1970   Niehaus, M.
     (with M. Niehaus)

Feustking, Friedrich Christian
   Almira   1705   Handel, G.F.
   Almira, Königen von   1704   Keiser, R.
     Castilien+
   Cleopatra   1704   Mattheson, J.
   Nero   1705   Handel, G.F.

Fiedler, Gottlieb
  Leonilde+   1703 Schürmann, G.C.
  Narcissus+   1692 Kusser, J.S.

Filistri (da Caramondani), Antonio de'
  Andromeda+   1788 Reichardt, J.F.

Fischer, E. Kurt
  Dame Kobold+   1940 Wolfurt, K. von

Flury, Richard (1896-1967)
  Florentinische Tragödie, 1929 Flury, R.
    Eine+

Forest, Jean Kurt (1909-1975)
  Arme Konrad, Der+   1959 Forest, J. K.
  Blumen von Hiroshima, Die+ 1967 Forest, J. K.
  Hamlet+   1973 Forest, J. K.
    (with S. Grammaticus)

Förg, Carl Josef
  Helena und Paris+   1782 Winter, P.

Forst, J. von
  Nacht zu Paluzzi, Die+   1840 Pentenrieder,
                                F. X.

Forster, Friedrich
  Alexander+   1960 Holterdorf, T.

Forster, Josef (1845-1917)
  Rose von Pontevedra, Die+ 1893 Forster, J.

Förtsch, J. P.
  Aeneas+   1680 Franck, J. W.

Fouqué, Friedrich Heinrich Karl de la Motte
  (1777-1843)
  Undine+   1830 Girschner, K. F.

Franck, Johann Wolfgang (1664-ca. 1710)
  Alceste+   1680 Franck, J. W.

Franke-Ruta, Walther
  Verirrte Taube, Die+   1953 Haug, H.

Frauendorf, Johann Christoph
  Telemaque+   1706 Schürmann, G. C.
  Verstöhrte Troja, Das+   1706 Schürmann, G. C.

Freska, Friedrich [Kurt Friedrich]
  Eifersüchtige Trinker, Der+ 1925 Ettinger, M.

Fried, Erich (1921-)
  Arden muss sterben   1967   Goehr, A.
  Teufel von Loudun, Die   1969   Penderecki, K.
    (with K. Penderecki)
  Unter dem Milchwald+   1972   Steffens, W.

Friedrich, Karl
  Brüderlein und   1949   Friedrich, K.
    Schwesterlein+

Friedrich, M.G. [Friedrich Melchior Gredy]
  Zwei Prinzen, Die+   1845   Esser, H.

Friedrich, W. [Friedrich Wilhelm Riese]
  Alessandro Stradella   1844   Flotow, F. von
  Martha   1847   Flotow, F. von
  Matrosen, Die+   1839   Flotow, F. von

Fritsch, Gerhard (1924-1969)
  Peter und Susanne+   1959   Kont, P.

Fröhlich, Michael
  Jakob Lenz   1980   Rihm, W.

Fuchs, Georg
  Don Quichotte+   1908   Beer-Walbrunn, A.

Gahlbeck, Rudolf
  Nachtigall, Die+   1939   Irmler, A.

Gans zu Putlitz, Gustav Heinrich von
  Rübezahl+   1852   Flotow, F. von

Gartner, Ernst
  Visiones amantes+   1964   Bresgen, C.

Gast, Peter [Johann Heinrich Köselitz] (1854-1918)
  Heimliche Ehe, Die+   1891   Gast, P.

Gehe, Eduard Heinrich
  Jessonda   1823   Spohr, L.
  Maja und Alpino+   1826   Wolfram, J. M.
  Schloss Candra+   1832   Wolfram, J. M.

Geibel, Emanuel (1815-1884)
  Loreley, Die   1863   Bruch, M.

Geissler, Fritz (1921-1984)
  Zerbrochene Krug, Der   1971   Geissler, F.

Genée, Richard (with F. Zell [Camillo Walzel])
  Apajune der Wassermann+   1880 Millöcker, C.
  Bettelstudent, Der   1882 Millöcker, C.
  Boccaccio   1879 Suppé, F. von
  Cagliostro in Wien+   1875 Strauss, J., Jr.
  Donna Juanita+   1880 Suppé, F. von
  Fatinitza+   1876 Suppé, F. von
  Gasparone+   1884 Millöcker, C.
  Karneval in Rom, Der+   1873 Strauss, J., Jr.
    (also with J. Braun)
  Königen Mariette+   1883 Brüll, I.
  Lustige Krieg, Der+   1881 Strauss, J., Jr.
  Nacht in Venedig, Eine 1883 Strauss, J., Jr.
  Seekadett, Der+   1876 Genée, R.
  Vice-Admiral, Der+   1886 Millöcker, C.

Gerber, E.
  Nibelungen, Die+   1854 Dorn, H.

Gerhäuser, Emil
  Moloch+   1906 Schillings, M.
                           von

Gerlach, Harald
  Preis, Der+   1980 Treibmann, K. P.

Gerlach, Theodor
  Liebeswogen+   1903 Gerlach, T.

Gide, André (1869-1951)
  Verlorene Sohn, Der+   1929 Reutter, H.
    (transl. Rilke)

Giesecke, Karl Ludwig
  Idris und Zenide+   1795 Süssmayr, F. X.
  Oberon   1789 Wranitzky, P.

Ginthum, Paul
  Uhrmacher von Strassburg, 1941 Brehme, H.
    Der+

Girzik, Franz Xaver
  Christliche Judenbraut,   1789 Paneck, J.B.
    Die+

Gitzinger, Oscar
  Des Kaisers neue Kleider+ 1957 Hummel, B.

Gleich, Josef Alois (1772-1841)
  Bezauberte Leyer, Die+   1809 Tuczek, V.F.
  Fuersten der Longobarden, 1808 Kauer, F.
    Die+

Gleich, J. A. (cont.)
  Graf von Gleichen, Der+   1815   Volkert, F.
  Inkle und Yariko+   1807   Kauer, F.
  Mohr von Semegonda, Der+   1805   Kauer, F.
  Wunderlampe, Die+   1811   Müller, W.

Goehr, Alexander (1932-)
  Wiedertäufer, Der+   1985   Goehr, A.
    (with J. McGrath)

Goeldner, Friedrich
  Schneider Fips, Der+   1928   Lorentz, A.

Goethe, Johann Wolfgang von (1749-1832)
  Claudine von Villa Bella   1789   Reichardt, J. F.
  Claudine von Villa Bella   1815   Schubert, F.
  Erwin und Elmire   1793   Reichardt, J. F.
  Erwin und Elmire   1916   Schoeck, O.
  Jery und Bätely   1801   Reichardt, J. F.
  Lieb' und Treue+   1800   Reichardt, J. F.
    (with J. Herder)

Goetz, Hermann (1840-1876)
  Francesca da Rimini   1877   Goetz, H.

Goldberg, Theo (1921-)
  Galatea Elettronica+   1969   Goldberg, T.

Goldschmidt, Adalbert von (1848-1906)
  Heliantus+   1884   Goldschmidt, A.
                                                von

Goldschmidt, Berthold (1903-)
  Gewaltige Hahnrei, Der+   1932   Goldschmidt, B.

Goldschmidt, Miriam
  Ophelia+   1969   Engelmann, H. U.

Goll, Ivan [Isaac Lang] (1891-1950)
  Royal Palace   1927   Weill, K.

Gollmick, Carl
  Zaïde   1779   Mozart, W. A.
    (with J. A. Schachtner)

Göting, Reinhard
  Opfer, Das+   1937   Zillig, W.

Gotter, Friedrich Wilhelm (1746-1797)
  Dorfgala, Der+   1772   Schweitzer, A.
  Geisterinsel, Die+   1798   Fleischmann, F.
    (with F. H. von Einsiedel)

Gotter, F. W. (cont.)
   Geisterinsel, Die   1798   Reichardt, J. F.
    (with F. H. von Einseidel)
   Geisterinsel, Die+   1798   Zumsteeg, J. R.
    (with F. H. von Einseidel)
   Holzhauer, Der+   1778   Benda, G.
   Jahrmarkt, Der   1775   Benda, G.
   Medea   1775   Benda, G.
   Romeo und Julie   1776   Benda, G.
   Tartarische Gesetz, Das+ 1779   André, J.
   Tartarische Gesetz, Das+ 1780   Zumsteeg, J.
   Walder+   1776   Benda, G.

Göttig, Willy Werner
   Yü-Nü+   1958   Riede, E.

Göz, Josef Franz von
   Lenardo und Blandine   1779   Winter, P.

Graener, Paul (1872-1944)
   Hanneles Himmelfahrt+   1927   Graener, P.
   Prinz von Homburg, Der+ 1935   Graener, P.

Grafe, Manfred (1935-)
   Bauer im Fegefeuer, Der+ 1958   Grafe, M.

Grammann, Karl (1842-1897)
   Melusina+   1875   Grammann, K.

Grandaur, Franz
   Junker Heinz+   1886   Perfall, K. von

Gräwe, Karl Dietrich
   Lou Salome+   1981   Sinopoli, G.

Gregor, Joseph (1888-1960)
   Daphne   1938   Strauss, R.
   Friedenstag   1938   Strauss, R.
    (with S. Zweig)
   Liebe der Danae, Die   1940   Strauss, R.

Griesbach, Karl-Rudi (1916-)
   Kolumbus+   1958   Griesbach, K. R.
   Marike Weiden+   1960   Griesbach, K. R.

Grillparzer, Franz (1791-1872)
   Melusina+   1833   Kreutzer, C.

Grossmann, G(ustav) F(riedrich) W(ilhelm) (1746-1796)
   Adelheit von Veltheim   1789   Neefe, C. G.
   Barbier von Sevilla, Der+ 1776   Benda, F. L.

Grothe, Wilhelm
   Sangeskönig Hiarne+   1863 Marschner, H.

Grun, James
   Arme Heinrich, Der   1895 Pfitzner, H.
   Rose von Liebesgarten,   1901 Pfitzner, H.
   Die+

Grünbaum, Fritz
   Don Quichote+   1910 Heuberger, R.
   (with H. Reichert)

Grünwald, Alfred
   Frau, die weiss was sie   1932 Straus, O.
   will, Eine+

Gumppenberg, Hanns von (1866-1928)
   Herzog Philipps   1909 Reuss, A.
   Brautfahrt+

Günther, Dorothee
   Orpheus+   1925 Orff, C. after
                                                  C. Monteverdi

Günther, Ernst
   Feuerprobe, Die+   1920 Dost, W.

Gurlitt, Manfred (1890-1972)
   Heilige, Die+   1920 Gurlitt, M.
   Soldaten+   1930 Gurlitt, M.

Guseck, B. von
   Faust und Yorick+   1977 Rihm, W.
   Konradin von   ca. 1810 Kreutzer, C.
   Schwaben+

Hackländer, Friedrich Wilhelm (1816-1877)
   Soldatenleben+   1848 Hackländer, F. W.

Hacks, Peter (1928-)
   Omphale   1976 Matthus, S.

Haffner, Karl
   Fledermaus, Die   1874 Strauss, J., Jr.
   (with R. Genée)

Hamel, Kurt Peter
   Tragödie der Menschheit,   1981 Hamel, P. M.
   Die+

Hanell, Robert (1925-)
   Dorian Gray+   1962 Hanell, R.

Hanisch, Carl
Bergkönig, Der+   1825   Lindpaintner, P.

Hardt, Ernst [Ernst Stöckhardt] (1876-1947)
Schirin und Getraude+   1920   Graener, P.

Hardt-Warden, Bruno
Eiserne Heiland, Der+   1917   Oberleithner, M.
  (with I. M. Welleminsky)   von
Entzückende Frau, Eine+   1940   Heuberger, R.
  (with R. Zindler)
Mann im Mond, Der+   1922   Brandt-Buys, J.
  (with I. M. Welleminsky
Rosen der Madonna, Die+   1964   Stolz, R.
  (with O. Tumtinz)
Schneider von Schönau,   1916   Brandts-Buys, J.
  Der+
  (with I. M. Welleminsky)

Harsdörffer, Georg Philipp (1607-1658)
Seelewig   1644   Staden, S. T.

Hartmann, Gerhard
Spiel von Liebe und   1982   Rosenfeld, G.
  Zufall, Das+

Hartmann, Karl Amadeus (1905-1963)
Des Simplicius   1949   Hartmann, K. A.
  Simplicissimus Jugend+
  (with W. Petzer)

Hartmann, Moritz (1821-1872)
Katakomben, Die+   1862   Hiller, F.

Hass, Frithjof
Faust und Yorick+   1977   Rihm, W.

Haug, C. F.
Elbondokani+   1803   Zumsteeg, J. R.

Haug, Hans (1900-1967)
Tartuffe+   1937   Haug, H.

Hauptmann, Elisabeth
Happy End   1929   Weill, K.
  (with B. Brecht)

Hausegger, Siegmund von (1872-1948)
Zinnober+   1898   Hausegger, S. von

Heermann, Gottlob Ephraim
Abend im Walde, Der+   1773   Wolf, E. W.

Heermann, G. E. (cont.)
    Dorfdeputierten, Die+   1772 Wolf, E. W.
    Dorfdeputierten, Die+   1783 Schubaur, J. L.
    Dorfdeputierten, Die   1786 Dieter, C. F.
    Rosenfest, Das+   1770 Wolf, E. W.
    Treuen Köhler, Die+   1786 Schubaur, J. L.
    Treuen Köhler, Die+   1773 Wolf, E. W.

Heger, Robert (1886-1978)
    Bettler Namenlos, Der+   1932 Heger, R.
    Fest auf Haderslev, Ein+   1919 Heger, R.
    Lady Hamilton+   1951 Heger, R.

Heggars
    Habemeajaja+   1929 Blacher, B.

Heigel, Cäsar Max
    Vampyr, Der+   1828 Lindpaintner, P.

Heimbacher, P.
    Maskerade im Serail, Die+ 1792 Volanek, A.

Heindl, Viktor
    Tante Simona   1913 Dohnányi, E. von

Heinrich, Hermann
    Viel Lärm um nichts+   1956 Heinrich, H.

Heiter, Theodor
    Ali Hitsch-Hatsch+   1844 Sechter, S.

Hell, Theodor [Karl Gottlieb Theodor Winkler]
    (1775-1856)
    Drei Pintos, Die   1821 Weber, C. M. von

Hellem, Charles
    Judith+ (with P. d'Estoc) 1848 Adam, F.

Helmund, Else
    Prinzessin und der   1938 Reutter, H.
      Schweinehirt, Die+

Henisch, Carl Friedrich
    Bassa von Tunis, Der+   1774 Holly, F. A.
    Lustige Schuster, Der+ 1770 Holly, F. A.

Henke, Eduard
    Prüfung, Die   1806 Spohr, L.

Henneberg, Claus H.
    Fettlöschen+   1976 Wahren, K. H.
    (with K. H. Wahren)

Henneberg, C. H. (cont.)
    Lear   1978 Reimann, A.
    Melusine+   1971 Reimann, A.

Hennies, Herbert
    Nachtigall, Die+   1947 Schanazara, H.

Henrion, Poly
    Schöne Galatea, Die   1865 Suppé, F. von

Henry, Marc [Achille d'Ailly-Vaucheret]
    Toten Augen, Die   1916 Albert, E. d'
    (with H. H. Ewers)

Hensler, Karl Friedrich (1759-1825)
    Bergfest, Das+   1803 Müller, W.
    Donauweibchen, Das   1798 Kauer, F.
    Friedliche Dörfchen, Das+   1803 Müller, W.
    Sonnenfest der Braminen,   1790 Müller, W.
      Das
    Sturm, Der+   1799 Müller, W.
    Teufelsmühle am   1799 Müller, W.
      Wienerberg, Die+

Henze, Hans Werner (1926-)
    Landarzt, Ein   1953 Henze, H. W.
    Langwienzige Weg, Der   1971 Henze, H. W.

Herbst, Walter
    Lukrezia Borgia+   1946 Herbst, W.

Herklots, Carl Alexander
    Alcidor+   1825 Spontini, G.
    Frohsinn und Schwärmerei+   1801 Himmel, F. H.
    Mudarra+   1800 Weber, B. A.
    Nurmahal   1822 Spontini, G.

Hermann, Heinrich
    Amphitryon+   1958 Hermann, H.

Hermann, Paul (1904-)
    Arme Gespenst, Das+   1961 Hermann, P.

Herrig, Hans
    Harald der Wiking+   1881 Hallen, A.
    Genesius+   1892 Weingartner, F.

Herzer, Ludwig [Ludwig Herzl] (with F. Löhner)
    Friederike+   1928 Lehár, F.
    Land des Lächelns, Das   1929 Lehár, F.
    Schön ist die Welt+   1930 Lehár, F.

Hess, Joachim
  Belagerungszustand, Der+   1970   Keleman, M.
  (with M. Keleman)

Hess, Ludwig (1877-1944)
  Was ihr wollt+   1941   Hess, L.

Hiemer, Franz Karl
  Silvana   1810   Weber, C. M. von
  Abu Hassan   1811   Weber, C. M. von
  Apollo's Wettgesang+   1808   Sutor, W.

Hildesheimer, Wolfgang (1916-)
  Ende einer Welt, Das   1965   Henze, H.W.

Hindemith, Paul (1895-1963)
  Harmonie der Welt, Die   1957   Hindemith, P.
  Lange Weihnachtsmahl, Das   1961   Hindemith, P.
  Mathis der Maler   1938   Hindemith, P.

Hinsch, Heinrich
  Beglückte Florindo, Der+   1708   Handel, G. F.
  Claudius   1703   Keiser, R.
  Dido   1707   Graupner, C.
  Dido, Königin von   1707   Graupner, C.
    Cathargo+
  Lucius Verus+   1728   Keiser, R.
  Semiramis+   1683   Franck, J. W.
  Verwandelte Daphne, Die+   1708   Handel, G. F.

Hinzelmann, H. H. [Karl Michael von Levetzow]
  Sandro der Narr+   1916   Bienstock, H.
    (with L. Hirschfeld)

Hirschfeld, Leo. See Leo Feld.

Hobein, E.
  Herzog Johann Albrecht   1857   Flotow, F. von
    von Mechlenberg+

Hoe, Johann Joachim
  Grossmüthige Tomyris, Die   1717   Keiser, R.
  Henrico IV+   1711   Mattheson, J.
  Julia+   1717   Keiser, R.

Hoernes, Moritz
  Manuel Venegas   1903   Wolf, H.

Hoffmann, E(rnst) T(heodor) A(madeus) (1776-1822)
  Liebe und Eifersucht+   1807   Hoffmann,
                                             E. T. A.

Hoffmann, E. T. A. (cont.)
   Maske, Die+   1799   Hoffmann,
                                          E. T. A.
   Olimpia+   1821   Spontini, G.
   Scherz, List und   ca. 1801   Hoffmann,
     Rache+   E. T. A.
   Undine   1816   Hoffmann,
                                            E. T. A.

Hoffmann, Hugo
   Ilsebill+   1903   Klose, F.

Hoffmann, Leopold Alois
   Kinder der Natur, Die+   1778   Aspelmayr, F.

Hoffmann, Ludwig
   Merlin+   1887   Rüfer, P.

Hofmann, Friedrich
   Rattenfänger von Hamelin, 1879   Nessler, V. E.
     Der+
   Wilde Jagd, Der+   1881   Nessler, V. E.

Hofmann, Georg Ernst von
   Baals Sturz+   1820   Weigl, J.
   Ochsenmenuette, Die+   1823   Haydn, F.J.
   Zauberharfe, Die   1820   Schubert, F.
   Zwillingsbrüder, Die   1820   Schubert, F.

Hofmann, Michel
   Carmina burana   1937   Orff, C.
    (with W. Schadewaldt)

Hofmannsthal, Hugo von (1874-1929)
   Ägyptische Helena, Die 1928   Strauss, R.
   Alkestis+   1924   Wellesz, E.
   Arabella   1933   Strauss, R.
   Ariadne auf Naxos   1912   Strauss, R.
   Elektra   1909   Strauss, R.
   Frau ohne Schatten, Die 1919   Strauss, R.
   Rosenkavalier, Der   1911   Strauss, R.

Hohenstatter, Ernst
   Grüne Heinrich, Der+   1922   Ebner, G.

Holbein, Franz Ignaz von
   Aloise+   1828   Maurer, L.
   Aurora   1812   Hoffmann,
                                        E. T. A.
   Ida, die Büssende+   1807   Gyrowetz, A.

Holberg, Ludwig
   Pfiffige Magd, Die+   1939 Weismann, J.

Hölderlin, Friedrich (1770-1843)
   Ödipus der Tyrann   1959 Orff, C.

Holm, Gustav (with E. Decsey)
   Dame im Traum+   1935 Salmhofer, F.

Holstein, Friedrich von (1837-1909)
   Erbe von Morley, Der+   1872 Holstein, F. von
   Haideschacht, Der+   1868 Holstein, F. von
   Hochländer, Die+   1876 Holstein, F. von

Holtei, Karl von (1798-1880)
   Adlers Horst, Der+   1832 Glaeser, F.

Honolka, Kurt
   Zweimal Alexander   1937 Martinů, B.

Hopffer, Emil
   Hermione+   1872 Bruch, M.

Hordt, S. tor
   Abdul und Erinieh+   1828 Curschmann, K. F.

Hornbostel (with Alberti)
   Heinrich IV und d'Aubigne+ 1820 Marschner, H.

Hospelt, Arthur
   Mira+   1925 Overhoff, K.

Hotter
   Stoertebecker und Joedge 1701 Keiser, R.
   Michaels+

Hotzel, C.
   Pulcinella+   1961 Krol, B.

Huber, Franz Xaver
   Bauernliebe+   1802 Kauer, F.
   Edle Rache, Die+   1795 Süssmayr, F. X.
   Robert/Die Prüfung+   1813 Gyrowetz, A.
   Samori+   1804 Vogler, G. J.
   Soliman der Zweyte   1799 Süssmayr, F. X.
   Unterbrochene Opferfest, 1796 Winter, P.
   Das+

Huber, Leopold
   Eiserne Mann, Der+   1801 Müller, W.

Hübner, Johannes
  Agamemnons Tod+   1949   Goldberg, T.
  Judith+   1950   Goldberg, T.
  Phaedra+   1950   Goldberg, T.

Hughes, Langston (1902-1967)
  Mauer, Die+   1955   Engelmann, H. U.

Humperdinck, Hedwig
  Heirat wider Willen, Die+   1905   Humperdinck, E.

Ihlee, Johann Jakob
  Fest der Winzer, Das   1793   Kunzen, F. L. A.
  Zemire und Azor   1819   Spohr, L.

Iliraz, Israel
  Versuchung, Die+   1976   Tal, J.

Ingrisch, Lotte
  Jesu Hochzeit   1980   Einem, G. von

Jacobi, Johann Greg
  Elysium+   1770   Schweitzer, A.

Jacobson, Leopold
  Tapfere Soldat, Der   1908   Straus, O.
  (with R. Bernauer)

Jacoby, Wilhelm
  Kaisertochter, Die+   1885   Haan, W. de

Jansen, Ferdinand
  Menandra+ (with H. Kaun)   1925   Kaun, H.

Jaroschek, Karl
  Zauberspiegel, Der+   1930   Gál, H.

Jenbach, Bela
  Paganini   1925   Lehár, F.
  (with P. Knepler)
  Zarewitsch, Der   1927   Lehár, F.
  (with H. Reichert)

Jenny, Albert (1912-)
  Rubin, Der+   1938   Jenny, A.
  Zerrissene, Der+   1942   Jenny, A.

Jester, Friedrich Ernst
  Triumph der Liebe, Der+   1796   Stegmann, C. D.

Jirasek, Alfred   and W. Pribil
   Krach im Offen, Der+   1961   Kaufmann, A.

John, Eva
   Frauen von Troia, Die+   1962   Röttger, H.

Jona, E.
   Atomtod+   1965   Manzoni, G.

Jünger, Johann Friedrich
   Gutsherr, Der+   1791   Dittersdorf, K.

Kabitz, Ulrich
   Ali Baba und die vierzig   1952   Dienel, J.
   Räuber+

Kafka, Hans
   Leonce und Lena+   1952   Zeisl, E.
   (with H. F. Königsgarten)

Kagel, Maurizio (1931-)
   Aus Deutschland+   1981   Kagel, M.
   Erschöpfung der Welt, Die+ 1980   Kagel, M.

Kaibel, Franz
   Mönch von Sendomir, Der+   1907   Lorentz, A.

Kaiser, Alfred (1872-1917)
   Stella Maris+   1910   Kaiser, A.

Kaiser, Georg
   Juana+   1925   Ettinger, M.
   Protagonist, Der   1926   Weill, K.
   Silbersee   1933   Weill, K.
   Spieldose, Die+   1957   Hanell, R.
   Zar lässt sich   1928   Weill, K.
   photographieren, Der

Kalbeck, Max
   Jabuka+   1894   Strauss, J., Jr.
   (with G. Davis)

Kallman, Chester (with W. H. Auden)
   Bassariden, Die   1966   Henze, H. W.

Kamer, Paul
   Ewige Arzt, Der+   1956   Bresgen, C.

Kaminski, Heinrich (1886-1946)
   Spiel von König Aphelius,   1950   Kaminski, H.
   Das+

Kamps, Johann M.
  Badewanne, Die   1973 Niehaus, M.

Karlev, M. See K. M. von Levetzow.

Kasack, Hermann
  Stadt hinter dem Strom, 1955 Vogt, H.
    Die+

Kastropp, Gustav
  Gernot+   1897 Albert, E. d'
  Improvisator, Der+   1902 Albert, E. d'

Kaufmann, Harald
  König Nicolo+   1972 Weishappel, R.
  Stella+   1951 Bloch, W.

Kaufmann, Otto (1927-)
  Des Kaisers neueste Kleider+ 1957 Kaufmann, O.

Kaun, Hugo (1863-1932)
  Menandra+ (with F. Jansen) 1925 Kaun, H.
  Sappho+   1917 Kaun, H.

Kelemen, Milko (1924-)
  Belagerungszustand, Der+ 1970 Keleman, M.

Kelterborn, Rudolf (1932-)
  Errettung Thebens, Die+ 1963 Kelterborn, R.

Kempe, Johann
  Taras Bulba+   1935 Richter, E.

Kessler, Richard
  Blonde Liselott, Die+   1927 Künneke, E.

Keussler, Gerhard von (1874-1949)
  Gefängnisse+   1914 Keussler, G. von

Kien, Peter (d. 1944)
  Kaiser von Atlantis, Der 1944 Ullmann, V.

Kienzl, Wilhelm (1857-1941)
  Don Quixote+   1898 Kienzl, W.
  Evangelimann, Der+   1895 Kienzl, W.
  Testament, Das+   1916 Kienzl, W.

Kind, Friedrich (1768-1843)
  Blanda+   1847 Kalliwoda, J. W.
  Freischütz, Der+   1821 Weber, C. M. von
  Holzdieb, Der+   1825 Marschner, H.

Kirchner, Anton
Mischelli und sein Sohn+   1806   Clasing, J. H.

Kirchner, Robert (1891-1946)
Abenteuer des Don Quichotte, 1941   Kirchner, R.
  Ein+

Kirchner, Volker David (1942-)
Fünf Minuten des Isaak   1980   Kirchner, V. D.
  Babel, Die+ (with H. Weirich)

Klabund [Alfred Henschke]
Kreiderkeis, Der+   1933   Zemlinsky, A. von

Klebe, A.
Haus ist zu verkaufen, Dies+ 1806   Hummel, J. N.

Klebe, Giselher (1925-)
  Alkmene   1961   Klebe, G.
  Ermordung Cäsars, Die+   1959   Klebe, G.
  Figaro lässt sich scheiden 1963   Klebe, G.
  Jacobowsky und der Oberst 1965   Klebe, G.
  Jüngste Tag, Der+   1980   Klebe, G.
  Mädchen aus Domrémy, Das   1976   Klebe, G.
  Märchen von der schönen   1969   Klebe, G.
    Lilie, Das+
  Räuber, Die   1957   Klebe, G.
  Tödlichen Wünsche, Die   1959   Klebe, G.
  Wahrer Held, Ein   1975   Klebe, G.

Kleemann, Ingeborg
  Bildnis des Dorian Gray,   1965   Kleemann, R.
    Das+

Klein, Anton
  Günther von Schwarzburg   1777   Holzbauer, I.

Klenau, Paul von (1883-1946)
  Elisabeth von England+   1939   Klenau, P. von
  Kjarten und Gudrun   1918   Klenau, P. von
  Rembrandt van Rijn+   1937   Klenau, P. von

Klett, Gertrud
  Gelöbnis, Das+   1910   Oosterzee, C. van
    (with L. Wittich)

Klingemann, August
  Schloss am Ätna, Das+   1836   Marschner, H.

Klingemann, Karl
  Heimkehr aus der Fremde, Die 1829 Mendelssohn, F.
  Hochzeit des Camacho, Die 1827   Mendelssohn, F.

Klopstock, Friedrich Gottlob (1724-1803)
    Abels Tod+   1778 Haydn, M.

Kluener, Johannes
    Odysseus und die Sirenen+   1950 Goldberg, T.

Kneisel, Rudolf
    Blindekuh+   1878 Strauss, J., Jr.

Knepler, Paul
    Belsazar+   1929 Peró, H.
    Drei Walzer+   1935 Strauss, O.
    (with A. Robinson)
    Giuditta (with F. Löhner)   1934 Lehár, F.
    Paganini (with B. Jenbach) 1925 Lehár, F.

Knorr von Rosenroth, J. C. (or Anton Ulrich
    of Brunswick)
    Salomon+   1701 Schürmann, G. C.

Knudsen, Paul
    Gondoliere des Dogen, Der+ 1931 Reznicek,
                                   E. N. von
    Spiel oder Ernst?+   1930 Reznicek,
                                     E. N. von

Koch, Karl
    Fürstin Tarakanowa   1941 Blacher, B.
    (with B. Blacher)

Koch, Paul
    Verzauberte ich, Das+   1949 Gerster, O.

Kokoschka, Oskar (1886-1980)
    Mörder, Hoffnung der Frauen 1921 Hindemith, P.
    Orpheus und Eurydike   1926 Krenek, E.

Köler, Johann Marti
    Esther+   1680 Strungk, N. A.

König, Eberhard
    Rübezahl und der   1904 Sommer, H.
      Sackpfeifer von Neisse+

König, Heinrich
    Bianca und Giuseppe+   1848 Kittl, J. F.
    (with R. Wagner)

König, Johann Ulrich (1688-1744)
    Diana+   1712 Keiser, R.
    Fredegunda+   1715 Keiser, R.
    Getreue Alceste, Die+   1719 Schürmann, G. C.

König, J. U. (cont.)
   Heinrich der Vogler+   1718   Schürmann, G. C.
   Inganno fedele, L'   1714   Keiser, R.
   Sancio und Sinilde+   1727   Graun, K. H.

Königsgarten, Hugo von
   Leonce und Lena+   1952   Zeisl, E.
   (with H. Kafka)
   Lord Spleen+   1930   Lothar, M.
   Tyll+   1928   Lothar, M.

Königsmarck, Aurora von
   Drey Töchter Cecrops, Die+   1679   Franck, J. W.

Kont, Paul (1920-)
   Inzwischen+   1967   Kont, P.
   Lysistrate   1961   Kont, P.
   Pluto+   1977   Kont, P.

Konta, Robert (1880-1953)
   Kalte Herz, Das+   1908   Konta, R.

Körner, Karin (with Thomas Körner)
   R. Hot+   1977   Goldmann, F.

Körner, Theodor (1791-1813)
   Vierjährige Posten, Der   1815   Schubert, F.

Körner, Thomas
   Fanferlieschen   1983   Schwertsik, K.
   Schönefüsschen+ (with K. Körner)
   R. Hot+   1977   Goldmann, F.

Korty, Sonia
   Weg nach Freudenstadt, Der+ 1948   Reutter, H.

Kotzebue, August von (1761-1819)
   Alpenhütte, Die+   1815   Kreutzer, C.
   Des Teufels Lustschloss+   1802   Dieter, C. F.
   Des Teufels Lustschloss   1814   Schubert, F.
   Dorf im Gebirge, Das+   1798   Weigl, J.
   Eremit auf Formentara, Der+ 1788   Ritter, P.
   Eremit auf Formentera, Der+ 1791   Dieter, C. F.
   Fanchon, das Leiermädchen+ 1804   Himmel, F. H.
   Feodora+   1812   Kreutzer, C.
   Kyffhäuserberg, Der+   1822   Marschner, H.
   Spiegelritter, Der   1811   Schubert, F.
   Spiegelritter, Der+   1791   Walter, I.

Krauss, Clemens (1893-1954)
   Capriccio   1942   Strauss, R.

Kremer, Hans M.
   Zerrissene, Der+   1941   Kreuder, P.

Krenek, Ernst (1900-)
   Ausgerechnet und verspielt+ 1962   Krenek, E.
   Das kommt davon+   1970   Krenek, E.
   Diktator, Der   1928   Krenek, E.
   Flaschenpost vom   1974   Krenek, E.
     Paradies, Die+
   Geheime Königreich, Das+   1928   Krenek, E.
   Goldene Bock, Der   1964   Krenek, E.
   Jonny spielt auf   1927   Krenek, E.
   Karl der Fünfte   1938   Krenek, E.
   Leben des Orest, Das   1930   Krenek, E.
   Pallas Athene weint   1955   Krenek, E.
   Schwergericht   1928   Krenek, E.
   Sprung über den   1924   Krenek, E.
     Schatten, Der+
   Vertrauenssache+   1962   Krenek, E.
   Zauberspiegel, Der+   1967   Krenek, E.

Krenn, Leopold (with C. Lindau)
   Drei Wünsche, Die+   1901   Ziehrer, C. M.
   Fremdenführer, Der+   1902   Ziehrer, C. M.
   Landstreicher, Die   1899   Ziehrer, C. M.

Kretchmer, Edmund
   Heinrich der Löwe+   1877   Kretschmer, E.

Krug, Hans-Hermann
   Bremer Stadtmusikanten, Die+ 1972   Auenmüller, H.

Kunad, Rainer
   Vincent+   1979   Kunad, R.

Kunhardt, David
   Aglaja+   1893   Blech, L.
   Cherubina+   1894   Blech, L.

Kunz, Ernst (1891-)
   Fächer, Der+   1929   Kunz, E.

Kunz, Harald
   Geisterliebe   1971   Yun, I.
   Sim Tjong   1972   Yun, I.
   Witwe des Schmetterlings,   1969   Yun, I.
     Die

Kupelwieser, Josef
   Fierrabras   1823   Schubert, F.

Kupfer, Harry
Schwarze Maske, Die+   1987   Penderecki, K.

Kurz, Johann Joseph
Neue krumme Teufel, Der+   1759   Haydn, F. J.

Kurz, Johann Joseph?
Krumme Teufel, Der+   1753   Haydn, F. J.

Kutter, Markus
Fall van Damm, Der+   1968   Engelmann, H. U.

Lambrecht, Matthias Georg
Mitternachtsstunde+   1788   Danzi, F.

Landgraf, Ludwig
Elegie für junge   1961   Henze, H. W.
  Liebende (with W. Schachtel)

Larska, J. (with G. Drechsel)
Don Juans Ende+   1930   Drechsel, G.

Lauckner, Rolf
Satuala+   1927   Reznicek,
                                                  E. N. von

Lavery, E.
Tarquin+   1941   Krenek, E.

Lax, Louis
Bibiana+   1829   Pixis, J. P.

Leen, Dora
Flammen+ (with F. Schreker)   1902   Schreker, F.

Lehner, Franz X. (1904-)
Liebeskette, Die+   1961   Lehner, F. X.
Schlaue Susanna, Die+   1952   Lehner, F. X.
  (with H. Schlegel)

Leitner, Gottfried von
Leonore+   1835   Hüttenbrenner, A.

Léon, Victor
Barfüssele+   1905   Heuberger, R.
Geschiedene Frau, Die+   1908   Fall, L.
Gringoire+   1892   Brüll, I.
Lustige Witwe, Die   1905   Lehár, F.
  (with L. Stein)
Opernball, Der   1898   Heuberger, R.
  (with Waldeberg)

Léon, V. (cont.)
Polnische Jude, Der+ 1901 Weis, K.
  (with R. Batka)
Schach dem König+ 1893 Brüll, I.
Simplizius, Der+ 1887 Strauss, J., Jr.
Strike der Schmiede, Der+ 1897 Beer, M. J.
Wiener Blut (with L. Stein) 1899 Strauss, J., Jr.

Leonhardt-Lysen, Caroline
Leila+ 1848 Piersen, H. H.

Lernet-Holenia, Alexander
Saul 1928 Reutter, H.

Lersner, Friedrich Maximilian
Ulysses+ 1722 Keiser, R.

Levetzow, Karl Michael von
  (sometimes used pseud. M. Karlev)
Enoch Arden+ 1936 Gerster, O.
Heilige Ente, Die+ 1923 Gál, H.
  (with L. Feld)
Lied der Nacht, Das+ 1926 Gál, H.
Mister Wü+ 1932 Albert, E. d'
Schwarze Orchidee, Die+ 1928 Albert, E. d'

Levi, J.
Eulenspiegel+ 1889 Kistler, C.
  (with L. Sauer)

Levitschnigg, H. von
Tannenhäuser, Der+ 1852 Suppé, F. von

Lewald, August
Agnes Bernauer+ 1858 Krebs, K. A.
Herzog Albrecht+ 1833 Krebs, K. A.

Leyda, Jay
Bartelby+ 1964 Aschaffenburg, W.

Lichtenberg, Christian Friedrich
Lampedo 1779 Vogler, G. J.

Lieck, Walter
Schwarzer Peter+ 1936 Schultze, N.

Lillie, Roland
König Ubü 1984 Hummel, Fr.

Lindau, Carl
Drei Wünsche, Die+ 1901 Ziehrer, C. M.
Fremdenführer, Der+ 1902 Ziehrer, C. M.

Lindau, C. (cont.)
  Landstreicher, Die   1899 Ziehrer, C. M.
  (with L. Krenn)

Lindau, M. E.
  Contarini+   1883 Pierson, H. H.

Lindemann
  Orpheus+   1785 Benda, F.

Lindemann, Friedrich
  Kluge Wirtin, Die+   1943 Hinrichs, H.

Lindemayr, M.
  Reisende Ceres, Die   1777? Haydn, F.J.

Lingen, Theo
  Mysteriöse Herr X, Der+   1966 Uhl, A.

Lion, Ferdinand
  Abenteuer des Casanova, Ein+ 1924 Andreae, V.
  Cardillac   1926 Hindemith, P.
  Fächer, Der+   1930 Toch, E.
  Golem, Der+   1926 Albert, E. d'
  Revolutionshochzeit+   1919 Albert, E. d'
  Zuleima+   1913 Bienstock, H.

Lipiner, Siegfried
  Merlin+   1886 Goldmark, K.

Lippert, Friedrich Karl
  Gülnare   1800 Süssmayr, F. X.

Lobe, Johann Christian (1797-1881)
  Fürstin von Granada, Die+   1833 Weimar
  (with P. C. C. Sonderhausen)

Loess, H. W.
  Alpenhirten, Die+   1811 Wollank, F.

Logau, Gotthold
  König Alfred+ (with J. Raff) 1851 Raff, J.

Lohmann, Peter
  Irene+   1881 Huber, J.

Löhner, Fritz (Beda-Löhner)
  Friederika+ (with L. Herzer) 1928 Lehár, F.
  Giuditta (with P. Knepler)   1934 Lehár, F.
  Schön ist die Welt+   1930 Lehár, F.
  (with L. Herzer)

Löhner, Johann (1645-1705)
Theseus+   1688   Löhner, J.

Lorenz, Karl Adolf (1837-1923)
Komödie der Irrungen, Die+   1939   Stettin

Lortzing, Albert (1801-1851)
Ali Pascha von Janina+   1816   Lortzing, A.
Beiden Schützen, Die   1837   Lortzing, A.
Cagliostro+   1850   Lortzing, A.
Caramo+   1839   Lortzing, A.
Casanova in Murano+   1841   Lortzing, A.
Hans Sachs (with P. Reger   1840   Lortzing, A.
   and P. J. Düringer)
Opernprobe, Die   1851   Lortzing, A.
Regina   1848   Lortzing, A.
Rolands Knappen+   1849   Lortzing, A.
   (with G. Meisinger and C. Haffner)
Undine   1845   Lortzing, A.
Waffenschmied, Der   1846   Lortzing, A.
Wildschütz, Der   1842   Lortzing, A.
Zar und Zimmermann   1837   Lortzing, A.
Zum Grossadmiral+   1847   Lortzing, A.

Lothar, Mark (1902-)
Widerspenstige Heilige, Der+ 1968   Lothar, M.

Lothar, Rudolf [Rudolf Spitzer]
Des Kaisers Dichter+   1920   Franckenstein,
                                             C. von
Freikorporal, Der+   1931   Vollerthun, G.
Friedemann Bach+   1931   Graener, P.
Izeyel+   1909   Albert, E. d'
Liebesketten+   1912   Albert, E. d'
Tiefland   1903   Albert, E. d'
Tote Gast, Der   1923   Berr, J. R.
Tragaldabas+   1907   Albert, E. d'
Verschenkte Frau, Die+   1912   Albert, E. d'

Löwenberg, H.
Rübezahl+   1917   Vogler, C.

Lyser, Johann Peter Theodor
Salvator Rosa+   1832   Rastrelli, J.

Magenburg, Ruth von
Gluckerich, Der+   1965   Urbanner, E.

Mai, Julius (1862-1938)
Braut von Messina, Die+   1904   Mai, J.

Marsano, Wilhelm
  Rübezahl+   1824 Würfel, W.

Marschner, Heinrich (1795-1861)
  Austin+   1852 Marschner, H.

Marti, Kurt
  Jot+ (with D. Rischl)   1973 Huber, K.

Martin, Rainer
  Schwarz auf weiss+   1968 Hüber, K.

Martinů, Bohuslav
  Griechische Passion, Die   1961 Martinů, B.

Matthus, Siegfried
  Letzte Schuss, Der+   1967 Matthus, S.

Maurice, Pierre (1868-1936)
  Andromeda+   1924 Maurice, P.

Mauritius, J. J. van
  Circe+ (with J. Praetorius)   1734 Keiser, R.

Mauthe, Jörg
  Indische Legende+   1952 Kont, P.
  Traumleben+   1963 Kont, P.

May, M.
  Giuditta+   1912 Dessau, P.

Mayer, Johann Cölestin
  Kaiser Hadrian+   1897 Weigl, J.

Mayreder-Obermeyer, Rosa
  Corregidor, Der   1896 Wolf, H.

Mayrhofer, Johann
  Adrast+   1819 Schubert, F.
  Freunde von Salamanca, Die   1815 Schubert, F.

Mazzola, Caterino
  Rübezahl+   1813 Danzi, F.

McGrath, John (with A. Goehr)
  Wiedertäufer, Der+   1985 Goehr, A.

Meck, Friedrich
  Kätchen von Heilbronn, Das+   1846 Lux, F.

Meier, Herbert
  Kaiser Jovian+   1967 Kelterborn, R.

Meyer, H. (cont.)
  Ophelia+   1984 Kelterborn, R.

Meisinger, Georg
  Rolands Knappen+   1849 Lortzing, A.
  (with A. Lortzing and C. Haffner)

Meisl, Karl
  Schwarze Frau, Die+   1826 Müller, A.E.
  Travistirte Zauberflöte,   1818 Müller, W.
    Die+

Meissner, August Gottlob
  Alchymist, Der   1778 Schuster, J.
  Alchymist, Der+   1778 Andre, J.
  Arsene+   1779 Seydelmann, F.
  Grab des Mufti, Das   1779 Hiller, J. A.

Meister
  Angenehme Betrug, Der+   1707 Keiser, R.
    (with M. Cuno)   and C. Graupner

Menantes
  Nebucadnezar   1704 Keiser, R.

Mendelssohn, Albrecht
  Simplicius, Der+   1912 Huber, H.

Mennicken, Peter
  Kalif Storch+   1885 Eidens, J.

Metzband, Harald
  Schneekönigen, Die+   1957 Thies, K.

Meyer, Krzystof (1943-)
  Kyberiade+   1970 Meyer, K.

Meyer, Wilhelm Christian Dieter
  Weinlese, Die+   1785 Schenk, J.

Meyer von Schauensee, Franz (1720-1789)
  Hans Hüttenstock+   1769 Meyer von
                                        Schauensee, F.
Meyerfeld, Max
  Florentinische Tragödie,   1917 Zemlinsky, A. von
    Eine

Meyerowitz, Jan (1913-)
  Doppelgängerin, Die+   1967 Meyerowitz, J.

Michaelis, J. B.
  Amors Guckkasten+   1772 Neefe, C. G.

Michel, Robert
   Geliebte Stimme, Die+   1931 Weinberger, J.

Mickel, Karl
   Einstein   1974 Dessau, P.

Middleton, Christopher
   Athener Komödie+   1964 Vogt, H.
   (with E. Fried)

Mikorey, Franz
   König von Samarkand, Der+ 1910 Mikorey, F.

Miltitz, Karl Borromäus von
   Bergmönch, Der+   1830 Wolfram, J. M.

Misch, Robert
   Gaudeamus+   1919 Humperdinck, E.
   Marketendieren, Die+   1914 Humperdinck, E.

Möckel, Karl
   Murieta   1984 Ostendorf, J. P.
   William Ratcliff   1982 Ostendorf, J. P.
   (with J. P. Ostendorf)

Mohaupt, Richard (1904-1957)
   Grüne Kakadu, Der+   1958 Mohaupt, R.
   Zwillingskomödie   1954 Mohaupt, R.

Mojsisovics, Roderich (1877-1953)
   Zauberer, Der+   1926 Mojsisovics, R.

Molen, Reinhard
   Robin Hood+   1879 Dietrich, A.

Mons, Hans Mahner
   Herz, Das+   1931 Pfitzner, H.

Montague, Elizabeth
   Schule der Frauen, Die   1957 Liebermann, R.
   (with H. Strobel)

Montowt, Reinhold (1842-1925)
   Letzte Tage von Pompeji, 1900 Montowt, R.
   Die+

Morgenstern, Christian (1871-1914)
   Egon und Emilie+   1928 Toch, E.

Möricke, Eduard (1804-1875)
   Regenbrüder, Die+   1839 Lachner, I.
   (with H. Kurz)

Morris, Maximilian
    Robins Ende+   1909   Künneke, E.

Mosenthal, S(alomon) H(ermann) (1821-1877)
    Abenteuer Carl des   1850   Hoven, J.
      Zweiten, Ein+
    Erste Falte, Die+   1867   Leschetizky, T.
    Folkunger, Die+   1874   Kretschmer, E.
    Goldene Kreuz, Das+   1875   Brüll, I.
    Judith+   1870   Doppler, A. F.
    Kinder der Heide, Die+   1861   Rubinstein, A.
    Königin von Saba, Die   1875   Goldmark, K.
    Landfriede, Der+   1877   Brüll, I.
    Lustigen Weiber von   1849   Nicolai, O.
      Windsor, Die
    Maccabäer, Die+   1875   Rubinstein, A.
    Reise, Die+ (with L. Rusen) 1969   Werle, L. J.

Mraczek, Joseph Gustav (1878-1944)
    Traum, Der+   1909   Mraczek, J. G.

Mühler, C.
    Psyche+   1790   Winter, P.

Müller, Dominique
    Don Juan in der Fremde+ 1930   Haug, H.

Müller, Gerhard
    Bankette, Die+   1988   Katzer, G.

Müller, Hans
    Im Weissen Rössl   1930   Benatzky, R.
      (with E. Charell)
    Violanta   1916   Korngold, E.
    Wunder der Heliane, Das+ 1927   Korngold, E.

Müller, Heiner (1927-)
    Hamletmaschine+   1987   Rihm, W.
    Lanzelot   1969   Dessau, P.
      (with G. Tscholakowa)

Müller, J. H. F.
    Insel der Liebe, Die+   ca. 1772   Umlauf, I.

Müller, Johann Samuel
    Eroberte Jerusalem, Die+ 1722   Schürmann, G. C.
    Miriways   1728   Telemann, G. P.

Müller, Max
    Dornröschen+   1918   Höfer, F.

Müller, Wilhelm
Kenilworth+   1895   Klein, B. O.

Müller-Schlösser, Hans
Schneider Wibbel   1938   Lothar, M.

Musäus, C. A.
Gärtnermädchen, Das+   1769   Wolf, E.W.

Naue, Kurt
Wirtin von Pinsk, Die+   1938   Mohaupt, R.

Neher, Caspar (1897-1962)
Bürgschaft, Die   1932   Weill, K.
Günstling, Der   1935   Wagner-Régeny, R.
Persische Episode+   1963   Wagner-Régeny, R.

Neidhardt, August
Strohwitwe, Die+   ca. 1920   Blech, L.

Netzband, Harald
Schneekönigin, Die+   1957   Thies, K.

Neuhaus, P.
Spielmann, Der+   1949   Striegler, K.

Neumann, Johann P.
Sakuntala+   1820   Schubert, F.

Niehaus, Manfred (1933-)
Bartelby+   1967   Niehaus, M.
Tartarin von Tarascon   1977   Niehaus, M.

Nodermann, Preben
König Magnus+   1898   Nodermann, P.

Nossig, Alfred
Manru+   1901   Paderewski, I.

Nötzel, Hermann
Meister Guido+   1918   Nötzel, H.

Oboussier, Robert (1900-1957)
Amphityron+   1951   Oboussier, R.

Opitz, Martin
Dafne   1627   Schütz, H.

Orff, Carl (1895-1982)
Antigonae   1949   Orff, C.

Orff, C. (cont.)
Astutuli+   1953 Orff, C.
Bernauerin, Die   1947 Orff, C.
Kluge, Die   1943 Orff, C.
Mond, Der   1939 Orff, C.

Ortel (with Elsner)
Gläserne Berg, Der+   1928 Braunfels, W.

Ortner, H. H.
Tobias Wunderlich+   1937 Haas, J.
  (with L. Andersen)

Osiander
Berenice und Lucilla+   1710 Graupner, C.

Ostendorf, Jens-Peter (1944-)
Murieta   1984 Ostendorf, J.-P.
  (with K. Möckel)
William Ratcliff   1982 Ostendorf, J.-P.

Ostermann, Arthur
Herrn Dürers Bild+   1927 Mraczek, J. G.

Ott, Georg
Höhle von Waverly, Die+   1837 Kreutzer, C.

Palffy-Wanick, Kamilla
Fremde Erde+   1930 Rathaus, K.

Palitzsch, Peter
Puntila   1966 Dessau, P.
  (with M. Werkwerth)

Pappenheim, Marie
Erwartung   1909 Schoenberg, A.

Pasqué, Ernst
Aleida von Holland+   1866 Thooft, W. F.
Astorga+   1866 Abert, J. J.
Hochzeit des Mönchs, Die+   1886 Klughardt, A.
Landgraf Ludwigs Brautfahrt+ 1857 Lassen, E.

Pasztor, Arpad
Dorf ohne Glocke, Das+   1919 Künneke, E.

Paulun, Dirks
Don Quijote+   1947 Maasz, G.

Paumgartner, Bernhard (1887-1971)
Heisse Eisen, Das+   1922 Paumgartner, B.

Paumgartner, B. (cont.)
   Höhle von Salamanca, Die+   1923   Paumgartner, B.

Pedersen, Olaf
   Dorian Gray+   1930   Flick-Steger, C.

Penderecki, Krzystof (1933-)
   Teufel von Loudun, Der   1969   Penderecki, K.
   (with E. Fried)

Perinet, Joachim (1763-1816)
   Durchmarsch, Der+   1808   Tuczek, V.F.
   Hamlet+   1807   Schuster, I.
   Liebe macht kurzen Prozess+   1798   Wölfl, J. et al.
   Neue Alceste, Die+   1806   Müller, W.
   Neue Semiramis, Die+   1808   Tuczek, V.F.
   Neusonntagskind, Das+   1793   Müller, W.
   Schwestern von Prag, Die   1794   Müller, W.
   Weinlese, Die+   1782   Beecke, I. von

Petzer, Wolfgang
   Des Simplicius Simplicissi-   1949   Hartmann, K. A.
   mus Jugend+ (with K. Hartmann)

Peucer
   Graf von Gleichen,   ca. 1822   Eberwein, K.
   Der+ (with Schmidt)

Pfeiffer, Karl
   Pietro von Abano   1827   Spohr, L.

Pfitzner, Hans (1869-1949)
   Christelflein, Das+   1917   Pfitzner, H.
   Palestrina   1917   Pfitzner, H.

Phil, Theo
   Bremer Stadtmusikanten, Die+ 1949   Mohaupt, R.

Pistor, Carl (1895-1951)
   Alchemist, Der+   1931   Pistor, C.

Planché, James Robinson (1796-1880)
   Oberon (transl. W. Sotheby) 1826   Weber, C. M. von

Plümicke, Karl M.
   Lanassa+ (with V. F. Tuczek) 1805   Tuczek, V. F.

Pohl, Richard
   Letzte Zauberer, Der+   1869   Viardot, P.

Poissl, Johann Nepomuk von (1783-1865)
   Wettkampf zu Olympia, Der+   1815   Poissl, J. N.

Poser, Hans (1917-1970)
  Auszeichnung, Die+   1959   Poser, H.
  (with K. Vibach)

Postel, Christian Heinrich (1658-1705)
  Adonis   1697   Keiser, R.
  Ariadne   1691   Conradi, J. G.
  Ariadne+   1722   Keiser, R.
  Augustus+   1698   Keiser, R.
  Gensericus+   1693   Conradi, J. G.
  Iphigenia in Aulis+   1731   Graun, K. H.
  Janus   1698   Keiser, R.
  Psyche+   1701   Keiser, R.

Praetorius, Johann
  Circe+ (with J. J.   1734   Keiser, R.
    van Mauritius)
  Lächerliche Printz   1726   Keiser, R.
    Jodelet, Der
  Pimpinone   1725   Telemann, G. P.

Prechtler, Otto
  Alidia+   1839   Lachner, F.
  Diana von Solange+   1858   Ernst II
  Guttenberg+   1846   Füchs, F.
  Johanna d'Arc+   1840   Hoven, J.
  Mara+   1841   Netzer, J.
  Rächer, Der+   1846   Schindelmeisser, L.

Pribil, Willi
  Krach im Offen, Der+   1961   Kaufmann, A.
  (with A. Jirasek)

Radermacher, Friedrich (1924-)
  Tartarin von Tarascon+   1965   Radermacher, F.

Raff, Johann (1822-1882)
  König Alfred+   1851   Raff, J.
  (with G. Logau)

Raimund, Ferdinand (1790-1836)
  Alpenkönig und   1828   Müller, W.
    Menschenfeind+
  Gefesselte Phantasie, Die+   1828   Müller, W.
  Verschwender, Der+   1834   Kreutzer, C.

Ramler, K. W.
  Cephalus und Prokris+   1777   Reichardt, J. F.

Rau, Heribert
  Kaiser Adolph von Nassau+   1845   Marschner, H.

Rau, H. (cont.)
Sicilianische Vesper, Die+   1843   Lindpaintner, P.

Rauch, Franz
Fremde, Der+   1920   Kaun, H.

Raupach, Ernst
Agnes von Hohenstaufen   1827   Spontini, G.
Drei Wünsche, Die+   1834   Loewe, C.

Reger, Karl
Marie von Montalban+   1800   Winter, P.

Reger, Philipp
Hans Sachs (with Lortzing   1840   Lortzing, A.
   and P. J. Düringer)

Rehbaum Theobald
Mirandolina+   1907   Scholz, B.

Reichert, Heinz
Don Quichote+   1910   Heuberger, R.
   (with F. Grünbaum)
Wo die Lerche singt+   1918   Vienna
   (with A. M. Willner)
Zarewitsch, Der   1927   Lehár, F.
   (with B. Jenbach)

Reil, Johann Anton Friedrich
Bergsturz, Der+   1812   Weigl, J.
Fridolin+   1837   Kreutzer, C.

Reimann, Aribert (1936-)
Gespenstersonate   1984   Reimann, A.
   (with U. Schendel)

Reinacher, Eduard
Geschichte vom schönen   1942   Kauffmann, L. J.
   Annerl, Die+ (with E. Bormann)

Reingold, Ingeborg
Hexenlied+   1948   Kleemann, R.

Reinhart, Hans
Spiel von der   1954   Braunfels, W.
   Auferstehung, Das+

Reinick, Robert
Genoveva   1850   Schumann, R.

Rellstab, Ludwig (1799-1860)
Dido+   1823   Klein, B.

Rellstab, L. (cont.)
   Feldlager in Schlesien, Ein+ 1844 Meyerbeer, G.

Rennert, Wolfgang
   Dame Kobold (with Wimberger) 1964 Wimberger, G.

Reuter, Florizel von
   Postmeister Wyrin+   1946 Reuter, F. von

Reuther, Otto
   Dornröschen+   1942 Bresgen, C.
   Urteil des Paris, Das+   1943 Bresgen, C.

Reutter, Hermann (1900-)
   Brücke von San Luis Rey,   1954 Reutter, H.
     Die+
   Don Juan und Faust+   1950 Reutter, H.
   Nausikaa+   1967 Reutter, H.

Reznicek, E[mil] N[ikolaus] von (1860-1945)
   Donna Diana   1894 Reznicek, E. N.
    (with C. A. West)   von
   Eros und Psyche+   1917 Reznicek, E. N.
                          von
   Holofernes+   1923 Reznicek, E. N.
                          von
   Jungfrau von Orleans,   1887 Reznicek, E. N.
     Die+   von
   Till Eulenspiegel+   1902 Reznicek, E. N.
                          von

Rhode, Johann Gottlieb
   Rübezahl   1805 Weber, C. M. von

Richter, Christian
   Erschaffene...Mensch, Der+ 1678 Theile, J.

Rideamus
   Lustigen Nibelungen, Die+ 1904 Straus, O.

Riedl, Peter
   Graf von Gleichen, Der+   1901 Mohaupt, R.

Riemann, Hugo (1849-1919)
   Meister Martin und   1897 Lacombe, L.
    seine Gesellen+

Riethmüller, Helmut
   Mitschuldigen, Die+   1957 Riethmüller, H.

Rihm, Wolfgang (1952-)
   Oedipus   1987 Rihm, W.

Rio, Marie-Noel
Liebestod+   1982 Aperghis, G.

Rischl, Dietrich
Jot+ (with K. Marti)   1973 Huber, K.

Ritter, Alexander (1833-1896)
Faule Hans, Der+   1885 Ritter, A.
Wem die Krone?+   1890 Ritter, A.

Ritter, Karl
Penthesilea+   1927 Ritter, R.

Robert, L.
Omar und Leila+   1824 Fesca, F. E.

Robinson, Armin
Drei Walzer+   1935 Straus, O.
   (with P. Knepler)

Rochlitz, Friedrich
Blumenmädchen, Das+   1806 Benda, F.

Rodenberg, Julius
Feramors+   1863 Rubinstein, A.
Sulamith+   1883 Rubinstein, A.

Roeber, Friedrich
König Manfred+   1867 Reinecke, C.

Rohrmann
Ungebetenen Gäste, Die+   1805 Hoffmann,
                                              E. T. A.

Roquette, Otto
Legende von der   1881 Liszt, F.
   heiligen Elisabeth, Die+

Rösler, Albert
Schwarze Spinne, Die+   1936 Sutermeister, H.

Rosmer, Ernst [Elsa Bernstein-Porges] (1866-1949)
Königskinder   1910 Humperdinck, E.

Rost, Alexander
Prinz Eugen+   1847 Schmidt, G.

Roth, H.
Bauernhochzeit+   1967 Reutter, H.

Röttger, Heinz (1909-1977)
Heiratsantrag, Der+   1960 Röttger, H.

Rubin, Marcel (1905-)
Kleider machen Leute+   1973   Rubin, M.

Rüeger, Armin
Don Ranudo   1919   Schoeck, O.
Massamilla Doni   1937   Schoeck, O.
Venus   1922   Schoeck, O.

Rullmann, Wilhelm
Albigenser, Die+   1878   Deswert, J.

Runge, Philipp Otto (1777-1810)
Vom Fischer un syner Fru   1930   Schoeck, O.

Rupel, Heinrich
Heimkehr, Die+   1954   Mihalovici, M.

Rusen, Lars
Maccabär, Die+   1875   Rubinstein, A.
  (with S. H. Mosenthal)
Reise, Die+   1969   Werle, L. J.

Salice-Contessa, C. W.
Liebhaber nach dem Tode,   1822   Hoffmann,
  Der+   E. T. A.

Sanden, Aline
Salambo+   1926   Böttcher, L.

Sauer, L.
Eulenspiegel+   1889   Kistler, C.
  (with J. Levi)

Savigny, Hans von
Fabel vom seligen   1964   Wagner-Régeny, R.
  Schächtermeister+

Schachtel, Werner
Elegie für junge Liebende   1961   Henze, H. W.
  (with L. Landgraf)

Schachtner, Johann Andreas
Zaïde (with C. Gollmick)   1779   Mozart, W. A.

Schack, Adolf Friedrich Graf von (1815-1894)
Wundertheater, Das   1949   Henze, H. W.

Schäfer, Anneliese
Undine+   1969   Fortner, W.

Schaldopler, Johann
  Königen der schwarzen   1801   Eberl, A.
  Insel, Die+

Schanzer, Rudolph
  Madame Pompadour+   1923   Fall, L.
  (with E. Welisch)

Scharnke, Reinhold
  König Lustig+   1952   Riede, E.

Schaum, Johann Otto Heinrich
  Tamerlan+   1800   Reichardt, J. F.

Schaumann, Franz
  Abenteuer einer   1886   Heuberger, R.
  Neujahrsnacht, Der+

Scheibe, Johann Adolf
  Thusnelde+   1749   not set

Schendel, Uwe
  Gespenstersonate   1984   Reimann, A.
  (with A. Reimann)

Schibler, Ernst (1920–)
  Füsse im Feuer, Die+   1955   Schibler, E.

Schiebeler, Daniel (1741–1771)
  Lisuarte und Darlioette+   1766   Hiller, J. A.
  Musen, Die+   1767   Hiller, J. A.

Schiffer, Marcellus
  Hin und zurück   1927   Hindemith, P.
  Neues vom Tage   1929   Hindemith, P.
  Rufen Sie Herr Plim!   ca. 1925   Spoliansky, M.

Schikaneder, Emanuel (1751–1812)
  Alexander+   1801   Teyber, F.
  Anton bei Hofe+   1791   Schack, B.?
  Babylons Pyramiden+   1797   Winter, P. and
                                            J. Mederitsch
  Dumme Gärtner aus dem   1789   Gerl, F. X.
  Gebirge, Der+
  Fall ist noch weit   1790   Schack, B.
  seltner, Der+
  Frühling, Der+   1790   Schack, B.?
  Häuschen im Walde, Das+   1795   Schack, B.
  Höllenberg, Der+   1795   Wölfl, J.
  Königssohn aus Ithaka,   1795   Hoffmeister,
  Der+   F. A.
  Labarint, Das   1798   Winter, P.

Schikaneder, E. (cont.)
  Spiegel von Arkadien, Der   1794 Süssmayr, F. X.
  Tiroler Wastel, Der+   1796 Haibel, J.
  Vestas Feuer   1803 Beethoven, L. van
  Vestas Feuer+   1805 Weigl, J.
  Zauberflöte, Die   1791 Mozart, W. A.

Schink, Johann Friedrich
  Ruinen vom Paluzzi, Die+   1811 Romberg, A.
  Zweikampf mit der   1811 Spohr, L.
    Geliebten, Der+

Schjelderup, Gerhard (1859-1933)
  Frühlingsnacht+   1934 Schjelderup, G.
  Norwegische Hochzeit+   1900 Schjelderup, G.
  Sturmvögel+   1926 Schjelderup, G.

Schleger, Hans
  Schlaue Susanna, Die+   1952 Lehner, F. X.
    (with F. X. Lehner)

Schlesinger, H.
  Schwarze Spinne, Die+   1932 Hauer, J. M.

Schlicht, Emil [Formey, Alfred]
  Kriegsgefangene, Die+   1899 Goldmark, K.

Schmezer, Friedrich
  Troubadour, Der+   1847 Fesca, A. E.

Schmidel, F. L.
  Unnutzte Vorsicht, Die+   1783 Weigl, J.

Schmidt
  Graf von Gleichen,   ca. 1822 Eberwein, K.
    Der+ (with Peucer)

Schmidt, Eberhard
  Schuhu, Der+   1976 Zimmermann, U.
    (with U. Zimmermann)

Schmidt, Fr. Georg [Karl Pfeiffer]
  Alchymist, Der   1830 Spohr, L.

Schmidt, Gustav (1816-1882)
  Weibertreue+   1858 Schmidt, G.

Schmidt, Heiner
  Almanzine+   1820 Pixis, J. P.
  Corinna+   1958 Fortner, W.

Schmidt, Heinrich?
   Junker in der Mühle, Der+   1813   Hummel, J. N.

Schmidt, M. A.
   Kaspar, der Fagottist+   1791   Müller, W.

Schmidtmann, Friedrich (1913-)
   Kain+   1952   Schmidtmann, F.

Schmiedel, Hans P.
   Käficht, Der+   1925   Kormann, H.

Schmieder, Heinrich Gottlieb
   Doktor Faust   1797   Walter, I.
   Heinrich der Löwe+   1792   Stegmann, C. D.
   Trojanische Pferd, Das+   1799   Wölf, J.

Schmilinski, H.
   Sakuntala+   1905   Zimmermann, B.

Schmolke, Annelies
   Bremer Stadtmusikanten, Die+ 1949   Bergese, H.

Schnabel, Ernst (1913-)
   Floss der Medusa, Das   1968   Henze, H. W.

Schneider, Rolf
   Aufsichtsrat, Der+   1970   Motte, D. de la

Schnell, Robert
   Bär, Der+   1963   Dressel, E.

Schnitzer, Ignaz
   Zigeunerbaron, Der   1885   Strauss, J., Jr.

Schnurre, Wolfdietrich (1920-)
   Anaximanders Ende+   1958   Thaerichen, W.

Schober, Franz von
   Alfonso und Estrella   1822   Schubert, F.

Schoeck, Othmar (1886-1957)
   Penthesilea   1927   Schoeck, O.

Schoenberg, Arnold (1874-1951)
   Glückliche Hand, Die   1924   Schoenberg, A.
   Moses und Aron   1932   Schoenberg, A.
   Sarema+   1897   Zemlinsky, A. von

Schoenbohm, Siegfried
   Bassgeige, Die+   1978   Kounadis, A.
      (with W. Reuter)

Schott, Paul
   Tote Stadt, Die   1920   Korngold, E.

Schrader, Julie
   Genoveva+   1977   Müller-Siemens,
                                        D.

Schreiber, Alois (1763-1841)
   Jephta's Gelübde+   1812   Meyerbeer, G.

Schreker, Franz (1878-1934)
   Christophorus   1927   Schreker, F.
   Ferne Klang, Der   1912   Schreker, F.
   Flammen+ (with D. Leen)   1902   Schreker, F.
   Gezeichneten, Die   1918   Schreker, F.
   Irrelohe   1924   Schreker, F.
   Schatzgräber, Der+   1920   Schreker, F.
   Schmied von Gent, Der   1932   Schreker, F.
   Singende Teufel, Der+   1928   Schreker, F.
   Spielwerk und die   1913   Schreker, F.
    Prinzessin, Das
   Tönenden Sphären, Die+ 1915   not perf

Schriefer, Wilhelm
   Eros und Psyche+   1901   Zenger, M.

Schriker, August
   Meister Martin und   1879   Weissheimer, W.
    seine Gesellen+

Schubert, Karl Emil
   Zemire und Azor+   1776   Baumgarten, C. G.
    (with C. G. von Baumgarten)   von

Schulz-Gellen, Christoph
   Andreas Wolius+   1940   Walter, F.

Schwaen, Kurt (1909-)
   Leonce und Lena+   1961   Schwaen, K.

Schwan, Christian Friedrich
   Azakia+   1778   Cannabich, C.
   Kaufmann von Smyrna, Der 1771   Vogler, G. J.
   Kaufmann von Smyrna, Der+ 1773   Holly, F. A.
   Kaufmann von Smyrna, Der+ 1773   Stegmann, C. D.

Schweitzer, Richard
   Casanova in der Schweiz+ 1943   Burkhard, P.

Schwenn, Günther
   Bad auf der Tenne, Das+ 1955   Schröder, F.

Schwitters, Kurt (1887-1948)
   Anna Blume+   1929   Wolpe, S.

Searle, Humphrey (1915-1982)
   Hamlet   1968   Searle, H.

Seitz, Robert
   Orpheus und der   1931   Dessau, P.
      Bürgermeister+
   Wir bauen eine Stadt   1930   Hindemith, P.

Semmler, Rudolf (1904-)
   Hansel und Gretel+   1956   Semmler, R.

Sendtner, Jacob
   Rodrigo und Zimene+   1821   Aiblinger, J. K.

Seuberlich, Rudolf
   Prinz wider Willen, Der+   1890   Lohse, O.

Seyfried, Joseph von
   Vestalin, Die+   1814   Guhr, K. W. F.

Sieberg, Wilhelm Dieter
   Untergang der Titanic, Der+   1979   Sieberg, W. D.

Simonetti, Christian Ernst
   Ludewig der Fromme   1726   Schürmann, G. C.
      (Ludovicus Pius)+

Singer, Maximilian
   Es war einmal+   1900   Zemlinsky, A. von

Smyth, Ethel (1858-1944)
   Fantasio+   1898   Smyth, E.
   Wald, Der+   1902   Smyth, E.

Soden, Julius von
   Lindor und Ismene+   1777   Schmittbauer,
                                                   J. A.

Sohlehrn, Edgar von
   Baldurs Tod+   1905   Kistler, C.

Sonderhausen, Philipp Carl Christian
   Fürstin von Granada,   1833   Lobe, J. C.
      Die+ (with J. C. Lobe)

Sonnleithner, Josef (1766-1835)
   Agnes Sorel+   1806   Gyrowetz, A.
   Leonore   1805   Beethoven, L. van

Spaun-Matthus, Lia
  Blaue Berg, Der+   1945 Lustgarten, E.

Specht, Richard
  Erlösung, Die+   1895 Scharrer, A.

Spiess, C. H.
  Im Dunkel ist nicht gut   1789 Dittersdorf, K.
  munkeln+

Spiess, Eric
  Bassgeige, Die+   1964 Poser, H.
  Hero und Leander   1966 Bialas, G.

Spohr, Ludwig (Louis) (1784-1859)
  Kreuzfahrer, Die   1845 Spohr, L.
    (with M. Spohr)

Spohr, Marianne
  Kreuzfahrer, Die   1845 Spohr, L.
    (with L. Spohr)

Sporck, Ferdinand Graf von
  Abreise, Die   1898 Albert, E. d'
  Ingewelde+   1894 Schillings, M.
  Kunihild+   1884 Kistler, C.
  Pfeifertag, Der+   1899 Schillings, M.
                                         von
  Scherz, List und Rache+   1961 Leinert, F.

Stadler, Albert
  Fernando   1815 Schubert, F.

Stauffer, Theodor (1826-1880)
  Touristen, Die+   1869 Stauffer, T.

Stegmayer, Matthäus
  Harald+   1814 Kleinheinz, F. X.
  Wladimir, Fürst von   1807 Bierey, G. B.
  Novgorod+

Stein, Leo [Leo Rosenstein] (with V. Léon)
  Lustige Witwe, Die   1905 Lehár, F.
  Wiener Blut   1899 Strauss, J., Jr.

Steiner, Maximilian
  Indigo und die vierzig   1871 Strauss, J., Jr.
  Räuber+

Steinsberg, Carl von
  Hochzeit auf dem Lande, Die+ 1798 Volanek, A.
  Waldmädchen, Das   1800 Weber, C.M. von

Stephanie, Christian Gottlob, Jr. (1733-1800)
    Doctor [Doktor] und   1786   Dittersdorf, K.
      Apotheker
    Entführung aus dem   1782   Mozart, W. A.
      Serail, Die
    Entführung aus dem   1787   Knecht, J.
      Serail, Die
    Liebe im Narrenhaus, Die   1787   Dittersdorf, K.
    Schauspieldirektor, Der   1786   Mozart, W. A.

Stern, Adolf
    Hagbarth und Signe+   1882   Mihalovich, Ö.

Stillmark, Alexander
    König Drosselbart+   1958   Noll, D.

Stockhausen, Karlheinz (1928-)
    Atmen gibt das Leben+   1977   Stockhausen, K.
    from **Licht:**
      Donnerstag   1981   Stockhausen, K.
      Montag   1988   Stockhausen, K.
      Samstag   1984   Stockhausen, K.
    Originale+   1961   Stockhausen, K.
    Sirius+   1977   Stockhausen, K.

Stramm, August
    Sancta Susanna   1922   Hindemith, P.

Strauss, Richard (1864-1949)
    Guntram   1894   Strauss, R.
    Intermezzo   1924   Strauss, R.
    Salome (after O. Wilde)   1905   Strauss, R.

Strobel, Heinrich
    Leonore 40/45   1952   Liebermann, R.
    Penelope   1954   Liebermann, R.
    Schule der Frauen, Die   1957   Liebermann, R.
      (with E. Montague)

Stucken, Franz von der
    Opferung des Gefangenen, 1926   Wellesz, E.
    Die+

Sutermeister, Heinrich (1910-)
    Fingerhütchen+   1950   Sutermeister, H.
    Füsse im Feuer, Die+   1950   Sutermeister, H.
    Gespenst von   1964   Sutermeister, H.
      Canterville, Das
    Jorinda und Jorgile+   1934   Sutermeister, H.
    Niobe+   1945   Sutermeister, H.
    Raskolnikoff+   1948   Sutermeister, H.
    Romeo und Julia   1940   Sutermeister, H.

Sutermeister, H. (cont.)
   Seraphine+   1959   Sutermeister, H.
   Titus Feuerfuchs+   1958   Sutermeister, H.
   Zauberinsel, Der+   1942   Sutermeister, H.

Telemann, Georg Philipp (1681-1767)
   Neu-modische Liebhaber   1724   Telemann, G. P.
   Damon, Der

Tenelli, N. [Johann Heinrich Millenet]
   Casilda+   1851   Ernst II

Teweles, Heinrich
   Ring des Polykrates, Der   1916   Korngold, E.

Thiemisch, Paul
   Alceste+   1693   Strungk, N. A.

Thierisch, Bertha
   Island-Saga+   1925   Vollerthun, G.

Thullen, Peter
   Alles ist Kismet+   1952   Hofmann, W.

Tiel, Walter
   Trauung, Die+   1975   Kirchner, V. D.

Trantow, Herbert
   Odysseus bei Circe+   1938   Trantow, H.

Treichlinger, Wilhelm M.
   Münchhausen+   1933   Lothar, M.
   Rappelkopf+   1958   Lothar, M.

Treitschke, Georg Friedrich
   Adrian von Ostade+   1807   Weigl, J.
   Beiden Figaro, Die+   1840   Kreutzer, C.
   (with J. F. Jünger)
   Fidelio   1814   Beethoven, L. van
   Jugend Peter des Grossen, 1814   Weigl, J.
   Die+
   Junggesellen-Wirtschaft,   1807   Gyrowetz, A.
   Die+
   Mitgefühl, Das+   1804   Wranitzky, P.
   Nachtigall und Rabe+   1818   Weigl, J.
   Uniform, Der+   1805   Weigl, J.
   Waisenhaus, Das+   1808   Weigl, J.

Treumann, Karl
   Prinz Methusalem+   1877   Strauss, J., Jr.
   Zehn Mädchen und kein Mann+ 1862   Suppé, F. von

Tschirsch, Emil
  Coeur As+ (with O. Berg)   1913   Künneke, E.

Tscholakowa, Gertrud
  Hamletmaschine+   1987   Rihm, W.
  Lanzelot (with H. Müller)   1969   Dessau, P.

Tschudi, Fridolin
  Spiegel der Agrippina, Das+   1937   Haug, H.

Tuczek, Vincenz Franz (1773-1821 or later)
  Lanassa+   1805   Tuczek, V. F.
    (with K. M. Plümicke)

Tumtinz, Otto
  Rosen der Madonna, Die+   1940? Heuberger, R.
    (with B. Hardt-Warden)

Türk[e], J.
  Peter Schmoll und seine   1802   Weber, C. M. von
  Nachbarn

Tyl, Josef Kajetán
  Dorfmusikanten, Die   1907   Weiss, K.

Ulrich, Anton
  Amelinde+   1657   Löwe, J. J.
  Orpheus aus Thracien+   1659   Löwe, J. J.

Umlauft, Paul (1853-1934)
  Evanthia+   1893   Umlauft, P.

Urspruch, Anton (1850-1907)
  Unmöglichste von allem,   1897   Urspruch, A.
  Das+

Veith, Johann Emanuel
  Augenarzt, Der+   1811   Gyrowetz, A.
  Rückfahrt des Kaisers, Die+   1814   Hummel, J. N.

Vesper, Will
  Herr Dandolo+   1914   Siegel, R.

Vibach, Karl
  Auszeichnung, Die+   1959   Poser, H.
    (with H. Poser)

Vogel, Wilhelm
  Carlos Fioras+   1810   Fränzl, F.

Vulpius, Christian August (1762-1827)
  Hieronymus Knicker   1789 Dittersdorf, K.
  Hokus-Pokus+   1790 Dittersdorf, K.

Wackernagel, Rudolf
  Weltfrühling+   1894 Huber, H.

Wagenseil, C. J.
  Ehrlichkeit und Liebe+   1776 Wolf, E. W.

Wagner, Helmut
  Dybuk, Der+   1970 Füssl, K.

Wagner, Richard (1813-1883)
  Bianca und Giuseppe+   1848 Kittl, J.F.
    (with H. König)
  Feen, Die   1833 Wagner, R.
  Fliegende Holländer, Der 1843 Wagner, R.
  Liebesverbot, Das   1836 Wagner, R.
  Lohengrin   1850 Wagner, R.
  Meistersinger von   1868 Wagner, R.
    Nürnberg, Die
  Parsifal   1882 Wagner, R.
  Rienzi   1842 Wagner, R.
  Ring des Nibelungen, Der: 1876 Wagner, R.
    Das Reingold   1869 Wagner, R.
    Die Walküre   1870 Wagner, R.
    Siegfried   1876 Wagner, R.
    Götterdämmerung   1876 Wagner, R.
  Tannhäuser   1845 Wagner, R.
  Tristan und Isolde   1865 Wagner, R.

Wagner, Siegfried (1869-1930)
  An allem ist Hütchen   1917 Wagner, S.
    schuld+
  Banadietrich+   1910 Wagner, S.
  Bärenhäuter, Der   1899 Wagner, S.
  Bruder Lustig+   1905 Wagner, S.
  Friedensengel, Der+   1926 Wagner, S.
  Heidenkönig, Der+   1933 Wagner, S.
  Herzog Wildfang+   1901 Wagner, S.
  Kobold, Der   1904 Wagner, S.
  Schmied von Marienburg, Der+ 1923 Wagner, S.
  Schwarzschwanreich+   1918 Wagner, S.
  Sonnenflammen+   1918 Wagner, S.
  Sterngebot, Das+   1908 Wagner, S.

Wagner-Régeny, Rudolf (1903-1969)
  Bergwerk zu Falun, Das   1961 Wagner-Régeny, R.
  Moschopulos+   1928 Wagner-Régeny, R.
  Prometheus+   1959 Wagner-Régeny, R.
  Sganarelle+   1929 Wagner-Régeny, R.

Wahren, Karl Heinz (1933-)
   Fettlösschen+   1976   Wahren, K. H.
   (with C. H. Henneberg)

Walter, Kurt E.
   Kalte Herz, Das   1943   Schultze, N.

Waltershausen, Hermann Wolfgang von (1882-1954)
   Doktor Eisenbart+   1922   Zilcher, H.
   Oberst Chabert+   1912   Waltershausen,
                                     H. W. von

Walther, Oscar [Oscar Friedrich Kunel]
   Don Cesar+   1885   Dellinger, R.

Wanja, Ivo
   Peter der Dritte+   1965   Schultze, N.
   (with K. Vibach)

Warden, Bruno. See Bruno Hardt-Warden

Wartisch, Otto (1893-1969)
   Cagliostro+   1924   Wartisch, O.

Wassermann, Jacob
   Prinzessin Ginara+   1921   Wellesz, E.

Wäterlin, Oscar
   Don Pedros Heimkehr+   1952   Erismann, H.
   (with W. Galusser)

Weichmann, C. F.
   Sieg der Schönheit+   1722   Conradi, J. G.
                                     and G. P.
                                     Telemann

Weichselbaumer, Karl
   Hermannsschlacht, Die+ 1835   Chelard, H.

Weidmann, F. K.
   Ring des Glückes, Der+ 1833   Kreutzer, C.

Weidmann, Joseph
   Dorfbarbier, Der   1796   Schenk, J.
   (with P. Weidmann)

Weidmann, Paul
   Bergknappen, Die   1778   Umlauf, I.
   Bettelstudent, Der+   1785   Winter, P.
   Dorfbarbier, Der   1796   Schenk, J.
   (with J. Weidmann)

Weidmann, P. (cont.)
   Ring der Liebe, Der+   1786   Umlauf, I.
      (with K. E. Schubert)

Weil, Greta
   Boulevard Solitude   1952   Henze, H. W.
      (with W. Jockisch)

Weingartner, Felix (1863-1942)
   Dame Kobold+   1916   Weingartner, F.
   Dorfschule, Die+   1920   Weingartner, F.
   Kain und Abel+   1914   Weingartner, F.
   Meister Andrea+   1920   Weingartner, F.
   Orestes+   1902   Weingartner, F.
   Sakuntala+   1884   Weingartner, F.

Weinstock
   Ödipus+   1960   Eder, H.

Weirich, Harald
   Belshazar+   1986   Kirchner, V. D.
   Fünf Minuten des Isaak   1980   Kirchner, V. D.
      Babel, Die+ (with V. D. Kirchner)

Weiser, I. A.
   Schuldigkeit des ersten   1767   Mozart, W. A.,
      Gebotes, Die+   M. Haydn, and
                                                A. C. Adlgasser

Weishappel, Rudolf (1921-)
   Elga+   1939   Weishappel, R.

Weiskern, Friedrich Wilhelm
   Bastien und Bastienne   1768   Mozart, W. A.

Weismann, Julius (1879-1950)
   Gespenstersonate, Die+   1930   Weismann, J.
   Leonce und Lena+   1925   Weismann, J.
   Schwanenweiss+   1923   Weismann, J.
   Traumspiel, Ein+   1925   Weismann, J.

Weiss, Peter (1916-1982)
   Traumspiel, Ein   1965   Reimann, A.

Weisse, Christian Felix (1726-1804)
   Aehrenleserin, Die+   1778   Haydn, M.
   Aerndtekranz, Der+   1771   Hiller, J. A.
   Dorfbarbier, Der+   1771   Hiller, J. A.
   Findelkind, Das+   ca. 1787   Benda, G.
   Jagd, Die   1770   Hiller, J. A.
   Jagd, Die+   1799   Schenk, J.
   Jubelhochzeit, Die+   1773   Hiller, J. A.

Weisse, C. F. (cont.)
   Jubelhochzeit, Die+   1782   Beecke, I. von
   Kleine Aehrenleserin, Die+   1778   Hiller, J. A.
   Krieg, Der+   1772   Hiller, J. A.
   Liebe auf dem Lande, Die+   1768   Hiller, J. A.
   Liebe auf dem Lande,   ca. 1789   Süssmayr, F. X.
      Die+
   Lottchen am Hofe+   1767   Hiller, J. A.
   Lustige Schuster, Der+   1759   Standfuss, J. C.
   Teufel ist los, Der   1743   Standfuss, J. C.
   Teufel ist los, Der   1766   Hiller, J. A.

Weissleder, Paul (1886-1960)
   Weg durchs Fesnter, Der+   1917   Weissleder, P.

Welisch, Ernst
   Liebe Augustin, Der+   1912   Fall, L.
      (with R. Bernauer)
   Madame Pompadour+   1923   Fall, L.
      (with R. Schanzer)

Welleminsky, Ignaz Michael
   Eiserne Heiland, Der+   1917   Oberleithner, M.
      (with B. Hardt-Warden)   von
   Mann im Mond, Der+   1922   Brandt-Buys, J.
      (with B. Hardt-Warden)
   Schneider von Schönau,   1916   Brandt-Buys, J.
      Der+
      (with B. Hardt-Warden)

Wellesz, Egon (1885-1974)
   Bakchantinnen, Die   1931   Wellesz, E.
   Scherz, List und Rache+   1928   Wellesz, E.

Werdin, Eberhard (1911-)
   Des Kaisers neue Kleider+   1948   Werdin, E.

Werfel, Franz (1890-1945)
   Weg der Verheissung, Der+   1935   Weill, K.
   Zwingburg+   1924   Krenek, E.

Werkwerth, Manfred
   Puntila   1966   Dessau, P.
      (with P. Palitzsch)

Werthes, F. A.
   Pfauenfest, Das+   1801   Zumsteeg, J.R.

Wessling, Bernd W.
   Palast Hotel Thanatos+   1972   Einfeldt, D.

West, Carl August [Joseph Schreyvogel]
  Donna Diana   1894 Reznicek, E. N.
    (with E. N. von Reznicek)   von

West, Moritz [Moritz Georg Nitzelberger]
  Obersteiger, Der+   1894 Zeller, C.
    (with L. Held)
  Vogelhändler, Der   1891 Zeller, C.
    (with L. Held)

Westermann, Gerhart von
  Rosamunde Floris   1960 Blacher, B.

Westien, Fritz (1925-)
  Des Kaisers neue   1957 Westien, F.
    Kleider+

Wette, Adelheid
  Hänsel und Gretel   1893 Humperdinck, E.
  Sieben Geislein+   1895 Humperdinck, E.

Wette, Hermann
  Bärenhäuter, Der+   1900 Mendelssohn, A.

Wetz, Richard (1875-1935)
  Ewige Feuer, Das+   1907 Wetz, R.

Wetzel, J.
  Kluge Jacob, Der+   1788 Kospoth, O. C. E.
                                           von

Wetzler, Lini
  Baskische Venus, Die+   1928 Wetzler, H. H.

Wichert, Ernst
  Unter Räubern+   1883 Rubinstein, A.

Widmann, Joseph Victor
  Steinerne Herz, Das+   1888 Brüll, I.
  Widerspenstigen Zähmung,   1874 Goetz, H.
    Die

Widowitz, Oskar
  Viola+   1934 Holenia, H.

Wieland, Christoph Martin (1733-1813)
  Alceste   1773 Schweitzer, A.
  Alceste+   1780 Wolf, E. W.
  Alceste+   1786 Benda, F.
  Rosamunde+   1780 Schweitzer, A.

Wiesinger, Herbert
  Kleine Stadt, Die+   1957 Lehner, F.

Wilde, Richard
  Porzia+   1916   Taubmann, O.

Wilhelm, Julius
  Goldene Vogel, Der+   1920   Fall, L.
    (with P. Frank)

Wilk, Leopold
  Notre Dame+   1914   Schmidt, F.

Willnau, Carl
  Dreispitz, Der+   1936   Korman, H.

Willner, Alfred Maria
  Dollarprinzessin, Die   1907   Fall, L.
    (with F. Grünbaum)
  Endlich allein+   1914   Lehár, F.
    (with A. Böckmann)
  Frasquita+   1922   Lehár, F.
    (with H. Reichert)
  Göttin der Vernunft, Die+   1897   Strauss, J., Jr.
    (with B. Buchbinder)
  Götz von Berlichingen+   1902   Goldmark, K.
  Graf von Luxemburg, Der   1909   Lehár, F.
    (with R. Bodanzky)
  Heimchen am Herd, Das+   1896   Goldmark, K.
  Walzer aus Wien+   1931   Strauss, J., Jr.
    (with H. Reichert, Marischka)
  Wintermärchen, Ein+   1908   Goldmark, K.
  Zigeunerliebe   1910   Lehár, F.
    (with R. Bodanzky)

Wimberger, Gerhard (1923-)
  Dame Kobold   1964   Wimberger, G.
    (with W. Rennert)

Windt, Herbert (1894-1965)
  Andromache+   1932   Windt, H.

Wittkowsky, Carl
  Boabdil+   1892   Moszkowski, M.
  Donna Diana+   1896   Hofmann, H.

Wittmann, Hugo
  Feldprediger, Der+   1884   Millöcker, C.
  Fürstin Ninetta+   1893   Strauss, J., Jr.
    (with J. Bauer)

Wohlbrück, Johann Gottfried
  Wirth und Gast   1813   Meyerbeer, G.

Wohlbrück, Wilhelm August
  Babü, Der+   1838 Marschner, H.
  Des Falkners Braut+   1832 Marschner, H.
  Schöffe von Paris, Der+   1836 Dorn, H.
  Templer und die Jüdin, Der   1829 Marschner, H.
  Vampyr, Der   1828 Marschner, H.

Wolf, Friedrich
  Nachtschwalbe, Die+   1948 Blacher, B.
  Tai Yang erwacht+   1960 Forest, J. K.

Wolf, Winfried
  Glückliche Ende, Das+   1954 Wolf, W.

Wolf-Ferrari, Ermanno (1876-1948)
  Himmelskleid, Das+   1927 Wolf-Ferrari, E.

Wolff, A.
  Polterabend+   ca. 1813 Müller, A. E.

Wolff, P. A.
  Preciosa   1821 Weber, C. M. von

Wolzogen, Ernst Freiherr von (1855-1934)
  Feuersnot   1901 Strauss, R.
  Flauto solo+   1905 Albert, E. d'

Woska, Elisabeth
  Niobe+   1977 Hiller, W.

Wunsch, Hermann (1884-1954)
  Don Juans Sohn+   1928 Wunsch, H.

Zehntner, Louis (1868-?)
  Dorval+   1913 Zehntner, L.

Zeitler, Andreas
  Cress ertrinkt+   1931 Fortner, W.

Zell, F. [Camillo Walzel] (with R. Genée)
  Apajune der Wassermann+   1880 Millöcker, C.
  Bettelstudent, Der   1882 Millöcker, C.
  Boccaccio   1879 Suppé, F. von
  Cagliostro in Wien+   1875 Strauss, J., Jr.
  Donna Juanita+   1880 Suppé, F. von
  Fatinitza+   1876 Suppé, F. von
  Gasparone+   1884 Millöcker, C.
  Karneval in Rom, Der+   1873 Strauss, J., Jr.
    (also with J. Braun)
  Königen Mariette+   1883 Brüll, I.
  Lustige Krieg, Der+   1881 Strauss, J., Jr.

Zell, F. (cont.)
   Nacht in Venedig, Eine   1883 Strauss, J., Jr.
   Seekadett, Der+   1876 Genée, R.
   Vice-Admiral, Der+   1886 Millöcker, C.

Zender, Hans (1936-)
   Stephan Climax+   1986 Zender, H.

Zillig, Winfried (1905-1963)
   Troilus und Cressida   1951 Zillig, W.
   Verlobung in San   1957 Zillig, W.
     Domingo, Die+

Zimmermann, Balduin (1867-1948)
   Wintermärchen, Das+   1900 Zimmermann, B.

Zimmermann, Inge
   Amphytiron+   1984 Kunad, R.
   Levins Mühle+   1973 Zimmermann, U.
   Weisse Rose, Die   1968 Zimmermann, U.
   Zweite Entscheidung, Die+ 1970 Zimmermann, U.

Zobeltitz, Martha von
   Elga+   1916 Lendvai, E.

Zöllner, Heinrich (1854-1941)
   Faust+   1887 Zöllner, H.
   Überfall, Der+   1895 Zöllner, H.
   Versunkene Glocke, Die+   1899 Zöllner, H.

Zoref, Fritz
   Arzt der Sobeide, Der+   1919 Gál, H.

Zweig, Stefan (1881-1942)
   Friedenstag   1938 Strauss, R.
     (with J. Gregor)
   Schweigsame Frau, Die   1935 Strauss, R.

Zweiniger, Arthur
   Armer Kolumbus+   1928 Dressel, E.

Zwerenz, Karl Georg
   Goldschmied von Toledo, 1919 Offenbach, J.
    Der+   (arr. Stern and
                             Zamara)

APPENDIX 4
AUTHORS

+See Appendix I.

Abrahams, P.
    Reiter der Nacht+   1973   Meyer, E. H.

Addison, Joseph (1672-1719)
   Inkle and Yariko (1711)
    Fernando und Yariko   1784   Schack, B.

Aeschylus, 525-456 B.C.
   Agamemnon
    Kassandras Tod+   1977   Chemin-Petit, H.
   Niobe
    Niobe   1977   Hiller, W.
   Orestes
    Orestes+   1902   Weingartner, F.
   Prometheus
    Prometheus+   1959   Wagner-Régeny, R.

Alarcón, Pedro Antonio de (1833-1891)
   Niño de la bola, El (1880)
    Manuel Venegas   1903   Wolf, H.
   Sombrero de tres picos, El
    (1784)
    Corregidor, Der   1896   Wolf, H.
    Dreispitz, Der+   1936   Korman, H.

Alechem, Sholem (1859-1916)
    Zweihunderttausend Taler+ 1969   Blacher, B.

Almquist (with Hauser)
    Don Juans Sohn+   1928   Wunsch, H.

An-Ski
    Dybuk, Der+   1970   Füssl, K.

Andersen, Hans Christian (1805-1875)
   Emperor's New Clothes, The (1888)
    Des Kaisers neue Kleider+ 1948   Werdin, E.
    Des Kaisers neue Kleider+ 1953   Lofer, H.
    Des Kaisers neue Kleider+ 1957   Hummel, B.
    Des Kaisers neueste   1954   Kaufmann, O.
     Kleider+
    Nackte König, Der+   1928   Wagner-Régeny, R.
   Improvisator, The (1835)
    Improvisator, Der+   1902   Albert, E. d'
   Lancelot
    Lanzelot   1969   Dessau, P.
   Nightingale, The (1912)
    Nachtigall, Die+   1939   Irmler, A.
    Nachtigall, Die+   1947   Schanazara, H.

Andersen, H. C. (cont.)
  Princess and the Pea, The (1900)
    Prinzessin auf der Erbse,   1927   Toch, E.
    Die+
  Princess and the Swineherd, The
    Prinzessin und der   1938   Reutter, H.
    Schweinehirt, Die+

Anseame, Louis
  Clochette, La
    Liebe auf dem Lande, Die+   1768   Hiller, J. A.

Antony, F.
    Verschenkte Frau, Die+   1912   Albert, E. d'

Apel, Johann August (1771-1816)
  Gespensterbuch (1811)
    Freischütz, Der   1821   Weber, C. M. von

Ariosto, Lodovico
  Orlando furioso (1516)
    Rinaldo und Alcina+   1797   Paradis, M. T.
                                           von

Aristophanes, 445 B.C.-380 B.C.
  Birds, The (414 B.C.)
    Vögel, Die   1920   Braunfels, W.
  Lysistrata (415 B.C.)
    Lysistrate   1961   Kont, P.
    Verschworenen, Die   1823   Schubert, F.

Auden, W[ystan] H[ugh] (1907-1973)
    Inzwischen+   1967   Kont, P.

Auerbach, Berthold [Moyses Baruch] (1812-1882)
  Barfüssele (1856)
    Barfüssele+   1905   Heuberger, R.

Aureli, Aurelio
  Antigona delusa da Alceste (1660)
    Alceste+   1693   Strungk, N.A.
  Teseo (1685)
    Theseus+   1688   Löhner, J.
  Also:
    Berenice und Lucilla+   1710   Graupner, C.

Balzac, Honoré de (1799-1850)
  Colonel Chabert, Le
    Oberst Chabert+   1912   Waltershausen,
                                           H. W. von

Balzac, H. de (cont.)
  Massimilla Doni (1839)
    Massimilla Doni   1937   Schoeck, O.
  Peau de chagrin, Le (1831)
    Tödlichen Wünsche, Die 1959   Klebe, G.

Banville, Théodore de
    Gringoire+   1892   Brüll, I.

Barbier, August
  Benvenuto Cellini (1838) (with A. F. L. Wailly)
    Benvenuto Cellini   1849   Lachner, F.

Barnet, Miguel
  Autobiography of a Runaway Slave
    Cimarrón, El   1970   Henze, H. W.
  Cancion de Rachel, La
    Cubana, La   1974   Henze, H. W.

Bartsch, Rudolf Hans (1873-1952)
    Kuhreigen, Der+   1911   Kienzl, W.

Bauernfeld, Eduard von (1802-1890)
  Landfrieden (1869)
    Landfriede, Der+   1877   Brüll, I.

Beaumarchais, Pierre Augustin Caron de (1732-1799)
  Barbier de Seville, Le (1775)
    Barbier von Sevilla,   1776   Benda, F. L.
      Der+
  Folle journée, La, ou
    Le Mariage de Figaro (1778)
    Hochzeit des Figaro,   1789   Dittersdorf, K.
      Die

Beck, Karl (1817-1879)
    Kinder der Heide, Die+ 1861   Rubinstein, A.

Belleforest, F. de
    Hamlet+   1973   Forest, J. K.

Benedix, Roderich (1811-1873)
  Gefängnis, Das (1859)
    Fledermaus, Die   1874   Strauss, J., Jr.

Bertati, Giovanni
  Matrimonio segreto
    Heimliche Ehe, Die+   1891   Gast, P.

Blumenthal, Oscar (1853-1917)
  Zum Weissen Rössl (1897) (with G. Kadelburg)
    Im Weissen Rössl   1930   Benatzky, R.

Boirie, Eugène Cantiran de
  Bourgemestre de Saardam, Le (with
    A. H. J. Mélesville and J. T. Merle)
  Zar und Zimmermann   1837 Lortzing, A.

Bouilly, Jean-Nicolas (1763-1842)
  Fanchon
  Fanchon, das Leiermädchen+ 1804 Himmel, F. H.
  Pierre le Grand (1790)
  Jugend Peter des Grossen, 1814 Weigl, J.
  Die+
  Léonore, ou L'Amour conjugal
    (1798)
  Fidelio   1814 Beethoven, L. van
  Leonore   1805 Beethoven, L. van

Brachvogel, Albert Emil (1824-1878)
  Friedemann Bach (1858)
  Friedemann Bach+   1931 Graener, P.

Brazier, Nicolas
  Cathérine (with A. H. J. Mélesville)
  Goldene Kreuz, Das+   1875 Brüll, I.

Brecht, Bertolt (1898-1956)
  Baal (1918)
  Baal   1981 Cerha, F.
  Persische Episode+   1963 Wagner-Régeny, R.
  Herr Puntila und Knecht Matti
    (1940)
  Puntila   1966 Dessau, P.
  Kreidekreis, Der
  Kreiderkeis, Der+   1933 Zemlinsky, A. von
  Verhör des Lukullus, Das
    (1939)
  Verhör des Lukullus, Das   1951 Dessau, P.

Brentano, Clemens (1778-1842)
  Geschichte vom braven Kasperl
    und dem schönen Annerl
    (1817)
  Geschichte vom schönen   1942 Kauffmann, L. J.
  Annerl, Die+

Bretzner, Christoph Friedrich (1748-1807)
  Belmont und Constanze (1782)
  Entführung aus dem Serail, 1782 Mozart, W. A.
  Die

Brobowski, Johannes
  Levins Mühle+   1973 Zimmermann, U.

Büchner, Georg (1813-1837)
   Dantons Tod (1835)
     Dantons Tod+   1929   Eisler, H.
     Dantons Tod   1947   Einem, G. von
   Leonce und Lena (1836)
     Leonce und Lena+   1925   Weismann, J.
     Leonce und Lena+   1961   Schwaen, K.
     Leonce und Lena   1979   Dessau, P.
   Lenz (1836)
     Jakob Lenz   1980   Rihm, W.
   Woyzeck (1837)
     Wozzeck   1925   Berg, A.
     Wozzeck+   1926   Gurlitt, M.
     Wozzeck+   1950   Pfister, K.

Bulwer-Lytton, Edward (1803-1873)
   Last Days of Pompeii (1834)
     Alidia+   1839   Lachner, F.
   Rienzi (1835)
     Rienzi   1842   Wagner, R.

Bürger, Gottfried August (1747-1794)
   Lenore (1774)
     Leonore+   1835   Hüttenbrenner, A.
   Lenardo und Blandine
     Lenardo und Blandine   1779   Winter, P.
   Münchhausen (1786)
     Münchhausen+   1933   Lothar, M.
   Also:
     Geisterbraut, Die+   1842   Eugen of
                                Württenberg

Busch, Wilhelm (1832-1908)
   Max und Moritz (1865)
     Max und Moritz+   1979   Willig, W.
   Also:
     Feindlichen Nachbarn, Die+ 1949   Breuer, P.
     Hansel und Gretel+   1956   Semmler, R.

Büsching, J. G.
   Ritterzeit
     Hochzeit, Die   1832   Wagner, R.

Bussani, Giacomo Francesco
     Julia+   1717   Keiser, R.

Byron, George Gordon (1788-1824)
   Corsair, The (1814)
     Corsair, Der+   1844   Schumann, R.

Caigniez, Louis Charles
  Forêt de Hermanstadt, La (1805)
    Elisene, Prinzessin von   1807 Rösler, J.
      Bulgarien+

Calderón de la Barca, Pedro (1600-1681)
  Alcaide de si mismo, El
    Lächerliche Printz   1726 Keiser, R.
      Jodelet, Der
  Dama Duende, La
    Dame Kobold+   1916 Weingartner, F.
    Dame Kobold+   1940 Wolfurt, K. von
    Dame Kobold   1964 Wimberger, G.
  Galan Fantasma, El
    Liebhaber nach dem Tode,   1822 Hoffmann,
      Der+   E. T. A.
  Mayor encanto amor, El
    Circe+   1948 Egk, W.
    Siebzehn Tage und vier   1966 Egk, W.
      Minuten
  Rendención de Breda, La (1625)
    Friedenstag   1938 Strauss, R.
  Schärpe und die Blüme, Die
    (transl. Schlegel)
    Liebe und Eifersucht+   1807 Hoffmann,
                                           E. T. A.

Camus, Albert (1913-1960)
  Etat du siège, L' (1948)
    Belagerungszustand, Der+   1970 Keleman, M.

Carmouche, Pierre François Adrien and E. Scribe
  Trilby (1823)
    Trilby+   1835 Truhn, F. H.
    Trilby+   1845 Schmitt, G. A.

Carpani, Giuseppe
    Uniform, Der+   1805 Weigl, J.

Carroll, P. V.
  Wayward Saint, The (1955)
    Widerspenstige Heilige,   1968 Lothar, M.
      Der+

Castet, Nicolas
  Bûcheron, Le (1763) (with J.-F. Guichard)
    Holzhauer, Der+   1778 Benda, G.

Cellini, Benvenuto (1500-1571)
  Autobiography (1562) (published 1728)
    Benvenuto Cellini   1849 Lachner, F.

Cervantes, Miguel de (1547-1616)
  Don Quixote (1605, 1615)
    Don Quichote+   1908 Beer-Walbrunn, A.
    Don Quichotte   1910 Heuberger, R.
    Don Quijote   1947 Maasz, G.
    Don Quixote+   1898 Kienzl, W.
    Don Quixote der Zweyte   1795 Dittersdorf, K.
    Don Quixote in dem   1727 Müller, A.
      Mohrengebirge
    Don Quixotte   1788 Beecke, I. von
    Hochzeit des Camacho, Die   1827 Mendelssohn, F.
  Cueva de salamanca, La
    (from *Ocho comedias y ocho
      entremesses nuevos*) (1615)
    Bettelstudent, Der+   1785 Winter, P.
    Höhle von Salamanca, Die+   1923 Paumgartner, B.
    Zauberer, Der+   1926 Mojsisovics, R.
  Gitanella, La (1913)
    Preciosa   1821 Weber, C. M. von
  Retablo de las maravillas (1605)
    Wundertheater, Das   1949 Henze, H. W.

Chabannes, Rochon de
  Alcidor+   1825 Spontini, G.

Chamfort, Nicolas (1741-1794)
  Jeune Indienne, La (1765)
    Fernando und Yariko   1784 Schack, B.
  Marchand de Smyrne, Le (1770)
    Kaufmann von Smyrna, Der   1771 Vogler, G. J.
    Kaufmann von Smyrna, Der+   1773 Holly, F. A.
    Kaufmann von Smyrna, Der+   1773 Stegmann, C. D.

Chateauvieux, Armand François
  Aveugles de Franconville, Les
    (with A. Croizette) (1802)
    Augenarzt, Der+   1811 Gyrowetz, A.

Chatrian, Pierre Alexandre (1826-1890)
    Polnische Jude, Der+   1901 Weis, K.
      (with E. Erckmann)

Chekhov, Anton (1860-1904)
  Bear, The (1888)
    Bär, Der+   1963 Dressel, E.
    Ungeheuer, Das+   1914 Walbrunn, A.
  Cherry Orchard (1904)
    Kirschgarten, Der+   1984 Kelterborn, R.
  Proposal, The (1888)
    Heiratsantrag, Der+   1960 Röttger, H.
  Romance with a Double-Bass (1896)
    Bassgeige, Die+   1978 Kounadis, A.

Choler, Adolphe
  Six Demoiselles à marier
    (with A. Jaime) (1856)
    Zehn Mädchen und kein   1862   Suppé, F. von
    Mann+

Claudel, Paul (1868-1955)
  Annonce faite à Marie, L' (1910)
    Verkündigung+   1948   Braunfels, W.

Coffey, Charles (late 17th century-1745)
  Devil to Pay, The (1731)
    Teufel ist los, Der   1743   Standfuss, J. C.
  Merry Cobbler, The
    Lustige Schuster, Der+   1759   Standfuss, J. C.
    Lustige Schuster, Der+   1770   Holly, F. A.

Collé, Charles (1709-1783)
  Partie de chasse de Henri IV, La
    (prod. 1774)
    Jagd, Die   1770   Hiller, J. A.

Coppée, François (1842-1908)
    Strike der Schmiede, Der+   1897   Beer, M.J.

Corneille, Pierre (1606-1684)
  Andromède (1647)
    Errettete Unschuld, Die+   1675   Franck, J. W.
  Bellerophon
    Bellerophon+   1708   Graupner, C.
  Cid, Le (1637)
    Cid, Der   1865   Cornelius, P.
    Rächer, Der+   1846   Schindelmeisser,
                                             L.
    Rodrigo und Zimene+   1821   Aiblinger, J. K.

Corradi, Giulio Cesare (d. ca. 1702)
  Gerusalemme liberata
    Eroberte Jerusalem, Die+   1722   Schürmann, G. C.

Coster, Charles de
  Smetse Smee
    Schmied von Gent, Der   1932   Schreker, F.
  Also:
    Uilenspiegel+   1913   Braunfels, W.

Coubier, Heinz
    Komödiantin, Die+   1970   Chemin-Petit, H.

Cramer, C. G. [Karl Gottlob Kramer]
  Peter Schmoll und seine   1802   Weber, C. M. von
    Nachbarn

Croizette, Armand
  Aveugles de Franconville, Les (1802)
    (with A. F. Chateauvrieux)
  Augenarzt, Der+   1811   Gyrowetz, A.

Crommelynck, Ferdinand (1886-1970)
  Cocu magnifique, Le (1921)
  Gewaltige Hahnrei, Der+   1932   Goldschmidt, B.

Cuno, Heinrich
  Bibiena+   1829   Pixis, J. P.

Dahn, Felix (1834-1912)
  Faule Hans, Der+   1885   Ritter, A.

Dante Alighieri (1265-1321)
  Divine Comedy (ca. 1307-21):
    L'Inferno, Francesca da Rimini episode, V (116-42)
  Francesca da Rimini   1877   Goetz, H.

Da Ponte, Lorenzo (1749-1838)
  Don Pedros Heimkehr+   1952   Erismann, H.
                                         after W. A. Mozart

Daudet, Alphonse (1840-1897)
  Tartarin de Tarascon (1885)
    Tartarin von Tarascon+   1965   Radermacher, F.
    Tartarin von Tarascon   1977   Niehaus, M.

David, Domenico
  Forza della virtù, La (1693)
  Forza della virtù, La   1700   Keiser, R.

Deinhardstein, Johann Ludwig Ferdinand (1794-1859)
  Hans Sachs (1829)
  Hans Sachs   1840   Lortzing, A.

Delacour, Alfred [Alfred Charlemagne Lartigue]
  Dominos roses, Les (with A. Hennequin) (1876)
  Opernball, Der   1898   Heuberger, R.
  Also:
  Prinz Methusalem+   1877   Strauss, J., Jr.
    (with V. Wilder)

Dickens, Charles (1812-1870)
  Cricket on the Hearth, The (1845)
  Heimchen am Herd, Das+   1896   Goldmark, K.

Dobrovensky, Roald G.
   Behind the Treble Clef
     Boom—Boom Land+   1978   Katzer, G.

Dorbeil, C.
     Liebhaber als Automat,   1782   André, J.
     Der+

Dostoevsky, Fyodor (1821–1881)
   Brothers Karamazov, The (1880)
     Karamasows, Die+   1945   Coenen, P.
   Crime and Punishment (1866)
     Raskolnikoff+   1848   Sutermeister, H.

Drachmann, Holger (1846–1908)
   Der var engag (1885)
     Es war einmal+   1900   Zemlinsky, A. von

Dumaniant, Antoine Jean
   Guerre ouverte, La
     Mitternachtsstunde+   1788   Danzi, F.

Dumanoir, Pinel
   Don César de Bazin (with A. P. d'Ennery)
     Don Cesar+   1885   Dellinger, R.

Dumas, Alexandre [Dumas père] (1802–1870)
   Demoiselles de Saint Cyr, Les (1843)
     Heirat wider Willen, Die+ 1905   Humperdinck, E.

Duport, Paul
   Alessandro Stradella (1837)
     (with P. A. P. Pittaud de Forges)
     Alessandro Stradella   1844   Flotow, F. von
   Cosimo (with A. Villain de
     Saint-Hilaire) (1835)
     Caramo+   1839   Lortzing, A.

Dürrenmatt, Friedrich (1921–)
   Besuch der alten Dame, Der (1956)
     Besuch der alten Dame, Der 1971   Einem, G. von
   Engel kommt nach Babylon, Ein (1953)
     Engel kommt nach Babylon, 1977   Kelterborn, R.
     Ein+

Duval, Alexandre (1767–1842)
   Jeunesse de Henri V, La
     Zum Grossadmiral+   1847   Lortzing, A.
   Maison à vendre
     Haus ist zu verkaufen,   1806   Hummel, J. N.
     Dies+

Duval, A. (cont.)
  Souper imprévu, Le
  Ungebetenen Gäste, Die+   1805 Hoffmann,
                                       E. T. A.

Eichendorff, Joseph Freiherr von (1788-1857)
  Schloss Dürande, Das (1837)
  Schloss Dürande, Das   1943 Schoeck, O.

Ennery, Adolphe Phillipe d' (1811-1899)
  Don César de Bazan (with P. Dumanoir)
  Don Cesar+   1885 Dellinger, R.

Erckmann, Emile (1822-1899)
  Polnische Jude, Der+   1901 Weis, K.
  (with P. E. Chatrian)

Etienne, Charles-Guillaume (1777-1845)
  Rossignol, Le
  Nachtigall und Rabe+   1818 Weigl, J.

Euripides (ca. 480 B.C.-ca. 405 B.C.)
  Alcestis, 438 B.C.
  Alceste+   1680 Franck, J.W.
  Alceste+   1693 Strungk, N. A.
  Alceste+   1773 Schweitzer, A.
  Alceste+   1780 Wolf, E. W.
  Alceste+   1786 Benda, F.
  Alkestis+   1924 Wellesz, E.
  Bacchae, The, 408-406 B.C.
  Bassariden, Die   1966 Henze, H. W.
  Bakchantinnen, Die   1931 Wellesz, E.
  Helen, 412 B.C.
  Ägyptische Helena, Die   1928 Strauss, R.

Falbaire, C. G. F. [Charles George Fenouillot de
  Falbères]
  Deux Avares, Les (1770)
  Grab des Mufti, Das   1779 Hiller, J. A.

Falckenberg, Otto
  Doktor Eisenbart+   1922 Zilcher, H.

Favart, Charles-Simon (1710-1792)
  Amours de Bastien et Bastienne, Les (1753)
    (with M. Favart)
  Bastien und Bastienne   1768 Mozart, W. A.
  Annette et Lubin
    (with M. Favart) (1762)
  Liebe auf dem Lande, Die+ 1768 Hiller, J. A.

Favart, C.-S. (cont.)
  Belle Arsène, La (1773)
    Arsene+   1779   Seydelmann, F.
  Fée Urgèle, La (1765)
    Lisuarte und Darlioette+   1766   Hiller, J. A.
  Fortune au village, La (1760)
    Grosse Loos, Das+   1774   Wolf, E. W.
  Rosière de Salency, Le (1769)
    Rosenfest, Das+   1770   Wolf, E. W.
  *Soliman II, ou Les trois
    sultanes* (1761)
    Soliman der Zweyte   1799   Süssmayr, F. X.

Favart, Marie (1727-1772)
  *Amours de Bastien et Bastienne,
    Les* (with C.-S. Favart) (1753)
    Bastien und Bastienne   1768   Mozart, W. A.
  Annette et Lubin (1762)
    (with C.-S. Favart)
    Liebe auf dem Lande, Die+ 1768   Hiller, J. A.
  Also:
    Bezauberten, Die+   1777   André, J.

Feutsking, Friedrich Christian
  Almira (1704)
    Almira+   1706   Keiser, R.

Fischart, Johann (1546-1590)
  Till Eulenspiegel Reimenweiss (1572)
    Till Eulenspiegel+   1902   Reznicek, E. N.
                                          von

Flaubert, Gustave (1821-1880)
  Madame Bovary (1856)
    Madame Bovary+   1967   Sutermeister, H.
  Salammbô (1862)
    Salambo+   1926   Böttcher, L.

Fouqué, Friedrich Heinrich Karl, Freiherr de la Motte
  (1777-1843)
  Undine (1811)
    Undine   1816   Hoffmann,
                                          E. T. A.
    Undine   1845   Lortzing, A.

Freytag, Gustav (1816-1895)
    Freikorporal, Der+   1931   Vollerthun, G.

García Lorca, Federico (1898-1936)
   Amor de Don Perlimplín con Belisa en su jardín
      (1931)
      In seinem Garten liebt   1962   Fortner, W.
      Don Perlimplín Belisa
   Bodas de sangre (1933)
      Bluthochzeit, Die   1957   Fortner, W.
   Zapatera prodigiosa, La (1931)
      Merkwürdige Frau des   1982   Zimmermann, U.
      Schusters, Die+
   Also:
      Wald, Der+   1953   Fortner, W.

Gatti, Emmerich von
      Dollarprinzessin, Die   1907   Fall, L.

Gay, John (1685-1732)
   Beggar's Opera, The (1728)
      Dreigroschenoper, Die   1928   Weill, K.

Geibel, Emanuel (1815-1884)
      Meister Andrea+   1920   Weingartner, F.

Gerstenberg, Heinrich Wilhelm von (1737-1823)
   Ariadne auf Naxos (1767)
      Ariadne auf Naxos   1775   Benda, G.

Ginzkey, Franz Karl von (1871-1963)
      Herrn Dürers Bild+   1927   Mraczek, J. G.

Giraud, Giovanni
      Herr Dandolo+   1914   Siegel, R.

Goethe, Johann Wolfgang von (1749-1832)
   Claudine von Villa Bella (1776)
      Claudine von Villa Bella+   1778   André, J.
      Claudine von Villa Bella+   1780   Kienlen, J. C.
      Claudine von Villa Bella   1789   Reichardt, J. F.
      Claudine von Villa Bella   1815   Schubert, F.
   Erwin und Elmire (1774)
      Erwin und Elmire+   1775   André, J.
      Erwin und Elmire+   1781   Vogler, G. J.
      Erwin und Elmire   1793   Reichardt, J. F.
      Erwin und Elmire   1916   Schoeck, O.
   Faust, Pt. 1 (1808), *Pt. 2*
      (1832)
      Doktor Faust+   1797   Walter, I.
      Faust+   1887   Zöllner, H.
      Faust I. Teil+   1905   Kistler, C.
   Götz von Berlichingen (1773)
      Götz von Berlichingen+   1902   Goldmark, K.

Goethe, J. W. von (cont.)
  Jery und Bätely (1780)
    Jery und Bäteli+   1790   Winter, P.
  Laune des Verliebten, Die
     (1767)
    Laune des Verliebten, Die+ 1949   Dressel, E.
  Märchen (1794)
    Märchen von der schönen   1969   Klebe, G.
      Lilie+
  Mitschuldigen, Die (1769)
    Mitschuldigen, Die+   1957   Riethmüller, H.
  Nausikaa (1827)
    Nausikaa+   1967   Reutter, H.
  Satyros (1773)
    Satyros+   1923   Baussnern, W. von
  Scherz, List und Rache (1784)
    Scherz, List und Rache+   1790   Winter, P.
    Scherz, List und   ca. 1801   Hoffmann,
      Rache+   E. T. A.
    Scherz, List und Rache+   1856   Bruch, M.
    Scherz, List und Rache+   1928   Wellesz, E.
    Scherz, List und Rache+   1961   Leinert, F.
  Stella (1776)
    Stella+   1951   Bloch, W.
  Zauberlehrling, Der (1797)
    Zauberlehrling, Der+   1907   Döbber, J.

Gogol, Nicolai (1809-1852)
  Inspector General, The (1836)
    Revisor, Der   1957   Egk, W.
  Taras Bulba (1835)
    Taras Bulba+   1935   Richter, E.

Goldoni, Carlo (1707-1793)
  Arcifano, Re dei Mattei
    Arcifano+   1777   Dittersdorf, K.
  Feudatario, Il
    Dorfdeputierten, Die+   1772   Wolf, E. W.
    Dorfdeputierten, Die+   1783   Schubaur, J. L.
    Dorfdeputierten, Die   1786   Dieter, C. F.
  Speziale, Lo (1755)
    Apotheke, Die+   1771   Neefe, C. G.
  Ventaglio, Il
    Fächer, Der+   1929   Kunz, E.
    Fächer, Der+   1930   Toch, E.
  Also:
    Diener zweier Herren, Der+ 1936   Bloch, W.
    Mirandolina+   1907   Scholz, B.
    Tartarische Gesetz, Das+   1780   Zumsteeg, J.
    Wirtin von Pinsk, Die+   1938   Mohaupt, R.

Goldoni, C. and C. Favart
  Ninette à la cour (1755)
    Lottchen am Hofe+   1767   Hiller, J. A.

Goldsmith, Oliver (1731-1774)
  Edwin and Angelina
    Erwin und Elmire   1793   Reichardt, J. F.

Goll, Yvan [Isaac Lang] (1891-1950)
  Melusine (publ. 1956)
    Melusine+   1971   Reimann, A.

Gombrowicz, Witold (1904-1969)
  Princess Ivona (1938)
    **Yvonne, Prinzessin von
      Burgund+**   1973   Blacher, B.

Gotter, Friedrich Wilhelm (1746-1797)
  Kobold, Der (1813)
    Kobold, Der+   1813   Himmel, F. H.

Gotthelf, Jeremias [Albert Bitzius] (1797-1854)
  Schwarze Spinne, Die (1842)
    Schwarze Spinne, Die+   1932   Hauer, J. M.
    Schwarze Spinne, Die+   1936   Sutermeister, H.
    Schwarze Spinne, Die   1949   Burkhard, W.

Gottschall, Rudolf von (1823-1909)
  Rose vom Kaukasus, Die
    Sarema+   1897   Zemlinsky, A. von

Gouffé, Armand
  Bouffe et le tailleur, Le (with P. Villiers) (1804)
    Sänger und der Schneider,   1814   Driesberg,
      Der+   F. von

Gozzi, Carlo (1720-1806)
  Arlecchino
    Arlecchino   1917   Busoni, F.
  Donna serpente, La (1762)
    Feen, Die   1833   Wagner, R.
  Pittochi fortunati, I
    Tartarische Gesetz, Das+   1779   André, J.
    Tartarische Gesetz, Das+   1780   Zumsteeg, J.
  Re Cervo, Il (1762)
    König Hirsch   1956   Henze, H.W.
  Re Turandot (1762)
    Turandot+   1817   Danzi, F.
    Turandot   1917   Busoni, F.

Grabbe, Christian Dieter (1801-1836)
  Don Juan und Faust (1829)
    Don Juan und Faust+   1950   Reutter, H.

Grillparzer, Franz (1791-1872)
  Des Meeres und der Liebe Wellen (1829)
    Hero und Leander+   1912   Caró, P.
    Hero und Leander   1966   Bialas, G.
  Kloster bei Sendomir, Das (1828)
    Mönch von Sendomir, Der+   1907   Lorentz, A.
  König von Samarkand, Der
    König von Samarkand, Der+   1910   Mikorey, F.
  Sappho (1817)
    Sappho+   1917   Kaun, H.
  Traum ein Leben (1831)
    Traum, Der+   1909   Mraczek, J.G.
    Traum ein Leben, Der   1937   Braunfels, W.
    Traumleben+   1963   Kont, P.

Grimm, Jacob (1785-1863) and Wilhelm Grimm (1786-1859)
  Bremer Stadtmusikanten, Die
    Bremer Stadtmusikanten,   1949   Bergese, H.
      Die+
    Bremer Stadtmusikanten,   1949   Mohaupt, R.
      Die+
    Bremer Stadtmusikanten,   1972   Auenmüller, H.
      Die+
  Ewige Arzt, Der
    Ewige Arzt, Der+   1956   Bresgen, C.
  Fischer un syne Fru, De
    Fischer un syne Fru,   1936   Brüggemann, K.
      De+
    Vom Fischer un syner Fru   1930   Schoeck, O.
  *Geschichte von dem König und
    der klugen Frau*
    Kluge, Die   1943   Orff, C.
  Gevatter Tod
    Fremde, Der+   1920   Kaun, H.
  Hänsel und Gretel
    Hänsel und Gretel   1893   Humperdinck, E.
  Ilsebill
    Ilsebill+   1903   Klose, F.
  Jorinda und Jorgile
    Jorinda und Jorgile+   1934   Sutermeister, H.
  König Drosselbart
    König Drosselbart+   1958   Noll, D.
  Mond, Der
    Mond, Der   1939   Orff, C.
  Rumpelstilzchen
    Rumpelstilzchen+   1911   Büttner, P.

Grimmelshausen, Johann Hans Jakob Christoffel von
  (1622–1676)
  Simplicissimus (1669)
    Des Simplicius			1949	Hartmann, K. A.
    Simplicissimus Jugend+
    Simplicius, Der+			1912	Huber, H.

Guichard, Henri
  Ulysses+				1722	Keiser, R.

Guichard, Jean-François
  Bûcheron, Le (with N. Castet) (1763)
    Holzhauer, Der+			1778	Benda, G.

Guillet, P.
  Quart-d'Heure de silence, Une (1804)
    Wette+				1805	Weber, B. A.

Guimerà, Angel (1849–1924)
  Filla del mar, El (1886)
    Liebesketten+			1912	Albert, E. d'
  Terra baixa (1896)
    Tiefland				1903	Albert, E. d'

Hacks, Peter (1928–)
  Schuhu und die fliegende Prinzessin, Der (1966)
    Schuhu, Der+			1976	Zimmermann, U.

Hafner, Philipp (1735–1764)
  Furchtsame, Der (1763)
    Neusonntagskind, Das+		1793	Müller, W.
  Reisenden Komödienten, Die
    (1762)
    Schwestern von Prag, Die		1794	Müller, W.

Hardt, Ernst [Ernst Stöckhardt]
  Schirin und Getraude (1913)
    Schirin und Getraude+		1920	Graener, P.

Hauff, Wilhelm (1802–1827)
  Kalif Storch
    Kalif Storch+			1885	Eidens, J.
  Kalte Herz, Das
    Kalte Herz, Das+			1908	Konta, R.
    Kalte Herz, Das+			1935	Lothar, M.
    Kalte Herz, Das+			1938	Brüggemann, K.
    Kalte Herz, Das			1943	Schultze, N.
  Lichtenstein (1826)
    Lichtenstein+			1846	Lindpaintner, P.
  Rote Stiefel, Der
    Rote Stiefel, Der+			1951	Sutermeister, H.

Hauff, W. (cont.)
  Scheik von Alexandria, Der (1827)
    Junge Lord, Der   1965   Henze, H.W.

Hauptmann, Carl (1858-1921)
    Heilige, Die+   1920   Gurlitt, M.

Hauptmann, Elisabeth
    Jasager, Der   1930   Weill, K.

Hauptmann, Gerhart (1862-1946)
  Elga (1905)
    Elga+   1916   Lendvai, E.
    Elga+   1939   Weishappel, R.
  Hanneles Himmelfahrt (1893)
    Hanneles Himmelfahrt+   1927   Graener, P.
  Versunkene Glocke, Die (1896)
    Versunkene Glocke, Die+   1899   Zöllner, H.
  Winterballade (1917)
    Doppelgängerin, Die+   1967   Meyerowitz, J.

Hauser
    Don Juans Sohn+   1928   Wunsch, H.
      (with Almquist)

Hebbel, Friedrich (1813-1863)
  Agnes Bernauer (1851)
    Agnes Bernauer+   ca. 1935   Messner, J.
  Genoveva (1843)
    Genoveva   1850   Schumann, R.
  Judith (1841)
    Holofernes+   1923   Reznicek, E. N.
                                                  von
    Judith+   1921   Ettinger, M.
  Moloch (1849)
    Moloch+   1906   Schillings, M.
  Rubin, Der (1851)
    Rubin, Der+   1893   Albert, E. d'
    Rubin, Der+   1938   Jenny, A.

Heine, Heinrich (1797-1856)
  Deutschland (1844)
    Aus Deutschland+   1981   Kagel, M.
  Memoiren des Herrn von Schabel
    Fliegende Holländer, Der   1843   Wagner, R.
  William Ratcliff (1823)
    Ratcliff+   1914   Andreae, V.
    William Ratcliff+   1909   Dopper, C.
    William Ratcliff   1982   Ostendorf, J.P.
  Also:
    Kain+   1952   Schmidtmann, F.
    Liebeswogen+   1903   Gerlach, T.

Hèle, Thomas d'
    Apollo's Wettgesang+   1808   Sutor, W.

Hennequin, Alfred
   Domino roses, Les (with A. Delacour) (1876)
   Opernball, Der   1898   Heuberger, R.

Henry, Marc [Achille d'Ailly-Vaucheret]
   Yeux morts, Les (1897)
   Toten Augen, Die   1916   Albert, E. d'

Herder, Johann Gottfried (1744-1803)
   Afrikanische Rechtspruch, Der
   Bürgschaft, Die   1932   Weill, K.

Hertz, Wilhelm (1835-1902)
   Heinrich von Schwaben
   Junker Heinz+   1886   Perfall, K. von

Hoffmann, E(rnst) T(heodor) A(madeus) (1776-1822)
   Bergwerke zu Falun, Die
     (1819)
   Haideschacht, Der+   1868   Holstein, F. von
   Brautwahl, Die (1820)
   Brautwahl, Die   1912   Busoni, F.
   Fräulein von Scuderi, Das
     (1819)
   Cardillac   1926   Hindemith, P.
   Goldschmied von Toledo,   1919   Offenbach, J.,
   Der+   Stern, and Zamara
   Klein Zaches (1819)
   Zinnober+   1898   Hausegger, S. von
   Majorat, Das (1817)
   Eiserne Pforte, Die+   1823   Weigl, J.
   Meister Martin der Küfner und
     seine Gesellen (1819)
   Meister Martin und seine
   Gesellen+   1879   Weissheimer, W.
   Prinzessin Brambilla (1820)
   Prinzessin Brambilla   1909   Braunfels, W.
   Signor Formica (1819)
   Salvator Rosa+   1832   Rastrelli, J.

Hofmannsthal, Hugo von (1874-1929)
   Lucidor (1910)
   Arabella   1933   Strauss, R.
   Bergwerk zu Falun, Das (1933)
   Bergwerk zu Falun, Das   1961   Wagner-Régeny, R.
   Tor und der Tod, Der (1893)
   Tor und der Tod, Der+   1928   Brehme, H.

Holberg, Ludvig
  Don Ranudo
    Don Ranudo   1919   Schoeck, O.

Hölderlin, Friedrich (1770-1843)
  Antigonae (transl. of Sophocles)
    Antigonae   1949   Orff, C.
  Tod des Empedokles, Der (1826)
    Tod des Empedokles, Der+   1966   Reutter, H.

Homer
  Iliad, The
    Penthesilea   1927   Schoeck, O.
  Odyssey, The
    Circe+   1734   Keiser, R.
    Circe+   1948   Egk, W.
    Circe (Des Ulysses   1696   Keiser, R.
      erster Theil)+
    Odysseus+   1942   Reutter, H.
    Odysseus bei Circe+   1938   Trantow, H.
    Odysseus' Tod+   1903   Bungert, A.
    Odysseus und die Sirenen+ 1950   Goldberg, T.

Horvath, Ödön von (1901-1938)
  Figaro lässt sich scheiden
    (1937)
    Figaro lässt sich scheiden 1963   Klebe, G.
  Jüngste Tag, Der (1937)
    Jüngste Tag, Der+   1980   Klebe, G.

Hugo, Victor (1892-1885)
  Marie Tudor (1833)
    Günstling, Der   1935   Wagner-Régeny, R.
  Notre Dame de Paris (1831)
    Notre Dame+   1914   Schmidt, F.

Hui Lan-Ki
    Kreidekreis, Der+   1933   Zemlinsky, A. von

Hutt, Johann
    Das war ich+   1902   Blech, L.

Huxley, Aldous (1894-1963)
  Devils of Loudun, The
    Teufel von Loudun, Der 1969   Penderecki, K.

Ibsen, Henrik (1828-1906)
  Ghosts (1881)
    Gespenstersonate, Die+ 1930   Weismann, J.
    Gespenstersonate, Die   1984   Reimann, A.

Ibsen, H. (cont.)
  Peer Gynt (1867)
    Peer Gynt   1938   Egk, W.
    Peer Gynt+   not perf   Ullmann, V.
  Also:
    Fest auf Solhaug, Das+   1899   Stenhammar, V.

Immermann, Karl (1796-1840)
  Merlin (1832)
    Merlin+   1887   Rüfer, P.
    Merlin+   1913   Draeseke, F.
  Also:
    Ghismonda+   1895   Albert, E. d'

Irving, Washington (1783-1859)
  Student of Salamanca, The
    Alchymist, Der   1830   Spohr, L.

Jaime, Adolphe
  Six Demoiselles à marier (with A. Choler) (1856)
    Zehn Mädchen und kein   1862   Suppé, F. von
      Mann+

Jansen, Ferdinand
  Hypatia
    Menandra+   1925   Kaun, H.

Jarry, Alfred (1873-1907)
  Ubu Roi (1896)
    König Ubü   1984   Hummel, F.

Jersild, Per Christian (1935-)
  To Warmer Lands (1961)
    Reise, Die+   1969   Werle, L. J.

Jókai, Maurus [Mór] (1825-1904)
  Saffi
    Zigeunerbaron, Der   1885   Strauss, J., Jr.

Jonson, Ben (1573-1637)
  Epicoene (1609)
    Lord Spleen+   1930   Lothar, M.
    Schweigsame Frau, Die   1935   Strauss, R.

Jouy, (Joseph)-Etienne de (1764-1846)
  Vestale, La (1807)
    Vestalin, Die+   1814   Guhr, K. W. F.

Joyce, James (1882-1941)
  Ulysses (1921)
    Stephan Climax+   1986   Zender, H.

Jünger, Johann Friedrich
   Komödie aus dem Stegreif, Die (1794)
     Opernprobe, Die   1851 Lortzing, A.

Justinius, Marcus Junianus
   Historiae Philippicae
     Lampedo   1779 Vogler, G. J.

Kadelburg, G.
   Zum Weissen Rössl (with O. Blumenthal) (1897)
     Im Weissen Rössl   1930 Benatzky, R.

Kafka, Franz (1883-1924)
   Landarzt, Ein (1919)
     Landarzt, Ein   1953 Henze, H. W.
   Prozess, Der (1915)
     Prozess, Der   1953 Einem, G. von
   Schloss, Das (1922)
     Schloss, Das+   ca. 1986 Laporte, A.

Kaiser, Georg (1878-1945)
   Protagonist, Der (1926)
     Protagonist, Der   1926 Weill, K.
   Rosamunde Floris (1940)
     Rosamunde Floris   1960 Blacher, B.

Kalidasa (5th century?)
   Shakuntala
     Sakuntala+   1884 Weingartner, F.

Kaltneker, Hans
     Wunder der Heliane, Das+ 1927 Korngold, E.

Kazantzakis, Nikos (1883-1957)
   Christ Recrucified (1938)
     Griechische Passion, Die 1961 Martinů, B.

Keller, Gottfried (1819-1890)
   Eugenia
     Claudia amata+   1952 Driessler, J.
   Grüne Heinrich, Der (1855)
     Grüne Heinrich, Der+   1922 Ebner, G.
   Kleider machen Leute (1874)
     Kleider machen Leute+ 1910 Zemlinsky, A. von
     Kleider machen Leute+ 1973 Rubin, M.

Kerner, Justinius (1786-1862)
     Bär, Der+   1938 Stierlin, J.
     (with L. Uhland)

Kind, Friedrich (1768-1843)
  Nachtlager in Granada, Das
  Nachtlager in Granada, Das 1834 Kreutzer, C.

Klabund [Alfred Henschke] (1890-1928)
  Doktor Fausts Höllenfahrt+ 1965 Engelmann, H. U.

Kleist, Heinrich von (1777-1811)
  Amphytryon (1807)
    Alkmene   1961 Klebe, G.
    Amphitryon+   1951 Oboussier, R.
    Amphitryon+   1958 Hermann, H.
  Julietta
    Julietta+   1959 Erbse, H.
  Kätchen von Heilbronn, Das
    (1810)
    Kätchen von Heilbronn,   1846 Lux, F.
    Das+
    Kätchen von Heilbronn,   1881 Reinthaler, K.
    Das+
    Kätchen von Heilbronn,   1958 Bloch, W.
    Das+
  Penthesilea (1807)
    Penthesilea+   1927 Ritter, R.
    Penthesilea   1927 Schoeck, O.
  Prinz Friedrich von Homburg,
    Der (1810)
    Prinz von Homburg, Der+   1935 Graener, P.
    Prinz von Homburg, Der   1960 Henze, H. W.
  Verlobung in San Domingo, Die
    (1811)
    Verlobung in San Domingo, 1957 Zillig, W.
    Die+
    Verlobung in San Domingo, 1963 Egk, W.
    Die
  Zerbrochene Krug, Der (1811)
    Zerbrochene Krug, Der   1971 Geissler, F.

Komarcek, Johann Nepomuk
  Marie von Montalban+   1800 Winter, P.

Körner, Theodor (1791-1813)
  Dorval
    Dorval+   1913 Zehntner, L.
  Hans Heilings Felsen (1811)
    Hans Heiling   1833 Marschner, H.

Kotzebue, August von (1761-1819)
  Kreuzfahrer, Die (1803)
    Kreuzfahrer, Die   1845 Spohr, L.

Kotzebue, A. von (cont.)
  Rehbock, Der
    Wildschütz, Der   1842 Lortzing, A.
  Also:
    Eulenspiegel+   1889 Kistler, C.
    Feuerprobe, Die+   1920 Dost, W.
    Käficht, Der+   1925 Kormann, H.

Kraszewski, Jozef Korwin
  Manru+   1901 Paderewski, I.

Lalli, Domenico [Sebastiano Biancardi]
  Amor di figlio, L' (1715)
    Grossmüthige Tomyris, Die 1717 Keiser, R.

Lane, Dorothy
  Happy End   1929 Weill, K.

Laube, Heinrich (1806-1884)
  Spanische Nacht+   1937 Bodart, E.

Laun, Friedrich
  Gespensterbuch (1811) (with J. Apel)
    Freischütz, Der   1826 Weber, C. M. von

Lautréamont, Comte de [Isidore Ducasse] (1846-1870)
  Chants de Maldoror, Les (1868)
    Maldoror+   1970 Niehaus, M.

Lavrenyov, Boris Andreyevich (1891-1959)
    Letzte Schuss, Der+   1967 Matthus, S.

Lem, Stanislav (1921-)
  Friend of the Automathias, The, and *The Story of the
      Three Storytelling Machines*
    Kyberiade+   1970 Meyer, K.

Lemierre, Antoine-Marin (1723-1793)
  Veuve de Malabar, La
    Jessonda   1823 Spohr, L.
  Also:
    Lanassa+   1805 Tuczek, V. F.

Lenz, Jakob Michael (1751-1792)
  Engländer, Der (1776)
    R. Hot+   1977 Goldmann, F.
  Soldaten, Die (1775)
    Soldaten+   1930 Gurlitt, M.
    Soldaten, Die   1965 Zimmermann, B. A.

Lesage, Alain-René (1668-1747)
Diable boîteux, Le (1707)
Neue krumme Teufel, 1759 Haydn, F. J.
Der+

Lilienfein, Heinrich
Stier von Olivera, Der+ 1918 Albert, E. d'

Livigni, Filippo
Giannina e Bernadone (1791)
Rothe Käppchen, Das 1790 Dittersdorf, K.

Lope de Vega Carpio, Félix (1562-1635)
Mejor imposible, El
Unmöglichste von allem, 1897 Urspruch, A.
Das+
Also:
Hirtenlegende+ 1936 Bodart, E.
Liebeskette, Die+ 1961 Lehner, F.
Schlaue Susanna, Die+ 1952 Lehner, F.

Ma-Chi-Yunn
Traum des Liu-Tung, Der 1965 Yun, I.

Madach, Imre
Tragedy of Mankind
Tragödie der Menschheit, 1981 Hamel, P. M.
Die+

Mann, Heinrich (1871-1950)
Kleine Stadt, Die (1909)
Kleine Stadt, Die+ 1957 Lehner, F.

Marivaux, Pierre Carlet de Chamblain de (1688-1763)
Jeu de l'amour et du hasard, Le (1730)
Spiel von Liebe und 1982 Rosenfeld, G.
Zufall, Das+
Also:
Kinder der Natur, Die+ 1778 Aspelmayr, F.

Marlowe, Christopher (1564-1593)
Doctor Faustus (1589)
Doktor Faust 1922 Busoni, F.

Marmontel, Jean-François (1723-1799)
Silvain (1770)
Walder+ 1776 Benda, G.
Zemire et Azor (1771)
Zemire und Azor+ 1776 Baumgarten, C. G.
von
Zemire und Azor 1819 Spohr, L.

Marsollier, Jean Baptiste
   Gulnare, ou l'Esclave persanne
   (1798)
    Gülnare+   1800   Süssmayr, F. X.

Matusche, Alfred
   Van Gogh (1966)
    Vincent+   1979   Kunad, R.

Maupassant, Guy de (1850-1893)
   Boule-de-suif, Le (1880)
    Fettlöschen+   1976   Wahren, K. H.
   Also:
    Auszeichnung, Die+   1959   Poser, H.
    Gluckerich, Der+   1965   Urbanner, E.
    Heimkehr, Die+   1954   Mihalovici, M.

Maurois, André (1885-1967)
    Palast Hotel Thanatos+   1972   Einfeldt, D.

Meissner, Leopold Florian
   Evangelimann, Der (1894)
    Evangelimann, Der   1895   Kienzl, W.

Mélesville, Anne Honoré Joseph
   Bourgemestre de Saardam, Le (1818)
    (with   Merle and de Boirie)
    Zar und Zimmermann   1837   Lortzing, A.
   Cathérine (with N. Brazier)
    Goldene Kreuz, Das+   1875   Brüll, I.
   Also:
    Zwei Prinzen, Die+   1845   Esser, H.
    (with E. Scribe)

Melville, Hermann (1819-1891)
   Bartleby the Scrivener (1853)
    Bartleby   1967   Niehaus, M.

Menachmi
   Plautus
    Zwillingskomödie   1954   Mohaupt, R.

Menander, 342-292 B.C.
    Athener Komödie+   1964   Vogt, H.

Menasci, Guido
   Redenzione, La
    Erlösung, Die+   1895   Scharrer, A.

Mercier-Dupaty, Emanuel
    Mathilde von Guise+   1810   Hummel, J. N.

Mérimée, Prosper (1830-1870)
Vénus d'Ille, La (1837)
   Baskische Venus, Die+   1928 Wetzler, H.H.
   Venus   1922 Schoeck, O.

Merle, Jean Toussaint
Bourgemestre de Saardam, Le (with Eugène Cantiran
   de Boirie and A. H. J. Mélesville)
   Zar und Zimmermann   1837 Lortzing, A.

Metastasio, Pietro (1698-1782)
Ciro riconosciuto, Il (1736)
   Cyrus und Astyages+   1818 Mosel, J. F. von

Meyer, Conrad Ferdinand (1825-1898)
Hochzeit des Mönchs, Die
   (1884)
   Hochzeit des Mönchs, Die+ 1886 Klughardt, A.
Jürg Jentsch (1876)
   Jürg Jentsch+   1929 Kaminski, H.
Also:
   Fingerhütchen+   1950 Sutermeister, H.
   Füsse im Feuer, Die+   1955 Schibler, E.
   Füsse im Feuer, Die+   1950 Sutermeister, H.

Michaelis, Sophus
   Revolutionshochzeit+   1919 Albert, E. d'

Miller, Henry (1891-1980)
Smile at the Foot of the Ladder, The
   Lächeln am Füsse der   1965 Bibalo, A.
    Leiter, Das+

Minato, Niccolò (ca. 1630-1698)
Patienza di Socrate, La (1680)
   Gedultige Sokrates, Der 1721 Telemann, G. P.
Scipione Africano (1664)
   Grossmüthige Scipio, Der+ 1690 Krieger, J. P.
Also:
   Croesus   1710 Keiser, R.

Mitford, Mary Russell (1787-1855)
Rienzi (1828)
   Rienzi   1842 Wagner, R.

Molière [Jean-Baptiste Poquelin] (1622-1673)
Amphytryon (1668)
   Amphitryon+   1951 Oboussier, R.
Bourgeois Gentilhomme, Le (1670)
   Ariadne auf Naxos   1912 Strauss, R.
Ecole des femmes, L' (1662)
   Schule der Frauen, Die   1955 Liebermann, R.

Molière (cont.)
  Fouberies de Scapan, Les (1671)
    Rosenkavalier, Der   1911   Strauss, R.
  Médecin malgré lui, Le (1666)
    Unsterbliche Kranke, Der+ 1947   Haug, H.
  Précieuses ridicules, Les
    (1659)
    Lächerlichen Preziösen,   1949   Behrend, F.
      Die+
    Zierpuppen+   1905   Goetzl, A.
  Sganarelle (1660)
    Sganarelle+   1929   Wagner-Régeny, R.
  Sicilien, Le (1666)
    Sizilianer, Der+   1924   David, K. H.
  Tartuffe (1664)
    Tartuffe+   1929   Eidens, J.
    Tartuffe+   1937   Haug, H.
  Also:
    Adrast und Isidore+   1779   Kospoth, O. C. E.
                               von

Moniglia, Giovanni Andrea
  Semiramide, La (with M. Noris) (1670)
    Semiramis+   1683   Franck, J.W.

Moore, Thomas (1870-1944)
  Lalla Rookh (1817)
    Feramors+   1863   Rubinstein, A.
    Nurmahal   1822   Spontini, G.

Morand, Eugène
    Izeyel+   1909   Albert, E. d'
      (with P. A. Silvestre)

Morel de Chédeville, Etienne
  Tamerlan (1786)
    Tamerlan+   1800   Reichardt, J. F.

Moreto y Cabena, Augustin
  Desdén con el desdén, El
    Donna Diana   1894   Reznicek, E. N.
                               von
    Donna Diana+   1896   Hofmann, H.

Mörike, Eduard Friedrich (1804-1875)
    Brüderlein und   1949   Friedrich, K.
      Schwesterlein+

Mörner, Birger
    König Magnus+   1898   Nodermann, P.

Morris, Editha
    Blumen von Hiroshima, Die+ 1967 Forest, J. K.

Müller, Hans
    Spiegel der Agrippina,   1937 Haug, H.
      Das+

Musset, Alfred de (1810-1857)
   Fantasio (1834)
    Fantasio+   1898 Smyth, E.

Neruda, Pablo [Neftali Ricardo Reyes Basualto]
   (1904-1973)
   Glory and Death of Joaquin Murieta
    Murieta   1984 Ostendorf, J. P.

Nerval, Gerhard (Gérard de, pseud. of Gérard Labrunie)
   (1808-1855)
    Corinna+   1958 Fortner, W.

Nestroy, Johann (1801-1862)
   Talismann, Der (1840)
    Titus Feuerfuchs+   1958 Sutermeister, H.
   Zerrissene, Der (1844)
    Zerrissene, Der+   1941 Kreuder, P.
    Zerrissene, Der+   1942 Jenny, A.
    Zerrissene, Der   1964 Einem, G. von

Nietzsche, Friedrich (1844-1900)
    Klage der Ariadne+   1973 Chemin-Petit, H.

Nivelle de la Causé
   Amour par amour
    Zemire und Azor   1819 Spohr, L.

Noris, Matteo
   Semiramide, La (with G. A. Moniglia) (1670)
    Semiramis+   1683 Franck, J. W.

Nuitter, Charles-Louis-Etienne (1828-1899)
   Tonnlier de Nurenberg, Le
    Meister Martin und seine 1897 Lacombe, L.
      Gesellen+

Oehlenschläger, Adam Gottlob (1779-1850)
    Hagbarth und Signe+ 1882 Mihalovich, Ö.
    Höhle von Waverly, Die+ 1837 Kreutzer, C.

Ossian (ca. 3rd century)
    Colmal+   1809 Winter, P.

Ovid (43 B.C. -A.D. 18)
  Metamorphoses, Book 1
    Beglückte Florindo, Der+   1708   Handel, G. F.
    Verwandelte Daphne, Die+   1708   Handel, G. F.
  Metamorphoses, Book 8
    Philemon und Baucis   1773   Haydn, F. J.

Oxman, Philip
  Jot oder **Wann kommt der**   1973   Huber, K.
    Herr+

Pain, Joseph Maria
  Fanchon, das Leiermädchen   1804   Himmel, F. H.

Palissot de Montenoy, Charles (1730-1814)
  Barbier de Bagdad, Le (1777)
    Barbier von Bagdad, Der   1783   André, J.

Pancieri, Giulio
  Almira (1691)
    Almira   1705   Handel, G. F.

Pariati, Pietro
  Pimpinone (1708)
    Pimpinone   1725   Telemann, G. P.

Parisetti, Flaminio
    Basilius+   1694   Keiser, R.

Patrat, Joseph
  Méprises par resemblance, Les (1786)
    Beiden Schützen, Die   1837   Lortzing, A.

Patzke, Johann Samuel
    Abels Tod+   1778   Haydn, M.

Pauersbach
  Neue Alceste, Die+
    (with Richter)   1806   Müller, W.

Perrault, Charles (1628-1703)
  Contes de ma mère l'Oye, Les (1697)
    Dornröschen+   1902   Humperdinck, E.
    Himmelskleid, Das+   1927   Wolf-Ferrari, E.

Perutz, Leo (d. 1957)
  Nachts unter der steinernen Brücke
    Engel von Prag, Der   1979   Bresgen, C.

Pétis de la Croix
  Milles et un jour, contes persanes, Les (1712)
    Turandot   1917 Busoni, F.

Petronius Gaius (d. A.D. 66)
  Witwe von Ephesus, Die+   1954 Reutter, H.

Pfeffel, Gottlob Konrad (1736-1809)
    Philemon und Baucis   1773 Haydn, F. J.

Pigault-Lebrun, Charles Antoine Guillaume (1753-1835)
  Major Palmer, Le
    Palmer und Amalia+   1893 Cannabich, C.

Pittaud de Forges, Philippe Auguste Alfred
  Alessandro Stradella (1837)
      (with P. Duport)
    Alessandro Stradella   1844 Flotow, F. von

Plato (ca. 427-347 B.C.)
    Bankette, Die+   1988 Katzer, G.

Pocci, Franz (1807-1876)
    Moschopulos+   1928 Wagner-Régeny, R.
    Zaubergeige, Die+   1935 Egk, W.

Poe, Edgar Allan (1809-1849)
  Purloined Letter, The (1845)
    Geheimnis des entwendeten 1975 Blacher, B.
    Briefes, Das+

Polidori, John William
  Vampire, The (1819)
    Vampyr, Der   1828 Marschner, H.

Prévost, Abbé (1697-1763)
  Manon Lescaut (1731)
    Boulevard Solitude   1952 Henze, H. W.

Pushkin, Alexander (1799-1837)
  Postmaster, The (1830)
    Postmeister Wyrin+   1946 Reutter, F. von

Quinault, Philippe (1635-1688)
  Alceste (1674)
    Getreue Alceste, Die+   1719 Schürmann, G. C.
    Theseus+   1683 Strungk, N. A.

Racine, Jean (1639-1699)
  Athalie (1691)
    Athalia+   1786   Schulz, J.A.P.
  Phèdre (1677)
    Phaedra+   1950   Goldberg, T.

Raimund, Ferdinand (1790-1836)
  Alpenkönig und Menschenfeind (1828)
    Alpenkönig und   1903   Blech, L.
      Menschenfeind
    Rappelkopf+   1958   Lothar, M.
  Also:
    Verzauberte ich, Das+   1949   Gerster, O.

Raupach, Ernst (1784-1852)
  Versiegelte Bürgermeister, Der
    Versiegelt   1908   Blech, L.
  Also:
    Liebe ist teuer+   1949   Brehme, H.

Rautenstrauch, J.
    Liebe macht kurzen   1798   Wölfl, J. et al.
      Prozess+

Reichssiegel, P. F.
    Rebekka als Braut+   1776   Haydn, M.

Revers, Henry
  Stella Maris
    Stella Maris+   1910   Kaiser, A.

Rinuccini, Ottavio (1552-1621)
  Dafne (1597)
    Dafne   1627   Schütz, H.

Rodenbach, Georges (1855-1898)
  Bruges la morte (1892)
    Tote Stadt, Die   1920   Korngold, E.

Romani, Felice (1788-1865)
    Prinzessin von Provence,   1825   Poissl, J. N.
      Die+

Rosegger, Peter (1843-1918)
    Testament, Das+   1916   Kienzl, W.

Rousseau, Jean-Jacques (1712-1778)
  Devin du village, Le (1752)
    Bastien und Bastienne   1768   Mozart, W. A.
  Galatée (1795)
    Galatea+   1930   Braunfels, W.
    Galatea Elettronica+   1969   Goldberg, T.

Rousseau, J.-J. (cont.)
    Schöne Galatea, Die   1865   Suppé, F. von
    Pygmalion (1775)
    Pygmalion+   1779   Benda, G.

Sachs, Hans (1494-1576)
    Bauer im Feg[e]feuer, Der (1552)
    Bauer im Fegefeuer, Der+   1958   Grafe, M.
    Heiss[e] Eisen, Das (1551)
    Heisse Eisen, Das+   1909   Wolff, M.
    Heiss[e] Eisen, Das+   1918   Wehrli, W.
    Heisse Eisen, Das+   1922   Paumgarten, B.
    Höllisch Gold, Das
    Höllisch Gold, Das+   1916   Bittner, J.
    Also:
    Böse Weib, Das+   1939   Hufeld, A.

Salis (-Seewis), Johann Gaudenz von (1762-1834)
    Lieb' und Treue+   1800   Reichardt, J. F.

Salvatore, Gastón
    Langwienzige Weg in die   1971   Henze, H. W.
    Wohnung Natascha
    Ungeheuer, Der

Sardou, Victorien (1831-1908)
    Karneval in Rom, Der+   1873   Strauss, J., Jr.

Scarron, Paul (1610-1660)
    Jodelet ou le Maître Valet
       (1645)
    Lächerliche Printz   1726   Keiser, R.
     Jodelet, Der

Schauffer
    Schach dem König+   1893   Brüll, I.

Scheffel, Joseph Viktor von (1826-1886)
    Ekkehard (1857)
    Ekkehard+   1878   Abert, J. J.
    Trompeter von Säckingen, Der
       (1854)
    Trompeter von Säckingen,   1884   Nessler, V. E.
    Der+

Schiller, Friedrich (1759-1805)
    Braut von Messina, Die (1803)
    Braut von Messina, Die+   1904   Mai, J.
    Bürgschaft, Die (1798)
    Bürgschaft, Die   1816   Schubert, F.
    Bürgschaft, Die   1838   Lachner, F.

Schiller, F. (cont.)
   Jungfrau von Orleans, Die
     (1801)

Johanna d'Arc+	1840	Hoven, J.
Jungfrau von Orleans,	1887	Reznicek, E. N.
Die+		von
Mädchen aus Domremy, Das	1976	Klebe, G.

   Kabale und Liebe (1784)

Kabale und Liebe	1976	Einem, G. von

   Räuber, Die (1782)

Räuber, Die	1957	Klebe, G.

   Taucher, Der (1797)

Taucher, Der+	1811	Reichardt, J. F.

   Wallenstein (1799)

Wallenstein+	1937	Weinberger, J.

   Also:

Fridolin+	1837	Kreutzer, C.

Schnitzler, Arthur (1862-1931)
   Grüne Kakadu, Der (1899)

Grüne Kakadu, Der+	1958	Mohaupt, R.

   Liebelei (1895)

Liebelei+	1910	Neumann, F.

Schopenhauer, Johanna (1766-1838)

Des Adlers Horst+	1832	Gläser, F.

Schulze, Ernst Konrad Friedrich (1789-1817)
   Bezauberte Rose, Die (1818)

Maja und Alpino+	1826	Wolfram, J. M.

Schwarz, Yevgeni
   Dragon, The (1943)

Lanzelot	1969	Dessau, P.

Scott, Sir Walter (1771-1832)
   Kenilworth (1821)

Kenilworth+	1895	Klein, B. O.

   Ivanhoe (1820)

Templer und die Jüdin, Der	1829	Marschner, H.

   Waverly (1814)

Hochländer, Die+	1876	Holstein, F. von

Scribe, Eugène (1791-1861)
   Circassienne, La (1861)

Fatinitza+	1876	Suppé, F. von

   Dame blanche, La (1815)

Schwarze Frau, Die+	1826	Müller, A. E.

   Deux Precepteurs, Les

Beiden Pädagogen, Die	1821	Mendelssohn, F.

   Also:

Cagliostro+	1850	Lortzing, A.

Scribe, E. (cont.)
    Coeur As+   1913 Künneke, E.
    Weg durchs Fenster, Der+ 1917 Weissleder, P.

Scribe, E. and P. F. A. Carmouche
  Trilby (1823)
    Trilby+   1845 Schmitt, G. A.
    Trilby+   1835 Truhn, F. H.

Scribe, E. and A. H. P Mélesville
    Zwei Prinzen, Die+   1845 Esser, H.

Sedaine, Jean-Michel (1719-1797)
  Blaise le savetier (1759)
    Dorfbarbier, Der+   1771 Hiller, J. A.
  Roi et le fermier, Le (1770
    Jagd, Die   1770 Hiller, J. A.
  Rose et Colas (1771)
    Hänschen und Gretschen+ 1727 Reichardt, J. F.

Seidel, Carl
  Brautkampf, Der
    Drei Pintos, Die   1821 Weber, C. M. von

Seneca (4 B.C.-A.D. 65)
    Andromeda+   1924 Maurice, P.

Seyler, Sophie
    Oberon   1789 Wranitzky, P.

Shakespeare, William (1564-1616)
  As You Like It (1600)
    Was ihr wollt+   1941 Hess, L.
  Comedy of Errors, The (1593)
    Komödie der Irrungen, Die+ 1939 Lorenz, K.
  Hamlet (1601)
    Hamlet+   1807 Schuster, I.
    Hamlet   1968 Searle, H.
    Ophelia+   1969 Engelmann, H. U.
    Ophelia+   1984 Kelterborn, R.
  Julius Caesar (1600)
    Ermordung Cäsars, Die+ 1959 Klebe, G.
  King Lear (1606)
    Lear   1978 Reimann, A.
  Macbeth (1606)
    Macbeth+   1858 Taubert, W.
  Measure for Measure (1605)
    Liebesverbot, Das   1836 Wagner, R.
  Merchant of Venice, The
    (1596)
    Porzia+   1916 Taubmann, O.

Shakespeare, W. (cont.)
  Merry Wives of Windsor, The
    (1601)

Lustigen Weiber von Windsor, Die+	1796	Dittersdorf, K.
Lustigen Weiber von Windsor, Die+	1849	Nicolai, O.

  Midsummer Night's Dream, A
    (1596)

Mitternachtstraum, Ein+	1988	Decker, W.

  Much Ado About Nothing (1599)

Viel Lärm um nichts+	1956	Heinrich, H.

  Romeo and Juliet (1595)

Romeo und Julia	1940	Sutermeister, H.
Romeo und Julia	1947	Blacher, B.
Romeo und Julie	1776	Benda, G.

  Taming of the Shrew, The
    (1594)

Widerspenstigen Zähmung, Der+	1874	Goetz, H.

  Tempest, The (1612)

Geisterinsel, Die+	1798	Fleischmann, F.
Geisterinsel, Die	1798	Reichardt, J. F.
Geisterinsel, Die+	1798	Zumsteeg, J. R.
Sturm, Der	1798	Winter, P.
Sturm, Der+	1799	Müller, W.
Sturm, Der+	1888	Urspruch, A.
Sturm, Der	1956	Martin, F.
Zauberinsel, Die+	1942	Sutermeister, H.

  Troilus and Cressida (1602)

Troilus und Cressida	1951	Zillig, W.

  Twelfth Night (1600)

Viola+	1934	Holenia, H.

  Winter's Tale, A (1611)

Hermione+	1872	Bruch, M.
Wintermärchen, Das+	1900	Zimmermann, B.
Wintermärchen, Ein+	1908	Goldmark, K.

Shaw, George Bernard (1856-1950)
  Arms and the Man (1894)

Tapfere Soldat, Der	1908	Straus, O.

Shelley, Percy Bysshe (1792-1822)

Beatrice Cenci+	1953	Goldschmidt, B.

Silvani, Francesco
  Miglior d'ogni Amore, Il (1703)

Sancio und Sinilde+	1727	Graun, K. H.

  Fredegonda, La

Fredegunda+	1715	Keiser, R.

Silvestre, Paul-Armand (1838-1901)
   Izeyel+ (with E. Morand)   1909 Albert, E. d'

Sophocles (496-406 B.C.)
   Antigone
     Antigonae   1949 Orff, C.
   Electra (414 B.C.)
     Elektra   1909 Strauss, R.
   Oedipus Tyrannos
     Oedipus+   1960 Eder, H.
     Oedipus+   1987 Rihm, W.
     Oedipus der Tyrann   1959 Orff, C.

Spindler, Karl (1796-1855)
   Des Falkners Braut+   1832 Marschner, H.

Stach, Ilse von
   Christelflein, Das+   1917 Pfitzner, H.

Stegentesch, August von
   Abreise, Die (1813)
     Abreise, Die   1898 Albert, E. d'

Steinel
   Poltis+   ca. 1777 Hiller, J. A.

Storm, Theodor (1817-1888)
   Dagmar+   1932 Stiegler, K.

Strassburg, Gottfried von
   Tristan (ca. 1210)
     Tristan und Isolde   1865 Wagner, R.

Strindberg, August (1849-1912)
   Dream Play, A (1902)
     Traumspiel, Ein+   1925 Weismann, J.
     Traumspiel, Ein   1965 Reimann, A.
   Ghosts (1907)
     Gespenstersonate, Die+ 1930 Weismann, J.
     Gespenstersonate   1984 Reimann, A.
   Miss Julie (1888)
     Miss Julie+   1975 Bibalo, A.
   Swanwhite (1901)
     Schwanenweiss+   1923 Weismann, J.

Swift, Jonathan (1667-1745)
   Schwarz auf weiss+ 1968 Hüber, K.

Synge, John Millington (1871-1909)
   Playboy of the Western World, The (1907)
     Wahrer Held, Ein   1975 Klebe, G.

Tardieu, Jean (1903-)
     Faust und Yorick+   1977 Rihm, W.

Tennyson, Alfred Lord (1809-1892)
     Enoch Arden (1864)
          Enoch Arden+   1936 Gerster, O.
     Lancelot
          Lanzelot und Elaine+   1917 Courvoisier, W.

Théâtre de la Foire (16th century)
     Achmed und Almanzine+   1795 Schenk, J.

Thomas, Dylan (1914-1953)
     Under Milk Wood (1974)
          Unter dem Milchwald+   1972 Steffens, W.

Thomas of Britain
     Tristram (ca. 1150)
          Tristan und Isolde   1865 Wagner, R.

Tieck, Ludwig (1773-1853)
     Gestiefelte Kater, Der (1797)
          Gestiefelte Kater, Der+   1975 Bialas, G.
     Pietro von Abano (1825)
          Pietro von Abano   1827 Spohr, L.

Tirso de Molina [Gabriel Téllez] (ca. 1583-1648)
     Don Gil de las calzas verdes
          Don Gil von den grünen   1924 Braunfels, W.
          Hosen+

Trakl, Georg (1887-1914)
     Blau Bart+   1977 Togni, C.

Traulsen, Heinrich
     Erica
          Schwarzer Peter+   1936 Schultze, N.

Trotha, T. F. W. von
     Dollarprinzessin, Die   1907 Fall, L.

Turgenev, Ivan Sergeyevich (1818-1883)
     Letzte Zauberer, Der+   1869 Viardot, P.
     Traumwandel+   1928 David, K. H.

Uhland, Ludwig (1787-1862)
     Bär, Der+ (with J. Kerner) 1938 Stierlin, K.

Vacquerie, Auguste (1819-1895)
     Tragaldabas+   1907 Albert, E. d'

Varesco, Giovanni Battista
   Don Pedros Heimkehr+   1952 Erismann, H.

Varin, Arago, Desvergers
   Casanova au Fort Saint-André
   Casanova in Murano+   1841 Lortzing, A.

Verneuil, L.
   Frau, die weiss was sie   1932 Straus, O.
   will, Eine+

Vernoy de Saint-Georges, Jules Henri
   Lady Henriette (1844)
   Martha   1847 Flotow, F. von
   Reine de Chypre, La (1841)
   Catharina Cornaro   1841 Lachner, F.
   Also:
   Cagliostro+   1850 Lortzing, A.

Villain de Saint-Hilaire, Amable
   Cosimo (with P. Duport) (1835)
   Caramo+   1839 Lortzing, A.

Villiers, Pierre
   Bouffe et le tailleur, Le (with A. Gouffé) (1804)
   Sänger und der Schneider, 1814 Driesberg, F. von
   Der+

Voltaire [François Marie Arouet] (1694-1778)
   Olympie (1764)
   Olympia+   1821 Spontini, G.

Voss, Richard (1851-1918)
   Gelöbnis, Das+   1910 Oosterzee, C. van

Vyxcoczyl, Ivan
   Badewanne, Die   1973 Niehaus, M.

Wailly, A. F. L. de
   Benvenuto Cellini (1838)
   Benvenuto Cellini   1849 Lachner, F.

Waley, Arthur (1889-1966)
   Taniko
   Jasager, Der   1930 Weill, K.

Wedekind, Frank (1864-1918)
   Büchse der Pandora, Die (1901)
   Lulu   1937 Berg, A.
   Erdgeist (1895)
   Lulu   1937 Berg, A.

Wedekind, F. (cont.)
  Frühlings Erwachen (1891)
    Frühlings Erwachen+   1928   Ettinger, M.
  König Nicolo oder *So ist das*
      Leben (1902)
    König Nicolo+   1962   Chemin-Petit, H.
    König Nicolo+   1972   Weishappel, R.

Weinberger, Jaromil (1896-1967)
    Geliebte Stimme, Die+   1931   Weinberger, J.

Weiss, Peter (1916-1982)
  Marat/Sade (1965)
    Marat+   1984   Haupt, W.

Weisse, Christian Felix (1726-1804)
  Aerndtekranz, Die (1771)
    Weinlese, Die+   1785   Schenk, J.

Werfel, Franz (1890-1945)
  Jacobowsky und der Oberst (1944)
    Jacobowsky und der Oberst   1965   Klebe, G.

Wieland, Christoph Martin (1733-1813)
  Abderiten, Die (1774)
    Des Esels Schatten+   1964   Strauss, R.
                                              (arr. Haussner)
  Dschinnistan (1786)
    Zauberflöte, Die   1791   Mozart, W. A.
  Oberon (1780)
    Oberon   1789   Wranitzky, P.
    Oberon   1826   Weber, C. M. von
  Also:
    Heilige Katharina, Die+   1919   Böhme, O.
    Idris und Zenide+   1795   Süssmayr, F. X.
    Königen der schwarzen   1801   Eberl, A.
      Insel, Die+

Wilde, Oscar (1854-1900)
  Birthday of the Infanta
    Zwerg, Der   1922   Zemlinsky, A. von
  Canterville Ghost, The
    Arme Gespenst, Das+   1961   Hermann, P.
    Gespenst von Canterville,   1964   Sutermeister, H.
      Das
  Florentine Tragedy, A
    Florentinische Tragödie,   1917   Zemlinsky, A.
      Eine   von
    Florentinische Tragödie,   1929   Flury, R.
      Eine+

Wilde, O. (cont.)
  Picture of Dorian Gray, The
    (1891)
    Dorian+   1939 Leger, H.
    Dorian Gray+   1930 Flick-Steger, C.
    Dorian Gray+   1962 Hanell, R.
  Salome (1894)
    Salome   1905 Strauss, R.

Wildenbruch, Ernst von (1845-1909)
  Danaide, Die
    Hexenlied+   1948 Kleemann, R.
    Überfall, Der+   1895 Zöllner, H.

Wilder, Thornton (1897-1975)
  Bridge of San Luis Rey, The
    (1927)
    Brücke von San Luis Rey+ 1954 Reutter, H.
  Long Christmas Dinner, The
    (1931)
    Lange Weihnachtsmahl, Das 1961 Hindemith, P.

Wilder, Victor (with A. Delacour)
    Prinz Methusalem+   1877 Strauss, J., Jr.

Wohlmuth, Alois
    Feldprediger, Der+   1884 Millöcker, C.

Wolf, Friedrich (1759-1824)
    Arme Konrad, Der+   1959 Forest, J. K.

Wolf, J. W.
  Sagas of the Netherlands (1843)
    Feuersnot   1901 Strauss, R.

Wolff, Julius
    Rattenfänger von Hamelin, 1879 Nessler, V.E.
      Der+
    Wilde Jagd, Der+   1881 Nessler, V. E.

Wolfram von Eschenbach (ca. 1170-ca. 1220)
  Parzival (ca. 1210)
    Parsifal   1882 Wagner, R.

Wollenstein, O. von
    Visiones amantes+   1964 Bresgen, C.

Wurmser, André
    Zweimal Alexander   1937 Martinů, B.

Yeats, William Butler (1865-1939)
  Countess Cathleen, The (1892)
    Irische Legende   1955   Egk, W.

Zola, Emile (1840-1902)
  Nana (1880)
    Nana+   1933   Gurlitt, M.

Zschokke, Heinrich (1771-1848)
    Tote Gast, Der   1923   Berr, J.R.

Zuckmayer, Carl (1896-1977)
  Hauptmann von Köpenick, Der (1931)
    Preussisches Märchen   1952   Blacher, B.
  Rattenfänger, Der (1975)
    Rattenfänger, Der+   1987   Cerha, F.

APPENDIX 5
SOURCES

APPENDIX V: Sources: A Selective List

+See Appendix I.

Abderiten, Die, 1774 (C. M. Wieland)
  Esels Schatten, Des+   1964 Strauss, R.
                                           (arr. Haussner)

Abreise, Die, 1813 (A. von Stegentesch)
  Abreise, Die   1898 Albert, E. d'

Aerndtekranz, Die, 1771 (C. F. Weisse)
  Weinlese, Die+   1785 Schenk, J.

Afrikanische Rechtspruch, Der (J. G. von Herder)
  Bürgschaft, Die   1932 Weill, K.

Alcaide de si mismo, El (P. Calderón)
  Lächerliche Printz Jodelet, 1726 Keiser, R.
  Der+

Alceste, 1674 (P. Quinault)
  Getreue Alceste, Die+   1719 Schürmann, G. C.

Alcestis, 438 B.C. (Euripides)
  Alceste+   1680 Franck, J. W.
  Alceste+   1693 Strungk, N. A.
  Alceste+   1773 Schweitzer, A.
  Alceste+   1780 Wolf, E. W.
  Alceste+   1786 Benda, F.
  Alkestis+   1924 Wellesz, E.

Almira, 1704 (F. C. Feutsking)
  Almira+   1706 Keiser, R.

Alpenkönig und Menschenfeind, 1828 (F. Raimund)
  Alpenkönig und Menschenfeind 1903 Blech, L.
  Verzauberte ich, Das+   1949 Gerster, O.

Alsfelder Passion play
  Spiel von der Auferstehung, 1954 Braunfels, W.
  Das+

Amor de Don Perlimplín con Belisa en su jardin, 1931
     (F. García Lorca)
  In seinem Garten liebt Don   1962 Fortner, W.
  Perlimplín Belisa

Amor di figlio, L', 1715 (D. Lalli)
  Grossmüthige Tomyris, Die   1717 Keiser, R.

Amour par amour (Nivelle de la Causée)
Zemire und Azor   1819   Spohr, L.

Amours de Bastien et Bastienne, Les, 1753 (C.-S. Favart
   and M. Favart)
Bastien und Bastienne   1768   Mozart, W. A.

Andromède, 1650 (P. Corneille)
Errettete Unschuld, Die+   1675   Franck, J. W.

Annette et Lubin, 1762 (C.-S. Favart and M. Favart)
Liebe auf dem Lande, Die+   1768   Hiller, J. A.

Annonce faite à Marie, L', 1910 (P. Claudel)
Verkündigung+   1948   Braunfels, W.

Antigona delusa da Alceste, 1660 (A. Aureli)
Alceste+   1693   Strungk, N. A.

Antigone (transl. Hölderlin) (Sophocles)
Antigonae   1949   Orff, C.

Arcifano, Re de Mattei (C. Goldoni)
Arcifano+   1777   Dittersdorf, K.

Arms and the Man, 1894 (G. B. Shaw)
Tapfere Soldat, Der   1908   Straus, O.

As You Like It, 1599 (W. Shakespeare)
Was ihr wollt+   1941   Hess, L.

Athalie, 1691 (J. Racine)
Athalia+   1786   Schulz, J. A. P.

Autobiography of a Runaway Slave (M. Barnet)
Cimarrón, El   1970   Henze, H. W.

Aztec legend
Opferung des Gefangenen,   1926   Wellesz, E.
   Die+

Baal, 1918 (B. Brecht)
Baal   1981   Cerha, F.
Persische Episode+   1963   Wagner-Régeny, R.

Bacchae, The (Euripides)
Bakchantinnen, Die   1931   Wellesz, E.
Bassariden, Die   1966   Henze, H. W.

Barbier de Bagdad, Le, 1777 (C. M. de Palissot)
Barbier von Bagdad, Der   1783   André, J.

Bartleby the Scrivener, 1853 (H. Melville)
  Bartleby   1967 Niehaus, M.

Bauer im Feg[e]feuer, Der, 1552 (H. Sachs)
  Bauer im Fegefeuer, Der+   1958 Grafe, M.

Bear, The, 1888 (A. Chekhov)
  Bär, Der+   1963 Dressel, E.
  Ungeheuer, Das+   1914 Walbrunn, A.

Beggar's Opera, The, 1728 (J. Gay)
  Dreigroschenoper, Die   1928 Weill, K.

Behind the Treble Clef (R. G. Dobrovensky)
  Boom-Boom Land+   1978 Katzer, G.

Belmont und Constanze, 1782 (C. F. Bretzner)
  Entführung aus dem Serail, 1782 Mozart, W. A.
    Die

Benediktbeuren codex
  Carmina burana   1937 Orff, C.

Benvenuto Cellini, 1838 (H. A. Barbier and A. F. L.
    de Wailly)
  Benvenuto Cellini   1849 Lachner, F.

Bergwerk zu Falun, Das, 1933 (H. von Hofmannsthal)
  Bergwerk zu Falun, Das   1961 Wagner-Régeny, R.

Bergwerke zu Falun, Die, 1819 (E. T. A. Hoffmann)
  Haideschacht, Der+   1868 Holstein, F. von

Besuch der alten Dame, Der, 1956 (F. Dürrenmatt)
  Besuch der alten Dame, Der 1971 Einem, G. von

Bezauberte Rose, Die, 1818 (E. K. F. Schulze)
  Maja und Alpino+   1826 Wolfram, J. M.

Bible, The. See New Testament, Old Testament

Birds, The (Aristophanes)
  Vögel, Die   1920 Braunfels, W.

Birthday of the Infanta (O. Wilde)
  Zwerg, Der   1922 Zemlinsky, A. von

Blaise le savetier, 1759 (J. M. Sedaine)
  Dorfbarbier, Der+   1771 Hiller, J. A.

Bodas de sangre, 1933 (F. García Lorca)
  Bluthochzeit, Die   1957 Fortner, W.

Bouffe et le tailleur, Le, 1804   (P. Villiers and
    A. Gouffé)
  Sänger und der Schneider,   1814   Driesberg, F. von
  Der+

Boule de Suif, 1880 (G. de Maupassant)
  Fettlöschen+   1976   Wahren, K. H.

Bourgemestre de Saardam, Le (A. H. J. Mélesville)
  Zar und Zimmermann   1837   Lortzing, A.

Bourgeois Gentilhomme, Le, 1670 (Molière)
  Ariadne auf Naxos   1912   Strauss, R.

Brautkampf, Der   (C. Seidel)
  Drei Pintos, Die   1821   Weber, C. M. von

Bremer Stadtmusikanten, Die (Grimm brothers)
  Bremer Stadtmusikanten,   1949   Bergese, H.
  Die+
  Bremer Stadtmusikanten,   1949   Mohaupt, R.
  Die+
  Bremer Stadtmusikanten,   1972   Auenmüller, H.
  Die+

Bruges la morte, 1892 (G. Rodenbach)
  Tote Stadt, Die   1920   Korngold, E.

Bûcheron, Le, 1763 (J.-F. Guichard and N. Castet)
  Holzhauer, Der+   1778   Benda, G.

Büchse der Pandora, Die, 1901 (F. Wedekind)
  Lulu   1937   Berg, A.

Bürgschaft, Die, 1798 (F. Schiller)
  Bürgschaft, Die   1816   Schubert, F.
  Bürgschaft, Die   1838   Lachner, F.

Cancion de Rachel, La (M. Barnet)
  Cubana, La   1974   Henze, H. W.

Canterville Ghost, The (O. Wilde)
  Gespenst von Canterville,   1964   Sutermeister, H.
  Das

Casanova au Fort Saint-André (A. Varin, E. Arago, and
    Desvergers)
  Casanova in Murano+   1841   Lortzing, A.

Cherry Orchard, The, 1904 (A. Chekhov)
  Kirschgarten, Der+   1984   Kelterborn, R.

Christ Recrucified (The Greek Passion), 1951 (M. Kazantzakis)
Griechische Passion, Die   1961 Martinů, B.

Cid, Le, 1637 (P. Corneille)
  Cid, Der   1865 Cornelius, P.
  Rächer, Der+   1846 Schindelmeisser, L.
  Rodrigo und Zimene+ 1821 Aiblinger, J. K.

Circassienne, La, 1861 (A. E. Scribe)
  Fatinitza+   1876 Suppé, F. von

Ciro riconosciuto, 1736 (P. Metastasio)
  Cyrus und Astyages+   1818 Mosel, J. F. von

Claudine von Villa Bella, 1775 (J. W. von Goethe)
  Claudine von Villa Bella+ 1778 André, J.
  Claudine von Villa Bella+ 1780 Beecke, I. von
  Claudine von Villa Bella+ 1780 Kienlen, J. C.
  Claudine von Villa Bella   1789 Reichardt, J. F.
  Claudine von Villa Bella   1815 Schubert, F.

Clochette, La (L. Anseame)
  Liebe auf dem Lande, Die+ 1768 Hiller, J. A.

Colonel Chabert, Le (H. de Balzac)
  Oberst Chabert+   1912 Waltershausen, H. W. von

Comedy of Errors, The, 1593 (W. Shakespeare)
  Komödie der Irrungen, Die+ 1949 Lorenz, K.

Contes de ma mère l'Oye, Les, 1697 (C. Perrault)
  Dornröschen+   1902 Humperdinck, E.
  Himmelskleid, Das+   1927 Wolf-Ferrari, E.

Corsair, The, 1814 (Lord Byron)
  Corsair, Der+   not perf Schumann, R.

Cosimo, 1835 (Saint-Hilaire and P. Duport)
  Caramo+   1839 Lortzing, A.

Countess Cathleen, The, 1892 (W. B. Yeats)
  Irische Legende   1955 Egk, W.

Cricket on the Hearth, 1845 (C. Dickens)
  Heimchen am Herd, Das+ 1896 Goldmark, K.

Crime and Punishment, 1866 (F. Dostoevsky)
  Raskolnikoff+   1948 Sutermeister, H.

Cueva de Salamanca, La (M. de Cervantes)
Bettelstudent, Der+   1785   Winter, P.

Dafne, 1597 (O. Rinuccini)
Dafne   1627   Schütz, H.

Dama Duende, La (P. Calderón)
Dame Kobold+   1916   Weingartner, F.
Dame Kobold+   1940   Wolfurt, K. von
Dame Kobold   1964   Wimberger, G.

Dame blanche, La, 1815 (A. Boieldieu)
Schwarze Frau, Die+   1826   Müller, A. E.

Danaide, Die (E. von Wildenbruch)
Überfall, Der+   1895   Zöllner, H.

Dantons Tod, 1835 (G. Büchner)
Dantons Tod+   1929   Eisler, H.
Dantons Tod   1947   Einem, G. von

Demoiselles de St. Cyr, Les, 1843 (A. Dumas)
Heirat wider Willen, Die+   1905   Humperdinck, E.

Des Meeres und der Liebe, 1831 (F. Grillparzer)
Hero und Leander   1966   Bialas, G.

Deux Avares, Les, 1777 (C. G. F. de Falbaire)
Grab des Mufti, Das   1779   Hiller, J. A.

Deux Precepteurs, Les (E. Scribe)
Beiden Pädagogen, Die   1821   Mendelssohn, F.

Deux Valentins, Les (vaudeville)
Zwillingsbrüder, Die   1820   Schubert, F.

Devil to Pay, The, 1731 (C. Coffey)
Teufel ist los, Der   1743   Standfuss, J. C.

Devils of Loudun, The, 1952 (A. Huxley)
Teufel von Loudun, Der   1969   Penderecki, K.

Devin du Village, Le, 1752 (J.-J. Rousseau)
Bastien und Bastienne   1768   Mozart, W. A.

Diable boîteux, Le (A. R. Lesage)
Neue krumme Teufel, Der+   1759   Haydn, F. J.

Divine Comedy, The, 1321 (Dante)
Francesca da Rimini   1877   Goetz, H.

Doctor Faustus, 1589 (C. Marlowe)
   Doktor Faust   1922 Busoni, F.

Dominos roses, Les (A. Delacour and A. Hennequin)
   Opernball, Der   1898 Heuberger, R.

Don Cesar de Bazan (A. P. de Ennery and P. Dumanoir)
   Don Cesar+   1885 Dellinger, R.

Don Quixote de la Mancha, 1605, 1615 (M. de Cervantes)
   Don Quichote+   1908 Beer-Walbrunn, A.
   Don Quichotte+   1910 Heuberger, R.
   Don Quijote+   1947 Maasz, G.
   Don Quixote+   1898 Kienzl, W.
   Don Quixote der Zweyte+   1795 Dittersdorf, K.
   Don Quixote in dem   1727 Müller, A.
    Mohrengebirge+
   Don Quixotte+   1788 Beecke, I. von
   Hochzeit des Camacho, Die   1827 Mendelssohn, F.

Donna serpente, La, 1762 (C. Gozzi)
   Feen, Die   1833 Wagner, R.

Dragon, The, 1943 (Y. Schwarz)
   Lanzelot   1969 Dessau, P.

Dream Play, A, 1902 (A. Strindberg)
   Traumspiel, Ein+   1925 Weismann, J.
   Traumspiel, Ein   1965 Reimann, A.

Dschinnistan, 1786 (C. M. Wieland)
   Zauberflöte, Die   1791 Mozart, W. A.

Edelstein-sklavin, Die
   Yü-Nü+   1958 Riede, E.

Edwin and Angelina (The Hermit), 1764 (O. Goldsmith)
   Erwin und Elmire   1793 Reichardt, J. F.

Eginhard und Emma, 12th c. (legend)
   Fierrabras   1835 Schubert, F.

Ekkehard, 1857 (J. V. von Scheffel)
   Ekkehard+   1878 Abert, J. J.

Electra, 414 B.C. (Sophocles)
   Elektra   1909 Strauss, R.

Emperor's New Clothes, The (H. C. Andersen)
   Des Kaisers neue Kleider+ 1948 Werdin, E.
   Des Kaisers neue Kleider+ 1957 Hummel, B.

Emperor's New Clothes, The (cont.)
   Des Kaisers neue Kleider+   1957 Westien F.
   Des Kaisers neueste   1954 Kaufmann, O.
    Kleider+

Engel kommt nach Babylon, Ein, 1953 (F. Dürrenmatt)
   Engel kommt nach Babylon, 1977 Kelterborn, R.
   Ein

Engländer, Der, 1776 (J. M. R. Lenz)
   R. Hot+   1977 Goldmann, F.

Epicoene, 1609 (B. Jonson)
   Lord Spleen+   1930 Lothar, M.
   Schweigsame Frau, Die   1935 Strauss, R.

Erdgeist, 1895 (F. Wedekind)
   Lulu   1937 Berg, A.

Erica (H. Traulsen)
   Schwarzer Peter+   1936 Schultze, N.

Erwin und Elmire, 1774   (J. W. von Goethe)
   Erwin und Elmira+   1775 André, J.
   Erwin und Elmire+   1781 Vogler, G. J.
   Erwin und Elmire   1793 Reichardt, J. F.
   Erwin und Elmire   1916 Schoeck, O.

Eugenia (G. Keller)
   Claudia amata+   1952 Driessler, J.

Eulenspiegel Reimenweiss, 1572 (J. Fischart)
   Till Eulenspiegel+   1902 Reznicek, E. N.
                        von

Evangelimann, Der, 1894 (L. F. Meissner)
   Evangelimann, Der   1895 Kienzl, W.

Faust, Pt. 1, 1808, Pt. 2, 1832 (J. W. von Goethe)
   Doktor Faust+   1797 Walter, I.
   Faust+   1887 Zöllner, H.
   Faust I. Teil+   1905 Kistler, C.

Fée Urgèle, La (C. S. Favart)
   Lisuarte und Darlioette+ 1766 Hiller, J. A.

Feudatario, Il (C. Goldoni)
   Dorfdeputierten, Die+   1772 Wolf, E. W.
   Dorfdeputierten, Die+   1783 Schubaur, J. L.
   Dorfdeputierten, Die   1786 Dieter, C. F.

Fierabras, 1533
Fierrabras 1835 Schubert, F.

Filla del mar (A. Guimerà)
Liebesketten+ 1912 Albert, E. d'

Florentine Tragedy, A (O. Wilde)
Florentinische Tragödie, 1917 Zemlinsky, A. von
Eine
Florentinische Tragödie, 1929 Flury, R.
Eine+

Folle journée, La (*Le Mariage de Figaro*), 1781
(Beaumarchais)
Hochzeit des Figaro, Die 1789 Dittersdorf, K.

Forêt de Hermanstadt, Le, 1805 (L. C. Caigniez)
Elisene, Prinzessin von 1807 Rösler, J.
Bulgarien+

Forza della virtù, La, 1693 (D. David)
Forza della virtù, La 1700 Keiser, R.

Fouberies de Scapan, Les, 1671 (Molière)
Rosenkavalier, Der 1911 Strauss, R.

Fraülein von Scuderie, Das (E. T. A. Hoffmann)
Cardillac 1926 Hindemith, P.
Goldschmied von Toledo, Der+ 1919 Offenbach (arr.
Stern and Zamara)

Fredegonda, La (F. Silvani)
Fredegunda+ 1715 Keiser, R.

Friend of the Automathias (S. Lem)
Kyberiade+ 1970 Meyer, K.

Furchtsame, Der (Philipp Hafner)
Neusonntagskind, Das+ 1793 Müller, W.

Galan Fantasma, El (P. Calderón)
Liebhaber nach dem Tode, 1822 Hoffmann,
Der+ E. T. A.

Galatée, 1795 (J.-J. Rousseau)
Galatea+ 1930 Braunfels, W.
Galatea Elettronica+ 1969 Goldberg, T.

Gefängnis, Das, 1851 (R. Bendix)
Fledermaus, Die 1874 Strauss, J., Jr.

Genoveva, 1843 (F. Hebbel)
Genoveva   1850   Schumann, R.

Gerusalemme liberata (G. C. Corradi)
Eroberte Jerusalem, Die+   1722   Schürmann, G. C.

Geschichte von dem König, Die (Grimm brothers)
Kluge, Die   1943   Orff, C.

Gespensterbuch (F. Laun and J. A. Apel)
Freischütz, Der   1821   Weber, C. M. von

Gevatter Tod (Grimm brothers)
Fremde, Der+   1920   Kaun, H.

Ghosts, 1881 (A. Strindberg)
Gespenstersonate   1984   Reimann, A.
Gespenstersonate, Die+   1930   Weismann, J.

Giannina e Bernadone, 1791 (F. Livigni)
Rothe Käppchen, Das   1790   Dittersdorf, K.

Gitanella, La, 1913 (Cervantes)
Preciosa   1821   Weber, C. M. von

Glory and Death of J. Murieta (P. Neruda)
Murieta   1984   Ostendorf, J.-P.

Golden Fleece, The (legend)
Goldene Bock, Der   1964   Krenek, E.

Götz von Berlichingen, 1773 (J.W. von Goethe)
Götz von Berlichingen+   1902   Goldmark, K.

Guerra, La (C. Goldoni)
Krieg, Der+   1772   Hiller, J. A.

Guerre ouverte, La (A. J. Dumaniant)
Mitternachtsstunde+   1788   Danzi, F.

Gulnare, ou l'Esclave persanne, 1798   (B. Marsollier)
Gülnare+   1800   Süssmayr, F. X.

Hamlet, 1601 (W. Shakespeare)
Hamlet+   1807   Schuster, I.
Hamlet   1968   Searle, H.
Ophelia+   1969   Engelmann, H. U.
Ophelia+   1984   Kelterborn, R.

Hanneles Himmelfahrt, 1893 (G. Hauptmann)
Hanneles Himmelfahrt+   1927   Graener, P.

Hauptmann von Koepenick, Der, 1931 (C. Zuckmayr)
Preussisches Märchen   1952   Blacher, B.

Heinrich von Schwaben (W. Hertz)
Junker Heinz+   1886   Perfall, K. von

Heiss[e] Eisen, Das, 1551 (H. Sachs)
Heisse Eisen, Das+   1909   Wolff, M.
Heiss[e] Eisen, Das+   1918   Wehrli, W.
Heisse Eisen, Das+   1922   Paumgartner, B.

Herr Puntila, 1940 (B. Brecht)
Puntila   1966   Dessau, P.

Historiae Philippicae (M. J. Justinius)
Lampedo   1779   Vogler, G. J.

Hypatia (F. Jansen)
Menandra+   1925   Kaun, H.

Iliad, The (Homer)
Penthesilea   1927   Schoeck, O.

Inferno, L', Francesca da Rimini episode (Dante)
Francesca da Rimini   1877   Goetz, H.

Inkle and Yariko, 1711 (J. Addison)
Fernando und Yariko   1784   Schack, B.

Inspector General, The, 1836 (N. Gogol)
Revisor, Der   1957   Egk, W.

Ivanhoe, 1820 (W. Scott).
Templer und die Jüdin, Der   1829   Marschner, H.

Jery und Bätely, 1780 (J. W. von Goethe)
Jery und Bäteli+   1790   Winter, P.

Jeu de l'amour et du hasard, 1730 (P. de Marivaux)
Spiel von Liebe und Zufall, 1982 Rosenfeld, G.
Das+

Jeune Indienne, La, 1765 (M. Chamfort)
Fernando und Yariko   1784   Schack, B.

Jeunesse de Henri V, La (A. Duval)
Zum Grossadmiral+   1847   Lortzing, A.

Jodelet ou le Maître Valet, 1645 (P. Scarron)
Lächerliche Printz Jodelet,   1726   Keiser, R.
Der

Judith, 1841 (F. Hebbel)
Holofernes+   1923   Reznicek, E. N.
                                             von

Julius Caesar, 1600 (W. Shakespeare)
Ermordung Cäsars, Die+   1959   Klebe, G.

Jungfrau von Orleans, Die, 1801 (F. Schiller)
Johanna d'Arc+   1840   Hoven, J.
Jungfrau von Orleans, Die+   1887   Reznicek, E. N.
                                             von
Mädchen aus Domrémy, Das   1976   Klebe, G.

Jüngste Tag, Der (Ö. von Horvath)
Jüngste Tag, Der+   1980   Klebe, G.

Kabale und Liebe, 1784 (F. Schiller)
Kabale und Liebe   1976   Einem, G. von

Kalte Herz, Das (W. Hauff)
Kalte Herz, Das+   1908   Konta, R.
Kalte Herz, Das+   1935   Lothar, M.
Kalte Herz, Das+   1938   Brüggemann, K.
Kalte Herz, Das   1943   Schultze, N.
Rote Stiefel, Der+   1951   Sutermeister, H.

Kenilworth, 1821 (W. Scott)
Kenilworth+   1895   Klein, B. O.

King Lear, 1606 (W. Shakespeare)
Lear   1978   Reimann, A.

Klein Zaches, 1818 (E. T. A. Hoffmann)
Zinnober+   1898   Hausegger, S.
                                             von

Komödie aus dem Stegreif, Die (J. F. Jünger)
Opernprobe, Die   1851   Lortzing, A.

Lady Henriette, 1844   (Vernoy de Saint-Georges)
Martha   1847   Flotow, F. von

Lalla Rookh, 1817 (T. Moore)
Feramors+   1863   Rubinstein, A.
Nurmahal   1822   Spontini, G.

Landarzt, Ein, 1919 (F. Kafka)
Landarzt, Ein   1953   Henze, H. W.

Last Days of Pompeii, The, 1834 (E. Bulwer-Lytton)
Alidia+   1839   Lachner, F.

Laune des Verliebten, Die, 1767 (J. W. Goethe)
Laune des Verliebten, Die+   1949   Dressel, E.

Lenardo und Blandine (G. A. Bürger)
Lenardo und Blandine   1779   Winter, P.

Lenz, 1836 (G. Büchner)
Jakob Lenz   1980   Rihm, W.

Leonce und Lena, 1836 (G. Büchner)
Leonce und Lena+   1925   Weissmann, J.
Leonce und Lena+   1961   Schwaen, K.
Leonce und Lena   1979   Dessau, P.

Léonore ou L'Amour conjugal, 1798 (J. N. Bouilly)
Fidelio   1814   Beethoven, L. van
Leonore   1805   Beethoven, L. van

Long Christmas Dinner, The (T. Wilder)
Lange Weihnachtsmahl, Das   1961   Hindemith, P.

Lucidor, 1910 (H. von Hofmannsthal)
Arabella   1933   Strauss, R.

Lysistrata (Aristophanes)
Verschworenen, Die   1823   Schubert, F.

Macbeth, 1606 (W. Shakespeare)
Macbeth+   1858   Taubert, W.

Maison à vendre (A. Duval)
Haus ist zu verkaufen, Dies+ 1806 Hummel, J. N.

Major Palmer, Le (C. A. G. Pigault-Lebrun)
Palmer und Amalia+   1893   Cannabich, C.

Manon Lescaut, 1731 (Abbé Prevost)
Boulevard Solitude   1952   Henze, H. W.

Marat/Sade, 1965 (P. Weiss)
Marat+   1984   Haupt, W.

Märchen, 1794 (J. W. von Goethe)
Märchen von der schönen   1969   Klebe, G.
  Lillie, Das+

Mariage de Figaro, Le. See *La Folle journée.*

Marie Tudor, 1833 (V. Hugo)
  Günstling, Der   1935 Wagner-Régeny, R.

Marienkirche poems
  Lübecker Totentanz, Der+   1948 Reutter, H.

Massimilla Doni, 1839 (H. de Balzac)
  Massimilla Doni   1937 Schoeck, O.

Matrimonio segreto, Il (G. Bertati)
  Heimliche Ehe, Die+   1891 Gast, P.

Mayor encanto amor, El (P. Calderón)
  Circe+   1948 Egk, W.
  Siebzehn Tage und vier   1966 Egk, W.
    Minuten

Measure for Measure, 1605 (W. Shakespeare)
  Liebesverbot, Das   1836 Wagner, R.

Médecin malgré lui, Le, 1666 (Molière)
  Unsterbliche Kranke, Der+   1947 Haug, H.

Mejor imposible, El (F. Lope de Vega)
  Unmöglichste von allem,   1897 Urspruch, A.
    Das+

Memoiren des Herrn von Schabel, Die (H. Heine)
  Fliegende Holländer, Der   1843 Wagner, R.

Méprises par resemblance, 1786 (J. Patrat)
  Beiden Schützen, Die   1837 Lortzing, A.

Merchant of Venice, The, 1596 (W. Shakespeare)
  Porzia+   1916 Taubmann, O.

Merry Cobbler, The (C. Coffey)
  Lustige Schuster, Der+   1759 Standfuss, J. C.
  Lustige Schuster, Der+   1770 Holly, F. A.

Merry Wives of Windsor, The, 1601 (W. Shakespeare)
  Lustigen Weiber von Windsor, 1796 Dittersdorf, K.
    Die+
  Lustigen Weiber von Windsor, 1849 Nicolai, O.
    Die

Metamorphoses, Book 1 (Ovid)
  Beglückte Florindo, Der+   1708 Handel, G. F.
  Verwandelte Daphne, Die+   1708 Handel, G. F.

Metamorphoses, Book 8 (Ovid)
Philemon und Baucis   1773   Haydn, F. J.

Midsummer Night's Dream, A, 1595 (W. Shakespeare)
Mitternachtstraum, Ein+   1988   Decker, W.

Miglior d'ogni Amore, Il, 1703 (F. Silvani)
Sancio und Sinilde+   1727   Graun, K. H.

Milles et un jour, Les, 1712 (Pétis de la Croix)
Turandot   1917   Busoni, F.

Mitschuldigen, Die, 1769 (J. W. von Goethe)
Mitschuldigen, Die+   1957   Riethmüller, H.

Mond, Der (Grimm brothers)
Mond, Der   1939   Orff, C.

Much Ado About Nothing, 1599 (W. Shakespeare)
Viel Lärm um nichts+   1956   Heinrich, H.

Nachts unter der steinernen Brücke (L. Perutz)
Engel von Prag, Der   1979   Bresgen, C.

Nachtstücke, 1815 (E. T. A. Hoffmann)
Sandmann, Der+   1987   Kounadis, A.

Nausikaa, 1827 (J. W. von Goethe)
Nausikaa+   1967   Reutter, H.

New Testament, The
Jesu Hochzeit   1980   Einem, G. von
Legende von der heiligen   1881   Liszt, F.
  Elisabeth, Die+

Nibelung saga
Ring des Nibelungen, Der   1876   Wagner, R.

Ninette à la cour (C. Goldoni and C.-S. Favart)
Lottchen am Hofe+   1767   Hiller, J. A.

Nino de la bola, El (P. Alacron)
Manuel Venegas   1903   Wolf, H.

Niobe (Aeschylus)
Niobe+   1977   Hiller, W.

Oberon, 1780 (C. M. Wieland)
Oberon   1789   Wranitzky, P.
Oberon   1826   Weber, C. M. von

Odyssey, The (Homer)
Circe+	1734	Keiser, R.
Circe+	1948	Egk, W.
Circe (Des Ulysses erster		
Theil)+	1696	Keiser, R.
Odysseus+	1942	Reutter, H.
Odysseus bei Circe+	1938	Trantow, H.
Odysseus' Tod+	1903	Bungert, A.
Odysseus und die Sirenen+	1950	Goldberg, T.

Oedipus Tyrannos (Sophocles)
Oedipus+	1960	Eder, H.
Oedipus+	1987	Rihm, W.
Oedipus der Tyrann	1959	Orff, C.

Old Testament, The
Abels Tod+	ca. 1778	Haydn, M.
Baal	1981	Cerha, F.
Baals Sturz+	not perf	Sehlbach, E.
Belsazar+	1723	Telemann, G. P.
Belsazar+	1929	Peró, H.
Belshazar+	1984	Kirchner, V. D.
Erschaffene...Mensch, Der+	1678	Theile, J.
Jephtas Gelübde+	1812	Meyerbeer, G.
Judith+	1870	Doppler, A. F.
Judith+	1921	Ettinger, M.
Judith+	1948	Adam, F.
Judith+	1950	Goldberg, T.
Kain+	1952	Schmidtmann, F.
Kain und Abel+	1914	Weingartner, F.
Maccabäer, Die+	1875	Rubinstein, A.
Moses und Aron	1932	Schoenberg, A.
Sulamith+	1913	Klenau, P. von

Orlando furioso (L. Ariosto)
Rinaldo und Alcina+	1797	Paradis, M. T. von

Partie de chasse de Henri IV, Le (C. Colle)
Jagd, Die	1770	Hiller, J. A.

Parzival, ca. 1210 (W. von Eschenbach)
Parsifal	1882	Wagner, R.

Patienza di Socrate, La, 1680 (N. Minato)
Gedultige Sokrates, Der	1721	Telemann, G. P.

Peau de chagrin, Le, 1831 (H. de Balzac)
Tödlichen Wünsche, Die	1959	Klebe, G.

Peer Gynt, 1867 (H. Ibsen)
    Peer Gynt   1938 Egk, W.
    Peer Gynt+   not perf Ullmann, V.

Penthesilea, 1807 (H. von Kleist)
    Penthesilea+   1927 Ritter, R.
    Penthesilea   1927 Schoeck, O.

Picture of Dorian Gray, The, 1891 (O. Wilde)
    Dorian+   1939 Leger, H.
    Dorian Gray+   1930 Flick-Steger, C.
    Dorian Gray+   1962 Hanell, R.

Pietro von Abano, 1825 (L. Tieck)
    Pietro von Abano   1827 Spohr, L.

Pimpinone, 1708 (P. Pariati)
    Pimpinone   1725 Telemann, G. P.

Pittochi fortunati, I (C. Gozzi)
    Tartarische Gesetz, Das+ 1779 André, J.
    Tartarische Gesetz, Das+ 1780 Zumsteeg, F.

Plautus (Menachmi)
    Zwillingskomödie   1954 Mohaupt, R.

Playboy of the Western World, The, 1907 (J. M. Synge)
    Wahrer Held, Ein   1975 Klebe, G.

Postmaster, The, 1830 (A. Pushkin)
    Postmeister Wyrin+   1946 Reutter, F. von

Precieuses ridicules, Les, 1659 (Molière)
    Zierpuppen+   1905 Goetzl, A.

Princess and the Pea, The (H. C. Andersen)
    Prinzessin auf der Erbse, 1927 Toch, E.
      Die+

Prinz Friedrich von Homburg, Der, 1810 (H. von Kleist)
    Prinz von Homburg, Der 1960 Henze, H. W.

Prinzessin Brambilla, 1820 (E. T. A. Hoffmann)
    Prinzessin Brambilla   1909 Braunfels, W.

Protagonist, Der (G. Kaiser)
    Protagonist, Der   1926 Weill, K.

Prozess, Der, 1915 (F. Kafka)
    Prozess, Der   1953 Einem, G. von

Purloined Letter, The, 1845 (E. A. Poe)
Geheimnis des entwendeten   1975   Blacher, B.
Briefes, Das+

Quart-d'Heure de Silence, Un, 1804 (P. Guillet)
Wette+   1805   Weber, B. A.

Rattenfänger, Der, 1975 (C. Zuckmayer)
Rattenfänger, Der+   1987   Cerha, F.

Räuber, Die, 1782 (F. Schiller)
Räuber, Die   1957   Klebe, G.

Re Cervo, Il (C. Gozzi)
König Hirsch   1956   Henze, H. W.

Redenzione, La (G. Menasci)
Erlösung, Die+   1895   Scharrer, A.

Rehbock, Der (A. von Kotzebue)
Wildschütz, Der   1842   Lortzing, A.

Reine de Chypre, La, 1841 (J. H. Saint-Georges)
Catharina Cornaro   1841   Lachner, F.

Reisenden Komödienten, Die, 1774 (P. Hafner)
Schwestern von Prag, Die   1794   Müller, W.

Rendencion de Breda, La, 1625 (P. Calderón)
Friedenstag   1938   Strauss, R.

Retablo de las maravillas, 1605 (M. de Cervantes)
Wundertheater, Das   1949   Henze, H. W.

Rienzi, 1828 (M. R. Mitford)
Rienzi   1842   Wagner, R.

Rienzi, 1835 (E. Bulwer-Lytton)
Rienzi   1842   Wagner, R.

Ritterzeit (J. G. Büsching)
Hochzeit, Die   1832   Wagner, R.

Roi et le fermier, Le, 1770 (J. M. Sedaine)
Jagd, Die   1770   Hiller, J. A.

Romeo and Juliet, 1595 (W. Shakespeare)
Romeo und Julia   1940   Sutermeister, H.
Romeo und Julia   1947   Blacher, B.
Romeo und Julie   1776   Benda, G.

Rosamunde Floris, 1940 (G. Kaiser)
Rosamunde Floris   1960   Blacher, B.

Rose et Colas, 1771 (J. M. Sedaine)
Hänschen und Gretschen+   1727   Reichardt, J. F.

Rose vom Kaukasus, Die (R. von Gottschall)
Sarema+   1897   Zemlinsky, A. von

Rossignol, Le (C. G. Etienne)
Nachtigall und Rabe+   1818   Weigl, J.

Rubin, Der, 1851 (F. Hebbel)
Rubin, Der+   1893   Albert, E. d'
Rubin, Der+   1938   Jenny, A.

Rumpelstiltzchen (Grimm brothers)
Rumpelstilzchen+   1911   Büttner, P.

Saffi (M. Jokai)
Zigeunerbaron, Der   1885   Strauss, J., Jr.

Sagas of the Netherlands, 1843 (J. W. Wolf)
Feuersnot   1901   Strauss, R.

Salambo, 1862 (G. Flaubert)
Salambo+   1926   Böttcher, L.

Salome, 1894 (O. Wilde)
Salome   1905   Strauss, R.

Sappho, 1817 (F. Grillparzer)
Sappho+   1917   Kaun, H.

Satyros, 1773 (J. W. von Goethe)
Satyros+   1923   Baussnern, W. von

Schärpe und die Blüme, Die (P. Calderón)
   (transl. Schlegel)
Liebe und Eifersucht+   1807   Hoffmann,
                                       E. T. A.

Scheik von Alexandria, Der, 1827 (W. Hauff)
Junge Lord, Der   1965   Henze, H. W.

Scherz, List und Rache, 1784 (J. W. von Goethe)
Scherz, List und Rache+   1790   Winter, P.
Scherz, List und Rache+ ca. 1801   Hoffmann,
                                       E. T. A.
Scherz, List und Rache+   1856   Bruch, M.
Scherz, List und Rache+   1928   Wellesz, E.

Scherz, List und Rache (cont.)
Scherz, List und Rache+   1961   Leinert, F.

Schirin und Getraude (E. Hardt)
Schirin und Getraude+   1920   Graener, P.

Schloss, Das, 1922 (F. Kafka)
Schloss, Das+   ca. 1986   Laporte, A.

Schloss Dürande, Das, 1837 (J. F. von Eichendorff)
Schloss Dürande, Das   1943   Schoeck, O.

Schuhu, 1966 (P. Hacks)
Schuhu, Der+   1976   Zimmermann, U.

Schwarze Spinne, Die, 1842 (J. Gotthelf)
Schwarze Spinne, Die+   1932   Hauer, J. M.
Schwarze Spinne, Die   1949   Burkhard, W.

Scipione Africano, 1664 (N. Minato)
Grossmüthige Scipio, Der+   1690   Krieger, J. P.

Semiramide, La, 1670 (P. A. Ziani)
Semiramis+   1683   Franck, J. W.
Sganarelle, 1660 (Molière)
Sganarelle+   1929   Wagner-Régeny, R.

Signor Formica, 1819 (E. T. A. Hoffmann)
Salvator Rosa+   1832   Rastrelli, J.

Silvain, 1770 (J. F. Marmontel)
Walder+   1776   Benda, G.

Simplicissimus, 1669 (J. H. C. Grimmelshausen)
Des Simplicius   1949   Hartmann, K. A.
  Simplicissimus Jugend+
Simplicius, Der+   1912   Huber, H.

Six Demoiselles à marier, 1856 (A. Jaime and A. Choler)
Zehn Mädchen und kein Mann+   1862   Suppé, F. von

Smetse Smee (C. de Coster)
Schmied von Gent, Der   1932   Schreker, F.

Smile at the Foot of the Ladder, The, 1948 (H. Miller)
Lächeln am Füsse der Leiter,   1965   Bibalo, A.
  Das+

Soldaten, Die, 1775 (J. M. Lenz)
Soldaten+   1930   Gurlitt, M.
Soldaten, Die   1965   Zimmermann, B. A.

Soliman II, 1761 (C.-S. Favart)
Soliman der Zweyte 1799 Süssmayr, F. X.

Sombrero de tres picos, El, 1784 (P. de Alarcón)
Corregidor, Der 1896 Wolf, H.

Souper imprévu, Le (A. Duval)
Unbetene Gäster, Die+ 1805 Hoffmann,
E. T. A.

Speziale, Lo (C. Goldoni)
Apotheke, Die+ 1771 Neefe, C. G.

Stella, 1776 (J. W. von Goethe)
Stella+ 1951 Bloch, W.

Stella Maris (H. Revers)
Stella Maris+ 1910 Kaiser, A.

Student of Salamanca, The (W. Irving)
Alchymist, Der 1830 Spohr, L.

Talismann, Der, 1840 (J. Nestroy)
Titus Feuerfuchs+ 1958 Sutermeister, H.

Taming of the Shrew, The, 1592 (W. Shakespeare)
Widerspänstigen Zähmung, Die 1874 Goetz, H.

Taniko (A. Waley)
Jasager, Der 1930 Weill, K.

Taras Bulba, 1835 (N. Gogol)
Taras Bulba+ 1935 Richter, E.

Tartarin de Tarascon, 1885 (A. Daudet)
Tartarin von Tarascon+ 1965 Radermacher, F.
Tartarin von Tarascon 1977 Niehaus, M.

Tartuffe, 1664 (Molière)
Tartuffe+ 1929 Eidens, J.
Tartuffe+ 1937 Haug, H.

Taucher, Der, 1797 (F. Schiller)
Taucher, Der+ 1811 Reichardt, J. F.

Tempest, The, 1612 (W. Shakespeare)
Geisterinsel, Die+ 1798 Fleischmann, F.
Geisterinsel, Die 1798 Reichardt, J. F.
Geisterinsel, Die+ 1798 Zumsteeg, J. R.
Sturm, Der 1798 Winter, P.

Tempest, The (cont.)
Sturm, Der+   1799   Müller, W.
Sturm, Der+   1888   Urspruch, A.
Sturm, Der   1956   Martin, F.
Zauberinsel, Die+   1942   Sutermeister, H.

Terra baixa (A. Guiméra)
Tiefland   1903   Albert, E. d'

Teseo, 1685 (A. Aureli)
Theseus+   1688   Löhner, J.

Thousand and One Nights
Abu Hassan   1811   Weber, C. M. von
Barbier von Bagdad, Der   1858   Cornelius, P.
Wirth und Gast   1813   Meyerbeer, G.

To Warmer Lands (P. C. Jersild)
Reise, Die+   1969   Werle, L. J.

Tod des Empedokles, Der, 1626 (F. Hölderlin)
Tod des Empedokles, Der+   1966   Reutter, H.

Tonnlier de Nurenberg, Le (C. Nuitter)
Meister Martin und seine   1897   Lacombe, L.
   Gesellen+

Tragedy of Mankind (I. Madach)
Tragödie der Menschheit,   1981   Hamel, P. M.
   Die+

Traum ein Leben, Der, 1831 (F. Grillparzer)
Traum, Der+   1909   Mraczek, J. G.
Traum ein Leben, Der   1937   Braunfels, W.
Traumleben+   1963   Kont, P.

Trauung, Die, 1946 (W. Gombrowicz)
Trauung, Die+   1975   Kirchner, V. D.

Trilby, 1823 (E. Scribe and P. F. A. Carmouche)
Trilby+   1835   Truhn, F. H.
Trilby+   1845   Schmitt, G. A.

Tristan, ca. 1210 (G. von Strassburg)
Tristan und Isolde   1865   Wagner, R.

Tristram, ca. 1150 (Thomas of Britain)
Tristan und Isolde   1865   Wagner, R.

Troilus and Cressida, 1602 (W. Shakespeare)
Troilus und Cressida   1951   Zillig, W.

Trompeter von Säckingen, Der, 1854 (J. V. von Scheffel)
    Trompeter von Säckingen,   1884   Nessler, V. E.
    Der+

Turandot (C. Gozzi)
    Turandot   1817   Danzi, F.
    Turandot   1917   Busoni, F.

Twelfth Night, 1601 (W. Shakespeare)
    Viola+   1934   Holenia, H.

Ulysses, 1921 (J. Joyce)
    Stephan Climax+   1986   Zender, H.

Under Milk Wood, 1974 (D. Thomas)
    Unter dem Milchwald+   1972   Steffens, W.

Vampire, The, 1819 (J. W. Polidori)
    Vampyr, Der   1828   Marschner, H.

Van Gogh, 1966 (A. Matusche)
    Vincent+   1979   Kunad, R.

Ventaglio, Il (C. Goldoni)
    Fächer, Der+   1929   Kunz, E.
    Fächer, Der+   1930   Toch, E.

Verlobung in San Domingo, Die, 1811 (H. von Kleist)
    Verlobung in San Domingo, 1957   Zillig, W.
    Die+
    Verlobung in San Domingo, 1963   Egk, W.
    Die

Versiegelte Bürgermeister, Der (E. Raupach)
    Versiegelt   1908   Blech, L.

Vestale, La, 1807 (E. de Jouy)
    Vestalin, Die+   1814   Guhr, K. W. F.

Veuve de Malabar, La (A. M. Lemierre)
    Jessonda   1823   Spohr, L.
    Lanassa+   1805   Tuczek, V. F.

Wallenstein, 1799 (F. Schiller)
    Wallenstein+   1937   Weinberger, J.

Wayward Saint, The, 1955 (P. V. Carroll)
    Widerspenstige Heilige, Der+ 1968   Lothar, M.

William Ratcliff, 1823 (H. Heine)
Ratcliff+   1914 Andreae, V.
William Ratcliff+   1909 Dopper, C.
William Ratcliff   1982 Ostendorf, J. P.

Winterballade, 1917 (G. Hauptmann)
Doppelgängerin, Die+   1967 Meyerowitz, J.

Winter's Tale, A, 1611 (W. Shakespeare)
Hermione+   1872 Bruch, M.
Wintermärchen, Das+   1900 Zimmermann, B.
Wintermärchen, Ein+   1908 Goldmark, K.

Woyzeck, 1837 (G. Büchner)
Wozzeck   1925 Berg, A.
Wozzeck+   1926 Gurlitt, M.

Yeux morts, Les, 1897 (M. Henry)
Toten Augen, Die   1916 Albert, E. d'

Zapatera prodigiosa, La, 1931 (F. García Lorca, F.)
Merkwürdige Frau des   1982 Zimmermann, U.
Schusters+

Zauberlehrling, Der, 1797 (J. W. von Goethe)
Zauberlehrling, Der+   1907 Döbber, J.

Zemire et Azor, 1771 (J. F. Marmontel)
Zemire und Azor   1819 Spohr, L.
Zemire und Azor+   1776 Baumgarten, C. G.
                                   von

Zerbrochene Krug, Der, 1811 (H. von Kleist)
Zerbrochene Krug, Der   1971 Geissler, F.

Zerrissene, Der, 1844 (J. Nestroy)
Zerrissene, Der+   1941 Kreuder, P.
Zerrissene, Der+   1942 Jenny, A.
Zerrissene, Der   1964 Einem, G. von

APPENDIX 6

CHRONOLOGY

*Date of premiere or composition.
+See Appendix I.

Year*	City, Date	Title	Composer
1627	Torgau, ?	Dafne	Schütz, H.
1644	Nuremberg, ?	Seelewig	Staden, S. T.
1657	Brunswick, April	Amelinde+	Loewe, J. J.
1659	Brunswick, Aug. 30	Orpheus aus Thracien+	Loewe, J. J.
1675	Ansbach, ?	Errettete Unschuld, Die+	Franck, J. W.
1678	Hamburg, Jan.	Erschaffene...Mensch, Der+	Theile, J.
	Hamburg, ?	Orontes+	Theile, J.
1679	Ansbach, ?	Drey Töchter Cecrops, Die+	Franck, J. W.
1680	Hamburg, ?	Aeneas+	Franck, J. W.
	Hamburg, ?	Alceste+	Franck, J. W.
	Hamburg, ?	Esther+	Strungk, N. A.
	Reval, ?	Beständige Argenis, Die+	Meder, J. V.
1681	Hamburg, ?	Geburth Christi, Die+	Theile, J.
	Hamburg, ?	Vespanius+	Franck, J. W.
1682	Hamburg, ?	Diocletianus+	Franck, J. W.

Year	Place, Date	Title	Composer
1683	Hamburg, ?	Semiramis+	Franck, J. W.
	Hamburg, ?	Theseus+	Strungk, N. A.
1686	Vienna, Jan.	Cara Mustapha+	Franck, J. W.
1688	Nuremberg, ?	Theseus+	Löhner, J.
1690	Brunswick, Aug.	Julia+	Kusser, J.
	Weissenfels, Nov. 20	Grossmüthige Scipio, Der+	Krieger, J. P.
1691	Brunswick, ?	Cleopatra+	Kusser, J. S.
	Hamburg, ?	Ariadne	Conradi, J. G.
1692	Brunswick, Feb. 15	Ariadne+	Kusser, J. S.
	Brunswick, Feb. 20	Andromeda+	Kusser, J. S.
	Brunswick, Sept.	Jason+	Kusser, J. S.
	Brunswick, Oct. 4	Narcissus+	Kusser, J. S.
1693	Leipzig, May 18	Alceste+	Strungk, N. A.
	Brunswick, ?	Echo und Narcissus+	Bronner, G.
	Hamburg, ?	Gensericus+	Conradi, J. G.
1694	Hamburg, Carnival?	Erindo+	Kusser, J. S.
	Hamburg, spring?	Basilius+	Keiser, R.
	Brunswick, ?	Procris und Cephalis+	Keiser, R.
1696	Brunswick, Feb.	Circe (Des Ulysses, pt. 1)	Keiser, R.
	Brunswick, Feb.	Penelope (Des Ulysses, pt. 2)+	Keiser, R.

Year	Place	Title	Composer
1697	Hamburg, ?	Adonis	Keiser, R.
1698	Hamburg, June	Augustus+	Keiser, R.
	Brunswick, ?	Orpheus+	Keiser, R.
	Hamburg, ?	Janus	Keiser, R.
1699	Brunswick, ?	Verwandelte Leyer, des Orpheus, Die+	Keiser, R.
1700	Hamburg, Carnival	Forza della virtù, La	Keiser, R.
1701	Brunswick, Aug.	Salomon+	Schürmann, J. C.
	Hamburg, ?	Psyche+	Keiser, R.
	Hamburg, ?	stoertebecker und Joedge Michael+	Keiser, R.
1702	Hamburg, ?	Orpheus ander Theil+	Keiser, R.
	Hamburg, ?	sterbende Eurydice, Die (Orpheus erster Theil)+	Keiser, R.
1703	Hamburg, spring	Claudius	Keiser, R.
	Brunswick, ?	Leonilde+	Schürmann, G. C.
1704	Hamburg, Carnival	Nebucadnezar	Keiser, R.
	Leipzig, Oct.	Germanicus+	Grünewald, G.
	Hamburg, Oct. 20	Cleopatra	Mattheson, J.
	Weissenfels, ?	Almira, Königen von Castilien+	Keiser, R.
1705	Hamburg, Aug.	Octavia	Keiser, R.

Year	Place, Date	Title	Composer
1705 (cont.)	Hamburg, ?	Almira	Handel, G. F.
	Hamburg, ?	Nero	Handel, G. F.
1706	Hamburg, June	Masagniello Furioso	Keiser, R.
	Naumburg, June-July	Telemaque+	Schürmann, G. C.
	Hamburg, Oct. 11	Costanza sforzata+	Keiser, R.
	Hamburg, ?	Almira+	Keiser, R.
	? ?	Verstöhrte Troja, Das+	Schürmann, G. C.
1707	Hamburg, spring	Dido, Königin von Carthago+	Graupner, C.
	Hamburg, summer	Angenehme Betrug, Der+	Keiser and Graupner
1708	Hamburg, Jan.	Beglückte Florindo, Der+	Handel, G. F.
	Hamburg, Feb.	Verwandelte Daphne, Die+	Handel, G. F.
	Hamburg, Nov. 28	Bellerophon+	Graupner, C.
	Hamburg, ?	Fido amico, Il+	Graupner, C.
	Hamburg, ?	Lustige Hochzeit, Die+	Keiser and Graupner
	? ?	Antiochus und Stratonica+	Graupner, C.
1709	Hamburg, July	Desiderius+	Keiser, R.
	Hamburg, ?	Fall des grossen Richters, Der+	Graupner, C.
1710	Darmstadt, March 10	Berenice und Lucilla+	Graupner, C.
	Hamburg, ?	Bon vivant, Le+	Keiser, R.
	Hamburg, ?	Boris Goudenow+	Mattheson, J.
	Hamburg, ?	Croesus	Keiser, R.
	Hamburg, ?	Julius Caesar+	Keiser, R.
	Hamburg, ?	Paris und Helena+	Heinichen, J. D.

1711	Forza dell'amore, La+	Hamburg, ?	Keiser, R.
	Henrico IV+	Hamburg, ?	Mattheson, J.
1712	Diana+	Hamburg, ?	Keiser, R.
1714	Romanische Lucretia, Die+	Durlach, ?	Schweitzelsperger, C.
	Inganno fedele, L'	Hamburg, ?	Keiser, R.
1715	Fredegunda+	Hamburg, ?	Keiser, R.
1716	Unglückliche Liebe+	Durlach, ?	Schweitzelsperger, C.
1717	Grossmüthige Tomyris, Die	Hamburg, July	Keiser, R.
	Julia+	Hamburg, ?	Keiser, R.
1718	Heinrich der Vogler+	Brunswick, July	Schürmann, G. C.
	Porsenna+	Brunswick, ?	Schürmann, G. C.
1719	Getreue Alceste, Die+	Brunswick, ?	Schürmann, G. C.
1720	Cadmus+	Brunswick? ?	Kunzen, J. P.
1721	Gedultige Sokrates, Der	Hamburg, ?	Telemann, G. P.
1722	Eroberte Jerusalem, Die+	Brunswick, Feb.	Schürmann, G. C.
	Ulysses+	Copenhagen, Nov.	Keiser, R.
	Sieg der Schönheit, Der+	Hamburg, ?	Conradi and Telemann
1723	Belsazar+	? ?	Telemann, G. P.

Year	Title	Place, Date	Composer
1724	Neu-modische Liebhaber Damon, Der	Hamburg, ?	Telemann, G. P.
1725	Pimpinone	Hamburg, ?	Telemann, G. P.
1726	Ludovicus Pius	Brunswick, Feb.	Schürmann, G. C.
	Lächerliche Printz Jodelet, Der	Hamburg, ?	Keiser, R.
1727	Sancio und Sinilde+	Brunswick, Feb.	Graun, K. H.
	Don Quixote+	Hamburg, ?	Müller, A. E.
	Hänschen und Gretschen+	Leipzig, ?	Reichardt, J. F.
1728	Miriways	Hamburg, May	Telemann, G. P.
	Last-tragende Liebe, Die	Hamburg, ?	Telemann, G. P.
	Verkehrte Welt, Die+	? ?	Telemann, G. P.
1729	Flavius Bertaridus+	? ?	Telemann, G. P.
1731	Iphigenia in Aulis+	Brunswick, ?	Graun, K. H.
1734	Circe+	Hamburg, ?	Keiser, R.
1743	Teufel ist los, Der	Berlin, Jan. 24	Standfuss, J. C.
1747	Doris+	Dresden, Feb. 13	Schürer, J. G.
1749	Thusnelde+	---	not set
1753	Krumme Teufel, Der+	Vienna, May 29	Haydn, F. J.

568

Year	Place, Date	Title	Composer
1759	Lübeck, Jan. 18	Lustige Schuster, Der+	Standfuss, J. C.
	Hamburg, ?	Jochem Tröbs+	Standfuss, J. C.
	Vienna	Neue krumme Teufel, Der+	Haydn, F. J.
1761	? ?	Don Quichotte der Löwenritter+	Telemann, G. P.
1766	Leipzig, May	Teufel ist los, Der	Hiller, J. A.
	Leipzig, Nov. 25	Lisuarte und Darlioette+	Hiller, J. A.
1767	Leipzig, April	Lottchen am Hofe	Hiller, J. A.
	Leipzig, Oct.	Musen, Die+	Hiller, J. A.
	Salzburg, May 1	Schuldigkeit des ersten Gebotes, Die, part I	Mozart, W. A.
	? ?	part II	Haydn, M.
	? ?	part III	Adlgasser, M.
1768	Leipzig, May	Liebe auf dem Lande, Die+	Hiller, J. A.
	Vienna, Sept.	Bastien und Bastienne	Mozart, W. A.
	Salzburg	Hochzeit auf der Alm, Die+	Haydn, M.
1769	Lucerne, ?	Hans Hüttenstock+	Meyer von Schauensee, F.
	Weimar, ?	Gärtnermädchen, Das+	Wolf, E. W.
	Salzburg	Wahrheit der Natur, Die+	Haydn, M.
1770	Hanover, Jan. 18	Elysium+	Schweitzer, A.
	Weimar, Jan. 29	Jagd, Die	Hiller, J. A.
	Weimar, Sept. 4	Rosenfest, Das+	Wolf, E. W.
	Prague, ?	Lustige Schuster, Der+	Holly, F. A.

Year	Place, Date	Title	Composer
1771	Leipzig, spring	Aerndtekranz, Der+	Hiller, J. A.
	Hamburg, Oct. 8	Clarisse	Roellig, K. L.
	Berlin, Dec.	Apotheke, Die+	Neefe, C. G.
	Leipzig, ?	Dorfbarbier, Der+	Hiller, J. A.
	Mannheim, ?	Kaufmann von Smyrna, Der+	Vogler, G. J.
1772	Prague, May 10	Jagd, Die+	Holly, F. A.
	Berlin, June 15	Dorfdeputierten, Die+	Wolf, E. W.
	Weimar, June 30	Dorfgala, Der+	Schweitzer, A.
	Leipzig, ?	Amors Guckkasten+	Neefe, C. G.
	Leipzig, ?	Krieg, Der+	Hiller, J. A.
ca. 1772	Vienna	Insel der Liebe, Die+	Umlauf, I.
1773	Hanau, Jan. 22	Töpfer, Der	André, J.
	Weimar, May 28	Alceste	Schweitzer, A.
	Berlin, Nov. 13	Kaufmann von Smyrna, Der+	Holly, F. A.
	Esterháza, ?	Philemon und Baucis	Haydn, F. J.
	Leipzig, ?	Jubelhochzeit, Die+	Hiller, J. A.
	Weimar, ?	Abend im Walde, Der+	Wolf, E. W.
	Weimar, ?	Treuen Köhler, Die+	Wolf, E. W.
	? ?	Hexen-schabbas+	Haydn, F. J.
	? ?	Kaufmann von Smyrna, Der+	Stegmann, C. D.
1774	Prague, Jan. 6	Bassa von Tunis, Der+	Holly, F. A.
	Weimar, ?	Grosse Loos, Das+	Wolf, E. W.
1775	Gotha, Jan. 27	Ariadne auf Naxos	Benda, G.
	Gotha, Feb.	Jahrmarkt, Der	Benda, G.

Year	Place, Date	Title	Composer
1775 (cont.)	Berlin, ?	Clarissa+	Schulz, J. A. P.
	Frankfurt, ?	Erwin und Elmira+	André, J.
	Leipzig, ?	Medea	Benda, G.
	premiere 1982	Feuersbrunst, Die	Haydn, F. J.
1776	Gotha, Sept.	Romeo und Julie	Benda, G.
	Berlin, ?	Alte Freyer, Der+	André, J.
	Breslau, ?	Andromeda+	Baumgarten, C. G. von
	Breslau, ?	Zemire und Azor+	Baumgarten, C. G. von
	Gotha, ?	Walder+	Benda, G.
	Leipzig, ?	Barbier von Sevilla, Der+	Benda, F. L.
	Weimar	Ehrlichkeit und Liebe+	Wolf, E. W.
	? ?	Rebekka als Braut+	Haydn, M.
1777	Mannheim, Jan.	Günther von Schwarzburg	Holzbauer, I.
	Lüneborg, June	Lindor und Ismene+	Schmittbauer, J. A.
	Hamburg, July 7	Cephalus und Prokris+	Reichardt, J. F.
	Berlin, ?	Bezauberten, Die+	André, J.
	? ?	Arcifano+	Dittersdorf, K.
ca. 1777	Esterháza? ?	Reisende Ceres, Die	Haydn, F. J.
	? ?	Poltis+	Hiller, J. A.
1778	Gotha, Jan. 2	Holzhauer, Der+	Benda, G.
	Vienna, Feb. 17	Bergknappen, Die	Umlauf, I.
	Dresden, March	Alchymist, Der	Schuster, J.
	Berlin, April 11	Alchymist, Der+	André, J.
	Vienna, July 15	Kinder der Natur, Die+	Aspelmayr, F.
	Berlin, ?	Freund deutscher sitten, Der+	Kosposth, O. C. E. von

Year	Place, Date	Work	Composer
1778 (cont.)	Berlin, ?	Laura Rosetti+	André, J.
	Gotha, ?	Claudine von Villa Bella+	André, J.
	Leipzig, ?	Kleine Aehrenleserin, Die+	Hiller, J. A.
	Mannheim, ?	Azakia+	Cannabich, C.
	Mannheim, ?	Sophonisbe+	Neefe, C. G.
	Salzburg, ?	Aehrenleserin, Die+	Haydn, M.
	Vienna, ?	Apotheke, Die+	Umlauf, I.
	? ?	Abels Tod+	Haydn, M.
	? ?	Dido+	Haydn, F. J.
1779	Dresden, May 3	Arsene+	Seydelmann, F.
	Berlin, May 31	Tartarische Gesetz, Das+	André, J.
	Vienna, June 22	Schöne Schusterin, Die+	Umlauf, I.
	Mannheim, June 25	Lenardo und Blandine	Winter, P.
	Darmstadt, July 11	Lampedo	Vogler, G. J.
	Leipzig, Sept. 4	Ino	Reichardt, J. F.
	Gotha, Sept. 20	Pygmalion+	Benda, G.
	Stuttgart, Oct. 2	Irrwisch, Der+	Dieter, C. F.
	Berlin, Oct. 16	Adrast und Isidore+	Kospoth, O. C. E. von
	Leipzig, ?	Grab des Mufti, Das	Hiller, J. A.
	Leipzig, ?	Wüste Insel, Die+	Schuster, J.
	? ?	Aesopus+	Telemann, G. P.
	premiere 1866	Zaïde	Mozart, W. A.
ca. 1779	?	Bestrafte Rachbegierde, Die+	Haydn, F. J.
1780	Mannheim, Jan. 20	Rosamunde+	Schweitzer, A.
	Stuttgart, March 28	Tartarische Gesetz, Das	Zumsteeg, J.
	Vienna, June 13	Claudine von Villa Bella+	Kienlen, J. C.

Year	Place, Date	Title	Composer
1780 (cont.)	Frankfurt, Sept. 23	Adelheit von Veltheim	Neefe, C. G.
	Berlin, Oct.	Irrwisch, Der+	Kospoth, O. C. E. von
	Weimar, ?	Alceste+	Wolf, E. W.
1781	Stuttgart, Feb.	Laura Rosetti+	Dieter, C. F.
	Vienna, April 1	Rauchfangkehrer, Die+	Salieri, A.
	Berlin, May 25	Belmont und Constanze	André, J.
	Mannheim, Sept. 1	Electra+	Cannabich, C.
	Darmstadt, Dec.	Erwin und Elmire+	Vogler, G. J.
	? ?	Engelberger Talhochzeit, Eine+	Meyer von Schauensee, F.
1782	Vienna, Jan.	Irrlicht, Das+	Umlauf, I.
	Munich, Feb.	Helena und Paris+	Winter, P.
	Vienna, July 16	Entführung aus dem Serail, Die	Mozart, W. A.
	Berlin, Sept. 11	Liebhaber als Automat, Der+	André, J.
	Mannheim, ?	Jubelhochzeit, Die+	Beecke, I. von
	Mannheim, ?	Weinlese, Die+	Beecke, I. von
1783	Vienna, Feb. 9	Rose+	Mederitsch, J.
	Berlin, Feb. 19	Barbier von Bagdad, Der	André, J.
	Vienna, Feb. 22	Unnutze Vorsicht, Die+	Weigl, J.
	Munich, May 8	Dorfdeputierten, Die+	Schubaur, J. L.
1784	Stuttgart, Aug. 27	Belmont und Constanze+	Dieter, C. F.
	Vienna, Dec. 3	Fernando und Yariko	Schack, B.
1785	Munich, Feb. 2	Bettelstudent, Der+	Winter, P.
	Vienna, Oct. 12	Weinlese, Die+	Schenk, J.
	Berlin, ?	Orpheus+	Benda, F.

Year	Place, Date	Title	Composer
1786	Berlin, Jan. 15	Alceste+	Benda, F.
	Vienna, Feb. 7	Schauspieldirektor, Der	Mozart, W. A.
	Vienna, July 11	Doctor (Doktor) und Apotheker	Dittersdorf, K.
	Munich, Sept. 29	Treuen Köhler, Die+	Schubaur, J. L.
	Stuttgart, Oct.	Dorfdeputierten, Die	Dieter, C. F.
	Vienna, Oct. 3	Betrug durch Aberglauben+	Dittersdorf, K.
	Vienna, Dec. 3	Ring der Liebe, Der+	Umlauf, I.
	Berlin, ?	Athalia+	Schulz, J. A. P.
1787	Biberach, Feb. 2	Entführung aus dem Serail, Die	Knecht, J. K.
	Vienna, April 12	Liebe im Narrenhaus, Die	Dittersdorf, K.
	Leipzig, ?	Tartarische Gesetz, Das+	Benda, G.
ca. 1787	not perf	Findelkind, Das+	Benda, G.
1788	Berlin, Jan. 11	Andromeda+	Reichardt, J. F.
	Berlin, Feb.	Kluge Jacob, Der+	Kospoth, O. C. E. von
	Munich, April	Mitternachtsstunde, Die+	Danzi, F.
	Mannheim, Dec. 14	Eremit auf Formentara, Der+	Ritter, P.
	Berlin, ?	Don Quixotte+	Beecke, I. von
	Stuttgart, ?	Tamira+	Zumsteeg, J. R.
1789	Vienna, Feb.	Im Dunkel ist nicht gut munkeln+	Dittersdorf, K.
	Vienna, July 7	Hieronymus Knicker	Dittersdorf, K.
	Vienna, July 12	Dumme Gärtner, Der+	Schack, B.
	Charlottenburg, July 29	Claudine von Villa Bella	Reichardt, J. F.
	Vienna, Sept. 26	Verdeckten Sachen, Die+	Schack, B.

Year	Place, Date	Title	Composer
1789 (cont.)	Budapest, Oct. 18	Christliche Judenbraut, Die+	Paneck, J. B.
	Vienna, Nov. 7	Oberon, König der Elfen	Wranitzky, P.
	Brünn, ?	Hochzeit des Figaro, Die	Dittersdorf, K.
ca. 1789	not perf	Liebe auf dem Lande, Die+	Süssmayr, F. X.
1790	Vienna, May 10	Fall ist noch weiter+	Schack, B.
	Breslau, May 26	Rothe Käppchen, Das	Dittersdorf, K.
	Vienna, June 18	Frühling, Der	Schack, B.
	Vienna, Sept. 9	Sonnenfest der Braminen, Das	Müller, W.
	Munich, ?	Jery und Bäteli+	Winter, P.
	Munich, ?	Psyche+	Winter, P.
	Munich, ?	Scherz, List und Rache+	Winter, P.
	Vienna, ?	Bastien und Bastienne+	Kauer, F.
	Vienna, ?	Hokus-Pokus+	Dittersdorf, K.
1791	Stuttgart, Jan. 10	Eremit auf Formentera, Der+	Dieter, C. F.
	Königsberg, Jan. 16	Louise+	Benda, F. L.
	Vienna, March 2	Gutsherr, Der+	Dittersdorf, K.
	Vienna, June 4	Anton bei Hofe	Schack, B.?
	Vienna, June 8	Kaspar, der Fagottist+	Müller, W.
	Frankfurt, Sept.11	Spiegelritter, Der+	Walter, I.
	Vienna, Sept. 30	Zauberflöte, Die	Mozart, W. A.
	Laxenburg, ?	Ariadne und Bacchus+	Paradis, M. T. von
1792	Frankfurt, July 15	Heinrich der Löwe+	Stegmann, C. D.
	Vienna, Sept. 15	Renegat, Der	Schack, B.?
	Kassel, ?	Titania+	Grosheim, G. C.
	Prague, ?	Maskarade im Serail, Die+	Volanek, A.

Year	Place, Date	Work	Composer
1792 (cont.)	Vienna, ?	Schulkandidat, Der+	Paradis, M. T. von
1793	Berlin, March	Erwin und Elmire	Reichardt, J. F.
	Frankfurt, May 3	Fest der Winzer, Das	Kunzen, F. L. A.
	Vienna, Oct. 10	Neusonntagskind, Das+	Müller, W.
	Prague, ?	Schuster-Feierabend, Der+	Volanek, A.
1794	Vienna, March 11	Schwestern von Prag, Die	Müller, W.
	Vienna, Nov. 14	Spiegel von Arkadien, Der	Süssmayr, F. X.
	Vienna, Dec. 7	Pyramus und Thisbe+	Eberl, A.
1795	Vienna, Jan. 6?	Häuschen im Walde, Das	Schack, B.?
	Oels, June 25	Don Quixote der Zweyte+	Dittersdorf, K.
	Vienna, May 11	Idris und Zenide+	Süssmayr, F. X.
	Vienna, June 27	Königssohn aus Ithaka, Der+	Hoffmeister, F. A.
	Vienna, Aug. 14	Achmed und Almanzine+	Schenk, J.
	Vienna, Aug. 27	Edle Rache, Die+	Süssmayr, F. X.
	Vienna, Nov. 21	Höllenberg, Der+	Wölfl, J.
1796	Hamburg, April 4	Triumph der Liebe, Der+	Stegmann, C. D.
	Vienna, May 4	Tiroler Wastel, Der+	Haibel, J.
	Vienna, June 14	Unterbrochene Opferfest, Das+	Winter, P.
	Oels, June 25	Lustigen Weiber von Windsor, Die+	Dittersdorf, K.
1797	Vienna, Oct. 30	Dorfbarbier, Der	Schenk, J.
	Prague, summer	Rinaldo und Alcina+	Paradis, M. T. von
	Vienna, Oct. 4	Wildfang, Der+	Süssmayr, F. X.
	Vienna, Oct. 25	Babylons Pyramiden+	Mederitsch, J. and P. Winter

Year	Place, Date	Title	Composer
1797 (cont.)	Bremen, Dec. 28	Doktor Faust+	Walter, I.
	Prague, ?	Zwei Klacheln von Przelautsch+	Tuczek, V. F.
1798	Vienna, Jan. 11	Donauweibchen, Das	Kauer, F.
	Vienna, March 26	Liebe macht kurzen Prozess+	Wölfl, J. et al.
	Vienna, April 17	Dorf im Gebirge, Das+	Weigl, J.
	Vienna, June 12	Labarint, Das	Winter, P.
	Berlin, July 6	Geisterinsel, Die+	Reichardt, J. F.
	Stuttgart, Nov. 7	Geisterinsel, Die+	Zumsteeg, J. R.
	Vienna, Nov. 8	Sturm, Der+	Müller, W.
	Munich, ?	Sturm, Der+	Winter, P.
	Prague, Leipzig, ?	Hochzeit auf dem Lande, Die+	Volanek, A.
1799	Vienna, Oct. 1	Soliman der Zweyte	Süssmayr, F. X.
	Vienna, Nov. 12	Teufelsmühle am Wienerberg, Die+	Müller, W.
	Vienna, ?	Dankgefühl einer Geretteten+	Hummel, J. N.
	Vienna, ?	Jagd, Die+	Schenk, J.
	Vienna, ?	Schreiner, Der+	Wranitzky, P.
	? ?	Trojanische Pferd, Das+	Wölfl, J.
	not perf	Maske, Die+	Hoffmann, E. T. A.
1800	Munich, Jan. 28	Marie von Montalban+	Winter, P.
	Berlin, March 31	Lieb' und Treue+	Reichardt, J. F.
	Vienna, July 5	Gülnare+	Süssmayr, F. X.
	Berlin, Oct. 16	Tamerlan+	Reichardt, J. F.
	Freiburg, Nov. 24	Waldmädchen, Das	Weber, C. M. von
	Berlin, ?	Mudarra+	Weber, B. A.

Year	Premiere	Work	Composer
1801	Berlin, March 9	Frohsinn und Schwärmerei+	Himmel, F. H.
	Berlin, March 30	Jery und Bätely	Reichardt, J. F.
	Vienna, May 23	Königin der schwarzen Insel, Die+	Eberl, A.
	Vienna, June 13	Alexander+	Teyber, F.
	Vienna, July 25	Phasma+	Süssmayr, F. X.
	Breslau, ?	Rübezahl+	Tuczek, V. F.
	Stuttgart, ?	Pfaufenfest, Das+	Zumsteeg, J. R.
	Vienna, ?	Eiserne Mann, Der+	Müller, W.
ca. 1801	Posen	Scherz, List und Rache+	Hoffmann, E. T. A.
1802	Vienna, Dec. 17	Fassbinder, Der+	Schenk, J.
	Stuttgart, ?	Des Teufels Lustschloss+	Dieter, C. F.
	Vienna, ?	Bauernliebe+	Kauer, F.
1803	Augsburg, March	Peter Schmoll und seine Nachbarn	Weber, C. M. von
	Munich, Aug.	Palmer und Amalia+	Cannabich, C.
	Stuttgart, ?	Elbondokani+	Zumsteeg, J. R.
	Vienna, ?	Bergfest, Das+	Müller, W.
	Vienna, ?	Friedliche Dörfchen, Das+	Müller, W.
	Vienna, ?	Hussiten von Naumberg, Die+	Salieri, A.
	premiere 1982	Vestas Feuer	Beethoven, L. van
1804	Vienna, April 21	Mitgefühl, Das+	Wranitzky, P.
	Berlin, May 16	Fanchon, das Leiermädchen+	Himmel, F. H.
	Vienna, May 17	Samori+	Vogler, G. J.

Year	Place, Date	Work	Composer
1805	Vienna, Feb. 15	Uniform, Der+	Weigl, J.
	Warsaw, April 6	Lustigen Musikanten, Die	Hoffmann, E. T. A.
	Pest, May 29	Dämona+	Tuczek, V. F.
	Vienna, Aug. 10	Vestas Feuer+	Weigl, J.
	Vienna, Nov. 20	Leonore	Beethoven, L. van
	Pest, Dec. 13	Lanassa+	Tuczek, V. F.
	Berlin, ?	Wette, Die+	Weber, B. A.
	Vienna, ?	Familie auf Isle de France, Die+	Kreutzer, C.
	Vienna, ?	Mohr von Semegonda, Der+	Kauer, F.
	not perf	Rübezahl	Weber, C. M. von
	not perf	Ungebetene Gäste, Die+	Hoffmann, E. T. A.
1806	Leipzig, Feb. 3	Rosette	Bierey, G. B.
	Vienna, March 29	Fidelio	Beethoven, L. van
	Berlin, April 14	Sylphen, Die+	Himmel, F. H.
	Vienna, June 12	Neue Alceste, Die+	Müller, W.
	Berlin, ?	Blumenmädchen, Das+	Benda, F.
	Eisenstadt, ?	Haus ist zu verkaufen, Dies+	Hummel, J. N.
	Hamburg, ?	Mischelli und sein Sohn+	Clasing, J. H.
	Vienna, ?	Agnes Sorel+	Gyrowetz, A.
	? ?	Julie oder Der Blumenkopf+	Spontini, G.
	not perf	Prüfung, Die	Spohr, L.
1807	Vienna, Feb. 26	Ida, die Büssende+	Gyrowetz, A.
	Vienna, May 21	Kaiser Hadrian	Weigl, J.
	Vienna, June 18	Junggesellen-Wirtschaft, Die+	Gyrowetz, A.
	Vienna, Oct. 3	Adrian von Ostade+	Weigl, J.
	Prague, Oct. 18	Elisene+	Rösler, J.

Year	Place, Date	Title	Composer
1807 (cont.)	Vienna, Nov. 25	Wladimir, Fürst von Novgorod+	Bierey, G. B.
	Vienna, ?	Emerike+	Gyrowetz, A.
	Vienna, ?	Hamlet+	Schuster, I.
	?	Inkle und Yariko+	Kauer, F.
	not perf	Liebe und Eifersucht+	Hoffmann, E. T. A.
1808	Stuttgart, March 27	Apollos Wettgesang+	Sutor, W.
	Vienna, June 25	Neue Semiramis, Die+	Tuczek, V. F.
	Vienna, Aug. 13	Samson, Richter in Israel+	Tuczek, V. F.
	Vienna, Oct. 4	Waisenhaus, Das+	Weigl, J.
	Vienna, Nov. 30	Durchmarsch, Der+	Tuczek, V. F.
	Vienna, ?	Fuersten der Longobarden, Die+	Kauer, F.
	not perf	Alruna, die Eulenkönigin	Spohr, L.
1809	Vienna, March 14	Schweizerfamilie, Die	Weigl, J.
	Vienna, May 6	Schöne Melusine, Die+	Tuczek, V. F.
	Hamburg, July 7	Unsichtbare, Die+	Eule, C. D.
	Munich, Sept. 15	Colmal+	Winter, P.
	Vienna, ?	Bezauberte Leyer, Die+	Tuczek, V. F.
1810	Vienna, March 26	Mathilde von Guise+	Hummel, J. N.
	Munich, Sept. 9	Claudine von Villa Bella	Kienlen, J. C.
	Frankfurt, Sept. 10	Silvana	Weber, C. M. von
	Munich, Oct. 16	Carlos Fioras	Fränzl, F.
ca. 1810	?	Konradin von Schwaben+	Kreutzer, C.
1811	Darmstadt, Jan.	Admiral, Der+	Vogler, G. J.
	Berlin, Feb. 19	Alpenhirten, Die+	Wollank, F.

Year	Place, Date	Title	Composer
1811 (cont.)	Berlin, March 18	Taucher, Der+	Reichardt, J. F.
	Munich, June 4	Abu Hassan	Weber, C. M. von
	Vienna, Oct. 1	Augenarzt, Der+	Gyrowetz, A.
	Hamburg, Nov. 15	Zweikampf mit der Geliebten, Der+	Spohr, L.
	Hamburg, Dec. 27	Ruinen vom Paluzzi, Die+	Romberg, A.
	Berlin, ?	Abenteuer des Ritters Don Quichotte, Ein+	Seidel, L.
	Vienna, ?	Wunderlampe, Die+	Müller, W.
	premiere 1949	Spiegelritter, Der	Schubert, F.
1812	Vienna, Dec. 19	Bergsturz, Der+	Weigl, J.
	Munich, Dec. 23	Jephtas Gelübde+	Meyerbeer, G.
	Stuttgart, ?	Feodora+	Kreutzer, C.
	premiere 1933	Aurora	Hoffmann, E. T. A.
1813	Stuttgart, Jan. 6	Wirth und Gast	Meyerbeer, G.
	Karlsruhe, April 19	Rübezahl+	Danzi, F.
	Vienna, May 22	Kobold, Der+	Himmel, F. H.
	Vienna, July 15	Robert+	Gyrowetz, A.
	Vienna, Nov.	Junker in der Mühle, Der+	Hummel, J. N.
ca. 1813	Weimar	Polterabend, Der+	Müller, A. E.
1814	Stuttgart, Feb. 24	Alimon und Zaide+	Kreutzer, C.
	Vienna, March 14	Eselhaut, Die+	Hummel, J. N.
	Budapest, March 22	Harald+	Kleinheinz, F. X.
	Vienna, May 23	Fidelio (rev. version)	Beethoven, L. van
	Kassel, June 3	Vestalin, Die+	Guhr, K. W. F.

Year	Place, Date	Title	Composer
1814 (cont.)	Munich, June 3	Athalia+	Poissl, J. N.
	Vienna, June 15	Rückfahrt des Kaisers, Die+	Hummel, J. N.
	Berlin, Nov. 23	Sänger und der Schneider, Der+	Driesberg, F. von
	Vienna, Dec. 10	Jugend Peter des Grossen, Die+	Weigl, J.
	Bamberg, ?	Frauenort oder Der Kaiser+	Lichtenstein, K. A.
	premiere 1879	Des Teufels Lustschloss	Schubert, F.
	not perf	Brandenburger Tor, Der+	Meyerbeer, G.
1815	Stuttgart, March 1	Alpenhütte, Die+	Kreutzer, C.
	Munich, April 21	Wettkampf zu Olympia, Der+	Poissl, J. N.
	Vienna, ?	Graf von Gleichen, Der+	Volkert, F.
	premiere 1875	Freunde von Salamanca, Die	Schubert, F.
	premiere 1896	Vierjährige Posten, Der	Schubert, F.
	premiere 1907	Fernando	Schubert, F.
	premiere 1916	Claudine von Villa Bella	Schubert, F.
1816	Berlin, Aug. 3	Undine	Hoffmann, E. T. A.
	Dresden, Sept. 1	Faust	Spohr, L.
	premiere 1908	Bürgschaft, Die	Schubert, F.
1817	Karlsruhe, April 17	Turandot+	Danzi, F.
	Vienna, April 25	Tankredi+	Müller, W.
1818	Vienna, April 20	Nachtigall und Rabe+	Weigl, J.
	Vienna, June 13	Cyrus und Astyages+	Mosel, J. F. von
	Vienna, Aug. 13	Travistirte Zauberflöte, Die+	Müller, W.
	Pest, Oct. 26	Arabella+	Tuczek, V. F.
	Bratislava, Nov. 26	Saidar und Zulima+	Marschner, H.

582

Year	Place, Date	Work	Composer
ca. 1818	Berlin	Zoraide+	Blum, K. L.
1819	Vienna, Feb. 7	Aladin+	Gyrowetz, A.
	Frankfurt, April 4	Zemire und Azor	Spohr, L.
	premiere 1868	Adrast+	Schubert, F.
1820	Vienna, April 11	Almanzine+	Pixis, J. P.
	Vienna, April 13	Baals Sturz+	Weigl, J.
	Vienna, April 19	Zauberharfe, Die	Schubert, F.
	Dresden, April 27	Bergknappen, Die+	Hellwig, K.
	Vienna, June 14	Zwillingsbrüder, Die	Schubert, F.
	Dresden, July 19	Heinrich IV und d'Aubigne+	Marschner, H.
	premiere 1962	Soldatenliebschaft, Die	Mendelssohn, F.
	premiere 1971	Sakuntala+	Schubert, F.
1821	Berlin, March 14	Preciosa	Weber, C. M. von
	Munich, May 1	Rodrigo und Zimene+	Aiblinger, J. K.
	Berlin, May 14	Olympia+	Spontini, G.
	Berlin, June 18	Freischütz, Der	Weber, C. M. von
	premiere 1888	Drei Pintos, Die	Weber, C. M. von
	premiere 1962	Beiden Pädagogen, Die	Mendelssohn, F.
1822	Zittau, Jan. 2	Kyffhäuserberg, Der+	Marschner, H.
	Berlin, May 27	Nurmahal	Spontini, G.
	Vienna, Dec. 4	Libussa	Kreutzer, C.
	premiere 1854	Alfonso und Estrella	Schubert, F.
	not perf	Liebhaber nach dem Tode, Der+	Hoffmann, E. T. A.
	not perf	Wandernden Komödianten, Die+	Mendelssohn, F.

Year	City, Date	Title	Composer
ca. 1822	Weimar	Graf von Gleichen, Der+	Eberwein, K.
1823	Vienna, Feb. 27	Eiserne Pforte, Die+	Weigl, J.
	Kassel, July 28	Jessonda	Spohr, L.
	Berlin, Oct. 15	Dido+	Klein, B.
	Vienna, Oct. 25	Euryanthe	Weber, C. M. von
	Vienna, Nov. 20	Siguna+	Kreutzer, C.
	Vienna, Dec. 13	Ochsensmenuette, Die+	Seygried, I. von
	Vienna, Dec. 20	Rosamunde, Fürstin von Cypern	Schubert, F.
	premiere 1835	Fierrabras	Schubert, F.
	premiere 1861	Die Verschworenen	Schubert, F.
1824	Berlin, Feb. 3	Onkel aus Boston, Der (Die beiden Neffen)+	Mendelssohn, F.
	Karlsruhe, Feb. 26	Omar und Leila+	Fesca, F. E.
	Prague, Oct. 7	Rübezahl+	Würfel, W.
1825	Munich, Jan. 23	Prinzessin von Provence, Die+	Poissl, J. N.
	Stuttgart, Jan. 30	Bergkönig, Der+	Lindpaintner, P.
	Dresden, Feb. 22	Holzdieb, Der+	Marschner, H.
	Kassel, March 24	Berggeist, Der	Spohr, L.
	Berlin, May 25	Alcidor+	Spontini, G.
1826	Hanover, Jan. 27	Neue Paris+	Maurer, L.
	London, April 12	Oberon	Weber, C. M. von
	Prague, May 24	Maja und Alpino+	Wolfram, J. M.
	Vienna, July 8	Besuch auf dem Lande, Der+	Kreutzer, C.
	Vienna, December	Schwarze Frau, Die+	Müller, A. E.

Year	Place, Date	Work	Composer
1827	Danzig, Jan. 17	Lukretia+	Marschner, H.
	Berlin, April 29	Hochzeit des Camacho, Die	Mendelssohn, F.
	Berlin, May 28	Agnes von Hohenstaufen	Spontini, G.
	Kassel, Oct. 13	Pietro von Abano	Spohr, L.
	Berlin, Dec. 26	Heimkehr aus der Fremde, Die+	Mendelssohn, F.
1828	Vienna, Jan. 8	Gefesselte Phantasie, Die+	Müller, W.
	Hanover, Jan. 16	Aloise+	Maurer, L.
	Münster, Feb. 1	Ali Pascha von Janina+	Lortzing, A.
	Leipzig, March 29	Vampyr, Der	Marschner, H.
	Stuttgart, Sept. 21	Vampyr, Der	Lindpaintner, P.
	Frankfurt, Oct. 15	Räuberbraut, Die+	Ries, F.
	Vienna, Oct. 28	Alpenkönig und Menschenfeind+	Müller, W.
	Kassel, Oct. 29	Abdul und Erinieh+	Curschmann, K. F.
1829	Aachen, Oct. 8	Bibiena+	Pixis, J. P.
	Leipzig, Dec. 22	Templer und die Jüdin, Der	Marschner, H.
	Berlin, Dec. 26	Heimkehr aus der Fremde, Die	Mendelssohn, F.
	Munich, ?	Untersberg, Der+	Poissl, J. N.
1830	Dresden, March 14	Bergmönch, Der+	Wolfram, J. M.
	Berlin, May 21	Undine+	Girschner, K. F.
	Kassel, July 28	Alchymist, Der	Spohr, L.
1831	Dresden, April 10	Felsenmühle zu Estalieres, Die+	Reissiger, K. G.
	Frankfurt, Oct. 2	Fortunat+	Wartensee, X. S.
	Leipzig, ?	Abu Kara+	Dorn, H.
1832	Berlin, Jan. 23	Kirmies, Die+	Taubert, W.

1832 (cont.)			
	Leipzig, March 10	Des Falkners Braut+	Marschner, H.
	Dresden, July 22	Salvator Rosa+	Rastrelli, J.
	Dresden, Dec. 1	Schloss Candra+	Wolfram, J. M.
	Berlin, Dec. 29	Des Adlers Horst+	Gläser, F.
	? ?	Szenen aus Mozarts Leben+	Lortzing, A.
1833			
	Berlin, Feb. 27	Melusina+	Kreutzer, C.
	Berlin, May 24	Hans Heiling	Marschner, H.
	Weimar, Sept. 28	Fürstin von Granada, Die+	Lobe, J. C.
	Hamburg, Oct. 8	Herzog Albrecht+	Krebs, K. A.
	Vienna, Dec. 19	Ring des Glückes, Der+	Kreutzer, C.
	premiere 1888	Feen, Die	Wagner, R.
1834			
	Vienna, Jan. 13	Nachtlager in Granada, Das	Kreutzer, C.
	Berlin, Feb. 18	Drei Wünsche, Die+	Loewe, C.
	Vienna, Feb. 20	Verschwender, Der+	Kreutzer, C.
	Dresden, ?	Hans Sachs+	Gyrowetz, A.
1835			
	Graz, April 22	Leonore+	Hüttenbrenner, A.
	Vienna, May 7	Fierrabras (comp. 1823)	Schubert, F.
	Berlin, May 22	Trilby+	Truhn, F. H.
	Munich, Sept. 12	Hermannsschlacht, Die+	Chélard, H.
1836			
	Leipzig, Jan. 29	Schloss am Ätna, Das+	Marschner, H.
	Magdeburg, March 29	Liebesverbot, Das	Wagner, R.
	Riga, Nov. 13	Schöffe von Paris, Der+	Dorn, H.
	Berlin, ?	Aurora+	Gläser, F.
1837			
	Leipzig, Feb. 20	Beiden Schützen, Die	Lortzing, A.

Year	Place, Date	Work	Composer
1837 (cont.)	Vienna, April 6	Höhle von Waverly, Die+	Kreutzer, C.
	Danzig, April 20	Undine	Girschner, K. F.
	Vienna, Dec. 16	Fridolin+	Kreutzer, C.
	Leipzig, Dec. 22	Zar und Zimmermann	Lortzing, A.
1838	Hanover, Feb. 19	Babü, Der+	Marschner, H.
	Dresden, May 6	Besuch in Saint-Cyr, Ein+	Dessauer, J.
	Pest, Oct. 30	Bürgschaft, Die	Lachner, F.
	Riga, Nov. 13	Schöffe von Paris, Der+	Dorn, H.
1839	Vienna, Feb. 8	Genüserin, Die+	Lindpaintner, P.
	Berlin, Feb. 26	Flucht nach der Schweiz, Die+	Kücken, F. W.
	Munich, April 12	Alidia+	Lachner, F.
	Stuttgart, May 20	Regenbrüder, Die+	Lachner, I.
	Leipzig, Sept. 20	Caramo+	Lortzing, A.
	Paris, Dec. 23	Matrosen, Die+	Flotow, F. von
1840	Leipzig, June 23	Hans Sachs	Lortzing, A.
	Brunswick, Aug. 13	Beiden Figaro, Die+	Kreutzer, C.
	Munich, Oct. 2	Nacht zu Paluzzi, Die+	Pentenrieder, F. X.
	Vienna, Dec. 30	Johanna d'Arc+	Hoven, J.
1841	Vienna, March 16	Mara+	Netzer, J.
	Munich, Dec. 3	Catharina Cornaro	Lachner, F.
	Leipzig, Dec. 31	Casanova in Murano+	Lortzing, A.
1842	Breslau, Feb. 22	Geisterbraut, Die+	Eugen of Württenberg
	Dresden, Oct. 20	Rienzi	Wagner, R.
	Leipzig, Dec. 31	Wildschütz, Der	Lortzing, A.

Year	Place, Date	Work	Composer
1843	Dresden, Jan. 2	Fliegende Holländer, Der	Wagner, R.
	Munich, ?	Zaide+	Poissl, J. N.
	? ?	Sicilianische Versper, Die+	Lindpaintner, P.
1844	Vienna, Nov. 12	Ali Hitsch-Hatsch+	Sechter, S.
	Berlin, Dec. 7	Feldlager in Schlesien, Ein+	Meyerbeer, G.
	Hamburg, Dec. 30	Alessandro Stradella	Flotow, F. von
1845	Kassel, Jan. 3	Kreuzfahrer, Die	Spohr, L.
	Dresden, Jan. 5	Kaiser Adolph von Nassau+	Marschner, H.
	Munich, April 11	Zwei Prinzen, Die+	Esser, H.
	Magdeburg, April 21	Undine	Lortzing, A.
	Frankfurt, May 22	Trilby+	Schmitt, G. A.
	Dresden, Oct. 9	Tannhäuser	Wagner, R.
1846	Dessau, March 23	Kätchen von Heilbronn, Das+	Lux, F.
	Graz, April 1	Guttenberg+	Füchs, F.
	Budapest, April 4	Rächer, Der+	Schindelmeisser, L.
	Vienna, May 3	Waffenschmied, Der	Lortzing, A.
	Darmstadt, May 17	Tan[n]häuser+	Mangold, K.
	Stuttgart, Aug. 26	Lichtenstein+	Lindpaintner, P.
	Munich, ?	Loreley, Die+	Lachner, I.
1847	Brunswick, July 25	Troubadour, Der+	Fesca, A. E.
	Frankfurt, July 26	Prinz Eugen+	Schmidt, G.
	Vienna, Nov. 25	Martha	Flotow, F. von
	Prague, Nov. 29	Blanda+	Kalliwoda, J. W.
	Leipzig, Dec. 13	Zum Grossadmiral+	Lortzing, A.
	Gotha, ?	Graf von Gleichen, Der+	Wandersleb, A.

Year	Place, Date	Work	Composer
1848	Prague, Feb. 19	Bianca und Giuseppe+	Kittl, J. F.
	Hamburg, Feb. 22	Leila+	Piersen, H. H.
	Strasbourg, May 8	Judith+	Adam, F.
	Stuttgart, June 4	Soldatenleben+	Hackländer, F. W.
	Vienna, Dec. 16	Martl+	Suppé, F. von
	premiere 1899	Regina	Lortzing, A.
1849	Berlin, March 9	Lustigen Weiber von Windsor, Die	Nicolai, O.
	Leipzig, May 25	Rolands Knappen+	Lortzing, A.
	Vienna, July 1	Gervinus+	Suppé, F. von
	Munich, Oct. 7	Benvenuto Cellini	Lachner, F.
1850	Vienna, Jan. 12	Abenteuer Carl des Zweiten, Ein+	Hoven, J.
	Vienna, Feb. 27	Cagliostro+	Lortzing, A.
	Leipzig, June 25	Genoveva	Schumann, R.
	Weimar, Aug. 28	Lohengrin	Wagner, R.
	Berlin, Nov. 19	Sophie Katharina+	Flotow, F. von
1851	Frankfurt, Jan. 20	Opernprobe, Die	Lortzing, A.
	Weimar, March 9	König Alfred+	Raff, J.
	Gotha, March 23	Casilda+	Ernst II
	Prague, Nov. 29	Meergeuse+	Skroup, F.
	Darmstadt, ?	Dornröschen+	Mangold, K.
	Darmstadt, ?	Gudrun+	Mangold, K.
1852	Hanover, Jan. 25	Austin+	Marschner, H.
	Vienna, Feb. 27	Tannenhäuser, Der+	Suppé, F. von

Year	Place, Date	Opera	Composer
1852 (cont.)	Retzien, Aug. 13	Rübezahl+	Flotow, F. von
1854	Berlin, March 27	Nibelungen, Die+	Dorn, H.
	Gotha, April 2	Santa Chiara+	Ernst II
	Weimar, June 24	Alfonso und Estrella (comp. 1822)	Schubert, F.
1856	Cologne, Dec. 14	Scherz, List und Rache+	Bruch, M.
1857	Weimar, May 10	Landgraf Ludwigs Brautfahrt+	Lassen, E.
	Schwerin, May 27	Herzog Johann Albrecht von Mecklenberg+	Flotow, F. von
1858	Dresden, Jan. 17	Agnes Bernauer+	Krebs, K.
	Weimar, Feb. 16	Weibertreue+	Schmidt, G.
	Berlin, Nov. 16	Macbeth+	Taubert, W.
	Coburg, Dec. 5	Diana von Solange+	Ernst II
	Weimar, Dec. 15	Barbier von Bagdad, Der	Cornelius, P.
1861	Vienna, Feb. 23	Kinder der Heide, Die+	Rubinstein, A.
	Frankfurt, Aug. 29	Verschworenen, Die (comp. 1823)	Schubert, F.
1862	Wiesbaden, Feb. 15	Katakomben, Die+	Hiller, F.
	Vienna, Oct. 25	Zehn Mädchen und kein Mann+	Suppé, F. von
1863	Dresden, Feb. 24	Feramors (Lallah Rookh)+	Rubinstein, A.
	Vienna, April 18	Flotte Bursche+	Suppé, F. von
	Mannheim, June 14	Loreley, Die	Bruch, M.
	Frankfurt, Sept. 13	Sangeskönig Hiarne+	Marschner, H.

Year	Place, Date	Title	Composer
1863 (cont.)	Munich, ?	Foscari, Die+	Zenger, M.
1864	Vienna, ?	Rheinnixen, Die+	Offenbach, J.
1865	Vienna, May 4	Dinorah+	Suppé, F. von
	Weimar, May 21	Cid, Der	Cornelius, P.
	Munich, June 10	Tristan und Isolde	Wagner, R.
	Berlin, June 30	Schöne Galatea, Die	Suppé, F. von
	Vienna, Dec. 15	Graf von Gleichen, Der (comp. 1815)	Schubert, F.
	?	Erbin von Montfort, Die+	Jensen, A.
1866	Frankfurt, Jan. 27	Zaïde (comp. 1779)	Mozart, W. A.
	Amsterdam, March 10	Aleida von Holland+	Thooft, W. F.
	Vienna, March 24	Leichte Cavallerie, Die+	Suppé, F. von
	Stuttgart, May 27	Astorga+	Abert, J. J.
1867	Wiesbaden, July 26	König Manfred+	Reinecke, C.
	Prague, Oct. 9	Erste Falte, Die+	Leschetizky, T.
1868	Munich, June 21	Meistersinger von Nürnberg, Die	Wagner, R.
	Dresden, Oct. 22	Haideschacht, Der+	Holstein, F. von
	Mannheim, ?	Ruy Blas+	Zenger, M.
1869	Lucerne, Jan.	Touristen, Die+	Stauffer, T.
	Weimar, April 8	Letzte Zauberer, Der+	Viardot, P.
	Munich, Sept. 22	Ring des Nibelungen, Der: Das Reingold	Wagner, R.
	Berlin, ?	Cartouche+	Hofmann, H.

1870	Munich, June 26	Ring des Nibelungen, Der: Die Walküre	Wagner, R.
	Vienna, Dec. 30	Judith+	Doppler, A. F.
1871	Vienna, Feb. 10	Indigo und die vierzig Räuber+	Strauss, J., Jr.
1872	Leipzig, Jan. 23	Erbe von Morley, Der+	Holstein, F. von
	Vienna, March 8	Fleurette+	Offenbach, J.
	Berlin, March 22	Hermione+	Bruch, M.
	Hamburg, April 16	Contarini+	Pierson, H. H.
	Vienna, Sept. 21	Schwarze Korsar, Der+	Offenbach, J.
	Dresden, ?	Armin+	Hofmann, H.
1873	Vienna, March 1	Karneval in Rom, Der+	Strauss, J., Jr.
1874	Dresden, March 21	Folkunger, Die+	Kretschmer, E.
	Vienna, April 5	Fledermaus, Die	Strauss, J., Jr.
	Mannheim, Oct. 11	Widerspenstigen Zähmung, Der	Goetz, H.
	premiere 1891	Gunlöd	Cornelius, P.
1875	Vienna, Feb. 27	Cagliostro in Wien+	Strauss, J., Jr.
	Vienna, March 10	Königin von Saba, Die	Goldmark, K.
	Berlin, April 17	Maccabäer, Die+	Rubinstein, A.
	Wiesbaden, Sept. 25	Melusina+	Grammann, K.
	Vienna, Dec. 19	Freunde von Salamanca, Die (comp. 1815)	Schubert, F.
	Berlin, Dec. 22	Goldene Kreuz, Das+	Brüll, I.

Year	Place, Date	Work	Composer
1876	Vienna, Jan. 5	**Fatinitza+**	Suppé, F. von
	Mannheim, Jan. 16	**Hochländer, Die+**	Holstein, F. von
	Bayreuth:	**Ring des Nibelungen, Der:**	Wagner, R.
	Aug. 13	**Das Rheingold** (prem. 1869)	
	Aug. 14	**Die Walküre** (prem. 1870)	
	Aug. 16	**Siegfried**	
	Aug. 17	**Götterdämmerung**	
	Vienna, Oct. 24	**Seekadett, Der+**	Genée, R.
1877	Vienna, Jan. 3	**Prinz Methusalem+**	Strauss, J., Jr.
	Vienna, March 10	**Nanon+**	Geneé, R.
	Mannheim, Sept. 30	**Francesca da Rimini**	Goetz, H.
	Vienna, Oct. 4	**Landfriede, Der+**	Brüll, I.
	Leipzig, ?	**Heinrich der Löwe+**	Kretschmer, E.
1878	Wiesbaden, Oct. 1	**Albigenser, Die+**	Deswert, J.
	Berlin, Oct. 11	**Ekkehard+**	Abert, J.J.
	Hamburg, Nov. 6	**Aennchen von Tharau+**	Hofmann, H.
	Vienna, Dec. 18	**Blindekuh+**	Strauss, J., Jr.
1879	Vienna, Feb. 1	**Boccaccio**	Suppé, F. von
	Leipzig, March 1	**Rattenfänger von Hamelin, Der+**	Nessler, V. E.
	Karlsruhe, March 7	**Meister Martin und seine Gesellen+**	Weissheimer, W.
	Hamburg, Nov. 1	**Nero+**	Rubinstein, A.
	Vienna, Dec. 12	**Des Teufels Lustschloss** (comp. 1814)	Schubert, F.
	Frankfurt, ?	**Robin Hood+**	Dietrich, A.

Year	Location, Date	Work	Composer
1879 (cont.)	Neustrelitz, ?	Iwein+	Klughardt, A.
	? ?	Lancelot+	Hentschel, T.
1880	Munich, Jan. 18	Wieland der Schmied+	Zenger, M.
	Vienna, Feb. 21	Donna Juanita+	Suppé, F. von
	Vienna, Oct. 1	Spitzentuch der Königin, Das+	Strauss, J., Jr.
	Vienna, Dec. 18	Apajune der Wassermann+	Millöcker, C.
1881	Munich, March 27	Raimondin+	Perfal, K. von
	Stuttgart, June 3	Irene+	Huber, J.
	Leipzig, Oct. 16	Harald der Wiking+	Hallén, A.
	Weimar, Oct. 23	Legende von der heiligen Elisabeth, Die+	Liszt, F.
	Vienna, Nov. 25	Lustige Krieg, Der+	Strauss, J., Jr.
	Frankfurt, Dec. 7	Kätchen von Heilbronn, Das+	Reinthaler, K.
	Leipzig, ?	Wilde Jagd, Der+	Nessler, V. E.
1882	Dresden, March 12	Hagbarth und Signe+	Mihalovich, Ö.
	Mainz, March 29	Schmied von Ruhla, Der+	Lux, F.
	Bayreuth, July 26	Parsifal	Wagner, R.
	Vienna, Dec. 6	Bettelstudent, Der	Millöcker, C.
	Hamburg, ?	Wilhelm von Oranien+	Hofmann, H.
1883	Hamburg, Jan.	Manon+	Kleinmichel, R.
	Berlin, Oct. 3	Nacht in Venedig, Eine	Strauss, J., Jr.
	Hamburg, Nov. 8	Sulamith+	Rubinstein, A.
	Hamburg, Nov. 8	Unter Räubern+	Rubinstein, A.
	Munich, ?	Königin Mariette+	Brüll, I.

Year	Place, Date	Work	Composer
1884	Vienna, Jan. 26	**Gasparone+**	Millöcker, C.
	Sonderhausen, March 20	**Kunihild+**	Kistler, C.
	Weimar, March 23	**Sakuntala+**	Weingartner, F.
	Leipzig, March 26	**Heliantus+**	Goldschmidt, A. von
	Leipzig, May 4	**Trompeter von Säckingen, Der+**	Nessler, V. E.
	Vienna, Oct. 31	**Feldprediger, Der+**	Millöcker, C.
	Mainz, ?	**Graf Hammerstein+**	Deswert, J.
1885	Darmstadt, Feb. 1	**Kaisertochter, Die+**	Haan, W. de
	Hamburg, March 28	**Don Cesar+**	Dellinger, R.
	Munich, Oct. 15	**Faule Hans, Der+**	Ritter, A.
	Vienna, Oct. 24	**Zigeunerbaron, Der**	Strauss, J., Jr.
	Darmstadt, Dec. 22	**Kalif Storch+**	Eidens, J.
	? ?	**Aurora+**	Bungert, A.
1886	Dresden, Feb. 20	**Urvasi+**	Kienzl, W.
	Munich, April 9	**Junker Heinz+**	Perfall, K. von
	Vienna, Oct. 9	**Vice-Admiral, Der+**	Millöcker, C.
	Dessau, Nov. 10	**Hochzeit des Mönchs, Die+**	Klughardt, A.
	Vienna, Nov. 19	**Merlin+**	Goldmark, K.
	Berlin, ?	**Donna Diana+**	Hofmann, H.
	Leipzig, ?	**Abenteuer einer Neujahrsnacht, Der+**	Heuberger, R.
1887	Berlin, Feb. 28	**Merlin+**	Rüfer, P.
	Prague, June 19	**Jungfrau von Orleans, Die+**	Reznicek, E. N. von
	Munich, June 29	**Feen, Die**	Wagner, R.
	Munich, Oct. 19	**Faust+**	Zöllner, H.

Year	Work	Place, Date	Composer
1887 (cont.)	Simplizius, Der+	Vienna, Dec. 17	Strauss, J., Jr.
1888	Drei Pintos, Die (comp. 1821)	Leipzig, Jan. 20	Weber, C. M. von
	Feen, Die (comp. 1833)	Munich, June 29	Wagner, R.
	Sturm, Der+	Frankfurt, ?	Urspruch, A.
	Steinerne Herz, Das+	Vienna, ?	Brüll, I.
1889	Manuel Venegas+	Leipzig, March 27	Heuberger, R.
	Eulenspiegel+	Würzburg, ?	Kistler, C.
1890	Arme Jonathan, Der+	Vienna, Jan. 4	Millöcker, C.
	Prinz wider Willen, Der+	Riga, Feb. 27	Lohse, O.
	Wem die Krone?+	Weimar, June 8	Ritter, A.
1891	Vogelhändler, Der	Vienna, Jan. 10	Zeller, C.
	Heimliche Ehe, Die+	Danzig, Jan. 23	Gast, P.
	Günlod (comp. 1874)	Weimar, May 6	Cornelius, P.
	Loreley, Die+	Brunswick, ?	Sommer, H.
1892	Ritter Pázmán+	Vienna, Jan. 1	Strauss, J., Jr.
	Herrat+	Dresden, March 10	Draeseke, F.
	Gringoire+	Munich, March 19	Brüll, I.
	Boabdil+	Berlin, April 21	Moszkowski, M.
	Genesius+	Berlin, Nov. 15	Weingartner, F.
1893	Fürstin Ninetta+	Vienna, Jan. 10	Strauss, J., Jr.
	Evanthia+	Gotha, July 30	Umlauft, P.
	Rose von Pontevedra, Die+	Gotha, July 30	Forster, J.
	Palmer und Amalia+	Munich, Aug.	Cannabich, C.

1893 (cont.)

Berlin, Oct. 11	**Mara+**	Hummel, Ferd.
Karslruhe, Oct. 12	**Rubin, Der+**	Albert, E. d'
Weimar, Dec. 23	**Hänsel und Gretel**	Humperdinck, E.
Munich, ?	**Schach dem König!+**	Brüll, I.
? ?	**Aglaja+**	Blech, L.

1894

Vienna, Jan. 5	**Obersteiger, Der+**	Zeller, C.
Vienna, Jan. 20	**Mirjam+**	Heuberger, R.
Basel, March 28	**Weltfrühling+**	Huber, H.
Gotha, March 29	**Seemannsbraut, Die+**	Aspestrand, S.
Weimar, May 10	**Guntram**	Strauss, R.
Vienna, Oct. 12	**Jabuka+**	Strauss, J., Jr.
Karlsruhe, Nov. 13	**Ingewelde+**	Schillings, M. von
Prague, Dec. 16	**Donna Diana+**	Reznicek, E. N. von
? ?	**Cherubina+**	Blech, L.

1895

Hamburg, Feb. 13	**Kenilworth+**	Klein, B. O.
Mainz, April 2	**Arme Heinrich, Der**	Pfitzner, H.
Vienna, April 4	**Waldmeister+**	Strauss, J., Jr.
Berlin, May 4	**Evangelimann, Der**	Kienzl, W.
Breslau, May 12	**Schwarze Kaschka, Die+**	Jarno, G.
Dresden, Sept. 7	**Überfall, Der+**	Zöllner, H.
Strasbourg, Nov. 21	**Erlösung, Die+**	Scharrer, A.
Dresden, Nov. 28	**Ghismonda+**	Albert, E. d'
Magdeburg, Dec. 19	**Sieben Geislein+**	Humperdinck, E.

1896

Basel, Jan. 29	**Kudrun+**	Huber, H.
Vienna, March 21	**Heimchen am Herd, Das+**	Goldmark, K.
Mannheim, June 7	**Corregidor, Der**	Wolf, H.

1896	(cont.)		
	Hamburg, Oct. 15	Runenzauber+	Hartmann, E.
	Karlsruhe, Nov. 14	Fluthgeist, Der+	Hillemacher, P. L.
	Leipzig, Nov. 27	Kukuska+	Lehár, F.
	Dresden, Dec. 12	Odysseus' Heimkehr+	Bungert, A.
1897	Karlsruhe, Feb. 9	Fierrabras (comp. 1823)	Schubert, F.
	Augsburg, Feb. 18	strike der schmiede, Der+	Beer, M. J.
	Koblenz, March 7	Meister Martin und seine Gesellen+	Lacombe, L.
	Vienna, March 13	Göttin der Vernunft, Die+	Strauss, J., Jr.
	Mannheim, April 11	Gernot+	Albert, E. d'
	Munich, Oct. 10	Sarema+	Zemlinsky, A. von
	Karlsruhe, Nov. 5	Unmöglichste von allem, Das+	Urspruch, A.
1898	Vienna, Jan. 5	Opernball, Der	Heuberger, R.
	Dresden, Jan. 29	Kirke+	Bungert, A.
	Karlsruhe, Feb. 6	Lobentanz+	Thuille, L.
	Weimar, May 24	Fantasio+	Smyth, E.
	Munich, June 19	Zinnober+	Hausegger, S. von
	Hamburg, Oct. 8	König Magnus+	Nodermann, P.
	Frankfurt, Oct. 20	Abreise, Die	Albert, E. d'
	Berlin, Nov. 18	Don Quixote+	Kienzl, W.
1899	Vienna, Jan. 17	Kriegsgefangene, Die+	Goldmark, K.
	Munich, Jan. 22	Bärenhäuter, Der	Wagner, S.
	Vienna, Jan. 28	Ihre Excellenz+	Heuberger, R.
	Berlin, March 21	Regina (comp. 1848)	Lortzing, A.
	Stuttgart, April 12	Fest auf Solhaug, Das+	Stenhammar, V.
	Munich, May 7	Fremdling, Der+	Vogl, H.

Year	Place, Date	Title	Composer
1899 (cont.)	Vienna, June 29	Landstreicher, Die	Ziehrer, C. M.
	Berlin, July 8	Versunkene Glocke, Die+	Zöllner, H.
	Vienna, Oct. 26	Wiener Blut	Strauss, J., Jr.
	Schwerin, Nov. 26	Pfeifertag, Der+	Schillings, M. von
1900	Vienna, Jan. 22	Es war einmal+	Zemlinsky, A. von
	Berlin, Feb. 9	Bärenhäuter, Der+	Mendelssohn, A.
	Berlin, Feb. 17	Kain+	Albert, E. d'
	Erfurt, March 11	Wintermärchen, Das+	Zimmermann, B.
	Prague, March 17	Norwegische Hochzeit+	Schjelderup, G.
	Lübeck, March 29	Letzte Tage von Pompeji, Die+	Montowt, R.
1901	Munich, Jan. 11	Eros und Psyche+	Zenger, M.
	Prague, March 3	Polnische Jude, Der+	Weis, K.
	Bremen, March 4	Gugeline+	Thuille, L.
	Vienna, March 9	Drei Wünsche, Die+	Ziehrer, C. M.
	Reichenberg, March 14	Graf von Gleichen, Der+	Mohaupt, F.
	Dresden, March 20	Nausikaa+	Bungert, A.
	Munich, March 23	Herzog Wildfang+	Wagner, S.
	Dresden, May 29	Manru+	Paderewski, I.
	Elberfeld, Nov. 9	Rose von Liebesgarten, Die+	Pfitzner, H.
	Dresden, Nov. 21	Feuersnot	Strauss, R.
1902	Karslruhe, Jan. 12	Till Eulenspiegel+	Reznicek, E. N. von
	Leipzig, Feb. 15	Orestes+	Weingartner, F.
	Cologne, Feb. 22	Pompadour, La+	Moór, E.
	Berlin, Feb. 26	Improvisator, Der+	Albert, E. d'
	Berlin, April 9	Wald, Der+	Smyth, E.

Year	Place, Date	Work	Composer
1905 (cont.)	Prague, Nov. 15	Zierpuppen+	Goetzl, A.
	Dresden, Dec. 9	Salome	Strauss, R.
	Prague, Dec. 26	Aschenbrödel+	Blech, L.
	Vienna, Dec. 30	Lustige Witwe, Die	Lehár, F.
	not perf	Faust I. Teil+	Kistler, C.
1906	Kassel, Nov. 6	Schöne Müllerin, Die+	Dorn, O.
	Dresden, Dec. 8	Moloch+	Schillings, M. von
	Posen, ?	Ali Pascha+	Goeldner, F.
	premiere 1980	Traumgörge, Der+	Zemlinsky, A. von
1907	Darmstadt, March 1	Mirandolina+	Scholz, B.
	Vienna, March 2	Walzertraum, Ein+	Straus, O.
	Düsseldorf, March 19	Ewige Feuer, Das+	Wetz, R.
	Karlsruhe, April 9	Mönch von Sendomir, Der+	Lorentz, A.
	Brunswick, July 25	Zauberlehrling, Der+	Döbber, J.
	Frankfurt, Oct. 26	Rote Gred, Die+	Bittner, J.
	Vienna, Nov. 2	Dollarprinzessin, Die	Fall, L.
	Hamburg, Dec. 3	Tragaldabas+	Albert, E. d'
1908	Munich, Jan. 1	Don Quichote+	Beer-Walbrunn, A.
	Vienna, Jan. 2	Wintermärchen, Ein+	Goldmark, K.
	Hamburg, Jan. 21	Sterngebot, Das+	Wagner, S.
	Dresden, May 1	Frühlingsnacht+	Schjelderup, G.
	Düsseldorf and Prague, Oct. 28	Kalte Herz, Das+	Konta, R.
	Hamburg, Nov. 4	Versiegelt	Blech, L.
	Vienna, Nov. 14	Tapfere Soldat, Der	Straus, O.

Year	Place, Date	Title	Composer
1908 (cont.)	Vienna, Dec. 23	Geschiedene Frau, Die+	Fall, L.
1909	Dresden, Jan. 25	Elektra	Strauss, R.
	Graz, Feb. 22	Herzog Philipps Brautfahrt+	Reuss, A.
	Brünn, Feb. 26	Traum, Der+	Mraczek, J. G.
	Stuttgart, March 25	Prinzessin Brambilla	Braunfels, W.
	Mannheim, May 5	Robins Ende+	Künneke, E.
	Frankfurt, Oct. 10	Heisse Eisen, Das+	Wolff, M.
	Weimar, Oct. 19	William Ratcliff+	Dopper, C.
	Hamburg, Nov. 6	Izeyel+	Albert, E. d'
	Vienna, Nov. 12	Graf von Luxemburg, Der	Lehár, F.
	premiere 1924	Erwartung	Schoenberg, A.
1910	Vienna, Jan. 8	Zigeunerliebe	Lehár, F.
	Karlsruhe, Jan. 23	Banadietrich+	Wagner, S.
	Dessau, March 27	König von Samarkand, Der+	Mikorey, F.
	Vienna, April 12	Musikant, Der+	Bittner, J.
	Weimar, May 1	Gelöbnis, Das+	Oosterzee, C. van
	Frankfurt, Sept. 18	Liebelei+	Neumann, F.
	Düsseldorf, Nov. 25	Stella Maris+	Kaiser, A.
	Vienna, Dec. 2	Kleider machen Leute+	Zemlinsky, A. von
	New York, Dec. 28	Königskinder	Humperdinck, E.
	Vienna, ?	Don Quichotte+	Heuberger, R.
1911	Dresden, Jan. 26	Rosenkavalier, Der	Strauss, R.
	Vienna, Nov. 9	Bergsee, Der+	Bittner, J.
	Vienna, Nov. 23	Kuhreigen, Der+	Kienzl, W.
1912	Frankfurt, Jan. 18	Oberst Chabert+	Waltershausen, H. W. von

1912 (cont.)

Berlin, Feb. 3	Liebe Augustin, Der+	Fall, L.
Troppau, Feb. 3	Verschenkte Frau, Die+	Albert, E. d'
Basel, Feb. 22	Simplicius, Der+	Huber, H.
Prague, March 29	Sturm auf die Mühle, Der+	Weis, K.
Hamburg, April 13	Brautwahl, Die	Busoni, F.
Breslau, May 31	Hero und Leander+	Caró, P.
Frankfurt, Aug. 18	Ferne Klang, Der	Schreker, F.
Vienna, Oct. 25	Ariadne auf Naxos	Strauss, R.
Vienna, Nov. 12	Liebesketten+	Albert, E. d'
not perf	Giuditta+	Dessau, P.

1913

Dresden, Jan. 23	Tante Simona+	Dohnányi, E.
Karlsruhe, Feb. 18	Zuleima+	Bienstock, H.
Frankfurt, March 15	Spielwerk und die Prinzessin, Das	Schreker, F.
Basel, April 4	Dorval+	Zehntner, L.
Gotha, April 18	Merlin+	Draeseke, F.
Hamburg, June	Daphnis und Chloe+	Nacke, E.
Cologne, Oct. 30	Abenteuer, Der+	Bittner, J.
Dresden, Oct. 31	Coeur As+	Künneke, E.
Stuttgart, Nov. 9	Uilenspiegel+	Braunfels, W.
Munich, ?	Sulamith+	Klenau, P. von

1914

Vienna, April 1	Notre Dame+	Schmidt, F.
Dessau, April 19	Heilige Berg, Der+	Sinding, C.
Prague, April 22	Gefängnisse+	Keussler, G. von
Karlsruhe, April 25	Ungeheuer, Das+	Walbrunn, A.
Cologne, May 10	Marketendieren, Die+	Humperdinck, E.
Darmstadt, May 17	Kain und Abel+	Weingartner, F.

Year	Place, Date	Work	Composer
1914 (cont.)	Essen, May 23	Herr Dandolo+	Siegel, R.
	Duisburg, May 25	Ratcliff+	Andreae, V.
	Leipzig, June 11	Don Juans letztes Abenteuer+	Graener, P.
1915	Stuttgart, Sept. 26	Mona Lisa	Schillings, M. von
	Vienna, Nov. 13	Csárdásfürstin, Die	Kálmán, E.
	not perf	Tönenden Sphären, Die+	Schreker, F.
1916	Halle, Feb. 20	Narrengericht, Das+	Graener, P.
	Darmstadt, Feb. 23	Dame Kobold+	Weingartner, F.
	Dresden, March 5	Toten Augen, Die	Albert, E. d'
	Munich, March 28	Ring des Polykrates, Der	Korngold, E.
	Munich, March 28	Violanta	Korngold, E.
	Dresden, April 1	Schneider von Schönau, Die+	Brandt-Buys, J.
	Bern, April 2	Schöne Bellinda, Die+	Huber, H.
	Vienna, June 11	Liebe Augustin, Der+	Bittner, J.
	Stuttgart, Sept. 24	Sandro der Narr+	Bienstock, H.
	Darmstadt, Oct. 15	Höllisch Gold, Das+	Bittner, J.
	Zurich, Nov. 11	Erwin und Elmire	Schoeck, O.
	Frankfurt, Nov. 14	Porzia+	Taubmann, O.
	Vienna, Dec. 2	Rose von Stambul, Die	Fall, L.
	Mannheim, Dec. 6	Elga+	Lendvai, E.
	Vienna, Dec. 6	Testament, Das+	Kienzl, W.
1917	Vienna, Jan. 20	Eiserne Heiland, Der+	Oberleithner, M. von
	Stuttgart, Jan. 30	Florentinische Tragödie, Eine	Zemlinsky, A. von
	Mainz, May 8	Weg durchs Fenster, Der+	Weissleder, P.
	Zurich, May 11	Turandot and Arlecchino	Busoni, F.
	Munich, June 12	Palestrina	Pfitzner, H.

Year	Place, Date	Work	Composer
1917 (cont.)	Leipzig, Oct. 27	Sappho+	Kaun, H.
	Mannheim, Nov. 2	Scharazade+	Sekles, B.
	Munich, Nov. 3	Lanzelot und Elaine+	Courvoisier, W.
	Stuttgart, Dec. 6	An allem ist Hütchen schuld+	Wagner, S.
	Munich, Dec. 11	Christelflein, Das+	Pfitzner, H.
	Zurich, ?	Rübezahl+	Vogler, C.
1918	Darmstadt, March 18	Gaudeamus+	Humperdinck, E.
	Vienna, March 27	Wo die Lerche singt+	Lehár, F.
	Mannheim, April 4	Kjarten und Gudrun+	Klenau, P. von
	Frankfurt, April 25	Gezeichneten, Die	Schreker, F.
	Munich, June 5	Theophano+	Graener, P.
	Magdeburg, Aug. 18	Fernando (comp. 1815)	Schubert, F.
	Karlsruhe, Sept. 15	Meister Guido+	Nötzel, H.
	Darmstadt, Oct. 30	Sonnenflammen+	Wagner, S.
	Karlsruhe, Nov. 5	Schwarzschwanreich+	Wagner, S.
	Nuremberg, Nov. 24	Dornröschen+	Höfer, F.
	Bern, Dec. 11	Heisse Eisen, Das+	Wehrli, W.
1919	Mannheim, Feb. 7	Goldschmied von Toledo, Der+ (arr. Stern and Zamara)	Offenbach, J.
	Zurich, April 16	Don Ranudo	Schoeck, O.
	Chemnitz, May 16	Heilige Katharina, Die+	Böhme, O.
	Leipzig, Sept. 26	Revolutionshochzeit+	Albert, E. d'
	Vienna, Oct. 10	Frau ohne Schatten, Die	Strauss, R.
	Breslau, Nov. 2	Arzt der Sobeide, Der+	Gál, H.
	Nuremberg, Nov. 12	Fest auf Haderslev, Ein+	Heger, R.
	Berlin, ?	Dorf ohne Glocke, Das+	Künneke, E.

Year	Place, Date	Title	Composer
1920	Frankfurt, Jan. 21	Schatzgräber, Der	Schreker, F.
	Darmstadt, Jan. 29	Ritter Blaubart+	Reznicek, E. N. von
	Berlin, Feb. 12	Letzte Walzer, Der+	Straus, O.
	Dresden, Feb. 23	Fremde, Der+	Kaun, H.
	Plauen, April 18	Feuerprobe, Die+	Dost, W.
	Dresden, April 28	Schirin und Getraude+	Graener, P.
	Vienna, May 13	Dorfschule, Die+	Weingartner, F.
	Vienna, May 13	Meister Andrea+	Weingartner, F.
	Dresden, May 21	Goldene Vogel, Der+	Fall, L.
	Frankfurt, July 20	Ersten Menschen, Die (posth.)	Stephan, R.
	Hamburg, Nov. 2	Des Kaisers Dichter+	Franckenstein, C. von
	Hamburg and Cologne, Dec. 4	Tote Stadt, Die	Korngold, E.
	Munich, Dec. 4	Vögel, Die	Braunfels, W.
	Bremen, ?	Heilige, Die+	Gurlitt, M.
ca. 1920	? ?	Strohwitwe, Die+	Blech, L.
1921	Vienna, April 9	Kohlhaymerin, Die+	Bittner, J.
	Berlin, April 15	Vetter aus Dingsda, Der+	Künneke, E.
	Münster, April 28	Berggeist, Der+	Stierlin, K.
	Hanover, May 15	Prinzessin Ginara+	Wellesz, E.
	Darmstadt, May 16	Scirocco+	Albert, E. d'
	Stuttgart, June 4	Mörder, Hoffnung der Frauen	Hindemith, P.
	Stuttgart, June 4	Nusch-Nuschi, Das	Hindemith, P.
	Nuremberg, Nov. 24	Judith+	Ettinger, M.
1922	Frankfurt, March 26	Sancta Susanna	Hindemith, P.
	Zurich, May 10	Venus	Schoeck, O.

Year	Place, Date	Work	Composer
1922 (cont.)	Munich, May 12	**Grüne Heinrich, Der+**	Ebner, G.
	Vienna, May 12	**Frasquita+**	Lehár, F.
	Mannheim, May 21	**Doktor Eisenbart+**	Zilcher, H.
	Leipzig and Cologne, May 28	**Zwerg, Der**	Zemlinsky, A. von
	Salzburg, July 24	**Heisse Eisen, Das+**	Paumgartner, B.
	? ?	**Mann im Mond, Der+**	Brandt-Buys, J.
	premiere 1925	**Doktor Faust**	Busoni, F.
1923	Basel, Jan. 31	**Satyros+**	Baussnern, W. von
	Mannheim, March 18	**Rosengärtlein, Das+**	Bittner, J.
	Basel, March 23	**Tote Gast, Der**	Berr, J. R.
	Düsseldorf, April 29	**Heilige Ente, Die+**	Gál, H.
	Berlin, Sept. 9	**Madame Pompadour+**	Fall, L.
	Duisburg, Sept. 23	**Schwanenweiss+**	Weismann, J.
	Berlin, Oct. 27	**Holofernes+**	Reznicek, E. N. von
	Hamburg, Oct. 31	**Mareike von Numwegen+**	Albert, E. d'
	Dresden, Nov. 20	**Höhle von Salamanca, Die+**	Paumgartner, B.
	Rostock, Dec. 16	**Schmied von Marienburg, Der+**	Wagner, S.
1924	Zurich, Jan. 29	**Wandbild, Das+**	Schoeck, O.
	Vienna, Feb. 28	**Gräfin Maritza**	Kálmán, E.
	Mannheim, March 20	**Alkestis+**	Wellesz, E.
	Cologne, March 27	**Irrelohe**	Schreker, F.
	Berlin, April 23	**Andromeda+**	Maurice, P.
	Gotha, April 23	**Cagliostro+**	Wartisch, O.
	Prague, June 6	**Erwartung** (comp. 1909)	Schoenberg, A.
	Frankfurt, June 9	**Sprung über den Schatten, Der+**	Krenek, E.
	Dresden, June 17	**Abenteuer des Casanova+**	Andreae, V.

Year	Place, Date	Title	Composer
1924 (cont.)			
	Vienna, Oct. 14	Glückliche Hand, Die	Schoenberg, A.
	Berlin, Oct. 21	Zwingburg+	Krenek, E.
	Zurich, Oct. 22	Sizilianer, Der+	David, K. H.
	Dresden, Nov. 4	Intermezzo	Strauss, R.
	Munich, Nov. 15	Don Gil von den grünen Hosen+	Braunfels, W.
1925	Leipzig, Jan. 16	Käficht, Der+	Kormann, H.
	Munich, Jan. 17	Island-Saga+	Vollerthun, G.
	Nuremberg, Feb. 7	Eifersüchtige Trinker, Der+ and Juana+	Ettinger, M.
	Essen, March 18	Mira+	Overhoff, K.
	Duisburg, April 23	Traumspiel, Ein+	Weismann, J.
	Dresden, May 21	Doktor Faust	Busoni, F.
	Freiburg, June 21	Leonce und Lena+	Weismann, J.
	Dresden, Oct. 4	Orpheus+	Orff, C. after C. Monteverdi
	Brunswick, etc., Oct. 29	Menandra+	Kaun, H.
	Vienna, Oct. 30	Paganini	Lehár, F.
	Berlin, Dec. 14	Wozzeck	Berg, A.
	Karlsruhe, ?	Klage der Ariadne+	Orff, C. after C. Monteverdi
ca. 1925	? ?	Rufen sie Herrn Plim!+	Spoliansky, M.
1926	Karlsruhe, March 4	Friedensengel, Der+	Wagner, S.
	Dresden, March 29	Protagonist, Der	Weill, K.
	Bremen, April 22	Wozzeck+	Gurlitt, M.
	Breslau, April 24	Lied der Nacht, Das+	Gál, H.

Year	Place/Date	Title	Composer
1926 (cont.)			
	Altenburg, May 1	Salambo+	Böttcher, L.
	Gera, May 22	Zauberer, Der+	Mojsisovics, R.
	Schwerin, Sept. 19	Sturmvögel+	Schjelderup, G.
	Dresden, Nov. 9	Cardillac	Hindemith, P.
	Frankfurt, Nov. 14	Golem, Der+	Albert, E. d'
	Kassel, Nov. 27	Orpheus und Eurydike	Krenek, E.
	Cologne, ?	Opferung des Gefangenen, Die+	Wellesz, E.
	Vienna, ?	Zirkusprinzessin, Die+	Kálmán, E.
1927			
	Dresden, Jan. 8	Penthesilea	Schoeck, O.
	Hanover, Jan. 29	Herrn Dürers Bild+	Mraczek, J. G.
	Leipzig, Feb. 10	Jonny spielt auf	Krenek, E.
	Dresden and Breslau, Feb. 17	Hanneles Himmelfahrt+	Graener, P.
	Berlin, Feb. 21	Zarewitsch, Der	Lehár, F.
	Berlin, March 2	Royal Palace	Weill, K.
	Munich, April 21	Himmelskleid, Das+	Wolf-Ferrari, E.
	Würzburg, June 14	Penthesilea+	Ritter, R.
	Baden-Baden, July 17	Hin und zurück	Hindemith, P.
	Baden-Baden, July 17	Prinzessin auf der Erbse, Die+	Toch, E.
	Baden-Baden, July 18	Mahagonny (Das kleine Mahagonny)	Weill, K.
	Hamburg, Oct. 7	Wunder der Heliane, Das+	Korngold, E.
	Altenburg, Dec. 25	Blonde Liselott, Die+	Künneke, E.
	Leipzig, Dec. 27	Satuala+	Reznicek, E. N. von
	premiere 1978	Christophorus	Schreker, F.
	not perf	König René's Tochter+	Behrend, F.

1928	Zurich, Jan. 29	Traumwandel+	David, K. H.
	Vienna, Jan. 31	Don Juans Sohn+	Wunsch, H.
	Leipzig, Feb. 18	Zar lässt sich photographien, Der	Weill, K.
	Kassel, Feb. 19	Armer Kolumbus+	Dressel, E.
	Stuttgart, March 1	Scherz, List und Rache+	Wellesz, E.
	Coburg, March 16	Schneider Fips+	Lorentz, A.
	Leipzig, April 14	Frühlings Erwachen+	Ettinger, M.
	Halle, May 6	Freunde von Salamanka, Die (comp. 1815)	Schubert, F.
	Wiesbaden, May 6	Schwergewicht, Das, Der geheime Königreich,+ and Der Diktator	Krenek, E.
	Dresden, June 16	Ägyptische Helena, Die	Strauss, R.
	Baden-Baden, July 15	Saul	Reutter, H.
	Berlin, Aug. 31	Dreigroschenoper, Die	Weill, K.
	Weimar, Oct. 4	Tyll+	Lothar, M.
	Mannheim, Oct. 21	Egon und Emilie+	Toch, E.
	Berlin, Nov. 13	Mondnacht+	Bittner, J.
	Leipzig, Nov. 18	Baskische Venus, Die	Wetzler, H.
	Berlin, Dec. 1	Casanova+	Benatzky, R.
	Gera, Dec. 1	Moschopulos+ and Der nackte König+	Wagner-Régeny, R.
	Leipzig, Dec. 1	Schwarze Orchidee, Die+	Albert, E. d'
	Berlin, Dec. 10	Singende Teufel, Der+	Schreker, F.
	Krefeld, ?	Gläserne Berg, Der+	Braunfels, W.
	not perf	Tor und der Tod, Der+	Brehme, H.
	not perf	Zeus und Elida+	Wolpe, S.

Year	Place, Date	Work	Composer
1929	Augsburg, March 3	Dornröschen+	Herre, M.
	Hamburg, March 12	Belsazar+	Peró, H.
	Stuttgart, March 20	Verlorene Sohn, Der+	Reutter, H.
	Elberfeld, April 7	Tartuffe+	Eidens, J.
	Solothurn, April 9	Florentinische Tragödie, Eine+	Flury, R.
	Duisburg, April 13	Maschinist Hopkins	Brand, M.
	Dresden, April 27	Jürg Jentsch+	Kaminski, H.
	Zurich, May 5	Fächer, Der+	Kunz, E.
	Berlin, June 25	Neues vom Tage	Hindemith, P.
	Berlin, Sept. 2	Happy End	Weill, K.
	Berlin, Oct. 10	Land des Lächelns, Das	Lehár, F.
	Berlin, ?	Dantons Tod+	Eisler, H.
	premiere 1987	Habemeajaja+	Blacher, B.
	not perf	Anna Blume+	Wolpe, S.
	not perf	Schöne Geschichten+	Wolpe, S.
1930	Leipzig, Jan. 19	Leben des Orest, Das	Krenek, E.
	Cologne, Jan. 26	Galatea+	Braunfels, W.
	Frankfurt, Feb. 1	Von heute auf morgen	Schoenberg, A.
	Aussig, March 1	Dorian Gray+	Flick-Steger, C.
	Leipzig, March 9	Aufsteig und Fall der stadt Mahagonny	Weill, K.
	Ansbach, May 15	Don Juans Ende+	Drechsel, G.
	Königsberg, June 8	Fächer, Der+	Toch, E.
	Berlin, June 21	Wir bauen eine Stadt	Hindemith, P.
	Berlin, June 23	Jasager, Der	Weill, K.
	Dresden, Oct. 3	Vom Fischer un syner Fru	Schoeck, O.
	Berlin, Nov. 8	Im Weissen Rössl	Benatzky, R.
	Düsseldorf, Nov. 9	Soldaten+	Gurlitt, M.

1930 (cont.)

Dresden, Nov. 11	Lord Spleen+	Lothar, M.
Dresden, Nov. 11	Spiel oder Ernst?+	Reznicek, E. N. von
Berlin, Dec. 3	Schön ist die Welt+	Lehár, F.
Basel, Dec. 5	Don Juan in der Fremde+	Haug, H.
Berlin, Dec. 10	Fremde Erde+	Rathaus, K.
Breslau, Dec. 19	Zauberspiegel, Der+	Gál, H.
Munich, Dec. 19	Gespenstersonate, Die+	Weismann, J.

1931

Munich, Feb. 28	Geliebte Stimme, Die+	Weinberger, J.
Kiel, March 12	Alchemist, Der+	Pistor, C.
Bad Pyrmont, June 4	Cress ertrinkt+	Fortner, W.
Vienna, June 20	Bakchantinnen, Die	Wellesz, E.
Stuttgart, Oct. 29	Gondoliere des Dogen, Der+	Reznicek, E. N. von
Hanover, Nov. 10	Freikorporal, Der+	Vollerthun, G.
Berlin, Nov. 12	Herz, Das+	Pfitzner, H.
Schwerin, Nov. 13	Friedemann Bach+	Graener, P.
Vienna	Walzer aus Wien+	Strauss, J., Jr.
? ?	Orpheus und der Bürgermeister+	Dessau, P.

1932

Mannheim, Feb. 14	Gewaltige Hahnrei, Der+	Goldschmidt, B.
Berlin, Feb. 16	Andromache+	Windt, H.
Berlin, March 10	Bürgschaft, Die	Weill, K.
Dresden, March 18	Dagmar+	Stiegler, K.
Munich, April 8	Bettler Namenlos, Der+	Heger, R.
Berlin, Sept. 1	Frau, die weiss was sie will, Eine+	Straus, O.
Dresden, Sept. 29	Mister Wü+	Albert, E. d'
Berlin, Oct. 29	Schmied von Gent, Der	Schreker, F.
premiere 1954	Moses und Aron	Schoenberg, A.

Year	Place, Date	Title	Composer
1932 (cont.)	premiere 1966	Schwarze Spinne, Die+	Hauer, J. M.
1933	Düsseldorf, Feb. 11	Rossenknecht+	Zillig, W.
	Leipzig, Feb. 18	Silbersee, Der	Weill, K.
	Darmstadt, April 26	Nana+	Gurlitt, M.
	Paris, July 1	Sieben Todsünden, Die	Weill, K.
	Vienna, July 1	Arabella	Strauss, R.
	Munich radio, July 13	Columbus	Egk, W.
	Zurich, Sept. 30	Zwei Herzen im 3/4 Takt+	Stolz, R.
	Zurich, Oct. 14	Kreiderkeis, Der+	Zemlinsky, A. von
	Dresden, Dec. 6	Münchhausen+	Lothar, M.
	Cologne, Dec. 16	Heidenkönig, Der+	Wagner, S.
1934	Vienna, Jan. 20	Giuditta	Lehár, F.
	Munich radio, April 13	Jorinda und Jorgile+	Sutermeister, H.
	Graz, Nov. 17	Viola+	Holenia, H.
	Vienna, Dec. 8	Veilchen, Das+	Bittner, J.
1935	Stettin, Jan. 21	Taras Bulba+	Richter, E.
	Dresden, Feb. 20	Günstling, Der	Wagner-Régeny, R.
	Berlin, March 14	Prinz von Homburg, Der+	Graener, P.
	Berlin radio, March 24	Kalte Herz, Das+	Lothar, M.
	Frankfurt, May 22	Zaubergeige, Die+	Egk, W.
	Dresden, June 2	Schweigsame Frau, Die	Strauss, R.
	Vienna, Dec. 26	Dame im Traum+	Salmhofer, F.
	Zurich, ?	Drei Walzer+	Straus, O.

Year	Place, Date	Work	Composer
1935 (cont.)	not perf	Agnes Bernauer+	Messner, J.
	not perf	Weg der Verheissung, Der+	Weill, K.
1936	Hamburg, Jan. 25	Fischer un syne Fru, De+	Brüggemann, K.
	Berlin radio, Feb. 9	Genoveva+	Ecklebe, A.
	Altenberg, Feb. 18	Dreispitz, Der+	Korman, H.
	Feiburg, March 3	Diener zweier Herren, Der+	Kusterer, A.
	Zurich, March 27	Rossini in Neapel+	Paumgartner, B.
	Bern radio, Oct. 15	Schwarze Spinne, Die+	Sutermeister, H.
	Düsseldorf, Nov. 15	Enoch Arden+	Gerster, O.
	Weimar, Nov. 26	Hirtenlegende+	Bodart, E.
	Hamburg, Dec. 6	Schwarzer Peter+	Schultze, N.
1937	Berlin, Jan. 23	Rembrandt van Rijn+	Klenau, P. von
	Dresden, March 2	Massimilla Doni	Schoeck, O.
	Basel, May 24	Tartuffe+ and Der Spiegel der Agrippina+	Haug, H.
	Zurich, June 2	Lulu	Berg, A.
	Frankfurt, June 8	Carmina burana	Orff, C.
	Mannheim, Oct. 16	Spanische Nacht+	Bodart, E.
	Hamburg, Nov. 12	Opfer, Das+	Zillig, W.
	Vienna, Nov. 18	Wallenstein+	Weinberger, J.
	Kassel, Nov. 24	Tobias Wunderlich+	Haas, J.
	premiere 1950	Traum ein Leben, Der	Braunfels, W.
	premiere 1964	Zweimal Alexander	Martinů, B.
1938	Hamburg, Jan. 28	Kalte Herz, Das+	Brüggemann, K.
	Dresden, Feb. 10	Wirtin von Pinsk, Die+	Mohaupt, R.
	Stans, Feb. 20	Rubin, Der+	Jenny, A.

Year	Place, Date	Title	Composer
1938 (cont.)	Berlin, May 12	Schneider Wibbel	Lothar, M.
	Zurich, May 28	Mathis der Maler	Hindemith, P.
	Brunswick, May 30	Odysseus bei Circe+	Trantow, H.
	Prague, June 15	Karl der Fünfte	Krenek, E.
	Munich, July 24	Friedenstag	Strauss, R.
	Stockholm, Oct. 7	Kathrin, Die+	Korngold, E.
	Dresden, Oct. 15	Daphne	Strauss, R.
	Berlin, Nov. 24	Peer Gynt	Egk, W.
	Osnabrück, Nov. 27	Bär, Der+	Stierlin, K.
	Mainz, Dec. 18	Prinzessin und der Schweinenhirt, Die+	Reutter, H.
1939	Munich, Feb. 5	Mond, Der	Orff, C.
	Tilsit, Feb. 5	Böse Weib, Das+	Hufeld, A.
	Leipzig, Feb. 11	Pfiffige Magd, Die+	Weismann, J.
	Stettin, March 11	Komödie der Irrungen, Die+	Lorenz, K.
	Karlsruhe, March 24	Dorian+	Leger, H.
	Kassel, March 29	Elisabeth von England+	Klenau, P. von
	Düsseldorf, May 17	Nachtigall, Die+	Irmler, A.
1940	Kassel, March 14	Dame Kobold+	Wolfurt, K. von
	Dresden, April 13	Romeo und Julia	Sutermeister, H.
	Berlin, Dec. 19	Andreas Wolius+	Walter, F.
	? ?	Entzückende Frau, Eine+	Heuberger, R.
	premiere 1952	Liebe der Danae, Die	Strauss, R.
1941	Wuppertal, Feb. 5	Fürstin Tarakanowa	Blacher, B.
	Kassel, Feb. 25	Uhrmacher von Strassburg, Der+	Brehme, H.
	Stettin, March 30	Was ihr wollt+	Hess, L.

Year	Location, Date	Title	Composer
1941 (cont.)	Leipzig, May 12	**Windsbraut, Die+**	Zillig, W.
	Poughkeepsie, N.Y., May 13	**Tarquin+**	Krenek, E.
	Stockholm, Sept. 15	**Zerrissene, Der+**	Kreuder, P.
	Düsseldorf, Oct. 11	**Hexe von Passau, Die+**	Gerster, O.
	Schwerin, Oct. 25	**Abenteuer des Don Quichotte, Ein+**	Kirchner, R.
1942	Cologne, Jan. 4	**Schwanhild+**	Graener, P.
	Stans, Feb. 12	**Zerrissene, Der+**	Jenny, A.
	Strasbourg, April 15	**Dornröschen+**	Bresgen, C.
	Frankfurt, Oct. 7	**Odysseus+**	Reutter, H.
	Munich, Oct. 28	**Capriccio**	Strauss, R.
	Dresden, Oct. 31	**Zauberinsel, Der+**	Sutermeister, H.
1943	Göttingen, Feb. 7	**Urteil des Paris, Das+**	Bresgen, C.
	Frankfurt, Feb. 20	**Kluge, Die**	Orff, C.
	Zurich, Feb. 20	**Casanova in der Schweiz+**	Burkhard, P.
	Berlin, April 1	**Schloss Dürande, Das**	Schoeck, O.
	Oldenburg, May 27	**Kluge Wirtin, Die+**	Hinrichs, H.
	Leipzig, Nov. 7	**Kalte Herz, Das**	Schultze, N.
	?	**Schlaue Müllerin, Die+**	Bresgen, C.
1944	Dresden, July 2	**Hochzeit des Jobs, Die+**	Haas, J.
	premiere 1975	**Kaiser von Atlantis, Der**	Ullmann, V.
1945	New York, May 4	**Blaue Berg, Der+**	Lustgarten, E.
	Zurich, June 22	**Niobe+**	Sutermeister, H.
	Berlin, Sept. 3	**Karamasows, Die+**	Coenen, P.

Year	Place, Date	Title	Composer
1946	Strelsund, July 4	Lukrezia Borgia+	Herbst, W.
	Berlin, Nov. 12	Postmeister Wyrin+	Reutter, F. von
	Radio Berlin, Dec. 20	Flut, Die	Blacher, B.
1947	Zurich, Feb. 8	Unsterbliche Kranke, Der+	Haug, H.
	Stuttgart, June 15	Bernauerin, Die	Orff, C.
	Salzburg, Aug. 6	Dantons Tod	Einem, G. von
	Hamburg, Oct. 24	Don Quijote+	Maasz, G.
	Cologne, Dec. 31	Nachtigall, Die+	Schanazara, H.
	Berlin-Zehlendorf, ?	Romeo und Julia	Blacher, B.
1948	Göttingen, Jan. 25	Weg nach Freudenstadt, Der+	Reutter, H.
	Leipzig, Feb. 22	Nachtschwalbe, Die+	Blacher, B.
	Zwickau, March 20	Hexenlied+	Kleemann, R.
	Cologne, April 4	Verkündigung+	Braunfels, W.
	Leverkusen, June 29	Des Kaisers neue Kleider+	Werdin, E.
	Stockholm, Oct. 14	Raskolnikoff+	Sutermeister, H.
	Berlin, Dec. 18	Circe+	Egk, W.
	Esslingen, ?	Igel als Bräutigam, Der+	Bresgen, C.
1949	Cologne, Jan. 21	Feindlichen Nachbarn, Die+	Breuer, P.
	Münster, Jan. 21	Liebe ist teuer+	Brehme, H.
	?, March 26	Brüderlein und schwesterlein+	Friedrich, K.
	Heidelberg, May 7	Wundertheater, Das	Henze, H. W.
	Berlin, May 22	Lächerlichen Preziösen, Die+	Behrend, F.
	Zurich, May 28	Schwarze Spinne, Die	Burkhard, W.
	Wuppertal, June 25	Verzauberte ich, Das+	Gerster, O.

1949	(cont.)		
	Bremen, July 15	**Bremer Stadtmusikanten, Die+**	Mohaupt, R.
	Salzburg, Aug. 9	**Antigonae**	Orff, C.
	Cologne, Oct. 22	**Des Simplicius Simplicisssimus+**	Hartmann, K. A.
	Leipzig, Oct. 30	**Laune des Verliebten, Die+**	Dressel, E.
	Coburg, Nov. 23	**Spielmann, Der+**	Striegler, K.
	Cologne, Dec. 20	**Bremer Stadtmusikanten, Die+**	Bergese, H.
	Berlin, ?	**Agamemnons Tod+**	Goldberg, T.
	Fischbachau, ?	**Till Eulenspiegel+**	Beckerath, A. von
1950	Göttingen, Jan. 29	**Spiel von König Aphelius, Das+**	Kaminski, H.
	Berlin, Feb. 12	**Füsse im Feuer, Die+** and **Fingerhütschen+**	Sutermeister, H.
	Berlin, Feb. 23	**Odysseus und die Sirenen+**	Goldberg, T.
	Regensburg, Feb. 25	**Wozzeck+**	Pfister, K.
	Frankfurt, Hessian radio, March 22	**Traum ein Leben, Der** (comp. 1937)	Braunfels, W.
	Reichenbach, June 13	**Kolumbus+**	Böhme, W.
	Stuttgart, June 14	**Don Juan und Faust+**	Reutter, H.
	Berlin, ?	**Judith+**	Goldberg, T.
	Berlin, ?	**Phaedra+**	Goldberg, T.
1951	Düsseldorf, Feb. 3	**Troilus und Cressida+**	Zillig, W.
	Nuremberg, Feb. 11	**Lady Hamilton+**	Heger, R.
	Berlin and Dresden, March 13	**Amphitryon+**	Oboussier, R.
	Hamburg Radio, June 11	**Doktor Fausts Höllenfahrt+**	Engelmann, H. U.
	Frankfurt, June 17	**Virgilius+**	Körpen, A.

Year	Place, Date	Title	Composer
1951 (cont.)	Berlin, RIAS, June 24	Robinson und Freitag+	Goldberg, T.
	Graz, July 5	Stella+	Bloch, W.
	Berlin (East), Oct. 12	Verhör des Lukullus, Das	Dessau, P.
	Stockholm, Nov. 22	Rote Stiefel, Der+	Sutermeister, H.
1952	Nuremberg, Jan. 13	Schlaue Susanna, Die+	Lehner, F. X.
	Zurich, Jan. 19	Don Pedros Heimkehr+	Erismann, H.
	Vienna, RDR, Jan. 30	Indische Legende+	Kont, P.
	Kassel, Feb. 1	König Lustig+	Riede, E.
	Hanover, Feb. 17	Boulevard Solitude	Henze, H. W.
	Cologne, March	Kain+	Schmidtmann, F.
	Basel, March 26	Leonore 40/45	Liebermann, R.
	Los Angeles, May 16	Leonore und Lena+	Zeisl, E.
	Fellbach, June 25	Ali Baba und die vierzig Räuber+	Dienel, J.
	Salzburg, Aug. 14	Liebe der Danae, Die (comp. 1940)	Strauss, R.
	Berlin, Sept. 2	Fabel in C+	Erbse, H.
	Berlin, Sept. 23	Preussisches Märchen	Blacher, B.
	Münster, Nov. 22	Claudia amata+	Driessler, J.
	Kaiserslautern, Nov. 29	Alles ist Kismet+	Hofmann, W.
	Karlsruhe, ?	Kleopatra+	Goldberg, T.
1953	Basel, Jan. 11	Verirrte Taube, Die+	Haug, H.
	London, April 13	Beatrice Cenci+	Goldschmidt, B.

Year	Place, Date	Title	Composer
1953 (cont.)			
	Cologne, May 27	Grossindustrielle, Die+	Driesch, K.
	Hamburg, May 27	Landarzt, Ein	Henze, H. W.
	Hessian radio, June 25	Wald, Der+	Fortner, W.
	Hessian radio, June 28	Abstrakte Oper Nr. 1	Blacher, B.
	Salzburg, Aug. 17	Prozess, Der	Einem, G. von
	Munich, Oct. 20	Astutuli+	Orff, C.
	Nuremberg, Nov. 12	Brüderlein Hund+	Bresgen, C.
	Münster, Nov. 13	Des Kaisers neueste Kleider+	Kaufmann, O.
	Frankfurt, NWDR, Dec. 3	Ende einer Welt, Das	Henze, H. W.
	not perf	Bergwerk von Falun, Das+	Schibler, A.
1954	Nuremberg, May 23	Glückliche Ende, Das+	Wolf, W.
	Hamburg, June 6	Moses und Aron (comp. 1932)	Schoenberg, A.
	Frankfurt radio, June 20	Brücke von San Luis Rey, Die+	Reutter, H.
	Cologne, June 23	Witwe von Ephesus, Die+	Reutter, H.
	Salzburg, Aug. 17	Penelope	Liebermann, R.
	Weimar, Sept. 4	Doktor Eisenbart+	Böckmann, A.
	Frankfurt radio, Nov. 9	Heimkehr, Die+	Mihalovici, M.
	Dortmund, Nov. 10	Stumme Serenade, Die+	Korngold, E.
	Louisville, Ky., Dec. 4	Zwillingskomödie	Mohaupt, R.
	Cologne radio, ?	Spiel von der Auferstehung, Das+	Braunfels, W.

Year	Place, Date	Work	Composer
1955	Nuremberg, March 26	Bad auf der Tenne, Das	Schröder, F.
	Zurich, April 25	Füsse im Feuer, Die+	Schibler, E.
	Wiesbaden, May 3	Stadt hinter dem Strom, Die+	Vogt, H.
	Salzburg, Aug. 17	Irische Legende	Egk, W.
	Hamburg, Oct. 4	Mauer, Die+	Engelmann, H. U.
	Hamburg, Oct. 17	Pallas Athene weint	Krenek, E.
1956	Schwyz, Switz., Feb. 10	Ewige Arzt, Der+	Bresgen, C.
	Zurich, June 9	Hansel und Gretel+	Semmler, R.
	Vienna, June 17	Sturm, Der	Martin, F.
	Frankfurt/Oder, Aug. 18	Viel Lärm um nichts+	Heinrich, H.
	Halle, Sept. 22	Till+	Wohlgemuth, G.
	Berlin, Sept. 23	König Hirsch	Henze, H.W.
1957	Trier, Jan. 18	Schneekönigin, Die+	Thies, K.
	Schwerin, Feb. 3	Mitschuldigen, Die+	Riethmüller, H.
	Freiburg/Bresgau, April 1	Des Kaisers neue Kleider+	Hummel, B.
	Weimar, April 1	Des Kaisers neue Kleider+	Westien, F.
	Schwetzingen, May 9	Revisor, Der	Egk, W.
	Nuremberg, May 26	Kleine Stadt, Die+	Lehner, F. X.
	Düsseldorf, June 3	Räuber, Die	Klebe, G.
	Cologne, June 8	Bluthochzeit, Die	Fortner, W.
	Hamburg, NDR, June 26	Verlobung in San Domingo, Die+	Zillig, W.
	Munich, Aug. 11	Harmonie der Welt, Die	Hindemith, P.
	Erfurt, Nov. 30	Spieldose, Die+	Hanell, R.

Year	Place, Date	Work	Composer
1957 (cont.)	Salzburg, Dec. 3	Schule der Frauen, Die	Liebermann, R.
1958	Erfurt, Jan. 15	König Drosselbart+	Noll, D.
	Meissen, Feb. 6	Bauer im Fegefeuer, Der+	Grafe, M.
	Dortmund, Feb. 25	Yü-Nü+	Riede, E.
	Basel, April 14	Titus Feuerfuchs+	Sutermeister, H.
	Graz, June 21	Kätchen von Heilbronn+	Bloch, W.
	Munich, Aug. 8	Rappelkopf+	Lothar, M.
	Magdeburg, Aug. 28	Amphitryon+	Hermann, H.
	Hamburg, Sept. 16	Grüne Kakadu, Der+	Mohaupt, R.
	Berlin, Oct. 3	Anaximanders Ende+	Thärichen, W.
	Berlin, Oct. 3	Corinna+	Fortner, W.
	Erfurt, Dec. 23	Kolumbus+	Griesbach, K. R.
1959	Bern, SRG, June 10	Seraphine+	Sutermeister, H.
	Düsseldorf, June 14	Tödlichen Wünsche, Die	Klebe, G.
	Vienna, ORF, June 26	Peter und Susanne+	Kont, P.
	Hamburg, ARD, Aug. 14	Auszeichnung, Die+	Poser, H.
	Salzburg, Aug. 17	Julietta+	Erbse, H.
	Kassel, Sept. 12	Prometheus+	Wagner-Régeny, R.
	Düsseldorf, Sept. 20	Ermordung Cäsars, Die+	Klebe, G.
	Berlin (East), Oct. 4	Arme Konrad, Der+	Forest, J. K.
	Stuttgart, Dec. 11	Oedipus der Tyrann	Orff, C.
1960	Hamburg, May 22	Prinz von Homburg, Der	Henze, H. W.
	Nuremberg, May 22	Mann im Mond, Der+	Bresgen, C.

Year	Date	Title	Composer
1960 (cont.)	Halberstadt, Sept. 4	**Tai Yang erwacht+**	Forest, J. K.
	Berlin, Sept. 21	**Rosamunde Floris**	Blacher, B.
	Schwerin, Sept. 27	**Erbschaft, Die+**	Nowka, D.
	Bremen, Sept. 29	**Alexander+**	Holterdorf, T.
	Linz, Sept. 30	**Ödipus+**	Eder, H.
	Weimar, Oct. 7	**Marike Weiden+**	Griesbach, K. R.
	Magdeburg, Oct. 31	**Heiratsantrag, Der+**	Röttger, H.
1961	Berlin, Jan. 18	**Arme Gespenst, Das+**	Hermann, P.
	Kaiserlautern, Jan. 24	**Pulcinella+**	Krol, B.
	Hanover, March 6	**Scherz, List und Rache+**	Leinert, F.
	Dresden, March 19	**Lysistrate**	Kont, P.
	Plauen, May 6	**Schweigende Dorf, Das+**	Neef, W.
	Schwetzingen, May 20	**Elegie für junge Liebende**	Henze, H. W.
	Vienna, May 27	**Krach im offen, Der+**	Kaufmann, A.
	Zurich, June 9	**Griechische Passion, Die**	Martinů, B.
	Wiesbaden, June 16	**Liebeskette, Die+**	Lehner, F. X.
	Salzburg, Aug. 16	**Bergwerk zu Falun, Das**	Wagner-Régeny, R.
	Berlin, Sept. 25	**Alkmene**	Klebe, G.
	Berlin, Oct. 15	**Leonce und Lena+**	Schwaen, K.
	Düsseldorf, Oct. 21	**Ameise, Die+**	Ronnenfeld, P.
	Cologne, Oct. 26	**Originale+**	Stockhausen, K.
	Mannheim, Dec. 17	**Lange Weihnachtsmahl, Das**	Hindemith, P.
1962	Dessau, Feb. 10	**Frauen von Troia, Die+**	Röttger, H.
	Nuremberg, March 16	**Glücksfischer, Der+**	Lothar, M.
	Aachen, May 6	**König Nicolo+**	Chemin-Petit, H.

Year	Place, Date	Work	Composer
1962 (cont.)	Schwetzingen, May 10	In seinem Garten liebt Don Perlimplín Belisa	Fortner, W.
	Saarbrücken, May 23	Vertrauenssache+	Krenek, E.
	Dresden, June 9	Dorian Gray+	Hanell, R.
	Vienna, ORF, June 15	Kardinal, Der+	Eder, H.
	Salzburg, ORF, July 25	Ausgerechnet und verspielt+	Krenek, E.
1963	Rostock, March 27	Persische Episode+	Wagner-Régeny, R.
	Radio Bern, June 23	Bär, Der+	Dressel, E.
	Zurich, June 23	Errettung Thebens, Die+	Kelterborn, R.
	Hamburg, June 28	Figaro lässt sich scheiden	Klebe, G.
	Linz, Nov. 23	Verlöbnis, Das+	Zillig, W.
	Munich, Nov. 27	Verlobung in San Domingo, Die	Egk, W.
	Salzburg, Dec. 25	Traumleben+	Kont, P.
1964	Radio Bremen, Feb. 17	Visiones amantes+	Bresgen, C.
	Mannheim, Feb. 18	Athener Komödie+	Vogt, H.
	Mannheim, Feb. 18	Zweimal Alexander (Alexander bis) (comp. 1937)	Martinů, B.
	Mainz, April 19	Bassgeige, Die+	Poser, H.
	Dresden, May 23	Fabel vom seligen Schlächtermeister, Die+	Wagner-Régeny, R.
	Ettal (Bavaria), June 7	Des Esels Schatten+	Strauss, R. (arr. Haussner)
	Hamburg, June 16	Goldene Bock, Der	Krenek, E.
	Mainz, ZDF, Sept. 6	Gespenst von Canterville, Das	Sutermeister, H.

Year	Location, Date	Work	Composer
1964 (cont.)	Hamburg, Sept. 17	Zerrissene, Der	Einem, G. von
	Frankfurt, Sept. 24	Dame Kobold	Wimberger, G.
	Vienna, ORF, Oct. 2	Rosen der Madonna, Die+	Stolz, R.
	Oberlin, Ohio, Nov. 23	Bartelby+	Aschaffenburg, W.
1965	Cologne, Feb. 15	Soldaten, Die	Zimmermann, B. A.
	Milan, March 17	Atomtod+	Manzoni, G.
	Kiel, ZDF, March 21	Peter der Dritte+	Schultze, N.
	Berlin, April 7	Junge Lord, Der	Henze, H. W.
	Radio Innsbruck, April 7	Gluckerich, Der+	Urbanner, E.
	Zwickau, May 21	Bildnis des Dorian Gray, Das+	Kleemann, R.
	Vienna, ORF, June 13	Elga+	Weishappel, R.
	Kiel, June 20	Traumspiel, Ein	Reimann, A.
	Cologne, July 6	Tartarin von Tarascon+	Radermacher, F.
	Berlin, Sept. 25	Traum des Liu-Tung, Der	Yun, I.
	Hamburg, Nov. 2	Jacobowsky und der Oberst	Klebe, G.
	Hamburg, ?	Lächeln am Füsse der Leiter, Das+	Bibalo, A.
1966	Hamburg, Feb. 4	Zwischenfälle bei einer Notlandung	Blacher, B.
	Vienna, May 23	Schwarze Spinne, Die+ (comp. 1932)	Hauer, J. M.
	Schwetzingen, May 29	Tod des Empedokles, Der+	Reutter, H.
	Stuttgart, June 2	Siebzehn Tage und 4 Minuten	Egk, W.
	Vienna, June 8	Mysteriöse Herr X, Der+	Uhl, A.
	Salzburg, Aug. 6	Bassariden, Die	Henze, H. W.

Year	Date/Location	Title	Composer
1966 (cont.)	Mannheim, Sept. 8	**Hero und Leander**	Bialas, G.
	Berlin (East), Oct. 10	**Esther+**	Hanell, R.
	Berlin (East), Nov. 15	**Puntila**	Dessau, P.
	? ?	**Herr in Grau, Der+**	Erbse, H.
1967	Vienna, ORF, Jan. 5	**Inzwischen+**	Kont, P.
	Hanover, Jan. 29	**Doppelgängerin, Die+**	Meyerowitz, J.
	Mainz, Feb. 15	**Bauernhochzeit+**	Reutter, H.
	Mainz, Feb. 15	**Nausikaa+**	Reutter, H.
	Karslruhe, March 4	**Kaiser Jovian+**	Kelterborn, R.
	Hamburg, March 5	**Arden muss sterben**	Goehr, A.
	Cologne and Berlin, May 5	**Bartelby**	Niehaus, M.
	Zurich, May 26	**Madame Bovary+**	Sutermeister, H.
	Weimar, June 21	**Blumen von Hiroshima, Die+**	Forest, J. K.
	Bavarian radio, Sept. 6	**Zauberspiegel, Der+**	Krenek, E.
	Berlin (East), Nov. 5	**Letzte Schuss, Der+**	Matthus, S.
	? ?	**Weisse Hut, Der+**	Killmayer, W.
1968	Munich, Feb. 8	**Widerspenstige Heilige, Der+**	Lothar, M.
	Hamburg, March 5	**Hamlet**	Searle, H.
	Cologne, WDR, June 11	**Fall van Damm, Der+**	Engelmann, H. U.
	Schwerin, Oct. 6	**Weisse Rose, Die**	Zimmermann, U.

Year / Place, Date	Title	Composer
1968 (cont.)		
Vienna, ORF, Nov. 19 premiere 1977	Schwarz auf weiss+	Hüber, K.
1969	Floss der Medusa, Das	Henze, H. W.
Hanover, Feb. 1	Ophelia+	Engelmann, H. U.
Nuremberg, Feb. 23	Witwe des Schmetterlings, Die	Yun, I.
Hamburg, March 2	Reise, Die+	Werle, L. J.
Bellingham, May 14	Galatea Elettronica+	Goldberg, T.
Schwetzingen, May 15	Märchen von der schönen Lilie, Das+	Klebe, G.
Ober Hambach, May 21	Undine+	Fortner, W.
Hamburg, June 20	Teufel von Loudun, Der	Penderecki, K.
Berlin, Sept. 25	Zweihunderttausend Taler+	Blacher, B.
Munich, Dec. 13	Geschichte von Aucassin und Nicolette, Die	Bialas, G.
Berlin (East), Dec. 19	Lanzelot	Dessau, P.
? ?	Libussa+	Kont, P.
1970		
Hamburg, Jan. 13	Belagerungszustand, Der+	Keleman, M.
Hanover, Feb. 1	Aufsichtsrat, Der+	Motte, D. de la
Munich, May 9	Yolimba+	Dorst, T.
Magdeburg, May 10	Zweite Entscheidung, Die+	Zimmermann, U.
Coburg, June 17	Komödiantin, Die+	Chemin-Petit, H.
Kiel, June 21	Maldoror+	Niehaus, M.
Aldeburgh Festival, June 22	Cimarrón, El	Henze, H. W.
Hamburg, June 27	Das kommt davon+	Krenek, E.
Hamburg, Dec. 6	Stern geht auf aus Jaakob, Ein+	Burkhard, P.
Karlsruhe, Sept. 26	Dybuk, Der+	Füssl, K.

1971	Berlin, April 29	Melusine+	Reimann, A.
	Vienna, May 23	Besuch der alten Dame, Der	Einem, G. von
	Kiel, June 20	Geisterliebe	Yun, I.
	Leipzig, Aug. 28	Zerbrochene Krug, Der	Geissler, F.
	Rome, Sept. 28	Langwienzige Weg in die Wohnung Natascha Ungeheuer, Der	Henze, H. W.
1972	Hamburg, Nov. 13	Aschmedai+	Tal, J.
	Vienna, Feb. 22	König Nicolo	Weishappel, R.
	Hanover, April 7	Palast Hotel Thanatos+	Einfeldt, D.
	Thale, July 22	Bremer Stadtmusikanten, Die+	Auenmüller, H.
	Munich, Aug. 1	Sim Tjong	Yun, I.
	Berlin, Oct. 23	Elisabeth Tudor	Fortner, W.
1973	Dresden, Weimar, March 23	Levins Mühle+	Zimmermann, U.
	Cologne, WDR, April 16	Badewanne, Die	Niehaus, M.
	Hamburg, May 10	Unter dem Milchwald+	Steffens, W.
	Berlin, Sept. 15	Klage der Ariadne+	Chemin-Petit, H.
	Berlin (East), Oct. 15	Hamlet+	Forest, J. K.
	Wuppertal, Nov. 15	Yvonne, Prinzessin von Burgund+	Blacher, B.
	Berlin (East), Nov. 17	Reiter der Nacht+	Meyer, E. H.
	Vienna, Dec. 14	Kleider machen Leute+	Rubin, M.
1974	Berlin (East), Feb. 16	Einstein	Dessau, P.

Year	City, Date	Work	Composer
1974 (cont.)			
	New York, WNET, March 4	Cubana, La	Henze, H. W.
	Vienna, ORF, March 7	Flaschenpost vom Paradies, Die+	Krenek, E.
	Tübingen, April 11	Johann Faustus+	Eisler, H.
1975			
	Zurich, Jan. 18	Wahrer Held, Ein	Klebe, G.
	Berlin, Feb. 16	Geheimnis des entwendeten Briefes, Das+	Blacher, B.
	Wiesbaden, April 27	Trauung, Die+	Kirchner, V. D.
	Philadelphia, May 10	Kaiser von Atlantis, Der (comp. 1944)	Ullmann, V.
	Schwetzingen, May 15	Gestiefelte Kater, Der+	Bialas, G.
	Aarhus, ?	Miss Julie+	Bibalo, A.
1976			
	Berlin (East), April 24	Fettlöschen+	Wahren, K. H.
	Stuttgart, June 19	Mädchen aus Domrémy, Das	Klebe, G.
	Munich, July 26	Versuchung, Die+	Tal, J.
	Weimar, Sept. 7	Omphale	Matthus, S.
	Vienna, Dec. 17	Kabale und Liebe	Einem, G. von
	Dresden, Dec. 30	Schuhu, Der+	Zimmermann, U.
1977			
	Klagenfurt, Feb. 10	Pluto+	Kont, P.
	Berlin (East), Feb. 27	R. Hot+	Goldmann, F.
	Nice, May 22	Atmen gib das Leben, Das+	Stockhausen, K.
	Zurich, June 5	Engel kommt nach Babylon, Ein+	Kelterborn, R.
	Vienna, ORF, Aug. 6	Niobe+	Hiller, W.

Year	Place, Date	Title	Composer
1977 (cont.)	Hanover, Oct. 7	Faust und Yorick+	Rihm, W.
	Berlin, Oct. 16	Kassandras Tod+	Chemin-Petit, H.
	Aix-en-Provence, April 8	Sirius+	Stockhausen, K.
	Hamburg, Dec. 4	Tartarin von Tarascon	Niehaus, M.
	Venice, Dec. 14	Blaubart+	Togni, C.
	London, Dec. 17	Floss der Medusa, Das (comp. 1968)	Henze, H. W.
		Genoveva+	Müller-Siemens, D.
1978	? ?	Lear	Reimann, A.
	Munich, July 9	Boom-Boom Land+	Katzer, G.
	Berlin (East), Sept. 30		
	Freiburg, Oct. 1	Christophorus (comp. 1927)	Schreker, F.
1979	Dresden, Feb. 22	Vincent+	Kunad, R.
	Berlin, Sept. 6	Untergang der Titanic+	Sieberg, W.
	Berlin (East) Nov. 27	Leonce und Lena	Dessau, P.
	Freiburg, Dec. 1	Max und Moritz+	Willig, W.
	Salzburg, ?	Engel von Prag, Der	Bresgen, C.
1980	Stuttgart, Feb. 8	Erschöpfung der Welt, Die+	Kagel, M.
	Karlsruhe, March 6	Jakob Lenz	Rihm, W.
	Vienna, May 18	Jesu Hochzeit	Einem, G. von
	Mannheim, July 16	Jüngste Tag, Der+	Klebe, G.
	Nuremberg, Oct. 11	Traumgörge, Der+ (comp. 1906)	Zemlinsky, A. von
	Erfurt, ?	Preis, Der+	Treibmann, K.

Year	Place, Date	Title	Composer
1980 (cont.)	Wuppertal, ?	Fünf Minuten des Isaak Babel, Die	Kirchner, V. D.
1981	Milan, April 3	Licht: Donnerstag	Stockhausen, K.
	Berlin, May 9	Aus Deutschland+	Kagel, M.
	Vienna, May 31	Netzwerk+	Cerha, F.
	Kassel, June 27	Tragödie der Menschheit, Die+	Hamel, P. M.
1982	Karslruhe, Feb. 27	Spiel von Liebe und Zufall, Das+	Rosenfeld, G.
	Strasbourg, March 16	Liebestod+	Aperghis, G.
	Schwetzingen, April 25	Merkwürdige Frau des Schusters, Die+	Zimmermann, U.
	Hamburg, Sept. 15	William Ratcliff	Ostendorf, J.-P.
1983	Munich, Feb. 6	Periander+	Antoniou, T.
	Schwetzingen, June 2	Englische Katze, Die	Henze, H. W.
	Stuttgart, Nov. 24	Fanferlieschen Schönefüsschen	Schwertsik, K.
1984	Salzburg, March 11	König Ubü+	Hummel, Fr.
	Schwetzingen, May 2	Ophelia+	Kelterborn, R.
	Milan, May 25	Licht: Samstag	Stockhausen, K.
	Berlin (East), May 26	Amphytrion+	Kunad, R.
	Kassel, June 23	Marat+	Haupt, W.
	Berlin, Sept. 30	Gespenstersonate+	Reimann, A.
	Cologne, Oct. 25	Murieta	Ostendorf, J.-P.
	Zurich, Dec. 6	Kirschgarten, Der+	Kelterborn, R.

1985	Munich, Feb. Duisburg, April 19 Berlin (East), Sept. 28	Gogolori, Der+ Wiedertäufer, Die+ Judith	Hiller, W. Goehr, A. Matthus, S.
1986	Munich, Jan. 25 Schwetzingen, April 30 Frankfurt, June 15 Brussels, Dec. ? ?	Belshazar+ Leiden des jungen Werthers, Das+ Stephan Climax+ Schloss, Das+ Kyberiade+	Kirchner, V. D. Bose, H. J. von Zender, M. Laporte, A. Meyer, K.
1987	Berlin, Jan. 30 Hamburg, Feb. 7 Salzburg, Aug. 15 Berlin, Oct. 4 Mannheim, ?	Habemeajaja+ (comp. 1929) Sandmann, Der+ Schwarze Maske, Die+ Oedipus+ Hamletmaschine+	Blacher, B. Kounadis, A. Penderecki, K. Rihm, W. Rihm, W.
1988	Berlin (East), April 30 Milan, May 7 Cologne, May 29 Berlin, Oct. 1	Bankette, Die+ Licht: Montag Mitternachtstraum, Ein+ Los Alamos+	Katzer, G. Stockhausen, K. Decker, W. Neikrug, M.
1989	Kassel, March 18 Cologne, May 29	Heisse Ofen, Der+ Mitternachtstraum, Ein+	Henze, H. W. et al. Decker, W.

BIBLIOGRAPHY

DICTIONARIES AND ENCYCLOPEDIAS

Clément, Félix, and Pierre Larousse. *Dictionnaire des opéras*. 2 volumes. Revised by Arthur Pougin. Paris: Larousse, 1905. Reprinted New York: Da Capo Press, 1969. 1293 pp. Operas listed by title; brief plots given occasionally.

Enciclopedia dello spettacolo. 9 volumes. Rome: Casa Ed. Le Maschere, 1954–1962. Supplements, 1963, 1966. Covers singers, composers, cities, countries, and terms.

Ewen, David. *The New Encyclopedia of the Opera*. 3rd edition. New York: Hill and Wang, 1971. 759 pp. Includes terms, cities, houses, plots, characters, and singers.

Hamilton, David, ed. *The Metropolitan Opera Encyclopedia*. New York: Simon & Schuster, 1987. 416 pp. Listing by title; includes operas, performers, terms; two dozen essays on most famous works; brief plots.

Orrey, Leslie. *The Encyclopedia of Opera*. New York: Scribner's, 1976. 376 pp. Listing by title; contains operas, performers, and terms; very brief plots.

Osborne, Charles. *The Dictionary of the Opera*. New York: Simon & Schuster, 1983. 382 pp. Listing by title; includes operas, performers, and terms; brief plots.

Pipers Enzyklopädie des Musik Theaters. Edited by Carl Dahlhaus. 8 volumes (projected). Münster: Akademischer Lexikadienst, 1986–. Detailed coverage of operas, operettas, musicals, and ballets, with information on premieres, plots, and stylistic elements. To date, the first three volumes have been issued: the first covers the works of Abbiati through Donizetti; the second, Donizetti through Henze; the third, Henze through Massine. Standard works, as well as more obscure ones.

Riemann, Hugo. *Opernhandbuch*. Leipzig: Hermann Seemann Nachfolger, 1886. Listing by title; brief plots.

Rosenthal, Harold, and John Warrack, eds. *The Concise Oxford Dictionary of Opera*. 2nd edition. London: Oxford University Press, 1979. 561 pp. Listing by title; includes operas, performers, and cities.

The Simon & Schuster Book of the Opera. New York: Simon & Schuster, 1978. An English translation of *L'Opera: repertorio della lirica dal 1597*, edited by Riccardo Mezzanote. Milan: Arnoldo Monadori Editore, 1977. 511 pp. Listings by year, then by title; brief plots.

Stieger, Franz. *Opernlexikon/Opera Catalogue* .... Part I (3 vols.): *Titelkatalog*; Part II (2 vols.): *Komponisten*; Part III (3 vols): *Librettisten*; Part IV (2 vols.): *Nachträge*. Tutzing: Hans Schneider, 1975–1983. Completed in 1934. Lists tittles of some 50,000 theater works with composer, librettist, and first performance.

Towers, John. *Dictionary Catalog of Operas and Operettas Which Have Been Performed on the Public Stage*. 2 volumes. Morgantown, W. Va.: Acme, 1910. Reprinted New York: Da Capo, 1967. Lists over 28,000 works with name of composer and nationality. Many errors.

PERFORMANCE INFORMATION

British Broadcasting Corporation. *BBC Music Library. Choral and Opera Catalogue*. Volume I: *Composers*. London: BBC, 1967.

Eaton, Quaintance. *Opera Production. A Handbook*. Minneapolis: University of Minnesota, 1961. Reprinted New York: Da Capo, 1974. By title. Includes brief plots, major and minor roles, orchestral forces needed, and available performance materials.

———. *Opera Production II. A Handbook*. Minneapolis: University of Minnesota Press, 1974. Same arrangement as volume I.

Gruber, Clemens M. *Opern-Uraufführungen*. Volume III. *Komponisten aus Deutschland ...1900–1977* [including East and West Germany, Austria, and Switzerland]. Vienna: Gesellschaft für Musiktheater, 1978. Listing by composer; includes title, librettist, number of acts, and city and date of first performance. If no premiere, only the title is given. Includes only composers born in German-speaking lands (excludes Busoni, for example).

Loewenberg, Alfred. *Annals of Opera 1597–1940*. 3rd revised edition. Totowa, N.J.: Rowman and Littlefield, 1978. Arranged by year; includes title, composer, librettist, city and date of first performance, and significant subsequent performances.

PLOTS

Cross, Milton and Karl Kohrs. *More Stories of the Great Operas*. Garden City, N.Y.: Doubleday & Co., 1971. 752 pp. Listing by title.

———. *The New Milton Cross Complete Stories of the Great Operas*. Garden City, N.Y.: Doubleday & Co., 1955. 688 pp. Standard repertoire. Listing by title.

Ewen, David. *The Book of European Light Opera*. New York: Holt, Rinehart and Winston, 1962. Listing by title.

Kobbé, Gustav. *The Definitive Kobbé's Opera Book*. Edited, revised, and updated by the Earl of Harewood. New York: G. Putnam's Sons, 1987.

Lubbock, Mark Hugh. *The Complete Book of Light Opera*. London: Putnam and New York: Appleton-Century-Crofts, 1962. 953 pp. About 300 works.

Newman, Ernest. *Stories of the Great Operas and their Composers*. New York: Alfred A. Knopf, 1930. 2 volumes. Reprinted New York: Dorset Press, n.d. Detailed synopses and musical analyses.

Schumann, Otto. *Handbuch der Opern*. 10th edition. Wilhelmshaven: Heinrichshofen's Verlag, 1972. 964 pp. Includes standard repertoire and lesser-known German composers.

The Victor Book of Operas. 13th edition. Revised by Henry W. Simon. New York: Simon & Schuster, 1968. 475 pp. Includes about 120 works.

Westerman, Gerhart von. *Knaurs Opernführer. Eine Geschichte der Oper.* Munich: Droemersche Verlagsanstalt, 1952. 546 pp. Chronological listings. Covers standard repertoire and lesser-known German composers.

BIBLIOGRAPHIES

Abert, Anna Amalie. "Die Oper zwischen Barock und Romantik." *AnMus* IL (1977), pp. 137–93.

Grout, Donald. *A Short History of Opera.* 2nd edition. New York: Columbia University Press, 1965, 585–768; 3rd edition, 1988, 731–835.

Marco, Guy A. *Opera: A Research and Information Guide.* New York and London: Garland Publishing, 1984.

CITIES

Berlin

Fetting, Hugo. *Die Geschichte der deutschen Staatsoper.* Berlin: Henschelverlag, 1955.

Kapp, Julius. *185 Jahre Staatsoper. Festschrift zum Wiederöffnung des Opernhauses Unter den Linden am 28. April 1928.* Berlin: Atlantis-Verlag [1928].

Dresden

Rank, Mathias, and Horst Seeger. *Leitmotive der Dresdner Operngeschichte II.* Berlin: Henschel, 1980.

Frankfurt

Mohr, Albert. *Das Frankfurter Opernhaus 1880–1980.* Frankfurt: Kramer, 1980.

Oven, A. H. E. von. *Das erse städtische Theater zu Frankfurt a.M.—Ein Beitrag zur aüsseren Geschichte des Frankfurter Theaters 1751–1872.* Frankfurt/M: Neujahrs-Blatt des Vereins für Geschichte und Alterthumskunde [1872].

Hamburg

Wolff, Hellmuth Christian. *Die Barockoper in Hamburg (1678–1738).* 2 volumes. Wolfenbüttel: Möseler, 1957.

London

Rosenthal, Harold. *Two Centuries of Opera at Covent Garden.* London: Putnam, 1958.

New York

Metropolitan Opera Annals. New York, 1947; Supplements, 1957, 1968, 1976.

Vienna

Bauer, Anton. *Opern und Operetten in Wien. Verzeichnis ihrer Erstaufführungen in der Zeit von 1629 bis zum Gegenwart.* Graz and Cologne: Hermann Böhlaus, 1955.

Prawy, Marcel. *Die Winer Oper.* 2 vols. Munich: Goldman, 1980.

HISTORY OF OPERAS IN GERMAN

Badura-Skoda, Eva. "The Influence of the Viennese Popular Comedy on Haydn and Mozart." *PRMA* C (1973–1974), 185–99.

Bauman, Thomas. *North German Opera in the Age of Goethe.* New York: Cambridge University Press, 1985.

Beckers, Paul. *Die nachwagner'sche Oper bis zum Ausgang des 19. Jahrhunderts im Spiegel der Münchener Presse.* Bielefeld: Beyer & Hausknecht, 1936.

Bittner, Werner. *Die deutsche komische Oper der Gegenwart.* Leipzig: Kistner & Siegel, 1932.

Branscombe, Peter. "Music in the Viennese Popular Theater of the Eighteenth and Nineteenth Centuries," *PRMA* XCVIII (1971–1972), 101–12.

Dietrich, Margret. *Goldene Vlies-Opern der Barockzeit. Ihre politische Bedeutung und ihr Publikum.* Vienna: Österreichische Akademie der Wissenschaften, 1975.

Draeger, Hans. "The Relation of Music to Words during the German Baroque Era," in *The German Baroque: Literature, Music, Art*, edited by George Schulz-Behrend. Austin, Tex.: University of Texas, 1972, 123–43.

Fargia, Franz. *Die Wiener Oper von ihren Anfängen bis 1938.* Vienna, 1947.

Flaherty, Maria Gloria. "Lessing and Opera—a Re-Evaluation." *Germanic Review* XLIV (1969), 95–109.

———. "Opera and Incipient Romantic Aesthetics in Germany," *Studies in Eighteenth-Century Culture* III (1973), 205–17.

———. *Opera in the Development of German Cultural Thought.* Princeton, N.J.: Princeton University Press, 1978.

Garlington, Aubrey S., Jr. "August Wilhelm von Schlegel and the Creation of German Romantic Opera," *JAMS* XXX (1977), 500–506.

———. "German Romantic Opera and the Problem of Origins," *MQ* LXIII (1977), 247–63.

Göpfert, Bernd. *Stimmtypen und Rollen-Charaktere in der deutschen Oper von 1815–1848.* Wiesbaden: B&H, 1977.

Goslich, Siegfried. *Die deutsche romantische Oper.* Berlin: Victor Otto Stomps, 1937. Reprinted Tutzing: Hans Schneider, 1975.

Grout, Donald Jay. "German Baroque Opera," *MQ* XXXII (1946), 574–87.

Haas, Robert. "Wiener deutsche Parodie-opern um 1730," *ZMW* VIII (1925–1926), 201–25.

———. *Die Wiener Oper.* Vienna-Budapest: Eligius, 1926.

Hadamovsky, Franz. *Die Wiener Operette: Ihre Theater- und Wirkungs-Geschichte.* Vienna: Bellaria Verlag, 1947.

Hennenberg, Fritz. *Musikdramatik und Dialektik: analytische Versuche*, in *Sammelbände zur Musikgeschichte der Deutschen Demokratischen Republik.* Volume IV. Edited by Heinz Brockhaus and Konrad Niemann. Berlin: Neue Musik, 1975.

Hortschansky, Klaus. "Der *Deus ex machina* im Opernlibretto der ersten Hälfte des 19. Jahrhunderts," in *Beiträge zur Geschichte der Oper.* Edited by Heinz Becker. Regensburg: Bosse, 1965, 45–76.

Höslinger, Clemens, comp. *Musik-Index zur "Wiener Zeitschrift für Kunst, Literatur, Theater und Mode" 1816–1848.* Munich and Salzburg: Katzbichler, 1980.

Istel, Edgar. *Die Blütezeit der musikalischen Romantik in Deutschland.* Leipzig: B. G. Teubner, 1909.

BIBLIOGRAPHY 637

————. *Die komische Oper*. Stuttgart: Carl Grüninger Verlag, 1906.

Kaindl-Hönig, Max. "Fest und Spiel am Lustort Hellbrunn," *ÖMZ* XXV (1970), 388–93.

Kanzog, Klaus, and Hans-Joachim Kreutzer, eds. *Werke Kleists auf dem modernen Musiktheater*. Berlin: Schmidt, 1977.

Kirby, F. E. "Herder and Opera." *JAMS* XV (1962), 316–29.

Kirsch, Winfried. "Die 'opera domestica.' Zur Dramaturgie des bürgerlichen Alltags im aktuellen Musiktheater der 20er Jahre." In *HJb* IX (1980), 179–82 (on the operas *Intermezzo, Neues vom Tage, and Von heute auf morgen*).

Klob, Karl Maria. *Beiträge zur Geschichte der deutschen komischen Oper*. Berlin: "Harmonie," [1903].

————. *Die komische Oper nach Lortzing*. Berlin: "Harmonie," 1904.

Krellmann, Hanspeter. "Moderne Oper—zeitgenössische Oper—zeitgerechte Oper?," *Musica* XXXI (1977), 119–25 [opera in Germany since World War II].

Lindberg, John. "The German Baroque Opera Libretto: A Forgotten Genre," in *The German Baroque: Literature, Music, Art*. Edited by Georg Schulze-Behrend. Austin, Tex.: University of Texas, 1972, 87–122.

Linke, Norbert. "Singspiel—Operette-Musical. Die heitere Muse in Böhmen/Mähren/Schlesien," in *Die musikalische Wechselbeziehungen Schlesien-Österreich*. Dülman: Laumann, 1977, 77–105.

Lüthge, Kurt. *Die deutsche Spieloper*. Brunswick: W. Piepenschneider Verlag, 1924.

Ott, Alfons. "Von der frühdeutschen Oper zum deutschen Singspiel," in *Musik in Bayern*. Volume I. Edited by Robert Münster and Hans Schmidt. Tutzing: Hans Schneider, 1972 [covers 1644 to 1870], 165–77.

Preibisch, Walther. *Quellenstudien zu Mozarts 'Entführung aus dem Serail.' Ein Beitrag zur Geschichte der Türkenoper*. Halle a.S.: Erhardt Karras, 1908 [also in *SIMG* X (1909), 430–76].

Redlich, Hans F. "Wagnerian Elements in Pre-Wagnerian Opera," in *Essays Presented to Egon Wellesz*. Edited by Jack Westrup. Oxford: Oxford University Press, 1966; 145–56.

Rienäcker, Gerd. "Zur Entwicklung des Opernschaffens der Deutschen Demokratischen Republik: Bemerkungen zur einigen Tendenzen," in *Sammelbände zur Musikgeschichte der DDR*. Volume IV. Edited by Heinz Brockhaus and Konrad Niemann. Berlin: Neue Musik, 1975, 9–41.

Ruhnke, Martin. "Das italienische Rezitativ bei den deutschen Komponisten des Spätbarok," *AnMus* XVII (1976), 29–120.

Schiedermair, Ludwig. *Die deutsche Oper: Grundzüge ihres Werdens und Wesens*. 3rd edition. Bonn and Berlin: Ferdinand Dümmlers Verlag, 1943.

Schöne, Günter. *Tausend Jahre deutsches Theater 914–1914*. Munich: Prestel Verlag, 1962.

Schulze, Walter. *Die Quellen der Hamburger Oper (1678–1738)*. Hamburg-Oldenburg: G. Stalling, 1938.

Schünemann, Georg. *Geschichte der deutschen Schulmusik*. Leipzig: Kistner & Siegel, 1928.

Stuckenschmidt, Hans Heinz. *Die grossen Komponisten unseres Jahrhunderts*. Volume I: *Deutschland-Mitteleuropa*. Munich: Piper, 1971. In English as *Twentieth-Century Composers*. Volume II: *Germany and Central Europe*. New York, 1971.

Unverricht, Hubert. "Das Berg- und Gebirgsmilieu und seine musikalischen Stilmittel in der Oper des 19. Jahrhunderts," in *Die 'Couleur locale' in der Oper des 19. Jahrhunderts*. Edited by Heinz Becker. Regensburg: Bosse, 1976, 99–119.

Vetter, Walther. "Deutschland und das Formgefühl Italiens: Betrachtungen über die Metastasianische Oper," *DJbMw* V (1960), 7–37.

Warrack, John. "German Operatic Ambitions at the Beginning of the 19th Century," *PRMA* CIV (1977–1978), 79–88.

Wolff, Hellmuth, and Günter Hausswald. "L'opera in Germania e in Austria," in *Storia dell'opera*. Volume II/1. Edited by Alberto Basso. Turin: UTET, 1977, 207–43.

COMPOSERS

André, Johann

Stauder, Wilhelm. "Johann André. Ein Beitrag zur Geschichte des deutschen Singspiels," *AfMw* I (1936), 318–60.

Benda, Georg

Bruckner, Fritz. "Georg Benda und das deutsche Singspiel," *SIMG* V (1903–1904), 571–621; also as book (Leipzig, B&H: 1904).

Berg, Alban

Jarman, Douglas. *The Music of Alban Berg*. Berkeley and Los Angeles: University of California Press, 1979.

Perle, George. *The Operas of Alban Berg*. 2 volumes. Berkeley: University of California Press, 1980.

Redlich, Hans. *Alban Berg: Versuch einer Würdigung*. Vienna: UE, 1957. Translated as *Alban Berg: The Man and his Music*. London: Calder, 1957 (abridged from the original).

Reich, Willi. *Alban Berg, Leben und Werk*. Zurich: Atlantis Verlag. 1963. Translated by Cornelius Cardew as *The Life and Works of Alban Berg*. New York: Harcourt, Brace & World, 1965.

Bialas, Günther

Goslich, Siegfried. "Wie man das Spiel spielt. Bialas und die Oper," in *Meilensteine eines Komponistenslebens*. Edited by Gotthard Speer et al. Kassel: Bärenreiter, 1977, 56–62.

Bresgen, Cesar

Lück, Rudolf. *Cesar Bresgen*. Vienna: Verlag Elisabeth Lafite, 1974.

Busoni, Ferruccio

Dent, Edward J. *Ferruccio Busoni: A Biography*. London: Oxford University Press, 1933; 2nd ed., 1984.

Kindermann, Jürgen. *Thematisch-chronologisch Verzeichnis der musikalischen Werke von Ferruccio Busoni*. Regensburg: Bosse, 1980.

Chemin-Petit, Hans

Buder, Marianne, and Dorett Gonschorek. *Hans Chemin-Petit*. Berlin: Stapp, 1977.

Cornelius, Peter

Federhofer, Hans, and Kurt Oehl, eds. *Peter Cornelius als Komponist. Dichter, Kritiker und Essayist*. Regensburg: Gustav Bosse Verlag, 1977.
Griffel, Margaret Ross. " 'Turkish' Opera from Mozart to Cornelius." Ph.D. dissertation, Columbia University, 1975, 391–429. Ann Arbor, Mich.: Xerox University Microfilms, order no. UM 75–27, 421.
Hasse, Max. *Der Dichtermusiker Peter Cornelius*. Leipzig: n.p., 1922.
Istel, Edgar. "Peter Cornelius," *MQ* XX (1934), 334–43.

Dessau, Paul

Henneberg, Fritz. *Paul Dessau*. Leipzig: Deutscher Verlag für Musik, 1965.
Nadar, Thomas Raymond. "The Music of Kurt Weill, Hanns Eisler and Paul Dessau in the Dramatic Works of Bertholt Brecht." Ph.D. dissertation, University of Michigan, 1974.

Dittersdorf, Karl Ditters von

Höll, Karl. *Carl Ditters von Dittersdorfs Opern für das wiedergestellte Johannisberger Theater*. Heidelberg: Carl Winters Universitätsbuchhandlung, 1913.

Egk, Werner

Krause, Ernst. *Werner Egk. Oper und Ballett*. Wilhelmshaven: Heinrichshofen's Verlag, 1971.
Wörner, Karl H. "Egk and Orff: Representatives of Contemporary German Opera," *MR* XIV (1953), 186–204.

Fortner, Wolfgang

Lindlar, Heinrich, ed. *Wolfgang Fortner*. Rodenkirchen/Rhein: P. J. Tonger, 1960.

Goetz, Hermann

Istel, Edgar. "Hermann Goetz," *ZIMG* III (1901–1902), 177–88.
Kreutzhage, Eduard. *Hermann Goetz' Leben und sein Schaffen auf dem Gebiet der Oper*. Leipzig: B&H, 1916.

Handel, George Frideric

Baselt, Bernd. "Zum Parodieverfahren in Händels frühen Opern." *Händel Jahrbuch* xxi–xxii (1975–1976), 19–39.
Harris, Ellen. *Handel and the Pastoral Tradition*. London: Oxford University Press, 1980.
———. *The Librettos of Handel's Operas*. Volume I, Introduction. New York: Garland Publishing, 1989, ix–xl.

Haug, Hans

Matthey, Jean-Louis, and Louis-Daniel Perret. *Catalogue de l'oeuvre de Hans Haug*. Lausanne: Bibliothèque cantonale et universitaire, 1971.

Haydn, Franz Joseph

Feder, Georg. "Haydns Opern und ihre Ausgaben," in *Musikalische Editions . . . Gunter Henle*. Edited by Martin Bente. Munich: Henle, 1980.
————. "Ein Kolloquium über Haydns Opern," in *Haydn-Studien* II (May 1969), 113–18, 126–30.
Robbins Landon, H. C. "Haydn's Marionette Operas," *Haydn Jahrbuch* I (1962), 111–97.
Rossi, Mick. "Joseph Haydn and Opera," *OQ* I (1983), 54–78.

Hiller, Johann Adam

Calmus, Gregory. *Die ersten deutschen Singspiele von Standfuss und Hiller*. Leipzig: B&H, 1908.

Himmel, Friedrich Heinrich

Odendahl, Laurenz. *Friedrich Heinrich Himmel*. Bonn: P. Rost & Co., 1917.

Hindemith, Paul

Epstein, Peter. "Paul Hindemiths Theatermusik," *Die Musik* XXIII (1931), 582–87.
Revue musicale de Suisse romande, XXVI (1973). [Hindemith issue.]
Rösner, Helmut. *Paul Hindemith. Katalog seiner Werke*. Frankfurt: Städtische Musik-bibliothek, 1970.

Hoffmann, E. T. A.

Allroggen, Gerhard. *E. T. A. Hoffmanns Kompositionen: ein chronologisch-thematisches Verzechnis*. Regensburg: G. Bosse, 1970.

Hummel, Johann Nepomuk

Zimmerschied, Dieter. *Thematisches Verzeichnis der Werke von Johann Nepomuk Hummel*. Hofheim am Taunus: F. Hofmeister, 1971.

Keiser, Reinhard

Deane, Basil. "Reinhard Keiser: An Interim Assessment," *Soundings* IV (1974), 30–41.
Zelm, Klaus. *Die Opern Reinhard Keisers*. Munich: Musikverlag Emil Katzbichler, 1975.

Klebe, Giselher

Lewinski, Wolf-Eberhard von. "Der Dramatiker Giselher Klebe," *Melos* XXVIII (1961), 4–7.

Krenek, Ernst

Maurer-Zenck, Claudia. *Ernst Krenek—ein Komponist in Exil*. Vienna: Lafite, 1980.
Molkow, Wolfgang. "Der Sprung über den Schatten. Zum Opernschaffen Ernst Kreneks in der 20er und 30er Jahren," *Musica* XXXIV (1980), 132–35.
Rogge, Wolfgang. *Ernst Kreneks Opern*. Wolfenbüttel and Zurich: Mosler Verlag, 1970.
Stewart, John. "Frauen in den Opern Ernst Kreneks," *Musica* XXXIV (1980), 136–38.

Lachner, Franz

Würz, Anton. *Franz Lachner als dramatischer Komponist*. Munich: Knorr & Hirth, 1927.

Lehár, Franz

Grun, Bernard. *Gold and Silver*. London: W. H. Allen, 1970.
Schönherr, Max. *Franz Lehár. Bibliographie zu Leben und Werk*. Vienna: Author, 1970.

Lortzing, Albert

Rosengard, Rose. "Popularity and Art in Lortzing's Operas: The Effects of Social Change on a National Operatic Genre." Ph.D. dissertation, Columbia University, 1973. Ann Arbor, Mich.: Xerox University Microfilms, order no. UM 76–28,498.

Marschner, Heinrich

Palmer, A. Dean. *Heinrich Marschner, 1795–1861. His Life and Works*. Ann Arbor, Mich.: UMI Research Press, 1980.

Mendelssohn, Felix

Köhler, Karl-Heinz, "Das Jugendwerk Felix Mendelssohns," *DJbMw* VII (1962), 18–35.
Schünemann, Georg. "Mendelssohns Jugendopern," *ZMw* V (1922–1923), 506–45.

Meyerbeer, Giacomo

Kruse, Georg Richard. "Meyerbeers Jugendopern," *ZMw* I (1918–1919), 399–413.

Mozart, Wolfgang Amadeus

Brophy, Brigid. *Mozart the Dramatist. A New View of Mozart, His Operas and His Age*. New York: Harcourt, Brace & Co., 1964.
Dent, Edward. *Mozart's Operas*. Second edition. London: Oxford University Press, 1947.
Einstein, Alfred. *Mozart, His Character, His Work*. Translated by Arthur Mendel and Nathan Broder. New York and London: Oxford University Press, 1945.
Hughes, Spike [Patrick]. *Famous Mozart Operas*. Second revised edition. New York: Dover, 1972.
Liebner, Janos. *Mozart on the Stage*. New York: Praeger, 1961.
Mann, William. *The Operas of Mozart*. London: Oxford University Press, 1977.
Noske, Frits. *The Signifier and the Signified: Studies in the Operas of Mozart and Verdi*. The Hague: Nijhoff, 1977.

Neefe, Christian Gottlob

Leux, Irmgard. *Christian Gottlob Neefe*. Leipzig: Kistner & Siegel, 1925.

Nicolai, Otto

Konrad, Ulrich. *Otto Nicolai (1810–1849): Studien zu Leben und Werk*. Sammlung musikwissenschaftlicher Abhandlungen, LXXIII. Baden-Baden: Verlag Valentin Koerner, 1986.
Kruse, Georg Richard. "Otto Nicolais Beziehungen zu den Tondichtern seiner Zeit," *Die Musik* XXXV, no. 18 (1909–1910), 340–66.

Orff, Carl

Helm, Everett. "Carl Orff," *MQ* XLI (1955), 285–304.
Liess, Andreas. *Carl Orff.* 2nd edition. Zurich: Atlantis, 1977.

Pfitzner, Hans

Osthoff, Wolfgang, ed. *Symposium Hans Pfitzner.* Tutzing: Schneider, 1984.

Schoeck, Othmar

Koenig, Charlotte. "Der Lyriker Othmar Schoeck," *ÖMZ* XXIV (1969), 141–46.
Vogel, Werner. *Thematisches Verzeichnis der Werke von Othmar Schoeck.* Zurich: Atlantis Verlag, 1956.

Schoenberg, Arnold

Lessem, Alan Philip. *Music and Text in the Works of Arnold Schoenberg. The Critical Years 1908–1922.* Ann Arbor, Mich.: University of Michigan Press, 1979.
Reich, Willi. *Schönberg, oder der konservative Revolutionär.* Vienna: Molden, 1968. Translated by Leo Black as *Schoenberg: A Critical Biography.* New York: Praeger; London, Longman, 1971.
Stuckenschmidt, Hans Heinz. *Arnold Schönberg.* Zurich and Freiburg: Atlantis-Verlag, 1959. English translation, New York: Grove Press, 1959.

Schreker, Franz

Budde, Elmar and Rudolf Stephan, eds. *Franz-Schreker Symposium.* Berlin: Colloquium, 1980.
Ermen, Reinhard, ed. *Franz Schreker (1872–1934) zum 50. Todestag.* Achen: Rimbaud, 1984.

Schubert, Franz

Citron, Marcia J. "Schubert's Seven Complete Operas: A Musico-Dramatic Study." Ph.D. dissertation. University of North Carolina, 1971. Ann Arbor, Mich.: University Microfilms, order no. UM 72–10, 699.
Hoorickx, P. Reinhard van. "Les opéras de Schubert," *Revue belge de musicologie* XXVIII-XXX (1974–1976), 238–59.
King, A. Hyatt. "Music for the Stage," in *The Music of Schubert.* Edited by Gerald Abraham. New York: W. W. Norton, 1947. Reprinted Port Washington, N.Y.: Kennikat Press, 1969, 198–216.

Schumann, Robert

Chissell, Joan. *Schumann.* London, 1948. Reprinted New York: Collier Books, 1962.

Spohr, Ludwig

Brown, Clive. *Louis Spohr. A Critical Biography.* Cambridge, England: Cambridge University Press, 1984.
Greiner, Dietrich. "Die Rolle des Rezitativs in den Opern Spohrs," *Louis Spohr. Festschrift und Ausstellungskatalog zum 200. Geburtstag.* Edited by Hartmut Becker and Rainer Krempien. Kassel: Georg Wenderoth, 1984, 35–52.
Wassermann, Rudolf. "Ludwig Spohr als Opernkomponist," *Die Musik* IX/2, no. 33 (1909–1910), 76–88.

Standfuss, J. C.

Calmus, Gregory. *Die ersten deutschen Singspiele von Standfuss und Hiller*. Leipzig: B&H, 1908.

Strauss, Richard

Abert, Anna Amalie. *Richard Strauss—Die Opern*. Hanover: Friedrich, 1972.
Del Mar, Norman. *Richard Strauss*. 3 volumes. New York, London, and Philadelphia: Chilton Books, 1962, 1969, 1972. Reprinted Ithaca, N.Y.: Cornell University Press, 1986.
Fähnrich, Hermann. "Richard Strauss über das Verhältnis von Dichtung und Musik (Wort und Ton) in seinem Opernschaffen," *Mf* XIV (1961), 22–35.
Mann, William. *Richard Strauss. A Critical Study of the Operas*. London: Cassell, 1964.
Ortner, Oswald. *Richard Strauss Bibliographie*. 2 volumes. I: 1882–1944; II: 1944–1964. Vienna: C. Pracher, 1964–1973.
Strauss, Richard, and Hugo von Hofmannsthal. *A Working Friendship. The Correspondence between Richard Strauss and Hugo von Hofmannsthal*. Translated by Hanns Hammelmann and Ewald Osers. New York: Random House, 1961. Reprinted New York: Vienna House, 1974.

Süssmayr, Franz Xaver

Lehner, Walter. "Franz Xaver Süssmayr als Opernkomponist," *SzMw* XVIII (1931), 66–96.

Telemann, Georg Philipp

Klessmann, Eckart. *Telemann in Hamburg 1721–1767*. Hamburg: Hoffmann & Campe, Wels, Welsermühle, 1980.
Peckham, Mary Adelaide. "The Operas of Georg Philipp Telemann." Ph.D. dissertation, Columbia University, 1972. Ann Arbor, Mich.: Xerox University Microfilm, order no. UM 72-28, 078.

Wagner, Richard

Adorno, Theodor. *Versuch über Wagner*. Berlin and Frankfurt: Suhrkamp, 1952.
Burbridge, Peter, and Richard Sutton, eds. *The Wagner Companion*. New York: Cambridge University Press, 1979.
Colloquium Verdi-Wagner: Rom 1969. AnMus, no. 11 (1972).
Dahlhaus, Carl, ed. *Das Drama Richard Wagners als musikalisches Kunstwerk*. Regensburg: Bosse, 1970.
———. *Die Musikdramen Richard Wagners*. Velber: Friedrich, 1971. Translated into English by Mary Whittall as *Richard Wagner's Music Dramas*. New York: Cambridge University Press, 1979.
Gregor-Dellin, Martin. *Richard Wagner: Sein Leben, Sein Werk*. Munich, Piper, 1980.
Gutman, Robert W. *Richard Wagner: The Man, His Mind, and His Music*. London: Secker & Warburg; New York: Harcourt, 1968.
Lorenz, Alfred. *Das Geheimnis der Form bei Richard Wagner*. 4 volumes. Berlin: Hesse, 1924–1933. Reprinted Tutzing: Hans Schneider Verlag, 1966.
Newman, Ernest. *The Wagner Operas*. New York: Knopf, 1949.

Stein, Jack M. *Richard Wagner and the Synthesis of the Arts*. Detroit: Wayne State
    University Press, 1960.
Westernhagen, Curt von. *Vom Holländer zum Parsifal: neue Wagner Studien*. Freiburg
    and Zurich: Atlantis, 1962.
————. *Wagner*. 2nd edition. Zurich: Atlantis Verlag, 1979. Translated by Mary Whittall
    as *Wagner: A Biography*. New York: Cambridge University Press, 1978. 2 vol-
    umes.

Wagner, Siegfried

Kraft, Zdenko von. *Der Sohn*. Graz: Leopold Stocker, 1969.
Pachl, Peter. *Siegfried Wagners musikdramatisches Schaffen*. Tutzing: Hans Schneider,
    1979.
Pretzsch, Paul. *Die Kunst Siegfried Wagners. Ein Führer durch seine Werke*. Wiesbaden:
    B&H, 1919. Reprinted Aachen: Reinhard Kiefer/Bernhard Albers, 1980.

Weber, Carl Maria von

Engländer, Richard. "The Struggle between German and Italian Opera at the Time of
    Weber," *MQ* XXXI (1945), 479–91.
Jähns, Friedrich Wilhelm. *Carl Maria von Weber in seinen Werken. Chronologisch-
    thematisches Verzeichnis seiner sämtlichen Werken*. Berlin: Verlag der Schlesin-
    ger'schen Buch- und Musik-handlung, 1871.
Kirby, Percival. "Weber's Operas in London, 1824–6," *MQ* XXXII (1946), 333–53.
Warrack, John. *Carl Maria von Weber*. 2nd edition. Cambridge, England: Cambridge
    University Press, 1976.

Weigl, Joseph

Bollert, Werner. "Joseph Weigl und das deutsche Singspiel." *Aufsätze zur Musikge-
    schichte* (Bottrop, 1938).

Weill, Kurt

Kowalke, Kim H., ed. *A New Orpheus. Essays on Kurt Weill*. New Haven: Yale Uni-
    versity Press, 1986.
Sanders, Ronald. *The Days Grow Short*. New York: Holt, Rinehart, and Winston, 1980.

Wellesz, Egon

Benser, Caroline. *Egon Wellesz (1885–1974)*. New York: Peter Lang, 1985.
Schollum, Robert. *Egon Wellesz*. Vienna: Österreichischer Bundesverlag, 1963.

Wolf, Hugo

Fellinger, Imogen. "Die Oper im kompositorischen Schaffen von Hugo Wolf," *Jahrbuch
    des Staatlichen Instituts für Musikforschung Preussischer Kulturbesitz 1971*.

Ziehrer, Carl Michael

Schönherr, Max. *Carl Michael Ziehrer. Sein Werk. . . . Dokumentation, Analysen und
    Kommentar*. Vienna: Österreichischer Verlag für Unterricht, Wissenschaft und
    Kunst, 1974.

INDEX OF CHARACTERS

Aase, Peer Gynt's mother (alto), **Peer Gynt**, 1938 (W. Egk)

Abbate Cospicuo (bar), **Arlecchino**, 1917 (F. Busoni)

Abednego, a Jewish prince (alto), **Nebucadnezar**, 1704 (R. Keiser)

Abu Hassan, favorite of the Caliph (ten), **Abu Hassan**, 1811 (C. M. von Weber)

Abul Hassan, the Barber of Bagdad (bass), **Der Barbier von Bagdad**, 1858 (P. Cornelius)

Achille (bar), **Penelope**, 1954 (R. Liebermann)

Achilles, a Greek king (bar), **Penthesilea**, 1927 (O. Schoeck)

Achilles (ten), **Troilus und Cressida**, 1951 (W. Zillig)

Achmet, Pasha of Tunis (ten), **Abu Hassan**, 1811 (C. G. Neefe)

Ada (sop), **Die Hochzeit**, 1832 (R. Wagner)

Ada (sop), **Die Feen**, 1833 (R. Wagner)

Adahm (Adam), **Die ersten Menschen**, 1920 (R. Stephan)

Adam, Lux's partner (ten), **Der Dorfbarbier**, 1796 (J. Schenk)

Adam, a Tyrolean birdseller (ten), **Der Vogelhändler**, 1891 (C. Zeller)

Adam, a chemist (ten), **Die Teufel von Loudun**, 1969 (K. Penderecki)

Adam, the town judge (bass), **Der zerbrochene Krug**, 1981 (F. Geissler)

Adam Ochsenschwanz, a boxer (buffo bass), **Schwergewicht**, 1928 (E. Krenek)

Adelaide, the mother of Arabella (mezzo), **Arabella**, 1933 (R. Strauss)

Adelaide, the mayor's daughter (sop), **Preussisches Märchen**, 1952 (B. Blacher)

Adele, Rosalinde's maid (sop), **Die Fledermaus**, 1874 (J. Strauss, Jr.)

Adelhart, a count (bass), **Silvana**, 1810 (C. M. von Weber)

Adelheid, royal princess (sop), **Ludivicus Pius**, 1726 (G. C. Schürmann)

Adelheit, a young German woman (sop), **Adelheit von Veltheim**, 1780 (C. G. Neefe)

Adelma, Turandot's servant (mezzo), **Turandot**, 1917 (F. Busoni)

Adhemar, Bishop of Puy (bar), **Die Kreuzfahrer**, 1845 (L. Spohr)

Adina, Nebucadnezar's wife (sop), **Nebucadnezar**, 1704 (R. Keiser)

Admet, king of Thessaly (ten), **Alceste**, 1773 (A. Schweitzer)

Admiral Orloff (bar), **Fürstin Tarakanowa**, 1941 (B. Blacher)

Admund (ten), **Die Hochzeit**, 1832 (R. Wagner)

Adolar, Count of Nevers (ten), **Euryanthe**, 1823 (C. M. von Weber)

Adolar Gilka, a prince, **Die Landstreicher**, 1899 (C. M. Ziehrer)

Adolf von Rheinthal (ten), **Die Opernprobe**, 1851 (A. Lortzing)

Adolfo, general of Mauregato (bass), **Alfonso und Estrella**, 1822 (F. Schubert)

Adonis (alto), **Adonis**, 1697 (R. Keiser)

Adriano, son of Stefano Colonna (mezzo), **Rienzi**, 1842 (R. Wagner)

Aeakos, supporter of the tyrant, **Die Bürgschaft**, 1838 (F. Lachner)

Aegist (ten), **Das Leben des Orest**, 1930 (E. Krenek)

Aegisthus, Klytemnestra's lover (ten), **Elektra**, 1909 (R. Strauss)

Aennchen, friend of Agathe (sop), **Der Freischütz**, 1821 (C. M. von Weber)

Agamemnon (ten), **Das Leben des Orest**, 1930 (E. Krenek)

Agathe, daughter of Cuno (sop), **Der Freischütz**, 1821 (C. M. von Weber)

Agathos, a genie (sop), **Der Spiegel von Arkadien**, 1794 (F. X. Süssmayr)

Agave, a queen, **Die Bakchantinnen**, 1931 (E. Wellesz)

Agave, daughter of Kadmos (mezzo), **Die Bassariden**, 1966 (H. W. Henze)

Agis, King of Sparta (bass), **Pallas Athene weint**, 1955 (E. Krenek)

Agnes, Countess Irmengard's daughter (sop), **Agnes von Hohenstaufen**, 1827 (G. Spontini)

Agnes, daughter of Dietrich and Hilde (sop), **Der arme Heinrich**, 1895 (H. Pfitzner)

Agnes (lyric sop), **Die Schule der Frauen**, 1955 (R. Liebermann)

Agnes Bernauer, **Die Bernauerin**, 1947 (C. Orff)

Agnes Sorel, Karl VII's mistress (sop), **Das Mädchen aus Domrémy**, 1976 (G. Klebe)

Agrippina, fiancée of Tiberius (sop), **Janus**, 1698 (R. Keiser)

Agrippina, Nero's mother, **Nero**, 1705 (G. F. Handel)

Ah-Hsiu, a fox (sop), **Geisterliebe**, 1971 (I. Yun)

Aithra, an Egyptian sorceress (sop), **Die ägyptische Helena**, 1928 (R. Strauss)

Albanus, leader of the citizens of Cyprus, **Rosamunde**, 1824 (F. Schubert)

Alberich, a Nibelung dwarf (bar/bass-bar), **Der Ring**: Das Rheingold, 1869, Siegfried, 1876, Götterdämmerung, 1876 (R. Wagner)

Albert, Constanze's lover (ten), **Die Liebe im Narrenhaus**, 1787 (K. Dittersdorf)

Albert von Cleeburg (ten), **Silvana**, 1810 (C. M. von Weber)

Albertine (sop), **Die Brautwahl**, 1912 (F. Busoni)

Alberto (ten), **La Cubana**, 1974 (H. W. Henze)

Albi, a young squire (ten), **Der Schatzgräber**, 1920 (F. Schreker)

Albrecht, Duke of Bavaria, **Die Bernauerin**, 1947 (C. Orff)

Albrecht von Brandenburg of Mainz (ten), **Mathis der Maler**, 1938 (P. Hindemith)

Albrecht von Waldsee (speaking role), **Das Donauweibchen**, 1798 (F. Kauer)

Alceste, wife of king of Thessaly (sop), **Alceste**, 1773 (A. Schweitzer)

Alcibiades, student of Socrates (ten), **Der geduldige Sokrates**, 1721 (G. P. Telemann)

Aleel (bar), **Irische Legende**, 1955 (W. Egk)

Alessandro Stradella, a composer (ten), **Alessandro Stradella**, 1844 (F. von Flotow)

Alexander, husband of Armande (bar), **Zweimal Alexander**, 1937 (B. Martinů)

Alfonso, captain of the guards (alto), **La forza della virtù**, 1700 (R. Keiser)

Alfonso, son of Troila (ten), **Alfonso und Estrella**, 1822 (F. Schubert)

Alfonso, prince of Candia, **Rosamunde**, 1824 (F. Schubert)

Alfonso (ten), **Violanta**, 1916 (E. Korngold)

Alfred (ten), **Die Fledermaus**, 1874 (J. Strauss, Jr.)

Alfred (ten), **Leonore 40/45**, 1952 (R. Liebermann)

Alfred III (bar), **Der Besuch der alten Dame**, 1971 (G. von Einem)

Ali, Sander's slave (ten), **Zemire und Azor**, 1819 (L. Spohr)

Alice, daughter of John Couder (sop), **Die Dollarprinzessin**, 1907 (L. Fall)

Alice Faversham, Arden's wife (mezzo), **Arden muss sterben**, 1967 (A. Goehr)

Alimelek, a young rich Moslem, **Wirth und Gast**, 1813 (G. Meyerbeer)

Alkibiades (ten), **Pallas Athene weint**, 1955 (E. Krenek)

Alkmene (mezzo), **Die Liebe der Danae**, 1944 (R. Strauss)

Alkmene (sop), **Alkmene**, 1961 (G. Klebe)

Allazim, a Turk (bass), **Zaïde**, 1779 (W. A. Mozart)

Alma (sop), **Der Berggeist**, 1825 (L. Spohr)

Almador, Prince (ten), **Der Spiegelritter**, ca. 1811 (F. Schubert)

Almansor, Emir of Tunis (speaking role), **Oberon**, 1826 (C. M. von Weber)

648   INDEX OF CHARACTERS

Apothecary, the (mezzo), **Puntila**, 1966 (P.
  Dessau)
Arabella (sop), **Arabella**, 1933 (R. Strauss)
Arbander, Count, **Das Waldmädchen**, 1800
  (C. M. von Weber)
Arcesius, a Roman senator (bar), **Die toten
  Augen**, 1916 (E. d'Albert)
Archbishop of Mainz (bass), **Die Loreley**,
  1863 (M. Bruch)
Arcimboldo, the Emperor's painter (bass), **Der
  Engel von Prag**, 1979 (C. Bresgen)
Arden, a rich businessman (bass), **Arden
  muss sterben**, 1967 (A. Goehr)
Aret, son of Philemon (ten), **Philemon und
  Baucis**, 1773 (F. J. Haydn)
Argabyses, Scythian king (speaking role),
  Lampedo, 1779 (G. J. Vogler)
Ariadne, **Ariadne**, 1722 (C. G. Conradi)
Ariadne, daughter of King Minos (speaking
  role), **Ariadne auf Naxos**, 1775 (G. Benda)
Ariadne (sop), **Ariadne auf Naxos**, 1912 (R.
  Strauss)
Ariel, a sylph (sop), **Die Geisterinsel**, 1798
  (J. F. Reichardt)
Ariel (dancer), **Der Sturm**, 1956 (F. Martin)
Arindal (ten), **Die Hochzeit**, 1832 (R. Wag-
  ner)
Arindal, a prince (ten), **Die Feen**, 1833 (R.
  Wagner)
Aristophanes, a poet (ten), **Der gedultige Sok-
  rates**, 1721 (G. P. Telemann)
Arkenholz, a student (ten), **Gespenstersonate**,
  1984 (A. Reimann)
Arlecchino (speaking role), **Arlecchino**, 1917
  (F. Busoni)
Armand, young count of Dürande (ten), **Das
  Schloss Dürande**, 1943 (O. Schoeck)
Armand des Grieux (ten), **Boulevard Soli-
  tude**, 1952 (H. W. Henze)
Armande, Alexander's wife (sop), **Zweimal
  Alexander**, 1937 (B. Martinů)
Arnold, nephew of Lord Puff (bass), **Die en-
  glische Katze**, 1983 (H. W. Henze)
Arnolphe, an old cynic (bar), **Die Schule der
  Frauen**, 1955 (R. Liebermann)
Arnulf (speaking role), **Die Zauberharfe**,
  1820 (F. Schubert)
Aron (ten), **Moses und Aron**, 1932 (A.
  Schoenberg)
Arsena, Kálmán's daughter (sop), **Der Zigeu-
  nerbaron**, 1885 (J. Strauss, Jr.)
Arsidas (ten), **Siebzehn Tage**, 1966 (W. Egk)

Arsinoë, Myrtocle's slave, **Die toten Augen**,
  1916 (E. d'Albert)
Arundel (ten), **Elisabeth Tudor**, 1972 (W.
  Fortner)
Asberta, Queen of Bohemia (sop), **Günther
  von Schwarzburg**, 1777 (I. Holzbauer)
Aseanio, **Benvenuto Cellini**, 1849 (F. Lach-
  ner)
Assad, favorite of Solomon (ten), **Die Königin
  von Saba**, 1875 (K. Goldmark)
Assistant, the (ten), **Der Zar lässt sich photo-
  graphieren**, 1928 (K .Weill)
Assistant, the false (ten), **Der Zar lässt sich
  photographieren**, 1928 (K. Weill)
Assistant, the (mezzo), **Zwischenfälle**, 1966
  (B. Blacher)
Astaroth, the Queen of Sheba's slave (sop),
  Die Königin von Saba, 1875 (K. Gold-
  mark)
Astarte, **Der Schmied von Gent**, 1932 (F.
  Schreker)
Asterie, a shepherdess, **L'inganno fedele**,
  1714 (R. Keiser)
Astolf von Reisenberg, Count (ten), **Die
  Verschworenen**, 1823 (F. Schubert)
Asträä (mezzo), **Siebzehn Tage**, 1966 (W.
  Egk)
Astragalus, the Alpenkönig (bar), **Alpenkönig**,
  1903 (L. Blech)
Athamas, husband of Ino (speaking role), **Ino**,
  1779 (J. F. Reichardt)
Athamas, king of Joklos (bar), **Der goldene
  Bock**, 1964 (E. Krenek)
Athlete, the (bass), **Lulu**, 1937 (A. Berg)
Atis, son of Croesus (bass/sop), **Croesus**,
  1711/1730 (R. Keiser)
Aubry, Count, a vampire (bar), **Der Vampyr**,
  1828 (P. Lindpaintner)
Aubry, Edgar (ten), **Der Vampyr**, 1828 (H.
  Marschner)
Aucassin (bar), **Die Geschichte von Aucassin**,
  1969 (G. Bialas)
August Fliederbusch, **Die Landstreicher**,
  1899 (C. M. Ziehrer)
Auguste, sister of Wilhelm (sop), **Preussisches
  Märchen**, 1952 (B. Blacher)
Augustus, Emperor of Rome (bass), **Janus**,
  1698 (R. Keiser)
Aurora (sop), **Aurora**, 1811–12 (E. T. A.
  Hoffmann)
Autonoë, sister of Agave (high sop), **Die Bas-
  sariden**, 1966 (H. W. Henze)

Beggar monk, a (bass), **Sim Tjong**, 1972 (I. Yun)

Belia, Kaleph's daughter (sop), **Das Sonnenfest der Braminen**, 1790 (W. Müller)

Belisa (sop), **In seinem Garten**, 1962 (W. Fortner)

Bella Giretti, a prima donna (sop), **Paganini**, 1925 (F. Lehár)

Bellante, Princess of Aranda (sop), **Almira**, 1705 (G. F. Handel)

Bellnitz, Louise's lover (ten), **Der Alchymist**, 1778 (J. Schuster)

Belmont, a Spaniard (ten), **Belmont und Constanze**, 1781 (J. André)

Belmonte, a young Spanish nobleman (ten), **Die Entführung**, 1782 (W. A. Mozart)

Beltsazar, son of Nebucadnezar (ten), **Nebucadnezar**, 1704 (R. Keiser)

Bemira, daughter of Miriways, **Miriways**, 1728 (G. P. Telemann)

Benito Repollo (bass), **Das Wundertheater**, 1949 (H. W. Henze)

Benler, Frau (sop), **Rosamunde Floris**, 1960 (B. Blacher)

Benler, Herr, **Rosamunde Floris**, 1960 (B. Blacher)

Benvenuto Cellini, **Benvenuto Cellini**, 1849 (F. Lachner)

Benvolo (bass), **Romeo und Julia**, 1944 (B. Blacher)

Beresynth, Pietro's servant (ten), **Pietro von Abano**, 1827 (L. Spohr)

Berggeist, the (bass), **Der Berggeist**, 1825 (L. Spohr)

Berkley, Sir John (bass), **Der Vampyr**, 1828 (H. Marschner)

Bernardo (bass), **Erwin und Elmire**, 1916 (O. Schoeck)

Beroe, an old slave (mezzo), **Die Bassariden**, 1966 (H. W. Henze)

Bertel, Frau Willmers' son (ten), **Versiegelt**, 1908 (L. Blech)

Bertha, Albrecht von Waldsee's wife (speaking role), **Das Donauweibchen**, 1798 (F. Kauer)

Bertha (sop), **Alruna**, 1808 (L. Spohr)

Bertha, the gatekeeper (mezzo), **Die Kreuzfahrer**, 1845 (L. Spohr)

Bertha, niece of the Archbishop (sop), **Die Loreley**, 1863 (M. Bruch)

Bertha Fliederbusch, **Die Landstreicher**, 1899 (C. M. Ziehrer)

Berthalda, the duke's daughter (sop), **Undine**, 1816 (E. T. A. Hoffmann)

Berthalda, Duke Heinrich's daughter (sop), **Undine**, 1845 (A. Lortzing)

Bessie (soubrette), **Mahagonny**, 1927 (K. Weill)

Bianca, **Benvenuto Cellini**, 1849 (F. Lachner)

Bianca, wife of Simone, **Eine florentinische Tragödie**, 1917 (A. von Zemlinsky)

Bianka, Baptista's daughter (sop), **Der widerspenstigen Zähmung**, 1874 (H. Goetz)

Bill, a gangster (male), **Happy End**, 1929 (K. Weill)

Bill, a machinist (ten), **Maschinist Hopkins**, 1929 (M. Brand)

Billy (ten), **Mahagonny**, 1927 (K. Weill)

Bishop of Beauvais (ten), **Das Mädchen aus Domrémy**, 1976 (G. Klebe)

Bishop of Padua (speaking role), **Pietro von Abano**, 1827 (L. Spohr)

Black Will, employee of Alice (bass), **Arden muss sterben**, 1967 (A. Goehr)

Blandine, the king's daughter (speaking role), **Lenardo und Blandine**, 1779 (P. Winter)

Blind, Dr., Eisenstein's attorney (ten), **Die Fledermaus**, 1874 (J. Strauss, Jr.)

Blonde, Constance's servant (sop), **Belmont und Constanze**, 1781 (J. André)

Blonde, maid of Constanze (sop), **Die Entführung**, 1782 (W. A. Mozart)

Bobby (bass), **Mahagonny**, 1927 (K. Weill)

Bobtschinski (ten), **Der Revisor**, 1957 (W. Egk)

Boccaccio, a writer (ten or sop), **Boccaccio**, 1879 (F. von Suppé)

Bodo von Triesnitz (speaking role), **Das Donauweibchen**, 1798 (F. Kauer)

Bohemund von Schwarzebeck (bass), **Die Kreuzfahrer**, 1845 (L. Spohr)

Bombasto, Dottore (bass), **Arlecchino**, 1917 (F. Busoni)

Bookkeeper, the (ten), **Aufsteig und Fall der Stadt Mahagonny**, 1930 (K. Weill)

Börg, Hans Sachs's apprentice (ten), **Hans Sachs**, 1840 (A. Lortzing)

Bostana, confidante of Margiana (alto), **Der Barbier von Bagdad**, 1858 (P. Cornelius)

Botak (bass), **Libussa**, 1822 (C. Kreutzer)

Boy, the (alto), **Der Zar lässt sich photographieren**, 1928 (K. Weill)

Boy, the false (alto), **Der Zar lässt sich photographieren**, 1928 (K. Weill)

Brambilla, a princess, **Prinzessin Brambilla**, 1909 (W. Braunfels)

Brandon (bass), **Das lange Weihnachtsmahl**, 1961 (P. Hindemith)

Brangäne, attendant of Isolde (sop), **Tristan und Isolde**, 1865 (R. Wagner)

Brasidas, a captain (bar), **Pallas Athene weint**, 1955 (E. Krenek)

Braun, the mayor (bar), **Versiegelt**, 1908 (L. Blech)

Brian de Bois-Guilbert (bar), **Der Templer und die Jüdin**, 1829 (H. Marschner)

Bride, a (sop), **Die Bluthochzeit**, 1957 (W. Fortner)

Bridegroom, a (speaking role), **Die Bluthochzeit**, 1957 (W. Fortner)

Brighella (bass), **Das Liebesverbot**, 1836 (R. Wagner)

Brighella (ten), **Ariadne auf Naxos**, 1912 (R. Strauss)

Brigitta (alto), **Die tote Stadt**, 1920 (E. Korngold)

Bronislawa, a countess (sop), **Der Bettelstudent**, 1882 (C. Millöcker)

Brown (bass), **Die Dreigroschenoper**, 1928 (K. Weill)

Brown, Widow (alto), **Zar und Zimmermann**, 1837 (A. Lortzing)

Brummer, Herr von (bass), **Die Schwestern von Prag**, 1794 (W. Müller)

Brünnhilde, daughter of Wotan (sop), **Der Ring: Die Walküre**, 1870, **Siegfried**, 1876, **Götterdämmerung**, 1876 (R. Wagner)

Bruno (bass), **Alruna**, 1808 (L. Spohr)

Bruno, Benler's son (ten), **Rosamunde Floris**, 1960 (B. Blacher)

Bumerli (ten), **Der tapfere Soldat**, 1908 (O. Straus)

Burgundy, Duke of (bar), **Agnes von Hohenstaufen**, 1827 (G. Spontini)

Burudusussu, a wizard (bass), **Der Spiegelritter**, ca. 1811 (F. Schubert)

Busch, an innkeeper (bass), **Die beiden Schützen**, 1837 (A. Lortzing)

Cäcilia, daughter of the Podesta (sop), **Pietro von Abano**, 1827 (L. Spohr)

Cadi, the (bass), **Der Barbier von Bagdad**, 1783 (J. André)

Cadmus. See Kadmus.

Cajus, Dr. (bass), **Die lustigen Weiber**, 1849 (O. Nicolai)

Caliban, a gnome (bass), **Die Geisterinsel**, 1798 (J. F. Reichardt)

Calicot, a poet (ten), **Madame Pompadour**, 1923 (L. Fall)

Caliph, the (bar), **Der Barbier von Bagdad**, 1858 (P. Cornelius)

Callistus, favorite of Claudius (alto), **Claudius**, 1703 (R. Keiser)

Calpurnia, betrothed of Callistus (sop), **Claudius**, 1703 (R. Keiser)

Camacho (bass), **Die Hochzeit des Camacho**, 1827 (F. Mendelssohn)

Camille de Rosillon (ten), **Die lustige Witwe**, 1905 (F. Lehár)

Camille Desmoulins (ten), **Dantons Tod**, 1947 (G. von Einem)

Canterville, Lord (speaking part), **Das Gespenst von Canterville**, 1964 (H. Sutermeister)

Capraja, Genovese's patron (bar), **Massimilla Doni**, 1937 (O. Schoeck)

Captain, the (ten), **Wozzeck**, 1925 (A. Berg)

Captain of the guards, the (bar), **Die Bassariden**, 1966 (H. W. Henze)

Capulet (bass), **Romeo und Julia**, 1944 (B. Blacher)

Capulet, Lady (alto), **Romeo und Julia**, 1944 (B. Blacher)

Caramello, a barber (ten/bar), **Eine Nacht in Venedig**, 1883 (J. Strauss, Jr.)

Cardillac, a goldsmith (bar), **Cardillac**, 1926 (P. Hindemith)

Carl, beloved of Minette (ten), **Peter Schmoll**, 1802 (C. M. von Weber)

Carl, son of Herr von Robert (ten), **Die beiden Pädagogen**, 1821 (F. Mendelssohn)

Carlo Borromeo, a cardinal (bar), **Palestrina**, 1917 (H. Pfitzner)

Carlotta (sop), **Die Gezeichneten**, 1918 (F. Schreker)

Carrasco (bass), **Die Hochzeit des Camacho**, 1827 (F. Mendelssohn)

Caspar, a young hunter (bass), **Der Freischütz**, 1821 (C. M. von Weber)

Cassandra, crown princess of Media, **Nero**, 1705 (G. F. Handel)

Catharina (Caterina) Cornaro (sop), **Catharina Cornaro**, 1841 (F. Lachner)

Cathleen (sop), **Irische Legende**, 1955 (W. Egk)

Cattaneo, an old duke (ten), **Massimilla Doni**, 1937 (O. Schoeck)

Desportes, a French baron (high ten), **Die Soldaten**, 1965 (B. A. Zimmermann)

Devil, the (buffo bass), **Der Bärenhäuter**, 1899 (S. Wagner)

Devil, the (bass-bar), **Die schwarze Spinne**, 1949 (W. Burkhard)

Dibdin, George, Davenaut's servant (ten), **Der Vampyr**, 1828 (H. Marschner)

Dick, nephew of John Couder, **Die Dollarprinzessin**, 1907 (L. Fall)

Dictator, the (bar), **Der Diktator**, 1928 (E. Krenek)

Diego (ten), **Die Freunde von Salamanka**, 1815 (F. Schubert)

Diemut, daughter of Ortlof Sentlinger (sop), **Feuersnot**, 1901 (R. Strauss)

Dietrich, one of Heinrich's men (bar), **Der arme Heinrich**, 1895 (H. Pfitzner)

Diomedes, a Greek king (ten), **Penthesilea**, 1927 (O. Schoeck)

Dionys (bass), **Die Bürgschaft**, 1816 (F. Schubert)

Dionysos, **Die Bakchantinnen**, 1931 (E. Wellesz)

Dionysus (ten), **Die Bassariden**, 1966 (H. W. Henze)

Director Hummel, the old man (bar), **Gespenstersonate**, 1984 (A. Reimann)

Dobra, a young woman at court (sop), **Libussa**, 1822 (C. Kreutzer)

Dobtschinski (bar), **Der Revisor**, 1957 (W. Egk)

Doctor, the (bass), **Der arme Heinrich**, 1895 (H. Pfitzner)

Doctor, the (bass), **Wozzeck**, 1925 (A. Berg)

Doktor Faust (bar), **Doktor Faust**, 1922 (F. Busoni)

Dombrowska (ten), **Das Ende einer Welt**, 1953 (H. W. Henze)

Domoslaw (bass), **Libussa**, 1822 (C. Kreutzer)

Don Alonzo, lover of Inez (ten), **Der Alchymist**, 1830 (L. Spohr)

Don Cesar, toreador (ten), **Donna Diana**, 1894 (E. N. von Reznicek)

Don Diego, mayor of Barcelona (bass), **Donna Diana**, 1894 (E. N. von Reznicek)

Don Eugenio de Zuniga, magistrate (ten), **Der Corregidor**, 1896 (H. Wolf)

Don Fernando, prime minister (bass), **Leonore/Fidelio**, 1805/1814 (L. van Beethoven)

Don Gaston (ten), **Die drei Pintos**, 1821 (C. M. von Weber)

Don Juan (bar), **Dame Kobold**, 1964 (G. Wimberger)

Don Luis, a sugar refiner (ten), **Donna Diana**, 1894 (E. N. von Reznicek)

Don Luis (high bass), **Dame Kobold**, 1964 (G. Wimberger)

Don Manuel (ten), **Dame Kobold**, 1964 (G. Wimberger)

Don Pantaleone, Clarissa's father (bar), **Die drei Pintos**, 1821 (C. M. von Weber)

Don Perlimplín (bar), **In seinem Garten**, 1962 (W. Fortner)

Don Pinto (bass), **Die drei Pintos**, 1821 (C. M. von Weber)

Don Pizarro, prison overseer (bass-bar), **Leonore/Fidelio**, 1805/1814 (L. van Beethoven)

Don Quixote (bass), **Die Hochzeit des Camacho**, 1827 (F. Mendelssohn)

Don Ramiro, lover of Inez (bass), **Der Alchymist**, 1830 (L. Spohr)

Don Ranudo di Colibrados (bass), **Don Ranudo**, 1919 (O. Schoeck)

Don Trinidad, a priest (bass), **Manuel Venegas**, 1903 (H. Wolf)

Dona Mercedes, wife of Don Eugenio (sop), **Der Corregidor**, 1896 (H. Wolf)

Dona Olympia (alto), **Don Ranudo**, 1919 (O. Schoeck)

Donna Angela, a young widow (sop), **Dame Kobold**, 1964 (G. Wimberger)

Donna Beatriz (mezzo), **Dame Kobold**, 1964 (G. Wimberger)

Donna Diana, Don Diego's daughter (sop), **Donna Diana**, 1894 (E. N. von Reznicek)

Donna Fenisa, Don Diego's niece (alto), **Donna Diana**, 1894 (E. N. von Reznicek)

Donna Laura, Don Diego's niece (sop), **Donna Diana**, 1894 (E. N. von Reznicek)

Donna Maria, Soledad's mother (alto), **Manuel Venegas**, 1903 (H. Wolf)

Donner, god of thunder (bar), **Der Ring: Das Rheingold**, 1869 (R. Wagner)

Doraspe, King of Damascus (bass), **Die grossmüthige Tomyris**, 1717 (R. Keiser)

Dorella, Isabella's former maid (sop), **Das Liebesverbot**, 1836 (R. Wagner)

Dornal, a Frenchman (ten), **Der Kaufmann von Smyrna**, 1771 (G. J. Vogler)

Douglas, Baron (speaking role), **William Ratcliff**, 1982 (J.-P. Ostendorf)

Dragon, the (bass), **Lanzelot**, 1969 (P. Dessau)

Dragotin, Peter (bar), **Zigeunerliebe**, 1910 (F. Lehár)

Dreifinger (bass), **Murieta**, 1984 (J.-P. Ostendorf)

Drolla, Laura's companion (sop), **Die Feen**, 1833 (R. Wagner)

Drum Major, the (ten), **Wozzeck**, 1925 (A. Berg)

Drummer, the (mezzo), **Der Kaiser von Atlantis**, 1944 (V. Ullmann)

Dryad, a nymph (alto), **Ariadne auf Naxos**, 1912 (R. Strauss)

Dryante, a shepherdess (sop), **Adonis**, 1697 (R. Keiser)

Dscheangir, a Mongolian emperor (ten), **Nurmahal**, 1822 (G. Spontini)

Duchess, the (sop), **Undine**, 1816 (E. T. A. Hoffmann)

Duke, the (ten), **Undine**, 1816 (E. T. A. Hoffmann)

Duménil, Georges (ten), **Der Opernball**, 1898 (R. Heuberger)

Dumristan, King of (bass), **Der Spiegelritter**, ca. 1811 (F. Schubert)

Dunois, bastard prince of Orléans (bar), **Das Mädchen aus Domrémy**, 1976 (G. Klebe)

Durmann (ten), **Die Schweizerfamilie**, 1828 (J. Weigl)

Dutchman, the (bar), **Der fliegende Holländer**, 1843 (R. Wagner)

Duval, a former soldier (ten), **Der vierjährige Posten**, 1815 (F. Schubert)

Dwarf, the (ten), **Der Zwerg**, 1922 (A. von Zemlinsky)

Dwarf, the (ten), **Siebzehn Tage**, 1966 (W. Egk)

Dyer's wife, the (sop), **Die Frau ohne Schatten**, 1918 (R. Strauss)

Eberbach, Count (bar), **Der Wildschütz**, 1842 (A. Lortzing)

Echo (sop), **Ariadne auf Naxos**, 1912 (R. Strauss)

Eckhart, **Der Kobold**, 1904 (S. Wagner)

Edgar (ten), **Lear**, 1978 (A. Reimann)

Edilla, a Castilian princess (sop), **Almira**, 1705 (G. F. Handel)

Edmund (ten), **Die Prüfung**, 1806 (L. Spohr)

Edmund (ten), **Lear**, 1978 (A. Reimann)

Edmund Lehsen, a young artist (ten), **Die Brautwahl**, 1912 (F. Busoni)

Edronica, Athenian princess (sop), **Der gedultige Sokrates**, 1721 (G. P. Telemann)

Eduard, **Der lächerliche Printz**, 1726 (R. Keiser)

Eduard, a young Englishman (ten), **Das Sonnenfest der Braminen**, 1790 (W. Müller)

Eduard (bar), **Neues vom Tage**, 1929 (P. Hindemith)

Edwin, a prince (ten), **Die Csárdásfürstin**, 1915 (E. Kálmán)

Eginhard, **Die last-tragende Liebe**, 1728 (G. P. Telemann)

Eginhard (ten), **Fierrabras**, 1823 (F. Schubert)

Eglantine of Puiset (mezzo), **Euryanthe**, 1823 (C. M. von Weber)

Ehrelob (ten/medium voice), **Seelewig**, 1644 (S. T. Staden)

Einstein (bar), **Einstein**, 1974 (P. Dessau)

Eisenstein, a wealthy socialite (ten), **Die Fledermaus**, 1874 (J. Strauss, Jr.)

Ekart, friend of Baal (bass), **Baal**, 1981 (F. Cerha)

Eleanore (sop), **Karl der Fünfte**, 1938 (E. Krenek)

Electress of Brandenburg, the (alto), **Der Prinz von Homburg**, 1960 (H. W. Henze)

Elektra (sop), **Elektra**, 1909 (R. Strauss)

Elektra (sop), **Das Leben des Orest**, 1930 (E. Krenek)

Elemer, a count, suitor of Arabella (ten), **Arabella**, 1933 (R. Strauss)

Eleonore (sop), **Fernando**, 1815 (F. Schubert)

Eliates, a Lydian prince (ten), **Croesus**, 1711 (R. Keiser)

Elis, a singer (ten), **Der Schatzgräber**, 1920 (F. Schreker)

Elisabeth, a princess, **Ludovicus Pius**, 1726 (G. C. Schürmann)

Elisabeth, niece of the Landgraf (sop), **Tannhäuser**, 1845 (R. Wagner)

Elisabeth (sop), **Elegie für junge Liebende**, 1961 (H. W. Henze)

Elisabeth Tudor (mezzo), **Elisabeth Tudor**, 1972 (W. Fortner)

Elise, niece of Herr von Robert (sop), **Die beiden Pädagogen**, 1821 (F. Mendelssohn)

Ellis, the Commisar (ten), **Die Bürgschaft**, 1932 (K. Weill)

Elmira, a Medean princess (sop), **Croesus**, 1711 (R. Keiser)

Elmire (sop), **Erwin und Elmire**, 1793 (J. F. Reichardt)

Elmire, a Spanish maiden, **Soliman der Zweyte**, 1799 (F. Süssmayr)

Elmire (sop), **Erwin und Elmire**, 1916 (O. Schoeck)

Elpin, an animal herder, **L'inganno fedele**, 1714 (R. Keiser)

Elpina, a nymph (sop), **Der neu-modische Liebhaber**, 1724 (G. P. Telemann)

Els (sop), **Der Schatzgräber**, 1920 (F. Schreker)

Elsa (sop), **Lanzelot**, 1969 (P. Dessau)

Elsa von Brabant (sop), **Lohengrin**, 1850 (R. Wagner)

Else, the mayor's daughter (sop), **Versiegelt**, 1908 (L. Blech)

Elvire, a widowed countess (sop), **Die Soldatenliebschaft**, 1820 (F. Mendelssohn)

Emillio Memmi, a young nobleman (ten), **Massimilla Doni**, 1937 (O. Schoeck)

Emir of the Seljuk Turks, the (bass), **Die Kreuzfahrer**, 1845 (L. Spohr)

Emma, **Die last-tragende Liebe**, 1728 (G. P. Telemann)

Emma (sop), **Fierrabras**, 1823 (F. Schubert)

Emma, a smuggler (alto), **Puntila**, 1966 (P. Dessau)

Emma of Falkenstein, a pilgrim (sop), **Die Kreuzfahrer**, 1845 (L. Spohr)

Emmeline (sop), **Die Schweizerfamilie**, 1828 (J. Weigl)

Emmy, John Perth's daughter (sop), **Der Vampyr**, 1828 (H. Marschner)

Emperor, the (ten), **Die Frau ohne Schatten**, 1918 (R. Strauss)

Emperor, the (bar), **Sim Tjong**, 1972 (I. Yun)

Empress, the (sop), **Die Frau ohne Schatten**, 1918 (R. Strauss)

Engineer, the (bar), **Zwischenfälle**, 1966 (B. Blacher)

Eoban Hesse, Augsburg councillor (ten), **Hans Sachs**, 1840 (A. Lortzing)

Erasmus, an old man from Naples (speaking role), **Der Günstling**, 1935 (R. Wagner-Régeny)

Ercole, Penelope's second husband (ten), **Penelope**, 1954 (R. Liebermann)

Erda, earth goddess (mezzo), **Der Ring: Das Rheingold**, 1869, **Siegfried**, 1876 (R. Wagner)

Erechtheus, King of the Athenians (bar), **Aurora**, 1811–1812 (E. T. A. Hoffmann)

Ergasto, a shepherd (bass), **Der neu-modische Liebhaber**, 1724 (G. P. Telemann)

Erich Siedler, a lawyer (bar), **Im Weissen Rössel**, 1930 (R. Benatzky)

Erik, a huntsman (ten), **Der fliegende Holländer**, 1843 (R. Wagner)

Erminde, a lady at the court, **Der lächerliche Printz**, 1726 (R. Keiser)

Ernst, a soldier (bar), **Die Soldatenliebschaft**, 1820 (F. Mendelssohn)

Ernst, the Duke, **Die Bernauerin**, 1947 (C. Orff)

Erotia, a courtesan (sop), **Zwillingskomödie**, 1954 (R. Mohaupt)

Erwin (ten), **Erwin und Elmire**, 1793 (J. F. Reichardt)

Erwin (ten), **Erwin und Elmire**, 1916 (O. Schoeck)

Erwin, Benler's son (ten), **Rosamunde Floris**, 1960 (B. Blacher)

Espali, an exiled prince (bar), **Der goldene Bock**, 1964 (E. Krenek)

Esteban (bar), **El Cimerrón**, 1970 (H. W. Henze)

Esther, wife of Mordechai Meisl (sop), **Der Engel von Prag**, 1979 (C. Bresgen)

Estrella, daughter of Mauregato (sop), **Alfonso und Estrella**, 1822 (F. Schubert)

Etienne, a gardener (bass), **Der Vampyr**, 1828 (P. Lindpaintner)

Eudoxia, wife of the Podesta (sop), **Pietro von Abano**, 1827 (L. Spohr)

Eumene, a shepherdess (sop), **Adonis**, 1697 (R. Keiser)

Europa (sop), **Die Liebe der Danae**, 1944 (R. Strauss)

Euryanthe of Savoy (sop), **Euryanthe**, 1823 (C. M. von Weber)

Eurydike (sop), **Orpheus und Eurydike**, 1926 (E. Krenek)

Eurydike (sop), **Antigonae**, 1949 (C. Orff)

Eurymachos, a freeman (buffo bass), **Penelope**, 1954 (R. Liebermann)

Eusebia (sop), **Die Freunde von Salamanka**, 1815 (F. Schubert)

Eusebio, a rich young man (bar), **La Cubana**, 1974 (H. W. Henze)

Eva, Lukas's mother (sop), **Der Jahrmarkt**, 1775 (G. Benda)

Eva (sop), **Die Meistersinger**, 1868 (R. Wagner)

Eva, the forester's daughter (sop), **Irrelohe**, 1924 (F. Schreker)

Eve, Marthe Rull's daughter (sop), **Der zerbrochene Krug**, 1971 (F. Geissler)

Eve, the mother (sop/basset hn/dancer), **Donnerstag**, 1981 (K. Stockhausen)

Gabriele, Zedlau's wife (sop), **Wiener Blut**, 1899 (J. Strauss, Jr.)

Gabriele, Renald's sister (sop), **Das Schloss Dürande**, 1943 (O. Schoeck)

Gaia, wife of Peneois (alto), **Daphne**, 1938 (R. Strauss)

Galatea, a statue (sop), **Die schöne Galatea**, 1865 (F. von Suppé)

Galba, Aurelius, a Roman captain (ten), **Die toten Augen**, 1916 (E. d'Albert)

Gamekeeper, a (bar), **Das Schloss Dürande**, 1943 (O. Schoeck)

Ganymed, a servant (alto), **Die schöne Galatea**, 1865 (F. von Suppé)

Garin von Beaucaire (bass), **Die Geschichte von Aucassin**, 1969 (G. Bialas)

Gaston, a dancing master (ten), **Schwergewicht**, 1928 (E. Krenek)

Gaston Salvatore (male voice), **Der langwienzige Weg**, 1971 (H. W. Henze)

Gelon, a shepherd (ten), **Adonis**, 1697 (R. Keiser)

Genevieve (mezzo), **Das lange Weihnachtsmahl**, 1961 (P. Hindemith)

Genoveva, a noblewoman (sop), **Genoveva**, 1850 (R. Schumann)

Gentleman, the young (bar), **Der Protagonist**, 1926 (K. Weill)

Georg, Liebenau's servant (ten), **Der Waffenschmied**, 1846 (A. Lortzing)

Georgette, Arnolphe's servant (alto), **Die Schule der Frauen**, 1955 (R. Liebermann)

Germaine (alto), **Leonore 40/45**, 1952 (R. Liebermann)

Gernot, Arindal's servant (bass), **Die Feen**, 1833 (R. Wagner)

Gerstenfeld, Herr von (ten), **Die Schwestern von Prag**, 1794 (W. Müller)

Gertrud (sop), **Die Schweizerfamilie**, 1828 (J. Weigl)

Gertrud, Anna's mother (alto), **Hans Heiling**, 1833 (H. Marschner)

Gertrud, **Der Kobold**, 1904 (S. Wagner)

Gertrud, Frau, a young widow (mezzo), **Versiegelt**, 1908 (L. Blech)

Geschwitz, a countess (mezzo), **Lulu**, 1937 (A. Berg)

Ghita, maid of the Infanta (sop), **Der Zwerg**, 1922 (A. von Zemlinsky)

Ghost, a (ten), **Die Feuersbrunst**, ca. 1776 (F. J. Haydn)

Ghost, a (ten), **Das Bergwerk zu Falun**, 1961 (R. Wagner-Régeny)

Ghost of Canterville, the (bar), **Das Gespenst von Canterville**, 1964 (H. Sutermeister)

Giacinta, a seamstress, **Prinzessin Brambilla**, 1909 (W. Braunfels)

Giaffer, Harun al Raschid's servant, **Wirth und Gast**, 1813 (G. Meyerbeer)

Giganie, Metallio's wife (sop), **Der Spiegel von Arkadien**, 1794 (F. Süssmayr)

Giglio, an actor, **Prinzessin Brambilla**, 1909 (W. Braunfels)

Gil, a man of the people (bar), **Der Günstling**, 1935 (R. Wagner-Régeny)

Gilfen (bar), **Die Abreise**, 1898 (E. d'Albert)

Giovanni de Salviati (ten), **Mona Lisa**, 1915 (M. von Schillings)

Girl, a (sop), **Der Kaiser von Atlantis**, 1944 (V. Ullmann)

Girl, the (sop), **Die Flut**, 1947 (B. Blacher)

Girl, the (sop), **Die tödlichen Wünsche**, 1959 (G. Klebe)

Girl friend, the (sop), **Von heute auf morgen**, 1930 (A. Schoenberg)

Giuditta (sop), **Giuditta**, 1934 (F. Lehár)

Glaukis, daughter of Espali (sop), **Der goldene Bock**, 1964 (E. Krenek)

Gloch, cultural dignitary (bass), **Das Ende einer Welt**, 1953 (H. W. Henze)

Gloster [Gloucester] (bass-bar), **Lear**, 1978 (A. Reimann)

Gluthammer, a locksmith (ten), **Der Zerrissene**, 1964 (G. von Einem)

Gobernador, the (bar), **Das Wundertheater**, 1949 (H. W. Henze)

Gold merchant, the (bass), **Cardillac**, 1926 (P. Hindemith)

Golo (ten), **Genoveva**, 1850 (R. Schumann)

Gomes, a Spanish slave (ten), **Zaïde**, 1779 (W. A. Mozart)

Gomez (ten), **Die drei Pintos**, 1821 (C. M. von Weber)

Gomez, a young hunter (ten), **Das Nachtlager in Granada**, 1834 (C. Kreutzer)

Goneril (dramatic sop), **Lear**, 1978 (A. Reimann)

Gonzalo de las Minas, Don (ten), **Don Ranudo**, 1919 (O. Schoeck)

Goose girl, the (sop), **Die Königskinder**, 1910 (E. Humperdinck)

Gottfried von Ried, Christoph's uncle (bass), **Die Verlobung in San Domingo**, 1963 (W. Egk)

Gotthold (ten), **Doctor und Apotheker**, 1785 (K. Dittersdorf)

Governor, the (bass-bar), **König Hirsch**, 1956 (H. W. Henze)

Graf von Gleichen (bass), **Der Graf von Gleichen**, 1827 (F. Schubert)

Grandier, Father (bar), **Die Teufel von Loudun**, 1969 (K. Penderecki)

Greene, a landowner (bar), **Arden muss sterben**, 1967 (A. Goehr)

Gregor Mittenhofer, poet (bar), **Elegie für junge Liebende**, 1961 (H. W. Henze)

Gresham (ten), **Elisabeth Tudor**, 1972 (W. Fortner)

Gretchen, Baculus' intended (sop), **Der Wildschütz**, 1842 (A. Lortzing)

Grete/Greta (sop), **Der ferne Klang**, 1912 (F. Schreker)

Gretel (sop), **Hänsel und Gretel**, 1893 (E. Humperdinck)

Grigoris (bass-bar), **Die griechische Passion**, 1971 (B. Martinů)

Gripon (bass), **Das Grab des Mufti**, 1779 (J. Hiller)

Grulla, Polidor's foster mother, **L'inganno fedele**, 1714 (R. Keiser)

Grumio, Petrucchio's servant (bass), **Der widerspenstigen Zähmung**, 1874 (H. Goehr)

Guido, a prince, **Eine florentinische Tragödie**, 1917 (A. von Zemlinsky)

Gulf, a knight, **Faust**, 1816 (L. Spohr)

Gülnare (sop), **Gülnare**, 1800 (F. Süssmayr)

Gülnare, the King of Sammarkand's daughter, **Der Traum ein Leben**, 1937 (W. Braunfels)

Gunlöd (mezzo), **Gunlöd**, 1874 (P. Cornelius)

Günther, Count of Schwarzburg (ten), **Günther von Schwarzburg**, 1777 (I. Holzbauer)

Gunther, half-brother of Hagen (bass/bass-bar), **Der Ring: Götterdämmerung**, 1876 (R. Wagner)

Guntram, a singer (ten), **Guntram**, 1894 (R. Strauss)

Gürge, a young peasant (ten), **Der Töpfer**, 1773 (J. André)

Gürge, a worker (ten), **Das Fest der Winzer**, 1793 (F. L. A. Kunzen)

Gurnemanz, an old knight of the Holy Grail (bass), **Parsifal**, 1882 (R. Wagner)

Gustav, a soldier (ten), **Die beiden Schützen**, 1837 (A. Lortzing)

Gustav, Count of Pottenstein (ten), **Das Land des Lächelns**, 1929 (F. Lehár)

Gustel, son of Tarnow (sop), **Der Alchymist**, 1778 (J. Schuster)

Gutrune, sister of Gunther (sop), **Der Ring: Götterdämmerung**, 1876 (R. Wagner)

Gwissulda, a matron (alto/high voice), **Seelewig**, 1644 (S. T. Staden)

Habicht, Frau von (sop), **Der Rauchfangkehrer**, 1781 (A. Salieri)

Hadmar (bass), **Die Hochzeit**, 1832 (R. Wagner)

Haemon, fiancé of Antigonae (ten), **Antigonae**, 1949 (C. Orff)

Hagen, son of Alberich (bass), **Der Ring: Götterdämmerung**, 1876 (R. Wagner)

Hamlet (bar), **Hamlet**, 1968 (H. Searle)

Hangman, the (bass), **Das Nusch-Nuschi**, 1921 (P. Hindemith)

Hanna Glawari (sop), **Die lustige Witwe**, 1905 (F. Lehár)

Hannchen, a farmer's daughter (sop), **Die Jagd**, 1770 (J. A. Hiller)

Hannchen, Michel's daughter (sop), **Der Töpfer**, 1773 (J. André)

Hannchen, Kinderschreck's niece (sop), **Die beiden Pädagogen**, 1821 (F. Mendelssohn)

Hannchen, the chamber maid (sop), **Die Opernprobe**, 1851 (A. Lortzing)

Hans, a young German (ten), **Die weisse Rose**, 1968 (U. Zimmermann)

Hans Heiling (bar), **Hans Heiling**, 1833 (H. Marschner)

Hans Kraft, a young soldier (ten), **Der Bärenhäuter**, 1899 (S. Wagner)

Hans Sachs. See Sachs, Hans.

Hans Schwalb, a peasant leader (ten), **Mathis der Maler**, 1938 (P. Hindemith)

Hänsel (mezzo), **Hänsel und Gretel**, 1893 (E. Humperdinck)

Hanswurst, a chimneysweep (bar), **Die Feuersbrunst**, ca. 1776 (F. J. Haydn)

Hanswurst (ten), **Einstein**, 1974 (P. Dessau)

Harald (ten), **Die Hochzeit**, 1832 (R. Wagner)

Harlequin (bar), **Ariadne auf Naxos**, 1912 (R. Strauss)

Harriet (Lady), Queen Anne's attendant (sop), **Martha**, 1847 (F. von Flotow)

Harun al Raschid, the Caliph of Bagdad (speaking role), **Abu Hassan**, 1811 (C. M. von Weber)

Harun al Raschid, the Caliph of Bagdad, **Wirth und Gast**, 1813 (G. Meyerbeer)

Horace, Zarandelle's nephew (ten), **Venus**, 1922 (O. Schoeck)

Horace (lyric ten), **Die Schule der Frauen**, 1955 (R. Liebermann)

Hortense, Duménil's chamber maid (sop), **Der Opernball**, 1898 (R. Heuberger)

Hortensio, Bianka's suitor (bar), **Der widerspenstigen Zähmung**, 1874 (H. Goehr)

Houdoux, Baron d' (bass), **Neues vom Tage**, 1929 (P. Hindemith)

Hubert, an innkeeper (bass), **Die Loreley**, 1863 (M. Bruch)

Hugo, Adelhart's servant (bass), **Silvana**, 1810 (C. M. von Weber)

Hugo, a count (ten), **Faust**, 1816 (L. Spohr)

Hugo von Ringstetten (ten), **Undine**, 1845 (A. Lortzing)

Huguette (sop), **Leonore 40/45**, 1952 (R. Liebermann)

Hulda, a water sprite (sop), **Das Donauweibchen**, 1798 (F. Kauer)

Huldbrand von Ringstetten, Knight (bar), **Undine**, 1816 (E. T. A. Hoffmann)

Hunding, husband of Sieglinde (bass), **Der Ring: Die Walküre**, 1870 (R. Wagner)

Hüon, a knight, **Oberon**, 1789 (P. Wranitzky)

Huon (Hüon) of Bordeaux, a knight (ten), **Oberon**, 1826 (C. M. von Weber)

Husband, the (bar), **Mörder, Hoffnung der Frauen**, 1921 (P. Hindemith)

Husband, the (bass), **Royal Hotel**, 1927 (K. Weill)

Husband, the (bass-bar), **Von heute auf morgen**, 1930 (A. Schoenberg)

Ibrahim, a high court official (bass), **Gülnare**, 1800 (F. X. Süssmayr)

Ibrahim, Alimelek's servant, **Wirth und Gast**, 1813 (G. Meyerbeer)

Ida (speaking role), **Die Zauberharfe**, 1820 (F. Schubert)

Ida, Adele's sister (sop), **Die Fledermaus**, 1874 (J. Strauss, Jr.)

Ighino, Palestrina's son (sop), **Palestrina**, 1917 (H. Pfitzner)

Ignerand, Count of Port d'Amour (bass), **Der Vampyr**, 1828 (P. Lindpaintner)

Ik-tjin, Sim Tjong's heavenly mother (sop), **Sim Tjong**, 1972 (I. Yun)

Ilona (sop), **Zigeunerliebe**, 1910 (F. Lehár)

Impresario, the (speaking part), **Der Schauspieldirektor**, 1786 (W. A. Mozart)

Inez, daughter of Felix de Vasquez (sop), **Der Alchymist**, 1830 (L. Spohr)

Infanta, the (sop), **Der Zwerg**, 1922 (A. von Zemlinsky)

Ingrid, Peer Gynt's former fiancée (sop), **Peer Gynt**, 1938 (W. Egk)

Inkle, a merchant (ten), **Fernando und Yariko**, 1784 (B. Schack)

Innkeeper, an (sop), **Des Teufels Lustschloss**, 1814 (F. Schubert)

Ino (speaking role), **Ino**, 1779 (J. F. Reichardt)

Iphigenie (mezzo), **Das Leben des Orest**, 1930 (E. Krenek)

Irene, Harun al Raschid's niece, **Wirth und Gast**, 1813 (G. Meyerbeer)

Irene, sister of Rienzi (sop), **Rienzi**, 1842 (R. Wagner)

Irmengard, a countess (sop), **Agnes von Hohenstaufen**, 1827 (G. Spontini)

Isabel, Donna Angela's maid (sop), **Dame Kobold**, 1964 (G. Wimberger)

Isabella, Princess of Salerno, **Der lächerliche Printz**, 1726 (R. Keiser)

Isabella, Claudio's sister (sop), **Das Liebesverbot**, 1836 (R. Wagner)

Isabella, Queen (sop), **Columbus**, 1933 (W. Egk)

Isella, Ludmilla's confidante (sop), **Die Verschworenen**, 1823 (F. Schubert)

Ismene, a shepherdess, **L'inganno fedele**, 1714 (R. Keiser)

Ismene (sop), **Die Bürgschaft**, 1816 (F. Schubert)

Ismene (alto), **Antigonae**, 1949 (C. Orff)

Isolde, Ignerand's daughter (sop), **Der Vampyr**, 1828 (P. Lindpaintner)

Isolde (sop), **Tristan und Isolde**, 1865 (R. Wagner)

Italian tenor, the (ten), **Der Rosenkavalier**, 1911 (R. Strauss)

Ivanhoe, a Saxon knight (ten), **Der Templer und die Jüdin**, 1829 (H. Marschner)

Jacob (ten), **Die Schweizerfamilie**, 1828 (J. Weigl)

Jacobowsky (bass), **Jacobowsky und der Oberst**, 1965 (G. Klebe)

Jäger (bass), **Fernando**, 1815 (F. Schubert)

Jakob, son of David Orth (ten), **Die Bürgschaft**, 1932 (K. Weill)

Jakob von Lusignan, King of Cyprus (ten), **Catharina Cornaro**, 1841 (F. Lachner)

Jan Janitzky (ten), **Der Bettelstudent**, 1882 (C. Millöcker)

Jane, an orphan (sop), **Der Günstling**, 1935 (R. Wagner-Régeny)

Jansen, Lord, a sea captain (bass), **Das Sonnenfest der Braminen**, 1790 (W. Müller)

Janthe, Berkley's daughter (sop), **Der Vampyr**, 1828 (H. Marschner)

Janthe (alto), **Hero und Leander**, 1966 (G. Bialas)

Jaquino, a turnkey (ten), **Leonore/Fidelio**, 1805/1814 (L. van Beethoven)

Jason (speaking role), **Medea**, 1775 (G. Benda)

Jason (bar), **Der goldene Bock**, 1964 (E. Krenek)

Jean-Charles (bar), **Das Floss der Medusa**, 1968 (H. W. Henze)

Jeanette, the maid, **Der Kobold**, 1904 (S. Wagner)

Jeanne, a young girl (sop), **Die Verlobung in San Domingo**, 1963 (W. Egk)

Jeanne, an Ursuline prioress (sop), **Die Teufel von Loudun**, 1969 (K. Penderecki)

Jenny (chanteuse), **Die Dreigroschenoper**, 1928 (K. Weill)

Jenny Hill (sop), **Aufsteig und Fall der Stadt Mahagonny**, 1930 (K. Weill)

Jery, **Jery und Bätely**, 1801 (J. F. Reichardt)

Jessie (soubrette), **Mahagonny**, 1927 (K. Weill)

Jessonda, a young widow (sop), **Jessonda**, 1823 (L. Spohr)

Jesus (ten), **Jesu Hochzeit**, 1980 (G. von Einem)

Jim, a foreman (bass), **Maschinist Hopkins**, 1929 (M. Brand)

Jimmy (bass), **Mahagonny**, 1927 (K. Weill)

Jimmy Mahoney (ten), **Aufsteig und Fall der Stadt Mahagonny**, 1930 (K. Weill)

Jocasta, Oedipus's mother (unspec.), **Oedipus der Tyrann**, 1959 (C. Orff)

Jodelet, a foolish person, **Der lächerliche Printz**, 1726 (R. Keiser)

Johann, a servant (bass), **Der Rauchfangkehrer**, 1781 (A. Salieri)

Johann, Adolf's servant (bar), **Die Opernprobe**, 1851 (A. Lortzing)

Johann, Maestro, **Christophorus**, 1927 (F. Schreker)

Johann Mattes (bar), **Die Bürgschaft**, 1932 (K. Weill)

Johanna (sop), **Das Mädchen aus Domrémy**, 1976 (G. Klebe)

Johannes Freudhofer, a schoolteacher (bar), **Der Evangelimann**, 1895 (W. Kienzl)

Jokanaan (John the Baptist) (bar), **Salome**, 1905 (R. Strauss)

Jonel Bolescu (ten), **Zigeunerliebe**, 1910 (F. Lehár)

Jonny, a Black jazz violinist (bar), **Jonny spielt auf**, 1927 (E. Krenek)

Joseph, son of a tenant farmer (ten), **Der Dorfbarbier**, 1796 (J. Schenk)

Joseph (bar), **Jesu Hochzeit**, 1980 (G. von Einem)

Joseph, St., **Der Schmied von Gent**, 1932 (F. Schreker)

Joseph K. (ten), **Der Prozess**, 1953 (G. von Einem)

Journalist, the (ten), **Zwischenfälle**, 1966 (B. Blacher)

Józsi, a gypsy violinist (ten), **Zigeunerliebe**, 1910 (F. Lehár)

Judge, the (bass), **Der Revisor**, 1957 (W. Egk)

Judge of Urb, the (ten), **Die Bürgschaft**, 1932 (K. Weill)

Judith, sister of Welfus, **Ludovicus Pius**, 1726 (G. C. Schürmann)

Judith (sop), **Judith**, 1985 (S. Matthus)

Julia, Augustus' daughter (sop), **Janus**, 1698 (R. Keiser)

Julia, confidante of Laura, **Der lächerliche Printz**, 1726 (R. Keiser)

Julia (sop), **Romeo und Julia**, 1944 (B. Blacher)

Julia, **Romeo und Julia**, 1953 (H. Sutermeister)

Julie, daughter of Kapellet (sop), **Romeo und Julie**, 1776 (G. Benda)

Julus (sop), **Die Bürgschaft**, 1816 (F. Schubert)

Juno (speaking part), **Ino**, 1779 (J. F. Reichardt)

Juno (sop), **Der Spiegel von Arkadien**, 1794 (F. X. Süssmayr)

Jupiter (speaking role), **Philemon und Baucis**, 1773 (F. J. Haydn)

Jupiter (bass), **Der Spiegel von Arkadien**, 1794 (F. X. Süssmayr)

Jupiter (bar), **Die Liebe der Danae**, 1944 (R. Strauss)

Jupiter (bar), **Alkmene**, 1961 (G. Klebe)

Krips, Rudolph's squire (bass), **Silvana**, 1810 (C. M. von Weber)

Ktesippos, son of Brasidas (ten), **Pallas Athene weint**, 1955 (E. Krenek)

Kühleborn, a water spirit (bass), **Undine**, 1816 (E. T. A. Hoffmann)

Kühleborn, a water prince (bar), **Undine**, 1845 (A. Lortzing)

Kundry, Klingsor's slave (sop), **Parsifal**, 1882 (R. Wagner)

Kunegunde, Brummer's wife (sop), **Die Schwestern von Prag**, 1794 (W. Müller)

Kunigunde, fiancée of Hugo (sop), **Faust**, 1816 (L. Spohr)

Kunigunde, Master Steffen's daughter (sop), **Hans Sachs**, 1840 (A. Lortzing)

Kunrad, an alchemist (bar), **Feuersnot**, 1901 (R. Strauss)

Künsteling, a shepherd (alto/high voice), **Seelewig**, 1644 (S. T. Staden)

Kuntz-Sartori, a professor (bar), **Das Ende einer Welt**, 1953 (H. W. Henze)

Kurt, Albert's squire (bass), **Silvana**, 1810 (C. M. von Weber)

Kurt (ten), **Der Graf von Gleichen**, 1827 (F. Schubert)

Kurwenal, Tristan's retainer (bar), **Tristan und Isolde**, 1865 (R. Wagner)

Kybbutz, tutor of Gustel (bass), **Der Alchymist**, 1778 (J. Schuster)

Kyce Waing, a field marshall (bass), **Das Nusch-Nuschi**, 1921 (P. Hindemith)

Lady, the (sop), **Cardillac**, 1926 (P. Hindemith)

Lady Milford (mezzo), **Kabale und Liebe**, 1976 (G. von Einem)

Lambertuccio, a Florentine (ten), **Boccaccio**, 1879 (F. von Suppé)

Lame boy, a (sop), **Die lustigen Musikanten**, 1805 (E. T. A. Hoffmann)

Lampe (bass), **Versiegelt**, 1908 (L. Blech)

Lampedo, Queen of the Amazons (speaking role), **Lampedo**, 1779 (G. J. Vogler)

Landowner, a (bass), **Das Fest der Winzer**, 1793 (F. L. A. Kunzen)

Lanzelot (bar), **Lanzelot**, 1969 (P. Dessau)

Lao-tse (ten), **Die Witwe des Schmetterlings**, 1969 (I. Yun)

Lara, a countess (sop), **Der Bettelstudent**, 1882 (C. Millöcker)

La Roche, director of a theater (bass), **Capriccio**, 1942 (R. Strauss)

Lasus, Lukullus' cook (ten), **Das Verhör des Lukullus**, 1951 (P. Dessau)

Laur, a baron, **Der Silbersee**, 1933 (K. Weill)

Laura, wife of Fernando, **Der lächerliche Printz**, 1726 (R. Keiser)

Laura, a friend of Julie (sop), **Romeo und Julie**, 1776 (G. Benda)

Laura (sop), **Die Freunde von Salamanka**, 1815 (F. Schubert)

Laura, wife of Wilhelm (sop), **Der Ring des Polykrates**, 1916 (E. Korngold)

Laura (sop), **Neues vom Tage**, 1929 (P. Hindemith)

Laura Windsor (sop), **Das Sonnenfest**, 1790 (W. Müller)

Laurindo, a shepherd (bar), **Der neu-modische Liebhaber**, 1724 (G. P. Telemann)

Lavigne, Lorette's fiancé (ten), **Der Vampyr**, 1828 (P. Lindpaintner)

Lawyer, the (bar), **Der Prozess**, 1953 (G. von Einem)

Laytyrus, confidant of Meroe (ten), **Die grossmüthige Tomyris**, 1717 (R. Keiser)

Leader of the chorus, the (bar), **Antigonae**, 1949 (C. Orff)

Leander, a dandy (ten), **Die Feuersbrunst**, ca. 1776 (F. J. Haydn)

Leander (bass), **Hero und Leander**, 1966 (G. Bialas)

Leandro, a fop (ten), **Arlecchino**, 1917 (F. Busoni)

Leandro, the king (ten), **König Hirsch**, 1965 (H. W. Henze)

Lear, the king (bar), **Lear**, 1978 (A. Reimann)

Leda (alto), **Die Liebe der Danae**, 1944 (R. Strauss)

Lefort, Admiral (bass), **Zar und Zimmermann**, 1837 (A. Lortzing)

Leicester, the Duke of (bar), **Elisabeth Tudor**, 1972 (W. Fortner)

Leiokritos, a freeman (bar), **Penelope**, 1954 (R. Liebermann)

Lejeune (buffo bass), **Leonore 40/45**, 1952 (R. Liebermann)

Lena, Princess of Pipi (sop), **Leonce und Lena**, 1979 (P. Dessau)

Lenardo, a noble in disguise (speaking role), **Lenardo und Blandine**, 1779 (P. Winter)

Lenchen, a Tyrolean (sop), **Der Jahrmarkt**, 1775 (G. Benda)

Lene, Zeckel's wife (sop), **Der Teufel ist los**, 1752 (J. C. Standfuss)

Lenore, Hubert's daughter (sop), **Die Loreley**, 1863 (R. Wagner)

Lenz, **Jakob Lenz**, 1980 (W. Rihm)

Leonardo (bar), **Die Bluthochzeit**, 1957 (W. Fortner)

Leonce, a prince (ten), **Leonce und Lena**, 1979 (P. Dessau)

Leonhard, a goldsmith (bar), **Die Brautwahl**, 1912 (F. Busoni)

Leonora, Alessandro Stradella's love (sop), **Alessandro Stradella**, 1844 (F. Flotow)

Leonora (high sop), **Das lange Weihnachts- mahl**, 1961 (P. Hindemith)

Leonore, Stössel's daughter (sop), **Doctor und Apotheker**, 1785 (K. Dittersdorf)

Leonore, wife of Florestan, going under the name of Fidelio (sop), **Leonore/Fidelio**, 1805/1814 (L. van Beethoven)

Leopold, the headwaiter (ten), **Im Weissen Rössl**, 1930 (R. Benatzky)

Leporell (bass), **Siebzehn Tage**, 1966 (W. Egk)

Lescaut (bar), **Boulevard Solitude**, 1952 (H. W. Henze)

Leukippos, a shepherd (ten), **Daphne**, 1938 (R. Strauss)

Li, Sim Tjong's mother (sop), **Sim Tjong**, 1972 (I. Yun)

Liang-Kung, a fox (mezzo), **Geisterliebe**, 1971 (I. Yun)

Libussa, Princess of Bohemia (sop), **Libussa**, 1822 (C. Kreutzer)

Licht, a writer (ten), **Der zerbrochene Krug**, 1971 (F. Geissler)

Liebenau, Count von (bar), **Der Waffen- schmied**, 1846 (A. Lortzing)

Liebreich, Frau von (sop), **Der Teufel ist los**, 1752 (J. C. Standfuss)

Liebreich, Herr von, a squire (ten), **Der Teu- fel ist los**, 1752 (J. C. Standfuss)

Lieschen (sop), **Die Zwillingsbrüder**, 1820 (F. Schubert)

Lieschen, Laura's maid (sop), **Der Ring des Polykrates**, 1916 (E. Korngold)

Liese, wife of Master Florian, **Das Spielwerk**, 1913 (F. Schreker)

Lieutenant, the (speaking part), **Der Jahr- markt**, 1775 (G. Benda)

Lilli, Hulda's daughter (sop), **Das Donau- weibchen**, 1798 (F. Kauer)

Lionel, Plunkett's foster brother (ten), **Mar- tha**, 1847 (F. von Flotow)

Lips, Herr von (bar), **Der Zerrissene**, 1964 (G. von Einem)

Lisa (sop), **Christophorus**, 1927 (F. Schreker)

Lisa (sop), **Das Land des Lächelns**, 1929 (F. Lehár)

Lisa, the milkmaid (sop), **Puntila**, 1966 (P. Dessau)

Lisbe (sop), **Zemire und Azor**, 1819 (L. Spohr)

Lisbeth, the ward (sop), **Die Heimkehr aus der Fremde**, 1829 (F. Mendelssohn)

Lisbeth (sop), **Das kalte Herz**, 1943 (N. Schultze)

Lisbus, servant of Welfus, **Ludovicus Pius**, 1726 (G. C. Schürmann)

Lisel, a cook (sop), **Der Rauchfangkehrer**, 1781 (A. Salieri)

Liu-Tung, a young student (bar), **Der Traum des Liu-Tung**, 1965 (I. Yun)

Livia, wife of Augustus (sop), **Janus**, 1698 (R. Keiser)

Loge, the god of fire (ten), **Der Ring: Das Rheingold**, 1869 (R. Wagner)

Lohengrin, a knight (ten), **Lohengrin**, 1850 (R. Wagner)

Lola, a barmaid (alto), **Irrelohe**, 1924 (F. Schreker)

Lora, Kaleph's daughter (sop), **Das Sonnen- fest der Braminen**, 1790 (W. Müller)

Lora (sop), **Die Hochzeit**, 1832 (R. Wagner)

Lora, sister of Prince Arindal (sop), **Die Feen**, 1833 (R. Wagner)

Lorette, Morton's daughter (sop), **Der Vam- pyr**, 1828 (P. Lindpaintner)

Lotharius, Ludwig's son (bass), **Ludovicus Pius**, 1726 (G. C. Schürmann)

Loudspeaker, the (bass), **Der Kaiser von At- lantis**, 1944 (V. Ullmann)

Louis XV (bar), **Madame Pompadour**, 1923 (L. Fall)

Louise, daughter of Tarnow (sop), **Der Alchy- mist**, 1778 (J. Schuster)

Louise, a mouse (sop), **Die englische Katze**, 1983 (H. W. Henze)

Luber, Frau von, a housekeeper, **Der Silber- see**, 1933 (K. Weill)

Lucentio, Bianka's suitor (ten), **Der wider- spenstigen Zähmung**, 1874 (H. Goetz)

Lucia (sop), **Das lange Weihnachtsmahl**, 1961 (P. Hindemith)

Lucian, a fox (ten), **Die englische Katze**, 1983 (H. W. Henze)

Lucifer, the father (bass/trombone/dancer/ mime), **Donnerstag**, 1981 (K. Stockhausen)

Lucile, wife of Desmoulins (sop), **Dantons Tod**, 1947 (G. von Einem)

Lucile, a young whore (mezzo), **La Cubana**, 1974 (H. W. Henze)

Lucinde (sop), **Claudine von Villa Bella**, 1815 (F. Schubert)

Lucio, Cynthia's lover (ten), **Zwillingskomödie**, 1954 (R. Mohaupt)

Lucy (sop), **Die Dreigroschenoper**, 1928 (K. Weill)

Ludmilla, Countess (sop), **Die Verschworenen**, 1823 (F. Schubert)

Ludmilla, Alma's maid (sop), **Der Berggeist**, 1825 (L. Spohr)

Ludwig (Ludovicus) the Pious, Roman Emperor (ten), **Ludovicus Pius**, 1726 (G. C. Schürmann)

Luftig, a servant (bar), **Die beiden Pädagogen**, 1821 (F. Mendelssohn)

Luise, daughter of the mayor (sop), **Das Fest der Winzer**, 1793 (F. K. A. Kunzen)

Luise, daughter of the Count (sop), **Die Opernprobe**, 1851 (A. Lortzing)

Luise, Gilfen's wife (sop), **Die Abreise**, 1898 (E. d'Albert)

Luise, the mayor's youngest daughter (sop), **Der Bärenhäuter**, 1899 (S. Wagner)

Luise, daughter of J. Mattes (sop), **Die Bürgschaft**, 1932 (K. Weill)

Luise, Baroness von Grünwiesel's ward (sop), **Der junge Lord**, 1965 (H. W. Henze)

Luise, the miller's daughter (sop), **Kabale und Liebe**, 1976 (G. von Einem)

Luitgarde (sop), **Des Teufels Lustschloss**, 1814 (F. Schubert)

Lukas, a young peasant (ten), **Der Jahrmarkt**, 1775 (G. Benda)

Lukullus, a Roman general (ten), **Das Verhör des Lukullus**, 1951 (P. Dessau)

Lulu (sop), **Lulu**, 1937 (A. Berg)

Luna (alto), **Die Harmonie der Welt**, 1957 (P. Hindemith)

Lux, the barber (bass), **Der Dorfbarbier**, 1796 (J. Schenk)

Luyn Calvo, the bishop (low bass), **Der Cid**, 1865 (P. Cornelius)

Luzifer, the devil, **Der Schmied von Gent**, 1932 (F. Schreker)

Luzio, a young noble (ten), **Das Liebesverbot**, 1836 (R. Wagner)

Lybia (sop), **Siebzehn Tage**, 1966 (W. Egk)

Lysander, a general (ten), **Pallas Athene weint**, 1955 (E. Krenek)

Lysiart, Count of Forêt (bar), **Euryanthe**, 1823 (C. M. von Weber)

Mac-Gregor, a Scottish laird (speaking role), **William Ratcliff**, 1982 (J.-P. Ostendorf)

Macheath (ten), **Die Dreigroschenoper**, 1928 (K. Weill)

Madame Pompadour (sop), **Madame Pompadour**, 1923 (L. Fall)

Madelon, Wilhelmine's confidante (sop), **Das Grab des Mufti**, 1779 (J. Hiller)

Mads, Ingrid's fiancé (ten), **Peer Gynt**, 1938 (W. Egk)

Magdalena, friend of Martha (alto), **Der Evangelimann**, 1895 (W. Kienzl)

Magdalene, Eva's nurse (sop/mezzo), **Die Meistersinger**, 1868 (R. Wagner)

Maggid, an angel (mezzo), **Der Engel von Prag**, 1979 (C. Bresgen)

Magistrate, the (bass), **Die Heimkehr aus der Fremde**, 1829 (F. Mendelssohn)

Mahon, old, Christy's father (bar), **Ein wahrer Held**, 1975 (G. Klebe)

Maiden, first (sop), **Mörder, Hoffnung der Frauen**, 1921 (P. Hindemith)

Maiden, second (alto), **Mörder, Hoffnung der Frauen**, 1921 (P. Hindemith)

Maiden, third (sop), **Mörder, Hoffnung der Frauen**, 1921 (P. Hindemith)

Maja, a shade (pantomime), **Die Geisterinsel**, 1798 (J. F. Reichardt)

Major-domo (speaking role), **Ariadne auf Naxos**, 1912 (R. Strauss)

Major-domo, the (bar), **Der Zwerg**, 1922 (A. von Zemlinsky)

Malaspina, a count (bass), **Der Engel von Prag**, 1979 (C. Bresgen)

Male nurse (bass), **Hin und zurück**, 1927 (P. Hindemith)

Malo, a slave of Porus (ten), **Vestas Feuer**, 1803 (L. van Beethoven)

Malwina, Sir Humphrey's daughter (sop), **Der Vampyr**, 1828 (H. Marschner)

Man, the (bar), **Die glückliche Hand**, 1924 (A. Schoenberg)

Man with the donkey, the (ten), **Die Kluge**, 1943 (C. Orff)

Man with the mule, the (bar), **Die Kluge**, 1943 (C. Orff)

Manasse, an old man (bass), **Die Brautwahl**, 1912 (F. Busoni)

Mandryka, a rich landowner (bar), **Arabella**, 1933 (R. Strauss)

Manolios (ten), **Die griechische Passion**, 1971 (B. Martinů)

Manon Lescaut (sop), **Boulevard Solitude**, 1952 (H. W. Henze)

Manuel Biffi (bar), **Giuditta**, 1934 (F. Lehár)

Manuel Venegas (ten), **Manuel Venegas**, 1903 (H. Wolf)

Marchesa Montetristo (alto), **Das Ende einer Welt**, 1953 (H. W. Henze)

Marco Vernero, a Venetian nobleman (ten), **Catharina Cornaro**, 1841 (F. Lachner)

Margarete, widow of a smith (sop), **Der Dorfbarbier**, 1796 (J. Schenk)

Margarete, Marie's nurse (alto), **William Ratcliff**, 1982 (J.-P. Ostendorf)

Margarethe, a sorceress (alto), **Genoveva**, 1850 (R. Schumann)

Margiana, daughter of Baba Mustapha (sop), **Der Barbier von Bagdad**, 1858 (P. Cornelius)

Margret (alto), **Wozzeck**, 1925 (A. Berg)

Marguérite, wife of Duménil (sop), **Der Opernball**, 1898 (R. Heuberger)

Maria, Don Ranudo's daughter (sop), **Don Ranudo**, 1919 (O. Schoeck)

Maria (sop), **Der Diktator**, 1928 (E. Krenek)

Maria, wife of the Commandant (sop), **Friedenstag**, 1938 (R. Strauss)

Maria, St., **Der Schmied von Gent**, 1932 (F. Schreker)

Maria Anna Elisa (sop), **Paganini**, 1925 (F. Lehár)

Maria Magdalene (alto), **Die toten Augen**, 1916 (E. d'Albert)

Maria Stuart (sop), **Elisabeth Tudor**, 1972 (W. Fortner)

Mariana, a novice (sop), **Das Liebesverbot**, 1836 (R. Wagner)

Marianne, Sander's wife (sop), **Das rothe Käppchen**, 1790 (K. Dittersdorf)

Marianne, a German girl, **Soliman der Zweyte**, 1799 (F. Süssmayr)

Marianne, Sophie's duenna (sop), **Der Rosenkavalier**, 1911 (R. Strauss)

Marianne (sop), **Jacobowsky und der Oberst**, 1965 (G. Klebe)

Marie, Van Bett's niece (sop), **Zar und Zimmermann**, 1837 (A. Lortzing)

Marie, Stadinger's daughter (sop), **Der Waffenschmied**, 1846 (A. Lortzing)

Marie, Countess (sop), **Der Vogelhändler**, 1891 (C. Zeller)

Marie (sop), **Die tote Stadt**, 1920 (E. Korngold)

Marie, Wozzeck's mistress (sop), **Wozzeck**, 1925 (A. Berg)

Marie, Mac-Gregor's daughter (sop), **William Ratcliff**, 1982 (J.-P. Ostendorf)

Marie Wesener (col sop), **Die Soldaten**, 1965 (B. A. Zimmermann)

Marietta (sop), **Die tote Stadt**, 1920 (E. Korngold)

Maritza, a countess (sop), **Gräfin Maritza**, 1924 (E. Kálmán)

Marja (sop), **Der Revisor**, 1957 (W. Egk)

Marke, King (bass), **Tristan und Isolde**, 1865 (R. Wagner)

Marquis de Chateauneuf (ten), **Zar und Zimmermann**, 1837 (A. Lortzing)

Mars (bass), **Adonis**, 1697 (R. Keiser)

Marschallin (Feldmarschallin), the (sop), **Der Rosenkavalier**, 1911 (R. Strauss)

Marta, Sebastiano's servant (sop), **Tiefland**, 1903 (E. d'Albert)

Martha, Michel's wife (sop), **Der Töpfer**, 1773 (J. André)

Martha, Tobias' wife (alto), **Undine**, 1845 (A. Lortzing)

Martha (sop), **Der Evangelimann**, 1895 (W. Kienzl)

Marthe, Michel's wife (sop), **Die Jagd**, 1770 (J. A. Hiller)

Marthe, Rappelkopf's daughter (sop), **Alpenkönig**, 1903 (L. Blech)

Marthe Rull, (alto), **Der zerbrochene Krug**, 1971 (F. Geissler)

Martin (ten), **Das Grab des Mufti**, 1779 (J. Hiller)

Martin Ladvenu, a priest (bar), **Das Mädchen aus Domrémy**, 1976 (G. Klebe)

Mary, Senta's nurse (alto), **Der fliegende Holländer**, 1843 (R. Wagner)

Mary (mezzo), **Jesu Hochzeit**, 1980 (G. von Einem)

Mary (Maria) Tudor of England (sop), **Der Günstling**, 1935 (R. Wagner-Régeny)

Marzelline, daughter of Rocco (sop), **Leonore/Fidelio**, 1805/1814 (L. van Beethoven)

Masdruscht, Bishop of Trent (bass), **Palestrina**, 1917 (H. Pfitzner)

Massimilla Doni, a duchess (sop), **Massamilla Doni**, 1937 (O. Schoeck)

Master Florian. See Florian, Master.

Master of ceremonies, the (bass), **Das Nusch-Nuschi**, 1921 (P. Hindemith)

Master Steffen. See Steffen, Master.

Mathias Freudhofer (ten), **Der Evangelimann**, 1895 (W. Kienzl)

Mathilde (sop), **Das Waldmädchen**, 1800 (C. M. von Weber)

Mathis, a painter (bar), **Mathis der Maler**, 1938 (P. Hindemith)

Matteo, suitor of Arabella (ten), **Arabella**, 1933 (R. Strauss)

Matti Altonen, Puntila's chauffeur (bar), **Puntila**, 1966 (P. Dessau)

Mauregato, father of Estrella (bass), **Alfonso und Estrella**, 1822 (F. Schubert)

Max, a young hunter (ten), **Der Freischütz**, 1821 (C. M. von Weber)

Max, a composer (ten), **Jonny spielt auf**, 1927 (E. Krenek)

Max, the circus clown (ten/sop), **Tartarin von Tarascon**, 1977 (M. Niehaus)

Maximilian I, emperor (bass-bar), **Hans Sachs**, 1840 (A. Lortzing)

Mayor, the (bar), **Das Fest der Winzer**, 1793 (F. L. A. Kunzen)

Mayor, the (bass), **Preussisches Märchen**, 1952 (B. Blacher)

Mayor, the (ten), **Lanzelot**, 1969 (P. Dessau)

Mayor, the (ten), **Der Besuch der alten Dame**, 1971 (G. von Einem)

Mechtilde, Rudolph's fiancée (sop), **Silvana**, 1810 (C. M. von Weber)

Medan Solana, the governor (bass), **Das Sonnenfest der Braminen**, 1790 (W. Müller)

Medea (speaking role), **Medea**, 1775 (G. Benda)

Medea (sop), **Der goldene Bock**, 1964 (E. Krenek)

Mehmet, overseer of the seraglio (bass), **Adelheit von Veltheim**, 1780 (C. G. Neefe)

Meletos (ten), **Pallas Athene weint**, 1955 (E. Krenek)

Melinde (speaking role), **Die Zauberharfe**, 1820 (F. Schubert)

Melito, Athenian prince (ten), **Der gedultige Sokrates**, 1721 (G. P. Telemann)

Menelaus (ten), **Die ägyptische Helena**, 1928 (R. Strauss)

Mephistofeles (bass), **Faust**, 1816 (L. Spohr)

Mephistopheles (ten), **Doktor Faust**, 1922 (F. Busoni)

Merkur (speaking role), **Philemon und Baucis**, 1773 (F. J. Haydn)

Meroe, Princess of Persia (sop), **Die grossmüthige Tomyris**, 1717 (R. Keiser)

Meroe, an Amazon princess (sop), **Penthesilea**, 1927 (O. Schoeck)

Mesach, a Jewish prince (alto), **Nebucadnezar**, 1704 (R. Keiser)

Messalina, wife of Claudius (sop), **Claudius**, 1703 (R. Keiser)

Messenger, the (bass), **Antigonae**, 1949 (C. Orff)

Metallio, a viper catcher (bass), **Der Spiegel von Arkadien**, 1794 (F. Süssmayr)

Meton (bar), **Pallas Athene weint**, 1955 (E. Krenek)

Mi, sister of Prince Sou-Chong (soubrette), **Das Land des Lächelns**, 1929 (F. Lehár)

Michael, the archangel (trumpet/ten/dancer), **Donnerstag**, 1981 (K. Stockhausen)

Michel, a village judge (ten), **Die Jagd**, 1770 (J. A. Hiller)

Michel, a potter (bass), **Der Töpfer**, 1773 (J. André)

Microscop, a magician (bass), **Der Teufel ist los**, 1752 (J. C. Standfuss)

Midas, King of Lydia (ten), **Die Liebe der Danae**, 1944 (R. Strauss)

Mikka, Pirokko's wife (sop), **Das Sonnenfest der Braminen**, 1790 (W. Müller)

Miller, the (bass), **Kabale und Liebe**, 1976 (G. von Einem)

Millionaire, the (bass), **Zwischenfälle**, 1966 (B. Blacher)

Mime, a Nibelung dwarf, (ten), **Der Ring: Das Reingold**, 1869, **Siegfried**, 1870 (R. Wagner)

Mimi, a dancer, **Die Landstreicher**, 1899 (C. M. Ziehrer)

Mine Queen, the (alto), **Das Bergwerk zu Falun**, 1961 (R. Wagner-Régeny)

Minette, Peter Schmoll's daughter (sop), **Peter Schmoll**, 1802 (C. M. von Weber)

Minette (sop), **Die englische Katze**, 1983 (H. W. Henze)

Minnewart, a singer (bar), **Das Donauweibchen**, 1798 (F. Kauer)

Miranda, daughter of Prospero (sop), **Die Geisterinsel**, 1798 (J. F. Reichardt)

Miranda, daughter of Prospero (sop), **Der Sturm**, 1956 (F. Martin)

Nicole, a servant (bass-bar), **Das Schloss Dürande**, 1943 (O. Schoeck)

Nicolette, a Moorish girl (sop), **Die Geschichte von Aucassin**, 1969 (G. Bialas)

Nicolo, Jodelet's neighbor, **Der lächerliche Printz**, 1726 (R. Keiser)

Nigella, an Egyptian gypsy (sop), **Der neumodische Liebhaber Damon**, 1724 (G. P. Telemann)

Nightingale, the (sop), **Die Vögel**, 1920 (W. Braunfels)

Nisibis, a widow, **Miriways**, 1728 (G. P. Telemann)

Nitsche, Hans Christoph (bass), **Das rothe Käppchen**, 1790 (K. Dittersdorf)

Norfolk, Duke of (bar), **Elisabeth Tudor**, 1972 (W. Fortner)

Norns, the three, sisters of fate (alto, mezzo, sop), **Der Ring: Götterdämmerung**, 1876 (R. Wagner)

Nostiz, a count (ten), **Der Engel von Prag**, 1979 (C. Bresgen)

Nun, an old (alto), **Sancta Susanna**, 1922 (P. Hindemith)

Nureddin, a wealthy young man (ten), **Der Barbier von Bagdad**, 1858 (P. Cornelius)

Nuri, Sebastiano's servant (sop), **Tiefland**, 1903 (E. d'Albert)

Nurmahal, Dscheangir's wife (sop), **Nurmahal**, 1822 (G. Spontini)

Nurse, the (mezzo), **Die Frau ohne Schatten**, 1918 (R. Strauss)

Nurse, the (alto), **Romeo und Julia**, 1944 (B. Blacher)

Oberlin, Pastor, **Jakob Lenz**, 1980 (W. Rihm)

Oberon, **Oberon**, 1789 (P. Wranitzky)

Oberon, King of the Elves (ten), **Oberon**, 1826 (C. M. von Weber)

Ochs, Baron of Lerchenau (bass), **Der Rosenkavalier**, 1911 (R. Strauss)

Octavia, Nero's wife, **Nero**, 1705 (G. F. Handel)

Octavia, **Octavia**, 1705 (R. Keiser)

Octavian, Count Rofrano, a young nobleman (mezzo), **Der Rosenkavalier**, 1911 (R. Strauss)

Octavio, a captain (ten), **Giuditta**, 1934 (F. Lehár)

Octavius, **Der lächerliche Printz**, 1726 (R. Keiser)

Odin, god of light (ten), **Gunlöd**, 1874 (P. Cornelius)

Odoardo, a rich peasant (ten), **Die Feuersbrunst**, ca. 1776 (F. J. Haydn)

Odysseus (bar), **Penelope**, 1954 (R. Liebermann)

Oedipus, a priest (unspec. voice), **Oedipus der Tyrann**, 1959 (C. Orff)

Officer, the (ten), **Cardillac**, 1926 (P. Hindemith)

Officer, the (ten), **Der Diktator**, 1928 (E. Krenek)

Old man, the (ten), **Peer Gynt**, 1938 (W. Egk)

Old man, an (bar), **Die tödlichen Wünsche**, 1959 (G. Klebe)

Olga Lambinski (comedienne), **Die Dollarprinzessin**, 1907 (L. Fall)

Olim, a policeman, **Der Silbersee**, 1933 (K. Weill)

Olivia (sop), **Die Freunde von Salamanka**, 1815 (F. Schubert)

Olivier, a poet (bar), **Capriccio**, 1942 (R. Strauss)

Ollendorf, Colonel (bass), **Der Bettelstudent**, 1882 (C. Millöcker)

Olympia (alto), **Erwin und Elmire**, 1916 (O. Schoeck)

Omar, a money changer (bass), **Abu Hassan**, 1811 (C. M. von Weber)

Omphale, Queen of Lydia (sop), **Omphale**, 1976 (S. Matthus)

Onofrio, member of the Venetian council (bass), **Catharina Cornaro**, 1841 (F. Lachner)

Oona, the nurse (alto), **Irische Legende**, 1955 (W. Egk)

Ophelia (sop), **Hamlet**, 1968 (H. Searle)

Orest (bar), **Das Leben des Orest**, 1930 (E. Krenek)

Orestes (bar), **Elektra**, 1909 (R. Strauss)

Orlovsky, a prince (mezzo/male voice), **Die Fledermaus**, 1874 (J. Strauss, Jr.)

Orpheus (ten), **Orpheus und Eurydike**, 1926 (E. Krenek)

Orsianes, a Lydian prince (bass), **Croesus**, 1711 (R. Keiser)

Ortrud, Telramund's wife (sop), **Lohengrin**, 1850 (R. Wagner)

Oscar, Alexander's cousin (ten), **Zweimal Alexander**, 1937 (B. Martinů)

Oskar (ten), **Der Berggeist**, 1825 (L. Spohr)

Osman, son of Consalvo (ten), **Almira**, 1705 (G. F. Handel)

Pius IV, the pope (bass), **Palestrina**, 1917 (H. Pfitzner)

Plato (bass), **Der gedultige Sokrates**, 1721 (G. P. Telemann)

Plunkett, a young farmer (bar), **Martha**, 1847 (F. von Flotow)

Pocus, twin of Hocus (bass-bar), **Zwillingskomödie**, 1954 (R. Mohaupt)

Poet/stranger, a (ten), **Die Rose von Stambul**, 1916 (L. Fall)

Pogner, Veit, a goldsmith (bass), **Die Meistersinger**, 1868 (R. Wagner)

Policares, King of Lydia (ten), **Die grossmüthige Tomyris**, 1717 (R. Keiser)

Polidor, **L'inganno fedele**, 1714 (R. Keiser)

Pollux, King of Eos (ten), **Die Liebe der Danae**, 1944 (R. Strauss)

Polly (sop), **Die Dreigroschenoper**, 1928 (K. Weill)

Polonius (bar), **Hamlet**, 1968 (H. Searle)

Polybius, Athenian general (bass), **Aurora**, 1811–1812 (E. T. A. Hoffmann)

Popoff, a colonel (bar), **Der tapfere Soldat**, 1908 (O. Straus)

Poppea, Sabina, a noble Roman woman, **Nero**, 1705 (G. F. Handel)

Poppea, **Octavia**, 1705 (R. Keiser)

Poquelin (bar), **Die Schule der Frauen**, 1955 (R. Liebermann)

Portrait (bass), **Zweimal Alexander**, 1937 (B. Martinů)

Porus, a noble Roman (bar), **Vestas Feuer**, 1803 (L. van Beethoven)

Postmaster, the (ten), **Der Revisor**, 1957 (W. Egk)

Preciosa, a gypsy, **Preciosa**, 1821 (C. M. von Weber)

President, the (bar), **Kabale und Liebe**, 1976 (G. von Einem)

Priest, a (ten), **Die Zauberflöte**, 1791, (W. A. Mozart)

Priest, a (bass), **Hero und Leander**, 1966 (G. Bialas)

Priest, the (bass-bar), **Der Besuch der alten Dame**, 1971 (G. von Einem)

Prima Donna, the (sop), **Ariadne auf Naxos**, 1912 (R. Strauss)

Prima Donna, the (sop), **Zwischenfälle**, 1966 (B. Blacher)

Prince, the (ten), **Königskinder**, 1910 (E. Humperdinck)

Princess, the, **Rübezahl**, 1805 (C. M. von Weber)

Princess, the, **Das Spielwerk**, 1913 (F. Schreker)

Prioress of Himmelpfort, the (alto), **Das Schloss Dürande**, 1943 (O. Schoeck)

Prison warden, the (bass), **Die Kluge**, 1943 (C. Orff)

Procris, daughter of Erechtheus (sop), **Aurora**, 1811–1812 (E. T. A. Hoffmann)

Professor, the (bar), **Hin und zurück**, 1927 (P. Hindemith)

Professor/host, the (ten), **Zwischenfälle**, 1966 (B. Blacher)

Prospero, former duke, magician (bass), **Die Geisterinsel**, 1798 (J. H. Reichardt)

Prospero (bass-bar), **Der Sturm**, 1956 (F. Martin)

Protagonist, the (ten), **Der Protagonist**, 1926 (K. Weill)

Proteus (bass), **Adonis**, 1697, (R. Keiser)

Prothoe, an Amazon princess (sop), **Penthesilea**, 1927 (O. Schoeck)

Psyche (sop), **Orpheus und Eurydike**, 1926 (E. Krenek)

Puck (mezzo), **Oberon**, 1826 (C. M. von Weber)

Puff, Lord (ten), **Die englische Katze**, 1983 (H. W. Henze)

Puntila, Johannes, a landowner (bass), **Puntila**, 1966 (P. Dessau)

Pygmalion, a young sculptor (ten), **Die schöne Galatea**, 1865 (F. von Suppé)

Queen, the (sop), **Der Spiegelritter**, ca. 1811 (F. Schubert)

Queen, the (sop), **Das Verhör des Lukullus**, 1951 (P. Dessau)

Queen, the (mezzo), **Hamlet**, 1968 (H. Searle)

Queen Mother of Samarkand (sop), **Turandot**, 1917 (F. Busoni)

Queen of the Earth Spirits (sop), **Hans Heiling**, 1833 (H. Marschner)

Queen of the Night, the (sop), **Die Zauberflöte**, 1791 (W. A. Mozart)

Queen of the Night, **Das Labarint**, 1798 (P. Winter)

Quin, Widow (sop), **Ein wahrer Held**, 1975 (G. Klebe)

Quiteria (sop), **Die Hochzeit des Camacho**, 1827 (F. Mendelssohn)

Rabbi Löw (bass), **Der Engel von Prag**, 1979 (C. Bresgen)

Walter, a lawyer (bar), **Der zerbrochene Krug**, 1971 (F. Geissler)

Walther, the town judge (bar), **Der vierjährige Posten**, 1815 (F. Schubert)

Walther von der Vogelweide (ten), **Tannhäuser**, 1845 (R. Wagner)

Walther von Stolzing, a knight (ten), **Die Meistersinger**, 1868 (R. Wagner)

Wanda (sop), **Rosamunde Floris**, 1960 (B. Blacher)

Wanderer (Wotan), the (bass/bass-bar), **Der Ring: Siegfried**, 1876 (R. Wagner)

Wang, Mrs., an innkeeper (mezzo), **Der Traum des Liu-Tung**, 1965 (I. Yun)

Warriors, first, second, third (ten, bass, ten), **Mörder, Hoffnung der Frauen**, 1921 (P. Hindemith)

Watchman, a (ten), **Antigonae**, 1949 (C. Orff)

Weiss, Mr. (bass), **Die Verlobung in San Domingo**, 1963 (W. Egk)

Welfus, a Swabian count (ten), **Ludovicus Pius**, 1726 (G. C. Schürmann)

Wellgunde, a Rhine Maiden (high sop), **Der Ring: Das Rheingold**, 1869, **Götterdämmerung**, 1876 (R. Wagner)

Wesener, a merchant (bass), **Die Soldaten**, 1965 (B. A. Zimmermann)

Wibbel, Anton, a master tailor (bass-bar), **Schneider Wibbel**, 1938 (M. Lothar)

Widow, a young (sop), **Der Revisor**, 1957 (W. Egk)

Widow, a young (sop), **Die Witwe des Schmetterlings**, 1969 (I. Yun)

Wife, the (sop), **Mörder, Hoffnung der Frauen**, 1921 (P. Hindemith)

Wife, the (sop), **Von heute auf morgen**, 1930 (A. Schoenberg)

Wife of the fisherman, the (mezzo), **Undine**, 1816 (E. T. A. Hoffmann)

Wife of the fisherman, the (sop), **Vom Fischer un syner Fru**, 1930 (O. Schoeck)

Wife of the jailor, the (mezzo), **Der Revisor**, 1957 (W. Egk)

Wife of the miller, the (mezzo), **Kabale und Liebe**, 1976 (G. von Einem)

Wilhelm, a soldier (bar), **Die beiden Schützen**, 1837 (A. Lortzing)

Wilhelm (bar), **Rosamunde Floris**, 1960 (B. Blacher)

Wilhelm (ten), **Der junge Lord**, 1965 (H. W. Henze)

Wilhelm Arndt, a conductor (ten), **Der Ring des Polykrates**, 1916 (E. Korngold)

Wilhelm Fadenkreutz (bar), **Preussisches Märchen**, 1952 (B. Blacher)

Wilhelmine (sop), **Das Grab des Mufti**, 1779 (J. Hiller)

Wilhelmine, Brummer's daughter (sop), **Die Schwestern von Prag**, 1794 (W. Müller)

William Ratcliff (ten), **William Ratcliff**, 1982 (J.-P. Ostendorf)

Willmers, Frau, Gertrud's neighbor (alto), **Versiegelt**, 1908 (L. Blech)

Wise woman, the (sop), **Die Kluge**, 1943 (C. Orff)

Witch, the (mezzo/male voice), **Hänsel und Gretel**, 1893 (E. Humperdinck)

Witch, the (alto), **Königskinder**, 1910 (E. Humperdinck)

Witch of Endor, the (sop), **Saul**, 1928 (H. Reutter)

Wladislaw (ten), **Libussa**, 1822 (C. Kreutzer)

Woglinde, a Rhine Maiden (high sop), **Der Ring: Das Rheingold**, 1869, **Götterdämmerung**, 1876 (R. Wagner)

Wohlhaldt (ten), **Faust**, 1816 (L. Spohr)

Wölf, Herr von, Nanette's lover (ten), **Der Rauchfangkehrer**, 1781 (A. Salieri)

Wolf, Liese's former lover, **Das Spielwerk**, 1913 (F. Schreker)

Wolfram von Eschenbach (bass), **Tannhäuser**, 1845 (R. Wagner)

Woman, a (sop), **Erwartung**, 1909 (A. Schoenberg)

Woman, a young (sop), **Die schwarze Spinne**, 1949 (W. Burkhard)

Woman, an old (sop), **Siebzehn Tage**, 1966 (W. Egk)

Woodsman, the (bass), **Königskinder**, 1910 (E. Humperdinck)

Wotan, ruler of the gods (bar), **Der Ring: Das Rheingold**, 1869, **Die Walküre**, 1870, **Siegfried** (as the Wanderer), 1876 (R. Wagner)

Wozzeck, a soldier (bar), **Wozzeck**, 1925 (A. Berg)

Xanthe, Danae's servant (sop), **Die Liebe der Danae**, 1944 (R. Strauss)

Xantippe (sop), **Der gedultige Sokrates**, 1721 (G. P. Telemann)

Xenephon, student of Socrates (ten), **Der gedultige Sokrates**, 1721 (G. P. Telemann)

Yannakos, a peddlar (ten), **Die griechische Passion**, 1971 (B. Martinů)

Yariko, a savage (sop), **Fernando und Yariko**, 1784 (B. Schack)

Yarini (ten), **La Cubana**, 1974 (H. W. Henze)

Yesterday's Lover (bar), **Royal Hotel**, 1927 (K. Weill)

Young lady, the (sop), **Gespenstersonate**, 1984 (A. Reimann)

Young man, the (ten), **Die Flut**, 1947 (B. Blacher)

Ypsheim-Gindelbach, Prince (bass), **Wiener Blut**, 1899 (J. Strauss, Jr.)

Yu-Chan, Pien-Fu's wife (sop), **Der Traum des Liu-Tung**, 1965 (I. Yun)

Yvonne, a chambermaid (sop), **Jonny spielt auf**, 1927 (E. Krenek)

Zaïde (sop), **Zaïde**, 1779 (W. A. Mozart)

Zanga, a slave, **Der Traum ein Leben**, 1937 (W. Braunfels)

Zarandelle, Baron de (ten), **Venus**, 1922 (O. Schoeck)

Zarewitsch, the (ten), **Der Zarewitsch**, 1927 (F. Lehár)

Zayde, wife of Hassan (sop), **Der Kaufmann von Smyrna**, 1771 (G. J. Vogler)

Zdenka, sister of Arabella (sop), **Arabella**, 1933 (R. Strauss)

Zdenko von Lobkowitz (bass), **Der Engel von Prag**, 1979 (C. Bresgen)

Zeckel, Jobsen, a cobbler (bass), **Der Teufel ist los**, 1752 (J. C. Standfuss)

Zedlau, Count (ten), **Wiener Blut**, 1899 (J. Strauss, Jr.)

Zelia, Bahar's sister, **Nurmahal**, 1822 (G. Spontini)

Zemir, an evil suitor of Bemira, **Miriways**, 1728 (G. P. Telemann)

Zemire, daughter of Sander (sop), **Zemire und Azor**, 1819 (L. Spohr)

Zerbinetta (sop), **Ariadne auf Naxos**, 1912 (R. Strauss)

Zerubine, Elvire's companion (sop), **Die Soldatenliebschaft**, 1820 (F. Mendelssohn)

Zimbel, Wibbel's apprentice (buffo ten), **Schneider Wibbel**, 1938 (M. Lothar)

Zimmerlein, Widow, a housekeeper (alto), **Die schweigsame Frau**, 1935 (R. Strauss)

Zobeide, wife of Harun al Raschid (speaking role), **Abu Hassan**, 1811 (C. M. von Weber)

Zorika, Dragotin's daughter (sop), **Zigeunerliebe**, 1910 (F. Lehár)

Zsupan, a baron (bar), **Gräfin Maritza**, 1924 (E. Kálmán)

Zulima, beloved of Almanzor (sop), **Der Barbier von Bagdad**, 1783 (J. André)

INDEX OF PERFORMERS

GENERAL INDEX

This General Index presents the titles of the operas in the main listing and Appendix I, and includes references not provided in the other Appendices and Indices.

About the Author

MARGARET ROSS GRIFFEL is a consultant with G. Schirmer, Inc. She was the consulting editor of the *Schirmer History of Music* and the consultant and translator for *Something to Sing About*. She also contributed to the *New Oxford History of Music*.